Database Systems:
The Complete Book

Hector Garcia-Molina
Jeffrey D. Ullman
Jennifer Widom

Department of Computer Science
Stanford University

An Alan R. Apt Book

Prentice Hall
Upper Saddle River, New Jersey 07458

Library of Congress Cataloging-in-Publication Data

Garcia-Molina, Hector.
    Database systems: the complete book / Hector
    Garcia-Molina, Jeffrey D. Ullman, and Jennifer Widom
    p.cm.
    Includes bibliographical references and index.
    ISBN 0-13-031995-3
    1. Database management. I. Ullman, Jeffrey D. II. Widom, Jennifer.
    III. Title.
    CIP Data available.

Vice President and Editorial Director, ECS: *Marcia J. Horton*
Publisher: *Alan R. Apt*
Associate Editor: *Toni Holm*
Editorial Assistant: *Patrick Lindner*
Vice President and Director of Production and Manufacturing, ESM: *David W. Riccardi*
Executive Managing Editor: *Vince O'Brien*
Managing Editor: *David A. George*
Production Editor: *Irwin Zucker*
Director of Creative Services: *Paul Belfanti*
Creative Director: *Carole Anson*
Art Director: *Heather Scott*
Cover Art and Design: *Tamara L. Newnam*
Manufacturing Manager: *Trudy Pisciotti*
Manufacturing Buyer: *Lisa McDowell*
Senior Marketing Manager: *Jennie Burger*
Marketing Assistant: *Barrie Reinhold*

 © 2002 by Prentice Hall
Prentice-Hall, Inc.
Upper Saddle River, New Jersey 07458

The author and publisher of this book have used their best efforts in preparing this book. These efforts include the development, research, and testing of the theories and programs to determine their effectiveness. The author and publisher make no warranty of any kind, expressed or implied, with regard to these programs or the documentation contained in this book. The author and publisher shall not be liable in any event for incidental or consequential damages in connection with, or arising out of, the furnishing, performance, or use of these programs

Printed in the United States of America

10 9 8 7 6 5 4 3

ISBN 0-13-031995-3

Pearson Education Ltd., *London*
Pearson Education Australia Pty. Ltd., *Sydney*
Pearson Education Singapore, Pte. Ltd.
Pearson Education North Asia Ltd., *Hong Kong*
Pearson Education Canada, Inc., *Toronto*
Pearson Educacíon de Mexico, S.A. de C.V.
Pearson Education—Japan, *Tokyo*
Pearson Education Malaysia, Pte. Ltd.

Preface

At Stanford, we are on the quarter system, and as a result, our introductory database instruction is divided into two courses. The first, CS145, is designed for students who will use database systems but not necessarily take a job implementing a DBMS. It is a prerequisite for CS245, which is the introduction to DBMS implementation. Students wishing to go further in the database field then take CS345 (theory), CS346 (DBMS implementation project), and CS347 (transaction processing and distributed databases).

Starting in 1997, we published a pair of books. *A First Course in Database Systems* was designed for CS145, and *Database System Implementation* was for CS245 and parts of CS346. Because many schools are on the semester system or combine the two kinds of database instruction into one introductory course, we felt that there was a need to produce the two books as a single volume. At the same time, the evolution of database systems has made a number of new topics imperative for a modern course. Thus, we have added, mostly to the application-programming area, topics such as object-relational data, SQL/PSM (stored programs), SQL/CLI (the emerging standard for the C/SQL interface), and JDBC (the same for Java/SQL).

Use of the Book

We recommend that two quarters be devoted to the material in this book. If you follow the Stanford approach, you would cover the first ten chapters in the first quarter and the last ten in the second quarter. Should you wish to cover the material in a single semester, then there will have to be some omitted portions. In general, we suggest that Chapters 2–7, 11–13, and 17–18 should be given highest priority, but there are pieces from each of these chapters that can be skipped.

If, as we do in CS145, you give students a substantial database-application design and implementation project, then you may have to reorder the material somewhat, so that SQL instruction occurs earlier in the book. You may wish to defer material such as dependencies, although students need normalization for design.

Prerequisites

We have used the book at the "mezzanine" level, in courses taken both by undergraduates and beginning graduate students. The formal prerequisites for the courses are Sophomore-level treatments of: (1) Data structures, algorithms, and discrete math, and (2) Software systems, software engineering, and programming languages. Of this material, it is important that students have at least a rudimentary understanding of such topics as: algebraic expressions and laws, logic, basic data structures such as search trees and graphs, object-oriented programming concepts, and programming environments. However, we believe that adequate background is surely acquired by the end of the Junior year in a typical computer science program.

Exercises

The book contains extensive exercises, with some for almost every section. We indicate harder exercises or parts of exercises with an exclamation point. The hardest exercises have a double exclamation point.

Some of the exercises or parts are marked with a star. For these exercises, we shall endeavor to maintain solutions accessible through the book's web page. These solutions are publicly available and should be used for self-testing. Note that in a few cases, one exercise B asks for modification or adaptation of your solution to another exercise A. If certain parts of A have solutions, then you should expect the corresponding parts of B to have solutions as well.

Support on the World Wide Web

The book's home page is

>   http://www-db.stanford.edu/~ullman/dscb.html

Here are solutions to starred exercises, errata as we learn of them, and backup materials. We are making available the notes for each offering of CS145 and CS245 as we teach them, including homeworks, projects and exams.

Acknowledgements

A large number of people have helped us, either with the initial vetting of the text for this book and its predecessors, or by contacting us with errata in the books and/or other Web-based materials. It is our pleasure to acknowledge them all here.

Marc Abromowitz, Joseph H. Adamski, Brad Adelberg, Gleb Ashimov, Donald Aingworth, Jonathan Becker, Margaret Benitez, Larry Bonham, Phillip Bonnet, David Brokaw, Ed Burns, Karen Butler, Christopher Chan, Sudarshan

Chawathe, Per Christensen, Ed Chang, Surajit Chaudhuri, Ken Chen, Rada Chirkova, Nitin Chopra, Bobbie Cochrane, Arturo Crespo, Linda DeMichiel, Tom Dienstbier, Pearl D'Souza, Oliver Duschka.

Also Xavier Faz, Greg Fichtenholtz, Bart Fisher, Jarl Friis, John Fry, Chi-ping Fu, Tracy Fujieda, Manish Godara, Meredith Goldsmith, Luis Gravano, Gerard Guillemette, Rafael Hernandez, Antti Hjelt, Ben Holtzman, Steve Huntsberry, Leonard Jacobson, Thulasiraman Jeyaraman, Dwight Joe, Seth Katz, Yeong-Ping Koh, Gyorgy Kovacs, Phillip Koza, Brian Kulman, Sang Ho Lee, Olivier Lobry, Lu Chao-Jun, Arun Marathe, Le-Wei Mo, Fabian Modoux, Peter Mork, Mark Mortensen.

Also Ramprakash Narayanaswami, Hankyung Na, Marie Nilsson, Torbjorn Norbye, Chang-Min Oh, Mehul Patel, Bert Porter, Limbek Reka, Prahash Ramanan, Ken Ross, Tim Roughgarten, Mema Roussopoulos, Richard Scherl, Catherine Tornabene, Anders Uhl, Jonathan Ullman, Mayank Upadhyay, Vassilis Vassalos, Qiang Wang, Kristian Widjaja, Janet Wu, Sundar Yamunachari, Takeshi Yokukawa, Min-Sig Yun, Torben Zahle, Sandy Zhang. The remaining errors are ours, of course.

H. G.-M.
J. D. U.
J. W.
Stanford, CA

About the Authors

JEFFREY D. ULLMAN is the Stanford W. Ascherman Professor of Computer Science at Stanford University. He is the author or co-author of 16 books, including *Elements of ML Programming* (Prentice Hall 1998). His research interests include data mining, information integration, and electronic education. He is a member of the National Academy of Engineering, and recipient of a Guggenheim Fellowship, the Karl V. Karlstrom Outstanding Educator Award, the SIGMOD Contributions Award, and the Knuth Prize.

JENNIFER WIDOM is Associate Professor of Computer Science and Electrical Engineering at Stanford University. Her research interests include query processing on data streams, data caching and replication, semistructured data and XML, and data warehousing. She is a former Guggenheim Fellow and has served on numerous program committees, advisory boards, and editorial boards.

HECTOR GARCIA-MOLINA is the L. Bosack and S. Lerner Professor of Computer Science and Electrical Engineering, and Chair of the Department of Computer Science at Stanford University. His research interests include digital libraries, information integration, and database application on the Internet. He was a recipient of the SIGMOD Innovations Award and is a member of PITAC (President's Information-Technology Advisory Council).

Table of Contents

Chapter 1

The Worlds of Database Systems

Databases today are essential to every business. They are used to maintain internal records, to present data to customers and clients on the World-Wide-Web, and to support many other commercial processes. Databases are likewise found at the core of many scientific investigations. They represent the data gathered by astronomers, by investigators of the human genome, and by biochemists exploring the medicinal properties of proteins, along with many other scientists.

The power of databases comes from a body of knowledge and technology that has developed over several decades and is embodied in specialized software called a *database management system*, or *DBMS*, or more colloquially a "database system." A DBMS is a powerful tool for creating and managing large amounts of data efficiently and allowing it to persist over long periods of time, safely. These systems are among the most complex types of software available. The capabilities that a DBMS provides the user are:

1. *Persistent storage.* Like a file system, a DBMS supports the storage of very large amounts of data that exists independently of any processes that are using the data. However, the DBMS goes far beyond the file system in providing flexibility, such as data structures that support efficient access to very large amounts of data.

2. *Programming interface.* A DBMS allows the user or an application program to access and modify data through a powerful query language. Again, the advantage of a DBMS over a file system is the flexibility to manipulate stored data in much more complex ways than the reading and writing of files.

3. *Transaction management.* A DBMS supports concurrent access to data, i.e., simultaneous access by many distinct processes (called "transac-

1

tions") at once. To avoid some of the undesirable consequences of simultaneous access, the DBMS supports *isolation*, the appearance that transactions execute one-at-a-time, and *atomicity*, the requirement that transactions execute either completely or not at all. A DBMS also supports *durability*, the ability to recover from failures or errors of many types.

1.1   The Evolution of Database Systems

What is a database? In essence a database is nothing more than a collection of information that exists over a long period of time, often many years. In common parlance, the term *database* refers to a collection of data that is managed by a DBMS. The DBMS is expected to:

1. Allow users to create new databases and specify their *schema* (logical structure of the data), using a specialized language called a *data-definition language*.

2. Give users the ability to *query* the data (a "query" is database lingo for a question about the data) and modify the data, using an appropriate language, often called a *query language* or *data-manipulation language*.

3. Support the storage of very large amounts of data — many gigabytes or more — over a long period of time, keeping it secure from accident or unauthorized use and allowing efficient access to the data for queries and database modifications.

4. Control access to data from many users at once, without allowing the actions of one user to affect other users and without allowing simultaneous accesses to corrupt the data accidentally.

1.1.1   Early Database Management Systems

The first commercial database management systems appeared in the late 1960's. These systems evolved from file systems, which provide some of item (3) above; file systems store data over a long period of time, and they allow the storage of large amounts of data. However, file systems do not generally guarantee that data cannot be lost if it is not backed up, and they don't support efficient access to data items whose location in a particular file is not known.

Further, file systems do not directly support item (2), a query language for the data in files. Their support for (1) — a schema for the data — is limited to the creation of directory structures for files. Finally, file systems do not satisfy (4). When they allow concurrent access to files by several users or processes, a file system generally will not prevent situations such as two users modifying the same file at about the same time, so the changes made by one user fail to appear in the file.

The first important applications of DBMS's were ones where data was composed of many small items, and many queries or modifications were made. Here are some of these applications.

Airline Reservations Systems

In this type of system, the items of data include:

1. Reservations by a single customer on a single flight, including such information as assigned seat or meal preference.

2. Information about flights — the airports they fly from and to, their departure and arrival times, or the aircraft flown, for example.

3. Information about ticket prices, requirements, and availability.

Typical queries ask for flights leaving around a certain time from one given city to another, what seats are available, and at what prices. Typical data modifications include the booking of a flight for a customer, assigning a seat, or indicating a meal preference. Many agents will be accessing parts of the data at any given time. The DBMS must allow such concurrent accesses, prevent problems such as two agents assigning the same seat simultaneously, and protect against loss of records if the system suddenly fails.

Banking Systems

Data items include names and addresses of customers, accounts, loans, and their balances, and the connection between customers and their accounts and loans, e.g., who has signature authority over which accounts. Queries for account balances are common, but far more common are modifications representing a single payment from, or deposit to, an account.

As with the airline reservation system, we expect that many tellers and customers (through ATM machines or the Web) will be querying and modifying the bank's data at once. It is vital that simultaneous accesses to an account not cause the effect of a transaction to be lost. Failures cannot be tolerated. For example, once the money has been ejected from an ATM machine, the bank must record the debit, even if the power immediately fails. On the other hand, it is not permissible for the bank to record the debit and then not deliver the money if the power fails. The proper way to handle this operation is far from obvious and can be regarded as one of the significant achievements in DBMS architecture.

Corporate Records

Many early applications concerned corporate records, such as a record of each sale, information about accounts payable and receivable, or information about employees — their names, addresses, salary, benefit options, tax status, and so on. Queries include the printing of reports such as accounts receivable or employees' weekly paychecks. Each sale, purchase, bill, receipt, employee hired, fired, or promoted, and so on, results in a modification to the database.

The early DBMS's, evolving from file systems, encouraged the user to visualize data much as it was stored. These database systems used several different data models for describing the structure of the information in a database, chief among them the "hierarchical" or tree-based model and the graph-based "network" model. The latter was standardized in the late 1960's through a report of CODASYL (Committee on Data Systems and Languages).[1]

A problem with these early models and systems was that they did not support high-level query languages. For example, the CODASYL query language had statements that allowed the user to jump from data element to data element, through a graph of pointers among these elements. There was considerable effort needed to write such programs, even for very simple queries.

1.1.2   Relational Database Systems

Following a famous paper written by Ted Codd in 1970,[2] database systems changed significantly. Codd proposed that database systems should present the user with a view of data organized as tables called *relations*. Behind the scenes, there might be a complex data structure that allowed rapid response to a variety of queries. But, unlike the user of earlier database systems, the user of a relational system would not be concerned with the storage structure. Queries could be expressed in a very high-level language, which greatly increased the efficiency of database programmers.

We shall cover the relational model of database systems throughout most of this book, starting with the basic relational concepts in Chapter 3. SQL ("Structured Query Language"), the most important query language based on the relational model, will be covered starting in Chapter 6. However, a brief introduction to relations will give the reader a hint of the simplicity of the model, and an SQL sample will suggest how the relational model promotes queries written at a very high level, avoiding details of "navigation" through the database.

Example 1.1 : Relations are tables. Their columns are headed by *attributes*, which describe the entries in the column. For instance, a relation named `Accounts`, recording bank accounts, their balance, and type might look like:

accountNo	*balance*	*type*
12345	1000.00	savings
67890	2846.92	checking
...	...	...

---

[1] *CODASYL Data Base Task Group April 1971 Report*, ACM, New York.

[2] Codd, E. F., "A relational model for large shared data banks," *Comm. ACM*, **13**:6, pp. 377–387, 1970.

Heading the columns are the three attributes: `accountNo`, `balance`, and `type`. Below the attributes are the rows, or *tuples*. Here we show two tuples of the relation explicitly, and the dots below them suggest that there would be many more tuples, one for each account at the bank. The first tuple says that account number 12345 has a balance of one thousand dollars, and it is a savings account. The second tuple says that account 67890 is a checking account with $2846.92.

Suppose we wanted to know the balance of account 67890. We could ask this query in SQL as follows:

```
SELECT balance
FROM Accounts
WHERE accountNo = 67890;
```

For another example, we could ask for the savings accounts with negative balances by:

```
SELECT accountNo
FROM Accounts
WHERE type = 'savings' AND balance < 0;
```

We do not expect that these two examples are enough to make the reader an expert SQL programmer, but they should convey the high-level nature of the SQL "select-from-where" statement. In principle, they ask the DBMS to

1. Examine all the tuples of the relation `Accounts` mentioned in the `FROM` clause,

2. Pick out those tuples that satisfy some criterion indicated in the `WHERE` clause, and

3. Produce as an answer certain attributes of those tuples, as indicated in the `SELECT` clause.

In practice, the system must "optimize" the query and find an efficient way to answer the query, even though the relations involved in the query may be very large. □

By 1990, relational database systems were the norm. Yet the database field continues to evolve, and new issues and approaches to the management of data surface regularly. In the balance of this section, we shall consider some of the modern trends in database systems.

1.1.3 Smaller and Smaller Systems

Originally, DBMS's were large, expensive software systems running on large computers. The size was necessary, because to store a gigabyte of data required a large computer system. Today, many gigabytes fit on a single disk, and it is quite feasible to run a DBMS on a personal computer. Thus, database systems based on the relational model have become available for even very small machines, and they are beginning to appear as a common tool for computer applications, much as spreadsheets and word processors did before them.

1.1.4   Bigger and Bigger Systems

On the other hand, a gigabyte isn't much data. Corporate databases often occupy hundreds of gigabytes. Further, as storage becomes cheaper people find new reasons to store greater amounts of data. For example, retail chains often store *terabytes* (a terabyte is 1000 gigabytes, or 10^{12} bytes) of information recording the history of every sale made over a long period of time (for planning inventory; we shall have more to say about this matter in Section 1.1.7).

Further, databases no longer focus on storing simple data items such as integers or short character strings. They can store images, audio, video, and many other kinds of data that take comparatively huge amounts of space. For instance, an hour of video consumes about a gigabyte. Databases storing images from satellites can involve *petabytes* (1000 terabytes, or 10^{15} bytes) of data.

Handling such large databases required several technological advances. For example, databases of modest size are today stored on arrays of disks, which are called *secondary storage devices* (compared to main memory, which is "primary" storage). One could even argue that what distinguishes database systems from other software is, more than anything else, the fact that database systems routinely assume data is too big to fit in main memory and must be located primarily on disk at all times. The following two trends allow database systems to deal with larger amounts of data, faster.

Tertiary Storage

The largest databases today require more than disks. Several kinds of *tertiary storage devices* have been developed. Tertiary devices, perhaps storing a terabyte each, require much more time to access a given item than does a disk. While typical disks can access any item in 10-20 milliseconds, a tertiary device may take several seconds. Tertiary storage devices involve transporting an object, upon which the desired data item is stored, to a reading device. This movement is performed by a robotic conveyance of some sort.

For example, compact disks (CD's) or digital versatile disks (DVD's) may be the storage medium in a tertiary device. An arm mounted on a track goes to a particular disk, picks it up, carries it to a reader, and loads the disk into the reader.

Parallel Computing

The ability to store enormous volumes of data is important, but it would be of little use if we could not access large amounts of that data quickly. Thus, very large databases also require speed enhancers. One important speedup is through index structures, which we shall mention in Section 1.2.2 and cover extensively in Chapter 13. Another way to process more data in a given time is to use parallelism. This parallelism manifests itself in various ways.

For example, since the rate at which data can be read from a given disk is fairly low, a few megabytes per second, we can speed processing if we use many disks and read them in parallel (even if the data originates on tertiary storage, it is "cached" on disks before being accessed by the DBMS). These disks may be part of an organized parallel machine, or they may be components of a distributed system, in which many machines, each responsible for a part of the database, communicate over a high-speed network when needed.

Of course, the ability to move data quickly, like the ability to store large amounts of data, does not by itself guarantee that queries can be answered quickly. We still need to use algorithms that break queries up in ways that allow parallel computers or networks of distributed computers to make effective use of all the resources. Thus, parallel and distributed management of very large databases remains an active area of research and development; we consider some of its important ideas in Section 15.9.

1.1.5   Client-Server and Multi-Tier Architectures

Many varieties of modern software use a *client-server* architecture, in which requests by one process (the *client*) are sent to another process (the *server*) for execution. Database systems are no exception, and it has become increasingly common to divide the work of a DBMS into a server process and one or more client processes.

In the simplest client-server architecture, the entire DBMS is a server, except for the query interfaces that interact with the user and send queries or other commands across to the server. For example, relational systems generally use the SQL language for representing requests from the client to the server. The database server then sends the answer, in the form of a table or relation, back to the client. The relationship between client and server can get more complex, especially when answers are extremely large. We shall have more to say about this matter in Section 1.1.6.

There is also a trend to put more work in the client, since the server will be a bottleneck if there are many simultaneous database users. In the recent proliferation of system architectures in which databases are used to provide dynamically-generated content for Web sites, the two-tier (client-server) architecture gives way to three (or even more) tiers. The DBMS continues to act as a server, but its client is typically an *application server*, which manages connections to the database, transactions, authorization, and other aspects. Application servers in turn have clients such as Web servers, which support end-users or other applications.

1.1.6   Multimedia Data

Another important trend in database systems is the inclusion of multimedia data. By "multimedia" we mean information that represents a signal of some sort. Common forms of multimedia data include video, audio, radar signals, satellite images, and documents or pictures in various encodings. These forms have in common that they are much larger than the earlier forms of data — integers, character strings of fixed length, and so on — and of vastly varying sizes.

The storage of multimedia data has forced DBMS's to expand in several ways. For example, the operations that one performs on multimedia data are not the simple ones suitable for traditional data forms. Thus, while one might search a bank database for accounts that have a negative balance, comparing each balance with the real number 0.0, it is not feasible to search a database of pictures for those that show a face that "looks like" a particular image.

To allow users to create and use complex data operations such as image-processing, DBMS's have had to incorporate the ability of users to introduce functions of their own choosing. Often, the object-oriented approach is used for such extensions, even in relational systems, which are then dubbed "object-relational." We shall take up object-oriented database programming in various places, including Chapters 4 and 9.

The size of multimedia objects also forces the DBMS to modify the storage manager so that objects or tuples of a gigabyte or more can be accommodated. Among the many problems that such large elements present is the delivery of answers to queries. In a conventional, relational database, an answer is a set of tuples. These tuples would be delivered to the client by the database server as a whole.

However, suppose the answer to a query is a video clip a gigabyte long. It is not feasible for the server to deliver the gigabyte to the client as a whole. For one reason it takes too long and will prevent the server from handling other requests. For another, the client may want only a small part of the film clip, but doesn't have a way to ask for exactly what it wants without seeing the initial portion of the clip. For a third reason, even if the client wants the whole clip, perhaps in order to play it on a screen, it is sufficient to deliver the clip at a fixed rate over the course of an hour (the amount of time it takes to play a gigabyte of compressed video). Thus, the storage system of a DBMS supporting multimedia data has to be prepared to deliver answers in an interactive mode, passing a piece of the answer to the client on request or at a fixed rate.

1.1.7   Information Integration

As information becomes ever more essential in our work and play, we find that existing information resources are being used in many new ways. For instance, consider a company that wants to provide on-line catalogs for all its products, so that people can use the World Wide Web to browse its products and place on-line orders. A large company has many divisions. Each division may have built its own database of products independently of other divisions. These divisions may use different DBMS's, different structures for information, perhaps even different terms to mean the same thing or the same term to mean different things.

Example 1.2 : Imagine a company with several divisions that manufacture disks. One division's catalog might represent rotation rate in revolutions per second, another in revolutions per minute. Another might have neglected to represent rotation speed at all. A division manufacturing floppy disks might refer to them as "disks," while a division manufacturing hard disks might call *them* "disks" as well. The number of tracks on a disk might be referred to as "tracks" in one division, but "cylinders" in another.   □

Central control is not always the answer. Divisions may have invested large amounts of money in their database long before information integration across divisions was recognized as a problem. A division may have been an independent company, recently acquired. For these or other reasons, these so-called *legacy databases* cannot be replaced easily. Thus, the company must build some structure on top of the legacy databases to present to customers a unified view of products across the company.

One popular approach is the creation of *data warehouses*, where information from many legacy databases is copied, with the appropriate translation, to a central database. As the legacy databases change, the warehouse is updated, but not necessarily instantaneously updated. A common scheme is for the warehouse to be reconstructed each night, when the legacy databases are likely to be less busy.

The legacy databases are thus able to continue serving the purposes for which they were created. New functions, such as providing an on-line catalog service through the Web, are done at the data warehouse. We also see data warehouses serving needs for planning and analysis. For example, company analysts may run queries against the warehouse looking for sales trends, in order to better plan inventory and production. *Data mining*, the search for interesting and unusual patterns in data, has also been enabled by the construction of data warehouses, and there are claims of enhanced sales through exploitation of patterns discovered in this way. These and other issues of information integration are discussed in Chapter 20.

1.2   Overview of a Database Management System

In Fig. 1.1 we see an outline of a complete DBMS. Single boxes represent system components, while double boxes represent in-memory data structures. The solid lines indicate control and data flow, while dashed lines indicate data flow only.

Since the diagram is complicated, we shall consider the details in several stages. First, at the top, we suggest that there are two distinct sources of commands to the DBMS:

1. Conventional users and application programs that ask for data or modify data.

2. A *database administrator*: a person or persons responsible for the structure or *schema* of the database.

1.2.1   Data-Definition Language Commands

The second kind of command is the simpler to process, and we show its trail beginning at the upper right side of Fig. 1.1. For example, the database administrator, or *DBA*, for a university registrar's database might decide that there should be a table or relation with columns for a student, a course the student has taken, and a grade for that student in that course. The DBA might also decide that the only allowable grades are A, B, C, D, and F. This structure and constraint information is all part of the schema of the database. It is shown in Fig. 1.1 as entered by the DBA, who needs special authority to execute schema-altering commands, since these can have profound effects on the database. These schema-altering *DDL commands* ("DDL" stands for "data-definition language") are parsed by a DDL processor and passed to the execution engine, which then goes through the index/file/record manager to alter the *metadata*, that is, the schema information for the database.

1.2.2   Overview of Query Processing

The great majority of interactions with the DBMS follow the path on the left side of Fig. 1.1. A user or an application program initiates some action that does not affect the schema of the database, but may affect the content of the database (if the action is a modification command) or will extract data from the database (if the action is a query). Remember from Section 1.1 that the language in which these commands are expressed is called a data-manipulation language (*DML*) or somewhat colloquially a query language. There are many data-manipulation languages available, but SQL, which was mentioned in Example 1.1, is by far the most commonly used. DML statements are handled by two separate subsystems, as follows.

Answering the query

The query is parsed and optimized by a *query compiler*. The resulting *query plan*, or sequence of actions the DBMS will perform to answer the query, is passed to the *execution engine*. The execution engine issues a sequence of requests for small pieces of data, typically records or tuples of a relation, to a resource manager that knows about *data files* (holding relations), the format

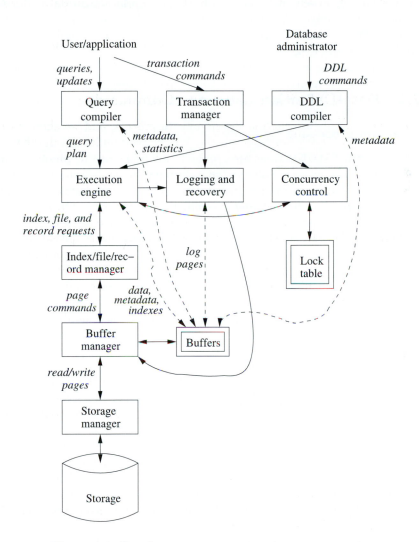

Figure 1.1: Database management system components

and size of records in those files, and *index files*, which help find elements of data files quickly.

The requests for data are translated into pages and these requests are passed to the *buffer manager*. We shall discuss the role of the buffer manager in Section 1.2.3, but briefly, its task is to bring appropriate portions of the data from secondary storage (disk, normally) where it is kept permanently, to main-memory buffers. Normally, the page or "disk block" is the unit of transfer between buffers and disk.

The buffer manager communicates with a storage manager to get data from disk. The storage manager might involve operating-system commands, but more typically, the DBMS issues commands directly to the disk controller.

Transaction processing

Queries and other DML actions are grouped into *transactions*, which are units that must be executed atomically and in isolation from one another. Often each query or modification action is a transaction by itself. In addition, the execution of transactions must be *durable*, meaning that the effect of any completed transaction must be preserved even if the system fails in some way right after completion of the transaction. We divide the transaction processor into two major parts:

1. A *concurrency-control manager*, or *scheduler*, responsible for assuring atomicity and isolation of transactions, and

2. A *logging and recovery manager*, responsible for the durability of transactions.

We shall consider these components further in Section 1.2.4.

1.2.3   Storage and Buffer Management

The data of a database normally resides in secondary storage; in today's computer systems "secondary storage" generally means magnetic disk. However, to perform any useful operation on data, that data must be in main memory. It is the job of the *storage manager* to control the placement of data on disk and its movement between disk and main memory.

In a simple database system, the storage manager might be nothing more than the file system of the underlying operating system. However, for efficiency purposes, DBMS's normally control storage on the disk directly, at least under some circumstances. The *storage manager* keeps track of the location of files on the disk and obtains the block or blocks containing a file on request from the buffer manager. Recall that disks are generally divided into *disk blocks*, which are regions of contiguous storage containing a large number of bytes, perhaps 2^{12} or 2^{14} (about 4000 to 16,000 bytes).

The *buffer manager* is responsible for partitioning the available main memory into *buffers*, which are page-sized regions into which disk blocks can be

transferred. Thus, all DBMS components that need information from the disk
will interact with the buffers and the buffer manager, either directly or through
the execution engine. The kinds of information that various components may
need include:

1. *Data*: the contents of the database itself.

2. *Metadata*: the database schema that describes the structure of, and constraints on, the database.

3. *Statistics*: information gathered and stored by the DBMS about data
properties such as the sizes of, and values in, various relations or other
components of the database.

4. *Indexes*: data structures that support efficient access to the data.

A more complete discussion of the buffer manager and its role appears in Section 15.7.

1.2.4 Transaction Processing

It is normal to group one or more database operations into a *transaction*, which
is a unit of work that must be executed atomically and in apparent isolation
from other transactions. In addition, a DBMS offers the guarantee of durability:
that the work of a completed transaction will never be lost. The *transaction
manager* therefore accepts *transaction commands* from an application, which
tell the transaction manager when transactions begin and end, as well as information about the expectations of the application (some may not wish to require
atomicity, for example). The transaction processor performs the following tasks:

1. *Logging*: In order to assure durability, every change in the database is
logged separately on disk. The *log manager* follows one of several policies
designed to assure that no matter when a system failure or "crash" occurs,
a *recovery manager* will be able to examine the log of changes and restore
the database to some consistent state. The log manager initially writes
the log in buffers and negotiates with the buffer manager to make sure that
buffers are written to disk (where data can survive a crash) at appropriate
times.

2. *Concurrency control*: Transactions must appear to execute in isolation.
But in most systems, there will in truth be many transactions executing
at once. Thus, the scheduler (concurrency-control manager) must assure
that the individual actions of multiple transactions are executed in such
an order that the net effect is the same as if the transactions had in
fact executed in their entirety, one-at-a-time. A typical scheduler does
its work by maintaining *locks* on certain pieces of the database. These
locks prevent two transactions from accessing the same piece of data in

---

The ACID Properties of Transactions

Properly implemented transactions are commonly said to meet the "ACID test," where:

- "A" stands for "atomicity," the all-or-nothing execution of transactions.

- "I" stands for "isolation," the fact that each transaction must appear to be executed as if no other transaction is executing at the same time.

- "D" stands for "durability," the condition that the effect on the database of a transaction must never be lost, once the transaction has completed.

The remaining letter, "C," stands for "consistency." That is, all databases have consistency constraints, or expectations about relationships among data elements (e.g., account balances may not be negative). Transactions are expected to preserve the consistency of the database. We discuss the expression of consistency constraints in a database schema in Chapter 7, while Section 18.1 begins a discussion of how consistency is maintained by the DBMS.

---

ways that interact badly. Locks are generally stored in a main-memory *lock table*, as suggested by Fig. 1.1. The scheduler affects the execution of queries and other database operations by forbidding the execution engine from accessing locked parts of the database.

3. *Deadlock resolution*: As transactions compete for resources through the locks that the scheduler grants, they can get into a situation where none can proceed because each needs something another transaction has. The transaction manager has the responsibility to intervene and cancel ("rollback" or "abort") one or more transactions to let the others proceed.

1.2.5   The Query Processor

The portion of the DBMS that most affects the performance that the user sees is the *query processor*. In Fig. 1.1 the query processor is represented by two components:

1. The *query compiler*, which translates the query into an internal form called a *query plan*. The latter is a sequence of operations to be performed on the data. Often the operations in a query plan are implementations of

"relational algebra" operations, which are discussed in Section 5.2. The query compiler consists of three major units:

(a) A *query parser*, which builds a tree structure from the textual form of the query.

(b) A *query preprocessor*, which performs semantic checks on the query (e.g., making sure all relations mentioned by the query actually exist), and performing some tree transformations to turn the parse tree into a tree of algebraic operators representing the initial query plan.

(c) A *query optimizer*, which transforms the initial query plan into the best available sequence of operations on the actual data.

The query compiler uses metadata and statistics about the data to decide which sequence of operations is likely to be the fastest. For example, the existence of an *index*, which is a specialized data structure that facilitates access to data, given values for one or more components of that data, can make one plan much faster than another.

2. The *execution engine*, which has the responsibility for executing each of the steps in the chosen query plan. The execution engine interacts with most of the other components of the DBMS, either directly or through the buffers. It must get the data from the database into buffers in order to manipulate that data. It needs to interact with the scheduler to avoid accessing data that is locked, and with the log manager to make sure that all database changes are properly logged.

1.3 Outline of Database-System Studies

Ideas related to database systems can be divided into three broad categories:

1. *Design of databases.* How does one develop a useful database? What kinds of information go into the database? How is the information structured? What assumptions are made about types or values of data items? How do data items connect?

2. *Database programming.* How does one express queries and other operations on the database? How does one use other capabilities of a DBMS, such as transactions or constraints, in an application? How is database programming combined with conventional programming?

3. *Database system implementation.* How does one build a DBMS, including such matters as query processing, transaction processing and organizing storage for efficient access?

How Indexes Are Implemented

The reader may have learned in a course on data structures that a hash table is a very efficient way to build an index. Early DBMS's did use hash tables extensively. Today, the most common data structure is called a *B-tree*; the "B" stands for "balanced." A B-tree is a generalization of a balanced binary search tree. However, while each node of a binary tree has up to two children, the B-tree nodes have a large number of children. Given that B-trees normally reside on disk rather than in main memory, the B-tree is designed so that each node occupies a full disk block. Since typical systems use disk blocks on the order of 2^{12} bytes (4096 bytes), there can be hundreds of pointers to children in a single block of a B-tree. Thus, search of a B-tree rarely involves more than a few levels.

The true cost of disk operations generally is proportional to the number of disk blocks accessed. Thus, searches of a B-tree, which typically examine only a few disk blocks, are much more efficient than would be a binary-tree search, which typically visits nodes found on many different disk blocks. This distinction, between B-trees and binary search trees, is but one of many examples where the most appropriate data structure for data stored on disk is different from the data structures used for algorithms that run in main memory.

1.3.1 Database Design

Chapter 2 begins with a high-level notation for expressing database designs, called the *entity-relationship model*. We introduce in Chapter 3 the relational model, which is the model used by the most widely adopted DBMS's, and which we touched upon briefly in Section 1.1.2. We show how to translate entity-relationship designs into relational designs, or "relational database schemas." Later, in Section 6.6, we show how to render relational database schemas formally in the data-definition portion of the SQL language.

Chapter 3 also introduces the reader to the notion of "dependencies," which are formally stated assumptions about relationships among tuples in a relation. Dependencies allow us to improve relational database designs, through a process known as "normalization" of relations.

In Chapter 4 we look at object-oriented approaches to database design. There, we cover the language ODL, which allows one to describe databases in a high-level, object-oriented fashion. We also look at ways in which object-oriented design has been combined with relational modeling, to yield the so-called "object-relational" model. Finally, Chapter 4 also introduces "semistructured data" as an especially flexible database model, and we see its modern embodiment in the document language XML.

1.3.2 Database Programming

Chapters 5 through 10 cover database programming. We start in Chapter 5 with an abstract treatment of queries in the relational model, introducing the family of operators on relations that form "relational algebra."

Chapters 6 through 8 are devoted to SQL programming. As we mentioned, SQL is the dominant query language of the day. Chapter 6 introduces basic ideas regarding queries in SQL and the expression of database schemas in SQL. Chapter 7 covers aspects of SQL concerning constraints and triggers on the data.

Chapter 8 covers certain advanced aspects of SQL programming. First, while the simplest model of SQL programming is a stand-alone, generic query interface, in practice most SQL programming is embedded in a larger program that is written in a conventional language, such as C. In Chapter 8 we learn how to connect SQL statements with a surrounding program and to pass data from the database to the program's variables and vice versa. This chapter also covers how one uses SQL features that specify transactions, connect clients to servers, and authorize access to databases by nonowners.

In Chapter 9 we turn our attention to standards for object-oriented database programming. Here, we consider two directions. The first, OQL (Object Query Language), can be seen as an attempt to make C++, or other object-oriented programming languages, compatible with the demands of high-level database programming. The second, which is the object-oriented features recently adopted in the SQL standard, can be viewed as an attempt to make relational databases and SQL compatible with object-oriented programming.

Finally, in Chapter 10, we return to the study of abstract query languages that we began in Chapter 5. Here, we study logic-based languages and see how they have been used to extend the capabilities of modern SQL.

1.3.3 Database System Implementation

The third part of the book concerns how one can implement a DBMS. The subject of database system implementation in turn can be divided roughly into three parts:

1. *Storage management*: how secondary storage is used effectively to hold data and allow it to be accessed quickly.

2. *Query processing*: how queries expressed in a very high-level language such as SQL can be executed efficiently.

3. *Transaction management*: how to support transactions with the ACID properties discussed in Section 1.2.4.

Each of these topics is covered by several chapters of the book.

Storage-Management Overview

Chapter 11 introduces the memory hierarchy. However, since secondary storage, especially disk, is so central to the way a DBMS manages data, we examine in the greatest detail the way data is stored and accessed on disk. The "block model" for disk-based data is introduced; it influences the way almost everything is done in a database system.

Chapter 12 relates the storage of data elements — relations, tuples, attribute-values, and their equivalents in other data models — to the requirements of the block model of data. Then we look at the important data structures that are used for the construction of indexes. Recall that an index is a data structure that supports efficient access to data. Chapter 13 covers the important one-dimensional index structures — indexed-sequential files, B-trees, and hash tables. These indexes are commonly used in a DBMS to support queries in which a value for an attribute is given and the tuples with that value are desired. B-trees also are used for access to a relation sorted by a given attribute. Chapter 14 discusses multidimensional indexes, which are data structures for specialized applications such as geographic databases, where queries typically ask for the contents of some region. These index structures can also support complex SQL queries that limit the values of two or more attributes, and some of these structures are beginning to appear in commercial DBMS's.

Query-Processing Overview

Chapter 15 covers the basics of query execution. We learn a number of algorithms for efficient implementation of the operations of relational algebra. These algorithms are designed to be efficient when data is stored on disk and are in some cases rather different from analogous main-memory algorithms.

In Chapter 16 we consider the architecture of the query compiler and optimizer. We begin with the parsing of queries and their semantic checking. Next, we consider the conversion of queries from SQL to relational algebra and the selection of a *logical query plan*, that is, an algebraic expression that represents the particular operations to be performed on data and the necessary constraints regarding order of operations. Finally, we explore the selection of a *physical query plan*, in which the particular order of operations and the algorithm used to implement each operation have been specified.

Transaction-Processing Overview

In Chapter 17 we see how a DBMS supports durability of transactions. The central idea is that a log of all changes to the database is made. Anything that is in main-memory but not on disk can be lost in a crash (say, if the power supply is interrupted). Therefore we have to be careful to move from buffer to disk, in the proper order, both the database changes themselves and the log of what changes were made. There are several log strategies available, but each limits our freedom of action in some ways.

Then, we take up the matter of concurrency control — assuring atomicity and isolation — in Chapter 18. We view transactions as sequences of operations that read or write database elements. The major topic of the chapter is how to manage locks on database elements: the different types of locks that may be used, and the ways that transactions may be allowed to acquire locks and release their locks on elements. Also studied are a number of ways to assure atomicity and isolation without using locks.

Chapter 19 concludes our study of transaction processing. We consider the interaction between the requirements of logging, as discussed in Chapter 17, and the requirements of concurrency that were discussed in Chapter 18. Handling of deadlocks, another important function of the transaction manager, is covered here as well. The extension of concurrency control to a distributed environment is also considered in Chapter 19. Finally, we introduce the possibility that transactions are "long," taking hours or days rather than milliseconds. A long transaction cannot lock data without causing chaos among other potential users of that data, which forces us to rethink concurrency control for applications that involve long transactions.

1.3.4   Information Integration Overview

Much of the recent evolution of database systems has been toward capabilities that allow different *data sources*, which may be databases and/or information resources that are not managed by a DBMS, to work together in a larger whole. We introduced you to these issues briefly, in Section 1.1.7. Thus, in the final Chapter 20, we study important aspects of information integration. We discuss the principal modes of integration, including translated and integrated copies of sources called a "data warehouse," and virtual "views" of a collection of sources, through what is called a "mediator."

1.4   Summary of Chapter 1

✦ *Database Management Systems*: A DBMS is characterized by the ability to support efficient access to large amounts of data, which persists over time. It is also characterized by support for powerful query languages and for durable transactions that can execute concurrently in a manner that appears atomic and independent of other transactions.

✦ *Comparison With File Systems*: Conventional file systems are inadequate as database systems, because they fail to support efficient search, efficient modifications to small pieces of data, complex queries, controlled buffering of useful data in main memory, or atomic and independent execution of transactions.

✦ *Relational Database Systems*: Today, most database systems are based on the relational model of data, which organizes information into tables. SQL is the language most often used in these systems.

✦ *Secondary and Tertiary Storage*: Large databases are stored on secondary storage devices, usually disks. The largest databases require tertiary storage devices, which are several orders of magnitude more capacious than disks, but also several orders of magnitude slower.

✦ *Client-Server Systems*: Database management systems usually support a client-server architecture, with major database components at the server and the client used to interface with the user.

✦ *Future Systems*: Major trends in database systems include support for very large "multimedia" objects such as videos or images and the integration of information from many separate information sources into a single database.

✦ *Database Languages*: There are languages or language components for defining the structure of data (data-definition languages) and for querying and modification of the data (data-manipulation languages).

✦ *Components of a DBMS*: The major components of a database management system are the storage manager, the query processor, and the transaction manager.

✦ *The Storage Manager*: This component is responsible for storing data, metadata (information about the schema or structure of the data), indexes (data structures to speed the access to data), and logs (records of changes to the database). This material is kept on disk. An important storage-management component is the buffer manager, which keeps portions of the disk contents in main memory.

✦ *The Query Processor*: This component parses queries, optimizes them by selecting a query plan, and executes the plan on the stored data.

✦ *The Transaction Manager*: This component is responsible for logging database changes to support recovery after a system crashes. It also supports concurrent execution of transactions in a way that assures atomicity (a transaction is performed either completely or not at all), and isolation (transactions are executed as if there were no other concurrently executing transactions).

1.5 References for Chapter 1

Today, on-line searchable bibliographies cover essentially all recent papers concerning database systems. Thus, in this book, we shall not try to be exhaustive in our citations, but rather shall mention only the papers of historical importance and major secondary sources or useful surveys. One searchable index of database research papers has been constructed by Michael Ley [5]. Alf-Christian Achilles maintains a searchable directory of many indexes relevant to the database field [1].

While many prototype implementations of database systems contributed to the technology of the field, two of the most widely known are the System R project at IBM Almaden Research Center [3] and the INGRES project at Berkeley [7]. Each was an early relational system and helped establish this type of system as the dominant database technology. Many of the research papers that shaped the database field are found in [6].

The 1998 "Asilomar report" [4] is the most recent in a series of reports on database-system research and directions. It also has references to earlier reports of this type.

You can find more about the theory of database systems than is covered here from [2], [8], and [9].

1. `http://liinwww.ira.uka.de/bibliography/Database` .

2. Abiteboul, S., R. Hull, and V. Vianu, *Foundations of Databases*, Addison-Wesley, Reading, MA, 1995.

3. M. M. Astrahan et al., "System R: a relational approach to database management," *ACM Trans. on Database Systems* **1**:2, pp. 97–137, 1976.

4. P. A. Bernstein et al., "The Asilomar report on database research," `http://www.acm.org/sigmod/record/issues/9812/asilomar.html` .

5. `http://www.informatik.uni-trier.de/~ley/db/index.html` . A mirror site is found at `http://www.acm.org/sigmod/dblp/db/index.html` .

6. Stonebraker, M. and J. M. Hellerstein (eds.), *Readings in Database Systems*, Morgan-Kaufmann, San Francisco, 1998.

7. M. Stonebraker, E. Wong, P. Kreps, and G. Held, "The design and implementation of INGRES," *ACM Trans. on Database Systems* **1**:3, pp. 189–222, 1976.

8. Ullman, J. D., *Principles of Database and Knowledge-Base Systems, Volume I*, Computer Science Press, New York, 1988.

9. Ullman, J. D., *Principles of Database and Knowledge-Base Systems, Volume II*, Computer Science Press, New York, 1989.

Chapter 2

The Entity-Relationship Data Model

The process of designing a database begins with an analysis of what information the database must hold and what are the relationships among components of that information. Often, the structure of the database, called the *database schema*, is specified in one of several languages or notations suitable for expressing designs. After due consideration, the design is committed to a form in which it can be input to a DBMS, and the database takes on physical existence.

In this book, we shall use several design notations. We begin in this chapter with a traditional and popular approach called the "entity-relationship" (E/R) model. This model is graphical in nature, with boxes and arrows representing the essential data elements and their connections.

In Chapter 3 we turn our attention to the relational model, where the world is represented by a collection of tables. The relational model is somewhat restricted in the structures it can represent. However, the model is extremely simple and useful, and it is the model on which the major commercial DBMS's depend today. Often, database designers begin by developing a schema using the E/R or an object-based model, then translate the schema to the relational model for implementation.

Other models are covered in Chapter 4. In Section 4.2, we shall introduce ODL (Object Definition Language), the standard for object-oriented databases. Next, we see how object-oriented ideas have affected relational DBMS's, yielding a model often called "object-relational."

Section 4.6 introduces another modeling approach, called "semistructured data." This model has an unusual amount of flexibility in the structures that the data may form. We also discuss, in Section 4.7, the XML standard for modeling data as a hierarchically structured document, using "tags" (like HTML tags) to indicate the role played by text elements. XML is an important embodiment of the semistructured data model.

Figure 2.1 suggests how the E/R model is used in database design. We

Figure 2.1: The database modeling and implementation process

start with ideas about the information we want to model and render them in the E/R model. The abstract E/R design is then converted to a schema in the data-specification language of some DBMS. Most commonly, this DBMS uses the relational model. If so, then by a fairly mechanical process that we shall discuss in Section 3.2, the abstract design is converted to a concrete, relational design, called a "relational database schema."

It is worth noting that, while DBMS's sometimes use a model other than relational or object-relational, there are no DBMS's that use the E/R model directly. The reason is that this model is not a sufficiently good match for the efficient data structures that must underlie the database.

2.1 Elements of the E/R Model

The most common model for abstract representation of the structure of a database is the *entity-relationship model* (or *E/R model*). In the E/R model, the structure of data is represented graphically, as an "entity-relationship diagram," using three principal element types:

1. Entity sets,

2. Attributes, and

3. Relationships.

We shall cover each in turn.

2.1.1 Entity Sets

An *entity* is an abstract object of some sort, and a collection of similar entities forms an *entity set*. There is some similarity between the entity and an "object" in the sense of object-oriented programming. Likewise, an entity set bears some resemblance to a class of objects. However, the E/R model is a static concept, involving the structure of data and not the operations on data. Thus, one would not expect to find methods associated with an entity set as one would with a class.

Example 2.1: We shall use as a running example a database about movies, their stars, the studios that produce them, and other aspects of movies. Each movie is an entity, and the set of all movies constitutes an entity set. Likewise, the stars are entities, and the set of stars is an entity set. A studio is another

---

E/R Model Variations

In some versions of the E/R model, the type of an attribute can be either:

1. Atomic, as in the version presented here.

2. A "struct," as in C, or tuple with a fixed number of atomic components.

3. A set of values of one type: either atomic or a "struct" type.

For example, the type of an attribute in such a model could be a set of pairs, each pair consisting of an integer and a string.

---

kind of entity, and the set of studios is a third entity set that will appear in our examples. □

2.1.2 Attributes

Entity sets have associated *attributes*, which are properties of the entities in that set. For instance, the entity set *Movies* might be given attributes such as *title* (the name of the movie) or *length*, the number of minutes the movie runs. In our version of the E/R model, we shall assume that attributes are atomic values, such as strings, integers, or reals. There are other variations of this model in which attributes can have some limited structure; see the box on "E/R Model Variations."

2.1.3 Relationships

Relationships are connections among two or more entity sets. For instance, if *Movies* and *Stars* are two entity sets, we could have a relationship *Stars-in* that connects movies and stars. The intent is that a movie entity m is related to a star entity s by the relationship *Stars-in* if s appears in movie m. While binary relationships, those between two entity sets, are by far the most common type of relationship, the E/R model allows relationships to involve any number of entity sets. We shall defer discussion of these multiway relationships until Section 2.1.7.

2.1.4 Entity-Relationship Diagrams

An *E/R diagram* is a graph representing entity sets, attributes, and relationships. Elements of each of these kinds are represented by nodes of the graph, and we use a special shape of node to indicate the kind, as follows:

- Entity sets are represented by rectangles.

- Attributes are represented by ovals.

- Relationships are represented by diamonds.

Edges connect an entity set to its attributes and also connect a relationship to its entity sets.

Example 2.2: In Fig. 2.2 is an E/R diagram that represents a simple database about movies. The entity sets are *Movies*, *Stars*, and *Studios*.

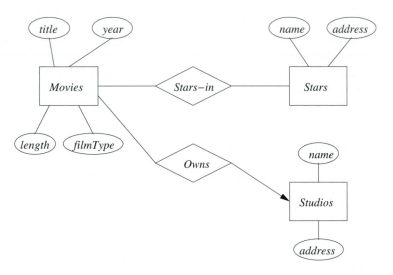

Figure 2.2: An entity-relationship diagram for the movie database

The *Movies* entity set has four attributes: *title*, *year* (in which the movie was made), *length*, and *filmType* (either "color" or "blackAndWhite"). The other two entity sets *Stars* and *Studios* happen to have the same two attributes: *name* and *address*, each with an obvious meaning. We also see two relationships in the diagram:

1. *Stars-in* is a relationship connecting each movie to the stars of that movie. This relationship consequently also connects stars to the movies in which they appeared.

2. *Owns* connects each movie to the studio that owns the movie. The arrow pointing to entity set *Studios* in Fig. 2.2 indicates that each movie is owned by a unique studio. We shall discuss uniqueness constraints such as this one in Section 2.1.6.

□

2.1.5   Instances of an E/R Diagram

E/R diagrams are a notation for describing the *schema* of databases, that is, their structure. A database described by an E/R diagram will contain particular data, which we call the database *instance*. Specifically, for each entity set, the database instance will have a particular finite set of entities. Each of these entities has particular values for each attribute. Remember, this data is abstract only; we do not store E/R data directly in a database. Rather, imagining this data exists helps us to think about our design, before we convert to relations and the data takes on physical existence.

The database instance also includes specific choices for the relationships of the diagram. A relationship R that connects n entity sets $E_1, E_2, \ldots, E_n$ has an instance that consists of a finite set of lists $(e_1, e_2, \ldots, e_n)$, where each e_i is chosen from the entities that are in the current instance of entity set E_i. We regard each of these lists of n entities as "connected" by relationship R.

This set of lists is called the *relationship set* for the current instance of R. It is often helpful to visualize a relationship set as a table. The columns of the table are headed by the names of the entity sets involved in the relationship, and each list of connected entities occupies one row of the table.

Example 2.3: An instance of the *Stars-in* relationship could be visualized as a table with pairs such as:

Movies	*Stars*
Basic Instinct	Sharon Stone
Total Recall	Arnold Schwarzenegger
Total Recall	Sharon Stone

The members of the relationship set are the rows of the table. For instance,

$$\text{(Basic Instinct, Sharon Stone)}$$

is a tuple in the relationship set for the current instance of relationship *Stars-in*.
□

2.1.6   Multiplicity of Binary E/R Relationships

In general, a binary relationship can connect any member of one of its entity sets to any number of members of the other entity set. However, it is common for there to be a restriction on the "multiplicity" of a relationship. Suppose R is a relationship connecting entity sets E and F. Then:

- If each member of E can be connected by R to at most one member of F, then we say that R is *many-one* from E to F. Note that in a many-one relationship from E to F, each entity in F can be connected to many members of E. Similarly, if instead a member of F can be connected by R to at most one member of E, then we say R is many-one from F to E (or equivalently, one-many from E to F).

- If R is both many-one from E to F and many-one from F to E, then we say that R is *one-one*. In a one-one relationship an entity of either entity set can be connected to at most one entity of the other set.

- If R is neither many-one from E to F or from F to E, then we say R is *many-many*.

As we mentioned in Example 2.2, arrows can be used to indicate the multiplicity of a relationship in an E/R diagram. If a relationship is many-one from entity set E to entity set F, then we place an arrow entering F. The arrow indicates that each entity in set E is related to at most one entity in set F. Unless there is also an arrow on the edge to E, an entity in F may be related to many entities in E.

Example 2.4: Following this principle, a one-one relationship between entity sets E and F is represented by arrows pointing to both E and F. For instance, Fig. 2.3 shows two entity sets, *Studios* and *Presidents*, and the relationship *Runs* between them (attributes are omitted). We assume that a president can run only one studio and a studio has only one president, so this relationship is one-one, as indicated by the two arrows, one entering each entity set.

Figure 2.3: A one-one relationship

Remember that the arrow means "at most one"; it does not guarantee existence of an entity of the set pointed to. Thus, in Fig. 2.3, we would expect that a "president" is surely associated with some studio; how could they be a "president" otherwise? However, a studio might not have a president at some particular time, so the arrow from *Runs* to *Presidents* truly means "at most one" and not "exactly one." We shall discuss the distinction further in Section 2.3.6. □

2.1.7 Multiway Relationships

The E/R model makes it convenient to define relationships involving more than two entity sets. In practice, ternary (three-way) or higher-degree relationships are rare, but they are occasionally necessary to reflect the true state of affairs. A multiway relationship in an E/R diagram is represented by lines from the relationship diamond to each of the involved entity sets.

Example 2.5: In Fig. 2.4 is a relationship *Contracts* that involves a studio, a star, and a movie. This relationship represents that a studio has contracted with a particular star to act in a particular movie. In general, the value of an E/R relationship can be thought of as a relationship set of tuples whose

> ## Implications Among Relationship Types
>
> We should be aware that a many-one relationship is a special case of a many-many relationship, and a one-one relationship is a special case of a many-one relationship. That is, any useful property of many-many relationships applies to many-one relationships as well, and a useful property of many-one relationships holds for one-one relationships too. For example, a data structure for representing many-one relationships will work for one-one relationships, although it might not work for many-many relationships.

Figure 2.4: A three-way relationship

components are the entities participating in the relationship, as we discussed in Section 2.1.5. Thus, relationship *Contracts* can be described by triples of the form

$$(\text{studio, star, movie})$$

In multiway relationships, an arrow pointing to an entity set E means that if we select one entity from each of the other entity sets in the relationship, those entities are related to at most one entity in E. (Note that this rule generalizes the notation used for many-one, binary relationships.) In Fig. 2.4 we have an arrow pointing to entity set *Studios*, indicating that for a particular star and movie, there is only one studio with which the star has contracted for that movie. However, there are no arrows pointing to entity sets *Stars* or *Movies*. A studio may contract with several stars for a movie, and a star may contract with one studio for more than one movie. □

2.1.8 Roles in Relationships

It is possible that one entity set appears two or more times in a single relationship. If so, we draw as many lines from the relationship to the entity set as the entity set appears in the relationship. Each line to the entity set represents a different *role* that the entity set plays in the relationship. We therefore label the edges between the entity set and relationship by names, which we call "roles."

Limits on Arrow Notation in Multiway Relationships

There are not enough choices of arrow or no-arrow on the lines attached to a relationship with three or more participants. Thus, we cannot describe every possible situation with arrows. For instance, in Fig. 2.4, the studio is really a function of the movie alone, not the star and movie jointly, since only one studio produces a movie. However, our notation does not distinguish this situation from the case of a three-way relationship where the entity set pointed to by the arrow is truly a function of both other entity sets. In Section 3.4 we shall take up a formal notation — functional dependencies — that has the capability to describe all possibilities regarding how one entity set can be determined uniquely by others.

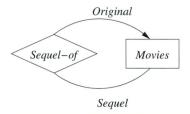

Figure 2.5: A relationship with roles

Example 2.6 : In Fig. 2.5 is a relationship *Sequel-of* between the entity set *Movies* and itself. Each relationship is between two movies, one of which is the sequel of the other. To differentiate the two movies in a relationship, one line is labeled by the role *Original* and one by the role *Sequel*, indicating the original movie and its sequel, respectively. We assume that a movie may have many sequels, but for each sequel there is only one original movie. Thus, the relationship is many-one from *Sequel* movies to *Original* movies, as indicated by the arrow in the E/R diagram of Fig. 2.5.   □

Example 2.7 : As a final example that includes both a multiway relationship and an entity set with multiple roles, in Fig. 2.6 is a more complex version of the *Contracts* relationship introduced earlier in Example 2.5. Now, relationship *Contracts* involves two studios, a star, and a movie. The intent is that one studio, having a certain star under contract (in general, not for a particular movie), may further contract with a second studio to allow that star to act in a particular movie. Thus, the relationship is described by 4-tuples of the form

$$(studio1, studio2, star, movie),$$

meaning that studio2 contracts with studio1 for the use of studio1's star by studio2 for the movie.

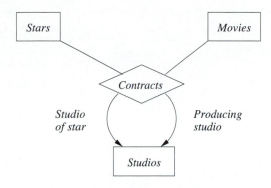

Figure 2.6: A four-way relationship

We see in Fig. 2.6 arrows pointing to *Studios* in both of its roles, as "owner" of the star and as producer of the movie. However, there are not arrows pointing to *Stars* or *Movies*. The rationale is as follows. Given a star, a movie, and a studio producing the movie, there can be only one studio that "owns" the star. (We assume a star is under contract to exactly one studio.) Similarly, only one studio produces a given movie, so given a star, a movie, and the star's studio, we can determine a unique producing studio. Note that in both cases we actually needed only one of the other entities to determine the unique entity—for example, we need only know the movie to determine the unique producing studio—but this fact does not change the multiplicity specification for the multiway relationship.

There are no arrows pointing to *Stars* or *Movies*. Given a star, the star's studio, and a producing studio, there could be several different contracts allowing the star to act in several movies. Thus, the other three components in a relationship 4-tuple do not necessarily determine a unique movie. Similarly, a producing studio might contract with some other studio to use more than one of their stars in one movie. Thus, a star is not determined by the three other components of the relationship. □

2.1.9   Attributes on Relationships

Sometimes it is convenient, or even essential, to associate attributes with a relationship, rather than with any one of the entity sets that the relationship connects. For example, consider the relationship of Fig. 2.4, which represents contracts between a star and studio for a movie.[1] We might wish to record the salary associated with this contract. However, we cannot associate it with the star; a star might get different salaries for different movies. Similarly, it does not make sense to associate the salary with a studio (they may pay different

---

[1] Here, we have reverted to the earlier notion of three-way contracts in Example 2.5, not the four-way relationship of Example 2.7.

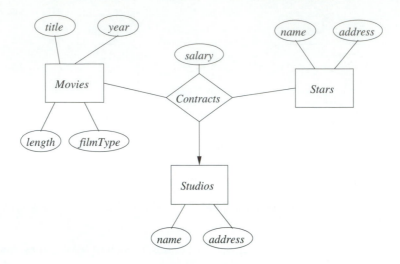

Figure 2.7: A relationship with an attribute

salaries to different stars) or with a movie (different stars in a movie may receive different salaries).

However, it is appropriate to associate a salary with the

$$(star, movie, studio)$$

triple in the relationship set for the *Contracts* relationship. In Fig. 2.7 we see Fig. 2.4 fleshed out with attributes. The relationship has attribute *salary*, while the entity sets have the same attributes that we showed for them in Fig. 2.2.

It is never necessary to place attributes on relationships. We can instead invent a new entity set, whose entities have the attributes ascribed to the relationship. If we then include this entity set in the relationship, we can omit the attributes on the relationship itself. However, attributes on a relationship are a useful convention, which we shall continue to use where appropriate.

Example 2.8 : Let us revise the E/R diagram of Fig. 2.7, which has the salary attribute on the *Contracts* relationship. Instead, we create an entity set *Salaries*, with attribute *salary*. *Salaries* becomes the fourth entity set of relationship *Contracts*. The whole diagram is shown in Fig. 2.8.   □

2.1.10   Converting Multiway Relationships to Binary

There are some data models, such as ODL (Object Definition Language), which we introduce in Section 4.2, that limit relationships to be binary. Thus, while the E/R model does not require binary relationships, it is useful to observe that any relationship connecting more than two entity sets can be converted to a collection of binary, many-one relationships. We can introduce a new entity set

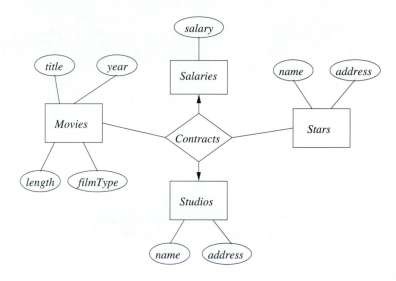

Figure 2.8: Moving the attribute to an entity set

whose entities we may think of as tuples of the relationship set for the multiway relationship. We call this entity set a *connecting* entity set. We then introduce many-one relationships from the connecting entity set to each of the entity sets that provide components of tuples in the original, multiway relationship. If an entity set plays more than one role, then it is the target of one relationship for each role.

Example 2.9: The four-way *Contracts* relationship in Fig. 2.6 can be replaced by an entity set that we may also call *Contracts*. As seen in Fig. 2.9, it participates in four relationships. If the relationship set for the relationship *Contracts* has a 4-tuple

(studio1, studio2, star, movie)

then the entity set *Contracts* has an entity *e*. This entity is linked by relationship *Star-of* to the entity *star* in entity set *Stars*. It is linked by relationship *Movie-of* to the entity *movie* in *Movies*. It is linked to entities *studio1* and *studio2* of *Studios* by relationships *Studio-of-star* and *Producing-studio*, respectively.

Note that we have assumed there are no attributes of entity set *Contracts*, although the other entity sets in Fig. 2.9 have unseen attributes. However, it is possible to add attributes, such as the date of signing, to entity set *Contracts*. □

2.1.11 Subclasses in the E/R Model

Often, an entity set contains certain entities that have special properties not associated with all members of the set. If so, we find it useful to define certain

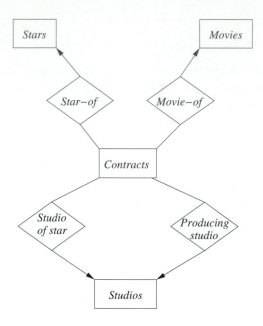

Figure 2.9: Replacing a multiway relationship by an entity set and binary relationships

special-case entity sets, or *subclasses*, each with its own special attributes and/or relationships. We connect an entity set to its subclasses using a relationship called *isa* (i.e., "an A is a B" expresses an "isa" relationship from entity set A to entity set B).

An isa relationship is a special kind of relationship, and to emphasize that it is unlike other relationships, we use for it a special notation. Each isa relationship is represented by a triangle. One side of the triangle is attached to the subclass, and the opposite point is connected to the superclass. Every isa relationship is one-one, although we shall not draw the two arrows that are associated with other one-one relationships.

Example 2.10 : Among the kinds of movies we might store in our example database are cartoons, murder mysteries, adventures, comedies, and many other special types of movies. For each of these movie types, we could define a subclass of the entity set *Movies*. For instance, let us postulate two subclasses: *Cartoons* and *Murder-Mysteries*. A cartoon has, in addition to the attributes and relationships of *Movies* an additional relationship called *Voices* that gives us a set of stars who speak, but do not appear in the movie. Movies that are not cartoons do not have such stars. Murder-mysteries have an additional attribute *weapon*. The connections among the three entity sets *Movies*, *Cartoons*, and *Murder-Mysteries* is shown in Fig. 2.10.   □

While, in principle, a collection of entity sets connected by *isa* relationships

---

Parallel Relationships Can Be Different

Figure 2.9 illustrates a subtle point about relationships. There are two different relationships, *Studio-of-Star* and *Producing-Studio*, that each connect entity sets *Contracts* and *Studios*. We should not presume that these relationships therefore have the same relationship sets. In fact, in this case, it is unlikely that both relationships would ever relate the same contract to the same studios, since a studio would then be contracting with itself.

More generally, there is nothing wrong with an E/R diagram having several relationships that connect the same entity sets. In the database, the instances of these relationships will normally be different, reflecting the different meanings of the relationships. In fact, if the relationship sets for two relationships are expected to be the same, then they are really the same relationship and should not be given distinct names.

---

could have any structure, we shall limit isa-structures to trees, in which there is one *root* entity set (e.g., *Movies* in Fig. 2.10) that is the most general, with progressively more specialized entity sets extending below the root in a tree.

Suppose we have a tree of entity sets, connected by *isa* relationships. A single entity consists of *components* from one or more of these entity sets, as long as those components are in a subtree including the root. That is, if an entity e has a component c in entity set E, and the parent of E in the tree is F, then entity e also has a component d in F. Further, c and d must be paired in the relationship set for the *isa* relationship from E to F. The entity e has whatever attributes any of its components has, and it participates in whatever relationships any of its components participate in.

Example 2.11: The typical movie, being neither a cartoon nor a murder-mystery, will have a component only in the root entity set *Movies* in Fig. 2.10. These entities have only the four attributes of *Movies* (and the two relationships of *Movies* — *Stars-in* and *Owns* — that are not shown in Fig. 2.10).

A cartoon that is not a murder-mystery will have two components, one in *Movies* and one in *Cartoons*. Its entity will therefore have not only the four attributes of *Movies*, but the relationship *Voices*. Likewise, a murder-mystery will have two components for its entity, one in *Movies* and one in *Murder-Mysteries* and thus will have five attributes, including *weapon*.

Finally, a movie like *Roger Rabbit*, which is both a cartoon and a murder-mystery, will have components in all three of the entity sets *Movies*, *Cartoons*, and *Murder-Mysteries*. The three components are connected into one entity by the *isa* relationships. Together, these components give the *Roger Rabbit* entity all four attributes of *Movies* plus the attribute *weapon* of entity set *Murder-Mysteries* and the relationship *Voices* of entity set *Cartoons*. □

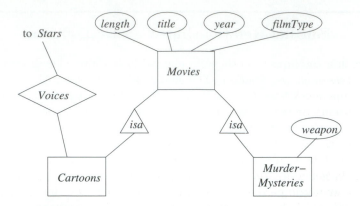

Figure 2.10: Isa relationships in an E/R diagram

2.1.12   Exercises for Section 2.1

* **Exercise 2.1.1 :** Let us design a database for a bank, including information about customers and their accounts. Information about a customer includes their name, address, phone, and Social Security number. Accounts have numbers, types (e.g., savings, checking) and balances. We also need to record the customer(s) who own an account. Draw the E/R diagram for this database. Be sure to include arrows where appropriate, to indicate the multiplicity of a relationship.

Exercise 2.1.2 : Modify your solution to Exercise 2.1.1 as follows:

a) Change your diagram so an account can have only one customer.

b) Further change your diagram so a customer can have only one account.

! c) Change your original diagram of Exercise 2.1.1 so that a customer can have a set of addresses (which are street-city-state triples) and a set of phones. Remember that we do not allow attributes to have nonatomic types, such as sets, in the E/R model.

! d) Further modify your diagram so that customers can have a set of addresses, and at each address there is a set of phones.

Exercise 2.1.3 : Give an E/R diagram for a database recording information about teams, players, and their fans, including:

1. For each team, its name, its players, its team captain (one of its players), and the colors of its uniform.

2. For each player, his/her name.

3. For each fan, his/her name, favorite teams, favorite players, and favorite color.

Subclasses in Object-Oriented Systems

There is a significant resemblance between "isa" in the E/R model and subclasses in object-oriented languages. In a sense, "isa" relates a subclass to its superclass. However, there is also a fundamental difference between the conventional E/R view and the object-oriented approach: entities are allowed to have representatives in a tree of entity sets, while objects are assumed to exist in exactly one class or subclass.

The difference becomes apparent when we consider how the movie *Roger Rabbit* was handled in Example 2.11. In an object-oriented approach, we would need for this movie a fourth entity set, "cartoon-murder-mystery," which inherited all the attributes and relationships of *Movies*, *Cartoons*, and *Murder-Mysteries*. However, in the E/R model, the effect of this fourth subclass is obtained by putting components of the movie *Roger Rabbit* in both the *Cartoons* and *Murder-Mysteries* entity sets.

Remember that a set of colors is not a suitable attribute type for teams. How can you get around this restriction?

Exercise 2.1.4: Suppose we wish to add to the schema of Exercise 2.1.3 a relationship *Led-by* among two players and a team. The intention is that this relationship set consists of triples

$$(player1, player2, team)$$

such that player 1 played on the team at a time when some other player 2 was the team captain.

a) Draw the modification to the E/R diagram.

b) Replace your ternary relationship with a new entity set and binary relationships.

! c) Are your new binary relationships the same as any of the previously existing relationships? Note that we assume the two players are different, i.e., the team captain is not self-led.

Exercise 2.1.5: Modify Exercise 2.1.3 to record for each player the history of teams on which they have played, including the start date and ending date (if they were traded) for each such team.

! **Exercise 2.1.6:** Suppose we wish to keep a genealogy. We shall have one entity set, *People*. The information we wish to record about persons includes their name (an attribute) and the following relationships: mother, father, and children. Give an E/R diagram involving the *People* entity set and all the relationships in which it is involved. Include relationships for mother, father, and children. Do not forget to indicate roles when an entity set is used more than once in a relationship.

! Exercise 2.1.7: Modify your "people" database design of Exercise 2.1.6 to include the following special types of people:

1. Females.

2. Males.

3. People who are parents.

You may wish to distinguish certain other kinds of people as well, so relationships connect appropriate subclasses of people.

Exercise 2.1.8: An alternative way to represent the information of Exercise 2.1.6 is to have a ternary relationship *Family* with the intent that a triple in the relationship set for *Family*

(person, mother, father)

is a person, their mother, and their father; all three are in the *People* entity set, of course.

  * a) Draw this diagram, placing arrows on edges where appropriate.

  b) Replace the ternary relationship *Family* by an entity set and binary relationships. Again place arrows to indicate the multiplicity of relationships.

Exercise 2.1.9: Design a database suitable for a university registrar. This database should include information about students, departments, professors, courses, which students are enrolled in which courses, which professors are teaching which courses, student grades, TA's for a course (TA's are students), which courses a department offers, and any other information you deem appropriate. Note that this question is more free-form than the questions above, and you need to make some decisions about multiplicities of relationships, appropriate types, and even what information needs to be represented.

! Exercise 2.1.10: Informally, we can say that two E/R diagrams "have the same information" if, given a real-world situation, the instances of these two diagrams that reflect this situation can be computed from one another. Consider the E/R diagram of Fig. 2.6. This four-way relationship can be decomposed into a three-way relationship and a binary relationship by taking advantage of the fact that for each movie, there is a unique studio that produces that movie. Give an E/R diagram without a four-way relationship that has the same information as Fig. 2.6.

2.2 Design Principles

We have yet to learn many of the details of the E/R model, but we have enough to begin study of the crucial issue of what constitutes a good design and what should be avoided. In this section, we offer some useful design principles.

2.2.1 Faithfulness

First and foremost, the design should be faithful to the specifications of the application. That is, entity sets and their attributes should reflect reality. You can't attach an attribute *number-of-cylinders* to *Stars*, although that attribute would make sense for an entity set *Automobiles*. Whatever relationships are asserted should make sense given what we know about the part of the real world being modeled.

Example 2.12: If we define a relationship *Stars-in* between *Stars* and *Movies*, it should be a many-many relationship. The reason is that an observation of the real world tells us that stars can appear in more than one movie, and movies can have more than one star. It is incorrect to declare the relationship *Stars-in* to be many-one in either direction or to be one-one. □

Example 2.13: On the other hand, sometimes it is less obvious what the real world requires us to do in our E/R model. Consider, for instance, entity sets *Courses* and *Instructors*, with a relationship *Teaches* between them. Is *Teaches* many-one from *Courses* to *Instructors*? The answer lies in the policy and intentions of the organization creating the database. It is possible that the school has a policy that there can be only one instructor for any course. Even if several instructors may "team-teach" a course, the school may require that exactly one of them be listed in the database as the instructor responsible for the course. In either of these cases, we would make *Teaches* a many-one relationship from *Courses* to *Instructors*.

Alternatively, the school may use teams of instructors regularly and wish its database to allow several instructors to be associated with a course. Or, the intent of the *Teaches* relationship may not be to reflect the current teacher of a course, but rather those who have ever taught the course, or those who are capable of teaching the course; we cannot tell simply from the name of the relationship. In either of these cases, it would be proper to make *Teaches* be many-many. □

2.2.2 Avoiding Redundancy

We should be careful to say everything once only. For instance, we have used a relationship *Owns* between movies and studios. We might also choose to have an attribute *studioName* of entity set *Movies*. While there is nothing illegal about doing so, it is dangerous for several reasons.

1. The two representations of the same owning-studio fact take more space, when the data is stored, than either representation alone.

2. If a movie were sold, we might change the owning studio to which it is related by relationship *Owns* but forget to change the value of its *studioName* attribute, or vice versa. Of course one could argue that one should never do such careless things, but in practice, errors are frequent, and by trying to say the same thing in two different ways, we are inviting trouble.

These problems will be described more formally in Section 3.6, and we shall also learn there some tools for redesigning database schemas so the redundancy and its attendant problems go away.

2.2.3   Simplicity Counts

Avoid introducing more elements into your design than is absolutely necessary.

Example 2.14 : Suppose that instead of a relationship between *Movies* and *Studios* we postulated the existence of "movie-holdings," the ownership of a single movie. We might then create another entity set *Holdings*. A one-one relationship *Represents* could be established between each movie and the unique holding that represents the movie. A many-one relationship from *Holdings* to *Studios* completes the picture shown in Fig. 2.11.

Figure 2.11: A poor design with an unnecessary entity set

Technically, the structure of Fig. 2.11 truly represents the real world, since it is possible to go from a movie to its unique owning studio via *Holdings*. However, *Holdings* serves no useful purpose, and we are better off without it. It makes programs that use the movie-studio relationship more complicated, wastes space, and encourages errors.   □

2.2.4   Choosing the Right Relationships

Entity sets can be connected in various ways by relationships. However, adding to our design every possible relationship is not often a good idea. First, it can lead to redundancy, where the connected pairs or sets of entities for one relationship can be deduced from one or more other relationships. Second, the resulting database could require much more space to store redundant elements, and modifying the database could become too complex, because one change in the data could require many changes to the stored relationships. The problems are essentially the same as those discussed in Section 2.2.2, although the cause of the problem is different from the problems we discussed there.

We shall illustrate the problem and what to do about it with two examples. In the first example, several relationships could represent the same information; in the second, one relationship could be deduced from several others.

Example 2.15 : Let us review Fig. 2.7, where we connected movies, stars, and studios with a three-way relationship *Contracts*. We omitted from that figure the two binary relationships *Stars-in* and *Owns* from Fig. 2.2. Do we also need these relationships, between *Movies* and *Stars*, and between *Movies* and *Studios*, respectively? The answer is: "we don't know; it depends on our assumptions regarding the three relationships in question."

It might be possible to deduce the relationship *Stars-in* from *Contracts*. If a star can appear in a movie only if there is a contract involving that star, that movie, and the owning studio for the movie, then there truly is no need for relationship *Stars-in*. We could figure out all the star-movie pairs by looking at the star-movie-studio triples in the relationship set for *Contracts* and taking only the star and movie components. However, if a star can work on a movie without there being a contract — or what is more likely, without there being a contract that we know about in our database — then there could be star-movie pairs in *Stars-in* that are not part of star-movie-studio triples in *Contracts*. In that case, we need to retain the *Stars-in* relationship.

A similar observation applies to relationship *Owns*. If for every movie, there is at least one contract involving that movie, its owning studio, and some star for that movie, then we can dispense with *Owns*. However, if there is the possibility that a studio owns a movie, yet has no stars under contract for that movie, or no such contract is known to our database, then we must retain *Owns*.

In summary, we cannot tell you whether a given relationship will be redundant. You must find out from those who wish the database created what to expect. Only then can you make a rational decision about whether or not to include relationships such as *Stars-in* or *Owns*. □

Example 2.16 : Now, consider Fig. 2.2 again. In this diagram, there is no relationship between stars and studios. Yet we can use the two relationships *Stars-in* and *Owns* to build a connection by the process of composing those two relationships. That is, a star is connected to some movies by *Stars-in*, and those movies are connected to studios by *Owns*. Thus, we could say that a star is connected to the studios that own movies in which the star has appeared.

Would it make sense to have a relationship *Works-for*, as suggested in Fig. 2.12, between *Stars* and *Studios* too? Again, we cannot tell without knowing more. First, what would the meaning of this relationship be? If it is to mean "the star appeared in at least one movie of this studio," then probably there is no good reason to include it in the diagram. We could deduce this information from *Stars-in* and *Owns* instead.

However, it is conceivable that we have other information about stars working for studios that is not entailed by the connection through a movie. In that

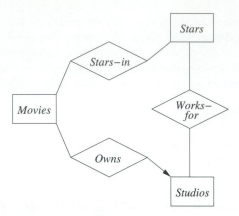

Figure 2.12: Adding a relationship between *Stars* and *Studios*

case, a relationship connecting stars directly to studios might be useful and
would not be redundant. Alternatively, we might use a relationship between
stars and studios to mean something entirely different. For example, it might
represent the fact that the star is under contract to the studio, in a manner
unrelated to any movie. As we suggested in Example 2.7, it is possible for a star
to be under contract to one studio and yet work on a movie owned by another
studio. In this case, the information found in the new *Works-for* relation would
be independent of the *Stars-in* and *Owns* relationships, and would surely be
nonredundant.   □

2.2.5   Picking the Right Kind of Element

Sometimes we have options regarding the type of design element used to represent a real-world concept. Many of these choices are between using attributes
and using entity set/relationship combinations. In general, an attribute is simpler to implement than either an entity set or a relationship. However, making
everything an attribute will usually get us into trouble.

Example 2.17 : Let us consider a specific problem. In Fig. 2.2, were we wise
to make studios an entity set? Should we instead have made the name and
address of the studio be attributes of movies and eliminated the *Studio* entity
set? One problem with doing so is that we repeat the address of the studio for
each movie. This situation is another instance of redundancy, similar to those
seen in Sections 2.2.2 and 2.2.4. In addition to the disadvantages of redundancy
discussed there, we also face the risk that, should we not have any movies owned
by a given studio, we lose the studio's address.

On the other hand, if we did not record addresses of studios, then there is
no harm in making the studio name an attribute of movies. We do not have
redundancy due to repeating addresses. The fact that we have to say the name
of a studio like `Disney` for each movie owned by Disney is not true redundancy,

since we must represent the owner of each movie somehow, and saying the name is a reasonable way to do so. □

We can abstract what we have observed in Example 2.17 to give the conditions under which we prefer to use an attribute instead of an entity set. Suppose E is an entity set. Here are conditions that E must obey, in order for us to replace E by an attribute or attributes of several other entity sets.

1. All relationships in which E is involved must have arrows entering E. That is, E must be the "one" in many-one relationships, or its generalization for the case of multiway relationships.

2. The attributes for E must collectively identify an entity. Typically, there will be only one attribute, in which case this condition is surely met. However, if there are several attributes, then no attribute must depend on the other attributes, the way *address* depends on *name* for *Studios*.

3. No relationship involves E more than once.

If these conditions are met, then we can replace entity set E as follows:

a) If there is a many-one relationship R from some entity set F to E, then remove R and make the attributes of E be attributes of F, suitably renamed if they conflict with attribute names for F. In effect, each F-entity takes, as attributes, the name of the unique, related E-entity,[2] as movie objects could take their studio name as an attribute, should we dispense with studio addresses.

b) If there is a multiway relationship R with an arrow to E, make the attributes of E be attributes of R and delete the arc from R to E. An example of transformation is replacing Fig. 2.8, where we had introduced a new entity set *Salaries*, with a number as its lone attribute, by its original diagram, in Fig. 2.7.

Example 2.18 : Let us consider a point where there is a tradeoff between using a multiway relationship and using a connecting entity set with several binary relationships. We saw a four-way relationship *Contracts* among a star, a movie, and two studios in Fig. 2.6. In Fig. 2.9, we mechanically converted it to an entity set *Contracts*. Does it matter which we choose?

As the problem was stated, either is appropriate. However, should we change the problem just slightly, then we are almost forced to choose a connecting entity set. Let us suppose that contracts involve one star, one movie, but any set of studios. This situation is more complex than the one in Fig. 2.6, where we had two studios playing two roles. In this case, we can have any number of

---

[2] In a situation where an F-entity is not related to any E-entity, the new attributes of F would be given special "null" values to indicate the absence of a related E-entity. A similar arrangement would be used for the new attributes of R in case (b).

studios involved, perhaps one to do production, one for special effects, one for distribution, and so on. Thus, we cannot assign roles for studios.

It appears that a relationship set for the relationship *Contracts* must contain triples of the form

(star, movie, set-of-studios)

and the relationship *Contracts* itself involves not only the usual *Stars* and *Movies* entity sets, but a new entity set whose entities are *sets of* studios. While this approach is unpreventable, it seems unnatural to think of sets of studios as basic entities, and we do not recommend it.

A better approach is to think of contracts as an entity set. As in Fig. 2.9, a contract entity connects a star, a movie and a set of studios, but now there must be no limit on the number of studios. Thus, the relationship between contracts and studios is many-many, rather than many-one as it would be if contracts were a true "connecting" entity set. Figure 2.13 sketches the E/R diagram. Note that a contract is associated with a single star and a single movie, but any number of studios.   □

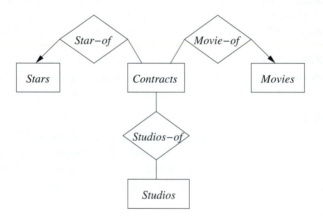

Figure 2.13: Contracts connecting a star, a movie, and a set of studios

2.2.6   Exercises for Section 2.2

* **Exercise 2.2.1:** In Fig. 2.14 is an E/R diagram for a bank database involving customers and accounts. Since customers may have several accounts, and accounts may be held jointly by several customers, we associate with each customer an "account set," and accounts are members of one or more account sets. Assuming the meaning of the various relationships and attributes are as expected given their names, criticize the design. What design rules are violated? Why? What modifications would you suggest?

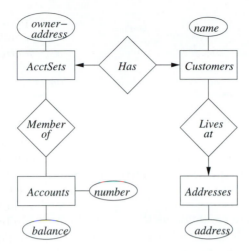

Figure 2.14: A poor design for a bank database

* Exercise 2.2.2 : Under what circumstances (regarding the unseen attributes of *Studios* and *Presidents*) would you recommend combining the two entity sets and relationship in Fig. 2.3 into a single entity set and attributes?

Exercise 2.2.3 : Suppose we delete the attribute *address* from *Studios* in Fig. 2.7. Show how we could then replace an entity set by an attribute. Where would that attribute appear?

Exercise 2.2.4 : Give choices of attributes for the following entity sets in Fig. 2.13 that will allow the entity set to be replaced by an attribute:

   a) *Stars.*

   b) *Movies.*

   ! c) *Studios.*

!! Exercise 2.2.5 : In this and following exercises we shall consider two design options in the E/R model for describing births. At a birth, there is one baby (twins would be represented by two births), one mother, any number of nurses, and any number of doctors. Suppose, therefore, that we have entity sets *Babies*, *Mothers*, *Nurses*, and *Doctors*. Suppose we also use a relationship *Births*, which connects these four entity sets, as suggested in Fig. 2.15. Note that a tuple of the relationship set for *Births* has the form

(baby, mother, nurse, doctor)

If there is more than one nurse and/or doctor attending a birth, then there will be several tuples with the same baby and mother, one for each combination of nurse and doctor.

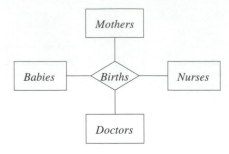

Figure 2.15: Representing births by a multiway relationship

There are certain assumptions that we might wish to incorporate into our design. For each, tell how to add arrows or other elements to the E/R diagram in order to express the assumption.

a) For every baby, there is a unique mother.

b) For every combination of a baby, nurse, and doctor, there is a unique mother.

c) For every combination of a baby and a mother there is a unique doctor.

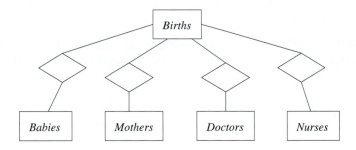

Figure 2.16: Representing births by an entity set

! **Exercise 2.2.6:** Another approach to the problem of Exercise 2.2.5 is to connect the four entity sets *Babies*, *Mothers*, *Nurses*, and *Doctors* by an entity set *Births*, with four relationships, one between *Births* and each of the other entity sets, as suggested in Fig. 2.16. Use arrows (indicating that certain of these relationships are many-one) to represent the following conditions:

a) Every baby is the result of a unique birth, and every birth is of a unique baby.

b) In addition to (a), every baby has a unique mother.

c) In addition to (a) and (b), for every birth there is a unique doctor.

In each case, what design flaws do you see?

!! Exercise 2.2.7 : Suppose we change our viewpoint to allow a birth to involve more than one baby born to one mother. How would you represent the fact that every baby still has a unique mother using the approaches of Exercises 2.2.5 and 2.2.6?

2.3 The Modeling of Constraints

We have seen so far how to model a slice of the real world using entity sets and relationships. However, there are some other important aspects of the real world that we cannot model with the tools seen so far. This additional information often takes the form of *constraints* on the data that go beyond the structural and type constraints imposed by the definitions of entity sets, attributes, and relationships.

2.3.1 Classification of Constraints

The following is a rough classification of commonly used constraints. We shall not cover all of these constraint types here. Additional material on constraints is found in Section 5.5 in the context of relational algebra and in Chapter 7 in the context of SQL programming.

1. *Keys* are attributes or sets of attributes that uniquely identify an entity within its entity set. No two entities may agree in their values for all of the attributes that constitute a key. It *is* permissible, however, for two entities to agree on some, but not all, of the key attributes.

2. *Single-value constraints* are requirements that the value in a certain context be unique. Keys are a major source of single-value constraints, since they require that each entity in an entity set has unique value(s) for the key attribute(s). However, there are other sources of single-value constraints, such as many-one relationships.

3. *Referential integrity constraints* are requirements that a value referred to by some object actually exists in the database. Referential integrity is analogous to a prohibition against dangling pointers, or other kinds of dangling references, in conventional programs.

4. *Domain constraints* require that the value of an attribute must be drawn from a specific set of values or lie within a specific range.

5. *General constraints* are arbitrary assertions that are required to hold in the database. For example, we might wish to require that no more than ten stars be listed for any one movie. We shall see general constraint-expression languages in Sections 5.5 and 7.4.

There are several ways these constraints are important. They tell us something about the structure of those aspects of the real world that we are modeling. For example, keys allow the user to identify entities without confusion. If we know that attribute *name* is a key for entity set *Studios*, then when we refer to a studio entity by its name we know we are referring to a unique entity. In addition, knowing a unique value exists saves space and time, since storing a single value is easier than storing a set, even when that set has exactly one member.[3] Referential integrity and keys also support certain storage structures that allow faster access to data, as we shall discuss in Chapter 13.

2.3.2 Keys in the E/R Model

A *key* for an entity set E is a set K of one or more attributes such that, given any two distinct entities e_1 and e_2 in E, e_1 and e_2 cannot have identical values for each of the attributes in the key K. If K consists of more than one attribute, then it is possible for e_1 and e_2 to agree in some of these attributes, but never in all attributes. Some important points to remember are:

- Every entity set must have a key.

- A key can consist of more than one attribute; see Example 2.19.

- There can also be more than one possible key for an entity set, as we shall see in Example 2.20. However, it is customary to pick one key as the "primary key," and to act as if that were the only key.

- When an entity set is involved in an isa-hierarchy, we require that the root entity set have all the attributes needed for a key, and that the key for each entity is found from its component in the root entity set, regardless of how many entity sets in the hierarchy have components for the entity.

Example 2.19 : Let us consider the entity set *Movies* from Example 2.1. One might first assume that the attribute *title* by itself is a key. However, there are several titles that have been used for two or even more movies, for example, *King Kong*. Thus, it would be unwise to declare that *title* by itself is a key. If we did so, then we would not be able to include information about both *King Kong* movies in our database.

A better choice would be to take the set of two attributes *title* and *year* as a key. We still run the risk that there are two movies made in the same year with the same title (and thus both could not be stored in our database), but that is unlikely.

For the other two entity sets, *Stars* and *Studios*, introduced in Example 2.1, we must again think carefully about what can serve as a key. For studios, it is reasonable to assume that there would not be two movie studios with the same

---

[3]In analogy, note that in a C program it is simpler to represent an integer than it is to represent a linked list of integers, even when that list contains only one integer.

Constraints Are Part of the Schema

We could look at the database as it exists at a certain time and decide erroneously that an attribute forms a key because no two entities have identical values for this attribute. For example, as we create our movie database we might not enter two movies with the same title for some time. Thus, it might look as if *title* were a key for entity set *Movies*. However, if we decided on the basis of this preliminary evidence that *title* is a key, and we designed a storage structure for our database that assumed *title* is a key, then we might find ourselves unable to enter a second *King Kong* movie into the database.

Thus, key constraints, and constraints in general, are part of the database schema. They are declared by the database designer along with the structural design (e.g., entities and relationships). Once a constraint is declared, insertions or modifications to the database that violate the constraint are disallowed.

Hence, although a particular instance of the database may satisfy certain constraints, the only "true" constraints are those identified by the designer as holding for all instances of the database that correctly model the real-world. These are the constraints that may be assumed by users and by the structures used to store the database.

---

name, so we shall take *name* to be a key for entity set *Studios*. However, it is less clear that stars are uniquely identified by their name. Surely name does not distinguish among people in general. However, since stars have traditionally chosen "stage names" at will, we might hope to find that *name* serves as a key for *Stars* too. If not, we might choose the pair of attributes *name* and *address* as a key, which would be satisfactory unless there were two stars with the same name living at the same address.   □

Example 2.20 : Our experience in Example 2.19 might lead us to believe that it is difficult to find keys or to be sure that a set of attributes forms a key. In practice the matter is usually much simpler. In the real-world situations commonly modeled by databases, people often go out of their way to create keys for entity sets. For example, companies generally assign employee ID's to all employees, and these ID's are carefully chosen to be unique numbers. One purpose of these ID's is to make sure that in the company database each employee can be distinguished from all others, even if there are several employees with the same name. Thus, the employee-ID attribute can serve as a key for employees in the database.

In US corporations, it is normal for every employee to also have a Social Security number. If the database has an attribute that is the Social Security number, then this attribute can also serve as a key for employees. Note that there is nothing wrong with there being several choices of key for an entity set, as there would be for employees having both employee ID's and Social Security numbers.

The idea of creating an attribute whose purpose is to serve as a key is quite widespread. In addition to employee ID's, we find student ID's to distinguish students in a university. We find drivers' license numbers and automobile registration numbers to distinguish drivers and automobiles, respectively, in the Department of Motor Vehicles. The reader can undoubtedly find more examples of attributes created for the primary purpose of serving as keys.   □

2.3.3   Representing Keys in the E/R Model

In our E/R diagram notation, we underline the attributes belonging to a key for an entity set. For example, Fig. 2.17 reproduces our E/R diagram for movies, stars, and studios from Fig. 2.2, but with key attributes underlined. Attribute *name* is the key for *Stars*. Likewise, *Studios* has a key consisting of only its own attribute *name*. These choices are consistent with the discussion in Example 2.19.

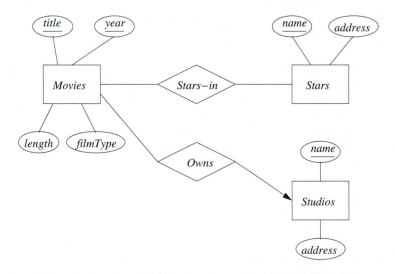

Figure 2.17: E/R diagram; keys are indicated by underlines

The attributes *title* and *year* together form the key for *Movies*, as we discussed in Example 2.19. Note that when several attributes are underlined, as in Fig. 2.17, then they are each members of the key. There is no notation for representing the situation where there are several keys for an entity set; we underline only the primary key. You should also be aware that in some unusual situations, the attributes forming the key for an entity set do not all belong to the entity set itself. We shall defer this matter, called "weak entity sets," until Section 2.4.

2.3.4 Single-Value Constraints

Often, an important property of a database design is that there is at most one value playing a particular role. For example, we assume that a movie entity has a unique title, year, length, and film type, and that a movie is owned by a unique studio.

There are several ways in which single-value constraints are expressed in the E/R model.

1. Each attribute of an entity set has a single value. Sometimes it is permissible for an attribute's value to be missing for some entities, in which case we have to invent a "null value" to serve as the value of that attribute. For example, we might suppose that there are some movies in our database for which the length is not known. We could use a value such as -1 for the length of a movie whose true length is unknown. On the other hand, we would not want the key attributes *title* or *year* to be null for any movie entity. A requirement that a certain attribute not have a null value does not have any special representation in the E/R model. We could place a notation beside the attribute stating this requirement if we wished.

2. A relationship R that is many-one from entity set E to entity set F implies a single-value constraint. That is, for each entity e in E, there is at most one associated entity f in F. More generally, if R is a multiway relationship, then each arrow out of R indicates a single value constraint. Specifically, if there is an arrow from R to entity set E, then there is at most one entity of set E associated with a choice of entities from each of the other related entity sets.

2.3.5 Referential Integrity

While single-value constraints assert that at most one value exists in a given role, a *referential integrity constraint* asserts that exactly one value exists in that role. We could see a constraint that an attribute have a non-null, single value as a kind of referential integrity requirement, but "referential integrity" is more commonly used to refer to relationships among entity sets.

Let us consider the many-one relationship *Owns* from *Movies* to *Studios* in Fig. 2.2. The many-one requirement simply says that no movie can be owned by more than one studio. It does *not* say that a movie must surely be owned by a studio, or that, even if it is owned by some studio, that the studio must be present in the *Studios* entity set, as stored in our database.

A referential integrity constraint on relationship *Owns* would require that for each movie, the owning studio (the entity "referenced" by the relationship for this movie) must exist in our database. There are several ways this constraint could be enforced.

1. We could forbid the deletion of a referenced entity (a studio in our example). That is, we could not delete a studio from the database unless it did not own any movies.

2. We could require that if a referenced entity is deleted, then all entities that reference it are deleted as well. In our example, this approach would require that if we delete a studio, we also delete from the database all movies owned by that studio.

In addition to one of these policies about deletion, we require that when a movie entity is inserted into the database, it is given an existing studio entity to which it is connected by relationship *Owns*. Further, if the value of that relationship changes, then the new value must also be an existing *Studios* entity. Enforcing these policies to assure referential integrity of a relationship is a matter for the implementation of the database, and we shall not discuss the details here.

2.3.6 Referential Integrity in E/R Diagrams

We can extend the arrow notation in E/R diagrams to indicate whether a relationship is expected to support referential integrity in one or more directions. Suppose R is a relationship from entity set E to entity set F. We shall use a rounded arrowhead pointing to F to indicate not only that the relationship is many-one or one-one from E to F, but that the entity of set F related to a given entity of set E is required to exist. The same idea applies when R is a relationship among more than two entity sets.

Example 2.21 : Figure 2.18 shows some appropriate referential integrity constraints among the entity sets *Movies*, *Studios*, and *Presidents*. These entity sets and relationships were first introduced in Figs. 2.2 and 2.3. We see a rounded arrow entering *Studios* from relationship *Owns*. That arrow expresses the referential integrity constraint that every movie must be owned by one studio, and this studio is present in the *Studios* entity set.

Figure 2.18: E/R diagram showing referential integrity constraints

Similarly, we see a rounded arrow entering *Studios* from *Runs*. That arrow expresses the referential integrity constraint that every president runs a studio that exists in the *Studios* entity set.

Note that the arrow to *Presidents* from *Runs* remains a pointed arrow. That choice reflects a reasonable assumption about the relationship between studios and their presidents. If a studio ceases to exist, its president can no longer be called a (studio) president, so we would expect the president of the studio to be deleted from the entity set *Presidents*. Hence there is a rounded arrow to *Studios*. On the other hand, if a president were deleted from the database, the studio would continue to exist. Thus, we place an ordinary, pointed arrow to *Presidents*, indicating that each studio has at most one president, but might have no president at some time. □

2.3.7 Other Kinds of Constraints

As mentioned at the beginning of this section, there are other kinds of constraints one could wish to enforce in a database. We shall only touch briefly on these here, with the meat of the subject appearing in Chapter 7.

Domain constraints restrict the value of an attribute to be in a limited set. A simple example would be declaring the type of an attribute. A stronger domain constraint would be to declare an enumerated type for an attribute or a range of values, e.g., the *length* attribute for a movie must be an integer in the range 0 to 240. There is no specific notation for domain constraints in the E/R model, but you may place a notation stating a desired constraint next to the attribute, if you wish.

There are also more general kinds of constraints that do not fall into any of the categories mentioned in this section. For example, we could choose to place a constraint on the degree of a relationship, such as that a movie entity cannot be connected by relationship *Stars-in* to more than 10 star entities. In the E/R model, we can attach a bounding number to the edges that connect a relationship to an entity set, indicating limits on the number of entities that can be connected to any one entity of the related entity set.

Figure 2.19: Representing a constraint on the number of stars per movie

Example 2.22: Figure 2.19 shows how we can represent the constraint that no movie has more than 10 stars in the E/R model. As another example, we can think of the arrow as a synonym for the constraint "≤ 1," and we can think of the rounded arrow of Fig. 2.18 as standing for the constraint "= 1." □

2.3.8 Exercises for Section 2.3

Exercise 2.3.1: For your E/R diagrams of:

* a) Exercise 2.1.1.

  b) Exercise 2.1.3.

    c) Exercise 2.1.6.

(i) Select and specify keys, and (ii) Indicate appropriate referential integrity constraints.

! **Exercise 2.3.2:** We may think of relationships in the E/R model as having keys, just as entity sets do. Let R be a relationship among the entity sets $E_1, E_2, \ldots, E_n$. Then a *key* for R is a set K of attributes chosen from the attributes of $E_1, E_2, \ldots, E_n$ such that if $(e_1, e_2, \ldots, e_n)$ and $(f_1, f_2, \ldots, f_n)$ are two different tuples in the relationship set for R, then it is not possible that these tuples agree in all the attributes of K. Now, suppose $n = 2$; that is, R is a binary relationship. Also, for each i, let K_i be a set of attributes that is a key for entity set E_i. In terms of E_1 and E_2, give a smallest possible key for R under the assumption that:

    a) R is many-many.

* b) R is many-one from E_1 to E_2.

    c) R is many-one from E_2 to E_1.

    d) R is one-one.

!! **Exercise 2.3.3:** Consider again the problem of Exercise 2.3.2, but with n allowed to be any number, not just 2. Using only the information about which arcs from R to the E_i's have arrows, show how to find a smallest possible key K for R in terms of the K_i's.

! **Exercise 2.3.4:** Give examples (other than those of Example 2.20) from real life of attributes created for the primary purpose of being keys.

2.4 Weak Entity Sets

There is an occasional condition in which an entity set's key is composed of attributes some or all of which belong to another entity set. Such an entity set is called a *weak entity set*.

2.4.1 Causes of Weak Entity Sets

There are two principal sources of weak entity sets. First, sometimes entity sets fall into a hierarchy based on classifications unrelated to the "isa hierarchy" of Section 2.1.11. If entities of set E are subunits of entities in set F, then it is possible that the names of E entities are not unique until we take into account the name of the F entity to which the E entity is subordinate. Several examples will illustrate the problem.

Example 2.23: A movie studio might have several film crews. The crews might be designated by a given studio as crew 1, crew 2, and so on. However, other studios might use the same designations for crews, so the attribute *number* is not a key for crews. Rather, to name a crew uniquely, we need to give both the name of the studio to which it belongs and the number of the crew. The situation is suggested by Fig. 2.20. The key for weak entity set *Crews* is its own *number* attribute and the *name* attribute of the unique studio to which the crew is related by the many-one *Unit-of* relationship.[4] □

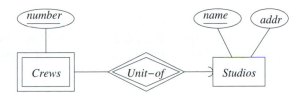

Figure 2.20: A weak entity set for crews, and its connections

Example 2.24: A species is designated by its genus and species names. For example, humans are of the species *Homo sapiens*; *Homo* is the genus name and *sapiens* the species name. In general, a genus consists of several species, each of which has a name beginning with the genus name and continuing with the species name. Unfortunately, species names, by themselves, are not unique. Two or more genera may have species with the same species name. Thus, to designate a species uniquely we need both the species name and the name of the genus to which the species is related by the *Belongs-to* relationship, as suggested in Fig. 2.21. *Species* is a weak entity set whose key comes partially from its genus. □

Figure 2.21: Another weak entity set, for species

The second common source of weak entity sets is the connecting entity sets that we introduced in Section 2.1.10 as a way to eliminate a multiway relationship.[5] These entity sets often have no attributes of their own. Their

---

[4]The double diamond and double rectangle will be explained in Section 2.4.3.

[5]Remember that there is no particular requirement in the E/R model that multiway relationships be eliminated, although this requirement exists in some other database design models.

key is formed from the attributes that are the key attributes for the entity sets they connect.

Example 2.25 : In Fig. 2.22 we see a connecting entity set *Contracts* that replaces the ternary relationship *Contracts* of Example 2.5. *Contracts* has an attribute *salary*, but this attribute does not contribute to the key. Rather, the key for a contract consists of the name of the studio and the star involved, plus the title and year of the movie involved.   □

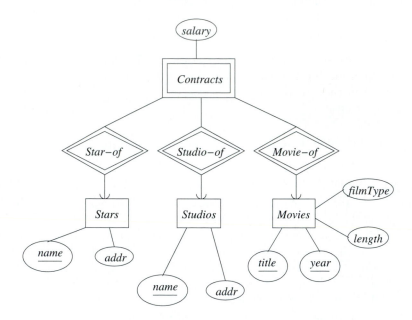

Figure 2.22: Connecting entity sets are weak

2.4.2   Requirements for Weak Entity Sets

We cannot obtain key attributes for a weak entity set indiscriminately. Rather, if E is a weak entity set then its key consists of:

1. Zero or more of its own attributes, and

2. Key attributes from entity sets that are reached by certain many-one relationships from E to other entity sets. These many-one relationships are called *supporting relationships* for E.

In order for R, a many-one relationship from E to some entity set F, to be a supporting relationship for E, the following conditions must be obeyed:

a) R must be a binary, many-one relationship[6] from E to F.

---

[6]Remember that a one-one relationship is a special case of a many-one relationship. When we say a relationship must be many-one, we always include one-one relationships as well.

b) R must have referential integrity from E to F. That is, for every E-entity, the F-entity related to it by R must actually exist in the database. Put another way, a rounded arrow from R to F must be justified.

c) The attributes that F supplies for the key of E must be key attributes of F.

d) However, if F is itself weak, then some or all of the key attributes of F supplied to E will be key attributes of one or more entity sets G to which F is connected by a supporting relationship. Recursively, if G is weak, some key attributes of G will be supplied from elsewhere, and so on.

e) If there are several different supporting relationships from E to F, then each relationship is used to supply a copy of the key attributes of F to help form the key of E. Note that an entity e from E may be related to different entities in F through different supporting relationships from E. Thus, the keys of several different entities from F may appear in the key values identifying a particular entity e from E.

The intuitive reason why these conditions are needed is as follows. Consider an entity in a weak entity set, say a crew in Example 2.23. Each crew is unique, abstractly. In principle we can tell one crew from another, even if they have the same number but belong to different studios. It is only the data about crews that makes it hard to distinguish crews, because the number alone is not sufficient. The only way we can associate additional information with a crew is if there is some deterministic process leading to additional values that make the designation of a crew unique. But the only unique values associated with an abstract crew entity are:

1. Values of attributes of the *Crews* entity set, and

2. Values obtained by following a relationship from a crew entity to a unique entity of some other entity set, where that other entity has a unique associated value of some kind. That is, the relationship followed must be many-one (or one-one as a special case) to the other entity set F, and the associated value must be part of a key for F.

2.4.3 Weak Entity Set Notation

We shall adopt the following conventions to indicate that an entity set is weak and to declare its key attributes.

1. If an entity set is weak, it will be shown as a rectangle with a double border. Examples of this convention are *Crews* in Fig. 2.20 and *Contracts* in Fig. 2.22.

2. Its supporting many-one relationships will be shown as diamonds with a double border. Examples of this convention are *Unit-of* in Fig. 2.20 and all three relationships in Fig. 2.22.

3. If an entity set supplies any attributes for its own key, then those attributes will be underlined. An example is in Fig. 2.20, where the number of a crew participates in its own key, although it is not the complete key for *Crews*.

We can summarize these conventions with the following rule:

- Whenever we use an entity set E with a double border, it is weak. E's attributes that are underlined, if any, plus the key attributes of those entity sets to which E is connected by many-one relationships with a double border, must be unique for the entities of E.

We should remember that the double-diamond is used only for supporting relationships. It is possible for there to be many-one relationships from a weak entity set that are not supporting relationships, and therefore do not get a double diamond.

Example 2.26: In Fig. 2.22, the relationship *Studio-of* need not be a supporting relationship for *Contracts*. The reason is that each movie has a unique owning studio, determined by the (not shown) many-one relationship from *Movies* to *Studios*. Thus, if we are told the name of a star and a movie, there is at most one contract with any studio for the work of that star in that movie. In terms of our notation, it would be appropriate to use an ordinary single diamond, rather than the double diamond, for *Studio-of* in Fig. 2.22.   □

2.4.4   Exercises for Section 2.4

* **Exercise 2.4.1:** One way to represent students and the grades they get in courses is to use entity sets corresponding to students, to courses, and to "enrollments." Enrollment entities form a "connecting" entity set between students and courses and can be used to represent not only the fact that a student is taking a certain course, but the grade of the student in the course. Draw an E/R diagram for this situation, indicating weak entity sets and the keys for the entity sets. Is the grade part of the key for enrollments?

Exercise 2.4.2: Modify your solution to Exercise 2.4.1 so that we can record grades of the student for each of several assignments within a course. Again, indicate weak entity sets and keys.

Exercise 2.4.3: For your E/R diagrams of Exercise 2.2.6(a)–(c), indicate weak entity sets, supporting relationships, and keys.

Exercise 2.4.4: Draw E/R diagrams for the following situations involving weak entity sets. In each case indicate keys for entity sets.

a) Entity sets *Courses* and *Departments*. A course is given by a unique department, but its only attribute is its number. Different departments can offer courses with the same number. Each department has a unique name.

*! b) Entity sets *Leagues*, *Teams*, and *Players*. League names are unique. No league has two teams with the same name. No team has two players with the same number. However, there can be players with the same number on different teams, and there can be teams with the same name in different leagues.

2.5   Summary of Chapter 2

✦ *The Entity-Relationship Model*: In the E/R model we describe entity sets, relationships among entity sets, and attributes of entity sets and relationships. Members of entity sets are called entities.

✦ *Entity-Relationship Diagrams*: We use rectangles, diamonds, and ovals to draw entity sets, relationships, and attributes, respectively.

✦ *Multiplicity of Relationships*: Binary relationships can be one-one, many-one, or many-many. In a one-one relationship, an entity of either set can be associated with at most one entity of the other set. In a many-one relationship, each entity of the "many" side is associated with at most one entity of the other side. Many-many relationships place no restriction on multiplicity.

✦ *Keys*: A set of attributes that uniquely determines an entity in a given entity set is a key for that entity set.

✦ *Good Design*: Designing databases effectively requires that we represent the real world faithfully, that we select appropriate elements (e.g., relationships, attributes), and that we avoid redundancy — saying the same thing twice or saying something in an indirect or overly complex manner.

✦ *Referential Integrity*: A requirement that an entity be connected, through a given relationship, to an entity of some other entity set, and that the latter entity exists in the database, is called a referential integrity constraint.

✦ *Subclasses*: The E/R model uses a special relationship *isa* to represent the fact that one entity set is a special case of another. Entity sets may be connected in a hierarchy with each child node a special case of its parent. Entities may have components belonging to any subtree of the hierarchy, as long as the subtree includes the root.

✦ *Weak Entity Sets*: An occasional complication that arises in the E/R model is a weak entity set that requires attributes of some related entity set(s) to identify its own entities. A special notation involving diamonds and rectangles with double borders is used to distinguish weak entity sets.

2.6   References for Chapter 2

The original paper on the Entity-Relationship model is [2]. Two modern books on the subject of E/R design are [1] and [3].

1. Batini, Carlo., S. Ceri, S. B. Navathe, and Carol Batini, *Conceptual Database Design: an Entity/Relationship Approach*, Addison-Wesley, Reading MA, 1991.

2. Chen, P. P., "The entity-relationship model: toward a unified view of data," *ACM Trans. on Database Systems* **1**:1, pp. 9–36, 1976.

3. Thalheim, B., "Fundamentals of Entity-Relationship Modeling," Springer-Verlag, Berlin, 2000.

Chapter 3

The Relational Data Model

While the entity-relationship approach to data modeling that we discussed in Chapter 2 is a simple and appropriate way to describe the structure of data, today's database implementations are almost always based on another approach, called the *relational model*. The relational model is extremely useful because it has but a single data-modeling concept: the "relation," a two-dimensional table in which data is arranged. We shall see in Chapter 6 how the relational model supports a very high-level programming language called SQL (structured query language). SQL lets us write simple programs that manipulate in powerful ways the data stored in relations. In contrast, the E/R model generally is not considered suitable as the basis of a data manipulation language.

On the other hand, it is often easier to design databases using the E/R notation. Thus, our first goal is to see how to translate designs from E/R notation into relations. We shall then find that the relational model has a design theory of its own. This theory, often called "normalization" of relations, is based primarily on "functional dependencies," which embody and expand the concept of "key" discussed informally in Section 2.3.2. Using normalization theory, we often improve our choice of relations with which to represent a particular database design.

3.1 Basics of the Relational Model

The relational model gives us a single way to represent data: as a two-dimensional table called a *relation*. Figure 3.1 is an example of a relation. The name of the relation is Movies, and it is intended to hold information about the entities in the entity set *Movies* of our running design example. Each row corresponds to one movie entity, and each column corresponds to one of the attributes of the entity set. However, relations can do much more than represent entity sets, as we shall see.

title	year	length	filmType
Star Wars	1977	124	color
Mighty Ducks	1991	104	color
Wayne's World	1992	95	color

Figure 3.1: The relation `Movies`

3.1.1   Attributes

Across the top of a relation we see *attributes*; in Fig. 3.1 the attributes are
`title`, `year`, `length`, and `filmType`. Attributes of a relation serve as names
for the columns of the relation. Usually, an attribute describes the meaning of
entries in the column below. For instance, the column with attribute `length`
holds the length in minutes of each movie.

Notice that the attributes of the relation `Movies` in Fig. 3.1 are the same as
the attributes of the entity set *Movies*. We shall see that turning one entity set
into a relation with the same set of attributes is a common step. However, in
general there is no requirement that attributes of a relation correspond to any
particular components of an E/R description of data.

3.1.2   Schemas

The name of a relation and the set of attributes for a relation is called the
schema for that relation. We show the schema for the relation with the relation
name followed by a parenthesized list of its attributes. Thus, the schema for
relation `Movies` of Fig. 3.1 is

$$\text{Movies(title, year, length, filmType)}$$

The attributes in a relation schema are a set, not a list. However, in order to
talk about relations we often must specify a "standard" order for the attributes.
Thus, whenever we introduce a relation schema with a list of attributes, as
above, we shall take this ordering to be the standard order whenever we display
the relation or any of its rows.

In the relational model, a design consists of one or more relation schemas.
The set of schemas for the relations in a design is called a *relational database
schema*, or just a *database schema*.

3.1.3   Tuples

The rows of a relation, other than the header row containing the attribute
names, are called *tuples*. A tuple has one *component* for each attribute of
the relation. For instance, the first of the three tuples in Fig. 3.1 has the
four components `Star Wars`, 1977, 124, and `color` for attributes `title`, `year`,

`length`, and `filmType`, respectively. When we wish to write a tuple in isolation, not as part of a relation, we normally use commas to separate components, and we use parentheses to surround the tuple. For example,

$$\texttt{(Star Wars, 1977, 124, color)}$$

is the first tuple of Fig. 3.1. Notice that when a tuple appears in isolation, the attributes do not appear, so some indication of the relation to which the tuple belongs must be given. We shall always use the order in which the attributes were listed in the relation schema.

3.1.4 Domains

The relational model requires that each component of each tuple be atomic; that is, it must be of some elementary type such as integer or string. It is not permitted for a value to be a record structure, set, list, array, or any other type that can reasonably have its values broken into smaller components.

It is further assumed that associated with each attribute of a relation is a *domain*, that is, a particular elementary type. The components of any tuple of the relation must have, in each component, a value that belongs to the domain of the corresponding column. For example, tuples of the `Movies` relation of Fig. 3.1 must have a first component that is a string, second and third components that are integers, and a fourth component whose value is one of the constants `color` and `blackAndWhite`. Domains are part of a relation's schema, although we shall not develop a notation for specifying domains until we reach Section 6.6.2.

3.1.5 Equivalent Representations of a Relation

Relations are sets of tuples, not lists of tuples. Thus the order in which the tuples of a relation are presented is immaterial. For example, we can list the three tuples of Fig. 3.1 in any of their six possible orders, and the relation is "the same" as Fig. 3.1.

Moreover, we can reorder the attributes of the relation as we choose, without changing the relation. However, when we reorder the relation schema, we must be careful to remember that the attributes are column headers. Thus, when we change the order of the attributes, we also change the order of their columns. When the columns move, the components of tuples change their order as well. The result is that each tuple has its components permuted in the same way as the attributes are permuted.

For example, Fig. 3.2 shows one of the many relations that could be obtained from Fig. 3.1 by permuting rows and columns. These two relations are considered "the same." More precisely, these two tables are different presentations of the same relation.

year	title	filmType	length
1991	Mighty Ducks	color	104
1992	Wayne's World	color	95
1977	Star Wars	color	124

Figure 3.2: Another presentation of the relation `Movies`

3.1.6   Relation Instances

A relation about movies is not static; rather, relations change over time. We expect that these changes involve the tuples of the relation, such as insertion of new tuples as movies are added to the database, changes to existing tuples if we get revised or corrected information about a movie, and perhaps deletion of tuples for movies that are expelled from the database for some reason.

It is less common for the schema of a relation to change. However, there are situations where we might want to add or delete attributes. Schema changes, while possible in commercial database systems, are very expensive, because each of perhaps millions of tuples needs to be rewritten to add or delete components. If we add an attribute, it may be difficult or even impossible to find the correct values for the new component in the existing tuples.

We shall call a set of tuples for a given relation an *instance* of that relation. For example, the three tuples shown in Fig. 3.1 form an instance of relation `Movies`. Presumably, the relation `Movies` has changed over time and will continue to change over time. For instance, in 1980, `Movies` did not contain the tuples for `Mighty Ducks` or `Wayne's World`. However, a conventional database system maintains only one version of any relation: the set of tuples that are in the relation "now." This instance of the relation is called the *current instance*.

3.1.7   Exercises for Section 3.1

Exercise 3.1.1: In Fig. 3.3 are instances of two relations that might constitute part of a banking database. Indicate the following:

a) The attributes of each relation.

b) The tuples of each relation.

c) The components of one tuple from each relation.

d) The relation schema for each relation.

e) The database schema.

f) A suitable domain for each attribute.

g) Another equivalent way to present each relation.

acctNo	type	balance
12345	savings	12000
23456	checking	1000
34567	savings	25

The relation Accounts

firstName	lastName	idNo	account
Robbie	Banks	901-222	12345
Lena	Hand	805-333	12345
Lena	Hand	805-333	23456

The relation Customers

Figure 3.3: Two relations of a banking database

!! **Exercise 3.1.2:** How many different ways (considering orders of tuples and attributes) are there to represent a relation instance if that instance has:

* a) Three attributes and three tuples, like the relation Accounts of Fig. 3.3?

b) Four attributes and five tuples?

c) n attributes and m tuples?

3.2 From E/R Diagrams to Relational Designs

Let us consider the process whereby a new database, such as our movie database, is created. We begin with a design phase, in which we address and answer questions about what information will be stored, how information elements will be related to one another, what constraints such as keys or referential integrity may be assumed, and so on. This phase may last for a long time, while options are evaluated and opinions are reconciled.

The design phase is followed by an implementation phase using a real database system. Since the great majority of commercial database systems use the relational model, we might suppose that the design phase should use this model too, rather than the E/R model or another model oriented toward design.

However, in practice it is often easier to start with a model like E/R, make our design, and then convert it to the relational model. The primary reason for doing so is that the relational model, having only one concept — the relation —

Schemas and Instances

Let us not forget the important distinction between the schema of a relation and an instance of that relation. The schema is the name and attributes for the relation and is relatively immutable. An instance is a set of tuples for that relation, and the instance may change frequently.

The schema/instance distinction is common in data modeling. For instance, entity set and relationship descriptions are the E/R model's way of describing a schema, while sets of entities and relationship sets form an instance of an E/R schema. Remember, however, that when designing a database, a database instance is not part of the design. We only imagine what typical instances would look like, as we develop our design.

---

rather than several complementary concepts (e.g., entity sets and relationships in the E/R model) has certain inflexibilities that are best handled after a design has been selected.

To a first approximation, converting an E/R design to a relational database schema is straightforward:

- Turn each entity set into a relation with the same set of attributes, and

- Replace a relationship by a relation whose attributes are the keys for the connected entity sets.

While these two rules cover much of the ground, there are also several special situations that we need to deal with, including:

1. Weak entity sets cannot be translated straightforwardly to relations.

2. "Isa" relationships and subclasses require careful treatment.

3. Sometimes, we do well to combine two relations, especially the relation for an entity set E and the relation that comes from a many-one relationship from E to some other entity set.

3.2.1   From Entity Sets to Relations

Let us first consider entity sets that are not weak. We shall take up the modifications needed to accommodate weak entity sets in Section 3.2.4. For each non-weak entity set, we shall create a relation of the same name and with the same set of attributes. This relation will not have any indication of the relationships in which the entity set participates; we'll handle relationships with separate relations, as discussed in Section 3.2.2.

Example 3.1 : Consider the three entity sets *Movies*, *Stars* and *Studios* from Fig. 2.17, which we reproduce here as Fig. 3.4. The attributes for the *Movies* entity set are *title*, *year*, *length*, and *filmType*. As a result, the relation Movies looks just like the relation Movies of Fig. 3.1 with which we began Section 3.1.

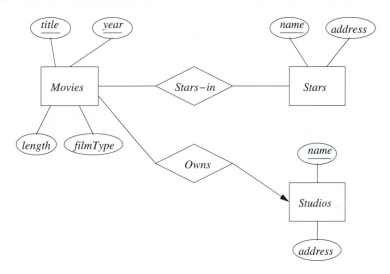

Figure 3.4: E/R diagram for the movie database

Next, consider the entity set *Stars* from Fig. 3.4. There are two attributes, *name* and *address*. Thus, we would expect the corresponding Stars relation to have schema Stars(name, address) and for a typical instance of the relation to look like:

name	address
Carrie Fisher	123 Maple St., Hollywood
Mark Hamill	456 Oak Rd., Brentwood
Harrison Ford	789 Palm Dr., Beverly Hills

□

3.2.2 From E/R Relationships to Relations

Relationships in the E/R model are also represented by relations. The relation for a given relationship R has the following attributes:

1. For each entity set involved in relationship R, we take its key attribute or attributes as part of the schema of the relation for R.

2. If the relationship has attributes, then these are also attributes of relation R.

A Note About Data Quality :-)

While we have endeavored to make example data as accurate as possible, we have used bogus values for addresses and other personal information about movie stars, in order to protect the privacy of members of the acting profession, many of whom are shy individuals who shun publicity.

If one entity set is involved several times in a relationship, in different roles, then its key attributes each appear as many times as there are roles. We must rename the attributes to avoid name duplication. More generally, should the same attribute name appear twice or more among the attributes of R itself and the keys of the entity sets involved in relationship R, then we need to rename to avoid duplication.

Example 3.2 : Consider the relationship *Owns* of Fig. 3.4. This relationship connects entity sets *Movies* and *Studios*. Thus, for the schema of relation Owns we use the key for *Movies*, which is *title* and *year*, and the key of *Studios*, which is *name*. That is, the schema for relation Owns is:

Owns(title, year, studioName)

A sample instance of this relation is:

title	year	studioName
Star Wars	1977	Fox
Mighty Ducks	1991	Disney
Wayne's World	1992	Paramount

We have chosen the attribute studioName for clarity; it corresponds to the attribute *name* of *Studios*. □

Example 3.3 : Similarly, the relationship *Stars-In* of Fig. 3.4 can be transformed into a relation with the attributes title and year (the key for *Movies*) and attribute starName, which is the key for entity set *Stars*. Figure 3.5 shows a sample relation Stars-In.

Because these movie titles are unique, it seems that the year is redundant in Fig. 3.5. However, had there been several movies of the same title, like "King Kong," we would see that the year was essential to sort out which stars appear in which version of the movie. □

Example 3.4 : Multiway relationships are also easy to convert to relations. Consider the four-way relationship *Contracts* of Fig. 2.6, reproduced here as Fig. 3.6, involving a star, a movie, and two studios — the first holding the

title	year	starName
Star Wars	1977	Carrie Fisher
Star Wars	1977	Mark Hamill
Star Wars	1977	Harrison Ford
Mighty Ducks	1991	Emilio Estevez
Wayne's World	1992	Dana Carvey
Wayne's World	1992	Mike Meyers

Figure 3.5: A relation for relationship *Stars-In*

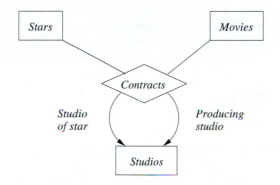

Figure 3.6: The relationship *Contracts*

star's contract and the second contracting for that star's services in that movie. We represent this relationship by a relation `Contracts` whose schema consists of the attributes from the keys of the following four entity sets:

1. The key `starName` for the star.

2. The key consisting of attributes `title` and `year` for the movie.

3. The key `studioOfStar` indicating the name of the first studio; recall we assume the studio name is a key for the entity set `Studios`.

4. The key `producingStudio` indicating the name of the studio that will produce the movie using that star.

That is, the schema is:

`Contracts(starName, title, year, studioOfStar, producingStudio)`

Notice that we have been inventive in choosing attribute names for our relation schema, avoiding "name" for any attribute, since it would be unobvious whether that referred to a star's name or studio's name, and in the latter case, which studio. Also, were there attributes attached to entity set *Contracts*, such as *salary*, these attributes would be added to the schema of relation Contracts. □

3.2.3 Combining Relations

Sometimes, the relations that we get from converting entity sets and relationships to relations are not the best possible choice of relations for the given data. One common situation occurs when there is an entity set E with a many-one relationship R from E to F. The relations from E and R will each have the key for E in their relation schema. In addition, the relation for E will have in its schema the attributes of E that are not in the key, and the relation for R will have the key attributes of F and any attributes of R itself. Because R is many-one, all these attributes have values that are determined uniquely by the key for E, and we can combine them into one relation with a schema consisting of:

1. All attributes of E.

2. The key attributes of F.

3. Any attributes belonging to relationship R.

For an entity e of E that is not related to any entity of F, the attributes of types (2) and (3) will have null values in the tuple for e. Null values were introduced informally in Section 2.3.4, in order to represent a situation where a value is missing or unknown. Nulls are not a formal part of the relational model, but a null value, denoted NULL, is available in SQL, and we shall use it where needed in our discussions of representing E/R designs as relational database schemas.

Example 3.5 : In our running movie example, *Owns* is a many-one relationship from *Movies* to *Studios*, which we converted to a relation in Example 3.2. The relation obtained from entity set *Movies* was discussed in Example 3.1. We can combine these relations by taking all their attributes and forming one relation schema. If we do, the relation looks like that in Fig. 3.7.   □

title	*year*	*length*	*filmType*	*studioName*
Star Wars	1977	124	color	Fox
Mighty Ducks	1991	104	color	Disney
Wayne's World	1992	95	color	Paramount

Figure 3.7: Combining relation Movies with relation Owns

Whether or not we choose to combine relations in this manner is a matter of judgement. However, there are some advantages to having all the attributes that are dependent on the key of entity set E together in one relation, even if there are a number of many-one relationships from E to other entity sets. For example, it is often more efficient to answer queries involving attributes of one relation than to answer queries involving attributes of several relations. In fact, some design systems based on the E/R model combine these relations automatically for the user.

On the other hand, one might wonder if it made sense to combine the relation for E with the relation of a relationship R that involved E but was not many-one from E to some other entity set. Doing so is risky, because it often leads to redundancy, an issue we shall take up in Section 3.6.

Example 3.6: To get a sense of what can go wrong, suppose we combined the relation of Fig. 3.7 with the relation that we get for the many-many relationship *Stars-in*; recall this relation was suggested by Fig. 3.5. Then the combined relation would look like Fig. 3.8.

title	year	length	filmType	studioName	starName
Star Wars	1977	124	color	Fox	Carrie Fisher
Star Wars	1977	124	color	Fox	Mark Hamill
Star Wars	1977	124	color	Fox	Harrison Ford
Mighty Ducks	1991	104	color	Disney	Emilio Estevez
Wayne's World	1992	95	color	Paramount	Dana Carvey
Wayne's World	1992	95	color	Paramount	Mike Meyers

Figure 3.8: The relation `Movies` with star information

Because a movie can have several stars, we are forced to repeat all the information about a movie, once for each star. For instance, we see in Fig. 3.8 that the length of *Star Wars* is repeated three times — once for each star — as is the fact that the movie is owned by Fox. This redundancy is undesirable, and the purpose of the relational-database design theory of Section 3.6 is to split relations such as that of Fig. 3.8 and thereby remove the redundancy. $\square$

3.2.4 Handling Weak Entity Sets

When a weak entity set appears in an E/R diagram, we need to do three things differently.

1. The relation for the weak entity set W itself must include not only the attributes of W but also the key attributes of the other entity sets that help form the key of W. These helping entity sets are easily recognized because they are reached by supporting (double-diamond) relationships from W.

2. The relation for any relationship in which the weak entity set W appears must use as a key for W all of its key attributes, including those of other entity sets that contribute to W's key.

3. However, a supporting relationship R, from the weak entity set W to another entity set that helps provide the key for W, need not be converted to a relation at all. The justification is that, as discussed in Section 3.2.3, the attributes of many-one relationship R's relation will either *be* attributes of the relation for W, or (in the case of attributes on R) can be combined with the schema for W's relation.

Of course, when introducing additional attributes to build the key of a weak entity set, we must be careful not to use the same name twice. If necessary, we rename some or all of these attributes.

Example 3.7: Let us consider the weak entity set *Crews* from Fig. 2.20, which we reproduce here as Fig. 3.9. From this diagram we get three relations, whose schemas are:

```
Studios(name, addr)
Crews(number, studioName)
Unit-of(number, studioName, name)
```

The first relation, `Studios`, is constructed in a straightforward manner from the entity set of the same name. The second, `Crews`, comes from the weak entity set *Crews*. The attributes of this relation are the key attributes of *Crews*; if there were any nonkey attributes for *Crews*, they would be included in the relation schema as well. We have chosen `studioName` as the attribute in relation `Crews` that corresponds to the attribute *name* in the entity set *Studios*.

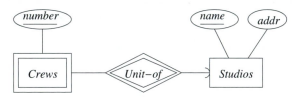

Figure 3.9: The crews example of a weak entity set

The third relation, `Unit-of`, comes from the relationship of the same name. As always, we represent an E/R relationship in the relational model by a relation whose schema has the key attributes of the related entity sets. In this case, `Unit-of` has attributes `number` and `studioName`, the key for weak entity set *Crews*, and attribute `name`, the key for entity set *Studios*. However, notice that since *Unit-of* is a many-one relationship, the studio `studioName` is surely the same as the studio `name`.

For instance, suppose Disney crew #3 is one of the crews of the Disney studio. Then the relationship set for E/R relationship *Unit-of* includes the pair

---

Relations With Subset Schemas

You might imagine from Example 3.7 that whenever one relation R has a set of attributes that is a subset of the attributes of another relation S, we can eliminate R. That is not exactly true. R might hold information that doesn't appear in S because the additional attributes of S do not allow us to extend a tuple from R to S.

For instance, the Internal Revenue Service tries to maintain a relation `People(name, ss#)` of potential taxpayers and their social-security numbers, even if the person had no income and did not file a tax return. They might also maintain a relation `TaxPayers(name, ss#, amount)` indicating the amount of tax paid by each person who filed a return in the current year. The schema of `People` is a subset of the schema of `TaxPayers`, yet there may be value in remembering the social-security number of those who are mentioned in `People` but not in `Taxpayers`.

In fact, even identical sets of attributes may have different semantics, so it is not possible to merge their tuples. An example would be two relations `Stars(name, addr)` and `Studios(name, addr)`. Although the schemas look alike, we cannot turn star tuples into studio tuples, or vice-versa.

On the other hand, when the two relations come from the weak-entity-set construction, then there can be no such additional value to the relation with the smaller set of attributes. The reason is that the tuples of the relation that comes from the supporting relationship correspond one-for-one with the tuples of the relation that comes from the weak entity set. Thus, we routinely eliminate the former relation.

$$\text{(Disney-crew-\#3, Disney)}$$

This pair gives rise to the tuple

$$\text{(3, Disney, Disney)}$$

for the relation `Unit-of`.

Notice that, as must be the case, the components of this tuple for attributes `studioName` and `name` are identical. As a consequence, we can "merge" the attributes `studioName` and `name` of `Unit-of`, giving us the simpler schema:

```
Unit-of(number, name)
```

However, now we can dispense with the relation `Unit-of` altogether, since it is now identical to the relation `Crews`. □

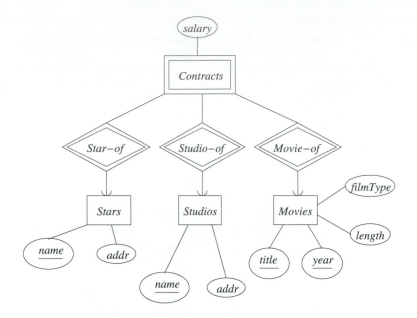

Figure 3.10: The weak entity set *Contracts*

Example 3.8 : Now consider the weak entity set *Contracts* from Example 2.25 and Fig. 2.22 in Section 2.4.1. We reproduce this diagram as Fig. 3.10. The schema for relation `Contracts` is

```
Contracts(starName, studioName, title, year, salary)
```

These attributes are the key for *Stars*, suitably renamed, the key for *Studios*, suitably renamed, the two attributes that form the key for *Movies*, and the lone attribute, *salary*, belonging to the entity set *Contracts* itself. There are no relations constructed for the relationships *Star-of*, *Studio-of*, or *Movie-of*. Each would have a schema that is a proper subset of that for `Contracts` above.

Incidentally, notice that the relation we obtain is exactly the same as what we would obtain had we started from the E/R diagram of Fig. 2.7. Recall that figure treats contracts as a three-way relationship among stars, movies, and studios, with a salary attribute attached to *Contracts*. □

The phenomenon observed in Examples 3.7 and 3.8 — that a supporting relationship needs no relation — is universal for weak entity sets. The following is a modified rule for converting to relations entity sets that are weak.

- If *W* is a weak entity set, construct for *W* a relation whose schema consists of:

  1. All attributes of *W*.

  2. All attributes of supporting relationships for *W*.

3. For each supporting relationship for W, say a many-one relationship from W to entity set E, all the *key* attributes of E.

Rename attributes, if necessary, to avoid name conflicts.

- Do *not* construct a relation for any supporting relationship for W.

3.2.5 Exercises for Section 3.2

* **Exercise 3.2.1:** Convert the E/R diagram of Fig. 3.11 to a relational database schema.

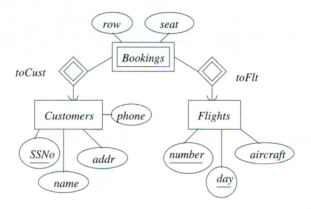

Figure 3.11: An E/R diagram about airlines

! **Exercise 3.2.2:** There is another E/R diagram that could describe the weak entity set *Bookings* in Fig. 3.11. Notice that a booking can be identified uniquely by the flight number, day of the flight, the row, and the seat; the customer is not then necessary to help identify the booking.

   a) Revise the diagram of Fig. 3.11 to reflect this new viewpoint.

   b) Convert your diagram from (a) into relations. Do you get the same database schema as in Exercise 3.2.1?

* **Exercise 3.2.3:** The E/R diagram of Fig. 3.12 represents ships. Ships are said to be *sisters* if they were designed from the same plans. Convert this diagram to a relational database schema.

Exercise 3.2.4: Convert the following E/R diagrams to relational database schemas.

   a) Figure 2.22.

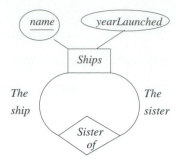

Figure 3.12: An E/R diagram about sister ships

b) Your answer to Exercise 2.4.1.

c) Your answer to Exercise 2.4.4(a).

d) Your answer to Exercise 2.4.4(b).

3.3   Converting Subclass Structures to Relations

When we have an isa-hierarchy of entity sets, we are presented with several choices of strategy for conversion to relations. Recall we assume that:

- There is a root entity set for the hierarchy,

- This entity set has a key that serves to identify every entity represented by the hierarchy, and

- A given entity may have *components* that belong to the entity sets of any subtree of the hierarchy, as long as that subtree includes the root.

The principal conversion strategies are:

1. *Follow the E/R viewpoint.* For each entity set E in the hierarchy, create a relation that includes the key attributes from the root and any attributes belonging to E.

2. *Treat entities as objects belonging to a single class.* For each possible subtree including the root, create one relation, whose schema includes all the attributes of all the entity sets in the subtree.

3. *Use null values.* Create one relation with all the attributes of all the entity sets in the hierarchy. Each entity is represented by one tuple, and that tuple has a null value for whatever attributes the entity does not have.

We shall consider each approach in turn.

3.3.1 E/R-Style Conversion

Our first approach is to create a relation for each entity set, as usual. If the entity set E is not the root of the hierarchy, then the relation for E will include the key attributes at the root, to identify the entity represented by each tuple, plus all the attributes of E. In addition, if E is involved in a relationship, then we use these key attributes to identify entities of E in the relation corresponding to that relationship.

Note, however, that although we spoke of "isa" as a relationship, it is unlike other relationships, in that it connects components of a single entity, not distinct entities. Thus, we do not create a relation for "isa."

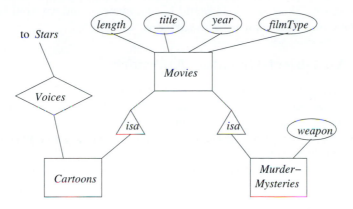

Figure 3.13: The movie hierarchy

Example 3.9: Consider the hierarchy of Fig. 2.10, which we reproduce here as Fig. 3.13. The relations needed to represent the four different kinds of entities in this hierarchy are:

1. `Movies(title, year, length, filmType)`. This relation was discussed in Example 3.1, and every movie is represented by a tuple here.

2. `MurderMysteries(title, year, weapon)`. The first two attributes are the key for all movies, and the last is the lone attribute for the corresponding entity set. Those movies that are murder mysteries have a tuple here as well as in `Movies`.

3. `Cartoons(title, year)`. This relation is the set of cartoons. It has no attributes other than the key for movies, since the extra information about cartoons is contained in the relationship *Voices*. Movies that are cartoons have a tuple here as well as in `Movies`.

Note that the fourth kind of movie — those that are both cartoons and murder mysteries — have tuples in all three relations.

In addition, we shall need the relation `Voices(title, year, starName)` that corresponds to the relationship *Voices* between *Stars* and *Cartoons*. The last attribute is the key for *Stars* and the first two form the key for *Cartoons*.

For instance, the movie *Roger Rabbit* would have tuples in all four relations. Its basic information would be in `Movies`, the murder weapon would appear in `MurderMysteries`, and the stars that provided voices for the movie would appear in `Voices`.

Notice that the relation `Cartoons` has a schema that is a subset of the schema for the relation `Voices`. In many situations, we would be content to eliminate a relation such as `Cartoons`, since it appears not to contain any information beyond what is in `Voices`. However, there may be silent cartoons in our database. Those cartoons would have no voices, and we would therefore lose the fact that these movies were cartoons.   □

3.3.2   An Object-Oriented Approach

An alternative strategy for converting isa-hierarchies to relations is to enumerate all the possible subtrees of the hierarchy. For each, create one relation that represents entities that have components in exactly those subtrees; the schema for this relation has all the attributes of any entity set in the subtree. We refer to this approach as "object-oriented," since it is motivated by the assumption that entities are "objects" that belong to one and only one class.

Example 3.10 : Consider the hierarchy of Fig. 3.13. There are four possible subtrees including the root:

1. *Movies* alone.

2. *Movies* and *Cartoons* only.

3. *Movies* and *Murder-Mysteries* only.

4. All three entity sets.

We must construct relations for all four "classes." Since only Murder-Mysteries contributes an attribute that is unique to its entities, there is actually some repetition, and these four relations are:

```
Movies(title, year, length, filmType)
MoviesC(title, year, length, filmType)
MoviesMM(title, year, length, filmType, weapon)
MoviesCMM(title, year, length, filmType, weapon)
```

Had *Cartoons* had attributes unique to that entity set, then all four relations would have different sets of attributes. As that is not the case here, we could combine `Movies` with `MoviesC` (i.e., create one relation for non-murder-mysteries) and combine `MoviesMM` with `MoviesCMM` (i.e., create one relation for all murder mysteries), although doing so loses some information — which movies are cartoons.

We also need to consider how to handle the relationship *Voices* from *Cartoons* to *Stars*. If *Voices* were many-one from *Cartoons*, then we could add a `voice` attribute to `MoviesC` and `MoviesCMM`, which would represent the *Voices* relationship and would have the side-effect of making all four relations different. However, *Voices* is many-many, so we need to create a separate relation for this relationship. As always, its schema has the key attributes from the entity sets connected; in this case

```
Voices(title, year, starName)
```

would be an appropriate schema.

One might consider whether it was necessary to create two such relations, one connecting cartoons that are not murder mysteries to their voices, and the other for cartoons that *are* murder mysteries. However, there does not appear to be any benefit to doing so in this case. □

3.3.3 Using Null Values to Combine Relations

There is one more approach to representing information about a hierarchy of entity sets. If we are allowed to use `NULL` (the null value as in SQL) as a value in tuples, we can handle a hierarchy of entity sets with a single relation. This relation has all the attributes belonging to any entity set of the hierarchy. An entity is then represented by a single tuple. This tuple has `NULL` in each attribute that is not defined for that entity.

Example 3.11: If we applied this approach to the diagram of Fig. 3.13, we would create a single relation whose schema is:

```
Movie(title, year, length, filmType, weapon)
```

Those movies that are not murder mysteries would have `NULL` in the `weapon` component of their tuple. It would also be necessary to have a relation `Voices` to connect those movies that are cartoons to the stars performing the voices, as in Example 3.10. □

3.3.4 Comparison of Approaches

Each of the three approaches, which we shall refer to as "straight-E/R," "object-oriented," and "nulls," respectively, have advantages and disadvantages. Here is a list of the principal issues.

1. It is expensive to answer queries involving several relations, so we would prefer to find all the attributes we needed to answer a query in one relation. The nulls approach uses only one relation for all the attributes, so it has an advantage in this regard. The other two approaches have advantages for different kinds of queries. For instance:

(a) A query like "what films of 1999 were longer than 150 minutes?" can be answered directly from the relation Movies in the straight-E/R approach of Example 3.9. However, in the object-oriented approach of Example 3.10, we need to examine Movies, MoviesC, MoviesMM, and MoviesCMM, since a long movie may be in any of these four relations.[1]

(b) On the other hand, a query like "what weapons were used in cartoons of over 150 minutes in length?" gives us trouble in the straight-E/R approach. We must access Movies to find those movies of over 150 minutes. We must access Cartoons to verify that a movie is a cartoon, and we must access MurderMysteries to find the murder weapon. In the object-oriented approach, we have only to access the relation MoviesCMM, where all the information we need will be found.

2. We would like not to use too many relations. Here again, the nulls method shines, since it requires only one relation. However, there is a difference between the other two methods, since in the straight-E/R approach, we use only one relation per entity set in the hierarchy. In the object-oriented approach, if we have a root and n children ($n + 1$ entity sets in all), then there are 2^n different classes of entities, and we need that many relations.

3. We would like to minimize space and avoid repeating information. Since the object-oriented method uses only one tuple per entity, and that tuple has components for only those attributes that make sense for the entity, this approach offers the minimum possible space usage. The nulls approach also has only one tuple per entity, but these tuples are "long"; i.e., they have components for all attributes, whether or not they are appropriate for a given entity. If there are many entity sets in the hierarchy, and there are many attributes among those entity sets, then a large fraction of the space could wind up not being used in the nulls approach. The straight-E/R method has several tuples for each entity, but only the key attributes are repeated. Thus, this method could use either more or less space than the nulls method.

3.3.5   Exercises for Section 3.3

* **Exercise 3.3.1:** Convert the E/R diagram of Fig. 3.14 to a relational database schema, using each of the following approaches:

a) The straight-E/R method.

b) The object-oriented method.

c) The nulls method.

---

[1] Even if we combine the four relations into two, we must still access both relations to answer the query.

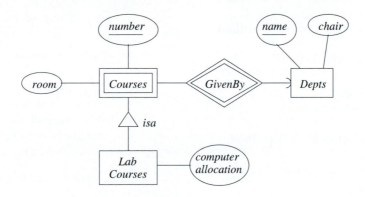

Figure 3.14: E/R diagram for Exercise 3.3.1

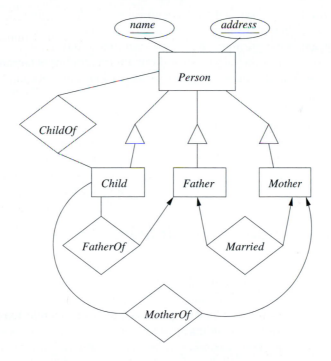

Figure 3.15: E/R diagram for Exercise 3.3.2

! **Exercise 3.3.2:** Convert the E/R diagram of Fig. 3.15 to a relational database schema, using:

   a) The straight-E/R method.

   b) The object-oriented method.

   c) The nulls method.

Exercise 3.3.3: Convert your E/R design from Exercise 2.1.7 to a relational database schema, using:

   a) The straight-E/R method.

   b) The object-oriented method.

   c) The nulls method.

! **Exercise 3.3.4:** Suppose that we have an isa-hierarchy involving e entity sets. Each entity set has a attributes, and k of those at the root form the key for all these entity sets. Give formulas for (i) the minimum and maximum number of relations used, and (ii) the minimum and maximum number of components that the tuple(s) for a single entity have all together, when the method of conversion to relations is:

 * a) The straight-E/R method.

   b) The object-oriented method.

   c) The nulls method.

3.4   Functional Dependencies

Sections 3.2 and 3.3 showed us how to convert E/R designs into relational schemas. It is also possible for database designers to produce relational schemas directly from application requirements, although doing so can be difficult. Regardless of how relational designs are produced, we shall see that frequently it is possible to improve designs systematically based on certain types of constraints. The most important type of constraint we use for relational schema design is a unique-value constraint called a "functional dependency" (often abbreviated FD). Knowledge of this type of constraint is vital for the redesign of database schemas to eliminate redundancy, as we shall see in Section 3.6. There are also some other kinds of constraints that help us design good databases schemas. For instance, multivalued dependencies are covered in Section 3.7, and referential-integrity constraints are mentioned in Section 5.5.

3.4.1 Definition of Functional Dependency

A *functional dependency* (FD) on a relation R is a statement of the form "If two tuples of R agree on attributes $A_1, A_2, \ldots, A_n$ (i.e., the tuples have the same values in their respective components for each of these attributes), then they must also agree on another attribute, B." We write this FD formally as $A_1 A_2 \cdots A_n \rightarrow B$ and say that "$A_1, A_2, \ldots, A_n$ functionally determine B."

If a set of attributes $A_1, A_2, \ldots, A_n$ functionally determines more than one attribute, say

$$A_1 A_2 \cdots A_n \rightarrow B_1$$
$$A_1 A_2 \cdots A_n \rightarrow B_2$$
$$\cdots$$
$$A_1 A_2 \cdots A_n \rightarrow B_m$$

then we can, as a shorthand, write this set of FD's as

$$A_1 A_2 \cdots A_n \rightarrow B_1 B_2 \cdots B_m$$

Figure 3.16 suggests what this FD tells us about any two tuples t and u in the relation R.

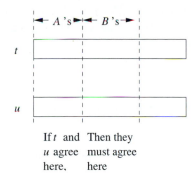

Figure 3.16: The effect of a functional dependency on two tuples.

Example 3.12 : Let us consider the relation

```
Movies(title, year, length, filmType, studioName, starName)
```

from Fig. 3.8, an instance of which we reproduce here as Fig. 3.17. There are several FD's that we can reasonably assert about the Movies relation. For instance, we can assert the three FD's:

```
title year → length
title year → filmType
title year → studioName
```

title	year	length	filmType	studioName	starName
Star Wars	1977	124	color	Fox	Carrie Fisher
Star Wars	1977	124	color	Fox	Mark Hamill
Star Wars	1977	124	color	Fox	Harrison Ford
Mighty Ducks	1991	104	color	Disney	Emilio Estevez
Wayne's World	1992	95	color	Paramount	Dana Carvey
Wayne's World	1992	95	color	Paramount	Mike Meyers

Figure 3.17: An instance of the relation Movies(title, year, length, filmType, studioName, starName)

Since the three FD's each have the same left side, title and year, we can summarize them in one line by the shorthand

$$\text{title year} \rightarrow \text{length filmType studioName}$$

Informally, this set of FD's says that if two tuples have the same value in their title components, and they also have the same value in their year components, then these two tuples must have the same values in their length components, the same values in their filmType components, and the same values in their studioName components. This assertion makes sense if we remember the original design from which this relation schema was developed. Attributes title and year form a key for the *Movies* entity set. Thus, we expect that given a title and year, there is a unique movie. Therefore, there is a unique length for the movie and a unique film type. Further, there is a many-one relationship from *Movies* to *Studios*. Consequently, we expect that given a movie, there is only one owning studio.

On the other hand, we observe that the statement

$$\text{title year} \rightarrow \text{starName}$$

is false; it is not a functional dependency. Given a movie, it is entirely possible that there is more than one star for the movie listed in our database.   □

3.4.2 Keys of Relations

We say a set of one or more attributes $\{A_1, A_2, \ldots, A_n\}$ is a *key* for a relation R if:

1. Those attributes functionally determine all other attributes of the relation. That is, because relations are sets, it is impossible for two distinct tuples of R to agree on all of $A_1, A_2, \ldots, A_n$.

Functional Dependencies Tell Us About the Schema

Remember that a FD, like any constraint, is an assertion about the schema of a relation, not about a particular instance. If we look at an instance, we cannot tell for certain that a FD holds. For example, looking at Fig. 3.17 we might suppose that a FD like `title` → `filmType` holds, because for every tuple in this particular instance of the relation `Movies` it happens that any two tuples agreeing on `title` also agree on `filmType`.

However, we cannot claim this FD for the relation `Movies`. Were our instance to include, for example, tuples for the two versions of *King Kong*, one of which was in color and the other in black-and-white, then the proposed FD would not hold.

---

2. No proper subset of $\{A_1, A_2, \ldots, A_n\}$ functionally determines all other attributes of R; i.e., a key must be *minimal*.

When a key consists of a single attribute A, we often say that A (rather than $\{A\}$) is a key.

Example 3.13: Attributes {`title`, `year`, `starName`} form a key for the relation `Movies` of Fig. 3.17. First, we must show that they functionally determine all the other attributes. That is, suppose two tuples agree on these three attributes: `title`, `year`, and `starName`. Because they agree on `title` and `year`, they must agree on the other attributes — `length`, `filmType`, and `studioName` — as we discussed in Example 3.12. Thus, two different tuples cannot agree on all of `title`, `year`, and `starName`; they would in fact be the same tuple.

Now, we must argue that no proper subset of {`title`, `year`, `starName`} functionally determines all other attributes. To see why, begin by observing that `title` and `year` do not determine `starName`, because many movies have more than one star. Thus, {`title`, `year`} is not a key.

{`year`, `starName`} is not a key because we could have a star in two movies in the same year; therefore

$$\text{year starName} \rightarrow \text{title}$$

is not a FD. Also, we claim that {`title`, `starName`} is not a key, because two movies with the same title, made in different years, occasionally have a star in common.[2] □

---

[2]Since we asserted in an earlier book that there were no known examples of this phenomenon, several people have shown us we were wrong. It's an interesting challenge to discover stars that appeared in two versions of the same movie.

Minimality of Keys

The requirement that a key be minimal was not present in the E/R model, although in the relational model, we *do* require keys to be minimal. While we suppose designers using the E/R model would not add unnecessary attributes to the keys they declare, we have no way of knowing whether an E/R key is minimal or not. Only when we have a formal representation such as FD's can we even ask the question whether a set of attributes is a minimal set that can serve as a key for some relation.

Incidentally, remember the difference between "minimal" — you can't throw anything out — and "minimum" — smallest of all possible. A minimal key may not have the minimum number of attributes of any key for the given relation. For example, we might find that ABC and DE are both keys (i.e., minimal), while only DE is of the minimum possible size for any key.

Sometimes a relation has more than one key. If so, it is common to designate one of the keys as the *primary key*. In commercial database systems, the choice of primary key can influence some implementation issues such as how the relation is stored on disk. A useful convention we shall follow is:

- Underline the attributes of the primary key when displaying its relation schema.

3.4.3 Superkeys

A set of attributes that contains a key is called a *superkey*, short for "superset of a key." Thus, every key is a superkey. However, some superkeys are not (minimal) keys. Note that every superkey satisfies the first condition of a key: it functionally determines all other attributes of the relation. However, a superkey need not satisfy the second condition: minimality.

Example 3.14 : In the relation of Example 3.13, there are many superkeys. Not only is the key

$$\{\texttt{title, year, starName}\}$$

a superkey, but any superset of this set of attributes, such as

$$\{\texttt{title, year, starName, length, studioName}\}$$

is a superkey.   □

What Is "Functional" About Functional Dependencies?

$A_1 A_2 \cdots A_n \rightarrow B$ is called a "functional" dependency because in principle there is a function that takes a list of values, one for each of attributes $A_1, A_2, \ldots, A_n$ and produces a unique value (or no value at all) for B. For example, in the `Movies` relation, we can imagine a function that takes a string like `"Star Wars"` and an integer like 1977 and produces the unique value of `length`, namely 124, that appears in the relation `Movies`. However, this function is not the usual sort of function that we meet in mathematics, because there is no way to compute it from first principles. That is, we cannot perform some operations on strings like `"Star Wars"` and integers like 1977 and come up with the correct length. Rather, the function is only computed by lookup in the relation. We look for a tuple with the given `title` and `year` values and see what value that tuple has for `length`.

3.4.4 Discovering Keys for Relations

When a relation schema was developed by converting an E/R design to relations, we can often predict the key of the relation. Our first rule about inferring keys is:

- If the relation comes from an entity set then the key for the relation is the key attributes of this entity set.

Example 3.15: In Example 3.1 we described how the entity sets *Movies* and *Stars* could be converted to relations. The keys for these entity sets were {*title, year*} and {*name*}, respectively. Thus, these are the keys for the corresponding relations, and

$$\text{Movies(\underline{title}, \underline{year}, length, filmType)}$$
$$\text{Stars(\underline{name}, address)}$$

are the schemas of the relations, with keys indicated by underline. □

Our second rule concerns binary relationships. If a relation R is constructed from a relationship, then the multiplicity of the relationship affects the key for R. There are three cases:

- If the relationship is many-many, then the keys of both connected entity sets are the key attributes for R.

- If the relationship is many-one from entity set E_1 to entity set E_2, then the key attributes of E_1 are key attributes of R, but those of E_2 are not.

Other Key Terminology

In some books and articles one finds different terminology regarding keys. One can find the term "key" used the way we have used the term "superkey," that is, a set of attributes that functionally determine all the attributes, with no requirement of minimality. These sources typically use the term "candidate key" for a key that is minimal — that is, a "key" in the sense we use the term.

- If the relationship is one-one, then the key attributes for either of the connected entity sets are key attributes of R. Thus, there is not a unique key for R.

Example 3.16: Example 3.2 discussed the relationship *Owns*, which is many-one from entity set *Movies* to entity set *Studios*. Thus, the key for the relation `Owns` is the key attributes `title` and `year`, which come from the key for *Movies*. The schema for `Owns`, with key attributes underlined, is thus

Owns(<u>title</u>, <u>year</u>, studioName)

In contrast, Example 3.3 discussed the many-many relationship *Stars-in* between *Movies* and *Stars*. Now, all attributes of the resulting relation

Stars-in(<u>title</u>, <u>year</u>, <u>starName</u>)

are key attributes. In fact, the only way the relation from a many-many relationship could not have all its attributes be part of the key is if the relationship itself has an attribute. Those attributes are omitted from the key.   □

Finally, let us consider multiway relationships. Since we cannot describe all possible dependencies by the arrows coming out of the relationship, there are situations where the key or keys will not be obvious without thinking in detail about which sets of entity sets functionally determine which other entity sets. One guarantee we can make, however, is

- If a multiway relationship R has an arrow to entity set E, then there is at least one key for the corresponding relation that excludes the key of E.

3.4.5 Exercises for Section 3.4

Exercise 3.4.1: Consider a relation about people in the United States, including their name, Social Security number, street address, city, state, ZIP code, area code, and phone number (7 digits). What FD's would you expect to hold? What are the keys for the relation? To answer this question, you need to know

---

Other Notions of Functional Dependencies

We take the position that a FD can have several attributes on the left but only a single attribute on the right. Moreover, the attribute on the right may not appear also on the left. However, we allow several FD's with a common left side to be combined as a shorthand, giving us a set of attributes on the right. We shall also find it occasionally convenient to allow a "trivial" FD whose right side is one of the attributes on the left.

Other works on the subject often start from the point of view that both left and right side are arbitrary sets of attributes, and attributes may appear on both left and right. There is no important difference between the two approaches, but we shall maintain the position that, unless stated otherwise, there is no attribute on both left and right of a FD.

---

something about the way these numbers are assigned. For instance, can an area code straddle two states? Can a ZIP code straddle two area codes? Can two people have the same Social Security number? Can they have the same address or phone number?

* Exercise 3.4.2: Consider a relation representing the present position of molecules in a closed container. The attributes are an ID for the molecule, the x, y, and z coordinates of the molecule, and its velocity in the x, y, and z dimensions. What FD's would you expect to hold? What are the keys?

! Exercise 3.4.3: In Exercise 2.2.5 we discussed three different assumptions about the relationship *Births*. For each of these, indicate the key or keys of the relation constructed from this relationship.

* Exercise 3.4.4: In your database schema constructed for Exercise 3.2.1, indicate the keys you would expect for each relation.

Exercise 3.4.5: For each of the four parts of Exercise 3.2.4, indicate the expected keys of your relations.

!! Exercise 3.4.6: Suppose R is a relation with attributes $A_1, A_2, \ldots, A_n$. As a function of n, tell how many superkeys R has, if:

* * a) The only key is A_1.

* b) The only keys are A_1 and A_2.

* c) The only keys are $\{A_1, A_2\}$ and $\{A_3, A_4\}$.

* d) The only keys are $\{A_1, A_2\}$ and $\{A_1, A_3\}$.

3.5   Rules About Functional Dependencies

In this section, we shall learn how to *reason* about FD's. That is, suppose we are told of a set of FD's that a relation satisfies. Often, we can deduce that the relation must satisfy certain other FD's. This ability to discover additional FD's is essential when we discuss the design of good relation schemas in Section 3.6.

Example 3.17: If we are told that a relation R with attributes A, B, and C, satisfies the FD's $A \rightarrow B$ and $B \rightarrow C$, then we can deduce that R also satisfies the FD $A \rightarrow C$. How does that reasoning go? To prove that $A \rightarrow C$, we must consider two tuples of R that agree on A and prove they also agree on C.

Let the tuples agreeing on attribute A be (a, b_1, c_1) and (a, b_2, c_2). We assume\the order of attributes in tuples is A, B, C. Since R satisfies $A \rightarrow B$, and these tuples agree on A, they must also agree on B. That is, $b_1 = b_2$, and the tuples are really (a, b, c_1) and (a, b, c_2), where b is both b_1 and b_2. Similarly, since R satisfies $B \rightarrow C$, and the tuples agree on B, they agree on C. Thus, $c_1 = c_2$; i.e., the tuples *do* agree on C. We have proved that any two tuples of R that agree on A also agree on C, and that is the FD $A \rightarrow C$.   □

FD's often can be presented in several different ways, without changing the set of legal instances of the relation. We say:

- Two sets of FD's S and T are *equivalent* if the set of relation instances satisfying S is exactly the same as the set of relation instances satisfying T.

- More generally, a set of FD's S *follows* from a set of FD's T if every relation instance that satisfies all the FD's in T also satisfies all the FD's in S.

Note then that two sets of FD's S and T are equivalent if and only if S follows from T, and T follows from S.

In this section we shall see several useful rules about FD's. In general, these rules let us replace one set of FD's by an equivalent set, or to add to a set of FD's others that follow from the original set. An example is the *transitive rule* that lets us follow chains of FD's, as in Example 3.17. We shall also give an algorithm for answering the general question of whether one FD follows from one or more other FD's.

3.5.1   The Splitting/Combining Rule

Recall that in Section 3.4.1 we defined the FD:

$$A_1 A_2 \cdots A_n \; \rightarrow \; B_1 B_2 \cdots B_m$$

to be a shorthand for the set of FD's:

$$A_1 A_2 \cdots A_n \to B_1$$
$$A_1 A_2 \cdots A_n \to B_2$$
$$\cdots$$
$$A_1 A_2 \cdots A_n \to B_m$$

That is, we may split attributes on the right side so that only one attribute appears on the right of each FD. Likewise, we can replace a collection of FD's with a common left side by a single FD with the same left side and all the right sides combined into one set of attributes. In either event, the new set of FD's is equivalent to the old. The equivalence noted above can be used in two ways.

- We can replace a FD $A_1 A_2 \cdots A_n \to B_1 B_2 \cdots B_m$ by a set of FD's $A_1 A_2 \cdots A_n \to B_i$ for $i = 1, 2, \ldots, m$. This transformation we call the *splitting rule*.

- We can replace a set of FD's $A_1 A_2 \cdots A_n \to B_i$ for $i = 1, 2, \ldots, m$ by the single FD $A_1 A_2 \cdots A_n \to B_1 B_2 \cdots B_m$. We call this transformation the *combining rule*.

For instance, we mentioned in Example 3.12 how the set of FD's:

$$\texttt{title year} \to \texttt{length}$$
$$\texttt{title year} \to \texttt{filmType}$$
$$\texttt{title year} \to \texttt{studioName}$$

is equivalent to the single FD:

$$\texttt{title year} \to \texttt{length filmType studioName}$$

One might imagine that splitting could be applied to the left sides of FD's as well as to right sides. However, there is no splitting rule for left sides, as the following example shows.

Example 3.18 : Consider one of the FD's such as:

$$\texttt{title year} \to \texttt{length}$$

for the relation `Movies` in Example 3.12. If we try to split the left side into

$$\texttt{title} \to \texttt{length}$$
$$\texttt{year} \to \texttt{length}$$

then we get two false FD's. That is, `title` does not functionally determine `length`, since there can be two movies with the same title (e.g., *King Kong*) but of different lengths. Similarly, `year` does not functionally determine `length`, because there are certainly movies of different lengths made in any one year. □

3.5.2   Trivial Functional Dependencies

A FD $A_1 A_2 \cdots A_n \rightarrow B$ is said to be *trivial* if B is one of the A's. For example,

$$\text{title year} \rightarrow \text{title}$$

is a trivial FD.

Every trivial FD holds in every relation, since it says that "two tuples that agree in all of $A_1, A_2, \ldots, A_n$ agree in one of them." Thus, we may assume any trivial FD, without having to justify it on the basis of what FD's are asserted for the relation.

In our original definition of FD's, we did not allow a FD to be trivial. However, there is no harm in including them, since they are always true, and they sometimes simplify the statement of rules.

When we allow trivial FD's, then we also allow (as shorthands) FD's in which some of the attributes on the right are also on the left. We say that a FD $A_1 A_2 \cdots A_n \rightarrow B_1 B_2 \cdots B_m$ is

- *Trivial* if the B's are a subset of the A's.

- *Nontrivial* if at least one of the B's is not among the A's.

- *Completely nontrivial* if none of the B's is also one of the A's.

Thus

$$\text{title year} \rightarrow \text{year length}$$

is nontrivial, but not completely nontrivial. By eliminating **year** from the right side we would get a completely nontrivial FD.

We can always remove from the right side of a FD those attributes that appear on the left. That is:

- The FD $A_1 A_2 \cdots A_n \rightarrow B_1 B_2 \cdots B_m$ is equivalent to

$$A_1 A_2 \cdots A_n \rightarrow C_1 C_2 \cdots C_k$$

where the C's are all those B's that are not also A's.

We call this rule, illustrated in Fig. 3.18, the *trivial-dependency rule*.

3.5.3   Computing the Closure of Attributes

Before proceeding to other rules, we shall give a general principle from which all rules follow. Suppose $\{A_1, A_2, \ldots, A_n\}$ is a set of attributes and S is a set of FD's. The *closure* of $\{A_1, A_2, \ldots, A_n\}$ under the FD's in S is the set of attributes B such that every relation that satisfies all the FD's in set S also satisfies $A_1 A_2 \cdots A_n \rightarrow B$. That is, $A_1 A_2 \cdots A_n \rightarrow B$ follows from the FD's of S. We denote the closure of a set of attributes $A_1 A_2 \cdots A_n$ by

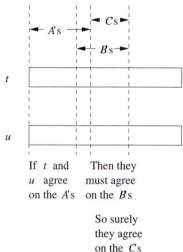

If t and   Then they
u agree   must agree
on the A's   on the Bs

So surely
they agree
on the Cs

Figure 3.18: The trivial-dependency rule

$\{A_1, A_2, \ldots, A_n\}^+$. To simplify the discussion of computing closures, we shall allow trivial FD's, so $A_1, A_2, \ldots, A_n$ are always in $\{A_1, A_2, \ldots, A_n\}^+$.

Figure 3.19 illustrates the closure process. Starting with the given set of attributes, we repeatedly expand the set by adding the right sides of FD's as soon as we have included their left sides. Eventually, we cannot expand the set any more, and the resulting set is the closure. The following steps are a more detailed rendition of the algorithm for computing the closure of a set of attributes $\{A_1, A_2, \ldots, A_n\}$ with respect to a set of FD's.

1. Let X be a set of attributes that eventually will become the closure. First, we initialize X to be $\{A_1, A_2, \ldots, A_n\}$.

2. Now, we repeatedly search for some FD $B_1 B_2 \cdots B_m \rightarrow C$ such that all of $B_1, B_2, \ldots, B_m$ are in the set of attributes X, but C is not. We then add C to the set X.

3. Repeat step 2 as many times as necessary until no more attributes can be added to X. Since X can only grow, and the number of attributes of any relation schema must be finite, eventually nothing more can be added to X.

4. The set X, after no more attributes can be added to it, is the correct value of $\{A_1, A_2, \ldots, A_n\}^+$.

Example 3.19: Let us consider a relation with attributes A, B, C, D, E, and F. Suppose that this relation has the FD's $AB \rightarrow C$, $BC \rightarrow AD$, $D \rightarrow E$, and $CF \rightarrow B$. What is the closure of $\{A, B\}$, that is, $\{A, B\}^+$?

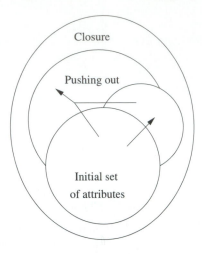

Figure 3.19: Computing the closure of a set of attributes

We start with $X = \{A, B\}$. First, notice that both attributes on the left side of FD $AB \rightarrow C$ are in X, so we may add the attribute C, which is on the right side of that FD. Thus, after one iteration of step 2, X becomes $\{A, B, C\}$.

Next, we see that the left side of $BC \rightarrow AD$ is now contained in X, so we may add to X the attributes A and D.[3] A is already there, but D is not, so X next becomes $\{A, B, C, D\}$. At this point, we may use the FD $D \rightarrow E$ to add E to X, which is now $\{A, B, C, D, E\}$. No more changes to X are possible. In particular, the FD $CF \rightarrow B$ can not be used, because its left side never becomes contained in X. Thus, $\{A, B\}^+ = \{A, B, C, D, E\}$.   □

If we know how to compute the closure of any set of attributes, then we can test whether any given FD $A_1 A_2 \cdots A_n \rightarrow B$ follows from a set of FD's S. First compute $\{A_1, A_2, \ldots, A_n\}^+$ using the set of FD's S. If B is in $\{A_1, A_2, \ldots, A_n\}^+$, then $A_1 A_2 \cdots A_n \rightarrow B$ does follow from S, and if B is not in $\{A_1, A_2, \ldots, A_n\}^+$, then this FD does not follow from S. More generally, a FD with a set of attributes on the right can be tested if we remember that this FD is a shorthand for a set of FD's. Thus, $A_1 A_2 \cdots A_n \rightarrow B_1 B_2 \cdots B_m$ follows from set of FD's S if and only if all of $B_1, B_2, \ldots, B_m$ are in $\{A_1, A_2, \ldots, A_n\}^+$.

Example 3.20 : Consider the relation and FD's of Example 3.19. Suppose we wish to test whether $AB \rightarrow D$ follows from these FD's. We compute $\{A, B\}^+$, which is $\{A, B, C, D, E\}$, as we saw in that example. Since D is a member of the closure, we conclude that $AB \rightarrow D$ does follow.

On the other hand, consider the FD $D \rightarrow A$. To test whether this FD follows from the given FD's, first compute $\{D\}^+$. To do so, we start with $X = \{D\}$. We can use the FD $D \rightarrow E$ to add E to the set X. However,

---

[3]Recall that $BC \rightarrow AD$ is shorthand for the pair of FD's $BC \rightarrow A$ and $BC \rightarrow D$. We could treat each of these FD's separately if we wished.

then we are stuck. We cannot find any other FD whose left side is contained in $X = \{D, E\}$, so $\{D\}^+ = \{D, E\}$. Since A is not a member of $\{D, E\}$, we conclude that $D \rightarrow A$ does not follow. $\square$

3.5.4 Why the Closure Algorithm Works

In this section, we shall show why the closure algorithm correctly decides whether or not a FD $A_1 A_2 \cdots A_n \rightarrow B$ follows from a given set of FD's S. There are two parts to the proof:

1. We must prove that the closure algorithm does not claim too much. That is, we must show that if $A_1 A_2 \cdots A_n \rightarrow B$ is asserted by the closure test (i.e., B is in $\{A_1, A_2, \ldots, A_n\}^+$), then $A_1 A_2 \cdots A_n \rightarrow B$ holds in any relation that satisfies all the FD's in S.

2. We must prove that the closure algorithm does not fail to discover a FD that truly follows from the set of FD's S.

Why the Closure Algorithm Claims only True FD's

We can prove by induction on the number of times that we apply the growing operation of step 2 that for every attribute D in X, the FD $A_1 A_2 \cdots A_n \rightarrow D$ holds (in the special case where D is among the A's, this FD is trivial). That is, every relation R satisfying all of the FD's in S also satisfies $A_1 A_2 \cdots A_n \rightarrow D$.

BASIS: The basis case is when there are zero steps. Then D must be one of $A_1, A_2, \ldots, A_n$, and surely $A_1 A_2 \cdots A_n \rightarrow D$ holds in any relation, because it is a trivial FD.

INDUCTION: For the induction, suppose D was added when we used the FD $B_1 B_2 \cdots B_m \rightarrow D$. We know by the inductive hypothesis that R satisfies $A_1 A_2 \cdots A_n \rightarrow B_i$ for all $i = 1, 2, \ldots, m$. Put another way, any two tuples of R that agree on all of $A_1, A_2, \ldots, A_n$ also agree on all of $B_1, B_2, \ldots, B_m$. Since R satisfies $B_1 B_2 \cdots B_m \rightarrow D$, we also know that these two tuples agree on D. Thus, R satisfies $A_1 A_2 \cdots A_n \rightarrow D$.

Why the Closure Algorithm Discovers All True FD's

Suppose $A_1 A_2 \cdots A_n \rightarrow B$ were a FD that the closure algorithm says does not follow from set S. That is, the closure of $\{A_1, A_2, \ldots, A_n\}$ using set of FD's S does not include B. We must show that FD $A_1 A_2 \cdots A_n \rightarrow B$ really doesn't follow from S. That is, we must show that there is at least one relation instance that satisfies all the FD's in S, and yet does not satisfy $A_1 A_2 \cdots A_n \rightarrow B$.

This instance I is actually quite simple to construct; it is shown in Fig. 3.20. I has only two tuples t and s. The two tuples agree in all the attributes of $\{A_1, A_2, \ldots, A_n\}^+$, and they disagree in all the other attributes. We must show first that I satisfies all the FD's of S, and then that it does not satisfy $A_1 A_2 \cdots A_n \rightarrow B$.

	$\{A_1, A_2, \ldots, A_n\}^+$	Other Attributes
t:	$1\,1\,1\,\cdots\,1\,1$	$0\,0\,0\,\cdots\,0\,0$
s:	$1\,1\,1\,\cdots\,1\,1$	$1\,1\,1\,\cdots\,1\,1$

Figure 3.20: An instance I satisfying S but not $A_1 A_2 \cdots A_n \to B$

Suppose there were some FD $C_1 C_2 \cdots C_k \to D$ in set S that instance I does not satisfy. Since I has only two tuples, t and s, those must be the two tuples that violate $C_1 C_2 \cdots C_k \to D$. That is, t and s agree in all the attributes of $\{C_1, C_2, \ldots, C_k\}$, yet disagree on D. If we examine Fig. 3.20 we see that all of $C_1, C_2, \ldots, C_k$ must be among the attributes of $\{A_1, A_2, \ldots, A_n\}^+$, because those are the only attributes on which t and s agree. Likewise, D must be among the other attributes, because only on those attributes do t and s disagree.

But then we did not compute the closure correctly. $C_1 C_2 \cdots C_k \to D$ should have been applied when X was $\{A_1, A_2, \ldots, A_n\}$ to add D to X. We conclude that $C_1 C_2 \cdots C_k \to D$ cannot exist; i.e., instance I satisfies S.

Second, we must show that I does not satisfy $A_1 A_2 \cdots A_n \to B$. However, this part is easy. Surely, $A_1, A_2, \ldots, A_n$ are among the attributes on which t and s agree. Also, we know that B is not in $\{A_1, A_2, \ldots, A_n\}^+$, so B is one of the attributes on which t and s disagree. Thus, I does not satisfy $A_1 A_2 \cdots A_n \to B$. We conclude that the closure algorithm asserts neither too few nor too many FD's; it asserts exactly those FD's that do follow from S.

3.5.5 The Transitive Rule

The transitive rule lets us cascade two FD's.

- If $A_1 A_2 \cdots A_n \to B_1 B_2 \cdots B_m$ and $B_1 B_2 \cdots B_m \to C_1 C_2 \cdots C_k$ hold in relation R, then $A_1 A_2 \cdots A_n \to C_1 C_2 \cdots C_k$ also holds in R.

If some of the C's are among the A's, we may eliminate them from the right side by the trivial-dependencies rule.

To see why the transitive rule holds, apply the test of Section 3.5.3. To test whether $A_1 A_2 \cdots A_n \to C_1 C_2 \cdots C_k$ holds, we need to compute the closure $\{A_1, A_2, \ldots, A_n\}^+$ with respect to the two given FD's.

The FD $A_1 A_2 \cdots A_n \to B_1 B_2 \cdots B_m$ tells us that all of $B_1, B_2, \ldots, B_m$ are in $\{A_1, A_2, \ldots, A_n\}^+$. Then, we can use the FD $B_1 B_2 \cdots B_m \to C_1 C_2 \cdots C_k$ to add $C_1, C_2, \ldots, C_k$ to $\{A_1, A_2, \ldots, A_n\}^+$. Since all the C's are in

$$\{A_1, A_2, \ldots, A_n\}^+$$

we conclude that $A_1 A_2 \cdots A_n \to C_1 C_2 \cdots C_k$ holds for any relation that satisfies both $A_1 A_2 \cdots A_n \to B_1 B_2 \cdots B_m$ and $B_1 B_2 \cdots B_m \to C_1 C_2 \cdots C_k$.

Closures and Keys

Notice that $\{A_1, A_2, \ldots, A_n\}^+$ is the set of all attributes of a relation if and only if $A_1, A_2, \ldots, A_n$ is a superkey for the relation. For only then does $A_1, A_2, \ldots, A_n$ functionally determine all the other attributes. We can test if $A_1, A_2, \ldots, A_n$ is a key for a relation by checking first that $\{A_1, A_2, \ldots, A_n\}^+$ is all attributes, and then checking that, for no set X formed by removing one attribute from $\{A_1, A_2, \ldots, A_n\}$, is X^+ the set of all attributes.

Example 3.21: Let us begin with the relation `Movies` of Fig. 3.7 that was constructed in Example 3.5 to represent the four attributes of entity set *Movies*, plus its relationship *Owns* with *Studios*. The relation and some sample data is:

title	*year*	*length*	*filmType*	*studioName*
Star Wars	1977	124	color	Fox
Mighty Ducks	1991	104	color	Disney
Wayne's World	1992	95	color	Paramount

Suppose we decided to represent some data about the owning studio in this same relation. For simplicity, we shall add only a city for the studio, representing its address. The relation might then look like

title	*year*	*length*	*filmType*	*studioName*	*studioAddr*
Star Wars	1977	124	color	Fox	Hollywood
Mighty Ducks	1991	104	color	Disney	Buena Vista
Wayne's World	1992	95	color	Paramount	Hollywood

Two of the FD's that we might reasonably claim to hold are:

$$\texttt{title year} \rightarrow \texttt{studioName}$$
$$\texttt{studioName} \rightarrow \texttt{studioAddr}$$

The first is justified because the *Owns* relationship is many-one. The second is justified because the address is an attribute of *Studios*, and the name of the studio is the key of *Studios*.

The transitive rule allows us to combine the two FD's above to get a new FD:

$$\texttt{title year} \rightarrow \texttt{studioAddr}$$

This FD says that a title and year (i.e., a movie) determines an address — the address of the studio owning the movie. □

3.5.6 Closing Sets of Functional Dependencies

As we have seen, given a set of FD's, we can often infer some other FD's, including both trivial and nontrivial FD's. We shall, in later sections, want to distinguish between *given* FD's that are stated initially for a relation and *derived* FD's that are inferred using one of the rules of this section or by using the algorithm for closing a set of attributes.

Moreover, we sometimes have a choice of which FD's we use to represent the full set of FD's for a relation. Any set of given FD's from which we can infer all the FD's for a relation will be called a *basis* for that relation. If no proper subset of the FD's in a basis can also derive the complete set of FD's, then we say the basis is *minimal*.

Example 3.22 : Consider a relation $R(A, B, C)$ such that each attribute functionally determines the other two attributes. The full set of derived FD's thus includes six FD's with one attribute on the left and one on the right; $A \rightarrow B$, $A \rightarrow C$, $B \rightarrow A$, $B \rightarrow C$, $C \rightarrow A$, and $C \rightarrow B$. It also includes the three nontrivial FD's with two attributes on the left: $AB \rightarrow C$, $AC \rightarrow B$, and $BC \rightarrow A$. There are also the shorthands for pairs of FD's such as $A \rightarrow BC$, and we might also include the trivial FD's such as $A \rightarrow A$ or FD's like $AB \rightarrow BC$ that are not completely nontrivial (although in our strict definition of what is a FD we are not required to list trivial or partially trivial FD's, or dependencies that have several attributes on the right).

This relation and its FD's have several minimal bases. One is

$$\{A \rightarrow B,\ B \rightarrow A,\ B \rightarrow C,\ C \rightarrow B\}$$

Another is

$$\{A \rightarrow B,\ B \rightarrow C,\ C \rightarrow A\}$$

There are many other bases, even minimal bases, for this example relation, and we leave their discovery as an exercise.   □

3.5.7 Projecting Functional Dependencies

When we study design of relation schemas, we shall also have need to answer the following question about FD's. Suppose we have a relation R with some FD's F, and we "project" R by eliminating certain attributes from the schema. Suppose S is the relation that results from R if we eliminate the components corresponding to the dropped attributes, in all R's tuples. Since S is a set, duplicate tuples are replaced by one copy. What FD's hold in S?

The answer is obtained in principle by computing all FD's that:

a) Follow from F, and

b) Involve only attributes of S.

A Complete Set of Inference Rules

If we want to know whether one FD follows from some given FD's, the closure computation of Section 3.5.3 will always serve. However, it is interesting to know that there is a set of rules, called *Armstrong's axioms*, from which it is possible to derive any FD that follows from a given set. These axioms are:

1. *Reflexivity.*   If $\{B_1, B_2, \ldots, B_m\} \subseteq \{A_1, A_2, \ldots, A_n\}$, then $A_1 A_2 \cdots A_n \to B_1 B_2 \cdots B_m$. These are what we have called trivial FD's.

2. *Augmentation.* If $A_1 A_2 \cdots A_n \to B_1 B_2 \cdots B_m$, then

$$A_1 A_2 \cdots A_n C_1 C_2 \cdots C_k \to B_1 B_2 \cdots B_m C_1 C_2 \cdots C_k$$

for any set of attributes $C_1, C_2, \ldots, C_k$.

3. *Transitivity.* If

$$A_1 A_2 \cdots A_n \to B_1 B_2 \cdots B_m \text{ and } B_1 B_2 \cdots B_m \to C_1 C_2 \cdots C_k$$

then $A_1 A_2 \cdots A_n \to C_1 C_2 \cdots C_k$.

Since there may be a large number of such FD's, and many of them may be redundant (i.e., they follow from other such FD's), we are free to simplify that set of FD's if we wish. However, in general, the calculation of the FD's for S is in the worst case exponential in the number of attributes of S.

Example 3.23: Suppose $R(A, B, C, D)$ has FD's $A \to B$, $B \to C$, and $C \to D$. Suppose also that we wish to project out the attribute B, leaving a relation $S(A, C, D)$. In principle, to find the FD's for S, we need to take the closure of all eight subsets of $\{A, C, D\}$, using the full set of FD's, including those involving B. However, there are some obvious simplifications we can make.

- Closing the empty set and the set of all attributes cannot yield a nontrivial FD.

- If we already know that the closure of some set X is all attributes, then we cannot discover any new FD's by closing supersets of X.

Thus, we may start with the closures of the singleton sets, and then move on to the doubleton sets if necessary. For each closure of a set X, we add the

FD $X \rightarrow E$ for each attribute E that is in X^+ and in the schema of S, but not in X.

First, $\{A\}^+ = \{A, B, C, D\}$. Thus, $A \rightarrow C$ and $A \rightarrow D$ hold in S. Note that $A \rightarrow B$ is true in R, but makes no sense in S because B is not an attribute of S.

Next, we consider $\{C\}^+ = \{C, D\}$, from which we get the additional FD $C \rightarrow D$ for S. Since $\{D\}^+ = \{D\}$, we can add no more FD's, and are done with the singletons.

Since $\{A\}^+$ includes all attributes of S, there is no point in considering any superset of $\{A\}$. The reason is that whatever FD we could discover, for instance $AC \rightarrow D$, follows by the rule for augmenting left sides [see Exercise 3.5.3(a)] from one of the FD's we already discovered for S by considering A alone as the left side. Thus, the only doubleton whose closure we need to take is $\{C, D\}^+ = \{C, D\}$. This observation allows us to add nothing. We are done with the closures, and the FD's we have discovered are $A \rightarrow C$, $A \rightarrow D$, and $C \rightarrow D$.

If we wish, we can observe that $A \rightarrow D$ follows from the other two by transitivity. Therefore a simpler, equivalent set of FD's for S is $A \rightarrow C$ and $C \rightarrow D$. □

3.5.8 Exercises for Section 3.5

* **Exercise 3.5.1:** Consider a relation with schema $R(A, B, C, D)$ and FD's $AB \rightarrow C$, $C \rightarrow D$, and $D \rightarrow A$.

   a) What are all the nontrivial FD's that follow from the given FD's? You should restrict yourself to FD's with single attributes on the right side.

   b) What are all the keys of R?

   c) What are all the superkeys for R that are not keys?

Exercise 3.5.2: Repeat Exercise 3.5.1 for the following schemas and sets of FD's:

   i) $S(A, B, C, D)$ with FD's $A \rightarrow B$, $B \rightarrow C$, and $B \rightarrow D$.

   ii) $T(A, B, C, D)$ with FD's $AB \rightarrow C$, $BC \rightarrow D$, $CD \rightarrow A$, and $AD \rightarrow B$.

   iii) $U(A, B, C, D)$ with FD's $A \rightarrow B$, $B \rightarrow C$, $C \rightarrow D$, and $D \rightarrow A$.

Exercise 3.5.3: Show that the following rules hold, by using the closure test of Section 3.5.3.

* a) *Augmenting left sides.* If $A_1 A_2 \cdots A_n \rightarrow B$ is a FD, and C is another attribute, then $A_1 A_2 \cdots A_n C \rightarrow B$ follows.

b) *Full augmentation.* If $A_1 A_2 \cdots A_n \rightarrow B$ is a FD, and C is another attribute, then $A_1 A_2 \cdots A_n C \rightarrow BC$ follows. Note: from this rule, the "augmentation" rule mentioned in the box of Section 3.5.6 on "A Complete Set of Inference Rules" can easily be proved.

c) *Pseudotransitivity.* Suppose FD's $A_1 A_2 \cdots A_n \rightarrow B_1 B_2 \cdots B_m$ and $C_1 C_2 \cdots C_k \rightarrow D$ hold, and the B's are each among the C's. Then $A_1 A_2 \cdots A_n E_1 E_2 \cdots E_j \rightarrow D$ holds, where the E's are all those of the C's that are not found among the B's.

d) *Addition.* If FD's $A_1 A_2 \cdots A_n \rightarrow B_1 B_2 \cdots B_m$ and

$$C_1 C_2 \cdots C_k \rightarrow D_1 D_2 \cdots D_j$$

hold, then FD $A_1 A_2 \cdots A_n C_1 C_2 \cdots C_k \rightarrow B_1 B_2 \cdots B_m D_1 D_2 \cdots D_j$ also holds. In the above, we should remove one copy of any attribute that appears among both the A's and C's or among both the B's and D's.

! **Exercise 3.5.4:** Show that each of the following are *not* valid rules about FD's by giving example relations that satisfy the given FD's (following the "if") but not the FD that allegedly follows (after the "then").

* a) If $A \rightarrow B$ then $B \rightarrow A$.

b) If $AB \rightarrow C$ and $A \rightarrow C$, then $B \rightarrow C$.

c) If $AB \rightarrow C$, then $A \rightarrow C$ or $B \rightarrow C$.

! **Exercise 3.5.5:** Show that if a relation has no attribute that is functionally determined by all the other attributes, then the relation has no nontrivial FD's at all.

! **Exercise 3.5.6:** Let X and Y be sets of attributes. Show that if $X \subseteq Y$, then $X^+ \subseteq Y^+$, where the closures are taken with respect to the same set of FD's.

! **Exercise 3.5.7:** Prove that $(X^+)^+ = X^+$.

!! **Exercise 3.5.8:** We say a set of attributes X is *closed* (with respect to a given set of FD's) if $X^+ = X$. Consider a relation with schema $R(A, B, C, D)$ and an unknown set of FD's. If we are told which sets of attributes are closed, we can discover the FD's. What are the FD's if:

* a) All sets of the four attributes are closed.

b) The only closed sets are $\emptyset$ and $\{A, B, C, D\}$.

c) The closed sets are $\emptyset$, $\{A,B\}$, and $\{A, B, C, D\}$.

! **Exercise 3.5.9:** Find all the minimal bases for the FD's and relation of Example 3.22.

! **Exercise 3.5.10 :** Suppose we have relation $R(A, B, C, D, E)$, with some set of FD's, and we wish to project those FD's onto relation $S(A, B, C)$. Give the FD's that hold in S if the FD's for R are:

* a) $AB \rightarrow DE$, $C \rightarrow E$, $D \rightarrow C$, and $E \rightarrow A$.

  b) $A \rightarrow D$, $BD \rightarrow E$, $AC \rightarrow E$, and $DE \rightarrow B$.

  c) $AB \rightarrow D$, $AC \rightarrow E$, $BC \rightarrow D$, $D \rightarrow A$, and $E \rightarrow B$.

  d) $A \rightarrow B$, $B \rightarrow C$, $C \rightarrow D$, $D \rightarrow E$, and $E \rightarrow A$.

In each case, it is sufficient to give a minimal basis for the full set of FD's of S.

!! **Exercise 3.5.11 :** Show that if a FD F follows from some given FD's, then we can prove F from the given FD's using Armstrong's axioms (defined in the box "A Complete Set of Inference Rules" in Section 3.5.6). *Hint*: Examine the algorithm for computing the closure of a set of attributes and show how each step of that algorithm can be mimicked by inferring some FD's by Armstrong's axioms.

3.6   Design of Relational Database Schemas

Careless selection of a relational database schema can lead to problems. For instance, Example 3.6 showed what happens if we try to combine the relation for a many-many relationship with the relation for one of its entity sets. The principal problem we identified is redundancy, where a fact is repeated in more than one tuple. This problem is seen in Fig. 3.17, which we reproduce here as Fig. 3.21; the length and film-type for *Star Wars* and *Wayne's World* are each repeated, once for each star of the movie.

   In this section, we shall tackle the problem of design of good relation schemas in the following stages:

1. We first explore in more detail the problems that arise when our schema is flawed.

2. Then, we introduce the idea of "decomposition," breaking a relation schema (set of attributes) into two smaller schemas.

3. Next, we introduce "Boyce-Codd normal form," or "BCNF," a condition on a relation schema that eliminates these problems.

4. These points are tied together when we explain how to assure the BCNF condition by decomposing relation schemas.

title	year	length	filmType	studioName	starName
Star Wars	1977	124	color	Fox	Carrie Fisher
Star Wars	1977	124	color	Fox	Mark Hamill
Star Wars	1977	124	color	Fox	Harrison Ford
Mighty Ducks	1991	104	color	Disney	Emilio Estevez
Wayne's World	1992	95	color	Paramount	Dana Carvey
Wayne's World	1992	95	color	Paramount	Mike Meyers

Figure 3.21: The relation `Movies` exhibiting anomalies

3.6.1 Anomalies

Problems such as redundancy that occur when we try to cram too much into a single relation are called *anomalies*. The principal kinds of anomalies that we encounter are:

1. *Redundancy.* Information may be repeated unnecessarily in several tuples. Examples are the length and film type for movies as in Fig. 3.21.

2. *Update Anomalies.* We may change information in one tuple but leave the same information unchanged in another. For example, if we found that *Star Wars* was really 125 minutes long, we might carelessly change the length in the first tuple of Fig. 3.21 but not in the second or third tuples. True, we might argue that one should never be so careless. But we shall see that it is possible to redesign relation `Movies` so that the risk of such mistakes does not exist.

3. *Deletion Anomalies.* If a set of values becomes empty, we may lose other information as a side effect. For example, should we delete Emilio Estevez from the set of stars of *Mighty Ducks*, then we have no more stars for that movie in the database. The last tuple for *Mighty Ducks* in the relation `Movies` would disappear, and with it information that it is 104 minutes long and in color.

3.6.2 Decomposing Relations

The accepted way to eliminate these anomalies is to *decompose* relations. Decomposition of R involves splitting the attributes of R to make the schemas of two new relations. Our decomposition rule also involves a way of populating those relations with tuples by "projecting" the tuples of R. After describing the decomposition process, we shall show how to pick a decomposition that eliminates anomalies.

Given a relation R with schema $\{A_1, A_2, \ldots, A_n\}$, we may *decompose* R into two relations S and T with schemas $\{B_1, B_2, \ldots, B_m\}$ and $\{C_1, C_2, \ldots, C_k\}$, respectively, such that

1. $\{A_1, A_2, \ldots, A_n\} = \{B_1, B_2, \ldots, B_m\} \cup \{C_1, C_2, \ldots, C_k\}$.

2. The tuples in relation S are the *projections* onto $\{B_1, B_2, \ldots, B_m\}$ of all the tuples in R. That is, for each tuple t in the current instance of R, take the components of t in the attributes $B_1, B_2, \ldots, B_m$. These components form a tuple, and this tuple belongs in the current instance of S. However, relations are sets, and the same tuple of S could result from projecting two different tuples of R. If so, we put into the current instance of S only one copy of each tuple.

3. Similarly, the tuples in relation T are the projections, onto set of attributes $\{C_1, C_2, \ldots, C_k\}$, of the tuples in the current instance of R.

Example 3.24 : Let us decompose the `Movies` relation of Fig. 3.21. First, we shall decompose the schema. Our choice, whose merit will be seen in Section 3.6.3, is to use

1. A relation called `Movies1`, whose schema is all the attributes except for `starName`.

2. A relation called `Movies2`, whose schema consists of the attributes `title`, `year`, and `starName`.

Now, let us illustrate the process of decomposing relation instances by decomposing the sample data of Fig. 3.21. First, let us construct the projection onto the `Movies1` schema:

$$\{\texttt{title}, \texttt{year}, \texttt{length}, \texttt{filmType}, \texttt{studioName}\}$$

The first three tuples of Fig. 3.21 each have the same components in these five attributes:

$$(\texttt{Star Wars}, \texttt{1977}, \texttt{124}, \texttt{color}, \texttt{Fox})$$

The fourth tuple yields a different tuple for the first five components, and the fifth and sixth tuple each yield the same five-component tuple. The resulting relation for `Movies1` is shown in Fig. 3.22.

title	*year*	*length*	*filmType*	*studioName*
Star Wars	1977	124	color	Fox
Mighty Ducks	1991	104	color	Disney
Wayne's World	1992	95	color	Paramount

Figure 3.22: The relation `Movies1`

Next, consider the projection of Fig. 3.21 onto the schema of `Movies2`. Each of the six tuples of that figure differ in at least one of the attributes `title`, `year`, and `starName`, so the result is the relation shown in Fig. 3.23. □

title	year	starName
Star Wars	1977	Carrie Fisher
Star Wars	1977	Mark Hamill
Star Wars	1977	Harrison Ford
Mighty Ducks	1991	Emilio Estevez
Wayne's World	1992	Dana Carvey
Wayne's World	1992	Mike Meyers

Figure 3.23: The relation `Movies2`

Notice how this decomposition eliminates the anomalies we mentioned in Section 3.6.1. The redundancy has been eliminated; for example, the length of each film appears only once, in relation `Movies1`. The risk of an update anomaly is gone. For instance, since we only have to change the length of *Star Wars* in one tuple of `Movies1`, we cannot wind up with two different lengths for that movie.

Finally, the risk of a deletion anomaly is gone. If we delete all the stars for *Mighty Ducks*, say, that deletion makes the movie disappear from `Movies2`. But all the other information about the movie can still be found in `Movies1`.

It might appear that `Movies2` still has redundancy, since the title and year of a movie can appear several times. However, these two attributes form a key for movies, and there is no more succinct way to represent a movie. Moreover, `Movies2` does not offer an opportunity for an update anomaly. For instance, one might suppose that if we changed to 2003 the year in the Carrie Fisher tuple, but not the other two tuples for *Star Wars*, then there would be an update anomaly. However, there is nothing in our assumed FD's that prevents there being a different movie named *Star Wars* in 2003, and Carrie Fisher may star in that one as well. Thus, we do not want to prevent changing the year in one *Star Wars* tuple, nor is such a change necessarily incorrect.

3.6.3 Boyce-Codd Normal Form

The goal of decomposition is to replace a relation by several that do not exhibit anomalies. There is, it turns out, a simple condition under which the anomalies discussed above can be guaranteed not to exist. This condition is called *Boyce-Codd normal form*, or *BCNF*.

- A relation R is in BCNF if and only if: whenever there is a nontrivial FD $A_1 A_2 \cdots A_n \rightarrow B$ for R, it is the case that $\{A_1, A_2, \ldots, A_n\}$ is a superkey for R.

That is, the left side of every nontrivial FD must be a superkey. Recall that a superkey need not be minimal. Thus, an equivalent statement of the BCNF condition is that the left side of every nontrivial FD must contain a key.

When we find a BCNF-violating FD, we sometimes wind up with a simpler complete decomposition into BCNF relations if we augment the right side of the FD to include the right sides of all the other FD's that have the same left side, whether or not they are BCNF violations. The following is an alternative definition of BCNF in which we look for a set of FD's with common left side, at least one of which is nontrivial and violates the BCNF condition.

- Relation R is in BCNF if and only if: whenever there is a nontrivial FD $A_1 A_2 \cdots A_n \rightarrow B_1 B_2 \cdots B_m$ for R, it is the case that $\{A_1, A_2, \ldots, A_n\}$ is a superkey for R.

This requirement is equivalent to the original BCNF condition. Recall that the FD $A_1 A_2 \cdots A_n \rightarrow B_1 B_2 \cdots B_m$ is shorthand for the set of FD's $A_1 A_2 \cdots A_n \rightarrow B_i$ for $i = 1, 2, \ldots, m$. Since there must be at least one B_i that is not among the A's (or else $A_1 A_2 \cdots A_n \rightarrow B_1 B_2 \cdots B_m$ would be trivial), $A_1 A_2 \cdots A_n \rightarrow B_i$ is a BCNF violation according to our original definition.

Example 3.25: Relation Movies, as in Fig. 3.21, is not in BCNF. To see why, we first need to determine what sets of attributes are keys. We argued in Example 3.13 why {title, year, starName} is a key. Thus, any set of attributes containing these three is a superkey. The same arguments we followed in Example 3.13 can be used to explain why no set of attributes that does not include all three of title, year, and starName could be a superkey. Thus, we assert that {title, year, starName} is the only key for Movies.

However, consider the FD

$$\text{title year} \rightarrow \text{length filmType studioName}$$

which holds in Movies according to our discussion in Example 3.13.

Unfortunately, the left side of the above FD is not a superkey. In particular, we know that title and year do not functionally determine the sixth attribute, starName. Thus, the existence of this FD violates the BCNF condition and tells us Movies is not in BCNF. Moreover, according to the original definition of BCNF, where a single attribute on the right side was required, we can offer any of the three FD's, such as title year $\rightarrow$ length, as a BCNF violation. □

Example 3.26: On the other hand, Movies1 of Fig. 3.22 is in BCNF. Since

$$\text{title year} \rightarrow \text{length filmType studioName}$$

holds in this relation, and we have argued that neither title nor year by itself functionally determines any of the other attributes, the only key for Movies1 is {title, year}. Moreover, the only nontrivial FD's must have at least title and year on the left side, and therefore their left sides must be superkeys. Thus, Movies1 is in BCNF. □

Example 3.27: We claim that any two-attribute relation is in BCNF. We need to examine the possible nontrivial FD's with a single attribute on the right. There are not too many cases to consider, so let us consider them in turn. In what follows, suppose that the attributes are A and B.

1. There are no nontrivial FD's. Then surely the BCNF condition must hold, because only a nontrivial FD can violate this condition. Incidentally, note that $\{A, B\}$ is the only key in this case.

2. $A \rightarrow B$ holds, but $B \rightarrow A$ does not hold. In this case, A is the only key, and each nontrivial FD contains A on the left (in fact the left can only be A). Thus there is no violation of the BCNF condition.

3. $B \rightarrow A$ holds, but $A \rightarrow B$ does not hold. This case is symmetric to case (2).

4. Both $A \rightarrow B$ and $B \rightarrow A$ hold. Then both A and B are keys. Surely any FD has at least one of these on the left, so there can be no BCNF violation.

It is worth noticing from case (4) above that there may be more than one key for a relation. Further, the BCNF condition only requires that *some* key be contained in the left side of any nontrivial FD, not that all keys are contained in the left side. Also observe that a relation with two attributes, each functionally determining the other, is not completely implausible. For example, a company may assign its employees unique employee ID's and also record their Social Security numbers. A relation with attributes `empID` and `ssNo` would have each attribute functionally determining the other. Put another way, each attribute is a key, since we don't expect to find two tuples that agree on either attribute. □

3.6.4 Decomposition into BCNF

By repeatedly choosing suitable decompositions, we can break any relation schema into a collection of subsets of its attributes with the following important properties:

1. These subsets are the schemas of relations in BCNF.

2. The data in the original relation is represented faithfully by the data in the relations that are the result of the decomposition, in a sense to be made precise in Section 3.6.5. Roughly, we need to be able to reconstruct the original relation instance exactly from the decomposed relation instances.

Example 3.27 suggests that perhaps all we have to do is break a relation schema into two-attribute subsets, and the result is surely in BCNF. However, such an arbitrary decomposition will not satisfy condition (2), as we shall see in

Section 3.6.5. In fact, we must be more careful and use the violating FD's to guide our decomposition.

The decomposition strategy we shall follow is to look for a nontrivial FD $A_1 A_2 \cdots A_n \rightarrow B_1 B_2 \cdots B_m$ that violates BCNF; i.e., $\{A_1, A_2, \ldots, A_n\}$ is not a superkey. As a heuristic, we shall generally add to the right side as many attributes as are functionally determined by $\{A_1, A_2, \ldots, A_n\}$. Figure 3.24 illustrates how the attributes are broken into two overlapping relation schemas. One is all the attributes involved in the violating FD, and the other is the left side of the FD plus all the attributes *not* involved in the FD, i.e., all the attributes except those B's that are not A's.

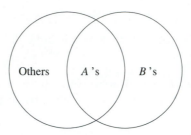

Figure 3.24: Relation schema decomposition based on a BCNF violation

Example 3.28 : Consider our running example, the `Movies` relation of Fig. 3.21. We saw in Example 3.25 that

> `title year` $\rightarrow$ `length filmType studioName`

is a BCNF violation. In this case, the right side already includes all the attributes functionally determined by `title` and `year`, so we shall use this BCNF violation to decompose `Movies` into:

1. The schema with all the attributes of the FD, that is:

   > {title, year, length, filmType, studioName}

2. The schema with all attributes of `Movies` except the three that appear on the right of the FD. Thus, we remove `length`, `filmType`, and `studioName`, leaving the second schema:

   > {title, year, starName}

Notice that these schemas are the ones selected for relations `Movies1` and `Movies2` in Example 3.24. We observed that these are each in BCNF in Example 3.26. □

title	year	length	filmType	studioName	studioAddr
Star Wars	1977	124	color	Fox	Hollywood
Mighty Ducks	1991	104	color	Disney	Buena Vista
Wayne's World	1992	95	color	Paramount	Hollywood
Addams Family	1991	102	color	Paramount	Hollywood

Figure 3.25: The relation `MovieStudio`

Example 3.29: Let us consider the relation that was introduced in Example 3.21. This relation, which we shall call `MovieStudio`, stores information about movies, their owning studios, and the addresses of those studios. The schema and some typical tuples for this relation are shown in Fig. 3.25.

Note that `MovieStudio` contains redundant information. Because we added to our usual sample data a second movie owned by Paramount, the address of Paramount is stated twice. However, the source of this problem is not the same as in Example 3.28. In the latter example, the problem was that a many-many relationship (the stars of a given movie) was being stored with other information about the movie. Here, everything is single-valued: the attributes `length` and `filmType` for a movie, the relationship *Owns* that relates a movie to its unique owning studio, and the attribute `studioAddr` for studios.

In this case, the problem is that there is a "transitive dependency." That is, as mentioned in Example 3.21, relation `MovieStudio` has the FD's:

$$\text{title year} \rightarrow \text{studioName}$$
$$\text{studioName} \rightarrow \text{studioAddr}$$

We may apply the transitive rule to these to get a new FD:

$$\text{title year} \rightarrow \text{studioAddr}$$

That is, a title and year (i.e., the key for movies) functionally determine a studio address — the address of the studio that owns the movie. Since

$$\text{title year} \rightarrow \text{length filmType}$$

is another obvious functional dependency, we conclude that {`title`, `year`} is a key for `MovieStudio`; in fact it is the only key.

On the other hand, FD:

$$\text{studioName} \rightarrow \text{studioAddr}$$

which is one of those used in the application of the transitive rule above, is non-trivial but its left side is not a superkey. This observation tells us `MovieStudio` is not in BCNF. We can fix the problem by following the decomposition rule, using the above FD. The first schema of the decomposition is the attributes of the FD itself, that is: {studioName, studioAddr}. The second schema is all the attributes of MovieStudio except for studioAddr, because the latter attribute is on the right of the FD used in the decomposition. Thus, the other schema is:

{title, year, length, filmType, studioName}

The projection of Fig. 3.25 onto these schemas gives us the two relations MovieStudio1 and MovieStudio2 shown in Figs. 3.26 and 3.27. Each of these is in BCNF. Recall from Section 3.5.7 that for each of the relations in the decomposition, we need to compute its FD's by computing the closure of each subset of its attributes, using the full set of given FD's. In general, the process is exponential in the number of attributes of the decomposed relations, but we also saw in Section 3.5.7 that there were some simplifications possible.

In our case, it is easy to determine that a basis for the FD's of MovieStudio1 is

title year → length filmType studioName

and for MovieStudio2 the only nontrivial FD is

studioName → studioAddr

Thus, the sole key for MovieStudio1 is {title, year}, and the sole key for MovieStudio2 is {studioName}. In each case, there are no nontrivial FD's that do not contain these keys on the left.   □

title	year	length	filmType	studioName
Star Wars	1977	124	color	Fox
Mighty Ducks	1991	104	color	Disney
Wayne's World	1992	95	color	Paramount
Addams Family	1991	102	color	Paramount

Figure 3.26: The relation MovieStudio1

studioName	studioAddr
Fox	Hollywood
Disney	Buena Vista
Paramount	Hollywood

Figure 3.27: The relation MovieStudio2

In each of the previous examples, one judicious application of the decomposition rule is enough to produce a collection of relations that are in BCNF. In general, that is not the case.

Example 3.30: We could generalize Example 3.29 to have a chain of FD's longer than two. Consider a relation with schema

$$\{\texttt{title, year, studioName, president, presAddr}\}$$

That is, each tuple of this relation tells about a movie, its studio, the president of the studio, and the address of the president of the studio. Three FD's that we would assume in this relation are

$$\texttt{title year} \rightarrow \texttt{studioName}$$
$$\texttt{studioName} \rightarrow \texttt{president}$$
$$\texttt{president} \rightarrow \texttt{presAddr}$$

The sole key for this relation is {`title, year`}. Thus the last two FD's above violate BCNF. Suppose we choose to decompose starting with

$$\texttt{studioName} \rightarrow \texttt{president}$$

First, we should add to the right side of this functional dependency any other attributes in the closure of `studioName`. By the transitive rule applied to `studioName` $\rightarrow$ `president` and `president` $\rightarrow$ `presAddr`, we know

$$\texttt{studioName} \rightarrow \texttt{presAddr}$$

Combining the two FD's with `studioName` on the left, we get:

$$\texttt{studioName} \rightarrow \texttt{president presAddr}$$

This FD has a maximally expanded right side, so we shall now decompose into the following two relation schemas.

$$\{\texttt{title, year, studioName}\}$$
$$\{\texttt{studioName, president, presAddr}\}$$

If we follow the projection algorithm of Section 3.5.7, we determine that the FD's for the first relation has a basis:

$$\texttt{title year} \rightarrow \texttt{studioName}$$

while the second has

$$\texttt{studioName} \rightarrow \texttt{president}$$
$$\texttt{president} \rightarrow \texttt{presAddr}$$

Thus, the sole key for the first relation is {`title, year`}, and it is therefore in BCNF. However, the second has {`studioName`} for its only key but also has the FD:

$$\texttt{president} \rightarrow \texttt{presAddr}$$

which is a BCNF violation. Thus, we must decompose again, this time using
the above FD. The resulting three relation schemas, all in BCNF, are:

$$\{\text{title, year, studioName}\}$$
$$\{\text{studioName, president}\}$$
$$\{\text{president, presAddr}\}$$

□

In general, we must keep applying the decomposition rule as many times as
needed, until all our relations are in BCNF. We can be sure of ultimate success,
because every time we apply the decomposition rule to a relation R, the two
resulting schemas each have fewer attributes than that of R. As we saw in
Example 3.27, when we get down to two attributes, the relation is sure to be
in BCNF; often relations with larger sets of attributes are also in BCNF.

3.6.5 Recovering Information from a Decomposition

Let us now turn our attention to the question of why the decomposition algorithm of Section 3.6.4 preserves the information that was contained in the
original relation. The idea is that if we follow this algorithm, then the projections of the original tuples can be "joined" again to produce all and only the
original tuples.

To simplify the situation, let us consider a relation $R(A, B, C)$ and a FD
$B \rightarrow C$, which we suppose is a BCNF violation. It is possible, for example,
that as in Example 3.29, there is a transitive dependency chain, with another
FD $A \rightarrow B$. In that case, $\{A\}$ is the only key, and the left side of $B \rightarrow C$
clearly is not a superkey. Another possibility is that $B \rightarrow C$ is the only
nontrivial FD, in which case the only key is $\{A, B\}$. Again, the left side of
$B \rightarrow C$ is not a superkey. In either case, the required decomposition based on
the FD $B \rightarrow C$ separates the attributes into schemas $\{A, B\}$ and $\{B, C\}$.

Let t be a tuple of R. We may write $t = (a, b, c)$, where a, b, and c are
the components of t for attributes A, B, and C, respectively. Tuple t projects
as (a, b) for the relation with schema $\{A, B\}$ and as (b, c) for the relation with
schema $\{B, C\}$.

It is possible to *join* a tuple from $\{A, B\}$ with a tuple from $\{B, C\}$, provided
they agree in the B component. In particular, (a, b) joins with (b, c) to give us
the original tuple $t = (a, b, c)$ back again. That is, regardless of what tuple t we
started with, we can always join its projections to get t back.

However, getting back those tuples we started with is not enough to assure
that the original relation R is truly represented by the decomposition. What
might happen if there were two tuples of R, say $t = (a, b, c)$ and $v = (d, b, e)$?
When we project t onto $\{A, B\}$ we get $u = (a, b)$, and when we project v onto
$\{B, C\}$ we get $w = (b, e)$, as suggested by Fig. 3.28.

Tuples u and w join, since they agree on their B components. The resulting
tuple is $x = (a, b, e)$. Is it possible that x is a bogus tuple? That is, could
(a, b, e) not be a tuple of R?

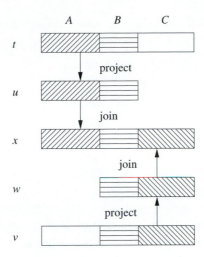

Figure 3.28: Joining two tuples from projected relations

Since we assume the FD $B \rightarrow C$ for relation R, the answer is "no." Recall that this FD says any two tuples of R that agree in their B components must also agree in their C components. Since t and v agree in their B components (they both have b there), they also agree on their C components. That means $c = e$; i.e., the two values we supposed were different are really the same. Thus, (a, b, e) is really (a, b, c); that is, $x = t$.

Since t is in R, it must be that x is in R. Put another way, as long as FD $B \rightarrow C$ holds, the joining of two projected tuples cannot produce a bogus tuple. Rather, every tuple produced by joining is guaranteed to be a tuple of R.

This argument works in general. We assumed A, B, and C were each single attributes, but the same argument would apply if they were any sets of attributes. That is, we take any BCNF-violating FD, let B be the attributes on the left side, let C be the attributes on the right but not the left, and let A be the attributes on neither side. We may conclude:

- If we decompose a relation according to the method of Section 3.6.4, then the original relation can be recovered exactly by joining the tuples of the new relations in all possible ways.

If we decompose relations in a way that is not based on a FD, then we might not be able to recover the original relation. Here is an example.

Example 3.31: Suppose we have the relation $R(A, B, C)$ as above, but that the FD $B \rightarrow C$ does not hold. Then R might consist of the two tuples

A	B	C
1	2	3
4	2	5

The projections of R onto the relations with schemas $\{A, B\}$ and $\{B, C\}$ are

A	B
1	2
4	2

and

B	C
2	3
2	5

respectively. Since all four tuples share the same B-value, 2, each tuple of one relation joins with both tuples of the other relation. Thus, when we try to reconstruct R by joining, we get

A	B	C
1	2	3
1	2	5
4	2	3
4	2	5

That is, we get "too much"; we get two bogus tuples, $(1, 2, 5)$ and $(4, 2, 3)$ that were not in the original relation R. □

3.6.6 Third Normal Form

Occasionally, one encounters a relation schema and its FD's that are not in BCNF but that one doesn't want to decompose further. The following example is typical.

Example 3.32: Suppose we have a relation `Bookings` with attributes:

1. `title`, the name of a movie.

2. `theater`, the name of a theater where the movie is being shown.

3. `city`, the city where the theater is located.

The intent behind a tuple (m, t, c) is that the movie with title m is currently being shown at theater t in city c.

We might reasonably assert the following FD's:

$$\text{theater} \rightarrow \text{city}$$
$$\text{title city} \rightarrow \text{theater}$$

The first says that a theater is located in one city. The second is not obvious but is based on the assumed practice of not booking a movie into two theaters in the same city. We shall assert this FD if only for the sake of the example.

Let us first find the keys. No single attribute is a key. For example, `title` is not a key because a movie can play in several theaters at once and in several cities at once.[4] Also, `theater` is not a key, because although `theater` functionally determines `city`, there are multiscreen theaters that show many movies at once. Thus, `theater` does not determine `title`. Finally, `city` is not a key because cities usually have more than one theater and more than one movie playing.

On the other hand, two of the three sets of two attributes are keys. Clearly {`title`, `city`} is a key because of the given FD that says these attributes functionally determine `theater`.

It is also true that {`theater`, `title`} is a key. To see why, start with the given FD `theater` → `city`. By the augmentation rule of Exercise 3.5.3(a), `theater title` → `city` follows. Intuitively, if `theater` alone functionally determines `city`, then surely `theatre` and `title` together will do so.

The remaining pair of attributes, `city` and `theater`, do not functionally determine `title`, and are therefore not a key. We conclude that the only two keys are

{`title`, `city`}
{`theater`, `title`}

Now we immediately see a BCNF violation. We were given functional dependency `theater` → `city`, but its left side, `theater`, is not a superkey. We are therefore tempted to decompose, using this BCNF-violating FD, into the two relation schemas:

{`theater`, `city`}
{`theater`, `title`}

There is a problem with this decomposition, concerning the FD

`title city` → `theater`

There could be current relations for the decomposed schemas that satisfy the FD `theater` → `city` (which can be checked in the relation {`theater`, `city`}) but that, when joined, yield a relation not satisfying `title city` → `theater`. For instance, the two relations

theater	city
Guild	Menlo Park
Park	Menlo Park

---

[4]In this example we assume that there are not two "current" movies with the same title, even though we have previously recognized that there could be two movies with the same title made in different years.

Other Normal Forms

If there is a "third normal form," what happened to the first two "normal forms"? They indeed were defined, but today there is little use for them. *First normal form* is simply the condition that every component of every tuple is an atomic value. *Second normal form* is less restrictive than 3NF. It permits transitive FD's in a relation but forbids a nontrivial FD with a left side that is a proper subset of a key. There is also a "fourth normal form" that we shall meet in Section 3.7.

---

and

theater	title
Guild	The Net
Park	The Net

are permissible according to the FD's that apply to each of the above relations, but when we join them we get two tuples

theater	city	title
Guild	Menlo Park	The Net
Park	Menlo Park	The Net

that violate the FD `title city → theater`. □

The solution to the above problem is to relax our BCNF requirement slightly, in order to allow the occasional relation schema, like that of Example 3.32, which cannot be decomposed into BCNF relations without our losing the ability to check each FD within one relation. This relaxed condition is called the *third normal form* condition:

- A relation R is in *third normal form* (3NF) if: whenever $A_1 A_2 \cdots A_n \rightarrow B$ is a nontrivial FD, either $\{A_1, A_2, \ldots, A_n\}$ is a superkey, or B is a member of some key.

An attribute that is a member of some key is often said to be *prime*. Thus, the 3NF condition can be stated as "for each nontrivial FD, either the left side is a superkey, or the right side is prime."

Note that the difference between this 3NF condition and the BCNF condition is the clause "or B is a member of some key (i.e., prime)." This clause "excuses" a FD like `theater → city` in Example 3.32, because the right side, `city`, is prime.

It is beyond the scope of this book to prove that 3NF is in fact adequate for its purposes. That is, we can always decompose a relation schema in a way that does not lose information, into schemas that are in 3NF and allow all FD's to be checked. When these relations are not in BCNF, there will be some redundancy left in the schema, however.

3.6.7 Exercises for Section 3.6

Exercise 3.6.1: For each of the following relation schemas and sets of FD's:

* a) $R(A, B, C, D)$ with FD's $AB \to C$, $C \to D$, and $D \to A$.

* b) $R(A, B, C, D)$ with FD's $B \to C$ and $B \to D$.

   c) $R(A, B, C, D)$ with FD's $AB \to C$, $BC \to D$, $CD \to A$, and $AD \to B$.

   d) $R(A, B, C, D)$ with FD's $A \to B$, $B \to C$, $C \to D$, and $D \to A$.

   e) $R(A, B, C, D, E)$ with FD's $AB \to C$, $DE \to C$, and $B \to D$.

   f) $R(A, B, C, D, E)$ with FD's $AB \to C$, $C \to D$, $D \to B$, and $D \to E$.

do the following:

   i) Indicate all the BCNF violations. Do not forget to consider FD's that are not in the given set, but follow from them. However, it is not necessary to give violations that have more than one attribute on the right side.

  ii) Decompose the relations, as necessary, into collections of relations that are in BCNF.

 iii) Indicate all the 3NF violations.

 iv) Decompose the relations, as necessary, into collections of relations that are in 3NF.

Exercise 3.6.2: We mentioned in Section 3.6.4 that we should expand the right side of a FD that is a BCNF violation if possible. However, it was deemed an optional step. Consider a relation R whose schema is the set of attributes $\{A, B, C, D\}$ with FD's $A \to B$ and $A \to C$. Either is a BCNF violation, because the only key for R is $\{A, D\}$. Suppose we begin by decomposing R according to $A \to B$. Do we ultimately get the same result as if we first expand the BCNF violation to $A \to BC$? Why or why not?

! **Exercise 3.6.3:** Let R be as in Exercise 3.6.2, but let the FD's be $A \to B$ and $B \to C$. Again compare decomposing using $A \to B$ first against decomposing by $A \to BC$ first.

! **Exercise 3.6.4:** Suppose we have a relation schema $R(A, B, C)$ with FD $A \to B$. Suppose also that we decide to decompose this schema into $S(A, B)$ and $T(B, C)$. Give an example of an instance of relation R whose projection onto S and T and subsequent rejoining as in Section 3.6.5 does not yield the same relation instance.

3.7   Multivalued Dependencies

A "multivalued dependency" is an assertion that two attributes or sets of attributes are independent of one another. This condition is, as we shall see, a generalization of the notion of a functional dependency, in the sense that every FD implies a corresponding multivalued dependency. However, there are some situations involving independence of attribute sets that cannot be explained as FD's. In this section we shall explore the cause of multivalued dependencies and see how they can be used in database schema design.

3.7.1   Attribute Independence and Its Consequent Redundancy

There are occasional situations where we design a relation schema and find it is in BCNF, yet the relation has a kind of redundancy that is not related to FD's. The most common source of redundancy in BCNF schemas is an attempt to put two or more many-many relationships in a single relation.

Example 3.33: In this example, we shall suppose that stars may have several addresses. We shall also break addresses of stars into street and city components. Along with star names and their addresses, we shall include in a single relation the usual *Stars-in* information about the titles and years of movies in which the star appeared. Then Fig. 3.29 is a typical instance of this relation.

name	street	city	title	year
C. Fisher	123 Maple St.	Hollywood	Star Wars	1977
C. Fisher	5 Locust Ln.	Malibu	Star Wars	1977
C. Fisher	123 Maple St.	Hollywood	Empire Strikes Back	1980
C. Fisher	5 Locust Ln.	Malibu	Empire Strikes Back	1980
C. Fisher	123 Maple St.	Hollywood	Return of the Jedi	1983
C. Fisher	5 Locust Ln.	Malibu	Return of the Jedi	1983

Figure 3.29: Sets of addresses independent from movies

We focus in Fig. 3.29 on Carrie Fisher's two hypothetical addresses and three best-known movies. There is no reason to associate an address with one movie and not another. Thus, the only way to express the fact that addresses and movies are independent properties of stars is to have each address appear with each movie. But when we repeat address and movie facts in all combinations, there is obvious redundancy. For instance, Fig. 3.29 repeats each of Carrie Fisher's addresses three times (once for each of her movies) and each movie twice (once for each address).

Yet there is no BCNF violation in the relation suggested by Fig. 3.29. There are, in fact, no nontrivial FD's at all. For example, attribute city is not functionally determined by the other four attributes. There might be a star with two homes that had the same street address in different cities. Then there would be two tuples that agreed in all attributes but `city` and disagreed in `city`. Thus,

$$\texttt{name street title year} \rightarrow \texttt{city}$$

is not a FD for our relation. We leave it to the reader to check that none of the five attributes is functionally determined by the other four. Since there are no nontrivial FD's, it follows that all five attributes form the only key and that there are no BCNF violations. $\quad\Box$

3.7.2 Definition of Multivalued Dependencies

A *multivalued dependency* (often abbreviated MVD) is a statement about some relation R that when you fix the values for one set of attributes, then the values in certain other attributes are independent of the values of all the other attributes in the relation. More precisely, we say the MVD

$$A_1 A_2 \cdots A_n \twoheadrightarrow B_1 B_2 \cdots B_m$$

holds for a relation R if when we restrict ourselves to the tuples of R that have particular values for each of the attributes among the A's, then the set of values we find among the B's is independent of the set of values we find among the attributes of R that are not among the A's or B's. Still more precisely, we say this MVD holds if

> For each pair of tuples t and u of relation R that agree on all the A's, we can find in R some tuple v that agrees:
>
> 1. With both t and u on the A's,
> 2. With t on the B's, and
> 3. With u on all attributes of R that are not among the A's or B's.

Note that we can use this rule with t and u interchanged, to infer the existence of a fourth tuple w that agrees with u on the B's and with t on the other attributes. As a consequence, for any fixed values of the A's, the associated values of the B's and the other attributes appear in all possible combinations in different tuples. Figure 3.30 suggests how v relates to t and u when a MVD holds.

In general, we may assume that the A's and B's (left side and right side) of a MVD are disjoint. However, as with FD's, it is permissible to add some of the A's to the right side if we wish. Also note that unlike FD's, where we started with single attributes on the right and allowed sets of attributes on the right as a shorthand, with MVD's, we must consider sets of attributes on the right immediately. As we shall see in Example 3.35, it is not always possible to break the right sides of MVD's into single attributes.

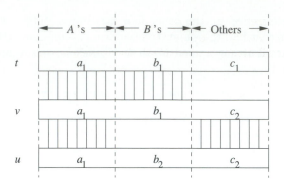

Figure 3.30: A multivalued dependency guarantees that v exists

Example 3.34: In Example 3.33 we encountered a MVD that in our notation is expressed:

$$name \twoheadrightarrow street\ city$$

That is, for each star's name, the set of addresses appears in conjunction with each of the star's movies. For an example of how the formal definition of this MVD applies, consider the first and fourth tuples from Fig. 3.29:

name	street	city	title	year
C. Fisher	123 Maple St.	Hollywood	Star Wars	1977
C. Fisher	5 Locust Ln.	Malibu	Empire Strikes Back	1980

If we let the first tuple be t and the second be u, then the MVD asserts that we must also find in R the tuple that has name C. Fisher, a street and city that agree with the first tuple, and other attributes (title and year) that agree with the second tuple. There is indeed such a tuple; it is the third tuple of Fig. 3.29.

Similarly, we could let t be the second tuple above and u be the first. Then the MVD tells us that there is a tuple of R that agrees with the second in attributes name, street, and city and with the first in name, title, and year. This tuple also exists; it is the second tuple of Fig. 3.29.   □

3.7.3   Reasoning About Multivalued Dependencies

There are a number of rules about MVD's that are similar to the rules we learned for FD's in Section 3.5. For example, MVD's obey

- The *trivial dependencies rule*, which says that if MVD

$$A_1 A_2 \cdots A_n \twoheadrightarrow B_1 B_2 \cdots B_m$$

holds for some relation, then so does $A_1 A_2 \cdots A_n \twoheadrightarrow C_1 C_2 \cdots C_k$, where the C's are the B's plus one or more of the A's. Conversely, we can also remove attributes from the B's if they are among the A's and infer the MVD $A_1 A_2 \cdots A_n \twoheadrightarrow D_1 D_2 \cdots D_r$ if the D's are those B's that are not among the A's.

- The *transitive rule*, which says that if $A_1 A_2 \cdots A_n \twoheadrightarrow B_1 B_2 \cdots B_m$ and $B_1 B_2 \cdots B_m \twoheadrightarrow C_1 C_2 \cdots C_k$ hold for some relation, then so does

$$A_1 A_2 \cdots A_n \twoheadrightarrow C_1 C_2 \cdots C_k$$

However, any C's that are also B's must be deleted from the right side.

On the other hand, MVD's do not obey the splitting part of the splitting/combining rule, as the following example shows.

Example 3.35: Consider again Fig. 3.29, where we observed the MVD:

$$\texttt{name} \twoheadrightarrow \texttt{street city}$$

If the splitting rule applied to MVD's, we would expect

$$\texttt{name} \twoheadrightarrow \texttt{street}$$

also to be true. This MVD says that each star's street addresses are independent of the other attributes, including `city`. However, that statement is false. Consider, for instance, the first two tuples of Fig. 3.29. The hypothetical MVD would allow us to infer that the tuples with the streets interchanged:

name	street	city	title	year
C. Fisher	5 Locust Ln.	Hollywood	Star Wars	1977
C. Fisher	123 Maple St.	Malibu	Star Wars	1977

were in the relation. But these are not true tuples, because, for instance, the home on 5 Locust Ln. is in Malibu, not Hollywood. □

However, there are several new rules dealing with MVD's that we can learn. First,

- Every FD is a MVD. That is, if $A_1 A_2 \cdots A_n \rightarrow B_1 B_2 \cdots B_m$, then $A_1 A_2 \cdots A_n \twoheadrightarrow B_1 B_2 \cdots B_m$.

To see why, suppose R is some relation for which the FD

$$A_1 A_2 \cdots A_n \rightarrow B_1 B_2 \cdots B_m$$

holds, and suppose t and u are tuples of R that agree on the A's. To show that the MVD $A_1 A_2 \cdots A_n \twoheadrightarrow B_1 B_2 \cdots B_m$ holds, we have to show that R

also contains a tuple v that agrees with t and u on the A's, with t on the B's, and with u on all other attributes. But v can be u. Surely u agrees with t and u on the A's, because we started by assuming that these two tuples agree on the A's. The FD $A_1 A_2 \cdots A_n \rightarrow B_1 B_2 \cdots B_m$ assures us that u agrees with t on the B's. And of course u agrees with itself on the other attributes. Thus, whenever a FD holds, the corresponding MVD holds.

Another rule that has no counterpart in the world of FD's is the *complementation rule*:

- If $A_1 A_2 \cdots A_n \twoheadrightarrow B_1 B_2 \cdots B_m$ is a MVD for relation R, then R also satisfies $A_1 A_2 \cdots A_n \twoheadrightarrow C_1 C_2 \cdots C_k$, where the C's are all attributes of R not among the A's and B's.

Example 3.36: Again consider the relation of Fig. 3.29, for which we asserted the MVD:

$$\texttt{name} \twoheadrightarrow \texttt{street city}$$

The complementation rule says that

$$\texttt{name} \twoheadrightarrow \texttt{title year}$$

must also hold in this relation, because `title` and `year` are the attributes not mentioned in the first MVD. The second MVD intuitively means that each star has a set of movies starred in, which are independent of the star's addresses. □

3.7.4 Fourth Normal Form

The redundancy that we found in Section 3.7.1 to be caused by MVD's can be eliminated if we use these dependencies in a new decomposition algorithm for relations. In this section we shall introduce a new normal form, called "fourth normal form." In this normal form, all "nontrivial" (in a sense to be defined below) MVD's are eliminated, as are all FD's that violate BCNF. As a result, the decomposed relations have neither the redundancy from FD's that we discussed in Section 3.6.1 nor the redundancy from MVD's that we discussed in Section 3.7.1.

A MVD $A_1 A_2 \cdots A_n \twoheadrightarrow B_1 B_2 \cdots B_m$ for a relation R is *nontrivial* if:

1. None of the B's is among the A's.

2. Not all the attributes of R are among the A's and B's.

The "fourth normal form" condition is essentially the BCNF condition, but applied to MVD's instead of FD's. Formally:

- A relation R is in *fourth normal form* (4NF) if whenever

$$A_1 A_2 \cdots A_n \twoheadrightarrow B_1 B_2 \cdots B_m$$

is a nontrivial MVD, $\{A_1, A_2, \ldots, A_n\}$ is a superkey.

That is, if a relation is in 4NF, then every nontrivial MVD is really a FD with a superkey on the left. Note that the notions of keys and superkeys depend on FD's only; adding MVD's does not change the definition of "key."

Example 3.37: The relation of Fig. 3.29 violates the 4NF condition. For example,

name $\twoheadrightarrow$ street city

is a nontrivial MVD, yet `name` by itself is not a superkey. In fact, the only key for this relation is all the attributes. $\Box$

Fourth normal form is truly a generalization of BCNF. Recall from Section 3.7.3 that every FD is also a MVD. Thus, every BCNF violation is also a 4NF violation. Put another way, every relation that is in 4NF is therefore in BCNF.

However, there are some relations that are in BCNF but not 4NF. Figure 3.29 is a good example. The only key for this relation is all five attributes, and there are no nontrivial FD's. Thus it is surely in BCNF. However, as we observed in Example 3.37, it is not in 4NF.

3.7.5 Decomposition into Fourth Normal Form

The 4NF decomposition algorithm is quite analogous to the BCNF decomposition algorithm. We find a 4NF violation, say $A_1 A_2 \cdots A_n \twoheadrightarrow B_1 B_2 \cdots B_m$, where $\{A_1, A_2, \ldots, A_n\}$ is not a superkey. Note this MVD could be a true MVD, or it could be derived from the corresponding FD $A_1 A_2 \cdots A_n \to B_1 B_2 \cdots B_m$, since every FD is a MVD. Then we break the schema for the relation R that has the 4NF violation into two schemas:

1. The A's and the B's.

2. The A's and all attributes of R that are not among the A's or B's.

Example 3.38: Let us continue Example 3.37. We observed that

name $\twoheadrightarrow$ street city

was a 4NF violation. The decomposition rule above tells us to replace the five-attribute schema by one schema that has only the three attributes in the above MVD and another schema that consists of the left side, `name`, plus the attributes that do not appear in the MVD. These attributes are `title` and `year`, so the following two schemas

---

Projecting Multivalued Dependencies

When we decompose into fourth normal form, we need to find the MVD's that hold in the relations that are the result of the decomposition. We wish it were easier to find these MVD's. However, there is no simple test analogous to computing the closure of a set of attributes (as in Section 3.5.3) for FD's. In fact, even a complete set of rules for reasoning about collections of functional and multivalued dependencies is quite complex and beyond the scope of this book. Section 3.9 mentions some places where the subject is treated.

Fortunately, we can often obtain the relevant MVD's for one of the products of a decomposition by using the transitive rule, the complementation rule, and the intersection rule [Exercise 3.7.7(b)]. We recommend that the reader try these in examples and exercises.

$$\{\text{name, street, city}\}$$
$$\{\text{name, title, year}\}$$

are the result of the decomposition. In each schema there are no nontrivial multivalued (or functional) dependencies, so they are in 4NF. Note that in the relation with schema {name, street, city}, the MVD:

$$\text{name} \twoheadrightarrow \text{street city}$$

is trivial since it involves all attributes. Likewise, in the relation with schema {name, title, year}, the MVD:

$$\text{name} \twoheadrightarrow \text{title year}$$

is trivial. Should one or both schemas of the decomposition not be in 4NF, we would have had to decompose the non-4NF schema(s). $\square$

As for the BCNF decomposition, each decomposition step leaves us with schemas that have strictly fewer attributes than we started with, so eventually we get to schemas that need not be decomposed further; that is, they are in 4NF. Moreover, the argument justifying the decomposition that we gave in Section 3.6.5 carries over to MVD's as well. When we decompose a relation because of a MVD $A_1 A_2 \cdots A_n \twoheadrightarrow B_1 B_2 \cdots B_m$, this dependency is enough to justify the claim that we can reconstruct the original relation from the relations of the decomposition.

3.7.6 Relationships Among Normal Forms

As we have mentioned, 4NF implies BCNF, which in turn implies 3NF. Thus, the sets of relation schemas (including dependencies) satisfying the three normal forms are related as in Fig. 3.31. That is, if a relation with certain dependencies is in 4NF, it is also in BCNF and 3NF. Also, if a relation with certain dependencies is in BCNF, then it is in 3NF.

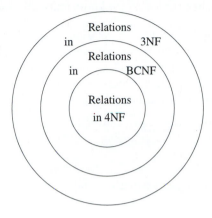

Figure 3.31: 4NF implies BCNF implies 3NF

Another way to compare the normal forms is by the guarantees they make about the set of relations that result from a decomposition into that normal form. These observations are summarized in the table of Fig. 3.32. That is, BCNF (and therefore 4NF) eliminates the redundancy and other anomalies that are caused by FD's, while only 4NF eliminates the additional redundancy that is caused by the presence of nontrivial MVD's that are not FD's. Often, 3NF is enough to eliminate this redundancy, but there are examples where it is not. A decomposition into 3NF can always be chosen so that the FD's are preserved; that is, they are enforced in the decomposed relations (although we have not discussed the algorithm to do so in this book). BCNF does not guarantee preservation of FD's, and none of the normal forms guarantee preservation of MVD's, although in typical cases the dependencies are preserved.

Property	3NF	BCNF	4NF
Eliminates redundancy due to FD's	Most	Yes	Yes
Eliminates redundancy due to MVD's	No	No	Yes
Preserves FD's	Yes	Maybe	Maybe
Preserves MVD's	Maybe	Maybe	Maybe

Figure 3.32: Properties of normal forms and their decompositions

3.7.7 Exercises for Section 3.7

* **Exercise 3.7.1:** Suppose we have a relation $R(A, B, C)$ with a MVD $A \twoheadrightarrow B$. If we know that the tuples (a, b_1, c_1), (a, b_2, c_2), and (a, b_3, c_3) are in the current instance of R, what other tuples do we know must also be in R?

* **Exercise 3.7.2:** Suppose we have a relation in which we want to record for each person their name, Social Security number, and birthdate. Also, for each child of the person, the name, Social Security number, and birthdate of the child, and for each automobile the person owns, its serial number and make. To be more precise, this relation has all tuples

$$(n, s, b, cn, cs, cb, as, am)$$

such that

1. n is the name of the person with Social Security number s.

2. b is n's birthdate.

3. cn is the name of one of n's children.

4. cs is cn's Social Security number.

5. cb is cn's birthdate.

6. as is the serial number of one of n's automobiles.

7. am is the make of the automobile with serial number as.

For this relation:

a) Tell the functional and multivalued dependencies we would expect to hold.

b) Suggest a decomposition of the relation into 4NF.

Exercise 3.7.3: For each of the following relation schemas and dependencies

* a) $R(A, B, C, D)$ with MVD's $A \twoheadrightarrow B$ and $A \twoheadrightarrow C$.

b) $R(A, B, C, D)$ with MVD's $A \twoheadrightarrow B$ and $B \twoheadrightarrow CD$.

c) $R(A, B, C, D)$ with MVD $AB \twoheadrightarrow C$ and FD $B \rightarrow D$.

d) $R(A, B, C, D, E)$ with MVD's $A \twoheadrightarrow B$ and $AB \twoheadrightarrow C$ and FD's $A \rightarrow D$ and $AB \rightarrow E$.

do the following:

i) Find all the 4NF violations.

ii) Decompose the relations into a collection of relation schemas in 4NF.

! Exercise 3.7.4: In Exercise 2.2.5 we discussed four different assumptions about the relationship *Births*. For each of these, indicate the MVD's (other than FD's) that would be expected to hold in the resulting relation.

Exercise 3.7.5: Give informal arguments why we would not expect any of the five attributes in Example 3.33 to be functionally determined by the other four.

! Exercise 3.7.6: Using the definition of MVD, show why the complementation rule holds.

! Exercise 3.7.7: Show the following rules for MVD's:

* a) The *union rule*. If X, Y, and Z are sets of attributes, $X \twoheadrightarrow Y$, and $X \twoheadrightarrow Z$, then $X \twoheadrightarrow (Y \cup Z)$.

  b) The *intersection rule*. If X, Y, and Z are sets of attributes, $X \twoheadrightarrow Y$, and $X \twoheadrightarrow Z$, then $X \twoheadrightarrow (Y \cap Z)$.

  c) The *difference rule*. If X, Y, and Z are sets of attributes, $X \twoheadrightarrow Y$, and $X \twoheadrightarrow Z$, then $X \twoheadrightarrow (Y - Z)$.

  d) *Trivial MVD's.* If $Y \subseteq X$, then $X \twoheadrightarrow Y$ holds in any relation.

  e) *Another source of trivial MVD's.* If $X \cup Y$ is all the attributes of relation R, then $X \twoheadrightarrow Y$ holds in R.

  f) *Removing attributes shared by left and right side.* If $X \twoheadrightarrow Y$ holds, then $X \twoheadrightarrow (Y - X)$ holds.

! Exercise 3.7.8: Give counterexample relations to show why the following rules for MVD's do *not* hold.

* a) If $A \twoheadrightarrow BC$, then $A \twoheadrightarrow B$.

  b) If $A \twoheadrightarrow B$, then $A \rightarrow B$.

  c) If $AB \twoheadrightarrow C$, then $A \twoheadrightarrow C$.

3.8 Summary of Chapter 3

✦ *Relational Model*: Relations are tables representing information. Columns are headed by attributes; each attribute has an associated domain, or data type. Rows are called tuples, and a tuple has one component for each attribute of the relation.

✦ *Schemas*: A relation name, together with the attributes of that relation, form the relation schema. A collection of relation schemas forms a database schema. Particular data for a relation or collection of relations is called an instance of that relation schema or database schema.

✦ *Converting Entity Sets to Relations*: The relation for an entity set has one attribute for each attribute of the entity set. An exception is a weak entity set E, whose relation must also have attributes for the key attributes of those other entity sets that help identify entities of E.

✦ *Converting Relationships to Relations*: The relation for an E/R relationship has attributes corresponding to the key attributes of each entity set that participates in the relationship. However, if a relationship is a supporting relationship for some weak entity set, it is not necessary to produce a relation for that relationship.

✦ *Converting Isa Hierarchies to Relations*: One approach is to partition entities among the various entity sets of the hierarchy and create a relation, with all necessary attributes, for each such entity set. A second approach is to create a relation for each possible subset of the entity sets in the hierarchy, and create for each entity one tuple; that tuple is in the relation for exactly the set of entity sets to which the entity belongs. A third approach is to create only one relation and to use null values for those attributes that do not apply to the entity represented by a given tuple.

✦ *Functional Dependencies*: A functional dependency is a statement that two tuples of a relation which agree on some particular set of attributes must also agree on some other particular attribute.

✦ *Keys of a Relation*: A superkey for a relation is a set of attributes that functionally determines all the attributes of the relation. A key is a superkey, no proper subset of which functionally determines all the attributes.

✦ *Reasoning About Functional Dependencies*: There are many rules that let us infer that one FD $X \rightarrow A$ holds in any relation instance that satisfies some other given set of FD's. The simplest approach to verifying that $X \rightarrow A$ holds usually is to compute the closure of X, using the given FD's to expand X until it includes A.

✦ *Decomposing Relations*: We can decompose one relation schema into two without losing information as long as the attributes that are common to both schemas form a superkey for at least one of the decomposed relations.

✦ *Boyce-Codd Normal Form*: A relation is in BCNF if the only nontrivial FD's say that some superkey functionally determines one of the other attributes. It is possible to decompose any relation into a collection of BCNF relations without losing information. A major benefit of BCNF is that it eliminates redundancy caused by the existence of FD's.

✦ *Third Normal Form*: Sometimes decomposition into BCNF can hinder us in checking certain FD's. A relaxed form of BCNF, called 3NF, allows a FD $X \rightarrow A$ even if X is not a superkey, provided A is a member of some key. 3NF does not guarantee to eliminate all redundancy due to FD's, but often does so.

✦ *Multivalued Dependencies*: A multivalued dependency is a statement that two sets of attributes in a relation have sets of values that appear in all possible combinations.

✦ *Fourth Normal Form*: MVD's can also cause redundancy in a relation. 4NF is like BCNF, but also forbids nontrivial MVD's (unless they are actually FD's that are allowed by BCNF). It is possible to decompose a relation into 4NF without losing information.

3.9 References for Chapter 3

The classic paper by Codd on the relational model is [4]. This paper introduces the idea of functional dependencies, as well as the basic relational concept. Third normal form was also described there, while Boyce-Codd normal form is described by Codd in a later paper [5].

Multivalued dependencies and fourth normal form were defined by Fagin in [7]. However, the idea of multivalued dependencies also appears independently in [6] and [9].

Armstrong was the first to study rules for inferring FD's [1]. The rules for FD's that we have covered here (including what we call "Armstrong's axioms") and rules for inferring MVD's as well, come from [2]. The technique for testing a FD by computing the closure for a set of attributes is from [3].

There are a number of algorithms and/or proofs that algorithms work which have not been given in this book, including how one infers multivalued dependencies, how one projects multivalued dependencies onto decomposed relations, and how one decomposes into 3NF without losing the ability to check functional dependencies. These and other matters concerned with dependencies are explained in [8].

1. Armstrong, W. W., "Dependency structures of database relationships," *Proceedings of the 1974 IFIP Congress*, pp. 580–583.

2. Beeri, C., R. Fagin, and J. H. Howard, "A complete axiomatization for functional and multivalued dependencies," *ACM SIGMOD International Conference on Management of Data*, pp. 47–61, 1977.

3. Bernstein, P. A., "Synthesizing third normal form relations from functional dependencies," *ACM Transactions on Database Systems* **1**:4, pp. 277–298, 1976.

4. Codd, E. F., "A relational model for large shared data banks," *Comm. ACM* **13**:6, pp. 377–387, 1970.

5. Codd, E. F., "Further normalization of the data base relational model," in *Database Systems* (R. Rustin, ed.), Prentice-Hall, Englewood Cliffs, NJ, 1972.

6. Delobel, C., "Normalization and hierarchical dependencies in the relational data model," *ACM Transactions on Database Systems* **3**:3, pp. 201–222, 1978.

7. Fagin, R., "Multivalued dependencies and a new normal form for relational databases," *ACM Transactions on Database Systems* **2**:3, pp. 262–278, 1977.

8. Ullman, J. D., *Principles of Database and Knowledge-Base Systems, Volume I*, Computer Science Press, New York, 1988.

9. Zaniolo, C. and M. A. Melkanoff, "On the design of relational database schemata," *ACM Transactions on Database Systems* **6**:1, pp. 1–47, 1981.

Chapter 4

Other Data Models

The entity-relationship and relational models are just two of the models that have importance in database systems today. In this chapter we shall introduce you to several other models of rising importance.

We begin with a discussion of object-oriented data models. One approach to object-orientation for a database system is to extend the concepts of object-oriented programming languages such as C++ or Java to include persistence. That is, the presumption in ordinary programming is that objects go away after the program finishes, while an essential requirement of a DBMS is that the objects are preserved indefinitely, unless changed by the user, as in a file system. We shall study a "pure" object-oriented data model, called ODL (object definition language), which has been standardized by the ODMG (object data management group).

Next, we consider a model called object-relational. This model, part of the most recent SQL standard, called SQL-99 (or SQL:1999, or SQL3), is an attempt to extend the relational model, as introduced in Chapter 3, to include many of the common object-oriented concepts. This standard forms the basis for object-relational DBMS's that are now available from essentially all the major vendors, although these vendors differ considerably in the details of how the concepts are implemented and made available to users. Chapter 9 includes a discussion of the object-relational model of SQL-99.

Then, we take up the "semistructured" data model. This recent innovation is an attempt to deal with a number of database problems, including the need to combine databases and other data sources, such as Web pages, that have different schemas. While an essential of object-oriented or object-relational systems is their insistence on a fixed schema for every class or every relation, semistructured data is allowed much more flexibility in what components are present. For instance, we could think of movie objects, some of which have a director listed, some of which might have several different lengths for several different versions, some of which may include textual reviews, and so on.

The most prominent implementation of semistructured data is XML (extensible markup language). Essentially, XML is a specification for "documents," which are really collections of nested data elements, each with a role indicated by a tag. We believe that XML data will serve as an essential component in systems that mediate among data sources or that transmit data among sources. XML may even become an important approach to flexible storage of data in databases.

4.1   Review of Object-Oriented Concepts

Before introducing object-oriented database models, let us review the major object-oriented concepts themselves. Object-oriented programming has been widely regarded as a tool for better program organization and, ultimately, more reliable software implementation. First popularized in the language Smalltalk, object-oriented programming received a big boost with the development of C++ and the migration to C++ of much software development that was formerly done in C. More recently, the language Java, suitable for sharing programs across the World Wide Web, has also focused attention on object-oriented programming.

The database world has likewise been attracted to the object-oriented paradigm, particularly for database design and for extending relational DBMS's with new features. In this section we shall review the ideas behind object orientation:

1. A powerful type system.

2. *Classes*, which are types associated with an *extent*, or set of *objects* belonging to the class. An essential feature of classes, as opposed to conventional data types is that classes may include *methods*, which are procedures that are applicable to objects belonging to the class.

3. *Object Identity*, the idea that each object has a unique identity, independent of its value.

4. *Inheritance*, which is the organization of classes into hierarchies, where each class inherits the properties of the classes above it.

4.1.1   The Type System

An object-oriented programming language offers the user a rich collection of types. Starting with *atomic types*, such as integers, real numbers, booleans, and character strings, one may build new types by using *type constructors*. Typically, the type constructors let us build:

1. *Record structures*. Given a list of types $T_1, T_2, \ldots, T_n$ and a corresponding list of *field names* (called *instance variables* in Smalltalk) $f_1, f_2, \ldots, f_n$, one can construct a record type consisting of n components. The ith

component has type T_i and is referred to by its field name f_i. Record structures are exactly what C or C++ calls "structs," and we shall frequently use that term in what follows.

2. *Collection types.* Given a type T, one can construct new types by applying a *collection operator* to type T. Different languages use different collection operators, but there are several common ones, including arrays, lists, and sets. Thus, if T were the atomic type integer, we might build the collection types "array of integers," "list of integers," or "set of integers."

3. *Reference types.* A reference to a type T is a type whose values are suitable for locating a value of the type T. In C or C++, a reference is a "pointer" to a value, that is, the virtual-memory address of the value pointed to.

Of course, record-structure and collection operators can be applied repeatedly to build ever more complex types. For instance, a bank might define a type that is a record structure with a first component named `customer` of type string and whose second component is of type set-of-integers and is named `accounts`. Such a type is suitable for associating bank customers with the set of their accounts.

4.1.2 Classes and Objects

A *class* consists of a type and possibly one or more functions or procedures (called *methods*; see below) that can be executed on objects of that class. The objects of a class are either values of that type (called *immutable objects*) or variables whose value is of that type (called *mutable objects*). For example, if we define a class C whose type is "set of integers," then $\{2, 5, 7\}$ is an immutable object of class C, while variable s could be declared to be a mutable object of class C and assigned a value such as $\{2, 5, 7\}$.

4.1.3 Object Identity

Objects are assumed to have an *object identity* (OID). No two objects can have the same OID, and no object has two different OID's. Object identity has some interesting effects on how we model data. For instance, it is essential that an entity set have a key formed from values of attributes possessed by it or a related entity set (in the case of weak entity sets). However, within a class, we assume we can distinguish two objects whose attributes all have identical values, because the OID's of the two objects are guaranteed to be different.

4.1.4 Methods

Associated with a class there are usually certain functions, often called *methods*. A method for a class C has at least one argument that is an object of class C; it may have other arguments of any class, including C. For example, associated with a class whose type is "set of integers," we might have methods to sum the elements of a given set, to take the union of two sets, or to return a boolean indicating whether or not the set is empty.

In some situations, classes are referred to as "abstract data types," meaning that they *encapsulate*, or restrict access to objects of the class so that only the methods defined for the class can modify objects of the class directly. This restriction assures that the objects of the class cannot be changed in ways that were not anticipated by the designer of the class. Encapsulation is regarded as one of the key tools for reliable software development.

4.1.5 Class Hierarchies

It is possible to declare one class C to be a *subclass* of another class D. If so, then class C *inherits* all the properties of class D, including the type of D and any functions defined for class D. However, C may also have additional properties. For example, new methods may be defined for objects of class C, and these methods may be either in addition to or in place of methods of D. It may even be possible to extend the type of D in certain ways. In particular, if the type of D is a record-structure type, then we can add new fields to this type that are present only in objects of type C.

Example 4.1: Consider a class of bank account objects. We might describe the type for this class informally as:

```
CLASS Account = {accountNo: integer;
                 balance: real;
                 owner: REF Customer;
                }
```

That is, the type for the `Account` class is a record structure with three fields: an integer account number, a real-number balance, and an owner that is a reference to an object of class `Customer` (another class that we'd need for a banking database, but whose type we have not introduced here).

We could also define some methods for the class. For example, we might have a method

```
deposit(a: Account, m: real)
```

that increases the `balance` for `Account` object a by amount m.

Finally, we might wish to have several subclasses of the `Account` subclass. For instance, a time-deposit account could have an additional field `dueDate`, the date at which the account balance may be withdrawn by the owner. There might also be an additional method for the subclass `TimeDeposit`

```
penalty(a: TimeDeposit)
```

that takes an account a belonging to the subclass `TimeDeposit` and calculates the penalty for early withdrawal, as a function of the `dueDate` field in object a and the current date; the latter would be obtainable from the system on which the method is run.   □

4.2   Introduction to ODL

ODL (Object Definition Language) is a standardized language for specifying the structure of databases in object-oriented terms. It is an extension of IDL (Interface Description Language), a component of CORBA (Common Object Request Broker Architecture). The latter is a standard for distributed, object-oriented computing.

4.2.1   Object-Oriented Design

In an object-oriented design, the world to be modeled is thought of as composed of *objects*, which are observable entities of some sort. For example, people may be thought of as objects; so may bank accounts, airline flights, courses at a college, buildings, and so on. Objects are assumed to have a unique *object identity* (OID) that distinguishes them from any other object, as we discussed in Section 4.1.3.

To organize information, we usually want to group objects into *classes* of objects with similar properties. However, when speaking of ODL object-oriented designs, we should think of "similar properties" of the objects in a class in two different ways:

- The real-world concepts represented by the objects of a class should be similar. For instance, it makes sense to group all customers of a bank into one class and all accounts at the bank into another class. It would not make sense to group customers and accounts together in one class, because they have little or nothing in common and play essentially different roles in the world of banking.

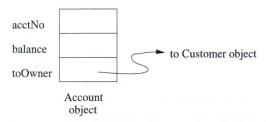

Figure 4.1: An object representing an account

- The properties of objects in a class must be the same. When programming in an object-oriented language, we often think of objects as records, like that suggested by Fig. 4.1. Objects have fields or slots in which values are placed. These values may be of common types such as integers, strings, or arrays, or they may be references to other objects.

When specifying the design of ODL classes, we describe properties of three kinds:

1. *Attributes*, which are values associated with the object. We discuss the legal types of ODL attributes in Section 4.2.8.

2. *Relationships*, which are connections between the object at hand and another object or objects.

3. *Methods*, which are functions that may be applied to objects of the class.

Attributes, relationships, and methods are collectively referred to as *properties*.

4.2.2   Class Declarations

A declaration of a class in ODL, in its simplest form, consists of:

1. The keyword `class`,

2. The name of the class, and

3. A bracketed list of properties of the class. These properties can be attributes, relationships, or methods, mixed in any order.

That is, the simple form of a class declaration is

```
class <name> {
    <list of properties>
}
```

4.2.3   Attributes in ODL

The simplest kind of property is the *attribute*. These properties describe some aspect of an object by associating a value of a fixed type with that object. For example, person objects might each have an attribute `name` whose type is string and whose value is the name of that person. Person objects might also have an attribute `birthdate` that is a triple of integers (i.e., a record structure) representing the year, month, and day of their birth.

In ODL, unlike the E/R model, attributes need not be of simple types, such as integers and strings. We just mentioned `birthdate` as an example of an attribute with a structured type. For another example, an attribute such as `phones` might have a set of strings as its type, and even more complex types are possible. We summarize the type system of ODL in Section 4.2.8.

Example 4.2: In Fig. 4.2 is an ODL declaration of the class of movies. It is not a complete declaration; we shall add more to it later. Line (1) declares `Movie` to be a class. Following line (1) are the declarations of four attributes that all `Movie` objects will have.

```
1)  class Movie {
2)      attribute string title;
3)      attribute integer year;
4)      attribute integer length;
5)      attribute enum Film {color,blackAndWhite} filmType;
    };
```

Figure 4.2: An ODL declaration of the class `Movie`

The first attribute, on line (2), is named `title`. Its type is `string`—a character string of unknown length. We expect the value of the `title` attribute in any `Movie` object to be the name of the movie. The next two attributes, `year` and `length` declared on lines (3) and (4), have integer type and represent the year in which the movie was made and its length in minutes, respectively. On line (5) is another attribute `filmType`, which tells whether the movie was filmed in color or black-and-white. Its type is an *enumeration,* and the name of the enumeration is `Film`. Values of enumeration attributes are chosen from a list of *literals,* `color` and `blackAndWhite` in this example.

An object in the class `Movie` as we have defined it so far can be thought of as a record or tuple with four components, one for each of the four attributes. For example,

```
("Gone With the Wind", 1939, 231, color)
```

is a `Movie` object. □

Example 4.3: In Example 4.2, all the attributes have atomic types. Here is an example with a nonatomic type. We can define the class `Star` by

```
1)  class Star {
2)      attribute string name;
3)      attribute Struct Addr
            {string street, string city} address;
    };
```

Line (2) specifies an attribute `name` (of the star) that is a string. Line (3) specifies another attribute `address`. This attribute has a type that is a *record structure.* The name of this structure is `Addr`, and the type consists of two fields: `street` and `city`. Both fields are strings. In general, one can define record structure types in ODL by the keyword `Struct` and curly braces around

---

Why Name Enumerations and Structures?

The name `Film` for the enumeration on line 5 of Fig. 4.2 doesn't seem to be necessary. However, by giving it a name, we can refer to it outside the scope of the declaration for class `Movie`. We do so by referring to it by the *scoped name* `Movie::Film`. For instance, in a declaration of a class of cameras, we could have a line:

```
attribute Movie::Film uses;
```

This line declares attribute `uses` to be of the same enumerated type with the values `color` and `blackAndWhite`.

Another reason for giving names to enumerated types (and structures as well, which are declared in a manner similar to enumerations) is that we can declare them in a "module" outside the declaration of any particular class, and have that type available to all the classes in the module.

---

the list of field names and their types. Like enumerations, structure types must have a name, which can be used elsewhere to refer to the same structure type. □

4.2.4 Relationships in ODL

While we can learn much about an object by examining its attributes, sometimes a critical fact about an object is the way it connects to other objects in the same or another class.

Example 4.4: Now, suppose we want to add to the declaration of the `Movie` class from Example 4.2 a property that is a set of stars. More precisely, we want each `Movie` object to connect the set of `Star` objects that are its stars. The best way to represent this connection between the `Movie` and `Star` classes is with a *relationship*. We may represent this relationship in `Movie` by a line:

```
relationship Set<Star> stars;
```

in the declaration of class `Movie`. This line may appear in Fig. 4.2 after any of the lines numbered (1) through (5). It says that in each object of class `Movie` there is a set of references to `Star` objects. The set of references is called `stars`. The keyword `relationship` specifies that `stars` contains references to other objects, while the keyword `Set` preceding `<Star>` indicates that `stars` references a set of `Star` objects, rather than a single object. In general, a type that is a set of elements of some other type T is defined in ODL by the keyword `Set` and angle brackets around the type T.   □

4.2.5 Inverse Relationships

Just as we might like to access the stars of a given movie, we might like to know the movies in which a given star acted. To get this information into `Star` objects, we can add the line

```
relationship Set<Movie> starredIn;
```

to the declaration of class `Star` in Example 4.3. However, this line and a similar declaration for `Movie` omits a very important aspect of the relationship between movies and stars. We expect that if a star S is in the `stars` set for movie M, then movie M is in the `starredIn` set for star S. We indicate this connection between the relationships `stars` and `starredIn` by placing in each of their declarations the keyword `inverse` and the name of the other relationship. If the other relationship is in some other class, as it usually is, then we refer to that relationship by the name of its class, followed by a double colon (`::`) and the name of the relationship.

Example 4.5 : To define the relationship `starredIn` of class `Star` to be the inverse of the relationship `stars` in class `Movie`, we revise the declarations of these classes, as shown in Fig. 4.3 (which also contains a definition of class `Studio` to be discussed later). Line (6) shows the declaration of relationship `stars` of movies, and says that its inverse is `Star::starredIn`. Since relationship `starredIn` is defined in another class, the relationship name is preceded by the name of that class (`Star`) and a double colon. Recall the double colon is used whenever we refer to something defined in another class, such as a property or type name.

Similarly, relationship `starredIn` is declared in line (11). Its inverse is declared by that line to be `stars` of class `Movie`, as it must be, because inverses always are linked in pairs.   □

As a general rule, if a relationship R for class C associates with object x of class C with objects $y_1, y_2, \ldots, y_n$ of class D, then the inverse relationship of R associates with each of the y_i's the object x (perhaps along with other objects). Sometimes, it helps to visualize a relationship R from class C to class D as a list of pairs, or tuples, of a relation. The idea is the same as the "relationship set" we used to describe E/R relationships in Section 2.1.5. Each pair consists of an object x from class C and an associated object y of class D, as:

C	D
x_1	y_1
x_2	y_2
$\ldots$	$\ldots$

Then the inverse relationship for R is the set of pairs with the components reversed, as:

```
1)   class Movie {
2)      attribute string title;
3)      attribute integer year;
4)      attribute integer length;
5)      attribute enum Film {color,blackAndWhite} filmType;
6)      relationship Set<Star> stars
                     inverse Star::starredIn;
7)      relationship Studio ownedBy
                     inverse Studio::owns;
     };

8)   class Star {
9)      attribute string name;
10)     attribute Struct Addr
            {string street, string city} address;
11)     relationship Set<Movie> starredIn
                     inverse Movie::stars;
     };

12)  class Studio {
13)     attribute string name;
14)     attribute string address;
15)     relationship Set<Movie> owns
                     inverse Movie::ownedBy;
     };
```

Figure 4.3: Some ODL classes and their relationships

D	C
y_1	x_1
y_2	x_2
$\ldots$	$\ldots$

Notice that this rule works even if C and D are the same class. There are some relationships that logically run from a class to itself, such as "child of" from the class "Persons" to itself.

4.2.6 Multiplicity of Relationships

Like the binary relationships of the E/R model, a pair of inverse relationships in ODL can be classified as either many-many, many-one in either direction, or one-one. The type declarations for the pair of relationships tells us which.

1. If we have a many-many relationship between classes C and D, then in class C the type of the relationship is `Set<D>`, and in class D the type is `Set<C>`.[1]

2. If the relationship is many-one from C to D, then the type of the relationship in C is just D, while the type of the relationship in D is `Set<C>`.

3. If the relationship is many-one from D to C, then the roles of C and D are reversed in (2) above.

4. If the relationship is one-one, then the type of the relationship in C is just D, and in D it is just C.

Note, that as in the E/R model, we allow a many-one or one-one relationship to include the case where for some objects the "one" is actually "none." For instance, a many-one relationship from C to D might have a missing or "null" value of the relationship in some of the C objects. Of course, since a D object could be associated with any set of C objects, it is also permissible for that set to be empty for some D objects.

Example 4.6: In Fig. 4.3 we have the declaration of three classes, `Movie`, `Star`, and `Studio`. The first two of these have already been introduced in Examples 4.2 and 4.3. We also discussed the relationship pair `stars` and `starredIn`. Since each of their types uses `Set`, we see that this pair represents a many-many relationship between `Star` and `Movie`.

   Studio objects have attributes `name` and `address`; these appear in lines (13) and (14). Notice that the type of addresses here is a string, rather than a structure as was used for the `address` attribute of class `Star` on line (10). There is nothing wrong with using attributes of the same name but different types in different classes.

   In line (7) we see a relationship `ownedBy` from movies to studios. Since the type of the relationship is `Studio`, and not `Set<Studio>`, we are declaring that for each movie there is one studio that owns it. The inverse of this relationship is found on line (15). There we see the relationship `owns` from studios to movies. The type of this relationship is `Set<Movie>`, indicating that each studio owns a set of movies—perhaps 0, perhaps 1, or perhaps a large number of movies. □

4.2.7 Methods in ODL

The third kind of property of ODL classes is the method. As in other object-oriented languages, a method is a piece of executable code that may be applied to the objects of the class.

   In ODL, we can declare the names of the methods associated with a class and the input/output types of those methods. These declarations, called *signatures*,

---

[1] Actually, the `Set` could be replaced by another "collection type," such as list or bag, as discussed in Section 4.2.8. We shall assume all collections are sets in our exposition of relationships, however.

Why Signatures?

The value of providing signatures is that when we implement the schema in a real programming language, we can check automatically that the implementation matches the design as was expressed in the schema. We cannot check that the implementation correctly implements the "meaning" of the operations, but we can at least check that the input and output parameters are of the correct number and of the correct type.

---

are like function declarations in C or C++ (as opposed to function *definitions*, which are the code to implement the function). The code for a method would be written in the host language; this code is not part of ODL.

Declarations of methods appear along with the attributes and relationships in a class declaration. As is normal for object-oriented languages, each method is associated with a class, and methods are invoked on an object of that class. Thus, the object is a "hidden" argument of the method. This style allows the same method name to be used for several different classes, because the object upon which the operation is performed determines the particular method meant. Such a method name is said to be *overloaded*.

The syntax of method declarations is similar to that of function declarations in C, with two important additions:

1. Method parameters are specified to be **in**, **out**, or **inout**, meaning that they are used as input parameters, output parameters, or both, respectively. The last two types of parameters can be modified by the method; **in** parameters cannot be modified. In effect, **out** and **inout** parameters are passed by reference, while **in** parameters may be passed by value. Note that a method may also have a return value, which is a way that a result can be produced by a method other than by assigning a value to an **out** or **inout** parameter.

2. Methods may raise *exceptions*, which are special responses that are outside the normal parameter-passing and return-value mechanisms by which methods communicate. An exception usually indicates an abnormal or unexpected condition that will be "handled" by some method that called it (perhaps indirectly through a sequence of calls). Division by zero is an example of a condition that might be treated as an exception. In ODL, a method declaration can be followed by the keyword **raises**, followed by a parenthesized list of one or more exceptions that the method can raise.

Example 4.7 : In Fig. 4.4 we see an evolution of the definition for class Movie, last seen in Fig. 4.3. The methods included with the class declaration are as follows.

Line (8) declares a method `lengthInHours`. We might imagine that it produces as a return value the length of the movie object to which it is applied, but converted from minutes (as in the attribute `length`) to a floating-point number that is the equivalent in hours. Note that this method takes no parameters. The `Movie` object to which the method is applied is the "hidden" argument, and it is from this object that a possible implementation of `lengthInHours` would obtain the length of the movie in minutes.[2]

Method `lengthInHours` may raise an exception called `noLengthFound`. Presumably this exception would be raised if the `length` attribute of the object to which the method `lengthInHours` was applied had an undefined value or a value that could not represent a valid length (e.g., a negative number).

```
 1)   class Movie {
 2)      attribute string title;
 3)      attribute integer year;
 4)      attribute integer length;
 5)      attribute enumeration(color,blackAndWhite) filmType;
 6)      relationship Set<Star> stars
                       inverse Star::starredIn;
 7)      relationship Studio ownedBy
                       inverse Studio::owns;
 8)      float lengthInHours() raises(noLengthFound);
 9)      void starNames(out Set<String>);
10)      void otherMovies(in Star, out Set<Movie>)
                       raises(noSuchStar);
      };
```

Figure 4.4: Adding method signatures to the `Movie` class

In line (9) we see another method signature, for a method called `starNames`. This method has no return value but has an output parameter whose type is a set of strings. We presume that the value of the output parameter is computed by `starNames` to be the set of strings that are the values of the attribute `name` for the stars of the movie to which the method is applied. However, as always there is no guarantee that the method definition behaves in this particular way.

Finally, at line (10) is a third method, `otherMovies`. This method has an input parameter of type `Star`. A possible implementation of this method is as follows. We may suppose that `otherMovies` expects this star to be one of the stars of the movie; if it is not, then the exception `noSuchStar` is raised. If it is one of the stars of the movie to which the method is applied, then the output parameter, whose type is a set of movies, is given as its value the set of all the

---

[2]In the actual definition of the method `lengthInHours` a special term such as `self` would be used to refer to the object to which the method is applied. This matter is of no concern as far as declarations of method signatures is concerned.

other movies of this star.   □

4.2.8   Types in ODL

ODL offers the database designer a type system similar to that found in C or other conventional programming languages. A type system is built from a basis of types that are defined by themselves and certain recursive rules whereby complex types are built from simpler types. In ODL, the basis consists of:

1. *Atomic types*: integer, float, character, character string, boolean, and *enumerations*. The latter are lists of names declared to be abstract values. We saw an example of an enumeration in line (5) of Fig. 4.3, where the names are `color` and `blackAndWhite`.

2. *Class names*, such as `Movie`, or `Star`, which represent types that are actually structures, with components for each of the attributes and relationships of that class.

These basic types are combined into structured types using the following *type constructors*:

1. *Set*. If T is any type, then `Set<T>` denotes the type whose values are finite sets of elements of type T. Examples using the set type-constructor occur in lines (6), (11), and (15) of Fig. 4.3.

2. *Bag*. If T is any type, then `Bag<T>` denotes the type whose values are finite bags or *multisets* of elements of type T. A bag allows an element to appear more than once. For example, $\{1, 2, 1\}$ is a bag but not a set, because 1 appears more than once.

3. *List*. If T is any type, then `List<T>` denotes the type whose values are finite lists of zero or more elements of type T. As a special case, the type `string` is a shorthand for the type `List<char>`.

4. *Array*. If T is a type and i is an integer, then `Array<T,i>` denotes the type whose elements are arrays of i elements of type T. For example, `Array<char,10>` denotes character strings of length 10.

5. *Dictionary*. If T and S are types, then `Dictionary<T,S>` denotes a type whose values are finite sets of pairs. Each pair consists of a value of the *key type* T and a value of the *range type* S. The dictionary may not contain two pairs with the same key value. Presumably, the dictionary is implemented in a way that makes it very efficient, given a value t of the key type T, to find the associated value of the range type S.

6. *Structures*. If $T_1, T_2, \ldots, T_n$ are types, and $F_1, F_2, \ldots, F_n$ are names of fields, then

---

Sets, Bags, and Lists

To understand the distinction between sets, bags, and lists, remember that a set has unordered elements, and only one occurrence of each element. A bag allows more than one occurrence of an element, but the elements and their occurrences are unordered. A list allows more than one occurrence of an element, but the occurrences are ordered. Thus, $\{1, 2, 1\}$ and $\{2, 1, 1\}$ are the same bag, but $(1, 2, 1)$ and $(2, 1, 1)$ are not the same list.

$$\texttt{Struct N } \{\texttt{T}_1 \texttt{ F}_1, \texttt{ T}_2 \texttt{ F}_2, \ldots, \texttt{ T}_n \texttt{ F}_n\}$$

denotes the type named N whose elements are structures with n fields. The ith field is named F_i and has type T_i. For example, line (10) of Fig. 4.3 showed a structure type named `Addr`, with two fields. Both fields are of type `string` and have names `street` and `city`, respectively.

The first five types — set, bag, list, array, and dictionary — are called *collection types*. There are different rules about which types may be associated with attributes and which with relationships.

- The type of a relationship is either a class type or a (single use of a) collection type constructor applied to a class type.

- The type of an attribute is built starting with an atomic type or types. Class types may also be used, but typically these will be classes that are used as "structures," much as the `Addr` structure was used in Example 4.3. We generally prefer to connect classes with relationships, because relationships are two-way, which makes queries about the database easier to express. In contrast, we can go from an object to its attributes, but not vice-versa. After beginning with atomic or class types, we may then apply the structure and collection type constructors as we wish, as many times as we wish.

Example 4.8: Some of the possible types of attributes are:

1. `integer`.

2. `Struct N {string field1, integer field2}`.

3. `List<real>`.

4. `Array<Struct N {string field1, integer field2}, 10>`.

Example (1) is an atomic type; (2) is a structure of atomic types, (3) a collection of an atomic type, and (4) a collection of structures built from atomic types.

Now, suppose the class names `Movie` and `Star` are available basic types. Then we may construct relationship types such as `Movie` or `Bag<Star>`. However, the following are illegal as relationship types:

1. `Struct N {Movie field1, Star field2}`. Relationship types cannot involve structures.

2. `Set<integer>`. Relationship types cannot involve atomic types.

3. `Set<Array<Star, 10>>`. Relationship types cannot involve two applications of collection types.

□

4.2.9   Exercises for Section 4.2

* **Exercise 4.2.1:** In Exercise 2.1.1 was the informal description of a bank database. Render this design in ODL.

Exercise 4.2.2: Modify your design of Exercise 4.2.1 in the ways enumerated in Exercise 2.1.2. Describe the changes; do not write a complete, new schema.

Exercise 4.2.3: Render the teams-players-fans database of Exercise 2.1.3 in ODL. Why does the complication about sets of team colors, which was mentioned in the original exercise, not present a problem in ODL?

*! **Exercise 4.2.4:** Suppose we wish to keep a genealogy. We shall have one class, `Person`. The information we wish to record about persons includes their name (an attribute) and the following relationships: mother, father, and children. Give an ODL design for the `Person` class. Be sure to indicate the inverses of the relationships that, like `mother`, `father`, and `children`, are also relationships from `Person` to itself. Is the inverse of the `mother` relationship the `children` relationship? Why or why not? Describe each of the relationships and their inverses as sets of pairs.

! **Exercise 4.2.5:** Let us add to the design of Exercise 4.2.4 the attribute `education`. The value of this attribute is intended to be a collection of the degrees obtained by each person, including the name of the degree (e.g., B.S.), the school, and the date. This collection of structs could be a set, bag, list, or array. Describe the consequences of each of these four choices. What information could be gained or lost by making each choice? Is the information lost likely to be important in practice?

Exercise 4.2.6: In Fig. 4.5 is an ODL definition for the classes `Ship` and `TG` (*task group*, a collection of ships). We would like to make some modifications to this definition. Each modification can be described by mentioning a line or lines to be changed and giving the replacement, or by inserting one or more new lines after one of the numbered lines. Describe the following modifications:

a) The type of the attribute `commander` is changed to be a pair of strings, the first of which is the rank and the second of which is the name.

b) A ship is allowed to be assigned to more than one task group.

c) *Sister ships* are identical ships made from the same plans. We wish to represent, for each ship, the set of its sister ships (other than itself). You may assume that each ship's sister ships are `Ship` objects.

```
1)   class Ship {
2)       attribute string name;
3)       attribute integer yearLaunched;
4)       relationship TG assignedTo inverse TG::unitsOf;
     };

5)   class TG {
6)       attribute real number;
7)       attribute string commander;
8)       relationship Set<Ship> unitsOf
             inverse Ship::assignedTo;
     };
```

Figure 4.5: An ODL description of ships and task groups

*!! Exercise 4.2.7: Under what circumstances is a relationship its own inverse? *Hint*: Think about the relationship as a set of pairs, as discussed in Section 4.2.5.

4.3 Additional ODL Concepts

There are a number of other features of ODL that we must learn if we are to express in ODL the things that we can express in the E/R or relational models. In this section, we shall cover:

1. Representing multiway relationships. Notice that all ODL relationships are binary, and we have to go to some lengths to represent 3-way or higher arity relationships that are simple to represent in E/R diagrams or relations.

2. Subclasses and inheritance.

3. Keys, which are optional in ODL.

4. Extents, the set of objects of a given class that exist in a database. These are the ODL equivalent of entity sets or relations, and must not be confused with the class itself, which is a schema.

4.3.1   Multiway Relationships in ODL

ODL supports only binary relationships. There is a trick, which we introduced in Section 2.1.7, to replace a multiway relationship by several binary, many-one relationships. Suppose we have a multiway relationship R among classes or entity sets $C_1, C_2, \ldots, C_n$. We may replace R by a class C and n many-one binary relationships from C to each of the C_i's. Each object of class C may be thought of as a tuple t in the relationship set for R. Object t is related, by the n many-one relationships, to the objects of the classes C_i that participate in the relationship-set tuple t.

Example 4.9: Let us consider how we would represent in ODL the 3-way relationship *Contracts*, whose E/R diagram was given in Fig. 2.7. We may start with the class definitions for `Movie`, `Star`, and `Studio`, the three classes that are related by *Contracts*, that we saw in Fig. 4.3.

We must create a class `Contract` that corresponds to the 3-way relationship *Contracts*. The three many-one relationships from `Contract` to the other three classes we shall call `theMovie`, `theStar`, and `theStudio`. Figure 4.6 shows the definition of the class `Contract`.

```
1)      class Contract {
2)          attribute integer salary;
3)          relationship Movie theMovie
                    inverse ... ;
4)          relationship Star theStar
                    inverse ... ;
5)          relationship Studio theStudio
                    inverse ... ;
        };
```

Figure 4.6: A class `Contract` to represent the 3-way relationship *Contracts*

There is one attribute of the class `Contract`, the salary, since that quantity is associated with the contract itself, not with any of the three participants. Recall that in Fig. 2.7 we made an analogous decision to place the attribute *salary* on the relationship *Contracts*, rather than on one of the participating entity sets. The other properties of `Contract` objects are the three relationships mentioned.

Note that we have not named the inverses of these relationships. We need to modify the declarations of `Movie`, `Star`, and `Studio` to include relationships from each of these to `Contract`. For instance, the inverse of `theMovie` might be named `contractsFor`. We would then replace line (3) of Fig. 4.6 by

```
3)    relationship Movie theMovie
          inverse Movie::contractsFor;
```

and add to the declaration of `Movie` the statement:

```
relationship Set<Contract> contractsFor
      inverse Contract::theMovie;
```

Notice that in `Movie`, the relationship `contractsFor` gives us a set of contracts, since there may be several contracts associated with one movie. Each contract in the set is essentially a triple consisting of that movie, a star, and a studio, plus the salary that is paid to the star by the studio for acting in that movie. □

4.3.2 Subclasses in ODL

Let us recall the discussion of subclasses in the E/R model from Section 2.1.11. There is a similar capability in ODL to declare one class C to be a subclass of another class D. We follow the name C in its declaration with the keyword `extends` and the name D.

Example 4.10: Recall Example 2.10, where we declared cartoons to be a subclass of movies, with the additional property of a relationship from a cartoon to a set of stars that are its "voices." We can create a subclass `Cartoon` for `Movie` with the ODL declaration:

```
class Cartoon extends Movie {
   relationship Set<Star> voices;
};
```

We have not indicated the name of the inverse of relationship `voices`, although technically we must do so.

A subclass *inherits* all the properties of its superclass. Thus, each cartoon object has attributes `title`, `year`, `length`, and `filmType` inherited from `Movie` (recall Fig. 4.3), and it inherits relationships `stars` and `ownedBy` from `Movie`, in addition to its own relationship `voices`.

Also in that example, we defined a class of murder mysteries with additional attribute `weapon`.

```
class MurderMystery extends Movie {
   attribute string weapon;
};
```

is a suitable declaration of this subclass. Again, all the properties of movies are inherited by `MurderMystery`. □

4.3.3   Multiple Inheritance in ODL

Sometimes, as in the case of a movie like "Roger Rabbit," we need a class that is a subclass of two or more other classes at the same time. In the E/R model, we were able to imagine that "Roger Rabbit" was represented by components in all three of the *Movies*, *Cartoons*, and *Murder-Mysteries* entity sets, which were connected in an isa-hierarchy. However, a principle of object-oriented systems is that objects belong to one and only one class. Thus, to represent movies that are both cartoons and murder mysteries, we need a fourth class for these movies.

The class `CartoonMurderMystery` must inherit properties from both `Cartoon` and `MurderMystery`, as suggested by Fig. 4.7. That is, a `CartoonMurderMystery` object has all the properties of a `Movie` object, plus the relationship `voices` and the attribute `weapon`.

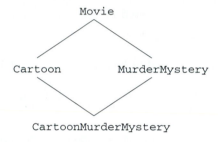

Figure 4.7: Diagram showing multiple inheritance

In ODL, we may follow the keyword `extends` by several classes, separated by colons.[3] Thus, we may declare the fourth class by:

```
class CartoonMurderMystery
    extends MurderMystery : Cartoon;
```

When a class C inherits from several classes, there is the potential for *conflicts* among property names. Two or more of the superclasses of C may have a property of the same name, and the types of these properties may differ. Class `CartoonMurderMystery` did not present such a problem, since the only properties in common between `Cartoon` and `MurderMystery` are the properties of `Movie`, which are the same property in both superclasses of `CartoonMurderMystery`. Here is an example where we are not so lucky.

Example 4.11: Suppose we have subclasses of `Movie` called `Romance` and `Courtroom`. Further suppose that each of these subclasses has an attribute called `ending`. In class `Romance`, attribute `ending` draws its values from the

---

[3]Technically, the second and subsequent names must be "interfaces," rather than classes. Roughly, an *interface* in ODL is a class definition without an associated set of objects, or "extent." We discuss the distinction further in Section 4.3.4.

enumeration {happy, sad}, while in class Courtroom, attribute ending draws its values from the enumeration {guilty, notGuilty}. If we create a further subclass, Courtroom-Romance, that has as superclasses both Romance and Courtroom, then the type for inherited attribute ending in class Courtroom-Romance is unclear. □

The ODL standard does not dictate how such conflicts are to be resolved. Some possible approaches to handling conflicts that arise from multiple inheritance are:

1. Disallow multiple inheritance altogether. This approach is generally regarded as too limiting.

2. Indicate which of the candidate definitions of the property applies to the subclass. For instance, in Example 4.11 we may decide that in a courtroom romance we are more interested in whether the movie has a happy or sad ending than we are in the verdict of the courtroom trial. In this case, we would specify that class Courtroom-Romance inherits attribute ending from superclass Romance, and not from superclass Courtroom.

3. Give a new name in the subclass for one of the identically named properties in the superclasses. For instance, in Example 4.11, if Courtroom-Romance inherits attribute ending from superclass Romance, then we may specify that class Courtroom-Romance has an additional attribute called verdict, which is a renaming of the attribute ending inherited from class Courtroom.

4.3.4 Extents

When an ODL class is part of the database being defined, we need to distinguish the class definition itself from the set of objects of that class that exist at a given time. The distinction is the same as that between a relation schema and a relation instance, even though both can be referred to by the name of the relation, depending on context. Likewise, in the E/R model we need to distinguish between the definition of an entity set and the set of existing entities of that kind.

In ODL, the distinction is made explicit by giving the class and its *extent*, or set of existing objects, different names. Thus, the class name is a schema for the class, while the extent is the name of the current set of objects of that class. We provide a name for the extent of a class by following the class name by a parenthesized expression consisting of the keyword extent and the name chosen for the extent.

Example 4.12: In general, we find it a useful convention to name classes by a singular noun and name the corresponding extent by the same noun in plural. Following this convention, we could call the extent for class Movie by the name

---

Interfaces

ODL provides for the definition of *interfaces*, which are essentially class definitions with no associated extent (and therefore, with no associated objects). We first mentioned interfaces in Section 4.3.3, where we pointed out that they could support inheritance by one class from several classes. Interfaces also are useful if we have several classes that have different extents, but the same properties; the situation is analogous to several relations that have the same schema but different sets of tuples.

If we define an interface I, we can then define several classes that inherit their properties from I. Each of those classes has a distinct extent, so we can maintain in our database several sets of objects that have the same type, yet belong to distinct classes.

`Movies`. To declare this name for the extent, we would begin the declaration of class `Movie` by:

```
class Movie (extent Movies) {
    attribute string title;
        ...
```

As we shall see when we study the query language OQL that is designed for querying ODL data, we refer to the extent `Movies`, not to the class `Movie`, when we want to examine the movies currently stored in our database. Remember that the choice of a name for the extent of a class is entirely arbitrary, although we shall follow the "make it plural" convention in this book.   □

4.3.5   Declaring Keys in ODL

ODL differs from the other models studied so far in that the declaration and use of keys is optional. That is, in the E/R model, entity sets need keys to distinguish members of the entity set from one another. In the relational model, where relations are sets, all attributes together form a key unless some proper subset of the attributes for a given relation can serve as a key. Either way, there must be at least one key for a relation.

However, objects have a unique object identity, as we discussed in Section 4.1.3. Consequently, in ODL, the declaration of a key or keys is optional. It is entirely appropriate for there to be several objects of a class that are indistinguishable by any properties we can observe; the system still keeps them distinct by their internal object identity.

In ODL we may declare one or more attributes to be a key for a class by using the keyword **key** or **keys** (it doesn't matter which) followed by the attribute or attributes forming keys. If there is more than one attribute in a key, the list of attributes must be surrounded by parentheses. The key declaration itself appears, along with the extent declaration, inside parentheses that may follow the name of the class itself in the first line of its declaration.

Example 4.13: To declare that the set of two attributes `title` and `year` form a key for class `Movie`, we could begin its declaration:

```
class Movie
    (extent Movies key (title, year))
{
    attribute string title;
        ...
```

We could have used `keys` in place of `key`, even though only one key is declared. Similarly, if `name` is a key for class `Star`, then we could begin its declaration:

```
class Star
    (extent Stars key name)
{
    attribute string name;
        ...
```

□

It is possible that several sets of attributes are keys. If so, then following the word `key(s)` we may place several keys separated by commas. As usual, a key that consists of more than one attribute must have parentheses around the list of its attributes, so we can disambiguate a key of several attributes from several keys of one attribute each.

Example 4.14: As an example of a situation where it is appropriate to have more than one key, consider a class `Employee`, whose complete set of attributes and relationships we shall not describe here. However, suppose that two of its attributes are `empID`, the employee ID, and `ssNo`, the Social Security number. Then we can declare each of these attributes to be a key by itself with

```
class Employee
    (extent Employees key empID, ssNo)
        ...
```

Because there are no parentheses around the list of attributes, ODL interprets the above as saying that each of the two attributes is a key by itself. If we put parentheses around the list (`empID`, `ssNo`), then ODL would interpret the two attributes together as forming one key. That is, the implication of writing

```
class Employee
    (extent Employees key (empID, ssNo))
        ...
```

is that no two employees could have both the same employee ID and the same Social Security number, although two employees might agree on one of these attributes.   □

The ODL standard also allows properties other than attributes to appear in keys. There is no fundamental problem with a method or relationship being declared a key or part of a key, since keys are advisory statements that the DBMS can take advantage of or not, as it wishes. For instance, one could declare a method to be a key, meaning that on distinct objects of the class the method is guaranteed to return distinct values.

When we allow many-one relationships to appear in key declarations, we can get an effect similar to that of weak entity sets in the E/R model. We can declare that the object O_1 referred to by an object O_2 on the "many" side of the relationship, perhaps together with other properties of O_2 that are included in the key, is unique for different objects O_2. However, we should remember that there is no requirement that classes have keys; we are never obliged to handle, in some special way, classes that lack attributes of their own to form a key, as we did for weak entity sets.

Example 4.15: Let us review the example of a weak entity set *Crews* in Fig. 2.20. Recall that we hypothesized that crews were identified by their number, and the studio for which they worked, although two studios might have crews with the same number. We might declare the class `Crew` as in Fig. 4.8. Note that we need to modify the declaration of `Studio` to include the relationship `crewsOf` that is an inverse to the relationship `unitOf` in `Crew`; we omit this change.

```
class Crew
    (extent Crews key (number, unitOf))
{
    attribute integer number;
    relationship Studio unitOf
        inverse Studio::crewsOf;
}
```

Figure 4.8: A ODL declaration for crews

What this key declaration asserts is that there cannot be two crews that both have the same value for the `number` attribute and are related to the same studio by `unitOf`. Notice how this assertion resembles the implication of the E/R diagram in Fig. 2.20, which is that the number of a crew and the name of the related studio (i.e., the key for studios) uniquely determine a crew entity. □

4.3.6 Exercises for Section 4.3

* **Exercise 4.3.1:** Add suitable extents and keys to your ODL schema from Exercise 4.2.1.

Exercise 4.3.2: Add suitable extents and keys to your ODL schema from Exercise 4.2.3.

! **Exercise 4.3.3:** Suppose we wish to modify the ODL declarations of Exercise 4.2.4, where we had a class of people with relationships `mother`, `father`, and `children`, to include certain subclasses of people: (1) Males (2) Females (3) People who are parents. In addition, we want the relationships `mother`, `father`, and `children` to run between the smallest classes for which all possible instances of the relationship appear. You may therefore wish to define other subclasses as well. Write these declarations, including multiple inheritances when appropriate.

Exercise 4.3.4: Is there a suitable key for the class `Contract` declared in Fig. 4.6? If so, what is it?

Exercise 4.3.5: In Exercise 2.4.4 we saw two examples of situations where weak entity sets were essential. Render these databases in ODL, including declarations for extents and suitable keys.

Exercise 4.3.6: Give an ODL design for the registrar's database described in Exercise 2.1.9.

4.4 From ODL Designs to Relational Designs

While the E/R model is intended to be converted into a model such as the relational model when we implement the design as an actual database, ODL was originally intended to be used as the specification language for real, object-oriented DBMS's. However ODL, like all object-oriented design systems, can also be used for preliminary design and converted to relations prior to implementation. In this section we shall consider how to convert ODL designs into relational designs. The process is similar in many ways to what we introduced in Section 3.2 for converting E/R diagrams to relational database schemas. Yet some new problems arise for ODL, including:

1. Entity sets must have keys, but there is no such guarantee for ODL classes. Therefore, in some situations we must invent a new attribute to serve as a key when we construct a relation for the class.

2. While we have required E/R attributes and relational attributes to be atomic, there is no such constraint for ODL attributes. The conversion of attributes that have collection types to relations is tricky and ad-hoc, often resulting in unnormalized relations that must be redesigned by the techniques of Section 3.6.

3. ODL allows us to specify methods as part of a design, but there is no simple way to convert methods directly into a relational schema. We shall visit the issue of methods in relational schemas in Section 4.5.5 and again in Chapter 9 covering the SQL-99 standard. For now, let us assume that any ODL design we wish to convert into a relational design does not include methods.

4.4.1   From ODL Attributes to Relational Attributes

As a starting point, let us assume that our goal is to have one relation for each class and for that relation to have one attribute for each property. We shall see many ways in which this approach must be modified, but for the moment, let us consider the simplest possible case, where we can indeed convert classes to relations and properties to attributes. The restrictions we assume are:

1. All properties of the class are attributes (not relationships or methods).

2. The types of the attributes are atomic (not structures or sets).

Example 4.16: Figure 4.9 is an example of such a class. There are four attributes and no other properties. These attributes each have an atomic type; `title` is a string, `year` and `length` are integers, and `filmType` is an enumeration of two values.

```
class Movie (extent Movies) {
    attribute string title;
    attribute integer year;
    attribute integer length;
    attribute enum Film {color,blackAndWhite} filmType;
};
```

Figure 4.9: Attributes of the class `Movie`

We create a relation with the same name as the extent of the class, `Movies` in this case. The relation has four attributes, one for each attribute of the class. The names of the relational attributes can be the same as the names of the corresponding class attributes. Thus, the schema for this relation is

```
Movies(title, year, length, filmType)
```

For each object in the extent `Movies`, there is one tuple in the relation `Movies`. This tuple has a component for each of the four attributes, and the value of each component is the same as the value of the corresponding attribute of the object.   □

4.4.2 Nonatomic Attributes in Classes

Unfortunately, even when a class' properties are all attributes we may have some difficulty converting the class to a relation. The reason is that attributes in ODL can have complex types such as structures, sets, bags, or lists. On the other hand, a fundamental principle of the relational model is that a relation's attributes have an atomic type, such as numbers and strings. Thus, we must find some way of representing nonatomic attribute types as relations.

Record structures whose fields are themselves atomic are the easiest to handle. We simply expand the structure definition, making one attribute of the relation for each field of the structure. The only possible problem is that two structures could have fields of the same name, in which case we have to invent new attribute names to distinguish them in the relation.

```
class Star (extent Stars) {
    attribute string name;
    attribute Struct Addr
        {string street, string city} address;
};
```

Figure 4.10: Class with a structured attribute

Example 4.17: In Fig. 4.10 is a declaration for class `Star`, with only attributes as properties. The attribute `name` is atomic, but attribute `address` is a structure with two fields, `street` and `city`. Thus, we can represent this class by a relation with three attributes. The first attribute, `name`, corresponds to the ODL attribute of the same name. The second and third attributes we shall call `street` and `city`; they correspond to the two fields of the `address` structure and together represent an address. Thus, the schema for our relation is

```
Stars(name, street, city)
```

Figure 4.11 shows some typical tuples of this relation. □

name	street	city
Carrie Fisher	123 Maple St.	Hollywood
Mark Hamill	456 Oak Rd.	Brentwood
Harrison Ford	789 Palm Dr.	Beverly Hills

Figure 4.11: A relation representing stars

4.4.3 Representing Set-Valued Attributes

However, record structures are not the most complex kind of attribute that can appear in ODL class definitions. Values can also be built using type constructors Set, Bag, List, Array, and Dictionary from Section 4.2.8. Each presents its own problems when migrating to the relational model. We shall only discuss the Set constructor, which is the most common, in detail.

One approach to representing a set of values for an attribute A is to make one tuple for each value. That tuple includes the appropriate values for all the other attributes besides A. Let us first see an example where this approach works well, and then we shall see a pitfall.

```
class Star (extent Stars) {
    attribute string name;
    attribute Set<
            Struct Addr {string street, string city}
        > address;
};
```

Figure 4.12: Stars with a set of addresses

Example 4.18: Suppose that class Star were defined so that for each star we could record a set of addresses, as in Fig. 4.12. Suppose next that Carrie Fisher also has a beach home, but the other two stars mentioned in Fig. 4.11 each have only one home. Then we may create two tuples with name attribute equal to "Carrie Fisher", as shown in Fig. 4.13. Other tuples remain as they were in Fig. 4.11. □

name	street	city
Carrie Fisher	123 Maple St.	Hollywood
Carrie Fisher	5 Locust Ln.	Malibu
Mark Hamill	456 Oak Rd.	Brentwood
Harrison Ford	789 Palm Dr.	Beverly Hills

Figure 4.13: Allowing a set of addresses

Unfortunately, this technique of replacing objects with one or more set-valued attributes by collections of tuples, one for each combination of values for these attributes, can lead to unnormalized relations, of the type discussed in Section 3.6. In fact, even one set-valued attribute can lead to a BCNF violation, as the next example shows.

Atomic Values: Bug or Feature?

It seems that the relational model puts obstacles in our way, while ODL is more flexible in allowing structured values as properties. One might be tempted to dismiss the relational model altogether or regard it as a primitive concept that has been superseded by more elegant "object-oriented" approaches such as ODL. However, the reality is that database systems based on the relational model are dominant in the marketplace. One of the reasons is that the simplicity of the model makes possible powerful programming languages for querying databases, especially SQL (see Chapter 6), the standard language used in most of today's database systems.

```
class Star (extent Stars) {
    attribute string name;
    attribute Set<
            Struct Addr {string street, string city}
        > address;
    attribute Date birthdate;
};
```

Figure 4.14: Stars with a set of addresses and a birthdate

Example 4.19: Suppose that we add `birthdate` as an attribute in the definition of the `Star` class; that is, we use the definition shown in Fig. 4.14. We have added to Fig. 4.12 the attribute `birthdate` of type `Date`, which is one of ODL's atomic types. The `birthdate` attribute can be an attribute of the `Stars` relation, whose schema now becomes:

```
Stars(name, street, city, birthdate)
```

Let us make another change to the data of Fig. 4.13. Since a set of addresses can be empty, let us assume that Harrison Ford has no address in the database. Then the revised relation is shown in Fig. 4.15. Two bad things have happened:

1. Carrie Fisher's birthdate has been repeated in each tuple, causing redundancy. Note that her name is also repeated, but that repetition is not true redundancy, because without the name appearing in each tuple we could not know that both addresses were associated with Carrie Fisher.

2. Because Harrison Ford has an empty set of addresses, we have lost all information about him. This situation is an example of a deletion anomaly that we discussed in Section 3.6.1.

name	street	city	birthdate
Carrie Fisher	123 Maple St.	Hollywood	9/9/99
Carrie Fisher	5 Locust Ln.	Malibu	9/9/99
Mark Hamill	456 Oak Rd.	Brentwood	8/8/88

Figure 4.15: Adding birthdates

Although `name` is a key for the class `Star`, our need to have several tuples for one star to represent all their addresses means that `name` is *not* a key for the relation `Stars`. In fact, the key for that relation is {`name, street, city`}. Thus, the functional dependency

$$\texttt{name} \rightarrow \texttt{birthdate}$$

is a BCNF violation. This fact explains why the anomalies mentioned above are able to occur.   □

There are several options regarding how to handle set-valued attributes that appear in a class declaration along with other attributes, set-valued or not. First, we may simply place all attributes, set-valued or not, in the schema for the relation, then use the normalization techniques of Sections 3.6 and 3.7 to eliminate the resulting BCNF and 4NF violations. Notice that a set-valued attribute in conjunction with a single-valued attribute leads to a BNCF violation, as in Example 4.19. Two set-valued attributes in the same class declaration will lead to a 4NF violation.

The second approach is to separate out each set-valued attribute as if it were a many-many relationship between the objects of the class and the values that appear in the sets. We shall discuss this approach for relationships in Section 4.4.5.

4.4.4 Representing Other Type Constructors

Besides record structures and sets, an ODL class definition could use `Bag`, `List`, `Array`, or `Dictionary` to construct values. To represent a bag (multiset), in which a single object can be a member of the bag n times, we cannot simply introduce into a relation n identical tuples.[4] Instead, we could add to the relation schema another attribute `count` representing the number of times that each element is a member of the bag. For instance, suppose that `address` in Fig. 4.12 were a bag instead of a set. We could say that 123 Maple St.,

---

[4]To be precise, we cannot introduce identical tuples into relations of the abstract relational model described in Chapter 3. However, SQL-based relational DBMS's *do* allow duplicate tuples; i.e., relations are bags rather than sets in SQL. See Sections 5.3 and 6.4. If queries are likely to ask for tuple counts, we advise using a scheme such as that described here, even if your DBMS allows duplicate tuples.

Hollywood is Carrie Fisher's address twice and 5 Locust Ln., Malibu is her address 3 times (whatever that may mean) by

name	street	city	count
Carrie Fisher	123 Maple St.	Hollywood	2
Carrie Fisher	5 Locust Ln.	Malibu	3

A list of addresses could be represented by a new attribute **position**, indicating the position in the list. For instance, we could show Carrie Fisher's addresses as a list, with Hollywood first, by:

name	street	city	position
Carrie Fisher	123 Maple St.	Hollywood	1
Carrie Fisher	5 Locust Ln.	Malibu	2

A fixed-length array of addresses could be represented by attributes for each position in the array. For instance, if **address** were to be an array of two street-city structures, we could represent **Star** objects as:

name	street1	city1	street2	city2
Carrie Fisher	123 Maple St.	Hollywood	5 Locust Ln.	Malibu

Finally, a dictionary could be represented as a set, but with attributes for both the key-value and range-value components of the pairs that are members of the dictionary. For instance, suppose that instead of star's addresses, we really wanted to keep, for each star, a dictionary giving the mortgage holder for each of their homes. Then the dictionary would have address as the key value and bank name as the range value. A hypothetical rendering of the Carrie-Fisher object with a dictionary attribute is:

name	street	city	mortgage-holder
Carrie Fisher	123 Maple St.	Hollywood	Bank of Burbank
Carrie Fisher	5 Locust Ln.	Malibu	Torrance Trust

Of course attribute types in ODL may involve more than one type constructor. If a type is any collection type besides dictionary applied to a structure (e.g., a set of structs), then we may apply the techniques from Sections 4.4.3 or 4.4.4 as if the struct were an atomic value, and then replace the single attribute representing the atomic value by several attributes, one for each field of the struct. This strategy was used in the examples above, where the address is a struct. The case of a dictionary applied to structs is similar and left as an exercise.

There are many reasons to limit the complexity of attribute types to an optional struct followed by an optional collection type. We mentioned in Section 2.1.1 that some versions of the E/R model allow exactly this much generality in the types of attributes, although we restricted ourselves to atomic

attributes in the E/R model. We recommend that, if you are going to use an
ODL design for the purpose of eventual translation to a relational database
schema, you similarly limit yourself. We take up in the exercises some options
for dealing with more complex types as attributes.

4.4.5   Representing ODL Relationships

Usually, an ODL class definition will contain relationships to other ODL classes.
As in the E/R model, we can create for each relationship a new relation that
connects the keys of the two related classes. However, in ODL, relationships
come in inverse pairs, and we must create only one relation for each pair.

```
class Movie
    (extent Movies key(title, year))
{
    attribute string title;
    attribute integer year;
    attribute integer length;
    attribute enum Film {color,blackAndWhite} filmType;
    relationship Set<Star> stars
                inverse Star::starredIn;
    relationship Studio ownedBy
                inverse Studio::owns;
};

class Studio
    (extent Studios key name)
{
    attribute string name;
    attribute string address;
    relationship Set<Movie> owns
                inverse Movie::ownedBy;
};
```

Figure 4.16: The complete definition of the `Movie` and `Studio` classes

Example 4.20: Consider the declarations of the classes `Movie` and `Studio`,
which we repeat in Fig. 4.16. We see that `title` and `year` form the key for
`Movie` and `name` is a key for class `Studio`. We may create a relation for the pair
of relationships `owns` and `ownedBy`. The relation needs a name, which can be
arbitrary; we shall pick `StudioOf` as the name. The schema for `StudioOf` has
attributes for the key of `Movie`, that is, `title` and `year`, and an attribute that
we shall call `studioName` for the key of `Studio`. This relation schema is thus:

```
StudioOf(title, year, studioName)
```

Some typical tuples that would be in this relation are:

title	year	studioName
Star Wars	1977	Fox
Mighty Ducks	1991	Disney
Wayne's World	1992	Paramount

□

When a relationship is many-one, we have an option to combine it with the relation that is constructed for the class on the "many" side. Doing so has the effect of combining two relations that have a common key, as we discussed in Section 3.2.3. It therefore does not cause a BCNF violation and is a legitimate and commonly followed option.

Example 4.21: Rather than creating a relation StudioOf for relationship pair owns and ownedBy, as we did in Example 4.20, we may instead modify our relation schema for relation Movies to include an attribute, say studioName, to represent the key of Studio. If we do, the schema for Movies becomes

```
Movies(title, year, length, filmType, studioName)
```

and some typical tuples for this relation are:

title	year	length	filmType	studioName
Star Wars	1977	124	color	Fox
Mighty Ducks	1991	104	color	Disney
Wayne's World	1992	95	color	Paramount

Note that title and year, the key for the Movie class, is also a key for relation Movies, since each movie has a unique length, film type, and owning studio. □

We should remember that it is possible but unwise to treat many-many relationships as we did many-one relationships in Example 4.21. In fact, Example 3.6 in Section 3.2.3 was based on what happens if we try to combine the many-many stars relationship between movies and their stars with the other information in the relation Movies to get a relation with schema:

```
Movies(title, year, length, filmType, studioName, starName)
```

There is a resulting BCNF violation, since {title, year, starName} is the key, yet attributes length, filmType, and studioName each are functionally determined by only title and year.

Likewise, if we do combine a many-one relationship with the relation for a class, it must be the class of the "many." For instance, combining owns and its inverse ownedBy with relation Studios will lead to a BCNF violation (see Exercise 4.4.4).

4.4.6   What If There Is No Key?

Since keys are optional in ODL, we may face a situation where the attributes available to us cannot serve to represent objects of a class C uniquely. That situation can be a problem if the class C participates in one or more relationships.

We recommend creating a new attribute or "certificate" that can serve as an identifier for objects of class C in relational designs, much as the hidden object-ID serves to identify those objects in an object-oriented system. The certificate becomes an additional attribute of the relation for the class C, as well as representing objects of class C in each of the relations that come from relationships involving class C. Notice that in practice, many important classes are represented by such certificates: university ID's for students, driver's-license numbers for drivers, and so on.

Example 4.22 : Suppose we accept that names are not a reliable key for movie stars, and we decide instead to adopt a "certificate number" to be assigned to each star as a way of identifying them uniquely. Then the `Stars` relation would have schema:

    Stars(cert#, name, street, city, birthdate)

If we wish to represent the many-many relationship between movies and their stars by a relation `StarsIn`, we can use the `title` and `year` attributes from `Movie` and the certificate to represent stars, giving us a relation with schema:

    StarsIn(title, year, cert#)

□

4.4.7   Exercises for Section 4.4

Exercise 4.4.1 : Convert your ODL designs from the following exercises to relational database schemas.

* a) Exercise 4.2.1.

  b) Exercise 4.2.2 (include all four of the modifications specified by that exercise).

  c) Exercise 4.2.3.

* d) Exercise 4.2.4.

  e) Exercise 4.2.5.

Exercise 4.4.2 : Convert the ODL description of Fig. 4.5 to a relational database schema. How does each of the three modifications of Exercise 4.2.6 affect your relational schema?

! **Exercise 4.4.3:** Consider an attribute of type dictionary with key and range types both structs of atomic types. Show how to convert a class with an attribute of this type to a relation.

* **Exercise 4.4.4:** We claimed that if you combine the relation for class `Studio`, as defined in Fig. 4.16, with the relation for the relationship pair `owns` and `ownedBy`, then there is a BCNF violation. Do the combination and show that there is, in fact, a BCNF violation.

Exercise 4.4.5: We mentioned that when attributes are of a type more complex than a collection of structs, it becomes tricky to convert them to relations; in particular, it becomes necessary to create some intermediate concepts and relations for them. The following sequence of questions will examine increasingly more complex types and how to represent them as relations.

* a) A *card* can be represented as a struct with fields `rank` (2, 3, ..., 10, Jack, Queen, King, and Ace) and `suit` (Clubs, Diamonds, Hearts, and Spades). Give a suitable definition of a structured type `Card`. This definition should be independent of any class declarations but available to them all.

* b) A *hand* is a set of cards. The number of cards may vary. Give a declaration of a class `Hand` whose objects are hands. That is, this class declaration has an attribute `theHand`, whose type is a hand.

*! c) Convert your class declaration `Hand` from (b) to a relation schema.

 d) A *poker hand* is a set of five cards. Repeat (b) and (c) for poker hands.

*! e) A *deal* is a set of pairs, each pair consisting of the name of a player and a hand for that player. Declare a class `Deal`, whose objects are deals. That is, this class declaration has an attribute `theDeal`, whose type is a deal.

 f) Repeat (e), but restrict hands of a deal to be hands of exactly five cards.

 g) Repeat (e), using a dictionary for a deal. You may assume the names of players in a deal are unique.

*!! h) Convert your class declaration from (e) to a relational database schema.

*! i) Suppose we defined deals to be sets of sets of cards, with no player associated with each hand (set of cards). It is proposed that we represent such deals by a relation schema

```
Deals(dealID, card)
```

meaning that the card was a member of one of the hands in the deal with the given ID. What, if anything, is wrong with this representation? How would you fix the problem?

Exercise 4.4.6: Suppose we have a class C defined by

```
class C (key a) {
    attribute string a;
    attribute T b;
}
```

where T is some type. Give the relation schema for the relation derived from C and indicate its key attributes if T is:

  a) `Set<Struct S {string f, string g}>`

*! b) `Bag<Struct S {string f, string g}>`

 ! c) `List<Struct S {string f, string g}>`

 ! d) `Dictionary<Struct K {string f, string g}, Struct R {string i, string j}>`

4.5   The Object-Relational Model

The relational model and the object-oriented model typified by ODL are two important points in a spectrum of options that could underlie a DBMS. For an extended period, the relational model was dominant in the commercial DBMS world. Object-oriented DBMS's made limited inroads during the 1990's, but have since died off. Instead of a migration from relational to object-oriented systems, as was widely predicted around 1990, the vendors of relational systems have moved to incorporate many of the ideas found in ODL or other object-oriented-database proposals. As a result, many DBMS products that used to be called "relational" are now called "object-relational."

In Chapter9 we shall meet the new SQL standard for object-relational data-bases. In this chapter, we cover the topic more abstractly. We introduce the concept of object-relations in Section 4.5.1, then discuss one of its earliest embodiments — nested relations — in Section 4.5.2. ODL-like references for object-relations are discussed in Section 4.5.3, and in Section 4.5.4 we compare the object-relational model against the pure object-oriented approach.

4.5.1   From Relations to Object-Relations

While the relation remains the fundamental concept, the relational model has been extended to the *object-relational model* by incorporation of features such as:

  1. *Structured types for attributes.* Instead of allowing only atomic types for attributes, object-relational systems support a type system like ODL's: types built from atomic types and type constructors for structs, sets, and

bags, for instance. Especially important is a type that is a set[5] of structs, which is essentially a relation. That is, a value of one component of a tuple can be an entire relation.

2. *Methods.* Special operations can be defined for, and applied to, values of a user-defined type. While we haven't yet addressed the question of how values or tuples are manipulated in the relational or object-oriented models, we shall find few surprises when we take up the subject beginning in Chapter 5. For example, values of numeric type are operated on by arithmetic operators such as addition or less-than. However, in the object-relational model, we have the option to define specialized operations for a type, such as those discussed in Example 4.7 on ODL methods for the Movie class.

3. *Identifiers for tuples.* In object-relational systems, tuples play the role of objects. It therefore becomes useful in some situations for each tuple to have a unique ID that distinguishes it from other tuples, even from tuples that have the same values in all components. This ID, like the object-identifier assumed in ODL, is generally invisible to the user, although there are even some circumstances where users can see the identifier for a tuple in an object-relational system.

4. *References.* While the pure relational model has no notion of references or pointers to tuples, object-relational systems can use these references in various ways.

In the next sections, we shall elaborate and illustrate each of these additional capabilities of object-relational systems.

4.5.2 Nested Relations

Relations extended by point (1) above are often called "nested relations." In the *nested-relational model*, we allow attributes of relations to have a type that is not atomic; in particular, a type can be a relation schema. As a result, there is a convenient, recursive definition of the types of attributes and the types (schemas) of relations:

BASIS: An atomic type (integer, real, string, etc.) can be the type of an attribute.

INDUCTION: A relation's type can be any *schema* consisting of names for one or more attributes, and any legal type for each attribute. In addition, a schema can also be the type of any attribute.

In our discussion of the relational model, we did not specify the particular atomic type associated with each attribute, because the distinctions among

---

[5]Strictly speaking, a bag rather than a set, since commercial relational DBMS's prefer to support relations with duplicate tuples, i.e. bags, rather than sets.

integers, reals, strings, and so on had little to do with the issues discussed, such as functional dependencies and normalization. We shall continue to avoid this distinction, but when describing the schema of a nested relation, we must indicate which attributes have relation schemas as types. To do so, we shall treat these attributes as if they were the names of relations and follow them by a parenthesized list of their attributes. Those attributes, in turn, may have associated lists of attributes, down for as many levels as we wish.

Example 4.23 : Let us design a nested relation schema for stars that incorporates within the relation an attribute `movies`, which will be a relation representing all the movies in which the star has appeared. The relation schema for attribute `movies` will include the title, year, and length of the movie. The relation schema for the relation `Stars` will include the name, address, and birthdate, as well as the information found in `movies`. Additionally, the `address` attribute will have a relation type with attributes `street` and `city`. We can record in this relation several addresses for the star. The schema for `Stars` can be written:

```
Stars(name, address(street, city), birthdate,
    movies(title, year, length))
```

An example of a possible relation for nested relation `Stars` is shown in Fig. 4.17. We see in this relation two tuples, one for Carrie Fisher and one for Mark Hamill. The values of components are abbreviated to conserve space, and the dashed lines separating tuples are only for convenience and have no notational significance.

name	address		birthdate	movies		
Fisher	*street*	*city*	9/9/99	*title*	*year*	*length*
	Maple	H'wood		Star Wars	1977	124
	Locust	Malibu		Empire	1980	127
				Return	1983	133
Hamill	*street*	*city*	8/8/88	*title*	*year*	*length*
	Oak	B'wood		Star Wars	1977	124
				Empire	1980	127
				Return	1983	133

Figure 4.17: A nested relation for stars and their movies

In the Carrie Fisher tuple, we see her name, an atomic value, followed by a relation for the value of the address component. That relation has two attributes, `street` and `city`, and there are two tuples, corresponding to her two houses. Next comes the birthdate, another atomic value. Finally, there is a component for the `movies` attribute; this attribute has a relation schema as its type, with components for the title, year, and length of a movie. The relation for the `movies` component of the Carrie Fisher tuple has tuples for her three best-known movies.

The second tuple, for Mark Hamill, has the same components. His relation for `address` has only one tuple, because in our imaginary data, he has only one house. His relation for `movies` looks just like Carrie Fisher's because their best-known movies happen, by coincidence, to be the same. Note that these two relations are two different tuple-components. These components happen to be identical, just like two components that happened to have the same integer value, e.g., 124. □

4.5.3 References

The fact that movies like *Star Wars* will appear in several relations that are values of the `movies` attribute in the nested relation `Stars` is a cause of redundancy. In effect, the schema of Example 4.23 has the nested-relation analog of not being in BCNF. However, decomposing this `Stars` relation will not eliminate the redundancy. Rather, we need to arrange that among all the tuples of all the `movies` relations, a movie appears only once.

To cure the problem, object-relations need the ability for one tuple t to refer to another tuple s, rather than incorporating s directly in t. We thus add to our model an additional inductive rule: the type of an attribute can also be a reference to a tuple with a given schema.

If an attribute A has a type that is a reference to a single tuple with a relation schema named R, we show the attribute A in a schema as $A(*R)$. Notice that this situation is analogous to an ODL relationship A whose type is R; i.e., it connects to a single object of type R. Similarly, if an attribute A has a type that is a set of references to tuples of schema R, then A will be shown in a schema as $A(\{*R\})$. This situation resembles an ODL relationship A that has type `Set<R>`.

Example 4.24: An appropriate way to fix the redundancy in Fig. 4.17 is to use two relations, one for stars and one for movies. The relation `Movies` will be an ordinary relation with the same schema as the attribute `movies` in Example 4.23. The relation `Stars` will have a schema similar to the nested relation `Stars` of that example, but the movies attribute will have a type that is a set of references to `Movies` tuples. The schemas of the two relations are thus:

```
Movies(title, year, length)
Stars(name, address(street, city), birthdate,
    movies({*Movies}))
```

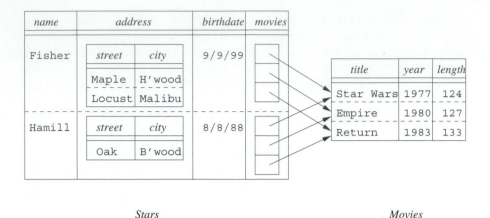

Stars   Movies

Figure 4.18: Sets of references as the value of an attribute

The data of Fig. 4.17, converted to this new schema, is shown in Fig. 4.18. Notice that, because each movie has only one tuple, although it can have many references, we have eliminated the redundancy inherent in the schema of Example 4.23.   □

4.5.4   Object-Oriented Versus Object-Relational

The object-oriented data model, as typified by ODL, and the object-relational model discussed here, are remarkably similar. Some of the salient points of comparison follow.

Objects and Tuples

An object's value is really a struct with components for its attributes and relationships. It is not specified in the ODL standard how relationships are to be represented, but we may assume that an object is connected to related objects by some collection of pointers. A tuple is likewise a struct, but in the conventional relational model, it has components for only the attributes. Relationships would be represented by tuples in another relation, as suggested in Section 3.2.2. However the object-relational model, by allowing sets of references to be a component of tuples, also allows relationships to be incorporated directly into the tuples that represent an "object" or entity.

Extents and Relations

ODL treats all objects in a class as living in an "extent" for that class. The object-relational model allows several different relations with identical schemas, so it might appear that there is more opportunity in the object-relational model to distinguish members of the same class. However, ODL allows the definition of interfaces, which are essentially class declarations without an extent (see the box on "Interfaces" in Section 4.3.4). Then, ODL allows you to define any number of classes that inherit this interface, while each class has a distinct extent. In that manner, ODL offers the same opportunity the object-relational approach when it comes to sharing the same declaration among several collections.

Methods

We did not discuss the use of methods as part of an object-relational schema. However, in practice, the SQL-99 standard and all implementations of object-relational ideas allow the same ability as ODL to declare and define methods associated with any class.

Type Systems

The type systems of the object-oriented and object-relational models are quite similar. Each is based on atomic types and construction of new types by struct- and collection-type-constructors. The selection of collection types may vary, but all variants include at least sets and bags. Moreover, the set (or bag) of structs type plays a special role in both models. It is the type of classes in ODL, and the type of relations in the object-relational model.

References and Object-ID's

A pure object-oriented model uses object-ID's that are completely hidden from the user, and thus cannot be seen or queried. The object-relational model allows references to be part of a type, and thus it is possible under some circumstances for the user to see their values and even remember them for future use. You may regard this situation as anything from a serious bug to a stroke of genius, depending on your point of view, but in practice it appears to make little difference.

Backwards Compatibility

With little difference in essential features of the two models, it is interesting to consider why object-relational systems have dominated the pure object-oriented systems in the marketplace. The reason, we believe, is that there was, by the time object-oriented systems were seriously proposed, an enormous number of installations running a relational database system. As relational DBMS's evolved into object-relational DBMS's, the vendors were careful to maintain backwards compatibility. That is, newer versions of the system would still run the old code and accept the same schemas, should the user not care to adopt any of the object-oriented features. On the other hand, migration to a pure object-oriented DBMS would require the installations to rewrite and reorganize extensively. Thus, whatever competitive advantage existed was not enough to convert many databases to a pure object-oriented DBMS.

4.5.5 From ODL Designs to Object-Relational Designs

In Section 4.4 we learned how to convert designs in ODL into schemas of the relational model. Difficulties arose primarily because of the richer modeling constructs of ODL: nonatomic attribute types, relationships, and methods. Some — but not all — of these difficulties are alleviated when we translate an ODL design into an object-relational design. Depending on the specific object-relational model used (we shall consider the concrete SQL-99 model in Chapter 9), we may be able to convert most of the nonatomic types of ODL directly into a corresponding object-relational type; structs, sets, bags, lists, and arrays all fall into this category.

   If a type in an ODL design is not available in our object-relational model, we can fall back on the techniques from Sections 4.4.2 through 4.4.4. The representation of relationships in an object-relational model is essentially the same as in the relational model (see Section 4.4.5), although we may prefer to use references in place of keys. Finally, although we were not able to translate ODL designs with methods into the pure relational model, most object-relational models include methods, so this restriction can be lifted.

4.5.6 Exercises for Section 4.5

Exercise 4.5.1: Using the notation developed for nested relations and relations with references, give one or more relation schemas that represent the following information. In each case, you may exercise some discretion regarding what attributes of a relation are included, but try to keep close to the attributes found in our running movie example. Also, indicate whether your schemas exhibit redundancy, and if so, what could be done to avoid it.

* a) Movies, with the usual attributes plus all their stars and the usual information about the stars.

*! b) Studios, all the movies made by that studio, and all the stars of each movie, including all the usual attributes of studios, movies, and stars.

  c) Movies with their studio, their stars, and all the usual attributes of these.

* **Exercise 4.5.2:** Represent the banking information of Exercise 2.1.1 in the object-relational model developed in this section. Make sure that it is easy, given the tuple for a customer, to find their account(s) and *also* easy, given the tuple for an account to find the customer(s) that hold that account. Also, try to avoid redundancy.

! **Exercise 4.5.3:** If the data of Exercise 4.5.2 were modified so that an account could be held by only one customer [as in Exercise 2.1.2(a)], how could your answer to Exercise 4.5.2 be simplified?

! **Exercise 4.5.4:** Render the players, teams, and fans of Exercise 2.1.3 in the object-relational model.

! **Exercise 4.5.5:** Render the genealogy of Exercise 2.1.6 in the object-relational model.

4.6 Semistructured Data

The *semistructured-data* model plays a special role in database systems:

1. It serves as a model suitable for *integration* of databases, that is, for describing the data contained in two or more databases that contain similar data with different schemas.

2. It serves as a document model in notations such as XML, to be taken up in Section 4.7, that are being used to share information on the Web.

In this section, we shall introduce the basic ideas behind "semistructured data" and how it can represent information more flexibly than the other models we have met previously.

4.6.1 Motivation for the Semistructured-Data Model

Let us begin by recalling the E/R model, and its two fundamental kinds of data — the entity set and the relationship. Remember also that the relational model has only one kind of data — the relation, yet we saw in Section 3.2 how both entity sets and relationships could be represented by relations. There is an advantage to having two concepts: we could tailor an E/R design to the real-world situation we were modeling, using whichever of entity sets or relationships most closely matched the concept being modeled. There is also some advantage to replacing two concepts by one: the notation in which we express schemas is thereby simplified, and implementation techniques that make querying of the database more efficient can be applied to all sorts of data. We shall begin to appreciate these advantages of the relational model when we study implementation of the DBMS, starting in Chapter 11.

Now, let us consider the object-oriented model we introduced in Section 4.2. There are two principal concepts: the class (or its extent) and the relationship. Likewise, the object-relational model of Section 4.5 has two similar concepts: the attribute type (which includes classes) and the relation.

We may see the semistructured-data model as blending the two concepts, class-and-relationship or class-and-relation, much as the relational model blends entity sets and relationships. However, the motivation for the blending appears to be different in each case. While, as we mentioned, the relational model owes some of its success to the fact that it facilitates efficient implementation, interest in the semistructured-data model appears motivated primarily by its flexibility. While the other models seen so far each start from a notion of a schema — E/R diagrams, relation schemas, or ODL declarations, for instance — semistructured data is "schemaless." More properly, the data itself carries information about what its schema is, and that schema can vary arbitrarily, both over time and within a single database.

4.6.2 Semistructured Data Representation

A database of *semistructured data* is a collection of *nodes*. Each node is either a *leaf* or *interior*. Leaf nodes have associated data; the type of this data can be any atomic type, such as numbers and strings. Interior nodes have one or more arcs out. Each arc has a *label*, which indicates how the node at the head of the arc relates to the node at the tail. One interior node, called the *root*, has no arcs entering and represents the entire database. Every node must be reachable from the root, although the graph structure is not necessarily a tree.

Example 4.25 : Figure 4.19 is an example of a semistructured database about stars and movies. We see a node at the top labeled *Root*; this node is the entry point to the data and may be thought of as representing all the information in the database. The central objects or entities — stars and movies in this case — are represented by nodes that are children of the root.

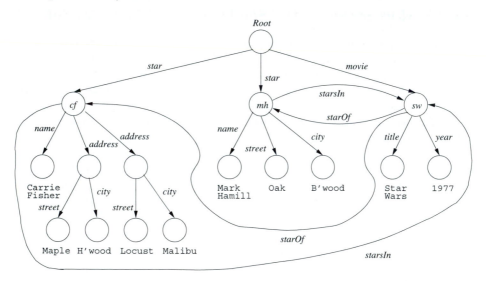

Figure 4.19: Semistructured data representing a movie and stars

We also see many leaf nodes. At the far left is a leaf labeled `Carrie Fisher`, and at the far right is a leaf labeled 1977, for instance. There are also many interior nodes. Three particular nodes we have labeled *cf*, *mh*, and *sw*, standing for "Carrie Fisher," "Mark Hamill," and "Star Wars," respectively. These labels are not part of the model, and we placed them on these nodes only so we would have a way of referring to the nodes, which otherwise would be nameless. We may think of node *sw*, for instance, as representing the concept "Star Wars":

the title and year of this movie, other information not shown, such as its length, and its stars, two of which are shown. □

The labels on arcs play two roles, and thus combine the information contained in class definitions and relationships. Suppose we have an arc labeled L from node N to node M.

1. It may be possible to think of N as representing an object or struct, while M represents one of the attributes of the object or fields of the struct. Then, L represents the name of the attribute or field, respectively.

2. We may be able to think of N and M as objects, and L as the name of a relationship from N to M.

Example 4.26 : Consider Fig. 4.19 again. The node indicated by *cf* may be thought of as representing the `Star` object for Carrie Fisher. We see, leaving this node, an arc labeled *name*, which represents the attribute `name` and properly leads to a leaf node holding the correct name. We also see two arcs, each labeled *address*. These arcs lead to unnamed nodes which we may think of as representing the two addresses of Carrie Fisher. Together, these arcs represent the set-valued attribute `address` as in Fig. 4.12.

Each of these addresses is a struct, with fields `street` and `city`. We notice in Fig. 4.19 how both nodes have out-arcs labeled *street* and *city*. Moreover, these arcs each lead to leaf nodes with the appropriate atomic values.

The other kind of arc also appears in Fig. 4.19. For instance, the node *cf* has an out-arc leading to the node *sw* and labeled *starsIn*. The node *mh* (for Mark Hamill) has a similar arc, and the node *sw* has arcs labeled *starOf* to both nodes *cf* and *mh*. These arcs represent the stars-in relationship between stars and movies. □

4.6.3 Information Integration Via Semistructured Data

Unlike the other models we have discussed, data in the semistructured model is *self-describing*; the schema is attached to the data itself. That is, each node (except the root) has an arc or arcs entering it, and the labels on these arcs tell what role the node is playing with respect to the node at the tail of the arc. In all the other models, data has a fixed schema, separate from the data, and the role(s) played by data items is implicit in the schema.

One might naturally wonder whether there is an advantage to creating a database without a schema, where one could enter data at will, and attach to the data whatever schema information you felt was appropriate for that data. There are actually some small-scale information systems such as Lotus Notes that take the self-describing-data approach. However, when people design databases to hold large amounts of data, it is generally accepted that the advantages of fixing the schema far outweigh the flexibility that comes from attaching the schema to the data. For instance, fixing the schema allows the data to be organized with data structures that support efficient answering of queries, as we shall discuss beginning in Chapter 13.

Yet the flexibility of semistructured data has made it important in two applications. We shall discuss its use in documents in Section 4.7, but here we shall consider its use as a tool for information integration. As databases have proliferated, it has become a common requirement that data in two or more of them be accessible as if they were one database. For instance, companies may merge; each has its own personnel database, its own database of sales, inventory, product designs, and perhaps many other matters. If corresponding databases had the same schemas, then combining them would be simple; for instance, we could take the union of the tuples in two relations that had the same schema and played the same roles in the the two databases.

However, life is rarely that simple. Independently developed databases are unlikely to share a schema, even if they talk about the same things, such as personnel. For instance, one employee database may record spouse-name, another not. One may have a way to represent several addresses, phones, or emails for an employee, another database may allow only one of each. One database might be relational, another object-oriented.

To make matters more complex, databases tend over time to be used in so many different applications that it is impossible to shut them down and copy or translate their data into another database, even if we could figure out an efficient way to transform the data from one schema to another. This situation is often referred to as the *legacy-database problem*; once a database has been in existence for a while, it becomes impossible to disentangle it from the applications that grow up around it, so the database can never be decommissioned.

A possible solution to the legacy-database problem is suggested in Fig. 4.20. We show two legacy databases with an interface; there could be many legacy systems involved. The legacy systems are each unchanged, so they can support their usual applications.

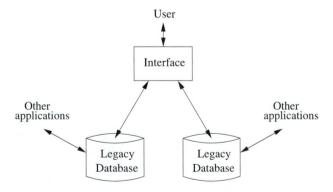

Figure 4.20: Integrating two legacy databases through an interface that supports semistructured data

For flexibility in integration, the interface supports semistructured data, and the user is allowed to query the interface using a query language that is suitable for such data. The semistructured data may be constructed by translating the data at the sources, using components called *wrappers* (or "adapters") that are each designed for the purpose of translating one source to semistructured data.

Alternatively, the semistructured data at the interface may not exist at all. Rather, the user queries the interface as if there were semistructured data, while the interface answers the query by posing queries to the sources, each referring to the schema found at that source.

Example 4.27: We can see in Fig. 4.19 a possible effect of information about stars being gathered from several sources. Notice that the address information for Carrie Fisher has an address concept, and the address is then broken into street and city. That situation corresponds roughly to data that had a nested-relation schema like `Stars(name, address(street, city))`.

On the other hand, the address information for Mark Hamill has no address concept at all, just street and city. This information may have come from a schema such as `Stars(name, street, city)` that only has the ability to represent one address for a star. Some of the other variations in schema that are not reflected in the tiny example of Fig. 4.19, but that could be present if movie information were obtained from several sources, include: optional film-type information, a director, a producer or producers, the owning studio, revenue, and information on where the movie is currently playing. □

4.6.4 Exercises for Section 4.6

Exercise 4.6.1: Since there is no schema to design in the semistructured-data model, we cannot ask you to design schemas to describe different situations. Rather, in the following exercises we shall ask you to suggest how particular data might be organized to reflect certain facts.

* a) Add to Fig. 4.19 the facts that *Star Wars* was directed by George Lucas and produced by Gary Kurtz.

  b) Add to Fig. 4.19 information about *Empire Strikes Back* and *Return of the Jedi*, including the facts that Carrie Fisher and Mark Hamill appeared in these movies.

  c) Add to (b) information about the studio (Fox) for these movies and the address of the studio (Hollywood).

* **Exercise 4.6.2:** Suggest how typical data about banks and customers, as in Exercise 2.1.1, could be represented in the semistructured model.

Exercise 4.6.3: Suggest how typical data about players, teams, and fans, as was described in Exercise 2.1.3, could be represented in the semistructured model.

Exercise 4.6.4: Suggest how typical data about a genealogy, as was described in Exercise 2.1.6, could be represented in the semistructured model.

! **Exercise 4.6.5:** The E/R model and the semistructured-data model are both "graphical" in nature, in the sense that they use nodes, labels, and connections among nodes as the medium of expression. Yet there is an essential difference between the two models. What is it?

4.7   XML and Its Data Model

XML (*Extensible Markup Language*) is a tag-based notation for "marking" documents, much like the familiar HTML or less familiar SGML. A *document* is nothing more nor less than a file of characters. However, while HMTL's tags talk about the presentation of the information contained in documents — for instance, which portion is to be displayed in italics or what the entries of a list are — XML tags talk about the meaning of substrings within the document.

In this section we shall introduce the rudiments of XML. We shall see that it captures, in a linear form, the same structure as do the graphs of semistructured data introduced in Section 4.6. In particular, tags play the same role as did the labels on the arcs of a semistructured-data graph. We then introduce the DTD ("document type definition"), which is a flexible form of schema that we can place on certain documents with XML tags.

4.7.1   Semantic Tags

Tags in XML are text surrounded by triangular brackets, i.e., `<...>`, as in HMTL. Also as in HTML, tags generally come in matching pairs, with a beginning tag like `<FOO>` and a matching ending tag that is the same word with a slash, like `</FOO>`. In HTML there is an option to have tags with no matching ender, like `<P>` for paragraphs, but such tags are not permitted in XML. When tags come in matching begin-end pairs, there is a requirement that the pairs be nested. That is, between a matching pair `<FOO>` and `</FOO>`, there can be any number of other matching pairs, but if the beginning of a pair is in this range, then the ending of the pair must also be in the range.

XML is designed to be used in two somewhat different modes:

1. *Well-formed* XML allows you to invent your own tags, much like the arc-labels in semistructured data. This mode corresponds quite closely to semistructured data, in that there is no schema, and each document is free to use whatever tags the author of the document wishes.

2. *Valid* XML involves a Document Type Definition that specifies the allowable tags and gives a grammar for how they may be nested. This form of XML is intermediate between the strict-schema models such as the relational or ODL models, and the completely schemaless world of

semistructured data. As we shall see in Section 4.7.3, DTD's generally allow more flexibility in the data than does a conventional schema; DTD's often allow optional fields or missing fields, for instance.

4.7.2 Well-Formed XML

The minimal requirement for well-formed XML is that the document begin with a declaration that it is XML, and that it have a *root tag* surrounding the entire body of the text. Thus, a well-formed XML document would have an outer structure like:

```
<? XML VERSION = "1.0" STANDALONE = "yes" ?>
<BODY>
    ...
</BODY>
```

The first line indicates that the file is an XML document. The parameter `STANDALONE = "yes"` indicates that there is no DTD for this document; i.e., it is well-formed XML. Notice that this initial declaration is delineated by special markers `<?...?>`.

```
<? XML VERSION = "1.0" STANDALONE = "yes" ?>
<STAR-MOVIE-DATA>
    <STAR><NAME>Carrie Fisher</NAME>
        <ADDRESS><STREET>123 Maple St.</STREET>
            <CITY>Hollywood</CITY></ADDRESS>
        <ADDRESS><STREET>5 Locust Ln.</STREET>
            <CITY>Malibu</CITY></ADDRESS>
    </STAR>
    <STAR><NAME>Mark Hamill</NAME>
        <STREET>456 Oak Rd.</STREET><CITY>Brentwood</CITY>
    </STAR>
    <MOVIE><TITLE>Star Wars</TITLE><YEAR>1977</YEAR>
    </MOVIE>
</STAR-MOVIE-DATA>
```

Figure 4.21: An XML document about stars and movies

Example 4.28: In Fig. 4.21 is an XML document that corresponds roughly to the data in Fig. 4.19. The root tag is `STAR-MOVIE-DATA`. We see two sections surrounded by the tag `<STAR>` and its matching `</STAR>`. Within each section are subsections giving the name of the star. One, for Carrie Fisher, has two subsections, each giving the address of one of her homes. These sections are surrounded by an `<ADDRESS>` tag and its ender. The section for Mark Hamill

has only entries for one street and one city, and does not use an `<ADDRESS>` tag
to group these. This distinction appeared as well in Fig. 4.19.

Notice that the document of Fig. 4.21 does not represent the relationship
"stars-in" between stars and movies. We could store information about each
movie of a star within the section devoted to that star, for instance:

```
<STAR><NAME>Mark Hamill</NAME>
    <STREET>Oak</STREET><CITY>Brentwood</CITY>
    <MOVIE><TITLE>Star Wars</TITLE><YEAR>1977</YEAR></MOVIE>
    <MOVIE><TITLE>Empire</TITLE><YEAR>1980</YEAR></MOVIE>
</STAR>
```

However, that approach leads to redundancy, since all information about the
movie is repeated for each of its stars (we have shown no information except a
movie's key — title and year — which does not actually represent an instance
of redundancy). We shall see in Section 4.7.5 how XML handles the problem
that tags inherently form a tree structure.   □

4.7.3   Document Type Definitions

In order for a computer to process XML documents automatically, there needs
to be something like a schema for the documents. That is, we need to be told
what tags can appear in a collection of documents and how tags can be nested.
The description of the schema is given by a grammar-like set of rules, called a
document type definition, or DTD. It is intended that companies or communities
wishing to share data will each create a DTD that describes the form(s) of the
documents they share and establishing a shared view of the semantics of their
tags. For instance, there could be a DTD for describing protein structures, a
DTD for describing the purchase and sale of auto parts, and so on.

The gross structure of a DTD is:

```
<!DOCTYPE root-tag [
        <!ELEMENT element-name (components)>
            more elements
]>
```

The *root-tag* is used (with its matching ender) to surround a document that
conforms to the rules of this DTD. An *element* is described by its name, which is
the tag used to surround portions of the document that represent that element,
and a parenthesized list of components. The latter are tags that may or must
appear within the tags for the element being described. The exact requirements
on each component are indicated in a manner we shall see shortly.

There is, however, an important special case. (`#PCDATA`) after an element
name means that element has a value that is text, and it has no tags nested
within.

Example 4.29 : In Fig. 4.22 we see a DTD for stars.[6] The name and surround-

---

[6]Note that the stars-and-movies data of Fig. 4.21 is not intended to conform to this DTD.

ing tag is STARS (XML, like HTML, is case-insensitive, so STARS is clearly the root-tag). The first element definition says that inside the matching pair of tags <STARS>...</STARS> we will find zero or more STAR tags, each representing a single star. It is the * in (STAR*) that says "zero or more," i.e., "any number of."

```
<!DOCTYPE Stars [
    <!ELEMENT STARS (STAR*)>
    <!ELEMENT STAR (NAME, ADDRESS+, MOVIES)>
    <!ELEMENT NAME (#PCDATA)>
    <!ELEMENT ADDRESS (STREET, CITY)>
    <!ELEMENT STREET (#PCDATA)>
    <!ELEMENT CITY (#PCDATA)>
    <!ELEMENT MOVIES (MOVIE*)>
    <!ELEMENT MOVIE (TITLE, YEAR)>
    <!ELEMENT TITLE (#PCDATA)>
    <!ELEMENT YEAR (#PCDATA)>
]>
```

Figure 4.22: A DTD for movie stars

The second element, STAR, is declared to consist of three kinds of subelements: NAME, ADDRESS, and MOVIES. They must appear in this order, and each must be present. However, the + following ADDRESS says "one or more"; that is, there can be any number of addresses listed for a star, but there must be at least one. The NAME element is then defined to be "PCDATA," i.e., simple text. The fourth element says that an address element consists of fields for a street and a city, in that order.

Then, the MOVIES element is defined to have zero or more elements of type MOVIE within it; again, the * says "any number of." A MOVIE element is defined to consist of title and year fields, each of which are simple text. Figure 4.23 is an example of a document that conforms to the DTD of Fig. 4.22. □

The components of an element E are generally other elements. They must appear between the tags $<E>$ and $</E>$ in the order listed. However, there are several operators that control the number of times elements appear.

1. A * following an element means that the element may occur any number of times, including zero times.

2. A + following an element means that the element may occur one or more times.

3. A ? following an element means that the element may occur either zero times or one time, but no more.

```
<STARS>
    <STAR><NAME>Carrie Fisher</NAME>
        <ADDRESS><STREET>123 Maple St.</STREET>
            <CITY>Hollywood</CITY></ADDRESS>
        <ADDRESS><STREET>5 Locust Ln.</STREET>
            <CITY>Malibu</CITY></ADDRESS>
        <MOVIES><MOVIE><TITLE>Star Wars</TITLE>
            <YEAR>1977</YEAR></MOVIE>
            <MOVIE><TITLE>Empire Strikes Back</TITLE>
            <YEAR>1980</YEAR></MOVIE>
            <MOVIE><TITLE>Return of the Jedi</TITLE>
            <YEAR>1983</YEAR></MOVIE>
        </MOVIES>
    </STAR>
    <STAR><NAME>Mark Hamill</NAME>
        <ADDRESS><STREET>456 Oak Rd.<STREET>
            <CITY>Brentwood</CITY></ADDRESS>
        <MOVIES><MOVIE><TITLE>Star Wars</TITLE>
            <YEAR>1977</YEAR></MOVIE>
            <MOVIE><TITLE>Empire Strikes Back</TITLE>
            <YEAR>1980</YEAR></MOVIE>
            <MOVIE><TITLE>Return of the Jedi</TITLE>
            <YEAR>1983</YEAR></MOVIE>
        </MOVIES>
    </STAR>
</STARS>
```

Figure 4.23: Example of a document following the DTD of Fig. 4.22

4. The symbol | may appear between elements, or between parenthesized groups of elements to signify "or"; that is, either the element(s) on the left appear or the element(s) on the right appear, but not both. For example, the expression (#PCDATA | (STREET, CITY)) as components for element ADDRESS would mean that an address could be either simple text, or consist of tagged street and city components.

4.7.4 Using a DTD

If a document is intended to conform to a certain DTD, we can either:

a) Include the DTD itself as a preamble to the document, or

b) In the opening line, refer to the DTD, which must be stored separately in the file system accessible to the application that is processing the document.

Example 4.30: Here is how we might introduce the document of Fig. 4.23 to assert that it is intended to conform to the DTD of Fig. 4.22.

```
<?XML VERSION = "1.0" STANDALONE = "no"?>
<!DOCTYPE Stars SYSTEM "star.dtd">
```

The parameter `STANDALONE = "no"` says that a DTD is being used. Recall we set this parameter to `"yes"` when we did not wish to specify a DTD for the document. The location from which the DTD can be obtained is given in the `!DOCTYPE` clause, where the keyword `SYSTEM` followed by a file name gives this location. □

4.7.5 Attribute Lists

There is a strong relationship between XML documents and semistructured data. Suppose that for some pair of matching tags $<T>$ and $</T>$ in a document we create a node n. Then, if $<S>$ and $</S>$ are matching tags nested directly within the pair $<T>$ and $</T>$ (i.e., there are no matched pairs surrounding the S-pair but surrounded by the T-pair), we draw an arc labeled S from node n to the node for the S-pair. Then the result will be an instance of semistructured data that has essentially the same structure as the document.

Unfortunately, the relationship doesn't go the other way, with the limited subset of XML we have described so far. We need a way to express in XML the idea that an instance of an element might have more than one arc leading to that element. Clearly, we cannot nest a tag-pair directly within more than one tag-pair, so nesting is not sufficient to represent multiple predecessors of a node. The additional features that allow us to represent all semistructured data in XML are attributes within tags, identifiers (ID's), and identifier references (IDREF's).

Opening tags can have *attributes* that appear within the tag, in analogy to constructs like `<A HREF = ...>` in HTML. Keyword `!ATTLIST` introduces a list of attributes and their types for a given element. One common use of attributes is to associate single, labeled values with a tag. This usage is an alternative to subtags that are simple text (i.e., declared as PCDATA).

Another important purpose of such attributes is to represent semistructured data that does not have a tree form. An attribute for elements of type E that is declared to be an *ID* will be given values that uniquely identify each portion of the document that is surrounded by an $<E>$ and matching $</E>$ tag. In terms of semistructured data, an ID provides a unique name for a node.

Other attributes may be declared to be *IDREF's*. Their values are the ID's associated with other tags. By giving one tag instance (i.e., a node in semistructured data) an ID with a value v and another tag instance an IDREF with value v, the latter is effectively given an arc or link to the former. The following example illustrates both the syntax for declaring ID's and IDREF's and the significance of using them in data.

```
<!DOCTYPE Stars-Movies [
    <!ELEMENT STARS-MOVIES (STAR*, MOVIE*)>
    <!ELEMENT STAR (NAME, ADDRESS+)>
        <!ATTLIST STAR
            starId ID
            starredIn IDREFS>
    <!ELEMENT NAME (#PCDATA)>
    <!ELEMENT ADDRESS (STREET, CITY)>
    <!ELEMENT STREET (#PCDATA)>
    <!ELEMENT CITY (#PCDATA)>
    <!ELEMENT MOVIE (TITLE, YEAR)>
        <!ATTLIST MOVIE
            movieId ID
            starsOf IDREFS>
    <!ELEMENT TITLE (#PCDATA)>
    <!ELEMENT YEAR (#PCDATA)>
]>
```

Figure 4.24: A DTD for stars and movies, using ID's and IDREF's

Example 4.31: Figure 4.24 shows a revised DTD, in which stars and movies are given equal status, and ID-IDREF correspondence is used to describe the many-many relationship between movies and stars. Analogously, the arcs between nodes representing stars and movies describe the same many-many relationship in the semistructured data of Fig. 4.19. The name of the root tag for this DTD has been changed to STARS-MOVIES, and its elements are a sequence of stars followed by a sequence of movies.

A star no longer has a set of movies as subelements, as was the case for the DTD of Fig. 4.22. Rather, its only subelements are a name and address, and in the beginning <STAR> tag we shall find an attribute starredIn whose value is a list of ID's for the movies of the star. Note that the attribute starredIn is declared to be of type IDREFS, rather than IDREF. The additional "S" allows the value of starredIn to be a list of ID's for movies, rather than a single movie, as would be the case if the type IDREF were used.

A <STAR> tag also has an attribute starId. Since it is declared to be of type ID, the value of starId may be referenced by <MOVIE> tags to indicate the stars of the movie. That is, when we look at the attribute list for MOVIE in Fig. 4.24, we see that it has an attribute movieId of type ID; these are the ID's that will appear on lists that are the values of starredIn tags. Symmetrically, the attribute starsOf of MOVIE is a list of ID's for stars.

Figure 4.25 is an example of a document that conforms to the DTD of Fig. 4.24. It is quite similar to the semistructured data of Fig. 4.19. It includes more data — three movies instead of only one. However, the only structural difference is that here, all stars have an **ADDRESS** subelement, even if they have only one address, while in Fig. 4.19 we went directly from the Mark-Hamill node to street and city nodes. □

```
<STARS-MOVIES>
    <STAR starId = "cf" starredIn = "sw, esb, rj">
        <NAME>Carrie Fisher</NAME>
        <ADDRESS><STREET>123 Maple St.</STREET>
            <CITY>Hollywood</CITY></ADDRESS>
        <ADDRESS><STREET>5 Locust Ln.</STREET>
            <CITY>Malibu</CITY></ADDRESS>
    </STAR>
    <STAR starId = "mh" starredIn = "sw, esb, rj">
        <NAME>Mark Hamill</NAME>
        <ADDRESS><STREET>456 Oak Rd.<STREET>
            <CITY>Brentwood</CITY></ADDRESS>
    </STAR>
    <MOVIE movieId = "sw" starsOf = "cf, mh">
        <TITLE>Star Wars</TITLE>
        <YEAR>1977</YEAR>
    </MOVIE>
    <MOVIE movieId = "esb" starsOf = "cf, mh">
        <TITLE>Empire Strikes Back</TITLE>
        <YEAR>1980</YEAR>
    </MOVIE>
    <MOVIE movieId = "rj" starsOf = "cf, mh">
        <TITLE>Return of the Jedi</TITLE>
        <YEAR>1983</YEAR>
    </MOVIE>
</STARS-MOVIES>
```

Figure 4.25: Example of a document following the DTD of Fig. 4.24

4.7.6 Exercises for Section 4.7

Exercise 4.7.1: Add to the document of Fig. 4.25 the following facts:

* a) Harrison Ford also starred in the three movies mentioned and the movie *Witness* (1985).

 b) Carrie Fisher also starred in *Hannah and Her Sisters* (1985).

 c) Liam Neeson starred in *The Phantom Menace* (1999).

* **Exercise 4.7.2:** Suggest how typical data about banks and customers, as was described in Exercise 2.1.1, could be represented as a DTD.

Exercise 4.7.3: Suggest how typical data about players, teams, and fans, as was described in Exercise 2.1.3, could be represented as a DTD.

Exercise 4.7.4: Suggest how typical data about a genealogy, as was described in Exercise 2.1.6, could be represented as a DTD.

4.8   Summary of Chapter 4

◆ *Object Definition Language*: This language is a notation for formally describing the schemas of databases in an object-oriented style. One defines classes, which may have three kinds of properties: attributes, methods, and relationships.

◆ *ODL Relationships*: A relationship in ODL must be binary. It is represented, in the two classes it connects, by names that are declared to be inverses of one another. Relationships can be many-many, many-one, or one-one, depending on whether the types of the pair are declared to be a single object or a set of objects.

◆ *The ODL Type System*: ODL allows types to be constructed, beginning with class names and atomic types such as integer, by applying any of the following type constructors: structure formation, set-of, bag-of, list-of, array-of, and dictionary-of.

◆ *Extents*: A class of objects can have an extent, which is the set of objects of that class currently existing in the database. Thus, the extent corresponds to a relation instance in the relational model, while the class declaration is like the schema of a relation.

◆ *Keys in ODL*: Keys are optional in ODL. One is allowed to declare one or more keys, but because objects have an object-ID that is not one of its properties, a system implementing ODL can tell the difference between objects, even if they have identical values for all properties.

◆ *Converting ODL Designs to Relations*: If we treat ODL as only a design language, whose designs are then converted to relations, the simplest approach is to create a relation for a the attributes of a class and a relation for each pair of inverse relationships. However, we can combine a many-one relationship with the relation intended for the attributes of the "many" class. It is also necessary to create new attributes to represent the key of a class that has no key.

◆ *The Object-Relational Model*: An alternative to pure object-oriented database models like ODL is to extend the relational model to include the major features of object-orientation. These extensions include nested relations, i.e., complex types for attributes of a relation, including relations as types. Other extensions include methods defined for these types, and the ability of one tuple to refer to another through a reference type.

✦ *Semistructured Data*: In this model, data is represented by a graph. Nodes are like objects or values of their attributes, and labeled arcs connect an object to both the values of its attributes and to other objects to which it is connected by a relationship.

✦ *XML*: The Extensible Markup Language is a World-Wide-Web Consortium standard that implements semistructured data in documents (text files). Nodes correspond to sections of the text, and (some) labeled arcs are represented in XML by pairs of beginning and ending tags.

✦ *Identifiers and References in XML*: To represent graphs that are not trees, XML allows attributes of type ID and IDREF within the beginning tags. A tag (corresponding to a node of semistructured data) can thus be given an identifier, and that identifier can be referred to by other tags, from which we would like to establish a link (arc in semistructured data).

4.9 References for Chapter 4

The manual defining ODL is [6]. It is the ongoing work of ODMG, the Object Data Management Group. One can also find more about the history of object-oriented database systems from [4], [5], and [8].

Semistructured data as a model developed from the TSIMMIS and LORE projects at Stanford. The original description of the model is in [9]. LORE and its query language are described in [3]. Recent surveys of work on semistructured data include [1], [10], and the book [2]. A bibliography of semistructured data is being compiled on the Web, at [7].

XML is a standard developed by the World-Wide-Web Consortium. The home page for information about XML is [11].

1. S. Abiteboul, "Querying semi-structured data," *Proc. Intl. Conf. on Database Theory* (1997), Lecture Notes in Computer Science 1187 (F. Afrati and P. Kolaitis, eds.), Springer-Verlag, Berlin, pp. 1–18.

2. Abiteboul, S., D. Suciu, and P. Buneman, *Data on the Web: From Relations to Semistructured Data and Xml*, Morgan-Kaufmann, San Francisco, 1999.

3. Abiteboul S., D. Quass, J. McHugh, J. Widom, and J. L. Weiner, "The LOREL query language for semistructured data," In *J. Digital Libraries* **1**:1, 1997.

4. Bancilhon, F., C. Delobel, and P. Kanellakis, *Building an Object-Oriented Database System*, Morgan-Kaufmann, San Francisco, 1992.

5. Cattell, R. G. G., *Object Data Management*, Addison-Wesley, Reading, MA, 1994.

6. Cattell, R. G. G. (ed.), *The Object Database Standard: ODMG–99*, Morgan-Kaufmann, San Francisco, 1999.

7. L. C. Faulstich,

   `http://www.inf.fu-berlin.de/~faulstic/bib/semistruct/`

8. Kim, W. (ed.), *Modern Database Systems: The Object Model, Interoperability, and Beyond*, ACM Press, New York, 1994.

9. Papakonstantinou, Y., H. Garcia-Molina, and J. Widom, "Object exchange across heterogeneous information sources," *IEEE Intl. Conf. on Data Engineering*, pp. 251–260, March 1995.

10. D. Suciu (ed.) Special issue on management of semistructured data, *SIGMOD Record* **26**:4 (1997).

11. World-Wide-Web Consortium, `http://www.w3.org/XML/`

Chapter 5

Relational Algebra

This chapter begins a study of database programming, that is, how the user can ask queries of the database and can modify the contents of the database. Our focus is on the relational model, and in particular on a notation for describing queries about the content of relations called "relational algebra."

While ODL uses methods that, in principle, can perform any operation on data, and the E/R model does not embrace a specific way of manipulating data, the relational model has a concrete set of "standard" operations on data. Surprisingly, these operations are not "Turing complete" the way ordinary programming languages are. Thus, there are operations we cannot express in relational algebra that could be expressed, for instance, in ODL methods written in C++. This situation is not a defect of the relational model or relational algebra, because the advantage of limiting the scope of operations is that it becomes possible to optimize queries written in a very high level language such as SQL, which we introduce in Chapter 6.

We begin by introducing the operations of relational algebra. This algebra formally applies to sets of tuples, i.e., relations. However, commercial DBMS's use a slightly different model of relations, which are bags, not sets. That is, relations in practice may contain duplicate tuples. While it is often useful to think of relational algebra as a set algebra, we also need to be conscious of the effects of duplicates on the results of the operations in relational algebra. In the final section of this chapter, we consider the matter of how constraints on relations can be expressed.

Later chapters let us see the languages and features that today's commercial DBMS's offer the user. The operations of relational algebra are all implemented by the SQL query language, which we study beginning in Chapter 6. These algebraic operations also appear in the OQL language, an object-oriented query language based on the ODL data model and introduced in Chapter 9.

5.1   An Example Database Schema

As we begin our focus on database programming in the relational model, it is useful to have a specific schema on which to base our examples of queries. Our chosen database schema draws upon the running example of movies, stars, and studios, and it uses normalized relations similar to the ones that we developed in Section 3.6. However, it includes some attributes that we have not used previously in examples, and it includes one relation — `MovieExec` — that has not appeared before. The purpose of these changes is to give us some opportunities to study different data types and different ways of representing information. Figure 5.1 shows the schema.

```
Movie(
    TITLE: string,
    YEAR: integer,
    length: integer,
    inColor: boolean,
    studioName: string,
    producerC#: integer)

StarsIn(
    MOVIETITLE: string,
    MOVIEYEAR: integer,
    STARNAME: string)

MovieStar(
    NAME: string,
    address: string,
    gender: char,
    birthdate: date)

MovieExec(
    name: string,
    address: string,
    CERT#: integer,
    netWorth: integer)

Studio(
    NAME: string,
    address: string,
    presC#: integer)
```

Figure 5.1: Example database schema about movies

Our schema has five relations. The attributes of each relation are listed, along with the intended domain for that attribute. The key attributes for a relation are shown in capitals in Fig. 5.1, although when we refer to them in text, they will be lower-case as they have been heretofore. For instance, all three attributes together form the key for relation StarsIn. Relation Movie has six attributes; title and year together constitute the key for Movie, as they have previously. Attribute title is a string, and year is an integer.

The major modifications to the schema compared with what we have seen so far are:

- There is a notion of a *certificate number* for movie executives — studio presidents and movie producers. This certificate is a unique integer that we imagine is maintained by some external authority, perhaps a registry of executives or a "union."

- We use certificate numbers as the key for movie executives, although movie stars do not always have certificates and we shall continue to use name as the key for stars. That decision is probably unrealistic, since two stars could have the same name, but we take this road in order to illustrate some different options.

- We introduced the producer as another property of movies. This information is represented by a new attribute, producerC#, of relation Movie. This attribute is intended to be the certificate number of the producer. Producers are expected to be movie executives, as are studio presidents. There may also be other executives in the MovieExec relation.

- Attribute filmType of Movie has been changed from an enumerated type to a boolean-valued attribute called inColor: true if the movie is in color and false if it is in black and white.

- The attribute gender has been added for movie stars. Its type is "character," either M for male or F for female. Attribute birthdate, of type "date" (a special type supported by many commercial database systems or just a character string if we prefer) has also been added.

- All addresses have been made strings, rather than pairs consisting of a street and city. The purpose is to make addresses in different relations comparable easily and to simplify operations on addresses.

5.2 An Algebra of Relational Operations

To begin our study of operations on relations, we shall learn about a special algebra, called *relational algebra*, that consists of some simple but powerful ways to construct new relations from given relations. When the given relations are stored data, then the constructed relations can be answers to queries about this data.

Why Bags Can Be More Efficient Than Sets

As a simple example of why bags can lead to implementation efficiency, if
you take the union of two relations but do not eliminate duplicates, then
you can just copy the relations to the output. If you insist that the result
be a set, you have to sort the relations, or do something similar to detect
identical tuples that come from the two relations.

The development of an algebra for relations has a history, which we shall
follow roughly in our presentation. Initially, relational algebra was proposed
by T. Codd as an algebra on sets of tuples (i.e., relations) that could be used
to express typical queries about those relations. It consisted of five operations
on sets: union, set difference, and Cartesian product, with which you might
already be familiar, and two unusual operations — selection and projection.
To these, several operations that can be defined in terms of these were added;
varieties of "join" are the most important.

When DBMS's that used the relational model were first developed, their
query languages largely implemented the relational algebra. However, for efficiency purposes, these systems regarded relations as bags, not sets. That is,
unless the user asked explicitly that duplicate tuples be condensed into one (i.e.,
that "duplicates be eliminated"), relations were allowed to contain duplicates.
Thus, in Section 5.3, we shall study the same relational operations on bags and
see the changes necessary.

Another change to the algebra that was necessitated by commercial implementations of the relational model is that several other operations are needed.
Most important is a way of performing aggregation, e.g., finding the average
value of some column of a relation. We shall study these additional operations
in Section 5.4.

5.2.1 Basics of Relational Algebra

An algebra, in general, consists of operators and atomic operands. For instance, in the algebra of arithmetic, the atomic operands are variables like x
and constants like 15. The operators are the usual arithmetic ones: addition,
subtraction, multiplication, and division. Any algebra allows us to build *expressions* by applying operators to atomic operands and/or other expressions
of the algebra. Usually, parentheses are needed to group operators and their
operands. For instance, in arithmetic we have expressions such as $(x + y) * z$ or
$((x + 7)/(y - 3)) + x$.

Relational algebra is another example of an algebra. Its atomic operands
are:

1. Variables that stand for relations.

2. Constants, which are finite relations.

As we mentioned, in the classical relational algebra, all operands and the results of expressions are sets. The operations of the traditional relational algebra fall into four broad classes:

a) The usual set operations — union, intersection, and difference — applied to relations.

b) Operations that remove parts of a relation: "selection" eliminates some rows (tuples), and "projection" eliminates some columns.

c) Operations that combine the tuples of two relations, including "Cartesian product," which pairs the tuples of two relations in all possible ways, and various kinds of "join" operations, which selectively pair tuples from two relations.

d) An operation called "renaming" that does not affect the tuples of a relation, but changes the relation schema, i.e., the names of the attributes and/or the name of the relation itself.

We shall generally refer to expressions of relational algebra as *queries*. While we don't yet have the symbols needed to show many of the expressions of relational algebra, you should be familiar with the operations of group (a), and thus recognize $(R \cup S)$ as an example of an expression of relational algebra. R and S are atomic operands standing for relations, whose sets of tuples are unknown. This query asks for the union of whatever tuples are in the relations named R and S.

5.2.2 Set Operations on Relations

The three most common operations on sets are union, intersection, and difference. We assume the reader is familiar with these operations, which are defined as follows on arbitrary sets R and S:

- $R \cup S$, the *union* of R and S, is the set of elements that are in R or S or both. An element appears only once in the union even if it is present in both R and S.

- $R \cap S$, the *intersection* of R and S, is the set of elements that are in both R and S.

- $R - S$, the *difference* of R and S, is the set of elements that are in R but not in S. Note that $R - S$ is different from $S - R$; the latter is the set of elements that are in S but not in R.

When we apply these operations to relations, we need to put some conditions on R and S:

1. R and S must have schemas with identical sets of attributes, and the types (domains) for each attribute must be the same in R and S.

2. Before we compute the set-theoretic union, intersection, or difference of sets of tuples, the columns of R and S must be ordered so that the order of attributes is the same for both relations.

Sometimes we would like to take the union, intersection, or difference of relations that have the same number of attributes, with corresponding domains, but that use different names for their attributes. If so, we may use the renaming operator to be discussed in Section 5.2.9 to change the schema of one or both relations and give them the same set of attributes.

name	*address*	*gender*	*birthdate*
Carrie Fisher	123 Maple St., Hollywood	F	9/9/99
Mark Hamill	456 Oak Rd., Brentwood	M	8/8/88

Relation R

name	*address*	*gender*	*birthdate*
Carrie Fisher	123 Maple St., Hollywood	F	9/9/99
Harrison Ford	789 Palm Dr., Beverly Hills	M	7/7/77

Relation S

Figure 5.2: Two relations

Example 5.1: Suppose we have the two relations R and S, instances of the relation MovieStar of Section 5.1. Current instances of R and S are shown in Fig. 5.2. Then the union $R \cup S$ is

name	*address*	*gender*	*birthdate*
Carrie Fisher	123 Maple St., Hollywood	F	9/9/99
Mark Hamill	456 Oak Rd., Brentwood	M	8/8/88
Harrison Ford	789 Palm Dr., Beverly Hills	M	7/7/77

Note that the two tuples for Carrie Fisher from the two relations appear only once in the result.

The intersection $R \cap S$ is

name	*address*	*gender*	*birthdate*
Carrie Fisher	123 Maple St., Hollywood	F	9/9/99

Now, only the Carrie Fisher tuple appears, because only it is in both relations. The difference $R - S$ is

name	address	gender	birthdate
Mark Hamill	456 Oak Rd., Brentwood	M	8/8/88

That is, the Fisher and Hamill tuples appear in R and thus are candidates for $R - S$. However, the Fisher tuple also appears in S and so is not in $R - S$. □

5.2.3 Projection

The *projection* operator is used to produce from a relation R a new relation that has only some of R's columns. The value of expression $\pi_{A_1, A_2, \ldots, A_n}(R)$ is a relation that has only the columns for attributes $A_1, A_2, \ldots, A_n$ of R. The schema for the resulting value is the set of attributes $\{A_1, A_2, \ldots, A_n\}$, which we conventionally show in the order listed.

title	year	length	inColor	studioName	producerC#
Star Wars	1977	124	true	Fox	12345
Mighty Ducks	1991	104	true	Disney	67890
Wayne's World	1992	95	true	Paramount	99999

Figure 5.3: The relation Movie

Example 5.2: Consider the relation Movie with the relation schema described in Section 5.1. An instance of this relation is shown in Fig. 5.3. We can project this relation onto the first three attributes with the expression

$$\pi_{title, year, length}(\text{Movie})$$

The resulting relation is

title	year	length
Star Wars	1977	124
Mighty Ducks	1991	104
Wayne's World	1992	95

As another example, we can project onto the attribute inColor with the expression $\pi_{inColor}(\text{Movie})$. The result is the single-column relation

inColor
true

Notice that there is only one tuple in the resulting relation, since all three tuples of Fig. 5.3 have the same value in their component for attribute inColor, and in the relational algebra of sets, duplicate tuples are always eliminated. □

5.2.4   Selection

The *selection* operator, applied to a relation R, produces a new relation with a subset of R's tuples. The tuples in the resulting relation are those that satisfy some condition C that involves the attributes of R. We denote this operation $\sigma_C(R)$. The schema for the resulting relation is the same as R's schema, and we conventionally show the attributes in the same order as we use for R.

C is a conditional expression of the type with which we are familiar from conventional programming languages; for example, conditional expressions follow the keyword `if` in programming languages such as C or Java. The only difference is that the operands in condition C are either constants or attributes of R. We apply C to each tuple t of R by substituting, for each attribute A appearing in condition C, the component of t for attribute A. If after substituting for each attribute of C the condition C is true, then t is one of the tuples that appear in the result of $\sigma_C(R)$; otherwise t is not in the result.

Example 5.3 : Let the relation `Movie` be as in Fig. 5.3. Then the value of expression $\sigma_{length \geq 100}(\texttt{Movie})$ is

title	year	length	inColor	studioName	producerC#
Star Wars	1977	124	true	Fox	12345
Mighty Ducks	1991	104	true	Disney	67890

The first tuple satisfies the condition $length \geq 100$ because when we substitute for *length* the value 124 found in the component of the first tuple for attribute `length`, the condition becomes $124 \geq 100$. The latter condition is true, so we accept the first tuple. The same argument explains why the second tuple of Fig. 5.3 is in the result.

The third tuple has a `length` component 95. Thus, when we substitute for *length* we get the condition $95 \geq 100$, which is false. Hence the last tuple of Fig. 5.3 is not in the result.   □

Example 5.4 : Suppose we want the set of tuples in the relation `Movie` that represent Fox movies at least 100 minutes long. We can get these tuples with a more complicated condition, involving the AND of two subconditions. The expression is

$$\sigma_{length \geq 100 \ \textbf{AND} \ studioName = \text{'Fox'}}(\texttt{Movie})$$

The tuple

title	year	length	inColor	studioName	producerC#
Star Wars	1977	124	true	Fox	12345

is the only one in the resulting relation.   □

5.2.5 Cartesian Product

The *Cartesian product* (or *cross-product*, or just *product*) of two sets R and S is the set of pairs that can be formed by choosing the first element of the pair to be any element of R and the second any element of S. This product is denoted $R \times S$. When R and S are relations, the product is essentially the same. However, since the members of R and S are tuples, usually consisting of more than one component, the result of pairing a tuple from R with a tuple from S is a longer tuple, with one component for each of the components of the constituent tuples. By convention, the components from R precede the components from S in the attribute order for the result.

The relation schema for the resulting relation is the union of the schemas for R and S. However, if R and S should happen to have some attributes in common, then we need to invent new names for at least one of each pair of identical attributes. To disambiguate an attribute A that is in the schemas of both R and S, we use $R.A$ for the attribute from R and $S.A$ for the attribute from S.

A	B
1	2
3	4

Relation R

B	C	D
2	5	6
4	7	8
9	10	11

Relation S

A	R.B	S.B	C	D
1	2	2	5	6
1	2	4	7	8
1	2	9	10	11
3	4	2	5	6
3	4	4	7	8
3	4	9	10	11

Result $R \times S$

Figure 5.4: Two relations and their Cartesian product

Example 5.5: For conciseness, let us use an abstract example that illustrates the product operation. Let relations R and S have the schemas and tuples shown in Fig. 5.4. Then the product $R \times S$ consists of the six tuples shown in that figure. Note how we have paired each of the two tuples of R with each of the three tuples of S. Since B is an attribute of both schemas, we have used $R.B$ and $S.B$ in the schema for $R \times S$. The other attributes are unambiguous, and their names appear in the resulting schema unchanged. □

5.2.6 Natural Joins

More often than we want to take the product of two relations, we find a need to *join* them by pairing only those tuples that match in some way. The simplest sort of match is the *natural join* of two relations R and S, denoted $R \bowtie S$, in which we pair only those tuples from R and S that agree in whatever attributes are common to the schemas of R and S. More precisely, let $A_1, A_2, \ldots, A_n$ be all the attributes that are in both the schema of R and the schema of S. Then a tuple r from R and a tuple s from S are successfully paired if and only if r and s agree on each of the attributes $A_1, A_2, \ldots, A_n$.

If the tuples r and s are successfully paired in the join $R \bowtie S$, then the result of the pairing is a tuple, called the *joined tuple*, with one component for each of the attributes in the union of the schemas of R and S. The joined tuple agrees with tuple r in each attribute in the schema of R, and it agrees with s in each attribute in the schema of S. Since r and s are successfully paired, the joined tuple is able to agree with both these tuples on the attributes they have in common. The construction of the joined tuple is suggested by Fig. 5.5.

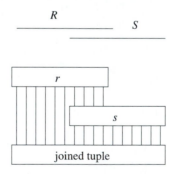

Figure 5.5: Joining tuples

Note also that this join operation is the same one that we used in Section 3.6.5 to recombine relations that had been projected onto two subsets of their attributes. There the motivation was to explain why BCNF decomposition made sense. In Section 5.2.8 we shall see another use for the natural join: combining two relations so that we can write a query that relates attributes of each.

Example 5.6 : The natural join of the relations R and S from Fig. 5.4 is

A	B	C	D
1	2	5	6
3	4	7	8

The only attribute common to R and S is B. Thus, to pair successfully, tuples need only to agree in their B components. If so, the resulting tuple has components for attributes A (from R), B (from either R or S), C (from S), and D (from S).

In this example, the first tuple of R successfully pairs with only the first tuple of S; they share the value 2 on their common attribute B. This pairing yields the first tuple of the result: $(1, 2, 5, 6)$. The second tuple of R pairs successfully only with the second tuple of S, and the pairing yields $(3, 4, 7, 8)$. Note that the third tuple of S does not pair with any tuple of R and thus has no effect on the result of $R \bowtie S$. A tuple that fails to pair with any tuple of the other relation in a join is said to be a *dangling tuple*. □

Example 5.7 : The previous example does not illustrate all the possibilities inherent in the natural join operator. For example, no tuple paired successfully with more than one tuple, and there was only one attribute in common to the two relation schemas. In Fig. 5.6 we see two other relations, U and V, that share two attributes between their schemas: B and C. We also show an instance in which one tuple joins with several tuples.

For tuples to pair successfully, they must agree in both the B and C components. Thus, the first tuple of U joins with the first two tuples of V, while the second and third tuples of U join with the third tuple of V. The result of these four pairings is shown in Fig. 5.6. □

5.2.7 Theta-Joins

The natural join forces us to pair tuples using one specific condition. While this way, equating shared attributes, is the most common basis on which relations are joined, it is sometimes desirable to pair tuples from two relations on some other basis. For that purpose, we have a related notation called the *theta-join*. Historically, the "theta" refers to an arbitrary condition, which we shall represent by C rather than θ.

The notation for a theta-join of relations R and S based on condition C is $R \underset{C}{\bowtie} S$. The result of this operation is constructed as follows:

1. Take the product of R and S.

2. Select from the product only those tuples that satisfy the condition C.

As with the product operation, the schema for the result is the union of the schemas of R and S, with "R." or "S." prefixed to attributes if necessary to indicate from which schema the attribute came.

A	B	C
1	2	3
6	7	8
9	7	8

Relation U

B	C	D
2	3	4
2	3	5
7	8	10

Relation V

A	B	C	D
1	2	3	4
1	2	3	5
6	7	8	10
9	7	8	10

Result $U \bowtie V$

Figure 5.6: Natural join of relations

Example 5.8 : Consider the operation $U \underset{A<D}{\bowtie} V$, where U and V are the relations from Fig. 5.6. We must consider all nine pairs of tuples, one from each relation, and see whether the A component from the U-tuple is less than the D component of the V-tuple. The first tuple of U, with an A component of 1, successfully pairs with each of the tuples from V. However, the second and third tuples from U, with A components of 6 and 9, respectively, pair successfully with only the last tuple of V. Thus, the result has only five tuples, constructed from the five successful pairings. This relation is shown in Fig. 5.7. □

Notice that the schema for the result in Fig. 5.7 consists of all six attributes, with U and V prefixed to their respective occurrences of attributes B and C to distinguish them. Thus, the theta-join contrasts with natural join, since in the latter common attributes are merged into one copy. Of course it makes sense to do so in the case of the natural join, since tuples don't pair unless they agree in their common attributes. In the case of a theta-join, there is no guarantee that compared attributes will agree in the result, since they may not be compared with =.

A	$U.B$	$U.C$	$V.B$	$V.C$	D
1	2	3	2	3	4
1	2	3	2	3	5
1	2	3	7	8	10
6	7	8	7	8	10
9	7	8	7	8	10

Figure 5.7: Result of $U \bowtie_{A<D} V$

Example 5.9: Here is a theta-join on the same relations U and V that has a more complex condition:

$$U \bowtie_{A<D \text{ AND } U.B \neq V.B} V$$

That is, we require for successful pairing not only that the A component of the U-tuple be less than the D component of the V-tuple, but that the two tuples disagree on their respective B components. The tuple

A	$U.B$	$U.C$	$V.B$	$V.C$	D
1	2	3	7	8	10

is the only one to satisfy both conditions, so this relation is the result of the theta-join above. $\square$

5.2.8 Combining Operations to Form Queries

If all we could do was to write single operations on one or two relations as queries, then relational algebra would not be as useful as it is. However, relational algebra, like all algebras, allows us to form expressions of arbitrary complexity by applying operators either to given relations or to relations that are the result of applying one or more relational operators to relations.

One can construct expressions of relational algebra by applying operators to subexpressions, using parentheses when necessary to indicate grouping of operands. It is also possible to represent expressions as expression trees; the latter often are easier for us to read, although they are less convenient as a machine-readable notation.

Example 5.10: Let us reconsider the decomposed `Movies` relation of Example 3.24. Suppose we want to know "What are the titles and years of movies made by Fox that are at least 100 minutes long?" One way to compute the answer to this query is:

1. Select those `Movies` tuples that have $length \geq 100$.

2. Select those Movies tuples that have *studioName =* 'Fox'.

3. Compute the intersection of (1) and (2).

4. Project the relation from (3) onto attributes title and year.

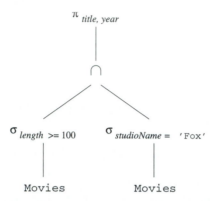

Figure 5.8: Expression tree for a relational algebra expression

In Fig. 5.8 we see the above steps represented as an expression tree. The two selection nodes correspond to steps (1) and (2). The intersection node corresponds to step (3), and the projection node is step (4).

Alternatively, we could represent the same expression in a conventional, linear notation, with parentheses. The formula

$$\pi_{title,year}\Big(\sigma_{length \geq 100}(\text{Movies}) \cap \sigma_{studioName=\text{'Fox'}}(\text{Movies})\Big)$$

represents the same expression.

Incidentally, there is often more than one relational algebra expression that represents the same computation. For instance, the above query could also be written by replacing the intersection by logical AND within a single selection operation. That is,

$$\pi_{title,year}\Big(\sigma_{length \geq 100 \text{ AND } studioName=\text{'Fox'}}(\text{Movies})\Big)$$

is an equivalent form of the query. □

Example 5.11 : One use of the natural join operation is to recombine relations that were decomposed to put them into BCNF. Recall the decomposed relations from Example 3.24:[1]

---

[1] Remember that the relation Movies of that example has a somewhat different relation schema from the relation Movie that we introduced in Section 5.1 and used in Examples 5.2, 5.3, and 5.4.

Equivalent Expressions and Query Optimization

All database systems have a query-answering system, and many of them are based on a language that is similar in expressive power to relational algebra. Thus, the query asked by a user may have many *equivalent expressions* (expressions that produce the same answer, whenever they are given the same relations as operands), and some of these may be much more quickly evaluated. An important job of the query "optimizer" discussed briefly in Section 1.2.5 is to replace one expression of relational algebra by an equivalent expression that is more efficiently evaluated. Optimization of relational-algebra expressions is covered extensively in Section 16.2.

Movies1 with schema {title, year, length, filmType, studioName}
Movies2 with schema {title, year, starName}

Let us write an expression to answer the query "Find the stars of movies that are at least 100 minutes long." This query relates the starName attribute of Movies2 with the length attribute of Movies1. We can connect these attributes by joining the two relations. The natural join successfully pairs only those tuples that agree on title and year; that is, pairs of tuples that refer to the same movie. Thus, Movies1 ⋈ Movies2 is an expression of relational algebra that produces the relation we called Movies in Example 3.24. That relation is the non-BCNF relation whose schema is all six attributes and that contains several tuples for the same movie when that movie has several stars.

To the join of Movies1 and Movies2 we must apply a selection that enforces the condition that the length of the movie is at least 100 minutes. We then project onto the desired attribute: starName. The expression

$$\pi_{starName}\Big(\sigma_{length \geq 100}(\text{Movies1} \bowtie \text{Movies2})\Big)$$

implements the desired query in relational algebra. □

5.2.9 Renaming

In order to control the names of the attributes used for relations that are constructed by applying relational-algebra operations, it is often convenient to use an operator that explicitly renames relations. We shall use the operator $\rho_{S(A_1,A_2,\ldots,A_n)}(R)$ to rename a relation R. The resulting relation has exactly the same tuples as R, but the name of the relation is S. Moreover, the attributes of the result relation S are named $A_1, A_2, \ldots, A_n$, in order from the left. If we only want to change the name of the relation to S and leave the attributes as they are in R, we can just say $\rho_S(R)$.

Example 5.12 : In Example 5.5 we took the product of two relations R and S from Fig. 5.4 and used the convention that when an attribute appears in both operands, it is renamed by prefixing the relation name to it. These relations R and S are repeated in Fig. 5.9.

Suppose, however, that we do not wish to call the two versions of B by names $R.B$ and $S.B$; rather we want to continue to use the name B for the attribute that comes from R, and we want to use X as the name of the attribute B coming from S. We can rename the attributes of S so the first is called X. The result of the expression $\rho_{S(X,C,D)}(S)$ is a relation named S that looks just like the relation S from Fig. 5.4, but its first column has attribute X instead of B.

A	B
1	2
3	4

Relation R

B	C	D
2	5	6
4	7	8
9	10	11

Relation S

A	B	X	C	D
1	2	2	5	6
1	2	4	7	8
1	2	9	10	11
3	4	2	5	6
3	4	4	7	8
3	4	9	10	11

Result $R \times \rho_{S(X,C,D)}(S)$

Figure 5.9: Renaming before taking a product

When we take the product of R with this new relation, there is no conflict of names among the attributes, so no further renaming is done. That is, the result of the expression $R \times \rho_{S(X,C,D)}(S)$ is the relation $R \times S$ from Fig. 5.4, except that the five columns are labeled A, B, X, C, and D, from the left. This relation is shown in Fig. 5.9.

As an alternative, we could take the product without renaming, as we did in Example 5.5, and then rename the result. The expression $\rho_{RS(A,B,X,C,D)}(R \times S)$ yields the same relation as in Fig. 5.9, with the same set of attributes. But this relation has a name, RS, while the result relation in Fig. 5.9 has no name. $\square$

5.2.10 Dependent and Independent Operations

Some of the operations that we have described in Section 5.2 can be expressed in terms of other relational-algebra operations. For example, intersection can be expressed in terms of set difference:

$$R \cap S = R - (R - S)$$

That is, if R and S are any two relations with the same schema, the intersection of R and S can be computed by first subtracting S from R to form a relation T consisting of all those tuples in R but not S. We then subtract T from R, leaving only those tuples of R that are also in S.

The two forms of join are also expressible in terms of other operations. Theta-join can be expressed by product and selection:

$$R \underset{C}{\bowtie} S = \sigma_C(R \times S)$$

The natural join of R and S can be expressed by starting with the product $R \times S$. We then apply the selection operator with a condition C of the form

$$R.A_1 = S.A_1 \text{ AND } R.A_2 = S.A_2 \text{ AND} \cdots \text{AND } R.A_n = S.A_n$$

where $A_1, A_2, \ldots, A_n$ are all the attributes appearing in the schemas of both R and S. Finally, we must project out one copy of each of the equated attributes. Let L be the list of attributes in the schema of R followed by those attributes in the schema of S that are not also in the schema of R. Then

$$R \bowtie S = \pi_L\Big(\sigma_C(R \times S)\Big)$$

Example 5.13: The natural join of the relations U and V from Fig. 5.6 can be written in terms of product, selection, and projection as:

$$\pi_{A,U.B,U.C,D}\Big(\sigma_{U.B=V.B \text{ AND } U.C=V.C}(U \times V)\Big)$$

That is, we take the product $U \times V$. Then we select for equality between each pair of attributes with the same name — B and C in this example. Finally, we project onto all the attributes except one of the B's and one of the C's; we have chosen to eliminate the attributes of V whose names also appear in the schema of U.

For another example, the theta-join of Example 5.9 can be written

$$\sigma_{A<D \text{ AND } U.B \neq V.B}(U \times V)$$

That is, we take the product of the relations U and V and then apply the condition that appeared in the theta-join. □

The rewriting rules mentioned in this section are the only "redundancies" among the operations that we have introduced. The six remaining operations — union, difference, selection, projection, product, and renaming — form an independent set, none of which can be written in terms of the other five.

5.2.11 A Linear Notation for Algebraic Expressions

In Section 5.2.8 we used trees to represent complex expressions of relational algebra. Another alternative is to invent names for the temporary relations that correspond to the interior nodes of the tree and write a sequence of assignments that create a value for each. The order of the assignments is flexible, as long as the children of a node N have had their values created before we attempt to create the value for N itself.

The notation we shall use for assignment statements is:

1. A relation name and parenthesized list of attributes for that relation. The name `Answer` will be used conventionally for the result of the final step; i.e., the name of the relation at the root of the expression tree.

2. The assignment symbol :=.

3. Any algebraic expression on the right. We can choose to use only one operator per assignment, in which case each interior node of the tree gets its own assignment statement. However, it is also permissible to combine several algebraic operations in one right side, if it is convenient to do so.

Example 5.14: Consider the tree of Fig. 5.8. One possible sequence of assignments to evaluate this expression is:

$$R(t,y,l,i,s,p) := \sigma_{length \geq 100}(\text{Movie})$$
$$S(t,y,l,i,s,p) := \sigma_{studioName='Fox'}(\text{Movie})$$
$$T(t,y,l,i,s,p) := R \cap S$$
$$\text{Answer}(title, year) := \pi_{t,i}(T)$$

The first step computes the relation of the interior node labeled $\sigma_{length \geq 100}$ in Fig. 5.8, and the second step computes the node labeled $\sigma_{studioName='Fox'}$. Notice that we get renaming "for free," since we can use any attributes and relation name we wish for the left side of an assignment. The last two steps compute the intersection and the projection in the obvious way.

It is also permissible to combine some of the steps. For instance, we could combine the last two steps and write:

$$R(t,y,l,i,s,p) := \sigma_{length \geq 100}(\text{Movie})$$
$$S(t,y,l,i,s,p) := \sigma_{studioName='Fox'}(\text{Movie})$$
$$\text{Answer}(title, year) := \pi_{t,i}(R \cap S)$$

□

5.2.12   Exercises for Section 5.2

Exercise 5.2.1: In this exercise we introduce one of our running examples of a relational database schema and some sample data.[2] The database schema consists of four relations, whose schemas are:

```
Product(maker, model, type)
PC(model, speed, ram, hd, rd, price)
Laptop(model, speed, ram, hd, screen, price)
Printer(model, color, type, price)
```

The Product relation gives the manufacturer, model number and type (PC, laptop, or printer) of various products. We assume for convenience that model numbers are unique over all manufacturers and product types; that assumption is not realistic, and a real database would include a code for the manufacturer as part of the model number. The PC relation gives for each model number that is a PC the speed (of the processor, in megahertz), the amount of RAM (in megabytes), the size of the hard disk (in gigabytes), the speed and type of the removable disk (CD or DVD), and the price. The Laptop relation is similar, except that the screen size (in inches) is recorded in place of information about the removable disk. The Printer relation records for each printer model whether the printer produces color output (true, if so), the process type (laser, ink-jet, or bubble), and the price.

Some sample data for the relation Product is shown in Fig. 5.10. Sample data for the other three relations is shown in Fig. 5.11. Manufacturers and model numbers have been "sanitized," but the data is typical of products on sale at the beginning of 2001.

Write expressions of relational algebra to answer the following queries. You may use the linear notation of Section 5.2.11 if you wish. For the data of Figs. 5.10 and 5.11, show the result of your query. However, your answer should work for arbitrary data, not just the data of these figures.

* a) What PC models have a speed of at least 1000?

  b) Which manufacturers make laptops with a hard disk of at least one gigabyte?

  c) Find the model number and price of all products (of any type) made by manufacturer B.

  d) Find the model numbers of all color laser printers.

  e) Find those manufacturers that sell Laptops, but not PC's.

*! f) Find those hard-disk sizes that occur in two or more PC's.

---

[2]Source: manufacturers' Web pages and Amazon.com.

maker	model	type
A	1001	pc
A	1002	pc
A	1003	pc
A	2004	laptop
A	2005	laptop
A	2006	laptop
B	1004	pc
B	1005	pc
B	1006	pc
B	2001	laptop
B	2002	laptop
B	2003	laptop
C	1007	pc
C	1008	pc
C	2008	laptop
C	2009	laptop
C	3002	printer
C	3003	printer
C	3006	printer
D	1009	pc
D	1010	pc
D	1011	pc
D	2007	laptop
E	1012	pc
E	1013	pc
E	2010	laptop
F	3001	printer
F	3004	printer
G	3005	printer
H	3007	printer

Figure 5.10: Sample data for Product

model	speed	ram	hd	rd	price
1001	700	64	10	48xCD	799
1002	1500	128	60	12xDVD	2499
1003	866	128	20	8xDVD	1999
1004	866	64	10	12xDVD	999
1005	1000	128	20	12xDVD	1499
1006	1300	256	40	16xDVD	2119
1007	1400	128	80	12xDVD	2299
1008	700	64	30	24xCD	999
1009	1200	128	80	16xDVD	1699
1010	750	64	30	40xCD	699
1011	1100	128	60	16xDVD	1299
1012	350	64	7	48xCD	799
1013	733	256	60	12xDVD	2499

(a) Sample data for relation PC

model	speed	ram	hd	screen	price
2001	700	64	5	12.1	1448
2002	800	96	10	15.1	2584
2003	850	64	10	15.1	2738
2004	550	32	5	12.1	999
2005	600	64	6	12.1	2399
2006	800	96	20	15.7	2999
2007	850	128	20	15.0	3099
2008	650	64	10	12.1	1249
2009	750	256	20	15.1	2599
2010	366	64	10	12.1	1499

(b) Sample data for relation Laptop

model	color	type	price
3001	true	ink-jet	231
3002	true	ink-jet	267
3003	false	laser	390
3004	true	ink-jet	439
3005	true	bubble	200
3006	true	laser	1999
3007	false	laser	350

(c) Sample data for relation Printer

Figure 5.11: Sample data for relations of Exercise 5.2.1

! g) Find those pairs of PC models that have both the same speed and RAM. A pair should be listed only once; e.g., list (i, j) but not (j, i).

*!! h) Find those manufacturers of at least two different computers (PC's or laptops) with speeds of at least 700.

!! i) Find the manufacturer(s) of the computer (PC or laptop) with the highest available speed.

!! j) Find the manufacturers of PC's with at least three different speeds.

!! k) Find the manufacturers who sell exactly three different models of PC.

Exercise 5.2.2: Draw expression trees for each of your expressions of Exercise 5.2.1.

Exercise 5.2.3: Write each of your expressions from Exercise 5.2.1 in the linear notation of Section 5.2.11.

Exercise 5.2.4: This exercise introduces another running example, concerning World War II capital ships. It involves the following relations:

```
Classes(class, type, country, numGuns, bore, displacement)
Ships(name, class, launched)
Battles(name, date)
Outcomes(ship, battle, result)
```

Ships are built in "classes" from the same design, and the class is usually named for the first ship of that class. The relation `Classes` records the name of the class, the type (`bb` for battleship or `bc` for battlecruiser), the country that built the ship, the number of main guns, the bore (diameter of the gun barrel, in inches) of the main guns, and the displacement (weight, in tons). Relation `Ships` records the name of the ship, the name of its class, and the year in which the ship was launched. Relation `Battles` gives the name and date of battles involving these ships, and relation `Outcomes` gives the result (sunk, damaged, or ok) for each ship in each battle.

Figures 5.12 and 5.13 give some sample data for these four relations.[3] Note that, unlike the data for Exercise 5.2.1, there are some "dangling tuples" in this data, e.g., ships mentioned in `Outcomes` that are not mentioned in `Ships`.

Write expressions of relational algebra to answer the following queries. For the data of Figs. 5.12 and 5.13, show the result of your query. However, your answer should work for arbitrary data, not just the data of these figures.

a) Give the class names and countries of the classes that carried guns of at least 16-inch bore.

---

[3]Source: J. N. Westwood, *Fighting Ships of World War II*, Follett Publishing, Chicago, 1975 and R. C. Stern, *US Battleships in Action*, Squadron/Signal Publications, Carrollton, TX, 1980.

class	type	country	numGuns	bore	displacement
Bismarck	bb	Germany	8	15	42000
Iowa	bb	USA	9	16	46000
Kongo	bc	Japan	8	14	32000
North Carolina	bb	USA	9	16	37000
Renown	bc	Gt. Britain	6	15	32000
Revenge	bb	Gt. Britain	8	15	29000
Tennessee	bb	USA	12	14	32000
Yamato	bb	Japan	9	18	65000

(a) Sample data for relation Classes

name	date
North Atlantic	5/24-27/41
Guadalcanal	11/15/42
North Cape	12/26/43
Surigao Strait	10/25/44

(b) Sample data for relation Battles

ship	battle	result
Bismarck	North Atlantic	sunk
California	Surigao Strait	ok
Duke of York	North Cape	ok
Fuso	Surigao Strait	sunk
Hood	North Atlantic	sunk
King George V	North Atlantic	ok
Kirishima	Guadalcanal	sunk
Prince of Wales	North Atlantic	damaged
Rodney	North Atlantic	ok
Scharnhorst	North Cape	sunk
South Dakota	Guadalcanal	damaged
Tennessee	Surigao Strait	ok
Washington	Guadalcanal	ok
West Virginia	Surigao Strait	ok
Yamashiro	Surigao Strait	sunk

(c) Sample data for relation Outcomes

Figure 5.12: Data for Exercise 5.2.4

name	class	launched
California	Tennessee	1921
Haruna	Kongo	1915
Hiei	Kongo	1914
Iowa	Iowa	1943
Kirishima	Kongo	1915
Kongo	Kongo	1913
Missouri	Iowa	1944
Musashi	Yamato	1942
New Jersey	Iowa	1943
North Carolina	North Carolina	1941
Ramillies	Revenge	1917
Renown	Renown	1916
Repulse	Renown	1916
Resolution	Revenge	1916
Revenge	Revenge	1916
Royal Oak	Revenge	1916
Royal Sovereign	Revenge	1916
Tennessee	Tennessee	1920
Washington	North Carolina	1941
Wisconsin	Iowa	1944
Yamato	Yamato	1941

Figure 5.13: Sample data for relation Ships

b) Find the ships launched prior to 1921.

c) Find the ships sunk in the battle of the North Atlantic.

d) The treaty of Washington in 1921 prohibited capital ships heavier than 35,000 tons. List the ships that violated the treaty of Washington.

e) List the name, displacement, and number of guns of the ships engaged in the battle of Guadalcanal.

f) List all the capital ships mentioned in the database. (Remember that all these ships may not appear in the Ships relation.)

! g) Find the classes that had only one ship as a member of that class.

! h) Find those countries that had both battleships and battlecruisers.

! i) Find those ships that "lived to fight another day"; they were damaged in one battle, but later fought in another.

Exercise 5.2.5: Draw expression trees for each of your expressions of Exercise 5.2.4.

Exercise 5.2.6: Write each of your expressions from Exercise 5.2.4 in the linear notation of Section 5.2.11.

* **Exercise 5.2.7:** What is the difference between the natural join $R \bowtie S$ and the theta-join $R \overset{\bowtie}{C} S$ where the condition C is that $R.A = S.A$ for each attribute A appearing in the schemas of both R and S?

! **Exercise 5.2.8:** An operator on relations is said to be *monotone* if whenever we add a tuple to one of its arguments, the result contains all the tuples that it contained before adding the tuple, plus perhaps more tuples. Which of the operators described in this section are monotone? For each, either explain why it is monotone or give an example showing it is not.

! **Exercise 5.2.9:** Suppose relations R and S have n tuples and m tuples, respectively. Give the minimum and maximum numbers of tuples that the results of the following expressions can have.

* a) $R \cup S$.

   b) $R \bowtie S$.

   c) $\sigma_C(R) \times S$, for some condition C.

   d) $\pi_L(R) - S$, for some list of attributes L.

*! **Exercise 5.2.10:** The *semijoin* of relations R and S, written $R \ltimes S$, is the bag of tuples t in R such that there is at least one tuple in S that agrees with t in all attributes that R and S have in common. Give three different expressions of relational algebra that are equivalent to $R \ltimes S$.

! **Exercise 5.2.11:** The *antisemijoin* $R \overline{\ltimes} S$ is the bag of tuples t in R that do *not* agree with any tuple of S in the attributes common to R and S. Give an expression of relational algebra equivalent to $R \overline{\ltimes} S$.

!! **Exercise 5.2.12:** Let R be a relation with schema

$$(A_1, A_2, \ldots, A_n, B_1, B_2, \ldots, B_m)$$

and let S be a relation with schema $(B_1, B_2, \ldots, B_m)$; that is, the attributes of S are a subset of the attributes of R. The *quotient* of R and S, denoted $R \div S$, is the set of tuples t over attributes $A_1, A_2, \ldots, A_n$ (i.e., the attributes of R that are not attributes of S) such that for every tuple s in S, the tuple ts, consisting of the components of t for $A_1, A_2, \ldots, A_n$ and the components of s for $B_1, B_2, \ldots, B_m$, is a member of R. Give an expression of relational algebra, using the operators we have defined previously in this section, that is equivalent to $R \div S$.

5.3   Relational Operations on Bags

While a set of tuples (i.e., a relation) is a simple, natural model of data as it might appear in a database, commercial database systems rarely, if ever, are based purely on sets. In some situations, relations as they appear in database systems are permitted to have duplicate tuples. Recall that if a "set" is allowed to have multiple occurrences of a member, then that set is called a *bag* or *multiset*. In this section, we shall consider relations that are bags rather than sets; that is, we shall allow the same tuple to appear more than once in a relation. When we refer to a "set," we mean a relation without duplicate tuples; a "bag" means a relation that may (or may not) have duplicate tuples.

Example 5.15: The relation in Fig. 5.14 is a bag of tuples. In it, the tuple $(1, 2)$ appears three times and the tuple $(3, 4)$ appears once. If Fig. 5.14 were a set-valued relation, we would have to eliminate two occurrences of the tuple $(1, 2)$. In a bag-valued relation, we *do* allow multiple occurrences of the same tuple, but like sets, the order of tuples does not matter.   □

A	B
1	2
3	4
1	2
1	2

Figure 5.14: A bag

5.3.1   Why Bags?

When we think about implementing relations efficiently, we can see several ways that allowing relations to be bags rather than sets can speed up operations on relations. We mentioned at the beginning of Section 5.2 how allowing the result to be a bag could speed up the union of two relations. For another example, when we do a projection, allowing the resulting relation to be a bag (even when the original relation is a set) lets us work with each tuple independently. If we want a set as the result, we need to compare each projected tuple with all the other projected tuples, to make sure that each projection appears only once. However, if we can accept a bag as the result, then we simply project each tuple and add it to the result; no comparison with other projected tuples is necessary.

Example 5.16: The bag of Fig. 5.14 could be the result of projecting the relation shown in Fig. 5.15 onto attributes A and B, provided we allow the result to be a bag and do not eliminate the duplicate occurrences of $(1, 2)$. Had

A	B	C
1	2	5
3	4	6
1	2	7
1	2	8

Figure 5.15: Bag for Example 5.16

we used the ordinary projection operator of relational algebra, and therefore eliminated duplicates, the result would be only:

A	B
1	2
3	4

Note that the bag result, although larger, can be computed more quickly, since there is no need to compare each tuple $(1, 2)$ or $(3, 4)$ with previously generated tuples.

Moreover, if we are projecting a relation in order to take an aggregate (discussed in Section 5.4), such as "Find the average value of A in Fig. 5.15," we could not use the set model to think of the relation projected onto attribute A. As a set, the average value of A is 2, because there are only two values of A — 1 and 3 — in Fig. 5.15, and their average is 2. However, if we treat the A-column in Fig. 5.15 as a bag $\{1, 3, 1, 1\}$, we get the correct average of A, which is 1.5, among the four tuples of Fig. 5.15. $\square$

5.3.2 Union, Intersection, and Difference of Bags

When we take the union of two bags, we add the number of occurrences of each tuple. That is, if R is a bag in which the tuple t appears n times, and S is a bag in which the tuple t appears m times, then in the bag $R \cup S$ tuple t appears $n + m$ times. Note that either n or m (or both) can be 0.

When we intersect two bags R and S, in which tuple t appears n and m times, respectively, in $R \cap S$ tuple t appears $\min(n, m)$ times. When we compute $R - S$, the difference of bags R and S, tuple t appears in $R - S$ $\max(0, n - m)$ times. That is, if t appears in R more times than it appears in S, then in $R - S$ tuple t appears the number of times it appears in R, minus the number of times it appears in S. However, if t appears at least as many times in S as it appears in R, then t does not appear at all in $R - S$. Intuitively, occurrences of t in S each "cancel" one occurrence in R.

Example 5.17: Let R be the relation of Fig. 5.14, that is, a bag in which tuple $(1, 2)$ appears three times and $(3, 4)$ appears once. Let S be the bag

$$
\begin{array}{c|c}
A & B \\
\hline\hline
1 & 2 \\
3 & 4 \\
3 & 4 \\
5 & 6 \\
\end{array}
$$

Then the bag union $R \cup S$ is the bag in which $(1,2)$ appears four times (three times for its occurrences in R and once for its occurrence in S); $(3,4)$ appears three times, and $(5,6)$ appears once.

The bag intersection $R \cap S$ is the bag

$$
\begin{array}{c|c}
A & B \\
\hline\hline
1 & 2 \\
3 & 4 \\
\end{array}
$$

with one occurrence each of $(1,2)$ and $(3,4)$. That is, $(1,2)$ appears three times in R and once in S, and $\min(3,1) = 1$, so $(1,2)$ appears once in $R \cap S$. Similarly, $(3,4)$ appears $\min(1,2) = 1$ time in $R \cap S$. Tuple $(5,6)$, which appears once in S but zero times in R appears $\min(0,1) = 0$ times in $R \cap S$.

The bag difference $R - S$ is the bag

$$
\begin{array}{c|c}
A & B \\
\hline\hline
1 & 2 \\
1 & 2 \\
\end{array}
$$

To see why, notice that $(1,2)$ appears three times in R and once in S, so in $R - S$ it appears $\max(0, 3 - 1) = 2$ times. Tuple $(3,4)$ appears once in R and twice in S, so in $R - S$ it appears $\max(0, 1 - 2) = 0$ times. No other tuple appears in R, so there can be no other tuples in $R - S$.

As another example, the bag difference $S - R$ is the bag

$$
\begin{array}{c|c}
A & B \\
\hline\hline
3 & 4 \\
5 & 6 \\
\end{array}
$$

Tuple $(3,4)$ appears once because that is the difference in the number of times it appears in S minus the number of times it appears in R. Tuple $(5,6)$ appears once in $S - R$ for the same reason. The resulting bag happens to be a set in this case. □

5.3.3 Projection of Bags

We have already illustrated the projection of bags. As we saw in Example 5.16, each tuple is processed independently during the projection. If R is the bag of Fig. 5.15 and we compute the bag-projection $\pi_{A,B}(R)$, then we get the bag of Fig. 5.14.

Bag Operations on Sets

Imagine we have two sets R and S. Every set may be thought of as a bag; the bag just happens to have at most one occurrence of any tuple. Suppose we intersect $R \cap S$, but we think of R and S as bags and use the bag intersection rule. Then we get the same result as we would get if we thought of R and S as sets. That is, thinking of R and S as bags, a tuple t is in $R \cap S$ the minimum of the number of times it is in R and S. Since R and S are sets, t can be in each only 0 or 1 times. Whether we use the bag or set intersection rules, we find that t can appear at most once in $R \cap S$, and it appears once exactly when it is in both R and S. Similarly, if we use the bag difference rule to compute $R - S$ or $S - R$ we get exactly the same result as if we used the set rule.

However, union behaves differently, depending on whether we think of R and S as sets or bags. If we use the bag rule to compute $R \cup S$, then the result may not be a set, even if R and S are sets. In particular, if tuple t appears in both R and S, then t appears twice in $R \cup S$ if we use the bag rule for union. But if we use the set rule then t appears only once in $R \cup S$. Thus, when taking unions, we must be especially careful to specify whether we are using the bag or set definition of union.

If the elimination of one or more attributes during the projection causes the same tuple to be created from several tuples, these duplicate tuples are not eliminated from the result of a bag-projection. Thus, the three tuples $(1, 2, 5)$, $(1, 2, 7)$, and $(1, 2, 8)$ of the relation R from Fig. 5.15 each gave rise to the same tuple $(1, 2)$ after projection onto attributes A and B. In the bag result, there are three occurrences of tuple $(1, 2)$, while in the set-projection, this tuple appears only once.

5.3.4 Selection on Bags

To apply a selection to a bag, we apply the selection condition to each tuple independently. As always with bags, we do not eliminate duplicate tuples in the result.

Example 5.18: If R is the bag

A	B	C
1	2	5
3	4	6
1	2	7
1	2	7

then the result of the bag-selection $\sigma_{C \geq 6}(R)$ is

---

Algebraic Laws for Bags

An algebraic law is an equivalence between two expressions of relational algebra whose arguments are variables standing for relations. The equivalence asserts that no matter what relations we substitute for these variables, the two expressions define the same relation. An example of a well-known law is the commutative law for union: $R \cup S = S \cup R$. This law happens to hold whether we regard relation-variables R and S as standing for sets or bags. However, there are a number of other laws that hold when relational algebra is applied to sets but that do not hold when relations are interpreted as bags. A simple example of such a law is the distributive law of set difference over union, $(R \cup S) - T = (R - T) \cup (S - T)$. This law holds for sets but not for bags. To see why it fails for bags, suppose R, S, and T each have one copy of tuple t. Then the expression on the left has one t, while the expression on the right has none. As sets, neither would have t. Some exploration of algebraic laws for bags appears in Exercises 5.3.4 and 5.3.5.

A	B	C
3	4	6
1	2	7
1	2	7

That is, all but the first tuple meets the selection condition. The last two tuples, which are duplicates in R, are each included in the result. □

5.3.5 Product of Bags

The rule for the Cartesian product of bags is the expected one. Each tuple of one relation is paired with each tuple of the other, regardless of whether it is a duplicate or not. As a result, if a tuple r appears in a relation R m times, and tuple s appears n times in relation S, then in the product $R \times S$, the tuple rs will appear mn times.

Example 5.19: Let R and S be the bags shown in Fig. 5.16. Then the product $R \times S$ consists of six tuples, as shown in Fig. 5.16(c). Note that the usual convention regarding attribute names that we developed for set-relations applies equally well to bags. Thus, the attribute B, which belongs to both relations R and S, appears twice in the product, each time prefixed by one of the relation names. □

A	B
1	2
1	2

(a) The relation R

B	C
2	3
4	5
4	5

(b) The relation S

A	R.B	S.B	C
1	2	2	3
1	2	2	3
1	2	4	5
1	2	4	5
1	2	4	5
1	2	4	5

(c) The product $R \times S$

Figure 5.16: Computing the product of bags

5.3.6 Joins of Bags

Joining bags also presents no surprises. We compare each tuple of one relation with each tuple of the other, decide whether or not this pair of tuples joins successfully, and if so we put the resulting tuple in the answer. When constructing the answer, we do not eliminate duplicate tuples.

Example 5.20 : The natural join $R \bowtie S$ of the relations R and S seen in Fig. 5.16 is

A	B	C
1	2	3
1	2	3

That is, tuple $(1, 2)$ of R joins with $(2, 3)$ of S. Since there are two copies of $(1, 2)$ in R and one copy of $(2, 3)$ in S, there are two pairs of tuples that join to give the tuple $(1, 2, 3)$. No other tuples from R and S join successfully.

As another example on the same relations R and S, the theta-join

$$R \underset{R.B<S.B}{\bowtie} S$$

produces the bag

A	$R.B$	$S.B$	C
1	2	4	5
1	2	4	5
1	2	4	5
1	2	4	5

The computation of the join is as follows. Tuple $(1,2)$ from R and $(4,5)$ from S meet the join condition. Since each appears twice in its relation, the number of times the joined tuple appears in the result is 2×2 or 4. The other possible join of tuples — $(1,2)$ from R with $(2,3)$ from S — fails to meet the join condition, so this combination does not appear in the result.   □

5.3.7   Exercises for Section 5.3

* **Exercise 5.3.1 :** Let PC be the relation of Fig. 5.11(a), and suppose we compute the projection $\pi_{speed}(\texttt{PC})$. What is the value of this expression as a set? As a bag? What is the average value of tuples in this projection, when treated as a set? As a bag?

Exercise 5.3.2 : Repeat Exercise 5.3.1 for the projection $\pi_{hd}(\texttt{PC})$.

Exercise 5.3.3 : This exercise refers to the "battleship" relations of Exercise 5.2.4.

   a) The expression $\pi_{bore}(\texttt{Classes})$ yields a single-column relation with the bores of the various classes. For the data of Exercise 5.2.4, what is this relation as a set? As a bag?

 ! b) Write an expression of relational algebra to give the bores of the ships (not the classes). Your expression must make sense for bags; that is, the number of times a value b appears must be the number of ships that have bore b.

! **Exercise 5.3.4 :** Certain algebraic laws for relations as sets also hold for relations as bags. Explain why each of the laws below hold for bags as well as sets.

   * a) The associative law for union: $(R \cup S) \cup T = R \cup (S \cup T)$.

   b) The associative law for intersection: $(R \cap S) \cap T = R \cap (S \cap T)$.

   c) The associative law for natural join: $(R \bowtie S) \bowtie T = R \bowtie (S \bowtie T)$.

d) The commutative law for union: $(R \cup S) = (S \cup R)$.

e) The commutative law for intersection: $(R \cap S) = (S \cap R)$.

f) The commutative law for natural join: $(R \bowtie S) = (S \bowtie R)$.

g) $\pi_L(R \cup S) = \pi_L(R) \cup \pi_L(S)$. Here, L is an arbitrary list of attributes.

* h) The distributive law of union over intersection: $R \cup (S \cap T) = (R \cup S) \cap (R \cup T)$.

i) $\sigma_{C \text{ AND } D}(R) = \sigma_C(R) \cap \sigma_D(R)$. Here, C and D are arbitrary conditions about the tuples of R.

!! **Exercise 5.3.5:** The following algebraic laws hold for sets but not for bags. Explain why they hold for sets and give counterexamples to show that they do not hold for bags.

* a) $(R \cap S) - T = R \cap (S - T)$.

b) The distributive law of intersection over union: $R \cap (S \cup T) = (R \cap S) \cup (R \cap T)$.

c) $\sigma_{C \text{ OR } D}(R) = \sigma_C(R) \cup \sigma_D(R)$. Here, C and D are arbitrary conditions about the tuples of R.

5.4 Extended Operators of Relational Algebra

Section 5.2 presented the classical relational algebra, and Section 5.3 introduced the modifications necessary to treat relations as bags of tuples rather than sets. The ideas of these two sections serve as a foundation for most of modern query languages. However, languages such as SQL have several other operations that have proved quite important in applications. Thus, a full treatment of relational operations must include a number of other operators, which we introduce in this section. The additions:

1. The *duplicate-elimination operator* δ turns a bag into a set by eliminating all but one copy of each tuple.

2. *Aggregation operators*, such as sums or averages, are not operations of relational algebra, but are used by the grouping operator (described next). Aggregation operators apply to attributes (columns) of a relation, e.g., the sum of a column produces the one number that is the sum of all the values in that column.

3. *Grouping* of tuples according to their value in one or more attributes has the effect of partitioning the tuples of a relation into "groups." Aggregation can then be applied to columns within each group, giving us the

ability to express a number of queries that are impossible to express in the classical relational algebra. The *grouping operator* γ is an operator that combines the effect of grouping and aggregation.

4. The *sorting operator* τ turns a relation into a list of tuples, sorted according to one or more attributes. This operator should be used judiciously, because other relational-algebra operators apply to sets or bags, but never to lists. Thus, τ only makes sense as the final step of a series of operations.

5. *Extended projection* gives additional power to the operator π. In addition to projecting out some columns, in its generalized form π can perform computations involving the columns of its argument relation to produce new columns.

6. The *outerjoin* operator is a variant of the join that avoids losing dangling tuples. In the result of the outerjoin, dangling tuples are "padded" with the null value, so the dangling tuples can be represented in the output.

5.4.1 Duplicate Elimination

Sometimes, we need an operator that converts a bag to a set. For that purpose, we use $\delta(R)$ to return the set consisting of one copy of every tuple that appears one or more times in relation R.

Example 5.21 : If R is the relation

A	B
1	2
3	4
1	2
1	2

from Fig. 5.14, then $\delta(R)$ is

A	B
1	2
3	4

Note that the tuple $(1, 2)$, which appeared three times in R, appears only once in $\delta(R)$. □

5.4.2 Aggregation Operators

There are several operators that apply to sets or bags of atomic values. These operators are used to summarize or "aggregate" the values in one column of a relation, and thus are referred to as *aggregation* operators. The standard operators of this type are:

1. SUM produces the sum of a column with numerical values.

2. AVG produces the average of a column with numerical values.

3. MIN and MAX, applied to a column with numerical values, produces the smallest or largest value, respectively. When applied to a column with character-string values, they produce the lexicographically (alphabetically) first or last value, respectively.

4. COUNT produces the number of (not necessarily distinct) values in a column. Equivalently, COUNT applied to any attribute of a relation produces the number of tuples of that relation, including duplicates.

Example 5.22: Consider the relation

A	B
1	2
3	4
1	2
1	2

Some examples of aggregations on the attributes of this relation are:

1. $\text{SUM(B)} = 2 + 4 + 2 + 2 = 10$.

2. $\text{AVG(A)} = (1 + 3 + 1 + 1)/4 = 1.5$.

3. $\text{MIN(A)} = 1$.

4. $\text{MAX(B)} = 4$.

5. $\text{COUNT(A)} = 4$.

□

5.4.3 Grouping

Often we do not want simply the average or some other aggregation of an entire column. Rather, we need to consider the tuples of a relation in groups, corresponding to the value of one or more other columns, and we aggregate only within each group. As an example, suppose we wanted to compute the total number of minutes of movies produced by each studio, i.e., a relation such as:

studio	sumOfLengths
Disney	12345
MGM	54321
...	...

Starting with the relation

```
Movie(title, year, length, inColor, studioName, producerC#)
```

from our example database schema of Section 5.1, we must group the tuples according to their value for attribute `studioName`. We must then sum the `length` column within each group. That is, we imagine that the tuples of `Movie` are grouped as suggested in Fig. 5.17, and we apply the aggregation `SUM(length)` to each group independently.

studioName	
Disney	
Disney	
Disney	
MGM	
MGM	
○	
○	
○	

Figure 5.17: A relation with imaginary division into groups

5.4.4 The Grouping Operator

We shall now introduce an operator that allows us to group a relation and/or aggregate some columns. If there is grouping, then the aggregation is within groups.

The subscript used with the γ operator is a list L of elements, each of which is either:

a) An attribute of the relation R to which the γ is applied; this attribute is one of the attributes by which R will be grouped. This element is said to be a *grouping attribute*.

b) An aggregation operator applied to an attribute of the relation. To provide a name for the attribute corresponding to this aggregation in the result, an arrow and new name are appended to the aggregation. The underlying attribute is said to be an *aggregated attribute*.

The relation returned by the expression $\gamma_L(R)$ is constructed as follows:

1. Partition the tuples of R into *groups*. Each group consists of all tuples having one particular assignment of values to the grouping attributes in the list L. If there are no grouping attributes, the entire relation R is one group.

2. For each group, produce one tuple consisting of:

δ is a Special Case of γ

Technically, the δ operator is redundant. If $R(A_1, A_2, \ldots, A_n)$ is a relation, then $\delta(R)$ is equivalent to $\gamma_{A_1, A_2, \ldots, A_n}(R)$. That is, to eliminate duplicates, we group on all the attributes of the relation and do no aggregation. Then each group corresponds to a tuple that is found one or more times in R. Since the result of γ contains exactly one tuple from each group, the effect of this "grouping" is to eliminate duplicates. However, because δ is such a common and important operator, we shall continue to consider it separately when we study algebraic laws and algorithms for implementing the operators.

One can also see γ as an extension of the projection operator on sets. That is, $\gamma_{A_1, A_2, \ldots, A_n}(R)$ is also the same as $\pi_{A_1, A_2, \ldots, A_n}(R)$, if R is a set. However, if R is a bag, then γ eliminates duplicates while π does not. For this reason, γ is often referred to as *generalized projection*.

---

i. The grouping attributes' values for that group and

ii. The aggregations, over all tuples of that group, for the aggregated attributes on list L.

Example 5.23: Suppose we have the relation

```
StarsIn(title, year, starName)
```

and we wish to find, for each star who has appeared in at least three movies, the earliest year in which they appeared. The first step is to group, using `starName` as a grouping attribute. We clearly must compute for each group the `MIN(year)` aggregate. However, in order to decide which groups satisfy the condition that the star appears in at least three movies, we must also compute the `COUNT(title)` aggregate for each group. We begin with the grouping expression

$$\gamma_{starName, \texttt{MIN}(year) \to minYear, \texttt{COUNT}(title) \to ctTitle}(\texttt{StarsIn})$$

The first two columns of the result of this expression are needed for the query result. The third column is an auxiliary attribute, which we have named `ctTitle`; it is needed to determine whether a star has appeared in at least three movies. That is, we continue the algebraic expression for the query by selecting for `ctTitle >= 3` and then projecting onto the first two columns. An expression tree for the query is shown in Fig. 5.18. □

Figure 5.18: Algebraic expression tree for the SQL query of Example 5.23

5.4.5   Extending the Projection Operator

Let us reconsider the projection operator $\pi_L(R)$ introduced in Section 5.2.3.
In the classical relational algebra, L is a list of (some of the) attributes of R.
We extend the projection operator to allow it to compute with components
of tuples as well as choose components. In *extended projection*, also denoted
$\pi_L(R)$, projection lists can have the following kinds of elements:

1. A single attribute of R.

2. An expression $x \rightarrow y$, where x and y are names for attributes. The
   element $x \rightarrow y$ in the list L asks that we take the attribute x of R and
   rename it y; i.e., the name of this attribute in the schema of the result
   relation is y.

3. An expression $E \rightarrow z$, where E is an expression involving attributes of
   R, constants, arithmetic operators, and string operators, and z is a new
   name for the attribute that results from the calculation implied by E. For
   example, $a+b \rightarrow x$ as a list element represents the sum of the attributes a
   and b, renamed x. Element $c|\,|d \rightarrow e$ means concatenate the (presumably
   string-valued) attributes c and d and call the result e.

The result of the projection is computed by considering each tuple of R in
turn. We evaluate the list L by substituting the tuple's components for the
corresponding attributes mentioned in L and applying any operators indicated
by L to these values. The result is a relation whose schema is the names of the
attributes on list L, with whatever renaming the list specifies. Each tuple of
R yields one tuple of the result. Duplicate tuples in R surely yield duplicate
tuples in the result, but the result can have duplicates even if R does not.

Example 5.24: Let R be the relation

A	B	C
0	1	2
0	1	2
3	4	5

Then the result of $\pi_{A,B+C\rightarrow X}(R)$ is

A	X
0	3
0	3
3	9

The result's schema has two attributes. One is A, the first attribute of R, not renamed. The second is the sum of the second and third attributes of R, with the name X.

For another example, $\pi_{B-A\rightarrow X,C-B\rightarrow Y}(R)$ is

X	Y
1	1
1	1
1	1

Notice that the calculation required by this projection list happens to turn different tuples $(0,1,2)$ and $(3,4,5)$ into the same tuple $(1,1)$. Thus, the latter tuple appears three times in the result. $\square$

5.4.6 The Sorting Operator

There are several contexts in which we want to sort the tuples of a relation by one or more of its attributes. Often, when querying data, one wants the result relation to be sorted. For instance, in a query about all the movies in which Sean Connery appeared, we might wish to have the list sorted by title, so we could more easily find whether a certain movie was on the list. We shall also see in Section 15.4 how execution of queries by the DBMS is often made more efficient if we sort the relations first.

The expression $\tau_L(R)$, where R is a relation and L a list of some of R's attributes, is the relation R, but with the tuples of R sorted in the order indicated by L. If L is the list $A_1, A_2, \ldots, A_n$, then the tuples of R are sorted first by their value of attribute A_1. Ties are broken according to the value of A_2; tuples that agree on both A_1 and A_2 are ordered according to their value of A_3, and so on. Ties that remain after attribute A_n is considered may be ordered arbitrarily.

Example 5.25 : If R is a relation with schema $R(A, B, C)$, then $\tau_{C,B}(R)$ orders the tuples of R by their value of C, and tuples with the same C-value are ordered by their B value. Tuples that agree on both B and C may be ordered arbitrarily. $\square$

The operator τ is anomalous, in that it is the only operator in our relational algebra whose result is a list of tuples, rather than a set. Thus, in terms of expressing queries, it only makes sense to talk about τ as the final operator in an algebraic expression. If another operator of relational algebra is applied after τ, the result of the τ is treated as a set or bag, and no ordering of the tuples is implied.[4]

5.4.7 Outerjoins

A property of the join operator is that it is possible for certain tuples to be "dangling"; that is, they fail to match any tuple of the other relation in the common attributes. Dangling tuples do not have any trace in the result of the join, so the join may not represent the data of the original relations completely. In cases where this behavior is undesirable, a variation on the join, called "outerjoin," has been proposed and appears in various commercial systems.

We shall consider the "natural" case first, where the join is on equated values of all attributes in common to the two relations. The *outerjoin* $R \stackrel{\circ}{\bowtie} S$ is formed by starting with $R \bowtie S$, and adding any dangling tuples from R or S. The added tuples must be padded with a special *null* symbol, $\perp$, in all the attributes that they do not possess but that appear in the join result.[5]

Example 5.26 : In Fig. 5.19 we see two relations U and V. Tuple $(1, 2, 3)$ of U joins with both $(2, 3, 10)$ and $(2, 3, 11)$ of V, so these three tuples are not dangling. However, the other three tuples — $(4, 5, 6)$ and $(7, 8, 9)$ of U and $(6, 7, 12)$ of V — are dangling. That is, for none of these three tuples is there a tuple of the other relation that agrees with it on both the B and C components. Thus, in $U \stackrel{\circ}{\bowtie} V$, the three dangling tuples are padded with $\perp$ in the attributes that they do not have: attribute D for the tuples of U and attribute A for the tuple of V. □

There are many variants of the basic (natural) outerjoin idea. The *left outerjoin* $R \stackrel{\circ}{\bowtie}_L S$ is like the outerjoin, but only dangling tuples of the left argument R are padded with $\perp$ and added to the result. The *right outerjoin* $R \stackrel{\circ}{\bowtie}_R S$ is like the outerjoin, but only the dangling tuples of the right argument S are padded with $\perp$ and added to the result.

Example 5.27 : If U and V are as in Fig. 5.19, then $U \stackrel{\circ}{\bowtie}_L V$ is:

A	B	C	D
1	2	3	10
1	2	3	11
4	5	6	$\perp$
7	8	9	$\perp$

---

[4]However, as we shall see in Chapter 15, it sometimes speeds execution of the query if we sort intermediate results.

[5]When we study SQL, we shall find that the null symbol $\perp$ is written out, as NULL. You may use NULL in place of $\perp$ here if you wish.

A	B	C
1	2	3
4	5	6
7	8	9

Relation U

B	C	D
2	3	10
2	3	11
6	7	12

Relation V

A	B	C	D
1	2	3	10
1	2	3	11
4	5	6	$\perp$
7	8	9	$\perp$
$\perp$	6	7	12

Result $U \overset{\circ}{\bowtie} V$

Figure 5.19: Outerjoin of relations

and $U \overset{\circ}{\bowtie}_R V$ is:

A	B	C	D
1	2	3	10
1	2	3	11
$\perp$	6	7	12

□

   In addition, all three natural outerjoin operators have theta-join analogs, where first a theta-join is taken and then those tuples that failed to join with any tuple of the other relation, when the condition of the theta-join was applied, are padded with $\perp$ and added to the result. We use $\overset{\circ}{\underset{C}{\bowtie}}$ to denote a theta-outerjoin with condition C. This operator can also be modified with L or R to indicate left- or right-outerjoin.

Example 5.28: Let U and V be the relations of Fig. 5.19, and consider $U \overset{\circ}{\underset{A>V.C}{\bowtie}} V$. Tuples $(4, 5, 6)$ and $(7, 8, 9)$ of U each satisfy the condition with both of the tuples $(2, 3, 10)$ and $(2, 3, 11)$ of V. Thus, none of these four tuples are dangling in this theta-join. However, the two other tuples — $(1, 2, 3)$ of U and $(6, 7, 12)$ of V — are dangling. They thus appear, padded, in the result shown in Fig. 5.20. □

A	$U.B$	$U.C$	$V.B$	$V.C$	D
4	5	6	2	3	10
4	5	6	2	3	11
7	8	9	2	3	10
7	8	9	2	3	11
1	2	3	⊥	⊥	⊥
⊥	⊥	⊥	6	7	12

Figure 5.20: Result of a theta-outerjoin

5.4.8   Exercises for Section 5.4

Exercise 5.4.1: Here are two relations:

$$R(A, B): \{(0,1),\ (2,3),\ (0,1),\ (2,4),\ (3,4)\}$$

$$S(B, C): \{(0,1),\ (2,4),\ (2,5),\ (3,4),\ (0,2),\ (3,4)\}$$

Compute the following: *a) $\pi_{A+B, A^2, B^2}(R)$; b) $\pi_{B+1, C-1}(S)$; *c) $\tau_{B,A}(R)$; d) $\tau_{B,C}(S)$; *e) $\delta(R)$; f) $\delta(S)$; *g) $\gamma_{A,\ \text{SUM}(B)}(R)$; h) $\gamma_{B,\text{AVG}(C)}(S)$; ! i) $\gamma_A(R)$; ! j) $\gamma_{A,\text{MAX}(C)}(R \bowtie S)$; *k) $R \underset{L}{\overset{\circ}{\bowtie}} S$; l) $R \overset{\circ}{\bowtie}_R S$; m) $R \overset{\circ}{\bowtie} S$; n) $R \underset{R.B < S.B}{\overset{\circ}{\bowtie}} S$.

! **Exercise 5.4.2:** A unary operator f is said to be *idempotent* if for all relations R, $f(f(R)) = f(R)$. That is, applying f more than once is the same as applying it once. Which of the following operators are idempotent? Either explain why or give a counterexample.
      *a) δ; *b) π_L; c) σ_C; d) γ_L; e) τ.

*! **Exercise 5.4.3:** One thing that can be done with an extended projection, but not with the original version of projection that we defined in Section 5.2.3, is to duplicate columns. For example, if $R(A, B)$ is a relation, then $\pi_{A,A}(R)$ produces the tuple (a, a) for every tuple (a, b) in R. Can this operation be done using only the classical operations of relation algebra from Section 5.2? Explain your reasoning.

5.5 Constraints on Relations

Relational algebra provides a means to express common constraints, such as the referential integrity constraints introduced in Section 2.3. In fact, we shall see that relational algebra offers us convenient ways to express a wide variety of other constraints. Even functional dependencies can be expressed in relational algebra, as we shall see in Example 5.31. Constraints are quite important in database programming, and we shall cover in Chapter 7 how SQL database systems can enforce the same sorts of constraints as we can express in relational algebra.

5.5.1 Relational Algebra as a Constraint Language

There are two ways in which we can use expressions of relational algebra to express constraints.

1. If R is an expression of relational algebra, then $R = \emptyset$ is a constraint that says "The value of R must be empty," or equivalently "There are no tuples in the result of R."

2. If R and S are expressions of relational algebra, then $R \subseteq S$ is a constraint that says "Every tuple in the result of R must also be in the result of S." Of course the result of S may contain additional tuples not produced by R.

These ways of expressing constraints are actually equivalent in what they can express, but sometimes one or the other is clearer or more succinct. That is, the constraint $R \subseteq S$ could just as well have been written $R - S = \emptyset$. To see why, notice that if every tuple in R is also in S, then surely $R - S$ is empty. Conversely, if $R - S$ contains no tuples, then every tuple in R must be in S (or else it would be in $R - S$).

On the other hand, a constraint of the first form, $R = \emptyset$, could just as well have been written $R \subseteq \emptyset$. Technically, $\emptyset$ is not an expression of relational algebra, but since there are expressions that evaluate to $\emptyset$, such as $R - R$, there is no harm in using $\emptyset$ as a relational-algebra expression. Note that these equivalences hold even if R and S are bags, provided we make the conventional interpretation of $R \subseteq S$: each tuple t appears in S at least as many times as it appears in R.

In the following sections, we shall see how to express significant constraints in one of these two styles. As we shall see in Chapter 7, it is the first style — equal-to-the-emptyset — that is most commonly used in SQL programming. However, as shown above, we are free to think in terms of set-containment if we wish and later convert our constraint to the equal-to-the-emptyset style.

5.5.2 Referential Integrity Constraints

A common kind of constraint, called "referential integrity" in Section 2.3, asserts that a value appearing in one context also appears in another, related context. We saw referential integrity as a matter of relationships "making sense." That is, if an object or entity A is related to object or entity B, then B must really exist. For example, in ODL terms, if a relationship in object A is represented physically by a pointer, then referential integrity of this relationship asserts that the pointer must not be null and must point to a genuine object.

In the relational model, referential integrity constraints look somewhat different. If we have a value v in a tuple of one relation R, then because of our design intentions we may expect that v will appear in a particular component of some tuple of another relation S. An example will illustrate how referential integrity in the relational model can be expressed in relational algebra.

Example 5.29: Let us think of our running movie database schema, particularly the two relations

```
Movie(title, year, length, inColor, studioName, producerC#)
MovieExec(name, address, cert#, netWorth)
```

We might reasonably assume that the producer of every movie would have to appear in the `MovieExec` relation. If not, there is something wrong, and we would at least want a system implementing a relational database to inform us that we had a movie with a producer of which the system had no knowledge.

To be more precise, the `producerC#` component of each `Movie` tuple must also appear in the `cert#` component of some `MovieExec` tuple. Since executives are uniquely identified by their certificate numbers, we would thus be assured that the movie's producer is found among the movie executives. We can express this constraint by the set-containment

$$\pi_{producerC\#}(\texttt{Movie}) \subseteq \pi_{cert\#}(\texttt{MovieExec})$$

The value of the expression on the left is the set of all certificate numbers appearing in `producerC#` components of `Movie` tuples. Likewise, the expression on the right's value is the set of all certificates in the `cert#` component of `MovieExec` tuples. Our constraint says that every certificate in the former set must also be in the latter set.

Incidentally, we could express the same constraint as an equality to the emptyset:

$$\pi_{producerC\#}(\texttt{Movie}) - \pi_{cert\#}(\texttt{MovieExec}) = \emptyset$$

□

Example 5.30: We can similarly express a referential integrity constraint where the "value" involved is represented by more than one attribute. For instance, we may want to assert that any movie mentioned in the relation

> ```
> StarsIn(movieTitle, movieYear, starName)
> ```

also appears in the relation

> ```
> Movie(title, year, length, inColor, studioName, producerC#)
> ```

Movies are represented in both relations by title-year pairs, because we agreed that one of these attributes alone was not sufficient to identify a movie. The constraint

$$\pi_{movieTitle,\ movieYear}(\text{StarsIn}) \subseteq \pi_{title,\ year}(\text{Movie})$$

expresses this referential integrity constraint by comparing the title-year pairs produced by projecting both relations onto the appropriate lists of components. □

5.5.3 Additional Constraint Examples

The same constraint notation allows us to express far more than referential integrity. For example, we can express any functional dependency as an algebraic constraint, although the notation is more cumbersome than the FD notation introduced in Section 3.4.

Example 5.31 : Let us express the FD:

$$\text{name} \rightarrow \text{address}$$

for the relation

> ```
> MovieStar(name, address, gender, birthdate)
> ```

as an algebraic constraint. The idea is that if we construct all pairs of `MovieStar` tuples (t_1, t_2), we must not find a pair that agree in the `name` component and disagree in the `address` component. To construct the pairs we use a Cartesian product, and to search for pairs that violate the FD we use a selection. We then assert the constraint by equating the result to ∅.

To begin, since we are taking the product of a relation with itself, we need to rename at least one copy, in order to have names for the attributes of the product. For succinctness, let us use two new names, MS1 and MS2, to refer to the `MovieStar` relation. Then the FD can be expressed by the algebraic constraint:

$$\sigma_{MS1.name=MS2.name\ \text{AND}\ MS1.address \neq MS2.address}(\text{MS1} \times \text{MS2}) = \emptyset$$

In the above, MS1 in the product MS1 × MS2 is shorthand for the renaming:

$$\rho_{MS1(name,address,gender,birthdate)}(\text{MovieStar})$$

and MS2 is a similar renaming of MovieStar. □

Some domain constraints can also be expressed in relational algebra. Often, a domain constraint simply requires that values for an attribute have a specific data type, such as integer or character string of length 30, so we may associate that domain with the attribute. However, often a domain constraint involves specific values that we require for an attribute. If the set of acceptable values can be expressed in the language of selection conditions, then this domain constraint can be expressed in the algebraic constraint language.

Example 5.32 : Suppose we wish to specify that the only legal values for the gender attribute of MovieStar are 'F' and 'M'. We can express this constraint algebraically by:

$$\sigma_{gender\neq 'F' \text{ AND } gender\neq 'M'}(\text{MovieStar}) = \emptyset$$

That is, the set of tuples in MovieStar whose gender component is equal to neither 'F' nor 'M' is empty. □

Finally, there are some constraints that fall into none of the categories outlined in Section 2.3, nor are they functional or multivalued dependencies. The algebraic constraint language lets us express many new kinds of constraints. We offer one example here.

Example 5.33 : Suppose we wish to require that one must have a net worth of at least \$10,000,000 to be the president of a movie studio. This constraint cannot be classified as a domain, single-value, or referential integrity constraint. Yet we can express it algebraically as follows. First, we need to theta-join the two relations

    MovieExec(name, address, cert#, netWorth)
    Studio(name, address, presC#)

using the condition that presC# from Studio and cert# from MovieExec are equal. That join combines pairs of tuples consisting of a studio and an executive, such that the executive is the president of the studio. If we select from this relation those tuples where the net worth is less than ten million, we have a set that, according to our constraint, must be empty. Thus, we may express the constraint as:

$$\sigma_{netWorth<10000000}(\text{Studio} \underset{presC\#=cert\#}{\bowtie} \text{MovieExec}) = \emptyset$$

An alternative way to express the same constraint is to compare the set of certificates that represent studio presidents with the set of certificates that represent executives with a net worth of at least \$10,000,000; the former must be a subset of the latter. The containment

$$\pi_{presC\#}(\text{Studio}) \subseteq \pi_{cert\#}\Big(\sigma_{netWorth\geq 10000000}(\text{MovieExec})\Big)$$

expresses the above idea. □

5.5.4 Exercises for Section 5.5

Exercise 5.5.1: Express the following constraints about the relations of Exercise 5.2.1, reproduced here:

```
Product(maker, model, type)
PC(model, speed, ram, hd, rd, price)
Laptop(model, speed, ram, hd, screen, price)
Printer(model, color, type, price)
```

You may write your constraints either as containments or by equating an expression to the empty set. For the data of Exercise 5.2.1, indicate any violations to your constraints.

* a) A PC with a processor speed less than 1000 must not sell for more than $1500.

  b) A laptop with a screen size less than 14 inches must have at least a 10 gigabyte hard disk or sell for less than $2000.

! c) No manufacturer of PC's may also make laptops.

*!! d) A manufacturer of a PC must also make a laptop with at least as great a processor speed.

! e) If a laptop has a larger main memory than a PC, then the laptop must also have a higher price than the PC.

Exercise 5.5.2: Express the following constraints in relational algebra. The constraints are based on the relations of Exercise 5.2.4:

```
Classes(class, type, country, numGuns, bore, displacement)
Ships(name, class, launched)
Battles(name, date)
Outcomes(ship, battle, result)
```

You may write your constraints either as containments or by equating an expression to the empty set. For the data of Exercise 5.2.4, indicate any violations to your constraints.

  a) No class of ships may have guns with larger than 16-inch bore.

  b) If a class of ships has more than 9 guns, then their bore must be no larger than 14 inches.

! c) No class may have more than 2 ships.

! d) No country may have both battleships and battlecruisers.

!! e) No ship with more than 9 guns may be in a battle with a ship having fewer than 9 guns that was sunk.

! **Exercise 5.5.3:** Suppose R and S are two relations. Let C be the referential integrity constraint that says: whenever R has a tuple with some values $v_1, v_2, \ldots, v_n$ in particular attributes $A_1, A_2, \ldots, A_n$, there must be a tuple of S that has the same values $v_1, v_2, \ldots, v_n$ in particular attributes $B_1, B_2, \ldots, B_n$. Show how to express constraint C in relational algebra.

! **Exercise 5.5.4:** Let R be a relation, and suppose $A_1 A_2 \cdots A_n \rightarrow B$ is a FD involving the attributes of R. Write in relational algebra the constraint that says this FD must hold in R.

!! **Exercise 5.5.5:** Let R be a relation, and suppose

$$A_1 A_2 \cdots A_n \twoheadrightarrow B_1 B_2 \cdots B_m$$

is a MVD involving the attributes of R. Write in relational algebra the constraint that says this MVD must hold in R.

5.6   Summary of Chapter 5

✦ *Classical Relational Algebra*: This algebra underlies most query languages for the relational model. Its principal operators are union, intersection, difference, selection, projection, Cartesian product, natural join, theta-join, and renaming.

✦ *Selection and Projection*: The selection operator produces a result consisting of all tuples of the argument relation that satisfy the selection condition. Projection removes undesired columns from the argument relation to produce the result.

✦ *Joins*: We join two relations by comparing tuples, one from each relation. In a natural join, we splice together those pairs of tuples that agree on all attributes common to the two relations. In a theta-join, pairs of tuples are concatenated if they meet a selection condition associated with the theta-join.

✦ *Relations as Bags*: In commercial database systems, relations are actually bags, in which the same tuple is allowed to appear several times. The operations of relational algebra on sets can be extended to bags, but there are some algebraic laws that fail to hold.

✦ *Extensions to Relational Algebra*: To match the capabilities of SQL or other query languages, some operators not present in the classical relational algebra are needed. Sorting of a relation is an example, as is an extended projection, where computation on columns of a relation is supported. Grouping, aggregation, and outerjoins are also needed.

✦ *Grouping and Aggregation*: Aggregations summarize a column of a relation. Typical aggregation operators are sum, average, count, minimum, and maximum. The grouping operator allows us to partition the tuples of a relation according to their value(s) in one or more attributes before computing aggregation(s) for each group.

✦ *Outerjoins*: The outerjoin of two relations starts with a join of those relations. Then, dangling tuples (those that failed to join with any tuple) from either relation are padded with null values for the attributes belonging only to the other relation, and the padded tuples are included in the result.

✦ *Constraints in Relational Algebra*: Many common kinds of constraints can be expressed as the containment of one relational algebra expression in another, or as the equality of a relational algebra expression to the empty set. These constraints include functional dependencies and referential-integrity constraints, for example.

5.7 References for Chapter 5

Relational algebra was another contribution of the fundamental paper [1] on the relational model. Extension of projection to include grouping and aggregation are from [2]. The original paper on the use of queries to express constraints is [3].

1. Codd, E. F., "A relational model for large shared data banks," *Comm. ACM* **13**:6, pp. 377–387, 1970.

2. A. Gupta, V. Harinarayan, and D. Quass, "Aggregate-query processing in data warehousing environments," *Proc. Intl. Conf. on Very Large Databases* (1995), pp. 358–369.

3. Nicolas, J.-M., "Logic for improving integrity checking in relational databases," *Acta Informatica* **18**:3, pp. 227–253, 1982.

Chapter 6

The Database Language SQL

The most commonly used relational DBMS's query and modify the database through a language called SQL (sometimes pronounced "sequel"). SQL stands for "Structured Query Language." The portion of SQL that supports queries has capabilities very close to that of relational algebra, as extended in Section 5.4. However, SQL also includes statements for modifying the database (e.g., inserting and deleting tuples from relations) and for declaring a database schema. Thus, SQL serves as both a data-manipulation language and as a data-definition language. SQL also standardizes many other database commands, covered in Chapters 7 and 8.

There are many different dialects of SQL. First, there are three major standards. There is ANSI (American National Standards Institute) SQL and an updated standard adopted in 1992, called SQL-92 or SQL2. The recent SQL-99 (previously referred to as SQL3) standard extends SQL2 with object-relational features and a number of other new capabilities. Then, there are versions of SQL produced by the principal DBMS vendors. These all include the capabilities of the original ANSI standard. They also conform to a large extent to the more recent SQL2, although each has its variations and extensions beyond SQL2, including some of the features in the SQL-99 standard.

In this and the next two chapters we shall emphasize the use of SQL as a query language. This chapter focuses on the generic (or "ad-hoc") query interface for SQL. That is, we consider SQL as a stand-alone query language, where we sit at a terminal and ask queries about a database or request database modifications, such as insertion of new tuples into a relation. Query answers are displayed for us at our terminal.

The next chapter discusses constraints and triggers, as another way of exerting user control over the content of the database. Chapter 8 covers database-related programming in conventional programming languages. Our discussion of SQL in this and the next two chapters will conform to the SQL-99 standard, emphasizing features found in almost all commercial systems as well as the earlier standards.

The intent of this chapter and the following two chapters is to provide the reader with a sense of what SQL is about, more at the level of a "tutorial" than a "manual." Thus, we focus on the most commonly used features only. The references mention places where more of the details of the language and its dialects can be found.

6.1 Simple Queries in SQL

Perhaps the simplest form of query in SQL asks for those tuples of some one relation that satisfy a condition. Such a query is analogous to a selection in relational algebra. This simple query, like almost all SQL queries, uses the three keywords, SELECT, FROM, and WHERE that characterize SQL.

```
Movie(title, year, length, inColor, studioName, producerC#)
StarsIn(movieTitle, movieYear, starName)
MovieStar(name, address, gender, birthdate)
MovieExec(name, address, cert#, netWorth)
Studio(name, address, presC#)
```

Figure 6.1: Example database schema, repeated

Example 6.1: In this and subsequent examples, we shall use the database schema described in Section 5.1. To review, these relation schemas are the ones shown in Fig. 6.1. We shall see in Section 6.6 how to express schema information in SQL, but for the moment, assume that each of the relations and domains (data types) mentioned in Section 5.1 apply to their SQL counterparts.

As our first query, let us ask about the relation

```
Movie(title, year, length, inColor, studioName, producerC#)
```

for all movies produced by Disney Studios in 1990. In SQL, we say

```
SELECT *
FROM Movie
WHERE studioName = 'Disney' AND year = 1990;
```

This query exhibits the characteristic select-from-where form of most SQL queries.

- The FROM clause gives the relation or relations to which the query refers. In our example, the query is about the relation Movie.

A Trick for Reading and Writing Queries

It is generally easist to examine a select-from-where query by first looking at the FROM clause, to learn which relations are involved in the query. Then, move to the WHERE clause, to learn what it is about tuples that is important to the query. Finally, look at the SELECT clause to see what the output is. The same order — from, then where, then select — is often useful when writing queries of your own, as well.

- The WHERE clause is a condition, much like a selection-condition in relational algebra. Tuples must satisfy the condition in order to match the query. Here, the condition is that the studioName attribute of the tuple has the value 'Disney' and the year attribute of the tuple has the value 1990. All tuples meeting both stipulations satisfy the condition; other tuples do not.

- The SELECT clause tells which attributes of the tuples matching the condition are produced as part of the answer. The * in this example indicates that the entire tuple is produced. The result of the query is the relation consisting of all tuples produced by this process.

One way to interpret this query is to consider each tuple of the relation mentioned in the FROM clause. The condition in the WHERE clause is applied to the tuple. More precisely, any attributes mentioned in the WHERE clause are replaced by the value in the tuple's component for that attribute. The condition is then evaluated, and if true, the components appearing in the SELECT clause are produced as one tuple of the answer. Thus, the result of the query is the Movie tuples for those movies produced by Disney in 1990, for example, *Pretty Woman*.

In detail, when the SQL query processor encounters the Movie tuple

title	year	length	inColor	studioName	producerC#
Pretty Woman	1990	119	true	Disney	999

(here, 999 is the imaginary certificate number for the producer of the movie), the value 'Disney' is substituted for attribute studioName and value 1990 is substituted for attribute year in the condition of the WHERE clause, because these are the values for those attributes in the tuple in question. The WHERE clause thus becomes

```
WHERE 'Disney' = 'Disney' AND 1990 = 1990
```

Since this condition is evidently true, the tuple for *Pretty Woman* passes the test of the WHERE clause and the tuple becomes part of the result of the query. □

6.1.1 Projection in SQL

We can, if we wish, eliminate some of the components of the chosen tuples; that is, we can project the relation produced by an SQL query onto some of its attributes. In place of the * of the SELECT clause, we may list some of the attributes of the relation mentioned in the FROM clause. The result will be projected onto the attributes listed.[1]

Example 6.2 : Suppose we wish to modify the query of Example 6.1 to produce only the movie title and length. We may write

```
SELECT title, length
FROM Movie
WHERE studioName = 'Disney' AND year = 1990;
```

The result is a table with two columns, headed title and length. The tuples in this table are pairs, each consisting of a movie title and its length, such that the movie was produced by Disney in 1990. For instance, the relation schema and one of its tuples looks like:

title	length
Pretty Woman	119
...	...

□

Sometimes, we wish to produce a relation with column headers different from the attributes of the relation mentioned in the FROM clause. We may follow the name of the attribute by the keyword AS and an *alias*, which becomes the header in the result relation. Keyword AS is optional. That is, an alias can immediately follow what it stands for, without any intervening punctuation.

Example 6.3 : We can modify Example 6.2 to produce a relation with attributes name and duration in place of title and length as follows.

```
SELECT title AS name, length AS duration
FROM Movie
WHERE studioName = 'Disney' AND year = 1990;
```

The result is the same set of tuples as in Example 6.2, but with the columns headed by attributes name and duration. For example, the result relation might begin:

name	duration
Pretty Woman	119
...	...

---

[1]Thus, the keyword SELECT in SQL actually corresponds most closely to the projection operator of relational algebra, while the selection operator of the algebra corresponds to the WHERE clause of SQL queries.

□

Another option in the `SELECT` clause is to use an expression in place of an attribute. Put another way, the `SELECT` list can function like the lists in an extended projection, which we discussed in Section 5.4.5. We shall see in Section 6.4 that the `SELECT` list can also include aggregates as in the γ operator of Section 5.4.4.

Example 6.4: Suppose we wanted output as in Example 6.3, but with the length in hours. We might replace the `SELECT` clause of that example with

```
SELECT title AS name, length*0.016667 AS lengthInHours
```

Then the same movies would be produced, but lengths would be calculated in hours and the second column would be headed by attribute `lengthInHours`, as:

name	lengthInHours
Pretty Woman	1.98334
...	...

□

Example 6.5: We can even allow a constant as an expression in the `SELECT` clause. It might seem pointless to do so, but one application is to put some useful words into the output that SQL displays. The following query:

```
SELECT title, length*0.016667 AS length, 'hrs.' AS inHours
FROM Movie
WHERE studioName = 'Disney' AND year = 1990;
```

produces tuples such as

title	length	inHours
Pretty Woman	1.98334	hrs.
...	...	...

We have arranged that the third column is called `inHours`, which fits with the column header `length` in the second column. Every tuple in the answer will have the constant `hrs.` in the third column, which gives the illusion of being the units attached to the value in the second column.   □

6.1.2   Selection in SQL

The selection operator of relational algebra, and much more, is available through the `WHERE` clause of SQL. The expressions that may follow `WHERE` include conditional expressions like those found in common languages such as C or Java.

Case Insensitivity

SQL is *case insensitive*, meaning that it treats upper- and lower-case letters as the same letter. For example, although we have chosen to write keywords like FROM in capitals, it is equally proper to write this keyword as From or from, or even FrOm. Names of attributes, relations, aliases, and so on are similarly case insensitive. Only inside quotes does SQL make a distinction between upper- and lower-case letters. Thus, 'FROM' and 'from' are different character strings. Of course, neither is the keyword FROM.

We may build expressions by comparing values using the six common comparison operators: =, <>, <, >, <=, and >=. These operators have the same meanings as in C, but <> is the SQL symbol for "not equal to"; it corresponds to != in C.

The values that may be compared include constants and attributes of the relations mentioned after FROM. We may also apply the usual arithmetic operators, +, *, and so on, to numeric values before we compare them. For instance, $(year - 1930) * (year - 1930) < 100$ is true for those years within 9 of 1930. We may apply the concatenation operator || to strings; for example 'foo' || 'bar' has value 'foobar'.

An example comparison is

```
studioName = 'Disney'
```

in Example 6.1. The attribute studioName of the relation Movie is tested for equality against the constant 'Disney'. This constant is string-valued; strings in SQL are denoted by surrounding them with single quotes. Numeric constants, integers and reals, are also allowed, and SQL uses the common notations for reals such as -12.34 or 1.23E45.

The result of a comparison is a boolean value: either TRUE or FALSE.[2] Boolean values may be combined by the logical operators AND, OR, and NOT, with their expected meanings. For instance, we saw in Example 6.1 how two conditions could be combined by AND. The WHERE clause of this example evaluates to true if and only if both comparisons are satisfied; that is, the studio name is 'Disney' and the year is 1990. Here are some more examples of queries with complex WHERE clauses.

Example 6.6: The following query asks for all the movies made after 1970 that are in black-and-white.

```
SELECT title
```

---

[2] Well there's a bit more to boolean values; see Section 6.1.6.

SQL Queries and Relational Algebra

The simple SQL queries that we have seen so far all have the form:

$$\text{SELECT } L$$
$$\text{FROM } R$$
$$\text{WHERE } C$$

in which L is a list of expressions, R is a relation, and C is a condition. The meaning of any such expression is the same as that of the relational-algebra expression

$$\pi_L\big(\sigma_C(R)\big)$$

That is, we start with the relation in the FROM clause, apply to each tuple whatever condition is indicated in the WHERE clause, and then project onto the list of attributes and/or expressions in the SELECT clause.

```
FROM Movie
WHERE year > 1970 AND NOT inColor;
```

In this condition, we again have the AND of two booleans. The first is an ordinary comparison, but the second is the attribute inColor, negated. The use of this attribute by itself makes sense, because inColor is of type boolean.

Next, consider the query

```
SELECT title
FROM Movie
WHERE (year > 1970 OR length < 90) AND studioName = 'MGM';
```

This query asks for the titles of movies made by MGM Studios that either were made after 1970 or were less than 90 minutes long. Notice that comparisons can be grouped using parentheses. The parentheses are needed here because the precedence of logical operators in SQL is the same as in most other languages: AND takes precedence over OR, and NOT takes precedence over both. □

6.1.3 Comparison of Strings

Two strings are equal if they are the same sequence of characters. SQL allows declarations of different types of strings, for example fixed-length arrays of characters and variable-length lists of characters.[3] If so, we can expect reasonable

---

[3] At least the strings may be thought of as stored as an array or list, respectively. How they are actually stored is an implementation-dependent matter, not specified in any SQL standard.

Representing Bit Strings

A string of bits is represented by B followed by a quoted string of 0's and 1's. Thus, B'011' represents the string of three bits, the first of which is 0 and the other two of which are 1. Hexadecimal notation may also be used, where an X is followed by a quoted string of hexadecimal digits (0 through 9, and a through f, with the latter representing "digits" 10 through 15). For instance, X'7ff' represents a string of twelve bits, a 0 followed by eleven 1's. Note that each hexadecimal digit represents four bits, and leading 0's are not suppressed.

---

coercions among string types. For example, a string like foo might be stored as a fixed-length string of length 10, with 7 "pad" characters, or it could be stored as a variable-length string. We would expect values of both types to be equal to each other and also equal to the constant string 'foo'. More about physical storage of character strings appears in Section 12.1.3.

When we compare strings by one of the "less than" operators, such as < or >=, we are asking whether one precedes the other in lexicographic order (i.e., in dictionary order, or alphabetically). That is, if $a_1 a_2 \cdots a_n$ and $b_1 b_2 \cdots b_m$ are two strings, then the first is "less than" the second if either $a_1 < b_1$, or if $a_1 = b_1$ and $a_2 < b_2$, or if $a_1 = b_1$, $a_2 = b_2$, and $a_3 < b_3$, and so on. We also say $a_1 a_2 \cdots a_n < b_1 b_2 \cdots b_m$ if $n < m$ and $a_1 a_2 \cdots a_n = b_1 b_2 \cdots b_n$; that is, the first string is a proper prefix of the second. For instance, 'fodder' < 'foo', because the first two characters of each string are the same, fo, and the third character of fodder precedes the third character of foo. Also, 'bar' < 'bargain' because the former is a proper prefix of the latter. As with equality, we may expect reasonable coercion among different string types.

SQL also provides the capability to compare strings on the basis of a simple pattern match. An alternative form of comparison expression is

```
s LIKE p
```

where s is a string and p is a *pattern*, that is, a string with the optional use of the two special characters % and _. Ordinary characters in p match only themselves in s. But % in p can match any sequence of 0 or more characters in s, and _ in p matches any one character in s. The value of this expression is true if and only if string s matches pattern p. Similarly, s NOT LIKE p is true if and only if string s does not match pattern p.

Example 6.7: We remember a movie "Star something," and we remember that the something has four letters. What could this movie be? We can retrieve all such names with the query:

```
SELECT title
```

```
    FROM Movie
    WHERE title LIKE 'Star ____';
```

This query asks if the title attribute of a movie has a value that is nine characters long, the first five characters being `Star` and a blank. The last four characters may be anything, since any sequence of four characters matches the four _ symbols. The result of the query is the set of complete matching titles, such as *Star Wars* and *Star Trek*. □

Example 6.8: Let us search for all movies with a possessive ('s) in their titles. The desired query is

```
    SELECT title
    FROM Movie
    WHERE title LIKE '%''s%';
```

To understand this pattern, we must first observe that the apostrophe, being the character that surrounds strings in SQL, cannot also represent itself. The convention taken by SQL is that two consecutive apostrophes in a string represent a single apostrophe and do not end the string. Thus, `''s` in a pattern is matched by a single apostrophe followed by an `s`.

The two `%` characters on either side of the `'s` match any strings whatsoever. Thus, any title with `'s` as a substring will match the pattern, and the answer to this query will include films such as *Logan's Run* or *Alice's Restaurant*. □

6.1.4 Dates and Times

Implementations of SQL generally support dates and times as special data types. These values are often representable in a variety of formats such as `5/14/1948` or `14 May 1948`. Here we shall describe only the SQL standard notation, which is very specific about format.

A *date* constant is represented by the keyword `DATE` followed by a quoted string of a special form. For example, `DATE '1948-05-14'` follows the required form. The first four characters are digits representing the year. Then come a hyphen and two digits representing the month. Note that, as in our example, a one-digit month is padded with a leading 0. Finally there is another hyphen and two digits representing the day. As with months, we pad the day with a leading 0 if that is necessary to make a two-digit number.

A *time* constant is represented similarly by the keyword `TIME` and a quoted string. This string has two digits for the hour, on the military (24-hour) clock. Then come a colon, two digits for the minute, another colon, and two digits for the second. If fractions of a second are desired, we may continue with a decimal point and as many significant digits as we like. For instance, `TIME '15:00:02.5'` represents the time at which all students will have left a class that ends at 3 PM: two and a half seconds past three o'clock.

Escape Characters in LIKE expressions

What if the pattern we wish to use in a LIKE expression involves the characters % or _? Instead of having a particular character used as the escape character (e.g., the backslash in most UNIX commands), SQL allows us to specify any one character we like as the escape character for a single pattern. We do so by following the pattern by the keyword ESCAPE and the chosen escape character, in quotes. A character % or _ preceded by the escape character in the pattern is interpreted literally as that character, not as a symbol for any sequence of characters or any one character, respectively. For example,

s LIKE 'x%%x%' ESCAPE 'x'

makes x the escape character in the pattern x%%x%. The sequence x% is taken to be a single %. This pattern matches any string that begins and ends with the character %. Note that only the middle % has its "any string" interpretation.

Alternatively, time can be expressed as the number of hours and minutes ahead of (indicated by a plus sign) or behind (indicated by a minus sign) Greenwich Mean Time (GMT). For instance, TIME '12:00:00-8:00' represents noon in Pacific Standard Time, which is eight hours behind GMT.

To combine dates and times we use a value of type TIMESTAMP. These values consist of the keyword TIMESTAMP, a date value, a space, and a time value. Thus, TIMESTAMP '1948-05-14 12:00:00' represents noon on May 14, 1948.

We can compare dates or times using the same comparison operators we use for numbers or strings. That is, < on dates means that the first date is earlier than the second; < on times means that the first is earlier (within the same day) than the second.

6.1.5 Null Values and Comparisons Involving NULL

SQL allows attributes to have a special value NULL, which is called the *null value*. There are many different interpretations that can be put on null values. Here are some of the most common:

1. *Value unknown*: that is, "I know there is some value that belongs here but I don't know what it is." An unknown birthdate is an example.

2. *Value inapplicable*: "There is no value that makes sense here." For example, if we had a spouse attribute for the MovieStar relation, then an unmarried star might have NULL for that attribute, not because we don't know the spouse's name, but because there is none.

3. *Value withheld*: "We are not entitled to know the value that belongs here." For instance, an unlisted phone number might appear as NULL in the component for a `phone` attribute.

We saw in Section 5.4.7 how the use of an outerjoin operator produces null values in some components of tuples; SQL allows outerjoins and also produces NULL's when a query involves outerjoins; see Section 6.3.8. There are other ways SQL produces NULL's as well. For example, certain insertions of tuples create null values, as we shall see in Section 6.5.1.

In WHERE clauses, we must be prepared for the possibility that a component of some tuple we are examining will be NULL. There are two important rules to remember when we operate upon a NULL value.

1. When we operate on a NULL and any value, including another NULL, using an arithmetic operator like × or +, the result is NULL.

2. When we compare a NULL value and any value, including another NULL, using a comparison operator like = or >, the result is UNKNOWN. The value UNKNOWN is another truth-value, like TRUE and FALSE; we shall discuss how to manipulate truth-value UNKNOWN shortly.

However, we must remember that, although NULL is a value that can appear in tuples, it is *not* a constant. Thus, while the above rules apply when we try to operate on an expression whose value is NULL, we cannot use NULL explicitly as an operand.

Example 6.9: Let x have the value NULL. Then the value of $x + 3$ is also NULL. However, NULL + 3 is not a legal SQL expression. Similarly, the value of $x = 3$ is UNKNOWN, because we cannot tell if the value of x, which is NULL, equals the value 3. However, the comparison NULL = 3 is not correct SQL. $\square$

Incidentally, the correct way to ask if x has the value NULL is with the expression x IS NULL. This expression has the value TRUE if x has the value NULL and it has value FALSE otherwise. Similarly, x IS NOT NULL has the value TRUE unless the value of x is NULL.

6.1.6 The Truth-Value UNKNOWN

In Section 6.1.2 we assumed that the result of a comparison was either TRUE or FALSE, and these truth-values were combined in the obvious way using the logical operators AND, OR, and NOT. We have just seen that when NULL values occur, comparisons can yield a third truth-value: UNKNOWN. We must now learn how the logical operators behave on combinations of all three truth-values.

The rule is easy to remember if we think of TRUE as 1 (i.e., fully true), FALSE as 0 (i.e., not at all true), and UNKNOWN as 1/2 (i.e., somewhere between true and false). Then:

Pitfalls Regarding Nulls

It is tempting to assume that NULL in SQL can always be taken to mean "a value that we don't know but that surely exists." However, there are several ways that intuition is violated. For instance, suppose x is a component of some tuple, and the domain for that component is the integers. We might reason that $0 * x$ surely has the value 0, since no matter what integer x is, its product with 0 is 0. However, if x has the value NULL, rule (1) of Section 6.1.5 applies; the product of 0 and NULL is NULL. Similarly, we might reason that $x - x$ has the value 0, since whatever integer x is, its difference with itself is 0. However, again rule (1) applies and the result is NULL.

---

1. The AND of two truth-values is the minimum of those values. That is, x AND y is FALSE if either x or y is FALSE; it is UNKNOWN if neither is FALSE but at least one is UNKNOWN, and it is TRUE only when both x and y are TRUE.

2. The OR of two truth-values is the maximum of those values. That is, x OR y is TRUE if either x or y is TRUE; it is UNKNOWN if neither is TRUE but at least one is UNKNOWN, and it is FALSE only when both are FALSE.

3. The negation of truth-value v is $1 - v$. That is, NOT x has the value TRUE when x is FALSE, the value FALSE when x is TRUE, and the value UNKNOWN when x has value UNKNOWN.

In Fig. 6.2 is a summary of the result of applying the three logical operators to the nine different combinations of truth-values for operands x and y. The value of the last operator, NOT, depends only on x.

x	y	x AND y	x OR y	NOT x
TRUE	TRUE	TRUE	TRUE	FALSE
TRUE	UNKNOWN	UNKNOWN	TRUE	FALSE
TRUE	FALSE	FALSE	TRUE	FALSE
UNKNOWN	TRUE	UNKNOWN	TRUE	UNKNOWN
UNKNOWN	UNKNOWN	UNKNOWN	UNKNOWN	UNKNOWN
UNKNOWN	FALSE	FALSE	UNKNOWN	UNKNOWN
FALSE	TRUE	FALSE	TRUE	TRUE
FALSE	UNKNOWN	FALSE	UNKNOWN	TRUE
FALSE	FALSE	FALSE	FALSE	TRUE

Figure 6.2: Truth table for three-valued logic

SQL conditions, as appear in WHERE clauses of select-from-where statements, apply to each tuple in some relation, and for each tuple, one of the three truth values, TRUE, FALSE, or UNKNOWN is produced. However, only the tuples for which the condition has the value TRUE become part of the answer; tuples with either UNKNOWN or FALSE as value are excluded from the answer. That situation leads to another surprising behavior similar to that discussed in the box on "Pitfalls Regarding Nulls," as the next example illustrates.

Example 6.10 : Suppose we ask about our running-example relation

```
Movie(title, year, length, inColor, studioName, producerC#)
```

the following query:

```
SELECT *
FROM Movie
WHERE length <= 120 OR length > 120;
```

Intuitively, we would expect to get a copy of the Movie relation, since each movie has a length that is either 120 or less or that is greater than 120.

However, suppose there are Movie tuples with NULL in the length component. Then both comparisons length <= 120 and length > 120 evaluate to UNKNOWN. The OR of two UNKNOWN's is UNKNOWN, by Fig. 6.2. Thus, for any tuple with a NULL in the length component, the WHERE clause evaluates to UNKNOWN. Such a tuple is *not* returned as part of the answer to the query. As a result, the true meaning of the query is "find all the Movie tuples with non-NULL lengths." □

6.1.7 Ordering the Output

We may ask that the tuples produced by a query be presented in sorted order. The order may be based on the value of any attribute, with ties broken by the value of a second attribute, remaining ties broken by a third, and so on, as in the τ operation of Section 5.4.6. To get output in sorted order, we add to the select-from-where statement a clause:

```
ORDER BY <list of attributes>
```

The order is by default ascending, but we can get the output highest-first by appending the keyword DESC (for "descending") to an attribute. Similarly, we can specify ascending order with the keyword ASC, but that word is unnecessary.

Example 6.11 : The following is a rewrite of our original query of Example 6.1, asking for the Disney movies of 1990 from the relation

```
Movie(title, year, length, inColor, studioName, producerC#)
```

To get the movies listed by length, shortest first, and among movies of equal length, alphabetically, we can say:

```
SELECT *
FROM Movie
WHERE studioName = 'Disney' AND year = 1990
ORDER BY length, title;
```

□

6.1.8   Exercises for Section 6.1

* **Exercise 6.1.1:** If a query has a SELECT clause

```
SELECT A B
```

how do we know whether A and B are two different attributes or B is an alias of A?

Exercise 6.1.2: Write the following queries, based on our running movie database example

```
Movie(title, year, length, inColor, studioName, producerC#)
StarsIn(movieTitle, movieYear, starName)
MovieStar(name, address, gender, birthdate)
MovieExec(name, address, cert#, netWorth)
Studio(name, address, presC#)
```

in SQL.

* a) Find the address of MGM studios.

  b) Find Sandra Bullock's birthdate.

* c) Find all the stars that appeared either in a movie made in 1980 or a movie with "Love" in the title.

  d) Find all executives worth at least $10,000,000.

  e) Find all the stars who either are male or live in Malibu (have string Malibu as a part of their address).

Exercise 6.1.3: Write the following queries in SQL. They refer to the database schema of Exercise 5.2.1:

```
Product(maker, model, type)
PC(model, speed, ram, hd, rd, price)
Laptop(model, speed, ram, hd, screen, price)
Printer(model, color, type, price)
```

Show the result of your queries using the data from Exercise 5.2.1.

* a) Find the model number, speed, and hard-disk size for all PC's whose price is under $1200.

* b) Do the same as (a), but rename the speed column megahertz and the hd column gigabytes.

  c) Find the manufacturers of printers.

  d) Find the model number, memory size, and screen size for laptops costing more than $2000.

* e) Find all the tuples in the Printer relation for color printers. Remember that color is a boolean-valued attribute.

  f) Find the model number, speed, and hard-disk size for those PC's that have either a 12x or 16x DVD and a price less than $2000. You may regard the rd attribute as having a string type.

Exercise 6.1.4: Write the following queries based on the database schema of Exercise 5.2.4:

```
Classes(class, type, country, numGuns, bore, displacement)
Ships(name, class, launched)
Battles(name, date)
Outcomes(ship, battle, result)
```

and show the result of your query on the data of Exercise 5.2.4.

  a) Find the class name and country for all classes with at least 10 guns.

  b) Find the names of all ships launched prior to 1918, but call the resulting column shipName.

  c) Find the names of ships sunk in battle and the name of the battle in which they were sunk.

  d) Find all ships that have the same name as their class.

  e) Find the names of all ships that begin with the letter "R."

! f) Find the names of all ships whose name consists of three or more words (e.g., King George V).

Exercise 6.1.5: Let a and b be integer-valued attributes that may be NULL in some tuples. For each of the following conditions (as may appear in a WHERE clause), describe exactly the set of (a, b) tuples that satisfy the condition, including the case where a and/or b is NULL.

* a) a = 10 OR b = 20

  b) a = 10 AND b = 20

  c) a < 10 OR a >= 10

*! d) a = b

 ! e) a <= b

! **Exercise 6.1.6:** In Example 6.10 we discussed the query

```
SELECT *
FROM Movie
WHERE length <= 120 OR length > 120;
```

which behaves unintuitively when the length of a movie is NULL. Find a simpler, equivalent query, one with a single condition in the WHERE clause (no AND or OR of conditions).

6.2   Queries Involving More Than One Relation

Much of the power of relational algebra comes from its ability to combine two or more relations through joins, products, unions, intersections, and differences. We get all of these operations in SQL. The set-theoretic operations — union, intersection, and difference — appear directly in SQL, as we shall learn in Section 6.2.5. First, we shall learn how the select-from-where statement of SQL allows us to perform products and joins.

6.2.1   Products and Joins in SQL

SQL has a simple way to couple relations in one query: list each relation in the FROM clause. Then, the SELECT and WHERE clauses can refer to the attributes of any of the relations in the FROM clause.

Example 6.12: Suppose we want to know the name of the producer of *Star Wars*. To answer this question we need the following two relations from our running example:

```
Movie(title, year, length, inColor, studioName, producerC#)
MovieExec(name, address, cert#, netWorth)
```

The producer certificate number is given in the Movie relation, so we can do a simple query on Movie to get this number. We could then do a second query on the relation MovieExec to find the name of the person with that certificate number.

However, we can phrase both these steps as one query about the pair of relations Movie and MovieExec as follows:

```
SELECT name
FROM Movie, MovieExec
WHERE title = 'Star Wars' AND producerC# = cert#;
```

This query asks us to consider all pairs of tuples, one from `Movie` and the other from `MovieExec`. The conditions on this pair are stated in the `WHERE` clause:

1. The `title` component of the tuple from `Movie` must have value `'Star Wars'`.

2. The `producerC#` attribute of the `Movie` tuple must be the same certificate number as the `cert#` attribute in the `MovieExec` tuple. That is, these two tuples must refer to the same producer.

Whenever we find a pair of tuples satisfying both conditions, we produce the `name` attribute of the tuple from `MovieExec` as part of the answer. If the data is what we expect, the only time both conditions will be met is when the tuple from `Movie` is for *Star Wars*, and the tuple from `MovieExec` is for George Lucas. Then and only then will the title be correct and the certificate numbers agree. Thus, `George Lucas` should be the only value produced. This process is suggested in Fig. 6.3. We take up in more detail how to interpret multirelation queries in Section 6.2.4. □

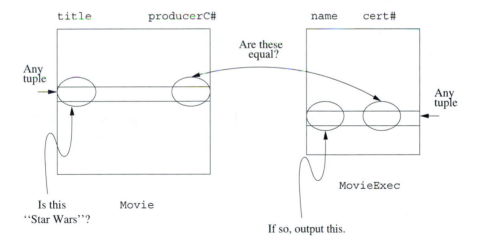

Figure 6.3: The query of Example 6.12 asks us to pair every tuple of `Movie` with every tuple of `MovieExec` and test two conditions

6.2.2 Disambiguating Attributes

Sometimes we ask a query involving several relations, and among these relations are two or more attributes with the same name. If so, we need a way to indicate

which of these attributes is meant by a use of their shared name. SQL solves
this problem by allowing us to place a relation name and a dot in front of an
attribute. Thus $R.A$ refers to the attribute A of relation R.

Example 6.13: The two relations

```
MovieStar(name, address, gender, birthdate)
MovieExec(name, address, cert#, netWorth)
```

each have attributes `name` and `address`. Suppose we wish to find pairs consisting of a star and an executive with the same address. The following query does
the job.

```
SELECT MovieStar.name, MovieExec.name
FROM MovieStar, MovieExec
WHERE MovieStar.address = MovieExec.address;
```

In this query, we look for a pair of tuples, one from `MovieStar` and the other
from `MovieExec`, such that their address components agree. The `WHERE` clause
enforces the requirement that the `address` attributes from each of the two
tuples agree. Then, for each matching pair of tuples, we extract the two `name`
attributes, first from the `MovieStar` tuple and then from the other. The result
would be a set of pairs such as

MovieStar.name	*MovieExec.name*
Jane Fonda	Ted Turner
. . .	. . .

□

The relation name, followed by a dot, is permissible even in situations where
there is no ambiguity. For instance, we are free to write the query of Example
6.12 as

```
SELECT MovieExec.name
FROM Movie, MovieExec
WHERE Movie.title = 'Star Wars'
      AND Movie.producerC# = MovieExec.cert#;
```

Alternatively, we may use relation names and dots in front of any subset of the
attributes in this query.

6.2.3 Tuple Variables

Disambiguating attributes by prefixing the relation name works as long as the
query involves combining several different relations. However, sometimes we
need to ask a query that involves two or more tuples from the same relation.

Tuple Variables and Relation Names

Technically, references to attributes in SELECT and WHERE clauses are *always* to a tuple variable. However, if a relation appears only once in the FROM clause, then we can use the relation name as its own tuple variable. Thus, we can see a relation name R in the FROM clause as shorthand for R AS R. Furthermore, as we have seen, when an attribute belongs unambiguously to one relation, the relation name (tuple variable) may be omitted.

We may list a relation R as many times as we need to in the FROM clause, but we need a way to refer to each occurrence of R. SQL allows us to define, for each occurrence of R in the FROM clause, an "alias" which we shall refer to as a *tuple variable*. Each use of R in the FROM clause is followed by the (optional) keyword AS and the name of the tuple variable; we shall generally omit the AS in this context.

In the SELECT and WHERE clauses, we can disambiguate attributes of R by preceding them by the appropriate tuple variable and a dot. Thus, the tuple variable serves as another name for relation R and can be used in its place when we wish.

Example 6.14: While Example 6.13 asked for a star and an executive sharing an address, we might similarly want to know about two stars who share an address. The query is essentially the same, but now we must think of two tuples chosen from relation MovieStar, rather than tuples from each of MovieStar and MovieExec. Using tuple variables as aliases for two uses of MovieStar, we can write the query as

```
SELECT Star1.name, Star2.name
FROM MovieStar Star1, MovieStar Star2
WHERE Star1.address = Star2.address
      AND Star1.name < Star2.name;
```

We see in the FROM clause the declaration of two tuple variables, Star1 and Star2; each is an alias for relation MovieStar. The tuple variables are used in the SELECT clause to refer to the **name** components of the two tuples. These aliases are also used in the WHERE clause to say that the two MovieStar tuples represented by Star1 and Star2 have the same value in their **address** components.

The second condition in the WHERE clause, Star1.name < Star2.name, says that the name of the first star precedes the name of the second star alphabetically. If this condition were omitted, then tuple variables Star1 and Star2 could both refer to the same tuple. We would find that the two tuple variables referred to tuples whose **address** components are equal, of course, and thus produce each star name paired with itself.[4] The second condition also forces us to produce each pair of stars with a common address only once, in alphabetical order. If we used <> (not-equal) as the comparison operator, then we would produce pairs of married stars twice, like

Star1.name	*Star2.name*
Alec Baldwin	Kim Basinger
Kim Basinger	Alec Baldwin
. . .	. . .

□

6.2.4 Interpreting Multirelation Queries

There are several ways to define the meaning of the select-from-where expressions that we have just covered. All are *equivalent*, in the sense that they each give the same answer for each query applied to the same relation instances. We shall consider each in turn.

Nested Loops

The semantics that we have implicitly used in examples so far is that of tuple variables. Recall that a tuple variable ranges over all tuples of the corresponding relation. A relation name that is not aliased is also a tuple variable ranging over the relation itself, as we mentioned in the box on "Tuple Variables and Relation Names." If there are several tuple variables, we may imagine nested loops, one for each tuple variable, in which the variables each range over the tuples of their respective relations. For each assignment of tuples to the tuple variables, we decide whether the WHERE clause is true. If so, we produce a tuple consisting of the values of the expressions following SELECT; note that each term is given a value by the current assignment of tuples to tuple variables. This query-answering algorithm is suggested by Fig. 6.4.

Parallel Assignment

There is an equivalent definition in which we do not explicitly create nested loops ranging over the tuple variables. Rather, we consider in arbitrary order, or in parallel, all possible assignments of tuples from the appropriate relations to the tuple variables. For each such assignment, we consider whether the WHERE clause becomes true. Each assignment that produces a true WHERE clause contributes a tuple to the answer; that tuple is constructed from the attributes of the SELECT clause, evaluated according to that assignment.

---

[4]A similar problem occurs in Example 6.13 when the same individual is both a star and an executive. We could solve that problem by requiring that the two names be unequal.

```
LET the tuple variables in the from-clause range over
        relations R₁, R₂, ..., Rₙ;
FOR each tuple t₁ in relation R₁ DO
    FOR each tuple t₂ in relation R₂ DO
        ...
            FOR each tuple tₙ in relation Rₙ DO
                IF the where-clause is satisfied when the values
                from t₁, t₂, ..., tₙ are substituted for all
                attribute references THEN
                    evaluate the expressions of the select-clause
                    according to t₁, t₂, ..., tₙ and produce the
                    tuple of values that results.
```

Figure 6.4: Answering a simple SQL query

Conversion to Relational Algebra

A third approach is to relate the SQL query to relational algebra. We start with the tuple variables in the FROM clause and take the Cartesian product of their relations. If two tuple variables refer to the same relation, then this relation appears twice in the product, and we rename its attributes so all attributes have unique names. Similarly, attributes of the same name from different relations are renamed to avoid ambiguity.

Having created the product, we apply a selection operator to it by converting the WHERE clause to a selection condition in the obvious way. That is, each attribute reference in the WHERE clause is replaced by the attribute of the product to which it corresponds. Finally, we create from the SELECT clause a list of expressions for a final (extended) projection operation. As we did for the WHERE clause, we interpret each attribute reference in the SELECT clause as the corresponding attribute in the product of relations.

Example 6.15 : Let us convert the query of Example 6.14 to relational algebra. First, there are two tuple variables in the FROM clause, both referring to relation MovieStar. Thus, our expression (without the necessary renaming) begins:

MovieStar × MovieStar

The resulting relation has eight attributes, the first four correspond to attributes name, address, gender, and birthdate from the first copy of relation MovieStar, and the second four correspond to the same attributes from the other copy of MovieStar. We could create names for these attributes with a dot and the aliasing tuple variable — e.g., Star1.gender — but for succinctness, let us invent new symbols and call the attributes simply $A_1, A_2, \ldots, A_8$. Thus, A_1 corresponds to Star1.name, A_5 corresponds to Star2.name, and so on.

An Unintuitive Consequence of SQL Semantics

Suppose R, S, and T are unary (one-component) relations, each having attribute A alone, and we wish to find those elements that are in R and also in either S or T (or both). That is, we want to compute $R \cap (S \cup T)$. We might expect the following SQL query would do the job.

```
SELECT R.A
FROM R, S, T
WHERE R.A = S.A OR R.A = T.A;
```

However, consider the situation in which T is empty. Since then $R.A = T.A$ can never be satisfied, we might expect the query to produce exactly $R \cap S$, based on our intuition about how "OR" operates. Yet whichever of the three equivalent definitions of Section 6.2.4 one prefers, we find that the result is empty, regardless of how many elements R and S have in common. If we use the nested-loop semantics of Figure 6.4, then we see that the loop for tuple variable T iterates 0 times, since there are no tuples in the relation for the tuple variable to range over. Thus, the if-statement inside the for-loops never executes, and nothing can be produced. Similarly, if we look for assignments of tuples to the tuple variables, there is no way to assign a tuple to T, so no assignments exist. Finally, if we use the Cartesian-product approach, we start with $R \times S \times T$, which is empty because T is empty.

Under this naming strategy for attributes, the selection condition obtained from the WHERE clause is $A_2 = A_6$ and $A_1 < A_5$. The projection list is A_1, A_5. Thus,

$$\pi_{A_1,A_5}\Big(\sigma_{A_2=A_6 \text{ AND } A_1<A_5}\big(\rho_{M(A_1,A_2,A_3,A_4)}(\texttt{MovieStar}) \times$$
$$\rho_{N(A_5,A_6,A_7,A_8)}(\texttt{MovieStar})\big)\Big)$$

renders the entire query in relational algebra.   □

6.2.5 Union, Intersection, and Difference of Queries

Sometimes we wish to combine relations using the set operations of relational algebra: union, intersection, and difference. SQL provides corresponding operators that apply to the results of queries, provided those queries produce relations with the same list of attributes and attribute types. The keywords used are UNION, INTERSECT, and EXCEPT for $\cup$, $\cap$, and $-$, respectively. Words like UNION are used between two queries, and those queries must be parenthesized.

Example 6.16: Suppose we wanted the names and addresses of all female movie stars who are also movie executives with a net worth over $10,000,000. Using the following two relations:

```
MovieStar(name, address, gender, birthdate)
MovieExec(name, address, cert#, netWorth)
```

we can write the query as in Fig. 6.5. Lines (1) through (3) produce a relation whose schema is (name, address) and whose tuples are the names and addresses of all female movie stars.

```
1)    (SELECT name, address
2)     FROM MovieStar
3)     WHERE gender = 'F')
4)          INTERSECT
5)    (SELECT name, address
6)     FROM MovieExec
7)     WHERE netWorth > 10000000);
```

Figure 6.5: Intersecting female movie stars with rich executives

Similarly, lines (5) through (7) produce the set of "rich" executives, those with net worth over $10,000,000. This query also yields a relation whose schema has the attributes name and address only. Since the two schemas are the same, we can intersect them, and we do so with the operator of line (4). □

Example 6.17: In a similar vein, we could take the difference of two sets of persons, each selected from a relation. The query

```
(SELECT name, address FROM MovieStar)
    EXCEPT
(SELECT name, address FROM MovieExec);
```

gives the names and addresses of movie stars who are not also movie executives, regardless of gender or net worth. □

In the two examples above, the attributes of the relations whose intersection or difference we took were conveniently the same. However, if necessary to get a common set of attributes, we can rename attributes as in Example 6.3.

Example 6.18: Suppose we wanted all the titles and years of movies that appeared in either the Movie or StarsIn relation of our running example:

```
Movie(title, year, length, inColor, studioName, producerC#)
StarsIn(movieTitle, movieYear, starName)
```

Readable SQL Queries

Generally, one writes SQL queries so that each important keyword like FROM or WHERE starts a new line. This style offers the reader visual clues to the structure of the query. However, when a query or subquery is short, we shall sometimes write it out on a single line, as we did in Example 6.17. That style, keeping a complete query compact, also offers good readability.

Ideally, these sets of movies would be the same, but in practice it is common for relations to diverge; for instance we might have movies with no listed stars or a StarsIn tuple that mentions a movie not found in the Movie relation.[5] Thus, we might write

```
(SELECT title, year FROM Movie)
    UNION
(SELECT movieTitle AS title, movieYear AS year FROM StarsIn);
```

The result would be all movies mentioned in either relation, with title and year as the attributes of the resulting relation.   □

6.2.6   Exercises for Section 6.2

Exercise 6.2.1: Using the database schema of our running movie example

```
Movie(title, year, length, inColor, studioName, producerC#)
StarsIn(movieTitle, movieYear, starName)
MovieStar(name, address, gender, birthdate)
MovieExec(name, address, cert#, netWorth)
Studio(name, address, presC#)
```

write the following queries in SQL.

* a) Who were the male stars in *Terms of Endearment*?

  b) Which stars appeared in movies produced by MGM in 1995?

  c) Who is the president of MGM studios?

*! d) Which movies are longer than *Gone With the Wind*?

! e) Which executives are worth more than Merv Griffin?

Exercise 6.2.2: Write the following queries, based on the database schema

---

[5]There are ways to prevent this divergence; see Section 7.1.4.

```
Product(maker, model, type)
PC(model, speed, ram, hd, rd, price)
Laptop(model, speed, ram, hd, screen, price)
Printer(model, color, type, price)
```

of Exercise 5.2.1, and evaluate your queries using the data of that exercise.

* a) Give the manufacturer and speed of laptops with a hard disk of at least thirty gigabytes.

* b) Find the model number and price of all products (of any type) made by manufacturer B.

  c) Find those manufacturers that sell Laptops, but not PC's.

! d) Find those hard-disk sizes that occur in two or more PC's.

! e) Find those pairs of PC models that have both the same speed and RAM. A pair should be listed only once; e.g., list (i, j) but not (j, i).

!! f) Find those manufacturers of at least two different computers (PC's or laptops) with speeds of at least 1000.

Exercise 6.2.3: Write the following queries, based on the database schema

```
Classes(class, type, country, numGuns, bore, displacement)
Ships(name, class, launched)
Battles(name, date)
Outcomes(ship, battle, result)
```

of Exercise 5.2.4, and evaluate your queries using the data of that exercise.

  a) Find the ships heavier than 35,000 tons.

  b) List the name, displacement, and number of guns of the ships engaged in the battle of Guadalcanal.

  c) List all the ships mentioned in the database. (Remember that all these ships may not appear in the Ships relation.)

! d) Find those countries that have both battleships and battlecruisers.

! e) Find those ships that were damaged in one battle, but later fought in another.

! f) Find those battles with at least three ships of the same country.

*! **Exercise 6.2.4:** A general form of relational-algebra query is

$$\pi_L\Big(\sigma_C(R_1 \times R_2 \times \cdots \times R_n)\Big)$$

Here, L is an arbitrary list of attributes, and C is an arbitrary condition. The list of relations $R_1, R_2, \ldots, R_n$ may include the same relation repeated several times, in which case appropriate renaming may be assumed applied to the R_i's. Show how to express any query of this form in SQL.

! **Exercise 6.2.5 :** Another general form of relational-algebra query is

$$\pi_L \Big(\sigma_C (R_1 \bowtie R_2 \bowtie \cdots \bowtie R_n) \Big)$$

The same assumptions as in Exercise 6.2.4 apply here; the only difference is that the natural join is used instead of the product. Show how to express any query of this form in SQL.

6.3 Subqueries

In SQL, one query can be used in various ways to help in the evaluation of another. A query that is part of another is called a *subquery*. Subqueries can have subqueries, and so on, down as many levels as we wish. We already saw one example of the use of subqueries; in Section 6.2.5 we built a union, intersection, or difference query by connecting two subqueries to form the whole query. There are a number of other ways that subqueries can be used:

1. Subqueries can return a single constant, and this constant can be compared with another value in a WHERE clause.

2. Subqueries can return relations that can be used in various ways in WHERE clauses.

3. Subqueries can have their relations appear in FROM clauses, just like any stored relation can.

6.3.1 Subqueries that Produce Scalar Values

An atomic value that can appear as one component of a tuple is referred to as a *scalar*. A select-from-where expression can produce a relation with any number of attributes in its schema, and there can be any number of tuples in the relation. However, often we are only interested in values of a single attribute. Furthermore, sometimes we can deduce from information about keys, or from other information, that there will be only a single value produced for that attribute.

   If so, we can use this select-from-where expression, surrounded by parentheses, as if it were a constant. In particular, it may appear in a WHERE clause any place we would expect to find a constant or an attribute representing a component of a tuple. For instance, we may compare the result of such a subquery to a constant or attribute.

Example 6.19 : Let us recall Example 6.12, where we asked for the producer of *Star Wars*. We had to query the two relations

```
Movie(title, year, length, inColor, studioName, producerC#)
MovieExec(name, address, cert#, netWorth)
```

because only the former has movie title information and only the latter has producer names. The information is linked by "certificate numbers." These numbers uniquely identify producers. The query we developed is:

```
SELECT name
FROM Movie, MovieExec
WHERE title = 'Star Wars' AND producerC# = cert#;
```

There is another way to look at this query. We need the `Movie` relation only to get the certificate number for the producer of *Star Wars*. Once we have it, we can query the relation `MovieExec` to find the name of the person with this certificate. The first problem, getting the certificate number, can be written as a subquery, and the result, which we expect will be a single value, can be used in the "main" query to achieve the same effect as the query above. This query is shown in Fig. 6.6.

```
1)   SELECT name
2)   FROM MovieExec
3)   WHERE cert# =
4)       (SELECT producerC#
5)        FROM Movie
6)        WHERE title = 'Star Wars'
         );
```

Figure 6.6: Finding the producer of *Star Wars* by using a nested subquery

Lines (4) through (6) of Fig. 6.6 are the subquery. Looking only at this simple query by itself, we see that the result will be a unary relation with attribute `producerC#`, and we expect to find only one tuple in this relation. The tuple will look like (12345), that is, a single component with some integer, perhaps 12345 or whatever George Lucas' certificate number is. If zero tuples or more than one tuple is produced by the subquery of lines (4) through (6), it is a run-time error.

Having executed this subquery, we can then execute lines (1) through (3) of Fig. 6.6, as if the value 12345 replaced the entire subquery. That is, the "main" query is executed as if it were

```
SELECT name
FROM MovieExec
WHERE cert# = 12345;
```

The result of this query should be `George Lucas`.   □

6.3.2   Conditions Involving Relations

There are a number of SQL operators that we can apply to a relation R and produce a boolean result. Typically, the relation R will be the result of a select-from-where subquery. Some of these operators — IN, ALL, and ANY — will be explained first in their simple form where a scalar value s is involved. In this situation, the relation R is required to be a one-column relation. Here are the definitions of the operators:

1. EXISTS R is a condition that is true if and only if R is not empty.

2. s IN R is true if and only if s is equal to one of the values in R. Likewise, s NOT IN R is true if and only if s is equal to no value in R. Here, we assume R is a unary relation. We shall discuss extensions to the IN and NOT IN operators where R has more than one attribute in its schema and s is a tuple in Section 6.3.3.

3. s > ALL R is true if and only if s is greater than every value in unary relation R. Similarly, the > operator could be replaced by any of the other five comparison operators, with the analogous meaning: s stands in the stated relationship to every tuple in R. For instance, s <> ALL R is the same as s NOT IN R.

4. s > ANY R is true if and only if s is greater than at least one value in unary relation R. Similarly, any of the other five comparisons could be used in place of >, with the meaning that s stands in the stated relationship to at least one tuple of R. For instance, s = ANY R is the same as s IN R.

The EXISTS, ALL, and ANY operators can be negated by putting NOT in front of the entire expression, just like any other boolean-valued expression. Thus, NOT EXISTS R is true if and only if R is empty. NOT s > ALL R is true if and only if s is not the maximum value in R, and NOT s > ANY R is true if and only if s is the minimum value in R. We shall see several examples of the use of these operators shortly.

6.3.3   Conditions Involving Tuples

A tuple in SQL is represented by a parenthesized list of scalar values. Examples are (123, 'foo') and (name, address, networth). The first of these has constants as components; the second has attributes as components. Mixing of constants and attributes is permitted.

If a tuple t has the same number of components as a relation R, then it makes sense to compare t and R in expressions of the type listed in Section 6.3.2. Examples are t IN R or t <> ANY R. The latter comparison means that there is some tuple in R other than t. Note that when comparing a tuple with members of a relation R, we must compare components using the assumed standard order for the attributes of R.

```
1)   SELECT name
2)   FROM MovieExec
3)   WHERE cert# IN
4)       (SELECT producerC#
5)        FROM Movie
6)        WHERE (title, year) IN
7)            (SELECT movieTitle, movieYear
8)             FROM StarsIn
9)             WHERE starName = 'Harrison Ford'
             )
         );
```

Figure 6.7: Finding the producers of Harrison Ford's movies

Example 6.20 : In Fig. 6.7 is an SQL query on the three relations

```
Movie(title, year, length, inColor, studioName, producerC#)
StarsIn(movieTitle, movieYear, starName)
MovieExec(name, address, cert#, netWorth)
```

asking for all the producers of movies in which Harrison Ford stars. It consists of a "main" query, a query nested within that, and a third query nested within the second.

We should analyze any query with subqueries from the inside out. Thus, let us start with the innermost nested subquery: lines (7) through (9). This query examines the tuples of the relation `StarsIn` and finds all those tuples whose `starName` component is `'Harrison Ford'`. The titles and years of those movies are returned by this subquery. Recall that title and year, not title alone, is the key for movies, so we need to produce tuples with both attributes to identify a movie uniquely. Thus, we would expect the value produced by lines (7) through (9) to look something like Fig. 6.8.

Now, consider the middle subquery, lines (4) through (6). It searches the `Movie` relation for tuples whose title and year are in the relation suggested by Fig. 6.8. For each tuple found, the producer's certificate number is returned, so the result of the middle subquery is the set of certificates of the producers of Harrison Ford's movies.

Finally, consider the "main" query of lines (1) through (3). It examines the tuples of the `MovieExec` relation to find those whose `cert#` component is one of the certificates in the set returned by the middle subquery. For each of these tuples, the name of the producer is returned, giving us the set of producers of Harrison Ford's movies, as desired. □

title	year
Star Wars	1977
Raiders of the Lost Ark	1981
The Fugitive	1993
...	...

Figure 6.8: Title-year pairs returned by inner subquery

Incidentally, the nested query of Fig. 6.7 can, like many nested queries, be written as a single select-from-where expression with relations in the FROM clause for each of the relations mentioned in the main query or a subquery. The IN relationships are replaced by equalities in the WHERE clause. For instance, the query of Fig. 6.9 is essentially that of Fig. 6.7. There is a difference regarding the way duplicate occurrences of a producer — e.g., George Lucas — are handled, as we shall discuss in Section 6.4.1.

```
SELECT name
FROM MovieExec, Movie, StarsIn
WHERE cert# = producerC# AND
      title = movieTitle AND
      year = movieYear AND
      starName = 'Harrison Ford';
```

Figure 6.9: Ford's producers without nested subqueries

6.3.4   Correlated Subqueries

The simplest subqueries can be evaluated once and for all, and the result used in a higher-level query. A more complicated use of nested subqueries requires the subquery to be evaluated many times, once for each assignment of a value to some term in the subquery that comes from a tuple variable outside the subquery. A subquery of this type is called a *correlated* subquery. Let us begin our study with an example.

Example 6.21: We shall find the titles that have been used for two or more movies. We start with an outer query that looks at all tuples in the relation

```
Movie(title, year, length, inColor, studioName, producerC#)
```

For each such tuple, we ask in a subquery whether there is a movie with the same title and a greater year. The entire query is shown in Fig. 6.10.

As with other nested queries, let us begin at the innermost subquery, lines (4) through (6). If `Old.title` in line (6) were replaced by a constant string such as `'King Kong'`, we would understand it quite easily as a query asking for the year or years in which movies titled *King Kong* were made. The present subquery differs little. The only problem is that we don't know what value `Old.title` has. However, as we range over `Movie` tuples of the outer query of lines (1) through (3), each tuple provides a value of `Old.title`. We then execute the query of lines (4) through (6) with this value for `Old.title` to decide the truth of the `WHERE` clause that extends from lines (3) through (6).

```
1)   SELECT title
2)   FROM Movie Old
3)   WHERE year < ANY
4)       (SELECT year
5)        FROM Movie
6)        WHERE title = Old.title
         );
```

Figure 6.10: Finding movie titles that appear more than once

The condition of line (3) is true if any movie with the same title as `Old.title` has a later year than the movie in the tuple that is the current value of tuple variable `Old`. This condition is true unless the year in the tuple `Old` is the last year in which a movie of that title was made. Consequently, lines (1) through (3) produce a title one fewer times than there are movies with that title. A movie made twice will be listed once, a movie made three times will be listed twice, and so on.[6] □

When writing a correlated query it is important that we be aware of the *scoping rules* for names. In general, an attribute in a subquery belongs to one of the tuple variables in that subquery's `FROM` clause if some tuple variable's relation has that attribute in its schema. If not, we look at the immediately surrounding subquery, then to the one surrounding that, and so on. Thus, `year` on line (4) and `title` on line (6) of Fig. 6.10 refer to the attributes of the tuple variable that ranges over all the tuples of the copy of relation `Movie` introduced on line (5) — that is, the copy of the `Movie` relation addressed by the subquery of lines (4) through (6).

However, we can arrange for an attribute to belong to another tuple variable if we prefix it by that tuple variable and a dot. That is why we introduced the alias `Old` for the `Movie` relation of the outer query, and why we refer to `Old.title` in line (6). Note that if the two relations in the `FROM` clauses of lines

---

[6]This example is the first occasion on which we've been reminded that relations in SQL are bags, not sets. There are several ways that duplicates may crop up in SQL relations. We shall discuss the matter in detail in Section 6.4.

(2) and (5) were different, we would not need an alias. Rather, in the subquery we could refer directly to attributes of a relation mentioned in line (2).

6.3.5   Subqueries in FROM Clauses

Another use for subqueries is as relations in a FROM clause. In a FROM list, instead of a stored relation, we may use a parenthesized subquery. Since we don't have a name for the result of this subquery, we must give it a tuple-variable alias. We then refer to tuples in the result of the subquery as we would tuples in any relation that appears in the FROM list.

Example 6.22 : Let us reconsider the problem of Example 6.20, where we wrote a query that finds the producers of Harrison Ford's movies. Suppose we had a relation that gave the certificates of the producers of those movies. It would then be a simple matter to look up the names of those producers in the relation MovieExec. Figure 6.11 is such a query.

```
1)   SELECT name
2)   FROM MovieExec, (SELECT producerC#
3)                     FROM Movie, StarsIn
4)                     WHERE title = movieTitle AND
5)                         year = movieYear AND
6)                         starName = 'Harrison Ford'
7)                    ) Prod
8)   WHERE cert# = Prod.producerC#;
```

Figure 6.11: Finding the producers of Ford's movies using a subquery in the FROM clause

Lines (2) through (7) are the FROM clause of the outer query. In addition to the relation MovieExec, it has a subquery. That subquery joins Movie and StarsIn on lines (3) through (5), adds the condition that the star is Harrison Ford on line (6), and returns the set of producers of the movies at line (2). This set is given the alias Prod on line (7).

At line (8), the relations MovieExec and the subquery aliased Prod are joined with the requirement that the certificate numbers be the same. The names of the producers from MovieExec that have certificates in the set aliased by Prod is returned at line (1).   □

6.3.6   SQL Join Expressions

We can construct relations by a number of variations on the join operator applied to two relations. These variants include products, natural joins, theta-joins, and outerjoins. The result can stand as a query by itself. Alternatively, all these expressions, since they produce relations, may be used as subqueries in the FROM clause of a select-from-where expression.

The simplest form of join expression is a *cross join*; that term is a synonym for what we called a Cartesian product or just "product" in Section 5.2.5. For instance, if we want the product of the two relations

```
Movie(title, year, length, inColor, studioName, producerC#)
StarsIn(movieTitle, movieYear, starName)
```

we can say

```
Movie CROSS JOIN StarsIn;
```

and the result will be a nine-column relation with all the attributes of Movie and StarsIn. Every pair consisting of one tuple of Movie and one tuple of StarsIn will be a tuple of the resulting relation.

The attributes in the product relation can be called $R.A$, where R is one of the two joined relations and A is one of its attributes. If only one of the relations has an attribute named A, then the R and dot can be dropped, as usual. In this instance, since Movie and StarsIn have no common attributes, the nine attribute names suffice in the product.

However, the product by itself is rarely a useful operation. A more conventional theta-join is obtained with the keyword ON. We put JOIN between two relation names R and S and follow them by ON and a condition. The meaning of JOIN...ON is that the product of $R \times S$ is followed by a selection for whatever condition follows ON.

Example 6.23: Suppose we want to join the relations

```
Movie(title, year, length, inColor, studioName, producerC#)
StarsIn(movieTitle, movieYear, starName)
```

with the condition that the only tuples to be joined are those that refer to the same movie. That is, the titles and years from both relations must be the same. We can ask this query by

```
Movie JOIN StarsIn ON
        title = movieTitle AND year = movieYear;
```

The result is again a nine-column relation with the obvious attribute names. However, now a tuple from Movie and one from StarsIn combine to form a tuple of the result only if the two tuples agree on both the title and year. As a result, two of the columns are redundant, because every tuple of the result will have the same value in both the title and movieTitle components and will have the same value in both year and movieYear.

If we are concerned with the fact that the join above has two redundant components, we can use the whole expression as a subquery in a FROM clause and use a SELECT clause to remove the undesired attributes. Thus, we could write

```
SELECT title, year, length, inColor, studioName,
       producerC#, starName
FROM Movie JOIN StarsIn ON
       title = movieTitle AND year = movieYear;
```

to get a seven-column relation which is the `Movie` relation's tuples, each extended in all possible ways with a star of that movie.   □

6.3.7   Natural Joins

As we recall from Section 5.2.6, a natural join differs from a theta-join in that:

1. The join condition is that all pairs of attributes from the two relations having a common name are equated, and there are no other conditions.

2. One of each pair of equated attributes is projected out.

The SQL natural join behaves exactly this way. Keywords `NATURAL JOIN` appear between the relations to express the ⋈ operator.

Example 6.24 : Suppose we want to compute the natural join of the relations

```
MovieStar(name, address, gender, birthdate)
MovieExec(name, address, cert#, netWorth)
```

The result will be a relation whose schema includes attributes `name` and `address` plus all the attributes that appear in one or the other of the two relations. A tuple of the result will represent an individual who is both a star and an executive and will have all the information pertinent to either: a name, address, gender, birthdate, certificate number, and net worth. The expression

```
MovieStar NATURAL JOIN MovieExec;
```

succinctly describes the desired relation.   □

6.3.8   Outerjoins

The outerjoin operator was introduced in Section 5.4.7 as a way to augment the result of a join by the dangling tuples, padded with null values. In SQL, we can specify an outerjoin; `NULL` is used as the null value.

Example 6.25 : Suppose we wish to take the outerjoin of the two relations

```
MovieStar(name, address, gender, birthdate)
MovieExec(name, address, cert#, netWorth)
```

SQL refers to the standard outerjoin, which pads dangling tuples from both of its arguments, as a *full* outerjoin. The syntax is unsurprising:

```
        MovieStar NATURAL FULL OUTER JOIN MovieExec;
```

The result of this operation is a relation with the same six-attribute schema as Example 6.24. The tuples of this relation are of three kinds. Those representing individuals who are both stars and executives have tuples with all six attributes non-NULL. These are the tuples that are also in the result of Example 6.24.

The second kind of tuple is one for an individual who is a star but not an executive. These tuples have values for attributes `name`, `address`, `gender`, and `birthdate` taken from their tuple in `MovieStar`, while the attributes belonging only to `MovieExec`, namely `cert#` and `netWorth`, have NULL values.

The third kind of tuple is for an executive who is not also a star. These tuples have values for the attributes of `MovieExec` taken from their `MovieExec` tuple and NULL's in the attributes `gender` and `birthdate` that come only from `MovieStar`. For instance, the three tuples of the result relation shown in Fig. 6.12 correspond to the three types of individuals, respectively. □

name	*address*	*gender*	*birthdate*	*cert#*	*networth*
Mary Tyler Moore	Maple St.	'F'	9/9/99	12345	$100···
Tom Hanks	Cherry Ln.	'M'	8/8/88	NULL	NULL
George Lucas	Oak Rd.	NULL	NULL	23456	$200···

Figure 6.12: Three tuples in the outerjoin of `MovieStar` and `MovieExec`

All the variations on the outerjoin that we mentioned in Section 5.4.7 are also available in SQL. If we want a left- or right-outerjoin, we add the appropriate word `LEFT` or `RIGHT` in place of `FULL`. For instance,

```
        MovieStar NATURAL LEFT OUTER JOIN MovieExec;
```

would yield the first two tuples of Fig. 6.12 but not the third. Similarly,

```
        MovieStar NATURAL RIGHT OUTER JOIN MovieExec;
```

would yield the first and third tuples of Fig. 6.12 but not the second.

Next, suppose we want a theta-outerjoin instead of a natural outerjoin. Instead of using the keyword `NATURAL`, we may follow the join by `ON` and a condition that matching tuples must obey. If we also specify `FULL OUTER JOIN`, then after matching tuples from the two joined relations, we pad dangling tuples of either relation with NULL's and include the padded tuples in the result.

Example 6.26 : Let us reconsider Example 6.23, where we joined the relations `Movie` and `StarsIn` using the conditions that the `title` and `movieTitle` attributes of the two relations agree and that the `year` and `movieYear` attributes of the two relations agree. If we modify that example to call for a full outerjoin:

```
Movie FULL OUTER JOIN StarsIn ON
    title = movieTitle AND year = movieYear;
```

then we shall get not only tuples for movies that have at least one star mentioned in `StarsIn`, but we shall get tuples for movies with no listed stars, padded with NULL's in attributes `movieTitle`, `movieYear`, and `starName`. Likewise, for stars not appearing in any movie listed in relation `Movie` we get a tuple with NULL's in the six attributes of `Movie`. □

   The keyword `FULL` can be replaced by either `LEFT` or `RIGHT` in outerjoins of the type suggested by Example 6.26. For instance,

```
Movie LEFT OUTER JOIN StarsIn ON
    title = movieTitle AND year = movieYear;
```

gives us the `Movie` tuples with at least one listed star and NULL-padded `Movie` tuples without a listed star, but will not include stars without a listed movie. Conversely,

```
Movie RIGHT OUTER JOIN StarsIn ON
    title = movieTitle AND year = movieYear;
```

will omit the tuples for movies without a listed star but will include tuples for stars not in any listed movies, padded with NULL's.

6.3.9 Exercises for Section 6.3

Exercise 6.3.1: Write the following queries, based on the database schema

```
Product(maker, model, type)
PC(model, speed, ram, hd, rd, price)
Laptop(model, speed, ram, hd, screen, price)
Printer(model, color, type, price)
```

of Exercise 5.2.1. You should use at least one subquery in each of your answers and write each query in two significantly different ways (e.g., using different sets of the operators `EXISTS`, `IN`, `ALL`, and `ANY`).

* a) Find the makers of PC's with a speed of at least 1200.

  b) Find the printers with the highest price.

! c) Find the laptops whose speed is slower than that of any PC.

! d) Find the model number of the item (PC, laptop, or printer) with the highest price.

! e) Find the maker of the color printer with the lowest price.

!! f) Find the maker(s) of the PC(s) with the fastest processor among all those PC's that have the smallest amount of RAM.

Exercise 6.3.2: Write the following queries, based on the database schema

```
Classes(class, type, country, numGuns, bore, displacement)
Ships(name, class, launched)
Battles(name, date)
Outcomes(ship, battle, result)
```

of Exercise 5.2.4. You should use at least one subquery in each of your answers and write each query in two significantly different ways (e.g., using different sets of the operators EXISTS, IN, ALL, and ANY).

a) Find the countries whose ships had the largest number of guns.

*! b) Find the classes of ships at least one of which was sunk in a battle.

c) Find the names of the ships with a 16-inch bore.

d) Find the battles in which ships of the Kongo class participated.

!! e) Find the names of the ships whose number of guns was the largest for those ships of the same bore.

! Exercise 6.3.3: Write the query of Fig. 6.10 without any subqueries.

! Exercise 6.3.4: Consider expression $\pi_L(R_1 \bowtie R_2 \bowtie \cdots \bowtie R_n)$ of relational algebra, where L is a list of attributes all of which belong to R_1. Show that this expression can be written in SQL using subqueries only. More precisely, write an equivalent SQL expression where no FROM clause has more than one relation in its list.

! Exercise 6.3.5: Write the following queries without using the intersection or difference operators:

* a) The intersection query of Fig. 6.5.

b) The difference query of Example 6.17.

!! Exercise 6.3.6: We have noticed that certain operators of SQL are redundant, in the sense that they always can be replaced by other operators. For example, we saw that s IN R can be replaced by s = ANY R. Show that EXISTS and NOT EXISTS are redundant by explaining how to replace any expression of the form EXISTS R or NOT EXISTS R by an expression that does not involve EXISTS (except perhaps in the expression R itself). *Hint:* Remember that it is permissible to have a constant in the SELECT clause.

Exercise 6.3.7: For these relations from our running movie database schema

```
StarsIn(movieTitle, movieYear, starName)
MovieStar(name, address, gender, birthdate)
MovieExec(name, address, cert#, netWorth)
Studio(name, address, presC#)
```

describe the tuples that would appear in the following SQL expressions:

a) `Studio CROSS JOIN MovieExec;`

b) `StarsIn NATURAL FULL OUTER JOIN MovieStar;`

c) `StarsIn FULL OUTER JOIN MovieStar ON name = starName;`

*! **Exercise 6.3.8:** Using the database schema

```
Product(maker, model, type)
PC(model, speed, ram, hd, rd, price)
Laptop(model, speed, ram, hd, screen, price)
Printer(model, color, type, price)
```

write an SQL query that will produce information about all products — PC's, laptops, and printers — including their manufacturer if available, and whatever information about that product is relevant (i.e., found in the relation for that type of product).

Exercise 6.3.9: Using the two relations

```
Classes(class, type, country, numGuns, bore, displacement)
Ships(name, class, launched)
```

from our database schema of Exercise 5.2.4, write an SQL query that will produce all available information about ships, including that information available in the `Classes` relation. You need not produce information about classes if there are no ships of that class mentioned in `Ships`.

! **Exercise 6.3.10:** Repeat Exercise 6.3.9, but also include in the result, for any class C that is not mentioned in `Ships`, information about the ship that has the same name C as its class.

! **Exercise 6.3.11:** The join operators (other than outerjoin) we learned in this section are redundant, in the sense that they can always be replaced by select-from-where expressions. Explain how to write expressions of the following forms using select-from-where:

* a) `R CROSS JOIN S;`

b) `R NATURAL JOIN S;`

c) `R JOIN S ON` C`;`, where C is an SQL condition.

6.4 Full-Relation Operations

In this section we shall study some operations that act on relations as a whole, rather than on tuples individually or in small numbers (as do joins of several relations, for instance). First, we deal with the fact that SQL uses relations that are bags rather than sets, and a tuple can appear more than once in a relation. We shall see how to force the result of an operation to be a set in Section 6.4.1, and in Section 6.4.2 we shall see that it is also possible to prevent the elimination of duplicates in circumstances where SQL systems would normally eliminate them.

Then, we discuss how SQL supports the grouping and aggregation operator γ that we introduced in Section 5.4.4. SQL has aggregation operators and a GROUP-BY clause. There is also a "HAVING" clause that allows selection of certain groups in a way that depends on the group as a whole, rather than on individual tuples.

6.4.1 Eliminating Duplicates

As mentioned in Section 6.3.4, SQL's notion of relations differs from the abstract notion of relations presented in Chapter 3. A relation, being a set, cannot have more than one copy of any given tuple. When an SQL query creates a new relation, the SQL system does not ordinarily eliminate duplicates. Thus, the SQL response to a query may list the same tuple several times.

Recall from Section 6.2.4 that one of several equivalent definitions of the meaning of an SQL select-from-where query is that we begin with the Cartesian product of the relations referred to in the FROM clause. Each tuple of the product is tested by the condition in the WHERE clause, and the ones that pass the test are given to the output for projection according to the SELECT clause. This projection may cause the same tuple to result from different tuples of the product, and if so, each copy of the resulting tuple is printed in its turn. Further, since there is nothing wrong with an SQL relation having duplicates, the relations from which the Cartesian product is formed may have duplicates, and each identical copy is paired with the tuples from the other relations, yielding a proliferation of duplicates in the product.

If we do not wish duplicates in the result, then we may follow the keyword SELECT by the keyword DISTINCT. That word tells SQL to produce only one copy of any tuple and is the SQL analog of applying the δ operator of Section 5.4.1 to the result of the query.

Example 6.27 : Let us reconsider the query of Fig. 6.9, where we asked for the producers of Harrison Ford's movies using no subqueries. As written, George Lucas will appear many times in the output. If we want only to see each producer once, we may change line (1) of the query to

```
1)   SELECT DISTINCT name
```

The Cost of Duplicate Elimination

One might be tempted to place DISTINCT after every SELECT, on the theory that it is harmless. In fact, it is very expensive to eliminate duplicates from a relation. The relation must be sorted or partitioned so that identical tuples appear next to each other. These algorithms are discussed starting in Section 15.2.2. Only by grouping the tuples in this way can we determine whether or not a given tuple should be eliminated. The time it takes to sort the relation so that duplicates may be eliminated is often greater than the time it takes to execute the query itself. Thus, duplicate elimination should be used judiciously if we want our queries to run fast.

Then, the list of producers will have duplicate occurrences of names eliminated before printing.

Incidentally, the query of Fig. 6.7, where we used subqueries, does not necessarily suffer from the problem of duplicate answers. True, the subquery at line (4) of Fig. 6.7 will produce the certificate number of George Lucas several times. However, in the "main" query of line (1), we examine each tuple of MovieExec once. Presumably, there is only one tuple for George Lucas in that relation, and if so, it is only this tuple that satisfies the WHERE clause of line (3). Thus, George Lucas is printed only once.   □

6.4.2 Duplicates in Unions, Intersections, and Differences

Unlike the SELECT statement, which preserves duplicates as a default and only eliminates them when instructed to by the DISTINCT keyword, the union, intersection, and difference operations, which we introduced in Section 6.2.5, normally eliminate duplicates. That is, bags are converted to sets, and the set version of the operation is applied. In order to prevent the elimination of duplicates, we must follow the operator UNION, INTERSECT, or EXCEPT by the keyword ALL. If we do, then we get the bag semantics of these operators as was discussed in Section 5.3.2.

Example 6.28: Consider again the union expression from Example 6.18, but now add the keyword ALL, as:

```
(SELECT title, year FROM Movie)
    UNION ALL
(SELECT movieTitle AS title, movieYear AS year FROM StarsIn);
```

Now, a title and year will appear as many times in the result as it appears in each of the relations Movie and StarsIn put together. For instance, if a movie appeared once in the Movie relation and there were three stars for that movie listed in `StarsIn` (so the movie appeared in three different tuples of `StarsIn`), then that movie's title and year would appear four times in the result of the union. □

As for union, the operators `INTERSECT ALL` and `EXCEPT ALL` are intersection and difference of bags. Thus, if R and S are relations, then the result of expression

$$R \text{ INTERSECT ALL } S$$

is the relation in which the number of times a tuple t appears is the minimum of the number of times it appears in R and the number of times it appears in S.

The result of expression

$$R \text{ EXCEPT ALL } S$$

has tuple t as many times as the difference of the number of times it appears in R minus the number of times it appears in S, provided the difference is positive. Each of these definitions is what we discussed for bags in Section 5.3.2.

6.4.3 Grouping and Aggregation in SQL

In Section 5.4.4, we introduced the grouping-and-aggregation operator γ for our extended relational algebra. Recall that this operator allows us to partition the tuples of a relation into "groups," based on the values of tuples in one or more attributes, as discussed in Section 5.4.3. We are then able to aggregate certain other columns of the relation by applying "aggregation" operators to those columns. If there are groups, then the aggregation is done separately for each group. SQL provides all the capability of the γ operator through the use of aggregation operators in `SELECT` clauses and a special `GROUP BY` clause.

6.4.4 Aggregation Operators

SQL uses the five aggregation operators `SUM`, `AVG`, `MIN`, `MAX`, and `COUNT` that we met in Section 5.4.2. These operators are used by applying them to a scalar-valued expression, typically a column name, in a `SELECT` clause. One exception is the expression `COUNT(*)`, which counts all the tuples in the relation that is constructed from the `FROM` clause and `WHERE` clause of the query.

In addition, we have the option of eliminating duplicates from the column before applying the aggregation operator by using the keyword `DISTINCT`. That is, an expression such as `COUNT(DISTINCT x)` counts the number of distinct values in column x. We could use any of the other operators in place of `COUNT` here, but expressions such as `SUM(DISTINCT x)` rarely make sense, since it asks us to sum the different values in column x.

Example 6.29: The following query finds the average net worth of all movie executives:

```
SELECT AVG(netWorth)
FROM MovieExec;
```

Note that there is no `WHERE` clause at all, so the keyword `WHERE` is properly omitted. This query examines the `netWorth` column of the relation

```
MovieExec(name, address, cert#, netWorth)
```

sums the values found there, one value for each tuple (even if the tuple is a duplicate of some other tuple), and divides the sum by the number of tuples. If there are no duplicate tuples, then this query gives the average net worth as we expect. If there were duplicate tuples, then a movie executive whose tuple appeared n times would have his or her net worth counted n times in the average. □

Example 6.30: The following query:

```
SELECT COUNT(*)
FROM StarsIn;
```

counts the number of tuples in the `StarsIn` relation. The similar query:

```
SELECT COUNT(starName)
FROM StarsIn;
```

counts the number of values in the `starName` column of the relation. Since duplicate values are not eliminated when we project onto the `starName` column in SQL, this count should be the same as the count produced by the query with `COUNT(*)`.

If we want to be certain that we do not count duplicate values more than once, we can use the keyword `DISTINCT` before the aggregated attribute, as:

```
SELECT COUNT(DISTINCT starName)
FROM StarsIn;
```

Now, each star is counted once, no matter in how many movies they appeared. □

6.4.5 Grouping

To group tuples, we use a `GROUP BY` clause, following the `WHERE` clause. The keywords `GROUP BY` are followed by a list of *grouping* attributes. In the simplest situation, there is only one relation reference in the `FROM` clause, and this relation has its tuples grouped according to their values in the grouping attributes. Whatever aggregation operators are used in the `SELECT` clause are applied only within groups.

Example 6.31 : The problem of finding, from the relation

    Movie(title, year, length, inColor, studioName, producerC#)

the sum of the lengths of all movies for each studio is expressed by

    SELECT studioName, SUM(length)
    FROM Movie
    GROUP BY studioName;

We may imagine that the tuples of relation Movie are reorganized and grouped so that all the tuples for Disney studios are together, all those for MGM are together, and so on, as was suggested in Fig. 5.17. The sums of the length components of all the tuples in each group are calculated, and for each group, the studio name is printed along with that sum. □

Observe in Example 6.31 how the SELECT clause has two kinds of terms.

1. Aggregations, where an aggregate operator is applied to an attribute or expression involving attributes. As mentioned, these terms are evaluated on a per-group basis.

2. Attributes, such as studioName in this example, that appear in the GROUP BY clause. In a SELECT clause that has aggregations, only those attributes that are mentioned in the GROUP BY clause may appear unaggregated in the SELECT clause.

While queries involving GROUP BY generally have both grouping attributes and aggregations in the SELECT clause, it is technically not necessary to have both. For example, we could write

    SELECT studioName
    FROM Movie
    GROUP BY studioName;

This query would group the tuples of Movie according to their studio name and then print the studio name for each group, no matter how many tuples there are with a given studio name. Thus, the above query has the same effect as

    SELECT DISTINCT studioName
    FROM Movie;

It is also possible to use a GROUP BY clause in a query about several relations. Such a query is interpreted by the following sequence of steps:

1. Evaluate the relation R expressed by the FROM and WHERE clauses. That is, relation R is the Cartesian product of the relations mentioned in the FROM clause, to which the selection of the WHERE clause is applied.

2. Group the tuples of R according to the attributes in the GROUP BY clause.

3. Produce as a result the attributes and aggregations of the SELECT clause, as if the query were about a stored relation R.

Example 6.32: Suppose we wish to print a table listing each producer's total length of film produced. We need to get information from the two relations

```
Movie(title, year, length, inColor, studioName, producerC#)
MovieExec(name, address, cert#, netWorth)
```

so we begin by taking their theta-join, equating the certificate numbers from the two relations. That step gives us a relation in which each MovieExec tuple is paired with the Movie tuples for all the movies of that producer. Note that an executive who is not a producer will not be paired with any movies, and therefore will not appear in the relation. Now, we can group the selected tuples of this relation according to the name of the producer. Finally, we sum the lengths of the movies in each group. The query is shown in Fig. 6.13.   □

```
SELECT name, SUM(length)
FROM MovieExec, Movie
WHERE producerC# = cert#
GROUP BY name;
```

Figure 6.13: Computing the length of movies for each producer

6.4.6   HAVING Clauses

Suppose that we did not wish to include all of the producers in our table of Example 6.32. We could restrict the tuples prior to grouping in a way that would make undesired groups empty. For instance, if we only wanted the total length of movies for producers with a net worth of more than $10,000,000, we could change the third line of Fig. 6.13 to

```
WHERE producerC# = cert# AND networth > 10000000
```

However, sometimes we want to choose our groups based on some aggregate property of the group itself. Then we follow the GROUP BY clause with a HAVING clause. The latter clause consists of the keyword HAVING followed by a condition about the group.

Example 6.33: Suppose we want to print the total film length for only those producers who made at least one film prior to 1930. We may append to Fig. 6.13 the clause

---

Grouping, Aggregation, and Nulls

When tuples have nulls, there are a few rules we must remember:

- The value NULL is ignored in any aggregation. It does not contribute to a sum, average, or count, nor can it be the minimum or maximum in its column. For example, COUNT(*) is always a count of the number of tuples in a relation, but COUNT(A) is the number of tuples with non-NULL values for attribute A.

- On the other hand, NULL is treated as an ordinary value in a grouped attribute. For example, SELECT a, AVG(b) FROM R GROUP BY a will produce a tuple with NULL for the value of a and the average value of b for the tuples with $a = $ NULL, if there is at least one tuple in R with a component NULL.

```
HAVING MIN(year) < 1930
```

The resulting query, shown in Fig. 6.14, would remove from the grouped relation all those groups in which every tuple had a **year** component 1930 or higher. □

```
SELECT name, SUM(length)
FROM MovieExec, Movie
WHERE producerC# = cert#
GROUP BY name
HAVING MIN(year) < 1930;
```

Figure 6.14: Computing the total length of film for early producers

There are several rules we must remember about HAVING clauses:

- An aggregation in a HAVING clause applies only to the tuples of the group being tested.

- Any attribute of relations in the FROM clause may be aggregated in the HAVING clause, but only those attributes that are in the GROUP BY list may appear unaggregated in the HAVING clause (the same rule as for the SELECT clause).

Order of Clauses in SQL Queries

We have now met all six clauses that can appear in an SQL "select-from-where" query: SELECT, FROM, WHERE, GROUP BY, HAVING, and ORDER BY. Only the first two are required, but you can't use a HAVING clause without a GROUP BY clause. Whichever additional clauses appear must be in the order listed above.

6.4.7 Exercises for Section 6.4

Exercise 6.4.1: Write each of the queries in Exercise 5.2.1 in SQL, making sure that duplicates are eliminated.

Exercise 6.4.2: Write each of the queries in Exercise 5.2.4 in SQL, making sure that duplicates are eliminated.

! **Exercise 6.4.3:** For each of your answers to Exercise 6.3.1, determine whether or not the result of your query can have duplicates. If so, rewrite the query to eliminate duplicates. If not, write a query without subqueries that has the same, duplicate-free answer.

! **Exercise 6.4.4:** Repeat Exercise 6.4.3 for your answers to Exercise 6.3.2.

*! **Exercise 6.4.5:** In Example 6.27, we mentioned that different versions of the query "find the producers of Harrison Ford's movies" can have different answers as bags, even though they yield the same set of answers. Consider the version of the query in Example 6.22, where we used a subquery in the FROM clause. Does this version produce duplicates, and if so, why?

Exercise 6.4.6: Write the following queries, based on the database schema

```
Product(maker, model, type)
PC(model, speed, ram, hd, rd, price)
Laptop(model, speed, ram, hd, screen, price)
Printer(model, color, type, price)
```

of Exercise 5.2.1, and evaluate your queries using the data of that exercise.

* a) Find the average speed of PC's.

  b) Find the average speed of laptops costing over $2000.

  c) Find the average price of PC's made by manufacturer "A."

! d) Find the average price of PC's and laptops made by manufacturer "D."

  e) Find, for each different speed the average price of a PC.

*! f) Find for each manufacturer, the average screen size of its laptops.

! g) Find the manufacturers that make at least three different models of PC.

! h) Find for each manufacturer who sells PC's the maximum price of a PC.

*! i) Find, for each speed of PC above 800, the average price.

!! j) Find the average hard disk size of a PC for all those manufacturers that make printers.

Exercise 6.4.7: Write the following queries, based on the database schema

```
Classes(class, type, country, numGuns, bore, displacement)
Ships(name, class, launched)
Battles(name, date)
Outcomes(ship, battle, result)
```

of Exercise 5.2.4, and evaluate your queries using the data of that exercise.

a) Find the number of battleship classes.

b) Find the average number of guns of battleship classes.

! c) Find the average number of guns of battleships. Note the difference between (b) and (c); do we weight a class by the number of ships of that class or not?

! d) Find for each class the year in which the first ship of that class was launched.

! e) Find for each class the number of ships of that class sunk in battle.

!! f) Find for each class with at least three ships the number of ships of that class sunk in battle.

!! g) The weight (in pounds) of the shell fired from a naval gun is approximately one half the cube of the bore (in inches). Find the average weight of the shell for each country's ships.

Exercise 6.4.8: In Example 5.23 we gave an example of the query: "find, for each star who has appeared in at least three movies, the earliest year in which they appeared." We wrote this query as a γ operation. Write it in SQL.

*! **Exercise 6.4.9:** The γ operator of extended relational algebra does not have a feature that corresponds to the HAVING clause of SQL. Is it possible to mimic an SQL query with a HAVING clause in relational algebra? If so, how would we do it in general?

6.5   Database Modifications

To this point, we have focused on the normal SQL query form: the select-from-where statement. There are a number of other statement forms that do not return a result, but rather change the state of the database. In this section, we shall focus on three types of statements that allow us to

1. Insert tuples into a relation.

2. Delete certain tuples from a relation.

3. Update values of certain components of certain existing tuples.

We refer to these three types of operations collectively as *modifications*.

6.5.1   Insertion

The basic form of insertion statement consists of:

1. The keywords INSERT INTO,

2. The name of a relation R,

3. A parenthesized list of attributes of the relation R,

4. The keyword VALUES, and

5. A tuple expression, that is, a parenthesized list of concrete values, one for each attribute in the list (3).

That is, the basic insertion form is

$$\text{INSERT INTO } R(A_1, \ldots, A_n) \text{ VALUES } (v_1, \ldots, v_n);$$

A tuple is created using the value v_i for attribute A_i, for $i = 1, 2, \ldots, n$. If the list of attributes does not include all attributes of the relation R, then the tuple created has default values for all missing attributes. The most common default value is NULL, the null value, but there are other options to be discussed in Section 6.6.4.

Example 6.34: Suppose we wish to add Sydney Greenstreet to the list of stars of *The Maltese Falcon*. We say:

```
1)  INSERT INTO StarsIn(movieTitle, movieYear, starName)
2)  VALUES('The Maltese Falcon', 1942, 'Sydney Greenstreet');
```

The effect of executing this statement is that a tuple with the three components on line (2) is inserted into the relation StarsIn. Since all attributes of StarsIn are mentioned on line (1), there is no need to add default components. The values on line (2) are matched with the attributes on line (1) in the order given, so 'The Maltese Falcon' becomes the value of the component for attribute movieTitle, and so on.   □

If, as in Example 6.34, we provide values for all attributes of the relation, then we may omit the list of attributes that follows the relation name. That is, we could just say:

```
INSERT INTO StarsIn
VALUES('The Maltese Falcon', 1942, 'Sydney Greenstreet');
```

However, if we take this option, we must be sure that the order of the values is the same as the standard order of attributes for the relation. We shall see in Section 6.6 how relation schemas are declared, and we shall see that as we do so we provide an order for the attributes. This order is assumed when matching values to attributes, if the list of attributes is missing from an INSERT statement.

- If you are not sure of the standard order for the attributes, it is best to list them in the INSERT clause in the order you choose for their values in the VALUES clause.

The simple INSERT described above only puts one tuple into a relation. Instead of using explicit values for one tuple, we can compute a set of tuples to be inserted, using a subquery. This subquery replaces the keyword VALUES and the tuple expression in the INSERT statement form described above.

Example 6.35 : Suppose we want to add to the relation

```
Studio(name, address, presC#)
```

all movie studios that are mentioned in the relation

```
Movie(title, year, length, inColor, studioName, producerC#)
```

but do not appear in Studio. Since there is no way to determine an address or a president for such a studio, we shall have to be content with value NULL for attributes address and presC# in the inserted Studio tuples. A way to make this insertion is shown in Fig. 6.15.

```
1)   INSERT INTO Studio(name)
2)       SELECT DISTINCT studioName
3)       FROM Movie
4)       WHERE studioName NOT IN
5)           (SELECT name
6)            FROM Studio);
```

Figure 6.15: Adding new studios

Like most SQL statements with nesting, Fig. 6.15 is easiest to examine from the inside out. Lines (5) and (6) generate all the studio names in the relation

---

The Timing of Insertions

Figure 6.15 illustrates a subtle point about the semantics of SQL statements. In principle, the evaluation of the query of lines (2) through (6) should be accomplished prior to executing the insertion of line (1). Thus, there is no possibility that new tuples added to Studio at line (1) will affect the condition on line (4). However, for efficiency purposes, it is possible that an implementation will execute this statement so that changes to Studio are made as soon as new studios are found, during the execution of lines (2) through (6).

In this particular example, it does not matter whether or not insertions are delayed until the query is completely evaluated. However, there are other queries where the result can be changed by varying the timing of insertions. For example, suppose DISTINCT were removed from line (2) of Fig. 6.15. If we evaluate the query of lines (2) through (6) before doing any insertion, then a new studio name appearing in several Movie tuples would appear several times in the result of this query and therefore would be inserted several times into relation Studio. However, if we inserted new studios into Studio as soon as we found them during the evaluation of the query of lines (2) through (6), then the same new studio would not be inserted twice. Rather, as soon as the new studio was inserted once, its name would no longer satisfy the condition of lines (4) through (6), and it would not appear a second time in the result of the query of lines (2) through (6).

Studio. Thus, line (4) tests that a studio name from the Movie relation is none of these studios.

Now, we see that lines (2) through (6) produce the set of studio names found in Movie but not in Studio. The use of DISTINCT on line (2) assures that each studio will appear only once in this set, no matter how many movies it owns. Finally, line (1) inserts each of these studios, with NULL for the attributes address and presC#, into relation Studio.   □

6.5.2   Deletion

A deletion statement consists of:

1. The keywords DELETE FROM,

2. The name of a relation, say R,

3. The keyword WHERE, and

4. A condition.

That is, the form of a deletion is

$$\text{DELETE FROM } R \text{ WHERE } <\text{condition}>;$$

The effect of executing this statement is that every tuple satisfying the condition (4) will be deleted from relation R.

Example 6.36: We can delete from relation

        StarsIn(movieTitle, movieYear, starName)

the fact that Sydney Greenstreet was a star in *The Maltese Falcon* by the SQL statement:

```
DELETE FROM StarsIn
WHERE movieTitle = 'The Maltese Falcon' AND
      movieYear = 1942 AND
      starName = 'Sydney Greenstreet';
```

Notice that unlike the insertion statement of Example 6.34, we cannot simply specify a tuple to be deleted. Rather, we must describe the tuple exactly by a WHERE clause. □

Example 6.37: Here is another example of a deletion. This time, we delete from relation

        MovieExec(name, address, cert#, netWorth)

several tuples at once by using a condition that can be satisfied by more than one tuple. The statement

```
DELETE FROM MovieExec
WHERE netWorth < 10000000;
```

deletes all movie executives whose net worth is low — less than ten million dollars. □

6.5.3 Updates

While we might think of both insertions and deletions of tuples as "updates" to the database, an *update* in SQL is a very specific kind of change to the database: one or more tuples that already exist in the database have some of their components changed. The general form of an update statement is:

1. The keyword UPDATE,

2. A relation name, say R,

3. The keyword SET,

4. A list of formulas that each set an attribute of the relation R equal to the value of an expression or constant,

5. The keyword WHERE, and

6. A condition.

That is, the form of an update is

UPDATE R SET <new-value assignments> WHERE <condition>;

Each new-value assignment (item 4 above) is an attribute, an equal sign, and a formula. If there is more than one assignment, they are separated by commas.

The effect of this statement is to find all the tuples in R that satisfy the condition (6). Each of these tuples are then changed by having the formulas of (4) evaluated and assigned to the components of the tuple for the corresponding attributes of R.

Example 6.38: Let us modify the relation

    MovieExec(name, address, cert#, netWorth)

by attaching the title Pres. in front of the name of every movie executive who is the president of a studio. The condition the desired tuples satisfy is that their certificate numbers appear in the presC# component of some tuple in the Studio relation. We express this update as:

    1) UPDATE MovieExec
    2) SET name = 'Pres. ' || name
    3) WHERE cert# IN (SELECT presC# FROM Studio);

Line (3) tests whether the certificate number from the MovieExec tuple is one of those that appear as a president's certificate number in Studio.

Line (2) performs the update on the selected tuples. Recall that the operator || denotes concatenation of strings, so the expression following the = sign in line (2) places the characters Pres. and a blank in front of the old value of the name component of this tuple. The new string becomes the value of the name component of this tuple; the effect is that 'Pres. ' has been prepended to the old value of name. □

6.5.4 Exercises for Section 6.5

Exercise 6.5.1: Write the following database modifications, based on the database schema

    Product(maker, model, type)
    PC(model, speed, ram, hd, rd, price)
    Laptop(model, speed, ram, hd, screen, price)
    Printer(model, color, type, price)

of Exercise 5.2.1. Describe the effect of the modifications on the data of that exercise.

a) Using two INSERT statements store in the database the fact that PC model 1100 is made by manufacturer C, has speed 1800, RAM 256, hard disk 80, a 20x DVD, and sells for $2499.

! b) Insert the facts that for every PC there is a laptop with the same manufacturer, speed, RAM, and hard disk, a 15-inch screen, a model number 1100 greater, and a price $500 more.

c) Delete all PC's with less than 20 gigabytes of hard disk.

d) Delete all laptops made by a manufacturer that doesn't make printers.

e) Manufacturer A buys manufacturer B. Change all products made by B so they are now made by A.

f) For each PC, double the amount of RAM and add 20 gigabytes to the amount of hard disk. (Remember that several attributes can be changed by one UPDATE statement.)

! g) For each laptop made by manufacturer B, add one inch to the screen size and subtract $100 from the price.

Exercise 6.5.2: Write the following database modifications, based on the database schema

> Classes(class, type, country, numGuns, bore, displacement)
> Ships(name, class, launched)
> Battles(name, date)
> Outcomes(ship, battle, result)

of Exercise 5.2.4. Describe the effect of the modifications on the data of that exercise.

* a) The two British battleships of the Nelson class — Nelson and Rodney — were both launched in 1927, had nine 16-inch guns, and a displacement of 34,000 tons. Insert these facts into the database.

b) Two of the three battleships of the Italian Vittorio Veneto class — Vittorio Veneto and Italia — were launched in 1940; the third ship of that class, Roma, was launched in 1942. Each had nine 15-inch guns and a displacement of 41,000 tons. Insert these facts into the database.

* c) Delete from Ships all ships sunk in battle.

* d) Modify the Classes relation so that gun bores are measured in centimeters (one inch = 2.5 centimeters) and displacements are measured in metric tons (one metric ton = 1.1 tons).

e) Delete all classes with fewer than three ships.

6.6 Defining a Relation Schema in SQL

In this section we shall begin a discussion of *data definition*, the portions of SQL that involve describing the structure of information in the database. In contrast, the aspects of SQL discussed previously — queries and modifications — are often called *data manipulation*.[7]

The subject of this section is declaration of the schemas of stored relations. We shall see how to describe a new relation or *table* as it is called in SQL. Section 6.7 covers the declaration of "views," which are virtual relations that are not really stored in the database, while some of the more complex issues regarding constraints on relations are deferred to Chapter 7.

6.6.1 Data Types

To begin, let us introduce the principal atomic data types that are supported by SQL systems. All attributes must have a data type.

1. Character strings of fixed or varying length. The type CHAR(n) denotes a fixed-length string of n characters. That is, if an attribute has type CHAR(n), then in any tuple the component for this attribute will be a string of n characters. VARCHAR(n) denotes a string of up to n characters. Components for an attribute of this type will be strings of between 0 and n characters. SQL permits reasonable coercions between values of character-string types. Normally, a string is padded by trailing blanks if it becomes the value of a component that is a fixed-length string of greater length. For example, the string 'foo', if it became the value of a component for an attribute of type CHAR(5), would assume the value 'foo ' (with two blanks following the second o). The padding blanks can then be ignored if the value of this component were compared (see Section 6.1.3) with another string.

2. Bit strings of fixed or varying length. These strings are analogous to fixed and varying-length character strings, but their values are strings of bits rather than characters. The type BIT(n) denotes bit strings of length n, while BIT VARYING(n) denotes bit strings of length up to n.

3. The type BOOLEAN denotes an attribute whose value is logical. The possible values of such an attribute are TRUE, FALSE, and — although it would surprise George Boole — UNKNOWN.

4. The type INT or INTEGER (these names are synonyms) denotes typical integer values. The type SHORTINT also denotes integers, but the number

---

[7]Technically, the material of this section is in the realm of database design, and thus should have been covered earlier in the book, like the analogous ODL for object-oriented databases. However, there are good reasons to group all SQL study together, so we took the liberty of violating our own organization.

of bits permitted may be less, depending on the implementation (as with the types `int` and `short int` in C).

5. Floating-point numbers can be represented in a variety of ways. We may use the type `FLOAT` or `REAL` (these are synonyms) for typical floating-point numbers. A higher precision can be obtained with the type `DOUBLE PRECISION`; again the distinction between these types is as in C. SQL also has types that are real numbers with a fixed decimal point. For example, `DECIMAL(n,d)` allows values that consist of n decimal digits, with the decimal point assumed to be d positions from the right. Thus, 0123.45 is a possible value of type `DECIMAL(6,2)`. `NUMERIC` is almost a synonym for `DECIMAL`, although there are possible implementation-dependent differences.

6. Dates and times can be represented by the data types `DATE` and `TIME`, respectively. Recall our discussion of date and time values in Section 6.1.4. These values are essentially character strings of a special form. We may, in fact, coerce dates and times to string types, and we may do the reverse if the string "makes sense" as a date or time.

6.6.2 Simple Table Declarations

The simplest form of declaration of a relation schema consists of the keywords `CREATE TABLE` followed by the name of the relation and a parenthesized list of the attribute names and their types.

Example 6.39: The relation schema for our example `MovieStar` relation, which was described informally in Section 5.1, is expressed in SQL as in Fig. 6.16. The first two attributes, `name` and `address`, have each been declared to be character strings. However, with the name, we have made the decision to use a fixed-length string of 30 characters, padding a name out with blanks at the end if necessary and truncating a name to 30 characters if it is longer. In contrast, we have declared addresses to be variable-length character strings of up to 255 characters.[8] It is not clear that these two choices are the best possible, but we use them to illustrate two kinds of string data types.

The `gender` attribute has values that are a single letter, `M` or `F`. Thus, we can safely use a single character as the type of this attribute. Finally, the `birthdate` attribute naturally deserves the data type `DATE`. If this type were not available in a system that did not conform to the SQL standard, we could use `CHAR(10)` instead, since all `DATE` values are actually strings of 10 characters: eight digits and two hyphens. □

---

[8]The number 255 is not the result of some weird notion of what typical addresses look like. A single byte can store integers between 0 and 255, so it is possible to represent a varying-length character string of up to 255 bytes by a single byte for the count of characters plus the bytes to store the string itself. Commercial systems generally support longer varying-length strings, however.

```
1)   CREATE TABLE MovieStar (
2)       name CHAR(30),
3)       address VARCHAR(255),
4)       gender CHAR(1),
5)       birthdate DATE
     );
```

Figure 6.16: Declaring the relation schema for the MovieStar relation

6.6.3 Modifying Relation Schemas

We can delete a relation R by the SQL statement:

```
DROP TABLE R;
```

Relation R is no longer part of the database schema, and we can no longer access any of its tuples.

More frequently than we would drop a relation that is part of a long-lived database, we may need to modify the schema of an existing relation. These modifications are done by a statement that begins with the keywords ALTER TABLE and the name of the relation. We then have several options, the most important of which are

1. ADD followed by a column name and its data type.

2. DROP followed by a column name.

Example 6.40 : Thus, for instance, we could modify the MovieStar relation by adding an attribute phone with

```
ALTER TABLE MovieStar ADD phone CHAR(16);
```

As a result, the MovieStar schema now has five attributes: the four mentioned in Fig. 6.16 and the attribute phone, which is a fixed-length string of 16 bytes. In the actual relation, tuples would all have components for phone, but we know of no phone numbers to put there. Thus, the value of each of these components would be NULL. In Section 6.6.4, we shall see how it is possible to choose another "default" value to be used instead of NULL for unknown values.

As another example, we could delete the birthdate attribute by

```
ALTER TABLE MovieStar DROP birthdate;
```

□

6.6.4 Default Values

When we create or modify tuples, we sometimes do not have values for all components. For example, we mentioned in Example 6.40 that when we add a column to a relation schema, the existing tuples do not have a known value, and it was suggested that NULL could be used in place of a "real" value. Or, we suggested in Example 6.35 that we could insert new tuples into the Studio relation knowing only the studio name and not the address or president's certificate number. Again, it would be necessary to use some value that says "I don't know" in place of real values for the latter two attributes.

To address these problems, SQL provides the NULL value, which becomes the value of any component whose value is not specified, with the exception of certain situations where the NULL value is not permitted (see Section 7.1). However, there are times when we would prefer to use another choice of *default* value, the value that appears in a column if no other value is known.

In general, any place we declare an attribute and its data type, we may add the keyword DEFAULT and an appropriate value. That value is either NULL or a constant. Certain other values that are provided by the system, such as the current time, may also be options.

Example 6.41: Let us consider Example 6.39. We might wish to use the character ? as the default for an unknown gender, and we might also wish to use the earliest possible date, DATE '0000-00-00' for an unknown birthdate. We could replace lines (4) and (5) of Fig. 6.16 by:

```
4)      gender CHAR(1) DEFAULT '?',
5)      birthdate DATE DEFAULT DATE '0000-00-00'
```

As another example, we could have declared the default value for new attribute phone to be 'unlisted' when we added this attribute in Example 6.40. The alteration statement would then look like:

```
ALTER TABLE MovieStar ADD phone CHAR(16) DEFAULT 'unlisted';
```

□

6.6.5 Indexes

An *index* on an attribute A of a relation is a data structure that makes it efficient to find those tuples that have a fixed value for attribute A. Indexes usually help with queries in which their attribute A is compared with a constant, for instance $A = 3$, or even $A \leq 3$. The technology of implementing indexes on large relations is of central importance in the implementation of DBMS's. Chapter 13 is devoted to this topic.

When relations are very large, it becomes expensive to scan all the tuples of a relation to find those (perhaps very few) tuples that match a given condition. For example, consider the first query we examined:

```
SELECT *
FROM Movie
WHERE studioName = 'Disney' AND year = 1990;
```

from Example 6.1. There might be 10,000 `Movie` tuples, of which only 200 were made in 1990.

The naive way to implement this query is to get all 10,000 tuples and test the condition of the `WHERE` clause on each. It would be much more efficient if we had some way of getting only the 200 tuples from the year 1990 and testing each of them to see if the studio was Disney. It would be even more efficient if we could obtain directly only the 10 or so tuples that satisfied both the conditions of the `WHERE` clause — that the studio be Disney and the year be 1990; see the discussion of "multiattribute indexes," below.

Although the creation of indexes is not part of any SQL standard up to and including SQL-99, most commercial systems have a way for the database designer to say that the system should create an index on a certain attribute for a certain relation. The following syntax is typical. Suppose we want to have an index on attribute `year` for the relation `Movie`. Then we say:

```
CREATE INDEX YearIndex ON Movie(year);
```

The result will be that an index whose name is `YearIndex` will be created on attribute `year` of the relation `Movie`. Henceforth, SQL queries that specify a year may be executed by the SQL query processor in such a way that only those tuples of `Movie` with the specified year are ever examined; there is a resulting decrease in the time needed to answer the query.

Often, a DBMS allows us to build a single index on multiple attributes. This type of index takes values for several attributes and efficiently finds the tuples with the given values for these attributes.

Example 6.42 : Since `title` and `year` form a key for `Movie`, we might expect it to be common that values for both these attributes will be specified, or neither will. The following is a typical declaration of an index on these two attributes:

```
CREATE INDEX KeyIndex ON Movie(title, year);
```

Since (`title`, `year`) is a key, then when we are given a title and year, we know the index will find only one tuple, and that will be the desired tuple. In contrast, if the query specifies both the title and year, but only `YearIndex` is available, then the best the system can do is retrieve all the movies of that year and check through them for the given title.

If, as is often the case, the key for the multiattribute index is really the concatenation of the attributes in some order, then we can even use this index to find all the tuples with a given value in the first of the the attributes. Thus, part of the design of a multiattribute index is the choice of the order in which the attributes are listed. For instance, if we were more likely to specify a title than a year for a movie, then we would prefer to order the attributes as above; if a year were more likely to be specified, then we would ask for an index on (year, title). □

If we wish to delete the index, we simply use its name in a statement like:

```
DROP INDEX YearIndex;
```

6.6.6 Introduction to Selection of Indexes

Selection of indexes requires a trade-off by the database designer, and in practice, this choice is one of the principal factors that influence whether a database design is acceptable. Two important factors to consider are:

- The existence of an index on an attribute greatly speeds up queries in which a value for that attribute is specified, and in some cases can speed up joins involving that attribute as well.

- On the other hand, every index built for an attribute of some relation makes insertions, deletions, and updates to that relation more complex and time-consuming.

Index selection is one of the hardest parts of database design, since it requires estimating what the typical mix of queries and other operations on the database will be. If a relation is queried much more frequently than it is modified, then indexes on the attributes that are most frequently specified in queries make sense. Indexes are useful for attributes that tend to be compared with constants in WHERE clauses of queries, but indexes also are useful for attributes that appear frequently in join conditions.

Example 6.43 : Recall Figure 6.3, where we suggested an exhaustive pairing of tuples to compute a join. An index on Movie.title would help us find the Movie tuple for *Star Wars* quickly, and then, after finding its producer-certificate-number, an index on MovieExec.cert# would help us quickly find that person in the MovieExec relation. □

If modifications are the predominant action, then we should be very conservative about creating indexes. Even then, it may be an efficiency gain to create an index on a frequently used attribute. In fact, since some modification commands involve querying the database (e.g., an INSERT with a select-from-where subquery or a DELETE with a condition) one must be very careful how one estimates the relative frequency of modifications and queries.

We do not yet have the details — how data is typically stored and how indexes are implemented — that are needed to see the complete picture. However, we can see part of the problem in the following example. We should be aware that the typical relation is stored over many disk blocks, and the principal cost of a query or modification is often the number of disk blocks that need to be brought to main memory (see Section 11.4.1). Thus, indexes that let us find a tuple without examining the entire relation can save a lot of time. However, the indexes themselves have to be stored, at least partially, on disk, so accessing and modifying the indexes themselves cost disk accesses. In fact, modification, since it requires one disk access to read a block and another disk access to write the changed block, is about twice as expensive as accessing the index or the data in a query.

Example 6.44: Let us consider the relation

> StarsIn(movieTitle, movieYear, starName)

Suppose that there are three database operations that we sometimes perform on this relation:

Q_1: We look for the title and year of movies in which a given star appeared. That is, we execute a query of the form:

> SELECT movieTitle, movieYear
> FROM StarsIn
> WHERE starName = s;

for some constant s.

Q_2: We look for the stars that appeared in a given movie. That is, we execute a query of the form:

> SELECT starName
> FROM StarsIn
> WHERE movieTitle = t AND movieYear = y;

for constants t and y.

I: We insert a new tuple into StarsIn. That is, we execute an insertion of the form:

> INSERT INTO StarsIn VALUES(t, y, s);

for constants t, y, and s.

Let us make the following assumptions about the data:

1. StarsIn is stored in 10 disk blocks, so if we need to examine the entire relation the cost is 10.

2. On the average, a star has appeared in 3 movies and a movie has 3 stars.

3. Since the tuples for a given star or a given movie are likely to be spread over the 10 disk blocks of StarsIn, even if we have an index on starName or on the combination of movieTitle and movieYear, it will take 3 disk accesses to find the (average of) 3 tuples for a star or movie. If we have no index on the star or movie, respectively, then 10 disk accesses are required.

4. One disk access is needed to read a block of the index every time we use that index to locate tuples with a given value for the indexed attribute(s). If the index block must be modified (in the case of an insertion), then another disk access is needed to write back the modified block.

5. Likewise, in the case of an insertion, one disk access is needed to read a block on which the new tuple will be placed, and another disk access is needed to write back this block. We assume that, even without an index, we can find some block on which an additional tuple will fit, without scanning the entire relation.

Action	No Index	Star Index	Movie Index	Both Indexes
Q_1	10	4	10	4
Q_2	10	10	4	4
I	2	4	4	6
	$2 + 8p_1 + 8p_2$	$4 + 6p_2$	$4 + 6p_1$	$6 - 2p_1 - 2p_2$

Figure 6.17: Costs associated with the three actions, as a function of which indexes are selected

Figure 6.17 gives the costs of each of the three operations; Q_1 (query given a star), Q_2 (query given a movie), and I (insertion). If there is no index, then we must scan the entire relation for Q_1 or Q_2 (cost 10), while an insertion requires merely that we access a block with free space and rewrite it with the new tuple (cost of 2, since we assume that block can be found without an index). These observations explain the column labeled "No Index."

If there is an index on stars only, then Q_2 still requires a scan of the entire relation (cost 10). However, Q_1 can be answered by accessing one index block to find the three tuples for a given star and then making three more accesses to find those tuples. Insertion I requires that we read and write both a disk block for the index and a disk block for the data, for a total of 4 disk accesses.

The case where there is an index on movies only is symmetric to the case for stars only. Finally, if there are indexes on both stars and movies, then it takes 4 disk accesses to answer either Q_1 or Q_2. However, insertion I requires that we read and write two index blocks as well as a data block, for a total of 6 disk accesses. That observation explains the last column in Fig. 6.17.

The final row in Fig. 6.17 gives the average cost of an action, on the assumption that the fraction of the time we do Q_1 is p_1 and the fraction of the time we do Q_2 is p_2; therefore, the fraction of the time we do I is $1 - p_1 - p_2$.

Depending on p_1 and p_2, any of the four choices of index/no index can yield the best average cost for the three actions. For example, if $p_1 = p_2 = 0.1$, then the expression $2 + 8p_1 + 8p_2$ is the smallest, so we would prefer not to create any indexes. That is, if we are doing mostly insertion, and very few queries, then we don't want an index. On the other hand, if $p_1 = p_2 = 0.4$, then the formula $6 - 2p_1 - 2p_2$ turns out to be the smallest, so we would prefer indexes on both starName and on the (movieTitle, movieYear) combination. Intuitively, if we are doing a lot of queries, and the number of queries specifying movies and stars are roughly equally frequent, then both indexes are desired.

If we have $p_1 = 0.5$ and $p_2 = 0.1$, then it turns out that an index on stars only gives the best average value, because $4 + 6p_2$ is the formula with the smallest value. Likewise, $p_1 = 0.1$ and $p_2 = 0.5$ tells us to create an index on only movies. The intuition is that if only one type of query is frequent, create only the index that helps that type of query. □

6.6.7   Exercises for Section 6.6

* **Exercise 6.6.1:** In this section, we gave a formal declaration for only the relation MovieStar among the five relations of our running example. Give suitable declarations for the other four relations:

```
Movie(title, year, length, inColor, studioName, producerC#)
StarsIn(movieTitle, movieYear, starName)
MovieExec(name, address, cert#, netWorth)
Studio(name, address, presC#)
```

Exercise 6.6.2: Below we repeat once again the informal database schema from Exercise 5.2.1.

```
Product(maker, model, type)
PC(model, speed, ram, hd, rd, price)
Laptop(model, speed, ram, hd, screen, price)
Printer(model, color, type, price)
```

Write the following declarations:

  a) A suitable schema for relation Product.

  b) A suitable schema for relation PC.

 * c) A suitable schema for relation Laptop.

  d) A suitable schema for relation Printer.

  e) An alteration to your Printer schema from (d) to delete the attribute color.

* f) An alteration to your `Laptop` schema from (c) to add the attribute `cd`. Let the default value for this attribute be `'none'` if the laptop does not have a CD reader.

Exercise 6.6.3: Here is the informal schema from Exercise 5.2.4.

```
Classes(class, type, country, numGuns, bore, displacement)
Ships(name, class, launched)
Battles(name, date)
Outcomes(ship, battle, result)
```

Write the following declarations:

a) A suitable schema for relation `Classes`.

b) A suitable schema for relation `Ships`.

c) A suitable schema for relation `Battles`.

d) A suitable schema for relation `Outcomes`.

e) An alteration to your `Classes` relation from (a) to delete the attribute `bore`.

f) An alteration to your `Ships` relation from (b) to include the attribute `yard` giving the shipyard where the ship was built.

! **Exercise 6.6.4:** Explain the difference between the statement `DROP R` and the statement `DELETE FROM R`.

Exercise 6.6.5: Suppose that the relation `StarsIn` discussed in Example 6.44 required 100 blocks rather than 10, but all other assumptions of that example continued to hold. Give formulas in terms of p_1 and p_2 to measure the cost of queries Q_1 and Q_2 and insertion I, under the four combinations of index/no index discussed there.

6.7 View Definitions

Relations that are defined with a `CREATE TABLE` statement actually exist in the database. That is, an SQL system stores tables in some physical organization. They are persistent, in the sense that they can be expected to exist indefinitely and not to change unless they are explicitly told to change by an `INSERT` or one of the other modification statements we discussed in Section 6.5.

There is another class of SQL relations, called *views*, that do not exist physically. Rather, they are defined by an expression much like a query. Views, in turn, can be queried as if they existed physically, and in some cases, we can even modify views.

6.7.1 Declaring Views

The simplest form of view definition is

1. The keywords CREATE VIEW,

2. The name of the view,

3. The keyword AS, and

4. A query Q. This query is the definition of the view. Any time we query the view, SQL behaves as if Q were executed at that time and the query were applied to the relation produced by Q.

That is, a simple view declaration has the form

CREATE VIEW <view-name> AS <view-definition>;

Example 6.45 : Suppose we want to have a view that is a part of the

Movie(title, year, length, inColor, studioName, producerC#)

relation, specifically, the titles and years of the movies made by Paramount Studios. We can define this view by

```
1)   CREATE VIEW ParamountMovie AS
2)       SELECT title, year
3)       FROM Movie
4)       WHERE studioName = 'Paramount';
```

First, the name of the view is ParamountMovie, as we see from line (1). The attributes of the view are those listed in line (2), namely title and year. The definition of the view is the query of lines (2) through (4).   □

6.7.2 Querying Views

Relation ParamountMovie does not contain tuples in the usual sense. Rather, if we query ParamountMovie, the appropriate tuples are obtained from the base table Movie, so the query can be answered. As a result, we can ask the same query about ParamountMovie twice and get different answers. The reason is that, even though we have not changed the definition of view ParamountMovie, the base table Movie may have changed in the interim.

Example 6.46 : We may query the view ParamountMovie just as if it were a stored table, for instance:

```
SELECT title
FROM ParamountMovie
WHERE year = 1979;
```

Relations, Tables, and Views

SQL programmers tend to use the term "table" instead of "relation." The reason is that it is important to make a distinction between stored relations, which are "tables," and virtual relations, which are "views." Now that we know the distinction between a table and a view, we shall use "relation" only where either a table or view could be used. When we want to emphasize that a relation is stored, rather than a view, we shall sometimes use the term "base relation" or "base table."

There is also a third kind of relation, one that is neither a view nor stored permanently. These relations are temporary results, as might be constructed for some subquery. Temporaries will also be referred to as "relations" subsequently.

The definition of the view `ParamountMovie` is used to turn the query above into a new query that addresses only the base table `Movie`. We shall illustrate how to convert queries on views to queries on base tables in Section 6.7.5. However, in this simple case it is not hard to deduce what the example query about the view means. We observe that `ParamountMovie` differs from `Movie` in only two ways:

1. Only attributes `title` and `year` are produced by `ParamountMovie`.

2. The condition `studioName = 'Paramount'` is part of any `WHERE` clause about `ParamountMovie`.

Since our query wants only the `title` produced, (1) does not present a problem. For (2), we need only to introduce the condition `studioName = 'Paramount'` into the `WHERE` clause of our query. Then, we can use `Movie` in place of `ParamountMovie` in the `FROM` clause, assured that the meaning of our query is preserved. Thus, the query:

```
SELECT title
FROM Movie
WHERE studioName = 'Paramount' AND year = 1979;
```

is a query about the base table `Movie` that has the same effect as our original query about the view `ParamountMovie`. Note that it is the job of the SQL system to do this translation. We show the reasoning process only to indicate what a query about a view means. □

Example 6.47: It is also possible to write queries involving both views and base tables. An example is

```
SELECT DISTINCT starName
FROM ParamountMovie, StarsIn
WHERE title = movieTitle AND year = movieYear;
```

This query asks for the name of all stars of movies made by Paramount. Note that the use of DISTINCT assures that stars will be listed only once, even if they appeared in several Paramount movies.   □

Example 6.48: Let us consider a more complicated query used to define a view. Our goal is a relation MovieProd with movie titles and the names of their producers. The query defining the view involves both relation

```
Movie(title, year, length, inColor, studioName, producerC#)
```

from which we get a producer's certificate number, and the relation

```
MovieExec(name, address, cert#, netWorth)
```

where we connect the certificate to the name. We may write:

```
CREATE VIEW MovieProd AS
    SELECT title, name
    FROM Movie, MovieExec
    WHERE producerC# = cert#;
```

We can query this view as if it were a stored relation. For instance, to find the producer of *Gone With the Wind*, ask:

```
SELECT name
FROM MovieProd
WHERE title = 'Gone With the Wind';
```

As with any view, this query is treated as if it were an equivalent query over the base tables alone, such as:

```
SELECT name
FROM Movie, MovieExec
WHERE producerC# = cert# AND title = 'Gone With the Wind';
```

□

6.7.3   Renaming Attributes

Sometimes, we might prefer to give a view's attributes names of our own choosing, rather than use the names that come out of the query defining the view. We may specify the attributes of the view by listing them, surrounded by parentheses, after the name of the view in the CREATE VIEW statement. For instance, we could rewrite the view definition of Example 6.48 as:

```
CREATE VIEW MovieProd(movieTitle, prodName) AS
    SELECT title, name
    FROM Movie, MovieExec
    WHERE producerC# = cert#;
```

The view is the same, but its columns are headed by attributes `movieTitle` and `prodName` instead of `title` and `name`.

6.7.4 Modifying Views

In limited circumstances it is possible to execute an insertion, deletion, or update to a view. At first, this idea makes no sense at all, since the view does not exist the way a base table (stored relation) does. What could it mean, say, to insert a new tuple into a view? Where would the tuple go, and how would the database system remember that it was supposed to be in the view?

For many views, the answer is simply "you can't do that." However, for sufficiently simple views, called *updatable views*, it is possible to translate the modification of the view into an equivalent modification on a base table, and the modification can be done to the base table instead. SQL provides a formal definition of when modifications to a view are permitted. The SQL rules are complex, but roughly, they permit modifications on views that are defined by selecting (using `SELECT`, not `SELECT DISTINCT`) some attributes from one relation R (which may itself be an updatable view). Two important technical points:

- The `WHERE` clause must not involve R in a subquery.

- The list in the `SELECT` clause must include enough attributes that for every tuple inserted into the view, we can fill the other attributes out with `NULL` values or the proper default and have a tuple of the base relation that will yield the inserted tuple of the view.

Example 6.49: Suppose we try to insert into view `ParamountMovie` of Example 6.45 a tuple like:

```
INSERT INTO ParamountMovie
VALUES('Star Trek', 1979);
```

View `ParamountMovie` almost meets the SQL updatability conditions, since the view asks only for some components of some tuples of one base table:

```
Movie(title, year, length, inColor, studioName, producerC#)
```

The only problem is that since attribute `studioName` of `Movie` is not an attribute of the view, the tuple we insert into `Movie` would have `NULL` rather than `'Paramount'` as its value for `studioName`. That tuple does not meet the condition that its studio be Paramount.

Thus, to make the view `ParamountMovie` updatable, we shall add attribute `studioName` to its SELECT clause, even though it is obvious to us that the studio name will be Paramount. The revised definition of view `ParamountMovie` is:

```
CREATE VIEW ParamountMovie AS
    SELECT studioName, title, year
    FROM Movie
    WHERE studioName = 'Paramount';
```

Then, we write the insertion into updatable view `ParamountMovie` as:

```
INSERT INTO ParamountMovie
VALUES('Paramount', 'Star Trek', 1979);
```

To effect the insertion, we invent a `Movie` tuple that yields the inserted view tuple when the view definition is applied to `Movie`. For the particular insertion above, the `studioName` component is 'Paramount', the `title` component is 'Star Trek', and the `year` component is 1979.

The other three attributes that do not appear in the view — `length`, `inColor`, and `producerC#` — surely exist in the inserted `Movie` tuple. However, we cannot deduce their values. As a result, the new `Movie` tuple must have in the components for each of these three attributes the appropriate default value: either `NULL` or some other default that was declared for an attribute. For example, if the default value 0 was declared for attribute `length`, but the other two use `NULL` for the default, then the resulting inserted `Movie` tuple would be:

title	year	length	inColor	studioName	producerC#
'Star Trek'	1979	0	NULL	'Paramount'	NULL

□

We may also delete from an updatable view. The deletion, like the insertion, is passed through to the underlying relation R and causes the deletion of every tuple of R that gives rise to a deleted tuple of the view.

Example 6.50: Suppose we wish to delete from the updatable `Paramount-Movie` view all movies with "Trek" in their titles. We may issue the deletion statement

```
DELETE FROM ParamountMovie
WHERE title LIKE '%Trek%';
```

This deletion is translated into an equivalent deletion on the `Movie` base table; the only difference is that the condition defining the view `ParamountMovie` is added to the conditions of the `WHERE` clause.

```
DELETE FROM Movie
WHERE title LIKE '%Trek%' AND studioName = 'Paramount';
```

Why Some Views Are Not Updatable

Consider the view `MovieProd` of Example 6.48, which relates movie titles and producers' names. This view is not updatable according to the SQL definition, because there are two relations in the `FROM` clause: `Movie` and `MovieExec`. Suppose we tried to insert a tuple like

> ('Greatest Show on Earth', 'Cecil B. DeMille')

We would have to insert tuples into both `Movie` and `MovieExec`. We could use the default value for attributes like `length` or `address`, but what could be done for the two equated attributes `producerC#` and `cert#` that both represent the unknown certificate number of DeMille? We could use `NULL` for both of these. However, when joining relations with `NULL`'s, SQL does not recognize two `NULL` values as equal (see Section 6.1.5). Thus, 'Greatest Show on Earth' would not be connected with 'Cecil B. DeMille' in the `MovieProd` view, and our insertion would not have been done correctly.

---

is the resulting delete statement. □

Similarly, an update on an updatable view is passed through to the underlying relation. The view update thus has the effect of updating all tuples of the underlying relation that give rise in the view to updated view tuples.

Example 6.51: The view update

```
UPDATE ParamountMovie
SET year = 1979
WHERE title = 'Star Trek the Movie';
```

is turned into the base-table update

```
UPDATE Movie
SET year = 1979
WHERE title = 'Star Trek the Movie' AND
    studioName = 'Paramount';
```

□

A final kind of modification of a view is to delete it altogether. This modification may be done whether or not the view is updatable. A typical `DROP` statement is

```
DROP VIEW ParamountMovie;
```

Note that this statement deletes the definition of the view, so we may no longer make queries or issue modification commands involving this view. However dropping the view does not affect any tuples of the underlying relation `Movie`. In contrast,

```
DROP TABLE Movie
```

would not only make the `Movie` table go away. It would also make the view `ParamountMovie` unusable, since a query that used it would indirectly refer to the nonexistent relation `Movie`.

6.7.5 Interpreting Queries Involving Views

We can get a good idea of what view queries mean by following the way a query involving a view would be processed. The matter is taken up in more generality in Section 16.2, when we examine query processing in general.

The basic idea is illustrated in Fig. 6.18. A query Q is there represented by its expression tree in relational algebra. This expression tree uses as leaves some relations that are views. We have suggested two such leaves, the views V and W. To interpret Q in terms of base tables, we find the definition of the views V and W. These definitions are also expressed as expression trees of relational algebra.

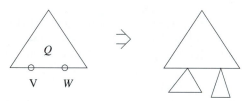

Figure 6.18: Substituting view definitions for view references

To form the query over base tables, we substitute, for each leaf in the tree for Q that is a view, the root of a copy of the tree that defines that view. Thus, in Fig. 6.18 we have shown the leaves labeled V and W replaced by the definitions of these views. The resulting tree is a query over base tables that is equivalent to the original query about views.

Example 6.52 : Let us consider the view definition and query of Example 6.46. Recall the definition of view `ParamountMovie` is:

```
CREATE VIEW ParamountMovie AS
    SELECT title, year
    FROM Movie
    WHERE studioName = 'Paramount';
```

An expression tree for the query that defines this view is shown in Fig. 6.19.

The query of Example 6.46 is

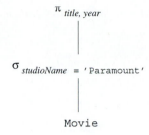

Figure 6.19: Expression tree for view `ParamountMovie`

```
SELECT title
FROM ParamountMovie
WHERE year = 1979;
```

asking for the Paramount movies made in 1979. This query has the expression tree shown in Fig. 6.20. Note that the one leaf of this tree represents the view `ParamountMovie`.

Figure 6.20: Expression tree for the query

We therefore interpret the query by substituting the tree of Fig. 6.19 for the leaf `ParamountMovie` in Fig. 6.20. The resulting tree is shown in Fig. 6.21.

The tree of Fig. 6.21 is an acceptable interpretation of the query. However, it is expressed in an unnecessarily complex way. An SQL system would apply transformations to this tree in order to make it look like the expression tree for the query we suggested in Example 6.46:

```
SELECT title
FROM Movie
WHERE studioName = 'Paramount' AND year = 1979;
```

For example, we can move the projection $\pi_{title,\ year}$ above the selection $\sigma_{year=1979}$. The reason is that delaying a projection until after a selection can never change the result of an expression. Then, we have two projections in a row, first onto `title` and `year` and then onto `title` alone. Clearly the first of these is redundant, and we can eliminate it. Thus, the two projections can be replaced by a single projection onto `title`.

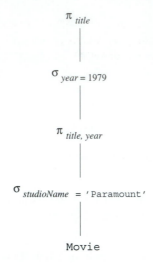

Figure 6.21: Expressing the query in terms of base tables

The two selections can also be combined. In general, two consecutive selections can be replaced by one selection for the AND of their conditions. The resulting expression tree is shown in Fig. 6.22. It is the tree that we would obtain from the query

```
SELECT title
FROM Movie
WHERE studioName = 'Paramount' AND year = 1979;
```

directly.   □

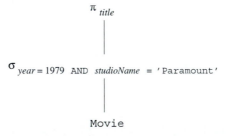

Figure 6.22: Simplifying the query over base tables

6.7.6   Exercises for Section 6.7

Exercise 6.7.1 : From the following base tables of our running example

```
MovieStar(name, address, gender, birthdate)
MovieExec(name, address, cert#, netWorth)
Studio(name, address, presC#)
```

Construct the following views:

* a) A view `RichExec` giving the name, address, certificate number and net worth of all executives with a net worth of at least $10,000,000.

  b) A view `StudioPres` giving the name, address, and certificate number of all executives who are studio presidents.

  c) A view `ExecutiveStar` giving the name, address, gender, birth date, certificate number, and net worth of all individuals who are both executives and stars.

Exercise 6.7.2: Which of the views of Exercise 6.7.1 are updatable?

Exercise 6.7.3: Write each of the queries below, using one or more of the views from Exercise 6.7.1 and no base tables.

  a) Find the names of females who are both stars and executives.

* b) Find the names of those executives who are both studio presidents and worth at least $10,000,000.

! c) Find the names of studio presidents who are also stars and are worth at least $50,000,000.

*! **Exercise 6.7.4:** For the view and query of Example 6.48:

  a) Show the expression tree for the view `MovieProd`.

  b) Show the expression tree for the query of that example.

  c) Build from your answers to (a) and (b) an expression for the query in terms of base tables.

  d) Explain how to change your expression from (c) so it is an equivalent expression that matches the suggested solution in Example 6.48.

! **Exercise 6.7.5:** For each of the queries of Exercise 6.7.3, express the query and views as relational-algebra expressions, substitute for the uses of the view in the query expression, and simplify the resulting expressions as best you can. Write SQL queries corresponding to your resulting expressions on the base tables.

Exercise 6.7.6: Using the base tables

```
Classes(class, type, country, numGuns, bore, displacement)
Ships(name, class, launched)
```

from Exercise 5.2.4:

a) Define a view `BritishShips` that gives for each ship of Great Britain its class, type, number of guns, bore, displacement, and year launched.

b) Write a query using your view from (a) asking for the number of guns and displacements of all British battleships launched before 1919.

! c) Express the query of (b) and view of (a) as relational-algebra expressions, substitute for the uses of the view in the query expression, and simplify the resulting expressions as best you can.

! d) Write an SQL query corresponding to your expression from (c) on the base tables `Classes` and `Ships`.

6.8   Summary of Chapter 6

◆ *SQL*: The language SQL is the principal query language for relational database systems. The current standard is called SQL-99 or SQL3. Commercial systems generally vary from this standard.

◆ *Select-From-Where Queries*: The most common form of SQL query has the form select-from-where. It allows us to take the product of several relations (the `FROM` clause), apply a condition to the tuples of the result (the `WHERE` clause), and produce desired components (the `SELECT` clause).

◆ *Subqueries*: Select-from-where queries can also be used as subqueries within a `WHERE` clause or `FROM` clause of another query. The operators `EXISTS`, `IN`, `ALL`, and `ANY` may be used to express boolean-valued conditions about the relations that are the result of a subquery in a `WHERE` clause.

◆ *Set Operations on Relations*: We can take the union, intersection, or difference of relations by connecting the relations, or connecting queries defining the relations, with the keywords `UNION`, `INTERSECT`, and `EXCEPT`, respectively.

◆ *Join Expressions*: SQL has operators such as `NATURAL JOIN` that may be applied to relations, either as queries by themselves or to define relations in a `FROM` clause.

◆ *Null Values*: SQL provides a special value `NULL` that appears in components of tuples for which no concrete value is available. The arithmetic and logic of `NULL` is unusual. Comparison of any value to `NULL`, even another `NULL`, gives the truth value `UNKNOWN`. That truth value, in turn, behaves in boolean-valued expressions as if it were halfway between `TRUE` and `FALSE`.

✦ *Outerjoins*: SQL provides an `OUTER JOIN` operator that joins relations but also includes in the result dangling tuples from one or both relations; the dangling tuples are padded with `NULL`'s in the resulting relation.

✦ *The Bag Model of Relations*: SQL actually regards relations as bags of tuples, not sets of tuples. We can force elimination of duplicate tuples with the keyword `DISTINCT`, while keyword `ALL` allows the result to be a bag in certain circumstances where bags are not the default.

✦ *Aggregations*: The values appearing in one column of a relation can be summarized (aggregated) by using one of the keywords `SUM`, `AVG` (average value), `MIN`, `MAX`, or `COUNT`. Tuples can be partitioned prior to aggregation with the keywords `GROUP BY`. Certain groups can be eliminated with a clause introduced by the keyword `HAVING`.

✦ *Modification Statements*: SQL allows us to change the tuples in a relation. We may `INSERT` (add new tuples), `DELETE` (remove tuples), or `UPDATE` (change some of the existing tuples), by writing SQL statements using one of these three keywords.

✦ *Data Definition*: SQL has statements to declare elements of a database schema. The `CREATE TABLE` statement allows us to declare the schema for stored relations (called tables), specifying the attributes and their types, and default values.

✦ *Altering Schemas*: We can change aspects of the database schema with an `ALTER` statement. These changes include adding and removing attributes from relation schemas and changing the default value associated with an attribute or domain. We may also use a `DROP` statement to completely eliminate relations or other schema elements.

✦ *Indexes*: While not part of the SQL standard, commerical SQL systems allow the declaration of indexes on attributes; these indexes speed up certain queries or modifications that involve specification of a value for the indexed attribute.

✦ *Views*: A view is a definition of how one relation (the view) may be constructed from tables stored in the database. Views may be queried as if they were stored relations, and an SQL system modifies queries about a view so the query is instead about the base tables that are used to define the view.

6.9 References for Chapter 6

The SQL2 and SQL-99 standards are published on-line via anonymous FTP. The primary site is `ftp://jerry.ece.umassd.edu/isowg3`, with mirror sites at `ftp://math0.math.ecu.edu/isowg3` and `ftp://tiu.ac.jp/iso/wg3`. In each case the subdirectory is `dbl/BASEdocs`. As of the time of the printing of this book, not all sites were accepting FTP requests. We shall endeavour to keep the reader up to date on the situation through this book's Web site (see the Preface).

Several books are available that give more details of SQL programming. Some of our favorites are [2], [4], and [6]. [5] is an early exposition of the recent SQL-99 standard.

SQL was first defined in [3]. It was implemented as part of System R [1], one of the first generation of relational database prototypes.

1. Astrahan, M. M. et al., "System R: a relational approach to data management," *ACM Transactions on Database Systems* **1**:2, pp. 97–137, 1976.

2. Celko, J., *SQL for Smarties*, Morgan-Kaufmann, San Francisco, 1999.

3. Chamberlin, D. D., et al., "SEQUEL 2: a unified approach to data definition, manipulation, and control," *IBM Journal of Research and Development* **20**:6, pp. 560–575, 1976.

4. Date, C. J. and H. Darwen, *A Guide to the SQL Standard*, Addison-Wesley, Reading, MA, 1997.

5. Gulutzan, P. and T. Pelzer, *SQL-99 Complete, Really*, R&D Books, Lawrence, KA, 1999.

6. Melton, J. and A. R. Simon, *Understanding the New SQL: A Complete Guide*, Morgan-Kaufmann, San Francisco, 1993.

Chapter 7

Constraints and Triggers

In this chapter we shall cover those aspects of SQL that let us create "active" elements. An *active* element is an expression or statement that we write once, store in the database, and expect the element to execute at appropriate times. The time of action might be when a certain event occurs, such as an insertion into a particular relation, or it might be whenever the database changes so that a certain boolean-valued condition becomes true.

One of the serious problems faced by writers of applications that update the database is that the new information could be wrong in a variety of ways. For example, there are often typographical or transcription errors in manually entered data. The most straightforward way to make sure that database modifications do not allow inappropriate tuples in relations is to write application programs so every insertion, deletion, and update command has associated with it the checks necessary to assure correctness. Unfortunately, the correctness requirements are frequently complex, and they are always repetitive; application programs must make the same tests after every modification.

Fortunately, SQL provides a variety of techniques for expressing *integrity constraints* as part of the database schema. In this chapter we shall study the principal methods. First are key constraints, where an attribute or set of attributes is declared to be a key for a relation. Next, we consider a form of referential integrity, called "foreign-key constraints," which are the requirement that a value in an attribute or attributes of one relation (e.g., a `presC#` in `Studio`) must also appear as a value in an attribute or attributes of another relation (e.g., `cert#` of `MovieExec`).

Then, we consider constraints on attributes, tuples, and relations as a whole, and we cover interrelation constraints called "assertions." Finally, we discuss "triggers," which are a form of active element that is called into play on certain specified events, such as insertion into a specific relation.

315

7.1 Keys and Foreign Keys

Perhaps the most important kind of constraint in a database is a declaration that a certain attribute or set of attributes forms a key for a relation. If a set of attributes S is a key for relation R, then any two tuples of R must disagree in at least one attribute in the set S. Note that this rule applies even to duplicate tuples; i.e., if R has a declared key, then R cannot have duplicates.

A key constraint, like many other constraints, is declared within the CREATE TABLE command of SQL. There are two similar ways to declare keys: using the keywords PRIMARY KEY or the keyword UNIQUE. However, a table may have only one primary key but any number of "unique" declarations.

SQL also uses the term "key" in connection with certain referential-integrity constraints. These constraints, called "foreign-key constraints," assert that a value appearing in one relation must also appear in the primary-key component(s) of another relation. We shall take up foreign-key constraints in Section 7.1.4.

7.1.1 Declaring Primary Keys

A relation may have only one primary key. There are two ways to declare a primary key in the CREATE TABLE statement that defines a stored relation.

1. We may declare one attribute to be a primary key when that attribute is listed in the relation schema.

2. We may add to the list of items declared in the schema (which so far have only been attributes) an additional declaration that says a particular attribute or set of attributes forms the primary key.

For method (1), we append the keywords PRIMARY KEY after the attribute and its type. For method (2), we introduce a new element in the list of attributes consisting of the keywords PRIMARY KEY and a parenthesized list of the attribute or attributes that form this key. Note that if the key consists of more than one attribute, we need to use method (2).

The effect of declaring a set of attributes S to be a primary key for relation R is twofold:

1. Two tuples in R cannot agree on all of the attributes in set S. Any attempt to insert or update a tuple that violates this rule causes the DBMS to reject the action that caused the violation.

2. Attributes in S are not allowed to have NULL as a value for their components.

Example 7.1: Let us reconsider the schema for relation MovieStar from Example 6.39. The primary key for this relation is name. Thus, we can add this

```
1)   CREATE TABLE MovieStar (
2)       name CHAR(30) PRIMARY KEY,
3)       address VARCHAR(255),
4)       gender CHAR(1),
5)       birthdate DATE
     );
```

Figure 7.1: Making `name` the primary key

fact to the line declaring `name`. Figure 7.1 is a revision of Fig. 6.16 that reflects this change.

Alternatively, we can use a separate definition of the primary key. After line (5) of Fig. 6.16 we add a declaration of the primary key, and we have no need to declare it in line (2). The resulting schema declaration would look like Fig. 7.2. □

```
1)   CREATE TABLE MovieStar (
2)       name CHAR(30),
3)       address VARCHAR(255),
4)       gender CHAR(1),
5)       birthdate DATE,
6)       PRIMARY KEY (name)
     );
```

Figure 7.2: A separate declaration of the primary key

Note that in Example 7.1, the form of either Fig. 7.1 or Fig. 7.2 is acceptable, because the primary key is a single attribute. However, in a situation where the primary key has more than one attribute, we must use the style of Fig. 7.2. For instance, if we declare the schema for relation `Movie`, whose key is the pair of attributes `title` and `year`, we should add, after the list of attributes, the line

```
PRIMARY KEY (title, year)
```

7.1.2 Keys Declared With UNIQUE

Another way to declare a key is to use the keyword `UNIQUE`. This word can appear exactly where `PRIMARY KEY` can appear: either following an attribute and its type or as a separate item within a `CREATE TABLE` statement. The meaning of a `UNIQUE` declaration is almost the same as the meaning of a `PRIMARY KEY` declaration. There are two distinctions, however:

1. We may have any number of `UNIQUE` declarations for a table, but only one primary key.

2. While `PRIMARY KEY` forbids NULL's in the attributes of the key, `UNIQUE` permits them. Moreover, the rule that two tuples may not agree in all of a set of attributes declared `UNIQUE` may be violated if one or more of the components involved have `NULL` as a value. In fact, it is even permitted for both tuples to have `NULL` in all corresponding attributes of the `UNIQUE` key.

The implementor of a DBMS has the option to make additional distinctions. For instance, a database vendor might always place an index on a key declared to be a primary key (even if that key consisted of more than one attribute), but require the user to call for an index explicitly on other attributes. Alternatively, a table might always be kept sorted on its primary key, if it had one.

Example 7.2: Line (2) of Fig. 7.1 could have been written

        2)   name CHAR(30) UNIQUE,

We could also change line (3) to

        3)   address VARCHAR(255) UNIQUE,

if we felt that two movie stars could not have the same address (a dubious assumption). Similarly, we could change line (6) of Fig. 7.2 to

        6)   UNIQUE (name)

should we choose. □

7.1.3 Enforcing Key Constraints

Recall our discussion of indexes in Section 6.6.5, where we learned that although they are not part of any SQL standard, each SQL implementation has a way of creating indexes as part of the database schema definition. It is normal to build an index on the primary key, in order to support the common type of query that specifies a value for the primary key. We may also want to build indexes on other attributes declared to be `UNIQUE`.

Then, when the `WHERE` clause of the query includes a condition that equates a key to a particular value — for instance `name = 'Audrey Hepburn'` in the case of the `MovieStar` relation of Example 7.1 — the matching tuple will be found very quickly, without a search through all the tuples of the relation.

Many SQL implementations offer an index-creation statement using the keyword `UNIQUE` that declares an attribute to be a key at the same time it creates an index on that attribute. For example, the statement

```
CREATE UNIQUE INDEX YearIndex ON Movie(year);
```

would have the same effect as the example index-creation statement in Section 6.6.5, but it would also declare a uniqueness constraint on attribute `year` of the relation `Movie` (not a reasonable assumption).

Let us consider for a moment how an SQL system would enforce a key constraint. In principle, the constraint must be checked every time we try to change the database. However, it should be clear that the only time a key constraint for a relation R can become violated is when R is modified. In fact, a deletion from R cannot cause a violation; only an insertion or update can. Thus, it is normal practice for the SQL system to check a key constraint only when an insertion or update to that relation occurs.

An index on the attribute(s) declared to be keys is vital if the SQL system is to enforce a key constraint efficiently. If the index is available, then whenever we insert a tuple into the relation or update a key attribute in some tuple, we use the index to check that there is not already a tuple with the same value in the attribute(s) declared to be a key. If so, the system must prevent the modification from taking place.

If there is no index on the key attribute(s), it is still possible to enforce a key constraint. Sorting the relation by key-value helps us search. However, in the absence of any aid to searching, the system must examine the entire relation, looking for a tuple with the given key value. That process is extremely time-consuming and would render database modification of large relations virtually impossible.

7.1.4 Declaring Foreign-Key Constraints

A second important kind of constraint on a database schema is that values for certain attributes must make sense. That is, an attribute like `presC#` of relation `Studio` is expected to refer to a particular movie executive. The implied "referential integrity" constraint is that if a studio's tuple has a certain certificate number c in the `presC#` component, then c is the certificate of a real movie executive. In terms of the database, a "real" executive is one mentioned in the `MovieExec` relation. Thus, there must be some `MovieExec` tuple that has c in the `cert#` attribute.

In SQL we may declare an attribute or attributes of one relation to be a *foreign key*, referencing some attribute(s) of a second relation (possibly the same relation). The implication of this declaration is twofold:

1. The referenced attribute(s) of the second relation must be declared `UNIQUE` or the `PRIMARY KEY` for their relation. Otherwise, we cannot make the foreign-key declaration.

2. Values of the foreign key appearing in the first relation must also appear in the referenced attributes of some tuple. More precisely, let there be a foreign-key F that references set of attributes G of some relation. Suppose a tuple t of the first relation has non-`NULL` values in all the attributes of F; call the list of t's values in these attributes $t[F]$. Then in the referenced

relation there must be some tuple s that agrees with $t[F]$ on the attributes G. That is, $s[G] = t[F]$.

As for primary keys, we have two ways to declare a foreign key.

a) If the foreign key is a single attribute we may follow its name and type by a declaration that it "references" some attribute (which must be a key — primary or unique) of some table. The form of the declaration is

REFERENCES <table>(<attribute>)

b) Alternatively, we may append to the list of attributes in a CREATE TABLE statement one or more declarations stating that a set of attributes is a foreign key. We then give the table and its attributes (which must be a key) to which the foreign key refers. The form of this declaration is:

FOREIGN KEY (<attributes>) REFERENCES <table>(<attributes>)

Example 7.3: Suppose we wish to declare the relation

    Studio(name, address, presC#)

whose primary key is name and which has a foreign key presC# that references cert# of relation

    MovieExec(name, address, cert#, netWorth)

We may declare presC# directly to reference cert# as follows:

```
CREATE TABLE Studio (
    name CHAR(30) PRIMARY KEY,
    address VARCHAR(255),
    presC# INT REFERENCES MovieExec(cert#)
);
```

An alternative form is to add the foreign key declaration separately, as

```
CREATE TABLE Studio (
    name CHAR(30) PRIMARY KEY,
    address VARCHAR(255),
    presC# INT,
    FOREIGN KEY (presC#) REFERENCES MovieExec(cert#)
);
```

Notice that the referenced attribute, cert# in MovieExec, is a key of that relation, as it must be. The meaning of either of these two foreign key declarations is that whenever a value appears in the presC# component of a Studio tuple, that value must also appear in the cert# component of some MovieExec tuple. The one exception is that, should a particular Studio tuple have NULL as the value of its presC# component, there is no requirement that NULL appear as the value of a cert# component (in fact, cert# is a primary key and therefore cannot have NULL's anyway). □

7.1.5 Maintaining Referential Integrity

We have seen how to declare a foreign key, and we learned that this declaration implies that any set of values for the attributes of the foreign key, none of which are NULL, must also appear in the corresponding attribute(s) of the referenced relation. But how is this constraint to be maintained in the face of modifications to the database? The database implementor may choose from among three alternatives.

The Default Policy: Reject Violating Modifications

SQL has a default policy that any modification violating the referential integrity constraint is rejected by the system. For instance, consider Example 7.3, where it is required that a presC# value in relation Studio also be a cert# value in MovieExec. The following actions will be rejected by the system (i.e., a run-time exception or error will be generated).

1. We try to insert a new Studio tuple whose presC# value is not NULL and is not the cert# component of any MovieExec tuple. The insertion is rejected by the system, and the tuple is never inserted into Studio.

2. We try to update a Studio tuple to change the presC# component to a non-NULL value that is not the cert# component of any MovieExec tuple. The update is rejected, and the tuple is unchanged.

3. We try to delete a MovieExec tuple, and its cert# component appears as the presC# component of one or more Studio tuples. The deletion is rejected, and the tuple remains in MovieExec.

4. We try to update a MovieExec tuple in a way that changes the cert# value, and the old cert# is the value of presC# of some movie studio. The system again rejects the change and leaves MovieExec as it was.

The Cascade Policy

There is another approach to handling deletions or updates to a referenced relation like MovieExec (i.e., the third and fourth types of modifications described above), called the *cascade policy*. Intuitively, changes to the referenced attribute(s) are mimicked at the foreign key.

Under the cascade policy, when we delete the MovieExec tuple for the president of a studio, then to maintain referential integrity the system will delete the referencing tuple(s) from Studio. Updates are handled analogously. If we change the cert# for some movie executive from c_1 to c_2, and there was some Studio tuple with c_1 as the value of its presC# component, then the system will also update this presC# component to have value c_2.

The Set-Null Policy

Yet another approach to handling the problem is to change the `presC#` value from that of the deleted or updated studio president to `NULL`; this policy is called *set-null*.

These options may be chosen for deletes and updates, independently, and they are stated with the declaration of the foreign key. We declare them with `ON DELETE` or `ON UPDATE` followed by our choice of `SET NULL` or `CASCADE`.

Example 7.4: Let us see how we might modify the declaration of

        Studio(name, address, presC#)

in Example 7.3 to specify the handling of deletes and updates in the

        MovieExec(name, address, cert#, netWorth)

relation. Figure 7.3 takes the first of the `CREATE TABLE` statements in that example and expands it with `ON DELETE` and `ON UPDATE` clauses. Line (5) says that when we delete a `MovieExec` tuple, we set the `presC#` of any studio of which he or she was the president to `NULL`. Line (6) says that if we update the `cert#` component of a `MovieExec` tuple, then any tuples in `Studio` with the same value in the `presC#` component are changed similarly.

```
1)   CREATE TABLE Studio (
2)      name CHAR(30) PRIMARY KEY,
3)      address VARCHAR(255),
4)      presC# INT REFERENCES MovieExec(cert#)
5)          ON DELETE SET NULL
6)          ON UPDATE CASCADE
     );
```

Figure 7.3: Choosing policies to preserve referential integrity

Note that in this example, the set-null policy makes more sense for deletes, while the cascade policy seems preferable for updates. We would expect that if, for instance, a studio president retires, the studio will exist with a "null" president for a while. However, an update to the certificate number of a studio president is most likely a clerical change. The person continues to exist and to be the president of the studio, so we would like the `presC#` attribute in `Studio` to follow the change.   □

Dangling Tuples and Modification Policies

A tuple with a foreign key value that does not appear in the referenced relation is said to be a *dangling tuple*. Recall that a tuple which fails to participate in a join is also called "dangling." The two ideas are closely related. If a tuple's foreign-key value is missing from the referenced relation, then the tuple will not participate in a join of its relation with the referenced relation.

The dangling tuples are exactly the tuples that violate referential integrity for this foreign-key constraint.

- The default policy for deletions and updates to the referenced relation is that the action is forbidden if and only if it creates one or more dangling tuples in the referencing relation.

- The cascade policy is to delete or update all dangling tuples created (depending on whether the modification is a delete or update to the referenced relation, respectively).

- The set-null policy is to set the foreign key to NULL in each dangling tuple.

7.1.6 Deferring the Checking of Constraints

Let us assume the situation of Example 7.3, where presC# in Studio is a foreign key referencing cert# of MovieExec. Bill Clinton decides, after his national presidency, to found a movie studio, called Redlight Studios, of which he will naturally be the president. If we execute the insertion:

```
INSERT INTO Studio
VALUES('Redlight', 'New York', 23456);
```

we are in trouble. The reason is that there is no tuple of MovieExec with certificate number 23456 (the presumed newly issued certificate for Bill Clinton), so there is an obvious violation of the foreign-key constraint.

One possible fix is first to insert the tuple for Redlight without a president's certificate, as:

```
INSERT INTO Studio(name, address)
VALUES('Redlight', 'New York');
```

This change avoids the constraint violation, because the Redlight tuple is inserted with NULL as the value of presC#, and NULL in a foreign key does not require that we check for the existence of any value in the referenced column.

However, we must insert a tuple for Bill Clinton into `MovieExec`, with his correct certificate number before we can apply an update statement such as

```
UPDATE Studio
SET presC# = 23456
WHERE name = 'Redlight';
```

If we do not fix `MovieExec` first, then this update statement will also violate the foreign-key constraint.

Of course, inserting Bill Clinton and his certificate number into `MovieExec` before inserting Redlight into `Studio` will surely protect us against a foreign-key violation in this case. However, there are cases of *circular constraints* that cannot be fixed by judiciously ordering the database modification steps we take.

Example 7.5: If movie executives were limited to studio presidents, then we might want to declare `cert#` to be a foreign key referencing `Studio(presC#)`; we would then have to declare `presC#` to be `UNIQUE`, but that declaration makes sense if you assume a person cannot be the president of two studios at the same time.

Now, it is impossible to insert new studios with new presidents. We can't insert a tuple with a new value of `presC#` into `Studio`, because that tuple would violate the foreign-key constraint from `presC#` to `MovieExec(cert#)`. We can't insert a tuple with a new value of `cert#` into `MovieExec`, because that would violate the foreign-key constraint from `cert#` to `Studio(presC#)`. □

The problem of Example 7.5 has a solution, but it involves several elements of SQL that we have not yet seen.

1. First, we need the ability to group several SQL statements (the two insertions — one into `Studio` and the other into `MovieExec`) into one unit, called a "transaction." We shall meet transactions as an indivisible unit of work in Section 8.6.

2. Then, we need a way to tell the SQL system not to check the constraints until after the whole transaction is finished ("committed" in the terminology of transactions).

We may take point (1) on faith for the moment, but there are two details we must learn to handle point (2):

a) Any constraint — key, foreign-key, or other constraint types we shall meet later in this chapter — may be declared `DEFERRABLE` or `NOT DEFERRABLE`. The latter is the default, and means that every time a database modification occurs, the constraint is checked immediately afterwards, if the modification requires that it be checked at all. However, if we declare a constraint to be `DEFERRABLE`, then we have the option of telling it to wait until a transaction is complete before checking the constraint.

b) If a constraint is deferrable, then we may also declare it to be INITIALLY DEFERRED or INITIALLY IMMEDIATE. In the former case, checking will be deferred to the end of the current transaction, unless we tell the system to stop deferring this constraint. If declared INITIALLY IMMEDIATE, the check will be made before any modification, but because the constraint is deferrable, we have the option of later deciding to defer checking.

Example 7.6: Figure 7.4 shows the declaration of Studio modified to allow the checking of its foreign-key constraint to be deferred until after each transaction. We have also declared presC# to be UNIQUE, in order that it may be referenced by other relations' foreign-key constraints.

```
CREATE TABLE Studio (
    name CHAR(30) PRIMARY KEY,
    address VARCHAR(255),
    presC# INT UNIQUE
        REFERENCES MovieExec(cert#)
        DEFERRABLE INITIALLY DEFERRED
);
```

Figure 7.4: Making presC# unique and deferring the checking of its foreign-key constraint

If we made a similar declaration for the hypothetical foreign-key constraint from MovieExec(cert#) to Studio(presC#) mentioned in Example 7.5, then we could write transactions that inserted two tuples, one into each relation, and the two foreign-key constraints would not be checked until after both insertions had been done. Then, if we insert both a new studio and its new president, and use the same certificate number in each tuple, we would avoid violation of any constraint. □

There are two additional points about deferring constraints that we should bear in mind:

- Constraints of any type can be given names. We shall discuss how to do so in Section 7.3.1.

- If a constraint has a name, say MyConstraint, then we can change a deferrable constraint from immediate to deferred by the SQL statement

    ```
    SET CONSTRAINT MyConstraint DEFERRED;
    ```

    and we can reverse the process by changing DEFERRED in the above to IMMEDIATE.

7.1.7 Exercises for Section 7.1

* **Exercise 7.1.1:** Our running example movie database of Section 5.1 has keys defined for all its relations.

```
Movie(title, year, length, inColor, studioName, producerC#)
StarsIn(movieTitle, movieYear, starName)
MovieStar(name, address, gender, birthdate)
MovieExec(name, address, cert#, netWorth)
Studio(name, address, presC#)
```

Modify your SQL schema declarations of Exercise 6.6.1 to include declarations of the keys for each of these relations. Recall that all three attributes are the key for StarsIn.

Exercise 7.1.2: Declare the following referential integrity constraints for the movie database as in Exercise 7.1.1.

* a) The producer of a movie must be someone mentioned in MovieExec. Modifications to MovieExec that violate this constraint are rejected.

  b) Repeat (a), but violations result in the producerC# in Movie being set to NULL.

  c) Repeat (a), but violations result in the deletion or update of the offending Movie tuple.

  d) A movie that appears in StarsIn must also appear in Movie. Handle violations by rejecting the modification.

  e) A star appearing in StarsIn must also appear in MovieStar. Handle violations by deleting violating tuples.

*! **Exercise 7.1.3:** We would like to declare the constraint that every movie in the relation Movie must appear with at least one star in StarsIn. Can we do so with a foreign-key constraint? Why or why not?

Exercise 7.1.4: Suggest suitable keys for the relations of the PC database:

```
Product(maker, model, type)
PC(model, speed, ram, hd, rd, price)
Laptop(model, speed, ram, hd, screen, price)
Printer(model, color, type, price)
```

of Exercise 5.2.1. Modify your SQL schema from Exercise 6.6.2 to include declarations of these keys.

Exercise 7.1.5: Suggest suitable keys for the relations of the battleships database

```
Classes(class, type, country, numGuns, bore, displacement)
Ships(name, class, launched)
Battles(name, date)
Outcomes(ship, battle, result)
```

of Exercise 5.2.4. Modify your SQL schema from Exercise 6.6.3 to include declarations of these keys.

Exercise 7.1.6: Write the following referential integrity constraints for the battleships database as in Exercise 7.1.5. Use your assumptions about keys from that exercise, and handle all violations by setting the referencing attribute value to NULL.

* a) Every class mentioned in Ships must be mentioned in Classes.

  b) Every battle mentioned in Outcomes must be mentioned in Battles.

  c) Every ship mentioned in Outcomes must be mentioned in Ships.

7.2 Constraints on Attributes and Tuples

We have seen key constraints, which force certain attributes to have distinct values among all the tuples of a relation, and we have seen foreign-key constraints, which enforce referential integrity between attributes of two relations. Now, we shall see a third important kind of constraint: one that limits the values that may appear in components for some attributes. These constraints may be expressed as either:

1. A constraint on the attribute in the definition of its relation's schema, or

2. A constraint on a tuple as a whole. This constraint is part of the relation's schema, not associated with any of its attributes.

In Section 7.2.1 we shall introduce a simple type of constraint on an attribute's value: the constraint that the attribute not have a NULL value. Then in Section 7.2.2 we cover the principal form of constraints of type (1): *attribute-based* CHECK *constraints.* The second type, the tuple-based constraints, are covered in Section 7.2.3.

There are other, more general kinds of constraints that we shall meet in Section 7.4. These constraints can be used to restrict changes to whole relations or even several relations, as well as to constrain the value of a single attribute or tuple.

7.2.1   Not-Null Constraints

One simple constraint to associate with an attribute is NOT NULL. The effect is to disallow tuples in which this attribute is NULL. The constraint is declared by the keywords NOT NULL following the declaration of the attribute in a CREATE TABLE statement.

Example 7.7 : Suppose relation Studio required presC# not to be NULL, perhaps by changing line (4) of Fig. 7.3 to:

```
4)      presC# INT REFERENCES MovieExec(cert#) NOT NULL
```

This change has several consequences. For instance:

- We could not insert a tuple into Studio by specifying only the name and address, because the inserted tuple would have NULL in the presC# component.

- We could not use the set-null policy in situations like line (5) of Fig. 7.3, which tells the system to fix foreign-key violations by making presC# be NULL.

□

7.2.2   Attribute-Based CHECK Constraints

More complex constraints can be attached to an attribute declaration by the keyword CHECK, followed by a parenthesized condition that must hold for every value of this attribute. In practice, an attribute-based CHECK constraint is likely to be a simple limit on values, such as an enumeration of legal values or an arithmetic inequality. However, in principle the condition can be anything that could follow WHERE in an SQL query. This condition may refer to the attribute being constrained, by using the name of that attribute in its expression. However, if the condition refers to any other relations or attributes of relations, then the relation must be introduced in the FROM clause of a subquery (even if the relation referred to is the one to which the checked attribute belongs).

An attribute-based CHECK constraint is checked whenever any tuple gets a new value for this attribute. The new value could be introduced by an update for the tuple, or it could be part of an inserted tuple. If the constraint is violated by the new value, then the modification is rejected. As we shall see in Example 7.9, the attribute-based CHECK constraint is not checked if a database modification does not change a value of the attribute with which the constraint is associated, and this limitation can result in the constraint becoming violated. First, let us consider a simple example of an attribute-based check.

Example 7.8 : Suppose we want to require that certificate numbers be at least six digits. We could modify line (4) of Fig. 7.3, a declaration of the schema for relation

```
    Studio(name, address, presC#)
```

to be

```
4)     presC# INT REFERENCES MovieExec(cert#)
              CHECK (presC# >= 100000)
```

For another example, the attribute gender of relation

```
    MovieStar(name, address, gender, birthdate)
```

was declared in Fig. 6.16 to be of data type CHAR(1) — that is, a single character. However, we really expect that the only characters that will appear there are 'F' and 'M'. The following substitute for line (4) of Fig. 6.16 enforces the rule:

```
4) gender CHAR(1) CHECK (gender IN ('F', 'M')),
```

The above condition uses an explicit relation with two tuples, and says that the value of any gender component must be in this set. □

It is permitted for the condition being checked to mention other attributes or tuples of the relation, or even to mention other relations, but doing so requires a subquery in the condition. As we said, the condition can be anything that could follow WHERE in a select-from-where SQL statement. However, we should be aware that the checking of the constraint is associated with the attribute in question only, not with every relation or attribute mentioned by the constraint. As a result, a complex condition can become false if some element other than the checked attribute changes.

Example 7.9: We might suppose that we could simulate a referential integrity constraint by an attribute-based CHECK constraint that requires the existence of the referred-to value. The following is an *erroneous* attempt to simulate the requirement that the presC# value in a

```
    Studio(name, address, presC#)
```

tuple must appear in the cert# component of some

```
    MovieExec(name, address, cert#, netWorth)
```

tuple. Suppose line (4) of Fig. 7.3 were replaced by

```
4)     presC# INT CHECK
          (presC# IN (SELECT cert# FROM MovieExec))
```

This statement is a legal attribute-based CHECK constraint, but let us look at its effect.

- If we attempt to insert a new tuple into `Studio`, and that tuple has a `presC#` value that is not the certificate of any movie executive, then the insertion is rejected.

- If we attempt to update the `presC#` component of a `Studio` tuple, and the new value is not the `cert#` of a movie executive, the update is rejected.

- However, if we change the `MovieExec` relation, say by deleting the tuple for the president of a studio, this change is invisible to the above `CHECK` constraint. Thus, the deletion is permitted, even though the attribute-based `CHECK` constraint on `presC#` is now violated.

We shall see in Section 7.4.1 how more powerful constraint forms can correctly express this condition. □

7.2.3 Tuple-Based `CHECK` Constraints

To declare a constraint on the tuples of a single table R, when we define that table with a `CREATE TABLE` statement we may add to the list of attributes and key or foreign-key declarations the keyword `CHECK` followed by a parenthesized condition. This condition can be anything that could appear in a `WHERE` clause. It is interpreted as a condition about a tuple in the table R, and the attributes of R may be referred to by name in this expression. However, as for attribute-based `CHECK` constraints, the condition may also mention, in subqueries, other relations or other tuples of the same relation R.

The condition of a tuple-based `CHECK` constraint is checked every time a tuple is inserted into R and every time a tuple of R is updated, and is evaluated for the new or updated tuple. If the condition is false for that tuple, then the constraint is violated and the insertion or update statement that caused the violation is rejected. However, if the condition mentions some relation (even R itself) in a subquery, and a change to that relation causes the condition to become false for some tuple of R, the check does not inhibit this change. That is, like an attribute-based `CHECK`, a tuple-based `CHECK` is invisible to other relations.

Although tuple-based checks can involve some very complex conditions, it is often best to leave complex checks to SQL's "assertions," which we discuss in Section 7.4.1. The reason is that, as discussed above, tuple-based checks can be violated under certain conditions. However, if the tuple-based check involves only attributes of the tuple being checked and has no subqueries, then its constraint will always hold. Here is one example of a simple tuple-based `CHECK` constraint that involves several attributes of one tuple.

Example 7.10: Recall Example 6.39, where we declared the schema of table `MovieStar`. Figure 7.5 repeats the `CREATE TABLE` statement with the addition of a primary-key declaration and one other constraint, which is one of several possible "consistency conditions" that we might wish to check. This constraint says that if the star's gender is male, then his name must not begin with `'Ms.'`.

```
1)   CREATE TABLE MovieStar (
2)       name CHAR(30) PRIMARY KEY,
3)       address VARCHAR(255),
4)       gender CHAR(1),
5)       birthdate DATE,
6)       CHECK (gender = 'F' OR name NOT LIKE 'Ms.%')
     );
```

Figure 7.5: A constraint on the table MovieStar

Writing Constraints Correctly

Many constraints are like Example 7.10, where we want to forbid tuples that satisfy two or more conditions. The expression that should follow the check is the OR of the negations, or opposites, of each condition; this transformation is one of "DeMorgan's laws": the negation of the AND of terms is the OR of the negations of the same terms. Thus, in Example 7.10 the first condition was that the star is male, and we used gender = 'F' as a suitable negation (although perhaps gender <> 'M' would be the more normal way to phrase the negation). The second condition is that the name begins with 'Ms.', and for this negation we used the NOT LIKE comparison. This comparison negates the condition itself, which would be name LIKE 'Ms.%' in SQL.

In line (2), name is declared the primary key for the relation. Then line (6) declares a constraint. The condition of this constraint is true for every female movie star and for every star whose name does not begin with 'Ms.'. The only tuples for which it is *not* true are those where the gender is male and the name *does* begin with 'Ms.'. Those are exactly the tuples we wish to exclude from MovieStar. □

7.2.4 Exercises for Section 7.2

Exercise 7.2.1: Write the following constraints for attributes of the relation

Movie(title, year, length, inColor, studioName, producerC#)

* a) The year cannot be before 1895.

  b) The length cannot be less than 60 nor more than 250.

* c) The studio name can only be Disney, Fox, MGM, or Paramount.

Limited Constraint Checking: Bug or Feature?

One might wonder why attribute- and tuple-based checks are allowed to be violated if they refer to other relations or other tuples of the same relation. The reason is that such constraints can be implemented more efficiently than more general constraints such as assertions (see Section 7.4.1) can. With attribute- or tuple-based checks, we only have to evaluate that constraint for the tuple(s) that are inserted or updated. On the other hand, assertions must be evaluated every time any one of the relations they mention is changed. The careful database designer will use attribute- and tuple-based checks only when there is no possibility that they will be violated, and will use another mechanism, such as assertions or triggers (Section 7.4.2) otherwise.

Exercise 7.2.2: Write the following constraints on attributes from our example schema

```
Product(maker, model, type)
PC(model, speed, ram, hd, rd, price)
Laptop(model, speed, ram, hd, screen, price)
Printer(model, color, type, price)
```

of Exercise 5.2.1.

   a) The speed of a laptop must be at least 800.

   b) A removable disk can only be a 32x or 40x CD, or a 12x or 16x DVD.

   c) The only types of printers are laser, ink-jet, and bubble.

   d) The only types of products are PC's, laptops, and printers.

 ! e) A model of a product must also be the model of a PC, a laptop, or a printer.

Exercise 7.2.3: We mentioned in Example 7.13 that the tuple-based CHECK constraint of Fig. 7.7 does only half the job of the assertion of Fig. 7.6. Write the CHECK constraint on MovieExec that is necessary to complete the job.

Exercise 7.2.4: Write the following constraints as tuple-based CHECK constraints on one of the relations of our running movies example:

```
Movie(title, year, length, inColor, studioName, producerC#)
StarsIn(movieTitle, movieYear, starName)
MovieStar(name, address, gender, birthdate)
MovieExec(name, address, cert#, netWorth)
Studio(name, address, presC#)
```

If the constraint actually involves two relations, then you should put constraints in both relations so that whichever relation changes, the constraint will be checked on insertions and updates. Assume no deletions; it is not possible to maintain tuple-based constraints in the face of deletions.

* a) A movie may not be in color if it was made before 1939.

  b) A star may not appear in a movie made before they were born.

! c) No two studios may have the same address.

*! d) A name that appears in `MovieStar` must not also appear in `MovieExec`.

! e) A studio name that appears in `Studio` must also appear in at least one `Movie` tuple.

!! f) If a producer of a movie is also the president of a studio, then they must be the president of the studio that made the movie.

Exercise 7.2.5: Write the following as tuple-based `CHECK` constraints about our "PC" schema.

  a) A PC with a processor speed less than 1200 must not sell for more than $1500.

  b) A laptop with a screen size less than 15 inches must have at least a 20 gigabyte hard disk or sell for less than $2000.

Exercise 7.2.6: Write the following as tuple-based `CHECK` constraints about our "battleships" schema Exercise 5.2.4:

```
Classes(class, type, country, numGuns, bore, displacement)
Ships(name, class, launched)
Battles(name, date)
Outcomes(ship, battle, result)
```

  a) No class of ships may have guns with larger than 16-inch bore.

  b) If a class of ships has more than 9 guns, then their bore must be no larger than 14 inches.

! c) No ship can be in battle before it is launched.

7.3 Modification of Constraints

It is possible to add, modify, or delete constraints at any time. The way to express such modifications depends on whether the constraint involved is associated with an attribute, a table, or (as in Section 7.4.1) a database schema.

7.3.1 Giving Names to Constraints

In order to modify or delete an existing constraint, it is necessary that the constraint have a name. To do so, we precede the constraint by the keyword CONSTRAINT and a name for the constraint.

Example 7.11: We could rewrite line (2) of Fig. 7.1 to name the constraint that says attribute name is a primary key, as

```
2)      name CHAR(30) CONSTRAINT NameIsKey PRIMARY KEY,
```

Similarly, we could name the attribute-based CHECK constraint that appeared in Example 7.8 by:

```
4) gender CHAR(1) CONSTRAINT NoAndro
              CHECK (gender IN ('F', 'M')),
```

Finally, the following constraint:

```
6)      CONSTRAINT RightTitle
              CHECK (gender = 'F' OR name NOT LIKE 'Ms.%');
```

is a rewriting of the tuple-based CHECK constraint in line (6) of Fig. 7.5 to give that constraint a name. □

7.3.2 Altering Constraints on Tables

We mentioned in Section 7.1.6 that we can switch the checking of a constraint from immediate to deferred or vice-versa with a SET CONSTRAINT statement. Other changes to constraints are effected with an ALTER TABLE statement. We previously discussed some uses of the ALTER TABLE statement in Section 6.6.3, where we used it to add and delete attributes.

These statements can also be used to alter constraints; ALTER TABLE is used for both attribute-based and tuple-based checks. We may drop a constraint with keyword DROP and the name of the constraint to be dropped. We may also add a constraint with the keyword ADD, followed by the constraint to be added. Note, however, that you cannot add a constraint to a table unless it holds for the current instance of that table.

Example 7.12: Let us see how we would drop and add the constraints of Example 7.11 on relation MovieStar. The following sequence of three statements drops them:

```
ALTER TABLE MovieStar DROP CONSTRAINT NameIsKey;
ALTER TABLE MovieStar DROP CONSTRAINT NoAndro;
ALTER TABLE MovieStar DROP CONSTRAINT RightTitle;
```

Should we wish to reinstate these constraints, we would alter the schema for relation MovieStar by adding the same constraints, for example:

Name Your Constraints

Remember, it is a good idea to give each of your constraints a name, even if you do not believe you will ever need to refer to it. Once the constraint is created without a name, it is too late to give it one later, should you wish to alter it. However, should you be faced with a situation of having to alter a nameless constraint, you will find that your DBMS probably has a way for you to query it for a list of all your constraints, and that it has given your unnamed constraint an internal name of its own, which you may use to refer to the constraint.

```
ALTER TABLE MovieStar ADD CONSTRAINT NameIsKey
    PRIMARY KEY (name);
ALTER TABLE MovieStar ADD CONSTRAINT NoAndro
    CHECK (gender IN ('F', 'M'));
ALTER TABLE MovieStar ADD CONSTRAINT RightTitle
    CHECK (gender = 'F' OR name NOT LIKE 'Ms.%');
```

These constraints are now tuple-based, rather than attribute-based checks. We could not bring them back as attribute-based constraints.

The name is optional for these reintroduced constraints. However, we cannot rely on SQL remembering the dropped constraints. Thus, when we add a former constraint we need to write the constraint again; we cannot refer to it by its former name. □

7.3.3 Exercises for Section 7.3

Exercise 7.3.1: Show how to alter your relation schemas for the movie example:

```
Movie(title, year, length, inColor, studioName, producerC#)
StarsIn(movieTitle, movieYear, starName)
MovieStar(name, address, gender, birthdate)
MovieExec(name, address, cert#, netWorth)
Studio(name, address, presC#)
```

in the following ways.

* a) Make `title` and `year` the key for `Movie`.

  b) Require the referential integrity constraint that the producer of every movie appear in `MovieExec`.

  c) Require that no movie length be less than 60 nor greater than 250.

*! d) Require that no name appear as both a movie star and movie executive (this constraint need not be maintained in the face of deletions).

! e) Require that no two studios have the same address.

Exercise 7.3.2: Show how to alter the schemas of the "battleships" database:

```
Classes(class, type, country, numGuns, bore, displacement)
Ships(name, class, launched)
Battles(name, date)
Outcomes(ship, battle, result)
```

to have the following tuple-based constraints.

a) `Class` and `country` form a key for relation `Classes`.

b) Require the referential integrity constraint that every ship appearing in `Battles` also appears in `Ships`.

c) Require the referential integrity constraint that every ship appearing in `Outcomes` appears in `Ships`.

d) Require that no ship has more than 14 guns.

! e) Disallow a ship being in battle before it is launched.

7.4 Schema-Level Constraints and Triggers

The most powerful forms of active elements in SQL are not associated with particular tuples or components of tuples. These elements, called "triggers" and "assertions," are part of the database schema, on a par with the relations and views themselves.

- An assertion is a boolean-valued SQL expression that must be true at all times.

- A trigger is a series of actions that are associated with certain events, such as insertions into a particular relation, and that are performed whenever these events arise.

While assertions are easier for the programmer to use, since they merely require the programmer to state what must be true, triggers are the feature DBMS's typically provide as general-purpose, active elements. The reason is that it is very hard to implement assertions efficiently. The DBMS must deduce whether any given database modification could affect the truth of an assertion. Triggers, on the other hand, tell exactly when the DBMS needs to deal with them.

7.4.1 Assertions

The SQL standard proposes a simple form of *assertion* (also called a "general constraint") that allows us to enforce any condition (expression that can follow `WHERE`). Like other schema elements, we declare an assertion with a `CREATE` statement. The form of an assertion is:

1. The keywords `CREATE ASSERTION`,

2. The name of the assertion,

3. The keyword `CHECK`, and

4. A parenthesized condition.

That is, the form of this statement is

> `CREATE ASSERTION <name> CHECK (<condition>)`

The condition in an assertion must be true when the assertion is created and must always remain true; any database modification whatsoever that causes it to become false will be rejected. Recall that the other types of `CHECK` constraints we have covered can be violated under certain conditions, if they involve subqueries.

There is a difference between the way we write tuple-based `CHECK` constraints and the way we write assertions. Tuple-based checks can refer to the attributes of that relation in whose declaration they appear. For instance, in line (6) of Fig. 7.5 we used attributes `gender` and `name` without saying where they came from. They refer to components of a tuple being inserted or updated in the table `MovieStar`, because that table is the one being declared in the `CREATE TABLE` statement.

The condition of an assertion has no such privilege. Any attributes referred to in the condition must be introduced in the assertion, typically by mentioning their relation in a select-from-where expression. Since the condition must have a boolean value, it is normal to aggregate the results of the condition in some way to make a single true/false choice. For example, we might write the condition as an expression producing a relation, to which `NOT EXISTS` is applied; that is, the constraint is that this relation is always empty. Alternatively, we might apply an aggregate operator like `SUM` to a column of a relation and compare it to a constant. For instance, this way we could require that a sum always be less than some limiting value.

Example 7.13 : Suppose we wish to require that no one can become the president of a studio unless their net worth is at least $10,000,000. We declare an assertion to the effect that the set of movie studios with presidents having a net worth less than $10,000,000 is empty. This assertion involves the two relations

```
MovieExec(name, address, cert#, netWorth)
Studio(name, address, presC#)
```

```
CREATE ASSERTION RichPres CHECK
    (NOT EXISTS
        (SELECT *
         FROM Studio, MovieExec
         WHERE presC# = cert# AND netWorth < 10000000
         )
    );
```

Figure 7.6: Assertion guaranteeing rich studio presidents

The assertion is shown in Fig. 7.6.

Incidentally, it is worth noting that even though this constraint involves two relations, we could write it as tuple-based **CHECK** constraints on the two relations rather than as a single assertion. For instance, we can add to the **CREATE TABLE** statement of Example 7.3 a constraint on **Studio** as shown in Fig. 7.7.

```
CREATE TABLE Studio (
    name CHAR(30) PRIMARY KEY,
    address VARCHAR(255),
    presC# INT REFERENCES MovieExec(cert#),
    CHECK (presC# NOT IN
        (SELECT cert# FROM MovieExec
         WHERE netWorth < 10000000)
    )
);
```

Figure 7.7: A constraint on **Studio** mirroring an assertion

Note, however, that the constraint of Fig. 7.7 will only be checked when a change to its relation, **Studio** occurs. It would not catch a situation where the net worth of some studio president, as recorded in relation **MovieExec**, dropped below $10,000,000. To get the full effect of the assertion, we would have to add another constraint to the declaration of the table **MovieExec**, requiring that the net worth be at least $10,000,000 if that executive is the president of a studio. □

Example 7.14: Here is another example of an assertion. It involves the relation

```
Movie(title, year, length, inColor, studioName, producerC#)
```

Comparison of Constraints

The following table lists the principal differences among attribute-based checks, tuple-based checks, and assertions.

Type of Constraint	Where Declared	When Activated	Guaranteed to Hold?
Attribute-based CHECK	With attribute	On insertion to relation or attribute update	Not if subqueries
Tuple-based CHECK	Element of relation schema	On insertion to relation or tuple update	Not if subqueries
Assertion	Element of database schema	On any change to any mentioned relation	Yes

---

and says the total length of all movies by a given studio shall not exceed 10,000 minutes.

```
CREATE ASSERTION SumLength CHECK (10000 >= ALL
    (SELECT SUM(length) FROM Movie GROUP BY studioName)
);
```

As this constraint involves only the relation `Movie`, it could have been expressed as a tuple-based `CHECK` constraint in the schema for `Movie` rather than as an assertion. That is, we could add to the definition of table `Movie` the tuple-based `CHECK` constraint

```
CHECK (10000 >= ALL
    (SELECT SUM(length) FROM Movie GROUP BY studioName));
```

Notice that in principle this condition applies to every tuple of table `Movie`. However, it does not mention any attributes of the tuple explicitly, and all the work is done in the subquery.

Also observe that if implemented as a tuple-based constraint, the check would not be made on deletion of a tuple from the relation `Movie`. In this example, that difference causes no harm, since if the constraint was satisfied before the deletion, then it is surely satisfied after the deletion. However, if the constraint were a lower bound on total length, rather than an upper bound as in this example, then we could find the constraint violated had we written it as a tuple-based check rather than an assertion. □

As a final point, it is possible to drop an assertion. The statement to do so follows the pattern for any database schema element:

DROP ASSERTION <assertion name>

7.4.2   Event-Condition-Action Rules

Triggers, sometimes called *event-condition-action rules* or *ECA rules*, differ from the kinds of constraints discussed previously in three ways.

1. Triggers are only awakened when certain *events*, specified by the database programmer, occur. The sorts of events allowed are usually insert, delete, or update to a particular relation. Another kind of event allowed in many SQL systems is a transaction end (we mentioned transactions briefly in Section 7.1.6 and cover them with more detail in Section 8.6).

2. Instead of immediately preventing the event that awakened it, a trigger tests a *condition*. If the condition does not hold, then nothing else associated with the trigger happens in response to this event.

3. If the condition of the trigger is satisfied, the *action* associated with the trigger is performed by the DBMS. The action may then prevent the event from taking place, or it could undo the event (e.g., delete the tuple inserted). In fact, the action could be any sequence of database operations, perhaps even operations not connected in any way to the triggering event.

7.4.3   Triggers in SQL

The SQL trigger statement gives the user a number of different options in the event, condition, and action parts. Here are the principal features.

1. The action may be executed either before or after the triggering event.

2. The action can refer to both old and/or new values of tuples that were inserted, deleted, or updated in the event that triggered the action.

3. Update events may be limited to a particular attribute or set of attributes.

4. A condition may be specified by a WHEN clause; the action is executed only if the rule is triggered *and* the condition holds when the triggering event occurs.

5. The programmer has an option of specifying that the action is performed either:

   (a) Once for each modified tuple, or

   (b) Once for all the tuples that are changed in one database operation.

Before giving the details of the syntax for triggers, let us consider an example that will illustrate the most important syntactic as well as semantic points. In this example, the trigger executes once for each tuple that is updated.

Example 7.15 : We shall write an SQL trigger that applies to the

```
MovieExec(name, address, cert#, netWorth)
```

table. It is triggered by updates to the `netWorth` attribute. The effect of this trigger is to foil any attempt to lower the net worth of a movie executive. The trigger declaration appears in Fig. 7.8.

```
1)  CREATE TRIGGER NetWorthTrigger
2)  AFTER UPDATE OF netWorth ON MovieExec
3)  REFERENCING
4)      OLD ROW AS OldTuple,
5)      NEW ROW AS NewTuple
6)  FOR EACH ROW
7)  WHEN (OldTuple.netWorth > NewTuple.netWorth)
8)      UPDATE MovieExec
9)      SET netWorth = OldTuple.netWorth
10)     WHERE cert# = NewTuple.cert#;
```

Figure 7.8: An SQL trigger

Line (1) introduces the declaration with the keywords `CREATE TRIGGER` and the name of the trigger. Line (2) then gives the triggering event, namely the update of the `netWorth` attribute of the `MovieExec` relation. Lines (3) through (5) set up a way for the condition and action portions of this trigger to talk about both the old tuple (the tuple before the update) and the new tuple (the tuple after the update). These tuples will be referred to as `OldTuple` and `NewTuple`, according to the declarations in lines (4) and (5), respectively. In the condition and action, these names can be used as if they were tuple variables declared in the `FROM` clause of an ordinary SQL query.

Line (6), the phrase `FOR EACH ROW`, expresses the requirement that this trigger is executed once for each updated tuple. If this phrase is missing or it is replaced by the default `FOR EACH STATEMENT`, then the triggering would occur once for an SQL statement, no matter how many triggering-event changes to tuples it made. We would not then declare alias for old and new rows, but we might use `OLD TABLE` and `NEW TABLE`, introduced below.

Line (7) is the condition part of the trigger. It says that we only perform the action when the new net worth is lower than the old net worth; i.e., the net worth of an executive has shrunk.

Lines (8) through (10) form the action portion. This action is an ordinary SQL update statement that has the effect of restoring the net worth of the

executive to what it was before the update. Note that in principle, every tuple of
`MovieExec` is considered for update, but the `WHERE`-clause of line (10) guarantees
that only the updated tuple (the one with the proper `cert#`) will be affected.
□

Of course Example 7.15 illustrates only some of the features of SQL triggers.
In the points that follow, we shall outline the options that are offered by triggers
and how to express these options.

- Line (2) of Fig. 7.8 says that the action of the rule is executed after the
  triggering event, as indicated by the keyword `AFTER`. We may replace
  `AFTER` by `BEFORE`, in which case the `WHEN` condition is tested before the
  triggering event, that is, before the modification that awakened the trigger
  has been made to the database. If the condition is true, then the action
  of the trigger is executed. Then, the event that awakened the trigger is
  executed, regardless of whether the condition is true.

- Besides `UPDATE`, other possible triggering events are `INSERT` and `DELETE`.
  The `OF netWorth` clause in line (2) of Fig. 7.8 is optional for `UPDATE`
  events, and if present defines the event to be only an update of the at-
  tribute(s) listed after the keyword `OF`. An `OF` clause is not permitted for
  `INSERT` or `DELETE` events; these events make sense for entire tuples only.

- The `WHEN` clause is optional. If it is missing, then the action is executed
  whenever the trigger is awakened.

- While we showed a single SQL statement as an action, there can be any
  number of such statements, separated by semicolons and surrounded by
  `BEGIN...END`.

- When the triggering event is an update, then there will be old and new tuples, which are the tuple before the update and after, respectively. We give
  these tuples names by the `OLD ROW AS` and `NEW ROW AS` clauses seen in
  lines (4) and (5). If the triggering event is an insertion, then we may use a
  `NEW ROW AS` clause to give a name for the inserted tuple, and `OLD ROW AS`
  is disallowed. Conversely, on a deletion `OLD ROW AS` is used to name the
  deleted tuple and `NEW ROW AS` is disallowed.

- If we omit the `FOR EACH ROW` on line (6), then a *row-level trigger* such
  as Fig. 7.8 becomes a *statement-level trigger*. A statement-level trigger is
  executed once whenever a statement of the appropriate type is executed,
  no matter how many rows — zero, one, or many — it actually affects.
  For instance, if we update an entire table with an SQL update statement,
  a statement-level update trigger would execute only once, while a tuple-
  level trigger would execute once for each tuple to which an update is
  applied. In a statement-level trigger, we cannot refer to old and new tuples
  directly, as we did in lines (4) and (5). However, any trigger — whether

row- or statement-level — can refer to the relation of *old tuples* (deleted tuples or old versions of updated tuples) and the relation of *new tuples* (inserted tuples or new versions of updated tuples), using declarations such as OLD TABLE AS OldStuff and NEW TABLE AS NewStuff.

Example 7.16: Suppose we want to prevent the average net worth of movie executives from dropping below \$500,000. This constraint could be violated by an insertion, a deletion, or an update to the netWorth column of

```
MovieExec(name, address, cert#, netWorth)
```

The subtle point is that we might, in one INSERT or UPDATE statement insert or change many tuples of MovieExec, and during the modification, the average net worth might temporarily dip below \$500,000 and then rise above it by the time all the modifications are made. We only want to reject the entire set of modifications if the net worth is below \$500,000 at the end of the statement.

It is necessary to write one trigger for each of these three events: insert, delete, and update of relation MovieExec. Figure 7.9 shows the trigger for the update event. The triggers for the insertion and deletion of tuples are similar but slightly simpler.

```
1)   CREATE TRIGGER AvgNetWorthTrigger
2)   AFTER UPDATE OF netWorth ON MovieExec
3)   REFERENCING
4)       OLD TABLE AS OldStuff,
5)       NEW TABLE AS NewStuff
6)   FOR EACH STATEMENT
7)   WHEN (500000 > (SELECT AVG(netWorth) FROM MovieExec))
8)   BEGIN
9)       DELETE FROM MovieExec
10)      WHERE (name, address, cert#, netWorth) IN NewStuff;
11)      INSERT INTO MovieExec
12)          (SELECT * FROM OldStuff);
13)  END;
```

Figure 7.9: Constraining the average net worth

Lines (3) through (5) declare that NewStuff and OldStuff are the names of relations containing the new tuples and old tuples that are involved in the database operation that awakened our trigger. Note that one database statement can modify many tuples of a relation, and if such a statement executes, there can be many tuples in NewStuff and OldStuff.

If the operation is an update, then NewStuff and OldStuff are the new and old versions of the updated tuples, respectively. If an analogous trigger were written for deletions, then the deleted tuples would be in OldStuff, and there would be no declaration of a relation name like `NewStuff` for `NEW TABLE` in this trigger. Likewise, in the analogous trigger for insertions, the new tuples would be in `NewStuff`, and there would be no declaration of `OldStuff`.

Line (6) tells us that this trigger is executed once for a statement, regardless of how many tuples are modified. Line (7) is the condition. This condition is satisfied if the average net worth *after* the update is less than $500,000.

The action of lines (8) through (13) consists of two statements that restore the old relation `MovieExec` if the condition of the `WHEN` clause is satisfied; i.e., the new average net worth is too low. Lines (9) and (10) remove all the new tuples, i.e., the updated versions of the tuples, while lines (11) and (12) restore the tuples as they were before the update. □

7.4.4 Instead-Of Triggers

There is a useful feature of triggers that did not make the SQL-99 standard, but figured into the discussion of the standard and is supported by some commercial systems. This extension allows `BEFORE` or `AFTER` to be replaced by `INSTEAD OF`; the meaning is that when an event awakens a trigger, the action of the trigger is done instead of the event itself.

This capability offers little when the trigger is on a stored table, but it is very powerful when used on a view. The reason is that we cannot really modify a view (see Section 6.7.4). An instead-of trigger intercepts attempts to modify the view and in its place performs whatever action the database designer deems appropriate. The following is a typical example.

Example 7.17: Let us recall the definition of the view of all movies owned by Paramount:

```
CREATE VIEW ParamountMovie AS
    SELECT title, year
    FROM Movie
    WHERE studioName = 'Paramount';
```

from Example 6.45. As we discussed in Example 6.49, this view is updatable, but it has the unexpected flaw that when you insert a tuple into `Paramount-Movie`, the system cannot deduce that the `studioName` attribute is surely Paramount, so that attribute is `NULL` in the inserted `Movie` tuple.

A better result can be obtained if we create an instead-of trigger on this view, as shown in Fig. 7.10. Much of the trigger is unsurprising. We see the keyword `INSTEAD OF` on line (2), establishing that an attempt to insert into `ParamountMovie` will never take place.

Rather, we see in lines (5) and (6) the action that replaces the attempted insertion. There is an insertion into `Movie`, and it specifies the three attributes that we know about. Attributes `title` and `year` come from the tuple we tried to insert into the view; we refer to these values by the tuple variable `NewRow` that was declared in line (3) to represent the tuple we are trying to insert. The

```
1)   CREATE TRIGGER ParamountInsert
2)   INSTEAD OF INSERT ON ParamountMovie
3)   REFERENCING NEW ROW AS NewRow
4)   FOR EACH ROW
5)   INSERT INTO Movie(title, year, studioName)
6)   VALUES(NewRow.title, NewRow.year, 'Paramount');
```

Figure 7.10: Trigger to replace an insertion on a view by an insertion on the underlying base table

value of attribute `studioName` is the constant `'Paramount'`. This value is not part of the inserted tuple. Rather, we assume it is the correct studio for the inserted movie, because the insertion came through the view `ParamountMovie`. □

7.4.5 Exercises for Section 7.4

Exercise 7.4.1: Write the triggers analogous to Fig. 7.9 for the insertion and deletion events on `MovieExec`.

Exercise 7.4.2: Write the following as triggers or assertions. In each case, disallow or undo the modification if it does not satisfy the stated constraint. The database schema is from the "PC" example of Exercise 5.2.1:

```
Product(maker, model, type)
PC(model, speed, ram, hd, rd, price)
Laptop(model, speed, ram, hd, screen, price)
Printer(model, color, type, price)
```

* a) When updating the price of a PC, check that there is no lower priced PC with the same speed.

* b) No manufacturer of PC's may also make laptops.

*! c) A manufacturer of a PC must also make a laptop with at least as great a processor speed.

  d) When inserting a new printer, check that the model number exists in `Product`.

! e) When making any modification to the `Laptop` relation, check that the average price of laptops for each manufacturer is at least $2000.

! f) When updating the RAM or hard disk of any PC, check that the updated PC has at least 100 times as much hard disk as RAM.

! g) If a laptop has a larger main memory than a PC, then the laptop must also have a higher price than the PC.

! h) When inserting a new PC, laptop, or printer, make sure that the model number did not previously appear in any of PC, Laptop, or Printer.

! i) If the relation Product mentions a model and its type, then this model must appear in the relation appropriate to that type.

Exercise 7.4.3: Write the following as triggers or assertions. In each case, disallow or undo the modification if it does not satisfy the stated constraint. The database schema is from the battleships example of Exercise 5.2.4.

```
Classes(class, type, country, numGuns, bore, displacement)
Ships(name, class, launched)
Battles(name, date)
Outcomes(ship, battle, result)
```

* a) When a new class is inserted into Classes, also insert a ship with the name of that class and a NULL launch date.

  b) When a new class is inserted with a displacement greater than 35,000 tons, allow the insertion, but change the displacement to 35,000.

  c) No class may have more than 2 ships.

! d) No country may have both battleships and battlecruisers.

! e) No ship with more than 9 guns may be in a battle with a ship having fewer than 9 guns that was sunk.

! f) If a tuple is inserted into Outcomes, check that the ship and battle are listed in Ships and Battles, respectively, and if not, insert tuples into one or both of these relations, with NULL components where necessary.

! g) When there is an insertion into Ships or an update of the class attribute of Ships, check that no country has more than 20 ships.

! h) No ship may be launched before the ship that bears the name of the first ship's class.

! i) For every class, there is a ship with the name of that class.

!! j) Check, under all circumstances that could cause a violation, that no ship fought in a battle that was at a later date than another battle in which that ship was sunk.

! **Exercise 7.4.4:** Write the following as triggers or assertions. In each case, disallow or undo the modification if it does not satisfy the stated constraint. The problems are based on our running movie example:

```
Movie(title, year, length, inColor, studioName, producerC#)
StarsIn(movieTitle, movieYear, starName)
MovieStar(name, address, gender, birthdate)
MovieExec(name, address, cert#, netWorth)
Studio(name, address, presC#)
```

You may assume that the desired condition holds before any change to the database is attempted. Also, prefer to modify the database, even if it means inserting tuples with NULL or default values, rather than rejecting the attempted modification.

a) Assure that at all times, any star appearing in StarsIn also appears in MovieStar.

b) Assure that at all times every movie executive appears as either a studio president, a producer of a movie, or both.

c) Assure that every movie has at least one male and one female star.

d) Assure that the number of movies made by any studio in any year is no more than 100.

e) Assure that the average length of all movies made in any year is no more than 120.

7.5 Summary of Chapter 7

✦ *Key Constraints*: We can declare an attribute or set of attributes to be a key with a UNIQUE or PRIMARY KEY declaration in a relation schema.

✦ *Referential Integrity Constraints*: We can declare that a value appearing in some attribute or set of attributes must also appear in the corresponding attributes of some tuple of another relation with a REFERENCES or FOREIGN KEY declaration in a relation schema.

✦ *Attribute-Based Check Constraints*: We can place a constraint on the value of an attribute by adding the keyword CHECK and the condition to be checked after the declaration of that attribute in its relation schema.

✦ *Tuple-Based Check Constraints*: We can place a constraint on the tuples of a relation by adding the keyword CHECK and the condition to be checked to the declaration of the relation itself.

✦ *Modifying Constraints*: A tuple-based check can be added or deleted with an ALTER statement for the appropriate table.

✦ *Assertions*: We can declare an assertion as an element of a database schema with the keyword CHECK and the condition to be checked. This condition may involve one or more relations of the database schema, and may involve the relation as a whole, e.g., with aggregation, as well as conditions about individual tuples.

✦ *Invoking the Checks*: Assertions are checked whenever there is a change to one of the relations involved. Attribute- and tuple-based checks are only checked when the attribute or relation to which they apply changes by insertion or update. Thus, these constraints can be violated if they have subqueries.

✦ *Triggers*: The SQL standard includes triggers that specify certain events (e.g., insertion, deletion, or update to a particular relation) that awaken them. Once awakened, a condition can be checked, and if true, a specified sequence of actions (SQL statements such as queries and database modifications) will be executed.

7.6   References for Chapter 7

The reader should go to the bibliographic notes for Chapter 6 for information about how to get the SQL2 or SQL-99 standards documents. References [5] and [4] survey all aspects of active elements in database systems. [1] discusses recent thinking regarding active elements in SQL-99 and future standards. References [2] and [3] discuss HiPAC, an early prototype system that offered active database elements.

1. Cochrane, R. J., H. Pirahesh, and N. Mattos, "Integrating triggers and declarative constraints in SQL database systems," *Intl. Conf. on Very Large Database Systems*, pp. 567–579, 1996.

2. Dayal, U., et al., "The HiPAC project: combining active databases and timing constraints," *SIGMOD Record* **17**:1, pp. 51–70, 1988.

3. McCarthy, D. R., and U. Dayal, "The architecture of an active database management system," *Proc. ACM SIGMOD Intl. Conf. on Management of Data*, pp. 215–224, 1989.

4. N. W. Paton and O. Diaz, "Active database systems," *Computing Surveys* **31**:1 (March, 1999), pp. 63–103.

5. Widom, J. and S. Ceri, *Active Database Systems*, Morgan-Kaufmann, San Francisco, 1996.

Chapter 8

System Aspects of SQL

We now turn to the question of how SQL fits into a complete programming environment. In Section 8.1 we see how to embed SQL in programs that are written in an ordinary programming language, such as C. A critical issue is how we move data between SQL relations and the variables of the surrounding, or "host," language.

Section 8.2 considers another way to combine SQL with general-purpose programming: persistent stored modules, which are pieces of code stored as part of a database schema and executable on command from the user. Section 8.3 covers additional system issues, such as support for a client-server model of computing.

A third programming approach is a "call-level interface," where we program in some conventional language and use a library of functions to access the database. In Section 8.4 we discuss the SQL-standard library called SQL/CLI, for making calls from C programs. Then, in Section 8.5 we meet Java's JDBC (database connectivity), which is an alternative call-level interface.

Then, Section 8.6 introduces us to the "transaction," an atomic unit of work. Many database applications, such as banking, require that operations on the data appear atomic, or indivisible, even though a large number of concurrent operations may be in progress at once. SQL provides features to allow us to specify transactions, and SQL systems have mechanisms to make sure that what we call a transaction is indeed executed atomically. Finally, Section 8.7 discusses how SQL controls unauthorized access to data, and how we can tell the SQL system what accesses are authorized.

8.1 SQL in a Programming Environment

To this point, we have used the *generic SQL interface* in our examples. That is, we have assumed there is an SQL interpreter, which accepts and executes the sorts of SQL queries and commands that we have learned. Although provided as an option by almost all DBMS's, this mode of operation is actually rare. In

---

The Languages of the SQL Standard

Implementations conforming to the SQL standard are required to support at least one of the following seven host languages: ADA, C, Cobol, Fortran, M (formerly called Mumps), Pascal, and PL/I. Each of these should be familiar to the student of computer science, with the possible exception of M or Mumps, which is a language used primarily in the medical community. We shall use C in our examples.

---

practice, most SQL statements are part of some larger piece of software. A more realistic view is that there is a program in some conventional *host* language such as C, but some of the steps in this program are actually SQL statements. In this section we shall describe one way SQL can be made to operate within a conventional program.

A sketch of a typical programming system that involves SQL statements is in Fig. 8.1. There, we see the programmer writing programs in a host language, but with some special "embedded" SQL statements that are not part of the host language. The entire program is sent to a preprocessor, which changes the embedded SQL statements into something that makes sense in the host language. The representation of the SQL could be as simple as a call to a function that takes the SQL statement as a character-string argument and executes that SQL statement.

The preprocessed host-language program is then compiled in the usual manner. The DBMS vendor normally provides a library that supplies the necessary function definitions. Thus, the functions that implement SQL can be executed, and the whole program behaves as one unit. We also show in Fig. 8.1 the possibility that the programmer writes code directly in the host language, using these function calls as needed. This approach, often referred to as a *call-level interface* or CLI, will be discussed in Section 8.4.

8.1.1   The Impedance Mismatch Problem

The basic problem of connecting SQL statements with those of a conventional programming language is *impedance mismatch*, the fact that the data model of SQL differs so much from the models of other languages. As we know, SQL uses the relational data model at its core. However, C and other common programming languages use a data model with integers, reals, arithmetic, characters, pointers, record structures, arrays, and so on. Sets are not represented directly in C or these other languages, while SQL does not use pointers, loops and branches, or many other common programming-language constructs. As a result, jumping or passing data between SQL and other languages is not straightforward, and a mechanism must be devised to allow the development of programs that use both SQL and another language.

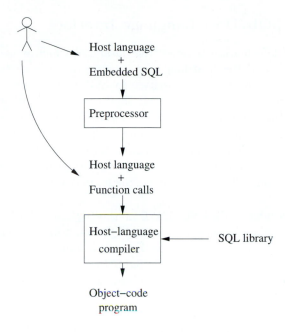

Figure 8.1: Processing programs with SQL statements embedded

One might first suppose that it is preferable to use a single language; either do all computation in SQL or forget SQL and do all computation in a conventional language. However, we can quickly dispense with the idea of omitting SQL when there are database operations involved. SQL systems greatly aid the programmer in writing database operations that can be executed efficiently, yet that can be expressed at a very high level. SQL takes from the programmer's shoulders the need to understand how data is organized in storage or how to exploit that storage structure to operate efficiently on the database.

On the other hand, there are many important things that SQL cannot do at all. For example, one cannot write an SQL query to compute the factorial of a number n [$n! = n \times (n-1) \times \cdots \times 2 \times 1$], something that is an easy exercise in C or similar languages.[1] As another example, SQL cannot format its output directly into a convenient form such as a graphic. Thus, real database programming requires both SQL and a conventional language; the latter is often referred to as the *host language*.

---

[1] We should be careful here. There are extensions to the basic SQL language, such as recursive SQL discussed in Section 10.4 or the SQL/PSM discussed in Section 8.2, that do offer "Turing completeness," i.e., the ability to compute anything that can be computed in any other programming language. However, these extensions were never intended for general purpose calculation, and we do not regard them as general-purpose languages.

8.1.2   The SQL/Host Language Interface

The transfer of information between the database, which is accessed only by SQL statements, and the host-language program is through variables of the host language that can be read or written by SQL statements. All such *shared variables* are prefixed by a colon when they are referred to within an SQL statement, but they appear without the colon in host-language statements.

When we wish to use an SQL statement within a host-language program, we warn that SQL code is coming with the keywords `EXEC SQL` in front of the statement. A typical system will preprocess those statements and replace them by suitable function calls in the host language, making use of an SQL-related library of functions.

A special variable, called `SQLSTATE` in the SQL standard, serves to connect the host-language program with the SQL execution system. The type of `SQLSTATE` is an array of five characters. Each time a function of the SQL library is called, a code is put in the variable `SQLSTATE` that indicates any problems found during that call. The SQL standard also specifies a large number of five-character codes and their meanings.

For example, `'00000'` (five zeroes) indicates that no error condition occurred, and `'02000'` indicates that a tuple requested as part of the answer to an SQL query could not be found. We shall see that the latter code is very important, since it allows us to create a loop in the host-language program that examines tuples from some relation one-at-a-time and to break the loop after the last tuple has been examined. The value of `SQLSTATE` can be read by the host-language program and a decision made on the basis of the value found there.

8.1.3   The `DECLARE` Section

To declare shared variables, we place their declarations between two embedded SQL statements:

```
EXEC SQL BEGIN DECLARE SECTION;
    ...
EXEC SQL END DECLARE SECTION;
```

What appears between them is called the *declare section*. The form of variable declarations in the declare section is whatever the host language requires. Moreover, it only makes sense to declare variables to have types that both the host language and SQL can deal with, such as integers, reals, and character strings or arrays.

Example 8.1: The following statements might appear in a C function that updates the `Studio` relation:

```
EXEC SQL BEGIN DECLARE SECTION;
    char studioName[50], studioAddr[256];
    char SQLSTATE[6];
EXEC SQL END DECLARE SECTION;
```

The first and last statements are the required beginning and end of the declare section. In the middle is a statement declaring two variables `studioName` and `studioAddr`. These are both character arrays and, as we shall see, they can be used to hold a name and address of a studio that are made into a tuple and inserted into the `Studio` relation. The third statement declares `SQLSTATE` to be a six-character array.[2] □

8.1.4 Using Shared Variables

A shared variable can be used in SQL statements in places where we expect or allow a constant. Recall that shared variables are preceded by a colon when so used. Here is an example in which we use the variables of Example 8.1 as components of a tuple to be inserted into relation `Studio`.

Example 8.2: In Fig. 8.2 is a sketch of a C function `getStudio` that prompts the user for the name and address of a studio, reads the responses, and inserts the appropriate tuple into `Studio`. Lines (1) through (4) are the declarations we learned about in Example 8.1. We omit the C code that prints requests and scans entered text to fill the two arrays `studioName` and `studioAddr`.

Then, in lines (5) and (6) is an embedded SQL statement that is a conventional `INSERT` statement. This statement is preceded by the keywords `EXEC SQL` to indicate that it is indeed an embedded SQL statement rather than ungrammatical C code. The preprocessor suggested in Fig. 8.1 will look for `EXEC SQL` to detect statements that must be preprocessed.

The values inserted by lines (5) and (6) are not explicit constants, as they were in previous examples such as in Example 6.34. Rather, the values appearing in line (6) are shared variables whose current values become components of the inserted tuple. □

There are many kinds of SQL statements besides an `INSERT` statement that can be embedded into a host language, using shared variables as an interface. Each embedded SQL statement is preceded by `EXEC SQL` in the host-language program and may refer to shared variables in place of constants. Any SQL statement that does not return a result (i.e., is not a query) can be embedded. Examples of embeddable SQL statements include delete- and update-statements and those statements that create, modify, or drop schema elements such as tables and views.

---

[2]We shall use six characters for the five-character value of `SQLSTATE` because in programs to follow we want to use the C function `strcmp` to test whether `SQLSTATE` has a certain value. Since `strcmp` expects strings to be terminated by `'\0'`, we need a sixth character for this endmarker. The sixth character must be set initially to `'\0'`, but we shall not show this assignment in programs to follow.

```
        void getStudio() {

1)          EXEC SQL BEGIN DECLARE SECTION;
2)              char studioName[50], studioAddr[256];
3)              char SQLSTATE[6];
4)          EXEC SQL END DECLARE SECTION;

            /* print request that studio name and address
               be entered and read response into variables
               studioName and studioAddr */

5)          EXEC SQL INSERT INTO Studio(name, address)
6)                  VALUES (:studioName, :studioAddr);
        }
```

Figure 8.2: Using shared variables to insert a new studio

However, select-from-where queries are not embeddable directly into a host language, because of the "impedance mismatch." Queries produce sets of tuples as a result, while none of the major host languages supports a set data type directly. Thus, embedded SQL must use one of two mechanisms for connecting the result of queries with a host-language program.

1. A query that produces a single tuple can have that tuple stored in shared variables, one variable for each component of the tuple. To do so, we use a modified form of select-from-where statement called a *single-row select*.

2. Queries producing more than one tuple can be executed if we declare a *cursor* for the query. The cursor ranges over all tuples in the answer relation, and each tuple in turn can be fetched into shared variables and processed by the host-language program.

We shall consider each of these mechanisms in turn.

8.1.5 Single-Row Select Statements

The form of a single-row select is the same as an ordinary select-from-where statement, except that following the SELECT clause is the keyword INTO and a list of shared variables. These shared variables are preceded by colons, as is the case for all shared variables within an SQL statement. If the result of the query is a single tuple, this tuple's components become the values of these variables. If the result is either no tuple or more than one tuple, then no assignment to the shared variables are made, and an appropriate error code is written in the variable SQLSTATE.

Example 8.3: We shall write a C function to read the name of a studio and print the net worth of the studio's president. A sketch of this function is shown in Fig. 8.3. It begins with a declare section, lines (1) through (5), for the variables we shall need. Next, C statements that we do not show explicitly obtain a studio name from the standard input.

Lines (6) through (9) are the single-row select statement. It is quite similar to queries we have already seen. The two differences are that the value of variable studioName is used in place of a constant string in the condition of line (9), and there is an INTO clause at line (7) that tells us where to put the result of the query. In this case, we expect a single tuple, and tuples have only one component, that for attribute netWorth. The value of this one component of one tuple is stored in the shared variable presNetWorth. □

```
        void printNetWorth() {

1)          EXEC SQL BEGIN DECLARE SECTION;
2)              char studioName[50];
3)              int presNetWorth;
4)              char SQLSTATE[6];
5)          EXEC SQL END DECLARE SECTION;

            /* print request that studio name be entered.
               read response into studioName */

6)          EXEC SQL SELECT netWorth
7)                  INTO :presNetWorth
8)                  FROM Studio, MovieExec
9)                  WHERE presC# = cert# AND
                            Studio.name = :studioName;

            /* check that SQLSTATE has all 0's and if so, print
               the value of presNetWorth */
        }
```

Figure 8.3: A single-row select embedded in a C function

8.1.6 Cursors

The most versatile way to connect SQL queries to a host language is with a cursor that runs through the tuples of a relation. This relation can be a stored table, or it can be something that is generated by a query. To create and use a cursor, we need the following statements:

1. A cursor declaration. The simplest form of a cursor declaration consists of:

   (a) An introductory EXEC SQL, like all embedded SQL statements.

   (b) The keyword DECLARE.

   (c) The name of the cursor.

   (d) The keywords CURSOR FOR.

   (e) An expression such as a relation name or a select-from-where expression, whose value is a relation. The declared cursor *ranges* over the tuples of this relation; that is, the cursor refers to each tuple of this relation, in turn, as we "fetch" tuples using the cursor.

   In summary, the form of a cursor declaration is

   ```
   EXEC SQL DECLARE <cursor> CURSOR FOR <query>
   ```

2. A statement EXEC SQL OPEN, followed by the cursor name. This statement initializes the cursor to a position where it is ready to retrieve the first tuple of the relation over which the cursor ranges.

3. One or more uses of a *fetch statement*. The purpose of a fetch statement is to get the next tuple of the relation over which the cursor ranges. If the tuples have been exhausted, then no tuple is returned, and the value of SQLSTATE is set to '02000', a code that means "no tuple found." The fetch statement consists of the following components:

   (a) The keywords EXEC SQL FETCH FROM.

   (b) The name of the cursor.

   (c) The keyword INTO.

   (d) A list of shared variables, separated by commas. If there is a tuple to fetch, then the components of this tuple are placed in these variables, in order.

   That is, the form of a fetch statement is:

   ```
   EXEC SQL FETCH FROM <cursor> INTO <list of variables>
   ```

4. The statement EXEC SQL CLOSE followed by the name of the cursor. This statement closes the cursor, which now no longer ranges over tuples of the relation. It can, however, be reinitialized by another OPEN statement, in which case it ranges anew over the tuples of this relation.

Example 8.4 : Suppose we wish to determine the number of movie executives whose net worths fall into a sequence of bands of exponentially growing size, each band corresponding to a number of digits in the net worth. We shall design a query that retrieves the `netWorth` field of all the `MovieExec` tuples into a shared variable called `worth`. A cursor called `execCursor` will range over all these one-component tuples. Each time a tuple is fetched, we compute the number of digits in the integer `worth` and increment the appropriate element of an array `counts`.

The C function `worthRanges` begins in line (1) of Fig. 8.4. Line (2) declares some variables used only by the C function, not by the embedded SQL. The array `counts` holds the counts of executives in the various bands, `digits` counts the number of digits in a net worth, and `i` is an index ranging over the elements of array `counts`.

```
1)  void worthRanges() {

2)      int i, digits, counts[15];
3)      EXEC SQL BEGIN DECLARE SECTION;
4)          int worth;
5)          char SQLSTATE[6];
6)      EXEC SQL END DECLARE SECTION;
7)      EXEC SQL DECLARE execCursor CURSOR FOR
8)          SELECT netWorth FROM MovieExec;

9)      EXEC SQL OPEN execCursor;
10)     for(i=0; i<15; i++) counts[i] = 0;
11)     while(1) {
12)         EXEC SQL FETCH FROM execCursor INTO :worth;
13)         if(NO_MORE_TUPLES) break;
14)         digits = 1;
15)         while((worth /= 10) > 0) digits++;
16)         if(digits <= 14) counts[digits]++;
        }
17)     EXEC SQL CLOSE execCursor;
18)     for(i=0; i<15; i++)
19)         printf("digits = %d: number of execs = %d\n",
                i, counts[i]);
    }
```

Figure 8.4: Grouping executive net worths into exponential bands

Lines (3) through (6) are an SQL declare section in which shared variable `worth` and the usual `SQLSTATE` are declared. Lines (7) and (8) declare `execCursor` to be a cursor that ranges over the values produced by the query on line (8). This query simply asks for the `netWorth` components of all the tuples in `MovieExec`. This cursor is then opened at line (9). Line (10) completes the initialization by zeroing the elements of array `counts`.

The main work is done by the loop of lines (11) through (16). At line (12) a tuple is fetched into shared variable `worth`. Since tuples produced by the query of line (8) have only one component, we need only one shared variable, although in general there would be as many variables as there are components of the retrieved tuples. Line (13) tests whether the fetch has been successful. Here, we use a macro `NO_MORE_TUPLES`, which we may suppose is defined by

```
#define NO_MORE_TUPLES !(strcmp(SQLSTATE,"02000"))
```

Recall that `"02000"` is the `SQLSTATE` code that means no tuple was found. Thus, line (13) tests if all the tuples returned by the query had previously been found and there was no "next" tuple to be obtained. If so, we break out of the loop and go to line (17).

If a tuple has been fetched, then at line (14) we initialize the number of digits in the net worth to 1. Line (15) is a loop that repeatedly divides the net worth by 10 and increments `digits` by 1. When the net worth reaches 0 after division by 10, `digits` holds the correct number of digits in the value of `worth` that was originally retrieved. Finally, line (16) increments the appropriate element of the array `counts` by 1. We assume that the number of digits is no more than 14. However, should there be a net worth with 15 or more digits, line (16) will not increment any element of the `counts` array, since there is no appropriate range; i.e., enormous net worths are thrown away and do not affect the statistics.

Line (17) begins the wrap-up of the function. The cursor is closed, and lines (18) and (19) print the values in the `counts` array. □

8.1.7 Modifications by Cursor

When a cursor ranges over the tuples of a base table (i.e., a relation that is stored in the database, rather than a view or a relation constructed by a query), then one can not only read and process the value of each tuple, but one can update or delete tuples. The syntax of these `UPDATE` and `DELETE` statements are the same as we encountered in Section 6.5, with the exception of the `WHERE` clause. That clause may only be `WHERE CURRENT OF` followed by the name of the cursor. Of course it is possible for the host-language program reading the tuple to apply whatever condition it likes to the tuple before deciding whether or not to delete or update it.

Example 8.5 : In Fig. 8.5 we see a C function that looks at each tuple of `MovieExec` and decides either to delete the tuple or to double the net worth. In lines (3) and (4) we declare variables that correspond to the four attributes of `MovieExec`, as well as the necessary `SQLSTATE`. Then, at line (6), `execCursor` is declared to range over the stored relation `MovieExec` itself. Note that, while we could try to modify tuples through a cursor that ranged over some temporary relation that was the result of some query, we can only have a lasting effect on the database if the cursor ranges over a stored relation such as `MovieExec`.

```
1)   void changeWorth() {

2)       EXEC SQL BEGIN DECLARE SECTION;
3)           int certNo, worth;
4)           char execName[31], execAddr[256], SQLSTATE[6];
5)       EXEC SQL END DECLARE SECTION;
6)       EXEC SQL DECLARE execCursor CURSOR FOR MovieExec;

7)       EXEC SQL OPEN execCursor;
8)       while(1) {
9)           EXEC SQL FETCH FROM execCursor INTO :execName,
                 :execAddr, :certNo, :worth;
10)          if(NO_MORE_TUPLES) break;
11)          if (worth < 1000)
12)              EXEC SQL DELETE FROM MovieExec
                         WHERE CURRENT OF execCursor;
13)          else
14)              EXEC SQL UPDATE MovieExec
                         SET netWorth = 2 * netWorth
                         WHERE CURRENT OF execCursor;
         }
15)      EXEC SQL CLOSE execCursor;
     }
```

Figure 8.5: Modifying executive net worths

Lines (8) through (14) are the loop, in which the cursor `execCursor` refers to each tuple of `MovieExec`, in turn. Line (9) fetches the current tuple into the four variables used for this purpose; note that only `worth` is actually used. Line (10) tests whether we have exhausted the tuples of `MovieExec`. We have again used the macro `NO_MORE_TUPLES` for the condition that variable `SQLSTATE` has the "no more tuples" code "02000".

In the test of line (11) we ask if the net worth is under \$1000. If so, the tuple is deleted by the `DELETE` statement of line (12). Note that the `WHERE` clause refers to the cursor, so the current tuple of `MovieExec`, the one we just fetched, is deleted from `MovieExec`. If the net worth is at least \$1000, then at line (14), the net worth in the same tuple is doubled, instead. □

8.1.8   Protecting Against Concurrent Updates

Suppose that as we examine the net worths of movie executives using the function `worthRanges` of Fig. 8.4, some other process is modifying the underlying `MovieExec` relation. We shall have more to say about several processes accessing a single database simultaneously when we discuss transactions in Section 8.6. However, for the moment, let us simply accept the possibility that there are other processes that could modify a relation as we use it.

What should we do about this possibility? Perhaps nothing. We might be happy with approximate statistics, and we don't care whether or not we count an executive who was in the process of being deleted, for example. Then, we simply accept what tuples we get through the cursor.

However, we may not wish to allow concurrent changes to affect the tuples we see through this cursor. Rather, we may insist on the statistics being taken on the relation as it exists at some point in time. We cannot control exactly which modifications to `MovieExec` occur before our gathering of statistics, but we can expect that all modification statements appear either to have occurred completely before or completely after the function `worthRanges` ran, regardless of how many executives were affected by one modification statement. To obtain this guarantee, we may declare the cursor *insensitive* to concurrent changes.

Example 8.6: We could modify lines (7) and (8) of Fig. 8.4 to be:

```
7)      EXEC SQL DECLARE execCursor INSENSITIVE CURSOR FOR
8)          SELECT netWorth FROM MovieExec;
```

If `execCursor` is so declared, then the SQL system will guarantee that changes to relation `MovieExec` made between one opening and closing of `execCursor` will not affect the set of tuples fetched.   □

An insensitive cursor could be expensive, in the sense that the SQL system might spend a lot of time managing data accesses to assure that the cursor is insensitive. Again, a discussion of managing concurrent operations on the database is deferred to Section 8.6. However, one simple way to support an insensitive cursor is for the SQL system to hold up any process that could access relations that our insensitive cursor's query uses.

There are certain cursors ranging over a relation R about which we may say with certainty that they will not change R. Such a cursor can run simultaneously with an insensitive cursor for R, without risk of changing the relation R that the insensitive cursor sees. If we declare a cursor `FOR READ ONLY`, then the database system can be sure that the underlying relation will not be modified because of access to the relation through this cursor.

Example 8.7: We could append after line (8) of Fig. 8.4 a line

```
FOR READ ONLY;
```

If so, then any attempt to execute a modification through cursor `execCursor` would cause an error.   □

8.1.9 Scrolling Cursors

Cursors give us a choice of how we move through the tuples of the relation. The default, and most common choice is to start at the beginning and fetch the tuples in order, until the end. However, there are other orders in which tuples may be fetched, and tuples could be scanned several times before the cursor is closed. To take advantage of these options, we need to do two things.

1. When declaring the cursor, put the keyword SCROLL before the keyword CURSOR. This change tells the SQL system that the cursor may be used in a manner other than moving forward in the order of tuples.

2. In a FETCH statement, follow the keyword FETCH by one of several options that tell where to find the desired tuple. These options are:

   (a) NEXT or PRIOR to get the next or previous tuple in the order. Recall that these tuples are relative to the current position of the cursor. NEXT is the default if no option is specified, and is the usual choice.

   (b) FIRST or LAST to get the first or last tuple in the order.

   (c) RELATIVE followed by a positive or negative integer, which indicates how many tuples to move forward (if the integer is positive) or backward (if negative) in the order. For instance, RELATIVE 1 is a synonym for NEXT, and RELATIVE -1 is a synonym for PRIOR.

   (d) ABSOLUTE followed by a positive or negative integer, which indicates the position of the desired tuple counting from the front (if positive) or back (if negative). For instance, ABSOLUTE 1 is a synonym for FIRST and ABSOLUTE -1 is a synonym for LAST.

Example 8.8 : Let us rewrite the function of Fig. 8.5 to begin at the last tuple and move backward through the list of tuples. First, we need to declare cursor execCursor to be scrollable, which we do by adding the keyword SCROLL in line (6), as:

```
6) EXEC SQL DECLARE execCursor SCROLL CURSOR FOR MovieExec;
```

Also, we need to initialize the fetching of tuples with a FETCH LAST statement, and in the loop we use FETCH PRIOR. The loop that was lines (8) through (14) in Fig. 8.5 is rewritten in Fig. 8.6. The reader should not assume that there is any advantage to reading tuples in the reverse of the order in which they are stored in MovieExec. □

8.1.10 Dynamic SQL

Our model of SQL embedded in a host language has been that of specific SQL queries and commands within a host-language program. An alternative style

```
EXEC SQL FETCH LAST FROM execCursor INTO :execName,
    :execAddr, :certNo, :worth;
while(1) {
    /* same as lines (10) through (14) */
    EXEC SQL FETCH PRIOR FROM execCursor INTO :execName,
        :execAddr, :certNo, :worth;
}
```

Figure 8.6: Reading `MovieExec` tuples backwards

of embedded SQL has the statements themselves be computed by the host language. Such statements are not known at compile time, and thus cannot be handled by an SQL preprocessor or a host-language compiler.

An example of such a situation is a program that prompts the user for an SQL query, reads the query, and then executes that query. The generic interface for ad-hoc SQL queries that we assumed in Chapter 6 is an example of just such a program; every commercial SQL system provides this type of generic SQL interface. If queries are read and executed at run-time, there is nothing that can be done at compile-time. The query has to be parsed and a suitable way to execute the query found by the SQL system, immediately after the query is read.

The host-language program must instruct the SQL system to take the character string just read, to turn it into an executable SQL statement, and finally to execute that statement. There are two *dynamic SQL* statements that perform these two steps.

1. `EXEC SQL PREPARE`, followed by an SQL variable V, the keyword `FROM`, and a host-language variable or expression of character-string type. This statement causes the string to be treated as an SQL statement. Presumably, the SQL statement is parsed and a good way to execute it is found by the SQL system, but the statement is not executed. Rather, the plan for executing the SQL statement becomes the value of V.

2. `EXEC SQL EXECUTE` followed by an SQL variable such as V in (1). This statement causes the SQL statement denoted by V to be executed.

Both steps can be combined into one, with the statement:

```
EXEC SQL EXECUTE IMMEDIATE
```

followed by a string-valued shared variable or a string-valued expression. The disadvantage of combining these two parts is seen if we prepare a statement once and then execute it many times. With `EXECUTE IMMEDIATE` the cost of preparing the statement is borne each time the statement is executed, rather than borne only once, when we prepare it.

Example 8.9: In Fig. 8.7 is a sketch of a C program that reads text from standard input into a variable `query`, prepares it, and executes it. The SQL variable `SQLquery` holds the prepared query. Since the query is only executed once, the line:

```
EXEC SQL EXECUTE IMMEDIATE :query;
```

could replace lines (6) and (7) of Fig. 8.7. □

```
1)  void readQuery() {

2)      EXEC SQL BEGIN DECLARE SECTION;
3)          char *query;
4)      EXEC SQL END DECLARE SECTION;

5)      /* prompt user for a query, allocate space (e.g.,
            use malloc) and make shared variable :query point
            to the first character of the query */
6)      EXEC SQL PREPARE SQLquery FROM :query;
7)      EXEC SQL EXECUTE SQLquery;
    }
```

Figure 8.7: Preparing and executing a dynamic SQL query

8.1.11   Exercises for Section 8.1

Exercise 8.1.1: Write the following embedded SQL queries, based on the database schema

```
Product(maker, model, type)
PC(model, speed, ram, hd, rd, price)
Laptop(model, speed, ram, hd, screen, price)
Printer(model, color, type, price)
```

of Exercise 5.2.1. You may use any host language with which you are familiar, and details of host-language programming may be replaced by clear comments if you wish.

* a) Ask the user for a price and find the PC whose price is closest to the desired price. Print the maker, model number, and speed of the PC.

  b) Ask the user for minimum values of the speed, RAM, hard-disk size, and screen size that they will accept. Find all the laptops that satisfy these requirements. Print their specifications (all attributes of `laptop`) and their manufacturer.

! c) Ask the user for a manufacturer. Print the specifications of all products by that manufacturer. That is, print the model number, product-type, and all the attributes of whichever relation is appropriate for that type.

!! d) Ask the user for a "budget" (total price of a PC and printer), and a minimum speed of the PC. Find the cheapest "system" (PC plus printer) that is within the budget and minimum speed, but make the printer a color printer if possible. Print the model numbers for the chosen system.

e) Ask the user for a manufacturer, model number, speed, RAM, hard-disk size, speed and kind or the removable disk, and price of a new PC. Check that there is no PC with that model number. Print a warning if so, and otherwise insert the information into tables `Product` and `PC`.

*! f) Lower the price of all "old" PC's by $100. Make sure that any "new" PC inserted during the time that your program is running does not have its price lowered.

Exercise 8.1.2: Write the following embedded SQL queries, based on the database schema

```
Classes(class, type, country, numGuns, bore, displacement)
Ships(name, class, launched)
Battles(name, date)
Outcomes(ship, battle, result)
```

of Exercise 5.2.4.

a) The firepower of a ship is roughly proportional to the number of guns times the cube of the bore of the guns. Find the class with the largest firepower.

! b) Ask the user for the name of a battle. Find the countries of the ships involved in the battle. Print the country with the most ships sunk and the country with the most ships damaged.

c) Ask the user for the name of a class and the other information required for a tuple of table `Classes`. Then ask for a list of the names of the ships of that class and their dates launched. However, the user need not give the first name, which will be the name of the class. Insert the information gathered into `Classes` and `Ships`.

! d) Examine the `Battles`, `Outcomes`, and `Ships` relations for ships that were in battle before they were launched. Prompt the user when there is an error found, offering the option to change the date of launch or the date of the battle. Make whichever change is requested.

*! **Exercise 8.1.3:** In this exercise, our goal is to find all PC's in the relation

```
PC(model, speed, ram, hd, rd, price)
```

for which there are at least two more expensive PC's of the same speed. While there are many ways we could approach the problem, you should use a scrolling cursor in this exercise. Read the tuples of PC ordered first by speed and then by price. *Hint*: For each tuple read, skip ahead two tuples to see if the speed has not changed.

8.2 Procedures Stored in the Schema

In this section, we introduce you to a recent SQL standard called *Persistent, Stored Modules* (SQL/PSM, or just PSM, or PSM-96). Each commercial DBMS offers a way for the user to store with a database schema some functions or procedures that can be used in SQL queries or other SQL statements. These pieces of code are written in a simple, general-purpose language, and allow us to perform, within the database itself, computations that cannot be expressed in the SQL query language. In this book, we shall describe the SQL/PSM standard, which captures the major ideas of these facilities, and which should help you understand the language associated with any particular system.

In PSM, you define *modules*, which are collections of function and procedure definitions, temporary relation declarations, and several other optional declarations. We discuss modules further in Section 8.3.7; here we shall discuss only the functions and procedures of PSM.

8.2.1 Creating PSM Functions and Procedures

The major elements of a procedure declaration are

```
CREATE PROCEDURE <name> (<parameters>)
    local declarations
    procedure body;
```

This form should be familiar from a number of programming languages; it consists of a procedure name, a parenthesized list of parameters, some optional local-variable declarations, and the executable body of code that defines the procedure. A function is defined in almost the same way, except that the keyword FUNCTION is used and there is a return-value type that must be specified. That is, the elements of a function definition are:

```
CREATE FUNCTION <name> (<parameters>) RETURNS <type>
    local declarations
    function body;
```

The parameters of a procedure are triples of mode-name-type, much like the parameters of ODL methods, which we discussed in Section 4.2.7. That is, the parameter name is not only followed by its declared type, as usual in programming languages, but it is preceded by a "mode," which is either IN, OUT, or INOUT. These three keywords indicate that the parameter is input-only, output-only, or both input and output, respectively. IN is the default, and can be omitted.

Function parameters, on the other hand, may only be of mode IN. That is, PSM forbids side-effects in functions, so the only way to obtain information from a function is through its return-value. We shall not specify the IN mode for function parameters, although we do so in procedure definitions.

Example 8.10 : While we have not yet learned the variety of statements that can appear in procedure and function bodies, one kind should not surprise us: an SQL statement. The limitation on these statements is the same as for embedded SQL, as we introduced in Section 8.1.4: only single-row-select statements and cursor-based accesses are permitted as queries. In Fig. 8.8 is a PSM procedure that takes two addresses — an old address and a new address — and changes to the new address the address attribute of every star who lived at the old address.

```
1)   CREATE PROCEDURE Move(
2)       IN oldAddr VARCHAR(255),
3)       IN newAddr VARCHAR(255)
     )
4)   UPDATE MovieStar
5)   SET address = newAddr
6)   WHERE address = oldAddr;
```

Figure 8.8: A procedure to change addresses

Line (1) introduces the procedure and its name, Move. Lines (2) and (3) contain the two parameters, both of which are input parameters whose type is variable-length character strings of length 255. Note that this type is consistent with the type we declared for the attribute address of MovieStar in Fig. 6.16. Lines (4) through (6) are a conventional UPDATE statement. However, notice that the parameter names can be used as if they were constants. Unlike host-language variables, which require a colon prefix when used in SQL (see Section 8.1.2), parameters and other local variables of PSM procedures and functions require no colon.   □

8.2.2   Some Simple Statement Forms in PSM

Let us begin with a potpourri of statement forms that are easy to master.

1. *The call-statement*: The form of a procedure call is:

```
CALL <procedure name> (<argument list>);
```

That is, the keyword **CALL** is followed by the name of the procedure and a parenthesized list of arguments, as in most any language. This call can, however, be made from a variety of places:

   i. From a host-language program, in which it might appear as

```
EXEC SQL CALL Foo(:x, 3);
```

   for instance.

  ii. As a statement of another PSM function or procedure.

 iii. As an SQL command issued to the generic SQL interface. For example, we can issue a statement such as

```
CALL Foo(1, 3);
```

   to such an interface, and have stored procedure **Foo** executed with its two parameters set equal to 1 and 3, respectively.

Note that it is not permitted to call a function. You invoke functions in PSM as you do in C: use the function name and suitable arguments as part of an expression.

2. *The return-statement*: Its form is

```
RETURN <expression>;
```

This statement can only appear in a function. It evaluates the expression and sets the return-value of the function equal to that result. However, at variance with common programming languages, the return-statement of PSM does *not* terminate the function. Rather, control continues with the following statement, and it is possible that the return-value will be changed before the function completes.

3. *Declarations of local variables*: The statement form

```
DECLARE <name> <type>;
```

declares a variable with the given name to have the given type. This variable is local, and its value is not preserved by the DBMS after a running of the function or procedure. Declarations must precede executable statements in the function or procedure body.

4. *Assignment Statements*: The form of an assignment is:

```
SET <variable> = <expression>;
```

Except for the introductory keyword SET, assignment in PSM is quite like assignment in other languages. The expression on the right of the equal-sign is evaluated, and its value becomes the value of the variable on the left. NULL is a permissible expression. The expression may even be a query, as long as it returns a single value.

5. *Statement groups*: We can form a list of statements ended by semicolons and surrounded by keywords BEGIN and END. This construct is treated as a single statement and can appear anywhere a single statement can. In particular, since a procedure or function body is expected to be a single statement, we can put any sequence of statements in the body by surrounding them by BEGIN...END.

6. *Statement labels*: We shall see in Section 8.2.5 one reason why certain statements need a label. We label a statement by prefixing it with a name (the label) and a colon.

8.2.3   Branching Statements

For our first complex PSM statement type, let us consider the if-statement. The form is only a little strange; it differs from C or similar languages in that:

1. The statement ends with keywords END IF.

2. If-statements nested within the else-clause are introduced with the single word ELSEIF.

Thus, the general form of an if-statement is as suggested by Fig. 8.9. The condition is any boolean-valued expression, as can appear in the WHERE clause of SQL statements. Each statement list consists of statements ended by semicolons, but does not need a surrounding BEGIN...END. The final ELSE and its statement(s) are optional; i.e., IF...THEN...END IF alone or with ELSEIF's is acceptable.

```
IF <condition> THEN
    <statement list>
ELSEIF <condition> THEN
    <statement list>
ELSEIF
    ...
ELSE <statement list>
END IF;
```

Figure 8.9: The form of an if-statement

Example 8.11: Let us write a function to take a year y and a studio s, and return a boolean that is TRUE if and only if studio s produced at least one black-and-white movie in year y or did not produce any movies at all in that year. The code appears in Fig. 8.10.

```
1)  CREATE FUNCTION BandW(y INT, s CHAR(15)) RETURNS BOOLEAN

2)  IF NOT EXISTS(
3)      SELECT * FROM Movie WHERE year = y AND
            studioName = s)
4)  THEN RETURN TRUE;
5)  ELSEIF 1 <=
6)      (SELECT COUNT(*) FROM Movie WHERE year = y AND
            studioName = s AND NOT inColor)
7)  THEN RETURN TRUE;
8)  ELSE RETURN FALSE;
9)  END IF;
```

Figure 8.10: If there are any movies at all, then at least one has to be in black-and-white

Line (1) introduces the function and includes its arguments. We do not need to specify a mode for the arguments, since that can only be IN for a function. Lines (2) and (3) test for the case where there are no movies at all by studio s in year y, in which case we set the return-value to TRUE at line (4). Note that line (4) does not cause the function to return. Technically, it is the flow of control dictated by the if-statements that causes control to jump from line (4) to line (9), where the function completes and returns.

If studio s made movies in year y, then lines (5) and (6) test if at least one of them was not in color. If so, the return-value is again set to true, this time at line (7). In the remaining case, studio s made movies but only in color, so we set the return-value to FALSE at line (8). □

8.2.4 Queries in PSM

There are several ways that select-from-where queries are used in PSM.

1. Subqueries can be used in conditions, or in general, any place a subquery is legal in SQL. We saw two examples of subqueries in lines (3) and (6) of Fig. 8.10, for instance.

2. Queries that return a single value can be used as the right sides of assignment statements.

3. A single-row select statement is a legal statement in PSM. Recall this statement has an INTO clause that specifies variables into which the components of the single returned tuple are placed. These variables could be local variables or parameters of a PSM procedure. The general form was discussed in the context of embedded SQL in Section 8.1.5.

4. We can declare and use a cursor, essentially as it was described in Section 8.1.6 for embedded SQL. The declaration of the cursor, OPEN, FETCH, and CLOSE statements are all as described there, with the exceptions that:

    (a) No EXEC SQL appears in the statements, and

    (b) The variables, being local, do not use a colon prefix.

```
CREATE PROCEDURE SomeProc(IN studioName CHAR(15))

DECLARE presNetWorth INTEGER;

SELECT netWorth
INTO presNetWorth
FROM Studio, MovieExec
WHERE presC# = cert# AND Studio.name = studioName;
    ...
```

Figure 8.11: A single-row select in PSM

Example 8.12 : In Fig. 8.11 is the single-row select of Fig. 8.3, redone for PSM and placed in the context of a hypothetical procedure definition. Note that, because the single-row select returns a one-component tuple, we could also get the same effect from an assignment statement, as:

```
SET presNetWorth = (SELECT netWorth
    FROM Studio, MovieExec
    WHERE presC# = cert# AND Studio.name = studioName);
```

We shall defer examples of cursor use until we learn the PSM loop statements in the next section. □

8.2.5 Loops in PSM

The basic loop construct in PSM is:

```
LOOP
    <statement list>
END LOOP;
```

One often labels the `LOOP` statement, so it is possible to break out of the loop, using a statement:

```
LEAVE <loop label>;
```

In the common case that the loop involves the fetching of tuples via a cursor, we often wish to leave the loop when there are no more tuples. It is useful to declare a *condition* name for the `SQLSTATE` value that indicates no tuple found (`'02000'`, recall); we do so with:

```
DECLARE Not_Found CONDITION FOR SQLSTATE '02000';
```

More generally, we can declare a condition with any desired name corresponding to any `SQLSTATE` value by

```
DECLARE <name> CONDITION FOR SQLSTATE <value>;
```

We are now ready to take up an example that ties together cursor operations and loops in PSM.

Example 8.13: Figure 8.12 shows a PSM procedure that takes a studio name s as an input argument and produces in output arguments **mean** and **variance** the mean and variance of the lengths of all the movies owned by studio s. Lines (1) through (4) declare the procedure and its parameters.

Lines (5) through (8) are local declarations. We define Not_Found to be the name of the condition that means a `FETCH` failed to return a tuple at line (5). Then, at line (6), the cursor `MovieCursor` is defined to return the set of the lengths of the movies by studio s. Lines (7) and (8) declare two local variables that we'll need. Integer `newLength` holds the result of a `FETCH`, while `movieCount` counts the number of movies by studio s. We need `movieCount` so that, at the end, we can convert a sum of lengths into an average (mean) of lengths and a sum of squares of the lengths into a variance.

The rest of the lines are the body of the procedure. We shall use **mean** and **variance** as temporary variables, as well as for "returning" the results at the end. In the major loop, **mean** actually holds the sum of the lengths, and **variance** actually holds the sum of the squares of the lengths. Thus, lines (9) through (11) initialize these variables and the count of the movies to 0. Line (12) opens the cursor, and lines (13) through (19) form the loop labeled `movieLoop`.

Line (14) performs a fetch, and at line (15) we check that another tuple was found. If not, we leave the loop. Lines (16) through (18) accumulate values; we add 1 to `movieCount`, add the length to **mean** (which, recall, is really computing the sum of lengths), and we add the square of the length to **variance**.

When all movies by studio s have been seen, we leave the loop, and control passes to line (20). At that line, we turn **mean** into its correct value by dividing the sum of lengths by the count of movies. At line (21), we make **variance** truly hold the variance by dividing the sum of squares of the lengths by the

```
1)   CREATE PROCEDURE MeanVar(
2)       IN s CHAR(15),
3)       OUT mean REAL,
4)       OUT variance REAL
     )
5)   DECLARE Not_Found CONDITION FOR SQLSTATE '02000';
6)   DECLARE MovieCursor CURSOR FOR
         SELECT length FROM Movie WHERE studioName = s;
7)   DECLARE newLength INTEGER;
8)   DECLARE movieCount INTEGER;

     BEGIN
9)       SET mean = 0.0;
10)      SET variance = 0.0;
11)      SET movieCount = 0;
12)      OPEN MovieCursor;
13)      movieLoop: LOOP
14)          FETCH MovieCursor INTO newLength;
15)          IF Not_Found THEN LEAVE movieLoop END IF;
16)          SET movieCount = movieCount + 1;
17)          SET mean = mean + newLength;
18)          SET variance = variance + newLength * newLength;
19)      END LOOP;
20)      SET mean = mean/movieCount;
21)      SET variance = variance/movieCount - mean * mean;
22)      CLOSE MovieCursor;
     END;
```

Figure 8.12: Computing the mean and variance of lengths of movies by one studio

number of movies and subtracting the square of the mean. See Exercise 8.2.4 for a discussion of why this calculation is correct. Line (22) closes the cursor, and we are done.   □

8.2.6   For-Loops

There is also in PSM a for-loop construct, but it is used for only one, important purpose: to iterate over a cursor. The form of the statement is:

```
FOR <loop name> AS <cursor name> CURSOR FOR
    <query>
DO
```

Other Loop Constructs

PSM also allows while- and repeat-loops, which have the expected meaning, as in C. That is, we can create a loop of the form

```
WHILE <condition> DO
    <statement list>
END WHILE;
```

or a loop of the form

```
REPEAT
    <statement list>
UNTIL <condition>
END REPEAT;
```

Incidentally, if we label these loops, or the loop formed by a loop-statement or for-statement, then we can place the label as well after the END LOOP or other ender. The advantage of doing so is that it makes clearer where each loop ends, and it allows the PSM interpreter to catch some syntactic errors involving the omission of an END.

```
        <statement list>
    END FOR;
```

This statement not only declares a cursor, but it handles for us a number of "grubby details": the opening and closing of the cursor, the fetching, and the checking whether there are no more tuples to be fetched. However, since we are not fetching tuples for ourselves, we can not specify the variable(s) into which component(s) of a tuple are placed. Thus, the names used for the attributes in the result of the query are also treated by PSM as local variables of the same type.

Example 8.14: Let us redo the procedure of Fig. 8.12 using a for-loop. The code is shown in Fig. 8.13. Many things have not changed. The declaration of the procedure in lines (1) through (4) of Fig. 8.13 are the same, as is the declaration of local variable `movieCount` at line (5).

However, we no longer need to declare a cursor in the declaration portion of the procedure, and we do not need to define the condition `Not_Found`. Lines (6) through (8) initialize the variables, as before. Then, in line (9) we see the for-loop, which also defines the cursor `MovieCursor`. Lines (11) through (13) are the body of the loop. Notice that in lines (12) and (13), we refer to the length retrieved via the cursor by the attribute name `length`, rather than by the local variable name `newLength`, which does not exist in this version of the procedure.

```
1)   CREATE PROCEDURE MeanVar(
2)        IN s CHAR(15),
3)        OUT mean REAL,
4)        OUT variance REAL
     )
5)   DECLARE movieCount INTEGER;

     BEGIN
6)       SET mean = 0.0;
7)       SET variance = 0.0;
8)       SET movieCount = 0;
9)       FOR movieLoop AS MovieCursor CURSOR FOR
             SELECT length FROM Movie WHERE studioName = s;
10)      DO
11)          SET movieCount = movieCount + 1;
12)          SET mean = mean + length;
13)          SET variance = variance + length * length;
14)      END FOR;
15)      SET mean = mean/movieCount;
16)      SET variance = variance/movieCount - mean * mean;
     END;
```

Figure 8.13: Computing the mean and variance of lengths using a for-loop

Lines (15) and (16) compute the correct values for the output variables, exactly as in the earlier version of this procedure.   □

8.2.7   Exceptions in PSM

An SQL system indicates error conditions by setting a nonzero sequence of digits in the five-character string SQLSTATE. We have seen one example of these codes: '02000' for "no tuple found." For another example, '21000' indicates that a single-row select has returned more than one row.

PSM allows us to declare a piece of code, called an *exception handler*, that is invoked whenever one of a list of these error codes appears in SQLSTATE during the execution of a statement or list of statements. Each exception handler is associated with a block of code, delineated by BEGIN...END. The handler appears within this block, and it applies only to statements within the block.

The components of the handler are:

1. A list of exception conditions that invoke the handler when raised.

2. Code to be executed when one of the associated exceptions is raised.

Why Do We Need Names in For-Loops?

Notice that `movieLoop` and `MovieCursor`, although declared at line (9) of Fig. 8.13, are never used in that procedure. Nonetheless, we have to invent names, both for the for-loop itself and for the cursor over which it iterates. The reason is that the PSM interpreter will translate the for-loop into a conventional loop, much like the code of Fig. 8.12, and in this code, there is a need for both names.

---

  3. An indication of where to go after the handler has finished its work.

The form of a handler declaration is:

```
DECLARE <where to go> HANDLER FOR <condition list>
    <statement>
```

The choices for "where to go" are:

  a) `CONTINUE`, which means that after executing the statement in the handler declaration, we execute the statement after the one that raised the exception.

  b) `EXIT`, which means that after executing the handler's statement, control leaves the `BEGIN...END` block in which the handler is declared. The statement after this block is executed next.

  c) `UNDO`, which is the same as `EXIT`, except that any changes to the database or local variables that were made by the statements of the block executed so far are "undone." That is, their effects are canceled, and it is as if those statements had not executed.

The "condition list" is a comma-separated list of conditions, which are either declared conditions, like `Not_Found` in line (5) of Fig. 8.12, or expressions of the form `SQLSTATE` and a five-character string.

Example 8.15: Let us write a PSM function that takes a movie title as argument and returns the year of the movie. If there is no movie of that title or more than one movie of that title, then `NULL` must be returned. The code is shown in Fig. 8.14.

  Lines (2) and (3) declare symbolic conditions; we do not have to make these definitions, and could as well have used the SQL states for which they stand in line (4). Lines (4), (5), and (6) are a block, in which we first declare a handler for the two conditions in which either zero tuples are returned, or more than one tuple is returned. The action of the handler, on line (5), is simply to set the return-value to `NULL`.

```
1)   CREATE FUNCTION GetYear(t VARCHAR(255)) RETURNS INTEGER

2)   DECLARE Not_Found CONDITION FOR SQLSTATE '02000';
3)   DECLARE Too_Many CONDITION FOR SQLSTATE '21000';

     BEGIN
4)       DECLARE EXIT HANDLER FOR Not_Found, Too_Many
5)            RETURN NULL;
6)       RETURN (SELECT year FROM Movie WHERE title = t);
     END;
```

Figure 8.14: Handling exceptions in which a single-row select returns other than one tuple

Line (6) is the statement that does the work of the function `GetYear`. It is a `SELECT` statement that is expected to return exactly one integer, since that is what the function `GetYear` returns. If there is exactly one movie with title t (the input parameter of the function), then this value will be returned. However, if an exception is raised at line (6), either because there is no movie with title t or several movies with that title, then the handler is invoked, and `NULL` instead becomes the return-value. Also, since the handler is an `EXIT` handler, control next passes to the point after the `END`. Since that point is the end of the function, `GetYear` returns at that time, with the return-value `NULL`. □

8.2.8   Using PSM Functions and Procedures

As we mentioned in Section 8.2.2, we can call a PSM function or procedure from a program with embedded SQL, from PSM code itself, or from ordinary SQL commands issued to the generic interface. The use of these procedures and functions is the same as in most programming languages, with procedures invoked by `CALL`, and functions appearing as part of an expression. We shall give one example of how a function can be called from the generic interface.

Example 8.16 : Suppose that our schema includes a module with the function `GetYear` of Fig. 8.14. Imagine that we are sitting at the generic interface, and we want to enter the fact that Denzel Washington was a star of *Remember the Titans*. However, we forget the year in which that movie was made. As long as there was only one movie of that name, and it is in the `Movie` relation, we don't have to look it up in a preliminary query. Rather, we can issue to the generic SQL interface the following insertion:

```
INSERT INTO StarsIn(movieTitle, movieYear, starName)
VALUES('Remember the Titans', GetYear('Remember the Titans'),
    'Denzel Washington');
```

Since `GetYear` returns `NULL` if there is not a unique movie by the name of *Remember the Titans*, it is possible that this insertion will have `NULL` in the middle component. □

8.2.9 Exercises for Section 8.2

Exercise 8.2.1: Using our running movie database:

```
Movie(title, year, length, inColor, studioName, producerC#)
StarsIn(movieTitle, movieYear, starName)
MovieStar(name, address, gender, birthdate)
MovieExec(name, address, cert#, netWorth)
Studio(name, address, presC#)
```

write PSM procedures or functions to perform the following tasks:

* a) Given the name of a movie studio, produce the net worth of its president.

* b) Given a name and address, return 1 if the person is a movie star but not an executive, 2 if the person is an executive but not a star, 3 if both, and 4 if neither.

*! c) Given a studio name, assign to output parameters the titles of the two longest movies by that studio. Assign `NULL` to one or both parameters if there is no such movie (e.g., if there is only one movie by a studio, there is no "second-longest").

! d) Given a star name, find the earliest (lowest year) movie of more than 120 minutes length in which they appeared. If there is no such movie, return the year 0.

  e) Given an address, find the name of the unique star with that address if there is exactly one, and return `NULL` if there is none or more than one.

  f) Given the name of a star, delete them from `MovieStar` and delete all their movies from `StarsIn` and `Movie`.

Exercise 8.2.2: Write the following PSM functions or procedures, based on the database schema

```
Product(maker, model, type)
PC(model, speed, ram, hd, rd, price)
Laptop(model, speed, ram, hd, screen, price)
Printer(model, color, type, price)
```

of Exercise 5.2.1.

* a) Take a price as argument and return the model number of the PC whose price is closest.

b) Take a maker and model as arguments, and return the price of whatever type of product that model is.

! c) Take model, speed, ram, hard-disk, removable-disk, and price information as arguments, and insert this information into the relation PC. However, if there is already a PC with that model number (tell by assuming that violation of a key constraint on insertion will raise an exception with SQLSTATE equal to '23000'), then keep adding 1 to the model number until you find a model number that is not already a PC model number.

! d) Given a price, produce the number of PC's, the number of laptops, and the number of printers selling for more than that price.

Exercise 8.2.3: Write the following PSM functions or procedures, based on the database schema

```
Classes(class, type, country, numGuns, bore, displacement)
Ships(name, class, launched)
Battles(name, date)
Outcomes(ship, battle, result)
```

of Exercise 5.2.4.

a) The firepower of a ship is roughly proportional to the number of guns times the cube of the bore. Given a class, find its firepower.

! b) Given the name of a battle, produce the two countries whose ships were involved in the battle. If there are more or fewer than two countries involved, produce NULL for both countries.

c) Take as arguments a new class name, type, country, number of guns, bore, and displacement. Add this information to Classes and also add the ship with the class name to Ships.

! d) Given a ship name, determine if the ship was in a battle with a date before the ship was launched. If so, set the date of the battle and the date the ship was launched to 0.

! **Exercise 8.2.4:** In Fig. 8.12, we used a tricky formula for computing the variance of a sequence of numbers $x_1, x_2, \ldots, x_n$. Recall that the variance is the average square of the deviation of these numbers from their mean. That is, the variance is $\left(\sum_{i=1}^{n}(x_i - \bar{x})^2\right)/n$, where the mean $\bar{x}$ is $\left(\sum_{i=1}^{n} x_i\right)/n$. Prove that the formula for the variance used in Fig. 8.12, which is

$$\left(\sum_{i=1}^{n}(x_i)^2\right)/n - \left(\left(\sum_{i=1}^{n} x_i\right)/n\right)^2$$

yields the same value.

8.3 The SQL Environment

In this section we shall take the broadest possible view of a DBMS and the databases and programs it supports. We shall see how databases are defined and organized into clusters, catalogs, and schemas. We shall also see how programs are linked with the data they need to manipulate. Many of the details depend on the particular implementation, so we shall concentrate on the general ideas that are contained in the SQL standard. Sections 8.4 and 8.5 illustrate how these high-level concepts appear in a "call-level interface," which requires the programmer to make explicit connections to databases.

8.3.1 Environments

An *SQL environment* is the framework under which data may exist and SQL operations on data may be executed. In practice, we should think of an SQL environment as a DBMS running at some installation. For example, ABC company buys a license for the Megatron 2002 DBMS to run on a collection of ABC's machines. The system running on these machines constitutes an SQL environment.

All the database elements we have discussed — tables, views, triggers, stored procedures, and so on — are defined within an SQL environment. These elements are organized into a hierarchy of structures, each of which plays a distinct role in the organization. The structures defined by the SQL standard are indicated in Fig. 8.15.

Briefly, the organization consists of the following structures:

1. *Schemas.*[3] These are collections of tables, views, assertions, triggers, PSM modules, and some other types of information that we do not discuss in this book (but see the box on "More Schema Elements" in Section 8.3.2). Schemas are the basic units of organization, close to what we might think of as a "database," but in fact somewhat less than a database as we shall see in point (3) below.

2. *Catalogs.* These are collections of schemas. They are the basic unit for supporting unique, accessible terminology. Each catalog has one or more schemas; the names of schemas within a catalog must be unique, and each catalog contains a special schema called INFORMATION_SCHEMA that contains information about all the schemas in the catalog.

3. *Clusters.* These are collections of catalogs. Each user has an associated cluster: the set of all catalogs accessible to the user (see Section 8.7 for an explanation of how access to catalogs and other elements is controlled). SQL is not very precise about what a cluster is, e.g., whether clusters for various users can overlap without being identical. A cluster is the

---

[3]Note that the term "schema" in this context refers to a database schema, not a relation schema.

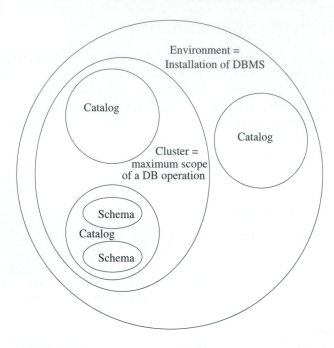

Figure 8.15: Organization of database elements within the environment

maximum scope over which a query can be issued, so in a sense, a cluster is "the database" as seen by a particular user.

8.3.2   Schemas

The simplest form of schema declaration consists of:

1. The keywords CREATE SCHEMA.

2. The name of the schema.

3. A list of declarations for schema elements such as base tables, views, and assertions.

That is, a schema may be declared by:

CREATE SCHEMA <schema name> <element declarations>

The element declarations are of the forms discussed in various places, such as Sections 6.6, 6.7.1, 7.4.3, and 8.2.1.

Example 8.17: We could declare a schema that includes the five relations about movies that we have been using in our running example, plus some of the other elements we have introduced, such as views. Figure 8.16 sketches the form of such a declaration. □

```
CREATE SCHEMA MovieSchema
    CREATE TABLE MovieStar ... as in Fig. 7.5
        Create-table statements for the four other tables
    CREATE VIEW MovieProd ... as in Example 6.48
        Other view declarations
    CREATE ASSERTION RichPres ... as in Example 7.13
```

Figure 8.16: Declaring a schema

It is not necessary to declare the schema all at once. One can modify or add to a schema using the appropriate CREATE, DROP, or ALTER statement, e.g., CREATE TABLE followed by the declaration of a new table for the schema. One problem is that the SQL system needs to know in which schema the new table belongs. If we alter or drop a table or other schema element, we may also need to disambiguate the name of the element, since two or more schemas may have distinct elements of the same name.

We change the "current" schema with a SET SCHEMA statement. For example,

```
SET SCHEMA MovieSchema;
```

makes the schema described in Fig. 8.16 the current schema. Then, any declarations of schema elements are added to that schema, and any DROP or ALTER statements refer to elements already in that schema.

8.3.3 Catalogs

Just as schema elements like tables are created within a schema, schemas are created and modified within a catalog. In principle, we would expect the process of creating and populating catalogs to be analogous to the process of creating and populating schemas. Unfortunately, SQL does not define a standard way to do so, such as a statement

```
CREATE CATALOG <catalog name>
```

followed by a list of schemas belonging to that catalog and the declarations of those schemas.

However, SQL does stipulate a statement

```
SET CATALOG <catalog name>
```

This statement allows us to set the "current" catalog, so new schemas will go into that catalog and schema modifications will refer to schemas in that catalog should there be a name ambiguity.

More Schema Elements

Some schema elements that we have not already mentioned, but that occasionally are useful are:

- *Domains*: These are sets of values or simple data types. They are little used today, because object-relational DBMS's provide more powerful type-creation mechanisms; see Section 9.4.

- *Character sets*: These are sets of symbols and methods for encoding them. ASCII is the best known character set, but an SQL implementation may support many others, such as sets for various foreign languages.

- *Collations*: Recall from Section 6.1.3 that character strings are compared lexicographically, assuming that any two characters can be compared by a "less than" relation we denoted <. A collation specifies which characters are "less than" which others. For example, we might use the ordering implied by the ASCII code, or we might treat lower-case and capital letters the same and not compare anything that isn't a letter.

- *Grant statements*: These concern who has access to schema elements. We shall discuss the granting of privileges in Section 8.7.

8.3.4 Clients and Servers in the SQL Environment

An SQL environment is more than a collection of catalogs and schemas. It contains elements whose purpose is to support operations on the database or databases represented by those catalogs and schemas. Within an SQL environment are two special kinds of processes: SQL clients and SQL servers. A server supports operations on the database elements, and a client allows a user to connect to a server and operate on the database. It is envisioned that the server runs on a large host that stores the database and the client runs on another host, perhaps a personal workstation remote from the server. However, it is also possible that both client and server run on the same host.

8.3.5 Connections

If we wish to run some program involving SQL at a host where an SQL client exists, then we may open a connection between the client and server by executing an SQL statement

---

Complete Names for Schema Elements

Formally, the name for a schema element such as a table is its catalog name, its schema name, and its own name, connected by dots in that order. Thus, the table `Movie` in the schema `MovieSchema` in the catalog `MovieCatalog` can be referred to as

`MovieCatalog.MovieSchema.Movie`

If the catalog is the default or current catalog, then we can omit that component of the name. If the schema is also the default or current schema, then that part too can be omitted, and we are left with the element's own name, as is usual. However, we have the option to use the full name if we need to access something outside the current schema or catalog.

```
CONNECT TO <server name> AS <connection name>
    AUTHORIZATION <name and password>
```

The server name is something that depends on the installation. The word `DEFAULT` can substitute for a name and will connect the user to whatever SQL server the installation treats as the "default server." We have shown an authorization clause followed by the user's name and password. The latter is the typical method by which a user would be identified to the server, although other strings following `AUTHORIZATION` might be used.

The connection name can be used to refer to the connection later on. The reason we might have to refer to the connection is that SQL allows several connections to be opened by the user, but only one can be active at any time. To switch among connections, we can make `conn1` become the active connection by the statement:

```
SET CONNECTION conn1;
```

Whatever connection was currently active becomes *dormant* until it is reactivated with another `SET CONNECTION` statement that mentions it explicitly.

We also use the name when we drop the connection. We can drop connection `conn1` by

```
DISCONNECT conn1;
```

Now, `conn1` is terminated; it is not dormant and cannot be reactivated.

However, if we shall never need to refer to the connection being created, then `AS` and the connection name may be omitted from the `CONNECT TO` statement. It is also permitted to skip the connection statements altogether. If we simply execute SQL statements at a host with an SQL client, then a default connection will be established on our behalf.

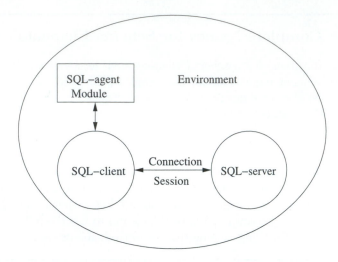

Figure 8.17: The SQL client-server interactions

8.3.6 Sessions

The SQL operations that are performed while a connection is active form a *session*. The session is coextensive with the connection that created it. For example, when a connection is made dormant, its session also becomes dormant, and reactivation of the connection by a `SET CONNECTION` statement also makes the session active. Thus, we have shown the session and connection as two aspects of the link between client and server in Fig. 8.17.

Each session has a current catalog and a current schema within that catalog. These may be set with statements `SET SCHEMA` and `SET CATALOG`, as discussed in Sections 8.3.2 and 8.3.3. There is also an authorized user for every session, as we shall discuss in Section 8.7.

8.3.7 Modules

A *module* is the SQL term for an application program. The SQL standard suggests that there are three kinds of modules, but insists only that an SQL implementation offer the user at least one of these types.

1. *Generic SQL Interface.* The user may type SQL statements that are executed by an SQL server. In this mode, each query or other statement is a module by itself. It is this mode that we imagined for most of our examples in this book, although in practice it is rarely used.

2. *Embedded SQL.* This style was discussed in Section 8.1, where SQL statements appear within host-language programs and are introduced by `EXEC SQL`. Presumably, a preprocessor turns the embedded SQL statements into

suitable function or procedure calls to the SQL system. The compiled host-language program, including these function calls, is a module.

3. *True Modules.* The most general style of modules envisioned by SQL is one in which there are a collection of stored functions or procedures, some of which are host-language code and some of which are SQL statements. They communicate among themselves by passing parameters and perhaps via shared variables. PSM modules (Section 8.2) are an example of this type of module.

An execution of a module is called an *SQL agent.* In Fig. 8.17 we have shown both a module and an SQL agent, as one unit, calling upon an SQL client to establish a connection. However, we should remember that the distinction between a module and an SQL agent is analogous to the distinction between a program and a process; the first is code, the second is an execution of that code.

8.4 Using a Call-Level Interface

In this section we return to the matter of coordinating SQL operations and host-language programs. We saw embedded SQL in Section 8.1 and we covered procedures stored in the schema (Section 8.2). In this section, we take up a third approach. When using a *call-level interface* (CLI), we write ordinary host-language code, and we use a library of functions that allow us to connect to and access a database, passing SQL statements to that database.

The differences between this approach and embedded SQL programming are, in one sense, cosmetic. If we observed what the preprocessor does with embedded SQL statements, we would find that they were replaced by calls to library functions much like the functions in the standard SQL/CLI. However, when SQL is passed by CLI functions directly to the database server, there is a certain level of system independence gained. That is, in principle, we could run the same host-language program at several sites that used different DBMS's. As long as those DBMS's accepted standard SQL (which unfortunately is not always the case), then the same code could run at all these sites, without a specially designed preprocessor.

We shall give two examples of call-level interfaces. In this section, we cover the standard SQL/CLI, which is an adaptation of ODBC (Open Database Connectivity). In Section 8.5, we consider JDBC (Java Database Connectivity), a similar standard that links Java programs to databases in an object-oriented style. In neither case do we cover the standard exhaustively, preferring to show the flavor only.

8.4.1 Introduction to SQL/CLI

A program written in C and using SQL/CLI (hereafter, just CLI) will include the header file sqlcli.h, from which it gets a large number of functions, type definitions, structures, and symbolic constants. The program is then able to create and deal with four kinds of records (structs, in C):

1. *Environments.* A record of this type is created by the application (client) program in preparation for one or more connections to the database server.

2. *Connections.* One of these records is created to connect the application program to the database. Each connection exists within some environment.

3. *Statements.* An application program can create one or more statement records. Each holds information about a single SQL statement, including an implied cursor if the statement is a query. At different times, the same CLI statement can represent different SQL statements. Every CLI statement exists within some connection.

4. *Descriptions.* These records hold information about either tuples or parameters. The application program or the database server, as appropriate, sets components of description records to indicate the names and types of attributes and/or their values. Each statement has several of these created implicitly, and the user can create more if needed. In our presentation of CLI, description records will generally be invisible.

Each of these records is represented in the application program by a *handle*, which is a pointer to the record.[4] The header file `sqlcli.h` provides types for the handles of environments, connections, statements, and descriptions: `SQLHENV`, `SQLHDBC`, `SQLHSTMT`, and `SQLHDESC`, respectively, although we may think of them as pointers or integers. We shall use these types and also some other defined types with obvious interpretations, such as `SQL_CHAR` and `SQL_INTEGER`, that are provided in `sqlcli.h`.

We shall not go into detail about how descriptions are set and used. However, (handles for) the other three types of records are created by the use of a function

$$\text{SQLAllocHandle}(hType, hIn, hOut)$$

Here, the three arguments are:

1. *hType* is the type of handle desired. Use `SQL_HANDLE_ENV` for a new environment, `SQL_HANDLE_DBC` for a new connection, or `SQL_HANDLE_STMT` for a new statement.

2. *hIn* is the handle of the higher-level element in which the newly allocated element lives. This parameter is `SQL_NULL_HANDLE` if you want an environment; the latter name is a defined constant telling `SQLAllocHandle`

---

[4]Do not confuse this use of the term "handle" with the handlers for exceptions that were discussed in Section 8.2.7.

that there is no relevant value here. If you want a connection handle, then *hIn* is the handle of the environment within which the connection will exist, and if you want a statement handle, then *hIn* is the handle of the connection within which the statement will exist.

3. *hOut* is the address of the handle that is created by `SQLAllocHandle`.

`SQLAllocHandle` also returns a value of type `SQLRETURN` (an integer). This value is 0 if no errors occurred, and there are certain nonzero values returned in the case of errors.

Example 8.18 : Let us see how the function `worthRanges` of Fig. 8.4, which we used as an example of embedded SQL, would begin in CLI. Recall this function examines all the tuples of `MovieExec` and breaks their net worths into ranges. The initial steps are shown in Fig. 8.18.

```
1)   #include sqlcli.h
2)   SQLHENV myEnv;
3)   SQLHDBC myCon;
4)   SQLHSTMT execStat;
5)   SQLRETURN errorCode1, errorCode2, errorCode3;

6)   errorCode1 = SQLAllocHandle(SQL_HANDLE_ENV,
         SQL_NULL_HANDLE, &myEnv);
7)   if(!errorCode1)
8)       errorCode2 = SQLAllocHandle(SQL_HANDLE_DBC,
             myEnv, &myCon);
9)   if(!errorCode2)
10)      errorCode3 = SQLAllocHandle(SQL_HANDLE_STMT,
             myCon, &execStat);
```

Figure 8.18: Declaring and creating an environment, a connection, and a statement

Lines (2) through (4) declare handles for an environment, connection, and statement, respectively; their names are `myEnv`, `myCon`, and `execStat`, respectively. We plan that `execStat` will represent the SQL statement

```
SELECT netWorth FROM MovieExec;
```

much as did the cursor `execCursor` in Fig. 8.4, but as yet there is no SQL statement associated with `execStat`. Line (5) declares three variables into which function calls can place their response and indicate an error. A value of 0 indicates no error occurred in the call, and we are counting on that being the case.

What is in Environments and Connections?

We shall not examine the contents of the records that represent environments and connections. However, there may be useful information contained in fields of these records. This information is generally not part of the standard, and may depend on the implementation. However, as an example, the environment record is required to indicate how character strings are represented, e.g., terminated by '\0' as in C, or fixed-length.

Line (6) calls `SQLAllocHandle`, asking for an environment handle (the first argument), providing a null handle in the second argument (because none is needed when we are requesting an environment handle), and providing the address of `myEnv` as the third argument; the generated handle will be placed there. If line (6) is successful, lines (7) and (8) use the environment handle to get a connection handle in `myCon`. Assuming that call is also successful, lines (9) and (10) get a statement handle for `execStat`. □

8.4.2   Processing Statements

At the end of Fig. 8.18, a statement record whose handle is `execStat`, has been created. However, there is as yet no SQL statement with which that record is associated. The process of associating and executing SQL statements with statement handles is analogous to the dynamic SQL described in Section 8.1.10. There, we associated the text of an SQL statement with what we called an "SQL variable," using `PREPARE`, and then executed it using `EXECUTE`.

The situation in CLI is quite analogous, if we think of the "SQL variable" as a statement handle. There is a function

$$\text{SQLPrepare}(sh, st, sl)$$

that takes:

1. A statement handle sh,

2. A pointer to an SQL statement st, and

3. A length sl for the character string pointed to by st. If we don't know the length, a defined constant `SQL_NTS` tells `SQLPrepare` to figure it out from the string itself. Presumably, the string is a "null-terminated string," and it is sufficient for `SQLPrepare` to scan it until encountering the endmarker '\0'.

The effect of this function is to arrange that the statement referred to by the handle sh now represents the particular SQL statement st.

Another function

$$\text{SQLExecute}(sh)$$

causes the statement to which handle *sh* refers to be executed. For many forms of SQL statement, such as insertions or deletions, the effect of executing this statement on the database is obvious. Less obvious is what happens when the SQL statement referred to by *sh* is a query. As we shall see in Section 8.4.3, there is an implicit cursor for this statement that is part of the statement record itself. The statement is in principle executed, so we can imagine that all the answer tuples are sitting somewhere, ready to be accessed. We can fetch tuples one at a time, using the implicit cursor, much as we did with real cursors in Sections 8.1 and 8.2.

Example 8.19: Let us continue with the function `worthRanges` that we began in Fig. 8.18. The following two function calls associate the query

```
SELECT netWorth FROM MovieExec;
```

with the statement referred to by handle `execStat`:

```
11)   SQLPrepare(execStat, "SELECT netWorth FROM MovieExec",
          SQL_NTS);
12)   SQLExecute(execStat);
```

They could appear right after line (10) of Fig. 8.18. Remember that `SQL_NTS` tells `SQLPrepare` to determine the length of the null-terminated string to which its second argument refers.   □

As with dynamic SQL, the prepare and execute steps can be combined into one if we use the function `SQLExecDirect`. An example that combines lines (11) and (12) above is:

```
SQLExecDirect(execStat, "SELECT netWorth FROM MovieExec",
    SQL_NTS);
```

8.4.3   Fetching Data From a Query Result

The function that corresponds to a `FETCH` command in embedded SQL or PSM is

$$\text{SQLFetch}(sh)$$

where *sh* is a statement handle. We presume the statement referred to by *sh* has been executed already, or the fetch will cause an error. `SQLFetch`, like all CLI functions, returns a value of type `SQLRETURN` that indicates either success or an error. We should be especially aware of the return value represented by the symbolic constant `SQL_NO_DATA`, which indicates that no more tuples were left in the query result. As in our previous examples of fetching, this value will be used to get us out of a loop in which we repeatedly fetch new tuples from the result.

However, if we follow the SQLExecute of Example 8.19 by one or more SQLFetch calls, where does the tuple appear? The answer is that its components go into one of the description records associated with the statement whose handle appears in the SQLFetch call. We can extract the same component at each fetch by binding the component to a host-language variable, before we begin fetching. The function that does this job is:

$$\text{SQLBindCol}(sh, \; colNo, \; colType, \; pVar, \; varSize, \; varInfo)$$

The meanings of these six arguments are:

1. *sh* is the handle of the statement involved.

2. *colNo* is the number of the component (within the tuple) whose value we obtain.

3. *colType* is a code for the type of the variable into which the value of the component is to be placed. Examples of codes provided by sqlcli.h are SQL_CHAR for character arrays and strings, and SQL_INTEGER for integers.

4. *pVar* is a pointer to the variable into which the value is to be placed.

5. *varSize* is the length in bytes of the value of the variable pointed to by *pVar*.

6. *varInfo* is a pointer to an integer that can be used by SQLBindCol to provide additional information about the value produced.

Example 8.20 : Let us redo the entire function worthRanges from Fig. 8.4, using CLI calls instead of embedded SQL. We begin as in Fig. 8.18, but for the sake of succinctness, we skip all error checking except for the test whether SQLFetch indicates that no more tuples are present. The code is shown in Fig. 8.19.

Line (3) declares the same local variables that the embedded-SQL version of the function uses, and lines (4) through (7) declare additional local variables using the types provided in sqlcli.h; these are variables that involve SQL in some way. Lines (4) through (6) are as in Fig. 8.18. New are the declarations on line (7) of worth (which corresponds to the shared variable of that name in Fig. 8.4) and worthInfo, which is required by SQLBindCol, but not used.

Lines (8) through (10) allocate the needed handles, as in Fig. 8.18, and lines (11) and (12) prepare and execute the SQL statement, as discussed in Example 8.19. In line (13), we see the binding of the first (and only) column of the result of this query to the variable worth. The first argument is the handle for the statement involved, and the second argument is the column involved, 1 in this case. The third argument is the type of the column, and the fourth argument is a pointer to the place where the value will be placed: the variable

```
1)   #include sqlcli.h
2)   void worthRanges() {

3)       int i, digits, counts[15];
4)       SQLHENV myEnv;
5)       SQLHDBC myCon;
6)       SQLHSTMT execStat;
7)       SQLINTEGER worth, worthInfo;

8)       SQLAllocHandle(SQL_HANDLE_ENV,
                 SQL_NULL_HANDLE, &myEnv);
9)       SQLAllocHandle(SQL_HANDLE_DBC, myEnv, &myCon);
10)      SQLAllocHandle(SQL_HANDLE_STMT, myCon, &execStat);
11)      SQLPrepare(execStat,
                 "SELECT netWorth FROM MovieExec", SQL_NTS);
12)      SQLExecute(execStat);
13)      SQLBindCol(execStat, 1, SQL_INTEGER, &worth,
                 sizeof(worth), &worthInfo);
14)      while(SQLFetch(execStat) != SQL_NO_DATA) {
15)          digits = 1;
16)          while((worth /= 10) > 0) digits++;
17)          if(digits <= 14) counts[digits]++;
         }
18)      for(i=0; i<15; i++)
19)          printf("digits = %d: number of execs = %d\n",
                 i, counts[i]);
     }
```

Figure 8.19: Grouping executive net worths: CLI version

worth. The fifth argument is the size of that variable, and the final argument points to worthInfo, a place for SQLBindCol to put additional information (which we do not use here).

The balance of the function resembles closely lines (11) through (19) of Fig. 8.4. The while-loop begins at line (14) of Fig. 8.19. Notice that we fetch a tuple and check that we are not out of tuples, all within the condition of the while-loop, on line (14). If there is a tuple, then in lines (15) through (17) we determine the number of digits the integer (which is bound to worth) has and increment the appropriate count. After the loop finishes, i.e., all tuples returned by the statement execution of line (12) have been examined, the resulting counts are printed out at lines (18) and (19). □

Extracting Components with `SQLGetData`

An alternative to binding a program variable to an output of a query's result relation is to fetch tuples without any binding and then transfer components to program variables as needed. The function to use is `SQLGetData`, and it takes the same arguments as `SQLBindCol`. However, it only copies data once, and it must be used after each fetch in order to have the same effect as initially binding the column to a variable.

8.4.4 Passing Parameters to Queries

Embedded SQL gives us the ability to execute an SQL statement, part of which consists of values determined by the current contents of shared variables. There is a similar capability in CLI, but it is rather more complicated. The steps needed are:

1. Use `SQLPrepare` to prepare a statement in which some portions, called *parameters*, are replaced by a question-mark. The ith question-mark represents the ith parameter.

2. Use function `SQLBindParameter` to bind values to the places where the question-marks are found. This function has ten arguments, of which we shall explain only the essentials.

3. Execute the query with these bindings, by calling `SQLExecute`. Note that if we change the values of one or more parameters, we need to call `SQLExecute` again.

The following example will illustrate the process, as well as indicate the important arguments needed by `SQLBindParameter`.

Example 8.21: Let us reconsider the embedded SQL code of Fig. 8.2, where we obtained values for two variables `studioName` and `studioAddr` and used them as the components of a tuple, which we inserted into `Studio`. Figure 8.20 sketches how this process would work in CLI. It assumes that we have a statement handle `myStat` to use for the insertion statement.

The code begins with steps (not shown) to give `studioName` and `studioAddr` values. Line (1) shows statement `myStat` being prepared to be an insertion statement with two parameters (the question-marks) in the `VALUE` clause. Then, lines (2) and (3) bind the first and second question-marks, to the current contents of `studioName` and `studioAddr`, respectively. Finally, line (4) executes the insertion. If the entire sequence of steps in Fig. 8.20, including the unseen work to obtain new values for `studioName` and `studioAddr`, are placed in a loop, then each time around the loop, a new tuple, with a new name and address for a studio, is inserted into `Studio`. □

```
          /* get values for studioName and studioAddr */

1)  SQLPrepare(myStat,
        "INSERT INTO Studio(name, address) VALUES(?, ?)",
        SQL_NTS);
2)  SQLBindParameter(myStat, 1,..., studioName,...);
3)  SQLBindParameter(myStat, 2,..., studioAddr,...);
4)  SQLExecute(myStat);
```

Figure 8.20: Inserting a new studio by binding parameters to values

8.4.5 Exercises for Section 8.4

Exercise 8.4.1: Repeat the problems of Exercise 8.1.1, but write the code in C with CLI calls.

Exercise 8.4.2: Repeat the problems of Exercise 8.1.2, but write the code in C with CLI calls.

8.5 Java Database Connectivity

JDBC, which stands for "Java Database Connectivity," is a facility similar to CLI for allowing Java programs to access SQL databases. The concepts are quite similar to those of CLI, although Java's object-oriented flavor is evident in JDBC.

8.5.1 Introduction to JDBC

The first steps we must take to use JDBC are:

1. Load a "driver" for the database system we shall use. This step may be installation- and implementation-dependent. The effect, however, is that an object called `DriverManager` is created. This object is analogous in many ways to the environment whose handle we get as the first step in using CLI.

2. Establish a connection to the database. A variable of type `Connection` is created if we apply the method `getConnection` to `DriverManager`.

The Java statement to establish a connection looks like:

```
Connection myCon = DriverManager.getConnection(<URL>,
    <name>, <password>);
```

That is, the method `getConnection` takes as arguments the URL for the database to which you wish to connect, your user name, and your password. It returns an object of type `Connection`, which we have chosen to call `myCon`. Note that in the Java style, `myCon` is given its type and value in one statement.

This connection is quite analogous to a CLI connection, and it serves the same purpose. By applying the appropriate methods to a connection like `myCon`, we can create statement objects, place SQL statements "in" those objects, bind values to SQL statement parameters, execute the SQL statements, and examine results a tuple at a time. Since the differences between JDBC and CLI are often more syntactic than semantic, we shall go only briefly through these steps.

8.5.2 Creating Statements in JDBC

There are two methods we can apply to a connection in order to create statements. They differ in the number of their arguments:

1. `createStatement()` returns an object of type `Statement`. This object has no associated SQL statement yet, so method `createStatement()` may be thought of as analogous to the CLI call to `SQLAllocHandle` that takes a connection handle and returns a statement handle.

2. `prepareStatement(Q)`, where Q is an SQL query passed as a string argument, returns an object of type `PreparedStatement`. Thus, we may draw an analogy between executing `prepareStatement(Q)` in JDBC with the two CLI steps in which we get a statement handle with `SQLAllocHandle` and then apply `SQLPrepare` to that handle and the query Q.

There are four different methods that execute SQL statements. Like the methods above, they differ in whether or not they take a statement as an argument. However, these methods also distinguish between SQL statements that are queries and other statements, which are collectively called "updates." Note that the SQL `UPDATE` statement is only one small example of what JDBC terms an "update." The latter include all modification statements, such as inserts, and all schema-related statements such as `CREATE TABLE`. The four "execute" methods are:

a) `executeQuery(Q)` takes a statement Q, which must be a query, and is applied to a `Statement` object. This method returns an object of type `ResultSet`, which is the set (bag, to be precise) of tuples produced by the query Q. We shall see how to access these tuples in Section 8.5.3.

b) `executeQuery()` is applied to a `PreparedStatement` object. Since a prepared statement already has an associated query, there is no argument. This method also returns an object of type `ResultSet`.

c) `executeUpdate(U)` takes a nonquery statement U and, when applied to a `Statement` object, executes U. The effect is felt on the database only; no result set is returned.

d) executeUpdate(), with no argument, is applied to a PreparedStatement. In that case, the SQL statement associated with the prepared statement is executed. This SQL statement must not be a query, of course.

Example 8.22 : Suppose we have a connection object myCon, and we wish to execute the query

```
SELECT netWorth FROM MovieExec;
```

One way to do so is to create a statement object execStat, and then use it to execute the query directly. The result set will be placed in an object Worths of type ResultSet; we'll see in Section 8.5.3 how to extract the net worths and process them. The Java code to accomplish this task is:

```
Statement execStat = myCon.createStatement();
ResultSet Worths = execStat.executeQuery(
    "SELECT netWorth FROM MovieExec");
```

An alternative is to prepare the query immediately and later execute it. This approach would be preferable, as in the analogous CLI situation, should we want to execute the same query repeatedly. Then, it makes sense to prepare it once and execute it many times, rather than having the DBMS prepare the same query repeatedly. The JDBC steps needed to follow this approach are:

```
PreparedStatement execStat = myCon.prepareStatement(
    "SELECT netWorth FROM MovieExec");
ResultSet Worths = execStat.executeQuery();
```

☐

Example 8.23 : If we want to execute a parameterless nonquery, we can perform analogous steps in both styles. There is no result set, however. For instance, suppose we want to insert into StarsIn the fact that Denzel Washington starred in *Remember the Titans* in the year 2000. We may create and use a statement starStat in either of the following ways:

```
Statement starStat = myCon.createStatement();
starStat.executeUpdate("INSERT INTO StarsIn VALUES(" +
    "'Remember the Titans', 2000, 'Denzel Washington')");
```

or

```
PreparedStatement starStat = myCon.prepareStatement(
    "INSERT INTO StarsIn VALUES('Remember the Titans'," +
    "2000, 'Denzel Washington')");
starStat.executeUpdate();
```

Notice that each of these sequences of Java statements takes advantage of the fact that + is a Java operator that concatenates strings. Thus, we are able to extend SQL statements over several lines of Java, as needed. ☐

8.5.3 Cursor Operations in JDBC

When we execute a query and obtain a result-set object, we may, in effect, run a cursor through the tuples of the result set. To do so, the `ResultSet` class provides the following useful methods:

1. `next()`, when applied to a result-set object, causes an implicit cursor to move to the next tuple (to the first tuple the first time it is applied). This method returns `FALSE` if there is no next tuple.

2. `getString(`i`)`, `getInt(`i`)`, `getFloat(`i`)`, and analogous methods for the other types that SQL values can take, each return the ith component of the tuple currently indicated by the cursor. The method appropriate to the type of the ith component must be used.

Example 8.24: Having obtained the result set `Worths` as in Example 8.22, we may access its tuples one at a time. Recall that these tuples have only one component, of type integer. The form of the loop is:

```
while(Worths.next()) {
    worth = Worths.getInt(1);
    /* process this net worth */
}
```

□

8.5.4 Parameter Passing

As in CLI, we can use a question-mark in place of a portion of a query, then bind values to those *parameters*. To do so in JDBC, we need to create a prepared statement, and we need to apply to that statement object methods such as `setString(`i`, `v`)` or `setInt(`i`, `v`)` that bind the value v, which must be of the appropriate type for the method, to the ith parameter in the query.

Example 8.25: Let us mimic the CLI code in Example 8.21, where we prepared a statement to insert a new studio into relation `Studio`, with parameters for the value of the name and address of that studio. The Java code to prepare this statement, set its parameters, and execute it is shown in Fig. 8.21. We continue to assume that connection object `myCon` is available to us.

In lines (1) and (2), we create and prepare the insertion statement. It has parameters for each of the values to be inserted. After line (2), we could begin a loop in which we repeatedly ask the user for a studio name and address, and place these strings in the variables `studioName` and `studioAddr`. This assignment is not shown, but represented by a comment. Lines (3) and (4) set the first and second parameters to the strings that are the current values of `studioName` and `studioAddr`, respectively. Finally, at line (5), we execute the insertion statement with the current values of its parameters. After line (5), we could go around the loop again, beginning with the steps represented by the comment. □

```
1)  PreparedStatement studioStat = myCon.prepareStatement(
2)      "INSERT INTO Studio(name, address) VALUES(?, ?)");
    /* get values for variables studioName and studioAddr
       from the user */
3)  studioStat.setString(1, studioName);
4)  studioStat.setString(2, studioAddr);
5)  studioStat.executeUpdate();
```

Figure 8.21: Setting and using parameters in JDBC

8.5.5 Exercises for Section 8.5

Exercise 8.5.1: Repeat Exercise 8.1.1, but write the code in Java using JDBC.

Exercise 8.5.2: Repeat Exercise 8.1.2, but write the code in Java using JDBC.

8.6 Transactions in SQL

To this point, our model of operations on the database has been that of one user querying or modifying the database. Thus, operations on the database are executed one at a time, and the database state left by one operation is the state upon which the next operation acts. Moreover, we imagine that operations are carried out in their entirety ("atomically"). That is, we assumed it is impossible for the hardware or software to fail in the middle of an operation, leaving the database in a state that cannot be explained as the result of the operations performed on it.

Real life is often considerably more complicated. We shall first consider what can happen to leave the database in a state that doesn't reflect the operations performed on it, and then we shall consider the tools SQL gives the user to assure that these problems do not occur.

8.6.1 Serializability

In applications like banking or airline reservations, hundreds of operations per second may be performed on the database. The operations initiate at any of hundreds or thousands of sites, such as automatic teller machines or machines on the desks of travel agents, airline employees, or airline customers themselves. It is entirely possible that we could have two operations affecting the same account or flight, and for those operations to overlap in time. If so, they might interact in strange ways. Here is an example of what could go wrong if the DBMS were completely unconstrained as to the order in which it operated upon the database. We emphasize that database systems do not normally behave in this manner, and that one has to go out of one's way to make these sorts of errors occur when using a commercial DBMS.

```
1)   EXEC SQL BEGIN DECLARE SECTION;
2)       int flight; /* flight number */
3)       char date[10]; /* flight date in SQL format */
4)       char seat[3]; /* two digits and a letter represents
                            a seat */
5)       int occ; /* boolean to tell if seat is occupied */
6)   EXEC SQL END DECLARE SECTION;

7)   void chooseSeat() {
8)       /* C code to prompt the user to enter a flight,
            date, and seat and store these in the three
            variables with those names */
9)       EXEC SQL SELECT occupied INTO :occ
10)               FROM Flights
11)               WHERE fltNum = :flight AND fltDate = :date
                        AND fltSeat = :seat;
12)      if (!occ) {
13)          EXEC SQL UPDATE Flights
14)                  SET occupied = TRUE
15)                  WHERE fltNum = :flight
                            AND fltDate = :date
                            AND fltSeat = :seat;
16)          /* C and SQL code to record the seat assignment
                and inform the user of the assignment */
         }
17)      else /* C code to notify user of unavailability and
                ask for another seat selection */
     }
```

Figure 8.22: Choosing a seat

Example 8.26 : Suppose that we write a function `chooseSeat()`, in C with embedded SQL, to read a relation about flights and the seats available, find if a particular seat is available, and make it occupied if so. The relation upon which we operate will be called `Flights`, and it has attributes `fltNum`, `fltDate`, `fltSeat`, and `occupied` with the obvious meanings. The seat-choosing program is sketched in Fig. 8.22.

Lines (9) through (11) of Fig. 8.22 are a single-row select that sets shared variable `occ` to true or false (1 or 0) depending on whether the specified seat is or is not occupied. Line (12) tests whether that seat is occupied, and if not, the tuple for that seat is updated to make it occupied. The update is done by lines (13) through (15), and at line (16) the seat is assigned to the customer who requested it. In practice, we would probably store seat-assignment information in another relation. Finally, at line (17), if the seat is occupied the customer is told that.

Now, remember that the function `chooseSeat()` may be executed simultaneously by two or more customers. Suppose by coincidence that two agents are trying to book the same seat for the same flight and date at approximately the same time, as suggested by Fig. 8.23. They both get to line (9) at the same time, and their copies of local variable `occ` both get value 0; that is, the seat is currently unassigned. At line (12), each execution of `chooseSeat()` decides to update `occupied` to `TRUE`, that is, to make the seat occupied. These updates execute, perhaps one after the other, and each execution tells its customer at line (16) that the seat belongs to them. □

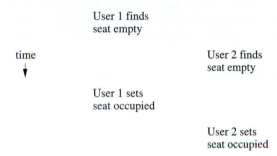

Figure 8.23: Two customers trying to book the same seat simultaneously

As we see from Example 8.26, it is conceivable that two operations could each be performed correctly, and yet the global result not be correct: both customers believe they have been granted the seat in question. The problem can be solved by several SQL mechanisms that serve to *serialize* the execution of the two function executions. We say an execution of functions operating on the same database is *serial* if one function executes completely before any other function begins. We say the execution is *serializable* if they behave as if they were run serially, even though their executions may overlap in time.

Clearly, if the two invocations of `chooseSeat()` are run serially (or serializably), then the error we saw cannot occur. One customer's invocation occurs first. This customer sees an empty seat and books it. The other customer's invocation then begins and sees that the seat is already occupied. It may matter to the customers who gets the seat, but to the database all that is important is that a seat is assigned only once.

8.6.2 Atomicity

In addition to nonserialized behavior that can occur if two or more database operations are performed about the same time, it is possible for a single operation to put the database in an unacceptable state if there is a hardware or software "crash" while the operation is executing. Here is another example suggesting

---

Assuring Serializable Behavior

In practice it is often impossible to require that operations run serially; there are just too many of them and some parallelism is required. Thus, DBMS's adopt a mechanism for assuring serializable behavior; even if the execution is not serial, the result looks to users as if operations were executed serially.

One common approach is for the DBMS to *lock* elements of the database so that two functions cannot access them at the same time. We mentioned locking in Section 1.2.4, and the idea will be covered extensively, starting in Section 18.3. For example, if the function `chooseSeat()` of Example 8.26 were written to lock other operations out of the `Flights` relation, then operations that did not access `Flights` could run in parallel with this invocation of `chooseSeat()`, but no other invocation of `chooseSeat()` could run.

---

what might occur. As in Example 8.26, we should remember that real database systems do not allow this sort of error to occur in properly designed application programs.

Example 8.27 : Let us picture another common sort of database: a bank's account records. We can represent the situation by a relation `Accounts` with attributes `acctNo` and `balance`. Pairs in this relation are an account number and the balance in that account.

We wish to write a function `transfer()` that reads two accounts and an amount of money, checks that the first account has at least that much money, and if so moves the money from the first account to the second. Figure 8.24 is a sketch of the function `transfer()`.

The working of Fig. 8.24 is straightforward. Lines (8) through (10) retrieve the balance of the first account. At line (11), it is determined whether this balance is sufficient to allow the desired amount to be subtracted from it. If so, then lines (12) through (14) add the amount to the second account, and lines (15) through (17) subtract the amount from the first account. If the amount in the first account is insufficient, then no transfer is made, and a warning is printed at line (18).

Now, consider what happens if there is a failure after line (14); perhaps the computer fails or the network connecting the database to the processor that is actually performing the transfer fails. Then the database is left in a state where money has been transferred into the second account, but the money has not been taken out of the first account. The bank has in effect given away the amount of money that was to be transferred. □

The problem illustrated by Example 8.27 is that certain combinations of database operations, like the two updates of Fig. 8.24, need to be done *atomi-*

```
1)   EXEC SQL BEGIN DECLARE SECTION;
2)       int acct1, acct2; /* the two accounts */
3)       int balance1; /* the amount of money in the
                          first account */
4)       int amount; /* the amount of money to transfer */
5)   EXEC SQL END DECLARE SECTION;

6)   void transfer() {
7)       /* C code to prompt the user to enter accounts
              1 and 2 and an amount of money to transfer,
           in variables acct1, acct2, and amount */
8)       EXEC SQL SELECT balance INTO :balance1
9)                FROM Accounts
10)                 WHERE acctNo = :acct1;
11)      if (balance1 >= amount) {
12)          EXEC SQL UPDATE Accounts
13)                    SET balance = balance + :amount
14)                    WHERE acctNo = :acct2;
15)          EXEC SQL UPDATE Accounts
16)                    SET balance = balance - :amount
17)                    WHERE acctNo = :acct1;
         }
18)      else /* C code to print a message that there were
                  insufficient funds to make the transfer */
     }
```

Figure 8.24: Transferring money from one account to another

cally; that is, either they are both done or neither is done. For example, a simple solution is to have all changes to the database done in a local workspace, and only after all work is done do we *commit* the changes to the database, whereupon all changes become part of the database and visible to other operations.

8.6.3 Transactions

The solution to the problems of serialization and atomicity posed in Sections 8.6.1 and 8.6.2 is to group database operations into *transactions*. A transaction is a collection of one or more operations on the database that must be executed atomically; that is, either all operations are performed or none are. In addition, SQL requires that, as a default, transactions are executed in a serializable manner. A DBMS may allow the user to specify a less stringent constraint on the interleaving of operations from two or more transactions. We shall discuss these modifications to the serializability condition in later sections.

When using the generic SQL interface, each statement is normally a transaction by itself.[5] However, when writing code with embedded SQL or code that uses the SQL/CLI or JDBC, we usually want to control transactions explicitly. Transactions begin automatically, when any SQL statement that queries or manipulates either the database or the schema begins. The SQL command START TRANSACTION may be used if we wish.

In the generic interface, unless started with a START TRANSACTION command, the transaction ends with the statement. In all other cases, there are two ways to end a transaction:

1. The SQL statement COMMIT causes the transaction to end successfully. Whatever changes to the database were caused by the SQL statement or statements since the current transaction began are installed permanently in the database (i.e., they are *committed*). Before the COMMIT statement is executed, changes are tentative and may or may not be visible to other transactions.

2. The SQL statement ROLLBACK causes the transaction to *abort*, or terminate unsuccessfully. Any changes made in response to the SQL statements of the transaction are undone (i.e., they are *rolled back*), so they no longer appear in the database.

There is one exception to the above points. If we attempt to commit a transaction, but there are deferred constraints (see Section 7.1.6) that need to be checked, and these constraints are now violated, then the transaction is *not* committed, even if we tell it to with a COMMIT statement. Rather, the transaction is rolled back, and an indication in SQLSTATE tells the application that the transaction was aborted for this reason.

Example 8.28: Suppose we want an execution of function transfer() of Fig. 8.24 to be a single transaction. The transaction begins at line (8) when we read the balance of the first account. If the test of line (11) is true, and we perform the transfer of funds, then we would like to commit the changes made. Thus, we put at the end of the if-block of lines (12) through (17) the additional SQL statement

```
EXEC SQL COMMIT;
```

If the test of line (11) is false — that is, there are insufficient funds to make the transfer — then we might prefer to abort the transaction. We can do so by placing

```
EXEC SQL ROLLBACK;
```

---

[5]However, any triggers awakened by the statement are also part of this same transaction. Some systems even allow triggers to awaken other triggers, and if so, all these actions form part of the transaction as well.

How the Database Changes During Transactions

Different systems may do different things to implement transactions. It is possible that as a transaction executes, it makes changes to the database. If the transaction aborts, then (without precautions) it is possible that these changes were seen by some other transaction. The most common solution is for the database system to lock the changed items until `COMMIT` or `ROLLBACK` is chosen, thus preventing other transactions from seeing the tentative change. Locks or an equivalent would surely be used if the user wants the transactions to run in a serializable fashion.

However, as we shall see starting in Section 8.6.4, SQL offers us several options regarding the treatment of tentative database changes. It is possible that the changed data is not locked and becomes visible even though a subsequent rollback makes the change disappear. It is up to the author of the transactions to decide whether visibility of tentative changes needs to be avoided. If so, all SQL implementations provide a method, such as locking, to keep changes invisible before commitment.

---

at the end of the else-block suggested by line (18). Actually, since in this branch there were no database modification statements executed, it doesn't matter whether we commit or abort, since there are no changes to be committed. □

8.6.4 Read-Only Transactions

Examples 8.26 and 8.27 each involved a transaction that read and then (possibly) wrote some data into the database. This sort of transaction is prone to serialization problems. Thus we saw in Example 8.26 what could happen if two executions of the function tried to book the same seat at the same time, and we saw in Example 8.27 what could happen if there was a crash in the middle of function execution. However, when a transaction only reads data and does not write data, we have more freedom to let the transaction execute in parallel with other transactions.[6]

Example 8.29: Suppose we wrote a function that read data to determine whether a certain seat was available; this function would behave like lines (1) through (11) of Fig. 8.22. We could execute many invocations of this function at once, without risk of permanent harm to the database. The worst that could happen is that while we were reading the availability of a certain seat, that

---

[6]There is a comparison to be made between transactions on one hand and the management of cursors on the other. For example, we noted in Section 8.1.8 that more parallelism was possible with read-only cursors than with general cursors. Similarly, read-only transactions enable parallelism; read/write transactions inhibit it.

Application- Versus System-Generated Rollbacks

In our discussion of transactions, we have presumed that the decision whether a transaction is committed or rolled back is made as part of the application issuing the transaction. That is, as in Examples 8.30 and 8.28, a transaction may perform a number of database operations, then decide whether to make any changes permanent by issuing `COMMIT`, or to return to the original state by issuing `ROLLBACK`. However, the system may also perform transaction rollbacks, to ensure that transactions are executed atomically and conform to their specified isolation level in the presence of other concurrent transactions or system crashes. Typically, if the system aborts a transaction then a special error code or exception is generated. If an application wishes to guarantee that its transactions are executed successfully, it must catch such conditions (e.g., through the `SQLSTATE` value) and reissue the transaction in question.

---

seat was being booked or was being released by the execution of some other function. Thus, we might get the answer "available" or "occupied," depending on microscopic differences in the time at which we executed the query, but the answer would make sense at some time.   □

If we tell the SQL execution system that our current transaction is *read-only*, that is, it will never change the database, then it is quite possible that the SQL system will be able to take advantage of that knowledge. Generally it will be possible for many read-only transactions accessing the same data to run in parallel, while they would not be allowed to run in parallel with a transaction that wrote the same data.

We tell the SQL system that the next transaction is read-only by:

```
SET TRANSACTION READ ONLY;
```

This statement must be executed before the transaction begins. For example, if we had a function consisting of lines (1) through (11) of Fig. 8.22, we could declare it read-only by placing

```
EXEC SQL SET TRANSACTION READ ONLY;
```

just prior to line (9), which begins the transaction. It would be too late to make the read-only declaration after line (9).

We can also inform SQL that the coming transaction may write data by the statement

```
SET TRANSACTION READ WRITE;
```

However, this option is the default and thus is unnecessary.

8.6.5 Dirty Reads

Dirty data is a common term for data written by a transaction that has not yet committed. A *dirty read* is a read of dirty data. The risk in reading dirty data is that the transaction that wrote it may eventually abort. If so, then the dirty data will be removed from the database, and the world is supposed to behave as if that data never existed. If some other transaction has read the dirty data, then that transaction might commit or take some other action that reflects its knowledge of the dirty data.

Sometimes the dirty read matters, and sometimes it doesn't. Other times it matters little enough that it makes sense to risk an occasional dirty read and thus avoid:

1. The time-consuming work by the DBMS that is needed to prevent dirty reads, and

2. The loss of parallelism that results from waiting until there is no possibility of a dirty read.

Here are some examples of what might happen when dirty reads are allowed.

Example 8.30: Let us reconsider the account transfer of Example 8.27. However, suppose that transfers are implemented by a program P that executes the following sequence of steps:

1. Add money to account 2.

2. Test if account 1 has enough money.

   (a) If there is not enough money, remove the money from account 2 and end.[7]

   (b) If there is enough money, subtract the money from account 1 and end.

If program P is executed serializably, then it doesn't matter that we have put money temporarily into account 2. No one will see that money, and it gets removed if the transfer can't be made.

However, suppose dirty reads are possible. Imagine there are three accounts: $A1$, $A2$, and $A3$, with \$100, \$200, and \$300, respectively. Suppose transaction T_1 executes program P to transfer \$150 from $A1$ to $A2$. At roughly the same time, transaction T_2 runs program P to transfer \$250 from $A2$ to $A3$. Here is a possible sequence of events:

1. T_2 executes step 1 and adds \$250 to $A3$, which now has \$550.

---

[7]You should be aware that the program P is trying to perform functions that would more typically be done by the DBMS. In particular, when P decides, as it has done at this step, that it must not complete the transaction, it would issue a rollback (abort) command to the DBMS and have the DBMS reverse the effects of this execution of P.

2. T_1 executes step 1 and adds $150 to $A2$, which now has $350.

3. T_2 executes the test of step 2 and finds that $A2$ has enough funds ($350) to allow the transfer of $250 from $A2$ to $A3$.

4. T_1 executes the test of step 2 and finds that $A1$ does not have enough funds ($100) to allow the transfer of $150 from $A1$ to $A2$.

5. T_2 executes step 2b. It subtracts $250 from $A2$, which now has $100, and ends.

6. T_1 executes step 2a. It subtracts $150 from $A2$, which now has $-$50, and ends.

The total amount of money has not changed; there is still $600 among the three accounts. But because T_2 read dirty data at the third of the six steps above, we have not protected against an account going negative, which supposedly was the purpose of testing the first account to see if it had adequate funds. □

Example 8.31 : Let us imagine a variation on the seat-choosing function of Example 8.26. In the new approach:

1. We find an available seat and reserve it by setting `occupied` to `TRUE` for that seat. If there is none, abort.

2. We ask the customer for approval of the seat. If so, we commit. If not, we release the seat by setting `occupied` to `FALSE` and repeat step 1 to get another seat.

If two transactions are executing this algorithm at about the same time, one might reserve a seat S, which later is rejected by the customer. If the second transaction executes step 1 at a time when seat S is marked occupied, the customer for that transaction is not given the option to take seat S.

As in Example 8.30, the problem is that a dirty read has occurred. The second transaction saw a tuple (with S marked occupied) that was written by the first transaction and later modified by the first transaction. □

How important is the fact that a read was dirty? In Example 8.30 it was very important; it caused an account to go negative despite apparent safeguards against that happening. In Example 8.31, the problem does not look too serious. Indeed, the second traveler might not get their favorite seat, or even be told that no seats existed. However, in the latter case, running the transaction again will almost certainly reveal the availability of seat S. It might well make sense to implement this seat-choosing function in a way that allowed dirty reads, in order to speed up the average processing time for booking requests.

SQL allows us to specify that dirty reads are acceptable for a given transaction. We use the `SET TRANSACTION` statement that we discussed in Section 8.6.4. The appropriate form for a transaction like that described in Example 8.31 is:

```
1)   SET TRANSACTION READ WRITE
2)       ISOLATION LEVEL READ UNCOMMITTED;
```

The statement above does two things:

1. Line (1) declares that the transaction may write data.

2. Line (2) declares that the transaction may run with the "isolation level" *read-uncommitted*. That is, the transaction is allowed to read dirty data. We shall discuss the four isolation levels in Section 8.6.6. So far, we have seen two of them: serializable and read-uncommitted.

Note that if the transaction is not read-only (i.e., it may modify the database), and we specify isolation level `READ UNCOMMITTED`, then we must also specify `READ WRITE`. Recall from Section 8.6.4 that the default assumption is that transactions are read-write. However, SQL makes an exception for the case where dirty reads are allowed. Then, the default assumption is that the transaction is read-only, because read-write transactions with dirty reads entail significant risks, as we saw. If we want a read-write transaction to run with read-uncommitted as the isolation level, then we need to specify `READ WRITE` explicitly, as above.

8.6.6   Other Isolation Levels

SQL provides a total of four *isolation levels*. Two of them we have already seen: serializable and read-uncommitted (dirty reads allowed). The other two are *read-committed* and *repeatable-read*. They can be specified for a given transaction by

```
    SET TRANSACTION ISOLATION LEVEL READ COMMITTED;
```

or

```
    SET TRANSACTION ISOLATION LEVEL REPEATABLE READ;
```

respectively. For each, the default is that transactions are read-write, so we can add `READ ONLY` to either statement, if appropriate. Incidentally, we also have the option of specifying

```
    SET TRANSACTION ISOLATION LEVEL SERIALIZABLE;
```

However, that is the SQL default and need not be stated explicitly.

The read-committed isolation level, as its name implies, forbids the reading of dirty (uncommitted) data. However, it does allow one transaction to issue the same query several times and get different answers, as long as the answers reflect data that has been written by transactions that already committed.

Interactions Among Transactions Running at Different Isolation Levels

A subtle point is that the isolation level of a transaction affects only what data *that* transaction may see; it does not affect what any other transaction sees. As a case in point, if a transaction T is running at level serializable, then the execution of T must appear as if all other transactions run either entirely before or entirely after T. However, if some of those transactions are running at another isolation level, then *they* may see the data written by T as T writes it. They may even see dirty data from T if they are running at isolation level read-uncommitted, and T aborts.

Example 8.32 : Let us reconsider the seat-choosing function of Example 8.31, but suppose we declare it to run with isolation level read-committed. Then when it searches for a seat at step 1, it will not see seats as booked if some other transaction is reserving them but not committed.[8] However, if the traveler rejects seats, and one execution of the function queries for available seats many times, it may see a different set of available seats each time it queries, as other transactions successfully book seats or cancel seats in parallel with our transaction. □

Now, let us consider isolation level repeatable-read. The term is something of a misnomer, since the same query issued more than once is not quite guaranteed to get the same answer. Under repeatable-read isolation, if a tuple is retrieved the first time, then we can be sure that the identical tuple will be retrieved again if the query is repeated. However, it is also possible that a second or subsequent execution of the same query will retrieve *phantom* tuples. The latter are tuples that are the result of insertions into the database while our transaction is executing.

Example 8.33 : Let us continue with the seat-choosing problem of Examples 8.31 and 8.32. If we execute this function under isolation level repeatable-read, then a seat that is available on the first query at step 1 will remain available at subsequent queries.

However, suppose some new tuples enter the relation `Flights`. For example, the airline may have switched the flight to a larger plane, creating some new tuples that weren't there before. Then under repeatable-read isolation, a subsequent query for available seats may also retrieve the new seats. □

---

[8]What actually happens may seem mysterious, since we have not addressed the algorithms for enforcing the various isolation levels. Possibly, should two transactions both see a seat as available and try to book it, one will be forced by the system to roll back in order to break the deadlock (see the box on 'Application- Versus System-Generated Rollbacks" in Section 8.6.3.

8.6.7 Exercises for Section 8.6

Exercise 8.6.1: This and the next exercises involve certain programs that operate on the two relations

```
Product(maker, model, type)
PC(model, speed, ram, hd, rd, price)
```

from our running PC exercise. Sketch the following programs, using embedded SQL and an appropriate host language. Do not forget to issue COMMIT and ROLLBACK statements at the proper times and to tell the system your transactions are read-only if they are.

a) Given a speed and amount of RAM (as arguments of the function), look up the PC's with that speed and RAM, printing the model number and price of each.

* b) Given a model number, delete the tuple for that model from both PC and Product.

c) Given a model number, decrease the price of that model PC by $100.

d) Given a maker, model number, processor speed, RAM size, hard-disk size, removable-disk type, and price, check that there is no product with that model. If there is such a model, print an error message for the user. If no such model existed, enter the information about that model into the PC and Product tables.

! **Exercise 8.6.2:** For each of the programs of Exercise 8.6.1, discuss the atomicity problems, if any, that could occur should the system crash in the middle of an execution of the program.

! **Exercise 8.6.3:** Suppose we execute as a transaction T one of the four programs of Exercise 8.6.1, while other transactions that are executions of the same or a different one of the four programs may also be executing at about the same time. What behaviors of transaction T may be observed if all the transactions run with isolation level READ UNCOMMITTED that would not be possible if they all ran with isolation level SERIALIZABLE? Consider separately the case that T is any of the programs (a) through (d) of Exercise 8.6.1.

*!! **Exercise 8.6.4:** Suppose we have a transaction T that is a function which runs "forever," and at each hour checks whether there is a PC that has a speed of 1500 or more and sells for under $1000. If it finds one, it prints the information and terminates. During this time, other transactions that are executions of one of the four programs described in Exercise 8.6.1 may run. For each of the four isolation levels — serializable, repeatable read, read committed, and read uncommitted — tell what the effect on T of running at this isolation level is.

8.7   Security and User Authorization in SQL

SQL postulates the existence of *authorization ID's*, which are essentially user names. SQL also has a special authorization ID, PUBLIC, which includes any user. Authorization ID's may be granted privileges, much as they would be in the file system environment maintained by an operating system. For example, a UNIX system generally controls three kinds of privileges: read, write, and execute. That list of privileges makes sense, because the protected objects of a UNIX system are files, and these three operations characterize well the things one typically does with files. However, databases are much more complex than file systems, and the kinds of privileges used in SQL are correspondingly more complex.

In this section, we shall first learn what privileges SQL allows on database elements. We shall then see how privileges may be acquired by users (by authorization ID's, that is). Finally, we shall see how privileges may be taken away.

8.7.1   Privileges

SQL defines nine types of privileges: SELECT, INSERT, DELETE, UPDATE, REFERENCES, USAGE, TRIGGER, EXECUTE, and UNDER. The first four of these apply to a relation, which may be either a base table or a view. As their names imply, they give the holder of the privilege the right to query (select from) the relation, insert into the relation, delete from the relation, and update tuples of the relation, respectively.

A module containing an SQL statement cannot be executed without the privilege appropriate to that statement; e.g., a select-from-where statement requires the SELECT privilege on every table it accesses. We shall see how the module can get those privileges shortly. SELECT, INSERT, and UPDATE may also have an associated list of attributes, for instance, SELECT(name, addr). If so, then it is only those attributes that may be seen in a selection, specified in an insertion, or changed in an update. Note that, when granted, privileges such as these will be associated with a particular relation, so it will be clear at that time to what relation attributes name and addr belong.

The REFERENCES privilege on a relation is the right to refer to that relation in an integrity constraint. These constraints may take any of the forms mentioned in Chapter 7, such as assertions, attribute- or tuple-based checks, or referential integrity constraints. The REFERENCES privilege may also have an attached list of attributes, in which case only those attributes may be referenced in a constraint. A constraint cannot be checked unless the owner of the schema in which the constraint appears has the REFERENCES privilege on all data involved in the constraint.

USAGE is a privilege that applies to several kinds of schema elements other than relations and assertions (see Section 8.3.2); it is the right to use that element in one's own declarations. The TRIGGER privilege on a relation is the

---

Triggers and Privileges

It is a bit subtle how privileges are handled for triggers. First, if you have the TRIGGER privilege for a relation, you can attempt to create any trigger you like on that relation. However, since the condition and action portions of the trigger are likely to query and/or modify portions of the database, the trigger creator must have the necessary privileges for those actions. When someone performs an activity that awakens the trigger, they do not need the privileges that the trigger condition and action require; the trigger is executed under the privileges of its creator.

---

right to define triggers on that relation. EXECUTE is the right to execute a piece of code, such as a PSM procedure or function. Finally, UNDER is the right to create subtypes of a given type. This matter has been deferred until Chapter 9, when we take up object-oriented features of SQL.

Example 8.34: Let us consider what privileges are needed to execute the insertion statement of Fig. 6.15, which we reproduce here as Fig. 8.25. First, it is an insertion into the relation Studio, so we require an INSERT privilege on Studio. However, since the insertion specifies only the component for attribute name, it is acceptable to have either the privilege INSERT or the privilege INSERT(name) on relation Studio. The latter privilege allows us to insert Studio tuples that specify only the name component and leave other components to take their default value or NULL, which is what Fig. 8.25 does.

```
1)  INSERT INTO Studio(name)
2)      SELECT DISTINCT studioName
3)      FROM Movie
4)      WHERE studioName NOT IN
5)          (SELECT name
6)           FROM Studio);
```

Figure 8.25: Adding new studios

However, notice that the insertion statement of Fig. 8.25 involves two subqueries, starting at lines (2) and (5). To carry out these selections we require the privileges needed for the subqueries. Thus, we need the SELECT privilege on both relations involved in FROM clauses: Movie and Studio. Note that just because we have the INSERT privilege on Studio doesn't mean we have the SELECT privilege on Studio, or vice versa. Since it is only particular attributes of Movie and Studio that get selected, it is sufficient to have the privilege

SELECT(studioName) on Movie and the privilege SELECT(name) on Studio, or privileges that included these attributes within a list of attributes.   □

8.7.2   Creating Privileges

We have seen what the SQL privileges are and observed that they are required to perform SQL operations. Now we must learn how one obtains the privileges needed to perform an operation. There are two aspects to the awarding of privileges: how they are created initially, and how they are passed from user to user. We shall discuss initialization here and the transmission of privileges in Section 8.7.4.

First, SQL elements such as schemas or modules have an owner. The owner of something has all privileges associated with that thing. There are three points at which ownership is established in SQL.

1. When a schema is created, it and all the tables and other schema elements in it are assumed owned by the user who created it. This user thus has all possible privileges on elements of the schema.

2. When a session is initiated by a CONNECT statement, there is an opportunity to indicate the user with an AUTHORIZATION clause. For instance, the connection statement

    ```
    CONNECT TO Starfleet-sql-server AS conn1
        AUTHORIZATION kirk;
    ```

    would create a connection called conn1 to an SQL server whose name is Starfleet-sql-server, on behalf of a user kirk. Presumably, the SQL implementation would verify that the user name is valid, for example by asking for a password. It is also possible to include the password in the AUTHORIZATION clause, as we discussed in Section 8.3.5. That approach is somewhat insecure, since passwords are then visible to someone looking over Kirk's shoulder.

3. When a module is created, there is an option to give it an owner by using an AUTHORIZATION clause. For instance, a clause

    ```
    AUTHORIZATION picard;
    ```

    in a module-creation statement would make user picard the owner of the module. It is also acceptable to specify no owner for a module, in which case the module is publicly executable, but the privileges necessary for executing any operations in the module must come from some other source, such as the user associated with the connection and session during which the module is executed.

8.7.3 The Privilege-Checking Process

As we saw above, each module, schema, and session has an associated user; in SQL terms, there is an associated authorization ID for each. Any SQL operation has two parties:

1. The database elements upon which the operation is performed and

2. The agent that causes the operation.

The privileges available to the agent derive from a particular authorization ID called the *current authorization ID*. That ID is either

a) The module authorization ID, if the module that the agent is executing has an authorization ID, or

b) The session authorization ID if not.

We may execute the SQL operation only if the current authorization ID possesses all the privileges needed to carry out the operation on the database elements involved.

Example 8.35: To see the mechanics of checking privileges, let us reconsider Example 8.34. We might suppose that the referenced tables — `Movie` and `Studio` — are part of a schema called `MovieSchema` that was created by, and owned by, user `janeway`. At this point, user `janeway` has all privileges on these tables and any other elements of the schema `MovieSchema`. She may choose to grant some privileges to others by the mechanism to be described in Section 8.7.4, but let us assume none have been granted yet. There are several ways that the insertion of Example 8.34 can be executed.

1. The insertion could be executed as part of a module created by user `janeway` and containing an `AUTHORIZATION janeway` clause. The module authorization ID, if there is one, always becomes the current authorization ID. Then, the module and its SQL insertion statement have exactly the same privileges user `janeway` has, which includes all privileges on the tables `Movie` and `Studio`.

2. The insertion could be part of a module that has no owner. User `janeway` opens a connection with an `AUTHORIZATION janeway` clause in the `CON-NECT` statement. Now, `janeway` is again the current authorization ID, so the insertion statement has all the privileges needed.

3. User `janeway` grants all privileges on tables `Movie` and `Studio` to user `sisko`, or perhaps to the special user `PUBLIC`, which stands for "all users." The insertion statement is in a module with the clause

   ```
   AUTHORIZATION sisko
   ```

Since the current authorization ID is now `sisko`, and this user has the needed privileges, the insertion is again permitted.

4. As in (3), user `janeway` has given user `sisko` the needed privileges. The insertion statement is in a module without an owner; it is executed in a session whose authorization ID was set by an `AUTHORIZATION sisko` clause. The current authorization ID is thus `sisko`, and that ID has the needed privileges.

□

There are several principles that are illustrated by Example 8.35. We shall summarize them below.

- The needed privileges are always available if the data is owned by the same user as the user whose ID is the current authorization ID. Scenarios (1) and (2) above illustrate this point.

- The needed privileges are available if the user whose ID is the current authorization ID has been granted those privileges by the owner of the data, or if the privileges have been granted to user `PUBLIC`. Scenarios (3) and (4) illustrate this point.

- Executing a module owned by the owner of the data, or by someone who has been granted privileges on the data, makes the needed privileges available. Of course, one needs the `EXECUTE` privilege on the module itself. Scenarios (1) and (3) illustrate this point.

- Executing a publicly available module during a session whose authorization ID is that of a user with the needed privileges is another way to execute the operation legally. Scenarios (2) and (4) illustrate this point.

8.7.4 Granting Privileges

We saw in Example 8.35 the importance to a user (i.e., an authorization ID) of having the needed privileges. But so far, the only way we have seen to have privileges on a database element is to be the creator and owner of that element. SQL provides a `GRANT` statement to allow one user to give a privilege to another. The first user retains the privilege granted, as well; thus `GRANT` can be thought of as "copy a privilege."

There is one important difference between granting privileges and copying. Each privilege has an associated *grant option*. That is, one user may have a privilege like `SELECT` on table `Movie` "with grant option," while a second user may have the same privilege, but without the grant option. Then the first user may grant the privilege `SELECT` on `Movie` to a third user, and moreover that grant may be with or without the grant option. However, the second user, who does not have the grant option, may not grant the privilege `SELECT` on `Movie` to anyone else. If the third user later gets this same privilege with the grant option, then that user may grant the privilege to a fourth user, again with or without the grant option, and so on.

A *grant statement* consists of the following elements:

1. The keyword `GRANT`.

2. A list of one or more privileges, e.g., `SELECT` or `INSERT(name)`. Optionally, the keywords `ALL PRIVILEGES` may appear here, as a shorthand for all the privileges that the grantor may legally grant on the database element in question (the element mentioned in item 4 below).

3. The keyword `ON`.

4. A database element. This element is typically a relation, either a base table or a view. It may also be a domain or other element we have not discussed (see the box "More Schema Elements" in Section 8.3.2), but in these cases the element name must be preceded by the keyword `DOMAIN` or another appropriate keyword.

5. The keyword `TO`.

6. A list of one or more users (authorization ID's).

7. Optionally, the keywords `WITH GRANT OPTION`

That is, the form of a grant statement is:

> `GRANT` <privilege list> `ON` <database element> `TO` <user list>

possibly followed by `WITH GRANT OPTION`.

In order to execute this grant statement legally, the user executing it must possess the privileges granted, and these privileges must be held with the grant option. However, the grantor may hold a more general privilege (with the grant option) than the privilege granted. For instance, the privilege `INSERT(name)` on table `Studio` might be granted, while the grantor holds the more general privilege `INSERT` on `Studio`, with grant option.

Example 8.36 : User `janeway`, who is the owner of the `MovieSchema` schema that contains tables

```
Movie(title, year, length, inColor, studioName, producerC#)
Studio(name, address, presC#)
```

grants the `INSERT` and `SELECT` privileges on table `Studio` and privilege `SELECT` on `Movie` to users `kirk` and `picard`. Moreover, she includes the grant option with these privileges. The grant statements are:

```
GRANT SELECT, INSERT ON Studio TO kirk, picard
    WITH GRANT OPTION;
GRANT SELECT ON Movie TO kirk, picard
    WITH GRANT OPTION;
```

Now, `picard` grants to user `sisko` the same privileges, but without the grant option. The statements executed by `picard` are:

```
GRANT SELECT, INSERT ON Studio TO sisko;
GRANT SELECT ON Movie TO sisko;
```

Also, `kirk` grants to `sisko` the minimal privileges needed for the insertion of Fig. 8.25, namely `SELECT` and `INSERT(name)` on `Studio` and `SELECT` on `Movie`. The statements are:

```
GRANT SELECT, INSERT(name) ON Studio TO sisko;
GRANT SELECT ON Movie TO sisko;
```

Note that `sisko` has received the `SELECT` privilege on `Movie` and `Studio` from two different users. He has also received the `INSERT(name)` privilege on `Studio` twice: directly from `kirk` and via the generalized privilege `INSERT` from `picard`. □

8.7.5 Grant Diagrams

Because of the complex web of grants and overlapping privileges that may result from a sequence of grants, it is useful to represent grants by a graph called a *grant diagram*. An SQL system maintains a representation of this diagram to keep track of both privileges and their origins (in case a privilege is revoked; see Section 8.7.6).

The nodes of a grant diagram correspond to a user and a privilege. Note that a privilege with and without the grant option must be represented by two different nodes. If user U grants privilege P to user V, and this grant was based on the fact that U holds privilege Q (Q could be P with the grant option, or it could be some generalization of P, again with the grant option), then we draw an arc from the node for U/Q to the node for V/P.

Example 8.37 : Figure 8.26 shows the grant diagram that results from the sequence of grant statements of Example 8.36. We use the convention that a *
after a user-privilege combination indicates that the privilege includes the grant option. Also, ** after a user-privilege combination indicates that the privilege derives from ownership of the database element in question and was not due to a grant of the privilege from elsewhere. This distinction will prove important when we discuss revoking privileges in Section 8.7.6. A doubly starred privilege automatically includes the grant option.   □

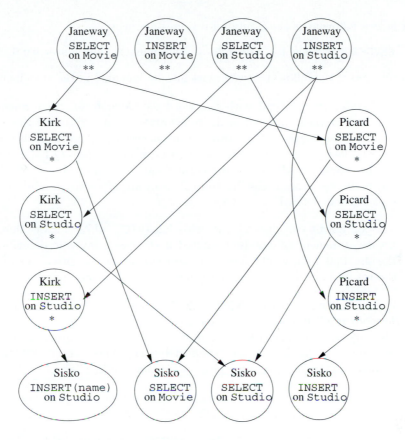

Figure 8.26: A grant diagram

8.7.6 Revoking Privileges

A granted privilege can be revoked at any time. In fact, the revoking of privileges may be required to *cascade*, in the sense that revoking a privilege with the grant option that has been passed on to other users may require those privileges to be revoked too. The simple form of a *revoke statement* is:

1. The keyword REVOKE.

2. A list of one or more privileges.

3. The keyword ON.

4. A database element, as discussed in item (4) in the description of a grant statement.

5. The keyword FROM.

6. A list of one or more users (authorization ID's).

That is, the following is the form of a revoke statement:

REVOKE <privilege list> ON <database element> FROM <user list>

However, one of the following items must also be included in the statement:

1. The statement can end with the word CASCADE. If so, then when the specified privileges are revoked, we also revoke any privileges that were granted *only* because of the revoked privileges. More precisely, if user U has revoked privilege P from user V, based on privilege Q belonging to U, then we delete the arc in the grant diagram from U/Q to V/P. Now, any node that is not accessible from some ownership node (doubly starred node) is also deleted.

2. The statement can instead end with RESTRICT, which means that the revoke statement cannot be executed if the cascading rule described in the previous item would result in the revoking of any privileges due to the revoked privileges having been passed on to others.

It is permissible to replace REVOKE by REVOKE GRANT OPTION FOR, in which case the core privileges themselves remain, but the option to grant them to others is removed. We may have to modify a node, redirect arcs, or create a new node to reflect the changes for the affected users. This form of REVOKE also must be made in combination with either CASCADE or RESTRICT.

Example 8.38 : Continuing with Example 8.36, suppose that janeway revokes the privileges she granted to picard with the statements:

    REVOKE SELECT, INSERT ON Studio FROM picard CASCADE;
    REVOKE SELECT ON Movie FROM picard CASCADE;

We delete the arcs of Fig. 8.26 from these janeway privileges to the corresponding picard privileges. Since CASCADE was stipulated, we also have to see if there are any privileges that are not reachable in the graph from a doubly starred (ownership-based) privilege. Examining Fig. 8.26, we see that picard's privileges are no longer reachable from a doubly starred node (they might have been, had there been another path to a picard node). Also, sisko's privilege to INSERT into Studio is no longer reachable. We thus delete not only picard's privileges from the grant diagram, but we delete sisko's INSERT privilege.

Note that we do not delete sisko's SELECT privileges on Movie and Studio or his INSERT(name) privilege on Studio, because these are all reachable from janeway's ownership-based privileges via kirk's privileges. The resulting grant diagram is shown in Fig. 8.27. □

Example 8.39 : There are a few subtleties that we shall illustrate with abstract examples. First, when we revoke a general privilege p, we do not also revoke a privilege that is a special case of p. For instance, consider the following sequence

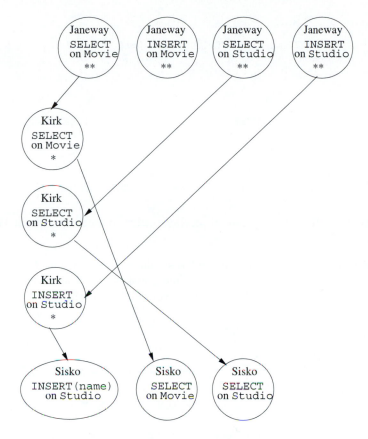

Figure 8.27: Grant diagram after revocation of `picard`'s privileges

of steps, whereby user U, the owner of relation R, grants the INSERT privilege on relation R to user V, and also grants the INSERT(A) privilege on the same relation.

Step	By	Action
1	U	GRANT INSERT ON R TO V
2	U	GRANT INSERT(A) ON R TO V
3	U	REVOKE INSERT ON R FROM V RESTRICT

When U revokes INSERT from V, the INSERT(A) privilege remains. The grant diagrams after steps (2) and (3) are shown in Fig. 8.28.

Notice that after step (2) there are two separate nodes for the two similar but distinct privileges that user V has. Also observe that the RESTRICT option in step (3) does not prevent the revocation, because V had not granted the option to any other user. In fact, V could not have granted either privilege, because V obtained them without grant option. □

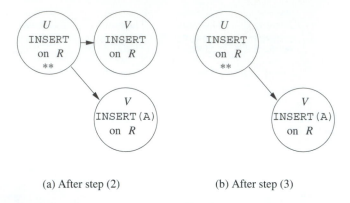

(a) After step (2)   (b) After step (3)

Figure 8.28: Revoking a general privilege leaves a more specific privilege

Example 8.40 : Now, let us consider a similar example where U grants V a privilege p with the grant option and then revokes only the grant option. In this case, we must change V's node to reflect the loss of the grant option, and any grants of p made by V must be cancelled by eliminating arcs out of the V/p node. The sequence of steps is as follows:

Step	By	Action
1	U	GRANT p TO V WITH GRANT OPTION
2	V	GRANT p TO W
3	U	REVOKE GRANT OPTION FOR p FROM V CASCADE

In step (1), U grants the privilege p to V with the grant option. In step (2), V uses the grant option to grant p to W. The diagram is then as shown in Fig. 8.29(a).

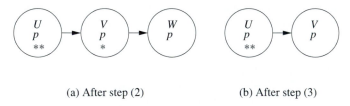

(a) After step (2)   (b) After step (3)

Figure 8.29: Revoking a grant option leaves the underlying privilege

Then in step (3), U revokes the grant option for privilege p from V, but does not revoke the privilege itself. Thus, the star is removed from the node for V and p. However, a node without a * may not have an arc out, because such a node cannot be the source of the granting of a privilege. Thus, we must also remove the arc out of the node V/p that goes to the node for W/p.

Now, the node W/p has no path to it from a ** node that represents the origin of privilege p. As a result, node W/p is deleted from the diagram. However, node V/p remains; it is just modified by removing the $*$ that represents the grant option. The resulting grant diagram is shown in Fig. 8.29(b). □

8.7.7 Exercises for Section 8.7

Exercise 8.7.1: Indicate what privileges are needed to execute the following queries. In each case, mention the most specific privileges as well as general privileges that are sufficient.

    a) The query of Fig. 6.5.

    b) The query of Fig. 6.7.

  * c) The insertion of Fig. 6.15.

    d) The deletion of Example 6.36.

    e) The update of Example 6.38.

    f) The tuple-based check of Fig. 7.5.

    g) The assertion of Example 7.13.

* Exercise 8.7.2: Show the grant diagrams after steps (4) through (6) of the sequence of actions listed in Fig. 8.30. Assume A is the owner of the relation to which privilege p refers.

Step	By	Action
1	A	GRANT p TO B WITH GRANT OPTION
2	A	GRANT p TO C
3	B	GRANT p TO D WITH GRANT OPTION
4	D	GRANT p TO B, C, E WITH GRANT OPTION
5	B	REVOKE p FROM D CASCADE
6	A	REVOKE p FROM C CASCADE

Figure 8.30: Sequence of actions for Exercise 8.7.2

Exercise 8.7.3: Show the grant diagrams after steps (5) and (6) of the sequence of actions listed in Fig. 8.31. Assume A is the owner of the relation to which privilege p refers.

! Exercise 8.7.4: Show the final grant diagram after the following steps, assuming A is the owner of the relation to which privilege p refers.

Step	By	Action
1	A	GRANT p TO B WITH GRANT OPTION
2	B	GRANT p TO B WITH GRANT OPTION
3	A	REVOKE p FROM B CASCADE

Step	By	Action
1	A	GRANT p TO B, E WITH GRANT OPTION
2	B	GRANT p TO C WITH GRANT OPTION
3	C	GRANT p TO D WITH GRANT OPTION
4	E	GRANT p TO C
5	E	GRANT p TO D WITH GRANT OPTION
6	A	REVOKE GRANT OPTION FOR p FROM B CASCADE

Figure 8.31: Sequence of actions for Exercise 8.7.3

8.8 Summary of Chapter 8

✦ *Embedded SQL*: Instead of using a generic query interface to express SQL queries and modifications, it is often more effective to write programs that embed SQL queries in a conventional host language. A preprocessor converts the embedded SQL statements into suitable function calls of the host language.

✦ *Impedance Mismatch*: The data model of SQL is quite different from the data models of conventional host languages. Thus, information passes between SQL and the host language through shared variables that can represent components of tuples in the SQL portion of the program.

✦ *Cursors*: A cursor is an SQL variable that indicates one of the tuples of a relation. Connection between the host language and SQL is facilitated by having the cursor range over each tuple of the relation, while the components of the current tuple are retrieved into shared variables and processed using the host language.

✦ *Dynamic SQL*: Instead of embedding particular SQL statements in a host-language program, the host program may create character strings that are interpreted by the SQL system as SQL statements and executed.

✦ *Persistent Stored Modules*: We may create collections of procedures and functions as part of a database schema. These are written in a special language that has all the familiar control primitives, as well as SQL statements. They may be invoked from either embedded SQL or through a generic query interface.

✦ *The Database Environment*: An installation using an SQL DBMS creates an SQL environment. Within the environment, database elements such as relations are grouped into (database) schemas, catalogs, and clusters. A catalog is a collection of schemas, and a cluster is the largest collection of elements that one user may see.

✦ *Client-Server Systems*: An SQL client connects to an SQL server, creating a connection (link between the two processes) and a session (sequence of operations). The code executed during the session comes from a module, and the execution of the module is called an SQL agent.

• *The Call-Level Interface*: There is a standard library of functions called SQL/CLI or ODBC, which can be linked into any C program. These allow capabilities similar to embedded SQL, but without the need for a preprocessor.

✦ *JDBC*: Java Database Connectivity is a system similar to CLI, but using the Java, object-oriented style.

✦ *Concurrency Control*: SQL provides two mechanisms to prevent concurrent operations from interfering with one another: transactions and restrictions on cursors. Restrictions on cursors include the ability to declare a cursor to be "insensitive," in which case no changes to its relation will be seen by the cursor.

✦ *Transactions*: SQL allows the programmer to group SQL statements into transactions, which may be committed or rolled back (aborted). Transactions may be rolled back by the application in order to undo changes, or by the system in order to guarantee atomicity and isolation.

✦ *Isolation Levels*: SQL allows transactions to run with four isolation levels called, from most stringent to least stringent: "serializable" (the transaction must appear to run either completely before or completely after each other transaction), "repeatable-read" (every tuple read in response to a query will reappear if the query is repeated), "read-committed" (only tuples written by transactions that have already committed may be seen by this transaction), and "read-uncommitted" (no constraint on what the transaction may see).

✦ *Read-Only Cursors and Transactions*: Either a cursor or a transaction may be declared read-only. This declaration is a guarantee that the cursor or transaction will not change the database, thus informing the SQL system that it will not affect other transactions or cursors in ways that may violate insensitivity, serializability, or other requirements.

✦ *Privileges*: For security purposes, SQL systems allow many different kinds of privileges to be obtained on database elements. These privileges include the right to select (read), insert, delete, or update relations, the right to reference relations (refer to them in a constraint), and the right to create triggers.

✦ *Grant Diagrams*: Privileges may be granted by owners to other users or to the general user PUBLIC. If granted with the grant option, then these privileges may be passed on to others. Privileges may also be revoked.

The grant diagram is a useful way to remember enough about the history of grants and revocations to keep track of who has what privilege and from whom they obtained those privileges.

8.9 References for Chapter 8

Again, the reader is referred to the bibliographic notes of Chapter 6 for information on obtaining the SQL standards. The PSM standard is [4], and [5] is a comprehensive book on the subject. [6] is a popular reference on JDBC.

There is a discussion of problems with this standard in the area of transactions and cursors in [1]. More about transactions and how they are implemented can be found in the bibliographic notes to Chapter 18.

The ideas behind the SQL authorization mechanism originated in [3] and [2].

1. Berenson, H., P. A. Bernstein, J. N. Gray, J. Melton, E. O'Neil, and P. O'Neil, "A critique of ANSI SQL isolation levels," *Proceedings of ACM SIGMOD Intl. Conf. on Management of Data*, pp. 1–10, 1995.

2. Fagin, R., "On an authorization mechanism," *ACM Transactions on Database Systems* **3**:3, pp. 310–319, 1978.

3. Griffiths, P. P. and B. W. Wade, "An authorization mechanism for a relational database system," *ACM Transactions on Database Systems* **1**:3, pp. 242–255, 1976.

4. ISO/IEC Report 9075-4, 1996.

5. Melton, J., *Understanding SQL's Stored Procedures: A Complete Guide to SQL/PSM*, Morgan-Kaufmann, San Francisco, 1998.

6. White, S., M. Fisher, R. Cattell, G. Hamilton, and M. Hapner, *JDBC API Tutorial and Reference*, Addison-Wesley, Boston, 1999.

Chapter 9

Object-Orientation in Query Languages

In this chapter, we shall discuss two ways in which object-oriented programming enters the world of query languages. OQL, or *Object Query Language*, is a standardized query language for object-oriented databases. It combines the high-level, declarative programming of SQL with the object-oriented programming paradigm. OQL is designed to operate on data described in ODL, the object-oriented data-description language that we introduced in Section 4.2.

If OQL is an attempt to bring the best of SQL into the object-oriented world, then the relatively new, object-relational features of the SQL-99 standard can be characterized as bringing the best of object-orientation into the relational world. In some senses, the two languages "meet in the middle," but there are differences in approach that make certain things easier in one language than the other.

In essence, the two approaches to object-orientation differ in their answer to the question: "how important is the relation?" For the object-oriented community centered around ODL and OQL, the answer is "not very." Thus, in OQL we find objects of all types, some of which are sets or bags of structures (i.e., relations). For the SQL community, the answer is that relations are still the fundamental data-structuring concept. In the object-relational approach that we introduced in Section 4.5, the relational model is extended by allowing more complex types for the tuples of relations and for attributes. Thus, objects and classes are introduced into the relational model, but always in the context of relations.

9.1 Introduction to OQL

OQL, the *Object Query Language*, gives us an SQL-like notation for expressing queries. It is intended that OQL will be used as an extension to some

425

object-oriented *host* language, such as C++, Smalltalk, or Java. Objects will be manipulated both by OQL queries and by the conventional statements of the host language. The ability to mix host-language statements and OQL queries without explicitly transferring values between the two languages is an advance over the way SQL is embedded into a host language, as was discussed in Section 8.1.

9.1.1   An Object-Oriented Movie Example

In order to illustrate the dictions of OQL, we need a running example. It will involve the familiar classes `Movie`, `Star`, and `Studio`. We shall use the definitions of `Movie`, `Star`, and `Studio` from Fig. 4.3, augmenting them with key and extent declarations. Only `Movie` has methods, gathered from Fig. 4.4. The complete example schema is in Fig. 9.1.

9.1.2   Path Expressions

We access components of objects and structures using a dot notation that is similar to the dot used in C and also related to the dot used in SQL. The general rule is as follows. If a denotes an object belonging to class C, and p is some property of the class — either an attribute, relationship, or method of the class — then $a.p$ denotes the result of "applying" p to a. That is:

1. If p is an attribute, then $a.p$ is the value of that attribute in object a.

2. If p is a relationship, then $a.p$ is the object or collection of objects related to a by relationship p.

3. If p is a method (perhaps with parameters), then $a.p(\cdots)$ is the result of applying p to a.

Example 9.1 : Let `myMovie` denote an object of type `Movie`. Then:

- The value of `myMovie.length` is the length of the movie, that is, the value of the `length` attribute for the `Movie` object denoted by `myMovie`.

- The value of `myMovie.lengthInHours()` is a real number, the length of the movie in hours, computed by applying the method `lengthInHours` to object `myMovie`.

- The value of `myMovie.stars` is the set of `Star` objects related to the movie `myMovie` by the relationship `stars`.

- Expression `myMovie.starNames(myStars)` returns no value (i.e., in C++ the type of this expression is `void`). As a side effect, however, it sets the value of the output variable `myStars` of the method `starNames` to be a set of strings; those strings are the names of the stars of the movie.

```
class Movie
    (extent Movies key (title, year))
{
   attribute string title;
   attribute integer year;
   attribute integer length;
   attribute enum Film {color,blackAndWhite} filmType;
   relationship Set<Star> stars
                 inverse Star::starredIn;
   relationship Studio ownedBy
                 inverse Studio::owns;
   float lengthInHours() raises(noLengthFound);
   void starNames(out Set<String>);
   void otherMovies(in Star, out Set<Movie>)
                 raises(noSuchStar);
};


class Star
    (extent Stars key name)
{
   attribute string name;
   attribute Struct Addr
       {string street, string city} address;
   relationship Set<Movie> starredIn
                 inverse Movie::stars;
};


class Studio
    (extent Studios key name)
{
   attribute string name;
   attribute string address;
   relationship Set<Movie> owns
                 inverse Movie::ownedBy;
};
```

Figure 9.1: Part of an object-oriented movie database

Arrows and Dots

OQL allows the arrow `->` as a synonym for the dot. This convention is partly in the spirit of C, where the dot and arrow both obtain components of a structure. However, in C, the arrow and dot operators have slightly different meanings; in OQL they are the same. In C, expression `a.f` expects `a` to be a structure, while `p->f` expects `p` to be a pointer to a structure. Both produce the value of the field `f` of that structure.

☐

If it makes sense, we can form expressions with several dots. For example, if `myMovie` denotes a movie object, then `myMovie.ownedBy` denotes the `Studio` object that owns the movie, and `myMovie.ownedBy.name` denotes the string that is the name of that studio.

9.1.3   Select-From-Where Expressions in OQL

OQL permits us to write expressions using a select-from-where syntax similar to SQL's familiar query form. Here is an example asking for the year of the movie *Gone With the Wind*.

```
SELECT m.year
FROM Movies m
WHERE m.title = "Gone With the Wind"
```

Notice that, except for the double-quotes around the string constant, this query could be SQL rather than OQL.

In general, the OQL select-from-where expression consists of:

1. The keyword `SELECT` followed by a list of expressions.

2. The keyword `FROM` followed by a list of one or more variable declarations. A variable is declared by giving

   (a) An expression whose value has a collection type, e.g. a set or bag.

   (b) The optional keyword `AS`, and

   (c) The name of the variable.

   Typically, the expression of (a) is the extent of some class, such as the extent `Movies` for class `Movie` in the example above. An extent is the analog of a relation in an SQL `FROM` clause. However, it is possible to use in a variable declaration any collection-producing expression, such as another select-from-where expression.

3. The keyword WHERE and a boolean-valued expression. This expression, like the expression following the SELECT, may only use as operands constants and those variables declared in the FROM clause. The comparison operators are like SQL's, except that !=, rather than <>, is used for "not equal to." The logical operators are AND, OR, and NOT, like SQL's.

The query produces a bag of objects. We compute this bag by considering all possible values of the variables in the FROM clause, in nested loops. If any combination of values for these variables satisfies the condition of the WHERE clause, then the object described by the SELECT clause is added to the bag that is the result of the select-from-where statement.

Example 9.2: Here is a more complex OQL query:

```
SELECT s.name
FROM Movies m, m.stars s
WHERE m.title = "Casablanca"
```

This query asks for the names of the stars of *Casablanca*. Notice the sequence of terms in the FROM clause. First we define m to be an arbitrary object in the class Movie, by saying m is in the extent of that class, which is Movies. Then, for each value of m we let s be a Star object in the set m.stars of stars of movie m. That is, we consider in two nested loops all pairs (m, s) such that m is a movie and s a star of that movie. The evaluation can be sketched as:

```
FOR each m in Movies DO
    FOR each s in m.stars DO
        IF m.title = "Casablanca" THEN
            add s.name to the output bag
```

The WHERE clause restricts our consideration to those pairs that have m equal to the Movie object whose title is *Casablanca*. Then, the SELECT clause produces the bag (which should be a set in this case) of all the name attributes of star objects s in the (m, s) pairs that satisfy the WHERE clause. These names are the names of the stars in the set m_c.stars, where m_c is the *Casablanca* movie object. □

9.1.4 Modifying the Type of the Result

A query like Example 9.2 produces a bag of strings as a result. That is, OQL follows the SQL default of not eliminating duplicates in its answer unless directed to do so. However, we can force the result to be a set or a list if we wish.

- To make the result a set, use the keyword DISTINCT after SELECT, as in SQL.

Alternative Form of FROM Lists

In addition to the SQL-style elements of FROM clauses, where the collection is followed by a name for a typical element, OQL allows a completely equivalent, more logical, yet less SQL-ish form. We can give the typical element name, then the keyword IN, and finally the name of the collection. For instance,

```
FROM m IN Movies, s IN m.stars
```

is an equivalent FROM clause for the query in Example 9.2.

- To make the result a list, add an ORDER BY clause at the end of the query, again as in SQL.

The following examples will illustrate the correct syntax.

Example 9.3 : Let us ask for the names of the stars of Disney movies. The following query does the job, eliminating duplicate names in the situation where a star appeared in several Disney movies.

```
SELECT DISTINCT s.name
FROM Movies m, m.stars s
WHERE m.ownedBy.name = "Disney"
```

The strategy of this query is similar to that of Example 9.2. We again consider all pairs of a movie and a star of that movie in two nested loops as in Example 9.2. But now, the condition on that pair (m, s) is that "Disney" is the name of the studio whose Studio object is m.ownedBy. □

The ORDER BY clause in OQL is quite similar to the same clause in SQL. Keywords ORDER BY are followed by a list of expressions. The first of these expressions is evaluated for each object in the result of the query, and objects are ordered by this value. Ties, if any, are broken by the value of the second expression, then the third, and so on. By default, the order is ascending, but a choice of ascending or descending order can be indicated by the keyword ASC or DESC, respectively, following an attribute, as in SQL.

Example 9.4 : Let us find the set of Disney movies, but let the result be a list of movies, ordered by length. If there are ties, let the movies of equal length be ordered alphabetically. The query is:

```
SELECT m
FROM Movies m
WHERE m.ownedBy.name = "Disney"
ORDER BY m.length, m.title
```

In the first three lines, we consider each `Movie` object m. If the name of the studio that owns this movie is "Disney," then the complete object m becomes a member of the output bag. The fourth line specifies that the objects m produced by the select-from-where query are to be ordered first by the value of `m.length` (i.e., the length of the movie) and then, if there are ties, by the value of `m.title` (i.e., the title of the movie). The value produced by this query is thus a list of `Movie` objects. □

9.1.5 Complex Output Types

The elements in the `SELECT` clause need not be simple variables. They can be any expression, including expressions built using type constructors. For example, we can apply the `Struct` type constructor to several expressions and get a select-from-where query that produces a set or bag of structures.

Example 9.5 : Suppose we want the set of pairs of stars living at the same address. We can get this set with the query:

```
SELECT DISTINCT Struct(star1: s1, star2: s2)
FROM Stars s1, Stars s2
WHERE s1.address = s2.address AND s1.name < s2.name
```

That is, we consider all pairs of stars, `s1` and `s2`. The `WHERE` clause checks that they have the same address. It also checks that the name of the first star precedes the name of the second in alphabetic order, so we don't produce pairs consisting of the same star twice and we don't produce the same pair of stars in two different orders.

For every pair that passes the two tests, we produce a record structure. The type of this structure is a record with two fields, named `star1` and `star2`. The type of each field is the class `Star`, since that is the type of the variables `s1` and `s2` that provide values for the two fields. That is, formally, the type of the structure is

```
Struct{star1: Star, star2: Star}
```

The type of the result of the query is a set of these structures, that is:

```
Set<Struct{star1: Star, star2: Star}>
```

□

9.1.6 Subqueries

We can use a select-from-where expression anywhere a collection is appropriate. We shall give one example: in the `FROM` clause. Several other examples of subquery use appear in Section 9.2.

SELECT Lists of Length One Are Special

Notice that when a SELECT list has only a single expression, the type of the result is a collection of values of the type of that expression. However, if we have more than one expression in the SELECT list, there is an implicit stucture formed with components for each expression. Thus, even had we started the query of Example 9.5 with

SELECT DISTINCT star1: s1, star2: s2

the type of the result would be

Set<Struct{star1: Star, star2: Star}>

However, in Example 9.3, the type of the result is Set<String>, not Set<Struct{name: String}>.

In the FROM clause, we may use a subquery to form a collection. We then allow a variable representing a typical element of that collection to range over each member of the collection.

Example 9.6 : Let us redo the query of Example 9.3, which asked for the stars of the movies made by Disney. First, the set of Disney movies could be obtained by the query, as was used in Example 9.4.

```
SELECT m
FROM Movies m
WHERE m.ownedBy.name = "Disney"
```

We can now use this query as a subquery to define the set over which a variable d, representing the Disney movies, can range.

```
SELECT DISTINCT s.name
FROM (SELECT m
      FROM Movies m
      WHERE m.ownedBy.name = "Disney") d,
     d.stars s
```

This expression of the query "Find the stars of Disney movies" is no more succinct than that of Example 9.3, and perhaps less so. However, it does illustrate a new form of building queries available in OQL. In the query above, the FROM clause has two nested loops. In the first, the variable d ranges over all Disney movies, the result of the subquery in the FROM clause. In the second loop, nested within the first, the variable s ranges over all stars of the Disney movie d. Notice that no WHERE clause is needed in the outer query.   □

9.1.7 Exercises for Section 9.1

Exercise 9.1.1: In Fig. 9.2 is an ODL description of our running products exercise. We have made each of the three types of products subclasses of the main `Product` class. The reader should observe that a type of a product can be obtained either from the attribute `type` or from the subclass to which it belongs. This arrangement is not an excellent design, since it allows for the possibility that, say, a PC object will have its `type` attribute equal to `"laptop"` or `"printer"`. However, the arrangement gives you some interesting options regarding how one expresses queries.

Because `type` is inherited by `Printer` from the superclass `Product`, we have had to rename the `type` attribute of `Printer` to be `printerType`. The latter attribute gives the process used by the printer (e.g., laser or inkjet), while `type` of `Product` will have values such as PC, laptop, or printer.

Add to the ODL code of Fig. 9.2 method signatures (see Section 4.2.7) appropriate for functions that do the following:

* a) Subtract x from the price of a product. Assume x is provided as an input parameter of the function.

* b) Return the speed of a product if the product is a PC or laptop and raise the exception `notComputer` if not.

  c) Set the screen size of a laptop to a specified input value x.

! d) Given an input product p, determine whether the product q to which the method is applied has a higher speed and a lower price than p. Raise the exception `badInput` if p is not a product with a speed (i.e., neither a PC nor laptop) and the exception `noSpeed` if q is not a product with a speed.

Exercise 9.1.2: Using the ODL schema of Exercise 9.1.1 and Fig. 9.2, write the following queries in OQL:

* a) Find the model numbers of all products that are PC's with a price under $2000.

  b) Find the model numbers of all the PC's with at least 128 megabytes of RAM.

*! c) Find the manufacturers that make at least two different models of laser printer.

  d) Find the set of pairs (r, h) such that some PC or laptop has r megabytes of RAM and h gigabytes of hard disk.

  e) Create a list of the PC's (objects, not model numbers) in ascending order of processor speed.

! f) Create a list of the model numbers of the laptops with at least 64 megabytes of RAM, in descending order of screen size.

```
class Product
    (extent Products
     key model)
 {
    attribute integer model;
    attribute string manufacturer;
    attribute string type;
    attribute real price;
 };


class PC extends Product
    (extent PCs)
 {
    attribute integer speed;
    attribute integer ram;
    attribute integer hd;
    attribute string rd;
 };


class Laptop extends Product
    (extent Laptops)
 {
    attribute integer speed;
    attribute integer ram;
    attribute integer hd;
    attribute real screen;
 };


class Printer extends Product
    (extent Printers)
 {
    attribute boolean color;
    attribute string printerType;
 };
```

Figure 9.2: Product schema in ODL

```
class Class
    (extent Classes
     key name)
  {
    attribute string name;
    attribute string country;
    attribute integer numGuns;
    attribute integer bore;
    attribute integer displacement;
    relationship Set<Ship> ships inverse Ship::classOf;
  };

class Ship
    (extent Ships
     key name)
  {
    attribute string name;
    attribute integer launched;
    relationship Class classOf inverse Class::ships;
    relationship Set<Outcome> inBattles
                inverse Outcome::theShip;
  };

class Battle
    (extent Battles
     key name)
  {
    attribute string name;
    attribute Date dateFought;
    relationship Set<Outcome> results
                inverse Outcome::theBattle;
  };

class Outcome
    (extent Outcomes)
  {
    attribute enum Stat {ok,sunk,damaged} status;
    relationship Ship theShip inverse Ship::inBattles;
    relationship Battle theBattle inverse Battle::results;
  };
```

Figure 9.3: Battleships database in ODL

Exercise 9.1.3: In Fig. 9.3 is an ODL description of our running "battleships" database. Add the following method signatures:

a) Compute the firepower of a ship, that is, the number of guns times the cube of the bore.

b) Find the sister ships of a ship. Raise the exception `noSisters` if the ship is the only one of its class.

c) Given a battle b as a parameter, and applying the method to a ship s, find the ships sunk in the battle b, provided s participated in that battle. Raise the exception `didNotParticipate` if ship s did not fight in battle b.

d) Given a name and a year launched as parameters, add a ship of this name and year to the class to which the method is applied.

! Exercise 9.1.4: Repeat each part of Exercise 9.1.2 using at least one subquery in each of your queries.

Exercise 9.1.5: Using the ODL schema of Exercise 9.1.3 and Fig. 9.3, write the following queries in OQL:

a) Find the names of the classes of ships with at least nine guns.

b) Find the ships (objects, not ship names) with at least nine guns.

c) Find the names of the ships with a displacement under 30,000 tons. Make the result a list, ordered by earliest launch year first, and if there are ties, alphabetically by ship name.

d) Find the pairs of objects that are sister ships (i.e., ships of the same class). Note that the objects themselves are wanted, not the names of the ships.

! e) Find the names of the battles in which ships of at least two different countries were sunk.

!! f) Find the names of the battles in which no ship was listed as damaged.

9.2   Additional Forms of OQL Expressions

In this section we shall see some of the other operators, besides select-from-where, that OQL provides to help us build expressions. These operators include logical quantifiers — for-all and there-exists — aggregation operators, the group-by operator, and set operators — union, intersection, and difference.

9.2.1 Quantifier Expressions

We can test whether all members of a collection satisfy some condition, and we can test whether at least one member of a collection satisfies a condition. To test whether all members x of a collection S satisfy condition $C(x)$, we use the OQL expression:

$$\text{FOR ALL } x \text{ IN } S : C(x)$$

The result of this expression is TRUE if every x in S satisfies $C(x)$ and is FALSE otherwise. Similarly, the expression

$$\text{EXISTS } x \text{ IN } S : C(x)$$

has value TRUE if there is at least one x in S such that $C(x)$ is TRUE and it has value FALSE otherwise.

Example 9.7: Another way to express the query "find all the stars of Disney movies" is shown in Fig. 9.4. Here, we focus on a star s and ask if they are the star of some movie m that is a Disney movie. Line (3) tells us to consider all movies m in the set of movies `s.starredIn`, which is the set of movies in which star s appeared. Line (4) then asks whether movie m is a Disney movie. If we find even one such movie m, the value of the EXISTS expression in lines (3) and (4) is TRUE; otherwise it is FALSE. □

```
1)   SELECT s
2)   FROM Stars s
3)   WHERE EXISTS m IN s.starredIn :
4)      m.ownedBy.name = "Disney"
```

Figure 9.4: Using an existential subquery

Example 9.8: Let us use the for-all operator to write a query asking for the stars that have appeared only in Disney movies. Technically, that set includes "stars" who appear in no movies at all (as far as we can tell from our database). It is possible to add another condition to our query, requiring that the star appear in at least one movie, but we leave that improvement as an exercise. Figure 9.5 shows the query. □

9.2.2 Aggregation Expressions

OQL uses the same five aggregation operators that SQL does: AVG, COUNT, SUM, MIN, and MAX. However, while these operators in SQL may be thought of as

```
SELECT s
FROM Stars s
WHERE FOR ALL m IN s.starredIn :
    m.ownedBy.name = "Disney"
```

Figure 9.5: Using a subquery with universal quantification

applying to a designated column of a table, the same operators in OQL apply to all collections whose members are of a suitable type. That is, COUNT can apply to any collection; SUM and AVG can be applied to collections of arithmetic types such as integers, and MIN and MAX can be applied to collections of any type that can be compared, e.g., arithmetic values or strings.

Example 9.9 : To compute the average length of all movies, we need to create a bag of all movie lengths. Note that we don't want the *set* of movie lengths, because then two movies that had the same length would count as one. The query is:

```
AVG(SELECT m.length FROM Movies m)
```

That is, we use a subquery to extract the length components from movies. Its result is the bag of lengths of movies, and we apply the AVG operator to this bag, giving the desired answer.   □

9.2.3   Group-By Expressions

The GROUP BY clause of SQL carries over to OQL, but with an interesting twist in perspective. The form of a GROUP BY clause in OQL is:

1. The keywords GROUP BY.

2. A comma-separated list of one or more *partition attributes*. Each of these consists of

    (a) A field name,

    (b) A colon, and

    (c) An expression.

That is, the form of a GROUP BY clause is:

$$\text{GROUP BY } f_1{:}e_1, \ f_2{:}e_2, \ldots, f_n{:}e_n$$

Each GROUP BY clause follows a select-from-where query. The expressions $e_1, e_2, \ldots, e_n$ may refer to variables mentioned in the FROM clause. To facilitate the explanation of how GROUP BY works, let us restrict ourselves to the common case where there is only one variable x in the FROM clause. The value of x ranges over some collection, C. For each member of C, say i, that satisfies the condition of the WHERE clause, we evaluate all the expressions that follow the GROUP BY, to obtain values $e_1(i), e_2(i), \ldots, e_n(i)$. This list of values is the group to which value i belongs.

The Intermediate Collection

The actual value returned by the GROUP BY is a set of structures, which we shall call the *intermediate collection*. The members of the intermediate collection have the form

$$\texttt{Struct}(f_1:v_1, \ f_2:v_2, \ldots, f_n:v_n, \ \texttt{partition}:P)$$

The first n fields indicate the group. That is, $(v_1, v_2, \ldots, v_n)$ must be the list of values $\big(e_1(i), e_2(i), \ldots, e_n(i)\big)$ for at least one value of i in the collection C that meets the condition of the WHERE clause.

The last field has the special name partition. Its value P is, intuitively, the values i that belong in this group. More precisely, P is a bag consisting of structures of the form Struct(x:i), where x is the variable of the FROM clause.

The Output Collection

The SELECT clause of a select-from-where expression that has a GROUP BY clause may refer only to the fields in the structures of the intermediate collection, namely $f_1, f_2, \ldots, f_n$ and partition. Through partition, we may refer to the field x that is present in the structures that are members of the bag P that forms the value of partition. Thus, we may refer to the variable x that appears in the FROM clause, but we may only do so within an aggregation operator that aggregates over all the members of a bag P. The result of the SELECT clause will be referred to as the *output collection*.

Example 9.10: Let us build a table of the total length of movies for each studio and for each year. In OQL, what we actually construct is a bag of structures, each with three components — a studio, a year, and the total length of movies for that studio and year. The query is shown in Fig. 9.6.

```
SELECT stdo, yr, sumLength: SUM(SELECT p.m.length
                                FROM partition p)
FROM Movies m
GROUP BY stdo: m.ownedBy.name, yr: m.year
```

Figure 9.6: Grouping movies by studio and year

To understand this query, let us start at the FROM clause. There, we find that variable m ranges over all Movie objects. Thus, m here plays the role of x

in our general discussion. In the GROUP BY clause are two fields stdo and yr, corresponding to the expressions m.ownedBy.name and m.year, respectively.

For instance, *Pretty Woman* is a movie made by Disney in 1990. When m is the object for this movie, the value of m.ownedBy.name is "Disney" and the value of m.year is 1990. As a result, the intermediate collection has, as one member, the structure:

$$\texttt{Struct(stdo:"Disney", yr:1990, partition:}P\texttt{)}$$

Here, P is a set of structures. It contains, for example,

$$\texttt{Struct(m:}m_{pw}\texttt{)}$$

where m_{pw} is the Movie object for *Pretty Woman*. Also in P are one-component structures with field name m for every other Disney movie of 1990.

Now, let us examine the SELECT clause. For each structure in the intermediate collection, we build one structure that is in the output collection. The first component of each output structure is stdo. That is, the field name is stdo and its value is the value of the stdo field of the corresponding structure in the intermediate collection. Similarly, the second component of the result has field name yr and a value equal to the yr component of the intermediate collection.

The third component of each structure in the output is

$$\texttt{SUM(SELECT p.m.length FROM partition p)}$$

To understand this select-from expression we first realize that variable p ranges over the members of the partition field of the structure in the GROUP BY result. Each value of p, recall, is a structure of the form Struct(m:o), where o is a movie object. The expression p.m therefore refers to this object o. Thus, p.m.length refers to the length component of this Movie object.

As a result, the select-from query produces the bag of lengths of the movies in a particular group. For instance, if stdo has the value "Disney" and yr has the value 1990, then the result of the select-from is the bag of the lengths of the movies made by Disney in 1990. When we apply the SUM operator to this bag we get the sum of the lengths of the movies in the group. Thus, one member of the output collection might be

$$\texttt{Struct(stdo:"Disney", yr:1990, sumLength:1234)}$$

if 1234 is the correct total length of all the Disney movies of 1990. □

Grouping When the FROM Clause has Multiple Collections

In the event that there is more than one variable in the FROM clause, a few changes to the interpretation of the query are necessary, but the principles remain the same as in the one-variable case above. Suppose that the variables appearing in the FROM clause are $x_1, x_2, \ldots, x_k$. Then:

1. All variables $x_1, x_2, \ldots, x_k$ may be used in the expressions $e_1, e_2, \ldots, e_n$ of the GROUP BY clause.

2. Structures in the bag that is the value of the **partition** field have fields named $x_1, x_2, \ldots, x_k$.

3. Suppose $i_1, i_2, \ldots, i_k$ are values for variables $x_1, x_2, \ldots, x_k$, respectively, that make the WHERE clause true. Then there is a structure in the intermediate collection of the form

$$\texttt{Struct}(f_1\!:\!e_1(i_1, \ldots, i_k), \ldots, f_n\!:\!e_n(i_1, \ldots, i_k), \ \texttt{partition:P})$$

and in bag P is the structure:

$$\texttt{Struct}(x_1\!:\!i_1, \ x_2\!:\!i_2, \ldots, x_k\!:\!i_k)$$

9.2.4 HAVING Clauses

A GROUP BY clause of OQL may be followed by a HAVING clause, with a meaning like that of SQL's HAVING clause. That is, a clause of the form

HAVING <condition>

serves to eliminate some of the groups created by the GROUP BY. The condition applies to the value of the **partition** field of each structure in the intermediate collection. If true, then this structure is processed as in Section 9.2.3, to form a structure of the output collection. If false, then this structure does not contribute to the output collection.

Example 9.11 : Let us repeat Example 9.10, but ask for the sum of the lengths of movies for only those studios and years such that the studio produced at least one movie of over 120 minutes. The query of Fig. 9.7 does the job. Notice that in the HAVING clause we used the same query as in the SELECT clause to obtain the bag of lengths of movies for a given studio and year. In the HAVING clause, we take the maximum of those lengths and compare it to 120. □

```
SELECT stdo, yr, sumLength: SUM(SELECT p.m.length
                                FROM partition p)
FROM Movies m
GROUP BY stdo: m.ownedBy.name, yr: m.year
HAVING MAX(SELECT p.m.length FROM partition p) > 120
```

Figure 9.7: Restricting the groups considered

9.2.5   Union, Intersection, and Difference

We may apply the union, intersection, and difference operators to two objects of set or bag type. These three operators are represented, as in SQL, by the keywords UNION, INTERSECT, and EXCEPT, respectively.

```
1)        (SELECT DISTINCT m
2)          FROM Movies m, m.stars s
3)          WHERE s.name = "Harrison Ford")
4)    EXCEPT
5)        (SELECT DISTINCT m
6)          FROM Movies m
7)          WHERE m.ownedBy.name = "Disney")
```

Figure 9.8: Query using the difference of two sets

Example 9.12: We can find the set of movies starring Harrison Ford that were not made by Disney with the difference of two select-from-where queries shown in Fig. 9.8. Lines (1) through (3) find the set of movies starring Ford, and lines (5) through (7) find the set of movies made by Disney. The EXCEPT at line (4) takes their difference.   □

We should notice the DISTINCT keywords in lines (1) and (5) of Fig. 9.8. This keyword forces the results of the two queries to be of set type; without DISTINCT, the result would be of bag (multiset) type. In OQL, the operators UNION, INTERSECT, and EXCEPT operate on either sets or bags. When both arguments are sets, then the operators have their usual set meaning.

However, when both arguments are of bag type, or one is a bag and one is a set, then the bag meaning of the operators is used. Recall Section 5.3.2, where the definitions of union, intersection, and difference for bags was explained.

For the particular query of Fig. 9.8, the number of times a movie appears in the result of either subquery is zero or one, so the result is the same regardless of whether DISTINCT is used. However, the *type* of the result differs. If DISTINCT is used, then the type of the result is Set<Movie>, while if DISTINCT is omitted in one or both places, then the result is of type Bag<Movie>.

9.2.6   Exercises for Section 9.2

Exercise 9.2.1: Using the ODL schema of Exercise 9.1.1 and Fig. 9.2, write the following queries in OQL:

* a) Find the manufacturers that make both PC's and printers.

* b) Find the manufacturers of PC's, all of whose PC's have at least 20 gigabytes of hard disk.

c) Find the manufacturers that make PC's but not laptops.

* d) Find the average speed of PC's.

* e) For each CD or DVD speed, find the average amount of RAM on a PC.

! f) Find the manufacturers that make some product with at least 64 megabytes of RAM and also make a product costing under $1000.

!! g) For each manufacturer that makes PC's with an average speed of at least 1200, find the maximum amount of RAM that they offer on a PC.

Exercise 9.2.2: Using the ODL schema of Exercise 9.1.3 and Fig. 9.3, write the following queries in OQL:

a) Find those classes of ship all of whose ships were launched prior to 1919.

b) Find the maximum displacement of any class.

! c) For each gun bore, find the earliest year in which any ship with that bore was launched.

*!! d) For each class of ships at least one of which was launched prior to 1919, find the number of ships of that class sunk in battle.

! e) Find the average number of ships in a class.

! f) Find the average displacement of a ship.

!! g) Find the battles (objects, not names) in which at least one ship from Great Britain took part and in which at least two ships were sunk.

! **Exercise 9.2.3:** We mentioned in Example 9.8 that the OQL query of Fig. 9.5 would return stars who starred in no movies at all, and therefore, technically appeared "only in Disney movies." Rewrite the query to return only those stars who have appeared in at least one movie and all movies in which they appeared where Disney movies.

! **Exercise 9.2.4:** Is it ever possible for FOR ALL x IN S : $C(x)$ to be true, while EXISTS x IN S : $C(x)$ is false? Explain your reasoning.

9.3 Object Assignment and Creation in OQL

In this section we shall consider how OQL connects to its host language, which we shall take to be C++ in examples, although another object-oriented, general-purpose programming language (e.g. Java) might be the host language in some systems.

9.3.1   Assigning Values to Host-Language Variables

Unlike SQL, which needs to move data between components of tuples and host-language variables, OQL fits naturally into its host language. That is, the expressions of OQL that we have learned, such as select-from-where, produce objects as values. It is possible to assign to any host-language variable of the proper type a value that is the result of one of these OQL expressions.

Example 9.13 : The OQL expression

```
SELECT DISTINCT m
FROM Movies m
WHERE m.year < 1920
```

produces the set of all those movies made before 1920. Its type is `Set<Movie>`. If `oldMovies` is a host-language variable of the same type, then we may write (in C++ extended with OQL):

```
oldMovies = SELECT DISTINCT m
            FROM Movies m
            WHERE m.year < 1920;
```

and the value of `oldMovies` will become the set of these `Movie` objects.   □

9.3.2   Extracting Elements of Collections

Since the select-from-where and group-by expressions each produce collections — either sets, bags, or lists — we must do something extra if we want a single element of that collection. This statement is true even if we have a collection that we are sure contains only one element. OQL provides the operator `ELEMENT` to turn a singleton collection into its lone member. This operator can be applied, for instance, to the result of a query that is known to return a singleton.

Example 9.14 : Suppose we would like to assign to the variable `gwtw`, of type `Movie` (i.e., the `Movie` class is its type) the object representing the movie *Gone With the Wind*. The result of the query

```
SELECT m
FROM Movies m
WHERE m.title = "Gone With the Wind"
```

is the bag containing just this one object. We cannot assign this bag to variable `gwtw` directly, because we would get a type error. However, if we apply the `ELEMENT` operator first,

```
gwtw = ELEMENT(SELECT m
               FROM Movies m
               WHERE m.title = "Gone With the Wind"
       );
```

then the type of the variable and the expression match, and the assignment is legal. □

9.3.3 Obtaining Each Member of a Collection

Obtaining each member of a set or bag is more complex, but still simpler than the cursor-based algorithms we needed in SQL. First, we need to turn our set or bag into a list. We do so with a select-from-where expression that uses ORDER BY. Recall from Section 9.1.4 that the result of such an expression is a list of the selected objects or values.

Example 9.15: Suppose we want a list of all the movie objects in the class Movie. We can use the title and (to break ties) the year of the movie, since (title, year) is a key for Movie. The statement

```
movieList = SELECT m
            FROM Movies m
            ORDER BY m.title, m.year;
```

assigns to host-language variable movieList a list of all the Movie objects, sorted by title and year. □

Once we have a list, sorted or not, we can access each element by number; the ith element of the list L is obtained by $L[i-1]$. Note that lists and arrays are assumed numbered starting at 0, as in C or C++.

Example 9.16: Suppose we want to write a C++ function that prints the title, year, and length of each movie. A sketch of the function is shown in Fig. 9.9.

```
1)  movieList = SELECT m
                FROM Movies m
                ORDER BY m.title, m.year;
2)  numberOfMovies = COUNT(Movies);
3)  for(i=0; i<numberOfMovies; i++) {
4)      movie = movieList[i];
5)      cout << movie.title << " " << movie.year << " "
6)          << movie.length << "\n";
    }
```

Figure 9.9: Examining and printing each movie

Line (1) sorts the Movie class, placing the result into variable movieList, whose type is List<Movie>. Line (2) computes the number of movies, using the OQL operator COUNT. Lines (3) through (6) are a for-loop in which integer variable i ranges over each position of the list. For convenience, the ith element of the list is assigned to variable `movie`. Then, at lines (5) and (6) the relevant attributes of the movie are printed.   □

9.3.4   Constants in OQL

Constants in OQL (sometimes referred to as *immutable objects*) are constructed from a basis and recursive constructors, in a manner analogous to the way ODL types are constructed.

1. *Basic values*, which are either

   (a) *Atomic values*: integers, floats, characters, strings, and booleans. These are represented as in SQL, with the exception that double-quotes are used to surround strings.

   (b) *Enumerations*. The values in an enumeration are actually declared in ODL. Any one of these values may be used as a constant.

2. *Complex values* built using the following type constructors:

   (a) `Set(...)`.
   (b) `Bag(...)`.
   (c) `List(...)`.
   (d) `Array(...)`.
   (e) `Struct(...)`.

   The first four of these are called *collection types*. The collection types and `Struct` may be applied at will to any values of the appropriate type(s), basic or complex. However, when applying the `Struct` operator, one needs to specify the field names and their corresponding values. Each field name is followed by a colon and the value, and field-value pairs are separated by commas. Note that the same type constructors are used in ODL, but here we use round, rather than triangular, brackets.

Example 9.17: The expression `Bag(2,1,2)` denotes the bag in which integer 2 appears twice and integer 1 appears once. The expression

```
Struct(foo: bag(2,1,2), bar: "baz")
```

denotes a structure with two fields. Field `foo`, has the bag described above as its value, and `bar`, has the string `"baz"` for its value.   □

9.3.5 Creating New Objects

We have seen that OQL expressions such as select-from-where allow us to create new objects. It is also possible to create objects by assembling constants or other expressions into structures and collections explicitly. We saw an example of this convention in Example 9.5, where the line

```
SELECT DISTINCT Struct(star1: s1, star2: s2)
```

was used to specify that the result of the query is a set of objects whose type is `Struct{star1: Star, star2: Star}`. We gave the field names `star1` and `star2` to specify the structure, while the types of these fields could be deduced from the types of the variables `s1` and `s2`.

Example 9.18: The construction of constants that we saw in Section 9.3.4 can be used with assignments to variables, in a manner similar to that of other programming languages. For instance, consider the following sequence of assignments:

```
x = Struct(a:1, b:2);
y = Bag(x, x, Struct(a:3, b:4));
```

The first line gives variable `x` a value of type

```
Struct(a:integer, b:integer)
```

a structure with two integer-valued fields named `a` and `b`. We may represent values of this type as pairs, with just the integers as components and not the field names `a` and `b`. Thus, the value of x may be represented by $(1, 2)$. The second line defines `y` to be a bag whose members are structures of the same type as x, above. The pair $(1, 2)$ appears twice in this bag, and $(3, 4)$ appears once. $\square$

Classes or other defined types can have instances created by *constructor functions*. Classes typically have several different forms of constructor functions, depending on which properties are initialized explicitly and which are given some default value. For example, methods are not initialized, most attributes will get initial values, and relationships might be initialized to the empty set and augmented later. The name for each of these constructor functions is the name of the class, and they are distinguished by the field names mentioned in their arguments. The details of how these constructor functions are defined depend on the host language.

Example 9.19: Let us consider a possible constructor function for `Movie` objects. This function, we suppose, takes values for the attributes `title`, `year`, `length`, and `ownedBy`, producing an object that has these values in the listed fields and an empty set of stars. Then, if `mgm` is a variable whose value is the MGM `Studio` object, we might create a *Gone With the Wind* object by:

```
gwtw = Movie(title: "Gone With the Wind",
             year: 1939,
             length: 239,
             ownedBy: mgm);
```

This statement has two effects:

1. It creates a new `Movie` object, which becomes part of the extent `Movies`.

2. It makes this object the value of host-language variable `gwtw`.

□

9.3.6   Exercises for Section 9.3

Exercise 9.3.1: Assign to a host-language variable x the following constants:

* a) The set $\{1, 2, 3\}$.

  b) The bag $\{1, 2, 3, 1\}$.

  c) The list $(1, 2, 3, 1)$.

  d) The structure whose first component, named a, is the set $\{1, 2\}$ and whose second component, named b, is the bag $\{1, 1\}$.

  e) The bag of structures, each with two fields named a and b. The respective pairs of values for the three structures in the bag are $(1, 2)$, $(2, 1)$, and $(1, 2)$.

Exercise 9.3.2: Using the ODL schema of Exercise 9.1.1 and Fig. 9.2, write statements of C++ (or an object-oriented host language of your choice) extended with OQL to do the following:

* a) Assign to host-language variable x the object for the PC with model number 1000.

  b) Assign to host-language variable y the set of all laptop objects with at least 64 megabytes of RAM.

  c) Assign to host-language variable z the average speed of PC's selling for less than \$1500.

! d) Find all the laser printers, print a list of their model numbers and prices, and follow it by a message indicating the model number with the lowest price.

!! e) Print a table giving, for each manufacturer of PC's, the minimum and maximum price.

Exercise 9.3.3: In this exercise, we shall use the ODL schema of Exercise 9.1.3 and Fig. 9.3. We shall assume that for each of the four classes of that schema, there is a constructor function of the same name that takes values for each of the attributes and single-valued relationships, but not the multivalued relationships, which are initialized to be empty. For the single-valued relationships to other classes, you may postulate a host-language variable whose current value is the related object. Create the following objects and assign the object to be the value of a host-language variable in each case.

* a) The battleship Colorado of the Maryland class, launched in 1923.

  b) The battleship Graf Spee of the Lützow class, launched in 1936.

  c) An outcome of the battle of Malaya was that the battleship Prince of Wales was sunk.

  d) The battle of Malaya was fought Dec. 10, 1941.

  e) The Hood class of British battlecruisers had eight 15-inch guns and a displacement of 41,000 tons.

9.4 User-Defined Types in SQL

We now turn to the way SQL-99 incorporates many of the object-oriented features that we have seen in ODL and OQL. Because of these recent extensions to SQL, a DBMS that follows this standard is often referred to as "object-relational." We met many of the object-relational concepts abstractly in Section 4.5. Now, it is time for us to study the details of the standard.

OQL has no specific notion of a relation; it is just a set (or bag) of structures. However, the relation is so central to SQL that objects in SQL keep relations as the core concept. The classes of ODL are transmogrified into *user-defined types*, or UDT's, in SQL. We find UDT's used in two distinct ways:

1. A UDT can be the type of a table.

2. A UDT can be the type of an attribute belonging to some table.

9.4.1 Defining Types in SQL

A user-defined type declaration in SQL can be thought of as roughly analogous to a class declaration in ODL, with some distinctions. First, key declarations for a relation with a user-defined type are part of the table definition, not the type definition; that is, many SQL relations can be declared to have the same (user-defined) type but different keys and other constraints. Second, in SQL we do not treat relationships as properties. A relationship must be represented by a separate relation, as was discussed in Section 4.4.5. A simple form of UDT definition is:

1. The keywords CREATE TYPE,

2. A name for the type,

3. The keyword AS,

4. A parenthesized, comma-separated list of attributes and their types.

5. A comma-separated list of methods, including their argument type(s), and return type.

That is, the definition of a type T has the form

CREATE TYPE T AS <attribute and method declarations> ;

Example 9.20: We can create a type representing movie stars, analogous to the class Star found in the OQL example of Fig. 9.1. However, we cannot represent directly a set of movies as a field within Star tuples. Thus, we shall start with only the name and address components of Star tuples.

To begin, note that the type of an address in Fig. 9.1 is itself a tuple, with components street and city. Thus, we need two type definitions, one for addresses and the other for stars. The necessary definitions are shown in Fig. 9.10.

```
CREATE TYPE AddressType AS (
    street  CHAR(50),
    city    CHAR(20)
);

CREATE TYPE StarType AS (
    name    CHAR(30),
    address AddressType
);
```

Figure 9.10: Two type definitions

A tuple of type AddressType has two components, whose attributes are street and city. The types of these components are character strings of length 50 and 20, respectively. A tuple of type StarType also has two components. The first is attribute name, whose type is a 30-character string, and the second is address, whose type is itself a UDT AddressType, that is, a tuple with street and city components.   □

9.4.2 Methods in User-Defined Types

The declaration of a method resembles the way a function in PSM is introduced; see Section 8.2.1. There is no analog of PSM procedures as methods. That is, every method returns a value of some type. While function declarations and definitions in PSM are combined, a method needs both a declaration, within the definition of its type, and a separate definition, in a `CREATE METHOD` statement.

A method declaration looks like a PSM function declaration, with the keyword `METHOD` replacing `CREATE FUNCTION`. However, SQL methods typically have no arguments; they are applied to rows, just as ODL methods are applied to objects. In the definition of the method, `SELF` refers to this tuple, if necessary.

Example 9.21: Let us extend the definition of the type `AddressType` of Fig. 9.10 with a method `houseNumber` that extracts from the `street` component the portion devoted to the house address. For instance, if the `street` component were '123 Maple St.', then `houseNumber` should return '123'. The revised type definition is thus:

```
CREATE TYPE AddressType AS (
    street  CHAR(50),
    city    CHAR(20)
    )
    METHOD houseNumber() RETURNS CHAR(10);
```

We see the keyword `METHOD`, followed by the name of the method and a parenthesized list of its arguments and their types. In this case, there are no arguments, but the parentheses are still needed. Had there been arguments, they would have appeared, followed by their types, such as `(a INT, b CHAR(5))`. □

Separately, we need to define the method. A simple form of method definition consists of:

1. The keywords `CREATE METHOD`.

2. The method name, arguments and their types, and the `RETURNS` clause, as in the declaration of the method.

3. The keyword `FOR` and the name of the UDT in which the method is declared.

4. The body of the method, which is written in the same language as the bodies of PSM functions.

For instance, we could define the method `houseNumber` from Example 9.21 as:

```
CREATE METHOD houseNumber() RETURNS CHAR(10)
FOR AddressType
```

```
BEGIN
    ...
END;
```

We have omitted the body of the method because accomplishing the intended separation of the string `string` as intended is nontrivial, even in PSM.

9.4.3   Declaring Relations with a UDT

Having declared a type, we may declare one or more relations whose tuples are of that type. The form of relation declarations is like that of Section 6.6.2, but we use

$$OF <\text{type name}>$$

in place of the list of attribute declarations in a normal SQL table declaration. Other elements of a table declaration, such as keys, foreign keys, and tuple-based constraints, may be added to the table declaration if desired, and apply only to this table, not to the UDT itself.

Example 9.22: We could declare `MovieStar` to be a relation whose tuples were of type `StarType` by

```
CREATE TABLE MovieStar OF StarType;
```

As a result, table `MovieStar` has two attributes, `name` and `address`. The first attribute, `name`, is an ordinary character string, but the second, `address`, has a type that is itself a UDT, namely the type `AddressType`.   □

It is common to have one relation for each type, and to think of that relation as the extent (in the sense of Section 4.3.4) of the class corresponding to that type. However, it is permissible to have many relations or none of a given type.

9.4.4   References

The effect of object identity in object-oriented languages is obtained in SQL through the notion of a *reference*. Tables whose type is a UDT may have a *reference column* that serves as its "identity." This column could be the primary key of the table, if there is one, or it could be a column whose values are generated and maintained unique by the DBMS, for example. We shall defer the matter of defining reference columns until we first see how reference types are used.

To refer to the tuples of a table with a reference column, an attribute may have as its type a reference to another type. If T is a UDT, then $REF(T)$ is the type of a reference to a tuple of type T. Further, the reference may be given a *scope*, which is the name of the relation whose tuples are referred to. Thus, an attribute A whose values are references to tuples in relation R, where R is a table whose type is the UDT T, would be declared by:

A REF(*T*) SCOPE *R*

If no scope is specified, the reference can go to any relation of type *T*.

Example 9.23: Reference attributes are not sufficient to record in `MovieStar` the set of all movies they starred in, but they let us record the best movie for each star. Assume that we have declared a relation `Movie`, and that the type of this relation is the UDT `MovieType`; we shall define both `MovieType` and `Movie` later, in Fig. 9.11. The following is a new definition of `StarType` that includes an attribute `bestMovie` that is a reference to a movie.

```
CREATE TYPE StarType AS (
    name        CHAR(30),
    address     AddressType,
    bestMovie   REF(MovieType) SCOPE Movie
);
```

Now, if relation `MovieStar` is defined to have the UDT above, then each star tuple will have a component that refers to a `Movie` tuple — the star's best movie. □

Next, we must arrange that a table such as `Movie` in Example 9.23 will have a reference column. Such a table is said to be *referenceable*. In a **CREATE TABLE** statement where the type of the table is a UDT (as in Section 9.4.3), we may append a clause of the form:

REF IS <attribute name> <how generated>

The attribute name is a name given to the column that will serve as an "object identifier" for tuples. The "how generated" clause is typically either:

1. SYSTEM GENERATED, meaning that the DBMS is responsible for maintaining a unique value in this column of each tuple, or

2. DERIVED, meaning that the DBMS will use the primary key of the relation to produce unique values for this column.

Example 9.24: Figure 9.11 shows how the UDT `MovieType` and relation `Movie` could be declared so that `Movie` is referenceable. The UDT is declared in lines (1) through (4). Then the relation `Movie` is defined to have this type in lines (5) through (7). Notice that we have declared `title` and `year`, together, to be the key for relation `Movie` in line (7).

We see in line (6) that the name of the "identity" column for `Movie` is `movieID`. This attribute, which automatically becomes a fourth attribute of `Movie`, along with `title`, `year`, and `inColor`, may be used in queries like any other attribute of `Movie`.

Line (6) also says that the DBMS is responsible for generating the value of `movieID` each time a new tuple is inserted into `Movie`. Had we replaced "SYSTEM

```
1)   CREATE TYPE MovieType AS (
2)        title   CHAR(30),
3)        year    INTEGER,
4)        inColor BOOLEAN
     );

5)   CREATE TABLE Movie OF MovieType (
6)        REF IS movieID SYSTEM GENERATED,
7)        PRIMARY KEY (title, year)
     );
```

Figure 9.11: Creating a referenceable table

GENERATED" by "DERIVED," then new tuples would get their value of `movieID` by some calculation, performed by the system, on the values of the primary-key attributes `title` and `year` from the same tuple.   □

Example 9.25: Now, let us see how to represent the many-many relationship between movies and stars using references. Previously, we represented this relationship by a relation like `StarsIn` that contains tuples with the keys of `Movie` and `MovieStar`. As an alternative, we may define `StarsIn` to have references to tuples from these two relations.

First, we need to redefine `MovieStar` so it is a referenceable table, thusly:

```
CREATE TABLE MovieStar OF StarType (
    REF IS starID SYSTEM GENERATED
);
```

Then, we may declare the relation `StarsIn` to have two attributes, which are references, one to a movie tuple and one to a star tuple. Here is a direct definition of this relation:

```
CREATE TABLE StarsIn (
    star    REF(StarType) SCOPE MovieStar,
    movie   REF(MovieType) SCOPE Movie
);
```

Optionally, we could have defined a UDT as above, and then declared `StarsIn` to be a table of that type.   □

9.4.5   Exercises for Section 9.4

Exercise 9.4.1: Write type declarations for the following types:

a) `NameType`, with components for first, middle, and last names and a title.

* b) `PersonType`, with a name of the person and references to the persons that are their mother and father. You must use the type from part (a) in your declaration.

  c) `MarriageType`, with the date of the marriage and references to the husband and wife.

Exercise 9.4.2: Redesign our running products database schema of Exercise 5.2.1 to use type declarations and reference attributes where appropriate. In particular, in the relations PC, `Laptop`, and `Printer` make the `model` attribute be a reference to the `Product` tuple for that model.

! **Exercise 9.4.3:** In Exercise 9.4.2 we suggested that model numbers in the tables PC, `Laptop`, and `Printer` could be references to tuples of the `Product` table. Is it also possible to make the `model` attribute in `Product` a reference to the tuple in the relation for that type of product? Why or why not?

* **Exercise 9.4.4:** Redesign our running battleships database schema of Exercise 5.2.4 to use type declarations and reference attributes where appropriate. The schema from Exercise 9.1.3 should suggest where reference attributes are useful. Look for many-one relationships and try to represent them using an attribute with a reference type.

9.5 Operations on Object-Relational Data

All appropriate SQL operations from previous chapters apply to tables that are declared with a UDT or that have attributes whose type is a UDT. There are also some entirely new operations we can use, such as reference-following. However, some familiar operations, especially those that access or modify columns whose type is a UDT, involve new syntax.

9.5.1 Following References

Suppose x is a value of type REF(T). Then x refers to some tuple t of type T. We can obtain tuple t itself, or components of t, by two means:

1. Operator `->` has essentially the same meaning as this operator does in C. That is, if x is a reference to a tuple t, and a is an attribute of t, then `x->a` is the value of the attribute a in tuple t.

2. The `DEREF` operator applies to a reference and produces the tuple referenced.

Example 9.26: Let us use the relation `StarsIn` from Example 9.25 to find the movies in which Mel Gibson starred. Recall that the schema is

    StarsIn(star, movie)

where `star` and `movie` are references to tuples of `MovieStar` and `Movie`, respectively. A possible query is:

```
1)  SELECT DEREF(movie)
2)  FROM StarsIn
3)  WHERE star->name = 'Mel Gibson';
```

In line (3), the expression `star->name` produces the value of the `name` component of the `MovieStar` tuple referred to by the `star` component of any given `StarsIn` tuple. Thus, the `WHERE` clause identifies those `StarsIn` tuples whose `star` component are references to the Mel-Gibson `MovieStar` tuple. Line (1) then produces the movie tuple referred to by the `movie` component of those tuples. All three attributes — `title`, `year`, and `inColor` — will appear in the printed result.

Note that we could have replaced line (1) by:

```
1)  SELECT  movie
```

However, had we done so, we would have gotten a list of system-generated gibberish that serves as the internal unique identifiers for those tuples. We would not see the information in the referenced tuples.   □

9.5.2 Accessing Attributes of Tuples with a UDT

When we define a relation to have a UDT, the tuples must be thought of as single objects, rather than lists with components corresponding to the attributes of the UDT. As a case in point, consider the relation `Movie` declared in Fig. 9.11. This relation has UDT `MovieType`, which has three attributes: `title`, `year`, and `inColor`. However, a tuple t in `Movie` has only *one* component, not three. That component is the object itself.

If we "drill down" into the object, we can extract the values of the three attributes in the type `MovieType`, as well as use any methods defined for that type. However, we have to access these attributes properly, since they are not attributes of the tuple itself. Rather, every UDT has an implicitly defined *observer method* for each attribute of that UDT. The name of the observer method for an attribute x is $x()$. We apply this method as we would any other method for this UDT; we attach it with a dot to an expression that evaluates to an object of this type. Thus, if t is a variable whose value is of type T, and x is an attribute of T, then $t.x()$ is the value of x in the tuple (object) denoted by t.

Example 9.27: Let us find, from the relation `Movie` of Fig. 9.11 the year(s) of movies with title *King Kong*. Here is one way to do so:

```
SELECT m.year()
FROM Movie m
WHERE m.title() = 'King Kong';
```

Even though the tuple variable m would appear not to be needed here, we need a variable whose value is an object of type `MovieType` — the UDT for relation `Movie`. The condition of the `WHERE` clause compares the constant `'King Kong'` to the value of `m.title()`. The latter is the observer method for attribute `title` of type `MovieType`. Similarly, the value in the `SELECT` clause is expressed `m.year()`; this expression applies the observer method for `year` to the object m. □

9.5.3 Generator and Mutator Functions

In order to create data that conforms to a UDT, or to change components of objects with a UDT, we can use two kinds of methods that are created automatically, along with the observer methods, whenever a UDT is defined. These are:

1. A *generator method.* This method has the name of the type and no argument. It also has the unusual property that it may be invoked without being applied to any object. That is, if T is a UDT, then $T()$ returns an object of type T, with no values in its various components.

2. *Mutator methods.* For each attribute x of UDT T, there is a mutator method $x(v)$. When applied to an object of type T, it changes the x attribute of that object to have value v. Notice that the mutator and observer method for an attribute each have the name of the attribute, but differ in that the mutator has an argument.

Example 9.28: We shall write a PSM procedure that takes as arguments a street, a city, and a name, and inserts into the relation `MovieStar` (of type `StarType` according to Example 9.22) an object constructed from these values, using calls to the proper generator and mutator functions. Recall from Example 9.20 that objects of `StarType` have a `name` component that is a character string, but an `address` component that is itself an object of type `AddressType`. The procedure `InsertStar` is shown in Fig. 9.12.

Lines (2) through (4) introduce the arguments s, c, and n, which will provide values for a street, city, and star name, respectively. Lines (5) and (6) declare two local variables. Each is of one of the UDT's involved in the type for objects that exist in the relation `MovieStar`. At lines (7) and (8) we create empty objects of each of these two types.

Lines (9) and (10) put real values in the object `newAddr`; these values are taken from the procedure arguments that provide a street and a city. Line (11) similarly installs the argument n as the value of the `name` component in the object `newStar`. Then line (12) takes the entire `newAddr` object and makes it the value of the `address` component in `newStar`. Finally, line (13) inserts the constructed object into relation `MovieStar`. Notice that, as always, a relation that has a UDT as its type has but a single component, even if that component has several attributes, such as `name` and `address` in this example.

```
1)   CREATE PROCEDURE InsertStar(
2)       IN s CHAR(50),
3)       IN c CHAR(20),
4)       IN n CHAR(30)
     )
5)   DECLARE newAddr AddressType;
6)   DECLARE newStar StarType;

     BEGIN
7)       SET newAddr = AddressType();
8)       SET newStar = StarType();
9)       newAddr.street(s);
10)      newAddr.city(c);
11)      newStar.name(n);
12)      newStar.address(newAddr);
13)      INSERT INTO MovieStar VALUES(newStar);
     END;
```

Figure 9.12: Creating and storing a `StarType` object

To insert a star into `MovieStar`, we can call procedure `InsertStar`.

```
CALL InsertStar('345 Spruce St.', 'Glendale', 'Gwyneth Paltrow');
```

is an example.   □

It is much simpler to insert objects into a relation with a UDT if your DBMS provides, or if you create, a generator function that takes values for the attributes of the UDT and returns a suitable object. For example, if we have functions `AddressType(s,c)` and `StarType(n,a)` that return objects of the indicated types, then we can make the insertion at the end of Example 9.28 with an `INSERT` statement of a familiar form:

```
INSERT INTO MovieStar VALUES(
    StarType('Gwyneth Paltrow',
        AddressType('345 Spruce St.', 'Glendale')));
```

9.5.4   Ordering Relationships on UDT's

Objects that are of some UDT are inherently abstract, in the sense that there is no way to compare two objects of the same UDT, either to test whether they are "equal" or whether one is less than another. Even two objects that have all components identical will not be considered equal unless we tell the system to regard them as equal. Similarly, there is no obvious way to sort the tuples of a relation that has a UDT unless we define a function that tells which of two objects of that UDT precedes the other.

Yet there are many SQL operations that require either an equality test or both an equality and a "less than" test. For instance, we cannot eliminate duplicates if we can't tell whether two tuples are equal. We cannot group by an attribute whose type is a UDT unless there is an equality test for that UDT. We cannot use an `ORDER BY` clause or a comparison like $<$ in a `WHERE` clause unless we can compare any two elements.

To specify an ordering or comparison, SQL allows us to issue a `CREATE ORDERING` statement for any UDT. There are a number of forms this statement may take, and we shall only consider the two simplest options:

1. The statement

   > `CREATE ORDERING FOR` T `EQUALS ONLY BY STATE;`

   says that two members of UDT T are considered equal if all of their corresponding components are equal. There is no $<$ defined on objects of UDT T.

2. The following statement

   > `CREATE ORDERING FOR` T
   > `ORDERING FULL BY RELATIVE WITH` F;

   says that any of the six comparisons (`<`, `<=`, `>`, `>=`, `=`, and `<>`) may be performed on objects of UDT T. To tell how objects x_1 and x_2 compare, we apply the function F to these objects. This function must be written so that $F(x_1, x_2) < 0$ whenever we want to conclude that $x_1 < x_2$; $F(x_1, x_2) = 0$ means that $x_1 = x_2$, and $F(x_1, x_2) > 0$ means that $x_1 > x_2$. If we replace "`ORDERING FULL`" with "`EQUALS ONLY`," then $F(x_1, x_2) = 0$ indicates that $x_1 = x_2$, while any other value of $F(x_1, x_2)$ means that $x_1 \neq x_2$. Comparison by $<$ is impossible in this case.

Example 9.29: Let us consider a possible ordering on the UDT `StarType` from Example 9.20. If we want only an equality on objects of this UDT, we could declare:

> `CREATE ORDERING FOR StarType EQUALS ONLY BY STATE;`

That statement says that two objects of `StarType` are equal if and only if their names are the same as character strings, and their addresses are the same as objects of UDT `AddressType`.

The problem is that, unless we define an ordering for `AddressType`, an object of that type is not even equal to itself. Thus, we also need to create at least an equality test for `AddressType`. A simple way to do so is to declare that two `AddressType` objects are equal if and only if their streets and cities are each the same. We could do so by:

CREATE ORDERING FOR AddressType EQUALS ONLY BY STATE;

Alternatively, we could define a complete ordering of AddressType objects. One reasonable ordering is to order addresses first by cities, alphabetically, and among addresses in the same city, by street address, alphabetically. To do so, we have to define a function, say AddrLEG, that takes two AddressType arguments and returns a negative, zero, or positive value to indicate that the first is less than, equal to, or greater than the second. We declare:

CREATE ORDERING FOR AddressType
ORDER FULL BY RELATIVE WITH AddrLEG;

The function AddrLEG is shown in Fig. 9.13. Notice that if we reach line (7), it must be that the two city components are the same, so we compare the street components. Likewise, if we reach line (9), the only remaining possibility is that the cities are the same and the first street precedes the second alphabetically.   □

```
1)    CREATE FUNCTION AddrLEG(
2)        x1 AddressType,
3)        x2 AddressType
4)    ) RETURNS INTEGER

5)    IF x1.city() < x2.city() THEN RETURN(-1)
6)    ELSEIF x1.city() > x2.city() THEN RETURN(1)
7)    ELSEIF x1.street() < x2.street() THEN RETURN(-1)
8)    ELSEIF x1.street() = x2.street() THEN RETURN(0)
9)    ELSE RETURN(1)
      END IF;
```

Figure 9.13: A comparison function for address objects

9.5.5   Exercises for Section 9.5

Exercise 9.5.1: Using the StarsIn relation of Example 9.25, and the Movie and MovieStar relations accessible through StarsIn, write the following queries:

* a) Find the names of the stars of *Ishtar*.

*! b) Find the titles and years of all movies in which at least one star lives in Malibu.

  c) Find all the movies (objects of type MovieType) that starred Melanie Griffith.

! d) Find the movies (title and year) with at least five stars.

Exercise 9.5.2 : Using your schema from Exercise 9.4.2, write the following queries. Don't forget to use references whenever appropriate.

a) Find the manufacturers of PC's with a hard disk larger than 60 gigabytes.

b) Find the manufacturers of laser printers.

! c) Produce a table giving for each model of laptop, the model of the laptop having the highest processor speed of any laptop made by the same manufacturer.

Exercise 9.5.3 : Using your schema from Exercise 9.4.4, write the following queries. Don't forget to use references whenever appropriate and avoid joins (i.e., subqueries or more than one tuple variable in the FROM clause).

* a) Find the ships with a displacement of more than 35,000 tons.

b) Find the battles in which at least one ship was sunk.

! c) Find the classes that had ships launched after 1930.

!! d) Find the battles in which at least one US ship was damaged.

Exercise 9.5.4 : Assuming the function AddrLEG of Fig. 9.13 is available, write a suitable function to compare objects of type StarType, and declare your function to be the basis of the ordering of StarType objects.

*! **Exercise 9.5.5 :** Write a procedure to take a star name as argument and delete from StarsIn and MovieStar all tuples involving that star.

9.6 Summary of Chapter 9

✦ *Select-From-Where Statements in OQL*: OQL offers a select-from-where expression that resembles SQL's. In the FROM clause, we can declare variables that range over any collection, including both extents of classes (analogous to relations) and collections that are the values of attributes in objects.

✦ *Common OQL Operators*: OQL offers for-all, there-exists, IN, union, intersection, difference, and aggregation operators that are similar in spirit to SQL's. However, aggregation is always over a collection, not a column of a relation.

✦ *OQL Group-By*: OQL also offers a GROUP BY clause in select-from-where statements that is similar to SQL's. However, in OQL, the collection of objects in each group is explicitly accessible through a field name called partition.

✦ *Extracting Elements From OQL Collections*: We can obtain the lone member of a collection that is a singleton by applying the ELEMENT operator. The elements of a collection with more than one member can be accessed by first turning the collection into a list, using an ORDER BY clause in a select-from-where statement, and then using a loop in the surrounding host-language program to visit each element of the list in turn.

✦ *User-Defined Types in SQL*: Object-relational capabilities of SQL are centered around the UDT, or user-defined type. These types may be declared by listing their attributes and other information, as in table declarations. In addition, methods may be declared for UDT's.

✦ *Relations With a UDT as Type*: Instead of declaring the attributes of a relation, we may declare that relation to have a UDT. If we do so, then its tuples have one component, and this component is an object of the UDT.

✦ *Reference Types*: A type of an attribute can be a reference to a UDT. Such attributes essentially are pointers to objects of that UDT.

✦ *Object Identity for UDT's*: When we create a relation whose type is a UDT, we declare an attribute to serve as the "object-ID" of each tuple. This component is a reference to the tuple itself. Unlike in object-oriented systems, this "OID" column may be accessed by the user, although it is rarely meaningful.

✦ *Accessing components of a UDT*: SQL provides observer and mutator functions for each attribute of a UDT. These functions, respectively, return and change the value of that attribute when applied to any object of that UDT.

9.7   References for Chapter 9

The reference for OQL is the same as for ODL: [1]. Material on object-relational features of SQL can be obtained as described in the bibliographic notes to Chapter 6.

1. Cattell, R. G. G. (ed.), *The Object Database Standard: ODMG–99*, Morgan-Kaufmann, San Francisco, 1999.

Chapter 10

Logical Query Languages

Some query languages for the relational model resemble a logic more than they do the algebra that we introduced in Section 5.2. However, logic-based languages appear to be difficult for many programmers to grasp. Thus, we have delayed our coverage of logic until the end of our study of query languages.

We shall introduce Datalog, which is the simplest form of logic devised for the relational model. In its nonrecursive form, Datalog has the same power as the classical relational algebra. However, by allowing recursion, we can express queries in Datalog that cannot be expressed in SQL2 (except by adding procedural programming such as PSM). We discuss the complexities that come up when we allow recursive negation, and finally, we see how the solution provided by Datalog has been used to provide a way to allow meaningful recursion in the most recent SQL-99 standard.

10.1   A Logic for Relations

As an alternative to abstract query languages based on algebra, one can use a form of logic to express queries. The logical query language *Datalog* ("database logic") consists of if-then rules. Each of these rules expresses the idea that from certain combinations of tuples in certain relations we may infer that some other tuple is in some other relation, or in the answer to a query.

10.1.1   Predicates and Atoms

Relations are represented in Datalog by *predicates*. Each predicate takes a fixed number of arguments, and a predicate followed by its arguments is called an *atom*. The syntax of atoms is just like that of function calls in conventional programming languages; for example $P(x_1, x_2, \ldots, x_n)$ is an atom consisting of the predicate P with arguments $x_1, x_2, \ldots, x_n$.

In essence, a predicate is the name of a function that returns a boolean value. If R is a relation with n attributes in some fixed order, then we shall

463

also use R as the name of a predicate corresponding to this relation. The atom $R(a_1, a_2, \ldots, a_n)$ has value TRUE if $(a_1, a_2, \ldots, a_n)$ is a tuple of R; the atom has value FALSE otherwise.

Example 10.1: Let R be the relation

A	B
1	2
3	4

Then $R(1, 2)$ is true and so is $R(3, 4)$. However, for any other values x and y, $R(x, y)$ is false. □

A predicate can take variables as well as constants as arguments. If an atom has variables for one or more of its arguments, then it is a boolean-valued function that takes values for these variables and returns TRUE or FALSE.

Example 10.2: If R is the predicate from Example 10.1, then $R(x, y)$ is the function that tells, for any x and y, whether the tuple (x, y) is in relation R. For the particular instance of R mentioned in Example 10.1, $R(x, y)$ returns TRUE when either

1. $x = 1$ and $y = 2$, or

2. $x = 3$ and $y = 4$

and FALSE otherwise. As another example, the atom $R(1, z)$ returns TRUE if $z = 2$ and returns FALSE otherwise. □

10.1.2 Arithmetic Atoms

There is another kind of atom that is important in Datalog: an *arithmetic atom*. This kind of atom is a comparison between two arithmetic expressions, for example $x < y$ or $x + 1 \geq y + 4 \times z$. For contrast, we shall call the atoms introduced in Section 10.1.1 *relational atoms*; both are "atoms."

Note that arithmetic and relational atoms each take as arguments the values of any variables that appear in the atom, and they return a boolean value. In effect, arithmetic comparisons like $<$ or $\geq$ are like the names of relations that contain all the true pairs. Thus, we can visualize the relation "$<$" as containing all the tuples, such as $(1, 2)$ or $(-1.5, 65.4)$, that have a first component less than their second component. Remember, however, that database relations are always finite, and usually change from time to time. In contrast, arithmetic-comparison relations such as $<$ are both infinite and unchanging.

10.1.3 Datalog Rules and Queries

Operations similar to those of the classical relational algebra of Section 5.2 are described in Datalog by *rules*, which consist of

1. A relational atom called the *head*, followed by

2. The symbol ←, which we often read "if," followed by

3. A *body* consisting of one or more atoms, called *subgoals*, which may be either relational or arithmetic. Subgoals are connected by AND, and any subgoal may optionally be preceded by the logical operator NOT.

Example 10.3: The Datalog rule

$$\text{LongMovie(t,y)} \leftarrow \text{Movie(t,y,l,c,s,p) AND l} \geq 100$$

defines the set of "long" movies, those at least 100 minutes long. It refers to our standard relation Movie with schema

```
Movie(title, year, length, inColor, studioName, producerC#)
```

The head of the rule is the atom *LongMovie(t, y)*. The body of the rule consists of two subgoals:

1. The first subgoal has predicate *Movie* and six arguments, corresponding to the six attributes of the Movie relation. Each of these arguments has a different variable: t for the title component, y for the year component, l for the length component, and so on. We can see this subgoal as saying: "Let (t, y, l, c, s, p) be a tuple in the current instance of relation Movie." More precisely, $Movie(t, y, l, c, s, p)$ is true whenever the six variables have values that are the six components of some one Movie tuple.

2. The second subgoal, $l \geq 100$, is true whenever the length component of a Movie tuple is at least 100.

The rule as a whole can be thought of as saying: *LongMovie(t, y)* is true whenever we can find a tuple in Movie with:

a) t and y as the first two components (for title and year),

b) A third component l (for length) that is at least 100, and

c) Any values in components 4 through 6.

Notice that this rule is thus equivalent to the "assignment statement" in relational algebra:

$$\text{LongMovie} := \pi_{title,year}\left(\sigma_{length \geq 100}(\text{Movie})\right)$$

Anonymous Variables

Frequently, Datalog rules have some variables that appear only once. The names used for these variables are irrelevant. Only when a variable appears more than once do we care about its name, so we can see it is the same variable in its second and subsequent appearances. Thus, we shall allow the common convention that an underscore, _, as an argument of an atom, stands for a variable that appears only there. Multiple occurrences of _ stand for different variables, never the same variable. For instance, the rule of Example 10.3 could be written

```
LongMovie(t,y) ← Movie(t,y,l,_,_,_) AND l ≥ 100
```

The three variables c, s, and p that appear only once have each been replaced by underscores. We cannot replace any of the other variables, since each appears twice in the rule.

---

whose right side is a relational-algebra expression.   □

A *query* in Datalog is a collection of one or more rules. If there is only one relation that appears in the rule heads, then the value of this relation is taken to be the answer to the query. Thus, in Example 10.3, LongMovie is the answer to the query. If there is more than one relation among the rule heads, then one of these relations is the answer to the query, while the others assist in the definition of the answer. We must designate which relation is the intended answer to the query, perhaps by giving it a name such as Answer.

10.1.4 Meaning of Datalog Rules

Example 10.3 gave us a hint of the meaning of a Datalog rule. More precisely, imagine the variables of the rule ranging over all possible values. Whenever these variables all have values that make all the subgoals true, then we see what the value of the head is for those variables, and we add the resulting tuple to the relation whose predicate is in the head.

For instance, we can imagine the six variables of Example 10.3 ranging over all possible values. The only combinations of values that can make all the subgoals true are when the values of (t, y, l, c, s, p) in that order form a tuple of Movie. Moreover, since the $l \geq 100$ subgoal must also be true, this tuple must be one where l, the value of the length component, is at least 100. When we find such a combination of values, we put the tuple (t, y) in the head's relation LongMovie.

There are, however, restrictions that we must place on the way variables are used in rules, so that the result of a rule is a finite relation and so that rules with arithmetic subgoals or with *negated* subgoals (those with NOT in front of them) make intuitive sense. This condition, which we call the *safety* condition, is:

- Every variable that appears anywhere in the rule must appear in some nonnegated, relational subgoal.

In particular, any variable that appears in the head, in a negated relational subgoal, or in any arithmetic subgoal, must also appear in a nonnegated, relational subgoal.

Example 10.4 : Consider the rule

$$\texttt{LongMovie(t,y)} \leftarrow \texttt{Movie(t,y,l,\_,\_,\_)} \text{ AND } l \geq 100$$

from Example 10.3. The first subgoal is a nonnegated, relational subgoal, and it contains all the variables that appear anywhere in the rule. In particular, the two variables t and y that appear in the head also appear in the first subgoal of the body. Likewise, variable l appears in an arithmetic subgoal, but it also appears in the first subgoal. □

Example 10.5 : The following rule has three safety violations:

$$\texttt{P(x,y)} \leftarrow \texttt{Q(x,z)} \text{ AND NOT } \texttt{R(w,x,z)} \text{ AND } \texttt{x<y}$$

1. The variable y appears in the head but not in any nonnegated, relational subgoal. Notice the fact that y appears in the arithmetic subgoal $x < y$ does not help to limit the possible values of y to a finite set. As soon as we find values a, b, and c for w, x, and z respectively that satisfy the first two subgoals, the infinite number of tuples (b, d) such that $d > b$ wind up in the head's relation P.

2. Variable w appears in a negated, relational subgoal but not in a non-negated, relational subgoal.

3. Variable y appears in an arithmetic subgoal, but not in a nonnegated, relational subgoal.

Thus, it is not a safe rule and cannot be used in Datalog. □

There is another way to define the meaning of rules. Instead of considering all of the possible assignments of values to variables, we consider the sets of tuples in the relations corresponding to each of the nonnegated, relational subgoals. If some assignment of tuples for each nonnegated, relational subgoal is *consistent*, in the sense that it assigns the same value to each occurrence of a variable, then consider the resulting assignment of values to all the variables of the rule. Notice that because the rule is safe, every variable is assigned a value.

For each consistent assignment, we consider the negated, relational subgoals and the arithmetic subgoals, to see if the assignment of values to variables makes them all true. Remember that a negated subgoal is true if its atom is false. If all the subgoals are true, then we see what tuple the head becomes under this assignment of values to variables. This tuple is added to the relation whose predicate is the head.

Example 10.6 : Consider the Datalog rule

$$\texttt{P(x,y)} \leftarrow \texttt{Q(x,z) AND R(z,y) AND NOT Q(x,y)}$$

Let relation Q contain the two tuples $(1, 2)$ and $(1, 3)$. Let relation R contain tuples $(2, 3)$ and $(3, 1)$. There are two nonnegated, relational subgoals, $Q(x, z)$ and $R(z, y)$, so we must consider all combinations of assignments of tuples from relations Q and R, respectively, to these subgoals. The table of Fig. 10.1 considers all four combinations.

	Tuple for $Q(x,z)$	Tuple for $R(z,y)$	Consistent Assignment?	NOT Q(x,y) True?	Resulting Head
1)	$(1, 2)$	$(2, 3)$	Yes	No	—
2)	$(1, 2)$	$(3, 1)$	No; $z = 2, 3$	Irrelevant	—
3)	$(1, 3)$	$(2, 3)$	No; $z = 3, 2$	Irrelevant	—
4)	$(1, 3)$	$(3, 1)$	Yes	Yes	$P(1, 1)$

Figure 10.1: All possible assignments of tuples to $Q(x, z)$ and $R(z, y)$

The second and third options in Fig. 10.1 are not consistent. Each assigns two different values to the variable z. Thus, we do not consider these tuple-assignments further.

The first option, where subgoal $Q(x, z)$ is assigned the tuple $(1, 2)$ and subgoal $R(z, y)$ is assigned tuple $(2, 3)$, yields a consistent assignment, with x, y, and z given the values 1, 3, and 2, respectively. We thus proceed to the test of the other subgoals, those that are not nonnegated, relational subgoals. There is only one: NOT Q(x,y). For this assignment of values to the variables, this subgoal becomes NOT Q(1,3). Since $(1, 3)$ is a tuple of Q, this subgoal is false, and no head tuple is produced for the tuple-assignment (1).

The final option is (4). Here, the assignment is consistent; x, y, and z are assigned the values 1, 1, and 3, respectively. The subgoal NOT Q(x,y) takes on the value NOT Q(1,1). Since $(1, 1)$ is not a tuple of Q, this subgoal is true. We thus evaluate the head $P(x, y)$ for this assignment of values to variables and find it is $P(1, 1)$. Thus the tuple $(1, 1)$ is in the relation P. Since we have exhausted all tuple-assignments, this is the only tuple in P.   □

10.1.5 Extensional and Intensional Predicates

It is useful to make the distinction between

- *Extensional* predicates, which are predicates whose relations are stored in a database, and

- *Intensional* predicates, whose relations are computed by applying one or more Datalog rules.

The difference is the same as that between the operands of a relational-algebra expression, which are "extensional" (i.e., defined by their *extension*, which is another name for the "current instance of a relation") and the relations computed by a relational-algebra expression, either as the final result or as an intermediate result corresponding to some subexpression; these relations are "intensional" (i.e., defined by the programmer's "intent").

When talking of Datalog rules, we shall refer to the relation corresponding to a predicate as "intensional" or "extensional," if the predicate is intensional or extensional, respectively. We shall also use the abbreviation *IDB* for "intensional database" to refer to either an intensional predicate or its corresponding relation. Similarly, we use abbreviation *EDB*, standing for "extensional database," for extensional predicates or relations.

Thus, in Example 10.3, `Movie` is an EDB relation, defined by its extension. The predicate *Movie* is likewise an EDB predicate. Relation and predicate `LongMovie` are both intensional.

An EDB predicate can never appear in the head of a rule, although it can appear in the body of a rule. IDB predicates can appear in either the head or the body of rules, or both. It is also common to construct a single relation by using several rules with the same predicate in the head. We shall see an illustration of this idea in Example 10.10, regarding the union of two relations.

By using a series of intensional predicates, we can build progressively more complicated functions of the EDB relations. The process is similar to the building of relational-algebra expressions using several operators.

10.1.6 Datalog Rules Applied to Bags

Datalog is inherently a logic of sets. However, as long as there are no negated, relational subgoals, the ideas for evaluating Datalog rules when relations are sets apply to bags as well. When relations are bags, it is conceptually simpler to use the second approach for evaluating Datalog rules that we gave in Section 10.1.4. Recall this technique involves looking at each of the nonnegated, relational subgoals and substituting for it all tuples of the relation for the predicate of that subgoal. If a selection of tuples for each subgoal gives a consistent value to each variable, and the arithmetic subgoals all become true,[1] then we see what

---

[1] Note that there must not be any negated relational subgoals in the rule. There is not a clearly defined meaning of arbitrary Datalog rules with negated, relational subgoals under the bag model.

the head becomes with this assignment of values to variables. The resulting tuple is put in the head relation.

Since we are now dealing with bags, we do not eliminate duplicates from the head. Moreover, as we consider all combinations of tuples for the subgoals, a tuple appearing n times in the relation for a subgoal gets considered n times as the tuple for that subgoal, in conjunction with all combinations of tuples for the other subgoals.

Example 10.7: Consider the rule

$$H(x,z) \leftarrow R(x,y) \text{ AND } S(y,z)$$

where relation $R(A,B)$ has the tuples:

A	B
1	2
1	2

and $S(B,C)$ has tuples:

B	C
2	3
4	5
4	5

The only time we get a consistent assignment of tuples to the subgoals (i.e., an assignment where the value of y from each subgoal is the same) is when the first subgoal is assigned the tuple $(1,2)$ from R and the second subgoal is assigned tuple $(2,3)$ from S. Since $(1,2)$ appears twice in R, and $(2,3)$ appears once in S, there will be two assignments of tuples that give the variable assignments $x = 1$, $y = 2$, and $z = 3$. The tuple of the head, which is (x,z), is for each of these assignments $(1,3)$. Thus the tuple $(1,3)$ appears twice in the head relation H, and no other tuple appears there. That is, the relation

1	3
1	3

is the head relation defined by this rule. More generally, had tuple $(1,2)$ appeared n times in R and tuple $(2,3)$ appeared m times in S, then tuple $(1,3)$ would appear nm times in H. □

If a relation is defined by several rules, then the result is the bag-union of whatever tuples are produced by each rule.

Example 10.8: Consider a relation H defined by the two rules

```
H(x,y) ← S(x,y) AND x>1
H(x,y) ← S(x,y) AND y<5
```

where relation $S(B,C)$ is as in Example 10.7; that is, $S = \{(2,3), (4,5), (4,5)\}$. The first rule puts each of the three tuples of S into H, since they each have a first component greater than 1. The second rule puts only the tuple $(2,3)$ into H, since $(4,5)$ does not satisfy the condition $y < 5$. Thus, the resulting relation H has two copies of the tuple $(2,3)$ and two copies of the tuple $(4,5)$. □

10.1.7 Exercises for Section 10.1

Exercise 10.1.1: Write each of the queries of Exercise 5.2.1 in Datalog. You should use only safe rules, but you may wish to use several IDB predicates corresponding to subexpressions of complicated relational-algebra expressions.

Exercise 10.1.2: Write each of the queries of Exercise 5.2.4 in Datalog. Again, use only safe rules, but you may use several IDB predicates if you like.

!! **Exercise 10.1.3:** The requirement we gave for safety of Datalog rules is sufficient to guarantee that the head predicate has a finite relation if the predicates of the relational subgoals have finite relations. However, this requirement is too strong. Give an example of a Datalog rule that violates the condition, yet whatever finite relations we assign to the relational predicates, the head relation will be finite.

10.2 From Relational Algebra to Datalog

Each of the relational-algebra operators of Section 5.2 can be mimicked by one or several Datalog rules. In this section we shall consider each operator in turn. We shall then consider how to combine Datalog rules to mimic complex algebraic expressions.

10.2.1 Intersection

The set intersection of two relations is expressed by a rule that has subgoals for both relations, with the same variables in corresponding arguments.

Example 10.9: Let us use the relations R:

name	address	gender	birthdate
Carrie Fisher	123 Maple St., Hollywood	F	9/9/99
Mark Hamill	456 Oak Rd., Brentwood	M	8/8/88

and S:

name	address	gender	birthdate
Carrie Fisher	123 Maple St., Hollywood	F	9/9/99
Harrison Ford	789 Palm Dr., Beverly Hills	M	7/7/77

as an example. Their intersection is computed by the Datalog rule

$$\text{I(n,a,g,b)} \leftarrow \text{R(n,a,g,b) AND S(n,a,g,b)}$$

Here, I is an IDB predicate, whose relation becomes $R \cap S$ when we apply this rule. That is, in order for a tuple (n, a, g, b) to make both subgoals true, that tuple must be in both R and S.   □

10.2.2   Union

The union of two relations is constructed by two rules. Each has an atom corresponding to one of the relations as its sole subgoal, and the heads of both rules have the same IDB predicate in the head. The arguments in each head are exactly the same as in the subgoal of its rule.

Example 10.10: To take the union of the relations R and S from Example 10.9 we use two rules

$$1. \text{ U(n,a,g,b)} \leftarrow \text{R(n,a,g,b)}$$
$$2. \text{ U(n,a,g,b)} \leftarrow \text{S(n,a,g,b)}$$

Rule (1) says that every tuple in R is a tuple in the IDB relation U. Rule (2) similarly says that every tuple in S is in U. Thus, the two rules together imply that every tuple in $R \cup S$ is in U. If we write no more rules with U in the head, then there is no way any other tuples can get into the relation U, in which case we can conclude that U is exactly $R \cup S$.[2] Note that, unlike the construction for intersection, which works only for sets, this pair of rules takes either the set- or bag-union, depending on how we interpret the union of the results of the two rules. We shall assume the "set" interpretation unless we say otherwise.   □

10.2.3   Difference

The set difference of relations R and S is computed by a single rule with a negated subgoal. That is, the nonnegated subgoal has predicate R and the negated subgoal has predicate S. These subgoals and the head all have the same variables for corresponding arguments.

Example 10.11: If R and S are the relations from Example 10.9 then the rule

$$\text{D(n,a,g,b)} \leftarrow \text{R(n,a,g,b) AND NOT S(n,a,g,b)}$$

defines D to be the relation $R - S$.   □

---

[2]In fact, we should assume in each of the examples of this section that there are no other rules for an IDB predicate besides those that we show explicitly. If there are other rules, then we cannot rule out the existence of other tuples in the relation for that predicate.

Variables Are Local to a Rule

Notice that the names we choose for variables in a rule are arbitrary and have no connection to the variables used in any other rule. The reason there is no connection is that each rule is evaluated alone and contributes tuples to its head's relation independent of other rules. Thus, for instance, we could replace the second rule of Example 10.10 by

$$U(w,x,y,z) \leftarrow S(w,x,y,z)$$

while leaving the first rule unchanged, and the two rules would still compute the union of R and S. Note, however, that when substituting one variable a for another variable b within a rule, we must substitute a for all occurrences of b within the rule. Moreover, the substituting variable a that we choose must not be a variable that already appears in the rule.

10.2.4 Projection

To compute a projection of a relation R, we use one rule with a single subgoal with predicate R. The arguments of this subgoal are distinct variables, one for each attribute of the relation. The head has an atom with arguments that are the variables corresponding to the attributes in the projection list, in the desired order.

Example 10.12: Suppose we want to project the relation

```
Movie(title, year, length, inColor, studioName, producerC#)
```

onto its first three attributes — `title`, `year`, and `length`. The rule

$$P(t,y,l) \leftarrow Movie(t,y,l,c,s,p)$$

serves, defining a relation called P to be the result of the projection. ☐

10.2.5 Selection

Selections can be somewhat more difficult to express in Datalog. The simple case is when the selection condition is the AND of one or more arithmetic comparisons. In that case, we create a rule with

1. One relational subgoal for the relation upon which we are performing the selection. This atom has distinct variables for each component, one for each attribute of the relation.

2. For each comparison in the selection condition, an arithmetic subgoal that is identical to this comparison. However, while in the selection condition an attribute name was used, in the arithmetic subgoal we use the corresponding variable, following the correspondence established by the relational subgoal.

Example 10.13: The selection

$$\sigma_{length \geq 100 \text{ AND } studioName = \text{'Fox'}}(\text{Movie})$$

from Example 5.4 can be written as a Datalog rule

```
S(t,y,l,c,s,p) ← Movie(t,y,l,c,s,p) AND l ≥ 100 AND s = 'Fox'
```

The result is the relation S. Note that l and s are the variables corresponding to attributes `length` and `studioName` in the standard order we have used for the attributes of `Movie`. □

Now, let us consider selections that involve the OR of conditions. We cannot necessarily replace such selections by single Datalog rules. However, selection for the OR of two conditions is equivalent to selecting for each condition separately and then taking the union of the results. Thus, the OR of n conditions can be expressed by n rules, each of which defines the same head predicate. The ith rule performs the selection for the ith of the n conditions.

Example 10.14: Let us modify the selection of Example 10.13 by replacing the AND by an OR to get the selection:

$$\sigma_{length \geq 100 \text{ OR } studioName = \text{'Fox'}}(\text{Movie})$$

That is, find all those movies that are either long or by Fox. We can write two rules, one for each of the two conditions:

```
1. S(t,y,l,c,s,p) ← Movie(t,y,l,c,s,p) AND l ≥ 100
2. S(t,y,l,c,s,p) ← Movie(t,y,l,c,s,p) AND s = 'Fox'
```

Rule (1) produces movies at least 100 minutes long, and rule (2) produces movies by Fox. □

Even more complex selection conditions can be formed by several applications, in any order, of the logical operators AND, OR, and NOT. However, there is a widely known technique, which we shall not present here, for rearranging any such logical expression into "disjunctive normal form," where the expression is the disjunction (OR) of "conjuncts." A *conjunct*, in turn, is the AND of "literals," and a *literal* is either a comparison or a negated comparison.[3]

---

[3]See, e.g., A. V. Aho and J. D. Ullman, *Foundations of Computer Science*, Computer Science Press, New York, 1992.

We can represent any literal by a subgoal, perhaps with a NOT in front of it. If the subgoal is arithmetic, the NOT can be incorporated into the comparison operator. For example, NOT $x \geq 100$ can be written as $x < 100$. Then, any conjunct can be represented by a single Datalog rule, with one subgoal for each comparison. Finally, every disjunctive-normal-form expression can be written by several Datalog rules, one rule for each conjunct. These rules take the union, or OR, of the results from each of the conjuncts.

Example 10.15: We gave a simple instance of this algorithm in Example 10.14. A more difficult example can be formed by negating the condition of that example. We then have the expression:

$$\sigma_{\text{NOT } (length \geq 100 \text{ OR } studioName='\text{Fox}')}(\text{Movie})$$

That is, find all those movies that are neither long nor by Fox.

Here, a NOT is applied to an expression that is itself not a simple comparison. Thus, we must push the NOT down the expression, using one form of *DeMorgan's law*, which says that the negation of an OR is the AND of the negations. That is, the selection can be rewritten:

$$\sigma_{(\text{NOT } (length \geq 100)) \text{ AND } (\text{NOT } (studioName='\text{Fox}'))}(\text{Movie})$$

Now, we can take the NOT's inside the comparisons to get the expression:

$$\sigma_{length < 100 \text{ AND } studioName \neq '\text{Fox}'}(\text{Movie})$$

This expression can be converted into the Datalog rule

```
S(t,y,l,c,s,p) ← Movie(t,y,l,c,s,p) AND l < 100 AND s ≠ 'Fox'
```

□

Example 10.16: Let us consider a similar example where we have the negation of an AND in the selection. Now, we use the second form of DeMorgan's law, which says that the negation of an AND is the OR of the negations. We begin with the algebraic expression

$$\sigma_{\text{NOT } (length \geq 100 \text{ AND } studioName='\text{Fox}')}(\text{Movie})$$

That is, find all those movies that are not both long and by Fox.

We apply DeMorgan's law to push the NOT below the AND, to get:

$$\sigma_{(\text{NOT } (length \geq 100)) \text{ OR } (\text{NOT } (studioName='\text{Fox}'))}(\text{Movie})$$

Again we take the NOT's inside the comparisons to get:

$$\sigma_{length < 100 \text{ OR } studioName \neq '\text{Fox}'}(\text{Movie})$$

Finally, we write two rules, one for each part of the OR. The resulting Datalog rules are:

```
1. S(t,y,l,c,s,p) ← Movie(t,y,l,c,s,p) AND l < 100
2. S(t,y,l,c,s,p) ← Movie(t,y,l,c,s,p) AND s ≠ 'Fox'
```

□

10.2.6   Product

The product of two relations $R \times S$ can be expressed by a single Datalog rule. This rule has two subgoals, one for R and one for S. Each of these subgoals has distinct variables, one for each attribute of R or S. The IDB predicate in the head has as arguments all the variables that appear in either subgoal, with the variables appearing in the R-subgoal listed before those of the S-subgoal.

Example 10.17: Let us consider the two four-attribute relations R and S from Example 10.9. The rule

$$P(a,b,c,d,w,x,y,z) \leftarrow R(a,b,c,d) \text{ AND } S(w,x,y,z)$$

defines P to be $R \times S$. We have arbitrarily used variables at the beginning of the alphabet for the arguments of R and variables at the end of the alphabet for S. These variables all appear in the rule head.   □

10.2.7   Joins

We can take the natural join of two relations by a Datalog rule that looks much like the rule for a product. The difference is that if we want $R \bowtie S$, then we must be careful to use the same variable for attributes of R and S that have the same name and to use different variables otherwise. For instance, we can use the attribute names themselves as the variables. The head is an IDB predicate that has each variable appearing once.

Example 10.18: Consider relations with schemas $R(A, B)$ and $S(B, C, D)$. Their natural join may be defined by the rule

$$J(a,b,c,d) \leftarrow R(a,b) \text{ AND } S(b,c,d)$$

Notice how the variables used in the subgoals correspond in an obvious way to the attributes of the relations R and S.   □

We also can convert theta-joins to Datalog. Recall from Section 5.2.10 how a theta-join can be expressed as a product followed by a selection. If the selection condition is a conjunct, that is, the AND of comparisons, then we may simply start with the Datalog rule for the product and add additional, arithmetic subgoals, one for each of the comparisons.

Example 10.19: Let us consider the relations $U(A, B, C)$ and $V(B, C, D)$ from Example 5.9, where we applied the theta-join

$$U \underset{A<D \text{ AND } U.B \neq V.B}{\bowtie} V$$

We can construct the Datalog rule

$$J(a,ub,uc,vb,vc,d) \leftarrow U(a,ub,uc) \text{ AND } V(vb,vc,d) \text{ AND}$$
$$a < d \text{ AND } ub \neq vb$$

to perform the same operation. We have used ub as the variable corresponding to attribute B of U, and similarly used vb, uc, and vc, although any six distinct variables for the six attributes of the two relations would be fine. The first two subgoals introduce the two relations, and the second two subgoals enforce the two comparisons that appear in the condition of the theta-join. $\square$

If the condition of the theta-join is not a conjunction, then we convert it to disjunctive normal form, as discussed in Section 10.2.5. We then create one rule for each conjunct. In this rule, we begin with the subgoals for the product and then add subgoals for each literal in the conjunct. The heads of all the rules are identical and have one argument for each attribute of the two relations being theta-joined.

Example 10.20 : In this example, we shall make a simple modification to the algebraic expression of Example 10.19. The AND will be replaced by an OR. There are no negations in this expression, so it is already in disjunctive normal form. There are two conjuncts, each with a single literal. The expression is:

$$U \overset{\bowtie}{_{A<D\ \text{OR}\ U.B\neq V.B}} V$$

Using the same variable-naming scheme as in Example 10.19, we obtain the two rules

1. `J(a,ub,uc,vb,vc,d) ← U(a,ub,uc) AND V(vb,vc,d) AND a < d`
2. `J(a,ub,uc,vb,vc,d) ← U(a,ub,uc) AND V(vb,vc,d) AND ub ≠ vb`

Each rule has subgoals for the two relations involved plus a subgoal for one of the two conditions $A < D$ or $U.B \neq V.B$. $\square$

10.2.8 Simulating Multiple Operations with Datalog

Datalog rules are not only capable of mimicking a single operation of relational algebra. We can in fact mimic any algebraic expression. The trick is to look at the expression tree for the relational-algebra expression and create one IDB predicate for each interior node of the tree. The rule or rules for each IDB predicate is whatever we need to apply the operator at the corresponding node of the tree. Those operands of the tree that are extensional (i.e., they are relations of the database) are represented by the corresponding predicate. Operands that are themselves interior nodes are represented by the corresponding IDB predicate.

Example 10.21 : Consider the algebraic expression

$$\pi_{title,year}\Big(\sigma_{length\geq 100}(\text{Movie}) \cap \sigma_{studioName='\text{Fox}'}(\text{Movie})\Big)$$

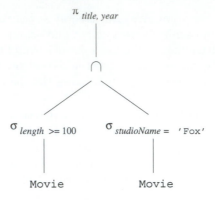

Figure 10.2: Expression tree

```
1. W(t,y,l,c,s,p) ← Movie(t,y,l,c,s,p) AND l ≥ 100
2. X(t,y,l,c,s,p) ← Movie(t,y,l,c,s,p) AND s = 'Fox'
3. Y(t,y,l,c,s,p) ← W(t,y,l,c,s,p) AND X(t,y,l,c,s,p)
4. Z(t,y) ← Y(t,y,l,c,s,p)
```

Figure 10.3: Datalog rules to perform several algebraic operations

from Example 5.10, whose expression tree appeared in Fig. 5.8. We repeat this tree as Fig. 10.2. There are four interior nodes, so we need to create four IDB predicates. Each of these predicates has a single Datalog rule, and we summarize all the rules in Fig. 10.3.

The lowest two interior nodes perform simple selections on the EDB relation Movie, so we can create the IDB predicates W and X to represent these selections. Rules (1) and (2) of Fig. 10.3 describe these selections. For example, rule (1) defines W to be those tuples of Movie that have a length at least 100.

Then rule (3) defines predicate Y to be the intersection of W and X, using the form of rule we learned for an intersection in Section 10.2.1. Finally, rule (4) defines predicate Z to be the projection of Y onto the title and year attributes. We here use the technique for simulating a projection that we learned in Section 10.2.4. The predicate Z is the "answer" predicate; that is, regardless of the value of relation Movie, the relation defined by Z is the same as the result of the algebraic expression with which we began this example.

Note that, because Y is defined by a single rule, we can substitute for the Y subgoal in rule (4) of Fig. 10.3, replacing it with the body of rule (3). Then, we can substitute for the W and X subgoals, using the bodies of rules (1) and (2). Since the Movie subgoal appears in both of these bodies, we can eliminate one copy. As a result, Z can be defined by the single rule:

```
Z(t,y) ← Movie(t,y,l,c,s,p) AND l ≥ 100 AND s = 'Fox'
```

However, it is not common that a complex expression of relational algebra is equivalent to a single Datalog rule. □

10.2.9 Exercises for Section 10.2

Exercise 10.2.1: Let $R(a,b,c)$, $S(a,b,c)$, and $T(a,b,c)$ be three relations. Write one or more Datalog rules that define the result of each of the following expressions of relational algebra:

a) $R \cup S$.

b) $R \cap S$.

c) $R - S$.

* d) $(R \cup S) - T$.

! e) $(R - S) \cap (R - T)$.

f) $\pi_{a,b}(R)$.

*! g) $\pi_{a,b}(R) \cap \rho_{U(a,b)}(\pi_{b,c}(S))$.

Exercise 10.2.2: Let $R(x,y,z)$ be a relation. Write one or more Datalog rules that define $\sigma_C(R)$, where C stands for each of the following conditions:

a) $x = y$.

* b) $x < y$ AND $y < z$.

c) $x < y$ OR $y < z$.

d) NOT $(x < y$ OR $x > y)$.

*! e) NOT $((x < y$ OR $x > y)$ AND $y < z)$.

! f) NOT $((x < y$ OR $x < z)$ AND $y < z)$.

Exercise 10.2.3: Let $R(a,b,c)$, $S(b,c,d)$, and $T(d,e)$ be three relations. Write single Datalog rules for each of the natural joins:

a) $R \bowtie S$.

b) $S \bowtie T$.

c) $(R \bowtie S) \bowtie T$. (*Note*: since the natural join is associative and commutative, the order of the join of these three relations is irrelevant.)

Exercise 10.2.4: Let $R(x,y,z)$ and $S(x,y,z)$ be two relations. Write one or more Datalog rules to define each of the theta-joins $R \underset{C}{\bowtie} S$, where C is one of the conditions of Exercise 10.2.2. For each of these conditions, interpret each arithmetic comparison as comparing an attribute of R on the left with an attribute of S on the right. For instance, $x < y$ stands for $R.x < S.y$.

! **Exercise 10.2.5:** It is also possible to convert Datalog rules into equivalent relational-algebra expressions. While we have not discussed the method of doing so in general, it is possible to work out many simple examples. For each of the Datalog rules below, write an expression of relational algebra that defines the same relation as the head of the rule.

* a) `P(x,y) ← Q(x,z) AND R(z,y)`

   b) `P(x,y) ← Q(x,z) AND Q(z,y)`

   c) `P(x,y) ← Q(x,z) AND R(z,y) AND x < y`

10.3 Recursive Programming in Datalog

While relational algebra can express many useful operations on relations, there are some computations that cannot be written as an expression of relational algebra. A common kind of operation on data that we cannot express in relational algebra involves an infinite, recursively defined sequence of similar expressions.

Example 10.22: Often, a successful movie is followed by a sequel; if the sequel does well, then the sequel has a sequel, and so on. Thus, a movie may be ancestral to a long sequence of other movies. Suppose we have a relation `SequelOf(movie, sequel)` containing pairs consisting of a movie and its immediate sequel. Examples of tuples in this relation are:

movie	*sequel*
`Naked Gun`	`Naked Gun 2`$_{1/2}$
`Naked Gun 2`$_{1/2}$	`Naked Gun 33`$_{1/3}$

We might also have a more general notion of a *follow-on* to a movie, which is a sequel, a sequel of a sequel, and so on. In the relation above, *Naked Gun 33*$_{1/3}$ is a follow-on to *Naked Gun*, but not a sequel in the strict sense we are using the term "sequel" here. It saves space if we store only the immediate sequels in the relation and construct the follow-ons if we need them. In the above example, we store only one fewer pair, but for the five *Rocky* movies we store six fewer pairs, and for the 18 *Friday the 13th* movies we store 136 fewer pairs.

However, it is not immediately obvious how we construct the relation of follow-ons from the relation `SequelOf`. We can construct the sequels of sequels by joining `SequelOf` with itself once. An example of such an expression in relational algebra, using renaming so that the join becomes a natural join, is:

$$\pi_{first,third}\big(\rho_{R(first,second)}(\texttt{SequelOf}) \bowtie \rho_{S(second,third)}(\texttt{SequelOf})\big)$$

In this expression, `SequelOf` is renamed twice, once so its attributes are called `first` and `second`, and again so its attributes are called `second` and `third`.

Thus, the natural join asks for tuples (m_1, m_2) and (m_3, m_4) in SequelOf such that $m_2 = m_3$. We then produce the pair (m_1, m_4). Note that m_4 is the sequel of the sequel of m_1.

Similarly, we could join three copies of SequelOf to get the sequels of sequels of sequels (e.g., *Rocky* and *Rocky IV*). We could in fact produce the ith sequels for any fixed value of i by joining SequelOf with itself $i - 1$ times. We could then take the union of SequelOf and a finite sequence of these joins to get all the sequels up to some fixed limit.

What we cannot do in relational algebra is ask for the "infinite union" of the infinite sequence of expressions that give the ith sequels for $i = 1, 2, \ldots$. Note that relational algebra's union allows us only to take the union of two relations, not an infinite number. By applying the union operator any finite number of times in an algebraic expression, we can take the union of any finite number of relations, but we cannot take the union of an unlimited number of relations in an algebraic expression. $\square$

10.3.1 Recursive Rules

By using an IDB predicate both in the head and the body of rules, we can express an infinite union in Datalog. We shall first see some examples of how to express recursions in Datalog. In Section 10.3.2 we shall examine the *least fixedpoint* computation of the relations for the IDB predicates of these rules. A new approach to rule-evaluation is needed for recursive rules, since the straightforward rule-evaluation approach of Section 10.1.4 assumes all the predicates in the body of rules have fixed relations.

Example 10.23: We can define the IDB relation FollowOn by the following two Datalog rules:

> 1. FollowOn(x,y) $\leftarrow$ SequelOf(x,y)
> 2. FollowOn(x,y) $\leftarrow$ SequelOf(x,z) AND FollowOn(z,y)

The first rule is the basis; it tells us that every sequel is a follow-on. The second rule says that every follow-on of a sequel of movie x is also a follow-on of x. More precisely: if z is a sequel of x, and we have found that y is a follow-on of z, then y is a follow-on of x. $\square$

10.3.2 Evaluating Recursive Datalog Rules

To evaluate the IDB predicates of recursive Datalog rules, we follow the principle that we never want to conclude that a tuple is in an IDB relation unless we are forced to do so by applying the rules as in Section 10.1.4. Thus, we:

1. Begin by assuming all IDB predicates have empty relations.

2. Perform a number of *rounds*, in which progressively larger relations are constructed for the IDB predicates. In the bodies of the rules, use the

IDB relations constructed on the previous round. Apply the rules to get new estimates for all the IDB predicates.

3. If the rules are safe, no IDB tuple can have a component value that does not also appear in some EDB relation. Thus, there are a finite number of possible tuples for all IDB relations, and eventually there will be a round on which no new tuples are added to any IDB relation. At this point, we can terminate our computation with the answer; no new IDB tuples will ever be constructed.

This set of IDB tuples is called the *least fixedpoint* of the rules.

Example 10.24: Let us show the computation of the least fixedpoint for relation FollowOn when the relation SequelOf consists of the following three tuples:

movie	sequel
Rocky	Rocky II
Rocky II	Rocky III
Rocky III	Rocky IV

At the first round of computation, FollowOn is assumed empty. Thus, rule (2) cannot yield any FollowOn tuples. However, rule (1) says that every SequelOf tuple is a FollowOn tuple. Thus, after the first round, the value of FollowOn is identical to the SequelOf relation above. The situation after round 1 is shown in Fig. 10.4(a).

In the second round, we use the relation from Fig. 10.4(a) as FollowOn and apply the two rules to this relation and the given SequelOf relation. The first rule gives us the three tuples that we already have, and in fact it is easy to see that rule (1) will never yield any tuples for FollowOn other than these three. For rule (2), we look for a tuple from SequelOf whose second component equals the first component of a tuple from FollowOn.

Thus, we can take the tuple (Rocky, Rocky II) from SequelOf and pair it with the tuple (Rocky II, Rocky III) from FollowOn to get the new tuple (Rocky, Rocky III) for FollowOn. Similarly, we can take the tuple

(Rocky II, Rocky III)

from SequelOf and tuple (Rocky III, Rocky IV) from FollowOn to get new tuple (Rocky II, Rocky IV) for FollowOn. However, no other pairs of tuples from SequelOf and FollowOn join. Thus, after the second round, FollowOn has the five tuples shown in Fig. 10.4(b). Intuitively, just as Fig. 10.4(a) contained only those follow-on facts that are based on a single sequel, Fig. 10.4(b) contains those follow-on facts based on one or two sequels.

In the third round, we use the relation from Fig. 10.4(b) for FollowOn and again evaluate the body of rule (2). We get all the tuples we already had, of course, and one more tuple. When we join the tuple (Rocky, Rocky II)

x	y
Rocky	Rocky II
Rocky II	Rocky III
Rocky III	Rocky IV

(a) After round 1

x	y
Rocky	Rocky II
Rocky II	Rocky III
Rocky III	Rocky IV
Rocky	Rocky III
Rocky II	Rocky IV

(b) After round 2

x	y
Rocky	Rocky II
Rocky II	Rocky III
Rocky III	Rocky IV
Rocky	Rocky III
Rocky II	Rocky IV
Rocky	Rocky IV

(c) After round 3 and subsequently

Figure 10.4: Recursive computation of relation FollowOn

from SequelOf with the tuple (Rocky II, Rocky IV) from the current value of FollowOn, we get the new tuple (Rocky, Rocky IV). Thus, after round 3, the value of FollowOn is as shown in Fig. 10.4(c).

When we proceed to round 4, we get no new tuples, so we stop. The true relation FollowOn is as shown in Fig. 10.4(c). □

There is an important trick that simplifies all recursive Datalog evaluations, such as the one above:

- At any round, the only new tuples added to any IDB relation will come from applications of rules in which at least one IDB subgoal is matched to a tuple that was added to its relation at the previous round.

Other Forms of Recursion

In Example 10.23 we used a *right-recursive* form for the recursion, where the use of the recursive relation FollowOn appears after the EDB relation SequelOf. We could also write similar *left-recursive* rules by putting the recursive relation first. These rules are:

    1. FollowOn(x,y) ← SequelOf(x,y)
    2. FollowOn(x,y) ← FollowOn(x,z) AND SequelOf(z,y)

Informally, y is a follow-on of x if it is either a sequel of x or a sequel of a follow-on of x.

We could even use the recursive relation twice, as in the *nonlinear* recursion:

    1. FollowOn(x,y) ← SequelOf(x,y)
    2. FollowOn(x,y) ← FollowOn(x,z) AND FollowOn(z,y)

Informally, y is a follow-on of x if it is either a sequel of x or a follow-on of a follow-on of x. All three of these forms give the same value for relation FollowOn: the set of pairs (x, y) such that y is a sequel of a sequel of $\cdots$ (some number of times) of x.

The justification for this rule is that should all subgoals be matched to "old" tuples, the tuple of the head would already have been added on the previous round. The next two examples illustrate this strategy and also show us more complex examples of recursion.

Example 10.25 : Many examples of the use of recursion can be found in a study of paths in a graph. Figure 10.5 shows a graph representing some flights of two hypothetical airlines — *Untried Airlines* (UA), and *Arcane Airlines* (AA) — among the cities San Francisco, Denver, Dallas, Chicago, and New York.

We may imagine that the flights are represented by an EDB relation:

$$\text{Flights(airline, from, to, departs, arrives)}$$

The tuples in this relation for the data of Fig. 10.5 are shown in Fig. 10.6.

The simplest recursive question we can ask is "For what pairs of cities (x, y) is it possible to get from city x to city y by taking one or more flights?" The following two rules describe a relation Reaches(x,y) that contains exactly these pairs of cities.

    1. Reaches(x,y) ← Flights(a,x,y,d,r)
    2. Reaches(x,y) ← Reaches(x,z) AND Reaches(z,y)

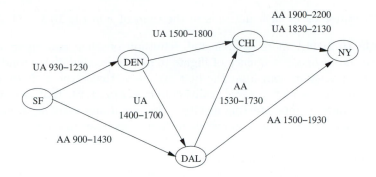

Figure 10.5: A map of some airline flights

airline	from	to	departs	arrives
UA	SF	DEN	930	1230
AA	SF	DAL	900	1430
UA	DEN	CHI	1500	1800
UA	DEN	DAL	1400	1700
AA	DAL	CHI	1530	1730
AA	DAL	NY	1500	1930
AA	CHI	NY	1900	2200
UA	CHI	NY	1830	2130

Figure 10.6: Tuples in the relation Flights

The first rule says that Reaches contains those pairs of cities for which there is a direct flight from the first to the second; the airline a, departure time d, and arrival time r are arbitrary in this rule. The second rule says that if you can reach from city x to city z and you can reach from z to y, then you can reach from x to y. Notice that we have used the nonlinear form of recursion here, as was described in the box on "Other Forms of Recursion." This form is slightly more convenient here, because another use of Flights in the recursive rule would involve three more variables for the unused components of Flights.

To evaluate the relation Reaches, we follow the same iterative process introduced in Example 10.24. We begin by using Rule (1) to get the following pairs in Reaches: (SF, DEN), (SF, DAL), (DEN, CHI), (DEN, DAL), (DAL, CHI), (DAL, NY), and (CHI, NY). These are the seven pairs represented by arcs in Fig. 10.5.

In the next round, we apply the recursive Rule (2) to put together pairs of arcs such that the head of one is the tail of the next. That gives us the additional pairs (SF, CHI), (DEN, NY), and (SF, NY). The third round combines all one- and two-arc pairs together to form paths of length up to four arcs. In this particular diagram, we get no new pairs. The relation Reaches thus consists of the ten pairs (x, y) such that y is reachable from x in the diagram of Fig. 10.5. Because of the way we drew the diagram, these pairs happen to be exactly those (x, y) such that y is to the right of x in Fig 10.5.   □

Example 10.26 : A more complicated definition of when two flights can be combined into a longer sequence of flights is to require that the second leaves an airport at least an hour after the first arrives at that airport. Now, we use an IDB predicate, which we shall call `Connects(x,y,d,r)`, that says we can take one or more flights, starting at city x at time d and arriving at city y at time r. If there are any connections, then there is at least an hour to make the connection.

The rules for `Connects` are:[4]

```
1.  Connects(x,y,d,r)    ←    Flights(a,x,y,d,r)
2.  Connects(x,y,d,r)    ←    Connects(x,z,d,t1) AND
                              Connects(z,y,t2,r) AND
                              t1 <= t2 - 100
```

In the first round, rule (1) gives us the eight `Connects` facts shown above the first line in Fig. 10.7 (the line is not part of the relation). Each corresponds to one of the flights indicated in the diagram of Fig. 10.5; note that one of the seven arcs of that figure represents two flights at different times.

We now try to combine these tuples using Rule (2). For example, the second and fifth of these tuples combine to give the tuple $(SF, CHI, 900, 1730)$. However, the second and sixth tuples do not combine because the arrival time in Dallas is 1430, and the departure time from Dallas, 1500, is only half an hour later. The `Connects` relation after the second round consists of all those tuples above the first or second line in Fig. 10.7. Above the top line are the original tuples from round 1, and the six tuples added on round 2 are shown between the first and second lines.

In the third round, we must in principle consider all pairs of tuples above one of the two lines in Fig. 10.7 as candidates for the two `Connects` tuples in the body of rule (2). However, if both tuples are above the first line, then they would have been considered during round 2 and therefore will not yield a `Connects` tuple we have not seen before. The only way to get a new tuple is if at least one of the two `Connects` tuple used in the body of rule (2) were added at the previous round; i.e., it is between the lines in Fig. 10.7.

The third round only gives us three new tuples. These are shown at the bottom of Fig. 10.7. There are no new tuples in the fourth round, so our computation is complete. Thus, the entire relation `Connects` is Fig. 10.7.   □

10.3.3   Negation in Recursive Rules

Sometimes it is necessary to use negation in rules that also involve recursion. There is a safe way and an unsafe way to mix recursion and negation. Generally, it is considered appropriate to use negation only in situations where the negation does not appear inside the fixedpoint operation. To see the difference, we shall

---

[4]These rules only work on the assumption that there are no connections spanning midnight.

x	y	d	r
SF	DEN	930	1230
SF	DAL	900	1430
DEN	CHI	1500	1800
DEN	DAL	1400	1700
DAL	CHI	1530	1730
DAL	NY	1500	1930
CHI	NY	1900	2200
CHI	NY	1830	2130
SF	CHI	900	1730
SF	CHI	930	1800
SF	DAL	930	1700
DEN	NY	1500	2200
DAL	NY	1530	2130
DAL	NY	1530	2200
SF	NY	900	2130
SF	NY	900	2200
SF	NY	930	2200

Figure 10.7: Relation `Connects` after third round

consider two examples of recursion and negation, one appropriate and the other paradoxical. We shall see that only "stratified" negation is useful when there is recursion; the term "stratified" will be defined precisely after the examples.

Example 10.27: Suppose we want to find those pairs of cities (x, y) in the map of Fig. 10.5 such that UA flies from x to y (perhaps through several other cities), but AA does not. We can recursively define a predicate `UAreaches` as we defined `Reaches` in Example 10.25, but restricting ourselves only to UA flights, as follows:

    1. `UAreaches(x,y) ← Flights(UA,x,y,d,r)`
    2. `UAreaches(x,y) ← UAreaches(x,z) AND UAreaches(z,y)`

Similarly, we can recursively define the predicate `AAreaches` to be those pairs of cities (x, y) such that one can travel from x to y using only AA flights, by:

    1. `AAreaches(x,y) ← Flights(AA,x,y,d,r)`
    2. `AAreaches(x,y) ← AAreaches(x,z) AND AAreaches(z,y)`

Now, it is a simple matter to compute the `UAonly` predicate consisting of those pairs of cities (x, y) such that one can get from x to y on UA flights but not on AA flights, with the nonrecursive rule:

    `UAonly(x,y) ← UAreaches(x,y) AND NOT AAreaches(x,y)`

This rule computes the set difference of UAreaches and AAreaches.

For the data of Fig. 10.5, UAreaches is seen to consist of the following pairs: (SF, DEN), (SF, DAL), (SF, CHI), (SF, NY), (DEN, DAL), (DEN, CHI), (DEN, NY), and (CHI, NY). This set is computed by the iterative fixedpoint process outlined in Section 10.3.2. Similarly, we can compute the value of AAreaches for this data; it is: (SF, DAL), (SF, CHI), (SF, NY), (DAL, CHI), (DAL, NY), and (CHI, NY). When we take the difference of these sets of pairs we get: (SF, DEN), (DEN, DAL), (DEN, CHI), and (DEN, NY). This set of four pairs is the relation UAonly.   □

Example 10.28 : Now, let us consider an abstract example where things don't work as well. Suppose we have a single EDB predicate R. This predicate is unary (one-argument), and it has a single tuple, (0). There are two IDB predicates, P and Q, also unary. They are defined by the two rules

> 1. P(x) ← R(x) AND NOT Q(x)
> 2. Q(x) ← R(x) AND NOT P(x)

Informally, the two rules tell us that an element x in R is either in P or in Q but not both. Notice that P and Q are defined recursively in terms of each other.

When we defined what recursive rules meant in Section 10.3.2, we said we want the least fixedpoint, that is, the smallest IDB relations that contain all tuples that the rules require us to allow. Rule (1), since it is the only rule for P, says that as relations, $P = R - Q$, and rule (2) likewise says that $Q = R - P$. Since R contains only the tuple (0), we know that only (0) can be in either P or Q. But where is (0)? It cannot be in neither, since then the equations are not satisfied; for instance $P = R - Q$ would imply that $\emptyset = \{(0)\} - \emptyset$, which is false.

If we let $P = \{(0)\}$ while $Q = \emptyset$, then we do get a solution to both equations. $P = R - Q$ becomes $\{(0)\} = \{(0)\} - \emptyset$, which is true, and $Q = R - P$ becomes $\emptyset = \{(0)\} - \{(0)\}$, which is also true.

However, we can also let $P = \emptyset$ and $Q = \{(0)\}$. This choice too satisfies both rules. We thus have two solutions:

> a) $P = \{(0)\}$ $Q = \emptyset$
> b) $P = \emptyset$ $Q = \{(0)\}$

Both are minimal, in the sense that if we throw any tuple out of any relation, the resulting relations no longer satisfy the rules. We cannot, therefore, decide between the two least fixedpoints (a) and (b), so we cannot answer a simple question such as "Is $P(0)$ true?"   □

In Example 10.28, we saw that our idea of defining the meaning of recursive rules by finding the least fixedpoint no longer works when recursion and negation are tangled up too intimately. There can be more than one least fixedpoint, and these fixedpoints can contradict each other. It would be good if some other approach to defining the meaning of recursive negation would work better, but unfortunately, there is no general agreement about what such rules should mean.

Thus, it is conventional to restrict ourselves to recursions in which negation is *stratified*. For instance, the SQL-99 standard for recursion discussed in Section 10.4 makes this restriction. As we shall see, when negation is stratified there is an algorithm to compute one particular least fixedpoint (perhaps out of many such fixedpoints) that matches our intuition about what the rules mean. We define the property of being stratified as follows.

1. Draw a graph whose nodes correspond to the IDB predicates.

2. Draw an arc from node A to node B if a rule with predicate A in the head has a negated subgoal with predicate B. Label this arc with a $-$ sign to indicate it is a *negative* arc.

3. Draw an arc from node A to node B if a rule with head predicate A has a non-negated subgoal with predicate B. This arc does not have a minus-sign as label.

If this graph has a cycle containing one or more negative arcs, then the recursion is not stratified. Otherwise, the recursion is stratified. We can group the IDB predicates of a stratified graph into *strata*. The stratum of a predicate A is the largest number of negative arcs on a path beginning from A.

If the recursion is stratified, then we may evaluate the IDB predicates in the order of their strata, lowest first. This strategy produces one of the least fixedpoints of the rules. More importantly, computing the IDB predicates in the order implied by their strata appears always to make sense and give us the "right" fixedpoint. In contrast, as we have seen in Example 10.28, unstratified recursions may leave us with no "right" fixedpoint at all, even if there are many to choose from.

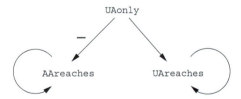

Figure 10.8: Graph constructed from a stratified recursion

Example 10.29: The graph for the predicates of Example 10.27 is shown in Fig. 10.8. `AAreaches` and `UAreaches` are in stratum 0, because none of the paths beginning at their nodes involves a negative arc. `UAonly` has stratum 1, because there are paths with one negative arc leading from that node, but no paths with more than one negative arc. Thus, we must completely evaluate `AAreaches` and `UAreaches` before we start evaluating `UAonly`.

Compare the situation when we construct the graph for the IDB predicates of Example 10.28. This graph is shown in Fig. 10.9. Since rule (1) has head P with negated subgoal Q, there is a negative arc from P to Q. Since rule (2) has head Q with negated subgoal P, there is also a negative arc in the opposite direction. There is thus a negative cycle, and the rules are not stratified. □

Figure 10.9: Graph constructed from an unstratified recursion

10.3.4   Exercises for Section 10.3

Exercise 10.3.1: If we add or delete arcs to the diagram of Fig. 10.5, we may change the value of the relation Reaches of Example 10.25, the relation Connects of Example 10.26, or the relations UAreaches and AAreaches of Example 10.27. Give the new values of these relations if we:

* a) Add an arc from CHI to SF labeled AA, 1900-2100.

  b) Add an arc from NY to DEN labeled UA, 900-1100.

  c) Add both arcs from (a) and (b).

  d) Delete the arc from DEN to DAL.

Exercise 10.3.2: Write Datalog rules (using stratified negation, if negation is necessary) to describe the following modifications to the notion of "follow-on" from Example 10.22. You may use EDB relation SequelOf and the IDB relation FollowOn defined in Example 10.23.

* a) P(x,y) meaning that movie y is a follow-on to movie x, but not a sequel of x (as defined by the EDB relation SequelOf).

  b) Q(x,y) meaning that y is a follow-on of x, but neither a sequel nor a sequel of a sequel.

! c) R(x) meaning that movie x has at least two follow-ons. Note that both could be sequels, rather than one being a sequel and the other a sequel of a sequel.

!! d) S(x,y), meaning that y is a follow-on of x but y has at most one follow-on.

Exercise 10.3.3: ODL classes and their relationships can be described by a relation Rel(class, rclass, mult). Here, mult gives the multiplicity of a relationship, either multi for a multivalued relationship, or single for a single-valued relationship. The first two attributes are the related classes; the relationship goes from class to rclass (related class). For example, the relation Rel representing the three ODL classes of our running movie example from Fig. 4.3 is shown in Fig. 10.10.

class	*rclass*	*mult*
Star	Movie	multi
Movie	Star	multi
Movie	Studio	single
Studio	Movie	multi

Figure 10.10: Representing ODL relationships by relational data

We can also see this data as a graph, in which the nodes are classes and the arcs go from a class to a related class, with label multi or single, as appropriate. Figure 10.11 illustrates this graph for the data of Fig. 10.10.

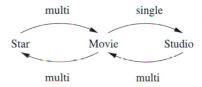

Figure 10.11: Representing relationships by a graph

For each of the following, write Datalog rules, using stratified negation if negation is necessary, to express the described predicate(s). You may use Rel as an EDB relation. Show the result of evaluating your rules, round-by-round, on the data from Fig. 10.10.

a) Predicate P(class, eclass), meaning that there is a path[5] in the graph of classes that goes from class to eclass. The latter class can be thought of as "embedded" in class, since it is in a sense part of a part of an ··· object of the first class.

*! b) Predicates S(class, eclass) and M(class, eclass). The first means that there is a "single-valued embedding" of eclass in class, that is, a path from class to eclass along which every arc is labeled single. The second, M, means that there is a "multivalued embedding" of eclass in class, i.e., a path from class to eclass with at least one arc labeled multi.

---

[5] We shall not consider empty paths to be "paths" in this exercise.

   c) Predicate Q(class, eclass) that says there is a path from class to
      eclass but no single-valued path. You may use IDB predicates defined
      previously in this exercise.

10.4 Recursion in SQL

The SQL-99 standard includes provision for recursive rules, based on the recursive Datalog described in Section 10.3. Although this feature is not part of the "core" SQL-99 standard that every DBMS is expected to implement, at least one major system — IBM's DB2 — does implement the SQL-99 proposal. This proposal differs from our description in two ways:

1. Only *linear* recursion, that is, rules with at most one recursive subgoal, is mandatory. In what follows, we shall ignore this restriction; you should remember that there could be an implementation of standard SQL that prohibits nonlinear recursion but allows linear recursion.

2. The requirement of stratification, which we discussed for the negation operator in Section 10.3.3, applies also to other operators of SQL that can cause similar problems, such as aggregations.

10.4.1 Defining IDB Relations in SQL

The WITH statement allows us to define the SQL equivalent of IDB relations. These definitions can then be used within the WITH statement itself. A simple form of the WITH statement is:

$$\text{WITH } R \text{ AS } <\text{definition of } R> \ <\text{query involving } R>$$

That is, one defines a temporary relation named R, and then uses R in some query. More generally, one can define several relations after the WITH, separating their definitions by commas. Any of these definitions may be recursive. Several defined relations may be mutually recursive; that is, each may be defined in terms of some of the other relations, optionally including itself. However, any relation that is involved in a recursion must be preceded by the keyword RECURSIVE. Thus, a WITH statement has the form:

1. The keyword WITH.

2. One or more definitions. Definitions are separated by commas, and each definition consists of

   (a) An optional keyword RECURSIVE, which is required if the relation being defined is recursive.

   (b) The name of the relation being defined.

   (c) The keyword AS.

(d) The query that defines the relation.

3. A query, which may refer to any of the prior definitions, and forms the result of the WITH statement.

It is important to note that, unlike other definitions of relations, the definitions inside a WITH statement are only available within that statement and cannot be used elsewhere. If one wants a persistent relation, one should define that relation in the database schema, outside any WITH statement.

Example 10.30: Let us reconsider the airline flights information that we used as an example in Section 10.3. The data about flights is in a relation[6]

    Flights(airline, frm, to, departs, arrives)

The actual data for our example was given in Fig. 10.5.

In Example 10.25, we computed the IDB relation Reaches to be the pairs of cities such that it is possible to fly from the first to the second using the flights represented by the EDB relation Flights. The two rules for Reaches are:

1. Reaches(x,y) ← Flights(a,x,y,d,r)
2. Reaches(x,y) ← Reaches(x,z) AND Reaches(z,y)

From these rules, we can develop an SQL query that produces the relation Reaches. This SQL query places the rules for Reaches in a WITH statement, and follows it by a query. In Example 10.25, the desired result was the entire Reaches relation, but we could also ask some query about Reaches, for instance the set of cities reachable from Denver.

```
1)  WITH RECURSIVE Reaches(frm, to) AS
2)         (SELECT frm, to FROM Flights)
3)      UNION
4)         (SELECT R1.frm, R2.to
5)          FROM Reaches R1, Reaches R2
6)          WHERE R1.to = R2.frm)
7)  SELECT * FROM Reaches;
```

Figure 10.12: Recursive SQL query for pairs of reachable cities

Figure 10.12 shows how to compute Reaches as an SQL query. Line (1) introduces the definition of Reaches, while the actual definition of this relation is in lines (2) through (6).

That definition is a union of two queries, corresponding to the two rules by which Reaches was defined in Example 10.25. Line (2) is the first term

---

[6]We changed the name of the second attribute to frm, since from in SQL is a keyword.

Mutual Recursion

There is a graph-theoretic way to check whether two relations or predicates are mutually recursive. Construct a *dependency graph* whose nodes correspond to the relations (or predicates if we are using Datalog rules). Draw an arc from relation A to relation B if the definition of B depends directly on the definition of A. That is, if Datalog is being used, then A appears in the body of a rule with B at the head. In SQL, A would appear somewhere in the definition of B, normally in a FROM clause, but possibly as a term in a union, intersection, or difference.

If there is a cycle involving nodes R and S, then R and S are *mutually recursive*. The most common case will be a loop from R to R, indicating that R depends recursively upon itself.

Note that the dependency graph is similar to the graph we introduced in Section 10.3.3 to define stratified negation. However, there we had to distinguish between positive and negative dependence, while here we do not make that distinction.

---

of the union and corresponds to the first, or basis rule. It says that for every tuple in the Flights relation, the second and third components (the frm and to components) are a tuple in Reaches.

Lines (4) through (6) correspond to the second, or inductive, rule in the definition of Reaches. The two Reaches subgoals are represented in the FROM clause by two aliases R1 and R2 for Reaches. The first component of R1 corresponds to x in Rule (2), and the second component of R2 corresponds to y. Variable z is represented by both the second component of R1 and the first component of R2; note that these components are equated in line (6).

Finally, line (7) describes the relation produced by the entire query. It is a copy of the Reaches relation. As an alternative, we could replace line (7) by a more complex query. For instance,

```
7)   SELECT to FROM Reaches WHERE frm = 'DEN';
```

would produce all those cities reachable from Denver.   □

10.4.2   Stratified Negation

The queries that can appear as the definition of a recursive relation are not arbitrary SQL queries. Rather, they must be restricted in certain ways; one of the most important requirements is that negation of mutually recursive relations be stratified, as discussed in Section 10.3.3. In Section 10.4.3, we shall see how the principle of stratification extends to other constructs that we find in SQL but not in Datalog, such as aggregation.

Example 10.31: Let us re-examine Example 10.27, where we asked for those pairs of cities (x, y) such that it is possible to travel from x to y on the airline UA, but not on AA. We need recursion to express the idea of traveling on one airline through an indefinite sequence of hops. However, the negation aspect appears in a stratified way: after using recursion to compute the two relations UAreaches and AAreaches in Example 10.27, we took their difference.

We could adopt the same strategy to write the query in SQL. However, to illustrate a different way of proceeding, we shall instead define recursively a single relation Reaches(airline, frm, to), whose triples (a, f, t) mean that one can fly from city f to city t, perhaps using several hops but using only flights of airline a. We shall also use a nonrecursive relation Triples(airline, frm, to) that is the projection of Flights onto the three relevant components. The query is shown in Fig. 10.13.

The definition of relation Reaches in lines (3) through (9) is the union of two terms. The basis term is the relation Triples at line (4). The inductive term is the query of lines (6) through (9) that produces the join of Triples with Reaches itself. The effect of these two terms is to put into Reaches all tuples (a, f, t) such that one can travel from city f to city t using one or more hops, but with all hops on airline a.

The query itself appears in lines (10) through (12). Line (10) gives the city pairs reachable via UA, and line (12) gives the city pairs reachable via AA. The result of the query is the difference of these two relations. □

```
1) WITH
2)      Triples AS SELECT airline, frm, to FROM Flights,

3)      RECURSIVE Reaches(airline, frm, to) AS
4)              (SELECT * FROM Triples)
5)          UNION
6)              (SELECT Triples.airline, Triples.frm, Reaches.to
7)               FROM Triples, Reaches
8)               WHERE Triples.to = Reaches.frm AND
9)                       Triples.airline = Reaches.airline)

10)     (SELECT frm, to FROM Reaches WHERE airline = 'UA')
11) EXCEPT
12)     (SELECT frm, to FROM Reaches WHERE airline = 'AA');
```

Figure 10.13: Stratified query for cities reachable by one of two airlines

Example 10.32: In Fig. 10.13, the negation represented by EXCEPT in line (11) is clearly stratified, since it applies only after the recursion of lines (3) through

(9) has been completed. On the other hand, the use of negation in Example 10.28, which we observed was unstratified, must be translated into a use of EXCEPT within the definition of mutually recursive relations. The straightforward translation of that example into SQL is shown in Fig. 10.14. This query asks only for the value of P, although we could have asked for Q, or some function of P and Q.

```
1)   WITH
2)       RECURSIVE P(x) AS
3)                 (SELECT * FROM R)
4)            EXCEPT
5)                 (SELECT * FROM Q),

6)       RECURSIVE Q(x) AS
7)                 (SELECT * FROM R)
8)            EXCEPT
9)                 (SELECT * FROM P)

10)  SELECT * FROM P;
```

Figure 10.14: Unstratified query, illegal in SQL

The two uses of EXCEPT, in lines (4) and (8) of Fig. 10.14 are illegal in SQL, since in each case the second argument is a relation that is mutually recursive with the relation being defined. Thus, these uses of negation are not stratified negation and therefore not permitted. In fact, there is no work-around for this problem in SQL, nor should there be, since the recursion of Fig. 10.14 does not define unique values for relations P and Q.   □

10.4.3   Problematic Expressions in Recursive SQL

We have seen in Example 10.32 that the use of EXCEPT to help define a recursive relation can violate SQL's requirement that negation be stratified. However, there are other unacceptable forms of query that do not use EXCEPT. For instance, negation of a relation can also be expressed by the use of NOT IN. Thus, lines (2) through (5) of Fig. 10.14 could also have been written

```
RECURSIVE P(x) AS
     SELECT x FROM R WHERE x NOT IN Q
```

This rewriting still leaves the recursion unstratified and therefore illegal.

On the other hand, simply using NOT in a WHERE clause, such as NOT x=y (which could be written x<>y anyway) does not automatically violate the condition that negation be stratified. What then is the general rule about what sorts of SQL queries can be used to define recursive relations in SQL?

The principle is that to be a legal SQL recursion, the definition of a recursive relation R may only involve the use of a mutually recursive relation S (S can be R itself) if that use is *monotone* in S. A use of S is monotone if adding an arbitrary tuple to S might add one or more tuples to R, or it might leave R unchanged, but it can never cause any tuple to be deleted from R.

This rule makes sense when one considers the least-fixedpoint computation outlined in Section 10.3.2. We start with our recursively defined IDB relations empty, and we repeatedly add tuples to them in successive rounds. If adding a tuple in one round could cause us to have to delete a tuple at the next round, then there is the risk of oscillation, and the fixedpoint computation might never converge. In the following examples, we shall see some constructs that are nonmonotone and therefore are outlawed in SQL recursion.

Example 10.33: Figure 10.14 is an implementation of the Datalog rules for the unstratified negation of Example 10.28. There, the rules allowed two different minimal fixedpoints. As expected, the definitions of P and Q in Fig. 10.14 are not monotone. Look at the definition of P in lines (2) through (5) for instance. P depends on Q, with which it is mutually recursive, but adding a tuple to Q can delete a tuple from P. To see why, suppose that R consists of the two tuples (a) and (b), and Q consists of the tuples (a) and (c). Then $P = \{(b)\}$. However, if we add (b) to Q, then P becomes empty. Addition of a tuple to Q has caused the deletion of a tuple from P, so we have a nonmonotone, illegal construct.

This lack of monotonicity leads directly to an oscillating behavior when we try to evaluate the relations P and Q by computing a minimal fixedpoint.[7] For instance, suppose that R has the two tuples $\{(a), (b)\}$. Initially, both P and Q are empty. Thus, in the first round, lines (3) through (5) of Fig. 10.14 compute P to have value $\{(a), (b)\}$. Lines (7) through (9) compute Q to have the same value, since the old, empty value of P is used at line (9).

Now, both R, P, and Q have the value $\{(a), (b)\}$. Thus, on the next round, P and Q are each computed to be empty at lines (3) through (5) and (7) through (9), respectively. On the third round, both would therefore get the value $\{(a), (b)\}$. This process continues forever, with both relations empty on even rounds and $\{(a), (b)\}$ on odd rounds. Therefore, we never obtain clear values for the two relations P and Q from their "definitions" in Fig. 10.14. □

Example 10.34: Aggregation can also lead to nonmonotonicity, although the connection may not be obvious at first. Suppose we have unary (one-attribute) relations P and Q defined by the following two conditions:

1. P is the union of Q and an EDB relation R.

---

[7] When the recursion is not monotone, then the order in which we evaluate the relations in a WITH clause can affect the final answer, although when the recursion is monotone, the result is independent of order. In this and the next example, we shall assume that on each round, P and Q are evaluated "in parallel." That is, the old value of each relation is used to compute the other at each round. See the box on "Using New Values in Fixedpoint Calculations."

2. Q has one tuple that is the sum of the members of P.

We can express these conditions by a WITH statement, although this statement violates the monotonicity requirement of SQL. The query shown in Fig. 10.15 asks for the value of P.

```
1)   WITH
2)       RECURSIVE P(x) AS
3)               (SELECT * FROM R)
4)           UNION
5)               (SELECT * FROM Q),

6)       RECURSIVE Q(x) AS
7)           SELECT SUM(x) FROM P

8)   SELECT * FROM P;
```

Figure 10.15: Nonmonotone query involving aggregation, illegal in SQL

Suppose that R consists of the tuples (12) and (34), and initially P and Q are both empty, as they must be at the beginning of the fixedpoint computation. Figure 10.16 summarizes the values computed in the first six rounds. Recall that we have adopted the strategy that all relations are computed in one round from the values at the previous round. Thus, P is computed in the first round to be the same as R, and Q is empty, since the old, empty value of P is used in line (7).

At the second round, the union of lines (3) through (5) is the set $R = \{(12), (34)\}$, so that becomes the new value of P. The old value of P was the same as the new value, so on the second round $Q = \{(46)\}$. That is, 46 is the sum of 12 and 34.

At the third round, we get $P = \{(12), (34), (46)\}$ at lines (2) through (5). Using the old value of P, $\{(12), (34)\}$, Q is defined by lines (6) and (7) to be

Round	P	Q
1)	$\{(12), (34)\}$	$\emptyset$
2)	$\{(12), (34)\}$	$\{(46)\}$
3)	$\{(12), (34), (46)\}$	$\{(46)\}$
4)	$\{(12), (34), (46)\}$	$\{(92)\}$
5)	$\{(12), (34), (92)\}$	$\{(92)\}$
6)	$\{(12), (34), (92)\}$	$\{(138)\}$

Figure 10.16: Iterative calculation of fixedpoint for a nonmonotone aggregation

---

Using New Values in Fixedpoint Calculations

One might wonder why we used the old values of P to compute Q in Examples 10.33 and 10.34, rather than the new values of P. If these queries were legal, and we used new values in each round, then the query results might depend on the order in which we listed the definitions of the recursive predicates in the WITH clause. In Example 10.33, P and Q would converge to one of the two possible fixedpoints, depending on the order of evaluation. In Example 10.34, P and Q would still not converge, and in fact they would change at every round, rather than every other round.

$\{(46)\}$ again.

At the fourth round, P has the same value, $\{(12), (34), (46)\}$, but Q gets the value $\{(92)\}$, since $12+34+46=92$. Notice that Q has lost the tuple (46), although it gained the tuple (92). That is, adding the tuple (46) to P has caused a tuple (by coincidence the same tuple) to be deleted from Q. That behavior is the nonmonotonicity that SQL prohibits in recursive definitions, confirming that the query of Fig. 10.15 is illegal. In general, at the $2i$th round, P will consist of the tuples (12), (34), and $(46i - 46)$, while Q consists only of the tuple $(46i)$. $\square$

10.4.4 Exercises for Section 10.4

Exercise 10.4.1 : In Example 10.23 we discussed a relation

```
SequelOf(movie, sequel)
```

that gives the immediate sequels of a movie. We also defined an IDB relation FollowOn whose pairs (x, y) were movies such that y was either a sequel of x, a sequel of a sequel, or so on.

a) Write the definition of FollowOn as an SQL recursion.

b) Write a recursive SQL query that returns the set of pairs (x, y) such that movie y is a follow-on to movie x, but not a sequel of x.

c) Write a recursive SQL query that returns the set of pairs (x, y) meaning that y is a follow-on of x, but neither a sequel nor a sequel of a sequel.

! d) Write a recursive SQL query that returns the set of movies x that have at least two follow-ons. Note that both could be sequels, rather than one being a sequel and the other a sequel of a sequel.

! e) Write a recursive SQL query that returns the set of pairs (x, y) such that movie y is a follow-on of x but y has at most one follow-on.

Exercise 10.4.2: In Exercise 10.3.3, we introduced a relation

```
Rel(class, eclass, mult)
```

that describes how one ODL class is related to other classes. Specifically, this relation has tuple (c, d, m) if there is a relation from class c to class d. This relation is multivalued if $m = $ 'multi' and it is single-valued if $m = $ 'single'. We also suggested in Exercise 10.3.3 that it is possible to view `Rel` as defining a graph whose nodes are classes and in which there is an arc from c to d labeled m if and only if (c, d, m) is a tuple of `Rel`. Write a recursive SQL query that produces the set of pairs (c, d) such that:

   a) There is a path from class c to class d in the graph described above.

 * b) There is a path from c to d along which every arc is labeled `single`.

*! c) There is a path from c to d along which at least one arc is labeled `multi`.

   d) There is a path from c to d but no path along which all arcs are labeled `single`.

 ! e) There is a path from c to d along which arc labels alternate `single` and `multi`.

   f) There are paths from c to d and from d to c along which every arc is labeled `single`.

10.5 Summary of Chapter 10

✦ *Datalog*: This form of logic allows us to write queries in the relational model. In Datalog, one writes rules in which a head predicate or relation is defined in terms of a body, consisting of subgoals.

✦ *Atoms*: The head and subgoals are each atoms, and an atom consists of an (optionally negated) predicate applied to some number of arguments. Predicates may represent relations or arithmetic comparisons such as $<$.

✦ *IDB and EDB Predicates*: Some predicates correspond to stored relations, and are called EDB (extensional database) predicates or relations. Other predicates, called IDB (intensional database), are defined by the rules. EDB predicates may not appear in rule heads.

✦ *Safe Rules*: We generally restrict Datalog rules to be safe, meaning that every variable in the rule appears in some nonnegated, relational subgoal of the body. Safe rules guarantee that if the EDB relations are finite, then the IDB relations will be finite.

✦ *Relational Algebra and Datalog*: All queries that can be expressed in relational algebra can also be expressed in Datalog. If the rules are safe and nonrecursive, then they define exactly the same set of queries as relational algebra.

✦ *Recursive Datalog*: Datalog rules can be recursive, allowing a relation to be defined in terms of itself. The meaning of recursive Datalog rules without negation is the least fixedpoint: the smallest set of tuples for the IDB relations that makes the heads of the rules exactly equal to what their bodies collectively imply.

✦ *Stratified Negation*: When a recursion involves negation, the least fixedpoint may not be unique, and in some cases there is no acceptable meaning to the Datalog rules. Therefore, uses of negation inside a recursion must be forbidden, leading to a requirement for stratified negation. For rules of this type, there is one (of perhaps several) least fixedpoint that is the generally accepted meaning of the rules.

✦ *SQL Recursive Queries*: In SQL, one can define temporary relations to be used in a manner similar to IDB relations in Datalog. These temporary relations may be used to construct answers to queries recursively.

✦ *Stratification in SQL*: Negations and aggregations involved in an SQL recursion must be monotone, a generalization of the requirement for stratified negation in Datalog. Intuitively, a relation may not be defined, directly or indirectly, in terms of a negation or aggregation of itself.

10.6 References for Chapter 10

Codd introduced a form of first-order logic called *relational calculus* in one of his early papers on the relational model [4]. Relational calculus is an expression language, much like relational algebra, and is in fact equivalent in expressive power to relational algebra, a fact proved in [4].

Datalog, looking more like logical rules, was inspired by the programming language Prolog. Because it allows recursion, it is more expressive than relational calculus. The book [6] originated much of the development of logic as a query language, while [2] placed the ideas in the context of database systems.

The idea that the stratified approach gives the correct choice of fixedpoint comes from [3], although using this approach to evaluating Datalog rules was the independent idea of [1], [8], and [10]. More on stratified negation, on the relationship between relational algebra, Datalog, and relational calculus, and on the evaluation of Datalog rules, with or without negation, can be found in [9].

[7] surveys logic-based query languages. The source of the SQL-99 proposal for recursion is [5].

1. Apt, K. R., H. Blair, and A. Walker, "Towards a theory of declarative knowledge," in *Foundations of Deductive Databases and Logic Programming* (J. Minker, ed.), pp. 89–148, Morgan-Kaufmann, San Francisco, 1988.

2. Bancilhon, F. and R. Ramakrishnan, "An amateur's introduction to recursive query-processing strategies," *ACM SIGMOD Intl. Conf. on Management of Data*, pp. 16–52, 1986.

3. Chandra, A. K. and D. Harel, "Structure and complexity of relational queries," *J. Computer and System Sciences* **25**:1 (1982), pp. 99–128.

4. Codd, E. F., "Relational completeness of database sublanguages," in *Database Systems* (R. Rustin, ed.), Prentice Hall, Engelwood Cliffs, NJ, 1972.

5. Finkelstein, S. J., N. Mattos, I. S. Mumick, and H. Pirahesh, "Expressing recursive queries in SQL," ISO WG3 report X3H2–96–075, March, 1996.

6. Gallaire, H. and J. Minker, *Logic and Databases*, Plenum Press, New York, 1978.

7. M. Liu, "Deductive database languages: problems and solutions," *Computing Surveys* **31**:1 (March, 1999), pp. 27–62.

8. Naqvi, S., "Negation as failure for first-order queries," *Proc. Fifth ACM Symp. on Principles of Database Systems*, pp. 114–122, 1986.

9. Ullman, J. D., *Principles of Database and Knowledge-Base Systems, Volume I*, Computer Science Press, New York, 1988.

10. Van Gelder, A., "Negation as failure using tight derivations for general logic programs," in *Foundations of Deductive Databases and Logic Programming* (J. Minker, ed.), pp. 149–176, Morgan-Kaufmann, San Francisco, 1988.

Chapter 11

Data Storage

This chapter begins our study of implementation of database management systems. The first issues we must address involve how a DBMS deals with very large amounts of data efficiently. The study can be divided into two parts:

1. How does a computer system store and manage very large amounts of data?

2. What representations and data structures best support efficient manipulations of this data?

We cover (1) in this chapter and (2) in Chapters 12 through 14.

This chapter explains the devices used to store massive amounts of information, especially rotating disks. We introduce the "memory hierarchy," and see how the efficiency of algorithms involving very large amounts of data depends on the pattern of data movement between main memory and secondary storage (typically disks) or even "tertiary storage" (robotic devices for storing and accessing large numbers of optical disks or tape cartridges). A particular algorithm — two-phase, multiway merge sort — is used as an important example of an algorithm that uses the memory hierarchy effectively.

We also consider, in Section 11.5, a number of techniques for lowering the time it takes to read or write data from disk. The last two sections discuss methods for improving the reliability of disks. Problems addressed include intermittent read- or write-errors, and "disk crashes," where data becomes permanently unreadable.

Our discussion begins with a fanciful examination of what goes wrong if one does not use the special methods developed for DBMS implementation.

11.1 The "Megatron 2002" Database System

If you have used a DBMS, you might imagine that implementing such a system is not hard. You might have in mind an implementation such as the recent (fictitious) offering from Megatron Systems Inc.: the Megatron 2002 Database Management System. This system, which is available under UNIX and other operating systems, and which uses the relational approach, supports SQL.

11.1.1 Megatron 2002 Implementation Details

To begin, Megatron 2002 uses the UNIX file system to store its relations. For example, the relation `Students(name, id, dept)` would be stored in the file `/usr/db/Students`. The file `Students` has one line for each tuple. Values of components of a tuple are stored as character strings, separated by the special marker character `#`. For instance, the file `/usr/db/Students` might look like:

```
Smith#123#CS
Johnson#522#EE
   . . .
```

The database schema is stored in a special file named `/usr/db/schema`. For each relation, the file `schema` has a line beginning with that relation name, in which attribute names alternate with types. The character `#` separates elements of these lines. For example, the `schema` file might contain lines such as

```
Students#name#STR#id#INT#dept#STR
Depts#name#STR#office#STR
   . . .
```

Here the relation `Students(name, id, dept)` is described; the types of attributes `name` and `dept` are strings while `id` is an integer. Another relation with schema `Depts(name, office)` is shown as well.

Example 11.1 : Here is an example of a session using the Megatron 2002 DBMS. We are running on a machine called `dbhost`, and we invoke the DBMS by the UNIX-level command `megatron2002`.

```
dbhost> megatron2002
```

produces the response

```
WELCOME TO MEGATRON 2002!
```

We are now talking to the Megatron 2002 user interface, to which we can type SQL queries in response to the Megatron prompt (`&`). A `#` ends a query. Thus:

```
& SELECT * FROM Students #
```

produces as an answer the table

name	id	dept
Smith	123	CS
Johnson	522	EE

Megatron 2002 also allows us to execute a query and store the result in a new file, if we end the query with a vertical bar and the name of the file. For instance,

```
& SELECT * FROM Students WHERE id >= 500 | HighId #
```

creates a new file `/usr/db/HighId` in which only the line

```
Johnson#522#EE
```

appears. □

11.1.2   How Megatron 2002 Executes Queries

Let us consider a common form of SQL query:

```
SELECT * FROM R WHERE <Condition>
```

Megatron 2002 will do the following:

1. Read the file `schema` to determine the attributes of relation R and their types.

2. Check that the <Condition> is semantically valid for R.

3. Display each of the attribute names as the header of a column, and draw a line.

4. Read the file named R, and for each line:

    (a) Check the condition, and

    (b) Display the line as a tuple, if the condition is true.

To execute

```
SELECT * FROM R WHERE <condition> | T
```

Megatron 2002 does the following:

1. Process query as before, but omit step (3), which generates column headers and a line separating the headers from the tuples.

2. Write the result to a new file `/usr/db/T`.

3. Add to the file `/usr/db/schema` an entry for T that looks just like the entry for R, except that relation name T replaces R. That is, the schema for T is the same as the schema for R.

Example 11.2: Now, let us consider a more complicated query, one involving a join of our two example relations `Students` and `Depts`:

```
SELECT office
FROM Students, Depts
WHERE Students.name = 'Smith' AND
      Students.dept = Depts.name #
```

This query requires that Megatron 2002 join relations Students and Depts. That is, the system must consider in turn each pair of tuples, one from each relation, and determine whether:

a) The tuples represent the same department, and

b) The name of the student is Smith.

The algorithm can be described informally as:

```
FOR each tuple s in Students DO
    FOR each tuple d in Depts DO
        IF s and d satisfy the where-condition THEN
            display the office value from Depts;
```

□

11.1.3   What's Wrong With Megatron 2002?

It may come as no surprise that a DBMS is not implemented like our imaginary Megatron 2002. There are a number of ways that the implementation described here is inadequate for applications involving significant amounts of data or multiple users of data. A partial list of problems follows:

- The tuple layout on disk is inadequate, with no flexibility when the database is modified. For instance, if we change EE to ECON in one Students tuple, the entire file has to be rewritten, as every subsequent character is moved two positions down the file.

- Search is very expensive. We always have to read an entire relation, even if the query gives us a value or values that enable us to focus on one tuple, as in the query of Example 11.2. There, we had to look at the entire Student relation, even though the only one we wanted was that for student Smith.

- Query-processing is by "brute force," and much cleverer ways of performing operations like joins are available. For instance, we shall see that in a query like that of Example 11.2, it is not necessary to look at all pairs of tuples, one from each relation, even if the name of one student (Smith) were not specified in the query.

- There is no way for useful data to be buffered in main memory; all data comes off the disk, all the time.

- There is no concurrency control. Several users can modify a file at the same time, with unpredictable results.

- There is no reliability; we can lose data in a crash or leave operations half done.

The remainder of this book will introduce you to the technology that addresses these questions. We hope that you enjoy the study.

11.2 The Memory Hierarchy

A typical computer system has several different components in which data may be stored. These components have data capacities ranging over at least seven orders of magnitude and also have access speeds ranging over seven or more orders of magnitude. The cost per byte of these components also varies, but more slowly, with perhaps three orders of magnitude between the cheapest and most expensive forms of storage. Not surprisingly, the devices with smallest capacity also offer the fastest access speed and have the highest cost per byte. A schematic of the memory hierarchy is shown in Fig. 11.1.

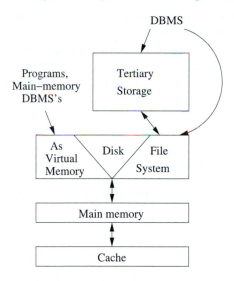

Figure 11.1: The memory hierarchy

11.2.1 Cache

At the lowest level of the hierarchy is a *cache*. *On-board cache* is found on the same chip as the microprocessor itself, and additional *level-2 cache* is found on another chip. The data items (including machine instructions) in the cache are copies of certain locations of main memory, the next higher level of the memory hierarchy. Sometimes, the values in the cache are changed, but the corresponding change to the main memory is delayed. Nevertheless, each value in the cache at any one time corresponds to one place in main memory. The unit of transfer between cache and main memory is typically a small number of bytes. We may therefore think of the cache as holding individual machine instructions, integers, floating-point numbers or short character strings.

When the machine executes instructions, it looks both for the instructions and for the data used by those instructions in the cache. If it doesn't find them there, it goes to main-memory and copies the instructions or data into the cache. Since the cache can hold only a limited amount of data, it is usually necessary to move something out of the cache in order to accommodate the new data. If what is moved out of cache has not changed since it was copied to cache, then nothing needs to be done. However, if the data being expelled from the cache has been modified, then the new value must be copied into its proper location in main memory.

When data in the cache is modified, a simple computer with a single processor has no need to update immediately the corresponding location in main memory. However, in a multiprocessor system that allows several processors to access the same main memory and keep their own private caches, it is often necessary for cache updates to *write through*, that is, to change the corresponding place in main memory immediately.

Typical caches in 2001 have capacities up to a megabyte. Data can be read or written between the cache and processor at the speed of the processor instructions, commonly a few nanoseconds (a *nanosecond* is 10^{-9} seconds). On the other hand, moving an instruction or data item between cache and main memory takes much longer, perhaps 100 nanoseconds.

11.2.2 Main Memory

In the center of the action is the computer's *main memory*. We may think of everything that happens in the computer — instruction executions and data manipulations — as working on information that is resident in main memory (although in practice, it is normal for what is used to migrate to the cache, as we discussed in Section 11.2.1).

In 2001, typical machines are configured with around 100 megabytes (10^8 bytes) of main memory. However, machines with much larger main memories, 10 gigabytes or more (10^{10} bytes) can be found.

Main memories are *random access*, meaning that one can obtain any byte in the same amount of time.[1] Typical times to access data from main memories are in the 10–100 nanosecond range (10^{-8} to 10^{-7} seconds).

---

[1] Although some modern parallel computers have a main memory shared by many processors in a way that makes the access time of certain parts of memory different, by perhaps a factor of 3, for different processors.

Computer Quantities are Powers of 2

It is conventional to talk of sizes or capacities of computer components as if they were powers of 10: megabytes, gigabytes, and so on. In reality, since it is most efficient to design components such as memory chips to hold a number of bits that is a power of 2, all these numbers are really shorthands for nearby powers of 2. Since $2^{10} = 1024$ is very close to a thousand, we often maintain the fiction that $2^{10} = 1000$, and talk about 2^{10} with the prefix "kilo," 2^{20} as "mega," 2^{30} as "giga," 2^{40} as "tera," and 2^{50} as "peta," even though these prefixes in scientific parlance refer to 10^3, 10^6, 10^9, 10^{12} and 10^{15}, respectively. The discrepancy grows as we talk of larger numbers. A "gigabyte" is really 1.074×10^9 bytes.

We use the standard abbreviations for these numbers: K, M, G, T, and P for kilo, mega, giga, tera, and peta, respectively. Thus, 16Gb is sixteen gigabytes, or strictly speaking 2^{34} bytes. Since we sometimes want to talk about numbers that are the conventional powers of 10, we shall reserve for these the traditional numbers, without the prefixes "kilo," "mega," and so on. For example, "one million bytes" is 1,000,000 bytes, while "one megabyte" is 1,048,576 bytes.

11.2.3 Virtual Memory

When we write programs, the data we use — variables of the program, files read, and so on — occupies a *virtual memory address space*. Instructions of the program likewise occupy an address space of their own. Many machines use a 32-bit address space; that is, there are 2^{32}, or about 4 billion, different addresses. Since each byte needs its own address, we can think of a typical virtual memory as 4 gigabytes.

Since a virtual memory space is much bigger than the usual main memory, most of the content of a fully occupied virtual memory is actually stored on the disk. We discuss the typical operation of a disk in Section 11.3, but for the moment we need only to be aware that the disk is divided logically into *blocks*. The block size on common disks is in the range 4K to 56K bytes, i.e., 4 to 56 kilobytes. Virtual memory is moved between disk and main memory in entire blocks, which are usually called *pages* in main memory. The machine hardware and the operating system allow pages of virtual memory to be brought into any part of the main memory and to have each byte of that block referred to properly by its virtual memory address.

The path in Fig. 11.1 involving virtual memory represents the treatment of conventional programs and applications. It does not represent the typical way data in a database is managed. However, there is increasing interest in *main-memory database systems*, which do indeed manage their data through virtual memory, relying on the operating system to bring needed data into main

---

Moore's Law

Gordon Moore observed many years ago that integrated circuits were improving in many ways, following an exponential curve that doubles about every 18 months. Some of these parameters that follow "Moore's law" are:

1. The speed of processors, i.e., the number of instructions executed per second and the ratio of the speed to cost of a processor.

2. The cost of main memory per bit and the number of bits that can be put on one chip.

3. The cost of disk per bit and the capacity of the largest disks.

On the other hand, there are some other important parameters that do not follow Moore's law; they grow slowly if at all. Among these slowly growing parameters are the speed of accessing data in main memory, or the speed at which disks rotate. Because they grow slowly, "latency" becomes progressively larger. That is, the time to move data between levels of the memory hierarchy appears to take progressively longer compared with the time to compute. Thus, in future years, we expect that main memory will appear much further away from the processor than cache, and data on disk will appear even further away from the processor. Indeed, these effects of apparent "distance" are already quite severe in 2001.

---

memory through the paging mechanism. Main-memory database systems, like most applications, are most useful when the data is small enough to remain in main memory without being swapped out by the operating system. If a machine has a 32-bit address space, then main-memory database systems are appropriate for applications that need to keep no more than 4 gigabytes of data in memory at once (or less if the machine's actual main memory is smaller than 2^{32} bytes). That amount of space is sufficient for many applications, but not for large, ambitious applications of DBMS's.

Thus, large-scale database systems will manage their data directly on the disk. These systems are limited in size only by the amount of data that can be stored on all the disks and other storage devices available to the computer system. We shall introduce this mode of operation next.

11.2.4 Secondary Storage

Essentially every computer has some sort of *secondary storage*, which is a form of storage that is both significantly slower and significantly more capacious than main memory, yet is essentially random-access, with relatively small differences among the times required to access different data items (these differences are discussed in Section 11.3). Modern computer systems use some form of disk as secondary memory. Usually this disk is magnetic, although sometimes optical or magneto-optical disks are used. The latter types are cheaper, but may not support writing of data on the disk easily or at all; thus they tend to be used only for archival data that doesn't change.

We observe from Fig. 11.1 that the disk is considered the support for both virtual memory and a file system. That is, while some disk blocks will be used to hold pages of an application program's virtual memory, other disk blocks are used to hold (parts of) files. Files are moved between disk and main memory in blocks, under the control of the operating system or the database system. Moving a block from disk to main memory is a *disk read*; moving the block from main memory to the disk is a *disk write*. We shall refer to either as a *disk I/O*. Certain parts of main memory are used to *buffer* files, that is, to hold block-sized pieces of these files.

For example, when you open a file for reading, the operating system might reserve a 4K block of main memory as a buffer for this file, assuming disk blocks are 4K bytes. Initially, the first block of the file is copied into the buffer. When the application program has consumed those 4K bytes of the file, the next block of the file is brought into the buffer, replacing the old contents. This process, illustrated in Fig. 11.2, continues until either the entire file is read or the file is closed.

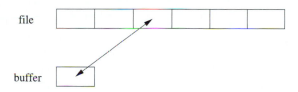

Figure 11.2: A file and its main-memory buffer

A DBMS will manage disk blocks itself, rather than relying on the operating system's file manager to move blocks between main and secondary memory. However, the issues in management are essentially the same whether we are looking at a file system or a DBMS. It takes roughly 10–30 milliseconds (.01 to .03 seconds) to read or write a block on disk. In that time, a typical machine can execute several million instructions. As a result, it is common for the time to read or write a disk block to dominate the time it takes to do whatever must be done with the contents of the block. Therefore it is vital that, whenever possible, a disk block containing data we need to access should already be in a main-memory buffer. Then, we do not have to pay the cost of a disk I/O. We shall return to this problem in Sections 11.4 and 11.5, where we see some examples of how to deal with the high cost of moving data between levels in the memory hierarchy.

In 2001, single disk units may have capacities of 100 gigabytes or more. Moreover, machines can use several disk units, so hundreds of gigabytes of secondary storage for a single machine is realistic. Thus, secondary memory is on the order of 10^5 times slower but at least 100 times more capacious than typical main memory. Secondary memory is also significantly cheaper than main memory. In 2001, prices for magnetic disk units are 1 to 2 cents per megabyte, while the cost of main memory is 1 to 2 dollars per megabyte.

11.2.5 Tertiary Storage

As capacious as a collection of disk units can be, there are databases much larger than what can be stored on the disk(s) of a single machine, or even of a substantial collection of machines. For example, retail chains accumulate many terabytes of data about their sales, while satellites return petabytes of information per year.

To serve such needs, *tertiary storage* devices have been developed to hold data volumes measured in terabytes. Tertiary storage is characterized by significantly higher read/write times than secondary storage, but also by much larger capacities and smaller cost per byte than is available from magnetic disks. While main memory offers uniform access time for any datum, and disk offers an access time that does not differ by more than a small factor for accessing any datum, tertiary storage devices generally offer access times that vary widely, depending on how close to a read/write point the datum is. Here are the principal kinds of tertiary storage devices:

1. *Ad-hoc Tape Storage*. The simplest — and in past years the only — approach to tertiary storage is to put data on tape reels or cassettes and to store the cassettes in racks. When some information from the tertiary store is wanted, a human operator locates and mounts the tape on a reader. The information is located by winding the tape to the correct position, and the information is copied from tape to secondary storage or to main memory. To write into tertiary storage, the correct tape and point on the tape is located, and the copy proceeds from disk to tape.

2. *Optical-Disk Juke Boxes*. A "juke box" consists of racks of CD-ROM's (CD = "compact disk"; ROM = "read-only memory." These are optical disks of the type used commonly to distribute software). Bits on an optical disk are represented by small areas of black or white, so bits can be read by shining a laser on the spot and seeing whether the light is reflected. A robotic arm that is part of the jukebox extracts any one CD-ROM and move it to a reader. The CD can then have its contents, or part thereof, read into secondary memory.

3. *Tape Silos* A "silo" is a room-sized device that holds racks of tapes. The tapes are accessed by robotic arms that can bring them to one of several tape readers. The silo is thus an automated version of the earlier ad-hoc storage of tapes. Since it uses computer control of inventory and automates the tape-retrieval process, it is at least an order of magnitude faster than human-powered systems.

The capacity of a tape cassette in 2001 is as high as 50 gigabytes. Tape silos can therefore hold many terabytes. CD's have a standard of about 2/3 of a gigabyte, with the next-generation standard of about 2.5 gigabytes (DVD's or *digital versatile disks*) becoming prevalent. CD-ROM jukeboxes in the multiterabyte range are also available.

The time taken to access data from a tertiary storage device ranges from a few seconds to a few minutes. A robotic arm in a jukebox or silo can find the desired CD-ROM or cassette in several seconds, while human operators probably require minutes to locate and retrieve tapes. Once loaded in the reader, any part of the CD can be accessed in a fraction of a second, while it can take many additional seconds to move the correct portion of a tape under the read-head of the tape reader.

In summary, tertiary storage access can be about 1000 times slower than secondary-memory access (milliseconds versus seconds). However, single tertiary-storage units can be 1000 times more capacious than secondary storage devices (gigabytes versus terabytes). Figure 11.3 shows, on a log-log scale, the relationship between access times and capacities for the four levels of memory hierarchy that we have studied. We include "Zip" and "floppy" disks ("diskettes"), which are common storage devices, although not typical of secondary storage used for database systems. The horizontal axis measures seconds in exponents of 10; e.g., -3 means 10^{-3} seconds, or one millisecond. The vertical axis measures bytes, also in exponents of 10; e.g., 8 means 100 megabytes.

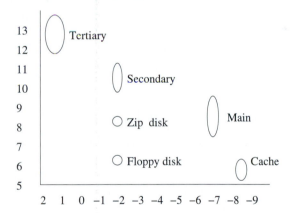

Figure 11.3: Access time versus capacity for various levels of the memory hierarchy

11.2.6 Volatile and Nonvolatile Storage

An additional distinction among storage devices is whether they are *volatile* or *nonvolatile*. A volatile device "forgets" what is stored in it when the power goes off. A nonvolatile device, on the other hand, is expected to keep its contents intact even for long periods when the device is turned off or there is a power failure. The question of volatility is important, because one of the characteristic capabilities of a DBMS is the ability to retain its data even in the presence of errors such as power failures.

Magnetic materials will hold their magnetism in the absence of power, so devices such as magnetic disks and tapes are nonvolatile. Likewise, optical devices such as CD's hold the black or white dots with which they are imprinted, even in the absence of power. Indeed, for many of these devices it is impossible to change what is written on their surface by any means. Thus, essentially all secondary and tertiary storage devices are nonvolatile.

On the other hand, main memory is generally volatile. It happens that a memory chip can be designed with simpler circuits if the value of the bit is allowed to degrade over the course of a minute or so; the simplicity lowers the cost per bit of the chip. What actually happens is that the electric charge that represents a bit drains slowly out of the region devoted to that bit. As a result, a so-called *dynamic random-access memory*, or DRAM, chip needs to have its entire contents read and rewritten periodically. If the power is off, then this refresh does not occur, and the chip will quickly lose what is stored.

A database system that runs on a machine with volatile main memory must back up every change on disk before the change can be considered part of the database, or else we risk losing information in a power failure. As a consequence, query and database modifications must involve a large number of disk writes, some of which could be avoided if we didn't have the obligation to preserve all information at all times. An alternative is to use a form of main memory that is not volatile. New types of memory chips, called *flash memory*, are nonvolatile and are becoming economical. An alternative is to build a so-called *RAM disk* from conventional memory chips by providing a battery backup to the main power supply.

11.2.7   Exercises for Section 11.2

Exercise 11.2.1 : Suppose that in 2001 the typical computer has a processor that runs at 1500 megahertz, has a disk of 40 gigabytes, and a main memory of 100 megabytes. Assume that Moore's law (these factors double every 18 months) continues to hold into the indefinite future.

* a) When will terabyte disks be common?

   b) When will gigabyte main memories be common?

   c) When will terahertz processors be common?

   d) What will be a typical configuration (processor, disk, memory) in the year 2008?

! **Exercise 11.2.2 :** Commander Data, the android from the 24th century on *Star Trek: The Next Generation* once proudly announced that his processor runs at "12 teraops." While an operation and a cycle may not be the same, let us suppose they are, and that Moore's law continues to hold for the next 300 years. If so, what would Data's true processor speed be?

11.3 Disks

The use of secondary storage is one of the important characteristics of a DBMS, and secondary storage is almost exclusively based on magnetic disks. Thus, to motivate many of the ideas used in DBMS implementation, we must examine the operation of disks in detail.

11.3.1 Mechanics of Disks

The two principal moving pieces of a disk drive are shown in Fig. 11.4; they are a *disk assembly* and a *head assembly*. The disk assembly consists of one or more circular *platters* that rotate around a central spindle. The upper and lower surfaces of the platters are covered with a thin layer of magnetic material, on which bits are stored. A 0 is represented by orienting the magnetism of a small area in one direction and a 1 by orienting the magnetism in the opposite direction. A common diameter for disk platters is 3.5 inches, although disks with diameters from an inch to several feet have been built.

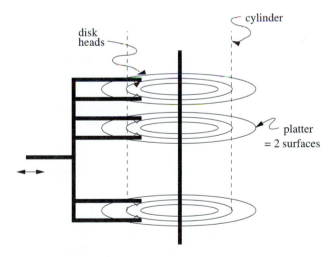

Figure 11.4: A typical disk

The locations where bits are stored are organized into *tracks*, which are concentric circles on a single platter. Tracks occupy most of a surface, except for the region closest to the spindle, as can be seen in the top view of Fig. 11.5. A track consists of many points, each of which represents a single bit by the direction of its magnetism.

Tracks are organized into *sectors*, which are segments of the circle separated by *gaps* that are not magnetized in either direction.[2] The sector is an indivisible unit, as far as reading and writing the disk is concerned. It is also indivisible as far as errors are concerned. Should a portion of the magnetic layer be corrupted in some way, so that it cannot store information, then the entire sector containing this portion cannot be used. Gaps often represent about 10% of the total track and are used to help identify the beginnings of sectors. As we mentioned in Section 11.2.3, blocks are logical units of data that are transferred between disk and main memory; blocks consist of one or more sectors.

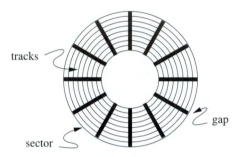

Figure 11.5: Top view of a disk surface

The second movable piece shown in Fig. 11.4, the head assembly, holds the *disk heads*. For each surface there is one head, riding extremely close to the surface but never touching it (or else a "head crash" occurs and the disk is destroyed, along with everything stored thereon). A head reads the magnetism passing under it, and can also alter the magnetism to write information on the disk. The heads are each attached to an arm, and the arms for all the surfaces move in and out together, being part of the rigid head assembly.

11.3.2   The Disk Controller

One or more disk drives are controlled by a *disk controller*, which is a small processor capable of:

1. Controlling the mechanical actuator that moves the head assembly, to position the heads at a particular radius. At this radius, one track from each surface will be under the head for that surface and will therefore be readable and writable. The tracks that are under the heads at the same time are said to form a *cylinder*.

2. Selecting a surface from which to read or write, and selecting a sector from the track on that surface that is under the head. The controller is

---

[2]We show each track with the same number of sectors in Fig. 11.5. However, as we shall discuss in Example 11.3, the number of sectors per track may vary, with the outer tracks having more sectors than inner tracks.

also responsible for knowing when the rotating spindle has reached the point where the desired sector is beginning to move under the head.

3. Transferring the bits read from the desired sector to the computer's main memory or transferring the bits to be written from main memory to the intended sector.

Figure 11.6 shows a simple, single-processor computer. The processor communicates via a data bus with the main memory and the disk controller. A disk controller can control several disks; we show three disks in this computer.

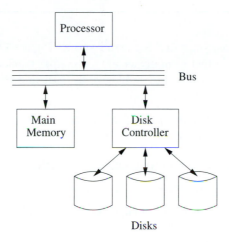

Figure 11.6: Schematic of a simple computer system

11.3.3 Disk Storage Characteristics

Disk technology is in flux, as the space needed to store a bit shrinks rapidly. In 2001, some of the typical measures associated with disks are:

- *Rotation Speed of the Disk Assembly.* 5400 RPM, i.e., one rotation every 11 milliseconds, is common, although higher and lower speeds are found.

- *Number of Platters per Unit.* A typical disk drive has about five platters and therefore ten surfaces. However, the common diskette ("floppy" disk) and "Zip" disk have a single platter with two surfaces, and disk drives with up to 30 surfaces are found.

- *Number of Tracks per Surface.* A surface may have as many as 20,000 tracks, although diskettes have a much smaller number; see Example 11.4.

- *Number of Bytes per Track.* Common disk drives may have almost a million bytes per track, although diskettes' tracks hold much less. As

---

Sectors Versus Blocks

Remember that a "sector" is a physical unit of the disk, while a "block" is a logical unit, a creation of whatever software system — operating system or DBMS, for example — is using the disk. As we mentioned, it is typical today for blocks to be at least as large as sectors and to consist of one or more sectors. However, there is no reason why a block cannot be a fraction of a sector, with several blocks packed into one sector. In fact, some older systems did use this strategy.

---

mentioned, tracks are divided into sectors. Figure 11.5 shows 12 sectors per track, but in fact as many as 500 sectors per track are found in modern disks. Sectors, in turn, may hold several thousand bytes.

Example 11.3 : The *Megatron 747* disk has the following characteristics, which are typical of a large, vintage-2001 disk drive.

- There are eight platters providing sixteen surfaces.

- There are 2^{14}, or 16,384 tracks per surface.

- There are (on average) $2^7 = 128$ sectors per track.

- There are $2^{12} = 4096$ bytes per sector.

The capacity of the disk is the product of 16 surfaces, times 16,384 tracks, times 128 sectors, times 4096 bytes, or 2^{37} bytes. The Megatron 747 is thus a 128-gigabyte disk. A single track holds 128×4096 bytes, or 512K bytes. If blocks are 2^{14}, or 16,384 bytes, then one block uses 4 consecutive sectors, and there are $128/4 = 32$ blocks on a track.

The Megatron 747 has surfaces of 3.5-inch diameter. The tracks occupy the outer inch of the surfaces, and the inner 0.75 inch is unoccupied. The density of bits in the radial direction is thus 16,384 per inch, because that is the number of tracks.

The density of bits around the tracks is far greater. Let us suppose at first that each track has the average number of sectors, 128. Suppose that the gaps occupy 10% of the tracks, so the 512K bytes per track (or 4M bits) occupy 90% of the track. The length of the outermost track is 3.5π or about 11 inches. Ninety percent of this distance, or about 9.9 inches, holds 4 megabits. Hence the density of bits in the occupied portion of the track is about 420,000 bits per inch.

On the other hand, the innermost track has a diameter of only 1.5 inches and would store the same 4 megabits in $0.9 \times 1.5 \times \pi$ or about 4.2 inches. The bit density of the inner tracks is thus around one megabit per inch.

Since the densities of inner and outer tracks would vary too much if the number of sectors and bits were kept uniform, the Megatron 747, like other modern disks, stores more sectors on the outer tracks than on inner tracks. For example, we could store 128 sectors per track on the middle third, but only 96 sectors on the inner third and 160 sectors on the outer third of the tracks. If we did, then the density would range from 530,000 bits to 742,000 bits per inch, at the outermost and innermost tracks, respectively. □

Example 11.4: At the small end of the range of disks is the standard 3.5-inch diskette. It has two surfaces with 40 tracks each, for a total of 80 tracks. The capacity of this disk, formatted in either the MAC or PC formats, is about 1.5 megabytes of data, or 150,000 bits (18,750 bytes) per track. About one quarter of the available space is taken up by gaps and other disk overhead in either format. □

11.3.4 Disk Access Characteristics

Our study of DBMS's requires us to understand not only the way data is stored on disks but the way it is manipulated. Since all computation takes place in main memory or cache, the only issue as far as the disk is concerned is how to move blocks of data between disk and main memory. As we mentioned in Section 11.3.2, blocks (or the consecutive sectors that comprise the blocks) are read or written when:

a) The heads are positioned at the cylinder containing the track on which the block is located, and

b) The sectors containing the block move under the disk head as the entire disk assembly rotates.

The time taken between the moment at which the command to read a block is issued and the time that the contents of the block appear in main memory is called the *latency* of the disk. It can be broken into the following components:

1. The time taken by the processor and disk controller to process the request, usually a fraction of a millisecond, which we shall neglect. We shall also neglect time due to contention for the disk controller (some other process might be reading or writing the disk at the same time) and other delays due to contention, such as for the bus.

2. *Seek time*: the time to position the head assembly at the proper cylinder. Seek time can be 0 if the heads happen already to be at the proper cylinder. If not, then the heads require some minimum time to start moving and to stop again, plus additional time that is roughly proportional to the distance traveled. Typical minimum times, the time to start, move by one track, and stop, are a few milliseconds, while maximum times to travel across all tracks are in the 10 to 40 millisecond range. Figure 11.7

suggests how seek time varies with distance. It shows seek time beginning at some value x for a distance of one cylinder and suggests that the
maximum seek time is in the range $3x$ to $20x$. The average seek time is
often used as a way to characterize the speed of the disk. We discuss how
to calculate this average in Example 11.5.

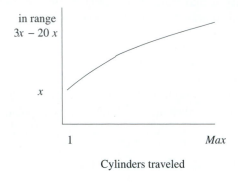

Figure 11.7: Seek time varies with distance traveled

3. *Rotational latency*: the time for the disk to rotate so the first of the sectors
   containing the block reaches the head. A typical disk rotates completely
   about once every 10 milliseconds. On the average, the desired sector will
   be about half way around the circle when the heads arrive at its cylinder,
   so the average rotational latency is around 5 milliseconds. Figure 11.8
   illustrates the problem of rotational latency.

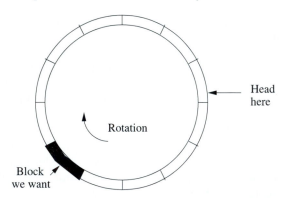

Figure 11.8: The cause of rotational latency

4. *Transfer time*: the time it takes the sectors of the block and any gaps
   between them to rotate past the head. If a disk has 250,000 bytes per
   track and rotates once in 10 milliseconds, we can read from the disk at
   25 megabytes per second. The transfer time for a 16,384-byte block is
   around two-thirds of a millisecond.

Example 11.5 : Let us examine the time it takes to read a 16,384-byte block from the Megatron 747 disk. First, we need to know some timing properties of the disk:

- The disk rotates at 7200 rpm; i.e., it makes one rotation in 8.33 milliseconds.

- To move the head assembly between cylinders takes one millisecond to start and stop, plus one additional millisecond for every 1000 cylinders traveled. Thus, the heads move one track in 1.001 milliseconds and move from the innermost to the outermost track, a distance of 16,383 tracks, in about 17.38 milliseconds.

Let us calculate the minimum, maximum, and average times to read that 16,384-byte block. The minimum time, since we are neglecting overhead and contention due to use of the controller, is just the transfer time. That is, the block might be on a track over which the head is positioned already, and the first sector of the block might be about to pass under the head.

Since there are 4096 bytes per sector on the Megatron 747 (see Example 11.3 for the physical specifications of the disk), the block occupies four sectors. The heads must therefore pass over four sectors and the three gaps between them. Recall that the gaps represent 10% of the circle and sectors the remaining 90%. There are 128 gaps and 128 sectors around the circle. Since the gaps together cover 36 degrees of arc and sectors the remaining 324 degrees, the total degrees of arc covered by 3 gaps and 4 sectors is:

$$36 \times \frac{3}{128} + 324 \times \frac{4}{128} = 10.97$$

degrees. The transfer time is thus $(10.97/360) \times 0.00833 = .000253$ seconds, or about a quarter of a millisecond. That is, $10.97/360$ is the fraction of a rotation needed to read the entire block, and $.00833$ seconds is the amount of time for a 360-degree rotation.

Now, let us look at the maximum possible time to read the block. In the worst case, the heads are positioned at the innermost cylinder, and the block we want to read is on the outermost cylinder (or vice versa). Thus, the first thing the controller must do is move the heads. As we observed above, the time it takes to move the Megatron 747 heads across all cylinders is about 17.38 milliseconds. This quantity is the seek time for the read.

The worst thing that can happen when the heads arrive at the correct cylinder is that the beginning of the desired block has just passed under the head. Assuming we must read the block starting at the beginning, we have to wait essentially a full rotation, or 8.33 milliseconds for the beginning of the block to reach the head again. Once that happens, we have only to wait an amount equal to the transfer time, 0.25 milliseconds, to read the entire block. Thus, the worst-case latency is $17.38 + 8.33 + 0.25 = 25.96$ milliseconds.

Trends in Disk-Controller Architecture

As the cost of digital hardware drops precipitously, disk controllers are beginning to look more like computers of their own, with general-purpose processors and substantial random-access memory. Among the many things that might be done with such additional hardware, disk controllers are beginning to read and store in their local memory entire tracks of a disk, even if only one block from that track is requested. This capability greatly reduces the average access time for blocks, as long as we need all or most of the blocks on a single track. Section 11.5.1 discusses some of the applications of full-track or full-cylinder reads and writes.

Last let us compute the average time to read a block. Two of the components of the latency are easy to compute: the transfer time is always 0.25 milliseconds, and the average rotational latency is the time to rotate the disk half way around, or 4.17 milliseconds. We might suppose that the average seek time is just the time to move across half the tracks. However, that is not quite right, since typically, the heads are initially somewhere near the middle and therefore will have to move less than half the distance, on average, to the desired cylinder.

A more detailed estimate of the average number of tracks the head must move is obtained as follows. Assume the heads are initially at any of the 16,384 cylinders with equal probability. If at cylinder 1 or cylinder 16,384, then the average number of tracks to move is $(1 + 2 + \cdots + 16383)/16384$, or about 8192 tracks. At the middle cylinder 8192, the head is equally likely to move in or out, and either way, it will move on average about a quarter of the tracks, or 4096 tracks. A bit of calculation shows that as the initial head position varies from cylinder 1 to cylinder 8192, the average distance the head needs to move decreases quadratically from 8192 to 4096. Likewise, as the initial position varies from 8192 up to 16,384, the average distance to travel increases quadratically back up to 8192, as suggested in Fig. 11.9.

If we integrate the quantity in Fig. 11.9 over all initial positions, we find that the average distance traveled is one third of the way across the disk, or 5461 cylinders. That is, the average seek time will be one millisecond, plus the time to travel 5461 cylinders, or $1 + 5461/1000 = 6.46$ milliseconds.[3] Our estimate of the average latency is thus $6.46 + 4.17 + 0.25 = 10.88$ milliseconds; the three terms represent average seek time, average rotational latency, and transfer time, respectively. □

---

[3]Note that this calculation ignores the possibility that we do not have to move the head at all, but that case occurs only once in 16,384 times assuming random block requests. On the other hand, random block requests is not necessarily a good assumption, as we shall see in Section 11.5.

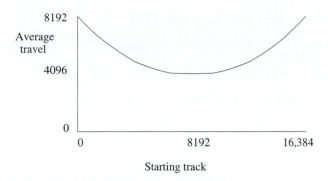

Figure 11.9: Average travel distance as a function of initial head position

11.3.5 Writing Blocks

The process of writing a block is, in its simplest form, quite analogous to reading a block. The disk heads are positioned at the proper cylinder, and we wait for the proper sector(s) to rotate under the head. But, instead of reading the data under the head we use the head to write new data. The minimum, maximum and average times to write would thus be exactly the same as for reading.

A complication occurs if we want to verify that the block was written correctly. If so, then we have to wait for an additional rotation and read each sector back to check that what was intended to be written is actually stored there. A simple way to verify correct writing by using checksums is discussed in Section 11.6.2.

11.3.6 Modifying Blocks

It is not possible to modify a block on disk directly. Rather, even if we wish to modify only a few bytes (e.g., a component of one of the tuples stored in the block), we must do the following:

1. Read the block into main memory.

2. Make whatever changes to the block are desired in the main-memory copy of the block.

3. Write the new contents of the block back onto the disk.

4. If appropriate, verify that the write was done correctly.

The total time for this block modification is thus the sum of time it takes to read, the time to perform the update in main memory (which is usually negligible compared to the time to read or write to disk), the time to write, and, if verification is performed, another rotation time of the disk.[4]

---

[4]We might wonder whether the time to write the block we just read is the same as the time to perform a "random" write of a block. If the heads stay where they are, then we know

11.3.7   Exercises for Section 11.3

Exercise 11.3.1: The *Megatron 777* disk has the following characteristics:

1. There are ten surfaces, with 10,000 tracks each.

2. Tracks hold an average of 1000 sectors of 512 bytes each.

3. 20% of each track is used for gaps.

4. The disk rotates at 10,000 rpm.

5. The time it takes the head to move n tracks is $1 + 0.001n$ milliseconds.

Answer the following questions about the Megatron 777.

* a) What is the capacity of the disk?

  b) If all tracks hold the same number of sectors, what is the density of bits in the sectors of a track?

* c) What is the maximum seek time?

* d) What is the maximum rotational latency?

  e) If a block is 16,384 bytes (i.e., 32 sectors), what is the transfer time of a block?

! f) What is the average seek time?

  g) What is the average rotational latency?

! **Exercise 11.3.2:** Suppose the Megatron 747 disk head is at track 2048, i.e., 1/8 of the way across the tracks. Suppose that the next request is for a block on a random track. Calculate the average time to read this block.

*!! **Exercise 11.3.3:** At the end of Example 11.5 we computed the average distance that the head travels moving from one randomly chosen track to another randomly chosen track, and found that this distance is 1/3 of the tracks. Suppose, however, that the number of sectors per track were proportional to the length (or radius) of the track, so the bit density is the same for all tracks. Suppose also that we need to move the head from a random *sector* to another random sector. Since the sectors tend to congregate at the outside of the disk, we might expect that the average head move would be less than 1/3 of the way across the tracks. Assuming, as in the Megatron 747, that tracks occupy radii from 0.75 inches to 1.75 inches, calculate the average number of tracks the head travels when moving between two random sectors.

---

we have to wait a full rotation to write, but the seek time is zero. However, since the disk controller does not know when the application will finish writing the new value of the block, the heads may well have moved to another track to perform some other disk I/O before the request to write the new value of the block is made.

!! **Exercise 11.3.4:** At the end of Example 11.3 we suggested that the maximum density of tracks could be reduced if we divided the tracks into three regions, with different numbers of sectors in each region. If the divisions between the three regions could be placed at any radius, and the number of sectors in each region could vary, subject only to the constraint that the total number of bytes on the 16,384 tracks of one surface be 8 gigabytes, what choice for the five parameters (radii of the two divisions between regions and the numbers of sectors per track in each of the three regions) minimizes the maximum density of any track?

11.4 Using Secondary Storage Effectively

In most studies of algorithms, one assumes that the data is in main memory, and access to any item of data takes as much time as any other. This model of computation is often called the "RAM model" or random-access model of computation. However, when implementing a DBMS, one must assume that the data does *not* fit into main memory. One must therefore take into account the use of secondary, and perhaps even tertiary storage in designing efficient algorithms. The best algorithms for processing very large amounts of data thus often differ from the best main-memory algorithms for the same problem.

In this section, we shall consider primarily the interaction between main and secondary memory. In particular, there is a great advantage in choosing an algorithm that uses few disk accesses, even if the algorithm is not very efficient when viewed as a main-memory algorithm. A similar principle applies at each level of the memory hierarchy. Even a main-memory algorithm can sometimes be improved if we remember the size of the cache and design our algorithm so that data moved to cache tends to be used many times. Likewise, an algorithm using tertiary storage needs to take into account the volume of data moved between tertiary and secondary memory, and it is wise to minimize this quantity even at the expense of more work at the lower levels of the hierarchy.

11.4.1 The I/O Model of Computation

Let us imagine a simple computer running a DBMS and trying to serve a number of users who are accessing the database in various ways: queries and database modifications. For the moment, assume our computer has one processor, one disk controller, and one disk. The database itself is much too large to fit in main memory. Key parts of the database may be buffered in main memory, but generally, each piece of the database that one of the users accesses will have to be retrieved initially from disk.

Since there are many users, and each user issues disk-I/O requests frequently, the disk controller often will have a queue of requests, which we assume it satisfies on a first-come-first-served basis. Thus, each request for a given user will appear random (i.e., the disk head will be in a random position before the request), even if this user is reading blocks belonging to a single relation, and that relation is stored on a single cylinder of the disk. Later in this section we shall discuss how to improve the performance of the system in various ways. However, in all that follows, the following rule, which defines the *I/O model of computation*, is assumed:

> **Dominance of I/O cost**: If a block needs to be moved between disk and main memory, then the time taken to perform the read or write is much larger than the time likely to be used manipulating that data in main memory. Thus, the number of block accesses (reads and writes) is a good approximation to the time needed by the algorithm and should be minimized.

In examples, we shall assume that the disk is a Megatron 747, with 16K-byte blocks and the timing characteristics determined in Example 11.5. In particular, the average time to read or write a block is about 11 milliseconds.

Example 11.6 : Suppose our database has a relation R and a query asks for the tuple of R that has a certain key value k. As we shall see, it is quite desirable that an index on R be created and used to identify the disk block on which the tuple with key value k appears. However it is generally unimportant whether the index tells us where on the block this tuple appears.

The reason is that it will take on the order of 11 milliseconds to read this 16K-byte block. In 11 milliseconds, a modern microprocessor can execute millions of instructions. However, searching for the key value k once the block is in main memory will only take thousands of instructions, even if the dumbest possible linear search is used. The additional time to perform the search in main memory will therefore be less than 1% of the block access time and can be neglected safely.   □

11.4.2   Sorting Data in Secondary Storage

As an extended example of how algorithms need to change under the I/O model of computation cost, let us consider sorting data that is much larger than main memory. To begin, we shall introduce a particular sorting problem and give some details of the machine on which the sorting occurs.

Example 11.7 : Let us assume that we have a large relation R consisting of 10,000,000 tuples. Each tuple is represented by a record with several fields, one of which is the *sort key* field, or just "key field" if there is no confusion with other kinds of keys. The goal of a sorting algorithm is to order the records by increasing value of their sort keys.

A sort key may or may not be a "key" in the usual SQL sense of a *primary key*, where records are guaranteed to have unique values in their primary key. If duplicate values of the sort key are permitted, then any order of records with equal sort keys is acceptable. For simplicity, we shall assume sort keys are unique.

The records (tuples) of R will be divided into disk blocks of 16,384 bytes per block. We assume that 100 records fit in one block. That is, records are about 160 bytes long. With the typical extra information needed to store records in a block (as discussed in Section 12.2, e.g.), 100 records of this size is about what can fit in one 16,384-byte block. Thus, R occupies 100,000 blocks totaling 1.64 billion bytes.

The machine on which the sorting occurs has one Megatron 747 disk and 100 megabytes of main memory available for buffering blocks of the relation. The actual main memory is larger, but the rest of main-memory is used by the system. The number of blocks that can fit in 100M bytes of memory (which, recall, is really 100×2^{20} bytes), is $100 \times 2^{20}/2^{14}$, or 6400 blocks. $\square$

If the data fits in main memory, there are a number of well-known algorithms that work well;[5] variants of "Quicksort" are generally considered the fastest. The preferred version of Quicksort sorts only the key fields, carrying pointers to the full records along with the keys. Only when the keys and their pointers were in sorted order, would we use the pointers to bring every record to its proper position.

Unfortunately, these ideas do not work very well when secondary memory is needed to hold the data. The preferred approaches to sorting, when the data is mostly in secondary memory, involve moving each block between main and secondary memory only a small number of times, in a regular pattern. Often, these algorithms operate in a small number of *passes*; in one pass every record is read into main memory once and written out to disk once. In Section 11.4.4, we see one such algorithm.

11.4.3 Merge-Sort

You may be familiar with a main-memory sorting algorithm called Merge-Sort that works by merging sorted lists into larger sorted lists. To *merge* two sorted lists, we repeatedly compare the smallest remaining keys of each list, move the record with the smaller key to the output, and repeat, until one list is exhausted. At that time, the output, in the order selected, followed by what remains of the nonexhausted list, is the complete set of records, in sorted order.

Example 11.8 : Suppose we have two sorted lists of four records each. To make matters simpler, we shall represent records by their keys and no other data, and we assume keys are integers. One of the sorted lists is $(1, 3, 4, 9)$ and the other is $(2, 5, 7, 8)$. In Fig. 11.10 we see the stages of the merge process.

At the first step, the head elements of the two lists, 1 and 2, are compared. Since $1 < 2$, the 1 is removed from the first list and becomes the first element of the output. At step (2), the heads of the remaining lists, now 3 and 2, are compared; 2 wins and is moved to the output. The merge continues until

---

[5]See D. E. Knuth, *The Art of Computer Programming, Vol. 3: Sorting and Searching, 2nd Edition*, Addison-Wesley, Reading MA, 1998.

Step	List 1	List 2	Output
start	$1, 3, 4, 9$	$2, 5, 7, 8$	none
1)	$3, 4, 9$	$2, 5, 7, 8$	1
2)	$3, 4, 9$	$5, 7, 8$	$1, 2$
3)	$4, 9$	$5, 7, 8$	$1, 2, 3$
4)	9	$5, 7, 8$	$1, 2, 3, 4$
5)	9	$7, 8$	$1, 2, 3, 4, 5$
6)	9	8	$1, 2, 3, 4, 5, 7$
7)	9	none	$1, 2, 3, 4, 5, 7, 8$
8)	none	none	$1, 2, 3, 4, 5, 7, 8, 9$

Figure 11.10: Merging two sorted lists to make one sorted list

step (7), when the second list is exhausted. At that point, the remainder of the first list, which happens to be only one element, is appended to the output and the merge is done. Note that the output is in sorted order, as must be the case, because at each step we chose the smallest of the remaining elements.   □

The time to merge in main memory is linear in the sum of the lengths of the lists. The reason is that, because the given lists are sorted, only the heads of the two lists are ever candidates for being the smallest unselected element, and we can compare them in a constant amount of time. The classic merge-sort algorithm sorts recursively, using $\log_2 n$ phases if there are n elements to be sorted. It can be described as follows:

BASIS: If there is a list of one element to be sorted, do nothing, because the list is already sorted.

INDUCTION: If there is a list of more than one element to be sorted, then divide the list arbitrarily into two lists that are either of the same length, or as close as possible if the original list is of odd length. Recursively sort the two sublists. Then merge the resulting sorted lists into one sorted list.

The analysis of this algorithm is well known and not too important here. Briefly $T(n)$, the time to sort n elements, is some constant times n (to split the list and merge the resulting sorted lists) plus the time to sort two lists of size $n/2$. That is, $T(n) = 2T(n/2) + an$ for some constant a. The solution to this recurrence equation is $T(n) = O(n \log n)$, that is, proportional to $n \log n$.

11.4.4   Two-Phase, Multiway Merge-Sort

We shall use a variant of Merge-Sort, called *Two-Phase, Multiway Merge-Sort* (often abbreviated TPMMS), to sort the relation of Example 11.7 on the machine described in that example. It is the preferred sorting algorithm in many database applications. Briefly, this algorithm consists of:

- *Phase 1*: Sort main-memory-sized pieces of the data, so every record is part of a sorted list that just fits in the available main memory. There may thus be any number of these *sorted sublists*, which we merge in the next phase.

- *Phase 2*: Merge all the sorted sublists into a single sorted list.

Our first observation is that with data on secondary storage, we do not want to start with a basis to the recursion that is one record or a few records. The reason is that Merge-Sort is not as fast as some other algorithms when the records to be sorted fit in main memory. Thus, we shall begin the recursion by taking an entire main memory full of records, and sorting them using an appropriate main-memory sorting algorithm such as Quicksort. We repeat the following process as many times as necessary:

1. Fill all available main memory with blocks from the original relation to be sorted.

2. Sort the records that are in main memory.

3. Write the sorted records from main memory onto new blocks of secondary memory, forming one sorted sublist.

At the end of this *first phase*, all the records of the original relation will have been read once into main memory, and become part of a main-memory-size *sorted sublist* that has been written onto disk.

Example 11.9: Consider the relation described in Example 11.7. We determined that 6400 of the 100,000 blocks will fill main memory. We thus fill memory 16 times, sort the records in main memory, and write the sorted sublists out to disk. The last of the 16 sublists is shorter than the rest; it occupies only 4000 blocks, while the other 15 sublists occupy 6400 blocks.

How long does this phase take? We read each of the 100,000 blocks once, and we write 100,000 new blocks. Thus, there are 200,000 disk I/O's. We have assumed, for the moment, that blocks are stored at random on the disk, an assumption that, as we shall see in Section 11.5, can be improved upon greatly. However, on our randomness assumption, each block read or write takes about 11 milliseconds. Thus, the I/O time for the first phase is 2200 seconds, or 37 minutes, or over 2 minutes per sorted sublist. It is not hard to see that, at a processor speed of hundreds of millions of instructions per second, we can create one sorted sublist in main memory in far less than the I/O time for that sublist. We thus estimate the total time for phase one as 37 minutes. □

Now, let us consider how we complete the sort by merging the sorted sublists. We could merge them in pairs, as in the classical Merge-Sort, but that would involve reading all data in and out of memory $2 \log_2 n$ times if there were n sorted sublists. For instance, the 16 sorted sublists of Example 11.9 would be read in and out of secondary storage once to merge into 8 lists; another complete reading and writing would reduce them to 4 sorted lists, and two more complete read/write operations would reduce them to one sorted list. Thus, each block would have 8 disk I/O's performed on it.

A better approach is to read the first block of each sorted sublist into a main-memory buffer. For some huge relations, there would be too many sorted sublists from phase one to read even one block per list into main memory, a problem we shall deal with in Section 11.4.5. But for data such as that of Example 11.7, there are relatively few lists, 16 in that example, and a block from each list fits easily in main memory.

We also use a buffer for an output block that will contain as many of the first elements in the complete sorted list as it can hold. Initially, the output block is empty. The arrangement of buffers is suggested by Fig. 11.11. We merge the sorted sublists into one sorted list with all the records as follows.

Input buffers, one for each sorted list

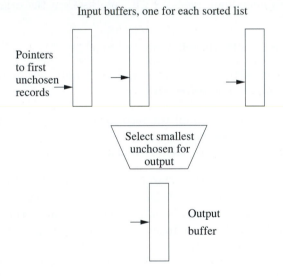

Figure 11.11: Main-memory organization for multiway merging

1. Find the smallest key among the first remaining elements of all the lists. Since this comparison is done in main memory, a linear search is sufficient, taking a number of machine instructions proportional to the number of sublists. However, if we wish, there is a method based on "priority queues"[6] that takes time proportional to the logarithm of the number of sublists to find the smallest element.

2. Move the smallest element to the first available position of the output block.

---

[6]See Aho, A. V. and J. D. Ullman *Foundations of Computer Science*, Computer Science Press, 1992.

How Big Should Blocks Be?

We have assumed a 16K byte block in our analysis of algorithms using the Megatron 747 disk. However, there are arguments that a larger block size would be advantageous. Recall from Example 11.5 that it takes about a quarter of a millisecond for transfer time of a 16K block and 10.63 milliseconds for average seek time and rotational latency. If we doubled the size of blocks, we would halve the number of disk I/O's for an algorithm like TPMMS. On the other hand, the only change in the time to access a block would be that the transfer time increases to 0.50 millisecond. We would thus approximately halve the time the sort takes. For a block size of 512K (i.e., an entire track of the Megatron 747) the transfer time is 8 milliseconds. At that point, the average block access time would be 20 milliseconds, but we would need only 12,500 block accesses, for a speedup in sorting by a factor of 14.

However, there are reasons to limit the block size. First, we cannot use blocks that cover several tracks effectively. Second, small relations would occupy only a fraction of a block, so large blocks would waste space on the disk. There are also certain data structures for secondary storage organization that prefer to divide data among many blocks and therefore work less well when the block size is too large. In fact, we shall see in Section 11.4.5 that the larger the blocks are, the fewer records we can sort by TPMMS. Nevertheless, as machines get faster and disks more capacious, there is a tendency for block sizes to grow.

---

3. If the output block is full, write it to disk and reinitialize the same buffer in main memory to hold the next output block.

4. If the block from which the smallest element was just taken is now exhausted of records, read the next block from the same sorted sublist into the same buffer that was used for the block just exhausted. If no blocks remain, then leave its buffer empty and do not consider elements from that list in any further competition for smallest remaining elements.

In the second phase, unlike the first phase, the blocks are read in an unpredictable order, since we cannot tell when an input block will become exhausted. However, notice that every block holding records from one of the sorted lists is read from disk exactly once. Thus, the total number of block reads is 100,000 in the second phase, just as for the first. Likewise, each record is placed once in an output block, and each of these blocks is written to disk. Thus, the number of block writes in the second phase is also 100,000. As the amount of second-phase computation in main memory can again be neglected compared to the I/O cost, we conclude that the second phase takes another 37 minutes, or 74 minutes for the entire sort.

11.4.5   Multiway Merging of Larger Relations

The Two-Phase, Multiway Merge-Sort (TPMMS) described above can be used to sort some very large sets of records. To see how large, let us suppose that:

1. The block size is B bytes.

2. The main memory available for buffering blocks is M bytes.

3. Records take R bytes.

The number of buffers available in main memory is thus M/B. On the second phase, all but one of these buffers may be devoted to one of the sorted sublists; the remaining buffer is for the output block. Thus, the number of sorted sublists that may be created in phase one is $(M/B) - 1$. This quantity is also the number of times we may fill main memory with records to be sorted. Each time we fill main memory, we sort M/R records. Thus, the total number of records we can sort is $(M/R)\big((M/B)-1\big)$, or approximately M^2/RB records.

Example 11.10 : If we use the parameters outlined in Example 11.7, then $M = 104{,}857{,}600$, $B = 16{,}384$, and $R = 160$. We can thus sort up to M^2/RB = 4.2 billion records, occupying two thirds of a terabyte. Note that relations this size will not fit on a Megatron 747 disk.   □

If we need to sort more records, we can add a third pass. Use TPMMS to sort groups of M^2/RB records, turning them into sorted sublists. Then, in a third phase, we merge up to $(M/B) - 1$ of these lists in a final multiway merge.

The third phase lets us sort approximately M^3/RB^2 records occupying M^3/B^3 blocks. For the parameters of Example 11.7, this amount is about 27 trillion records occupying 4.3 petabytes. Such an amount is unheard of to-day. Since even the 0.67 terabyte limit for TPMMS is unlikely to be carried out in secondary storage, we suggest that the two-phase version of Multiway Merge-Sort is likely to be enough for all practical purposes.

11.4.6   Exercises for Section 11.4

Exercise 11.4.1 : Using TPMMS, how long would it take to sort the relation of Example 11.7 if the Megatron 747 disk were replaced by the Megatron 777 disk described in Exercise 11.3.1, and all other characteristics of the machine and data remained the same?

Exercise 11.4.2 : Suppose we use TPMMS on the machine and relation R of Example 11.7, with certain modifications. Tell how many disk I/O's are needed for the sort if the relation R and/or machine characteristics are changed as follows:

* a) The number of tuples in R is doubled (all else remains the same).

  b) The length of tuples is doubled to 320 bytes (and everything else remains as in Example 11.7).

* c) The size of blocks is doubled, to 32,768 bytes (again, as throughout this exercise, all other parameters are unchanged).

  d) The size of available main memory is doubled to 200 megabytes.

! **Exercise 11.4.3:** Suppose the relation R of Example 11.7 grows to have as many tuples as can be sorted using TPMMS on the machine described in that example. Also assume that the disk grows to accommodate R, but all other characteristics of the disk, machine, and relation R remain the same. How long would it take to sort R?

* **Exercise 11.4.4:** Let us again consider the relation R of Example 11.7, but assume that it is stored sorted by the sort key (which is in fact a "key" in the usual sense, and uniquely identifies records). Also, assume that R is stored in a sequence of blocks whose locations are known, so that for any i it is possible to locate and retrieve the ith block of R using one disk I/O. Given a key value K, we can find the tuple with that key value by using a standard binary search technique. What is the maximum number of disk I/O's needed to find the tuple with key K?

!! **Exercise 11.4.5:** Suppose we have the same situation as in Exercise 11.4.4, but we are given 10 key values to find. What is the maximum number of disk I/O's needed to find all 10 tuples?

* **Exercise 11.4.6:** Suppose we have a relation whose n tuples each require R bytes, and we have a machine whose main memory M and disk-block size B are just sufficient to sort the n tuples using TPMMS. How would the maximum n change if we doubled: (a) B (b) R (c) M?

! **Exercise 11.4.7:** Repeat Exercise 11.4.6 if it is just possible to perform the sort using Three-Phase, Multiway Merge-Sort.

*! **Exercise 11.4.8:** As a function of parameters R, M, and B (as in Exercise 11.4.6) and the integer k, how many records can be sorted using a k-phase, Multiway Merge-Sort?

11.5 Accelerating Access to Secondary Storage

The analysis of Section 11.4.4 assumed that data was stored on a single disk and that blocks were chosen randomly from the possible locations on the disk. That assumption may be appropriate for a system that is executing a large number of small queries simultaneously. But if all the system is doing is sorting a large relation, then we can save a significant amount of time by being judicious about where we put the blocks involved in the sort, thereby taking advantage of the way disks work. In fact, even if the load on the system is from a large number of unrelated queries accessing "random" blocks on disk, we can do a number of things to make the queries run faster and/or allow the system to process more queries in the same time ("increase the *throughput*"). Among the strategies we shall consider in this section are:

- Place blocks that are accessed together on the same cylinder so we can often avoid seek time, and possibly rotational latency as well.

- Divide the data among several smaller disks rather than one large one. Having more head assemblies that can go after blocks independently can increase the number of block accesses per unit time.

- "Mirror" a disk: making two or more copies of the data on single disk. In addition to saving the data in case one of the disks fails, this strategy, like dividing the data among several disks, lets us access several blocks at once.

- Use a disk-scheduling algorithm, either in the operating system, in the DBMS, or in the disk controller, to select the order in which several requested blocks will be read or written.

- Prefetch blocks to main memory in anticipation of their later use.

In our discussion, we shall emphasize the improvements possible when the system is dedicated, at least momentarily, to doing a particular task such as the sorting operation we introduced in Example 11.7. However, there are at least two other viewpoints with which to measure the performance of systems and their use of secondary storage:

1. What happens when there are a large number of processes being supported simultaneously by the system? An example is an airline reservation system that accepts queries about flights and new bookings from many agents at the same time.

2. What do we do if we have a fixed budget for a computer system, or we must execute a mix of queries on a system that is already in place and not easily changed?

We address these questions in Section 11.5.6 after exploring the options.

11.5.1 Organizing Data by Cylinders

Since seek time represents about half the average time to access a block, there are a number of applications where it makes sense to store data that is likely to be accessed together, such as relations, on a single cylinder. If there is not enough room, then several adjacent cylinders can be used.

In fact, if we choose to read all the blocks on a single track or on a cylinder consecutively, then we can neglect all but the first seek time (to move to the cylinder) and the first rotational latency (to wait until the first of the blocks moves under the head). In that case, we can approach the theoretical transfer rate for moving data on or off the disk.

Example 11.11: Let us review the performance of TPMMS (Section 11.4.4). Recall from Example 11.5 that we determined the average block transfer time, seek time, and rotational latency to be 0.25 milliseconds, 6.46 milliseconds, and 4.17 milliseconds, respectively, for the Megatron 747 disk. We also found that the sorting of 10,000,000 records occupying a gigabyte took about 74 minutes. This time was divided into four components, one for reading and one for writing in each of the two phases of the algorithm.

Let us consider whether the organization of data by cylinders can improve the time of these operations. The first operation was the reading of the original records into main memory. Recall from Example 11.9 that we loaded main memory 16 times, with 6400 blocks each time.

The original 100,000 blocks of data may be stored on consecutive cylinders. Each of the 16,384 cylinders of the Megatron 747 stores about eight megabytes on 512 blocks; technically this figure is an average, because inner tracks store less and outer tracks more, but for simplicity we shall assume all tracks and cylinders are average. We must thus store the initial data on 196 cylinders, and we must read from 13 different cylinders to fill main memory once.

We can read one cylinder with a single seek time. We do not even have to wait for any particular block of the cylinder to pass under the head, because the order of records read is not important at this phase. We must move the heads 12 times to adjacent cylinders, but recall that a move of one track takes only one millisecond according to the parameters of Example 11.5. The total time to fill main memory is thus:

1. 6.46 milliseconds for one average seek.

2. 12 milliseconds for 12 one-cylinder seeks.

3. 1.60 seconds for the transfer of 6400 blocks.

All but the last quantity can be neglected. Since we fill memory 16 times, the total reading time for phase 1 is about 26 seconds. This number should be compared with the 18 minutes that the reading part of phase 1 takes in Example 11.9 when we assumed blocks were distributed randomly on disk. The writing part of phase 1 can likewise use adjacent cylinders to store the 16 sorted sublists of records. They can be written out onto another 196 cylinders, using the same head motions as for reading: one random seek and 12 one-cylinder seeks for each of the 16 lists. Thus, the writing time for phase 1 is also about

26 seconds, or 52 seconds for all of phase 1, compared with 37 minutes when randomly distributed blocks were used.

On the other hand, storage by cylinders does not help with the second phase of the sort. Recall that in the second phase, blocks are read from the fronts of the 16 sorted sublists in an order that is determined by the data and by which list next exhausts its current block. Likewise, output blocks, containing the complete sorted list, are written one at a time, interspersed with block reads. Thus, the second phase will still take about 37 minutes. We have consequently cut the sorting time almost in half, but cannot do better by judicious use of cylinders alone. □

11.5.2 Using Multiple Disks

We can often improve the speed of our system if we replace one disk, with many heads locked together, by several disks with their independent heads. The arrangement was suggested in Fig. 11.6, where we showed three disks connected to a single controller. As long as the disk controller, bus, and main memory can handle the data transferred at a higher rate, the effect will be approximately as if all times associated with reading and writing the disk were divided by the number of disks. An example should illustrate the difference.

Example 11.12 : The Megatron 737 disk has all the characteristics of the Megatron 747 outlined in Examples 11.3 and 11.5, but it has only two platters and four surfaces. Thus, each Megatron 737 holds 32 gigabytes. Suppose that we replace our one Megatron 747 by four Megatron 737's. Let us consider how TPMMS can be conducted.

First, we can divide the given records among the four disks; the data will occupy 196 adjacent cylinders on each disk. When we want to load main memory from disk during phase 1, we shall fill 1/4 of main memory from each of the four disks. We still get the benefit observed in Example 11.11 that the seek time and rotational latency go essentially to zero. However, we can read enough blocks to fill 1/4 of main memory, which is 1600 blocks, from a disk in about 400 milliseconds. As long as the system can handle data at this rate coming from four disks, we can fill the 100 megabytes of main memory in 0.4 seconds, compared with 1.6 seconds when we used one disk.

Similarly, when we write out main memory during phase 1, we can distribute each sorted sublist onto the four disks, occupying about 13 adjacent cylinders on each disk. Thus, there is a factor-of-4 speedup for the writing part of phase 1 too, and the entire phase 1 takes about 13 seconds, compared with 52 seconds using only the cylinder-based improvement of Section 11.5.1 and 37 minutes for the original, random approach.

Now, let us consider the second phase of TPMMS. We must still read blocks from the fronts of the various lists in a seemingly random, data-dependent way. If the core algorithm of phase 2 — the selection of smallest remaining elements from the 16 sublists — requires that all 16 lists be represented by blocks completely loaded into main memory, then we cannot use the four disks to advantage. Every time a block is exhausted, we must wait until a new block is read from the same list to replace it. Thus, only one disk at a time gets used.

However, if we write our code more carefully, we can resume comparisons among the 16 smallest elements as soon as the first element of the new block appears in main memory.[7] If so, then several lists might be having their blocks loaded into main memory at the same time. As long as they are on separate disks, then we can perform several block reads at the same time, and we have the potential of a factor-of-4 increase in the speed of the reading part of phase 2. We are also limited by the random order in which blocks must be read; if the next two blocks we need happen to be on the same disk, then one has to wait for the other, and all main-memory processing stops until at least the beginning of the second arrives in main memory.

The writing part of phase 2 is easier to speed up. We can use four output buffers and fill each in turn. Each buffer, when full, is written to one particular disk, filling cylinders in order. We can thus fill one of the buffers while the other three are written out.

Nevertheless, we cannot possibly write out the complete sorted list faster than we can read the data from the 16 intermediate lists. As we saw above, it is not possible to keep all four disks doing useful work all the time, and our speedup for phase 2 is probably in the 2-3 times range. However, even a factor of 2 saves us 18 minutes. By using cylinders to organize data and four disks to hold data, we can reduce the time for our sorting example from 37 minutes for each of the two phases to 13 seconds for the first phase and 18 minutes for the second.   □

11.5.3 Mirroring Disks

There are situations where it makes sense to have two or more disks hold identical copies of data. The disks are said to be *mirrors* of each other. One important motivation is that the data will survive a head crash by either disk, since it is still readable on a mirror of the disk that crashed. Systems designed to enhance reliability often use pairs of disks as mirrors of each other.

However, mirror disks can also speed up access to data. Recall our discussion of phase 2 in Example 11.12, where we observed that if we were very careful about timing, we could arrange to load up to four blocks from four different sorted lists whose previous blocks were exhausted. However, we could not choose which four lists would get new blocks. Thus, we could be unlucky and find that the first two lists were on the same disk, or two of the first three lists were on the same disk.

If we are willing to buy and use four copies of a single large disk, then we

---

[7]We should emphasize that this approach requires extremely delicate implementation and should only be attempted if there is an important benefit to doing so. There is a significant risk that, if we are not careful, there will be an attempt to read a record before it actually arrives in main memory.

can guarantee that the system can always be retrieving four blocks at once. That is, no matter which four blocks we need, we can assign each block to any of the four disks and read the block off of that disk.

In general, if we make n copies of a disk, we can read any n blocks in parallel. Moreover, if we have fewer than n blocks to read at once, then we can often obtain a speed increase by judiciously choosing which disk to read from. That is, we can pick the available disk whose head is closest to the cylinder from which we desire to read.

Using mirror disks does not speed up writing, but neither does it slow writing down, when compared with using a single disk. That is, whenever we need to write a block, we write it on all disks that have a copy. Since the writing can take place in parallel, the elapsed time is about the same as for writing to a single disk. There is a slight opportunity for differences among the writing times for the various mirror disks, because we cannot rely on them rotating in exact synchronism. Thus, one disk's head might just miss a block, while another disk's head might be about to pass over the position for the same block. However, these differences in rotational latency average out, and if we are using the cylinder-based strategy of Section 11.5.1, then the rotational latency can be neglected anyway.

11.5.4 Disk Scheduling and the Elevator Algorithm

Another effective way to speed up disk accesses in some situations is to have the disk controller choose which of several requests to execute first. This opportunity is not useful when the system needs to read or write disk blocks in a certain sequence, such as is the case in parts of our running merge-sort example. However, when the system is supporting many small processes that each access a few blocks, one can often increase the throughput by choosing which process' request to honor first.

A simple and effective way to schedule large numbers of block requests is known as the *elevator algorithm*. We think of the disk head as making sweeps across the disk, from innermost to outermost cylinder and then back again, just as an elevator makes vertical sweeps from the bottom to top of a building and back again. As heads pass a cylinder, they stop if there are one or more requests for blocks on that cylinder. All these blocks are read or written, as requested. The heads then proceed in the same direction they were traveling until the next cylinder with blocks to access is encountered. When the heads reach a position where there are no requests ahead of them in their direction of travel, they reverse direction.

Example 11.13: Suppose we are scheduling a Megatron 747 disk, which we recall has average seek, rotational latency, and transfer times of 6.46, 4.17, and 0.25, respectively (in this example, all times are in milliseconds). Suppose that at some time there are pending requests for block accesses at cylinders 2000, 6000, and 14,000. The heads are located at cylinder 2000. In addition, there are three more requests for block accesses that come in at later times, as summarized in Fig. 11.12. For instance, the request for a block from cylinder 4000 is made at time 10 milliseconds.

Cylinder of Request	First time available
2000	0
6000	0
14000	0
4000	10
16000	20
10000	30

Figure 11.12: Arrival times for six block-access requests

We shall assume that each block access incurs time 0.25 for transfer and 4.17 for average rotational latency, i.e., we need 4.42 milliseconds plus whatever the seek time is for each block access. The seek time can be calculated by the rule for the Megatron 747 given in Example 11.5: 1 plus the number of tracks divided by 1000. Let us see what happens if we schedule by the elevator algorithm. The first request at cylinder 2000 requires no seek, since the heads are already there. Thus, at time 4.42 the first access will be complete. The request for cylinder 4000 has not arrived at this point, so we move the heads to cylinder 6000, the next requested "stop" on our sweep to the highest-numbered tracks. The seek from cylinder 2000 to 6000 takes 5 milliseconds, so we arrive at time 9.42 and complete the access in another 4.42. Thus, the second access is complete at time 13.84. By this time, the request for cylinder 4000 has arrived, but we passed that cylinder at time 7.42 and will not come back to it until the next pass.

We thus move next to cylinder 14,000, taking time 9 to seek and 4.42 for rotation and transfer. The third access is thus complete at time 27.26. Now, the request for cylinder 16,000 has arrived, so we continue outward. We require 3 milliseconds for seek time, so this access is complete at time $27.26+3+4.42 = 34.68$.

At this time, the request for cylinder 10,000 has been made, so it and the request at cylinder 4000 remain. We thus sweep inward, honoring these two requests. Figure 11.13 summarizes the times at which requests are honored.

Let us compare the performance of the elevator algorithm with a more naive approach such as first-come-first-served. The first three requests are satisfied in exactly the same manner, assuming that the order of the first three requests was 2000, 6000, and 14,000. However, at that point, we go to cylinder 4000, because that was the fourth request to arrive. The seek time is 11 for this request, since we travel from cylinder 14,000 to 4000, more than half way across the disk. The fifth request, at cylinder 16,000, requires a seek time of 13, and the last,

Cylinder of Request	Time completed
2000	4.42
6000	13.84
14000	27.26
16000	34.68
10000	46.10
4000	57.52

Figure 11.13: Finishing times for block accesses using the elevator algorithm

at 10,000, uses seek time 7. Figure 11.14 summarizes the activity caused by first-come-first-serve scheduling. The difference between the two algorithms — 14 milliseconds — may not appear significant, but recall that the number of requests in this simple example is small and the algorithms were assumed not to deviate until the fourth of the six requests.   □

Cylinder of Request	Time completed
2000	4.42
6000	13.84
14000	27.26
4000	42.68
16000	60.10
10000	71.52

Figure 11.14: Finishing times for block accesses using the first-come-first-served algorithm

If the average number of requests waiting for the disk increases, the elevator algorithm further improves the throughput. For instance, should the pool of waiting requests equal the number of cylinders, then each seek will cover but a few cylinders, and the average seek time will approximate the minimum. If the pool of requests grows beyond the number of cylinders, then there will typically be more than one request at each cylinder. The disk controller can then order the requests around the cylinder, reducing the average rotational latency as well as the average seek time. However, should request pools grow that big, the time taken to serve any request becomes extremely large. An example should illustrate the situation.

Example 11.14 : Suppose again we are operating a Megatron 747 disk, with its 16,384 cylinders. Imagine that there are 1000 disk access requests waiting. For

---

Waiting for the Last of Two Blocks

Suppose there are two blocks at random positions around a cylinder. Let x_1 and x_2 be the positions, in fractions of the full circle, so these are numbers between 0 and 1. The probability that both x_1 and x_2 are less than some number y between 0 and 1 is y^2. Thus, the probability density for y is the derivative of y^2, or $2y$. That is, the probability that y has a given value increases linearly, as y grows from 0 to 1. The average of y is the integral of y times the probability density of y, that is $\int_0^1 2y^2$ or $2/3$.

---

simplicity, assume that these are all for blocks on different cylinders, spaced 16 apart. If we start at one end of the disk and sweep across, each of the 1000 requests has just a fraction more than 1 millisecond for seek time, 4.17 milliseconds for rotational latency, and 0.25 milliseconds for transfer. We can thus satisfy one request every 5.42 milliseconds, about half the 10.88 millisecond average time for random block accesses. However, the entire 1000 accesses take 5.42 seconds, so the average delay in satisfying a request is half that, or 2.71 seconds, a quite noticeable delay.

Now, suppose the pool of requests is as large as 32,768, which we shall assume for simplicity is exactly two accesses per cylinder. In this case, each seek time is one millisecond (0.5 per access), and of course the transfer time is 0.25 millisecond. Since there are two blocks accessed on each cylinder, on average the further of the two blocks will be 2/3 of the way around the disk when the heads arrive at that track. The proof of this estimate is tricky; we explain it in the box entitled "Waiting for the Last of Two Blocks."

Thus the average latency for these two blocks will be half of 2/3 of the time for a single revolution, or $\frac{1}{2} \times \frac{2}{3} \times 8.33 = 2.78$ milliseconds. We thus have reduced the average time to access a block to $0.5 + 0.25 + 2.78 = 3.53$ milliseconds, about a third the average time for first-come-first-served scheduling. On the other hand, the 32,768 accesses take a total of 116 seconds, so the average delay in satisfying a request is almost a minute. □

11.5.5 Prefetching and Large-Scale Buffering

Our final suggestion for speeding up some secondary-memory algorithms is called *prefetching* or sometimes *double buffering*. In some applications we can predict the order in which blocks will be requested from disk. If so, then we can load them into main memory buffers before they are needed. One advantage to doing so is that we are thus better able to schedule the disk, such as by using the elevator algorithm, to reduce the average time needed to access a block. We could gain the speedup in block access suggested by Example 11.14 without the long delay in satisfying requests that we also saw in that example.

Example 11.15: For an example of the use of double buffering, let us again focus on the second phase of TPMMS. Recall that we merged 16 sorted sublists by bringing into main memory one block from each list. If we had so many sorted sublists to merge that one block from each would fill main memory, then we could not do any better. But in our example, there is plenty of main memory left over. For instance, we could devote two block buffers to each list and fill one buffer while records were being selected from the other during the merge. When a buffer is exhausted, we switch to the other buffer for the same list, with no delay. □

However, the scheme of Example 11.15 still takes whatever time is required to read all 100,000 blocks of the sorted sublists. We could combine prefetching with the cylinder-based strategy of Section 11.5.1 if we:

1. Store the sorted sublists on whole, consecutive cylinders, with the blocks on each track being consecutive blocks of the sorted sublist.

2. Read whole tracks or whole cylinders whenever we need some more records from a given list.

Example 11.16: To appreciate the benefit of track-sized or cylinder-sized reads, again let us consider the second phase of TPMMS. We have room in main memory for two track-sized buffers for each of the 16 lists. Recall a track of the Megatron 747 holds half a megabyte, so the total space requirement is 16 megabytes of main memory. We can read a track starting at any sector, so the time to read a track is essentially the average seek time plus the time for the disk to rotate once, or $6.46 + 8.33 = 14.79$ milliseconds. Since we must read all the blocks on 196 cylinders, or 3136 tracks, to read the 16 sorted sublists, the total time for reading of all data is about 46 seconds.

We can do even better if we use two cylinder-sized buffers per sorted sublist, and fill one while the other is being used. Since there are 16 tracks on a cylinder of the Megatron 747, we would need 32 buffers of 4 megabytes each, or 128 megabytes. We said that there was only 100 megabytes of main memory available, but 128 megabytes is quite reasonable as a main-memory size.

Using cylinder-sized buffers, we need only do a seek once per cylinder. The time to seek and read all 16 tracks of a cylinder is thus $6.46 + 16 \times 8.33 = 140$ milliseconds. The time to read all 196 cylinders is 196 times as long, or about 27 seconds. □

The ideas just discussed for reading have their analogs for writing. In the spirit of prefetching, we can delay the writing of buffered blocks, as long as we don't need to reuse the buffer immediately. This strategy allows us to avoid delays while we wait for a block to be written out.

However, much more powerful is the strategy of using large output buffers — track-sized or cylinder-sized. If our application permits us to write in such large chunks, then we can essentially eliminate seek time and rotational latency, and write to disk at the maximum transfer rate of the disk. For instance, if we modified the writing part of the second phase of our sorting algorithm so there were two output buffers of 4 megabytes each, then we could fill one buffer with sorted records, and write it to a cylinder at the same time we filled the other output buffer with the next sorted records. Then, the writing time would be 27 seconds, like the reading time in Example 11.16, and the entire phase 2 would take under a minute, just like the improved phase 1 of Example 11.11. A combination of the tricks of storing data on whole cylinders, cylinder-sized buffering, and prefetching has given us a sort in less than two minutes that takes 74 minutes by a naive disk-management strategy.

11.5.6 Summary of Strategies and Tradeoffs

We have seen five different "tricks" that can sometimes improve the performance of a disk system. They are:

1. Organizing data by cylinders.

2. Using several disks in place of one.

3. Mirroring disks.

4. Scheduling requests by the elevator algorithm.

5. Prefetching data in track- or cylinder-sized chunks.

We also considered their effect on two situations, which represent the extremes of disk-access requirements:

a) A very regular situation, exemplified by phase 1 of TPMMS, where blocks can be read and written in a sequence that can be predicted in advance, and there is only one process using the disk.

b) A collection of short processes, such as airline reservations or bank-account changes, that execute in parallel, share the same disk(s), and cannot be predicted in advance. Phase 2 of TPMMS has some of these characteristics.

Below we summarize the advantages and disadvantages of each of these methods for these applications and those in between.

Cylinder-Based Organization

- Advantage: Excellent for type (a) applications, where accesses can be predicted in advance, and only one process is using the disk.

- Disadvantage: No help for type (b) applications, where accesses are unpredictable.

Multiple Disks

- Advantage: Increases the rate at which read/write requests can be satisfied, for both types of applications.

- Problem: Read or write requests for the same disk cannot be satisfied at the same time, so speedup factor may be less than the factor by which the number of disks increases.

- Disadvantage: The cost of several small disks exceeds the cost of a single disk with the same total capacity.

Mirroring

- Advantage: Increases the rate at which read/write requests can be satisfied, for both types of applications; does not have the problem of colliding accesses mentioned for multiple disks.

- Advantage: Improves fault tolerance for all applications.

- Disadvantage: We must pay for two or more disks but get the storage capacity of only one.

Elevator Algorithm

- Advantage: Reduces the average time to read/write blocks when the accesses to blocks are unpredictable.

- Problem: The algorithm is most effective in situations where there are many waiting disk-access requests and therefore the average delay for the requesting processes is high.

Prefetching/Double Buffering

- Advantage: Speeds up access when the needed blocks are known but the timing of requests is data-dependent, as in phase 2 of TPMMS.

- Disadvantage: Requires extra main-memory buffers. No help when accesses are random.

11.5.7   Exercises for Section 11.5

Exercise 11.5.1: Suppose we are scheduling I/O requests for a Megatron 747 disk, and the requests in Fig. 11.15 are made, with the head initially at track 8000. At what time is each request seviced fully if:

a) We use the elevator algorithm (it is permissible to start moving in either direction at first).

Cylinder of Request	First time available
2000	0
12000	1
1000	10
10000	20

Figure 11.15: Arrival times for six block-access requests

b) We use first-come, first-served scheduling.

*! Exercise 11.5.2: Suppose we use two Megatron 747 disks as mirrors of one another. However, instead of allowing reads of any block from either disk, we keep the head of the first disk in the inner half of the cylinders, and the head of the second disk in the outer half of the cylinders. Assuming read requests are on random tracks, and we never have to write:

a) What is the average rate at which this system can read blocks?

b) How does this rate compare with the average rate for mirrored Megatron 747 disks with no restriction?

c) What disadvantages do you forsee for this system?

! Exercise 11.5.3: Let us explore the relationship between the arrival rate of requests, the throughput of the elevator algorithm, and the average delay of requests. To simplify the problem, we shall make the following assumptions:

1. A pass of the elevator algorithm always proceeds from the innermost to outermost track, or vice-versa, even if there are no requests at the extreme cylinders.

2. When a pass starts, only those requests that are already pending will be honored, not requests that come in while the pass is in progress, even if the head passes their cylinder.[8]

3. There will never be two requests for blocks on the same cylinder waiting on one pass.

Let A be the interarrival rate, that is the time between requests for block accesses. Assume that the system is in steady state, that is, it has been accepting and answering requests for a long time. For a Megatron 747 disk, compute as a function of A:

---

[8]The purpose of this assumption is to avoid having to deal with the fact that a typical pass of the elevator algorithm goes fast as first, as there will be few waiting requests where the head has recently been, and speeds up as it moves into an area of the disk where it has not recently been. The analysis of the way request density varies during a pass is an interesting exercise in its own right.

* a) The average time taken to perform one pass.

 b) The number of requests serviced on one pass.

 c) The average time a request waits for service.

*!! **Exercise 11.5.4 :** In Example 11.12, we saw how dividing the data to be sorted among four disks could allow more than one block to be read at a time. On the assumption that the merging phase generates read requests for blocks that are on random disks, and that all read requests are honored unless they are for a disk that is currently serving another request, what is the average number of disks that are serving requests at any time? Note: there are a two observations that simplify the problem:

 1. Once a request to read a block is unable to proceed, then the merging must stop and generate no more requests, because there is no data from the exhausted sublist that generated the unsatisfied read request.

 2. As soon as merging is able to proceed, it will generate a read request, since main-memory merging takes essentially no time compared with the time to satisfy a read request.

! **Exercise 11.5.5 :** If we are to read k randomly chosen blocks from one cylinder, on the average how far around the cylinder must we go before we pass all of the blocks?

11.6 Disk Failures

In this and the next section we shall consider the ways in which disks can fail and what can be done to mitigate these failures.

 1. The most common form of failure is an *intermittent failure*, where an attempt to read or write a sector is unsuccessful, but with repeated tries we are able to read or write successfully.

 2. A more serious form of failure is one in which a bit or bits are permanently corrupted, and it becomes impossible to read a sector correctly no matter how many times we try. This form of error is called *media decay*.

 3. A related type of error is a *write failure*, where we attempt to write a sector, but we can neither write successfully nor can we retrieve the previously written sector. A possible cause is that there was a power outage during the writing of the sector.

 4. The most serious form of disk failure is a *disk crash*, where the entire disk becomes unreadable, suddenly and permanently.

In this section we consider a simple model of disk failures. We cover parity checks as a way to detect intermittent failures. We also discuss "stable storage," a technique for organizing a disk so that media decays or failed writes do not result in permanent loss. In Section 11.7 we examine techniques collectively known as "RAID" for coping with disk crashes.

11.6.1 Intermittent Failures

Disk sectors are ordinarily stored with some redundant bits, which we discuss in Section 11.6.2. The purpose of these bits is to enable us to tell whether what we are reading from the sector is correct or not; they similarly allow us to tell whether a sector we wrote has been written correctly.

A useful model of disk reads is that the reading function returns a pair (w, s), where w is the data in the sector that is read, and s is a *status* bit that tells whether or not the read was successful; i.e., whether or not we can rely on w being the true contents of the sector. In an intermittent failure, we may get a status "bad" several times, but if the read function is repeated enough times (100 times is a typical limit), then eventually a status "good" will be returned, and we rely on the data returned with this status to be the correct contents of the disk sector. As we shall see in Section 11.6.2, there is a chance that we are being fooled; the status is "good" but the data returned is wrong. However, we can make the probability of this event as low as we like, if we add more redundancy to the sectors.

Writing of sectors can also profit by observing the status of what we write. As we mentioned in Section 11.3.5, we may try to read each sector after we write it and determine whether the write was successful. A straightforward way to perform the check is to read the sector and compare it with the sector we intended to write. However, instead of performing the complete comparison at the disk controller, it is simpler to attempt to read the sector and see if its status is "good." If so, we assume the write was correct, and if the status is "bad" then the write was apparently unsuccessful and must be repeated. Notice that, as with reading, we can be fooled if the status is "good" but the write was actually unsuccessful. Also as with reading, we can make the probability of such an event as small as we like.

11.6.2 Checksums

How a reading operation can determine the good/bad status of a sector may appear mysterious at first. Yet the technique used in modern disk drives is quite simple: each sector has some additional bits, called the *checksum*, that are set depending on the values of the data bits stored in that sector. If, on reading, we find that the checksum is not proper for the data bits, then we return status "bad"; otherwise we return "good." While there is a small probability that the data bits may be misread, but the incorrect bits happen to have the same checksum as the correct bits (and therefore incorrect bits will be given the status "good"), by using a sufficiently large number of checksum bits, we can reduce this probability to whatever small level we wish.

A simple form of checksum is based on the *parity* of all the bits in the sector. If there is an odd number of 1's among a collection of bits, we say the bits have *odd* parity, or that their parity bit is 1. Similarly, if there is an even number of 1's among the bits, then we say the bits have *even* parity, or that their parity bit is 0. As a result:

- The number of 1's among a collection of bits and their parity bit is always even.

When we write a sector, the disk controller can compute the parity bit and append it to the sequence of bits written in the sector. Thus, every sector will have even parity.

Example 11.17: If the sequence of bits in a sector were 01101000, then there is an odd number of 1's, so the parity bit is 1. If we follow this sequence by its parity bit we have 011010001. If the given sequence of bits were 11101110, we have an even number of 1's, and the parity bit is 0. The sequence followed by its parity bit is 111011100. Note that each of the nine-bit sequences constructed by adding a parity bit has even parity. □

Any one-bit error in reading or writing the bits and their parity bit results in a sequence of bits that has *odd parity*; i.e., the number of 1's is odd. It is easy for the disk controller to count the number of 1's and to determine the presence of an error if a sector has odd parity.

Of course, more than one bit of the sector may be corrupted. If so, the probability is 50% that the number of 1-bits will be even, and the error will not be detected. We can increase our chances of detecting even large numbers of errors if we keep several parity bits. For example, we could keep eight parity bits, one for the first bit of every byte, one for the second bit of every byte, and so on, up to the eighth and last bit of every byte. Then, on a massive error, the probability is 50% that any one parity bit will detect an error, and the chance that none of the eight do so is only one in 2^8, or 1/256. In general, if we use n independent bits as a checksum, then the chance of missing an error is only $1/2^n$. For instance, if we devote 4 bytes to a checksum, then there is only one chance in about four billion that the error will go undetected.

11.6.3   Stable Storage

While checksums will almost certainly detect the existence of a media failure or a failure to read or write correctly, it does not help us correct the error. Moreover, when writing we could find ourselves in a position where we overwrite the previous contents of a sector and yet cannot read the new contents. That situation could be serious in a situation where, say, we were adding a small increment to an account balance and have now lost both the original balance and the new balance. If we could be assured that the contents of the sector contained either the new or old balance, then we would only have to determine whether the write was successful or not.

To deal with the problems above, we can implement a policy known as *stable storage* on a disk or on several disks. The general idea is that sectors are paired, and each pair represents one sector-contents X. We shall refer to the pair of sectors representing X as the "left" and "right" copies, X_L and X_R. We continue to assume that the copies are written with a sufficient number of parity-check bits so that we can rule out the possibility that a bad sector looks good when the parity checks are considered. Thus, we shall assume that if the read function returns (w, good) for either X_L or X_R, then w is the true value of X. The stable-storage writing policy is:

1. Write the value of X into X_L. Check that the value has status "good"; i.e., the parity-check bits are correct in the written copy. If not, repeat the write. If after a set number of write attempts, we have not successfully written X into X_L, assume that there is a media failure in this sector. A fix-up such as substituting a spare sector for X_L must be adopted.

2. Repeat (1) for X_R.

The stable-storage reading policy is:

1. To obtain the value of X, read X_L. If status "bad" is returned, repeat the read a set number of times. If a value with status "good" is eventually returned, take that value as X.

2. If we cannot read X_L, repeat (1) with X_R.

11.6.4 Error-Handling Capabilities of Stable Storage

The policies described in Section 11.6.3 are capable of compensating for several different kinds of errors. We shall outline them here.

1. *Media failures.* If, after storing X in sectors X_L and X_R, one of them undergoes a media failure and becomes permanently unreadable, we can always read X from the other. If X_R has failed but X_L has not, then the read policy will correctly read X_L and not even look at X_R; we shall discover that X_R is failed when we next try to write a new value for X. If only X_L has failed, then we shall not be able to get a "good" status for X in any of our attempts to read X_L (recall that we assume a bad sector will always return status "bad," even though in reality there is a tiny chance that "good" will be returned because all the parity-check bits happen to match). Thus, we proceed to step (2) of the read algorithm and correctly read X from X_R. Note that if both X_L and X_R have failed, then we cannot read X, but the probability of both failing is extremely small.

2. *Write failure.* Suppose that as we write X, there is a system failure —
    e.g., a power outage. It is possible that X will be lost in main memory,
    and also the copy of X being written at the time will be garbled. For
    example, half the sector may be written with part of the new value of X,
    while the other half remains as it was. When the system becomes available
    and we examine X_L and X_R, we are sure to be able to determine either
    the old or new value of X. The possible cases are:

    (a) The failure occurred as we were writing X_L. Then we shall find that
        the status of X_L is "bad." However, since we never got to write X_R,
        its status will be "good" (unless there is a coincident media failure at
        X_R, which we rule out as extremely unlikely). Thus, we can obtain
        the old value of X. We may also copy X_R into X_L to repair the
        damage to X_L.

    (b) The failure occurred after we wrote X_L. Then we expect that X_L
        will have status "good," and we may read the new value of X from
        X_L. Note that X_R may have status bad, and we should copy X_L
        into X_R if so.

11.6.5 Exercises for Section 11.6

Exercise 11.6.1: Compute the parity bit for the following bit sequences:

* a) 00111011.

  b) 00000000.

  c) 10101101.

Exercise 11.6.2: We can have two parity bits associated with a string if we
follow the string by one bit that is a parity bit for the odd positions and a
second that is the parity bit for the even positions. For each of the strings in
Exercise 11.6.1, find the two bits that serve in this way.

11.7 Recovery from Disk Crashes

In this section, we shall consider the most serious mode of failure for disks — the
"head crash," where data is permanently destroyed. In this event, if data is not
backed up on another medium, such as a tape backup system, or on a mirror disk
as we discussed in Section 11.5.3, then there is nothing we can do to recover the
data. This situation represents a disaster for major DBMS applications, such
as banking and other financial applications, airline or other reservation-booking
databases, inventory-management systems, and many others.

There are a number of schemes that have been developed to reduce the risk
of data loss by disk crashes. They generally involve redundancy, extending
the idea of parity checks, as discussed in Section 11.6.2, or duplicated sectors,

as in Section 11.6.3. The common term for this class of strategies is RAID, or *Redundant Arrays of Independent Disks.*[9] Here, we shall discuss primarily three schemes, called RAID levels 4, 5, and 6. These RAID schemes also handle failures in the modes discussed in Section 11.6: media failures and corruption of data in a single sector due to a temporary system failure.

11.7.1 The Failure Model for Disks

To begin our discussion of disk crashes, we need to consider first the statistics of such failures. The simplest way to describe failure behavior is through a measurement known as *mean time to failure.* This number is the length of time by which 50% of a population of disks will have failed catastrophically, i.e., had a head crash so they are no longer readable. For modern disks, the mean time to failure is about 10 years.

The simplest way to use this number is to assume that one-tenth of all disks fail in a given year, in which case the survival percentage would be an exponentially decaying function. More realistically, the survival percentage of disks looks more like Fig. 11.16. As for most types of electronic equipment, many disk failures occur early in the life cycle, due to tiny defects in the manufacture of that disk. Hopefully, most of these are caught before the disk leaves the factory, but some do not show up for months. A disk that does not suffer an early failure will probably serve for many years. Later in the life cycle, factors such as "wear-and-tear" and the accumulated effects of tiny dust particles increase the chances of a crash.

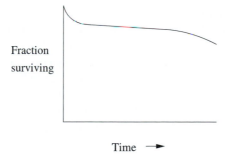

Figure 11.16: A survival rate curve for disks

However, the mean time to a disk crash does not have to be the same as the mean time to data loss. The reason is that there are a number of schemes available for assuring that if one disk fails, there are others to help recover the data of the failed disk. In the balance of this section, we shall study the most common schemes.

---

[9]Previously, the acronym RAID was translated as "Redundant Array of Inexpensive Disks," and this meaning may still appear in literature.

Each of these schemes starts with one or more disks that hold the data (we'll call these the *data disks*) and adding one or more disks that hold information that is completely determined by the contents of the data disks. The latter are called *redundant disks*. When there is a disk crash of either a data disk or a redundant disk, the other disks can be used to restore the failed disk, and there is no permanent information loss.

11.7.2 Mirroring as a Redundancy Technique

The simplest scheme is to mirror each disk, as discussed in Section 11.5.3. We shall call one of the disks the *data disk*, while the other is the *redundant disk*; which is which doesn't matter in this scheme. Mirroring, as a protection against data loss, is often referred to as *RAID level 1*. It gives a mean time to memory loss that is much greater than the mean time to disk failure, as the following example illustrates. Essentially, with mirroring and the other redundancy schemes we discuss, the only way data can be lost is if there is a second disk crash while the first crash is being repaired.

Example 11.18: Suppose each disk has a 10 year mean time to failure, which we shall take to mean that the probability of failure in any given year is 10%. If disks are mirrored, then when a disk fails, we have only to replace it with a good disk and copy the mirror disk to the new one. At the end, we have two disks that are mirrors of each other, and the system is restored to its former state.

The only thing that could go wrong is that during the copying the mirror disk fails. Now, both copies of at least part of the data have been lost, and there is no way to recover.

But how often will this sequence of events occur? Suppose that the process of replacing the failed disk takes 3 hours, which is 1/8 of a day, or 1/2920 of a year. Since we assume the average disk lasts 10 years, the probability that the mirror disk will fail during copying is $(1/10) \times (1/2920)$, or one in 29,200. If one disk fails every 10 years, then one of the two disks will fail once in 5 years on the average. One in every 29,200 of these failures results in data loss. Put another way, the mean time to a failure involving data loss is $5 \times 29,200 = 146,000$ years. □

11.7.3 Parity Blocks

While mirroring disks is an effective way to reduce the probability of a disk crash involving data loss, it uses as many redundant disks as there are data disks. Another approach, often called *RAID level 4*, uses only one redundant disk no matter how many data disks there are. We assume the disks are identical, so we can number the blocks on each disk from 1 to some number n. Of course, all the blocks on all the disks have the same number of bits; for instance, the 16,384-byte blocks in our Megatron 747 running example have $8 \times 16,384 = 131,072$ bits. In the redundant disk, the ith block consists of parity checks for the ith blocks of all the data disks. That is, the jth bits of all the ith blocks, including both the data disks and the redundant disk, must have an even number of 1's among them, and we always choose the bit of the redundant disk to make this condition true.

We saw in Example 11.17 how to force the condition to be true. In the redundant disk, we choose bit j to be 1 if an odd number of the data disks have 1 in that bit, and we choose bit j of the redundant disk to be 0 if there are an even number of 1's in that bit among the data disks. The term for this calculation is the *modulo-2 sum*. That is, the modulo-2 sum of bits is 0 if there are an even number of 1's among those bits, and 1 if there are an odd number of 1's.

Example 11.19 : Suppose for sake of an extremely simple example that blocks consist of only one byte — eight bits. Let there be three data disks, called 1, 2, and 3, and one redundant disk, called disk 4. Focus on, say, the first block of all these disks. If the data disks have in their first blocks the following bit sequences:

$$\text{disk 1: } 11110000$$
$$\text{disk 2: } 10101010$$
$$\text{disk 3: } 00111000$$

then the redundant disk will have in block 1 the parity check bits:

$$\text{disk 4: } 01100010$$

Notice how in each position, an even number of the four 8-bit sequences have 1's. There are two 1's in positions 1, 2, 4, 5, and 7, four 1's in position 3, and zero 1's in positions 6 and 8. □

Reading

Reading blocks from a data disk is no different from reading blocks from any disk. There is generally no reason to read from the redundant disk, but we could. In some circumstances, we can actually get the effect of two simultaneous reads from one of the data disks; the following example shows how, although the conditions under which it could be used are expected to be rare.

Example 11.20 : Suppose we are reading a block of the first data disk, and another request comes in to read a different block, say block 1, of the same data disk. Ordinarily, we would have to wait for the first request to finish. However, if none of the other disks are busy, we could read block 1 from each of them, and compute block 1 of the first disk by taking the modulo-2 sum.

Specifically, if the disks and their first blocks were as in Example 11.19, then we could read the second and third data disks and the redundant disk, to get the following blocks:

disk 2: 10101010
disk 3: 00111000
disk 4: 01100010

If we take the modulo-2 sum of the bits in each column, we get

disk 1: 11110000

which is the same as block 1 of the first disk.   □

Writing

When we write a new block of a data disk, we need not only to change that block, but we need to change the corresponding block of the redundant disk so it continues to hold the parity checks for the corresponding blocks of all the data disks. A naive approach would read the corresponding blocks of the n data disks, take their modulo-2 sum, and rewrite the block of the redundant disk. That approach requires a write of the data block that is rewritten, the reading of the $n - 1$ other data blocks, and a write of the block of the redundant disk. The total is thus $n + 1$ disk I/O's.

A better approach is to look only at the old and new versions of the data block i being rewritten. If we take their modulo-2 sum, we know in which positions there is a change in the number of 1's among the blocks numbered i on all the disks. Since these changes are always by one, any even number of 1's changes to an odd number. If we change the same positions of the redundant block, then the number of 1's in each position becomes even again. We can perform these calculations using four disk I/O's:

1. Read the old value of the data block being changed.

2. Read the corresponding block of the redundant disk.

3. Write the new data block.

4. Recalculate and write the block of the redundant disk.

Example 11.21 : Suppose the three first blocks of the data disks are as in Example 11.19:

disk 1: 11110000
disk 2: 10101010
disk 3: 00111000

Suppose also that the block on the second disk changes from 10101010 to 11001100. We take the modulo-2 sum of the old and new values of the block on disk 2, to get 01100110. That tells us we must change positions 2, 3, 6, and 7 of the first block of the redundant disk. We read that block: 01100010. We

---

The Algebra of Modulo-2 Sums

It may be helpful for understanding some of the tricks used with parity checks to know the algebraic rules involving the modulo-2 sum operation on bit vectors. We shall denote this operation $\oplus$. As an example, $1100 \oplus 1010 = 0110$. Here are some useful rules about $\oplus$:

- The *commutative law*: $x \oplus y = y \oplus x$.

- The *associative law*: $x \oplus (y \oplus z) = (x \oplus y) \oplus z$.

- The all-0 vector of the appropriate length, which we denote $\bar{0}$, is the *identity* for $\oplus$; that is, $x \oplus \bar{0} = \bar{0} \oplus x = x$.

- $\oplus$ is its own inverse: $x \oplus x = \bar{0}$. As a useful consequence, if $x \oplus y = z$, then we can "add" x to both sides and get $y = x \oplus z$.

---

replace this block by a new block that we get by changing the appropriate positions; in effect we replace the redundant block by the modulo-2 sum of itself and 01100110, to get 00000100. Another way to express the new redundant block is that it is the modulo-2 sum of the old and new versions of the block being rewritten and the old value of the redundant block. In our example, the first blocks of the four disks — three data disks and one redundant — have become

$$
\begin{aligned}
&\text{disk 1: } 11110000 \\
&\text{disk 2: } 11001100 \\
&\text{disk 3: } 00111000 \\
&\text{disk 4: } 00000100
\end{aligned}
$$

after the write to the block on the second disk and the necessary recomputation of the redundant block. Notice that in the blocks above, each column continues to have an even number of 1's.

Incidentally, notice that this write of a data block, like all writes of data blocks using the scheme described above, takes four disk I/O's. The naive scheme — read all but the rewritten block and recompute the redundant block directly — would also require four disk I/O's in this example: two to read data from the first and third data disks, and two to write the second data disk and the redundant disk. However, if we had more than three data disks, the number of I/O's for the naive scheme rises linearly with the number of data disks, while the cost of the scheme advocated here continues to require only four. □

Failure Recovery

Now, let us consider what we would do if one of the disks crashed. If it is the redundant disk, we swap in a new disk, and recompute the redundant blocks. If the failed disk is one of the data disks, then we need to swap in a good disk and recompute its data from the other disks. The rule for recomputing any missing data is actually simple, and doesn't depend on which disk, data or redundant, is failed. Since we know that the number of 1's among corresponding bits of all disks is even, it follows that:

- The bit in any position is the modulo-2 sum of all the bits in the corresponding positions of all the other disks.

If one doubts the above rule, one has only to consider the two cases. If the bit in question is 1, then the number of corresponding bits that are 1 must be odd, so their modulo-2 sum is 1. If the bit in question is 0, then there are an even number of 1's among the corresponding bits, and their modulo-2 sum is 0.

Example 11.22: Suppose that disk 2 fails. We need to recompute each block of the replacement disk. Following Example 11.19, let us see how to recompute the first block of the second disk. We are given the corresponding blocks of the first and third data disks and the redundant disk, so the situation looks like:

$$
\begin{aligned}
&\text{disk 1: } 11110000\\
&\text{disk 2: } ????????\\
&\text{disk 3: } 00111000\\
&\text{disk 4: } 01100010
\end{aligned}
$$

If we take the modulo-2 sum of each column, we deduce that the missing block is 10101010, as was initially the case in Example 11.19.   □

11.7.4   An Improvement: RAID 5

The RAID level 4 strategy described in Section 11.7.3 effectively preserves data unless there are two, almost-simultaneous disk crashes. However, it suffers from a bottleneck defect that we can see when we re-examine the process of writing a new data block. Whatever scheme we use for updating the disks, we need to read and write the redundant disk's block. If there are n data disks, then the number of disk writes to the redundant disk will be n times the average number of writes to any one data disk.

However, as we observed in Example 11.22, the rule for recovery is the same as for the data disks and redundant disks: take the modulo-2 sum of corresponding bits of the other disks. Thus, we do not have to treat one disk as the redundant disk and the others as data disks. Rather, we could treat each disk as the redundant disk for some of the blocks. This improvement is often called *RAID level 5*.

For instance, if there are $n + 1$ disks numbered 0 through n, we could treat the ith cylinder of disk j as redundant if j is the remainder when i is divided by $n + 1$.

Example 11.23 : In our running example, $n = 3$ so there are 4 disks. The first disk, numbered 0, is redundant for its cylinders numbered 4, 8, 12, and so on, because these are the numbers that leave remainder 0 when divided by 4. The disk numbered 1 is redundant for blocks numbered 1, 5, 9, and so on; disk 2 is redundant for blocks 2, 6, 10,..., and disk 3 is redundant for 3, 7, 11,.... .

As a result, the reading and writing load for each disk is the same. If all blocks are equally likely to be written, then for one write, each disk has a 1/4 chance that the block is on that disk. If not, then it has a 1/3 chance that it will be the redundant disk for that block. Thus, each of the four disks is involved in $\frac{1}{4} + \frac{3}{4} \times \frac{1}{3} = \frac{1}{2}$ of the writes. □

11.7.5 Coping With Multiple Disk Crashes

There is a theory of error-correcting codes that allows us to deal with any number of disk crashes — data or redundant — if we use enough redundant disks. This strategy leads to the highest RAID "level," *RAID level 6.* We shall give only a simple example here, where two simultaneous crashes are correctable, and the strategy is based on the simplest error-correcting code, known as a *Hamming code.*

In our description we focus on a system with seven disks, numbered 1 through 7. The first four are data disks, and disks 5 through 7 are redundant. The relationship between data and redundant disks is summarized by the 3×7 matrix of 0's and 1's in Fig. 11.17. Notice that:

a) Every possible column of three 0's and 1's, except for the all-0 column, appears in the matrix of Fig. 11.17.

b) The columns for the redundant disks have a single 1.

c) The columns for the data disks each have at least two 1's.

		Data				Redundant	
Disk number	1	2	3	4	5	6	7
	1	1	1	0	1	0	0
	1	1	0	1	0	1	0
	1	0	1	1	0	0	1

Figure 11.17: Redundancy pattern for a system that can recover from two simultaneous disk crashes

The meaning of each of the three rows of 0's and 1's is that if we look at the corresponding bits from all seven disks, and restrict our attention to those disks that have 1 in that row, then the modulo-2 sum of these bits must be 0. Put another way, the disks with 1 in a given row of the matrix are treated as if they were the entire set of disks in a RAID level 4 scheme. Thus, we can compute the bits of one of the redundant disks by finding the row in which that disk has 1, and taking the modulo-2 sum of the corresponding bits of the other disks that have 1 in the same row.

For the matrix of Fig. 11.17, this rule implies:

1. The bits of disk 5 are the modulo-2 sum of the corresponding bits of disks 1, 2, and 3.

2. The bits of disk 6 are the modulo-2 sum of the corresponding bits of disks 1, 2, and 4.

3. The bits of disk 7 are the modulo-2 sum of the corresponding bits of disks 1, 3, and 4.

We shall see shortly that the particular choice of bits in this matrix gives us a simple rule by which we can recover from two simultaneous disk crashes.

Reading

We may read data from any data disk normally. The redundant disks can be ignored.

Writing

The idea is similar to the writing strategy outlined in Section 11.7.4, but now several redundant disks may be involved. To write a block of some data disk, we compute the modulo-2 sum of the new and old versions of that block. These bits are then added, in a modulo-2 sum, to the corresponding blocks of all those redundant disks that have 1 in a row in which the written disk also has 1.

Example 11.24: Let us again assume that blocks are only eight bits long, and focus on the first blocks of the seven disks involved in our RAID level 6 example. First, suppose the data and redundant first blocks are as given in Fig. 11.18. Notice that the block for disk 5 is the modulo-2 sum of the blocks for the first three disks, the sixth row is the modulo-2 sum of rows 1, 2, and 4, and the last row is the modulo-2 sum of rows 1, 3, and 4.

Suppose we rewrite the first block of disk 2 to be 00001111. If we sum this sequence of bits modulo-2 with the sequence 10101010 that is the old value of this block, we get 10100101. If we look at the column for disk 2 in Fig. 11.17, we find that this disk has 1's in the first two rows, but not the third. Since redundant disks 5 and 6 have 1 in rows 1 and 2, respectively, we must perform the sum modulo-2 operation on the current contents of their first blocks and

Disk	Contents
1)	11110000
2)	10101010
3)	00111000
4)	01000001
5)	01100010
6)	00011011
7)	10001001

Figure 11.18: First blocks of all disks

the sequence 10100101 just calculated. That is, we flip the values of positions 1, 3, 6, and 8 of these two blocks. The resulting contents of the first blocks of all disks is shown in Fig. 11.19. Notice that the new contents continue to satisfy the constraints implied by Fig. 11.17: the modulo-2 sum of corresponding blocks that have 1 in a particular row of the matrix of Fig. 11.17 is still all 0's. □

Disk	Contents
1)	11110000
2)	00001111
3)	00111000
4)	01000001
5)	11000111
6)	10111110
7)	10001001

Figure 11.19: First blocks of all disks after rewriting disk 2 and changing the redundant disks

Failure Recovery

Now, let us see how the redundancy scheme outlined above can be used to correct up to two simultaneous disk crashes. Let the failed disks be a and b. Since all columns of the matrix of Fig. 11.17 are different, we must be able to find some row r in which the columns for a and b are different. Suppose that a has 0 in row r, while b has 1 there.

Then we can compute the correct b by taking the modulo-2 sum of corresponding bits from all the disks other than b that have 1 in row r. Note that a is not among these, so none of them have failed. Having done so, we must recompute a, with all other disks available. Since every column of the matrix

of Fig. 11.17 has a 1 in some row, we can use this row to recompute disk a by
taking the modulo-2 sum of bits of those other disks with a 1 in this row.

Disk	Contents
1)	11110000
2)	????????
3)	00111000
4)	01000001
5)	????????
6)	10111110
7)	10001001

Figure 11.20: Situation after disks 2 and 5 fail

Example 11.25 : Suppose that disks 2 and 5 fail at about the same time.
Consulting the matrix of Fig. 11.17, we find that the columns for these two
disks differ in row 2, where disk 2 has 1 but disk 5 has 0. We may thus
reconstruct disk 2 by taking the modulo-2 sum of corresponding bits of disks
1, 4, and 6, the other three disks with 1 in row 2. Notice that none of these
three disks has failed. For instance, following from the situation regarding the
first blocks in Fig. 11.19, we would initially have the data of Fig. 11.20 available
after disks 2 and 5 failed.

If we take the modulo-2 sum of the contents of the blocks of disks 1, 4, and
6, we find that the block for disk 2 is 00001111. This block is correct as can be
verified from Fig. 11.19. The situation is now as in Fig. 11.21.

Disk	Contents
1)	11110000
2)	00001111
3)	00111000
4)	01000001
5)	????????
6)	10111110
7)	10001001

Figure 11.21: After recovering disk 2

Now, we see that disk 5's column in Fig. 11.17 has a 1 in the first row. We
can therefore recompute disk 5 by taking the modulo-2 sum of corresponding
bits from disks 1, 2, and 3, the other three disks that have 1 in the first row.
For block 1, this sum is 11000111. Again, the correctness of this calculation
can be confirmed by Fig. 11.19. □

Additional Observations About RAID Level 6

1. We can combine the ideas of RAID levels 5 and 6, by varying the redundant disks according to the block or cylinder number. Doing so will avoid bottlenecks when writing; the scheme described in Section 11.7.5 will cause bottlenecks at the redundant disks.

2. The scheme described in Section 11.7.5 is not restricted to four data disks. The number of disks can be one less than any power of 2, say $2^k - 1$. Of these disks, k are redundant, and the remaining $2^k - k - 1$ are data disks, so the redundancy grows roughly as the logarithm of the number of data disks. For any k, we can construct the matrix corresponding to Fig. 11.17 by writing all possible columns of k 0's and 1's, except the all-0's column. The columns with a single 1 correspond to the redundant disks, and the columns with more than one 1 are the data disks.

11.7.6 Exercises for Section 11.7

Exercise 11.7.1: Suppose we use mirrored disks as in Example 11.18, the failure rate is 4% per year, and it takes 8 hours to replace a disk. What is the mean time to a disk failure involving loss of data?

*! **Exercise 11.7.2:** Suppose that a disk has probability F of failing in a given year, and it takes H hours to replace a disk.

    a) If we use mirrored disks, what is the mean time to data loss, as a function of F and H?

    b) If we use a RAID level 4 or 5 scheme, with N disks, what is the mean time to data loss?

!! **Exercise 11.7.3:** Suppose we use three disks as a mirrored group; i.e., all three hold identical data. If the yearly probability of failure for one disk is F, and it takes H hours to restore a disk, what is the mean time to data loss?

Exercise 11.7.4: Suppose we are using a RAID level 4 scheme with four data disks and one redundant disk. As in Example 11.19 assume blocks are a single byte. Give the block of the redundant disk if the corresponding blocks of the data disks are:

  * a) 01010110, 11000000, 00111011, and 11111011.

    b) 11110000, 11111000, 00111111, and 00000001.

Error-Correcting Codes and RAID Level 6

There is a theory that guides our selection of a suitable matrix, like that of Fig. 11.17, to determine the content of redundant disks. A *code* of length n is a set of bit-vectors (called *code words*) of length n. The *Hamming distance* between two code words is the number of positions in which they differ, and the *minimum distance* of a code is the smallest Hamming distance of any two different code words.

If C is any code of length n, we can require that the corresponding bits on n disks have one of the sequences that are members of the code. As a very simple example, if we are using a disk and its mirror, then $n = 2$, and we can use the code $C = \{00, 11\}$. That is, the corresponding bits of the two disks must be the same. For another example, the matrix of Fig. 11.17 defines the code consisting of the 16 bit-vectors of length 7 that have arbitrary values for the first four bits and have the remaining three bits determined by the rules for the three redundant disks.

If the minimum distance of a code is d, then disks whose corresponding bits are required to be a vector in the code will be able to tolerate $d - 1$ simultaneous disk crashes. The reason is that, should we obscure $d - 1$ positions of a code word, and there were two different ways these positions could be filled in to make a code word, then the two code words would have to differ in at most the $d - 1$ positions. Thus, the code could not have minimum distance d. As an example, the matrix of Fig. 11.17 actually defines the well-known *Hamming code*, which has minimum distance 3. Thus, it can handle two disk crashes.

Exercise 11.7.5: Using the same RAID level 4 scheme as in Exercise 11.7.4, suppose that data disk 1 has failed. Recover the block of that disk under the following circumstances:

* a) The contents of disks 2 through 4 are 01010110, 11000000, and 00111011, while the redundant disk holds 11111011.

  b) The contents of disks 2 through 4 are 11110000, 11111000, and 00111111, while the redundant disk holds 00000001.

Exercise 11.7.6: Suppose the block on the first disk in Exercise 11.7.4 is changed to 10101010. What changes to the corresponding blocks on the other disks must be made?

Exercise 11.7.7: Suppose we have the RAID level 6 scheme of Example 11.24, and the blocks of the four data disks are 00111100, 11000111, 01010101, and 10000100, respectively.

a) What are the corresponding blocks of the redundant disks?

b) If the third disk's block is rewritten to be 10000000, what steps must be taken to change other disks?

Exercise 11.7.8: Describe the steps taken to recover from the following failures using the RAID level 6 scheme with seven disks:

* a) Disks 1 and 7.

b) Disks 1 and 4.

c) Disks 3 and 6.

Exercise 11.7.9: Find a RAID level 6 scheme using 15 disks, four of which are redundant. *Hint*: Generalize the 7-disk Hamming matrix.

Exercise 11.7.10: List the 16 code words for the Hamming code of length 7. That is, what are the 16 lists of bits that could be corresponding bits on the seven disks of the RAID level 6 scheme based on the matrix of Fig. 11.17?

Exercise 11.7.11: Suppose we have four disks, of which disks 1 and 2 are data disks, and disks 3 and 4 are redundant. Disk 3 is a mirror of disk 1. Disk 4 holds the parity check bits for the corresponding bits of disks 2 and 3.

a) Express this situation by giving a parity check matrix analogous to Fig. 11.17.

!! b) It is possible to recover from *some* but not all situations where two disks fail at the same time. Determine for which pairs it is possible to recover and for which pairs it is not.

*! **Exercise 11.7.12:** Suppose we have eight data disks numbered 1 through 8, and three redundant disks: 9, 10, and 11. Disk 9 is a parity check on disks 1 through 4, and disk 10 is a parity check on disks 5 through 8. If all pairs of disks are equally likely to fail simultaneously, and we want to maximize the probability that we can recover from the simultaneous failure of two disks, then on which disks should disk 11 be a parity check?

!! **Exercise 11.7.13:** Find a RAID level 6 scheme with ten disks, such that it is possible to recover from the failure of any three disks simultaneously. You should use as many data disks as you can.

11.8 Summary of Chapter 11

✦ *Memory Hierarchy*: A computer system uses storage components ranging over many orders of magnitude in speed, capacity, and cost per bit. From the smallest/most expensive to largest/cheapest, they are: cache, main memory, secondary memory (disk), and tertiary memory.

♦ *Tertiary Storage*: The principal devices for tertiary storage are tape cassettes, tape silos (mechanical devices for managing tape cassettes), and "juke boxes" (mechanical devices for managing CD-ROM disks). These storage devices have capacities of many terabytes, but are the slowest available storage devices.

♦ *Disks/Secondary Storage*: Secondary storage devices are principally magnetic disks with multigigabyte capacities. Disk units have several circular platters of magnetic material, with concentric tracks to store bits. Platters rotate around a central spindle. The tracks at a given radius from the center of a platter form a cylinder.

♦ *Blocks and Sectors*: Tracks are divided into sectors, which are separated by unmagnetized gaps. Sectors are the unit of reading and writing from the disk. Blocks are logical units of storage used by an application such as a DBMS. Blocks typically consist of several sectors.

♦ *Disk Controller*: The disk controller is a processor that controls one or more disk units. It is responsible for moving the disk heads to the proper cylinder to read or write a requested track. It also may schedule competing requests for disk access and buffers the blocks to be read or written.

♦ *Disk Access Time*: The latency of a disk is the time between a request to read or write a block, and the time the access is completed. Latency is caused principally by three factors: the seek time to move the heads to the proper cylinder, the rotational latency during which the desired block rotates under the head, and the transfer time, while the block moves under the head and is read or written.

♦ *Moore's Law*: A consistent trend sees parameters such as processor speed and capacities of disk and main memory doubling every 18 months. However, disk access times shrink little if at all in a similar period. An important consequence is that the (relative) cost of accessing disk appears to grow as the years progress.

♦ *Algorithms Using Secondary Storage*: When the data is so large it does not fit in main memory, the algorithms used to manipulate the data must take into account the fact that reading and writing disk blocks between disk and memory often takes much longer than it does to process the data once it is in main memory. The evaluation of algorithms for data in secondary storage thus focuses on the number of disk I/O's required.

♦ *Two-Phase, Multiway Merge-Sort*: This algorithm for sorting is capable of sorting enormous amounts of data on disk using only two disk reads and two disk writes of each datum. It is the sorting method of choice in most database applications.

✦ *Speeding Up Disk Access*: There are several techniques for accessing disk blocks faster for some applications. They include dividing the data among several disks (to allow parallel access), mirroring disks (maintaining several copies of the data, also to allow parallel access), organizing data that will be accessed together by tracks or cylinders, and prefetching or double buffering by reading or writing entire tracks or cylinders together.

✦ *Elevator Algorithm*: We can also speed accesses by queueing access requests and handling them in an order that allows the heads to make one sweep across the disk. The heads stop to handle a request each time it reaches a cylinder containing one or more blocks with pending access requests.

✦ *Disk Failure Modes*: To avoid loss of data, systems must be able to handle errors. The principal types of disk failure are intermittent (a read or write error that will not reoccur if repeated), permanent (data on the disk is corrupted and cannot be properly read), and the disk crash, where the entire disk becomes unreadable.

✦ *Checksums*: By adding a parity check (extra bit to make the number of 1's in a bit string even), intermittent failures and permanent failures can be detected, although not corrected.

✦ *Stable Storage*: By making two copies of all data and being careful about the order in which those copies are written, a single disk can be used to protect against almost all permanent failures of a single sector.

✦ *RAID*: There are several schemes for using an extra disk or disks to enable data to survive a disk crash. RAID level 1 is mirroring of disks; level 4 adds a disk whose contents are a parity check on corresponding bits of all other disks, level 5 varies the disk holding the parity bit to avoid making the parity disk a writing bottleneck. Level 6 involves the use of error-correcting codes and may allow survival after several simultaneous disk crashes.

11.9 References for Chapter 11

The RAID idea can be traced back to [6] on disk striping. The name and error-correcting capability is from [5].

The model of disk failures in Section 11.6 appears in unpublished work of Lampson and Sturgis [4].

There are several useful surveys of material relevant to this chapter. [2] discusses trends in disk storage and similar systems. A study of RAID systems is in [1]. [7] surveys algorithms suitable for the secondary storage model (block model) of computation.

[3] is an important study of how one optimizes a system involving processor, memory, and disk, to perform specific tasks.

1. P. M. Chen et al., "RAID: high-performance, reliable secondary storage," *Computing Surveys* **26**:2 (1994), pp. 145–186.

2. G. A. Gibson et al., "Strategic directions in storage I/O issues in large-scale computing," *Computing Surveys* **28**:4 (1996), pp. 779–793.

3. J. N. Gray and F. Putzolo, "The five minute rule for trading memory for disk accesses and the 10 byte rule for trading memory for CPU time," *Proc. ACM SIGMOD Intl. Conf. on Management of Data* (1987), pp. 395–398.

4. B. Lampson and H. Sturgis, "Crash recovery in a distributed data storage system," Technical report, Xerox Palo Alto Research Center, 1976.

5. D. A. Patterson, G. A. Gibson, and R. H. Katz, "A case for redundant arrays of inexpensive disks," *Proc. ACM SIGMOD Intl. Conf. on Management of Data*, pp. 109–116, 1988.

6. K. Salem and H. Garcia-Molina, "Disk striping," *Proc. Second Intl. Conf. on Data Engineering*, pp. 336–342, 1986.

7. J. S. Vitter, "External memory algorithms," *Proc. Seventeenth Annual ACM Symposium on Principles of Database Systems*, pp. 119–128, 1998.

Chapter 12

Representing Data Elements

This chapter relates the block model of secondary storage that we covered in Section 11.4 to the requirements of a DBMS. We begin by looking at the way that relations or sets of objects are represented in secondary storage.

- Attributes need to be represented by fixed- or variable-length sequences of bytes, called "fields."

- Fields, in turn, are put together in fixed- or variable-length collections called "records," which correspond to tuples or objects.

- Records need to be stored in physical blocks. Various data structures are useful, especially if blocks of records need to be reorganized when the database is modified.

- A collection of records that forms a relation or the extent of a class is stored as a collection of blocks, called a *file*.[1] To support efficient querying and modification of these collections, we put one of a number of "index" structures on the file; these structures are the subject of Chapters 13 and 14.

12.1 Data Elements and Fields

We shall begin by looking at the representation of the most basic data elements: the values of attributes found in relational or object-oriented database systems. These are represented by "fields." Subsequently, we shall see how fields are put

---

[1] The database notion of a "file" is somewhat more general than the "file" in an operating system. While a database file could be an unstructured stream of bytes, it is more common for the file to consist of a collection of blocks organized in some useful way, with indexes or other specialized access methods. We discuss these organizations in Chapter 13.

together to form the larger elements of a storage system: records, blocks, and files.

12.1.1 Representing Relational Database Elements

Suppose we have declared a relation in an SQL system, by a CREATE TABLE statement such as that of Fig. 12.1, which repeats the definition in Fig. 6.16. The DBMS has the job of representing and storing the relation described by this declaration. Since a relation is a set of tuples, and tuples are similar to records or "structs" (the C or C++ term), we may imagine that each tuple will be stored on disk as a record. The record will occupy (part of) some disk block, and within the record there will be one field for every attribute of the relation.

```
CREATE TABLE MovieStar(
    name CHAR(30) PRIMARY KEY,
    address VARCHAR(255),
    gender CHAR(1),
    birthdate DATE
);
```

Figure 12.1: An SQL table declaration

While the general idea appears simple, the "devil is in the details," and we shall have to discuss a number of issues:

1. How do we represent SQL datatypes as fields?

2. How do we represent tuples as records?

3. How do we represent collections of records or tuples in blocks of memory?

4. How do we represent and store relations as collections of blocks?

5. How do we cope with record sizes that may be different for different tuples or that do not divide the block size evenly, or both?

6. What happens if the size of a record changes because some field is updated? How do we find space within its block, especially when the record grows?

The first item is the subject of this section. The next two items are covered in Section 12.2. We shall discuss the last two in Sections 12.4 and 12.5, respectively. The fourth question — representing relations so their tuples can be accessed efficiently — will be studied in Chapter 13.

Further, we need to consider how to represent certain kinds of data that are found in modern object-relational or object-oriented systems, such as object identifiers (or other pointers to records) and "blobs" (binary, large objects, such as a 2-gigabyte MPEG video). These matters are addressed in Sections 12.3 and 12.4.

12.1.2 Representing Objects

To a first approximation, an object is a tuple, and its fields or "instance variables" are attributes. Likewise, tuples in object-relational systems resemble tuples in ordinary, relational systems. However, there are two important extensions beyond what we discussed in Section 12.1.1:

1. Objects can have *methods* or special-purpose functions associated with them. The code for these functions is part of the schema for a class of objects.

2. Objects may have an *object identifier* (OID), which is an address in some global address space that refers uniquely to that object. Moreover, objects can have relationships to other objects, and these relationships are represented by pointers or lists of pointers.

Methods are generally stored with the schema, since they properly belong to the database as a whole, rather than any particular object. However, to access methods, the record for an object needs to have a field that indicates what class it belongs to.

Techniques for representing addresses, whether object ID's or references to other objects, are discussed in Section 12.3. Relationships that are part of an object, as are permitted in ODL, also require care in storage. Since we don't know how many related objects there can be (at least not in the case of a many-many relationship or the "many" side of a many-one relationship), we must represent the relationship by a "variable-length record," the subject of Section 12.4.

12.1.3 Representing Data Elements

Let us begin by considering how the principal SQL datatypes are represented as fields of a record. Ultimately, all data is represented as a sequence of bytes. For example, an attribute of type INTEGER is normally represented by two or four bytes, and an attribute of type FLOAT is normally represented by four or eight bytes. The integers and real numbers are represented by bit strings that are specially interpreted by the machine's hardware so the usual arithmetic operations can be performed on them.

Fixed-Length Character Strings

The simplest kind of character strings to represent are those described by the SQL type CHAR(n). These are fixed-length character strings of length n. The

A Note on Terminology

Depending on whether you have experience with file systems, conventional programming languages like C, with relational database languages (SQL in particular), or object-oriented languages (e.g., Smalltalk, C++, or the object-oriented database language OQL), you may know different terms for essentially the same concepts. The following table summarizes the correspondence, although there are some differences, e.g., a class can have methods; a relation cannot.

	Data Element	Record	Collection
Files	field	record	file
C	field	struct	array, file
SQL	attribute	tuple	relation
OQL	attribute, relationship	object	extent (of a class)

We shall tend to use file-system terms — fields and records — unless we are referring to specific uses of these concepts in database applications. In the latter case we shall use relational and/or object-oriented terms.

field for an attribute with this type is an array of n bytes. Should the value for this attribute be a string of length shorter than n, then the array is filled out with a special *pad* character, whose 8-bit code is not one of the legal characters for SQL strings.

Example 12.1: If an attribute A were declared to have type CHAR(5), then the field corresponding to A in all tuples is an array of five characters. If in one tuple the component for attribute A were 'cat', then the value of the array would be:

$$c \; a \; t \; \perp \; \perp$$

Here, $\perp$ is the "pad" character, which occupies the fourth and fifth bytes of the array. Note that the quote marks, which are needed to indicate a character string in SQL programs, are not stored with the value of the string. □

Variable-Length Character Strings

Sometimes the values in a column of a relation are character strings whose length may vary widely. The SQL type VARCHAR(n) is often used as the type of such a column. However, there is an intended implementation of attributes declared this way, in which $n + 1$ bytes are dedicated to the value of the string regardless of how long it is. Thus, the SQL VARCHAR type actually represents fields of fixed length, although its value has a length that varies. We shall examine character strings whose representation's length varies in Section 12.4. There are two common representations for `VARCHAR` strings:

1. *Length plus content.* We allocate an array of $n+1$ bytes. The first byte holds, as an 8-bit integer, the number of bytes in the string. The string cannot exceed n characters, and n itself cannot exceed 255, or we shall not be able to represent the length in a single byte.[2] The second and subsequent bytes hold the characters of the string. Any bytes of the array that are not used, because the string is shorter than the maximum possible, are ignored. These bytes cannot possibly be construed as part of the value, because the first byte tells us when the string ends.

2. *Null-terminated string.* Again allocate an array of $n+1$ bytes for the value of the string. Fill this array with the characters of the string, followed by a *null* character, which is not one of the legal characters that can appear in character strings. As with the first method, unused positions of the array cannot be construed as part of the value; here the null terminator warns us not to look further, and also makes the representation of `VARCHAR` strings compatible with that of character strings in C.

Example 12.2 : Suppose attribute A is declared `VARCHAR(10)`. We allocate an array of 11 characters in each tuple's record for the value of A. Suppose `'cat'` is the string to represent. Then in method 1, we would put 3 in the first byte to represent the length of the string, and the next three characters would be the string itself. The final seven positions are irrelevant. Thus, the value appears as:

$$3\ \text{c}\ \text{a}\ \text{t}$$

Note that the "3" is the 8-bit integer 3, i.e., 00000011, not the character '3'.

In the second method, we fill the first three positions with the string; the fourth is the null character (for which we use the symbol $\perp$, as we did for the "pad" character), and the remaining seven positions are irrelevant. Thus,

$$\text{c}\ \text{a}\ \text{t}\ \perp$$

is the representation of `'cat'` as a null-terminated string. □

Dates and Times

A date is usually represented as a fixed-length character string, as discussed in Section 6.1.4. Thus, a date can be represented just as we would represent any other fixed-length character string. Times may similarly be represented as if they were character strings. However, the SQL standard also allows a value of type `TIME` to include fractions of a second. Since such strings are of arbitrary length, we have two choices:

---

[2]Of course we could use a scheme in which two or more bytes are dedicated to the length.

1. The system can put a limit on the precision of times, and times can then be stored as if they were type VARCHAR(n), where n is the greatest length a time can have: 9 plus the number of fractional digits allowed in seconds.

2. Times can be stored as true variable-length values and dealt with as discussed in Section 12.4.

Bits

A sequence of bits — that is, data described in SQL by the type BIT(n) — can be packed eight to a byte. If n is not divisible by 8, then we are best off ignoring the unused bits of the last byte. For instance, the bit sequence 010111110011 might be represented by 01011111 as the first byte and 00110000 as the second; the final four 0's are not part of any field. As a special case, we can represent a boolean value, that is, a single bit, as 10000000 for true and 00000000 for false. However, it may in some contexts be easier to test a boolean if we make the distinction appear in all bits; i.e., use 11111111 for true and 00000000 for false.

Enumerated Types

Sometimes it is useful to have an attribute whose values take on a small, fixed set of values. These values are given symbolic names, and the type consisting of all those names is an *enumerated type*. Common examples of enumerated types are days of the week, e.g., {SUN, MON, TUE, WED, THU, FRI, SAT}, or a set of colors, e.g., {RED, GREEN, BLUE, YELLOW}.

We can represent the values of an enumerated type by integer codes, using only as many bytes as needed. For instance, we could represent RED by 0, GREEN by 1, BLUE by 2, and YELLOW by 3. These integers can each be represented by two bits, 00, 01, 10, and 11, respectively. It is more convenient, however, to use full bytes for representing integers chosen from a small set. For example, YELLOW is represented by the integer 3, which is 00000011 as an eight-bit byte. Any enumerated type with up to 256 values can be represented by a single byte. If the enumerated type has up to 2^{16} values, a short integer of two bytes will suffice, and so on.

12.2 Records

We shall now begin the discussion of how fields are grouped together into records. The study continues in Section 12.4, where we look at variable-length fields and records.

In general, each type of record used by a database system must have a *schema*, which is stored by the database. The schema includes the names and data types of fields in the record, and their offsets within the record. The schema is consulted when it is necessary to access components of the record.

Packing Fields Into a Single Byte

One may be tempted to take advantage of fields that have small enumerated types or that are boolean-valued, to pack several fields into a single byte. For instance, if we had three fields that were a boolean, a day of the week, and one of four colors, respectively, we could use one bit for the first, 3 bits for the second, and two bits for the third, put them all in a single byte and still have two bits left over. There is no impediment to doing so, but it makes retrieval of values from one of the fields or the writing of new values for one of the fields more complex and error-prone. Such packing of fields used to be more important when storage space was more expensive. Today, we do not advise it in common situations.

12.2.1 Building Fixed-Length Records

Tuples are represented by records consisting of the sorts of fields discussed in Section 12.1.3. The simplest situation occurs when all the fields of the record have a fixed length. We may then concatenate the fields to form the record.

Example 12.3: Consider the declaration of the `MovieStar` relation in Fig. 12.1. There are four fields:

1. `name`, a 30-byte string of characters.

2. `address`, of type `VARCHAR(255)`. This field will be represented by 256 bytes, using the schema discussed in Example 12.2.

3. `gender`, a single byte, which we suppose will always hold either the character 'F' or the character 'M'.

4. `birthdate`, of type `DATE`. We shall assume that the 10-byte SQL representation of dates is used for this field.

Thus, a record of type `MovieStar` takes $30 + 256 + 1 + 10 = 297$ bytes. It looks as suggested in Fig. 12.2. We have indicated the *offset* of each field, which is the number of bytes from the beginning of the record at which the field itself begins. Thus, field `name` begins at offset 0; `address` begins at offset 30, `gender` at 286, and `birthdate` at offset 287. □

Some machines allow more efficient reading and writing of data that begins at a byte of main memory whose address is a multiple of 4 (or 8 if the machine has a 64-bit processor). Certain types of data, such as integers, may be absolutely required to begin at an address that is a multiple of 4, while others, such as double-precision reals, may need to begin with a multiple of 8.

Figure 12.2: A `MovieStar` record

While the tuples of a relation are stored on disk and not in main memory, we have to be aware of this issue. The reason is that when we read a block from disk to main memory, the first byte of the block will surely be placed at a memory address that is a multiple of 4, and in fact will be a multiple of some high power of 2, such as 2^{12} if blocks and pages have length $4096 = 2^{12}$. Requirements that certain fields be loaded into a main-memory position whose first byte address is a multiple of 4 or 8 thus translate into the requirement that those fields have an offset within their block that has the same divisor.

For simplicity, let us assume that the only requirement on data is that fields start at a main-memory byte whose address is a multiple of 4. Then it is sufficient that

a) Each record start at a byte within its block that is a multiple of 4, and

b) All fields within the record start at a byte that is offset from the beginning of the record by a multiple of 4.

Put another way, we round all field and record lengths up to the next multiple of 4.

Example 12.4: Suppose that the tuples of the `MovieStar` relation need to be represented so each field starts at a byte that is a multiple of 4. Then the offsets of the four fields would be 0, 32, 288, and 292, and the entire record would take 304 bytes. The format is suggested by Fig. 12.3.

Figure 12.3: The layout of `MovieStar` tuples when fields are required to start at multiple of 4 bytes

For instance, the first field, `name`, takes 30 bytes, but we cannot start the second field until the next multiple of 4, or offset 32. Thus, `address` has offset 32 in this record format. The second field is of length 256 bytes, which means the first available byte following `address` is 288. The third field, `gender`, needs

---

The Need for a Record Schema

We might wonder why we need to indicate the record schema in the record itself, since currently we are only considering fixed-format records. For example, fields in a "struct," as used in C or similar languages, do not have their offsets stored when the program is running; rather the offsets are compiled into the application programs that access the struct.

However, there are several reasons why the record schema must be stored and accessible to the DBMS. For one, the schema of a relation (and therefore the schema of the records that represent its tuples) can change. Queries need to use the current schema for these records, and so need to know what the schema currently is. In other situations, we may not be able to tell immediately what the record type is simply from its location in the storage system. For example, some storage organizations permit tuples of different relations to appear in the same block of storage.

---

only one byte, but we cannot start the last field until a total of 4 bytes later, at 292. The fourth field, `birthdate`, being 10 bytes long, ends at byte 301, which makes the record length 302 (notice that the first byte is 0). However if all fields of all records must start at a multiple of 4, the bytes numbered 302 and 303 are useless, and effectively, the record consumes 304 bytes. We shall assign bytes 302 and 303 to the `birthdate` field, so they do not get used for any other purpose accidentally. $\Box$

12.2.2 Record Headers

There is another issue that must be raised when we design the layout of a record. Often, there is information that must be kept in the record but that is not the value of any field. For example, we may want to keep in the record:

1. The record schema, or more likely, a pointer to a place where the DBMS stores the schema for this type of record,

2. The length of the record,

3. Timestamps indicating the time the record was last modified, or last read,

among other possible pieces of information. Thus, many record layouts include a *header* of some small number of bytes to provide this additional information.

The database system maintains *schema information*, which is essentially what appears in the `CREATE TABLE` statement for that relation:

1. The attributes of the relation,

2. Their types,

3. The order in which attributes appear in the tuple,

4. Constraints on the attributes and the relation itself, such as primary key declarations, or a constraint that some integer attribute must have a value in a certain range.

We do not have to put all this information in the header of a tuple's record. It is sufficient to put there a pointer to the place where the information about the tuple's relation is stored. Then all this information can be obtained when needed.

As another example, even though the length of the tuple may be deducible from its schema, it may be convenient to have the length in the record itself. For instance, we may not wish to examine the record contents, but just find the beginning of the next record quickly. A length field lets us avoid accessing the record's schema, which may involve a disk I/O.

Example 12.5 : Let us modify the layout of Example 12.4 to include a header of 12 bytes. The first four bytes are the type. It is actually an offset in an area where the schemas for all the relations are kept. The second is the record length, a 4-byte integer, and the third is a timestamp indicating when the tuple was inserted or last updated. The timestamp is also a 4-byte integer. The resulting layout is shown in Fig. 12.4. The length of the record is now 316 bytes. □

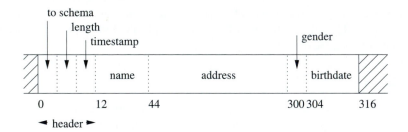

Figure 12.4: Adding some header information to records representing tuples of the `MovieStar` relation

12.2.3   Packing Fixed-Length Records into Blocks

Records representing tuples of a relation are stored in blocks of the disk and moved into main memory (along with their entire block) when we need to access or update them. The layout of a block that holds records is suggested in Fig. 12.5.

There is an optional *block header* that holds information such as:

1. Links to one or more other blocks that are part of a network of blocks such as those described in Chapter 13 for creating indexes to the tuples of a relation.

Figure 12.5: A typical block holding records

2. Information about the role played by this block in such a network.

3. Information about which relation the tuples of this block belong to.

4. A "directory" giving the offset of each record in the block.

5. A "block ID"; see Section 12.3.

6. Timestamp(s) indicating the time of the block's last modification and/or access.

By far the simplest case is when the block holds tuples from one relation, and the records for those tuples have a fixed format. In that case, following the header, we pack as many records as we can into the block and leave the remaining space unused.

Example 12.6 : Suppose we are storing records with the layout developed in Example 12.5. These records are 316 bytes long. Suppose also that we use 4096-byte blocks. Of these bytes, say 12 will be used for a block header, leaving 4084 bytes for data. In this space we can fit twelve records of the given 316-byte format, and 292 bytes of each block are wasted space. □

12.2.4 Exercises for Section 12.2

* **Exercise 12.2.1 :** Suppose a record has the following fields in this order: A character string of length 15, an integer of 2 bytes, an SQL date, and an SQL time (no decimal point). How many bytes does the record take if:

   a) Fields can start at any byte.

   b) Fields must start at a byte that is a multiple of 4.

   c) Fields must start at a byte that is a multiple of 8.

Exercise 12.2.2 : Repeat Exercise 12.2.1 for the list of fields: A real of 8 bytes, a character string of length 17, a single byte, and an SQL date.

* **Exercise 12.2.3 :** Assume fields are as in Exercise 12.2.1, but records also have a record header consisting of two 4-byte pointers and a character. Calculate the record length for the three situations regarding field alignment (a) through (c) in Exercise 12.2.1.

Exercise 12.2.4: Repeat Exercise 12.2.2 if the records also include a header consisting of an 8-byte pointer, and ten 2-byte integers.

* **Exercise 12.2.5:** Suppose records are as in Exercise 12.2.3, and we wish to pack as many records as we can into a block of 4096 bytes, using a block header that consists of ten 4-byte integers. How many records can we fit in the block in each of the three situations regarding field alignment (a) through (c) of Exercise 12.2.1?

Exercise 12.2.6: Repeat Exercise 12.2.5 for the records of Exercise 12.2.4, assuming that blocks are 16,384 bytes long, and that block headers consist of three 4-byte integers and a directory that has a 2-byte integer for every record in the block.

12.3   Representing Block and Record Addresses

Before proceeding with the study of how records with more complex structure are represented, we must consider how addresses, pointers, or references to records and blocks can be represented, since these pointers often form part of complex records. There are other reasons for knowing about secondary-storage address representation as well. When we look at efficient structures for representing files or relations in Chapter 13, we shall see several important uses for the address of a block or the address of a record.

The address of a block when it is loaded into a buffer of main memory can be taken to be the virtual-memory address of its first byte, and the address of a record within that block is the virtual-memory address of the first byte of that record. However, in secondary storage, the block is not part of the application's virtual-memory address space. Rather, a sequence of bytes describes the location of the block within the overall system of data accessible to the DBMS: the device ID for the disk, the cylinder number, and so on. A record can be identified by giving its block and the offset of the first byte of the record within the block.

To complicate further the matter of representing addresses, a recent trend toward "object brokers" allows independent creation of objects by many cooperating systems. These objects may be represented by records that are part of an object-oriented DBMS, although we can think of them as tuples of relations without losing the principal idea. However, the capability for independent creation of objects or records puts additional stress on the mechanism that maintains addresses of these records.

In this section, we shall begin with a discussion of address spaces, especially as they pertain to the common "client-server" architecture for DBMS's. We then discuss the options for representing addresses, and finally look at "pointer swizzling," the ways in which we can convert addresses in the data server's world to the world of the client application programs.

12.3.1   Client-Server Systems

Commonly, a database consists of a *server* process that provides data from secondary storage to one or more *client* processes that are applications using the data. The server and client processes may be on one machine, or the server and the various clients can be distributed over many machines. See Section 8.3.4, where the idea was first introduced.

The client application uses a conventional "virtual" address space, typically 32 bits, or about 4 billion different addresses. The operating system or DBMS decides which parts of the address space are currently located in main memory, and hardware maps the virtual address space to physical locations in main memory. We shall not think further of this virtual-to-physical translation, and shall think of the client address space as if it were main memory itself.

The server's data lives in a *database address space*. The addresses of this space refer to blocks, and possibly to offsets within the block. There are several ways that addresses in this address space can be represented:

1. *Physical Addresses.* These are byte strings that let us determine the place within the secondary storage system where the block or record can be found. One or more bytes of the physical address are used to indicate each of:

   (a) The host to which the storage is attached (if the database is stored across more than one machine),

   (b) An identifier for the disk or other device on which the block is located,

   (c) The number of the cylinder of the disk,

   (d) The number of the track within the cylinder (if the disk has more than one surface),

   (e) The number of the block within the track.

   (f) (In some cases) the offset of the beginning of the record within the block.

2. *Logical Addresses.* Each block or record has a "logical address," which is an arbitrary string of bytes of some fixed length. A *map table*, stored on disk in a known location, relates logical to physical addresses, as suggested in Fig. 12.6.

Notice that physical addresses are long. Eight bytes is about the minimum we could use if we incorporate all the listed elements, and some systems use up to 16 bytes. For example, imagine a database of objects that is designed to last for 100 years. In the future, the database may grow to encompass one million machines, and each machine might be fast enough to create one object every nanosecond. This system would create around 2^{77} objects, which requires a minimum of ten bytes to represent addresses. Since we would probably prefer

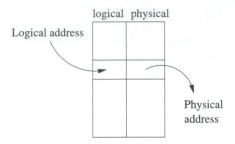

logical physical

Logical address

Physical
address

Figure 12.6: A map table translates logical to physical addresses

to reserve some bytes to represent the host, others to represent the storage unit, and so on, a rational address notation would use considerably more than 10 bytes for a system of this scale.

12.3.2 Logical and Structured Addresses

One might wonder what the purpose of logical addresses could be. All the information needed for a physical address is found in the map table, and following logical pointers to records requires consulting the map table and then going to the physical address. However, the level of indirection involved in the map table allows us considerable flexibility. For example, many data organizations require us to move records around, either within a block or from block to block. If we use a map table, then all pointers to the record refer to this map table, and all we have to do when we move or delete the record is to change the entry for that record in the table.

Many combinations of logical and physical addresses are possible as well, yielding *structured* address schemes. For instance, one could use a physical address for the block (but not the offset within the block), and add the key value for the record being referred to. Then, to find a record given this structured address, we use the physical part to reach the block containing that record, and we examine the records of the block to find the one with the proper key.

Of course, to survey the records of the block, we need enough information to locate them. The simplest case is when the records are of a known, fixed-length type, with the key field at a known offset. Then, we only have to find in the block header a count of how many records are in the block, and we know exactly where to find the key fields that might match the key that is part of the address. However, there are many other ways that blocks might be organized so that we could survey the records of the block; we shall cover others shortly.

A similar, and very useful, combination of physical and logical addresses is to keep in each block an *offset table* that holds the offsets of the records within the block, as suggested in Fig. 12.7. Notice that the table grows from the front end of the block, while the records are placed starting at the end of the block. This strategy is useful when the records need not be of equal length. Then, we do not know in advance how many records the block will hold, and we do not have to allocate a fixed amount of the block header to the table initially.

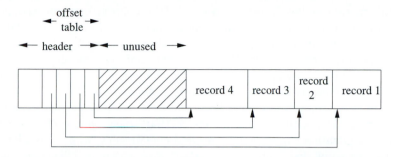

Figure 12.7: A block with a table of offsets telling us the position of each record within the block

The address of a record is now the physical address of its block plus the offset of the entry in the block's offset table for that record. This level of indirection within the block offers many of the advantages of logical addresses, without the need for a global map table.

- We can move the record around within the block, and all we have to do is change the record's entry in the offset table; pointers to the record will still be able to find it.

- We can even allow the record to move to another block, if the offset table entries are large enough to hold a "forwarding address" for the record.

- Finally, we have an option, should the record be deleted, of leaving in its offset-table entry a *tombstone*, a special value that indicates the record has been deleted. Prior to its deletion, pointers to this record may have been stored at various places in the database. After record deletion, following a pointer to this record leads to the tombstone, whereupon the pointer can either be replaced by a null pointer, or the data structure otherwise modified to reflect the deletion of the record. Had we not left the tombstone, the pointer might lead to some new record, with surprising, and erroneous, results.

12.3.3 Pointer Swizzling

Often, pointers or addresses are part of records. This situation is not typical for records that represent tuples of a relation, but it is common for tuples that represent objects. Also, modern object-relational database systems allow attributes of pointer type (called references), so even relational systems need the ability to represent pointers in tuples. Finally, index structures are composed of blocks that usually have pointers within them. Thus, we need to study

---

Ownership of Memory Address Spaces

In this section we have presented a view of the transfer between secondary and main memory in which each client owns its own memory address space, and the database address space is shared. This model is common in object-oriented DBMS's. However, relational systems often treat the memory address space as shared; the motivation is to support recovery and concurrency as we shall discuss in Chapters 17 and 18.

A useful compromise is to have a shared memory address space on the server side, with copies of parts of that space on the clients' side. That organization supports recovery and concurrency, while also allowing processing to be distributed in "scalable" way: the more clients the more processors can be brought to bear.

---

the management of pointers as blocks are moved between main and secondary memory; we do so in this section.

As we mentioned earlier, every block, record, object, or other referenceable data item has two forms of address:

1. Its address in the server's database address space, which is typically a sequence of eight or so bytes locating the item in the secondary storage of the system. We shall call this address the *database address*.

2. An address in virtual memory (provided that item is currently buffered in virtual memory). These addresses are typically four bytes. We shall refer to such an address as the *memory address* of the item.

When in secondary storage, we surely must use the database address of the item. However, when the item is in the main memory, we can refer to the item by either its database address or its memory address. It is more efficient to put memory addresses wherever an item has a pointer, because these pointers can be followed using single machine instructions.

In contrast, following a database address is much more time-consuming. We need a table that translates from all those database addresses that are currently in virtual memory to their current memory address. Such a *translation table* is suggested in Fig. 12.8. It may be reminiscent of the map table of Fig. 12.6 that translates between logical and physical addresses. However:

a) Logical and physical addresses are both representations for the database address. In contrast, memory addresses in the translation table are for copies of the corresponding object in memory.

b) All addressable items in the database have entries in the map table, while only those items currently in memory are mentioned in the translation table.

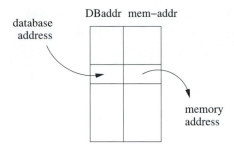

Figure 12.8: The translation table turns database addresses into their equivalents in memory

To avoid the cost of translating repeatedly from database addresses to memory addresses, several techniques have been developed that are collectively known as *pointer swizzling*. The general idea is that when we move a block from secondary to main memory, pointers within the block may be "swizzled," that is, translated from the database address space to the virtual address space. Thus, a pointer actually consists of:

1. A bit indicating whether the pointer is currently a database address or a (swizzled) memory address.

2. The database or memory pointer, as appropriate. The same space is used for whichever address form is present at the moment. Of course, not all the space may be used when the memory address is present, because it is typically shorter than the database address.

Example 12.7 : Figure 12.9 shows a simple situation in which the Block 1 has a record with pointers to a second record on the same block and to a record on another block. The figure also shows what might happen when Block 1 is copied to memory. The first pointer, which points within Block 1, can be swizzled so it points directly to the memory address of the target record.

However, if Block 2 is not in memory at this time, then we cannot swizzle the second pointer; it must remain unswizzled, pointing to the database address of its target. Should Block 2 be brought to memory later, it becomes theoretically possible to swizzle the second pointer of Block 1. Depending on the swizzling strategy used, there may or may not be a list of such pointers that are in memory, referring to Block 2; if so, then we have the option of swizzling the pointer at that time. □

There are several strategies we can use to determine when to swizzle pointers.

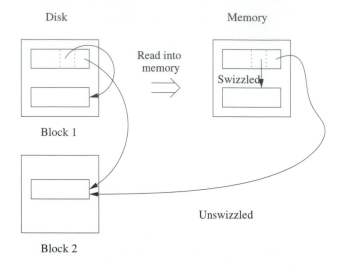

Figure 12.9: Structure of a pointer when swizzling is used

Automatic Swizzling

As soon as a block is brought into memory, we locate all its pointers and addresses and enter them into the translation table if they are not already there. These pointers include both the pointers *from* records in the block to elsewhere and the addresses of the block itself and/or its records, if these are addressable items. We need some mechanism to locate the pointers within the block. For example:

1. If the block holds records with a known schema, the schema will tell us where in the records the pointers are found.

2. If the block is used for one of the index structures we shall discuss in Chapter 13, then the block will hold pointers at known locations.

3. We may keep within the block header a list of where the pointers are.

When we enter into the translation table the addresses for the block just moved into memory, and/or its records, we know where in memory the block has been buffered. We may thus create the translation-table entry for these database addresses straightforwardly. When we insert one of these database addresses A into the translation table, we may find it in the table already, because its block is currently in memory. In this case, we replace A in the block just moved to memory by the corresponding memory address, and we set the "swizzled" bit to true. On the other hand, if A is not yet in the translation table, then its block has not been copied into main memory. We therefore cannot swizzle this pointer and leave it in the block as a database pointer.

If we try to follow a pointer P from a block, and we find that pointer P is still unswizzled, i.e., in the form of a database pointer, then we need to make sure the block B containing the item that P points to is in memory (or else why are we following that pointer?). We consult the translation table to see if database address P currently has a memory equivalent. If not, we copy block B into a memory buffer. Once B is in memory, we can "swizzle" P by replacing its database form by the equivalent memory form.

Swizzling on Demand

Another approach is to leave all pointers unswizzled when the block is first brought into memory. We enter its address, and the addresses of its pointers, into the translation table, along with their memory equivalents. If and when we follow a pointer P that is inside some block of memory, we swizzle it, using the same strategy that we followed when we found an unswizzled pointer using automatic swizzling.

The difference between on-demand and automatic swizzling is that the latter tries to get all the pointers swizzled quickly and efficiently when the block is loaded into memory. The possible time saved by swizzling all of a block's pointers at one time must be weighed against the possibility that some swizzled pointers will never be followed. In that case, any time spent swizzling and unswizzling the pointer will be wasted.

An interesting option is to arrange that database pointers look like invalid memory addresses. If so, then we can allow the computer to follow any pointer as if it were in its memory form. If the pointer happens to be unswizzled, then the memory reference will cause a hardware trap. If the DBMS provides a function that is invoked by the trap, and this function "swizzles" the pointer in the manner described above, then we can follow swizzled pointers in single instructions, and only need to do something more time consuming when the pointer is unswizzled.

No Swizzling

Of course it is possible never to swizzle pointers. We still need the translation table, so the pointers may be followed in their unswizzled form. This approach does offer the advantage that records cannot be pinned in memory, as discussed in Section 12.3.5, and decisions about which form of pointer is present need not be made.

Programmer Control of Swizzling

In some applications, it may be known by the application programmer whether the pointers in a block are likely to be followed. This programmer may be able to specify explicitly that a block loaded into memory is to have its pointers swizzled, or the programmer may call for the pointers to be swizzled only as needed. For example, if a programmer knows that a block is likely to be accessed heavily, such as the root block of a B-tree (discussed in Section 13.3), then the pointers would be swizzled. However, blocks that are loaded into memory, used once, and then likely dropped from memory, would not be swizzled.

12.3.4   Returning Blocks to Disk

When a block is moved from memory back to disk, any pointers within that block must be "unswizzled"; that is, their memory addresses must be replaced by the corresponding database addresses. The translation table can be used to associate addresses of the two types in either direction, so in principle it is possible to find, given a memory address, the database address to which the memory address is assigned.

However, we do not want each unswizzling operation to require a search of the entire translation table. While we have not discussed the implementation of this table, we might imagine that the table of Fig. 12.8 has appropriate indexes. If we think of the translation table as a relation, then the problem of finding the memory address associated with a database address x can be expressed as the query:

```
SELECT memAddr
FROM TranslationTable
WHERE dbAddr = x;
```

For instance, a hash table using the database address as the key might be appropriate for an index on the `dbAddr` attribute; Chapter 13 suggests many possible data structures.

If we want to support the reverse query,

```
SELECT dbAddr
FROM TranslationTable
WHERE memAddr = y;
```

then we need to have an index on attribute `memAddr` as well. Again, Chapter 13 suggests data structures suitable for such an index. Also, Section 12.3.5 talks about linked-list structures that in some circumstances can be used to go from a memory address to all main-memory pointers to that address.

12.3.5   Pinned Records and Blocks

A block in memory is said to be *pinned* if it cannot at the moment be written back to disk safely. A bit telling whether or not a block is pinned can be located in the header of the block. There are many reasons why a block could be pinned, including requirements of a recovery system as discussed in Chapter 17. Pointer swizzling introduces an important reason why certain blocks must be pinned.

If a block B_1 has within it a swizzled pointer to some data item in block B_2, then we must be very careful about moving block B_2 back to disk and reusing its main-memory buffer. The reason is that, should we follow the pointer in B_1, it will lead us to the buffer, which no longer holds B_2; in effect, the pointer has become dangling. A block, like B_2, that is referred to by a swizzled pointer from somewhere else is therefore pinned.

When we write a block back to disk, we not only need to "unswizzle" any pointers in that block. We also need to make sure it is not pinned. If it is pinned, we must either unpin it, or let the block remain in memory, occupying space that could otherwise be used for some other block. To unpin a block that is pinned because of swizzled pointers from outside, we must "unswizzle" any pointers to it. Consequently, the translation table must record, for each database address whose data item is in memory, the places in memory where swizzled pointers to that item exist. Two possible approaches are:

1. Keep the list of references to a memory address as a linked list attached to the entry for that address in the translation table.

2. If memory addresses are significantly shorter than database addresses, we can create the linked list in the space used for the pointers themselves. That is, each space used for a database pointer is replaced by

   (a) The swizzled pointer, and

   (b) Another pointer that forms part of a linked list of all occurrences of this pointer.

Figure 12.10 suggests how all the occurrences of a memory pointer y could be linked, starting at the entry in the translation table for database address x and its corresponding memory address y.

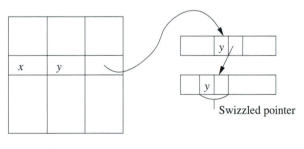

Figure 12.10: A linked list of occurrences of a swizzled pointer

12.3.6 Exercises for Section 12.3

* **Exercise 12.3.1:** If we represent physical addresses for the Megatron 747 disk by allocating a separate byte or bytes to each of the cylinder, track within

a cylinder, and block within a track, how many bytes do we need? Make a reasonable assumption about the maximum number of blocks on each track; recall that the Megatron 747 has a variable number of sectors/track.

Exercise 12.3.2: Repeat Exercise 12.3.1 for the Megatron 777 disk described in Exercise 11.3.1

Exercise 12.3.3: If we wish to represent record addresses as well as block addresses, we need additional bytes. Assuming we want addresses for a single Megatron 747 disk as in Exercise 12.3.1, how many bytes would we need for record addresses if we:

* a) Included the number of the byte within a block as part of the physical address.

  b) Used structured addresses for records. Assume that the stored records have a 4-byte integer as a key.

Exercise 12.3.4: Today, IP addresses have four bytes. Suppose that block addresses for a world-wide address system consist of an IP address for the host, a device number between 1 and 1000, and a block address on an individual device (assumed to be a Megatron 747 disk). How many bytes would block addresses require?

Exercise 12.3.5: In IP version 6, IP addresses are 16 bytes long. In addition, we may want to address not only blocks, but records, which may start at any byte of a block. However, devices will have their own IP address, so there will be no need to represent a device within a host, as we suggested was necessary in Exercise 12.3.4. How many bytes would be needed to represent addresses in these circumstances, again assuming devices were Megatron 747 disks?

! **Exercise 12.3.6:** Suppose we wish to represent the addresses of blocks on a Megatron 747 disk logically, i.e., using identifiers of k bytes for some k. We also need to store on the disk itself a map table, as in Fig. 12.6, consisting of pairs of logical and physical addresses. The blocks used for the map table itself are not part of the database, and therefore do not have their own logical addresses in the map table. Assuming that physical addresses use the minimum possible number of bytes for physical addresses (as calculated in Exercise 12.3.1), and logical addresses likewise use the minimum possible number of bytes for logical addresses, how many blocks of 4096 bytes does the map table for the disk occupy?

*! **Exercise 12.3.7:** Suppose that we have 4096-byte blocks in which we store records of 100 bytes. The block header consists of an offset table, as in Fig. 12.7, using 2-byte pointers to records within the block. On an average day, two records per block are inserted, and one record is deleted. A deleted record must have its pointer replaced by a "tombstone," because there may be dangling

pointers to it. For specificity, assume the deletion on any day always occurs before the insertions. If the block is initially empty, after how many days will there be no room to insert any more records?

! Exercise 12.3.8: Repeat Exercise 12.3.7 on the assumption that each day there is one deletion and 1.1 insertions on the average.

Exercise 12.3.9: Repeat Exercise 12.3.7 on the assumption that instead of deleting records, they are moved to another block and must be given an 8-byte forwarding address in their offset-table entry. Assume either:

> **!** a) All offset-table entries are given the maximum number of bytes needed in an entry.

> **!!** b) Offset-table entries are allowed to vary in length in such a way that all entries can be found and interpreted properly.

* Exercise 12.3.10: Suppose that if we swizzle all pointers automatically, we can perform the swizzling in half the time it would take to swizzle each one separately. If the probability that a pointer in main memory will be followed at least once is p, for what values of p is it more efficient to swizzle automatically than on demand?

! Exercise 12.3.11: Generalize Exercise 12.3.10 to include the possibility that we never swizzle pointers. Suppose that the important actions take the following times, in some arbitrary time units:

> *i.* On-demand swizzling of a pointer: 30.

> *ii.* Automatic swizzling of pointers: 20 per pointer.

> *iii.* Following a swizzled pointer: 1.

> *iv.* Following an unswizzled pointer: 10.

Suppose that in-memory pointers are either not followed (probability $1 - p$) or are followed k times (probability p). For what values of k and p do no-swizzling, automatic-swizzling, and on-demand-swizzling each offer the best average performance?

12.4 Variable-Length Data and Records

Until now, we have made the simplifying assumptions that every data item has a fixed length, that records have a fixed schema, and that the schema is a list of fixed-length fields. However, in practice, life is rarely so simple. We may wish to represent:

1. *Data items whose size varies.* For instance, in Fig. 12.1 we considered a `MovieStar` relation that had an address field of up to 255 bytes. While there might be some addresses that long, the vast majority of them will probably be 50 bytes or less. We could probably save more than half the space used for storing `MovieStar` tuples if we used only as much space as the actual address needed.

2. *Repeating fields.* If we try to represent a many-many relationship in a record representing an object, we shall have to store references to as many objects as are related to the given object.

3. *Variable-format records.* Sometimes we do not know in advance what the fields of a record will be, or how many occurrences of each field there will be. For example, some movie stars also direct movies, and we might want to add fields to their record referring to the movies they directed. Likewise, some stars produce movies or participate in other ways, and we might wish to put this information into their record as well. However, since most stars are neither producers nor directors, we would not want to reserve space for this information in every star's record.

4. *Enormous fields.* Modern DBMS's support attributes whose value is a very large data item. For instance, we might want to include a `picture` attribute with a movie-star record that is a GIF image of the star. A movie record might have a field that is a 2-gigabyte MPEG encoding of the movie itself, as well as more mundane fields such as the title of the movie. These fields are so large, that our intuition that records fit within blocks is contradicted.

12.4.1 Records With Variable-Length Fields

If one or more fields of a record have variable length, then the record must contain enough information to let us find any field of the record. A simple but effective scheme is to put all fixed-length fields ahead of the variable-length fields. We then place in the record header:

1. The length of the record.

2. Pointers to (i.e., offsets of) the beginnings of all the variable-length fields. However, if the variable-length fields always appear in the same order, then the first of them needs no pointer; we know it immediately follows the fixed-length fields.

Example 12.8 : Suppose that we have movie-star records with name, address, gender, and birthdate. We shall assume that the gender and birthdate are fixed-length fields, taking 4 and 12 bytes, respectively. However, both name and address will be represented by character strings of whatever length is appropriate. Figure 12.11 suggests what a typical movie-star record would look like. We shall always put the name before the address. Thus, no pointer to the beginning of the name is needed; that field will always begin right after the fixed-length portion of the record. □

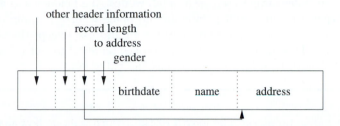

Figure 12.11: A `MovieStar` record with `name` and `address` implemented as variable-length character strings

12.4.2 Records With Repeating Fields

A similar situation occurs if a record contains a variable number of occurrences of a field F, but the field itself is of fixed length. It is sufficient to group all occurrences of field F together and put in the record header a pointer to the first. We can locate all the occurrences of the field F as follows. Let the number of bytes devoted to one instance of field F be L. We then add to the offset for the field F all integer multiples of L, starting at 0, then L, $2L$, $3L$, and so on. Eventually, we reach the offset of the field following F, whereupon we stop.

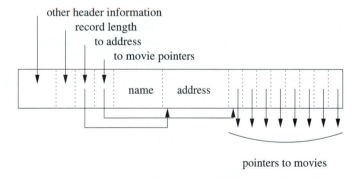

Figure 12.12: A record with a repeating group of references to movies

Example 12.9 : Suppose that we redesign our movie-star records to hold only the name and address (which are variable-length strings) and pointers to all the movies of the star. Figure 12.12 shows how this type of record could be represented. The header contains pointers to the beginning of the address field (we assume the name field always begins right after the header) and to the

---

Representing Null Values

Tuples often have fields that may be NULL. The record format of Fig. 12.11 offers a convenient way to represent NULL values. If a field such as address is null, then we put a null pointer in the place where the pointer to an address goes. Then, we need no space for an address, except the place for the pointer. This arrangement can save space on average, even if address is a fixed-length field but frequently has the value NULL.

---

first of the movie pointers. The length of the record tells us how many movie pointers there are.   □

An alternative representation is to keep the record of fixed length, and put the variable-length portion — be it fields of variable length or fields that repeat an indefinite number of times — on a separate block. In the record itself we keep:

1. Pointers to the place where each repeating field begins, and

2. Either how many repetitions there are, or where the repetitions end.

Figure 12.13 shows the layout of a record for the problem of Example 12.9, but with the variable-length fields name and address, and the repeating field starredIn (a set of movie references) kept on a separate block or blocks.

There are advantages and disadvantages to using indirection for the variable-length components of a record:

- Keeping the record itself fixed-length allows records to be searched more efficiently, minimizes the overhead in block headers, and allows records to be moved within or among blocks with minimum effort.

- On the other hand, storing variable-length components on another block increases the number of disk I/O's needed to examine all components of a record.

A compromise strategy is to keep in the fixed-length portion of the record enough space for:

1. Some reasonable number of occurrences of the repeating fields,

2. A pointer to a place where additional occurrences could be found, and

3. A count of how many additional occurrences there are.

If there are fewer than this number, some of the space would be unused. If there are more than can fit in the fixed-length portion, then the pointer to additional space will be nonnull, and we can find the additional occurrences by following this pointer.

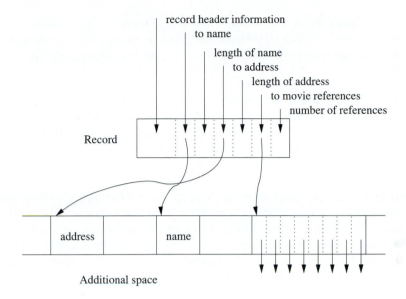

Figure 12.13: Storing variable-length fields separately from the record

12.4.3 Variable-Format Records

An even more complex situation occurs when records do not have a fixed schema. That is, the fields or their order are not completely determined by the relation or class whose tuple or object the record represents. The simplest representation of variable-format records is a sequence of *tagged fields*, each of which consists of:

1. Information about the role of this field, such as:

   (a) The attribute or field name,

   (b) The type of the field, if it is not apparent from the field name and some readily available schema information, and

   (c) The length of the field, if it is not apparent from the type.

2. The value of the field.

There are at least two reasons why tagged fields would make sense.

1. *Information-integration applications.* Sometimes, a relation has been constructed from several earlier sources, and these sources have different kinds of information; see Section 20.1 for a discussion. For instance, our movie-star information may have come from several sources, one of which records birthdates and the others do not, some give addresses, others not, and so on. If there are not too many fields, we are probably best off leaving NULL

those values we do not know. However, if there are many sources, with many different kinds of information, then there may be too many NULL's, and we can save significant space by tagging and listing only the nonnull fields.

2. *Records with a very flexible schema.* If many fields of a record can repeat and/or not appear at all, then even if we know the schema, tagged fields may be useful. For instance, medical records may contain information about many tests, but there are thousands of possible tests, and each patient has results for relatively few of them.

Example 12.10: Suppose some movie stars have information such as movies directed, former spouses, restaurants owned, and a number of other fixed but unusual pieces of information. In Fig. 12.14 we see the beginning of a hypothetical movie-star record using tagged fields. We suppose that single-byte codes are used for the various possible field names and types. Appropriate codes are indicated on the figure, along with lengths for the two fields shown, both of which happen to be of type string.   □

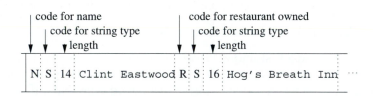

Figure 12.14: A record with tagged fields

12.4.4   Records That Do Not Fit in a Block

We shall now address another problem whose importance has been increasing as DBMS's are more frequently used to manage datatypes with large values: often values do not fit in one block. Typical examples are video or audio "clips." Often, these large values have a variable length, but even if the length is fixed for all values of the type, we need to use some special techniques to represent these values. In this section we shall consider a technique called "spanned records" that can be used to manage records that are larger than blocks. The management of extremely large values (megabytes or gigabytes) is addressed in Section 12.4.5.

Spanned records also are useful in situations where records are smaller than blocks, but packing whole records into blocks wastes significant amounts of space. For instance, the waste space in Example 12.6 was only 7%, but if records are just slightly larger than half a block, the wasted space can approach 50%. The reason is that then we can pack only one record per block.

For both these reasons, it is sometimes desirable to allow records to be split across two or more blocks. The portion of a record that appears in one block is called a *record fragment*. A record with two or more fragments is called *spanned*, and records that do not cross a block boundary are *unspanned*.

If records can be spanned, then every record and record fragment requires some extra header information:

1. Each record or fragment header must contain a bit telling whether or not it is a fragment.

2. If it is a fragment, then it needs bits telling whether it is the first or last fragment for its record.

3. If there is a next and/or previous fragment for the same record, then the fragment needs pointers to these other fragments.

Example 12.11 : Figure 12.15 suggests how records that were about 60% of a block in size could be stored with three records for every two blocks. The header for record fragment 2*a* contains an indicator that it is a fragment, an indicator that it is the first fragment for its record, and a pointer to next fragment, 2*b*. Similarly, the header for 2*b* indicates it is the last fragment for its record and holds a back-pointer to the previous fragment 2*a*. □

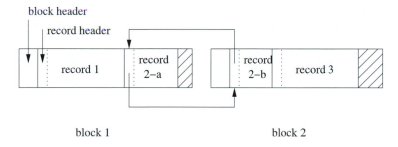

Figure 12.15: Storing spanned records across blocks

12.4.5 BLOBS

Now, let us consider the representation of truly large values for records or fields of records. The common examples include images in various formats (e.g., GIF, or JPEG), movies in formats such as MPEG, or signals of all sorts: audio, radar, and so on. Such values are often called *binary, large objects*, or BLOBS. When a field has a BLOB as value, we must rethink at least two issues.

Storage of BLOBS

A BLOB must be stored on a sequence of blocks. Often we prefer that these blocks are allocated consecutively on a cylinder or cylinders of the disk, so the BLOB may be retrieved efficiently. However, it is also possible to store the BLOB on a linked list of blocks.

Moreover, it is possible that the BLOB needs to be retrieved so quickly (e.g., a movie that must be played in real time), that storing it on one disk does not allow us to retrieve it fast enough. Then, it is necessary to *stripe* the BLOB across several disks, that is, to alternate blocks of the BLOB among these disks. Thus, several blocks of the BLOB can be retrieved simultaneously, increasing the retrieval rate by a factor approximately equal to the number of disks involved in the striping.

Retrieval of BLOBS

Our assumption that when a client wants a record, the block containing the record is passed from the database server to the client in its entirety may not hold. We may want to pass only the "small" fields of the record, and allow the client to request blocks of the BLOB one at a time, independently of the rest of the record. For instance, if the BLOB is a 2-hour movie, and the client requests that the movie be played, the BLOB could be shipped several blocks at a time to the client, at just the rate necessary to play the movie.

In many applications, it is also important that the client be able to request interior portions of the BLOB without having to receive the entire BLOB. Examples would be a request to see the 45th minute of a movie, or the ending of an audio clip. If the DBMS is to support such operations, then it requires a suitable index structure, e.g., an index by seconds on a movie BLOB.

12.4.6   Exercises for Section 12.4

* **Exercise 12.4.1:** A patient record consists of the following fixed-length fields: the patient's date of birth, social-security number, and patient ID, each 10 bytes long. It also has the following variable-length fields: name, address, and patient history. If pointers within a record require 4 bytes, and the record length is a 4-byte integer, how many bytes, exclusive of the space needed for the variable-length fields, are needed for the record? You may assume that no alignment of fields is required.

* **Exercise 12.4.2:** Suppose records are as in Exercise 12.4.1, and the variable-length fields name, address, and history each have a length that is uniformly distributed. For the name, the range is 10–50 bytes; for address it is 20–80 bytes, and for history it is 0–1000 bytes. What is the average length of a patient record?

Exercise 12.4.3: Suppose that the patient records of Exercise 12.4.1 are augmented by an additional repeating field that represents cholesterol tests. Each cholesterol test requires 16 bytes for a date and an integer result of the test. Show the layout of patient records if:

a) The repeating tests are kept with the record itself.

b) The tests are stored on a separate block, with pointers to them in the record.

Exercise 12.4.4: Starting with the patient records of Exercise 12.4.1, suppose we add fields for tests and their results. Each test consists of a test name, a date, and a test result. Assume that each such test requires 40 bytes. Also, suppose that for each patient and each test a result is stored with probability p.

a) Assuming pointers and integers each require 4 bytes, what is the average number of bytes devoted to test results in a patient record, assuming that all test results are kept within the record itself, as a variable-length field?

b) Repeat (a), if test results are represented by pointers within the record to test-result fields kept elsewhere.

! c) Suppose we use a hybrid scheme, where room for k test results are kept within the record, and additional test results are found by following a pointer to another block (or chain of blocks) where those results are kept. As a function of p, what value of k minimizes the amount of storage used for test results?

!! d) The amount of space used by the repeating test-result fields is not the only issue. Let us suppose that the figure of merit we wish to minimize is the number of bytes used, plus a penalty of 10,000 if we have to store some results on another block (and therefore will require a disk I/O for many of the test-result accesses we need to do. Under this assumption, what is the best value of k as a function of p?

*!! **Exercise 12.4.5:** Suppose blocks have 1000 bytes available for the storage of records, and we wish to store on them fixed-length records of length r, where $500 < r \leq 1000$. The value of r includes the record header, but a record fragment requires an additional 16 bytes for the fragment header. For what values of r can we improve space utilization by spanning records?

!! **Exercise 12.4.6:** An MPEG movie uses about one gigabyte per hour of play. If we carefully organized several movies on a Megatron 747 disk, how many could we deliver with only small delay (say 100 milliseconds) from one disk. Use the timing estimates of Example 11.5, but remember that you can choose how the movies are laid out on the disk.

12.5 Record Modifications

Insertions, deletions, and update of records often create special problems. These problems are most severe when the records change their length, but they come up even when records and fields are all of fixed length.

12.5.1 Insertion

First, let us consider insertion of new records into a relation (or equivalently, into the current extent of a class). If the records of a relation are kept in no particular order, we can just find a block with some empty space, or get a new block if there is none, and put the record there. Usually, there is some mechanism for finding all the blocks holding tuples of a given relation or objects of a class, but we shall defer the question of how to keep track of these blocks until Section 13.1.

There is more of a problem when the tuples must be kept in some fixed order, such as sorted by their primary key. There is good reason to keep records sorted, since it facilitates answering certain kinds of queries, as we shall see in Section 13.1. If we need to insert a new record, we first locate the appropriate block for that record. Fortuitously, there may be space in the block to put the new record. Since records must be kept in order, we may have to slide records around in the block to make space available at the proper point.

If we need to slide records, then the block organization that we showed in Fig. 12.7, which we reproduce here as Fig. 12.16, is useful. Recall from our discussion in Section 12.3.2 that we may create an "offset table" in the header of each block, with pointers to the location of each record in the block. A pointer to a record from outside the block is a "structured address," that is, the block address and the location of the entry for the record in the offset table.

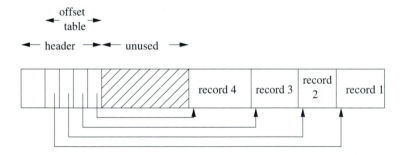

Figure 12.16: An offset table lets us slide records within a block to make room for new records

If we can find room for the inserted record in the block at hand, then we simply slide the records within the block and adjust the pointers in the offset table. The new record is inserted into the block, and a new pointer to the record is added to the offset table for the block.

However, there may be no room in the block for the new record, in which case we have to find room outside the block. There are two major approaches to solving this problem, as well as combinations of these approaches.

1. *Find space on a "nearby" block.* For example, if block B_1 has no available space for a record that needs to be inserted in sorted order into that block, then look at the following block B_2 in the sorted order of the blocks. If there is room in B_2, move the highest record(s) of B_1 to B_2, and slide the records around on both blocks. However, if there are external pointers to records, then we have to be careful to leave a *forwarding address* in the offset table of B_1 to say that a certain record has been moved to B_2 and where its entry in the offset table of B_2 is. Allowing forwarding addresses typically increases the amount of space needed for entries of the offset table.

2. *Create an overflow block.* In this scheme, each block B has in its header a place for a pointer to an *overflow* block where additional records that theoretically belong in B can be placed. The overflow block for B can point to a second overflow block, and so on. Figure 12.17 suggests the structure. We show the pointer for overflow blocks as a nub on the block, although it is in fact part of the block header.

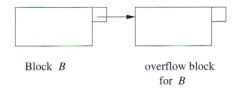

Block *B*   overflow block
                               for *B*

Figure 12.17: A block and its first overflow block

12.5.2 Deletion

When we delete a record, we may be able to reclaim its space. If we use an offset table as in Fig. 12.16 and records can slide around the block, then we can compact the space in the block so there is always one unused region in the center, as suggested by that figure.

If we cannot slide records, we should maintain an available-space list in the block header. Then we shall know where, and how large, the available regions are, when a new record is inserted into the block. Note that the block header normally does not need to hold the entire available space list. It is sufficient to put the list head in the block header, and use the available regions themselves to hold the links in the list, much as we did in Fig. 12.10.

When a record is deleted, we may be able to do away with an overflow block. If the record is deleted either from a block B or from any block on its overflow chain, we can consider the total amount of used space on all the blocks of that chain. If the records can fit on fewer blocks, and we can safely move records among blocks of the chain, then a reorganization of the entire chain can be performed.

However, there is one additional complication involved in deletion, which we must remember regardless of what scheme we use for reorganizing blocks. There may be pointers to the deleted record, and if so, we don't want these pointers to dangle or wind up pointing to a new record that is put in the place of the deleted record. The usual technique, which we pointed out in Section 12.3.2, is to place a *tombstone* in place of the record. This tombstone is permanent; it must exist until the entire database is reconstructed.

Where the tombstone is placed depends on the nature of record pointers. If pointers go to fixed locations from which the location of the record is found, then we put the tombstone in that fixed location. Here are two examples:

1. We suggested in Section 12.3.2 that if the offset-table scheme of Fig. 12.16 were used, then the tombstone could be a null pointer in the offset table, since pointers to the record were really pointers to the offset table entries.

2. If we are using a map table, as in Fig. 12.6, to translate logical record addresses to physical addresses, then the tombstone can be a null pointer in place of the physical address.

If we need to replace records by tombstones, it would be wise to have at the very beginning of the record header a bit that serves as a tombstone; i.e., it is 0 if the record is *not* deleted, while 1 means that the record has been deleted. Then, only this bit must remain where the record used to begin, and subsequent bytes can be reused for another record, as suggested by Fig. 12.18.[3] When we follow a pointer to the deleted record, the first thing we see is the "tombstone" bit telling us that the record was deleted. We then know not to look at the following bytes.

Figure 12.18: Record 1 can be replaced, but the tombstone remains; record 2 has no tombstone and can be seen when we follow a pointer to it

---

[3]However, the field-alignment problem discussed in Section 12.2.1 may force us to leave four bytes or more unused.

12.5.3 Update

When a fixed-length record is updated, there is no effect on the storage system, because we know it can occupy exactly the same space it did before the update. However, when a variable-length record is updated, we have all the problems associated with both insertion and deletion, except that it is never necessary to create a tombstone for the old version of the record.

If the updated record is longer than the old version, then we may need to create more space on its block. This process may involve sliding records or even the creation of an overflow block. If variable-length portions of the record are stored on another block, as in Fig. 12.13, then we may need to move elements around that block or create a new block for storing variable-length fields. Conversely, if the record shrinks because of the update, we have the same opportunities as with a deletion to recover or consolidate space, or to eliminate overflow blocks.

12.5.4 Exercises for Section 12.5

Exercise 12.5.1: Suppose we have blocks of records sorted by their sort key field and partitioned among blocks in order. Each block has a range of sort keys that is known from outside (the sparse-index structure in Section 13.1.3 is an example of this situation). There are no pointers to records from outside, so it is possible to move records between blocks if we wish. Here are some of the ways we could manage insertions and deletions.

- *i.* Split blocks whenever there is an overflow. Adjust the range of sort keys for a block when we do.

- *ii.* Keep the range of sort keys for a block fixed, and use overflow blocks as needed. Keep for each block and each overflow block an offset table for the records in that block alone.

- *iii.* Same as (*ii*), but keep the offset table for the block and all its overflow blocks in the first block (or overflow blocks if the offset table needs the space). Note that if more space for the offset table is needed, we can move records from the first block to an overflow block to make room.

- *iv.* Same as (*ii*), but keep the sort key along with a pointer in the offset tables.

- *v.* Same as (*iii*), but keep the sort key along with a pointer in the offset table.

Answer the following questions:

* a) Compare methods (*i*) and (*ii*) for the average numbers of disk I/O's needed to retrieve the record, once the block (or first block in a chain with overflow blocks) that could have a record with a given sort key is

found. Are there any disadvantages to the method with the fewer average disk I/O's?

b) Compare methods (*ii*) and (*iii*) for their average numbers of disk I/O's per record retrieval, as a function of b, the total number of blocks in the chain. Assume that the offset table takes 10% of the space, and the records take the remaining 90%.

! c) Include methods (*iv*) and (*v*) in the comparison from part (b). Assume that the sort key is 1/9 of the record. Note that we do not have to repeat the sort key in the record if it is in the offset table. Thus, in effect, the offset table uses 20% of the space and the remainders of the records use 80% of the space.

Exercise 12.5.2: Relational database systems have always preferred to use fixed-length tuples if possible. Give three reasons for this preference.

12.6 Summary of Chapter 12

✦ *Fields*: Fields are the most primitive data elements. Many, such as integers or fixed-length character strings, are simply given an appropriate number of bytes in secondary storage. Variable-length character strings are stored either in a fixed sequence of bytes containing an endmarker, or in an area for varying strings, with a length indicated by an integer at the beginning or an endmarker at the end.

✦ *Records*: Records are composed of several fields plus a record header. The header contains information about the record, possibly including such matters as a timestamp, schema information, and a record length.

✦ *Variable-Length Records*: If records contain one or more variable-length fields or contain an unknown number of repetitions of a field, then additional structure is necessary. A directory of pointers in the record header can be used to locate variable-length fields within the record. Alternatively, we can replace the variable-length or repeating fields by (fixed-length) pointers to a place outside the record where the field's value is kept.

✦ *Blocks*: Records are generally stored within blocks. A block header, with information about that block, consumes some of the space in the block, with the remainder occupied by one or more records.

✦ *Spanned Records*: Generally, a record exists within one block. However, if records are longer than blocks, or we wish to make use of leftover space within blocks, then we can break records into two or more fragments, one on each block. A fragment header is then needed to link the fragments of a record.

✦ *BLOBS*: Very large values, such as images and videos, are called BLOBS (binary, large objects). These values must be stored across many blocks. Depending on the requirements for access, it may be desirable to keep the BLOB on one cylinder, to reduce the access time for the BLOB, or it may be necessary to stripe the BLOB across several disks, to allow parallel retrieval of its contents.

✦ *Offset Tables*: To support insertions and deletions of records, as well as records that change their length due to modification of varying-length fields, we can put in the block header an offset table that has pointers to each of the records in the block.

✦ *Overflow Blocks*: Also to support insertions and growing records, a block may have a link to an overflow block or chain of blocks, wherein are kept some records that logically belong in the first block.

✦ *Database Addresses*: Data managed by a DBMS is found among several storage devices, typically disks. To locate blocks and records in this storage system, we can use physical addresses, which are a description of the device number, cylinder, track, sector(s), and possibly byte within a sector. We can also use logical addresses, which are arbitrary character strings that are translated into physical addresses by a map table.

✦ *Structured Addresses*: We may also locate records by using part of the physical address, e.g., the location of the block whereon a record is found, plus additional information such as a key for the record or a position in the offset table of a block that locates the record.

✦ *Pointer Swizzling*: When disk blocks are brought to main memory, the database addresses need to be translated to memory addresses, if pointers are to be followed. The translation is called swizzling, and can either be done automatically, when blocks are brought to memory, or on-demand, when a pointer is first followed.

✦ *Tombstones*: When a record is deleted, pointers to it will dangle. A tombstone in place of (part of) the deleted record warns the system that the record is no longer there.

✦ *Pinned Blocks*: For various reasons, including the fact that a block may contain swizzled pointers, it may be unacceptable to copy a block from memory back to its place on disk. Such a block is said to be pinned. If the pinning is due to swizzled pointers, then they must be unswizzled before returning the block to disk.

12.7 References for Chapter 12

The classic 1968 text on the subject of data structures [2] has been updated recently. [4] has information on structures relevant to this chapter and also

Chapter 13.

Tombstones as a technique for dealing with deletion is from [3]. [1] covers data representation issues, such as addresses and swizzling in the context of object-oriented DBMS's.

1. R. G. G. Cattell, *Object Data Management*, Addison-Wesley, Reading MA, 1994.

2. D. E. Knuth, *The Art of Computer Programming, Vol. I, Fundamental Algorithms, Third Edition*, Addison-Wesley, Reading MA, 1997.

3. D. Lomet, "Scheme for invalidating free references," *IBM J. Research and Development* **19**:1 (1975), pp. 26–35.

4. G. Wiederhold, *File Organization for Database Design*, McGraw-Hill, New York, 1987.

Chapter 13

Index Structures

Having seen the options available for representing records, we must now consider how whole relations, or the extents of classes, are represented. It is not sufficient simply to scatter the records that represent tuples of the relation or objects of the extent among various blocks. To see why, ask how we would answer even the simplest query, such as SELECT * FROM R. We would have to examine every block in the storage system and hope there is enough information in block headers to identify where in the block records begin and enough information in record headers to tell in what relation the record belongs.

A slightly better organization is to reserve some blocks, perhaps several whole cylinders, for a given relation. All blocks in those cylinders may be assumed to hold records that represent tuples of our relation. Now, at least we can find the tuples of the relation without scanning the entire data store.

However, this organization offers no help should we want to answer the next-simplest query, such as SELECT * FROM R WHERE a=10. Section 6.6.6 introduced us to the importance of creating *indexes* on a relation, in order to speed up the discovery of those tuples of a relation that have a particular value for a particular attribute. As suggested in Fig. 13.1, an index is any data structure that takes as input a property of records — typically the value of one or more fields — and finds the records with that property "quickly." In particular, an index lets us find a record without having to look at more than a small fraction of all possible records. The field(s) on whose values the index is based is called the *search key*, or just "key" if the index is understood.

Many different data structures can serve as indexes. In the remainder of this chapter we consider the following methods:

1. Simple indexes on sorted files.

2. Secondary indexes on unsorted files.

3. B-trees, a commonly used way to build indexes on any file.

4. Hash tables, another useful and important index structure.

605

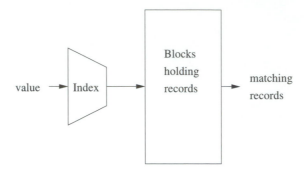

Figure 13.1: An index takes a value for some field(s) and finds records with the matching value

---

Keys and More Keys

There are many meanings of the term "key." We used it in Section 7.1.1 to mean the primary key of a relation. In Section 11.4.4 we learned about "sort keys," the attribute(s) on which a file of records is sorted. Now, we shall speak of "search keys," the attribute(s) for which we are given values and asked to search, through an index, for tuples with matching values. We try to use the appropriate adjective — "primary," "sort," or "search" — when the meaning of "key" is unclear. However, notice in sections such as 13.1.2 and 13.1.3 that there are many times when the three kinds of keys are one and the same.

13.1 Indexes on Sequential Files

We begin our study of index structures by considering what is probably the simplest structure: A sorted file, called the *data file*, is given another file, called the *index file*, consisting of key-pointer pairs. A search key K in the index file is associated with a pointer to a data-file record that has search key K. These indexes can be "dense," meaning there is an entry in the index file for every record of the data file, or "sparse," meaning that only some of the data records are represented in the index, often one index entry per block of the data file.

13.1.1 Sequential Files

One of the simplest index types relies on the file being sorted on the attribute(s) of the index. Such a file is called a *sequential file*. This structure is especially useful when the search key is the primary key of the relation, although it can be used for other attributes. Figure 13.2 suggests a relation represented as a sequential file.

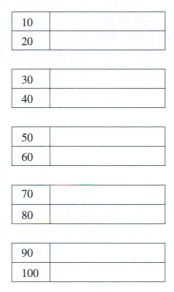

Figure 13.2: A sequential file

In this file, the tuples are sorted by their primary key. We imagine that keys are integers; we show only the key field, and we make the atypical assumption that there is room for only two records in one block. For instance, the first block of the file holds the records with keys 10 and 20. In this and many other examples, we use integers that are sequential multiples of 10 as keys, although there is surely no requirement that keys be multiples of 10 or that records with all multiples of 10 appear.

13.1.2 Dense Indexes

Now that we have our records sorted, we can build on them a *dense index*, which is a sequence of blocks holding only the keys of the records and pointers to the records themselves; the pointers are addresses in the sense discussed in Section 12.3. The index is called "dense" because every key from the data file is represented in the index. In comparison, "sparse" indexes, to be discussed in Section 13.1.3, normally keep only one key per data block in the index.

The index blocks of the dense index maintain these keys in the same sorted order as in the file itself. Since keys and pointers presumably take much less space than complete records, we expect to use many fewer blocks for the index than for the file itself. The index is especially advantageous when it, but not the data file, can fit in main memory. Then, by using the index, we can find any record given its search key, with only one disk I/O per lookup.

Example 13.1 : Figure 13.3 suggests a dense index on a sorted file that begins as Fig. 13.2. For convenience, we have assumed that the file continues with a key every 10 integers, although in practice we would not expect to find such a regular pattern of keys. We have also assumed that index blocks can hold only four key-pointer pairs. Again, in practice we would find typically that there were many more pairs per block, perhaps hundreds.

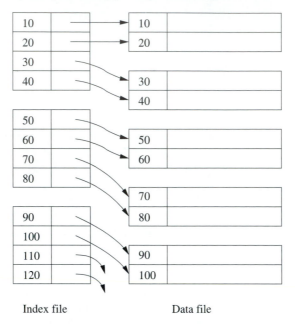

Index file   Data file

Figure 13.3: A dense index (left) on a sequential data file (right)

The first index block contains pointers to the first four records, the second block has pointers to the next four, and so on. For reasons that we shall discuss in Section 13.1.6, in practice we may not want to fill all the index blocks completely. □

The dense index supports queries that ask for records with a given search key value. Given key value K, we search the index blocks for K, and when we find it, we follow the associated pointer to the record with key K. It might appear that we need to examine every block of the index, or half the blocks of the index, on average, before we find K. However, there are several factors that make the index-based search more efficient than it seems.

1. The number of index blocks is usually small compared with the number of data blocks.

2. Since keys are sorted, we can use binary search to find K. If there are n blocks of the index, we only look at $\log_2 n$ of them.

3. The index may be small enough to be kept permanently in main memory buffers. If so, the search for key K involves only main-memory accesses, and there are no expensive disk I/O's to be performed.

Locating Index Blocks

We have assumed that some mechanism exists for locating the index blocks, from which the individual tuples (if the index is dense) or blocks of the data file (if the index is sparse) can be found. Many ways of locating the index can be used. For example, if the index is small, we may store it in reserved locations of memory or disk. If the index is larger, we can build another layer of index on top of it as we discuss in Section 13.1.4 and keep that in fixed locations. The ultimate extension of this idea is the B-tree of Section 13.3, where we need to know the location of only a single root block.

Example 13.2: Imagine a relation of 1,000,000 tuples that fit ten to a 4096-byte block. The total space required by the data is over 400 megabytes, probably too much to keep in main memory. However, suppose that the key field is 30 bytes, and pointers are 8 bytes. Then with a reasonable amount of block-header space we can keep 100 key-pointer pairs in a 4096-byte block.

A dense index therefore requires 10,000 blocks, or 40 megabytes. We might be able to allocate main-memory buffers for these blocks, depending on what else we needed in main memory, and how much main memory there was. Further, $\log_2(10000)$ is about 13, so we only need to access 13 or 14 blocks in a binary search for a key. And since all binary searches would start out accessing only a small subset of the blocks (the block in the middle, those at the 1/4 and 3/4 points, those at 1/8, 3/8, 5/8, and 7/8, and so on), even if we could not afford to keep the whole index in memory, we might be able to keep the most important blocks in main memory, thus retrieving the record for any key with significantly fewer than 14 disk I/O's. □

13.1.3 Sparse Indexes

If a dense index is too large, we can use a similar structure, called a *sparse index*, that uses less space at the expense of somewhat more time to find a record given its key. A sparse index, as seen in Fig. 13.4, holds only one key-pointer per data block. The key is for the first record on the data block.

Example 13.3: As in Example 13.1, we assume that the data file is sorted, and keys are all the integers divisible by 10, up to some large number. We also continue to assume that four key-pointer pairs fit on an index block. Thus, the first index block has entries for the first keys on the first four blocks, which are 10, 30, 50, and 70. Continuing the assumed pattern of keys, the second index block has the first keys of the fifth through eighth blocks, which we assume are 90, 110, 130, and 150. We also show a third index block with first keys from the hypothetical ninth through twelfth data blocks. □

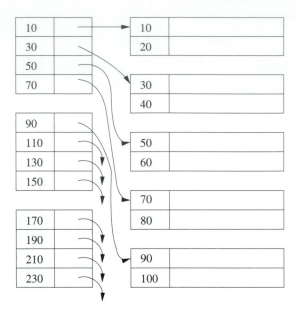

Figure 13.4: A sparse index on a sequential file

Example 13.4 : A sparse index can require many fewer blocks than a dense index. Using the more realistic parameters of Example 13.2, where there are 100,000 data blocks and 100 key-pointer pairs fit on one index block, we need only 1000 index blocks if a sparse index is used. Now the index uses only four megabytes, an amount that surely could be allocated in main memory.

On the other hand, the dense index allows us to answer queries of the form "does there exist a record with key value K?" without having to retrieve the block containing the record. The fact that K exists in the dense index is enough to guarantee the existence of the record with key K. On the other hand, the same query, using a sparse index, requires a disk I/O to retrieve the block on which key K *might* be found. □

To find the record with key K, given a sparse index, we search the index for the largest key less than or equal to K. Since the index file is sorted by key, a modified binary search will locate this entry. We follow the associated pointer to a data block. Now, we must search this block for the record with key K. Of course the block must have enough format information that the records and their contents can be identified. Any of the techniques from Sections 12.2 and 12.4 can be used, as appropriate.

13.1.4   Multiple Levels of Index

An index itself can cover many blocks, as we saw in Examples 13.2 and 13.4. Even if we use a binary search to find the desired index entry, we still may need to do many disk I/O's to get to the record we want. By putting an index on the index, we can make the use of the first level of index more efficient.

Figure 13.5 extends Fig. 13.4 by adding a second index level (as before, we assume the unusual pattern of keys every 10 integers). The same idea would let us place a third-level index on the second level, and so on. However, this idea has its limits, and we prefer the B-tree structure described in Section 13.3 over building many levels of index.

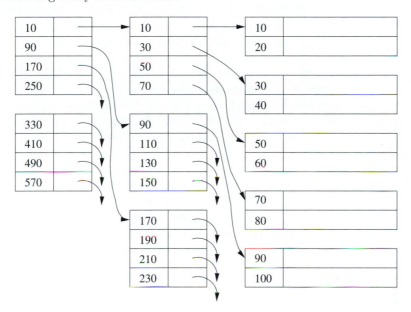

Figure 13.5: Adding a second level of sparse index

In this example, the first-level index is sparse, although we could have chosen a dense index for the first level. However, the second and higher levels must be sparse. The reason is that a dense index on an index would have exactly as many key-pointer pairs as the first-level index, and therefore would take exactly as much space as the first-level index. A second-level dense index thus introduces additional structure for no advantage.

Example 13.5: Continuing with a study of the hypothetical relation of Example 13.4, suppose we put a second-level index on the first-level sparse index. Since the first-level index occupies 1000 blocks, and we can fit 100 key-pointer pairs in a block, we need 10 blocks for the second-level index.

It is very likely that these 10 blocks can remain buffered in memory. If so, then to find the record with a given key K, we look up in the second-level index to find the largest key less than or equal to K. The associated pointer leads to a block B of the first-level index that will surely guide us to the desired record. We read block B into memory if it is not already there; this read is the first disk I/O we need to do. We look in block B for the greatest key less than or equal to K, and that key gives us a data block that will contain the record with key K if such a record exists. That block requires a second disk I/O, and we are done, having used only two I/O's. □

13.1.5 Indexes With Duplicate Search Keys

Until this point we have supposed that the search key, upon which the index is based, was also a key of the relation, so there could be at most one record with any key value. However, indexes are often used for nonkey attributes, so it is possible that more than one record has a given key value. If we sort the records by the search key, leaving records with equal search key in any order, then we can adapt the previous ideas when the search key is not a key of the relation.

Perhaps the simplest extension of previous ideas is to have a dense index with one entry with key K for each record of the data file that has search key K. That is, we allow duplicate search keys in the index file. Finding all the records with a given search key K is thus simple: Look for the first K in the index file, find all the other K's, which must immediately follow, and pursue all the associated pointers to find the records with search key K.

A slightly more efficient approach is to have only one record in the dense index for each search key K. This key is associated with a pointer to the first of the records with K. To find the others, move forward in the data file to find any additional records with K; these must follow immediately in the sorted order of the data file. Figure 13.6 illustrates this idea.

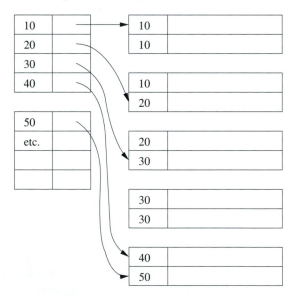

Figure 13.6: A dense index when duplicate search keys are allowed

Example 13.6 : Suppose we want to find all the records with search key 20 in Fig. 13.6. We find the 20 entry in the index and follow its pointer to the first record with search key 20. We then search forward in the data file. Since we are at the last record of the second block of this file, we move forward to the third block.[1] We find the first record of this block has 20, but the second has 30. Thus, we need search no further; we have found the only two records with search key 20. □

Figure 13.7 shows a sparse index on the same data file as Fig. 13.6. The sparse index is quite conventional; it has key-pointer pairs corresponding to the first search key on each block of the data file.

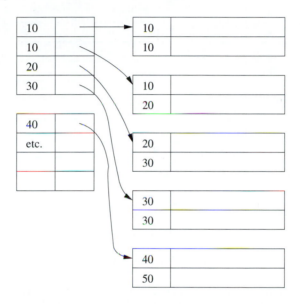

Figure 13.7: A sparse index indicating the lowest search key in each block

To find the records with search key K in this data structure, we find the last entry of the index, call it E_1, that has a key less than or equal to K. We then move towards the front of the index until we either come to the first entry or we come to an entry E_2 with a key strictly less than K. E_2 could be E_1. All the data blocks that might have a record with search key K are pointed to by the index entries from E_2 to E_1, inclusive.

Example 13.7 : Suppose we want to look up key 20 in Fig. 13.7. The third entry in the first index block is E_1; it is the last entry with a key ≤ 20. When we search backward, we see the previous entry has a key smaller than 20. Thus, the second entry of the first index block is E_2. The two associated pointers take

---

[1]To find the next block of the data file, chain the blocks in a linked list; i.e., give each block header a pointer to the next block.

us to the second and third data blocks, and it is on these two blocks that we find records with search key 20.

For another example, if $K = 10$, then E_1 is the second entry of the first index block, and E_2 doesn't exist because we never find a smaller key. Thus, we follow the pointers in all index entries up to and including the second. That takes us to the first two data blocks, where we find all of the records with search key 10.   □

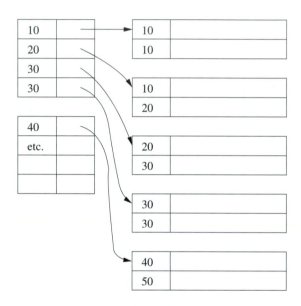

Figure 13.8: A sparse index indicating the lowest new search key in each block

A slightly different scheme is shown in Fig. 13.8. There, the index entry for a data block holds the smallest search key that is *new*; i.e., it did not appear in a previous block. If there is no new search key in a block, then its index entry holds the lone search key found in that block. Under this scheme, we can find the records with search key K by looking in the index for the first entry whose key is either

a) Equal to K, or

b) Less than K, but the next key is greater than K.

We follow the pointer in this entry, and if we find at least one record with search key K in that block, then we search forward through additional blocks until we find all records with search key K.

Example 13.8 : Suppose that $K = 20$ in the structure of Fig. 13.8. The second index entry is selected by the above rule, and its pointer leads us to the first block with 20. We must search forward, since the following block also has a 20.

If $K = 30$, the rule selects the third entry. Its pointer leads us to the third data block, where the records with search key 30 begin. Finally, if $K = 25$, then part (b) of the selection rule indicates the second index entry. We are thus led to the second data block. If there were any records with search key 25, at least one would have to follow the records with 20 on that block, because we know that the first new key in the third data block is 30. Since there are no 25's, we fail in our search. □

13.1.6 Managing Indexes During Data Modifications

Until this point, we have shown data files and indexes as if they were sequences of blocks, fully packed with records of the appropriate type. Since data evolves with time, we expect that records will be inserted, deleted, and sometimes updated. As a result, an organization like a sequential file will evolve so that what once fit in one block no longer does. We can use the techniques discussed in Section 12.5 to reorganize the data file. Recall that the three big ideas from that section are:

1. Create overflow blocks if extra space is needed, or delete overflow blocks if enough records are deleted that the space is no longer needed. Overflow blocks do not have entries in a sparse index. Rather, they should be considered as extensions of their primary block.

2. Instead of overflow blocks, we may be able to insert new blocks in the sequential order. If we do, then the new block needs an entry in a sparse index. We should remember that changing an index can create the same kinds of problems on the index file that insertions and deletions to the data file create. If we create new index blocks, then these blocks must be located somehow, e.g., with another level of index as in Section 13.1.4.

3. When there is no room to insert a tuple into a block, we can sometimes slide tuples to adjacent blocks. Conversely, if adjacent blocks grow too empty, they can be combined.

However, when changes occur to the data file, we must often change the index to adapt. The correct approach depends on whether the index is dense or sparse, and on which of the three strategies enumerated above is used. However, one general principle should be remembered:

- An index file is an example of a sequential file; the key-pointer pairs can be treated as records sorted by the value of the search key. Thus, the same strategies used to maintain data files in the face of modifications can be applied to its index file.

In Fig. 13.9, we summarize the actions that must be taken on a sparse or dense index when seven different actions on the data file are taken. These seven actions include creating or deleting empty overflow blocks, creating or deleting empty blocks of the sequential file, inserting, deleting, and moving records. Notice that we assume only empty blocks can be created or destroyed. In particular, if we want to delete a block that contains records, we must first delete the records or move them to another block.

Action	Dense Index	Sparse Index
Create empty overflow block	none	none
Delete empty overflow block	none	none
Create empty sequential block	none	insert
Delete empty sequential block	none	delete
Insert record	insert	update(?)
Delete record	delete	update(?)
Slide record	update	update(?)

Figure 13.9: How actions on the sequential file affect the index file

In this table, we notice the following:

- Creating or destroying an empty overflow block has no effect on either type of index. It has no effect on a dense index, because that index refers to records. It has no effect on a sparse index, because it is only the primary blocks, not the overflow blocks, that have entries in the sparse index.

- Creating or destroying blocks of the sequential file has no effect on a dense index, again because that index refers to records, not blocks. It *does* affect a sparse index, since we must insert or delete an index entry for the block created or destroyed, respectively.

- Inserting or deleting records results in the same action on a dense index: a key-pointer pair for that record is inserted or deleted. However, there is typically no effect on a sparse index. The exception is when the record is the first of its block, in which case the corresponding key value in the sparse index must be updated. Thus, we have put a question mark after "update" for these actions in the table of Fig. 13.9, indicating that the update is possible, but not certain.

- Similarly, sliding a record, whether within a block or between blocks, results in an update to the corresponding entry of a dense index, but only affects a sparse index if the moved record was or becomes the first of its block.

We shall illustrate the family of algorithms implied by these rules in a series of examples. These examples involve both sparse and dense indexes and both "record sliding" and overflow-block approaches.

Preparing for Evolution of Data

Since it is common for relations or class extents to grow with time, it is often wise to distribute extra space among blocks — both data and index blocks. If blocks are, say, 75% full to begin with, then we can run for some time before having to create overflow blocks or slide records between blocks. The advantage to having no overflow blocks, or few overflow blocks, is that the average record access then requires only one disk I/O. The more overflow blocks, the higher will be the average number of blocks we need to look at in order to find a given record.

Example 13.9 : First, let us consider the deletion of a record from a sequential file with a dense index. We begin with the file and index of Fig. 13.3. Suppose that the record with key 30 is deleted. Figure 13.10 shows the result of the deletion.

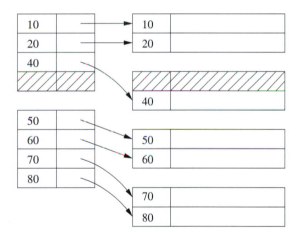

Figure 13.10: Deletion of record with search key 30 in a dense index

First, the record 30 is deleted from the sequential file. We assume that there are possible pointers from outside the block to records in the block, so we have elected not to slide the remaining record, 40, forward in the block. Rather, we suppose that a tombstone has been left in place of the record 30.

In the index, we delete the key-pointer pair for 30. We suppose that there cannot be pointers to index records from outside, so there is no need to leave a tombstone for the pair. Therefore, we have taken the option to consolidate the index block and move following records of the block forward. □

Example 13.10 : Now, let us consider two deletions from a file with a sparse index. We begin with the structure of Fig. 13.4 and again suppose that the record with key 30 is deleted. We also assume that there is no impediment to sliding records around within blocks — either we know there are no pointers to records from anywhere, or we are using an offset table as in Fig. 12.16 to support such sliding.

The effect of the deletion of record 30 is shown in Fig. 13.11. The record has been deleted, and the following record, 40, slides forward to consolidate the block at the front. Since 40 is now the first key on the second data block, we need to update the index record for that block. We see in Fig. 13.11 that the key associated with the pointer to the second data block has been updated from 30 to 40.

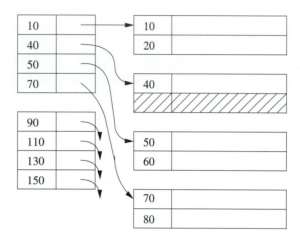

Figure 13.11: Deletion of record with search key 30 in a sparse index

Now, suppose that record 40 is also deleted. We see the effect of this action in Fig. 13.12. The second data block now has no records at all. If the sequential file is stored on arbitrary blocks (rather than, say, consecutive blocks of a cylinder), then we may link the unused block to a list of available space.

We complete the deletion of record 40 by adjusting the index. Since the second data block no longer exists, we delete its entry from the index. We also show in Fig 13.12 the consolidation of the first index block, by moving forward the following pairs. That step is optional.   □

Example 13.11 : Now, let us consider the effect of an insertion. Begin at Fig. 13.11, where we have just deleted record 30 from the file with a sparse index, but the record 40 remains. We now insert a record with key 15. Consulting the sparse index, we find that this record belongs in the first data block. But that block is full; it holds records 10 and 20.

One thing we can do is look for a nearby block with some extra space, and in this case we find it in the second data block. We thus slide records backward in the file to make room for record 15. The result is shown in Fig. 13.13. Record 20 has been moved from the first to the second data block, and 15 put in its

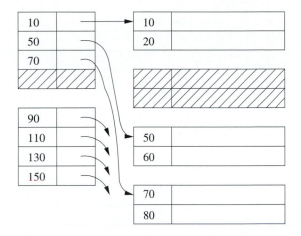

Figure 13.12: Deletion of record with search key 40 in a sparse index

place. To fit record 20 on the second block and keep records sorted, we slide record 40 back in the second block and put 20 ahead of it.

Our last step is to modify the index entries of the changed blocks. We might have to change the key in the index pair for block 1, but we do not in this case, because the inserted record is not the first in its block. We do, however, change the key in the index entry for the second data block, since the first record of that block, which used to be 40, is now 20. □

Example 13.12 : The problem with the strategy exhibited in Example 13.11 is that we were lucky to find an empty space in an adjacent data block. Had the record with key 30 not been deleted previously, we would have searched in vain for an empty space. In principle, we would have had to slide every record from 20 to the end of the file back until we got to the end of the file and could create an additional block.

Because of this risk, it is often wiser to allow overflow blocks to supplement the space of a primary block that has too many records. Figure 13.14 shows the effect of inserting a record with key 15 into the structure of Fig. 13.11. As in Example 13.11, the first data block has too many records. Instead of sliding records to the second block, we create an overflow block for the data block. We have shown in Fig. 13.14 a "nub" on each block, representing a place in the block header where a pointer to an overflow block may be placed. Any number of overflow blocks may be linked in a chain using these pointer spaces.

In our example, record 15 is inserted in its rightful place, after record 10. Record 20 slides to the overflow block to make room. No changes to the index are necessary, since the first record in data block 1 has not changed. Notice that no index entry is made for the overflow block, which is considered an extension of data block 1, not a block of the sequential file on its own. □

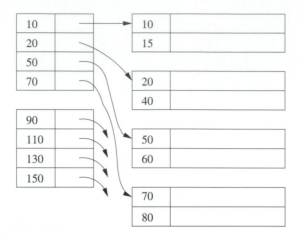

Figure 13.13: Insertion into a file with a sparse index, using immediate reorganization

13.1.7 Exercises for Section 13.1

* Exercise 13.1.1 : Suppose blocks hold either three records, or ten key-pointer pairs. As a function of n, the number of records, how many blocks do we need to hold a data file and:

    a) A dense index?

    b) A sparse index?

Exercise 13.1.2 : Repeat Exercise 13.1.1 if blocks can hold up to 30 records or 200 key-pointer pairs, but neither data- nor index-blocks are allowed to be more than 80% full.

! Exercise 13.1.3 : Repeat Exercise 13.1.1 if we use as many levels of index as is appropriate, until the final level of index has only one block.

*!! Exercise 13.1.4 : Suppose that blocks hold three records or ten key-pointer pairs, as in Exercise 13.1.1, but duplicate search keys are possible. To be specific, 1/3 of all search keys in the database appear in one record, 1/3 appear in exactly two records, and 1/3 appear in exactly three records. Suppose we have a dense index, but there is only one key-pointer pair per search-key value, to the first of the records that has that key. If no blocks are in memory initially, compute the average number of disk I/O's needed to find all the records with a given search key K. You may assume that the location of the index block containing key K is known, although it is on disk.

! Exercise 13.1.5 : Repeat Exercise 13.1.4 for:

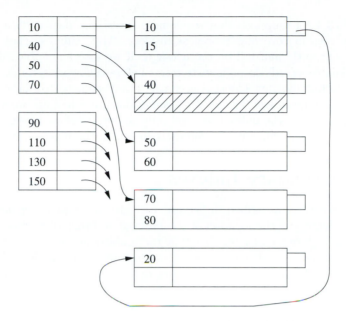

Figure 13.14: Insertion into a file with a sparse index, using overflow blocks

   a) A dense index with a key-pointer pair for each record, including those
      with duplicated keys.

   b) A sparse index indicating the lowest key on each data block, as in Fig. 13.7.

   c) A sparse index indicating the lowest *new* key on each data block, as in
      Fig. 13.8.

! Exercise 13.1.6: If we have a dense index on the primary key attribute of
a relation, then it is possible to have pointers to tuples (or the records that
represent those tuples) go to the index entry rather than to the record itself.
What are the advantages of each approach?

Exercise 13.1.7: Continue the changes to Fig. 13.13 if we next delete the
records with keys 60, 70, and 80, then insert records with keys 21, 22, and so
on, up to 29. Assume that extra space is obtained by:

  * a) Adding overflow blocks to either the data file or index file.

   b) Sliding records as far back as necessary, adding additional blocks to the
      end of the data file and/or index file if needed.

   c) Inserting new data or index blocks into the middle of these files as neces-
      sary.

*! Exercise 13.1.8 : Suppose that we handle insertions into a data file of n records by creating overflow blocks as needed. Also, suppose that the data blocks are currently half full on the average. If we insert new records at random, how many records do we have to insert before the average number of data blocks (including overflow blocks if necessary) that we need to examine to find a record with a given key reaches 2? Assume that on a lookup, we search the block pointed to by the index first, and only search overflow blocks, in order, until we find the record, which is definitely in one of the blocks of the chain.

13.2 Secondary Indexes

The data structures described in Section 13.1 are called *primary indexes*, because they determine the location of the indexed records. In Section 13.1, the location was determined by the fact that the underlying file was sorted on the search key. Section 13.4 will discuss another common example of a primary index: a hash table in which the search key determines the "bucket" into which the record goes.

However, frequently we want several indexes on a relation, to facilitate a variety of queries. For instance, since `name` is the primary key of the `MovieStar` relation (see Fig. 12.1), we expect that the DBMS will create a primary index structure to support queries that specify the name of the star. However, suppose we also want to use our database to acknowledge stars on milestone birthdays. We may then run queries like

```
SELECT name, address
FROM MovieStar
WHERE birthdate = DATE '1952-01-01';
```

We need a *secondary index* on `birthdate` to help with such queries. In an SQL system, we might call for such an index by an explicit command such as

```
CREATE INDEX BDIndex ON MovieStar(birthdate);
```

A secondary index serves the purpose of any index: it is a data structure that facilitates finding records given a value for one or more fields. However, the secondary index is distinguished from the primary index in that a secondary index does not determine the placement of records in the data file. Rather the secondary index tells us the current locations of records; that location may have been decided by a primary index on some other field. An important consequence of the distinction between primary and secondary indexes is that:

- It makes no sense to talk of a sparse, secondary index. Since the secondary index does not influence location, we could not use it to predict the location of any record whose key was not mentioned in the index file explicitly.

- Thus, secondary indexes are always dense.

13.2.1   Design of Secondary Indexes

A secondary index is a dense index, usually with duplicates. As before, this index consists of key-pointer pairs; the "key" is a search key and need not be unique. Pairs in the index file are sorted by key value, to help find the entries given a key. If we wish to place a second level of index on this structure, then that index would be sparse, for the reasons discussed in Section 13.1.4.

Example 13.13: Figure 13.15 shows a typical secondary index. The data file is shown with two records per block, as has been our standard for illustration. The records have only their search key shown; this attribute is integer valued, and as before we have taken the values to be multiples of 10. Notice that, unlike the data file in Section 13.1.5, here the data is not sorted by the search key.

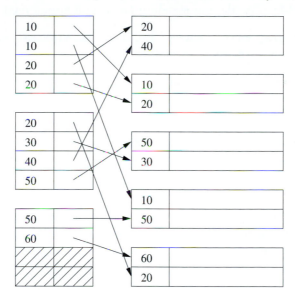

Figure 13.15: A secondary index

However, the keys in the index file *are* sorted. The result is that the pointers in one index block can go to many different data blocks, instead of one or a few consecutive blocks. For example, to retrieve all the records with search key 20, we not only have to look at two index blocks, but we are sent by their pointers to three different data blocks. Thus, using a secondary index may result in many more disk I/O's than if we get the same number of records via a primary index. However, there is no help for this problem; we cannot control the order of tuples in the data block, because they are presumably ordered according to some other attribute(s).

It would be possible to add a second level of index to Fig. 13.15. This level would be sparse, with pairs corresponding to the first key or first new key of each index block, as discussed in Section 13.1.4.   □

13.2.2 Applications of Secondary Indexes

Besides supporting additional indexes on relations (or extents of classes) that
are organized as sequential files, there are some data structures where secondary
indexes are needed for even the primary key. One of these is the "heap" structure, where the records of the relation are kept in no particular order.

A second common structure needing secondary indexes is the *clustered file*.
Suppose there are relations R and S, with a many-one relationship from the
tuples of R to tuples of S. It may make sense to store each tuple of R with the
tuple of S to which it is related, rather than according to the primary key of R.
An example will illustrate why this organization makes good sense in special
situations.

Example 13.14 : Consider our standard movie and studio relations:

```
Movie(title, year, length, inColor, studioName, producerC#)
Studio(name, address, presC#)
```

Suppose further that the most common form of query is:

```
SELECT title, year
FROM Movie, Studio
WHERE presC# = zzz AND Movie.studioName = Studio.name;
```

Here, *zzz* represents any possible certificate number for a studio president. That
is, given the president of a studio, we need to find all the movies made by that
studio.

If we are convinced that the above query is typical, then instead of ordering
`Movie` tuples by the primary key `title` and `year`, we can create a *clustered
file structure* for both relations `Studio` and `Movie`, as suggested by Fig. 13.16.
Following each `Studio` tuple are all the `Movie` tuples for all the movies owned
by that studio.

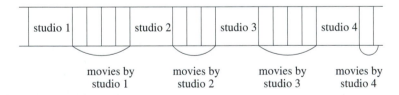

Figure 13.16: A clustered file with each studio clustered with the movies made
by that studio

If we create an index for `Studio` with search key `presC#`, then whatever the
value of `zzz` is, we can quickly find the tuple for the proper studio. Moreover,
all the `Movie` tuples whose value of attribute `studioName` matches the value
of `name` for that studio will follow the studio's tuple in the clustered file. As a
result, we can find the movies for this studio by making almost as few disk I/O's

as possible. The reason is that the desired `Movie` tuples are packed almost as densely as possible onto the following blocks. □

13.2.3 Indirection in Secondary Indexes

There is some wasted space, perhaps a significant amount of wastage, in the structure suggested by Fig. 13.15. If a search-key value appears n times in the data file, then the value is written n times in the index file. It would be better if we could write the key value once for all the pointers to data records with that value.

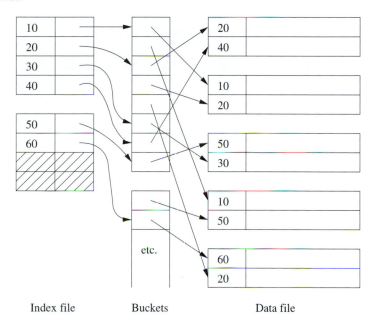

Index file   Buckets   Data file

Figure 13.17: Saving space by using indirection in a secondary index

A convenient way to avoid repeating values is to use a level of indirection, called *buckets*, between the secondary index file and the data file. As shown in Fig. 13.17, there is one pair for each search key K. The pointer of this pair goes to a position in a "bucket file," which holds the "bucket" for K. Following this position, until the next position pointed to by the index, are pointers to all the records with search-key value K.

Example 13.15: For instance, let us follow the pointer from search key 50 in the index file of Fig. 13.17 to the intermediate "bucket" file. This pointer happens to take us to the last pointer of one block of the bucket file. We search forward, to the first pointer of the next block. We stop at that point, because the next pointer of the index file, associated with search key 60, points to the second pointer of the second block of the bucket file. □

The scheme of Fig. 13.17 saves space as long as search-key values are larger than pointers, and the average key appears at least twice. However, even if not, there is an important advantage to using indirection with secondary indexes: often, we can use the pointers in the buckets to help answer queries without ever looking at most of the records in the data file. Specifically, when there are several conditions to a query, and each condition has a secondary index to help it, we can find the bucket pointers that satisfy all the conditions by intersecting sets of pointers in memory, and retrieving only the records pointed to by the surviving pointers. We thus save the I/O cost of retrieving records that satisfy some, but not all, of the conditions.[2]

Example 13.16: Consider the usual `Movie` relation:

```
Movie(title, year, length, inColor, studioName, producerC#)
```

Suppose we have secondary indexes with indirect buckets on both `studioName` and `year`, and we are asked the query

```
SELECT title
FROM Movie
WHERE studioName = 'Disney' AND year = 1995;
```

that is, find all the Disney movies made in 1995.

Figure 13.18 shows how we can answer this query using the indexes. Using the index on `studioName`, we find the pointers to all records for Disney movies, but we do not yet bring any of those records from disk to memory. Instead, using the index on `year`, we find the pointers to all the movies of 1995. We then intersect the two sets of pointers, getting exactly the movies that were made by Disney in 1995. Finally, we retrieve from disk all data blocks holding one or more of these movies, thus retrieving the minimum possible number of blocks. □

13.2.4 Document Retrieval and Inverted Indexes

For many years, the information-retrieval community has dealt with the storage of documents and the efficient retrieval of documents with a given set of key-words. With the advent of the World-Wide Web and the feasibility of keeping all documents on-line, the retrieval of documents given keywords has become one of the largest database problems. While there are many kinds of queries that one can use to find relevant documents, the simplest and most common form can be seen in relational terms as follows:

---

[2]We could also use this pointer-intersection trick if we got the pointers directly from the index, rather than from buckets. However, the use of buckets often saves disk I/O's, since the pointers use less space than key-pointer pairs.

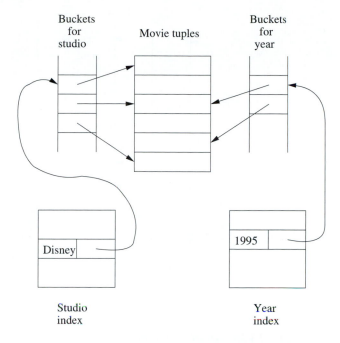

Figure 13.18: Intersecting buckets in main memory

- A document may be thought of as a tuple in a relation Doc. This relation has very many attributes, one corresponding to each possible word in a document. Each attribute is boolean — either the word is present in the document, or it is not. Thus, the relation schema may be thought of as

      Doc(hasCat, hasDog, ...)

  where hasCat is true if and only if the document has the word "cat" at least once.

- There is a secondary index on each of the attributes of Doc. However, we save the trouble of indexing those tuples for which the value of the attribute is FALSE; instead, the index only leads us to the documents for which the word is present. That is, the index has entries only for the search-key value TRUE.

- Instead of creating a separate index for each attribute (i.e., for each word), the indexes are combined into one, called an *inverted index*. This index uses indirect buckets for space efficiency, as was discussed in Section 13.2.3.

Example 13.17: An inverted index is illustrated in Fig. 13.19. In place of a data file of records is a collection of documents, each of which may be stored

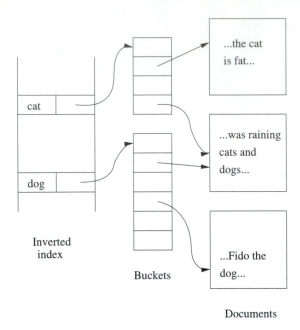

Figure 13.19: An inverted index on documents

on one or more disk blocks. The inverted index itself consists of a set of word-pointer pairs; the words are in effect the search key for the index. The inverted index is kept in a sequence of blocks, just like any of the indexes discussed so far. However, in some document-retrieval applications, the data may be more static than the typical database, so there may be no provision for overflow of blocks or changes to the index in general.

The pointers refer to positions in a "bucket" file. For instance, we have shown in Fig. 13.19 the word "cat" with a pointer to the bucket file. That pointer leads us to the beginning of a list of pointers to all the documents that contain the word "cat." We have shown some of these in the figure. Similarly, the word "dog" is shown leading to a list of pointers to all the documents with "dog."   □

Pointers in the bucket file can be:

1. Pointers to the document itself.

2. Pointers to an occurrence of the word. In this case, the pointer might be a pair consisting of the first block for the document and an integer indicating the number of the word in the document.

When we use "buckets" of pointers to occurrences of each word, we may extend the idea to include in the bucket array some information about each occurrence. Now, the bucket file itself becomes a collection of records with

---

More About Information Retrieval

There are a number of techniques for improving the effectiveness of retrieval of documents given keywords. While a complete treatment is beyond the scope of this book, here are two useful techniques:

1. *Stemming.* We remove suffixes to find the "stem" of each word, before entering its occurrence into the index. For example, plural nouns can be treated as their singular versions. Thus, in Example 13.17, the inverted index evidently uses stemming, since the search for word "dog" got us not only documents with "dog," but also a document with the word "dogs."

2. *Stop words.* The most common words, such as "the" or "and," are called *stop words* and often are excluded from the inverted index. The reason is that the several hundred most common words appear in too many documents to make them useful as a way to find documents about specific subjects. Eliminating stop words also reduces the size of the index significantly.

---

important structure. Early uses of the idea distinguished occurrences of a word in the title of a document, the abstract, and the body of text. With the growth of documents on the Web, especially documents using HTML, XML, or another markup language, we can also indicate the markings associated with words. For instance, we can distinguish words appearing in titles headers, tables, or anchors, as well as words appearing in different fonts or sizes.

Example 13.18: Figure 13.20 illustrates a bucket file that has been used to indicate occurrences of words in HTML documents. The first column indicates the type of occurrence, i.e., its marking, if any. The second and third columns are together the pointer to the occurrence. The third column indicates the document, and the second column gives the number of the word in the document.

We can use this data structure to answer various queries about documents without having to examine the documents in detail. For instance, suppose we want to find documents about dogs that compare them with cats. Without a deep understanding of the meaning of text, we cannot answer this query precisely. However, we could get a good hint if we searched for documents that

a) Mention dogs in the title, and

b) Mention cats in an anchor — presumably a link to a document about cats.

Insertion and Deletion From Buckets

We show buckets in figures such as Fig. 13.19 as compacted arrays of appropriate size. In practice, they are records with a single field (the pointer) and are stored in blocks like any other collection of records. Thus, when we insert or delete pointers, we may use any of the techniques seen so far, such as leaving extra space in blocks for expansion of the file, overflow blocks, and possibly moving records within or among blocks. In the latter case, we must be careful to change the pointer from the inverted index to the bucket file, as we move the records it points to.

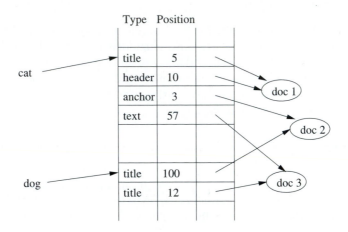

Figure 13.20: Storing more information in the inverted index

We can answer this query by intersecting pointers. That is, we follow the pointer associated with "cat" to find the occurrences of this word. We select from the bucket file the pointers to documents associated with occurrences of "cat" where the type is "anchor." We then find the bucket entries for "dog" and select from them the document pointers associated with the type "title." If we intersect these two sets of pointers, we have the documents that meet the conditions: they mention "dog" in the title and "cat" in an anchor. □

13.2.5 Exercises for Section 13.2

* **Exercise 13.2.1:** As insertions and deletions are made on a data file, a secondary index file needs to change as well. Suggest some ways that the secondary index can be kept up to date as the data file changes.

! **Exercise 13.2.2:** Suppose we have blocks that can hold three records or ten key-pointer pairs, as in Exercise 13.1.1. Let these blocks be used for a data file and a secondary index on search key K. For each K-value v present in the file, there are either 1, 2, or three records with v in field K. Exactly 1/3 of the values appear once, 1/3 appear twice, and 1/3 appear three times. Suppose further that the index blocks and data blocks are all on disk, but there is a structure that allows us to take any K-value v and get pointers to all the index blocks that have search-key value v in one or more records (perhaps there is a second level of index in main memory). Calculate the average number of disk I/O's necessary to retrieve all the records with search-key value v.

*! **Exercise 13.2.3:** Consider a clustered file organization like Fig. 13.16, and suppose that ten records, either studio records or movie records, will fit on one block. Also assume that the number of movies per studio is uniformly distributed between 1 and m. As a function of m, what is the averge number of disk I/O's needed to retrieve a studio and all its movies? What would the number be if movies were randomly distributed over a large number of blocks?

Exercise 13.2.4: Suppose that blocks can hold either three records, ten key-pointer pairs, or fifty pointers. If we use the indirect-buckets scheme of Fig. 13.17:

* a) If the average search-key value appears in 10 records, how many blocks do we need to hold 3000 records and its secondary index structure? How many blocks would be needed if we did *not* use buckets?

! b) If there are no constraints on the number of records that can have a given search-key value, what are the minimum and maximum number of blocks needed?

! **Exercise 13.2.5:** On the assumptions of Exercise 13.2.4(a), what is the average number of disk I/O's to find and retrieve the ten records with a given search-key value, both with and without the bucket structure? Assume nothing is in memory to begin, but it is possible to locate index or bucket blocks without incurring additional I/O's beyond what is needed to retrieve these blocks into memory.

Exercise 13.2.6: Suppose that as in Exercise 13.2.4, a block can hold either three records, ten key-pointer pairs, or fifty pointers. Let there be secondary indexes on `studioName` and `year` of the relation `Movie`, as in Example 13.16. Suppose there are 51 Disney movies, and 101 movies made in 1995. Only one of these movies was a Disney movie. Compute the number of disk I/O's needed to answer the query of Example 13.16 (find the Disney movies made in 1995) if we:

* a) Use buckets for both secondary indexes, retrieve the pointers from the buckets, intersect them in main memory, and retrieve only the one record for the Disney movie of 1995.

b) Do not use buckets, use the index on `studioName` to get the pointers to Disney movies, retrieve them, and select those that were made in 1995. Assume no two Disney movie records are on the same block.

c) Proceed as in (b), but starting with the index on `year`. Assume no two movies of 1995 are on the same block.

Exercise 13.2.7: Suppose we have a repository of 1000 documents, and we wish to build an inverted index with 10,000 words. A block can hold ten word-pointer pairs or 50 pointers to either a document or a position within a document. The distribution of words is Zipfian (see the box on "The Zipfian Distribution" in Section 16.4.3); the number of occurrences of the ith most frequent word is $100000/\sqrt{i}$, for $i = 1, 2, \ldots, 10000$.

* a) What is the averge number of words per document?

* b) Suppose our inverted index only records for each word all the documents that have that word. What is the maximum number of blocks we could need to hold the inverted index?

c) Suppose our inverted index holds pointers to each occurrence of each word. How many blocks do we need to hold the inverted index?

d) Repeat (b) if the 400 most common words ("stop" words) are *not* included in the index.

e) Repeat (c) if the 400 most common words are not included in the index.

Exercise 13.2.8: If we use an augmented inverted index, such as in Fig. 13.20, we can perform a number of other kinds of searches. Suggest how this index could be used to find:

* a) Documents in which "cat" and "dog" appeared within five positions of each other in the same type of element (e.g., title, text, or anchor).

b) Documents in which "dog" followed "cat" separated by exactly one position.

c) Documents in which "dog" and "cat" both appear in the title.

13.3 B-Trees

While one or two levels of index are often very helpful in speeding up queries, there is a more general structure that is commonly used in commercial systems. This family of data structures is called *B-trees*, and the particular variant that is most often used is known as a *B+ tree*. In essence:

- B-trees automatically maintain as many levels of index as is appropriate for the size of the file being indexed.

- B-trees manage the space on the blocks they use so that every block is between half used and completely full. No overflow blocks are needed.

In the following discussion, we shall talk about "B-trees," but the details will all be for the B+ tree variant. Other types of B-tree are discussed in exercises.

13.3.1 The Structure of B-trees

As implied by the name, a B-tree organizes its blocks into a tree. The tree is *balanced*, meaning that all paths from the root to a leaf have the same length. Typically, there are three layers in a B-tree: the root, an intermediate layer, and leaves, but any number of layers is possible. To help visualize B-trees, you may wish to look ahead at Figs. 13.21 and 13.22, which show nodes of a B-tree, and Fig. 13.23, which shows a small, complete B-tree.

There is a parameter n associated with each B-tree index, and this parameter determines the layout of all blocks of the B-tree. Each block will have space for n search-key values and $n + 1$ pointers. In a sense, a B-tree block is similar to the index blocks introduced in Section 13.1, except that the B-tree block has an extra pointer, along with n key-pointer pairs. We pick n to be as large as will allow $n + 1$ pointers and n keys to fit in one block.

Example 13.19 : Suppose our blocks are 4096 bytes. Also let keys be integers of 4 bytes and let pointers be 8 bytes. If there is no header information kept on the blocks, then we want to find the largest integer value of n such that $4n + 8(n + 1) \leq 4096$. That value is $n = 340$. □

There are several important rules about what can appear in the blocks of a B-tree:

- The keys in leaf nodes are copies of keys from the data file. These keys are distributed among the leaves in sorted order, from left to right.

- At the root, there are at least two used pointers.[3] All pointers point to B-tree blocks at the level below.

- At a leaf, the last pointer points to the next leaf block to the right, i.e., to the block with the next higher keys. Among the other n pointers in a leaf block, at least $\lfloor \frac{n+1}{2} \rfloor$ of these pointers are used and point to data records; unused pointers may be thought of as null and do not point anywhere. The ith pointer, if it is used, points to a record with the ith key.

- At an interior node, all $n + 1$ pointers can be used to point to B-tree blocks at the next lower level. At least $\lceil \frac{n+1}{2} \rceil$ of them are actually used

---

[3]Technically, there is a possibility that the entire B-tree has only one pointer because it is an index into a data file with only one record. In this case, the entire tree is a root block that is also a leaf, and this block has only one key and one pointer. We shall ignore this trivial case in the descriptions that follow.

(but if the node is the root, then we require only that at least 2 be used, regardless of how large n is). If j pointers are used, then there will be $j-1$ keys, say $K_1, K_2, \ldots, K_{j-1}$. The first pointer points to a part of the B-tree where some of the records with keys less than K_1 will be found. The second pointer goes to that part of the tree where all records with keys that are at least K_1, but less than K_2 will be found, and so on. Finally, the jth pointer gets us to the part of the B-tree where some of the records with keys greater than or equal to K_{j-1} are found. Note that some records with keys far below K_1 or far above K_{j-1} may not be reachable from this block at all, but will be reached via another block at the same level.

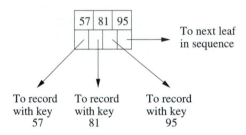

Figure 13.21: A typical leaf of a B-tree

Example 13.20: In this and our running examples of B-trees, we shall use $n = 3$. That is, blocks have room for three keys and four pointers, which are atypically small numbers. Keys are integers. Figure 13.21 shows a leaf that is completely used. There are three keys, 57, 81, and 95. The first three pointers go to records with these keys. The last pointer, as is always the case with leaves, points to the next leaf to the right in the order of keys; it would be null if this leaf were the last in sequence.

A leaf is not necessarily full, but in our example with $n = 3$, there must be at least two key-pointer pairs. That is, the key 95 in Fig. 13.21 might be missing, and with it the third of the pointers, the one labeled "to record with key 95."

Figure 13.22 shows a typical interior node. There are three keys; we have picked the same keys as in our leaf example: 57, 81, and 95.[4] There are also four pointers in this node. The first points to a part of the B-tree from which we can reach only records with keys less than 57 — the first of the keys. The second pointer leads to all records with keys between the first and second keys of the B-tree block; the third pointer is for those records between the second and third keys of the block, and the fourth pointer lets us reach some of the records with keys equal to or above the third key of the block.

---

[4]Although the keys are the same, the leaf of Fig. 13.21 and the interior node of Fig. 13.22 have no relationship. In fact, they could never appear in the same B-tree.

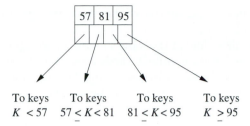

Figure 13.22: A typical interior node of a B-tree

As with our example leaf, it is not necessarily the case that all slots for keys and pointers are occupied. However, with $n = 3$, at least one key and two pointers must be present in an interior node. The most extreme case of missing elements would be if the only key were 57, and only the first two pointers were used. In that case, the first pointer would be to keys less than 57, and the second pointer would be to keys greater than or equal to 57. □

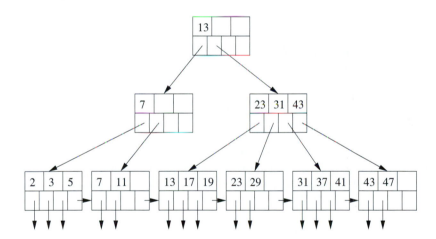

Figure 13.23: A B-tree

Example 13.21: Figure 13.23 shows a complete, three-level B-tree, using the nodes described in Example 13.20. We have assumed that the data file consists of records whose keys are all the primes from 2 to 47. Notice that at the leaves, each of these keys appears once, in order. All leaf blocks have two or three key-pointer pairs, plus a pointer to the next leaf in sequence. The keys are in sorted order as we look across the leaves from left to right.

The root has only two pointers, the minimum possible number, although it could have up to four. The one key at the root separates those keys reachable via the first pointer from those reachable via the second. That is, keys up to

12 could be found in the first subtree of the root, and keys 13 and up are in the second subtree.

If we look at the first child of the root, with key 7, we again find two pointers, one to keys less than 7 and the other to keys 7 and above. Note that the second pointer in this node gets us only to keys 7 and 11, not to *all* keys ≥ 7, such as 13 (although we could reach the larger keys by following the next-block pointers in the leaves).

Finally, the second child of the root has all four pointer slots in use. The first gets us to some of the keys less than 23, namely 13, 17, and 19. The second pointer gets us to all keys K such that $23 \leq K < 31$; the third pointer lets us reach all keys K such that $31 \leq K < 43$, and the fourth pointer gets us to some of the keys ≥ 43 (in this case, to all of them).   □

13.3.2   Applications of B-trees

The B-tree is a powerful tool for building indexes. The sequence of pointers to records at the leaves can play the role of any of the pointer sequences coming out of an index file that we learned about in Sections 13.1 or 13.2. Here are some examples:

1. The search key of the B-tree is the primary key for the data file, and the index is dense. That is, there is one key-pointer pair in a leaf for every record of the data file. The data file may or may not be sorted by primary key.

2. The data file is sorted by its primary key, and the B-tree is a sparse index with one key-pointer pair at a leaf for each block of the data file.

3. The data file is sorted by an attribute that is not a key, and this attribute is the search key for the B-tree. For each key value K that appears in the data file there is one key-pointer pair at a leaf. That pointer goes to the first of the records that have K as their sort-key value.

There are additional applications of B-tree variants that allow multiple occurrences of the search key[5] at the leaves. Figure 13.24 suggests what such a B-tree might look like. The extension is analogous to the indexes with duplicates that we discussed in Section 13.1.5.

If we do allow duplicate occurrences of a search key, then we need to change slightly the definition of what the keys at interior nodes mean, which we discussed in Section 13.3.1. Now, suppose there are keys $K_1, K_2, \ldots, K_n$ at an interior node. Then K_i will be the smallest new key that appears in the part of the subtree accessible from the $(i+1)$st pointer. By "new," we mean that there are no occurrences of K_i in the portion of the tree to the left of the $(i+1)$st subtree, but at least one occurrence of K_i in that subtree. Note that in some situations, there will be no such key, in which case K_i can be taken to be null.

---

[5]Remember that a "search key" is not necessarily a "key" in the sense of being unique.

Its associated pointer is still necessary, as it points to a significant portion of the tree that happens to have only one key value within it.

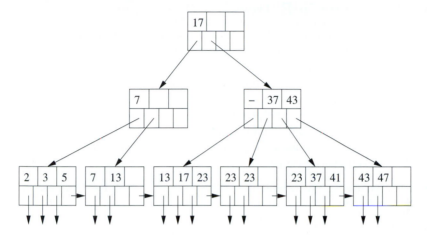

Figure 13.24: A B-tree with duplicate keys

Example 13.22 : Figure 13.24 shows a B-tree similar to Fig. 13.23, but with duplicate values. In particular, key 11 has been replaced by 13, and keys 19, 29, and 31 have all been replaced by 23. As a result, the key at the root is 17, not 13. The reason is that, although 13 is the lowest key in the second subtree of the root, it is not a *new* key for that subtree, since it also appears in the first subtree.

We also had to make some changes to the second child of the root. The second key is changed to 37, since that is the first new key of the third child (fifth leaf from the left). Most interestingly, the first key is now null. The reason is that the second child (fourth leaf) has no new keys at all. Put another way, if we were searching for any key and reached the second child of the root, we would never want to start at its second child. If we are searching for 23 or anything lower, we want to start at its first child, where we will either find what we are looking for (if it is 17), or find the first of what we are looking for (if it is 23). Note that:

- We would not reach the second child of the root searching for 13; we would be directed at the root to its first child instead.

- If we are looking for any key between 24 and 36, we are directed to the third leaf, but when we don't find even one occurrence of what we are looking for, we know not to search further right. For example, if there were a key 24 among the leaves, it would either be on the 4th leaf, in which case the null key in the second child of the root would be 24 instead, or it would be in the 5th leaf, in which case the key 37 at the second child of the root would be 24.

☐

13.3.3 Lookup in B-Trees

We now revert to our original assumption that there are no duplicate keys at the leaves. We also suppose that the B-tree is a dense index, so every search-key value that appears in the data file will also appear at a leaf. These assumptions make the discussion of B-tree operations simpler, but is not essential for these operations. In particular, modifications for sparse indexes are similar to the changes we introduced in Section 13.1.3 for indexes on sequential files.

Suppose we have a B-tree index and we want to find a record with search-key value K. We search for K recursively, starting at the root and ending at a leaf. The search procedure is:

BASIS: If we are at a leaf, look among the keys there. If the ith key is K, then the ith pointer will take us to the desired record.

INDUCTION: If we are at an interior node with keys $K_1, K_2, \ldots, K_n$, follow the rules given in Section 13.3.1 to decide which of the children of this node should next be examined. That is, there is only one child that could lead to a leaf with key K. If $K < K_1$, then it is the first child, if $K_1 \leq K < K_2$, it is the second child, and so on. Recursively apply the search procedure at this child.

Example 13.23: Suppose we have the B-tree of Fig. 13.23, and we want to find a record with search key 40. We start at the root, where there is one key, 13. Since $13 \leq 40$, we follow the second pointer, which leads us to the second-level node with keys 23, 31, and 43.

At that node, we find $31 \leq 40 < 43$, so we follow the third pointer. We are thus led to the leaf with keys 31, 37, and 41. If there had been a record in the data file with key 40, we would have found key 40 at this leaf. Since we do not find 40, we conclude that there is no record with key 40 in the underlying data.

Note that had we been looking for a record with key 37, we would have taken exactly the same decisions, but when we got to the leaf we would find key 37. Since it is the second key in the leaf, we follow the second pointer, which will lead us to the data record with key 37.   ☐

13.3.4 Range Queries

B-trees are useful not only for queries in which a single value of the search key is sought, but for queries in which a range of values are asked for. Typically, *range queries* have a term in the WHERE-clause that compares the search key with a value or values, using one of the comparison operators other than = or <>. Examples of range queries using a search-key attribute k could look like

```
SELECT *
FROM R
WHERE R.k > 40;
```

or

```
SELECT *
FROM R
WHERE R.k >= 10 AND R.k <= 25;
```

If we want to find all keys in the range $[a, b]$ at the leaves of a B-tree, we do a lookup to find the key a. Whether or not it exists, we are led to a leaf where a could be, and we search the leaf for keys that are a or greater. Each such key we find has an associated pointer to one of the records whose key is in the desired range.

If we do not find a key higher than b, we use the pointer in the current leaf to the next leaf, and keep examining keys and following the associated pointers, until we either

1. Find a key higher than b, at which point we stop, or

2. Reach the end of the leaf, in which case we go to the next leaf and repeat the process.

The above search algorithm also works if b is infinite; i.e., there is only a lower bound and no upper bound. In that case, we search all the leaves from the one that would hold key a to the end of the chain of leaves. If a is $-\infty$ (that is, there is an upper bound on the range but no lower bound), then the search for "minus infinity" as a search key will always take us to the first child of whatever B-tree node we are at; i.e., we eventually find the first leaf. The search then proceeds as above, stopping only when we pass the key b.

Example 13.24 : Suppose we have the B-tree of Fig. 13.23, and we are given the range $(10, 25)$ to search for. We look for key 10, which leads us to the second leaf. The first key is less than 10, but the second, 11, is at least 10. We follow its associated pointer to get the record with key 11.

Since there are no more keys in the second leaf, we follow the chain to the third leaf, where we find keys 13, 17, and 19. All are less than or equal to 25, so we follow their associated pointers and retrieve the records with these keys. Finally, we move to the fourth leaf, where we find key 23. But the next key of that leaf, 29, exceeds 25, so we are done with our search. Thus, we have retrieved the five records with keys 11 through 23.   □

13.3.5 Insertion Into B-Trees

We see some of the advantage of B-trees over the simpler multilevel indexes introduced in Section 13.1.4 when we consider how to insert a new key into a B-tree. The corresponding record will be inserted into the file being indexed by the B-tree, using any of the methods discussed in Section 13.1; here we consider how the B-tree changes in response. The insertion is, in principle, recursive:

- We try to find a place for the new key in the appropriate leaf, and we put it there if there is room.

- If there is no room in the proper leaf, we split the leaf into two and divide the keys between the two new nodes, so each is half full or just over half full.

- The splitting of nodes at one level appears to the level above as if a new key-pointer pair needs to be inserted at that higher level. We may thus recursively apply this strategy to insert at the next level: if there is room, insert it; if not, split the parent node and continue up the tree.

- As an exception, if we try to insert into the root, and there is no room, then we split the root into two nodes and create a new root at the next higher level; the new root has the two nodes resulting from the split as its children. Recall that no matter how large n (the number of slots for keys at a node) is, it is always permissible for the root to have only one key and two children.

When we split a node and insert into its parent, we need to be careful how the keys are managed. First, suppose N is a leaf whose capacity is n keys. Also suppose we are trying to insert an $(n + 1)$st key and its associated pointer. We create a new node M, which will be the sibling of N, immediately to its right. The first $\lceil \frac{n+1}{2} \rceil$ key-pointer pairs, in sorted order of the keys, remain with N, while the other key-pointer pairs move to M. Note that both nodes N and M are left with a sufficient number of key-pointer pairs — at least $\lfloor \frac{n+1}{2} \rfloor$ pairs.

Now, suppose N is an interior node whose capacity is n keys and $n + 1$ pointers, and N has just been assigned $n+2$ pointers because of a node splitting below. We do the following:

1. Create a new node M, which will be the sibling of N, immediately to its right.

2. Leave at N the first $\lceil \frac{n+2}{2} \rceil$ pointers, in sorted order, and move to M the remaining $\lfloor \frac{n+2}{2} \rfloor$ pointers.

3. The first $\lceil \frac{n}{2} \rceil$ keys stay with N, while the last $\lfloor \frac{n}{2} \rfloor$ keys move to M. Note that there is always one key in the middle left over; it goes with neither N nor M. The leftover key K indicates the smallest key reachable via the first of M's children. Although this key doesn't appear in N or M, it is associated with M, in the sense that it represents the smallest key reachable via M. Therefore K will be used by the parent of N and M to divide searches between those two nodes.

Example 13.25 : Let us insert key 40 into the B-tree of Fig. 13.23. We find the proper leaf for the insertion by the lookup procedure of Section 13.3.3. As found in Example 13.23, the insertion goes into the fifth leaf. Since $n = 3$, but this leaf now has four key-pointer pairs — 31, 37, 40, and 41 — we need to split the leaf. Our first step is to create a new node and move the highest two keys, 40 and 41, along with their pointers, to that node. Figure 13.25 shows this split.

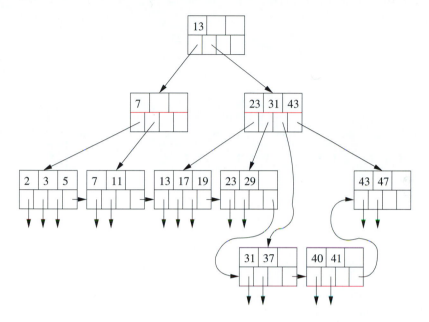

Figure 13.25: Beginning the insertion of key 40

Notice that although we now show the nodes on four ranks, there are still only three levels to the tree, and the seven leaves occupy the last two ranks of the diagram. They are linked by their last pointers, which still form a chain from left to right.

We must now insert a pointer to the new leaf (the one with keys 40 and 41) into the node above it (the node with keys 23, 31, and 43). We must also associate with this pointer the key 40, which is the least key reachable through the new leaf. Unfortunately, the parent of the split node is already full; it has no room for another key or pointer. Thus, it too must be split.

We start with pointers to the last five leaves and the list of keys representing the least keys of the last four of these leaves. That is, we have pointers P_1, P_2, P_3, P_4, P_5 to the leaves whose least keys are 13, 23, 31, 40, and 43, and we have the key sequence 23, 31, 40, 43 to separate these pointers. The first three pointers and first two keys remain with the split interior node, while the last two pointers and last key go to the new node. The remaining key, 40, represents the least key accessible via the new node.

Figure 13.26 shows the completion of the insert of key 40. The root now has three children; the last two are the split interior node. Notice that the key 40, which marks the lowest of the keys reachable via the second of the split nodes, has been installed in the root to separate the keys of the root's second

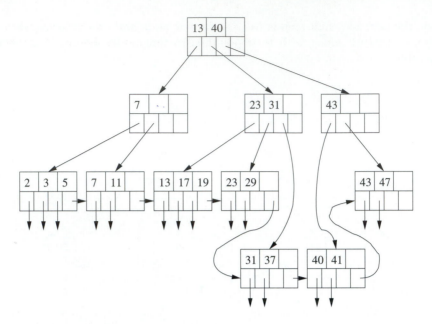

Figure 13.26: Completing the insertion of key 40

and third children.   □

13.3.6   Deletion From B-Trees

If we are to delete a record with a given key K, we must first locate that record
and its key-pointer pair in a leaf of the B-tree. This part of the deletion process
is essentially a lookup, as in Section 13.3.3. We then delete the record itself
from the data file and we delete the key-pointer pair from the B-tree.

If the B-tree node from which a deletion occurred still has at least the
minimum number of keys and pointers, then there is nothing more to be done.[6]
However, it is possible that the node was right at the minimum occupancy
before the deletion, so after deletion the constraint on the number of keys is
violated. We then need to do one of two things for a node N whose contents
are subminimum; one case requires a recursive deletion up the tree:

1. If one of the adjacent siblings of node N has more than the minimum
   number of keys and pointers, then one key-pointer pair can be moved to
   N, keeping the order of keys intact. Possibly, the keys at the parent of N
   must be adjusted to reflect the new situation. For instance, if the right
   sibling of N, say node M, provides an extra key and pointer, then it must

---

[6]If the data record with the least key at a leaf is deleted, then we have the option of raising
the appropriate key at one of the ancestors of that leaf, but there is no requirement that we
do so; all searches will still go to the appropriate leaf.

be the smallest key that is moved from M to N. At the parent of M and N, there is a key that represents the smallest key accessible via M; that key must be raised.

2. The hard case is when neither adjacent sibling can be used to provide an extra key for N. However, in that case, we have two adjacent nodes, N and one of its siblings M, one with the minimum number of keys and one with less than that. Therefore, together they have no more keys and pointers than are allowed in a single node (which is why half-full was chosen as the minimum allowable occupancy of B-tree nodes). We merge these two nodes, effectively deleting one of them. We need to adjust the keys at the parent, and then delete a key and pointer at the parent. If the parent is still full enough, then we are done. If not, then we recursively apply the deletion algorithm at the parent.

Example 13.26: Let us begin with the original B-tree of Fig. 13.23, before the insertion of key 40. Suppose we delete key 7. This key is found in the second leaf. We delete it, its associated pointer, and the record that pointer points to.

Unfortunately, the second leaf now has only one key, and we need at least two in every leaf. But we are saved by the sibling to the left, the first leaf, because that leaf has an extra key-pointer pair. We may therefore move the highest key, 5, and its associated pointer to the second leaf. The resulting B-tree is shown in Fig. 13.27. Notice that because the lowest key in the second leaf is now 5, the key in the parent of the first two leaves has been changed from 7 to 5.

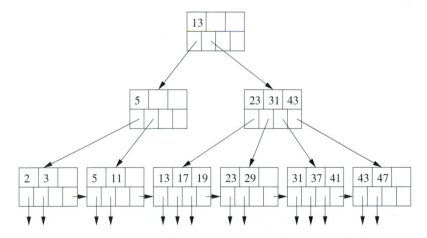

Figure 13.27: Deletion of key 7

Next, suppose we delete key 11. This deletion has the same effect on the second leaf; it again reduces the number of its keys below the minimum. This time, however, we cannot borrow from the first leaf, because the latter is down to the minimum number of keys. Additionally, there is no sibling to the right from which to borrow.[7] Thus, we need to merge the second leaf with a sibling, namely the first leaf.

The three remaining key-pointer pairs from the first two leaves fit in one leaf, so we move 5 to the first leaf and delete the second leaf. The pointers and keys in the parent are adjusted to reflect the new situation at its children; specifically, the two pointers are replaced by one (to the remaining leaf) and the key 5 is no longer relevant and is deleted. The situation is now as shown in Fig. 13.28.

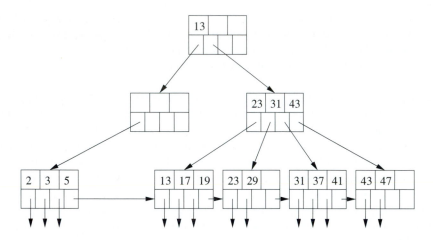

Figure 13.28: Beginning the deletion of key 11

Unfortunately, the deletion of a leaf has adversely affected the parent, which is the left child of the root. That node, as we see in Fig. 13.28, now has no keys and only one pointer. Thus, we try to obtain an extra key and pointer from an adjacent sibling. This time we have the easy case, since the other child of the root can afford to give up its smallest key and a pointer.

The change is shown in Fig. 13.29. The pointer to the leaf with keys 13, 17, and 19 has been moved from the second child of the root to the first child. We have also changed some keys at the interior nodes. The key 13, which used to reside at the root and represented the smallest key accessible via the pointer that was transferred, is now needed at the first child of the root. On the other hand, the key 23, which used to separate the first and second children of the second child of the root now represents the smallest key accessible from the second child of the root. It therefore is placed at the root itself.   □

---

[7]Notice that the leaf to the right, with keys 13, 17, and 19, is not a sibling, because it has a different parent. We could "borrow" from that node anyway, but then the algorithm for adjusting keys throughout the tree becomes more complex. We leave this enhancement as an exercise.

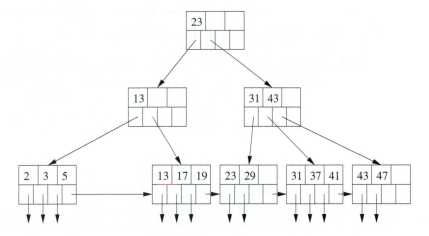

Figure 13.29: Completing the deletion of key 11

13.3.7 Efficiency of B-Trees

B-trees allow lookup, insertion, and deletion of records using very few disk I/O's per file operation. First, we should observe that if n, the number of keys per block is reasonably large, say 10 or more, then it will be a rare event that calls for splitting or merging of blocks. Further, when such an operation is needed, it almost always is limited to the leaves, so only two leaves and their parent are affected. Thus, we can essentially neglect the I/O cost of B-tree reorganizations.

However, every search for the record(s) with a given search key requires us to go from the root down to a leaf, to find a pointer to the record. Since we are only reading B-tree blocks, the number of disk I/O's will be the number of levels the B-tree has, plus the one (for lookup) or two (for insert or delete) disk I/O's needed for manipulation of the record itself. We must thus ask: how many levels does a B-tree have? For the typical sizes of keys, pointers, and blocks, three levels are sufficient for all but the largest databases. Thus, we shall generally take 3 as the number of levels of a B-tree. The following example illustrates why.

Example 13.27: Recall our analysis in Example 13.19, where we determined that 340 key-pointer pairs could fit in one block for our example data. Suppose that the average block has an occupancy midway between the minimum and maximum, i.e., a typical block has 255 pointers. With a root, 255 children, and $255^2 = 65025$ leaves, we shall have among those leaves 255^3, or about 16.6 million pointers to records. That is, files with up to 16.6 million records can be accommodated by a 3-level B-tree. □

However, we can use even fewer than three disk I/O's per search through the B-tree. The root block of a B-tree is an excellent choice to keep permanently buffered in main memory. If so, then every search through a 3-level B-tree

---

Should We Delete From B-Trees?

There are B-tree implementations that don't fix up deletions at all. If a leaf has too few keys and pointers, it is allowed to remain as it is. The rationale is that most files grow on balance, and while there might be an occasional deletion that makes a leaf become subminimum, the leaf will probably soon grow again and attain the minimum number of key-pointer pairs once again.

Further, if records have pointers from outside the B-tree index, then we need to replace the record by a "tombstone," and we don't want to delete its pointer from the B-tree anyway. In certain circumstances, when it can be guaranteed that all accesses to the deleted record will go through the B-tree, we can even leave the tombstone in place of the pointer to the record at a leaf of the B-tree. Then, space for the record can be reused.

---

requires only two disk reads. In fact, under some circumstances it may make sense to keep second-level nodes of the B-tree buffered in main memory as well, reducing the B-tree search to a single disk I/O, plus whatever is necessary to manipulate the blocks of the data file itself.

13.3.8 Exercises for Section 13.3

Exercise 13.3.1: Suppose that blocks can hold either ten records or 99 keys and 100 pointers. Also assume that the average B-tree node is 70% full; i.e., it will have 69 keys and 70 pointers. We can use B-trees as part of several different structures. For each structure described below, determine (i) the total number of blocks needed for a 1,000,000-record file, and (ii) the average number of disk I/O's to retrieve a record given its search key. You may assume nothing is in memory initially, and the search key is the primary key for the records.

* a) The data file is a sequential file, sorted on the search key, with 10 records per block. The B-tree is a dense index.

  b) The same as (a), but the data file consists of records in no particular order, packed 10 to a block.

  c) The same as (a), but the B-tree is a sparse index.

! d) Instead of the B-tree leaves having pointers to data records, the B-tree leaves hold the records themselves. A block can hold ten records, but on average, a leaf block is 70% full; i.e., there are seven records per leaf block.

* e) The data file is a sequential file, and the B-tree is a sparse index, but each primary block of the data file has one overflow block. On average, the

primary block is full, and the overflow block is half full. However, records
are in no particular order within a primary block and its overflow block.

Exercise 13.3.2: Repeat Exercise 13.3.1 in the case that the query is a range
query that is matched by 1000 records.

Exercise 13.3.3: Suppose pointers are 4 bytes long, and keys are 12 bytes
long. How many keys and pointers will a block of 16,384 bytes have?

Exercise 13.3.4: What are the minimum numbers of keys and pointers in
B-tree (*i*) interior nodes and (*ii*) leaves, when:

* a) $n = 10$; i.e., a block holds 10 keys and 11 pointers.

  b) $n = 11$; i.e., a block holds 11 keys and 12 pointers.

Exercise 13.3.5: Execute the following operations on Fig. 13.23. Describe
the changes for operations that modify the tree.

  a) Lookup the record with key 41.

  b) Lookup the record with key 40.

  c) Lookup all records in the range 20 to 30.

  d) Lookup all records with keys less than 30.

  e) Lookup all records with keys greater than 30.

  f) Insert a record with key 1.

  g) Insert records with keys 14 through 16.

  h) Delete the record with key 23.

  i) Delete all the records with keys 23 and higher.

! **Exercise 13.3.6:** We mentioned that the leaf of Fig. 13.21 and the interior
node of Fig. 13.22 could never appear in the same B-tree. Explain why.

Exercise 13.3.7: When duplicate keys are allowed in a B-tree, there are some
necessary modifications to the algorithms for lookup, insertion, and deletion
that we described in this section. Give the changes for:

* a) Lookup.

  b) Insertion.

  c) Deletion.

! **Exercise 13.3.8:** In Example 13.26 we suggested that it would be possible to borrow keys from a nonsibling to the right (or left) if we used a more complicated algorithm for maintaining keys at interior nodes. Describe a suitable algorithm that rebalances by borrowing from adjacent nodes at a level, regardless of whether they are siblings of the node that has too many or too few key-pointer pairs.

Exercise 13.3.9: If we use the 3-key, 4-pointer nodes of our examples in this section, how many different B-trees are there when the data file has:

*! a) 6 records.

!! b) 10 records.

!! c) 15 records.

*! **Exercise 13.3.10:** Suppose we have B-tree nodes with room for three keys and four pointers, as in the examples of this section. Suppose also that when we split a leaf, we divide the pointers 2 and 2, while when we split an interior node, the first 3 pointers go with the first (left) node, and the last 2 pointers go with the second (right) node. We start with a leaf containing pointers to records with keys 1, 2, and 3. We then add in order, records with keys 4, 5, 6, and so on. At the insertion of what key will the B-tree first reach four levels?

!! **Exercise 13.3.11:** Consider an index organized as a B-tree. The leaf nodes contain pointers to a total of N records, and each block that makes up the index has m pointers. We wish to choose the value of m that will minimize search times on a particular disk with the following characteristics:

> *i.* The time to read a given block into memory can be approximated by $70 + .05m$ milliseconds. The 70 milliseconds represent the seek and latency components of the read, and the $.05m$ milliseconds is the transfer time. That is, as m becomes larger, the block will be larger, and it will take more time to read it into memory.

> *ii.* Once the block is in memory, a binary search is used to find the correct pointer. Thus, the time to process a block in main memory is $a + b \log_2 m$ milliseconds, for some constants a and b.

> *iii.* The main memory time constant a is much smaller than the disk seek and latency time of 70 milliseconds.

> *iv.* The index is full, so that the number of blocks that must be examined per search is $\log_m N$.

Answer the following:

> a) What value of m minimizes the time to search for a given record?

> b) What happens as the seek and latency constant (70ms) decreases? For instance, if this constant is cut in half, how does the optimum m value change?

13.4 Hash Tables

There are a number of data structures involving a hash table that are useful as indexes. We assume the reader has seen the hash table used as a main-memory data structure. In such a structure there is a *hash function* that takes a search key (which we may call the *hash key*) as an argument and computes from it an integer in the range 0 to $B - 1$, where B is the number of *buckets*. A *bucket array*, which is an array indexed from 0 to $B - 1$, holds the headers of B linked lists, one for each bucket of the array. If a record has search key K, then we store the record by linking it to the bucket list for the bucket numbered $h(K)$, where h is the hash function.

13.4.1 Secondary-Storage Hash Tables

A hash table that holds a very large number of records, so many that they must be kept mainly in secondary storage, differs from the main-memory version in small but important ways. First, the bucket array consists of blocks, rather than pointers to the headers of lists. Records that are hashed by the hash function h to a certain bucket are put in the block for that bucket. If a bucket *overflows*, meaning that it cannot hold all the records that belong in that bucket, then a chain of *overflow blocks* can be added to the bucket to hold more records.

We shall assume that the location of the first block for any bucket i can be found given i. For example, there might be a main-memory array of pointers to blocks, indexed by the bucket number. Another possibility is to put the first block for each bucket in fixed, consecutive disk locations, so we can compute the location of bucket i from the integer i.

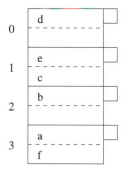

Figure 13.30: A hash table

Example 13.28 : Figure 13.30 shows a hash table. To keep our illustrations manageable, we assume that a block can hold only two records, and that $B = 4$; i.e., the hash function h returns values from 0 to 3. We show certain records populating the hash table. Keys are letters a through f in Fig. 13.30. We

---

Choice of Hash Function

The hash function should "hash" the key so the resulting integer is a seemingly random function of the key. Thus, buckets will tend to have equal numbers of records, which improves the average time to access a record, as we shall discuss in Section 13.4.4. Also, the hash function should be easy to compute, since we shall compute it many times.

- A common choice of hash function when keys are integers is to compute the remainder of K/B, where K is the key value and B is the number of buckets. Often, B is chosen to be a prime, although there are reasons to make B a power of 2, as we discuss starting in Section 13.4.5.

- For character-string search keys, we may treat each character as an integer, sum these integers, and take the remainder when the sum is divided by B.

---

assume that $h(d) = 0$, $h(c) = h(e) = 1$, $h(b) = 2$, and $h(a) = h(f) = 3$. Thus, the six records are distributed into blocks as shown. □

Note that we show each block in Fig. 13.30 with a "nub" at the right end. This nub represents additional information in the block's header. We shall use it to chain overflow blocks together, and starting in Section 13.4.5, we shall use it to keep other critical information about the block.

13.4.2 Insertion Into a Hash Table

When a new record with search key K must be inserted, we compute $h(K)$. If the bucket numbered $h(K)$ has space, then we insert the record into the block for this bucket, or into one of the overflow blocks on its chain if there is no room in the first block. If none of the blocks of the chain for bucket $h(K)$ has room, we add a new overflow block to the chain and store the new record there.

Example 13.29: Suppose we add to the hash table of Fig. 13.30 a record with key g, and $h(g) = 1$. Then we must add the new record to the bucket numbered 1, which is the second bucket from the top. However, the block for that bucket already has two records. Thus, we add a new block and chain it to the original block for bucket 1. The record with key g goes in that block, as shown in Fig. 13.31. □

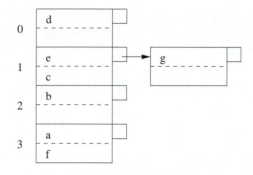

Figure 13.31: Adding an additional block to a hash-table bucket

13.4.3 Hash-Table Deletion

Deletion of the record (or records) with search key K follows the same pattern. We go to the bucket numbered $h(K)$ and search for records with that search key. Any that we find are deleted. If we are able to move records around among blocks, then after deletion we may optionally consolidate the blocks of a chain into one fewer block.[8]

Example 13.30: Figure 13.32 shows the result of deleting the record with key c from the hash table of Fig. 13.31. Recall $h(c) = 1$, so we go to the bucket numbered 1 (i.e., the second bucket) and search all its blocks to find a record (or records if the search key were not the primary key) with key c. We find it in the first block of the chain for bucket 1. Since there is now room to move the record with key g from the second block of the chain to the first, we can do so and remove the second block.

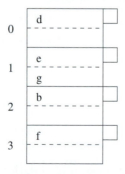

Figure 13.32: Result of deletions from a hash table

---

[8]A risk of consolidating blocks of a chain whenever possible is that an oscillation, where we alternately insert and delete records from a bucket will cause a block to be created or destroyed at each step.

We also show the deletion of the record with key a. For this key, we found our way to bucket 3, deleted it, and "consolidated" the remaining record at the beginning of the block.   □

13.4.4   Efficiency of Hash Table Indexes

Ideally, there are enough buckets that most of them fit on one block. If so, then the typical lookup takes only one disk I/O, and insertion or deletion from the file takes only two disk I/O's. That number is significantly better than straightforward sparse or dense indexes, or B-tree indexes (although hash tables do not support range queries as B-trees do; see Section 13.3.4).

However, if the file grows, then we shall eventually reach a situation where there are many blocks in the chain for a typical bucket. If so, then we need to search long lists of blocks, taking at least one disk I/O per block. Thus, there is a good reason to try to keep the number of blocks per bucket low.

The hash tables we have examined so far are called *static hash tables*, because B, the number of buckets, never changes. However, there are several kinds of *dynamic hash tables*, where B is allowed to vary so it approximates the number of records divided by the number of records that can fit on a block; i.e., there is about one block per bucket. We shall discuss two such methods:

1. Extensible hashing in Section 13.4.5, and

2. Linear hashing in Section 13.4.7.

The first grows B by doubling it whenever it is deemed too small, and the second grows B by 1 each time statistics of the file suggest some growth is needed.

13.4.5   Extensible Hash Tables

Our first approach to dynamic hashing is called *extensible hash tables*. The major additions to the simpler static hash table structure are:

1. There is a level of indirection introduced for the buckets. That is, an array of pointers to blocks represents the buckets, instead of the array consisting of the data blocks themselves.

2. The array of pointers can grow. Its length is always a power of 2, so in a growing step the number of buckets doubles.

3. However, there does not have to be a data block for each bucket; certain buckets can share a block if the total number of records in those buckets can fit in the block.

4. The hash function h computes for each key a sequence of k bits for some large k, say 32. However, the bucket numbers will at all times use some

smaller number of bits, say i bits, from the beginning of this sequence. That is, the bucket array will have 2^i entries when i is the number of bits used.

Example 13.31 : Figure 13.33 shows a small extensible hash table. We suppose, for simplicity of the example, that $k = 4$; i.e., the hash function produces a sequence of only four bits. At the moment, only one of these bits is used, as indicated by $i = 1$ in the box above the bucket array. The bucket array therefore has only two entries, one for 0 and one for 1.

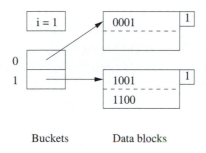

Figure 13.33: An extensible hash table

The bucket array entries point to two blocks. The first holds all the current records whose search keys hash to a bit sequence that begins with 0, and the second holds all those whose search keys hash to a sequence beginning with 1. For convenience, we show the keys of records as if they were the entire bit sequence that the hash function converts them to. Thus, the first block holds a record whose key hashes to 0001, and the second holds records whose keys hash to 1001 and 1100. □

We should notice the number 1 appearing in the "nub" of each of the blocks in Fig. 13.33. This number, which would actually appear in the block header, indicates how many bits of the hash function's sequence is used to determine membership of records in this block. In the situation of Example 13.31, there is only one bit considered for all blocks and records, but as we shall see, the number of bits considered for various blocks can differ as the hash table grows. That is, the bucket array size is determined by the maximum number of bits we are now using, but some blocks may use fewer.

13.4.6 Insertion Into Extensible Hash Tables

Insertion into an extensible hash table begins like insertion into a static hash table. To insert a record with search key K, we compute $h(K)$, take the first i bits of this bit sequence, and go to the entry of the bucket array indexed by these i bits. Note that we can determine i because it is kept as part of the hash data structure.

We follow the pointer in this entry of the bucket array and arrive at a block B. If there is room to put the new record in block B, we do so and we are done. If there is no room, then there are two possibilities, depending on the number j, which indicates how many bits of the hash value are used to determine membership in block B (recall the value of j is found in the "nub" of each block in figures).

1. If $j < i$, then nothing needs to be done to the bucket array. We:

   (a) Split block B into two.

   (b) Distribute records in B to the two blocks, based on the value of their $(j+1)$st bit — records whose key has 0 in that bit stay in B and those with 1 there go to the new block.

   (c) Put $j+1$ in each block's "nub" to indicate the number of bits used to determine membership.

   (d) Adjust the pointers in the bucket array so entries that formerly pointed to B now point either to B or the new block, depending on their $(j+1)$st bit.

   Note that splitting block B may not solve the problem, since by chance all the records of B may go into one of the two blocks into which it was split. If so, we need to repeat the process with the next higher value of j and the block that is still overfull.

2. If $j = i$, then we must first increment i by 1. We double the length of the bucket array, so it now has 2^{i+1} entries. Suppose w is a sequence of i bits indexing one of the entries in the previous bucket array. In the new bucket array, the entries indexed by both $w0$ and $w1$ (i.e., the two numbers derived from w by extending it with 0 or 1) each point to the same block that the w entry used to point to. That is, the two new entries share the block, and the block itself does not change. Membership in the block is still determined by whatever number of bits was previously used. Finally, we proceed to split block B as in case 1. Since i is now greater than j, that case applies.

Example 13.32 : Suppose we insert into the table of Fig. 13.33 a record whose key hashes to the sequence 1010. Since the first bit is 1, this record belongs in the second block. However, that block is already full, so it needs to be split. We find that $j = i = 1$ in this case, so we first need to double the bucket array, as shown in Fig. 13.34. We have also set $i = 2$ in this figure.

Notice that the two entries beginning with 0 each point to the block for records whose hashed keys begin with 0, and that block still has the integer 1 in its "nub" to indicate that only the first bit determines membership in the block. However, the block for records beginning with 1 needs to be split, so we partition its records into those beginning 10 and those beginning 11. A 2 in each of these blocks indicates that two bits are used to determine membership.

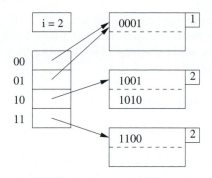

Figure 13.34: Now, two bits of the hash function are used

Fortunately, the split is successful; since each of the two new blocks gets at least one record, we do not have to split recursively.

Now suppose we insert records whose keys hash to 0000 and 0111. These both go in the first block of Fig. 13.34, which then overflows. Since only one bit is used to determine membership in this block, while $i = 2$, we do not have to adjust the bucket array. We simply split the block, with 0000 and 0001 staying, and 0111 going to the new block. The entry for 01 in the bucket array is made to point to the new block. Again, we have been fortunate that the records did not all go in one of the new blocks, so we have no need to split recursively.

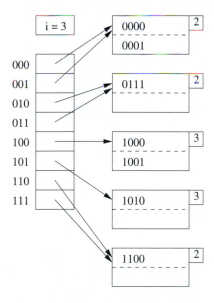

Figure 13.35: The hash table now uses three bits of the hash function

Now suppose a record whose key hashes to 1000 is inserted. The block for 10 overflows. Since it already uses two bits to determine membership, it is time to split the bucket array again and set $i = 3$. Figure 13.35 shows the data structure at this point. Notice that the block for 10 has been split into blocks for 100 and 101, while the other blocks continue to use only two bits to determine membership. □

13.4.7   Linear Hash Tables

Extensible hash tables have some important advantages. Most significant is the fact that when looking for a record, we never need to search more than one data block. We also have to examine an entry of the bucket array, but if the bucket array is small enough to be kept in main memory, then there is no disk I/O needed to access the bucket array. However, extensible hash tables also suffer from some defects:

1. When the bucket array needs to be doubled in size, there is a substantial amount of work to be done (when i is large). This work interrupts access to the data file, or makes certain insertions appear to take a long time.

2. When the bucket array is doubled in size, it may no longer fit in main memory, or may crowd out other data that we would like to hold in main memory. As a result, a system that was performing well might suddenly start using many more disk I/O's per operation and exhibit a noticeably degraded performance.

3. If the number of records per block is small, then there is likely to be one block that needs to be split well in advance of the logical time to do so. For instance, if there are two records per block as in our running example, there might be one sequence of 20 bits that begins the keys of three records, even though the total number of records is much less than 2^{20}. In that case, we would have to use $i = 20$ and a million-bucket array, even though the number of blocks holding records was much smaller than a million.

Another strategy, called *linear hashing*, grows the number of buckets more slowly. The principal new elements we find in linear hashing are:

- The number of buckets n is always chosen so the average number of records per bucket is a fixed fraction, say 80%, of the number of records that fill one block.

- Since blocks cannot always be split, overflow blocks are permitted, although the average number of overflow blocks per bucket will be much less than 1.

- The number of bits used to number the entries of the bucket array is $\lceil \log_2 n \rceil$, where n is the current number of buckets. These bits are always taken from the *right* (low-order) end of the bit sequence that is produced by the hash function.

- Suppose i bits of the hash function are being used to number array entries, and a record with key K is intended for bucket $a_1 a_2 \cdots a_i$; that is, $a_1 a_2 \cdots a_i$ are the last i bits of $h(K)$. Then let $a_1 a_2 \cdots a_i$ be m, treated as an i-bit binary integer. If $m < n$, then the bucket numbered m exists, and we place the record in that bucket. If $n \leq m < 2^i$, then the bucket m does not yet exist, so we place the record in bucket $m - 2^{i-1}$, that is, the bucket we would get if we changed a_1 (which must be 1) to 0.

Example 13.33: Figure 13.36 shows a linear hash table with $n = 2$. We currently are using only one bit of the hash value to determine the buckets of records. Following the pattern established in Example 13.31, we assume the hash function h produces 4 bits, and we represent records by the value produced by h when applied to the search key of the record.

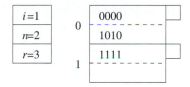

Figure 13.36: A linear hash table

We see in Fig. 13.36 the two buckets, each consisting of one block. The buckets are numbered 0 and 1. All records whose hash value ends in 0 go in the first bucket, and those whose hash value ends in 1 go in the second.

Also part of the structure are the parameters i (the number of bits of the hash function that currently are used), n (the current number of buckets), and r (the current number of records in the hash table). The ratio r/n will be limited so that the typical bucket will need about one disk block. We shall adopt the policy of choosing n, the number of buckets, so that there are no more than $1.7n$ records in the file; i.e., $r \leq 1.7n$. That is, since blocks hold two records, the average occupancy of a bucket does not exceed 85% of the capacity of a block. □

13.4.8 Insertion Into Linear Hash Tables

When we insert a new record, we determine its bucket by the algorithm outlined in Section 13.4.7. We compute $h(K)$, where K is the key of the record, and we use the i bits at the end of bit sequence $h(K)$ as the bucket number, m. If $m < n$, we put the record in bucket m, and if $m \geq n$, we put the record in bucket $m - 2^{i-1}$. If there is no room in the designated bucket, then we create an overflow block, add it to the chain for that bucket, and put the record there.

Each time we insert, we compare the current number of records r with the threshold ratio of r/n, and if the ratio is too high, we add the next bucket to the table. Note that the bucket we add bears no relationship to the bucket into which the insertion occurs! If the binary representation of the number of the bucket we add is $1a_2 \cdots a_i$, then we split the bucket numbered $0a_2 \cdots a_i$, putting records into one or the other bucket, depending on their last i bits. Note that all these records will have hash values that end in $a_2 \cdots a_i$, and only the ith bit from the right end will vary.

The last important detail is what happens when n exceeds 2^i. Then, i is incremented by 1. Technically, all the bucket numbers get an additional 0 in front of their bit sequences, but there is no need to make any physical change, since these bit sequences, interpreted as integers, remain the same.

Example 13.34: We shall continue with Example 13.33 and consider what happens when a record whose key hashes to 0101 is inserted. Since this bit sequence ends in 1, the record goes into the second bucket of Fig. 13.36. There is room for the record, so no overflow block is created.

However, since there are now 4 records in 2 buckets, we exceed the ratio 1.7, and we must therefore raise n to 3. Since $\lceil \log_2 3 \rceil = 2$, we should begin to think of buckets 0 and 1 as 00 and 01, but no change to the data structure is necessary. We add to the table the next bucket, which would have number 10. Then, we split the bucket 00, that bucket whose number differs from the added bucket only in the first bit. When we do the split, the record whose key hashes to 0000 stays in 00, since it ends with 00, while the record whose key hashes to 1010 goes to 10 because it ends that way. The resulting hash table is shown in Fig. 13.37.

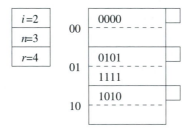

Figure 13.37: Adding a third bucket

Next, let us suppose we add a record whose search key hashes to 0001. The last two bits are 01, so we put it in this bucket, which currently exists. Unfortunately, the bucket's block is full, so we add an overflow block. The three records are distributed among the two blocks of the bucket; we chose to keep them in numerical order of their hashed keys, but order is not important. Since the ratio of records to buckets for the table as a whole is 5/3, and this ratio is less than 1.7, we do not create a new bucket. The result is seen in Fig. 13.38.

Finally, consider the insertion of a record whose search key hashes to 0111. The last two bits are 11, but bucket 11 does not yet exist. We therefore redirect this record to bucket 01, whose number differs by having a 0 in the first bit. The new record fits in the overflow block of this bucket.

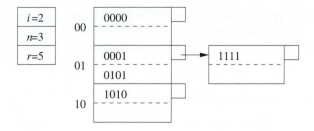

Figure 13.38: Overflow blocks are used if necessary

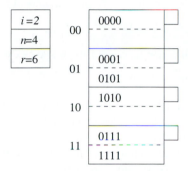

Figure 13.39: Adding a fourth bucket

However, the ratio of the number of records to buckets has exceeded 1.7, so we must create a new bucket, numbered 11. Coincidentally, this bucket is the one we wanted for the new record. We split the four records in bucket 01, with 0001 and 0101 remaining, and 0111 and 1111 going to the new bucket. Since bucket 01 now has only two records, we can delete the overflow block. The hash table is now as shown in Fig. 13.39.

Notice that the next time we insert a record into Fig. 13.39, we shall exceed the 1.7 ratio of records to buckets. Then, we shall raise n to 5 and i becomes 3. □

Example 13.35 : Lookup in a linear hash table follows the procedure we described for selecting the bucket in which an inserted record belongs. If the record we wish to look up is not in that bucket, it cannot be anywhere. For illustration, consider the situation of Fig. 13.37, where we have $i = 2$ and $n = 3$.

First, suppose we want to look up a record whose key hashes to 1010. Since $i = 2$, we look at the last two bits, 10, which we interpret as a binary integer, namely $m = 2$. Since $m < n$, the bucket numbered 10 exists, and we look there. Notice that just because we find a record with hash value 1010 doesn't mean that this record is the one we want; we need to examine the complete key of that record to be sure.

Second, consider the lookup of a record whose key hashes to 1011. Now, we must look in the bucket whose number is 11. Since that bucket number as a binary integer is $m = 3$, and $m \geq n$, the bucket 11 does not exist. We redirect to bucket 01 by changing the leading 1 to 0. However, bucket 01 has no record whose key has hash value 1011, and therefore surely our desired record is not in the hash table.   □

13.4.9   Exercises for Section 13.4

Exercise 13.4.1: Show what happens to the buckets in Fig. 13.30 if the following insertions and deletions occur:

  i. Records g through j are inserted into buckets 0 through 3, respectively.

  ii. Records a and b are deleted.

  iii. Records k through n are inserted into buckets 0 through 3, respectively.

  iv. Records c and d are deleted.

Exercise 13.4.2: We did not discuss how deletions can be carried out in a linear or extensible hash table. The mechanics of locating the record(s) to be deleted should be obvious. What method would you suggest for executing the deletion? In particular, what are the advantages and disadvantages of restructuring the table if its smaller size after deletion allows for compression of certain blocks?

! **Exercise 13.4.3:** The material of this section assumes that search keys are unique. However, only small modifications are needed to allow the techniques to work for search keys with duplicates. Describe the necessary changes to insertion, deletion, and lookup algorithms, and suggest the major problems that arise when there are duplicates in:

 * a) A simple hash table.

   b) An extensible hash table.

   c) A linear hash table.

! **Exercise 13.4.4:** Some hash functions do not work as well as theoretically possible. Suppose that we use the hash function on integer keys i defined by $h(i) = i^2 \bmod B$.

 * a) What is wrong with this hash function if $B = 10$?

   b) How good is this hash function if $B = 16$?

   c) Are there values of B for which this hash function is useful?

Exercise 13.4.5: In an extensible hash table with n records per block, what is the probability that an overflowing block will have to be handled recursively; i.e., all members of the block will go into the same one of the two blocks created in the split?

Exercise 13.4.6: Suppose keys are hashed to four-bit sequences, as in our examples of extensible and linear hashing in this section. However, also suppose that blocks can hold three records, rather than the two-record blocks of our examples. If we start with a hash table with two empty blocks (corresponding to 0 and 1), show the organization after we insert records with keys:

* a) $0000, 0001, \ldots, 1111$, and the method of hashing is extensible hashing.

  b) $0000, 0001, \ldots, 1111$, and the method of hashing is linear hashing with a capacity threshold of 100%.

  c) $1111, 1110, \ldots, 0000$, and the method of hashing is extensible hashing.

  d) $1111, 1110, \ldots, 0000$, and the method of hashing is linear hashing with a capacity threshold of 75%.

* **Exercise 13.4.7:** Suppose we use a linear or extensible hashing scheme, but there are pointers to records from outside. These pointers prevent us from moving records between blocks, as is sometimes required by these hashing methods. Suggest several ways that we could modify the structure to allow pointers from outside.

!! **Exercise 13.4.8:** A linear-hashing scheme with blocks that hold k records uses a threshold constant c, such that the current number of buckets n and the current number of records r are related by $r = ckn$. For instance, in Example 13.33 we used $k = 2$ and $c = 0.85$, so there were 1.7 records per bucket; i.e., $r = 1.7n$.

  a) Suppose for convenience that each key occurs exactly its expected number of times.[9] As a function of c, k, and n, how many blocks, including overflow blocks, are needed for the structure?

  b) Keys will not generally distribute equally, but rather the number of records with a given key (or suffix of a key) will be *Poisson distributed*. That is, if λ is the expected number of records with a given key suffix, then the actual number of such records will be i with probability $e^{-\lambda}\lambda^i/i!$. Under this assumption, calculate the expected number of blocks used, as a function of c, k, and n.

*! **Exercise 13.4.9:** Suppose we have a file of 1,000,000 records that we want to hash into a table with 1000 buckets. 100 records will fit in a block, and we wish to keep blocks as full as possible, but not allow two buckets to share a block. What are the minimum and maximum number of blocks that we could need to store this hash table?

---

[9] This assumption does not mean all buckets have the same number of records, because some buckets represent twice as many keys as others.

13.5   Summary of Chapter 13

✦ *Sequential Files*: Several simple file organizations begin by sorting the data file according to some search key and placing an index on this file.

✦ *Dense Indexes*: These indexes have a key-pointer pair for every record in the data file. The pairs are kept in sorted order of their key values.

✦ *Sparse Indexes*: These indexes have one key-pointer pair for each block of the data file. The key associated with a pointer to a block is the first key found on that block.

✦ *Multilevel Indexes*: It is sometimes useful to put an index on the index file itself, an index file on that, and so on. Higher levels of index must be sparse.

✦ *Expanding Files*: As a data file and its index file(s) grow, some provision for adding additional blocks to the file must be made. Adding overflow blocks to the original blocks is one possibility. Inserting additional blocks in the sequence for the data or index file may be possible, unless the file itself is required to be in sequential blocks of the disk.

✦ *Secondary Indexes*: An index on a search key K can be created even if the data file is not sorted by K. Such an index must be dense.

✦ *Inverted Indexes*: The relation between documents and the words they contain is often represented by an index structure with word-pointer pairs. The pointer goes to a place in a "bucket" file where is found a list of pointers to places where that word occurs.

✦ *B-trees*: These structures are essentially multilevel indexes, with graceful growth capabilities. Blocks with n keys and $n + 1$ pointers are organized in a tree, with the leaves pointing to records. All blocks are between half-full and completely full at all times.

✦ *Range Queries*: Queries in which we ask for all records whose search-key value lies in a given range are facilitated by indexed sequential files and B-tree indexes, although not by hash-table indexes.

✦ *Hash Tables*: We can create hash tables out of blocks in secondary memory, much as we can create main-memory hash tables. A hash function maps search-key values to buckets, effectively partitioning the records of a data file into many small groups (the buckets). Buckets are represented by a block and possible overflow blocks.

✦ *Dynamic Hashing*: Since performance of a hash table degrades if there are too many records in one bucket, the number of buckets may need to grow as time goes on. Two important methods of allowing graceful growth are extensible and linear hashing. Both begin by hashing search-key values to long bit-strings and use a varying number of those bits to determine the bucket for records.

✦ *Extensible Hashing*: This method allows the number of buckets to double whenever any bucket has too many records. It uses an array of pointers to blocks that represent the buckets. To avoid having too many blocks, several buckets can be represented by the same block.

✦ *Linear Hashing*: This method grows the number of buckets by 1 each time the ratio of records to buckets exceeds a threshold. Since the population of a single bucket cannot cause the table to expand, overflow blocks for buckets are needed in some situations.

13.6 References for Chapter 13

The B-tree was the original idea of Bayer and McCreight [2]. Unlike the B+ tree described here, this formulation had pointers to records at the interior nodes as well as at the leaves. [3] is a survey of B-tree varieties.

Hashing as a data structure goes back to Peterson [8]. Extensible hashing was developed by [4], while linear hashing is from [7]. The book by Knuth [6] contains much information on data structures, including techniques for selecting hash functions and designing hash tables, as well as a number of ideas concerning B-tree variants. The B+ tree formulation (without key values at interior nodes) appeared in the 1973 edition of [6].

Secondary indexes and other techniques for retrieval of documents are covered by [9]. Also, [5] and [1] are surveys of index methods for text documents.

1. R. Baeza-Yates, "Integrating contents and structure in text retrieval," *SIGMOD Record* **25**:1 (1996), pp. 67–79.

2. R. Bayer and E. M. McCreight, "Organization and maintenance of large ordered indexes," *Acta Informatica* **1**:3 (1972), pp. 173–189.

3. D. Comer, "The ubiquitous B-tree," *Computing Surveys* **11**:2 (1979), pp. 121–137.

4. R. Fagin, J. Nievergelt, N. Pippenger, and H. R. Strong, "Extendible hashing — a fast access method for dynamic files," *ACM Trans. on Database Systems* **4**:3 (1979), pp. 315–344.

5. C. Faloutsos, "Access methods for text," *Computing Surveys* **17**:1 (1985), pp. 49–74.

6. D. E. Knuth, *The Art of Computer Programming, Vol. III, Sorting and Searching, Third Edition*, Addison-Wesley, Reading MA, 1998.

7. W. Litwin, "Linear hashing: a new tool for file and table addressing," *Proc. Intl. Conf. on Very Large Databases* (1980) pp. 212–223.

8. W. W. Peterson, "Addressing for random access storage," *IBM J. Research and Development* **1**:2 (1957), pp. 130–146.

9. G. Salton, *Introduction to Modern Information Retrieval*, McGraw-Hill, New York, 1983.

Chapter 14

Multidimensional and Bitmap Indexes

All the index structures discussed so far are *one dimensional*; that is, they assume a single search key, and they retrieve records that match a given search-key value. We have imagined that the search key was a single attribute or field. However, an index whose search key is a combination of fields can still be one-dimensional. If we want a one-dimensional index whose search key is the fields $(F_1, F_2, \ldots, F_k)$, then we can take the search-key value to be the concatenation of values, the first from F_1, the second from F_2, and so on. We can separate these values by special marker symbols to make the association between search-key values and lists of values for the fields $F_1, \ldots, F_k$ unambiguous.

Example 14.1: If fields F_1 and F_2 are a string and an integer, respectively, and # is a character that cannot appear in strings, then the combination of values $F_1 = $ 'abcd' and $F_2 = 123$ can be represented by the string 'abcd#123'. □

In Chapter 13, we took advantage of a one-dimensional key space in several ways:

- Indexes on sequential files and B-trees both take advantage of having all keys in a single, sorted order.

- Hash tables require that the search key be completely known for any lookup. If a key consists of several fields, and even one is unknown, we cannot apply the hash function, but must instead search all the buckets.

There are a number of applications that require us to view data as existing in a 2-dimensional space, or sometimes in higher dimensions. Some of these applications can be supported by conventional DBMS's, but there are also some specialized systems designed for multidimensional applications. One important way in which these specialized systems distinguish themselves is by using data structures that support certain kinds of queries that are not common in SQL applications. Section 14.1 introduces us to the typical queries that benefit from an index that is designed to support multidimensional data and multidimensional queries. Then, in Sections 14.2 and 14.3 we discuss the following data structures:

1. *Grid files*, a multidimensional extension of one-dimensional hash-tables.

2. *Partitioned hash functions*, another way that brings hash-table ideas to multidimensional data.

3. *Multiple-key indexes*, in which the index on one attribute A leads to indexes on another attribute B for each possible value of A.

4. *kd-trees*, an approach to generalizing B-trees to sets of points.

5. *Quad trees*, which are multiway trees in which each child of a node represents a quadrant of a larger space.

6. *R-trees*, a B-tree generalization suitable for collections of regions.

Finally, Section 14.4 discusses an index structure called *bitmap indexes*. These indexes are succinct codes for the location of records with a given value in a given field. They are beginning to appear in the major commercial DBMS's, and they sometimes are an excellent choice for a one-dimensional index. However, they also can be a powerful tool for answering certain kinds of multidimensional queries.

14.1 Applications Needing Multiple Dimensions

We shall consider two general classes of multidimensional applications. One is *geographic* in nature, where the data is elements in a two-dimensional world, or sometimes a three-dimensional world. The second involves more abstract notions of dimensions. Roughly, every attribute of a relation can be thought of as a dimension, and all tuples are points in a space defined by those dimensions.

Also in this section is an analysis of how conventional indexes, such as B-trees, could be used to support multidimensional queries. While in some cases they are adequate, there are also examples where they are clearly dominated by more specialized structures.

14.1.1 Geographic Information Systems

A *geographic information system* stores objects in a (typically) two-dimensional space. The objects may be points or shapes. Often, these databases are maps, where the stored objects could represent houses, roads, bridges, pipelines, and many other physical objects. A suggestion of such a map is in Fig. 14.1.

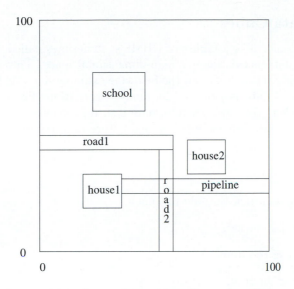

Figure 14.1: Some objects in 2-dimensional space

However, there are many other uses as well. For instance, an integrated-circuit design is a two-dimensional map of regions, often rectangles, composed of specific materials, called "layers." Likewise, we can think of the windows and icons on a screen as a collection of objects in two-dimensional space.

The queries asked of geographic information systems are not typical of SQL queries, although many can be expressed in SQL with some effort. Examples of these types of queries are:

1. *Partial match queries.* We specify values for one or more dimensions and look for all points matching those values in those dimensions.

2. *Range queries.* We give ranges for one or more of the dimensions, and we ask for the set of points within those ranges. If shapes are represented, then we may ask for the shapes that are partially or wholly within the range. These queries generalize the one-dimensional range queries that we considered in Section 13.3.4.

3. *Nearest-neighbor queries.* We ask for the closest point to a given point. For instance, if points represent cities, we might want to find the city of over 100,000 population closest to a given small city.

4. *Where-am-I queries.* We are given a point and we want to know in which shape, if any, the point is located. A familiar example is what happens when you click your mouse, and the system determines which of the displayed elements you were clicking.

14.1.2 Data Cubes

A recent development is a family of DBMS's, sometimes called *data cube* systems, that see data as existing in a high-dimensional space. These are discussed in more detail in Section 20.5, but the following example suggests the main idea. Multidimensional data is gathered by many corporations for *decision-support* applications, where they analyze information such as sales to better understand company operations. For example, a chain store may record each sale made, including:

1. The day and time.

2. The store at which the sale was made.

3. The item purchased.

4. The color of the item.

5. The size of the item.

and perhaps other properties of the sale.

It is common to view the data as a relation with an attribute for each property. These attributes can be seen as dimensions of a multidimensional space, the "data cube." Each tuple is a point in the space. Analysts then ask queries that typically group the data along some of the dimensions and summarize the groups by an aggregation. A typical example would be "give the sales of pink shirts for each store and each month of 1998."

14.1.3 Multidimensional Queries in SQL

It is possible to set up each of the applications suggested above as a conventional, relational database and to issue the suggested queries in SQL. Here are some examples.

Example 14.2 : Suppose we wish to answer nearest-neighbor queries about a set of points in two-dimensional space. We may represent the points as a relation consisting of a pair of reals:

```
Points(x, y)
```

That is, there are two attributes, x and y, representing the x- and y-coordinates of the point. Other, unseen, attributes of relation `Points` may represent properties of the point.

Suppose we want the nearest point to the point $(10.0, 20.0)$. The query of Fig. 14.2 finds the nearest point, or points if there is a tie. It asks, for each point p, whether there exists another point q that is closer to $(10.0, 20.0)$. Comparison of distances is carried out by computing the sum of the squares of the differences in the x- and y-coordinates between the point $(10.0, 20.0)$ and the points in question. Notice that we do not have to take the square roots of the sums to get the actual distances; comparing the squares of the distances is the same as comparing the distances themselves. □

```
SELECT *
FROM POINTS p
WHERE NOT EXISTS(
    SELECT *
    FROM POINTS q
    WHERE (q.x-10.0)*(q.x-10.0) + (q.y-20.0)*(q.y-20.0) <
        (p.x-10.0)*(p.x-10.0) + (p.y-20.0)*(p.y-20.0)
);
```

Figure 14.2: Finding the points with no point nearer to $(10.0, 20.0)$

Example 14.3: Rectangles are a common form of shape used in geographic systems. We can represent a rectangle in several ways; a popular one is to give the coordinates of the lower-left and upper-right corners. We then represent a collection of rectangles by a relation `Rectangles` with attributes for a rectangle-ID, the four coordinates that describe the rectangle, and any other properties of the rectangle that we wished to record. We shall use the relation:

```
Rectangles(id, xll, yll, xur, yur)
```

in this example. The attributes are the rectangle's ID, the x-coordinate of its lower-left corner, the y-coordinate of that corner, and the two coordinates of the upper-right corner, respectively.

Figure 14.3 is a query that asks for the rectangle(s) enclosing the point $(10.0, 20.0)$. The where-clause condition is straightforward. For the rectangle to enclose $(10.0, 20.0)$, the lower-left corner must have its x-coordinate at or to the left of 10.0, and its y-coordinate at or below 20.0. Also, the upper right corner must be at or to the right of $x = 10.0$ and at or above $y = 20.0$. □

```
SELECT id
FROM Rectangles
WHERE xll <= 10.0 AND yll <= 20.0 AND
      xur >= 10.0 AND yur >= 20.0;
```

Figure 14.3: Finding the rectangles that contain a given point

Example 14.4: Data suitable for a data-cube system is typically organized into a *fact table*, which gives the basic elements being recorded (e.g., each sale), and *dimension tables*, which give properties of the values along each dimension. For instance, if the store at which a sale was made is a dimension, the dimension table for stores might give the address, phone, and name of the store's manager.

In this example, we shall deal only with the fact table, which we assume has the dimensions suggested in Section 14.1.2. That is, the fact table is the relation:

```
Sales(day, store, item, color, size)
```

The query "summarize the sales of pink shirts by day and store" is shown in Fig. 14.4. It uses grouping to organize sales by the dimensions `day` and `store`, while summarizing the other dimensions through the `COUNT` aggregation operator. We focus on only those points of the data cube that we care about by using the `WHERE`-clause to select only the tuples for pink shirts. □

```
SELECT day, store, COUNT(*) AS totalSales
FROM Sales
WHERE item = 'shirt' AND color = 'pink'
GROUP BY day, store;
```

Figure 14.4: Summarizing the sales of pink shirts

14.1.4 Executing Range Queries Using Conventional Indexes

Now, let us consider to what extent the indexes described in Chapter 13 would help in answering range queries. Suppose for simplicity that there are two dimensions. We could put a secondary index on each of the dimensions, x and y. Using a B-tree for each would make it especially easy to get a range of values for each dimension.

Given ranges in both dimensions, we could begin by using the B-tree for x to get pointers to all of the records in the range for x. Next, we use the B-tree for y to get pointers to the records for all points whose y-coordinate is in the range for y. Then, we intersect these pointers, using the idea of Section 13.2.3. If the pointers fit in main memory, then the total number of disk I/O's is the number of leaf nodes of each B-tree that need to be examined, plus a few I/O's for finding our way down the B-trees (see Section 13.3.7). To this amount we must add the disk I/O's needed to retrieve all the matching records, however many they may be.

Example 14.5 : Let us consider a hypothetical set of 1,000,000 points distributed randomly in a space in which both the x- and y-coordinates range from 0 to 1000. Suppose that 100 point records fit on a block, and an average B-tree leaf has about 200 key-pointer pairs (recall that not all slots of a B-tree block are necessarily occupied, at any given time). We shall assume there are B-tree indexes on both x and y.

Imagine we are given the range query asking for points in the square of side 100 surrounding the center of the space, that is, $450 \leq x \leq 550$ and $450 \leq y \leq 550$. Using the B-tree for x, we can find pointers to all the records with x in the range; there should be about 100,000 pointers, and this number of pointers should fit in main memory. Similarly, we use the B-tree for y to get the pointers to all the records with y in the desired range; again there are about 100,000 of them. Approximately 10,000 pointers will be in the intersection of these two sets, and it is the records reached by the 10,000 pointers in the intersection that form our answer.

Now, let us estimate the number of disk I/O's needed to answer the range query. First, as we pointed out in Section 13.3.7, it is generally feasible to keep the root of any B-tree in main memory. Since we are looking for a range of search-key values in each B-tree, and the pointers at the leaves are sorted by this search key, all we have to do to access the 100,000 pointers in either dimension is examine one intermediate-level node and all the leaves that contain the desired pointers. Since we assumed leaves have about 200 key-pointer pairs each, we shall have to look at about 500 leaf blocks in each of the B-trees. When we add in one intermediate node per B-tree, we have a total of 1002 disk I/O's.

Finally, we have to retrieve the blocks containing the 10,000 desired records. If they are stored randomly, we must expect that they will be on almost 10,000 different blocks. Since the entire file of a million records is assumed stored over 10,000 blocks, packed 100 to a block, we essentially have to look at every block of the data file anyway. Thus, in this example at least, conventional indexes have been little if any help in answering the range query. Of course, if the range were smaller, then constructing the intersection of the two pointer sets would allow us to limit the search to a fraction of the blocks in the data file. □

14.1.5 Executing Nearest-Neighbor Queries Using Conventional Indexes

Almost any data structure we use will allow us to answer a nearest-neighbor query by picking a range in each dimension, asking the range query, and selecting the point closest to the target within that range. Unfortunately, there are two things that could go wrong:

1. There is no point within the selected range.

2. The closest point within the range might not be the closest point overall.

Let us consider each of these problems in the context of the nearest-neighbor query of Example 14.2, using the hypothetical indexes on dimensions x and y

introduced in Example 14.5. If we had reason to believe that a point within distance d of $(10.0, 20.0)$ existed, we could use the B-tree for x to get pointers to all the records for points whose x-coordinate is between $10 - d$ and $10 + d$. We could then use the B-tree for y to get pointers to all the records whose y-coordinate is between $20 - d$ and $20 + d$.

If we have one or more points in the intersection, and we have recorded with each pointer its x- or y-coordinate (whichever is the search key for the index), then we have the coordinates of all the points in the intersection. We can thus determine which of these points is closest to $(10.0, 20.0)$ and retrieve only its record. Unfortunately, we cannot be certain that there are any points within distance d of the given point, so we may have to repeat the entire process with a higher value of d.

However, even if there is a point in the range we have searched, there are some circumstances where the closest point in the range is further than distance d from the target point, e.g., $(10.0, 20.0)$ in our example. The situation is suggested by Fig. 14.5. If that is the case, then we must expand our range and search again, to make sure that no closer point exists. If the distance from the target to the closest point found so far is d', and $d' > d$, then we must repeat the search with d' in place of d.

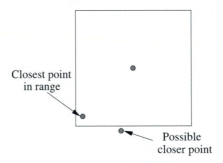

Figure 14.5: The point is in the range, but there could be a closer point outside the range

Example 14.6 : Let us consider the same data and indexes as in Example 14.5. If we want the nearest neighbor to target point $P = (10.0, 20.0)$, we might pick $d = 1$. Then, there will be one point per unit of area on the average, and with $d = 1$ we find every point within a square of side 2.0 around the point P, wherein the expected number of points is 4.

If we examine the B-tree for the x-coordinate with the range query $9.0 \le x \le 11.0$, then we shall find about 2,000 points, so we need to traverse at least 10 leaves, and most likely 11 (since the points with $x = 9.0$ are unlikely to start just at the beginning of a leaf). As in Example 14.5, we can probably keep the roots of the B-trees in main memory, so we only need one disk I/O for an intermediate node and 11 disk I/O's for the leaves. Another 12 disk I/O's search the B-tree index on the y-coordinate for the points whose y-coordinate is between 19.0 and 21.0.

If we intersect the approximately 4000 pointers in main memory, we shall find about four records that are candidates for the nearest neighbor of point $(10.0, 20.0)$. Assuming there is at least one, we can determine from the associated x- and y-coordinates of the pointers which is the nearest neighbor. One more disk I/O to retrieve the desired record, for a total of 25 disk I/O's, completes the query. However, if there is no point in the square with $d = 1$, or the closest point is more than distance 1 from the target, then we have to repeat the search with a larger value of d. □

The conclusion to draw from Example 14.6 is that conventional indexes might not be terrible for a nearest-neighbor query, but they use significantly more disk I/O's than would be used, say, to find a record given its key and a B-tree index on that key (which would probably take only two or three disk I/O's). The methods suggested in this chapter will generally provide better performance and are used in specialized DBMS's that support multidimensional data.

14.1.6 Other Limitations of Conventional Indexes

The previously mentioned structures fare no better for range queries than for nearest-neighbor queries. In fact, our approach to solving a nearest-neighbor query in Example 14.6 was really to convert it to a range-query with a small range in each dimension and hope the range was sufficient to include at least one point. Thus, if we were to tackle a range query with larger ranges, and the data structure were indexes in each dimension, then the number of disk I/O's necessary to retrieve the pointers to candidate records in each dimension would be even greater than what we found in Example 14.6.

The multidimensional aggregation of the query in Fig. 14.4 is likewise not well supported. If we have indexes on item and color, we can find all the records representing sales of pink shirts and intersect them, as we did in Example 14.6. However, queries in which other attributes besides item and color were specified would require indexes on those attributes instead.

Worse, while we can keep the data file sorted on one of the five attributes, we cannot keep it sorted on two attributes, let alone five. Thus, most queries of the form suggested by Fig. 14.4 would require that records from all or almost all of the blocks of the data file be retrieved. These queries of this type would be extremely expensive to execute if data was in secondary memory.

14.1.7 Overview of Multidimensional Index Structures

Most data structures for supporting queries on multidimensional data fall into one of two categories:

1. Hash-table-like approaches.

2. Tree-like approaches.

For each of these structures, we give up something that we have in the one-dimensional structures of Chapter 13.

- With the hash-bashed schemes — grid files and partitioned hash functions in Section 14.2 — we no longer have the advantage that the answer to our query is in exactly one bucket. However, each of these schemes limit our search to a subset of the buckets.

- With the tree-based schemes, we give up at least one of these important properties of B-trees:

  1. The balance of the tree, where all leaves are at the same level.
  2. The correspondence between tree nodes and disk blocks.
  3. The speed with which modifications to the data may be performed.

As we shall see in Section 14.3, trees often will be deeper in some parts than in others; often the deep parts correspond to regions that have many points. We shall also see that it is common that the information corresponding to a tree node is considerably smaller than what fits in one block. It is thus necessary to group nodes into blocks in some useful way.

14.1.8   Exercises for Section 14.1

Exercise 14.1.1: Write SQL queries using the relation

```
Rectangles(id, xll, yll, xur, yur)
```

from Example 14.3 to answer the following questions:

* a) Find the set of rectangles that intersect the rectangle whose lower-left corner is at $(10.0, 20.0)$ and whose upper-right corner is at $(40.0, 30.0)$.

  b) Find the pairs of rectangles that intersect.

  c) Find the rectangles that completely contain the rectangle mentioned in (a).

  d) Find the rectangles that are completely contained within the rectangle mentioned in (a).

! e) Find the "rectangles" in the relation `Rectangles` that are not really rectangles; i.e., they cannot exist physically.

For each of these queries, tell what indexes, if any, would help retrieve the desired tuples.

Exercise 14.1.2: Using the relation

    Sales(day, store, item, color, size)

from Example 14.4, write the following queries in SQL:

* a) List all colors of shirts and their total sales, provided there are more than 1000 sales for that color.

  b) List sales of shirts by store and color.

  c) List sales of all items by store and color.

! d) List for each item and color the store with the largest sales and the amount of those sales.

For each of these queries, tell what indexes, if any, would help retrieve the desired tuples.

Exercise 14.1.3: Redo Example 14.5 under the assumption that the range query asks for a square in the middle that is $n \times n$ for some n between 1 and 1000. How many disk I/O's are needed? For which values of n do indexes help?

* **Exercise 14.1.4:** Repeat Exercise 14.1.3 if the file of records is sorted on x.

!! **Exercise 14.1.5:** Suppose that we have points distributed randomly in a square, as in Example 14.6, and we want to perform a nearest neighbor query. We choose a distance d and find all points in the square of side $2d$ with the center at the target point. Our search is successful if we find within this square at least one point whose distance from the target point is d or less.

* a) If there is on average one point per unit of area, give as a function of d the probability that we will be successful.

  b) If we are unsuccessful, we must repeat the search with a larger d. Assume for simplicity that each time we are unsuccessful, we double d and pay twice as much as we did for the previous search. Again assuming that there is one point per unit area, what initial value of d gives us the minimum expected search cost?

14.2 Hash-Like Structures for Multidimensional Data

In this section we shall consider two data structures that generalize hash tables built using a single key. In each case, the bucket for a point is a function of all the attributes or dimensions. One scheme, called the "grid file," usually doesn't "hash" values along the dimensions, but rather partitions the dimensions by sorting the values along that dimension. The other, called "partitioned hashing," does "hash" the various dimensions, with each dimension contributing to the bucket number.

14.2.1   Grid Files

One of the simplest data structures that often outperforms single-dimension indexes for queries involving multidimensional data is the *grid file*. Think of the space of points partitioned in a grid. In each dimension, *grid lines* partition the space into *stripes*. Points that fall on a grid line will be considered to belong to the stripe for which that grid line is the lower boundary. The number of grid lines in different dimensions may vary, and there may be different spacings between adjacent grid lines, even between lines in the same dimension.

Example 14.7 : Let us introduce a running example for this chapter: the question "who buys gold jewelry?" We shall imagine a database of customers for gold jewelry that tells us many things about each customer — their name, address, and so on. However, to make things simpler, we assume that the only relevant attributes are the customer's age and salary. Our example database has twelve customers, which we can represent by the following age-salary pairs:

$$(25, 60) \quad (45, 60) \quad (50, 75) \quad (50, 100)$$
$$(50, 120) \quad (70, 110) \quad (85, 140) \quad (30, 260)$$
$$(25, 400) \quad (45, 350) \quad (50, 275) \quad (60, 260)$$

In Fig. 14.6 we see these twelve points located in a 2-dimensional space. We have also selected some grid lines in each dimension. For this simple example, we have chosen two lines in each dimension, dividing the space into nine rectangular regions, but there is no reason why the same number of lines must be used in each dimension. We have also allowed the spacing between the lines to vary. For instance, in the age dimension, the three regions into which the two vertical lines divide the space have width 40, 15, and 45.

In this example, no points are exactly on a grid line. But in general, a rectangle includes points on its lower and left boundaries, but not on its upper and right boundaries. For instance, the central rectangle in Fig. 14.6 represents points with $40 \leq age < 55$ and $90 \leq salary < 225$.   □

14.2.2   Lookup in a Grid File

Each of the regions into which a space is partitioned can be thought of as a bucket of a hash table, and each of the points in that region has its record placed in a block belonging to that bucket. If needed, overflow blocks can be used to increase the size of a bucket.

Instead of a one-dimensional array of buckets, as is found in conventional hash tables, the grid file uses an array whose number of dimensions is the same as for the data file. To locate the proper bucket for a point, we need to know, for each dimension, the list of values at which the grid lines occur. Hashing a point is thus somewhat different from applying a hash function to the values of its components. Rather, we look at each component of the point and determine the position of the point in the grid for that dimension. The positions of the point in each of the dimensions together determine the bucket.

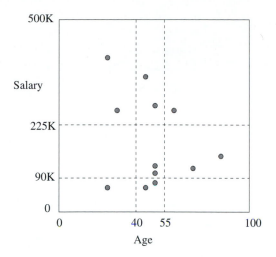

Figure 14.6: A grid file

Example 14.8: Figure 14.7 shows the data of Fig. 14.6 placed in buckets. Since the grids in both dimensions divide the space into three regions, the bucket array is a 3×3 matrix. Two of the buckets:

1. Salary between $90K and $225K and age between 0 and 40, and

2. Salary below $90K and age above 55

are empty, and we do not show a block for that bucket. The other buckets are shown, with the artificially low maximum of two data points per block. In this simple example, no bucket has more than two members, so no overflow blocks are needed. □

14.2.3 Insertion Into Grid Files

When we insert a record into a grid file, we follow the procedure for lookup of the record, and we place the new record in that bucket. If there is room in the block for the bucket then there is nothing more to do. The problem occurs when there is no room in the bucket. There are two general approaches:

1. Add overflow blocks to the buckets, as needed. This approach works well as long as the chains of blocks for a bucket do not get too long. If they do, then the number of disk I/O's needed for lookup, insertion, or deletion eventually grows unacceptably large.

2. Reorganize the structure by adding or moving the grid lines. This approach is similar to the dynamic hashing techniques discussed in Section 13.4, but there are additional problems because the contents of buckets are linked across a dimension. That is, adding a grid line splits all the

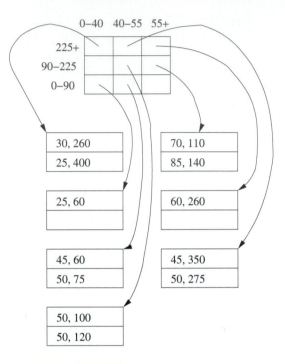

Figure 14.7: A grid file representing the points of Fig. 14.6

buckets along that line. As a result, it may not be possible to select a new grid line that does the best for all buckets. For instance, if one bucket is too big, we might not be able to choose either a dimension along which to split or a point at which to split, without making many empty buckets or leaving several very full ones.

Example 14.9 : Suppose someone 52 years old with an income of $200K buys gold jewelry. This customer belongs in the central rectangle of Fig. 14.6. However, there are now three records in that bucket. We could simply add an overflow block. If we want to split the bucket, then we need to choose either the age or salary dimension, and we need to choose a new grid line to create the division. There are only three ways to introduce a grid line that will split the central bucket so two points are on one side and one on the other, which is the most even possible split in this case.

1. A vertical line, such as age $= 51$, that separates the two 50's from the 52. This line does nothing to split the buckets above or below, since both points of each of the other buckets for age 40–55 are to the left of the line age $= 51$.

2. A horizontal line that separates the point with salary $= 200$ from the other two points in the central bucket. We may as well choose a number

---

Accessing Buckets of a Grid File

While finding the proper coordinates for a point in a three-by-three grid like Fig. 14.7 is easy, we should remember that the grid file may have a very large number of stripes in each dimension. If so, then we must create an index for each dimension. The search key for an index is the set of partition values in that dimension.

Given a value v in some coordinate, we search for the greatest key value w less than or equal to v. Associated with w in that index will be the row or column of the matrix into which v falls. Given values in each dimension, we can find where in the matrix the pointer to the bucket falls. We may then retrieve the block with that pointer directly.

In extreme cases, the matrix is so big, that most of the buckets are empty and we cannot afford to store all the empty buckets. Then, we must treat the matrix as a relation whose attributes are the corners of the nonempty buckets and a final attribute representing the pointer to the bucket. Lookup in this relation is itself a multidimensional search, but its size is smaller than the size of the data file itself.

---

like 130, which also splits the bucket to the right (that for age 55–100 and salary 90–225).

3. A horizontal line that separates the point with salary = 100 from the other two points. Again, we would be advised to pick a number like 115 that also splits the bucket to the right.

Choice (1) is probably not advised, since it doesn't split any other bucket; we are left with more empty buckets and have not reduced the size of any occupied buckets, except for the one we had to split. Choices (2) and (3) are equally good, although we might pick (2) because it puts the horizontal grid line at salary = 130, which is closer to midway between the upper and lower limits of 90 and 225 than we get with choice (3). The resulting partition into buckets is shown in Fig. 14.8. □

14.2.4 Performance of Grid Files

Let us consider how many disk I/O's a grid file requires on various types of queries. We have been focusing on the two-dimensional version of grid files, although they can be used for any number of dimensions. One major problem in the high-dimensional case is that the number of buckets grows exponentially with the dimension. If large portions of a space are empty, then there will be many empty buckets. We can envision the problem even in two dimensions. Suppose that there were a high correlation between age and salary, so all points

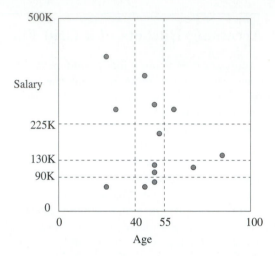

Figure 14.8: Insertion of the point $(52, 200)$ followed by splitting of buckets

in Fig. 14.6 lay along the diagonal. Then no matter where we placed the grid lines, the buckets off the diagonal would have to be empty.

However, if the data is well distributed, and the data file itself is not too large, then we can choose grid lines so that:

1. There are sufficiently few buckets that we can keep the bucket matrix in main memory, thus not incurring disk I/O to consult it, or to add rows or columns to the matrix when we introduce a new grid line.

2. We can also keep in memory indexes on the values of the grid lines in each dimension (as per the box "Accessing Buckets of a Grid File"), or we can avoid the indexes altogether and use main-memory binary search of the values defining the grid lines in each dimension.

3. The typical bucket does not have more than a few overflow blocks, so we do not incur too many disk I/O's when we search through a bucket.

Under those assumptions, here is how the grid file behaves on some important classes of queries.

Lookup of Specific Points

We are directed to the proper bucket, so the only disk I/O is what is necessary to read the bucket. If we are inserting or deleting, then an additional disk write is needed. Inserts that require the creation of an overflow block cause an additional write.

Partial-Match Queries

Examples of this query would include "find all customers aged 50," or "find all customers with a salary of $200K." Now, we need to look at all the buckets in a row or column of the bucket matrix. The number of disk I/O's can be quite high if there are many buckets in a row or column, but only a small fraction of all the buckets will be accessed.

Range Queries

A range query defines a rectangular region of the grid, and all points found in the buckets that cover that region will be answers to the query, with the exception of some of the points in buckets on the border of the search region. For example, if we want to find all customers aged 35–45 with a salary of 50–100, then we need to look in the four buckets in the lower left of Fig. 14.6. In this case, all buckets are on the border, so we may look at a good number of points that are not answers to the query. However, if the search region involves a large number of buckets, then most of them must be interior, and all their points are answers. For range queries, the number of disk I/O's may be large, as we may be required to examine many buckets. However, since range queries tend to produce large answer sets, we typically will examine not too many more blocks than the minimum number of blocks on which the answer could be placed by any organization whatsoever.

Nearest-Neighbor Queries

Given a point P, we start by searching the bucket in which that point belongs. If we find at least one point there, we have a candidate Q for the nearest neighbor. However, it is possible that there are points in adjacent buckets that are closer to P than Q is; the situation is like that suggested in Fig. 14.5. We have to consider whether the distance between P and a border of its bucket is less than the distance from P to Q. If there are such borders, then the adjacent buckets on the other side of each such border must be searched also. In fact, if buckets are severely rectangular — much longer in one dimension than the other — then it may be necessary to search even buckets that are not adjacent to the one containing point P.

Example 14.10 : Suppose we are looking in Fig. 14.6 for the point nearest $P = (45, 200)$. We find that $(50, 120)$ is the closest point in the bucket, at a distance of 80.2. No point in the lower three buckets can be this close to $(45, 200)$, because their salary component is at most 90, so we can omit searching them. However, the other five buckets must be searched, and we find that there are actually two equally close points: $(30, 260)$ and $(60, 260)$, at a distance of 61.8 from P. Generally, the search for a nearest neighbor can be limited to a few buckets, and thus a few disk I/O's. However, since the buckets nearest the point P may be empty, we cannot easily put an upper bound on how costly the search is. □

14.2.5 Partitioned Hash Functions

Hash functions can take a list of attribute values as an argument, although typically they hash values from only one attribute. For instance, if a is an integer-valued attribute and b is a character-string-valued attribute, then we could add the value of a to the value of the ASCII code for each character of b, divide by the number of buckets, and take the remainder. The result could be used as the bucket number of a hash table suitable as an index on the pair of attributes (a, b).

However, such a hash table could only be used in queries that specified values for both a and b. A preferable option is to design the hash function so it produces some number of bits, say k. These k bits are divided among n attributes, so that we produce k_i bits of the hash value from the ith attribute, and $\sum_{i=1}^{n} k_i = k$. More precisely, the hash function h is actually a list of hash functions $(h_1, h_2, \ldots, h_n)$, such that h_i applies to a value for the ith attribute and produces a sequence of k_i bits. The bucket in which to place a tuple with values $(v_1, v_2, \ldots, v_n)$ for the n attributes is computed by concatenating the bit sequences: $h_1(v_1)h_2(v_2) \cdots h_n(v_n)$.

Example 14.11: If we have a hash table with 10-bit bucket numbers (1024 buckets), we could devote four bits to attribute a and the remaining six bits to attribute b. Suppose we have a tuple with a-value A and b-value B, perhaps with other attributes that are not involved in the hash. We hash A using a hash function h_a associated with attribute a to get four bits, say 0101. We then hash B, using a hash function h_b, perhaps receiving the six bits 111000. The bucket number for this tuple is thus 0101111000, the concatenation of the two bit sequences.

By partitioning the hash function this way, we get some advantage from knowing values for any one or more of the attributes that contribute to the hash function. For instance, if we are given a value A for attribute a, and we find that $h_a(A) = 0101$, then we know that the only tuples with a-value A are in the 64 buckets whose numbers are of the form $0101 \cdots$, where the $\cdots$ represents any six bits. Similarly, if we are given the b-value B of a tuple, we can isolate the possible buckets of the tuple to the 16 buckets whose number ends in the six bits $h_b(B)$. □

Example 14.12: Suppose we have the "gold jewelry" data of Example 14.7, which we want to store in a partitioned hash table with eight buckets (i.e., three bits for bucket numbers). We assume as before that two records are all that can fit in one block. We shall devote one bit to the age attribute and the remaining two bits to the salary attribute.

For the hash function on age, we shall take the age modulo 2; that is, a record with an even age will hash into a bucket whose number is of the form $0xy$ for some bits x and y. A record with an odd age hashes to one of the buckets with a number of the form $1xy$. The hash function for salary will be the salary (in thousands) modulo 4. For example, a salary that leaves a remainder of 1

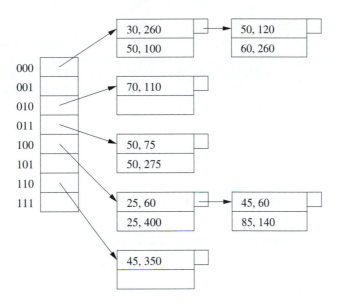

Figure 14.9: A partitioned hash table

when divided by 4, such as 57K, will be in a bucket whose number is $z01$ for some bit z.

In Fig. 14.9 we see the data from Example 14.7 placed in this hash table. Notice that, because we have used mostly ages and salaries divisible by 10, the hash function does not distribute the points too well. Two of the eight buckets have four records each and need overflow blocks, while three other buckets are empty. □

14.2.6 Comparison of Grid Files and Partitioned Hashing

The performance of the two data structures discussed in this section are quite different. Here are the major points of comparison.

- Partitioned hash tables are actually quite useless for nearest-neighbor queries or range queries. The problem is that physical distance between points is not reflected by the closeness of bucket numbers. Of course we could design the hash function on some attribute a so the smallest values were assigned the first bit string (all 0's), the next values were assigned the next bit string $(00\cdots01)$, and so on. If we do so, then we have reinvented the grid file.

- A well chosen hash function will randomize the buckets into which points fall, and thus buckets will tend to be equally occupied. However, grid files, especially when the number of dimensions is large, will tend to leave many buckets empty or nearly so. The intuitive reason is that when there are many attributes, there is likely to be some correlation among at least some of them, so large regions of the space are left empty. For instance, we mentioned in Section 14.2.4 that a correlation between age and salary would cause most points of Fig. 14.6 to lie near the diagonal, with most of the rectangle empty. As a consequence, we can use fewer buckets, and/or have fewer overflow blocks in a partitioned hash table than in a grid file.

Thus, if we are only required to support partial match queries, where we specify some attributes' values and leave the other attributes completely unspecified, then the partitioned hash function is likely to outperform the grid file. Conversely, if we need to do nearest-neighbor queries or range queries frequently, then we would prefer to use a grid file.

14.2.7   Exercises for Section 14.2

model	speed	ram	hd
1001	700	64	10
1002	1500	128	60
1003	866	128	20
1004	866	64	10
1005	1000	128	20
1006	1300	256	40
1007	1400	128	80
1008	700	64	30
1009	1200	128	80
1010	750	64	30
1011	1100	128	60
1013	733	256	60

Figure 14.10: Some PC's and their characteristics

Exercise 14.2.1: In Fig. 14.10 are specifications for twelve of the thirteen PC's introduced in Fig. 5.11. Suppose we wish to design an index on speed and hard-disk size only.

* a) Choose five grid lines (total for the two dimensions), so that there are no more than two points in any bucket.

! b) Can you separate the points with at most two per bucket if you use only four grid lines? Either show how or argue that it is not possible.

! c) Suggest a partitioned hash function that will partition these points into four buckets with at most four points per bucket.

Handling Tiny Buckets

We generally think of buckets as containing about one block's worth of data. However, there are reasons why we might need to create so many buckets that the average bucket has only a small fraction of the number of records that will fit in a block. For example, high-dimensional data will require many buckets if we are to partition significantly along each dimension. Thus, in the structures of this section and also for the tree-based schemes of Section 14.3, we might choose to pack several buckets (or nodes of trees) into one block. If we do so, there are some important points to remember:

- The block header must contain information about where each record is, and to which bucket it belongs.

- If we insert a record into a bucket, we may not have room in the block containing that bucket. If so, we need to split the block in some way. We must decide which buckets go with each block, find the records of each bucket and put them in the proper block, and adjust the bucket table to point to the proper block.

! Exercise 14.2.2: Suppose we wish to place the data of Fig. 14.10 in a three-dimensional grid file, based on the speed, ram, and hard-disk attributes. Suggest a partition in each dimension that will divide the data well.

Exercise 14.2.3: Choose a partitioned hash function with one bit for each of the three attributes speed, ram, and hard-disk that divides the data of Fig. 14.10 well.

Exercise 14.2.4: Suppose we place the data of Fig. 14.10 in a grid file with dimensions for speed and ram only. The partitions are at speeds of 720, 950, 1150, and 1350, and ram of 100 and 200. Suppose also that only two points can fit in one bucket. Suggest good splits if we insert points at:

* a) Speed = 1000 and ram = 192.

  b) Speed = 800, ram = 128, and then speed = 833, ram = 96.

Exercise 14.2.5: Suppose we store a relation $R(x,y)$ in a grid file. Both attributes have a range of values from 0 to 1000. The partitions of this grid file happen to be uniformly spaced; for x there are partitions every 20 units, at 20, 40, 60, and so on, while for y the partitions are every 50 units, at 50, 100, 150, and so on.

a) How many buckets do we have to examine to answer the range query

```
SELECT *
FROM R
WHERE 310 < x AND x < 400 AND 520 < y AND y < 730;
```

*! b) We wish to perform a nearest-neighbor query for the point $(110, 205)$. We begin by searching the bucket with lower-left corner at $(100, 200)$ and upper-right corner at $(120, 250)$, and we find that the closest point in this bucket is $(115, 220)$. What other buckets must be searched to verify that this point is the closest?

! **Exercise 14.2.6 :** Suppose we have a grid file with three lines (i.e., four stripes) in each dimension. However, the points (x, y) happen to have a special property. Tell the largest possible number of nonempty buckets if:

* a) The points are on a line; i.e., there is are constants a and b such that $y = ax + b$ for every point (x, y).

b) The points are related quadratically; i.e., there are constants a, b, and c such that $y = ax^2 + bx + c$ for every point (x, y).

Exercise 14.2.7 : Suppose we store a relation $R(x, y, z)$ in a partitioned hash table with 1024 buckets (i.e., 10-bit bucket addresses). Queries about R each specify exactly one of the attributes, and each of the three attributes is equally likely to be specified. If the hash function produces 5 bits based only on x, 3 bits based only on y, and 2 bits based only on z, what is the average number of buckets that need to be searched to answer a query?

!! **Exercise 14.2.8 :** Suppose we have a hash table whose buckets are numbered 0 to $2^n - 1$; i.e., bucket addresses are n bits long. We wish to store in the table a relation with two attributes x and y. A query will either specify a value for x or y, but never both. With probability p, it is x whose value is specified.

a) Suppose we partition the hash function so that m bits are devoted to x and the remaining $n - m$ bits to y. As a function of m, n, and p, what is the expected number of buckets that must be examined to answer a random query?

b) For what value of m (as a function of n and p) is the expected number of buckets minimized? Do not worry that this m is unlikely to be an integer.

*! **Exercise 14.2.9 :** Suppose we have a relation $R(x, y)$ with 1,000,000 points randomly distributed. The range of both x and y is 0 to 1000. We can fit 100 tuples of R in a block. We decide to use a grid file with uniformly spaced grid lines in each dimension, with m as the width of the stripes. we wish to select m in order to minimize the number of disk I/O's needed to read all the necessary

buckets to ask a range query that is a square 50 units on each side. You may assume that the sides of this square *never* align with the grid lines. If we pick m too large, we shall have a lot of overflow blocks in each bucket, and many of the points in a bucket will be outside the range of the query. If we pick m too small, then there will be too many buckets, and blocks will tend not to be full of data. What is the best value of m?

14.3   Tree-Like Structures for Multidimensional Data

We shall now consider four more structures that are useful for range queries or nearest-neighbor queries on multidimensional data. In order, we shall consider:

1. Multiple-key indexes.

2. *kd*-trees.

3. Quad trees.

4. R-trees.

The first three are intended for sets of points. The R-tree is commonly used to represent sets of regions; it is also useful for points.

14.3.1   Multiple-Key Indexes

Suppose we have several attributes representing dimensions of our data points, and we want to support range queries or nearest-neighbor queries on these points. A simple tree-like scheme for accessing these points is an index of indexes, or more generally a tree in which the nodes at each level are indexes for one attribute.

The idea is suggested in Fig. 14.11 for the case of two attributes. The "root of the tree" is an index for the first of the two attributes. This index could be any type of conventional index, such as a B-tree or a hash table. The index associates with each of its search-key values — i.e., values for the first attribute — a pointer to another index. If V is a value of the first attribute, then the index we reach by following key V and its pointer is an index into the set of points that have V for their value in the first attribute and any value for the second attribute.

Example 14.13: Figure 14.12 shows a multiple-key index for our running "gold jewelry" example, where the first attribute is age, and the second attribute is salary. The root index, on age, is suggested at the left of Fig. 14.12. We have not indicated how the index works. For example, the key-pointer pairs forming the seven rows of that index might be spread among the leaves of a B-tree. However, what is important is that the only keys present are the ages for which

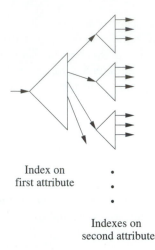

Index on
first attribute

Indexes on
second attribute

Figure 14.11: Using nested indexes on different keys

there is one or more data point, and the index makes it easy to find the pointer associated with a given key value.

At the right of Fig. 14.12 are seven indexes that provide access to the points themselves. For example, if we follow the pointer associated with age 50 in the root index, we get to a smaller index where salary is the key, and the four key values in the index are the four salaries associated with points that have age 50. Again, we have not indicated in the figure how the index is implemented, just the key-pointer associations it makes. When we follow the pointers associated with each of these values (75, 100, 120, and 275), we get to the record for the individual represented. For instance, following the pointer associated with 100, we find the person whose age is 50 and whose salary is $100K. □

In a multiple-key index, some of the second or higher rank indexes may be very small. For example, Fig 14.12 has four second-rank indexes with but a single pair. Thus, it may be appropriate to implement these indexes as simple tables that are packed several to a block, in the manner suggested by the box "Handling Tiny Buckets" in Section 14.2.5.

14.3.2   Performance of Multiple-Key Indexes

Let us consider how a multiple key index performs on various kinds of multidimensional queries. We shall concentrate on the case of two attributes, although the generalization to more than two attributes is unsurprising.

Partial-Match Queries

If the first attribute is specified, then the access is quite efficient. We use the root index to find the one subindex that leads to the points we want. For

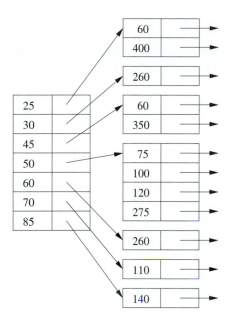

Figure 14.12: Multiple-key indexes for age/salary data

example, if the root is a B-tree index, then we shall do two or three disk I/O's to get to the proper subindex, and then use whatever I/O's are needed to access all of that index and the points of the data file itself. On the other hand, if the first attribute does not have a specified value, then we must search every subindex, a potentially time-consuming process.

Range Queries

The multiple-key index works quite well for a range query, provided the individual indexes themselves support range queries on their attribute — B-trees or indexed sequential files, for instance. To answer a range query, we use the root index and the range of the first attribute to find all of the subindexes that might contain answer points. We then search each of these subindexes, using the range specified for the second attribute.

Example 14.14: Suppose we have the multiple-key index of Fig. 14.12 and we are asked the range query $35 \leq$ age ≤ 55 and $100 \leq$ salary ≤ 200. When we examine the root index, we find that the keys 45 and 50 are in the range for age. We follow the associated pointers to two subindexes on salary. The index for age 45 has no salary in the range 100 to 200, while the index for age 50 has two such salaries: 100 and 120. Thus, the only two points in the range are $(50, 100)$ and $(50, 120)$. □

Nearest-Neighbor Queries

The answering of a nearest-neighbor query with a multiple-key index uses the same strategy as for almost all the data structures of this chapter. To find the nearest neighbor of point (x_0, y_0), we find a distance d such that we can expect to find several points within distance d of (x_0, y_0). We then ask the range query $x_0 - d \leq x \leq x_0 + d$ and $y_0 - d \leq y \leq y_0 + d$. If there turn out to be no points in this range, or if there is a point, but distance from (x_0, y_0) of the closest point is greater than d (and therefore there could be a closer point outside the range, as was discussed in Section 14.1.5), then we must increase the range and search again. However, we can order the search so the closest places are searched first.

14.3.3 kd-Trees

A kd-tree (k-dimensional search tree) is a main-memory data structure generalizing the binary search tree to multidimensional data. We shall present the idea and then discuss how the idea has been adapted to the block model of storage. A kd-tree is a binary tree in which interior nodes have an associated attribute a and a value V that splits the data points into two parts: those with a-value less than V and those with a-value equal to or greater than V. The attributes at different levels of the tree are different, with levels rotating among the attributes of all dimensions.

In the classical kd-tree, the data points are placed at the nodes, just as in a binary search tree. However, we shall make two modifications in our initial presentation of the idea to take some limited advantage of the block model of storage.

1. Interior nodes will have only an attribute, a dividing value for that attribute, and pointers to left and right children.

2. Leaves will be blocks, with space for as many records as a block can hold.

Example 14.15: In Fig. 14.13 is a kd-tree for the twelve points of our running gold-jewelry example. We use blocks that hold only two records for simplicity; these blocks and their contents are shown as square leaves. The interior nodes are ovals with an attribute — either age or salary — and a value. For instance, the root splits by salary, with all records in the left subtree having a salary less than \$150K, and all records in the right subtree having a salary at least \$150K.

At the second level, the split is by age. The left child of the root splits at age 60, so everything in its left subtree will have age less than 60 and salary less than \$150K. Its right subtree will have age at least 60 and salary less than \$150K. Figure 14.14 suggests how the various interior nodes split the space of points into leaf blocks. For example, the horizontal line at salary = 150 represents the split at the root. The space below that line is split vertically at age 60, while the space above is split at age 47, corresponding to the decision at the right child of the root.   □

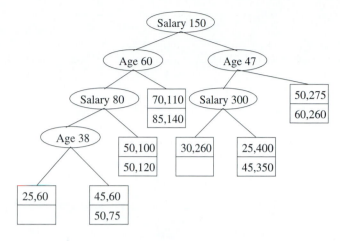

Figure 14.13: A kd-tree

14.3.4 Operations on kd-Trees

A lookup of a tuple given values for all dimensions proceeds as in a binary search tree. We make a decision which way to go at each interior node and are directed to a single leaf, whose block we search.

To perform an insertion, we proceed as for a lookup. We are eventually directed to a leaf, and if its block has room we put the new data point there. If there is no room, we split the block into two, and we divide its contents according to whatever attribute is appropriate at the level of the leaf being split. We create a new interior node whose children are the two new blocks, and we install at that interior node a splitting value that is appropriate for the split we have just made.[1]

Example 14.16: Suppose someone 35 years old with a salary of $500K buys gold jewelry. Starting at the root, since the salary is at least $150K we go to the right. There, we compare the age 35 with the age 47 at the node, which directs us to the left. At the third level, we compare salaries again, and our salary is greater than the splitting value, $300K. We are thus directed to a leaf containing the points $(25, 400)$ and $(45, 350)$, along with the new point $(35, 500)$.

There isn't room for three records in this block, so we must split it. The fourth level splits on age, so we have to pick some age that divides the records as evenly as possible. The median value, 35, is a good choice, so we replace the leaf by an interior node that splits on age = 35. To the left of this interior node is a leaf block with only the record $(25, 400)$, while to the right is a leaf block with the other two records, as shown in Fig. 14.15. □

---

[1]One problem that might arise is a situation where there are so many points with the same value in a given dimension that the bucket has only one value in that dimension and cannot be split. We can try splitting along another dimension, or we can use an overflow block.

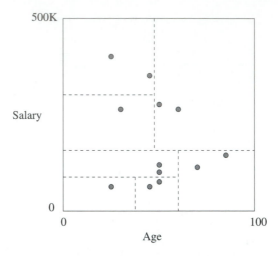

Figure 14.14: The partitions implied by the tree of Fig. 14.13

The more complex queries discussed in this chapter are also supported by a *kd*-tree. Here are the key ideas and synopses of the algorithms:

Partial-Match Queries

If we are given values for some of the attributes, then we can go one way when we are at a level belonging to an attribute whose value we know. When we don't know the value of the attribute at a node, we must explore both of its children. For example, if we ask for all points with age = 50 in the tree of Fig. 14.13, we must look at both children of the root, since the root splits on salary. However, at the left child of the root, we need go only to the left, and at the right child of the root we need only explore its right subtree. Suppose, for instance, that the tree were perfectly balanced, had a large number of levels, and had two dimensions, of which one was specified in the search. Then we would have to explore both ways at every other level, ultimately reaching about the square root of the total number of leaves.

Range Queries

Sometimes, a range will allow us to move to only one child of a node, but if the range straddles the splitting value at the node then we must explore both children. For example, given the range of ages 35 to 55 and the range of salaries from $100K to $200K, we would explore the tree of Fig. 14.13 as follows. The salary range straddles the $150K at the root, so we must explore both children. At the left child, the range is entirely to the left, so we move to the node with salary $80K. Now, the range is entirely to the right, so we reach the leaf with records (50, 100) and (50, 120), both of which meet the range query. Returning

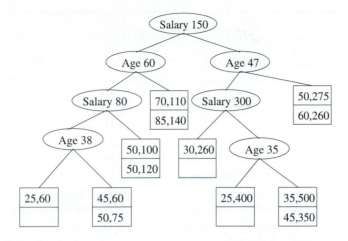

Figure 14.15: Tree after insertion of $(35, 500)$

to the right child of the root, the splitting value age = 47 tells us to look at both subtrees. At the node with salary \$300K, we can go only to the left, finding the point $(30, 260)$, which is actually outside the range. At the right child of the node for age = 47, we find two other points, both of which are outside the range.

Nearest-Neighbor Queries

Use the same approach as was discussed in Section 14.3.2. Treat the problem as a range query with the appropriate range and repeat with a larger range if necessary.

14.3.5 Adapting *kd*-Trees to Secondary Storage

Suppose we store a file in a *kd*-tree with n leaves. Then the average length of a path from the root to a leaf will be about $\log_2 n$, as for any binary tree. If we store each node in a block, then as we traverse a path we must do one disk I/O per node. For example, if $n = 1000$, then we shall need about 10 disk I/O's, much more than the 2 or 3 disk I/O's that would be typical for a B-tree, even on a much larger file. In addition, since interior nodes of a *kd*-tree have relatively little information, most of the block would be wasted space.

We cannot solve the twin problems of long paths and unused space completely. However, here are two approaches that will make some improvement in performance.

Multiway Branches at Interior Nodes

Interior nodes of a *kd*-tree could look more like B-tree nodes, with many key-pointer pairs. If we had n keys at a node, we could split values of an attribute a

---

Nothing Lasts Forever

Each of the data structures discussed in this chapter allow insertions and deletions that make local decisions about how to reorganize the structure. After many database updates, the effects of these local decisions may make the structure unbalanced in some way. For instance, a grid file may have too many empty buckets, or a kd-tree may be greatly unbalanced.

It is quite usual for any database to be restructured after a while. By reloading the database, we have the opportunity to create index structures that, at least for the moment, are as balanced and efficient as is possible for that type of index. The cost of such restructuring can be amortized over the large number of updates that led to the imbalance, so the cost per update is small. However, we do need to be able to "take the database down"; i.e., make it unavailable for the time it is being reloaded. That situation may or may not be a problem, depending on the application. For instance, many databases are taken down overnight, when no one is accessing them.

---

into $n + 1$ ranges. If there were $n + 1$ pointers, we could follow the appropriate one to a subtree that contained only points with attribute a in that range. Problems enter when we try to reorganize nodes, in order to keep distribution and balance as we do for a B-tree. For example, suppose a node splits on age, and we need to merge two of its children, each of which splits on salary. We cannot simply make one node with all the salary ranges of the two children, because these ranges will typically overlap. Notice how much easier it would be if (as in a B-tree) the two children both further refined the range of ages.

Group Interior Nodes Into Blocks

We may, instead, retain the idea that tree nodes have only two children. We could pack many interior nodes into a single block. In order to minimize the number of blocks that we must read from disk while traveling down one path, we are best off including in one block a node and all its descendants for some number of levels. That way, once we retrieve the block with this node, we are sure to use some additional nodes on the same block, saving disk I/O's. For instance, suppose we can pack three interior nodes into one block. Then in the tree of Fig. 14.13, we would pack the root and its two children into one block. We could then pack the node for salary = 80 and its left child into another block, and we are left with the node salary = 300, which belongs on a separate block; perhaps it could share a block with the latter two nodes, although sharing requires us to do considerable work when the tree grows or shrinks. Thus, if we wanted to look up the record $(25, 60)$, we would need to traverse only two blocks, even though we travel through four interior nodes.

14.3.6 Quad Trees

In a *quad tree*, each interior node corresponds to a square region in two dimensions, or to a k-dimensional cube in k dimensions. As with the other data structures in this chapter, we shall consider primarily the two-dimensional case. If the number of points in a square is no larger than what will fit in a block, then we can think of this square as a leaf of the tree, and it is represented by the block that holds its points. If there are too many points to fit in one block, then we treat the square as an interior node, with children corresponding to its four quadrants.

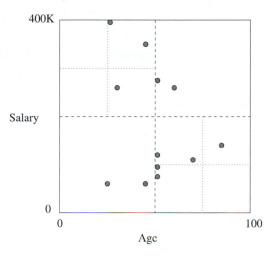

Figure 14.16: Data organized in a quad tree

Example 14.17: Figure 14.16 shows the gold-jewelry data points organized into regions that correspond to nodes of a quad tree. For ease of calculation, we have restricted the usual space so salary ranges between 0 and \$400K, rather than up to \$500K as in other examples of this chapter. We continue to make the assumption that only two records can fit in a block.

Figure 14.17 shows the tree explicitly. We use the compass designations for the quadrants and for the children of a node (e.g., SW stands for the southwest quadrant — the points to the left and below the center). The order of children is always as indicated at the root. Each interior node indicates the coordinates of the center of its region.

Since the entire space has 12 points, and only two will fit in one block, we must split the space into quadrants, which we show by the dashed line in Fig. 14.16. Two of the resulting quadrants — the southwest and northeast — have only two points. They can be represented by leaves and need not be split further.

The remaining two quadrants each have more than two points. Both are split into subquadrants, as suggested by the dotted lines in Fig. 14.16. Each of the

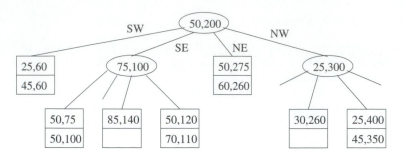

Figure 14.17: A quad tree

resulting quadrants has two or fewer points, so no more splitting is necessary.
□

   Since interior nodes of a quad tree in k dimensions have 2^k children, there is a range of k where nodes fit conveniently into blocks. For instance, if 128, or 2^7, pointers can fit in a block, then $k = 7$ is a convenient number of dimensions. However, for the 2-dimensional case, the situation is not much better than for kd-trees; an interior node has four children. Moreover, while we can choose the splitting point for a kd-tree node, we are constrained to pick the center of a quad-tree region, which may or may not divide the points in that region evenly. Especially when the number of dimensions is large, we expect to find many null pointers (corresponding to empty quadrants) in interior nodes. Of course we can be somewhat clever about how high-dimension nodes are represented, and keep only the non-null pointers and a designation of which quadrant the pointer represents, thus saving considerable space.
   We shall not go into detail regarding the standard operations that we discussed in Section 14.3.4 for kd-trees. The algorithms for quad trees resemble those for kd-trees.

14.3.7   R-Trees

An *R-tree* (region tree) is a data structure that captures some of the spirit of a B-tree for multidimensional data. Recall that a B-tree node has a set of keys that divide a line into segments. Points along that line belong to only one segment, as suggested by Fig. 14.18. The B-tree thus makes it easy for us to find points; if we think the point is somewhere along the line represented by a B-tree node, we can determine a unique child of that node where the point could be found.

Figure 14.18: A B-tree node divides keys along a line into disjoint segments

An R-tree, on the other hand, represents data that consists of 2-dimensional, or higher-dimensional regions, which we call *data regions*. An interior node of an R-tree corresponds to some *interior region*, or just "region," which is not normally a data region. In principle, the region can be of any shape, although in practice it is usually a rectangle or other simple shape. The R-tree node has, in place of keys, subregions that represent the contents of its children. Figure 14.19 suggests a node of an R-tree that is associated with the large solid rectangle. The dotted rectangles represent the subregions associated with four of its children. Notice that the subregions do not cover the entire region, which is satisfactory as long as all the data regions that lie within the large region are wholly contained within one of the small regions. Further, the subregions are allowed to overlap, although it is desirable to keep the overlap small.

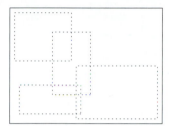

Figure 14.19: The region of an R-tree node and subregions of its children

14.3.8 Operations on R-trees

A typical query for which an R-tree is useful is a "where-am-I" query, which specifies a point P and asks for the data region or regions in which the point lies. We start at the root, with which the entire region is associated. We examine the subregions at the root and determine which children of the root correspond to interior regions that contain point P. Note that there may be zero, one, or several such regions.

If there are zero regions, then we are done; P is not in any data region. If there is at least one interior region that contains P, then we must recursively search for P at the child corresponding to *each* such region. When we reach one or more leaves, we shall find the actual data regions, along with either the complete record for each data region or a pointer to that record.

When we insert a new region R into an R-tree, we start at the root and try to find a subregion into which R fits. If there is more than one such region, then we pick one, go to its corresponding child, and repeat the process there. If there is no subregion that contains R, then we have to expand one of the subregions. Which one to pick may be a difficult decision. Intuitively, we want to expand regions as little as possible, so we might ask which of the children's subregions would have their area increased as little as possible, change the boundary of that region to include R, and recursively insert R at the corresponding child.

Eventually, we reach a leaf, where we insert the region R. However, if there is no room for R at that leaf, then we must split the leaf. How we split the leaf is subject to some choice. We generally want the two subregions to be as small as possible, yet they must, between them, cover all the data regions of the original leaf. Having split the leaf, we replace the region and pointer for the original leaf at the node above by a pair of regions and pointers corresponding to the two new leaves. If there is room at the parent, we are done. Otherwise, as in a B-tree, we recursively split nodes going up the tree.

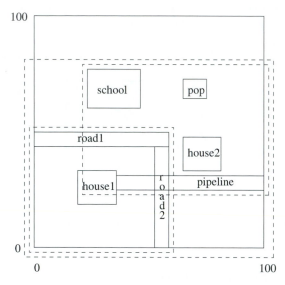

Figure 14.20: Splitting the set of objects

Example 14.18 : Let us consider the addition of a new region to the map of Fig. 14.1. Suppose that leaves have room for six regions. Further suppose that the six regions of Fig. 14.1 are together on one leaf, whose region is represented by the outer (solid) rectangle in Fig. 14.20.

Now, suppose the local cellular phone company adds a POP (point of presence) at the position shown in Fig. 14.20. Since the seven data regions do not fit on one leaf, we shall split the leaf, with four in one leaf and three in the other. Our options are many; we have picked in Fig. 14.20 the division (indicated by the inner, dashed rectangles) that minimizes the overlap, while splitting the leaves as evenly as possible.

We show in Fig. 14.21 how the two new leaves fit into the R-tree. The parent of these nodes has pointers to both leaves, and associated with the pointers are the lower-left and upper-right corners of the rectangular regions covered by each leaf. □

Example 14.19 : Suppose we inserted another house below house2, with lower-left coordinates $(70, 5)$ and upper-right coordinates $(80, 15)$. Since this house is

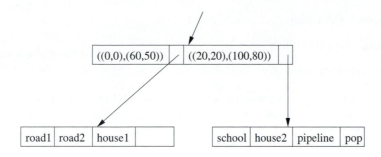

Figure 14.21: An R-tree

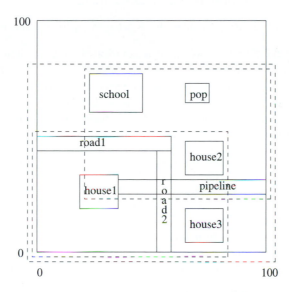

Figure 14.22: Extending a region to accommodate new data

not wholly contained within either of the leaves' regions, we must choose which region to expand. If we expand the lower subregion, corresponding to the first leaf in Fig. 14.21, then we add 1000 square units to the region, since we extend it 20 units to the right. If we extend the other subregion by lowering its bottom by 15 units, then we add 1200 square units. We prefer the first, and the new regions are changed in Fig. 14.22. We also must change the description of the region in the top node of Fig. 14.21 from $((0,0),\ (60,50))$ to $((0,0),\ (80,50))$. □

14.3.9 Exercises for Section 14.3

Exercise 14.3.1: Show a multiple-key index for the data of Fig. 14.10 if the indexes are on:

a) Speed, then ram.

b) Ram then hard-disk.

c) Speed, then ram, then hard-disk.

Exercise 14.3.2: Place the data of Fig. 14.10 in a *kd*-tree. Assume two records can fit in one block. At each level, pick a separating value that divides the data as evenly as possible. For an order of the splitting attributes choose:

a) Speed, then ram, alternating.

b) Speed, then ram, then hard-disk, alternating.

c) Whatever attribute produces the most even split at each node.

Exercise 14.3.3: Suppose we have a relation $R(x, y, z)$, where the pair of attributes x and y together form the key. Attribute x ranges from 1 to 100, and y ranges from 1 to 1000. For each x there are records with 100 different values of y, and for each y there are records with 10 different values of x. Note that there are thus 10,000 records in R. We wish to use a multiple-key index that will help us to answer queries of the form

```
SELECT z
FROM R
WHERE x = C AND y = D;
```

where C and D are constants. Assume that blocks can hold ten key-pointer pairs, and we wish to create dense indexes at each level, perhaps with sparse higher-level indexes above them, so that each index starts from a single block. Also assume that initially all index and data blocks are on disk.

* a) How many disk I/O's are necessary to answer a query of the above form if the first index is on x?

b) How many disk I/O's are necessary to answer a query of the above form if the first index is on y?

! c) Suppose you were allowed to buffer 11 blocks in memory at all times. Which blocks would you choose, and would you make x or y the first index, if you wanted to minimize the number of additional disk I/O's needed?

Exercise 14.3.4: For the structure of Exercise 14.3.3(a), how many disk I/O's are required to answer the range query in which $20 \leq x \leq 35$ and $200 \leq y \leq 350$. Assume data is distributed uniformly; i.e., the expected number of points will be found within any given range.

Exercise 14.3.5: In the tree of Fig. 14.13, what new points would be directed to:

* a) The block with point $(30, 260)$?

  b) The block with points $(50, 100)$ and $(50, 120)$?

Exercise 14.3.6: Show a possible evolution of the tree of Fig. 14.15 if we insert the points $(20, 110)$ and then $(40, 400)$.

! **Exercise 14.3.7:** We mentioned that if a *kd*-tree were perfectly balanced, and we execute a partial-match query in which one of two attributes has a value specified, then we wind up looking at about $\sqrt{n}$ out of the n leaves.

   a) Explain why.

   b) If the tree split alternately in d dimensions, and we specified values for m of those dimensions, what fraction of the leaves would we expect to have to search?

   c) How does the performance of (b) compare with a partitioned hash table?

Exercise 14.3.8: Place the data of Fig. 14.10 in a quad tree with dimensions speed and ram. Assume the range for speed is 100 to 500, and for ram it is 0 to 256.

Exercise 14.3.9: Repeat Exercise 14.3.8 with the addition of a third dimension, hard-disk, that ranges from 0 to 32.

*! **Exercise 14.3.10:** If we are allowed to put the central point in a quadrant of a quad tree wherever we want, can we always divide a quadrant into subquadrants with an equal number of points (or as equal as possible, if the number of points in the quadrant is not divisible by 4)? Justify your answer.

! **Exercise 14.3.11:** Suppose we have a database of 1,000,000 regions, which may overlap. Nodes (blocks) of an R-tree can hold 100 regions and pointers. The region represented by any node has 100 subregions, and the overlap among these regions is such that the total area of the 100 subregions is 150% of the area of the region. If we perform a "where-am-I" query for a given point, how many blocks do we expect to retrieve?

! **Exercise 14.3.12:** In the R-tree represented by Fig. 14.22, a new region might go into the subregion containing the school or the subregion containing house3. Describe the rectangular regions for which we would prefer to place the new region in the subregion with the school (i.e., that choice minimizes the increase in the subregion size).

14.4   Bitmap Indexes

Let us now turn to a type of index that is rather different from the kinds seen so far. We begin by imagining that records of a file have permanent numbers, $1, 2, \ldots, n$. Moreover, there is some data structure for the file that lets us find the ith record easily for any i.

A *bitmap index* for a field F is a collection of bit-vectors of length n, one for each possible value that may appear in the field F. The vector for value v has 1 in position i if the ith record has v in field F, and it has 0 there if not.

Example 14.20: Suppose a file consists of records with two fields, F and G, of type integer and string, respectively. The current file has six records, numbered 1 through 6, with the following values in order: $(30, \texttt{foo})$, $(30, \texttt{bar})$, $(40, \texttt{baz})$, $(50, \texttt{foo})$, $(40, \texttt{bar})$, $(30, \texttt{baz})$.

A bitmap index for the first field, F, would have three bit-vectors, each of length 6. The first, for value 30, is 110001, because the first, second, and sixth records have $F = 30$. The other two, for 40 and 50, respectively, are 001010 and 000100.

A bitmap index for G would also have three bit-vectors, because there are three different strings appearing there. The three bit-vectors are:

Value	Vector
foo	100100
bar	010010
baz	001001

In each case, the 1's indicate in which records the corresponding string appears. □

14.4.1   Motivation for Bitmap Indexes

It might at first appear that bitmap indexes require much too much space, especially when there are many different values for a field, since the total number of bits is the product of the number of records and the number of values. For example, if the field is a key, and there are n records, then n^2 bits are used among all the bit-vectors for that field. However, compression can be used to make the number of bits closer to n, independent of the number of different values, as we shall see in Section 14.4.2.

You might also suspect that there are problems managing the bitmap indexes. For example, they depend on the number of a record remaining the same throughout time. How do we find the ith record as the file adds and deletes records? Similarly, values for a field may appear or disappear. How do we find the bitmap for a value efficiently? These and related questions are discussed in Section 14.4.4.

The compensating advantage of bitmap indexes is that they allow us to answer partial-match queries very efficiently in many situations. In a sense they offer the advantages of buckets that we discussed in Example 13.16, where we found the `Movie` tuples with specified values in several attributes without first retrieving all the records that matched in each of the attributes. An example will illustrate the point.

Example 14.21: Recall Example 13.16, where we queried the `Movie` relation with the query

```
SELECT title
FROM Movie
WHERE studioName = 'Disney' AND year = 1995;
```

Suppose there are bitmap indexes on both attributes `studioName` and `year`. Then we can intersect the vectors for `year` = 1995 and `studioName` = 'Disney'; that is, we take the bitwise AND of these vectors, which will give us a vector with a 1 in position i if and only if the ith `Movie` tuple is for a movie made by Disney in 1995.

If we can retrieve tuples of `Movie` given their numbers, then we need to read only those blocks containing one or more of these tuples, just as we did in Example 13.16. To intersect the bit vectors, we must read them into memory, which requires a disk I/O for each block occupied by one of the two vectors. As mentioned, we shall later address both matters: accessing records given their numbers in Section 14.4.4 and making sure the bit-vectors do not occupy too much space in Section 14.4.2. □

Bitmap indexes can also help answer range queries. We shall consider an example next that both illustrates their use for range queries and shows in detail with short bit-vectors how the bitwise AND and OR of bit-vectors can be used to discover the answer to a query without looking at any records but the ones we want.

Example 14.22: Consider the gold jewelry data first introduced in Example 14.7. Suppose that the twelve points of that example are records numbered from 1 to 12 as follows:

1: $(25, 60)$	2: $(45, 60)$	3: $(50, 75)$	4: $(50, 100)$
5: $(50, 120)$	6: $(70, 110)$	7: $(85, 140)$	8: $(30, 260)$
9: $(25, 400)$	10: $(45, 350)$	11: $(50, 275)$	12: $(60, 260)$

For the first component, age, there are seven different values, so the bitmap index for age consists of the following seven vectors:

25: 100000001000	30: 000000010000	45: 010000000100
50: 001110000010	60: 000000000001	70: 000001000000
85: 000000100000		

For the salary component, there are ten different values, so the salary bitmap index has the following ten bit-vectors:

60:	110000000000	75:	001000000000	100:	000100000000
110:	000001000000	120:	000010000000	140:	000000100000
260:	000000010001	275:	000000000010	350:	000000000100
400:	000000001000				

Suppose we want to find the jewelry buyers with an age in the range 45-55 and a salary in the range 100-200. We first find the bit-vectors for the age values in this range; in this example there are only two: 010000000100 and 001110000010, for 45 and 50, respectively. If we take their bitwise OR, we have a new bit-vector with 1 in position i if and only if the ith record has an age in the desired range. This bit-vector is 011110000110.

Next, we find the bit-vectors for the salaries between 100 and 200 thousand. There are four, corresponding to salaries 100, 110, 120, and 140; their bitwise OR is 000111100000.

The last step is to take the bitwise AND of the two bit-vectors we calculated by OR. That is:

$$011110000110 \text{ AND } 000111100000 = 000110000000$$

We thus find that only the fourth and fifth records, which are $(50, 100)$ and $(50, 120)$, are in the desired range. □

14.4.2 Compressed Bitmaps

Suppose we have a bitmap index on field F of a file with n records, and there are m different values for field F that appear in the file. Then the number of bits in all the bit-vectors for this index is mn. If, say, blocks are 4096 bytes long, then we can fit 32,768 bits in one block, so the number of blocks needed is $mn/32768$. That number can be small compared to the number of blocks needed to hold the file itself, but the larger m is, the more space the bitmap index takes.

But if m is large, then 1's in a bit-vector will be very rare; precisely, the probability that any bit is 1 is $1/m$. If 1's are rare, then we have an opportunity to encode bit-vectors so that they take much fewer than n bits on the average. A common approach is called *run-length encoding*, where we represent a *run*, that is, a sequence of i 0's followed by a 1, by some suitable binary encoding of the integer i. We concatenate the codes for each run together, and that sequence of bits is the encoding of the entire bit-vector.

We might imagine that we could just represent integer i by expressing i as a binary number. However, that simple a scheme will not do, because it is not possible to break a sequence of codes apart to determine uniquely the lengths of the runs involved (see the box on "Binary Numbers Won't Serve as a Run-Length Encoding"). Thus, the encoding of integers i that represent a run length must be more complex than a simple binary representation.

We shall study one of many possible schemes for encoding. There are some better, more complex schemes that can improve on the amount of compression

> ## Binary Numbers Won't Serve as a Run-Length Encoding
>
> Suppose we represented a run of i 0's followed by a 1 with the integer i in binary. Then the bit-vector 000101 consists of two runs, of lengths 3 and 1, respectively. The binary representations of these integers are 11 and 1, so the run-length encoding of 000101 is 111. However, a similar calculation shows that the bit-vector 010001 is also encoded by 111; bit-vector 010101 is a third vector encoded by 111. Thus, 111 cannot be decoded uniquely into one bit-vector.

achieved here, by almost a factor of 2, but only when typical runs are very long. In our scheme, we first determine how many bits the binary representation of i has. This number j, which is approximately $\log_2 i$, is represented in "unary," by $j - 1$ 1's and a single 0. Then, we can follow with i in binary.[2]

Example 14.23: If $i = 13$, then $j = 4$; that is, we need 4 bits in the binary representation of i. Thus, the encoding for i begins with 1110. We follow with i in binary, or 1101. Thus, the encoding for 13 is 11101101.

The encoding for $i = 1$ is 01, and the encoding for $i = 0$ is 00. In each case, $j = 1$, so we begin with a single 0 and follow that 0 with the one bit that represents i. $\square$

If we concatenate a sequence of integer codes, we can always recover the sequence of run lengths and therefore recover the original bit-vector. Suppose we have scanned some of the encoded bits, and we are now at the beginning of a sequence of bits that encodes some integer i. We scan forward to the first 0, to determine the value of j. That is, j equals the number of bits we must scan until we get to the first 0 (including that 0 in the count of bits). Once we know j, we look at the next j bits; i is the integer represented there in binary. Moreover, once we have scanned the bits representing i, we know where the next code for an integer begins, so we can repeat the process.

Example 14.24: Let us decode the sequence 11101101001011. Starting at the beginning, we find the first 0 at the 4th bit, so $j = 4$. The next 4 bits are 1101, so we determine that the first integer is 13. We are now left with 001011 to decode.

Since the first bit is 0, we know the next bit represents the next integer by itself; this integer is 0. Thus, we have decoded the sequence 13, 0, and we must decode the remaining sequence 1011.

---

[2] Actually, except for the case that $j = 1$ (i.e., $i = 0$ or $i = 1$), we can be sure that the binary representation of i begins with 1. Thus, we can save about one bit per number if we omit this 1 and use only the remaining $j - 1$ bits.

We find the first 0 in the second position, whereupon we conclude that the final two bits represent the last integer, 3. Our entire sequence of run-lengths is thus 13, 0, 3. From these numbers, we can reconstruct the actual bit-vector, 0000000000000110001.   □

Technically, every bit-vector so decoded will end in a 1, and any trailing 0's will not be recovered. Since we presumably know the number of records in the file, the additional 0's can be added. However, since 0 in a bit-vector indicates the corresponding record is not in the described set, we don't even have to know the total number of records, and can ignore the trailing 0's.

Example 14.25 : Let us convert some of the bit-vectors from Example 14.23 to our run-length code. The vectors for the first three ages, 25, 30, and 45, are 100000001000, 000000010000, and 010000000100, respectively. The first of these has the run-length sequence $(0, 7)$. The code for 0 is 00, and the code for 7 is 110111. Thus, the bit-vector for age 25 becomes 00110111.

Similarly, the bit-vector for age 30 has only one run, with seven 0's. Thus, its code is 110111. The bit-vector for age 45 has two runs, $(1, 7)$. Since 1 has the code 01, and we determined that 7 has the code 110111, the code for the third bit-vector is 01110111.   □

The compression in Example 14.25 is not great. However, we cannot see the true benefits when n, the number of records, is small. To appreciate the value of the encoding, suppose that $m = n$, i.e., each value for the field on which the bitmap index is constructed, has a unique value. Notice that the code for a run of length i has about $2\log_2 i$ bits. If each bit-vector has a single 1, then it has a single run, and the length of that run cannot be longer than n. Thus, $2\log_2 n$ bits is an upper bound on the length of a bit-vector's code in this case.

Since there are n bit-vectors in the index (because $m = n$), the total number of bits to represent the index is at most $2n\log_2 n$. Notice that without the encoding, n^2 bits would be required. As long as $n > 4$, we have $2n\log_2 n < n^2$, and as n grows, $2n\log_2 n$ becomes arbitrarily smaller than n^2.

14.4.3 Operating on Run-Length-Encoded Bit-Vectors

When we need to perform bitwise AND or OR on encoded bit-vectors, we have little choice but to decode them and operate on the original bit-vectors. However, we do not have to do the decoding all at once. The compression scheme we have described lets us decode one run at a time, and we can thus determine where the next 1 is in each operand bit-vector. If we are taking the OR, we can produce a 1 at that position of the output, and if we are taking the AND we produce a 1 if and only if both operands have their next 1 at the same position. The algorithms involved are complex, but an example may make the idea adequately clear.

Example 14.26 : Consider the encoded bit-vectors we obtained in Example 14.25 for ages 25 and 30: 00110111 and 110111, respectively. We can decode their first runs easily; we find they are 0 and 7, respectively. That is, the first 1 of the bit-vector for 25 occurs in position 1, while the first 1 in the bit-vector for 30 occurs at position 8. We therefore generate 1 in position 1.

Next, we must decode the next run for age 25, since that bit-vector may produce another 1 before age 30's bit-vector produces a 1 at position 8. However, the next run for age 25 is 7, which says that this bit-vector next produces a 1 at position 9. We therefore generate six 0's and the 1 at position 8 that comes from the bit-vector for age 30. Now, that bit-vector contributes no more 1's to the output. The 1 at position 9 from age 25's bit-vector is produced, and that bit-vector too produces no subsequent 1's.

We conclude that the OR of these bit-vectors is 100000011. Referring to the original bit-vectors of length 12, we see that is almost right; there are three trailing 0's omitted. If we know that the number of records in the file is 12, we can append those 0's. However, it doesn't matter whether or not we append the 0's, since only a 1 can cause a record to be retrieved. In this example, we shall not retrieve any of records 10 through 12 anyway. □

14.4.4 Managing Bitmap Indexes

We have described operations on bitmap indexes without addressing three important issues:

1. When we want to find the bit-vector for a given value, or the bit-vectors corresponding to values in a given range, how do we find these efficiently?

2. When we have selected a set of records that answer our query, how do we retrieve those records efficiently?

3. When the data file changes by insertion or deletion of records, how do we adjust the bitmap index on a given field?

Finding Bit-Vectors

The first question can be answered based on techniques we have already learned. Think of each bit-vector as a record whose key is the value corresponding to this bit-vector (although the value itself does not appear in this "record"). Then any secondary index technique will take us efficiently from values to their bit-vectors. For example, we could use a B-tree, whose leaves contain key-pointer pairs; the pointer leads to the bit-vector for the key value. The B-tree is often a good choice, because it supports range queries easily, but hash tables or indexed-sequential files are other options.

We also need to store the bit-vectors somewhere. It is best to think of them as variable-length records, since they will generally grow as more records are added to the data file. If the bit-vectors, perhaps in compressed form, are typically shorter than blocks, then we can consider packing several to a block and moving them around as needed. If bit-vectors are typically longer than blocks, we should consider using a chain of blocks to hold each one. The techniques of Section 12.4 are useful.

Finding Records

Now let us consider the second question: once we have determined that we need record k of the data file, how do we find it. Again, techniques we have seen already may be adapted. Think of the kth record as having search-key value k (although this key does not actually appear in the record). We may then create a secondary index on the data file, whose search key is the number of the record.

If there is no reason to organize the file any other way, we can even use the record number as the search key for a primary index, as discussed in Section 13.1. Then, the file organization is particularly simple, since record numbers never change (even as records are deleted), and we only have to add new records to the end of the data file. It is thus possible to pack blocks of the data file completely full, instead of leaving extra space for insertions into the middle of the file as we found necessary for the general case of an indexed-sequential file in Section 13.1.6.

Handling Modifications to the Data File

There are two aspects to the problem of reflecting data-file modifications in a bitmap index.

1. Record numbers must remain fixed once assigned.

2. Changes to the data file require the bitmap index to change as well.

The consequence of point (1) is that when we delete record i, it is easiest to "retire" its number. Its space is replaced by a "tombstone" in the data file. The bitmap index must also be changed, since the bit-vector that had a 1 in position i must have that 1 changed to 0. Note that we can find the appropriate bit-vector, since we know what value record i had before deletion.

Next consider insertion of a new record. We keep track of the next available record number and assign it to the new record. Then, for each bitmap index, we must determine the value the new record has in the corresponding field and modify the bit-vector for that value by appending a 1 at the end. Technically, all the other bit-vectors in this index get a new 0 at the end, but if we are using a compression technique such as that of Section 14.4.2, then no change to the compressed values is needed.

As a special case, the new record may have a value for the indexed field that has not been seen before. In that case, we need a new bit-vector for this value, and this bit-vector and its corresponding value need to be inserted into the secondary-index structure that is used to find a bit-vector given its corresponding value.

Last, let us consider a modification to a record i of the data file that changes the value of a field that has a bitmap index, say from value v to value w. We must find the bit-vector for v and change the 1 in position i to 0. If there is a bit-vector for value w, then we change its 0 in position i to 1. If there is not yet a bit-vector for w, then we create it as discussed in the paragraph above for the case when an insertion introduces a new value.

14.4.5 Exercises for Section 14.4

Exercise 14.4.1 : For the data of Fig. 14.10 show the bitmap indexes for the attributes:

* a) Speed,

  b) Ram, and

  c) Hard-disk,

both in (*i*) uncompressed form, and (*ii*) compressed form using the scheme of Section 14.4.2.

Exercise 14.4.2 : Using the bitmaps of Example 14.22, find the jewelry buyers with an age in the range 20–40 and a salary in the range 0–100.

Exercise 14.4.3 : Consider a file of 1,000,000 records, with a field F that has m different values.

  a) As a function of m, how many bytes does the bitmap index for F have?

! b) Suppose that the records numbered from 1 to 1,000,000 are given values for the field F in a round-robin fashion, so each value appears every m records. How many bytes would be consumed by a compressed index?

!! **Exercise 14.4.4 :** We suggested in Section 14.4.2 that it was possible to reduce the number of bits taken to encode number i from the $2\log_2 i$ that we used in that section until it is close to $\log_2 i$. Show how to approach that limit as closely as you like, as long as i is large. *Hint*: We used a unary encoding of the length of the binary encoding that we used for i. Can you encode the length of the code in binary?

Exercise 14.4.5 : Encode, using the scheme of Section 14.4.2, the following bitmaps:

* a) 0110000000100000100.

  b) 10000010000001001101.

  c) 000100000000010000010000.

*! Exercise 14.4.6: We pointed out that compressed bitmap indexes consume about $2n \log_2 n$ bits for a file of n records. How does this number of bits compare with the number of bits consumed by a B-tree index? Remember that the B-tree index's size depends on the size of keys and pointers, as well as (to a small extent) on the size of blocks. However, make some reasonable estimates of these parameters in your calculations. Why might we prefer a B-tree, even if it takes more space than compressed bitmaps?

14.5   Summary of Chapter 14

✦ *Multidimensional Data*: Many applications, such as geographic databases or sales and inventory data, can be thought of as points in a space of two or more dimensions.

✦ *Queries Needing Multidimensional Indexes*: The sorts of queries that need to be supported on multidimensional data include partial-match (all points with specified values in a subset of the dimensions), range queries (all points within a range in each dimension), nearest-neighbor (closest point to a given point), and where-am-i (region or regions containing a given point).

✦ *Executing Nearest-Neighbor Queries*: Many data structures allow nearest-neighbor queries to be executed by performing a range query around the target point, and expanding the range if there is no point in that range. We must be careful, because finding a point within a rectangular range may not rule out the possibility of a closer point outside that rectangle.

✦ *Grid Files*: The grid file slices the space of points in each of the dimensions. The grid lines can be spaced differently, and there can be different numbers of lines for each dimension. Grid files support range queries, partial-match queries, and nearest-neighbor queries well, as long as data is fairly uniform in distribution.

✦ *Partitioned Hash Tables*: A partitioned hash function constructs some bits of the bucket number from each dimension. They support partial-match queries well, and are not dependent on the data being uniformly distributed.

✦ *Multiple-Key Indexes*: A simple multidimensional structure has a root that is an index on one attribute, leading to a collection of indexes on a second attribute, which can lead to indexes on a third attribute, and so on. They are useful for range and nearest-neighbor queries.

✦ *kd-Trees*: These trees are like binary search trees, but they branch on different attributes at different levels. They support partial-match, range, and nearest-neighbor queries well. Some careful packing of tree nodes into blocks must be done to make the structure suitable for secondary-storage operations.

✦ *Quad Trees*: The quad tree divides a multidimensional cube into quadrants, and recursively divides the quadrants the same way if they have too many points. They support partial-match, range, and nearest-neighbor queries.

✦ *R-Trees*: This form of tree normally represents a collection of regions by grouping them into a hierarchy of larger regions. It helps with where-am-i queries and, if the atomic regions are actually points, will support the other types of queries studied in this chapter, as well.

✦ *Bitmap Indexes*: Multidimensional queries are supported by a form of index that orders the points or records and represents the positions of the records with a given value in an attribute by a bit vector. These indexes support range, nearest-neighbor, and partial-match queries.

✦ *Compressed Bitmaps*: In order to save space, the bitmap indexes, which tend to consist of vectors with very few 1's, are compressed by using a run-length encoding.

14.6 References for Chapter 14

Most of the data structures discussed in this section were the product of research in the 1970's or early 1980's. The *kd*-tree is from [2]. Modifications suitable for secondary storage appeared in [3] and [13]. Partitioned hashing and its use in partial-match retieval is from [12] and [5]. However, the design idea from Exercise 14.2.8 is from [14].

Grid files first appeared in [9] and the quad tree in [6]. The R-tree is from [8], and two extensions [15] and [1] are well known.

The bitmap index has an interesting history. There was a company called Nucleus, founded by Ted Glaser, that patented the idea and developed a DBMS in which the bitmap index was both the index structure and the data representation. The company failed in the late 1980's, but the idea has recently been incorporated into several major commercial database systems. The first published work on the subject was [10]. [11] is a recent expansion of the idea.

There are a number of surveys of multidimensional storage structures. One of the earliest is [4]. More recent surveys are found in [16] and [7]. The former also includes surveys of several other important database topics.

1. N. Beckmann, H.-P. Kriegel, R. Schneider, and B. Seeger, "The R*-tree: an efficient and robust access method for points and rectangles," *Proc. ACM SIGMOD Intl. Conf. on Management of Data* (1990), pp. 322–331.

2. J. L. Bentley, "Multidimensional binary search trees used for associative searching," *Comm. ACM* **18**:9 (1975), pp. 509–517.

3. J. L. Bentley, "Multidimensional binary search trees in database applications," *IEEE Trans. on Software Engineering* **SE-5**:4 (1979), pp. 333-340.

4. J. L. Bentley and J. H. Friedman, "Data structures for range searching," *Computing Surveys* **13**:3 (1979), pp. 397–409.

5. W. A. Burkhard, "Hashing and trie algorithms for partial match retrieval," *ACM Trans. on Database Systems* **1**:2 (1976), pp. 175–187.

6. R. A. Finkel and J. L. Bentley, "Quad trees, a data structure for retrieval on composite keys," *Acta Informatica* **4**:1 (1974), pp. 1–9.

7. V. Gaede and O. Gunther, "Multidimensional access methods," *Computing Surveys* **30**:2 (1998), pp. 170–231.

8. A. Guttman, "R-trees: a dynamic index structure for spatial searching," *Proc. ACM SIGMOD Intl. Conf. on Management of Data* (1984), pp. 47–57.

9. J. Nievergelt, H. Hinterberger, and K. Sevcik, "The grid file: an adaptable, symmetric, multikey file structure," *ACM Trans. on Database Systems* **9**:1 (1984), pp. 38–71.

10. P. O'Neil, "Model 204 architecture and performance," *Proc. Second Intl. Workshop on High Performance Transaction Systems*, Springer-Verlag, Berlin, 1987.

11. P. O'Neil and D. Quass, "Improved query performance with variant indexes," *Proc. ACM SIGMOD Intl. Conf. on Management of Data* (1997), pp. 38–49.

12. R. L. Rivest, "Partial match retrieval algorithms," *SIAM J. Computing* **5**:1 (1976), pp. 19–50.

13. J. T. Robinson, "The K-D-B-tree: a search structure for large multidimensional dynamic indexes," *Proc. ACM SIGMOD Intl. Conf. on Mamagement of Data* (1981), pp. 10–18.

14. J. B. Rothnie Jr. and T. Lozano, "Attribute based file organization in a paged memory environment, *Comm. ACM* **17**:2 (1974), pp. 63–69.

15. T. K. Sellis, N. Roussopoulos, and C. Faloutsos, "The R+-tree: a dynamic index for multidimensional objects," *Proc. Intl. Conf. on Very Large Databases* (1987), pp. 507–518.

16. C. Zaniolo, S. Ceri, C. Faloutsos, R. T. Snodgrass, V. S. Subrahmanian, and R. Zicari, *Advanced Database Systems*, Morgan-Kaufmann, San Francisco, 1997.

Chapter 15

Query Execution

Previous chapters gave us data structures that allow efficient execution of basic database operations such as finding tuples given a search key. We are now ready to use these structures to support efficient algorithms for answering queries. The broad topic of query processing will be covered in this chapter and Chapter 16. The *query processor* is the group of components of a DBMS that turns user queries and data-modification commands into a sequence of database operations and executes those operations. Since SQL lets us express queries at a very high level, the query processor must supply a lot of detail regarding how the query is to be executed. Moreover, a naive execution strategy for a query may lead to an algorithm for executing the query that takes far more time than necessary.

Figure 15.1 suggests the division of topics between Chapters 15 and 16. In this chapter, we concentrate on query execution, that is, the algorithms that manipulate the data of the database. We focus on the operations of the extended relational algebra, described in Section 5.4. Because SQL uses a bag model, we also assume that relations are bags, and thus use the bag versions of the operators from Section 5.3.

We shall cover the principal methods for execution of the operations of relational algebra. These methods differ in their basic strategy; scanning, hashing, sorting, and indexing are the major approaches. The methods also differ on their assumption as to the amount of available main memory. Some algorithms assume that enough main memory is available to hold at least one of the relations involved in an operation. Others assume that the arguments of the operation are too big to fit in memory, and these algorithms have significantly different costs and structures.

Preview of Query Compilation

Query compilation is divided into the three major steps shown in Fig. 15.2.

  a) *Parsing*, in which a *parse tree*, representing the query and its structure, is constructed.

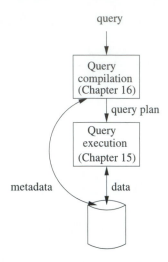

Figure 15.1: The major parts of the query processor

b) *Query rewrite*, in which the parse tree is converted to an initial query plan, which is usually an algebraic representation of the query. This initial plan is then transformed into an equivalent plan that is expected to require less time to execute.

c) *Physical plan generation*, where the abstract query plan from (b), often called a *logical query plan*, is turned into a *physical query plan* by selecting algorithms to implement each of the operators of the logical plan, and by selecting an order of execution for these operators. The physical plan, like the result of parsing and the logical plan, is represented by an expression tree. The physical plan also includes details such as how the queried relations are accessed, and when and if a relation should be sorted.

Parts (b) and (c) are often called the *query optimizer*, and these are the hard parts of query compilation. Chapter 16 is devoted to query optimization; we shall learn there how to select a "query plan" that takes as little time as possible. To select the best query plan we need to decide:

1. Which of the algebraically equivalent forms of a query leads to the most efficient algorithm for answering the query?

2. For each operation of the selected form, what algorithm should we use to implement that operation?

3. How should the operations pass data from one to the other, e.g., in a pipelined fashion, in main-memory buffers, or via the disk?

Each of these choices depends on the metadata about the database. Typical metadata that is available to the query optimizer includes: the size of each

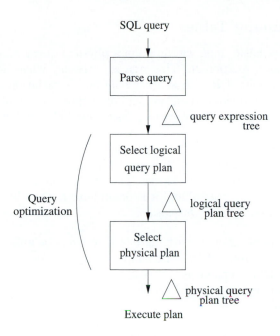

Figure 15.2: Outline of query compilation

relation; statistics such as the approximate number and frequency of different values for an attribute; the existence of certain indexes; and the layout of data on disk.

15.1 Introduction to Physical-Query-Plan Operators

Physical query plans are built from operators, each of which implements one step of the plan. Often, the physical operators are particular implementations for one of the operators of relational algebra. However, we also need physical operators for other tasks that do not involve an operator of relational algebra. For example, we often need to "scan" a table, that is, bring into main memory each tuple of some relation that is an operand of a relational-algebra expression. In this section, we shall introduce the basic building blocks of physical query plans. Later sections cover the more complex algorithms that implement operators of relational algebra efficiently; these algorithms also form an essential part of physical query plans. We also introduce here the "iterator" concept, which is an important method by which the operators comprising a physical query plan can pass requests for tuples and answers among themselves.

15.1.1 Scanning Tables

Perhaps the most basic thing we can do in a physical query plan is to read the entire contents of a relation R. This step is necessary when, for example, we take the union or join of R with another relation. A variation of this operator involves a simple predicate, where we read only those tuples of the relation R that satisfy the predicate. There are two basic approaches to locating the tuples of a relation R.

1. In many cases, the relation R is stored in an area of secondary memory, with its tuples arranged in blocks. The blocks containing the tuples of R are known to the system, and it is possible to get the blocks one by one. This operation is called *table-scan*.

2. If there is an index on any attribute of R, we may be able to use this index to get all the tuples of R. For example, a sparse index on R, as discussed in Section 13.1.3, can be used to lead us to all the blocks holding R, even if we don't know otherwise which blocks these are. This operation is called *index-scan*.

We shall take up index-scan again in Section 15.6.2, when we talk about implementation of the σ operator. However, the important observation for now is that we can use the index not only to get *all* the tuples of the relation it indexes, but to get only those tuples that have a particular value (or sometimes a particular range of values) in the attribute or attributes that form the search key for the index.

15.1.2 Sorting While Scanning Tables

There are a number of reasons why we might want to sort a relation as we read its tuples. For one, the query could include an ORDER BY clause, requiring that a relation be sorted. For another, various algorithms for relational-algebra operations require one or both of their arguments to be sorted relations. These algorithms appear in Section 15.4 and elsewhere.

The physical-query-plan operator *sort-scan* takes a relation R and a specification of the attributes on which the sort is to be made, and produces R in that sorted order. There are several ways that sort-scan can be implemented:

a) If we are to produce a relation R sorted by attribute a, and there is a B-tree index on a, or R is stored as an indexed-sequential file ordered by a, then a scan of the index allows us to produce R in the desired order.

b) If the relation R that we wish to retrieve in sorted order is small enough to fit in main memory, then we can retrieve its tuples using a table scan or index scan, and then use one of many possible efficient, main-memory sorting algorithms.

c) If R is too large to fit in main memory, then the multiway merging approach covered in Section 11.4.3 is a good choice. However, instead of storing the final sorted R back on disk, we produce one block of the sorted R at a time, as its tuples are needed.

15.1.3 The Model of Computation for Physical Operators

A query generally consists of several operations of relational algebra, and the corresponding physical query plan is composed of several physical operators. Often, a physical operator is an implementation of a relational-algebra operator, but as we saw in Section 15.1.1, other physical plan operators correspond to operations like scanning that may be invisible in relational algebra.

Since choosing physical plan operators wisely is an essential of a good query processor, we must be able to estimate the "cost" of each operator we use. We shall use the number of disk I/O's as our measure of cost for an operation. This measure is consistent with our view (see Section 11.4.1) that it takes longer to get data from disk than to do anything useful with it once the data is in main memory. The one major exception is when answering a query involves communicating data across a network. We discuss costs for distributed query processing in Sections 15.9 and 19.4.4.

When comparing algorithms for the same operations, we shall make an assumption that may be surprising at first:

- We assume that the arguments of any operator are found on disk, but the result of the operator is left in main memory.

If the operator produces the final answer to a query, and that result is indeed written to disk, then the cost of doing so depends only on the size of the answer, and not on how the answer was computed. We can simply add the final write-back cost to the total cost of the query. However, in many applications, the answer is not stored on disk at all, but printed or passed to some formatting program. Then, the disk I/O cost of the output either is zero or depends upon what some unknown application program does with the data.

Similarly, the result of an operator that forms part of a query (rather than the whole query) often is not written to disk. In Section 15.1.6 we shall discuss "iterators," where the result of one operator is constructed in main memory, perhaps a small piece at a time, and passed as an argument to another operator. In this situation, we never have to write the result to disk, and moreover, we save the cost of reading from disk this argument of the operator that uses the result. This saving is an excellent opportunity for the query optimizer.

15.1.4 Parameters for Measuring Costs

Now, let us introduce the parameters (sometimes called statistics) that we use to express the cost of an operator. Estimates of cost are essential if the optimizer is to determine which of the many query plans is likely to execute fastest. Section 16.5 introduces the exploitation of these cost estimates.

We need a parameter to represent the portion of main memory that the operator uses, and we require other parameters to measure the size of its argument(s). Assume that main memory is divided into buffers, whose size is the same as the size of disk blocks. Then M will denote the number of main-memory buffers available to an execution of a particular operator. When evaluating the cost of an operator, we shall not count the cost — either memory used or disk I/O's — of producing the output; thus M includes only the space used to hold the input and any intermediate results of the operator.

Sometimes, we can think of M as the entire main memory, or most of the main memory, as we did in Section 11.4.4. However, we shall also see situations where several operations share the main memory, so M could be much smaller than the total main memory. In fact, as we shall discuss in Section 15.7, the number of buffers available to an operation may not be a predictable constant, but may be decided during execution, based on what other processes are executing at the same time. If so, M is really an estimate of the number of buffers available to the operation. If the estimate is wrong, then the actual execution time will differ from the predicted time used by the optimizer. We could even find that the chosen physical query plan would have been different, had the query optimizer known what the true buffer availability would be during execution.

Next, let us consider the parameters that measure the cost of accessing argument relations. These parameters, measuring size and distribution of data in a relation, are often computed periodically to help the query optimizer choose physical operators.

We shall make the simplifying assumption that data is accessed one block at a time from disk. In practice, one of the techniques discussed in Section 11.5 might be able to speed up the algorithm if we are able to read many blocks of the relation at once, and they can be read from consecutive blocks on a track. There are three parameter families, B, T, and V:

- When describing the size of a relation R, we most often are concerned with the number of blocks that are needed to hold all the tuples of R. This number of blocks will be denoted $B(R)$, or just B if we know that relation R is meant. Usually, we assume that R is *clustered*; that is, it is stored in B blocks or in approximately B blocks. As discussed in Section 13.1.6, we may in fact wish to keep a small fraction of each block holding R empty for future insertions into R. Nevertheless, B will often be a good-enough approximation to the number of blocks that we must read from disk to see all of R, and we shall use B as that estimate uniformly.

- Sometimes, we also need to know the number of tuples in R, and we denote this quantity by $T(R)$, or just T if R is understood. If we need the number of tuples of R that can fit in one block, we can use the ratio T/B. Further, there are some instances where a relation is stored distributed among blocks that are also occupied by tuples of other relations. If so, then a simplifying assumption is that each tuple of R requires a separate disk read, and we shall use T as an estimate of the disk I/O's needed to read R in this situation.

- Finally, we shall sometimes want to refer to the number of distinct values that appear in a column of a relation. If R is a relation, and one of its attributes is a, then $V(R, a)$ is the number of distinct values of the column for a in R. More generally, if $[a_1, a_2, \ldots, a_n]$ is a list of attributes, then $V(R, [a_1, a_2, \ldots, a_n])$ is the number of distinct n-tuples in the columns of R for attributes $a_1, a_2, \ldots, a_n$. Put formally, it is the number of tuples in $\delta\big(\pi_{a_1,a_2,\ldots,a_n}(R)\big)$.

15.1.5 I/O Cost for Scan Operators

As a simple application of the parameters that were introduced, we can represent the number of disk I/O's needed for each of the table-scan operators discussed so far. If relation R is clustered, then the number of disk I/O's for the table-scan operator is approximately B. Likewise, if R fits in main-memory, then we can implement sort-scan by reading R into memory and performing an in-memory sort, again requiring only B disk I/O's.

If R is clustered but requires a two-phase multiway merge sort, then, as discussed in Section 11.4.4, we require about $3B$ disk I/O's, divided equally among the operations of reading R in sublists, writing out the sublists, and rereading the sublists. Remember that we do not charge for the final writing of the result. Neither do we charge memory space for accumulated output. Rather, we assume each output block is immediately consumed by some other operation; possibly it is simply written to disk.

However, if R is not clustered, then the number of required disk I/O's is generally much higher. If R is distributed among tuples of other relations, then a table-scan for R may require reading as many blocks as there are tuples of R; that is, the I/O cost is T. Similarly, if we want to sort R, but R fits in memory, then T disk I/O's are what we need to get all of R into memory. Finally, if R is not clustered and requires a two-phase sort, then it takes T disk I/O's to read the subgroups initially. However, we may store and reread the sublists in clustered form, so these steps require only $2B$ disk I/O's. The total cost for performing sort-scan on a large, unclustered relation is thus $T + 2B$.

Finally, let us consider the cost of an index-scan. Generally, an index on a relation R occupies many fewer than $B(R)$ blocks. Therefore, a scan of the entire R, which takes at least B disk I/O's, will require significantly more I/O's than does examining the entire index. Thus, even though index-scan requires examining both the relation and its index,

- We continue to use B or T as an estimate of the cost of accessing a clustered or unclustered relation in its entirety, using an index.

Why Iterators?

We shall see in Section 16.7 how iterators support efficient execution when
they are composed within query plans. They contrast with a *materialization* strategy, where the result of each operator is produced in its entirety — and either stored on disk or allowed to take up space in main
memory. When iterators are used, many operations are active at once. Tuples pass between operators as needed, thus reducing the need for storage.
Of course, as we shall see, not all physical operators support the iteration
approach, or "pipelining," in a useful way. In some cases, almost all the
work would need to be done by the `Open` function, which is tantamount
to materialization.

However, if we only want part of R, we often are able to avoid looking at the
entire index and the entire R. We shall defer analysis of these uses of indexes
to Section 15.6.2.

15.1.6   Iterators for Implementation of Physical Operators

Many physical operators can be implemented as an *iterator*, which is a group
of three functions that allows a consumer of the result of the physical operator
to get the result one tuple at a time. The three functions forming the iterator
for an operation are:

1. `Open`. This function starts the process of getting tuples, but does not get
   a tuple. It initializes any data structures needed to perform the operation
   and calls `Open` for any arguments of the operation.

2. `GetNext`. This function returns the next tuple in the result and adjusts
   data structures as necessary to allow subsequent tuples to be obtained. In
   getting the next tuple of its result, it typically calls `GetNext` one or more
   times on its argument(s). If there are no more tuples to return, `GetNext`
   returns a special value `NotFound`, which we assume cannot be mistaken
   for a tuple.

3. `Close`. This function ends the iteration after all tuples, or all tuples that
   the consumer wanted, have been obtained. Typically, it calls `Close` on
   any arguments of the operator.

When describing iterators and their functions, we shall assume that there
is a "class" for each type of iterator (i.e., for each type of physical operator
implemented as an iterator), and the class supports `Open`, `GetNext`, and `Close`
methods on instances of the class.

Example 15.1: Perhaps the simplest iterator is the one that implements the table-scan operator. The iterator is implemented by a class `TableScan`, and a table-scan operator in a query plan is an instance of this class parameterized by the relation R we wish to scan. Let us assume that R is a relation clustered in some list of blocks, which we can access in a convenient way; that is, the notion of "get the next block of R" is implemented by the storage system and need not be described in detail. Further, we assume that within a block there is a directory of records (tuples) so that it is easy to get the next tuple of a block or tell that the last tuple has been reached.

```
Open() {
    b := the first block of R;
    t := the first tuple of block b;
}

GetNext() {
    IF (t is past the last tuple on block b) {
        increment b to the next block;
        IF (there is no next block)
            RETURN NotFound;
        ELSE /* b is a new block */
            t := first tuple on block b;
    }  /* now we are ready to return t and increment */
    oldt := t;
    increment t to the next tuple of b;
    RETURN oldt;
}

Close() {
}
```

Figure 15.3: Iterator functions for the table-scan operator over relation R

Figure 15.3 sketches the three functions for this iterator. We imagine a block pointer b and a tuple pointer t that points to a tuple within block b. We assume that both pointers can point "beyond" the last block or last tuple of a block, respectively, and that it is possible to identify when these conditions occur. Notice that `Close` in this example does nothing. In practice, a `Close` function for an iterator might clean up the internal structure of the DBMS in various ways. It might inform the buffer manager that certain buffers are no longer needed, or inform the concurrency manager that the read of a relation has completed. □

Example 15.2: Now, let us consider an example where the iterator does most of the work in its `Open` function. The operator is sort-scan, where we read the tuples of a relation R but return them in sorted order. Further, let us suppose that R is so large that we need to use a two-phase, multiway merge-sort, as in Section 11.4.4.

We cannot return even the first tuple until we have examined each tuple of R. Thus, `Open` must do at least the following:

1. Read all the tuples of R in main-memory-sized chunks, sort them, and store them on disk.

2. Initialize the data structure for the second (merge) phase, and load the first block of each sublist into the main-memory structure.

Then, `GetNext` can run a competition for the first remaining tuple at the heads of all the sublists. If the block from the winning sublist is exhausted, `GetNext` reloads its buffer. □

Example 15.3 : Finally, let us consider a simple example of how iterators can be combined by calling other iterators. It is not a good example of how many iterators can be active simultaneously, but that will have to wait until we have considered algorithms for physical operators like selection and join, which exploit this capability of iterators better.

Our operation is the bag union $R \cup S$, in which we produce first all the tuples of R and then all the tuples of S, without regard for the existence of duplicates. Let $\mathcal{R}$ and $\mathcal{S}$ denote the iterators that produce relations R and S, and thus are the "children" of the union operator in a query plan for $R \cup S$. Iterators $\mathcal{R}$ and $\mathcal{S}$ could be table scans applied to stored relations R and S, or they could be iterators that call a network of other iterators to compute R and S. Regardless, all that is important is that we have available functions `R.Open`, `R.GetNext`, and `R.Close`, and analogous functions for iterator $\mathcal{S}$. The iterator functions for the union are sketched in Fig. 15.4. One subtle point is that the functions use a shared variable `CurRel` that is either $\mathcal{R}$ or $\mathcal{S}$, depending on which relation is being read from currently. □

15.2   One-Pass Algorithms for Database Operations

We shall now begin our study of a very important topic in query optimization: how should we execute each of the individual steps — for example, a join or selection — of a logical query plan? The choice of an algorithm for each operator is an essential part of the process of transforming a logical query plan into a physical query plan. While many algorithms for operators have been proposed, they largely fall into three classes:

1. Sorting-based methods. These are covered primarily in Section 15.4.

```
Open() {
    R.Open();
    CurRel := R;
}

GetNext() {
    IF (CurRel = R) {
        t := R.GetNext();
        IF (t <> NotFound) /* R is not exhausted */
            RETURN t;
        ELSE /* R is exhausted */ {
            S.Open();
            CurRel := S;
        }
    }
    /* here, we must read from S */
    RETURN S.GetNext();
    /* notice that if S is exhausted, S.GetNext()
       will return NotFound, which is the correct
       action for our GetNext as well */
}

Close() {
    R.Close();
    S.Close();
}
```

Figure 15.4: Building a union iterator from iterators $\mathcal{R}$ and $\mathcal{S}$

2. Hash-based methods. These are mentioned in Section 15.5 and Section 15.9, among other places.

3. Index-based methods. These are emphasized in Section 15.6.

In addition, we can divide algorithms for operators into three "degrees" of difficulty and cost:

a) Some methods involve reading the data only once from disk. These are the *one-pass* algorithms, and they are the topic of this section. Usually, they work only when at least one of the arguments of the operation fits in main memory, although there are exceptions, especially for selection and projection as discussed in Section 15.2.1.

b) Some methods work for data that is too large to fit in available main memory but not for the largest imaginable data sets. An example of such an algorithm is the two-phase, multiway merge sort of Section 11.4.4. These *two-pass* algorithms are characterized by reading data a first time from disk, processing it in some way, writing all, or almost all of it to disk, and then reading it a second time for further processing during the second pass. We meet these algorithms in Sections 15.4 and 15.5.

c) Some methods work without a limit on the size of the data. These methods use three or more passes to do their jobs, and are natural, recursive generalizations of the two-pass algorithms; we shall study multipass methods in Section 15.8.

In this section, we shall concentrate on the one-pass methods. However, both in this section and subsequently, we shall classify operators into three broad groups:

1. *Tuple-at-a-time, unary operations.* These operations — selection and projection — do not require an entire relation, or even a large part of it, in memory at once. Thus, we can read a block at a time, use one main-memory buffer, and produce our output.

2. *Full-relation, unary operations.* These one-argument operations require seeing all or most of the tuples in memory at once, so one-pass algorithms are limited to relations that are approximately of size M (the number of main-memory buffers available) or less. The operations of this class that we consider here are γ (the grouping operator) and δ (the duplicate-elimination operator).

3. *Full-relation, binary operations.* All other operations are in this class: set and bag versions of union, intersection, difference, joins, and products. Except for bag union, each of these operations requires at least one argument to be limited to size M, if we are to use a one-pass algorithm.

15.2.1 One-Pass Algorithms for Tuple-at-a-Time Operations

The tuple-at-a-time operations $\sigma(R)$ and $\pi(R)$ have obvious algorithms, regardless of whether the relation fits in main memory. We read the blocks of R one at a time into an input buffer, perform the operation on each tuple, and move the selected tuples or the projected tuples to the output buffer, as suggested by Fig. 15.5. Since the output buffer may be an input buffer of some other operator, or may be sending data to a user or application, we do not count the output buffer as needed space. Thus, we require only that $M \geq 1$ for the input buffer, regardless of B.

The disk I/O requirement for this process depends only on how the argument relation R is provided. If R is initially on disk, then the cost is whatever it takes to perform a table-scan or index-scan of R. The cost was discussed in Section 15.1.5; typically it is B if R is clustered and T if it is not clustered.

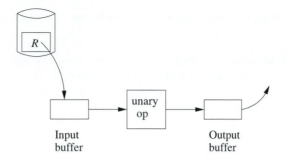

Figure 15.5: A selection or projection being performed on a relation R

Extra Buffers Can Speed Up Operations

Although tuple-at-a-time operations can get by with only one input buffer and one output buffer, as suggested by Fig. 15.5, we can often speed up processing if we allocate more input buffers. The idea appeared first in Section 11.5.1. If R is stored on consecutive blocks within cylinders, then we can read an entire cylinder into buffers, while paying for the seek time and rotational latency for only one block per cylinder. Similarly, if the output of the operation can be stored on full cylinders, we waste almost no time writing.

However, we should remind the reader again of the important exception when the operation being performed is a selection, and the condition compares a constant to an attribute that has an index. In that case, we can use the index to retrieve only a subset of the blocks holding R, thus improving performance, often markedly.

15.2.2 One-Pass Algorithms for Unary, Full-Relation Operations

Now, let us consider the unary operations that apply to relations as a whole, rather than to one tuple at a time: duplicate elimination (δ) and grouping (γ).

Duplicate Elimination

To eliminate duplicates, we can read each block of R one at a time, but for each tuple we need to make a decision as to whether:

1. It is the first time we have seen this tuple, in which case we copy it to the output, or

2. We have seen the tuple before, in which case we must not output this tuple.

To support this decision, we need to keep in memory one copy of every tuple we have seen, as suggested in Fig. 15.6. One memory buffer holds one block of R's tuples, and the remaining $M - 1$ buffers can be used to hold a single copy of every tuple seen so far.

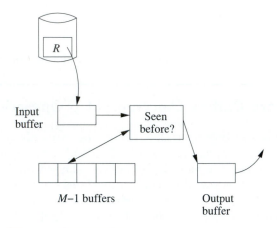

Figure 15.6: Managing memory for a one-pass duplicate-elimination

When storing the already-seen tuples, we must be careful about the main-memory data structure we use. Naively, we might just list the tuples we have seen. When a new tuple from R is considered, we compare it with all tuples seen so far, and if it is not equal to any of these tuples we both copy it to the output and add it to the in-memory list of tuples we have seen.

However, if there are n tuples in main memory, each new tuple takes processor time proportional to n, so the complete operation takes processor time proportional to n^2. Since n could be very large, this amount of time calls into serious question our assumption that only the disk I/O time is significant. Thus, we need a main-memory structure that allows each of the operations:

1. Add a new tuple, and

2. Tell whether a given tuple is already there

to be done in time that is close to a constant, independent of the number of tuples n that we currently have in memory. There are many such structures known. For example, we could use a hash table with a large number of buckets, or some form of balanced binary search tree.[1] Each of these structures has some

---

[1]See Aho, A. V., J. E. Hopcroft, and J. D. Ullman *Data Structures and Algorithms*, Addison-Wesley, 1984 for discussions of suitable main-memory structures. In particular, hashing takes on average $O(n)$ time to process n items, and balanced trees take $O(n \log n)$ time; either is sufficiently close to linear for our purposes.

space overhead in addition to the space needed to store the tuples; for instance, a main-memory hash table needs a bucket array and space for pointers to link the tuples in a bucket. However, the overhead tends to be small compared with the space needed to store the tuples. We shall thus make the simplifying assumption of no overhead space and concentrate on what is required to store the tuples in main memory.

On this assumption, we may store in the $M - 1$ available buffers of main memory as many tuples as will fit in $M - 1$ blocks of R. If we want one copy of each distinct tuple of R to fit in main memory, then $B(\delta(R))$ must be no larger than $M - 1$. Since we expect M to be much larger than 1, a simpler approximation to this rule, and the one we shall generally use, is:

- $B(\delta(R)) \leq M$

Note that we cannot in general compute the size of $\delta(R)$ without computing $\delta(R)$ itself. Should we underestimate that size, so $B(\delta(R))$ is actually larger than M, we shall pay a significant penalty due to thrashing, as the blocks holding the distinct tuples of R must be brought into and out of main memory frequently.

Grouping

A grouping operation γ_L gives us zero or more grouping attributes and presumably one or more aggregated attributes. If we create in main memory one entry for each group — that is, for each value of the grouping attributes — then we can scan the tuples of R, one block at a time. The *entry* for a group consists of values for the grouping attributes and an accumulated value or values for each aggregation. The accumulated value is, except in one case, obvious:

- For a `MIN(a)` or `MAX(a)` aggregate, record the minimum or maximum value, respectively, of attribute a seen for any tuple in the group so far. Change this minimum or maximum, if appropriate, each time a tuple of the group is seen.

- For any `COUNT` aggregation, add one for each tuple of the group that is seen.

- For `SUM(a)`, add the value of attribute a to the accumulated sum for its group.

- `AVG(a)` is the hard case. We must maintain two accumulations: the count of the number of tuples in the group and the sum of the a-values of these tuples. Each is computed as we would for a `COUNT` and `SUM` aggregation, respectively. After all tuples of R are seen, we take the quotient of the sum and count to obtain the average.

When all tuples of R have been read into the input buffer and contributed to the aggregation(s) for their group, we can produce the output by writing the tuple for each group. Note that until the last tuple is seen, we cannot begin to create output for a γ operation. Thus, this algorithm does not fit the iterator framework very well; the entire grouping has to be done by the Open function before the first tuple can be retrieved by GetNext.

In order that the in-memory processing of each tuple be efficient, we need to use a main-memory data structure that lets us find the entry for each group, given values for the grouping attributes. As discussed above for the δ operation, common main-memory data structures such as hash tables or balanced trees will serve well. We should remember, however, that the search key for this structure is the grouping attributes only.

The number of disk I/O's needed for this one-pass algorithm is B, as must be the case for any one-pass algorithm for a unary operator. The number of required memory buffers M is not related to B in any simple way, although typically M will be less than B. The problem is that the entries for the groups could be longer or shorter than tuples of R, and the number of groups could be anything equal to or less than the number of tuples of R. However, in most cases, group entries will be no longer than R's tuples, and there will be many fewer groups than tuples.

15.2.3 One-Pass Algorithms for Binary Operations

Let us now take up the binary operations: union, intersection, difference, product, and join. Since in some cases we must distinguish the set- and bag-versions of these operators, we shall subscript them with B or S for "bag" and "set," respectively; e.g., $\cup_B$ for bag union or $-_S$ for set difference. To simplify the discussion of joins, we shall consider only the natural join. An equijoin can be implemented the same way, after attributes are renamed appropriately, and theta-joins can be thought of as a product or equijoin followed by a selection for those conditions that cannot be expressed in an equijoin.

Bag union can be computed by a very simple one-pass algorithm. To compute $R \cup_B S$, we copy each tuple of R to the output and then copy every tuple of S, as we did in Example 15.3. The number of disk I/O's is $B(R) + B(S)$, as it must be for a one-pass algorithm on operands R and S, while $M = 1$ suffices regardless of how large R and S are.

Other binary operations require reading the smaller of the operands R and S into main memory and building a suitable data structure so tuples can be both inserted quickly and found quickly, as discussed in Section 15.2.2. As before, a hash table or balanced tree suffices. The structure requires a small amount of space (in addition to the space for the tuples themselves), which we shall neglect. Thus, the approximate requirement for a binary operation on relations R and S to be performed in one pass is:

- $\min\big(B(R), B(S)\big) \leq M$

Operations on Nonclustered Data

Remember that all our calculations regarding the number of disk I/O's required for an operation are predicated on the assumption that the operand relations are clustered. In the (typically rare) event that an operand R is not clustered, then it may take us $T(R)$ disk I/O's, rather than $B(R)$ disk I/O's to read all the tuples of R. Note, however, that any relation that is the result of an operator may always be assumed clustered, since we have no reason to store a temporary relation in a nonclustered fashion.

This rule assumes that one buffer will be used to read the blocks of the larger relation, while approximately M buffers are needed to house the entire smaller relation and its main-memory data structure.

We shall now give the details of the various operations. In each case, we assume R is the larger of the relations, and we house S in main memory.

Set Union

We read S into $M - 1$ buffers of main memory and build a search structure where the search key is the entire tuple. All these tuples are also copied to the output. We then read each block of R into the Mth buffer, one at a time. For each tuple t of R, we see if t is in S, and if not, we copy t to the output. If t is also in S, we skip t.

Set Intersection

Read S into $M - 1$ buffers and build a search structure with full tuples as the search key. Read each block of R, and for each tuple t of R, see if t is also in S. If so, copy t to the output, and if not, ignore t.

Set Difference

Since difference is not commutative, we must distinguish between $R -_S S$ and $S -_S R$, continuing to assume that R is the larger relation. In each case, read S into $M - 1$ buffers and build a search structure with full tuples as the search key.

To compute $R -_S S$, we read each block of R and examine each tuple t on that block. If t is in S, then ignore t; if it is not in S then copy t to the output.

To compute $S -_S R$, we again read the blocks of R and examine each tuple t in turn. If t is in S, then we delete t from the copy of S in main memory, while if t is not in S we do nothing. After considering each tuple of R, we copy to the output those tuples of S that remain.

Bag Intersection

We read S into $M-1$ buffers, but we associate with each distinct tuple a *count*, which initially measures the number of times this tuple occurs in S. Multiple copies of a tuple t are not stored individually. Rather we store one copy of t and associate with it a count equal to the number of times t occurs.

This structure could take slightly more space than $B(S)$ blocks if there were few duplicates, although frequently the result is that S is compacted. Thus, we shall continue to assume that $B(S) \le M$ is sufficient for a one-pass algorithm to work, although the condition is only an approximation.

Next, we read each block of R, and for each tuple t of R we see whether t occurs in S. If not we ignore t; it cannot appear in the intersection. However, if t appears in S, and the count associated with t is still positive, then we output t and decrement the count by 1. If t appears in S, but its count has reached 0, then we do not output t; we have already produced as many copies of t in the output as there were copies in S.

Bag Difference

To compute $S -_B R$, we read the tuples of S into main memory, and count the number of occurrences of each distinct tuple, as we did for bag intersection. When we read R, for each tuple t we see whether t occurs in S, and if so, we decrement its associated count. At the end, we copy to the output each tuple in main memory whose count is positive, and the number of times we copy it equals that count.

To compute $R -_B S$, we also read the tuples of S into main memory and count the number of occurrences of distinct tuples. We may think of a tuple t with a count of c as c reasons not to copy t to the output as we read tuples of R. That is, when we read a tuple t of R, we see if t occurs in S. If not, then we copy t to the output. If t does occur in S, then we look at the current count c associated with t. If $c = 0$, then copy t to the output. If $c > 0$, do not copy t to the output, but decrement c by 1.

Product

Read S into $M-1$ buffers of main memory; no special data structure is needed. Then read each block of R, and for each tuple t of R concatenate t with each tuple of S in main memory. Output each concatenated tuple as it is formed.

This algorithm may take a considerable amount of processor time per tuple of R, because each such tuple must be matched with $M-1$ blocks full of tuples. However, the output size is also large, and the time per output tuple is small.

Natural Join

In this and other join algorithms, let us take the convention that $R(X, Y)$ is being joined with $S(Y, Z)$, where Y represents all the attributes that R and S

What if M is not Known?

While we present algorithms as if M, the number of available memory blocks, were fixed and known in advance, remember that the available M is often unknown, except within some obvious limits like the total memory of the machine. Thus, a query optimizer, when choosing between a one-pass and a two-pass algorithm, might estimate M and make the choice based on this estimate. If the optimizer is wrong, the penalty is either thrashing of buffers between disk and memory (if the guess of M was too high), or unnecessary passes if M was underestimated.

There are also some algorithms that degrade gracefully when there is less memory than expected. For example, we can behave like a one-pass algorithm, unless we run out of space, and then start behaving like a two-pass algorithm. Sections 15.5.6 and 15.7.3 discuss some of these approaches.

---

have in common, X is all attributes of R that are not in the schema of S, and Z is all attributes of S that are not in the schema of R. We continue to assume that S is the smaller relation. To compute the natural join, do the following:

1. Read all the tuples of S and form them into a main-memory search structure with the attributes of Y as the search key. As usual, a hash table or balanced tree are good examples of such structures. Use $M - 1$ blocks of memory for this purpose.

2. Read each block of R into the one remaining main-memory buffer. For each tuple t of R, find the tuples of S that agree with t on all attributes of Y, using the search structure. For each matching tuple of S, form a tuple by joining it with t, and move the resulting tuple to the output.

Like all the one-pass, binary algorithms, this one takes $B(R) + B(S)$ disk I/O's to read the operands. It works as long as $B(S) \leq M - 1$, or approximately, $B(S) \leq M$. Also as for the other algorithms we have studied, the space required by the main-memory search structure is not counted but may lead to a small, additional memory requirement.

We shall not discuss joins other than the natural join. Remember that an equijoin is executed in essentially the same way as a natural join, but we must account for the fact that "equal" attributes from the two relations may have different names. A theta-join that is not an equijoin can be replaced by an equijoin or product followed by a selection.

15.2.4   Exercises for Section 15.2

Exercise 15.2.1: For each of the operations below, write an iterator that uses the algorithm described in this section.

* a) Projection.

* b) Distinct (δ).

  c) Grouping (γ_L).

* d) Set union.

  e) Set intersection.

  f) Set difference.

  g) Bag intersection.

  h) Bag difference.

  i) Product.

  j) Natural join.

Exercise 15.2.2: For each of the operators in Exercise 15.2.1, tell whether the operator is *blocking*, by which we mean that the first output cannot be produced until all the input has been read. Put another way, a blocking operator is one whose only possible iterators have all the important work done by `Open`.

Exercise 15.2.3: Figure 15.9 summarizes the memory and disk-I/O requirements of the algorithms of this section and the next. However, it assumes all arguments are clustered. How would the entries change if one or both arguments were not clustered?

! **Exercise 15.2.4:** Give one-pass algorithms for each of the following join-like operators:

* a) $R \ltimes S$, assuming R fits in memory (see Exercise 5.2.10 for a definition of the semijoin).

* b) $R \ltimes S$, assuming S fits in memory.

  c) $R \overline{\ltimes} S$, assuming R fits in memory (see Exercise 5.2.11 for a definition of the antisemijoin).

  d) $R \overline{\ltimes} S$, assuming S fits in memory.

* e) $R \underset{L}{\overset{\circ}{\bowtie}} S$, assuming R fits in memory (see Section 5.4.7 for definitions involving outerjoins).

  f) $R \underset{L}{\overset{\circ}{\bowtie}} S$, assuming S fits in memory.

g) $R \overset{\circ}{\bowtie}_R S$, assuming R fits in memory.

h) $R \overset{\circ}{\bowtie}_R S$, assuming S fits in memory.

i) $R \overset{\circ}{\bowtie} S$, assuming R fits in memory.

15.3 Nested-Loop Joins

Before proceeding to the more complex algorithms in the next sections, we shall turn our attention to a family of algorithms for the join operator called "nested-loop" joins. These algorithms are, in a sense, "one-and-a-half" passes, since in each variation one of the two arguments has its tuples read only once, while the other argument will be read repeatedly. Nested-loop joins can be used for relations of any size; it is not necessary that one relation fit in main memory.

15.3.1 Tuple-Based Nested-Loop Join

The simplest variation of nested-loop join has loops that range over individual tuples of the relations involved. In this algorithm, which we call *tuple-based nested-loop join*, we compute the join $R(X,Y) \bowtie S(Y,Z)$ as follows:

```
FOR each tuple s in S DO
    FOR each tuple r in R DO
        IF r and s join to make a tuple t THEN
            output t;
```

If we are careless about how we buffer the blocks of relations R and S, then this algorithm could require as many as $T(R)T(S)$ disk I/O's. However, there are many situations where this algorithm can be modified to have much lower cost. One case is when we can use an index on the join attribute or attributes of R to find the tuples of R that match a given tuple of S, without having to read the entire relation R. We discuss index-based joins in Section 15.6.3. A second improvement looks much more carefully at the way tuples of R and S are divided among blocks, and uses as much of the memory as it can to reduce the number of disk I/O's as we go through the inner loop. We shall consider this block-based version of nested-loop join in Section 15.3.3.

15.3.2 An Iterator for Tuple-Based Nested-Loop Join

One advantage of a nested-loop join is that it fits well into an iterator framework, and thus, as we shall see in Section 16.7.3, allows us to avoid storing intermediate relations on disk in some situations. The iterator for $R \bowtie S$ is easy to build from the iterators for R and S, which support functions R.Open(), and so on, as in Section 15.1.6. The code for the three iterator functions for nested-loop join is in Fig. 15.7. It makes the assumption that neither relation R nor S is empty.

```
Open() {
    R.Open();
    S.Open();
    s := S.GetNext();
}

GetNext() {
    REPEAT {
        r := R.GetNext();
        IF (r = NotFound) { /* R is exhausted for
                the current s */
            R.Close();
            s := S.GetNext();
            IF (s = NotFound) RETURN NotFound;
                /* both R and S are exhausted */
            R.Open();
            r := R.GetNext();
        }
    }
    UNTIL(r and s join);
    RETURN the join of r and s;
}

Close() {
    R.Close();
    S.Close();
}
```

Figure 15.7: Iterator functions for tuple-based nested-loop join of R and S

15.3.3 A Block-Based Nested-Loop Join Algorithm

We can improve on the tuple-based nested-loop join of Section 15.3.1 if we compute $R \bowtie S$ by:

1. Organizing access to both argument relations by blocks, and

2. Using as much main memory as we can to store tuples belonging to the relation S, the relation of the outer loop.

Point (1) makes sure that when we run through the tuples of R in the inner loop, we use as few disk I/O's as possible to read R. Point (2) enables us to join each tuple of R that we read with not just one tuple of S, but with as many tuples of S as will fit in memory.

As in Section 15.2.3, let us assume $B(S) \leq B(R)$, but now let us also assume that $B(S) > M$; i.e., neither relation fits entirely in main memory. We repeatedly read $M-1$ blocks of S into main-memory buffers. A search structure, with search key equal to the common attributes of R and S, is created for the tuples of S that are in main memory. Then we go through all the blocks of R, reading each one in turn into the last block of memory. Once there, we compare all the tuples of R's block with all the tuples in all the blocks of S that are currently in main memory. For those that join, we output the joined tuple. The nested-loop structure of this algorithm can be seen when we describe the algorithm more formally, in Fig. 15.8.

```
FOR each chunk of M-1 blocks of S DO BEGIN
    read these blocks into main-memory buffers;
    organize their tuples into a search structure whose
        search key is the common attributes of R and S;
    FOR each block b of R DO BEGIN
        read b into main memory;
        FOR each tuple t of b DO BEGIN
            find the tuples of S in main memory that
                join with t;
            output the join of t with each of these tuples;
        END;
    END;
END;
```

Figure 15.8: The nested-loop join algorithm

The program of Fig. 15.8 appears to have three nested loops. However, there really are only two loops if we look at the code at the right level of abstraction. The first, or outer loop, runs through the tuples of S. The other two loops run through the tuples of R. However, we expressed the process as two loops to emphasize that the order in which we visit the tuples of R is not arbitrary. Rather, we need to look at these tuples a block at a time (the role of the second loop), and within one block, we look at all the tuples of that block before moving on to the next block (the role of the third loop).

Example 15.4: Let $B(R) = 1000$, $B(S) = 500$, and $M = 101$. We shall use 100 blocks of memory to buffer S in 100-block chunks, so the outer loop of Fig. 15.8 iterates five times. At each iteration, we do 100 disk I/O's to read the chunk of S, and we must read R entirely in the second loop, using 1000 disk I/O's. Thus, the total number of disk I/O's is 5500.

Notice that if we reversed the roles of R and S, the algorithm would use slightly more disk I/O's. We would iterate 10 times through the outer loop and do 600 disk I/O's at each iteration, for a total of 6000. In general, there is a slight advantage to using the smaller relation in the outer loop. □

The algorithm of Fig. 15.8 is sometimes called "nested-block join." We shall continue to call it simply *nested-loop join*, since it is the variant of the nested-loop idea most commonly implemented in practice. If necessary to distinguish it from the tuple-based nested-loop join of Section 15.3.1, we can call Fig. 15.8 "block-based nested-loop join."

15.3.4   Analysis of Nested-Loop Join

The analysis of Example 15.4 can be repeated for any $B(R)$, $B(S)$, and M. Assuming S is the smaller relation, the number of chunks, or iterations of the outer loop is $B(S)/(M-1)$. At each iteration, we read $M-1$ blocks of S and $B(R)$ blocks of R. The number of disk I/O's is thus

$$\frac{B(S)}{M-1}\bigl(M-1+B(R)\bigr)$$

or

$$B(S) + \frac{B(S)B(R)}{M-1}$$

Assuming all of M, $B(S)$, and $B(R)$ are large, but M is the smallest of these, an approximation to the above formula is $B(S)B(R)/M$. That is, the cost is proportional to the product of the sizes of the two relations, divided by the amount of available main memory. We can do much better than a nested-loop join when both relations are large. But for reasonably small examples such as Example 15.4, the cost of the nested-loop join is not much greater than the cost of a one-pass join, which is 1500 disk I/O's for this example. In fact, if $B(S) \leq M-1$, the nested-loop join becomes identical to the one-pass join algorithm of Section 15.2.3.

Although nested-loop join is generally not the most efficient join algorithm possible, we should note that in some early relational DBMS's, it was the only method available. Even today, it is needed as a subroutine in more efficient join algorithms in certain situations, such as when large numbers of tuples from each relation share a common value for the join attribute(s). For an example where nested-loop join is essential, see Section 15.4.5.

15.3.5   Summary of Algorithms so Far

The main-memory and disk I/O requirements for the algorithms we have discussed in Sections 15.2 and 15.3 are shown in Fig. 15.9. The memory requirements for γ and δ are actually more complex than shown, and $M = B$ is only a loose approximation. For γ, M grows with the number of groups, and for δ, M grows with the number of distinct tuples.

15.3.6   Exercises for Section 15.3

Exercise 15.3.1: Give the three iterator functions for the block-based version of nested-loop join.

Operators	Approximate M required	Disk I/O	Section
σ, π	1	B	15.2.1
γ, δ	B	B	15.2.2
$\cup$, $\cap$, $-$, $\times$, $\bowtie$	$\min(B(R), B(S))$	$B(R) + B(S)$	15.2.3
$\bowtie$	any $M \geq 2$	$B(R)B(S)/M$	15.3.3

Figure 15.9: Main memory and disk I/O requirements for one-pass and nested-loop algorithms

* **Exercise 15.3.2 :** Suppose $B(R) = B(S) = 10,000$, and $M = 1000$. Calculate the disk I/O cost of a nested-loop join.

Exercise 15.3.3 : For the relations of Exercise 15.3.2, what value of M would we need to compute $R \bowtie S$ using the nested-loop algorithm with no more than a) 100,000   ! b) 25,000   ! c) 15,000 disk I/O's?

! **Exercise 15.3.4 :** If R and S are both unclustered, it seems that nested-loop join would require about $T(R)T(S)/M$ disk I/O's.

a) How can you do significantly better than this cost?

b) If only one of R and S is unclustered, how would you perform a nested-loop join? Consider both the cases that the larger is unclustered and that the smaller is unclustered.

! **Exercise 15.3.5 :** The iterator of Fig. 15.7 will not work properly if either R or S is empty. Rewrite the functions so they will work, even if one or both relations are empty.

15.4   Two-Pass Algorithms Based on Sorting

We shall now begin the study of multipass algorithms for performing relational-algebra operations on relations that are larger than what the one-pass algorithms of Section 15.2 can handle. We concentrate on *two-pass algorithms*, where data from the operand relations is read into main memory, processed in some way, written out to disk again, and then reread from disk to complete the operation. We can naturally extend this idea to any number of passes, where the data is read many times into main memory. However, we concentrate on two-pass algorithms because:

a) Two passes are usually enough, even for very large relations,

b) Generalizing to more than two passes is not hard; we discuss these extensions in Section 15.8.

In this section, we consider sorting as a tool for implementing relational operations. The basic idea is as follows. If we have a large relation R, where $B(R)$ is larger than M, the number of memory buffers we have available, then we can repeatedly:

1. Read M blocks of R into main memory.

2. Sort these M blocks in main memory, using an efficient, main-memory sorting algorithm. Such an algorithm will take an amount of processor time that is just slightly more than linear in the number of tuples in main memory, so we expect that the time to sort will not exceed the disk I/O time for step (1).

3. Write the sorted list into M blocks of disk. We shall refer to the contents of these blocks as one of the *sorted sublists* of R.

All the algorithms we shall discuss then use a second pass to "merge" the sorted sublists in some way to execute the desired operator.

15.4.1 Duplicate Elimination Using Sorting

To perform the $\delta(R)$ operation in two passes, we sort the tuples of R in sublists as described above. We then use the available main memory to hold one block from each sorted sublist, as we did for the multiway merge sort of Section 11.4.4. However, instead of sorting the tuples from these sublists, we repeatedly copy one to the output and ignore all tuples identical to it. The process is suggested by Fig. 15.10.

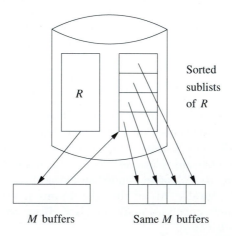

Figure 15.10: A two-pass algorithm for eliminating duplicates

More precisely, we look at the first unconsidered tuple from each block, and we find among them the first in sorted order, say t. We make one copy of t in the output, and we remove from the fronts of the various input blocks all copies of t. If a block is exhausted, we bring into its buffer the next block from the same sublist, and if there are t's on that block we remove them as well.

Example 15.5 : Suppose for simplicity that tuples are integers, and only two tuples fit on a block. Also, $M = 3$; i.e., there are three blocks in main memory. The relation R consists of 17 tuples:

$$2, 5, 2, 1, 2, 2, 4, 5, 4, 3, 4, 2, 1, 5, 2, 1, 3$$

We read the first six tuples into the three blocks of main memory, sort them, and write them out as the sublist R_1. Similarly, tuples seven through twelve are then read in, sorted and written as the sublist R_2. The last five tuples are likewise sorted and become the sublist R_3.

To start the second pass, we can bring into main memory the first block (two tuples) from each of the three sublists. The situation is now:

Sublist	In memory	Waiting on disk
R_1:	1 2	2 2, 2 5
R_2:	2 3	4 4, 4 5
R_3:	1 1	2 3, 5

Looking at the first tuples of the three blocks in main memory, we find that 1 is the first tuple in sorted order. We therefore make one copy of 1 on the output, and we remove all 1's from the blocks in memory. When we do so, the block from R_3 is exhausted, so we bring in the next block, with tuples 2 and 3, from that sublist. Had there been more 1's on this block, we would eliminate them. The situation is now:

Sublist	In memory	Waiting on disk
R_1:	2	2 2, 2 5
R_2:	2 3	4 4, 4 5
R_3:	2 3	5

Now, 2 is the least tuple at the fronts of the lists, and in fact it happens to appear on each list. We write one copy of 2 to the output and eliminate 2's from the in-memory blocks. The block from R_1 is exhausted and the next block from that sublist is brought to memory. That block has 2's, which are eliminated, again exhausting the block from R_1. The third block from that sublist is brought to memory, and its 2 is eliminated. The present situation is:

Sublist	In memory	Waiting on disk
R_1:	5	
R_2:	3	4 4, 4 5
R_3:	3	5

Now, 3 is selected as the least tuple, one copy of 3 is written to the output, and the blocks from R_2 and R_3 are exhausted and replaced from disk, leaving:

Sublist	In memory	Waiting on disk
R_1:	5	
R_2:	4 4	4 5
R_3:	5	

To complete the example, 4 is next selected, consuming most of list R_2. At the final step, each list happens to consist of a single 5, which is output once and eliminated from the input buffers. □

   The number of disk I/O's performed by this algorithm, as always ignoring the handling of the output, is:

1. $B(R)$ to read each block of R when creating the sorted sublists.

2. $B(R)$ to write each of the sorted sublists to disk.

3. $B(R)$ to read each block from the sublists at the appropriate time.

Thus, the total cost of this algorithm is $3B(R)$, compared with $B(R)$ for the single-pass algorithm of Section 15.2.2.

   On the other hand, we can handle much larger files using the two-pass algorithm than with the one-pass algorithm. Assuming M blocks of memory are available, we create sorted sublists of M blocks each. For the second pass, we need one block from each sublist in main memory, so there can be no more than M sublists, each M blocks long. Thus, $B \leq M^2$ is required for the two-pass algorithm to be feasible, compared with $B \leq M$ for the one-pass algorithm. Put another way, to compute $\delta(R)$ with the two-pass algorithm requires only $\sqrt{B(R)}$ blocks of main memory, rather than $B(R)$ blocks.

15.4.2 Grouping and Aggregation Using Sorting

The two-pass algorithm for $\gamma_L(R)$ is quite similar to the algorithm of Section 15.4.1 for $\delta(R)$. We summarize it as follows:

1. Read the tuples of R into memory, M blocks at a time. Sort each M blocks, using the grouping attributes of L as the sort key. Write each sorted sublist to disk.

2. Use one main-memory buffer for each sublist, and initially load the first block of each sublist into its buffer.

3. Repeatedly find the least value of the sort key (grouping attributes) present among the first available tuples in the buffers. This value, v, becomes the next group, for which we:

   (a) Prepare to compute all the aggregates on list L for this group. As in Section 15.2.2, use a count and sum in place of an average.

(b) Examine each of the tuples with sort key v, and accumulate the needed aggregates.

(c) If a buffer becomes empty, replace it with the next block from the same sublist.

When there are no more tuples with sort key v available, output a tuple consisting of the grouping attributes of L and the associated values of the aggregations we have computed for the group.

As for the δ algorithm, this two-pass algorithm for γ takes $3B(R)$ disk I/O's, and will work as long as $B(R) \leq M^2$.

15.4.3 A Sort-Based Union Algorithm

When bag-union is wanted, the one-pass algorithm of Section 15.2.3, where we simply copy both relations, works regardless of the size of the arguments, so there is no need to consider a two-pass algorithm for $\cup_B$. However, the one-pass algorithm for $\cup_S$ only works when at least one relation is smaller than the available main memory, so we should consider a two-pass algorithm for set union. The methodology we present works for the set and bag versions of intersection and difference as well, as we shall see in Section 15.4.4. To compute $R \cup_S S$, we do the following:

1. Repeatedly bring M blocks of R into main memory, sort their tuples, and write the resulting sorted sublist back to disk.

2. Do the same for S, to create sorted sublists for relation S.

3. Use one main-memory buffer for each sublist of R and S. Initialize each with the first block from the corresponding sublist.

4. Repeatedly find the first remaining tuple t among all the buffers. Copy t to the output, and remove from the buffers all copies of t (if R and S are sets there should be at most two copies). If a buffer becomes empty, reload it with the next block from its sublist.

We observe that each tuple of R and S is read twice into main memory, once when the sublists are being created, and the second time as part of one of the sublists. The tuple is also written to disk once, as part of a newly formed sublist. Thus, the cost in disk I/O's is $3\big(B(R) + B(S)\big)$.

The algorithm works as long as the total number of sublists among the two relations does not exceed M, because we need one buffer for each sublist. Since each sublist is M blocks long, that says the sizes of the two relations must not exceed M^2; that is, $B(R) + B(S) \leq M^2$.

15.4.4 Sort-Based Intersection and Difference

Whether the set version or the bag version is wanted, the algorithms are essentially the same as that of Section 15.4.3, except that the way we handle the copies of a tuple t at the fronts of the sorted sublists differs. In general we create the sorted sublists of M blocks each for both argument relations R and S. We use one main-memory buffer for each sublist, initially loaded with the first block of the sublist.

We then repeatedly consider the least tuple t among the remaining tuples in all the buffers. We count the number of tuples of R that are identical to t and we also count the number of tuples of S that are identical to t. Doing so requires that we reload buffers from any sublists whose currently buffered block is exhausted. The following indicates how we determine whether t is output, and if so, how many times:

- For set intersection, output t if it appears in both R and S.

- For bag intersection, output t the minimum of the number of times it appears in R and in S. Note that t is not output if either of these counts is 0; that is, if t is missing from one or both of the relations.

- For set difference, $R -_S S$, output t if and only if it appears in R but not in S.

- For bag difference, $R -_B S$, output t the number of times it appears in R minus the number of times it appears in S. Of course, if t appears in S at least as many times as it appears in R, then do not output t at all.

Example 15.6: Let us make the same assumptions as in Example 15.5: $M = 3$, tuples are integers, and two tuples fit in a block. The data will be almost the same as in that example as well. However, here we need two arguments, so we shall assume that R has 12 tuples and S has 5 tuples. Since main memory can fit six tuples, in the first pass we get two sublists from R, which we shall call R_1 and R_2, and only one sorted sublist from S, which we refer to as S_1.[2] After creating the sorted sublists (from unsorted relations similar to the data from Example 15.5), the situation is:

Sublist	In memory	Waiting on disk
R_1:	1 2	2 2, 2 5
R_2:	2 3	4 4, 4 5
S_1:	1 1	2 3, 5

Suppose we want to take the bag difference $R -_B S$. We find that the least tuple among the main-memory buffers is 1, so we count the number of 1's among the sublists of R and among the sublists of S. We find that 1 appears once in R

---

[2]Since S fits in main memory, we could actually use the one-pass algorithms of Section 15.2.3, but we shall use the two-pass approach for illustration.

and twice in S. Since 1 does not appear more times in R than in S, we do not output any copies of tuple 1. Since the first block of S_1 was exhausted counting 1's, we loaded the next block of S_1, leaving the following situation:

Sublist	In memory	Waiting on disk
R_1:	2	2 2, 2 5
R_2:	2 3	4 4, 4 5
S_1:	2 3	5

We now find that 2 is the least remaining tuple, so we count the number of its occurrences in R, which is five occurrences, and we count the number of its occurrences in S, which is one. We thus output tuple 2 four times. As we perform the counts, we must reload the buffer for R_1 twice, which leaves:

Sublist	In memory	Waiting on disk
R_1:	5	
R_2:	3	4 4, 4 5
S_1:	3	5

Next, we consider tuple 3, and find it appears once in R and once in S. We therefore do not output 3 and remove its copies from the buffers, leaving:

Sublist	In memory	Waiting on disk
R_1:	5	
R_2:	4 4	4 5
S_1:	5	

Tuple 4 occurs three times in R and not at all in S, so we output three copies of 4. Last, 5 appears twice in R and once in S, so we output 5 once. The complete output is 2, 2, 2, 2, 4, 4, 4, 5. □

The analysis of this family of algorithms is the same as for the set-union algorithm described in Section 15.4.3:

- $3\big(B(R) + B(S)\big)$ disk I/O's.

- Approximately $B(R) + B(S) \leq M^2$ for the algorithm to work.

15.4.5 A Simple Sort-Based Join Algorithm

There are several ways that sorting can be used to join large relations. Before examining the join algorithms, let us observe one problem that can occur when we compute a join but was not an issue for the binary operations considered so far. When taking a join, the number of tuples from the two relations that share a common value of the join attribute(s), and therefore need to be in main memory simultaneously, can exceed what fits in memory. The extreme example is when there is only one value of the join attribute(s), and every tuple of one relation joins with every tuple of the other relation. In this situation, there is really no choice but to take a nested-loop join of the two sets of tuples with a common value in the join-attribute(s).

To avoid facing this situation, we can try to reduce main-memory use for other aspects of the algorithm, and thus make available a large number of buffers to hold the tuples with a given join-attribute value. In this section we shall discuss the algorithm that makes the greatest possible number of buffers available for joining tuples with a common value. In Section 15.4.7 we consider another sort-based algorithm that uses fewer disk I/O's, but can present problems when there are large numbers of tuples with a common join-attribute value.

Given relations $R(X, Y)$ and $S(Y, Z)$ to join, and given M blocks of main memory for buffers, we do the following:

1. Sort R, using a two-phase, multiway merge sort, with Y as the sort key.

2. Sort S similarly.

3. Merge the sorted R and S. We generally use only two buffers, one for the current block of R and the other for the current block of S. The following steps are done repeatedly:

   (a) Find the least value y of the join attributes Y that is currently at the front of the blocks for R and S.

   (b) If y does not appear at the front of the other relation, then remove the tuple(s) with sort key y.

   (c) Otherwise, identify all the tuples from both relations having sort key y. If necessary, read blocks from the sorted R and/or S, until we are sure there are no more y's in either relation. As many as M buffers are available for this purpose.

   (d) Output all the tuples that can be formed by joining tuples from R and S with a common Y-value y.

   (e) If either relation has no more unconsidered tuples in main memory, reload the buffer for that relation.

Example 15.7: Let us consider the relations R and S from Example 15.4. Recall these relations occupy 1000 and 500 blocks, respectively, and there are $M = 101$ main-memory buffers. When we use two-phase, multiway merge sort on a relation, we do four disk I/O's per block, two in each of the two phases. Thus, we use $4(B(R) + B(S))$ disk I/O's to sort R and S, or 6000 disk I/O's.

When we merge the sorted R and S to find the joined tuples, we read each block of R and S a fifth time, using another 1500 disk I/O's. In this merge we generally need only two of the 101 blocks of memory. However, if necessary, we could use all 101 blocks to hold the tuples of R and S that share a common Y-value y. Thus, it is sufficient that for no y do the tuples of R and S that have Y-value y together occupy more than 101 blocks.

Notice that the total number of disk I/O's performed by this algorithm is 7500, compared with 5500 for nested-loop join in Example 15.4. However, nested-loop join is inherently a quadratic algorithm, taking time proportional to $B(R)B(S)$, while sort-join has linear I/O cost, taking time proportional to $B(R) + B(S)$. It is only the constant factors and the small size of the example (each relation is only 5 or 10 times larger than a relation that fits entirely in the allotted buffers) that make nested-loop join preferable. Moreover, we shall see in Section 15.4.7 that it is usually possible to perform a sort-join in $3\big(B(R) + B(S)\big)$ disk I/O's, which would be 4500 in this example and which is below the cost of nested-loop join. □

If there is a Y-value y for which the number of tuples with this Y-value does not fit in M buffers, then we need to modify the above algorithm.

1. If the tuples from one of the relations, say R, that have Y-value y fit in $M-1$ buffers, then load these blocks of R into buffers, and read the blocks of S that hold tuples with y, one at a time, into the remaining buffer. In effect, we do the one-pass join of Section 15.2.3 on only the tuples with Y-value y.

2. If neither relation has sufficiently few tuples with Y-value y that they all fit in $M - 1$ buffers, then use the M buffers to perform a nested-loop join on the tuples with Y-value y from both relations.

Note that in either case, it may be necessary to read blocks from one relation and then ignore them, having to read them later. For example, in case (1), we might first read the blocks of S that have tuples with Y-value y and find that there are too many to fit in $M - 1$ buffers. However, if we then read the tuples of R with that Y-value we find that they do fit in $M - 1$ buffers.

15.4.6 Analysis of Simple Sort-Join

As we noted in Example 15.7, our algorithm performs five disk I/O's for every block of the argument relation. The exception would be if there were so many tuples with a common Y-value that we needed to do one of the specialized joins on these tuples. In that case, the number of extra disk I/O's depends on whether one or both relations have so many tuples with a common Y-value that they require more than $M - 1$ buffers by themselves. We shall not go into all the cases here; the exercises contain some examples to work out.

We also need to consider how big M needs to be in order for the simple sort-join to work. The primary constraint is that we need to be able to perform the two-phase, multiway merge sorts on R and S. As we observed in Section 11.4.4, we need $B(R) \leq M^2$ and $B(S) \leq M^2$ to perform these sorts. Once done, we shall not run out of buffers, although as discussed before, we may have to deviate from the simple merge if the tuples with a common Y-value cannot fit in M buffers. In summary, assuming no such deviations are necessary:

- The simple sort-join uses $5\big(B(R) + B(S)\big)$ disk I/O's.

- It requires $B(R) \leq M^2$ and $B(S) \leq M^2$ to work.

15.4.7   A More Efficient Sort-Based Join

If we do not have to worry about very large numbers of tuples with a common value for the join attribute(s), then we can save two disk I/O's per block by combining the second phase of the sorts with the join itself. We call this algorithm *sort-join*; other names by which it is known include "merge-join" and "sort-merge-join." To compute $R(X, Y) \bowtie S(Y, Z)$ using M main-memory buffers:

1. Create sorted sublists of size M, using Y as the sort key, for both R and S.

2. Bring the first block of each sublist into a buffer; we assume there are no more than M sublists in all.

3. Repeatedly find the least Y-value y among the first available tuples of all the sublists. Identify all the tuples of both relations that have Y-value y, perhaps using some of the M available buffers to hold them, if there are fewer than M sublists. Output the join of all tuples from R with all tuples from S that share this common Y-value. If the buffer for one of the sublists is exhausted, then replenish it from disk.

Example 15.8: Let us again consider the problem of Example 15.4: joining relations R and S of sizes 1000 and 500 blocks, respectively, using 101 buffers. We divide R into 10 sublists and S into 5 sublists, each of length 100, and sort them.[3] We then use 15 buffers to hold the current blocks of each of the sublists. If we face a situation in which many tuples have a fixed Y-value, we can use the remaining 86 buffers to store these tuples, but if there are more tuples than that we must use a special algorithm such as was discussed at the end of Section 15.4.5.

Assuming that we do not need to modify the algorithm for large groups of tuples with the same Y-value, then we perform three disk I/O's per block of data. Two of those are to create the sorted sublists. Then, every block of every sorted sublist is read into main memory one more time in the multiway merging process. Thus, the total number of disk I/O's is 4500.   □

This sort-join algorithm is more efficient than the algorithm of Section 15.4.5 when it can be used. As we observed in Example 15.8, the number of disk I/O's is $3\big(B(R) + B(S)\big)$. We can perform the algorithm on data that is almost as large as that of the previous algorithm. The sizes of the sorted sublists are

---

[3]Technically, we could have arranged for the sublists to have length 101 blocks each, with the last sublist of R having 91 blocks and the last sublist of S having 96 blocks, but the costs would turn out exactly the same.

M blocks, and there can be at most M of them among the two lists. Thus, $B(R) + B(S) \leq M^2$ is sufficient.

We might wonder whether we can avoid the trouble that arises when there are many tuples with a common Y-value. Some important considerations are:

1. Sometimes we can be sure the problem will not arise. For example, if Y is a key for R, then a given Y-value y can appear only once among all the blocks of the sublists for R. When it is y's turn, we can leave the tuple from R in place and join it with all the tuples of S that match. If blocks of S's sublists are exhausted during this process, they can have their buffers reloaded with the next block, and there is never any need for additional space, no matter how many tuples of S have Y-value y. Of course, if Y is a key for S rather than R, the same argument applies with R and S switched.

2. If $B(R) + B(S)$ is much less than M^2, we shall have many unused buffers for storing tuples with a common Y-value, as we suggested in Example 15.8.

3. If all else fails, we can use a nested-loop join on just the tuples with a common Y-value, using extra disk I/O's but getting the job done correctly. This option was discussed in Section 15.4.5.

15.4.8 Summary of Sort-Based Algorithms

In Fig. 15.11 is a table of the analysis of the algorithms we have discussed in Section 15.4. As discussed in Sections 15.4.5 and 15.4.7, modifications to the time and memory requirements are necessary if we join two relations that have many tuples with the same value in the join attribute(s).

Operators	Approximate M required	Disk I/O	Section
γ, δ	$\sqrt{B}$	$3B$	15.4.1, 15.4.2
$\cup, \cap, -$	$\sqrt{B(R) + B(S)}$	$3\big(B(R) + B(S)\big)$	15.4.3, 15.4.4
$\bowtie$	$\sqrt{\max\big(B(R), B(S)\big)}$	$5\big(B(R) + B(S)\big)$	15.4.5
$\bowtie$	$\sqrt{B(R) + B(S)}$	$3\big(B(R) + B(S)\big)$	15.4.7

Figure 15.11: Main memory and disk I/O requirements for sort-based algorithms

15.4.9 Exercises for Section 15.4

Exercise 15.4.1: Using the assumptions of Example 15.5 (two tuples per block, etc.),

a) Show the behavior of the two-pass duplicate-elimination algorithm on the sequence of thirty one-component tuples in which the sequence 0, 1, 2, 3, 4 repeats six times.

b) Show the behavior of the two-pass grouping algorithm computing the relation $\gamma_{a,AVG(b)}(R)$. Relation $R(a,b)$ consists of the thirty tuples t_0 through t_{29}, and the tuple t_i has i modulo 5 as its grouping component a, and i as its second component b.

Exercise 15.4.2: For each of the operations below, write an iterator that uses the algorithm described in this section.

* a) Distinct (δ).

  b) Grouping (γ_L).

* c) Set intersection.

  d) Bag difference.

  e) Natural join.

Exercise 15.4.3: If $B(R) = B(S) = 10,000$ and $M = 1000$, what are the disk I/O requirements of:

  a) Set union.

* b) Simple sort-join.

  c) The more efficient sort-join of Section 15.4.7.

! **Exercise 15.4.4:** Suppose that the second pass of an algorithm described in this section does not need all M buffers, because there are fewer than M sublists. How might we save disk I/O's by using the extra buffers?

! **Exercise 15.4.5:** In Example 15.7 we discussed the join of two relations R and S, with 1000 and 500 blocks, respectively, and $M = 101$. However, we pointed out that there would be additional disk I/O's if there were so many tuples with a given value that neither relation's tuples could fit in main memory. Calculate the total number of disk I/O's needed if:

* a) There are only two Y-values, each appearing in half the tuples of R and half the tuples of S (recall Y is the join attribute or attributes).

  b) There are five Y-values, each equally likely in each relation.

c) There are 10 Y-values, each equally likely in each relation.

! **Exercise 15.4.6:** Repeat Exercise 15.4.5 for the more efficient sort-join of Section 15.4.7.

Exercise 15.4.7: How much memory do we need to use a two-pass, sort-based algorithm for relations of 10,000 blocks each, if the operation is:

* a) δ.

b) γ.

c) A binary operation such as join or union.

Exercise 15.4.8: Describe a two-pass, sort-based algorithm for each of the join-like operators of Exercise 15.2.4.

! **Exercise 15.4.9:** Suppose records could be larger than blocks, i.e., we could have spanned records. How would the memory requirements of two-pass, sort-based algorithms change?

!! **Exercise 15.4.10:** Sometimes, it is possible to save some disk I/O's if we leave the last sublist in memory. It may even make sense to use sublists of fewer than M blocks to take advantage of this effect. How many disk I/O's can be saved this way?

!! **Exercise 15.4.11:** OQL allows grouping of objects according to arbitrary, user-specified functions of the objects. For example, one could group tuples according to the sum of two attributes. How would we perform a sort-based grouping operation of this type on a set of objects?

15.5 Two-Pass Algorithms Based on Hashing

There is a family of hash-based algorithms that attack the same problems as in Section 15.4. The essential idea behind all these algorithms is as follows. If the data is too big to store in main-memory buffers, hash all the tuples of the argument or arguments using an appropriate hash key. For all the common operations, there is a way to select the hash key so all the tuples that need to be considered together when we perform the operation have the same hash value.

We then perform the operation by working on one bucket at a time (or on a pair of buckets with the same hash value, in the case of a binary operation). In effect, we have reduced the size of the operand(s) by a factor equal to the number of buckets. If there are M buffers available, we can pick M as the number of buckets, thus gaining a factor of M in the size of the relations we can handle. Notice that the sort-based algorithms of Section 15.4 also gain a factor of M by preprocessing, although the sorting and hashing approaches achieve their similar gains by rather different means.

15.5.1   Partitioning Relations by Hashing

To begin, let us review the way we would take a relation R and, using M buffers, partition R into $M - 1$ buckets of roughly equal size. We shall assume that h is the hash function, and that h takes complete tuples of R as its argument (i.e., all attributes of R are part of the hash key). We associate one buffer with each bucket. The last buffer holds blocks of R, one at a time. Each tuple t in the block is hashed to bucket $h(t)$ and copied to the appropriate buffer. If that buffer is full, we write it out to disk, and initialize another block for the same bucket. At the end, we write out the last block of each bucket if it is not empty. The algorithm is given in more detail in Fig. 15.12. Note that it assumes that tuples, while they may be variable-length, are never too large to fit in an empty buffer.

```
initialize M-1 buckets using M-1 empty buffers;
FOR each block b of relation R DO BEGIN
    read block b into the Mth buffer;
    FOR each tuple t in b DO BEGIN
        IF the buffer for bucket h(t) has no room for t THEN
            BEGIN
                copy the buffer to disk;
                initialize a new empty block in that buffer;
            END;
        copy t to the buffer for bucket h(t);
    END;
END;
FOR each bucket DO
    IF the buffer for this bucket is not empty THEN
        write the buffer to disk;
```

Figure 15.12: Partitioning a relation R into $M - 1$ buckets

15.5.2   A Hash-Based Algorithm for Duplicate Elimination

We shall now consider the details of hash-based algorithms for the various operations of relational algebra that might need two-pass algorithms. First, consider duplicate elimination, that is, the operation $\delta(R)$. We hash R to $M - 1$ buckets, as in Fig. 15.12. Note that two copies of the same tuple t will hash to the same bucket. Thus, δ has the essential property we need: we can examine one bucket at a time, perform δ on that bucket in isolation, and take as the answer the union of $\delta(R_i)$, where R_i is the portion of R that hashes to the ith bucket. The one-pass algorithm of Section 15.2.2 can be used to eliminate duplicates from each R_i in turn and write out the resulting unique tuples.

This method will work as long as the individual R_i's are sufficiently small to fit in main memory and thus allow a one-pass algorithm. Since we assume the hash function h partitions R into equal-sized buckets, each R_i will be approximately $B(R)/(M-1)$ blocks in size. If that number of blocks is no larger than M, i.e., $B(R) \leq M(M-1)$, then the two-pass, hash-based algorithm will work. In fact, as we discussed in Section 15.2.2, it is only necessary that the number of distinct tuples in one bucket fit in M buffers, but we cannot be sure that there are any duplicates at all. Thus, a conservative estimate, with a simple form in which M and $M-1$ are considered the same, is $B(R) \leq M^2$, exactly as for the sort-based, two-pass algorithm for δ.

The number of disk I/O's is also similar to that of the sort-based algorithm. We read each block of R once as we hash its tuples, and we write each block of each bucket to disk. We then read each block of each bucket again in the one-pass algorithm that focuses on that bucket. Thus, the total number of disk I/O's is $3B(R)$.

15.5.3 Hash-Based Grouping and Aggregation

To perform the $\gamma_L(R)$ operation, we again start by hashing all the tuples of R to $M-1$ buckets. However, in order to make sure that all tuples of the same group wind up in the same bucket, we must choose a hash function that depends only on the grouping attributes of the list L.

Having partitioned R into buckets, we can then use the one-pass algorithm for γ from Section 15.2.2 to process each bucket in turn. As we discussed for δ in Section 15.5.2, we can process each bucket in main memory provided $B(R) \leq M^2$.

However, on the second pass, we only need one record per group as we process each bucket. Thus, even if the size of a bucket is larger than M, we can handle the bucket in one pass provided the records for all the groups in the bucket take no more than M buffers. Normally, a group's record will be no larger than a tuple of R. If so, then a better upper bound on $B(R)$ is M^2 times the average number of tuples per group.

As a consequence, if there are are few groups, then we may actually be able to handle much larger relations R than is indicated by the $B(R) \leq M^2$ rule. On the other hand, if M exceeds the number of groups, then we cannot fill all buckets. Thus, the actual limitation on the size of R as a function of M is complex, but $B(R) \leq M^2$ is a conservative estimate. Finally, we observe that the number of disk I/O's for γ, as for δ, is $3B(R)$.

15.5.4 Hash-Based Union, Intersection, and Difference

When the operation is binary, we must make sure that we use the same hash function to hash tuples of both arguments. For example, to compute $R \cup_S S$, we hash both R and S to $M-1$ buckets each, say $R_1, R_2, \ldots, R_{M-1}$ and

$S_1, S_2, \ldots, S_{M-1}$. We then take the set-union of R_i with S_i for all i, and output the result. Notice that if a tuple t appears in both R and S, then for some i we shall find t in both R_i and S_i. Thus, when we take the union of these two buckets, we shall output only one copy of t, and there is no possibility of introducing duplicates into the result. For $\cup_B$, the simple bag-union algorithm of Section 15.2.3 is preferable to any other approach for that operation.

To take the intersection or difference of R and S, we create the $2(M-1)$ buckets exactly as for set-union and apply the appropriate one-pass algorithm to each pair of corresponding buckets. Notice that all these algorithms require $B(R) + B(S)$ disk I/O's. To this quantity we must add the two disk I/O's per block that are necessary to hash the tuples of the two relations and store the buckets on disk, for a total of $3\big(B(R) + B(S)\big)$ disk I/O's.

In order for the algorithms to work, we must be able to take the one-pass union, intersection, or difference of R_i and S_i, whose sizes will be approximately $B(R)/(M-1)$ and $B(S)/(M-1)$, respectively. Recall that the one-pass algorithms for these operations require that the smaller operand occupies at most $M-1$ blocks. Thus, the two-pass, hash-based algorithms require that $\min\big(B(R), B(S)\big) \leq M^2$, approximately.

15.5.5   The Hash-Join Algorithm

To compute $R(X, Y) \bowtie S(Y, Z)$ using a two-pass, hash-based algorithm, we act almost as for the other binary operations discussed in Section 15.5.4. The only difference is that we must use as the hash key just the join attributes, Y. Then we can be sure that if tuples of R and S join, they will wind up in corresponding buckets R_i and S_i for some i. A one-pass join of all pairs of corresponding buckets completes this algorithm, which we call *hash-join*.[4]

Example 15.9: Let us renew our discussion of the two relations R and S from Example 15.4, whose sizes were 1000 and 500 blocks, respectively, and for which 101 main-memory buffers are made available. We may hash each relation to 100 buckets, so the average size of a bucket is 10 blocks for R and 5 blocks for S. Since the smaller number, 5, is much less than the number of available buffers, we expect to have no trouble performing a one-pass join on each pair of buckets.

The number of disk I/O's is 1500 to read each of R and S while hashing into buckets, another 1500 to write all the buckets to disk, and a third 1500 to read each pair of buckets into main memory again while taking the one-pass join of corresponding buckets. Thus, the number of disk I/O's required is 4500, just as for the efficient sort-join of Section 15.4.7.   □

We may generalize Example 15.9 to conclude that:

---

[4]Sometimes, the term "hash-join" is reserved for the variant of the one-pass join algorithm of Section 15.2.3 in which a hash table is used as the main-memory search structure. Then, the two-pass hash-join algorithm described here is called "partition hash-join."

- Hash join requires $3\big(B(R) + B(S)\big)$ disk I/O's to perform its task.

- The two-pass hash-join algorithm will work as long as approximately $\min\big(B(R), B(S)\big) \leq M^2$.

The argument for the latter point is the same as for the other binary operations: one of each pair of buckets must fit in $M - 1$ buffers.

15.5.6 Saving Some Disk I/O's

If there is more memory available on the first pass than we need to hold one block per bucket, then we have some opportunities to save disk I/O's. One option is to use several blocks for each bucket, and write them out as a group, in consecutive blocks of disk. Strictly speaking, this technique doesn't save disk I/O's, but it makes the I/O's go faster, since we save seek time and rotational latency when we write.

However, there are several tricks that have been used to avoid writing some of the buckets to disk and then reading them again. The most effective of them, called *hybrid hash-join*, works as follows. In general, suppose we decide that to join $R \bowtie S$, with S the smaller relation, we need to create k buckets, where k is much less than M, the available memory. When we hash S, we can choose to keep m of the k buckets entirely in main memory, while keeping only one block for each of the other $k - m$ buckets. We can manage to do so provided the expected size of the buckets in memory, plus one block for each of the other buckets, does not exceed M; that is:

$$\frac{mB(S)}{k} + k - m \leq M \tag{15.1}$$

In explanation, the expected size of a bucket is $B(S)/k$, and there are m buckets in memory.

Now, when we read the tuples of the other relation, R, to hash that relation into buckets, we keep in memory:

1. The m buckets of S that were never written to disk, and

2. One block for each of the $k - m$ buckets of R whose corresponding buckets of S were written to disk.

If a tuple t of R hashes to one of the first m buckets, then we immediately join it with all the tuples of the corresponding S-bucket, as if this were a one-pass, hash-join. The result of any successful joins is immediately output. It is necessary to organize each of the in-memory buckets of S into an efficient search structure to facilitate this join, just as for the one-pass hash-join. If t hashes to one of the buckets whose corresponding S-bucket is on disk, then t is sent to the main-memory block for that bucket, and eventually migrates to disk, as for a two-pass, hash-based join.

On the second pass, we join the corresponding buckets of R and S as usual. However, there is no need to join the pairs of buckets for which the S-bucket was left in memory; these buckets have already been joined and their result output.

The savings in disk I/O's is equal to two for every block of the buckets of S that remain in memory, and their corresponding R-buckets. Since m/k of the buckets are in memory, the savings is $2(m/k)\big(B(R) + B(S)\big)$. We must thus ask how to maximize m/k, subject to the constraint of equation (15.1). The surprising answer is: pick $m = 1$, and then make k as small as possible.

The intuitive justification is that all but $k - m$ of the main-memory buffers can be used to hold tuples of S in main memory, and the more of these tuples, the fewer the disk I/O's. Thus, we want to minimize k, the total number of buckets. We do so by making each bucket about as big as can fit in main memory; that is, buckets are of size M, and therefore $k = B(S)/M$. If that is the case, then there is only room for one bucket in the extra main memory; i.e., $m = 1$.

In fact, we really need to make the buckets slightly smaller than $B(S)/M$, or else we shall not quite have room for one full bucket and one block for the other $k - 1$ buckets in memory at the same time. Assuming, for simplicity, that k is about $B(S)/M$ and $m = 1$, the savings in disk I/O's is

$$\left(\frac{2M}{B(S)}\right)\big(B(R) + B(S)\big)$$

and the total cost is

$$\left(3 - \frac{2M}{B(S)}\right)\big(B(R) + B(S)\big)$$

Example 15.10: Consider the problem of Example 15.4, where we had to join relations R and S, of 1000 and 500 blocks, respectively, using $M = 101$. If we use a hybrid hash-join, then we want k, the number of buckets, to be about $500/101$. Suppose we pick $k = 5$. Then the average bucket will have 100 blocks of S's tuples. If we try to fit one of these buckets and four extra blocks for the other four buckets, we need 104 blocks of main memory, and we cannot take the chance that the in-memory bucket will overflow memory.

Thus, we are advised to choose $k = 6$. Now, when hashing S on the first pass, we have five buffers for five of the buckets, and we have up to 96 buffers for the in-memory bucket, whose expected size is $500/6$ or 83. The number of disk I/O's we use for S on the first pass is thus 500 to read all of S, and $500 - 83 = 417$ to write five buckets to disk. When we process R on the first pass, we need to read all of R (1000 disk I/O's) and write 5 of its 6 buckets (833 disk I/O's).

On the second pass, we read all the buckets written to disk, or $417 + 833 = 1250$ additional disk I/O's. The total number of disk I/O's is thus 1500 to read R and S, 1250 to write 5/6 of these relations, and another 1250 to read those tuples again, or 4000 disk I/O's. This figure compares with the 4500 disk I/O's needed for the straightforward hash-join or sort-join.   □

15.5.7 Summary of Hash-Based Algorithms

Figure 15.13 gives the memory requirements and disk I/O's needed by each of the algorithms discussed in this section. As with other types of algorithms, we should observe that the estimates for γ and δ may be conservative, since they really depend on the number of duplicates and groups, respectively, rather than on the number of tuples in the argument relation.

Operators	Approximate M required	Disk I/O	Section
γ, δ	$\sqrt{B}$	$3B$	15.5.2, 15.5.3
$\cup, \cap, -$	$\sqrt{B(S)}$	$3(B(R) + B(S))$	15.5.4
$\bowtie$	$\sqrt{B(S)}$	$3(B(R) + B(S))$	15.5.5
$\bowtie$	$\sqrt{B(S)}$	$(3 - 2M/B(S))(B(R) + B(S))$	15.5.6

Figure 15.13: Main memory and disk I/O requirements for hash-based algorithms; for binary operations, assume $B(S) \le B(R)$

Notice that the requirements for sort-based and the corresponding hash-based algorithms are almost the same. The significant differences between the two approaches are:

1. Hash-based algorithms for binary operations have a size requirement that depends only on the smaller of two arguments rather than on the sum of the argument sizes, as for sort-based algorithms.

2. Sort-based algorithms sometimes allow us to produce a result in sorted order and take advantage of that sort later. The result might be used in another sort-based algorithm later, or it could be the answer to a query that is required to be produced in sorted order.

3. Hash-based algorithms depend on the buckets being of equal size. Since there is generally at least a small variation in size, it is not possible to use buckets that, on average, occupy M blocks; we must limit them to a somewhat smaller figure. This effect is especially prominent if the number of different hash keys is small, e.g., performing a group-by on a relation with few groups or a join with very few values for the join attributes.

4. In sort-based algorithms, the sorted sublists may be written to consecutive blocks of the disk if we organize the disk properly. Thus, one of the three disk I/O's per block may require little rotational latency or seek time

and therefore may be much faster than the I/O's needed for hash-based algorithms.

5. Moreover, if M is much larger than the number of sorted sublists, then we may read in several consecutive blocks at a time from a sorted sublist, again saving some latency and seek time.

6. On the other hand, if we can choose the number of buckets to be less than M in a hash-based algorithm, then we can write out several blocks of a bucket at once. We thus obtain the same benefit on the write step for hashing that the sort-based algorithms have for the second read, as we observed in (5). Similarly, we may be able to organize the disk so that a bucket eventually winds up on consecutive blocks of tracks. If so, buckets can be read with little latency or seek time, just as sorted sublists were observed in (4) to be writable efficiently.

15.5.8   Exercises for Section 15.5

Exercise 15.5.1: The hybrid-hash-join idea, storing one bucket in main memory, can also be applied to other operations. Show how to save the cost of storing and reading one bucket from each relation when implementing a two-pass, hash-based algorithm for: *a) δ b) γ c) $\cap_B$ d) $-_S$.

Exercise 15.5.2: If $B(S) = B(R) = 10{,}000$ and $M = 1000$, what is the number of disk I/O's required for a hybrid hash join?

Exercise 15.5.3: Write iterators that implement the two-pass, hash-based algorithms for   a) δ b) γ c) $\cap_B$ d) $-_S$ e) $\bowtie$.

*! **Exercise 15.5.4:** Suppose we are performing a two-pass, hash-based grouping operation on a relation R of the appropriate size; i.e., $B(R) \le M^2$. However, there are so few groups, that some groups are larger than M; i.e., they will not fit in main memory at once. What modifications, if any, need to be made to the algorithm given here?

! **Exercise 15.5.5:** Suppose that we are using a disk where the time to move the head to a block is 100 milliseconds, and it takes 1/2 millisecond to read one block. Therefore, it takes $k/2$ milliseconds to read k consecutive blocks, once the head is positioned. Suppose we want to compute a two-pass hash-join $R \bowtie S$, where $B(R) = 1000$, $B(S) = 500$, and $M = 101$. To speed up the join, we want to use as few buckets as possible (assuming tuples distribute evenly among buckets), and read and write as many blocks as we can to consecutive positions on disk. Counting 100.5 milliseconds for a random disk I/O and $100 + k/2$ milliseconds for reading or writing k consecutive blocks from or to disk:

a) How much time does the disk I/O take?

b) How much time does the disk I/O take if we use a hybrid hash-join as described in Example 15.10?

c) How much time does a sort-based join take under the same conditions, assuming we write sorted sublists to consecutive blocks of disk?

15.6 Index-Based Algorithms

The existence of an index on one or more attributes of a relation makes available some algorithms that would not be feasible without the index. Index-based algorithms are especially useful for the selection operator, but algorithms for join and other binary operators also use indexes to very good advantage. In this section, we shall introduce these algorithms. We also continue with the discussion of the index-scan operator for accessing a stored table with an index that we began in Section 15.1.1. To appreciate many of the issues, we first need to digress and consider "clustering" indexes.

15.6.1 Clustering and Nonclustering Indexes

Recall from Section 15.1.3 that a relation is "clustered" if its tuples are packed into roughly as few blocks as can possibly hold those tuples. All the analyses we have done so far assume that relations are clustered.

We may also speak of *clustering indexes*, which are indexes on an attribute or attributes such that all the tuples with a fixed value for the search key of this index appear on roughly as few blocks as can hold them. Note that a relation that isn't clustered cannot have a clustering index,[5] but even a clustered relation can have nonclustering indexes.

Example 15.11: A relation $R(a, b)$ that is sorted on attribute a and stored in that order, packed into blocks, is surely clustered. An index on a is a clustering index, since for a given a-value a_1, all the tuples with that value for a are consecutive. They thus appear packed into blocks, except possibly for the first and last blocks that contain a-value a_1, as suggested in Fig. 15.14. However, an index on b is unlikely to be clustering, since the tuples with a fixed b-value will be spread all over the file unless the values of a and b are very closely correlated. □

---

[5]Technically, if the index is on a key for the relation, so only one tuple with a given value in the index key exists, then the index is always "clustering," even if the relation is not clustered. However, if there is only one tuple per index-key value, then there is no advantage from clustering, and the performance measure for such an index is the same as if it were considered nonclustering.

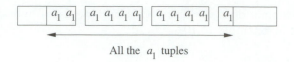

All the a_1 tuples

Figure 15.14: A clustering index has all tuples with a fixed value packed into (close to) the minimum possible number of blocks

15.6.2   Index-Based Selection

In Section 15.1.1 we discussed implementing a selection $\sigma_C(R)$ by reading all the tuples of relation R, seeing which meet the condition C, and outputting those that do. If there are no indexes on R, then that is the best we can do; the number of disk I/O's used by the operation is $B(R)$, or even $T(R)$, the number of tuples of R, should R not be a clustered relation.[6] However, suppose that the condition C is of the form $a = v$, where a is an attribute for which an index exists, and v is a value. Then one can search the index with value v and get pointers to exactly those tuples of R that have a-value v. These tuples constitute the result of $\sigma_{a=v}(R)$, so all we have to do is retrieve them.

If the index on $R.a$ is clustering, then the number of disk I/O's to retrieve the set $\sigma_{a=v}(R)$ will average $B(R)/V(R,a)$. The actual number may be somewhat higher, because:

1. Often, the index is not kept entirely in main memory, and therefore some disk I/O's are needed to support the index lookup.

2. Even though all the tuples with $a = v$ might fit in b blocks, they could be spread over $b + 1$ blocks because they don't start at the beginning of a block.

3. Although the index is clustering, the tuples with $a = v$ may be spread over several extra blocks. Two reasons why that situation might occur are:

   (a) We might not pack blocks of R as tightly as possible because we want to leave room for growth of R, as discussed in Section 13.1.6.

   (b) R might be stored with some other tuples that do not belong to R, say in a clustered-file organization.

Moreover, we of course must round up if the ratio $B(R)/V(R,a)$ is not an integer. Most significant is that should a be a key for R, then $V(R,a) = T(R)$, which is presumably much bigger than $B(R)$, yet we surely require one disk I/O to retrieve the tuple with key value v, plus whatever disk I/O's are needed to access the index.

---

[6]Recall from Section 15.1.3 the notation we developed: $T(R)$ for the number of tuples in R, $B(R)$ for the number of blocks in which R fits, and $V(R,L)$ for the number of distinct tuples in $\pi_L(R)$.

Notions of Clustering

We have seen three different, although related, concepts called "clustering" or "clustered."

1. In Section 13.2.2 we spoke of the "clustered-file organization," where tuples of one relation R are placed with a tuple of some other relation S with which they share a common value; the example was grouping movie tuples with the tuple of the studio that made the movie.

2. In Section 15.1.3 we spoke of a "clustered relation," meaning that the tuples of the relation are stored in blocks that are exclusively, or at least predominantly, devoted to storing that relation.

3. Here, we have introduced the notion of a clustering index — an index in which the tuples having a given value of the search key appear in blocks that are largely devoted to storing tuples with that search-key value. Typically, the tuples with a fixed value will be stored consecutively, and only the first and last blocks with tuples of that value will also have tuples of another search-key value.

The clustered-file organization is one example of a way to have a clustered relation that is not packed into blocks which are exclusively its own. Suppose that one tuple of the relation S is associated with many R-tuples in a clustered file. Then, while the tuples of R are not packed in blocks exclusively devoted to R, these blocks are "predominantly" devoted to R, and we call R clustered. On the other hand, S will typically *not* be a clustered relation, since its tuples are usually on blocks devoted predominantly to R-tuples rather than S-tuples.

Now, let us consider what happens when the index on $R.a$ is nonclustering. To a first approximation, each tuple we retrieve will be on a different block, and we must access $T(R)/V(R,a)$ tuples. Thus, $T(R)/V(R,a)$ is an estimate of the number of disk I/O's we need. The number could be higher because we may also need to read some index blocks from disk; it could be lower because fortuitously some retrieved tuples appear on the same block, and that block remains buffered in memory.

Example 15.12: Suppose $B(R) = 1000$, and $T(R) = 20{,}000$. That is, R has 20,000 tuples that are packed 20 to a block. Let a be one of the attributes of R, suppose there is an index on a, and consider the operation $\sigma_{a=0}(R)$. Here are some possible situations and the worst-case number of disk I/O's required. We shall ignore the cost of accessing the index blocks in all cases.

1. If R is clustered, but we do not use the index, then the cost is 1000 disk

I/O's. That is, we must retrieve every block of R.

2. If R is not clustered and we do not use the index, then the cost is 20,000 disk I/O's.

3. If $V(R, a) = 100$ and the index is clustering, then the index-based algorithm uses $1000/100 = 10$ disk I/O's.

4. If $V(R, a) = 10$ and the index is nonclustering, then the index-based algorithm uses $20,000/10 = 2000$ disk I/O's. Notice that this cost is higher than scanning the entire relation R, if R is clustered but the index is not.

5. If $V(R, a) = 20,000$, i.e., a is a key, then the index-based algorithm takes 1 disk I/O plus whatever is needed to access the index, regardless of whether the index is clustering or not.

□

Index-scan as an access method can help in several other kinds of selection operations.

a) An index such as a B-tree lets us access the search-key values in a given range efficiently. If such an index on attribute a of relation R exists, then we can use the index to retrieve just the tuples of R in the desired range for selections such as $\sigma_{a \geq 10}(R)$, or even $\sigma_{a \geq 10 \text{ AND } a \leq 20}(R)$.

b) A selection with a complex condition C can sometimes be implemented by an index-scan followed by another selection on only those tuples retrieved by the index-scan. If C is of the form $a = v$ AND C', where C' is any condition, then we can split the selection into a cascade of two selections, the first checking only for $a = v$, and the second checking condition C'. The first is a candidate for use of the index-scan operator. This splitting of a selection operation is one of many improvements that a query optimizer may make to a logical query plan; it is discussed particularly in Section 16.7.1.

15.6.3 Joining by Using an Index

All the binary operations we have considered, and the unary full-relation operations of γ and δ as well, can use certain indexes profitably. We shall leave most of these algorithms as exercises, while we focus on the matter of joins. In particular, let us examine the natural join $R(X, Y) \bowtie S(Y, Z)$; recall that X, Y, and Z can stand for sets of attributes, although it is adequate to think of them as single attributes.

For our first index-based join algorithm, suppose that S has an index on the attribute(s) Y. Then one way to compute the join is to examine each block of R, and within each block consider each tuple t. Let t_Y be the component or components of t corresponding to the attribute(s) Y. Use the index to find all those tuples of S that have t_Y in their Y-component(s). These are exactly the tuples of S that join with tuple t of R, so we output the join of each of these tuples with t.

The number of disk I/O's depends on several factors. First, assuming R is clustered, we shall have to read $B(R)$ blocks to get all the tuples of R. If R is not clustered, then up to $T(R)$ disk I/O's may be required.

For each tuple t of R we must read an average of $T(S)/V(S,Y)$ tuples of S. If S has a nonclustered index on Y, then the number of disk I/O's required to read S is $T(R)T(S)/V(S,Y)$, but if the index is clustered, then only $T(R)B(S)/V(S,Y)$ disk I/O's suffice.[7] In either case, we may have to add a few disk I/O's per Y-value, to account for the reading of the index itself.

Regardless of whether or not R is clustered, the cost of accessing tuples of S dominates. Ignoring the cost of reading R, we shall take $T(R)T(S)/V(S,Y)$ or $T(R)\big(\max(1, B(S)/V(S,Y))\big)$ as the cost of this join method, for the cases of nonclustered and clustered indexes on S, respectively.

Example 15.13: Let us consider our running example, relations $R(X,Y)$ and $S(Y,Z)$ covering 1000 and 500 blocks, respectively. Assume ten tuples of either relation fit on one block, so $T(R) = 10{,}000$ and $T(S) = 5000$. Also, assume $V(S,Y) = 100$; i.e., there are 100 different values of Y among the tuples of S.

Suppose that R is clustered, and there is a clustering index on Y for S. Then the approximate number of disk I/O's, excluding what is needed to access the index itself, is 1000 to read the blocks of R (neglected in the formulas above) plus $10{,}000 \times 500 / 100 = 50{,}000$ disk I/O's. This number is considerably above the cost of other methods for the same data discussed previously. If either R or the index on S is not clustered, then the cost is even higher. □

While Example 15.13 makes it look as if an index-join is a very bad idea, there are other situations where the join $R \bowtie S$ by this method makes much more sense. Most common is the case where R is very small compared with S, and $V(S,Y)$ is large. We discuss in Exercise 15.6.5 a typical query in which selection before a join makes R tiny. In that case, most of S will never be examined by this algorithm, since most Y-values don't appear in R at all. However, both sort- and hash-based join methods will examine every tuple of S at least once.

15.6.4 Joins Using a Sorted Index

When the index is a B-tree, or any other structure from which we easily can extract the tuples of a relation in sorted order, we have a number of other opportunities to use the index. Perhaps the simplest is when we want to compute $R(X,Y) \bowtie S(Y,Z)$, and we have such an index on Y for either R or S. We

---

[7] But remember that $B(S)/V(S,Y)$ must be replaced by 1 if it is less, as discussed in Section 15.6.2.

can then perform an ordinary sort-join, but we do not have to perform the intermediate step of sorting one of the relations on Y.

As an extreme case, if we have sorting indexes on Y for both R and S, then we need to perform only the final step of the simple sort-based join of Section 15.4.5. This method is sometimes called *zig-zag join*, because we jump back and forth between the indexes finding Y-values that they share in common. Notice that tuples from R with a Y-value that does not appear in S need never be retrieved, and similarly, tuples of S whose Y-value does not appear in R need not be retrieved.

Example 15.14: Suppose that we have relations $R(X, Y)$ and $S(Y, Z)$ with indexes on Y for both relations. In a tiny example, let the search keys (Y-values) for the tuples of R be in order $1, 3, 4, 4, 4, 5, 6$, and let the search key values for S be $2, 2, 4, 4, 6, 7$. We start with the first keys of R and S, which are 1 and 2, respectively. Since $1 < 2$, we skip the first key of R and look at the second key, 3. Now, the current key of S is less than the current key of R, so we skip the two 2's of S to reach 4.

At this point, the key 3 of R is less than the key of S, so we skip the key of R. Now, both current keys are 4. We follow the pointers associated with all the keys 4 from both relations, retrieve the corresponding tuples, and join them. Notice that until we met the common key 4, no tuples of the relation were retrieved.

Having dispensed with the 4's, we go to key 5 of R and key 6 of S. Since $5 < 6$, we skip to the next key of R. Now the keys are both 6, so we retrieve the corresponding tuples and join them. Since R is now exhausted, we know there are no more pairs of tuples from the two relations that join. $\Box$

If the indexes are B-trees, then we can scan the leaves of the two B-trees in order from the left, using the pointers from leaf to leaf that are built into the structure, as suggested in Fig. 15.15. If R and S are clustered, then retrieval of all the tuples with a given key will result in a number of disk I/O's proportional to the fractions of these two relations read. Note that in extreme cases, where there are so many tuples from R and S that neither fits in the available main memory, we shall have to use a fixup like that discussed in Section 15.4.5. However, in typical cases, the step of joining all tuples with a common Y-value can be carried out with only as many disk I/O's as it takes to read them.

Example 15.15: Let us continue with Example 15.13, to see how joins using a combination of sorting and indexing would typically perform on this data. First, assume that there is an index on Y for S that allows us to retrieve the tuples of S sorted by Y. We shall, in this example, also assume both relations and the index are clustered. For the moment, we assume there is no index on R.

Assuming 101 available blocks of main memory, we may use them to create 10 sorted sublists for the 1000-block relation R. The number of disk I/O's is 2000 to read and write all of R. We next use 11 blocks of memory — 10 for

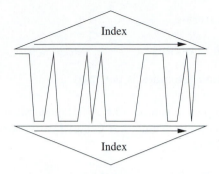

Figure 15.15: A zig-zag join using two indexes

the sublists of R and one for a block of S's tuples, retrieved via the index. We neglect disk I/O's and memory buffers needed to manipulate the index, but if the index is a B-tree, these numbers will be small anyway. In this second pass, we read all the tuples of R and S, using a total of 1500 disk I/O's, plus the small amount needed for reading the index blocks once each. We thus estimate the total number of disk I/O's at 3500, which is less than that for other methods considered so far.

Now, assume that both R and S have indexes on Y. Then there is no need to sort either relation. We use just 1500 disk I/O's to read the blocks of R and S through their indexes. In fact, if we determine from the indexes alone that a large fraction of R or S cannot match tuples of the other relation, then the total cost could be considerably less than 1500 disk I/O's. However, in any event we should add the small number of disk I/O's needed to read the indexes themselves. $\square$

15.6.5 Exercises for Section 15.6

Exercise 15.6.1: Suppose there is an index on attribute $R.a$. Describe how this index could be used to improve the execution of the following operations. Under what circumstances would the index-based algorithm be more efficient than sort- or hash-based algorithms?

* a) $R \cup_S S$ (assume that R and S have no duplicates, although they may have tuples in common).

  b) $R \cap_S S$ (again, with R and S sets).

  c) $\delta(R)$.

Exercise 15.6.2: Suppose $B(R) = 10{,}000$ and $T(R) = 500{,}000$. Let there be an index on $R.a$, and let $V(R, a) = k$ for some number k. Give the cost of $\sigma_{a=0}(R)$, as a function of k, under the following circumstances. You may neglect disk I/O's needed to access the index itself.

* a) The index is clustering.

  b) The index is not clustering.

  c) R is clustered, and the index is not used.

Exercise 15.6.3: Repeat Exercise 15.6.2 if the operation is the range query $\sigma_{C \leq a \text{ AND } a \leq D}(R)$. You may assume that C and D are constants such that $k/10$ of the values are in the range.

! Exercise 15.6.4: If R is clustered, but the index on $R.a$ is *not* clustering, then depending on k we may prefer to implement a query by performing a table-scan of R or using the index. For what values of k would we prefer to use the index if the relation and query are as in:

  a) Exercise 15.6.2.

  b) Exercise 15.6.3.

* Exercise 15.6.5: Consider the SQL query:

```
SELECT birthdate
FROM StarsIn, MovieStar
WHERE movieTitle = 'King Kong' AND starName = name;
```

This query uses the "movie" relations:

```
StarsIn(movieTitle, movieYear, starName)
MovieStar(name, address, gender, birthdate)
```

If we translate it to relational algebra, the heart is an equijoin between

$$\sigma_{movieTitle='King Kong'}(\text{StarsIn})$$

and `MovieStar`, which can be implemented much as a natural join $R \bowtie S$. Since there were only two movies named "King Kong," $T(R)$ is very small. Suppose that S, the relation `MovieStar`, has an index on `name`. Compare the cost of an index-join for this $R \bowtie S$ with the cost of a sort- or hash-based join.

! Exercise 15.6.6: In Example 15.15 we discussed the disk-I/O cost of a join $R \bowtie S$ in which one or both of R and S had sorting indexes on the join attribute(s). However, the methods described in that example can fail if there are too many tuples with the same value in the join attribute(s). What are the limits (in number of blocks occupied by tuples with the same value) under which the methods described will not need to do additional disk I/O's?

15.7 Buffer Management

We have assumed that operators on relations have available some number M of main-memory buffers that they can use to store needed data. In practice, these buffers are rarely allocated in advance to the operator, and the value of M may vary depending on system conditions. The central task of making main-memory buffers available to processes, such as queries, that act on the database is given to the *buffer manager*. It is the responsibility of the buffer manager to allow processes to get the memory they need, while minimizing the delay and unsatisfiable requests. The role of the buffer manager is illustrated in Fig. 15.16.

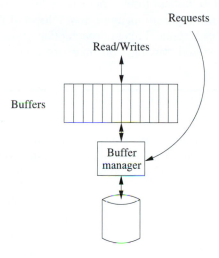

Figure 15.16: The buffer manager responds to requests for main-memory access to disk blocks

15.7.1 Buffer Management Architecture

There are two broad architectures for a buffer manager:

1. The buffer manager controls main memory directly, as in many relational DBMS's, or

2. The buffer manager allocates buffers in virtual memory, allowing the operating system to decide which buffers are actually in main memory at any time and which are in the "swap space" on disk that the operating system manages. Many "main-memory" DBMS's and "object-oriented" DBMS's operate this way.

Whichever approach a DBMS uses, the same problem arises: the buffer manager should limit the number of buffers in use so they fit in the available

---

Memory Management for Query Processing

We are assuming that the buffer manager allocates to an operator M main-memory buffers, where the value for M depends on system conditions (including other operators and queries underway), and may vary dynamically. Once an operator has M buffers, it may use some of them for bringing in disk pages, others for index pages, and still others for sort runs or hash tables. In some DBMS's, memory is not allocated from a single pool, but rather there are separate pools of memory — with separate buffer managers — for different purposes. For example, an operator might be allocated D buffers from a pool to hold pages brought in from disk, S buffers from a separate memory area allocated for sorting, and H buffers to build a hash table. This approach offers more opportunities for system configuration and "tuning," but may not make the best global use of memory.

---

main memory. When the buffer manager controls main memory directly, and requests exceed available space, it has to select a buffer to empty, by returning its contents to disk. If the buffered block has not been changed, then it may simply be erased from main memory, but if the block has changed it must be written back to its place on the disk. When the buffer manager allocates space in virtual memory, it has the option to allocate more buffers than can fit in main memory. However, if all these buffers are really in use, then there will be "thrashing," a common operating-system problem, where many blocks are moved in and out of the disk's swap space. In this situation, the system spends most of its time swapping blocks, while very little useful work gets done.

Normally, the number of buffers is a parameter set when the DBMS is initialized. We would expect that this number is set so that the buffers occupy the available main memory, regardless of whether the buffers are allocated in main or virtual memory. In what follows, we shall not concern ourselves with which mode of buffering is used, and simply assume that there is a fixed-size *buffer pool*, a set of buffers available to queries and other database actions.

15.7.2 Buffer Management Strategies

The critical choice that the buffer manager must make is what block to throw out of the buffer pool when a buffer is needed for a newly requested block. The *buffer-replacement strategies* in common use may be familiar to you from other applications of scheduling policies, such as in operating systems. These include:

Least-Recently Used (LRU)

The LRU rule is to throw out the block that has not been read or written for the longest time. This method requires that the buffer manager maintain a table indicating the last time the block in each buffer was accessed. It also requires that each database access make an entry in this table, so there is significant effort in maintaining this information. However, LRU is an effective strategy; intuitively, buffers that have not been used for a long time are less likely to be accessed sooner than those that have been accessed recently.

First-In-First-Out (FIFO)

When a buffer is needed, under the FIFO policy the buffer that has been occupied the longest by the same block is emptied and used for the new block. In this approach, the buffer manager needs to know only the time at which the block currently occupying a buffer was loaded into that buffer. An entry into a table can thus be made when the block is read from disk, and there is no need to modify the table when the block is accessed. FIFO requires less maintenance than LRU, but it can make more mistakes. A block that is used repeatedly, say the root block of a B-tree index, will eventually become the oldest block in a buffer. It will be written back to disk, only to be reread shortly thereafter into another buffer.

The "Clock" Algorithm ("Second Chance")

This algorithm is a commonly implemented, efficient approximation to LRU. Think of the buffers as arranged in a circle, as suggested by Fig. 15.17. A "hand" points to one of the buffers, and will rotate clockwise if it needs to find a buffer in which to place a disk block. Each buffer has an associated "flag," which is either 0 or 1. Buffers with a 0 flag are vulnerable to having their contents sent back to disk; buffers with a 1 are not. When a block is read into a buffer, its flag is set to 1. Likewise, when the contents of a buffer is accessed, its flag is set to 1.

When the buffer manager needs a buffer for a new block, it looks for the first 0 it can find, rotating clockwise. If it passes 1's, it sets them to 0. Thus, a block is only thrown out of its buffer if it remains unaccessed for the time it takes the hand to make a complete rotation to set its flag to 0 and then make another complete rotation to find the buffer with its 0 unchanged. For instance, in Fig. 15.17, the hand will set to 0 the 1 in the buffer to its left, and then move clockwise to find the buffer with 0, whose block it will replace and whose flag it will set to 1.

System Control

The query processor or other components of a DBMS can give advice to the buffer manager in order to avoid some of the mistakes that would occur with

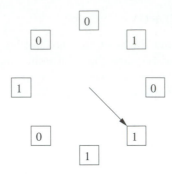

Figure 15.17: The clock algorithm visits buffers in a round-robin fashion and replaces $01\cdots 1$ with $10\cdots 0$

More Tricks Using the Clock Algorithm

The "clock" algorithm for choosing buffers to free is not limited to the scheme described in Section 15.7.2, where flags had values 0 and 1. For instance, one can start an important page with a number higher than 1 as its flag, and decrement the flag by 1 each time the "hand" passes that page. In fact, one can incorporate the concept of pinning blocks by giving the pinned block an infinite value for its flag, and then having the system release the pin at the appropriate time by setting the flag to 0.

---

a strict policy such as LRU, FIFO, or Clock. Recall from Section 12.3.5 that there are sometimes technical reasons why a block in main memory can *not* be moved to disk without first modifying certain other blocks that point to it. These blocks are called "pinned," and any buffer manager has to modify its buffer-replacement strategy to avoid expelling pinned blocks. This fact gives us the opportunity to force other blocks to remain in main memory by declaring them "pinned," even if there is no technical reason why they could not be written to disk. For example, a cure for the problem with FIFO mentioned above regarding the root of a B-tree is to "pin" the root, forcing it to remain in memory at all times. Similarly, for an algorithm like a one-pass hash-join, the query processor may "pin" the blocks of the smaller relation in order to assure that it will remain in main memory during the entire time.

15.7.3   The Relationship Between Physical Operator Selection and Buffer Management

The query optimizer will eventually select a set of physical operators that will be used to execute a given query. This selection of operators may assume that a certain number of buffers M is available for execution of each of these operators.

However, as we have seen, the buffer manager may not be willing or able to guarantee the availability of these M buffers when the query is executed. There are thus two related questions to ask about the physical operators:

1. Can the algorithm adapt to changes in the value of M, the number of main-memory buffers available?

2. When the expected M buffers are not available, and some blocks that are expected to be in memory have actually been moved to disk by the buffer manager, how does the buffer-replacement strategy used by the buffer manager impact the number of additional I/O's that must be performed?

Example 15.16: As an example of the issues, let us consider the block-based nested-loop join of Fig. 15.8. The basic algorithm does not really depend on the value of M, although its performance depends on M. Thus, it is sufficient to find out what M is just before execution begins.

It is even possible that M will change at different iterations of the outer loop. That is, each time we load main memory with a portion of the relation S (the relation of the outer loop), we can use all but one of the buffers available at that time; the remaining buffer is reserved for a block of R, the relation of the inner loop. Thus, the number of times we go around the outer loop depends on the average number of buffers available at each iteration. However, as long as M buffers are available *on average*, then the cost analysis of Section 15.3.4 will hold. In the extreme, we might have the good fortune to find that at the first iteration, enough buffers are available to hold all of S, in which case nested-loop join gracefully becomes the one-pass join of Section 15.2.3.

If we pin the $M - 1$ blocks we use for S on one iteration of the outer loop, then we shall not lose their buffers during the round. On the other hand, more buffers may become available during that iteration. These buffers allow more than one block of R to be kept in memory at the same time, but unless we are careful, the extra buffers will not improve the running time of the nested-loop join.

For instance, suppose that we use an LRU buffer-replacement strategy, and there are k buffers available to hold blocks of R. As we read each block of R, in order, the blocks that remain in buffers at the end of this iteration of the outer loop will be the last k blocks of R. We next reload the $M - 1$ buffers for S with new blocks of S and start reading the blocks of R again, in the next iteration of the outer loop. However, if we start from the beginning of R again, then the k buffers for R will need to be replaced, and we do not save disk I/O's just because $k > 1$.

A better implementation of nested-loop join, when an LRU buffer-replacement strategy is used, visits the blocks of R in an order that alternates: first-to-last and then last-to-first (called *rocking*). In that way, if there are k buffers available to R, we save k disk I/O's on each iteration of the outer loop except the first. That is, the second and subsequent iterations require only $B(R) - k$

disk I/O's for R. Notice that even if $k = 1$ (i.e., no *extra* buffers are available to R), we save one disk I/O per iteration.   □

Other algorithms also are impacted by the fact that M can vary and by the buffer-replacement strategy used by the buffer manager. Here are some useful observations.

- If we use a sort-based algorithm for some operator, then it is possible to adapt to changes in M. If M shrinks, we can change the size of a sublist, since the sort-based algorithms we discussed do not depend on the sublists being the same size. The major limitation is that as M shrinks, we could be forced to create so many sublists that we cannot then allocate a buffer for each sublist in the merging process.

- The main-memory sorting of sublists can be performed by a number of different algorithms. Since algorithms like merge-sort and quicksort are recursive, most of the time is spent on rather small regions of memory. Thus, either LRU or FIFO will perform well for this part of a sort-based algorithm.

- If the algorithm is hash-based, we can reduce the number of buckets if M shrinks, as long as the buckets do not then become so large that they do not fit in allotted main memory. However, unlike sort-based algorithms, we cannot respond to changes in M while the algorithm runs. Rather, once the number of buckets is chosen, it remains fixed throughout the first pass, and if buffers become unavailable, the blocks belonging to some of the buckets will have to be swapped out.

15.7.4   Exercises for Section 15.7

Exercise 15.7.1: Suppose that we wish to execute a join $R \bowtie S$, and the available memory will vary between M and $M/2$. In terms of M, $B(R)$, and $B(S)$, give the conditions under which we can guarantee that the following algorithms can be executed:

* a) A one-pass join.

* b) A two-pass, hash-based join.

  c) A two-pass, sort-based join.

! **Exercise 15.7.2:** How would the number of disk I/O's taken by a nested-loop join improve if extra buffers became available and the buffer-replacement policy were:

  a) First-in-first-out.

  b) The clock algorithm.

!! Exercise 15.7.3: In Example 15.16, we suggested that it was possible to take advantage of extra buffers becoming available during the join by keeping more than one block of R buffered and visiting the blocks of R in reverse order on even-numbered iterations of the outer loop. However, we could also maintain only one buffer for R and increase the number of buffers used for S. Which strategy yields the fewest disk I/O's?

15.8 Algorithms Using More Than Two Passes

While two passes are enough for operations on all but the largest relations, we should observe that the principal techniques discussed in Sections 15.4 and 15.5 generalize to algorithms that, by using as many passes as necessary, can process relations of arbitrary size. In this section we shall consider the generalization of both sort- and hash-based approaches.

15.8.1 Multipass Sort-Based Algorithms

In Section 11.4.5 we alluded to how the two-phase multiway merge sort could be extended to a three-pass algorithm. In fact, there is a simple recursive approach to sorting that will allow us to sort a relation, however large, completely, or if we prefer, to create n sorted sublists for any particular n.

Suppose we have M main-memory buffers available to sort a relation R, which we shall assume is stored clustered. Then do the following:

BASIS: If R fits in M blocks (i.e., $B(R) \leq M$), then read R into main memory, sort it using your favorite main-memory sorting algorithm, and write the sorted relation to disk.

INDUCTION: If R does not fit into main memory, partition the blocks holding R into M groups, which we shall call $R_1, R_2, \ldots, R_M$. Recursively sort R_i for each $i = 1, 2, \ldots, M$. Then, merge the M sorted sublists, as in Section 11.4.4.

If we are not merely sorting R, but performing a unary operation such as γ or δ on R, then we modify the above so that at the final merge we perform the operation on the tuples at the front of the sorted sublists. That is,

- For a δ, output one copy of each distinct tuple, and skip over copies of the tuple.

- For a γ, sort on the grouping attributes only, and combine the tuples with a given value of these grouping attributes in the appropriate manner, as discussed in Section 15.4.2.

When we want to perform a binary operation, such as intersection or join, we use essentially the same idea, except that the two relations are first divided into a total of M sublists. Then, each sublist is sorted by the recursive algorithm above. Finally, we read each of the M sublists, each into one buffer, and we perform the operation in the manner described by the appropriate subsection of Section 15.4.

We can divide the M buffers between relations R and S as we wish. However, to minimize the total number of passes, we would normally divide the buffers in proportion to the number of blocks taken by the relations. That is, R gets $M \times B(R)/\big(B(R) + B(S)\big)$ of the buffers, and S gets the rest.

15.8.2   Performance of Multipass, Sort-Based Algorithms

Now, let us explore the relationship between the number of disk I/O's required, the size of the relation(s) operated upon, and the size of main memory. Let $s(M, k)$ be the maximum size of a relation that we can sort using M buffers and k passes. Then we can compute $s(M, k)$ as follows:

BASIS: If $k = 1$, i.e., one pass is allowed, then we must have $B(R) \leq M$. Put another way, $s(M, 1) = M$.

INDUCTION: Suppose $k > 1$. Then we partition R into M pieces, each of which must be sortable in $k - 1$ passes. If $B(R) = s(M, k)$, then $s(M, k)/M$, which is the size of each of the M pieces of R, cannot exceed $s(M, k - 1)$. That is: $s(M, k) = M s(M, k - 1)$.

If we expand the above recursion, we find

$$s(M, k) = M s(M, k - 1) = M^2 s(M, k - 2) = \cdots = M^{k-1} s(M, 1)$$

Since $s(M, 1) = M$, we conclude that $s(M, k) = M^k$. That is, using k passes, we can sort a relation R if $B(R) \leq s(M, k)$, which says that $B(R) \leq M^k$. Put another way, if we want to sort R in k passes, then the minimum number of buffers we can use is $M = \big(B(R)\big)^{1/k}$.

Each pass of a sorting algorithm reads all the data from disk and writes it out again. Thus, a k-pass sorting algorithm requires $2kB(R)$ disk I/O's.

Now, let us consider the cost of a multipass join $R(X, Y) \bowtie S(Y, Z)$, as representative of a binary operation on relations. Let $j(M, k)$ be the largest number of blocks such that in k passes, using M buffers, we can join relations of $j(M, k)$ or fewer total blocks. That is, the join can be accomplished provided $B(R) + B(S) \leq j(M, k)$.

On the final pass, we merge M sorted sublists from the two relations. Each of the sublists is sorted using $k - 1$ passes, so they can be no longer than $s(M, k - 1) = M^{k-1}$ each, or a total of $M s(M, k - 1) = M^k$. That is, $B(R) + B(S)$ can be no larger than M^k, or put another way, $j(M, k) = M^k$. Reversing the role of the parameters, we can also state that to compute the join in k passes requires $\big(B(R) + B(S)\big)^{1/k}$ buffers.

To calculate the number of disk I/O's needed in the multipass algorithms, we should remember that, unlike for sorting, we do not count the cost of writing the final result to disk for joins or other relational operations. Thus, we use $2(k-1)\big(B(R)+B(S)\big)$ disk I/O's to sort the sublists, and another $B(R)+B(S)$

disk I/O's to read the sorted sublists in the final pass. The result is a total of $(2k - 1)\big(B(R) + B(S)\big)$ disk I/O's.

15.8.3 Multipass Hash-Based Algorithms

There is a corresponding recursive approach to using hashing for operations on large relations. We hash the relation or relations into $M - 1$ buckets, where M is the number of available memory buffers. We then apply the operation to each bucket individually, in the case of a unary operation. If the operation is binary, such as a join, we apply the operation to each pair of corresponding buckets, as if they were the entire relations. For the common relational operations we have considered — duplicate-elimination, grouping, union, intersection, difference, natural join, and equijoin — the result of the operation on the entire relation(s) will be the union of the results on the bucket(s). We can describe this approach recursively as:

BASIS: For a unary operation, if the relation fits in M buffers, read it into memory and perform the operation. For a binary operation, if either relation fits in $M - 1$ buffers, perform the operation by reading this relation into main memory and then read the second relation, one block at a time, into the Mth buffer.

INDUCTION: If no relation fits in main memory, then hash each relation into $M - 1$ buckets, as discussed in Section 15.5.1. Recursively perform the operation on each bucket or corresponding pair of buckets, and accumulate the output from each bucket or pair.

15.8.4 Performance of Multipass Hash-Based Algorithms

In what follows, we shall make the assumption that when we hash a relation, the tuples divide as evenly as possible among the buckets. In practice, this assumption will be met approximately if we choose a truly random hash function, but there will always be some unevenness in the distribution of tuples among buckets.

First, consider a unary operation, like γ or δ on a relation R using M buffers. Let $u(M, k)$ be the number of blocks in the largest relation that a k-pass hashing algorithm can handle. We can define u recursively by:

BASIS: $u(M, 1) = M$, since the relation R must fit in M buffers; i.e., $B(R) \leq M$.

INDUCTION: We assume that the first step divides the relation R into $M - 1$ buckets of equal size. Thus, we can compute $u(M, k)$ as follows. The buckets for the next pass must be sufficiently small that they can be handled in $k - 1$ passes; that is, the buckets are of size $u(M, k-1)$. Since R is divided into $M - 1$ buckets, we must have $u(M, k) = (M - 1)u(M, k - 1)$.

If we expand the recurrence above, we find that $u(M, k) = M(M - 1)^{k-1}$, or approximately, assuming M is large, $u(M, k) = M^k$. Equivalently, we can perform one of the unary relational operations on relation R in k passes with M buffers, provided $M \le (B(R))^{1/k}$.

We may perform a similar analysis for binary operations. As in Section 15.8.2, let us consider the join. Let $j(M, k)$ be an upper bound on the size of the smaller of the two relations R and S involved in $R(X, Y) \bowtie S(Y, Z)$. Here, as before, M is the number of available buffers and k is the number of passes we can use.

BASIS: $j(M, 1) = M - 1$; that is, if we use the one-pass algorithm to join, then either R or S must fit in $M - 1$ blocks, as we discussed in Section 15.2.3.

INDUCTION: $j(M, k) = (M - 1)j(M, k - 1)$; that is, on the first of k passes, we can divide each relation into $M - 1$ buckets, and we may expect each bucket to be $1/(M - 1)$ of its entire relation, but we must then be able to join each pair of corresponding buckets in $M - 1$ passes.

By expanding the recurrence for $j(M, k)$, we conclude that $j(M, k) = (M - 1)^k$. Again assuming M is large, we can say approximately $j(M, k) = M^k$. That is, we can join $R(X, Y) \bowtie S(Y, Z)$ using k passes and M buffers provided $M^k \ge \min(B(R), B(S))$.

15.8.5 Exercises for Section 15.8

Exercise 15.8.1: Suppose $B(R) = 20,000$, $B(S) = 50,000$, and $M = 101$. Describe the behavior of the following algorithms to compute $R \bowtie S$:

* a) A three-pass, sort-based algorithm.

  b) A three-pass, hash-based algorithm.

! **Exercise 15.8.2:** There are several "tricks" we have discussed for improving the performance of two-pass algorithms. For the following, tell whether the trick could be used in a multipass algorithm, and if so, how?

  a) The hybrid-hash-join trick of Section 15.5.6.

  b) Improving a sort-based algorithm by storing blocks consecutively on disk (Section 15.5.7).

  c) Improving a hash-based algorithm by storing blocks consecutively on disk (Section 15.5.7).

15.9 Parallel Algorithms for Relational Operations

Database operations, frequently being time-consuming and involving a lot of data, can generally profit from parallel processing. In this section, we shall review the principal architectures for parallel machines. We then concentrate on the "shared-nothing" architecture, which appears to be the most cost effective for database operations, although it may not be superior for other parallel applications. There are simple modifications of the standard algorithms for most relational operations that will exploit parallelism almost perfectly. That is, the time to complete an operation on a p-processor machine is about $1/p$ of the time it takes to complete the operation on a uniprocessor.

15.9.1 Models of Parallelism

At the heart of all parallel machines is a collection of processors. Often the number of processors p is large, in the hundreds or thousands. We shall assume that each processor has its own local cache, which we do not show explicitly in our diagrams. In most organizations, each processor also has local memory, which we do show. Of great importance to database processing is the fact that along with these processors are many disks, perhaps one or more per processor, or in some architectures a large collection of disks accessible to all processors directly.

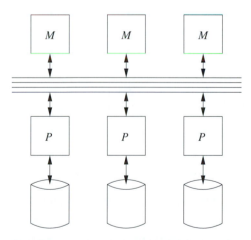

Figure 15.18: A shared-memory machine

Additionally, parallel computers all have some communications facility for passing information among processors. In our diagrams, we show the communication as if there were a shared bus for all the elements of the machine. However, in practice a bus cannot interconnect as many processors or other elements as are found in the largest machines, so the interconnection system is in many architectures a powerful switch, perhaps augmented by busses that connect subsets of the processors in local *clusters*.

The three most important classes of parallel machines are:

1. *Shared Memory.* In this architecture, illustrated in Fig. 15.18, each processor has access to all the memory of all the processors. That is, there is a single physical address space for the entire machine, rather than one address space for each processor. The diagram of Fig. 15.18 is actually too extreme, suggesting that processors have no private memory at all. Rather, each processor has some local main memory, which it typically uses whenever it can. However, it has direct access to the memory of other processors when it needs to. Large machines of this class are of the *NUMA* (nonuniform memory access) type, meaning that it takes somewhat more time for a processor to access data in a memory that "belongs" to some other processor than it does to access its "own" memory, or the memory of processors in its local cluster. However, the difference in memory-access times are not great in current architectures. Rather, all memory accesses, no matter where the data is, take much more time than a cache access, so the critical issue is whether or not the data a processor needs is in its own cache.

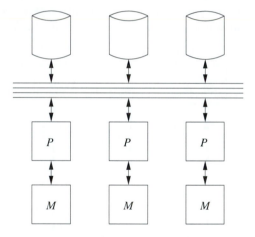

Figure 15.19: A shared-disk machine

2. *Shared Disk.* In this architecture, suggested by Fig. 15.19, every processor has its own memory, which is not accessible directly from other processors. However, the disks are accessible from any of the processors through the communication network. Disk controllers manage the potentially competing requests from different processors. The number of disks and processors need not be identical, as it might appear from Fig. 15.19.

3. *Shared Nothing.* Here, all processors have their own memory and their

own disk or disks, as in Fig. 15.20. All communication is via the communication network, from processor to processor. For example, if one processor P wants to read tuples from the disk of another processor Q, then processor P sends a message to Q asking for the data. Then, Q obtains the tuples from its disk and ships them over the network in another message, which is received by P.

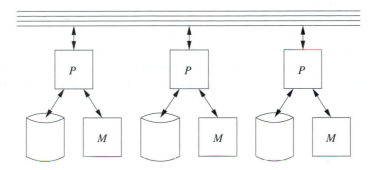

Figure 15.20: A shared-nothing machine

As we mentioned in the introduction to this section, the shared-nothing architecture is the most commonly used architecture for high-performance database systems. Shared-nothing machines are relatively inexpensive to build, but when we design algorithms for these machines we must be aware that it is costly to send data from one processor to another.

Normally, data must be sent between processors in a message, which has considerable overhead associated with it. Both processors must execute a program that supports the message transfer, and there may be contention or delays associated with the communication network as well. Typically, the cost of a message can be broken into a large fixed overhead plus a small amount of time per byte transmitted. Thus, there is a significant advantage to designing a parallel algorithm so that communications between processors involve large amounts of data sent at once. For instance, we might buffer several blocks of data at processor P, all bound for processor Q. If Q does not need the data immediately, it may be much more efficient to wait until we have a long message at P and then send it to Q.

15.9.2 Tuple-at-a-Time Operations in Parallel

Let us begin our discussion of parallel algorithms for a shared-nothing machine by considering the selection operator. First, we must consider how data is best stored. As first suggested by Section 11.5.2, it is useful to distribute our data across as many disks as possible. For convenience, we shall assume there is one disk per processor. Then if there are p processors, divide any relation R's tuples evenly among the p processor's disks.

Algorithms on Other Parallel Architectures

The shared-disk machine favors long messages, just like the shared-nothing machine does. If all communication is via a disk, then we need to move data in block-sized chunks, and if we can organize the data to be moved so it is together on one track or cylinder, then we can save much of the latency, as discussed in Section 11.5.1.

On the other hand, a shared-memory machine allows communication to occur between any two processors via the memory. There is no extensive software needed to send a message, and the cost of reading or writing main memory is proportional to the number of bytes involved. Thus, shared-memory machines can take advantage of algorithms that require fast, frequent, and short communications between processors. It is interesting that, while such algorithms are known in other domains, database processing does not seem to require such algorithms.

To compute $\sigma_C(R)$, we may use each processor to examine the tuples of R on its own disk. For each, it finds those tuples satisfying condition C and copies those to the output. To avoid communication among processors, we store those tuples t in $\sigma_C(R)$ at the same processor that has t on its disk. Thus, the result relation $\sigma_C(R)$ is divided among the processors, just like R is.

Since $\sigma_C(R)$ may be the input relation to another operation, and since we want to minimize the elapsed time and keep all the processors busy all the time, we would like $\sigma_C(R)$ to be divided evenly among the processors. If we were doing a projection, rather than a selection, then the number of tuples in $\pi_L(R)$ at each processor would be the same as the number of tuples of R at that processor. Thus, if R is distributed evenly, so would be its projection. However, a selection could radically change the distribution of tuples in the result, compared to the distribution of R.

Example 15.17 : Suppose the selection is $\sigma_{a=10}(R)$, that is, find all the tuples of R whose value in the attribute a (assumed to be one of R's attributes) is 10. Suppose also that we have divided R according to the value of the attribute a. Then all the tuples of R with $a = 10$ are at one of the processors, and the entire relation $\sigma_{a=10}(R)$ is at one processor. $\square$

To avoid the problem suggested by Example 15.17, we need to think carefully about the policy for partitioning our stored relations among the processors. Probably the best we can do is to use a hash function h that involves all the components of a tuple in such a way that changing one component of a tuple t can change $h(t)$ to be any possible bucket number.[8] For example, if we want B buckets, we might convert each component somehow to an integer between

---

[8]In particular, we do *not* want to use a partitioned hash function (which was discussed in

0 and $B - 1$, add the integers for each component, divide the result by B, and take the remainder as the bucket number. If B is also the number of processors, then we can associate each processor with a bucket and give that processor the contents of its bucket.

15.9.3   Parallel Algorithms for Full-Relation Operations

First, let us consider the operation $\delta(R)$, which is somewhat atypical of the full-relation operations. If we use a hash function to distribute the tuples of R as suggested in Section 15.9.2, then we shall place duplicate tuples of R at the same processor. If so, then we can produce $\delta(R)$ in parallel by applying a standard, uniprocessor algorithm (as in Section 15.4.1 or 15.5.2, e.g.) to the portion of R at each processor. Likewise, if we use the same hash functions to distribute the tuples of both R and S, then we can take the union, intersection, or difference of R and S by working in parallel on the portions of R and S at each processor.

However, suppose that R and S are not distributed using the same hash function, and we wish to take their union.[9] In this case, we must first make copies of all the tuples of R and S and distribute them according to a single hash function h.[10]

In parallel, we hash the tuples of R and S at each processor, using hash function h. The hashing proceeds as described in Section 15.5.1, but when the buffer corresponding to a bucket i at one processor j is filled, instead of moving it to the disk at j, we ship the contents of the buffer to processor i. If we have room for several blocks per bucket in main memory, then we may wait to fill several buffers with tuples of bucket i before shipping them to processor i.

Thus, processor i receives all the tuples of R and S that belong in bucket i. In the second stage, each processor performs the union of the tuples from R and S belonging to its bucket. As a result, the relation $R \cup S$ will be distributed over all the processors. If hash function h truly randomizes the placement of tuples in buckets, then we expect approximately the same number of tuples of $R \cup S$ to be at each processor.

The operations of intersection and difference may be performed just like a union; it does not matter whether these are set or bag versions of these operations. Moreover:

- To take a join $R(X, Y) \bowtie S(Y, Z)$, we hash the tuples of R and S to a number of buckets equal to the number of processors. However, the hash function h we use must depend only on the attributes of Y, not all the

---

Section 14.2.5), because that would place all the tuples with a given value of an attribute, say $a = 10$, among only a small subset of the buckets.

[9]In principle, this union could be either a set- or bag-union. But the simple bag-union technique from Section 15.2.3 of copying all the tuples from both arguments works in parallel, so we probably would not want to use the algorithm described here for a bag-union.

[10]If the hash function used to distribute tuples of R or S is known, we can use that hash function for the other and not distribute both relations.

attributes, so that joining tuples are always sent to the same bucket. As with union, we ship tuples of bucket i to processor i. We may then perform the join at each processor using any of the uniprocessor join algorithms we have discussed in this chapter.

- To perform grouping and aggregation $\gamma_L(R)$, we distribute the tuples of R using a hash function h that depends only on the grouping attributes in list L. If each processor has all the tuples corresponding to one of the buckets of h, then we can perform the γ_L operation on these tuples locally, using any uniprocessor γ algorithm.

15.9.4   Performance of Parallel Algorithms

Now, let us consider how the running time of a parallel algorithm on a p-processor machine compares with the time to execute an algorithm for the same operation on the same data, using a uniprocessor. The total work — disk I/O's and processor cycles — cannot be smaller for a parallel machine than a uniprocessor. However, because there are p processors working with p disks, we can expect the elapsed, or wall-clock, time to be much smaller for the multiprocessor than for the uniprocessor.

A unary operation such as $\sigma_C(R)$ can be completed in $1/p$th of the time it would take to perform the operation at a single processor, provided relation R is distributed evenly, as was supposed in Section 15.9.2. The number of disk I/O's is essentially the same as for a uniprocessor selection. The only difference is that there will, on average, be p half-full blocks of R, one at each processor, rather than a single half-full block of R had we stored all of R on one processor's disk.

Now, consider a binary operation, such as join. We use a hash function on the join attributes that sends each tuple to one of p buckets, where p is the number of processors. To send the tuples of bucket i to processor i, for all i, we must read each tuple from disk to memory, compute the hash function, and ship all tuples except the one out of p tuples that happens to belong to the bucket at its own processor. If we are computing $R(X, Y) \bowtie S(Y, Z)$, then we need to do $B(R) + B(S)$ disk I/O's to read all the tuples of R and S and determine their buckets.

We then must ship $\left(\frac{p-1}{p}\right)\big(B(R) + B(S)\big)$ blocks of data across the machine's internal interconnection network to their proper processors; only the $(1/p)$th of the tuples already at the right processor need not be shipped. The cost of shipment can be greater or less than the cost of the same number of disk I/O's, depending on the architecture of the machine. However, we shall assume that shipment across the internal network is significantly cheaper than movement of data between disk and memory, because no physical motion is involved in shipment among processors, while it is for disk I/O.

In principle, we might suppose that the receiving processor has to store the data on its own disk, then execute a local join on the tuples received. For example, if we used a two-pass sort-join at each processor, a naive parallel algorithm would use $3(B(R) + B(S))/p$ disk I/O's at each processor, since the sizes of the relations in each bucket would be approximately $B(R)/p$ and $B(S)/p$, and this type of join takes three disk I/O's per block occupied by each of the argument relations. To this cost we would add another $2(B(R) + B(S))/p$ disk I/O's per processor, to account for the first read of each tuple and the storing away of each tuple by the processor receiving the tuple during the hash and distribution of tuples. We should also add the cost of shipping the data, but we have elected to consider that cost negligible compared with the cost of disk I/O for the same data.

The above comparison demonstrates the value of the multiprocessor. While we do more disk I/O in total — five disk I/O's per block of data, rather than three — the elapsed time, as measured by the number of disk I/O's performed at each processor has gone down from $3(B(R) + B(S))$ to $5(B(R) + B(S))/p$, a significant win for large p.

Moreover, there are ways to improve the speed of the parallel algorithm so that the total number of disk I/O's is not greater than what is required for a uniprocessor algorithm. In fact, since we operate on smaller relations at each processor, we may be able to use a local join algorithm that uses fewer disk I/O's per block of data. For instance, even if R and S were so large that we need a two-pass algorithm on a uniprocessor, we may be able to use a one-pass algorithm on $(1/p)$th of the data.

We can avoid two disk I/O's per block if, when we ship a block to the processor of its bucket, that processor can use the block immediately as part of its join algorithm. Most of the algorithms known for join and the other relational operators allow this use, in which case the parallel algorithm looks just like a multipass algorithm in which the first pass uses the hashing technique of Section 15.8.3.

Example 15.18: Consider our running example $R(X, Y) \bowtie S(Y, Z)$, where R and S occupy 1000 and 500 blocks, respectively. Now, let there be 101 buffers at each processor of a 10-processor machine. Also, assume that R and S are distributed uniformly among these 10 processors.

We begin by hashing each tuple of R and S to one of 10 "buckets," using a hash function h that depends only on the join attributes Y. These 10 "buckets" represent the 10 processors, and tuples are shipped to the processor corresponding to their "bucket." The total number of disk I/O's needed to read the tuples of R and S is 1500, or 150 per processor. Each processor will have about 15 blocks worth of data for each other processor, so it ships 135 blocks to the other nine processors. The total communication is thus 1350 blocks.

We shall arrange that the processors ship the tuples of S before the tuples of R. Since each processor receives about 50 blocks of tuples from S, it can store those tuples in a main-memory data structure, using 50 of its 101 buffers. Then, when processors start sending R-tuples, each one is compared with the local S-tuples, and any resulting joined tuples are output.

Biiig Mistake

When using hash-based algorithms to distribute relations among processors and to execute operations, as in Example 15.18, we must be careful not to overuse one hash function. For instance, suppose we used a hash function h to hash the tuples of relations R and S among processors, in order to take their join. We might be tempted to use h to hash the tuples of S locally into buckets as we perform a one-pass hash-join at each processor. But if we do so, all those tuples will go to the same bucket, and the main-memory join suggested in Example 15.18 will be extremely inefficient.

In this way, the only cost of the join is 1500 disk I/O's, much less than for any other method discussed in this chapter. Moreover, the elapsed time is primarily the 150 disk I/O's performed at each processor, plus the time to ship tuples between processors and perform the main-memory computations. Note that 150 disk I/O's is less than 1/10th of the time to perform the same algorithm on a uniprocessor; we have not only gained because we had 10 processors working for us, but the fact that there are a total of 1010 buffers among those 10 processors gives us additional efficiency.

Of course, one might argue that had there been 1010 buffers at a single processor, then our example join could have been done in one pass, using 1500 disk I/O's. However, since multiprocessors usually have memory in proportion to the number of processors, we have only exploited two advantages of multiprocessing simultaneously to get two independent speedups: one in proportion to the number of processors and one because the extra memory allows us to use a more efficient algorithm.   □

15.9.5 Exercises for Section 15.9

Exercise 15.9.1: Suppose that a disk I/O takes 100 milliseconds. Let $B(R) = 100$, so the disk I/O's for computing $\sigma_C(R)$ on a uniprocessor machine will take about 10 seconds. What is the speedup if this selection is executed on a parallel machine with p processors, where: *a) $p = 8$ b) $p = 100$ c) $p = 1000$.

! **Exercise 15.9.2:** In Example 15.18 we described an algorithm that computed the join $R \bowtie S$ in parallel by first hash-distributing the tuples among the processors and then performing a one-pass join at the processors. In terms of $B(R)$ and $B(S)$, the sizes of the relations involved, p (the number of processors), and M (the number of blocks of main memory at each processor), give the condition under which this algorithm can be executed successfully.

15.10   Summary of Chapter 15

◆ *Query Processing*: Queries are compiled, which involves extensive optimization, and then executed. The study of query execution involves knowing methods for executing operations of relational algebra with some extensions to match the capabilities of SQL.

◆ *Query Plans*: Queries are compiled first into logical query plans, which are often like expressions of relational algebra, and then converted to a physical query plan by selecting an implementation for each operator, ordering joins and making other decisions, as will be discussed in Chapter 16.

◆ *Table Scanning*: To access the tuples of a relation, there are several possible physical operators. The table-scan operator simply reads each block holding tuples of the relation. Index-scan uses an index to find tuples, and sort-scan produces the tuples in sorted order.

◆ *Cost Measures for Physical Operators*: Commonly, the number of disk I/O's taken to execute an operation is the dominant component of the time. In our model, we count only disk I/O time, and we charge for the time and space needed to read arguments, but not to write the result.

◆ *Iterators*: Several operations involved in the execution of a query can be meshed conveniently if we think of their execution as performed by an iterator. This mechanism consists of three functions, to open the construction of a relation, to produce the next tuple of the relation, and to close the construction.

◆ *One-Pass Algorithms*: As long as one of the arguments of a relational-algebra operator can fit in main memory, we can execute the operator by reading the smaller relation to memory, and reading the other argument one block at a time.

◆ *Nested-Loop Join*: This simple join algorithm works even when neither argument fits in main memory. It reads as much as it can of the smaller relation into memory, and compares that with the entire other argument; this process is repeated until all of the smaller relation has had its turn in memory.

◆ *Two-Pass Algorithms*: Except for nested-loop join, most algorithms for arguments that are too large to fit into memory are either sort-based, hash-based, or index-based.

◆ *Sort-Based Algorithms*: These partition their argument(s) into main-memory-sized, sorted sublists. The sorted sublists are then merged appropriately to produce the desired result.

- ✦ *Hash-Based Algorithms*: These use a hash function to partition the argument(s) into buckets. The operation is then applied to the buckets individually (for a unary operation) or in pairs (for a binary operation).

- ✦ *Hashing Versus Sorting*: Hash-based algorithms are often superior to sort-based algorithms, since they require only one of their arguments to be "small." Sort-based algorithms, on the other hand, work well when there is another reason to keep some of the data sorted.

- ✦ *Index-Based Algorithms*: The use of an index is an excellent way to speed up a selection whose condition equates the indexed attribute to a constant. Index-based joins are also excellent when one of the relations is small, and the other has an index on the join attribute(s).

- ✦ *The Buffer Manager*: The availability of blocks of memory is controlled by the buffer manager. When a new buffer is needed in memory, the buffer manager uses one of the familiar replacement policies, such as least-recently-used, to decide which buffer is returned to disk.

- ✦ *Coping With Variable Numbers of Buffers*: Often, the number of main-memory buffers available to an operation cannot be predicted in advance. If so, the algorithm used to implement an operation needs to degrade gracefully as the number of available buffers shrinks.

- ✦ *Multipass Algorithms*: The two-pass algorithms based on sorting or hashing have natural recursive analogs that take three or more passes and will work for larger amounts of data.

- ✦ *Parallel Machines*: Today's parallel machines can be characterized as shared-memory, shared-disk, or shared-nothing. For database applications, the shared-nothing architecture is generally the most cost-effective.

- ✦ *Parallel Algorithms*: The operations of relational algebra can generally be sped up on a parallel machine by a factor close to the number of processors. The preferred algorithms start by hashing the data to buckets that correspond to the processors, and shipping data to the appropriate processor. Each processor then performs the operation on its local data.

15.11   References for Chapter 15

Two surveys of query optimization are [6] and [2]. [8] is a survey of distributed query optimization.

An early study of join methods is in [5]. Buffer-pool management was analyzed, surveyed, and improved by [3].

The use of sort-based techniques was pioneered by [1]. The advantage of hash-based algorithms for join was expressed by [7] and [4]; the latter is the origin of the hybrid hash-join. The use of hashing in parallel join and other operations has been proposed several times. The earliest source we know of is [9].

1. M. W. Blasgen and K. P. Eswaran, "Storage access in relational databases," *IBM Systems J.* **16**:4 (1977), pp. 363–378.

2. S. Chaudhuri, "An overview of query optimization in relational systems," *Proc. Seventeenth Annual ACM Symposium on Principles of Database Systems*, pp. 34–43, June, 1998.

3. H.-T. Chou and D. J. DeWitt, "An evaluation of buffer management strategies for relational database systems," *Proc. Intl. Conf. on Very Large Databases* (1985), pp. 127–141.

4. D. J. DeWitt, R. H. Katz, F. Olken, L. D. Shapiro, M. Stonebraker, and D. Wood, "Implementation techniques for main-memory database systems," *Proc. ACM SIGMOD Intl. Conf. on Management of Data* (1984), pp. 1–8.

5. L. R. Gotlieb, "Computing joins of relations," *Proc. ACM SIGMOD Intl. Conf. on Management of Data* (1975), pp. 55–63.

6. G. Graefe, "Query evaluation techniques for large databases," *Computing Surveys* **25**:2 (June, 1993), pp. 73–170.

7. M. Kitsuregawa, H. Tanaka, and T. Moto-oka, "Application of hash to data base machine and its architecture," *New Generation Computing* **1**:1 (1983), pp. 66–74.

8. D. Kossman, "The state of the art in distributed query processing," *Computing Surveys* **32**:4 (Dec., 2000), pp. 422–469.

9. D. E. Shaw, "Knowledge-based retrieval on a relational database machine," Ph. D. thesis, Dept. of CS, Stanford Univ. (1980).

Chapter 16

The Query Compiler

Having seen the basic algorithms for executing physical-query-plan operators in Chapter 15, we shall now take up the architecture of the query compiler and its optimizer. As we noted in Fig. 15.2, there are three broad steps that the query processor must take:

1. The query, written in a language like SQL, is *parsed*, that is, turned into a parse tree representing the structure of the query in a useful way.

2. The parse tree is transformed into an expression tree of relational algebra (or a similar notation), which we term a *logical query plan*.

3. The logical query plan must be turned into a *physical query plan*, which indicates not only the operations performed, but the order in which they are performed, the algorithm used to perform each step, and the ways in which stored data is obtained and data is passed from one operation to another.

The first step, parsing, is the subject of Section 16.1. The result of this step is a parse tree for the query. The other two steps involve a number of choices. In picking a logical query plan, we have opportunities to apply many different algebraic operations, with the goal of producing the best logical query plan. Section 16.2 discusses the algebraic laws for relational algebra in the abstract. Then, Section 16.3 discusses the conversion of parse trees to initial logical query plans and shows how the algebraic laws from Section 16.2 can be used in strategies to improve the initial logical plan.

When producing a physical query plan from a logical plan, we must evaluate the predicted cost of each possible option. Cost estimation is a science of its own, which we discuss in Section 16.4. We show how to use cost estimates to evaluate plans in Section 16.5, and the special problems that come up when we order the joins of several relations are the subject of Section 16.6. Finally, Section 16.7 covers additional issues and strategies for selecting the physical query plan: algorithm choice and pipelining versus materialization.

16.1   Parsing

The first stages of query compilation are illustrated in Fig. 16.1. The four boxes
in that figure correspond to the first two stages of Fig. 15.2. We have isolated a
"preprocessing" step, which we shall discuss in Section 16.1.3, between parsing
and conversion to the initial logical query plan.

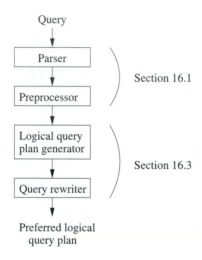

Figure 16.1: From a query to a logical query plan

In this section, we discuss parsing of SQL and give rudiments of a grammar
that can be used for that language. Section 16.2 is a digression from the line
of query-compilation steps, where we consider extensively the various laws or
transformations that apply to expressions of relational algebra. In Section 16.3,
we resume the query-compilation story. First, we consider how a parse tree
is turned into an expression of relational algebra, which becomes our initial
logical query plan. Then, we consider ways in which certain transformations
of Section 16.2 can be applied in order to improve the query plan, rather than
simply to change the plan into an equivalent plan of ambiguous merit.

16.1.1   Syntax Analysis and Parse Trees

The job of the parser is to take text written in a language such as SQL and
convert it to a *parse tree*, which is a tree whose nodes correspond to either:

1. *Atoms*, which are lexical elements such as keywords (e.g., SELECT), names
    of attributes or relations, constants, parentheses, operators such as + or
    <, and other schema elements, or

2. *Syntactic categories*, which are names for families of query subparts that
    all play a similar role in a query. We shall represent syntactic categories

by triangular brackets around a descriptive name. For example, <SFW> will be used to represent any query in the common select-from-where form, and <Condition> will represent any expression that is a condition; i.e., it can follow `WHERE` in SQL.

If a node is an atom, then it has no children. However, if the node is a syntactic category, then its children are described by one of the *rules* of the grammar for the language. We shall present these ideas by example. The details of how one designs grammars for a language, and how one "parses," i.e., turns a program or query into the correct parse tree, is properly the subject of a course on compiling.[1]

16.1.2 A Grammar for a Simple Subset of SQL

We shall illustrate the parsing process by giving some rules that could be used for a query language that is a subset of SQL. We shall include some remarks about what additional rules would be necessary to produce a complete grammar for SQL.

Queries

The syntactic category <Query> is intended to represent all well-formed queries of SQL. Some of its rules are:

```
<Query> ::= <SFW>
<Query> ::= ( <Query> )
```

Note that we use the symbol `::=` conventionally to mean "can be expressed as." The first of these rules says that a query can be a select-from-where form; we shall see the rules that describe <SFW> next. The second rule says that a query can be a pair of parentheses surrounding another query. In a full SQL grammar, we would also need rules that allowed a query to be a single relation or an expression involving relations and operations of various types, such as `UNION` and `JOIN`.

Select-From-Where Forms

We give the syntactic category <SFW> one rule:

```
<SFW> ::= SELECT <SelList> FROM <FromList> WHERE <Condition>
```

---

[1]Those unfamiliar with the subject may wish to examine A. V. Aho, R. Sethi, and J. D. Ullman, *Compilers: Principles, Techniques, and Tools*, Addison-Wesley, Reading MA, 1986, although the examples of Section 16.1.2 should be sufficient to place parsing in the context of the query processor.

This rule allows a limited form of SQL query. It does not provide for the various optional clauses such as GROUP BY, HAVING, or ORDER BY, nor for options such as DISTINCT after SELECT. Remember that a real SQL grammar would have a much more complex structure for select-from-where queries.

Note our convention that keywords are capitalized. The syntactic categories <SelList> and <FromList> represent lists that can follow SELECT and FROM, respectively. We shall describe limited forms of such lists shortly. The syntactic category <Condition> represents SQL conditions (expressions that are either true or false); we shall give some simplified rules for this category later.

Select-Lists

```
<SelList> ::= <Attribute> , <SelList>
<SelList> ::= <Attribute>
```

These two rules say that a select-list can be any comma-separated list of attributes: either a single attribute or an attribute, a comma, and any list of one or more attributes. Note that in a full SQL grammar we would also need provision for expressions and aggregation functions in the select-list and for aliasing of attributes and expressions.

From-Lists

```
<FromList> ::= <Relation> , <FromList>
<FromList> ::= <Relation>
```

Here, a from-list is defined to be any comma-separated list of relations. For simplification, we omit the possibility that elements of a from-list can be expressions, e.g., R JOIN S, or even a select-from-where expression. Likewise, a full SQL grammar would have to provide for aliasing of relations mentioned in the from-list; here, we do not allow a relation to be followed by the name of a tuple variable representing that relation.

Conditions

The rules we shall use are:

```
<Condition> ::= <Condition> AND <Condition>
<Condition> ::= <Tuple> IN <Query>
<Condition> ::= <Attribute> = <Attribute>
<Condition> ::= <Attribute> LIKE <Pattern>
```

Although we have listed more rules for conditions than for other categories, these rules only scratch the surface of the forms of conditions. We have omitted rules introducing operators OR, NOT, and EXISTS, comparisons other than equality and LIKE, constant operands, and a number of other structures that are needed in a full SQL grammar. In addition, although there are several forms that a tuple may take, we shall introduce only the one rule for syntactic category <Tuple> that says a tuple can be a single attribute:

```
<Tuple> ::= <Attribute>
```

Base Syntactic Categories

Syntactic categories <Attribute>, <Relation>, and <Pattern> are special, in that they are not defined by grammatical rules, but by rules about the atoms for which they can stand. For example, in a parse tree, the one child of <Attribute> can be any string of characters that identifies an attribute in whatever database schema the query is issued. Similarly, <Relation> can be replaced by any string of characters that makes sense as a relation in the current schema, and <Pattern> can be replaced by any quoted string that is a legal SQL pattern.

Example 16.1 : Our study of the parsing and query rewriting phase will center around two versions of a query about relations of the running movies example:

```
StarsIn(movieTitle, movieYear, starName)
MovieStar(name, address, gender, birthdate)
```

Both variations of the query ask for the titles of movies that have at least one star born in 1960. We identify stars born in 1960 by asking if their birthdate (an SQL string) ends in '1960', using the LIKE operator.

One way to ask this query is to construct the set of names of those stars born in 1960 as a subquery, and ask about each StarsIn tuple whether the starName in that tuple is a member of the set returned by this subquery. The SQL for this variation of the query is shown in Fig. 16.2.

```
SELECT movieTitle
FROM StarsIn
WHERE starName IN (
    SELECT name
    FROM MovieStar
    WHERE birthdate LIKE '%1960'
);
```

Figure 16.2: Find the movies with stars born in 1960

The parse tree for the query of Fig. 16.2, according to the grammar we have sketched, is shown in Fig. 16.3. At the root is the syntactic category <Query>, as must be the case for any parse tree of a query. Working down the tree, we see that this query is a select-from-where form; the select-list consists of only the attribute title, and the from-list is only the one relation StarsIn.

Figure 16.3: The parse tree for Fig. 16.2

The condition in the outer WHERE-clause is more complex. It has the form of tuple-IN-query, and the query itself is a parenthesized subquery, since all subqueries must be surrounded by parentheses in SQL. The subquery itself is another select-from-where form, with its own singleton select- and from-lists and a simple condition involving a LIKE operator. □

Example 16.2: Now, let us consider another version of the query of Fig. 16.2, this time without using a subquery. We may instead equijoin the relations StarsIn and MovieStar, using the condition starName = name, to require that the star mentioned in both relations be the same. Note that starName is an attribute of relation StarsIn, while name is an attribute of MovieStar. This form of the query of Fig. 16.2 is shown in Fig. 16.4.[2]

The parse tree for Fig. 16.4 is seen in Fig. 16.5. Many of the rules used in this parse tree are the same as in Fig. 16.3. However, notice how a from-list with more than one relation is expressed in the tree, and also observe how a condition can be several smaller conditions connected by an operator, AND in this case. □

---

[2]There is a small difference between the two queries in that Fig. 16.4 can produce duplicates if a movie has more than one star born in 1960. Strictly speaking, we should add DISTINCT to Fig. 16.4, but our example grammar was simplified to the extent of omitting that option.

```
SELECT movieTitle
FROM StarsIn, MovieStar
WHERE starName = name AND
      birthdate LIKE '%1960';
```

Figure 16.4: Another way to ask for the movies with stars born in 1960

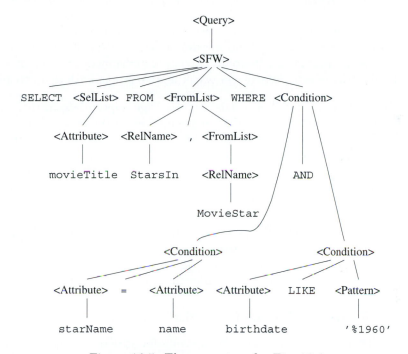

Figure 16.5: The parse tree for Fig. 16.4

16.1.3 The Preprocessor

What we termed the *preprocessor* in Fig. 16.1 has several important functions. If a relation used in the query is actually a view, then each use of this relation in the from-list must be replaced by a parse tree that describes the view. This parse tree is obtained from the definition of the view, which is essentially a query.

The preprocessor is also responsible for *semantic checking*. Even if the query is valid syntactically, it actually may violate one or more semantic rules on the use of names. For instance, the preprocessor must:

1. *Check relation uses.* Every relation mentioned in a FROM-clause must be a relation or view in the schema against which the query is executed. For instance, the preprocessor applied to the parse tree of Fig. 16.3 will

check that the two relations `StarsIn` and `MovieStar`, mentioned in the two from-lists, are legitimate relations in the schema.

2. *Check and resolve attribute uses.* Every attribute that is mentioned in the `SELECT`- or `WHERE`-clause must be an attribute of some relation in the current scope; if not, the parser must signal an error. For instance, attribute `title` in the first select-list of Fig. 16.3 is in the scope of only relation `StarsIn`. Fortunately, `title` is an attribute of `StarsIn`, so the preprocessor validates this use of `title`. The typical query processor would at this point *resolve* each attribute by attaching to it the relation to which it refers, if that relation was not attached explicitly in the query (e.g., `StarsIn.title`). It would also check ambiguity, signaling an error if the attribute is in the scope of two or more relations with that attribute.

3. *Check types.* All attributes must be of a type appropriate to their uses. For instance, `birthdate` in Fig. 16.3 is used in a `LIKE` comparison, which requires that `birthdate` be a string or a type that can be coerced to a string. Since `birthdate` is a date, and dates in SQL can normally be treated as strings, this use of an attribute is validated. Likewise, operators are checked to see that they apply to values of appropriate and compatible types.

If the parse tree passes all these tests, then it is said to be *valid*, and the tree, modified by possible view expansion, and with attribute uses resolved, is given to the logical query-plan generator. If the parse tree is not valid, then an appropriate diagnostic is issued, and no further processing occurs.

16.1.4 Exercises for Section 16.1

Exercise 16.1.1: Add to or modify the rules for <SFW> to include simple versions of the following features of SQL select-from-where expressions:

* a) The ability to produce a set with the `DISTINCT` keyword.

  b) A `GROUP BY` clause and a `HAVING` clause.

  c) Sorted output with the `ORDER BY` clause.

  d) A query with no where-clause.

Exercise 16.1.2: Add to the rules for <Condition> to allow the following features of SQL conditionals:

* a) Logical operators OR and NOT.

  b) Comparisons other than =.

  c) Parenthesized conditions.

    d) `EXISTS` expressions.

Exercise 16.1.3: Using the simple SQL grammar exhibited in this section, give parse trees for the following queries about relations $R(a, b)$ and $S(b, c)$:

a)   `SELECT a, c FROM R, S WHERE R.b = S.b;`

b)   `SELECT a FROM R WHERE b IN`
           `(SELECT a FROM R, S WHERE R.b = S.b);`

16.2   Algebraic Laws for Improving Query Plans

We resume our discussion of the query compiler in Section 16.3, where we first transform the parse tree into an expression that is wholly or mostly operators of the extended relational algebra from Sections 5.2 and 5.4. Also in Section 16.3, we see how to apply heuristics that we hope will improve the algebraic expression of the query, using some of the many algebraic laws that hold for relational algebra. As a preliminary, this section catalogs algebraic laws that turn one expression tree into an equivalent expression tree that may have a more efficient physical query plan.

    The result of applying these algebraic transformations is the logical query plan that is the output of the query-rewrite phase. The logical query plan is then converted to a physical query plan, as the optimizer makes a series of decisions about implementation of operators. Physical query-plan generation is taken up starting with Section 16.4. An alternative (not much used in practice) is for the query-rewrite phase to generate several good logical plans, and for physical plans generated from each of these to be considered when choosing the best overall physical plan.

16.2.1   Commutative and Associative Laws

The most common algebraic laws, used for simplifying expressions of all kinds, are commutative and associative laws. A *commutative law* about an operator says that it does not matter in which order you present the arguments of the operator; the result will be the same. For instance, $+$ and $\times$ are commutative operators of arithmetic. More precisely, $x + y = y + x$ and $x \times y = y \times x$ for any numbers x and y. On the other hand, $-$ is not a commutative arithmetic operator: $x - y \neq y - x$.

    An *associative law* about an operator says that we may group two uses of the operator either from the left or the right. For instance, $+$ and $\times$ are associative arithmetic operators, meaning that $(x + y) + z = x + (y + z)$ and $(x \times y) \times z = x \times (y \times z)$. On the other hand, $-$ is not associative: $(x - y) - z \neq x - (y - z)$. When an operator is both associative and commutative, then any number of operands connected by this operator can be grouped and ordered as we wish without changing the result. For example, $\big((w + x) + y\big) + z = (y + x) + (z + w)$.

Several of the operators of relational algebra are both associative and commutative. Particularly:

- $R \times S = S \times R$; $(R \times S) \times T = R \times (S \times T)$.

- $R \bowtie S = S \bowtie R$; $(R \bowtie S) \bowtie T = R \bowtie (S \bowtie T)$.

- $R \cup S = S \cup R$; $(R \cup S) \cup T = R \cup (S \cup T)$.

- $R \cap S = S \cap R$; $(R \cap S) \cap T = R \cap (S \cap T)$.

Note that these laws hold for both sets and bags.

We shall not prove each of these laws, although we give one example of a proof, below. The general method for verifying an algebraic law involving relations is to check that every tuple produced by the expression on the left must also be produced by the expression on the right, and also that every tuple produced on the right is likewise produced on the left.

Example 16.3: Let us verify the commutative law for $\bowtie$: $R \bowtie S = S \bowtie R$. First, suppose a tuple t is in the result of $R \bowtie S$, the expression on the left. Then there must be a tuple r in R and a tuple s in S that agree with t on every attribute that each shares with t. Thus, when we evaluate the expression on the right, $S \bowtie R$, the tuples s and r will again combine to form t.

We might imagine that the order of components of t will be different on the left and right, but formally, tuples in relational algebra have no fixed order of attributes. Rather, we are free to reorder components, as long as we carry the proper attributes along in the column headers, as was discussed in Section 3.1.5.

We are not done yet with the proof. Since our relational algebra is an algebra of bags, not sets, we must also verify that if t appears n times on the left, then it appears n times on the right, and vice-versa. Suppose t appears n times on the left. Then it must be that the tuple r from R that agrees with t appears some number of times n_R, and the tuple s from S that agrees with t appears some n_S times, where $n_R n_S = n$. Then when we evaluate the expression $S \bowtie R$ on the right, we find that s appears n_S times, and r appears n_R times, so we get $n_S n_R$ copies of t, or n copies.

We are still not done. We have finished the half of the proof that says everything on the left appears on the right, but we must show that everything on the right appears on the left. Because of the obvious symmetry, the argument is essentially the same, and we shall not go through the details here. □

We did not include the theta-join among the associative-commutative operators. True, this operator is commutative:

- $R \underset{C}{\overset{\bowtie}{}} S = S \underset{C}{\overset{\bowtie}{}} R$.

Moreover, if the conditions involved make sense where they are positioned, then the theta-join is associative. However, there are examples, such as the following, where we cannot apply the associative law because the conditions do not apply to attributes of the relations being joined.

Laws for Bags and Sets Can Differ

We should be careful about trying to apply familiar laws about sets to relations that are bags. For instance, you may have learned set-theoretic laws such as $A \cap_S (B \cup_S C) = (A \cap_S B) \cup_S (A \cap_S C)$, which is formally the "distributive law of intersection over union." This law holds for sets, but not for bags.

As an example, suppose bags A, B, and C were each $\{x\}$. Then $A \cap_B (B \cup_B C) = \{x\} \cap_B \{x, x\} = \{x\}$. But $(A \cap_B B) \cup_B (A \cap_B C) = \{x\} \cup_b \{x\} = \{x, x\}$, which differs from the left-hand-side, $\{x\}$.

Example 16.4: Suppose we have three relations $R(a, b)$, $S(b, c)$, and $T(c, d)$. The expression

$$(R \underset{R.b > S.b}{\bowtie} S) \underset{a < d}{\bowtie} T$$

is transformed by a hypothetical associative law into:

$$R \underset{R.b > S.b}{\bowtie} (S \underset{a < d}{\bowtie} T)$$

However, we cannot join S and T using the condition $a < d$, because a is an attribute of neither S nor T. Thus, the associative law for theta-join cannot be applied arbitrarily. □

16.2.2 Laws Involving Selection

Selections are crucial operations from the point of view of query optimization. Since selections tend to reduce the size of relations markedly, one of the most important rules of efficient query processing is to move the selections down the tree as far as they will go without changing what the expression does. Indeed early query optimizers used variants of this transformation as their primary strategy for selecting good logical query plans. As we shall point out shortly, the transformation of "push selections down the tree" is not quite general enough, but the idea of "pushing selections" is still a major tool for the query optimizer.

In this section we shall study the laws involving the σ operator. To start, when the condition of a selection is complex (i.e., it involves conditions connected by AND or OR), it helps to break the condition into its constituent parts. The motivation is that one part, involving fewer attributes than the whole condition, may be moved to a convenient place that the entire condition cannot go. Thus, our first two laws for σ are the *splitting laws*:

- $\sigma_{C_1 \text{ AND } C_2}(R) = \sigma_{C_1}\big(\sigma_{C_2}(R)\big).$

- $\sigma_{C_1 \text{ OR } C_2}(R) = \big(\sigma_{C_1}(R)\big) \cup_S \big(\sigma_{C_2}(R)\big).$

However, the second law, for OR, works only if the relation R is a set. Notice that if R were a bag, the set-union would have the effect of eliminating duplicates incorrectly.

Notice that the order of C_1 and C_2 is flexible. For example, we could just as well have written the first law above with C_2 applied after C_1, as $\sigma_{C_2}(\sigma_{C_1}(R))$. In fact, more generally, we can swap the order of any sequence of σ operators:

- $\sigma_{C_1}(\sigma_{C_2}(R)) = \sigma_{C_2}(\sigma_{C_1}(R))$.

Example 16.5 : Let $R(a, b, c)$ be a relation. Then $\sigma_{(a=1 \text{ OR } a=3) \text{ AND } b<c}(R)$ can be split as $\sigma_{a=1 \text{ OR } a=3}(\sigma_{b<c}(R))$. We can then split this expression at the OR into $\sigma_{a=1}(\sigma_{b<c}(R)) \cup \sigma_{a=3}(\sigma_{b<c}(R))$. In this case, because it is impossible for a tuple to satisfy both $a = 1$ and $a = 3$, this transformation holds regardless of whether or not R is a set, as long as $\cup_B$ is used for the union. However, in general the splitting of an OR requires that the argument be a set and that $\cup_S$ be used.

Alternatively, we could have started to split by making $\sigma_{b<c}$ the outer operation, as $\sigma_{b<c}(\sigma_{a=1 \text{ OR } a=3}(R))$. When we then split the OR, we would get $\sigma_{b<c}(\sigma_{a=1}(R) \cup \sigma_{a=3}(R))$, an expression that is equivalent to, but somewhat different from the first expression we derived. $\square$

The next family of laws involving σ allow us to push selections through the binary operators: product, union, intersection, difference, and join. There are three types of laws, depending on whether it is optional or required to push the selection to each of the arguments:

1. For a union, the selection *must* be pushed to both arguments.

2. For a difference, the selection must be pushed to the first argument and optionally may be pushed to the second.

3. For the other operators it is only required that the selection be pushed to one argument. For joins and products, it may not make sense to push the selection to both arguments, since an argument may or may not have the attributes that the selection requires. When it is possible to push to both, it may or may not improve the plan to do so; see Exercise 16.2.1.

Thus, the law for union is:

- $\sigma_C(R \cup S) = \sigma_C(R) \cup \sigma_C(S)$.

Here, it is mandatory to move the selection down both branches of the tree.

For difference, one version of the law is:

- $\sigma_C(R - S) = \sigma_C(R) - S$.

However, it is also permissible to push the selection to both arguments, as:

- $\sigma_C(R - S) = \sigma_C(R) - \sigma_C(S)$.

The next laws allow the selection to be pushed to one or both arguments. If the selection is σ_C, then we can only push this selection to a relation that has all the attributes mentioned in C, if there is one. We shall show the laws below assuming that the relation R has all the attributes mentioned in C.

- $\sigma_C(R \times S) = \sigma_C(R) \times S$.

- $\sigma_C(R \bowtie S) = \sigma_C(R) \bowtie S$.

- $\sigma_C(R \overset{\bowtie}{_D} S) = \sigma_C(R) \overset{\bowtie}{_D} S$.

- $\sigma_C(R \cap S) = \sigma_C(R) \cap S$.

If C has only attributes of S, then we can instead write:

- $\sigma_C(R \times S) = R \times \sigma_C(S)$.

and similarly for the other three operators $\bowtie$, $\overset{\bowtie}{_D}$, and $\cap$. Should relations R and S both happen to have all attributes of C, then we can use laws such as:

- $\sigma_C(R \bowtie S) = \sigma_C(R) \bowtie \sigma_C(S)$.

Note that it is impossible for this variant to apply if the operator is $\times$ or $\overset{\bowtie}{_D}$, since in those cases R and S have no shared attributes. On the other hand, for $\cap$ the law always applies since the schemas of R and S must then be the same.

Example 16.6: Consider relations $R(a, b)$ and $S(b, c)$ and the expression

$$\sigma_{(a=1 \text{ OR } a=3) \text{ AND } b<c}(R \bowtie S)$$

The condition $b < c$ can be applied to S alone, and the condition $a = 1$ OR $a = 3$ can be applied to R alone. We thus begin by splitting the AND of the two conditions as we did in the first alternative of Example 16.5:

$$\sigma_{a=1 \text{ OR } a=3}\left(\sigma_{b<c}(R \bowtie S)\right)$$

Next, we can push the selection $\sigma_{b<c}$ to S, giving us the expression:

$$\sigma_{a=1 \text{ OR } a=3}\left(R \bowtie \sigma_{b<c}(S)\right)$$

Lastly, we push the first condition to R, yielding: $\sigma_{a=1 \text{ OR } a=3}(R) \bowtie \sigma_{b<c}(S)$. Optionally, we can split the OR of two conditions as we did in Example 16.5. However, it may or may not be advantageous to do so. $\quad\square$

Some Trivial Laws

We are not going to state every true law for the relational algebra. The reader should be alert, in particular, for laws about extreme cases: a relation that is empty, a selection or theta-join whose condition is always true or always false, or a projection onto the list of all attributes, for example. A few of the many possible special-case laws:

- Any selection on an empty relation is empty.

- If C is an always-true condition (e.g., $x > 10$ OR $x \leq 10$ on a relation that forbids $x =$ NULL), then $\sigma_C(R) = R$.

- If R is empty, then $R \cup S = S$.

16.2.3 Pushing Selections

As was illustrated in Example 6.52, pushing a selection down an expression tree — that is, replacing the left side of one of the rules in Section 16.2.2 by its right side — is one of the most powerful tools of the query optimizer. It was long assumed that we could optimize by applying the laws for σ only in that direction. However, when systems that supported the use of views became common, it was found that in some situations it was essential first to move a selection as far *up* the tree as it would go, and *then* push the selections down all possible branches. An example should illustrate the proper selection-pushing approach.

Example 16.7 : Suppose we have the relations

```
StarsIn(title, year, starName)
Movie(title, year, length, inColor, studioName, producerC#)
```

Note that we have altered the first two attributes of StarsIn from the usual movieTitle and movieYear to make this example simpler to follow. Define view MoviesOf1996 by:

```
CREATE VIEW MoviesOf1996 AS
    SELECT *
    FROM Movie
    WHERE year = 1996;
```

We can ask the query "which stars worked for which studios in 1996?" by the SQL query:

```
SELECT starName, studioName
FROM MoviesOf1996 NATURAL JOIN StarsIn;
```

The view `MoviesOf1996` is defined by the relational-algebra expression

$$\sigma_{year=1996}(\texttt{Movie})$$

Thus, the query, which is the natural join of this expression with `StarsIn`, followed by a projection onto attributes `starName` and `studioName`, has the expression, or "logical query plan," shown in Fig. 16.6.

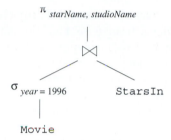

Figure 16.6: Logical query plan constructed from definition of a query and view

In this expression, the one selection is already as far down the tree as it will go, so there is no way to "push selections down the tree." However, the rule $\sigma_C(R \bowtie S) = \sigma_C(R) \bowtie S$ can be applied "backwards," to bring the selection $\sigma_{year=1996}$ above the join in Fig. 16.6. Then, since *year* is an attribute of both `Movie` and `StarsIn`, we may push the selection down to *both* children of the join node. The resulting logical query plan is shown in Fig. 16.7. It is likely to be an improvement, since we reduce the size of the relation `StarsIn` before we join it with the movies of 1996. □

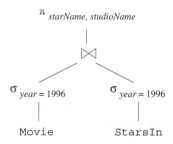

Figure 16.7: Improving the query plan by moving selections up and down the tree

16.2.4 Laws Involving Projection

Projections, like selections, can be "pushed down" through many other operators. Pushing projections differs from pushing selections in that when we push projections, it is quite usual for the projection also to remain where it is. Put another way, "pushing" projections really involves introducing a new projection somewhere below an existing projection.

Pushing projections is useful, but generally less so than pushing selections. The reason is that while selections often reduce the size of a relation by a large factor, projection keeps the number of tuples the same and only reduces the length of tuples. In fact, the extended projection operator of Section 5.4.5 can actually increase the length of tuples.

To describe the transformations of extended projection, we need to introduce some terminology. Consider a term $E \to x$ on the list for a projection, where E is an attribute or an expression involving attributes and constants. We say all attributes mentioned in E are *input* attributes of the projection, and x is an *output* attribute. If a term is a single attribute, then it is both an input and output attribute. Note that it is not possible to have an expression other than a single attribute without an arrow and renaming, so we have covered all the cases.

If a projection list consists only of attributes, with no renaming or expressions other than a single attribute, then we say the projection is *simple*. In the classical relational algebra, all projections are simple.

Example 16.8 : Projection $\pi_{a,b,c}(R)$ is simple; a, b, and c are both its input attributes and its output attributes. On the other hand, $\pi_{a+b \to x,\ c}(R)$ is not simple. It has input attributes a, b, and c, and its output attributes are x and c. $\square$

The principle behind laws for projection is that:

- We may introduce a projection anywhere in an expression tree, as long as it eliminates only attributes that are never used by any of the operators above, and are not in the result of the entire expression.

In the most basic form of these laws, the introduced projections are always simple, although other projections, such as L below, need not be.

- $\pi_L(R \bowtie S) = \pi_L\big(\pi_M(R) \bowtie \pi_N(S)\big)$, where M is the list of all attributes of R that are either join attributes (in the schema of both R and S) or are input attributes of L, and N is the list of attributes of S that are either join attributes or input attributes of L.

- $\pi_L(R \underset{C}{\bowtie} S) = \pi_L\big(\pi_M(R) \underset{C}{\bowtie} \pi_N(S)\big)$, where M is the list of all attributes of R that are either join attributes (i.e., are mentioned in condition C) or are input attributes of L, and N is the list of attributes of S that are either join attributes or input attributes of L.

- $\pi_L(R \times S) = \pi_L\big(\pi_M(R) \times \pi_N(S)\big)$, where M and N are the lists of all attributes of R and S, respectively, that are input attributes of L.

Example 16.9: Let $R(a, b, c)$ and $S(c, d, e)$ be two relations. Consider the expression $\pi_{a+e \to x,\ b \to y}(R \bowtie S)$. The input attributes of the projection are a, b, and e, and c is the only join attribute. We may apply the law for pushing projections below joins to get the equivalent expression:

$$\pi_{a+e \to x,\ b \to y}\big(\pi_{a,b,c}(R) \bowtie \pi_{c,e}(S)\big)$$

Notice that the projection $\pi_{a,b,c}(R)$ is trivial; it projects onto all the attributes of R. We may thus eliminate this projection and get a third equivalent expression: $\pi_{a+e \to x,\ b \to y}(R \bowtie \pi_{c,e}(S))$. That is, the only change from the original is that we remove the attribute d from S before the join. $\square$

In addition, we can perform a projection entirely before a bag union. That is:

- $\pi_L(R \cup_B S) = \pi_L(R) \cup_B \pi_L(S)$.

On the other hand, projections cannot be pushed below set unions or either the set or bag versions of intersection or difference at all.

Example 16.10: Let $R(a, b)$ consist of the one tuple $\{(1, 2)\}$ and $S(a, b)$ consist of the one tuple $\{(1, 3)\}$. Then $\pi_a(R \cap S) = \pi_a(\emptyset) = \emptyset$. However, $\pi_a(R) \cap \pi_a(S) = \{(1)\} \cap \{(1)\} = \{(1)\}$. $\square$

If the projection involves some computations, and the input attributes of a term on the projection list belong entirely to one of the arguments of a join or product below the projection, then we have the option, although not the obligation, to perform the computation directly on that argument. An example should help illustrate the point.

Example 16.11: Again let $R(a, b, c)$ and $S(c, d, e)$ be relations, and consider the join and projection $\pi_{a+b \to x,\ d+e \to y}(R \bowtie S)$. We can move the sum $a + b$ and its renaming to x directly onto the relation R, and move the sum $d + e$ to S similarly. The resulting equivalent expression is

$$\pi_{x,y}\big(\pi_{a+b \to x,\ c}(R) \bowtie \pi_{d+e \to y,\ c}(S)\big)$$

One special case to handle is if x or y were c. Then, we could not rename a sum to c, because a relation cannot have two attributes named c. Thus, we would have to invent a temporary name and do another renaming in the projection above the join. For example, $\pi_{a+b \to c,\ d+e \to y}(R \bowtie S)$ could become $\pi_{z \to c,\ y}\big(\pi_{a+b \to z,\ c}(R) \bowtie \pi_{d+e \to y,\ c}(S)\big)$. $\square$

It is also possible to push a projection below a selection.

- $\pi_L\big(\sigma_C(R)\big) = \pi_L\Big(\sigma_C\big(\pi_M(R)\big)\Big)$, where M is the list of all attributes that are either input attributes of L or mentioned in condition C.

As in Example 16.11, we have the option of performing computations on the list L in the list M instead, provided the condition C does not need the input attributes of L that are involved in a computation.

Often, we wish to push projections down expression trees, even if we have to leave another projection above, because projections tend to reduce the size of tuples and therefore to reduce the number of blocks occupied by an intermediate relation. However, we must be careful when doing so, because there are some common examples where pushing a projection down costs time.

Example 16.12: Consider the query asking for those stars that worked in 1996:

```
SELECT starName
FROM StarsIn
WHERE year = 1996;
```

about the relation `StarsIn(movieTitle, movieYear, starName)`. The direct translation of this query to a logical query plan is shown in Fig. 16.8.

Figure 16.8: Logical query plan for the query of Example 16.12

We can add below the selection a projection onto the attributes

1. `starName`, because that attribute is needed in the result, and

2. `movieYear`, because that attribute is needed for the selection condition.

The result is shown in Fig. 16.9.

If `StarsIn` were not a stored relation, but a relation that was constructed by another operation, such as a join, then the plan of Fig. 16.9 makes sense. We can "pipeline" the projection (see Section 16.7.3) as tuples of the join are generated, by simply dropping the useless `title` attribute.

However, in this case `StarsIn` is a stored relation. The lower projection in Fig. 16.9 could actually waste a lot of time, especially if there were an index on `movieYear`. Then a physical query plan based on the logical query plan of Fig. 16.8 would first use the index to get only those tuples of `StarsIn` that have `movieYear` equal to 1996, presumably a small fraction of the tuples. If we do

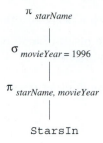

$\pi_{starName}$

$\sigma_{movieYear = 1996}$

$\pi_{starName, movieYear}$

StarsIn

Figure 16.9: Result of introducing a projection

the projection first, as in Fig. 16.9, then we have to read every tuple of StarsIn and project it. To make matters worse, the index on movieYear is probably useless in the projected relation $\pi_{starName, movieYear}(\texttt{StarsIn})$, so the selection now involves a scan of all the tuples that result from the projection. $\square$

16.2.5 Laws About Joins and Products

We saw in Section 16.2.1 many of the important laws involving joins and products: their commutative and associative laws. However, there are a few additional laws that follow directly from the definition of the join, as was mentioned in Section 5.2.10.

- $R \underset{C}{\bowtie} S = \sigma_C(R \times S)$.

- $R \bowtie S = \pi_L\big(\sigma_C(R \times S)\big)$, where C is the condition that equates each pair of attributes from R and S with the same name, and L is a list that includes one attribute from each equated pair and all the other attributes of R and S.

In practice, we usually want to apply these rules from right to left. That is, we identify a product followed by a selection as a join of some kind. The reason for doing so is that the algorithms for computing joins are generally much faster than algorithms that compute a product followed by a selection on the (very large) result of the product.

16.2.6 Laws Involving Duplicate Elimination

The operator δ, which eliminates duplicates from a bag, can be pushed through many, but not all operators. In general, moving a δ down the tree reduces the size of intermediate relations and may therefore be beneficial. Moreover, we can sometimes move the δ to a position where it can be eliminated altogether, because it is applied to a relation that is known not to possess duplicates:

- $\delta(R) = R$ if R has no duplicates. Important cases of such a relation R include

a) A stored relation with a declared primary key, and

b) A relation that is the result of a γ operation, since grouping creates a relation with no duplicates.

Several laws that "push" δ through other operators are:

- $\delta(R \times S) = \delta(R) \times \delta(S)$.

- $\delta(R \bowtie S) = \delta(R) \bowtie \delta(S)$.

- $\delta(R \underset{C}{\bowtie} S) = \delta(R) \underset{C}{\bowtie} \delta(S)$.

- $\delta\big(\sigma_C(R)\big) = \sigma_C\big(\delta(R)\big)$.

We can also move the δ to either or both of the arguments of an intersection:

- $\delta(R \cap_B S) = \delta(R) \cap_B S = R \cap_B \delta(S) = \delta(R) \cap_B \delta(S)$.

On the other hand, δ cannot be moved across the operators $\cup_B$, $-_B$, or π in general.

Example 16.13 : Let R have two copies of the tuple t and S have one copy of t. Then $\delta(R \cup_B S)$ has one copy of t, while $\delta(R) \cup_B \delta(S)$ has two copies of t. Also, $\delta(R -_B S)$ has one copy of t, while $\delta(R) -_B \delta(S)$ has no copy of t.

Now, consider relation $T(a,b)$ with one copy each of the tuples $(1,2)$ and $(1,3)$, and no other tuples. Then $\delta\big(\pi_a(T)\big)$ has one copy of the tuple (1), while $\pi_a\big(\delta(T)\big)$ has two copies of (1). $\square$

Finally, note that commuting δ with $\cup_S$, $\cap_S$, or $-_S$ makes no sense. Since producing a set is one way to guarantee there are no duplicates, we can eliminate the δ instead. For example:

- $\delta(R \cup_S S) = R \cup_S S$.

Note, however, that an implementation of $\cup_S$ or the other set operators involves a duplicate-elimination process that is tantamount to applying δ; see Section 15.2.3, for example.

16.2.7   Laws Involving Grouping and Aggregation

When we consider the operator γ, we find that the applicability of many transformations depends on the details of the aggregate operators used. Thus, we cannot state laws in the generality that we used for the other operators. One exception is the law, mentioned in Section 16.2.6, that a γ absorbs a δ. Precisely:

- $\delta\big(\gamma_L(R)\big) = \gamma_L(R)$.

Another general rule is that we may project useless attributes from the argument should we wish, prior to applying the γ operation. This law can be written:

- $\gamma_L(R) = \gamma_L\big(\pi_M(R)\big)$ if M is a list containing at least all those attributes of R that are mentioned in L.

The reason that other transformations depend on the aggregation(s) involved in a γ is that some aggregations — MIN and MAX in particular — are not affected by the presence or absence of duplicates. The other aggregations — SUM, COUNT, and AVG — generally produce different values if duplicates are eliminated prior to application of the aggregation.

Thus, let us call an operator γ_L *duplicate-impervious* if the only aggregations in L are MIN and/or MAX. Then:

- $\gamma_L(R) = \gamma_L\big(\delta(R)\big)$ provided γ_L is duplicate-impervious.

Example 16.14: Suppose we have the relations

```
MovieStar(name, addr, gender, birthdate)
StarsIn(movieTitle, movieYear, starName)
```

and we want to know for each year the birthdate of the youngest star to appear in a movie that year. We can express this query as

```
SELECT movieYear, MAX(birthdate)
FROM MovieStar, StarsIn
WHERE name = starName
GROUP BY movieYear;
```

Figure 16.10: Initial logical query plan for the query of Example 16.14

An initial logical query plan constructed directly from the query is shown in Fig. 16.10. The FROM list is expressed by a product, and the WHERE clause by a selection above it. The grouping and aggregation are expressed by the γ operator above those. Some transformations that we could apply to Fig. 16.10 if we wished are:

1. Combine the selection and product into an equijoin.

2. Generate a δ below the γ, since the γ is duplicate-impervious.

3. Generate a π between the γ and the introduced δ to project onto movie-Year and birthdate, the only attributes relevant to the γ.

The resulting plan is shown in Fig. 16.11.

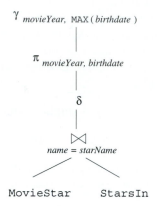

Figure 16.11: Another query plan for the query of Example 16.14

We can now push the δ below the $\bowtie$ and introduce π's below that if we wish. This new query plan is shown in Fig. 16.12. If name is a key for MovieStar, the δ can be eliminated along the branch leading to that relation. □

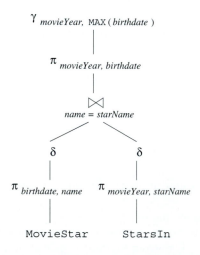

Figure 16.12: A third query plan for Example 16.14

16.2.8 Exercises for Section 16.2

* Exercise 16.2.1: When it is possible to push a selection to both arguments of a binary operator, we need to decide whether or not to do so. How would the existence of indexes on one of the arguments affect our choice? Consider, for instance, an expression $\sigma_C(R \cap S)$, where there is an index on S.

Exercise 16.2.2: Give examples to show that:

*   a) Projection cannot be pushed below set union.

   b) Projection cannot be pushed below set or bag difference.

   c) Duplicate elimination (δ) cannot be pushed below projection.

   d) Duplicate elimination cannot be pushed below bag union or difference.

! Exercise 16.2.3: Prove that we can always push a projection below both branches of a bag union.

! Exercise 16.2.4: Some laws that hold for sets hold for bags; others do not. For each of the laws below that are true for sets, tell whether or not it is true for bags. Either give a proof the law for bags is true, or give a counterexample.

*   a) $R \cup R = R$ (the idempotent law for union).

   b) $R \cap R = R$ (the idempotent law for intersection).

   c) $R - R = \emptyset$.

   d) $R \cup (S \cap T) = (R \cup S) \cap (R \cup T)$ (distribution of union over intersection).

! Exercise 16.2.5: We can define $\subseteq$ for bags by: $R \subseteq S$ if and only if for every element x, the number of times x appears in R is less than or equal to the number of times it appears in S. Tell whether the following statements (which are all true for sets) are true for bags; give either a proof or a counterexample:

   a) If $R \subseteq S$, then $R \cup S = S$.

   b) If $R \subseteq S$, then $R \cap S = R$.

   c) If $R \subseteq S$ and $S \subseteq R$, then $R = S$.

Exercise 16.2.6: Starting with an expression $\pi_L(R(a, b, c) \bowtie S(b, c, d, e))$, push the projection down as far as it can go if L is:

*   a) $b + c \to x$, $c + d \to y$.

   b) a, b, $a + d \to z$.

! **Exercise 16.2.7:** We mentioned in Example 16.14 that none of the plans we showed is necessarily the best plan. Can you think of a better plan?

! **Exercise 16.2.8:** The following are possible equalities involving operations on a relation $R(a, b)$. Tell whether or not they are true; give either a proof or a counterexample.

a) $\gamma_{MIN(a) \to y, \ x}\big(\gamma_{a, \ SUM(b) \to x}(R)\big) = \gamma_{y, SUM(b) \to x}\big(\gamma_{MIN(a) \to y, \ b}(R)\big)$.

b) $\gamma_{MIN(a) \to y, \ x}\big(\gamma_{a, \ MAX(b) \to x}(R)\big) = \gamma_{y, MAX(b) \to x}\big(\gamma_{MIN(a) \to y, \ b}(R)\big)$.

!! **Exercise 16.2.9:** The join-like operators of Exercise 15.2.4 obey some of the familiar laws, and others do not. Tell whether each of the following is or is not true. Give either a proof that the law holds or a counterexample.

* a) $\sigma_C(R \bowtie S) = \sigma_C(R) \bowtie S$.

* b) $\sigma_C(R \overset{\circ}{\bowtie} S) = \sigma_C(R) \overset{\circ}{\bowtie} S$.

c) $\sigma_C(R \overset{\circ}{\bowtie}_L S) = \sigma_C(R) \overset{\circ}{\bowtie}_L S$, where C involves only attributes of R.

d) $\sigma_C(R \overset{\circ}{\bowtie}_L S) = R \overset{\circ}{\bowtie}_L \sigma_C(S)$, where C involves only attributes of S.

e) $\pi_L(R \overline{\bowtie} S) = \pi_L(R) \overline{\bowtie} S$.

* f) $(R \overset{\circ}{\bowtie} S) \overset{\circ}{\bowtie} T = R \overset{\circ}{\bowtie} (S \overset{\circ}{\bowtie} T)$.

g) $R \overset{\circ}{\bowtie} S = S \overset{\circ}{\bowtie} R$.

h) $R \overset{\circ}{\bowtie}_L S = S \overset{\circ}{\bowtie}_L R$.

i) $R \bowtie S = S \bowtie R$.

16.3 From Parse Trees to Logical Query Plans

We now resume our discussion of the query compiler. Having constructed a parse tree for a query in Section 16.1, we next need to turn the parse tree into the preferred logical query plan. There are two steps, as was suggested in Fig. 16.1.

The first step is to replace the nodes and structures of the parse tree, in appropriate groups, by an operator or operators of relational algebra. We shall suggest some of these rules and leave some others for exercises. The second step is to take the relational-algebra expression produced by the first step and to turn it into an expression that we expect can be converted to the most efficient physical query plan.

16.3.1 Conversion to Relational Algebra

We shall now describe informally some rules for transforming SQL parse trees to algebraic logical query plans. The first rule, perhaps the most important, allows us to convert all "simple" select-from-where constructs to relational algebra directly. Its informal statement:

- If we have a <Query> that is a <SFW> construct, and the <Condition> in this construct has no subqueries, then we may replace the entire construct — the select-list, from-list, and condition — by a relational-algebra expression consisting, from bottom to top, of:

  1. The product of all the relations mentioned in the <FromList>, which is the argument of:

  2. A selection σ_C, where C is the <Condition> expression in the construct being replaced, which in turn is the argument of:

  3. A projection π_L, where L is the list of attributes in the <SelList>.

Example 16.15: Let us consider the parse tree of Fig. 16.5. The select-from-where transformation applies to the entire tree of Fig. 16.5. We take the product of the two relations `StarsIn` and `MovieStar` of the from-list, select for the condition in the subtree rooted at <Condition>, and project onto the select-list, `movieTitle`. The resulting relational-algebra expression is Fig. 16.13.

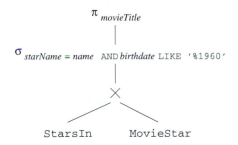

Figure 16.13: Translation of a parse tree to an algebraic expression tree

The same transformation does not apply to the outer query of Fig. 16.3. The reason is that the condition involves a subquery. We shall discuss in Section 16.3.2 how to deal with conditions that have subqueries, and you should examine the box on "Limitations on Selection Conditions" for an explanation of why we make the distinction between conditions that have subqueries and those that do not.

However, we could apply the select-from-where rule to the subquery in Fig. 16.3. The expression of relational algebra that we get from the subquery is $\pi_{name}\left(\sigma_{birthdate \text{ LIKE } '\%1960'}(\texttt{MovieStar})\right)$. $\square$

Limitations on Selection Conditions

One might wonder why we do not allow C, in a selection operator σ_C, to involve a subquery. It is conventional in relational algebra for the *arguments* of an operator — the elements that do not appear in subscripts — to be expressions that yield relations. On the other hand, *parameters* — the elements that appear in subscripts — have a type other than relations. For instance, parameter C in σ_C is a boolean-valued condition, and parameter L in π_L is a list of attributes or formulas.

If we follow this convention, then whatever calculation is implied by a parameter can be applied to each tuple of the relation argument(s). That limitation on the use of parameters simplifies query optimization. Suppose, in contrast, that we allowed an operator like $\sigma_C(R)$, where C involves a subquery. Then the application of C to each tuple of R involves computing the subquery. Do we compute it anew for every tuple of R? That would be unnecessarily expensive, unless the subquery were *correlated*, i.e., its value depends on something defined outside the query, as the subquery of Fig. 16.3 depends on the value of `starName`. Even correlated subqueries can be evaluated without recomputation for each tuple, in most cases, provided we organize the computation correctly.

16.3.2   Removing Subqueries From Conditions

For parse trees with a <Condition> that has a subquery, we shall introduce an intermediate form of operator, between the syntactic categories of the parse tree and the relational-algebra operators that apply to relations. This operator is often called *two-argument selection*. We shall represent a two-argument selection in a transformed parse tree by a node labeled σ, with no parameter. Below this node is a left child that represents the relation R upon which the selection is being performed, and a right child that is an expression for the condition applied to each tuple of R. Both arguments may be represented as parse trees, as expression trees, or as a mixture of the two.

Example 16.16: In Fig. 16.14 is a rewriting of the parse tree of Fig. 16.3 that uses a two-argument selection. Several transformations have been made to construct Fig. 16.14 from Fig. 16.3:

1. The subquery in Fig. 16.3 has been replaced by an expression of relational algebra, as discussed at the end of Example 16.15.

2. The outer query has also been replaced, using the rule for select-from-where expressions from Section 16.3.1. However, we have expressed the necessary selection as a two-argument selection, rather than by the conventional σ operator of relational algebra. As a result, the upper node of

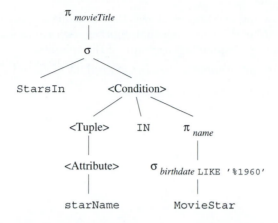

Figure 16.14: An expression using a two-argument σ, midway between a parse tree and relational algebra

the parse tree labeled <Condition> has not been replaced, but remains as an argument of the selection, with part of *its* expression replaced by relational algebra, per point (1).

This tree needs further transformation, which we discuss next. □

We need rules that allow us to replace a two-argument selection by a one-argument selection and other operators of relational algebra. Each form of condition may require its own rule. In common situations, it is possible to remove the two-argument selection and reach an expression that is pure relational algebra. However, in extreme cases, the two-argument selection can be left in place and considered part of the logical query plan.

We shall give, as an example, the rule that lets us deal with the condition in Fig. 16.14 involving the IN operator. Note that the subquery in this condition is uncorrelated; that is, the subquery's relation can be computed once and for all, independent of the tuple being tested. The rule for eliminating such a condition is stated informally as follows:

- Suppose we have a two-argument selection in which the first argument represents some relation R and the second argument is a <Condition> of the form t IN S, where expression S is an uncorrelated subquery, and t is a tuple composed of (some) attributes of R. We transform the tree as follows:

  a) Replace the <Condition> by the tree that is the expression for S. If S may have duplicates, then it is necessary to include a δ operation at the root of the expression for S, so the expression being formed does not produce more copies of tuples than the original query does.

   b) Replace the two-argument selection by a one-argument selection σ_C, where C is the condition that equates each component of the tuple t to the corresponding attribute of the relation S.

   c) Give σ_C an argument that is the product of R and S.

Figure 16.15 illustrates this transformation.

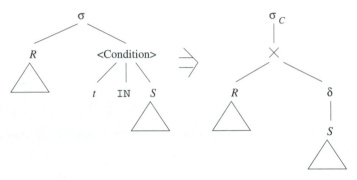

Figure 16.15: This rule handles a two-argument selection with a condition involving IN

Example 16.17 : Consider the tree of Fig. 16.14, to which we shall apply the rule for IN conditions described above. In this figure, relation R is StarsIn, and relation S is the result of the relational-algebra expression consisting of the subtree rooted at π_{name}. The tuple t has one component, the attribute starName.

    The two-argument selection is replaced by $\sigma_{starName=name}$; its condition C equates the one component of tuple t to the attribute of the result of query S. The child of the σ node is a $\times$ node, and the arguments of the $\times$ node are the node labeled StarsIn and the root of the expression for S. Notice that, because name is the key for MovieStar, there is no need to introduce a duplicate-eliminating δ in the expression for S. The new expression is shown in Fig. 16.16. It is completely in relational algebra, and is equivalent to the expression of Fig. 16.13, although its structure is quite different. □

    The strategy for translating subqueries to relational algebra is more complex when the subquery is correlated. Since correlated subqueries involve unknown values defined outside themselves, they cannot be translated in isolation. Rather, we need to translate the subquery so that it produces a relation in which certain extra attributes appear — the attributes that must later be compared with the externally defined attributes. The conditions that relate attributes from the subquery to attributes outside are then applied to this relation, and the extra attributes that are no longer necessary can then be projected out. During this process, we must be careful about accidentally introducing duplicate tuples, if the query does not eliminate duplicates at the end. The following example illustrates this technique.

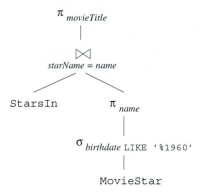

Figure 16.16: Applying the rule for IN conditions

```
SELECT DISTINCT m1.movieTitle, m1.movieYear
FROM StarsIn m1
WHERE m1.movieYear - 40 <= (
    SELECT AVG(birthdate)
    FROM StarsIn m2, MovieStar s
    WHERE m2.starName = s.name AND
        m1.movieTitle = m2.movieTitle AND
        m1.movieYear = m2.movieYear
);
```

Figure 16.17: Finding movies with high average star age

Example 16.18: Figure 16.17 is an SQL rendition of the query: "find the movies where the average age of the stars was at most 40 when the movie was made." To simplify, we treat `birthdate` as a birth year, so we can take its average and get a value that can be compared with the `movieYear` attribute of `StarsIn`. We have also written the query so that each of the three references to relations has its own tuple variable, in order to help remind us where the various attributes come from.

Fig. 16.18 shows the result of parsing the query and performing a partial translation to relational algebra. During this initial translation, we split the WHERE-clause of the subquery in two, and used part of it to convert the product of relations to an equijoin. We have retained the aliases m1, m2, and s in the nodes of this tree, in order to make clearer the origin of each attribute. Alternatively, we could have used projections to rename attributes and thus avoid conflicting attribute names, but the result would be harder to follow.

In order to remove the <Condition> node and eliminate the two-argument σ, we need to create an expression that describes the relation in the right branch of the <Condition>. However, because the subquery is correlated, there

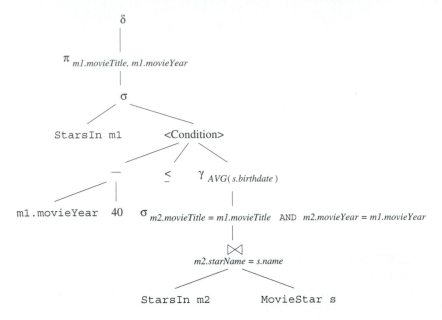

Figure 16.18: Partially transformed parse tree for Fig. 16.17

is no way to obtain the attributes `m1.movieTitle` or `m1.movieYear` from the relations mentioned in the subquery, which are `StarsIn` (with alias m2) and `MovieStar`. Thus, we need to defer the selection

$$\sigma_{m2.movieTitle=m1.movieTitle \text{ AND } m2.movieYear=m1.movieYear}$$

until after the relation from the subquery is combined with the copy of `StarsIn` from the outer query (the copy aliased m1). To transform the logical query plan in this way, we need to modify the γ to group by the attributes `m2.movieTitle` and `m2.movieYear`, so these attributes will be available when needed by the selection. The net effect is that we compute for the subquery a relation consisting of movies, each represented by its title and year, and the average star birth year for that movie.

The modified group-by operator appears in Fig. 16.19; in addition to the two grouping attributes, we need to rename the average `abd` (average birthdate) so we can refer to it later. Figure 16.19 also shows the complete translation to relational algebra. Above the γ, the `StarsIn` from the outer query is joined with the result of the subquery. The selection from the subquery is then applied to the product of `StarsIn` and the result of the subquery; we show this selection as a theta-join, which it would become after normal application of algebraic laws. Above the theta-join is another selection, this one corresponding to the selection of the outer query, in which we compare the movie's year to the average birth year of its stars. The algebraic expression finishes at the top like the expression of Fig. 16.18, with the projection onto the desired attributes and the elimination

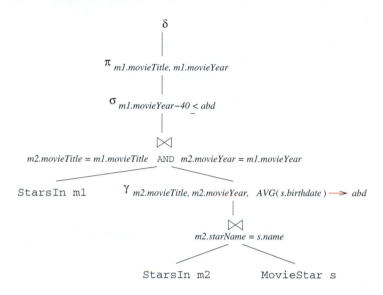

Figure 16.19: Translation of Fig. 16.18 to a logical query plan

of duplicates.

As we shall see in Section 16.3.3, there is much more that a query optimizer can do to improve the query plan. This particular example satisfies three conditions that let us improve the plan considerably. The conditions are:

1. Duplicates are eliminated at the end,

2. Star names from `StarsIn m1` are projected out, and

3. The join between `StarsIn m1` and the rest of the expression equates the title and year attributes from `StarsIn m1` and `StarsIn m2`.

Because these conditions hold, we can replace all uses of `m1.movieTitle` and `m1.movieYear` by `m2.movieTitle` and `m2.movieYear`, respectively. Thus, the upper join in Fig. 16.19 is unnecessary, as is the argument `StarsIn m1`. This logical query plan is shown in Fig. 16.20. □

16.3.3 Improving the Logical Query Plan

When we convert our query to relational algebra we obtain one possible logical query plan. The next step is to rewrite the plan using the algebraic laws outlined in Section 16.2. Alternatively, we could generate more than one logical plan, representing different orders or combinations of operators. But in this book we shall assume that the query rewriter chooses a single logical query plan that it believes is "best," meaning that it is likely to result ultimately in the cheapest physical plan.

Figure 16.20: Simplification of Fig. 16.19

We do, however, leave open the matter of what is known as "join ordering," so a logical query plan that involves joining relations can be thought of as a family of plans, corresponding to the different ways a join could be ordered and grouped. We discuss choosing a join order in Section 16.6. Similarly, a query plan involving three or more relations that are arguments to the other associative and commutative operators, such as union, should be assumed to allow reordering and regrouping as we convert the logical plan to a physical plan. We begin discussing the issues regarding ordering and physical plan selection in Section 16.4.

There are a number of algebraic laws from Section 16.2 that tend to improve logical query plans. The following are most commonly used in optimizers:

- Selections can be pushed down the expression tree as far as they can go. If a selection condition is the AND of several conditions, then we can split the condition and push each piece down the tree separately. This strategy is probably the most effective improvement technique, but we should recall the discussion in Section 16.2.3, where we saw that in some circumstances it was necessary to push the selection up the tree first.

- Similarly, projections can be pushed down the tree, or new projections can be added. As with selections, the pushing of projections should be done with care, as discussed in Section 16.2.4.

- Duplicate eliminations can sometimes be removed, or moved to a more convenient position in the tree, as discussed in Section 16.2.6.

- Certain selections can be combined with a product below to turn the pair of operations into an equijoin, which is generally much more efficient to evaluate than are the two operations separately. We discussed these laws in Section 16.2.5.

Example 16.19: Let us consider the query of Fig. 16.13. First, we may split the two parts of the selection into $\sigma_{starName=name}$ and $\sigma_{birthdate}$ LIKE '%1960'. The latter can be pushed down the tree, since the only attribute involved, `birthdate`, is from the relation `MovieStar`. The first condition involves attributes from both sides of the product, but they are equated, so the product and selection is really an equijoin. The effect of these transformations is shown in Fig. 16.21. □

Figure 16.21: The effect of query rewriting

16.3.4 Grouping Associative/Commutative Operators

Conventional parsers do not produce trees whose nodes can have an unlimited number of children. Thus, it is normal for operators to appear only in their unary or binary form. However, associative and commutative operators may be thought of as having any number of operands. Moreover, thinking of an operator such as join as a multiway operator offers us opportunities to reorder the operands so that when the join is executed as a sequence of binary joins, they take less time than if we had executed the joins in the order implied by the parse tree. We discuss ordering multiway joins in Section 16.6.

Thus, we shall perform a last step before producing the final logical query plan: for each portion of the subtree that consists of nodes with the same associative and commutative operator, we group the nodes with these operators into a single node with many children. Recall that the usual associative/commutative operators are natural join, union, and intersection. Natural joins and theta-joins can also be combined with each other under certain circumstances:

1. We must replace the natural joins with theta-joins that equate the attributes of the same name.

2. We must add a projection to eliminate duplicate copies of attributes involved in a natural join that has become a theta-join.

3. The theta-join conditions must be associative. Recall there are cases, as discussed in Section 16.2.1, where theta-joins are not associative.

In addition, products can be considered as a special case of natural join and combined with joins if they are adjacent in the tree. Figure 16.22 illustrates this transformation in a situation where the logical query plan has a cluster of two union operators and a cluster of three natural join operators. Note that the letters R through W stand for any expressions, not necessarily for stored relations.

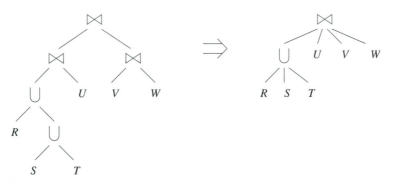

Figure 16.22: Final step in producing the logical query plan: group the associative and commutative operators

16.3.5 Exercises for Section 16.3

Exercise 16.3.1: Replace the natural joins in the following expressions by equivalent theta-joins and projections. Tell whether the resulting theta-joins form a commutative and associative group.

* a) $\big(R(a,b) \bowtie S(b,c)\big) \underset{S.c>T.c}{\bowtie} T(c,d)$.

 b) $\big(R(a,b) \bowtie S(b,c)\big) \bowtie \big(T(c,d) \bowtie U(d,e)\big)$.

 c) $\big(R(a,b) \bowtie S(b,c)\big) \bowtie \big(T(c,d) \bowtie U(a,d)\big)$.

Exercise 16.3.2: Convert to relational algebra your parse trees from Exercise 16.1.3(a) and (b). For (b), show both the form with a two-argument selection and its eventual conversion to a one-argument (conventional σ_C) selection.

! **Exercise 16.3.3:** Give a rule for converting each of the following forms of <Condition> to relational algebra. All conditions may be assumed to be applied (by a two-argument selection) to a relation R. You may assume that the subquery is not correlated with R. Be careful that you do not introduce or eliminate duplicates in opposition to the formal definition of SQL.

* a) A condition of the form EXISTS(<Query>).

  b) A condition of the form $a = $ ANY <Query>, where a is an attribute of R.

  c) A condition of the form $a = $ ALL <Query>, where a is an attribute of R.

!! **Exercise 16.3.4 :** Repeat Exercise 16.3.3, but allow the subquery to be corollated with R. For simplicity, you may assume that the subquery has the simple form of select-from-where expression described in this section, with *no* further subqueries.

!! **Exercise 16.3.5 :** From how many different expression trees could the grouped tree on the right of Fig. 16.22 have come? Remember that the order of children after grouping is not necessarily reflective of the ordering in the original expression tree.

16.4 Estimating the Cost of Operations

Suppose we have parsed a query and transformed it into a logical query plan. Suppose further that whatever transformations we choose have been applied to construct the preferred logical query plan. We must next turn our logical plan into a physical plan. We normally do so by considering many different physical plans that are derived from the logical plan, and evaluating or estimating the cost of each. After this evaluation, often called *cost-based enumeration*, we pick the physical query plan with the least estimated cost; that plan is the one passed to the query-execution engine. When enumerating possible physical plans derivable from a given logical plan, we select for each physical plan:

1. An order and grouping for associative-and-commutative operations like joins, unions, and intersections.

2. An algorithm for each operator in the logical plan, for instance, deciding whether a nested-loop join or a hash-join should be used.

3. Additional operators — scanning, sorting, and so on — that are needed for the physical plan but that were not present explicitly in the logical plan.

4. The way in which arguments are passed from one operator to the next, for instance, by storing the intermediate result on disk or by using iterators and passing an argument one tuple or one main-memory buffer at a time.

We shall consider each of these issues subsequently. However, in order to answer the questions associated with each of these choices, we need to understand what the costs of the various physical plans are. We cannot know these costs exactly without executing the plan. In almost all cases, the cost of executing a query plan is significantly greater than all the work done by the query compiler

---

Review of Notation

Recall from Section 15.1.3 the conventions we use for representing sizes of relations:

- $B(R)$ is the number of blocks needed to hold all the tuples of relation R.

- $T(R)$ is the number of tuples of relation R.

- $V(R, a)$ is the *value count* for attribute a of relation R, that is, the number of distinct values relation R has in attribute a. Also, $V(R, [a_1, a_2, \ldots, a_n])$ is the number of distinct values R has when all of attributes $a_1, a_2, \ldots, a_n$ are considered together, that is, the number of tuples in $\delta\big(\pi_{a_1, a_2, \ldots, a_n}(R)\big)$.

---

in selecting a plan. As a consequence, we surely don't want to execute more than one plan for one query, and we are forced to estimate the cost of any plan without executing it.

Preliminary to our discussion of physical plan enumeration, then, is a consideration of how to estimate costs of such plans accurately. Such estimates are based on parameters of the data (see the box on "Review of Notation") that must be either computed exactly from the data or estimated by a process of "statistics gathering" that we discuss in Section 16.5.1. Given values for these parameters, we may make a number of reasonable estimates of relation sizes that can be used to predict the cost of a complete physical plan.

16.4.1 Estimating Sizes of Intermediate Relations

The physical plan is selected to minimize the estimated cost of evaluating the query. No matter what method is used for executing query plans, and no matter how costs of query plans are estimated, the sizes of intermediate relations of the plan have a profound influence on costs. Ideally, we want rules for estimating the number of tuples in an intermediate relation so that the rules:

1. Give accurate estimates.

2. Are easy to compute.

3. Are logically consistent; that is, the size estimate for an intermediate relation should not depend on how that relation is computed. For instance, the size estimate for a join of several relations should not depend on the order in which we join the relations.

There is no universally agreed-upon way to meet these three conditions. We shall give some simple rules that serve in most situations. Fortunately, the goal of size estimation is not to predict the exact size; it is to help select a physical query plan. Even an inaccurate size-estimation method will serve that purpose well if it errs consistently, that is, if the size estimator assigns the least cost to the best physical query plan, even if the actual cost of that plan turns out to be different from what was predicted.

16.4.2 Estimating the Size of a Projection

The projection is different from the other operators, in that the size of the result is computable. Since a projection produces a result tuple for every argument tuple, the only change in the output size is the change in the lengths of the tuples. Recall that the projection operator used here is a bag operator and does not eliminate duplicates; if we want to eliminate duplicates produced during a projection, we need to follow with the δ operator.

Normally, tuples shrink during a projection, as some components are eliminated. However, the general form of projection we introduced in Section 5.4.5 allows the creation of new components that are combinations of attributes, and so there are situations where a π operator actually increases the size of the relation.

Example 16.20: Suppose $R(a, b, c)$ is a relation, where a and b are integers of four bytes each, and c is a string of 100 bytes. Let tuple headers require 12 bytes. Then each tuple of R requires 120 bytes. Let blocks be 1024 bytes long, with block headers of 24 bytes. We can thus fit 8 tuples in one block. Suppose $T(R) = 10,000$; i.e., there are 10,000 tuples in R. Then $B(R) = 1250$.

Consider $S = \pi_{a+b,c}(R)$; that is, we replace a and b by their sum. Tuples of S require 116 bytes: 12 for header, 4 for the sum, and 100 for the string. Although tuples of S are slightly smaller than tuples of R, we can still fit only 8 tuples in a block. Thus, $T(S) = 10,000$ and $B(S) = 1250$.

Now consider $U = \pi_{a,b}(R)$, where we eliminate the string component. Tuples of U are only 20 bytes long. $T(U)$ is still 10,000. However, we can now pack 50 tuples of U into one block, so $B(U) = 200$. This projection thus shrinks the relation by a factor slightly more than 6. $\square$

16.4.3 Estimating the Size of a Selection

When we perform a selection, we generally reduce the number of tuples, although the sizes of tuples remain the same. In the simplest kind of selection, where an attribute is equated to a constant, there is an easy way to estimate the size of the result, provided we know, or can estimate, the number of different values the attribute has. Let $S = \sigma_{A=c}(R)$, where A is an attribute of R and c is a constant. Then we recommend as an estimate:

- $T(S) = T(R)/V(R, A)$

The rule above surely holds if all values of attribute A occur equally often in the database. However, as discussed in the box on "The Zipfian Distribution," the formula above is still the best estimate on the average, even if values of A are not uniformly distributed in the database, but all values of A are equally likely to appear in queries that specify the value of A. Better estimates can be obtained, however, if the DBMS maintains more detailed statistics ("histograms") on the data, as discussed in Section 16.5.1.

The size estimate is more problematic when the selection involves an inequality comparison, for instance, $S = \sigma_{a<10}(R)$. One might think that on the average, half the tuples would satisfy the comparison and half not, so $T(R)/2$ would estimate the size of S. However, there is an intuition that queries involving an inequality tend to retrieve a small fraction of the possible tuples.[3] Thus, we propose a rule that acknowledges this tendency, and assumes the typical inequality will return about one third of the tuples, rather than half the tuples. If $S = \sigma_{a<c}(R)$, then our estimate for $T(S)$ is:

- $T(S) = T(R)/3$

The case of a "not equals" comparison is rare. However, should we encounter a selection like $S = \sigma_{a \neq 10}(R)$, we recommend assuming that essentially all tuples will satisfy the condition. That is, take $T(S) = T(R)$ as an estimate. Alternatively, we may use $T(S) = T(R)\big(V(R,a) - 1\big)/V(R,a)$, which is slightly less, as an estimate, acknowledging that about fraction $1/V(R,a)$ tuples of R will fail to meet the condition because their a-value *does* equal the constant.

When the selection condition C is the AND of several equalities and inequalities, we can treat the selection $\sigma_C(R)$ as a cascade of simple selections, each of which checks for one of the conditions. Note that the order in which we place these selections doesn't matter. The effect will be that the size estimate for the result is the size of the original relation multiplied by the *selectivity* factor for each condition. That factor is $1/3$ for any inequality, 1 for $\neq$, and $1/V(R,A)$ for any attribute A that is compared to a constant in the condition C.

Example 16.21 : Let $R(a, b, c)$ be a relation, and $S = \sigma_{a=10 \text{ AND } b<20}(R)$. Also, let $T(R) = 10{,}000$, and $V(R,a) = 50$. Then our best estimate of $T(S)$ is $T(R)/(50 \times 3)$, or 67. That is, 1/50th of the tuples of R will survive the $a = 10$ filter, and 1/3 of those will survive the $b < 20$ filter.

An interesting special case where our analysis breaks down is when the condition is contradictory. For instance, consider $S = \sigma_{a=10 \text{ AND } a>20}(R)$. According to our rule, $T(S) = T(R)/3V(R,a)$, or 67 tuples. However, it should be clear that no tuple can have both $a = 10$ and $a > 20$, so the correct answer is $T(S) = 0$. When rewriting the logical query plan, the query optimizer can look for instances of many special-case rules. In the above instance, the optimizer can apply a rule that finds the selection condition logically equivalent to FALSE and replaces the expression for S by the empty set.   □

---

[3]For instance, if you had data about faculty salaries, would you be more likely to query for those faculty who made *less* than \$200,000 or *more* than \$200,000?

The Zipfian Distribution

When we assume that one out of $V(R, a)$ tuples of R will satisfy a condition like $a = 10$, we appear to be making the tacit assumption that all values of attribute a are equally likely to appear in a given tuple of R. We also assume that 10 is one of these values, but that is a reasonable assumption, since most of the time one looks in a database for things that actually exist. However, the assumption that values distribute equally is rarely upheld, even approximately.

Many attributes have values whose occurrences follow a *Zipfian distribution*, where the frequencies of the ith most common values are in proportion to $1/\sqrt{i}$. For example, if the most common value appears 1000 times, then the second most common value would be expected to appear about $1000/\sqrt{2}$ times, or 707 times, and the third most common value would appear about $1000/\sqrt{3}$ times, or 577 times. Originally postulated as a way to describe the relative frequencies of words in English sentences, this distribution has been found to appear in many sorts of data. For example, in the US, state populations follow an approximate Zipfian distribution, with, say, the second most populous state, New York, having about 70% of the population of the most populous, California. Thus, if `state` were an attribute of a relation describing US people, say a list of magazine subscribers, we would expect the values of `state` to distribute in the Zipfian, rather than uniform manner.

As long as the constant in the selection condition is chosen randomly, it doesn't matter whether the values of the attribute involved have a uniform, Zipfian, or other distribution; the *average* size of the matching set will still be $T(R)/V(R, a)$. However, if the constants are also chosen with a Zipfian distribution, then we would expect the average size of the selected set to be somewhat larger than $T(R)/V(R, a)$.

When a selection involves an `OR` of conditions, say $S = \sigma_{C_1 \text{ OR } C_2}(R)$, then we have less certainty about the size of the result. One simple assumption is that no tuple will satisfy both conditions, so the size of the result is the sum of the number of tuples that satisfy each. That measure is generally an overestimate, and in fact can sometimes lead us to the absurd conclusion that there are more tuples in S than in the original relation R. Thus, another simple approach is to take the smaller of the size of R and the sum of the number of tuples satisfying C_1 and those satisfying C_2.

A less simple, but possibly more accurate estimate of the size of

$$S = \sigma_{C_1 \text{ OR } C_2}(R)$$

is to assume that C_1 and C_2 are independent. Then, if R has n tuples, m_1 of which satisfy C_1 and m_2 of which satisfy C_2, we would estimate the number of tuples in S as

$$n\left(1 - (1 - \frac{m_1}{n})(1 - \frac{m_2}{n})\right)$$

In explanation, $1 - m_1/n$ is the fraction of tuples that do not satisfy C_1, and $1 - m_2/n$ is the fraction that do not satisfy C_2. The product of these numbers is the fraction of R's tuples that are *not* in S, and 1 minus this product is the fraction that are in S.

Example 16.22: Suppose $R(a, b)$ has $T(R) = 10,000$ tuples, and

$$S = \sigma_{a=10 \text{ OR } b<20}(R)$$

Let $V(R, a) = 50$. Then the number of tuples that satisfy $a = 10$ we estimate at 200, i.e., $T(R)/V(R, a)$. The number of tuples that satisfy $b < 20$ we estimate at $T(R)/3$, or 3333.

The simplest estimate for the size of S is the sum of these numbers, or 3533. The more complex estimate based on independence of the conditions $a = 10$ and $b < 20$ gives

$$10000\left(1 - (1 - \frac{200}{10000})(1 - \frac{3333}{10000})\right)$$

or 3466. In this case, there is little difference between the two estimates, and it is very unlikely that choosing one over the other would change our estimate of the best physical query plan.   □

The final operator that could appear in a selection condition is NOT. The estimated number of tuples of R that satisfy condition NOT C is $T(R)$ minus the estimated number that satisfy C.

16.4.4   Estimating the Size of a Join

We shall consider here only the natural join. Other joins can be handled according to the following outline:

1. The number of tuples in the result of an equijoin can be computed exactly as for a natural join, after accounting for the change in variable names. Example 16.24 will illustrate this point.

2. Other theta-joins can be estimated as if they were a selection following a product, with the following additional observations:

   (a) The number of tuples in a product is the product of the number of tuples in the relations involved.

   (b) An equality comparison can be estimated using the techniques to be developed for natural joins.

(c) An inequality comparison between two attributes, such as $R.a <$ $S.b$, can be handled as for the inequality comparisons of the form $R.a < 10$, discussed in Section 16.4.3. That is, we can assume this condition has selectivity factor $1/3$ (if you believe that queries tend to ask for relatively rare conditions) or $1/2$ (if you do not make that assumption).

We shall begin our study with the assumption that the natural join of two relations involves only the equality of two attributes. That is, we study the join $R(X, Y) \bowtie S(Y, Z)$, but initially we assume that Y is a single attribute although X and Z can represent any set of attributes.

The problem is that we don't know how the Y-values in R and S relate. For instance:

1. The two relations could have disjoint sets of Y-values, in which case the join is empty and $T(R \bowtie S) = 0$.

2. Y might be the key of S and a foreign key of R, so each tuple of R joins with exactly one tuple of S, and $T(R \bowtie S) = T(R)$.

3. Almost all the tuples of R and S could have the same Y-value, in which case $T(R \bowtie S)$ is about $T(R)T(S)$.

To focus on the most common situations, we shall make two simplifying assumptions:

- *Containment of Value Sets.* If Y is an attribute appearing in several relations, then each relation chooses its values from the front of a fixed list of values $y_1, y_2, y_3, \ldots$ and has all the values in that prefix. As a consequence, if R and S are two relations with an attribute Y, and $V(R, Y) \le V(S, Y)$, then every Y-value of R will be a Y-value of S.

- *Preservation of Value Sets.* If we join a relation R with another relation, then an attribute A that is not a join attribute (i.e., not present in both relations) does not lose values from its set of possible values. More precisely, if A is an attribute of R but not of S, then $V(R \bowtie S, A) = V(R, A)$. Note that the order of joining R and S is not important, so we could just as well have said that $V(S \bowtie R, A) = V(R, A)$.

Assumption (1), containment of value sets, clearly might be violated, but it *is* satisfied when Y is a key in S and a foreign key in R. It also is approximately true in many other cases, since we would intuitively expect that if S has many Y-values, then a given Y-value that appears in R has a good chance of appearing in S.

Assumption (2), preservation of value sets, also might be violated, but it is true when the join attribute(s) of $R \bowtie S$ are a key for S and a foreign key for R. In fact, (2) can only be violated when there are "dangling tuples" in R, that is, tuples of R that join with no tuple of S; and even if there *are* dangling tuples in R, the assumption might still hold.

Under these assumptions, we can estimate the size of $R(X, Y) \bowtie S(Y, Z)$ as follows. Let $V(R, Y) \le V(S, Y)$. Then every tuple t of R has a chance $1/V(S, Y)$ of joining with a given tuple of S. Since there are $T(S)$ tuples in S, the expected number of tuples that t joins with is $T(S)/V(S, Y)$. As there are $T(R)$ tuples of R, the estimated size of $R \bowtie S$ is $T(R)T(S)/V(S, Y)$. If, on the other hand, $V(R, Y) \ge V(S, Y)$, then a symmetric argument gives us the estimate $T(R \bowtie S) = T(R)T(S)/V(R, Y)$. In general, we divide by whichever of $V(R, Y)$ and $V(S, Y)$ is larger. That is:

- $T(R \bowtie S) = T(R)T(S)/\max\big(V(R, Y), V(S, Y)\big)$

Example 16.23 : Let us consider the following three relations and their important statistics:

$R(a, b)$	$S(b, c)$	$U(c, d)$
$T(R) = 1000$	$T(S) = 2000$	$T(U) = 5000$
$V(R, b) = 20$	$V(S, b) = 50$	
	$V(S, c) = 100$	$V(U, c) = 500$

Suppose we want to compute the natural join $R \bowtie S \bowtie U$. One way is to group R and S first, as $(R \bowtie S) \bowtie U$. Our estimate for $T(R \bowtie S)$ is $T(R)T(S)/\max\big(V(R, b), V(S, b)\big)$, which is $1000 \times 2000/50$, or 40,000.

We then need to join $R \bowtie S$ with U. Our estimate for the size of the result is $T(R \bowtie S)T(U)/\max\big(V(R \bowtie S, c), V(U, c)\big)$. By our assumption that value sets are preserved, $V(R \bowtie S, c)$ is the same as $V(S, c)$, or 100; that is no values of attribute c disappeared when we performed the join. In that case, we get as our estimate for the number of tuples in $R \bowtie S \bowtie U$ the value $40,000 \times 5000/\max(100, 500)$, or 400,000.

We could also start by joining S and U. If we do, then we get the estimate $T(S \bowtie U) = T(S)T(U)/\max\big(V(S, c), V(U, c)\big) = 2000 \times 5000/500 = 20,000$. By our assumption that value sets are preserved, $V(S \bowtie U, b) = V(S, b) = 50$, so the estimated size of the result is

$$T(R)T(S \bowtie U)/\max\big(V(R, b), V(S \bowtie U, b)\big)$$

which is $1000 \times 20,000/50$, or 400,000. □

It is no coincidence that in Example 16.23 the estimate of the size of the join $R \bowtie S \bowtie U$ is the same whether we start by joining $R \bowtie S$ or by joining $S \bowtie U$. Recall that one of our desiderata of Section 16.4.1 is that the estimate for the result of an expression should not depend on order of evaluation. It can be shown that the two assumptions we have made — containment and preservation of value sets — guarantee that the estimate of any natural join is the same, regardless of how we order the joins.

16.4.5 Natural Joins With Multiple Join Attributes

Now, let us see what happens when Y represents several attributes in the join $R(X,Y) \bowtie S(Y,Z)$. For a specific example, suppose we want to join $R(x,y_1,y_2) \bowtie S(y_1,y_2,z)$. Consider a tuple r in R. The probability that r joins with a given tuple s of S can be calculated as follows.

First, what is the probability that r and s agree on attribute y_1? Suppose that $V(R,y_1) \geq V(S,y_1)$. Then the y_1-value of s is surely one of the y_1 values that appear in R, by the containment-of-value-sets assumption. Hence, the chance that r has the same y_1-value as s is $1/V(R,y_1)$. Similarly, if $V(R,y_1) < V(S,y_1)$, then the value of y_1 in r will appear in S, and the probability is $1/V(S,y_1)$ that r and s will share the same y_1-value. In general, we see that the probability of agreement on the y_1 value is $1/\max(V(R,y_1),V(S,y_1))$.

A similar argument about the probability of r and s agreeing on y_2 tells us this probability is $1/\max(V(R,y_2),V(S,y_2))$. As the values of y_1 and y_2 are independent, the probability that tuples will agree on both y_1 and y_2 is the product of these fractions. Thus, of the $T(R)T(S)$ pairs of tuples from R and S, the expected number of pairs that match in both y_1 and y_2 is

$$\frac{T(R)T(S)}{\max(V(R,y_1),V(S,y_1))\max(V(R,y_2),V(S,y_2))}$$

In general, the following rule can be used to estimate the size of a natural join when there are any number of attributes shared between the two relations.

- The estimate of the size of $R \bowtie S$ is computed by multiplying $T(R)$ by $T(S)$ and dividing by the larger of $V(R,y)$ and $V(S,y)$ for each attribute y that is common to R and S.

Example 16.24: The following example uses the rule above. It also illustrates that the analysis we have been doing for natural joins applies to any equijoin. Consider the join

$$R(a,b,c) \underset{R.b=S.d \text{ AND } R.c=S.e}{\bowtie} S(d,e,f)$$

Suppose we have the following size parameters:

$R(a,b,c)$	$S(d,e,f)$
$T(R) = 1000$	$T(S) = 2000$
$V(R,b) = 20$	$V(S,d) = 50$
$V(R,c) = 100$	$V(S,e) = 50$

We can think of this join as a natural join if we regard $R.b$ and $S.d$ as the same attribute and also regard $R.c$ and $S.e$ as the same attribute. Then the rule given above tells us the estimate for the size of $R \bowtie S$ is the product 1000×2000 divided by the larger of 20 and 50 and also divided by the larger of 100 and 50. Thus, the size estimate for the join is $1000 \times 2000/(50 \times 100) = 400$ tuples. $\square$

Numbers of Tuples is not Enough

Although our analysis of relation sizes has focused on the number of tuples in the result, sometimes we also have to take into account the size of each tuple. For instance, joins of relations produce tuples that are longer than the tuples of either relation. As an example, joining two relations $R \bowtie S$, each with 1000 tuples, might yield a result that also has 1000 tuples. However, the result would occupy more blocks than either R or S.

Example 16.24 is an interesting case in point. Although we can use natural-join techniques to estimate the number of tuples in a theta-join, as we did there, the tuples in a theta-join have more components than tuples of the corresponding natural join. Specifically, the theta-join $R(a, b, c) \overset{\bowtie}{\underset{R.b=S.d \text{ AND } R.c=S.e}{}} S(d, e, f)$ produces tuples with six components, one each for a through f, while the natural join $R(a, b, c) \bowtie S(b, c, d)$ produces the same number of tuples, but each tuple has only four components.

Example 16.25 : Let us reconsider Example 16.23, but consider the third possible order for the joins, where we first take $R(a, b) \bowtie U(c, d)$. This join is actually a product, and the number of tuples in the result is $T(R)T(U) = 1000 \times 5000 = 5{,}000{,}000$. Note that the number of different b's in the product is $V(R, b) = 20$, and the number of different c's is $V(U, c) = 500$.

When we join this product with $S(b, c)$, we multiply the numbers of tuples and divide by both $\max(V(R, b), V(S, b))$ and $\max(V(U, c), V(S, c))$. This quantity is $2000 \times 5{,}000{,}000/(50 \times 500) = 400{,}000$. Note that this third way of joining gives the same estimate for the size of the result that we found in Example 16.23. $\Box$

16.4.6 Joins of Many Relations

Finally, let us consider the general case of a natural join:

$$S = R_1 \bowtie R_2 \bowtie \cdots \bowtie R_n$$

Suppose that attribute A appears in k of the R_i's, and the numbers of its sets of values in these k relations — that is, the various values of $V(R_i, A)$ for $i = 1, 2, \ldots, k$ — are $v_1 \leq v_2 \leq \cdots \leq v_k$, in order from smallest to largest. Suppose we pick a tuple from each relation. What is the probability that all tuples selected agree on attribute A?

In answer, consider the tuple t_1 chosen from the relation that has the smallest number of A-values, v_1. By the containment-of-value-sets assumption, each of these v_1 values is among the A-values found in the other relations that have attribute A. Consider the relation that has v_i values in attribute A. Its selected tuple t_i has probability $1/v_i$ of agreeing with t_1 on A. Since this claim is true for all $i = 2, 3, \ldots, k$, the probability that all k tuples agree on A is the product $1/v_2 v_3 \cdots v_k$. This analysis gives us the rule for estimating the size of any join.

- Start with the product of the number of tuples in each relation. Then, for each attribute A appearing at least twice, divide by all but the least of the $V(R, A)$'s.

Likewise, we can estimate the number of values that will remain for attribute A after the join. By the preservation-of-value-sets assumption, it is the least of these $V(R, A)$'s.

Example 16.26 : Consider the join $R(a, b, c) \bowtie S(b, c, d) \bowtie U(b, e)$, and suppose the important statistics are as given in Fig. 16.23. To estimate the size of this join, we begin by multiplying the relation sizes; $1000 \times 2000 \times 5000$. Next, we look at the attributes that appear more than once; these are b, which appears three times, and c, which appears twice. We divide by the two largest of $V(R, b)$, $V(S, b)$, and $V(U, b)$; these are 50 and 200. Finally, we divide by the larger of $V(R, c)$ and $V(S, c)$, which is 200. The resulting estimate is

$$1000 \times 2000 \times 5000 / (50 \times 200 \times 200) = 5000$$

$R(a, b, c)$	$S(b, c, d)$	$U(b, e)$
$T(R) = 1000$	$T(S) = 2000$	$T(U) = 5000$
$V(R, a) = 100$		
$V(R, b) = 20$	$V(S, b) = 50$	$V(U, b) = 200$
$V(R, c) = 200$	$V(S, c) = 100$	
	$V(S, d) = 400$	
		$V(U, e) = 500$

Figure 16.23: Parameters for Example 16.26

We can also estimate the number of values for each of the attributes in the join. Each estimate is the least value count for the attribute among all the relations in which it appears. These numbers are, for a, b, c, d, e respectively: 100, 20, 100, 400, and 500. □

Based on the two assumptions we have made — containment and preservation of value sets — we have a surprising and convenient property of the estimating rule given above.

- No matter how we group and order the terms in a natural join of n relations, the estimation rules, applied to each join individually, yield the same estimate for the size of the result. Moreover, this estimate is the same that we get if we apply the rule for the join of all n relations as a whole.

> ## Why is the Join Size Estimate Independent of Order?
>
> A formal proof of this claim is by induction on the number of relations involved in the join. We shall not give this proof, but this box contains the intuition. Suppose we join some relations, and the final step is
>
> $$(R_1 \bowtie \cdots \bowtie R_n) \bowtie (S_1 \bowtie \cdots \bowtie S_m)$$
>
> We may assume that no matter how the join of the R's was taken, the size estimate for this join is the product of the sizes of the R's divided by all but the smallest value count for each attribute that appears more than once among the R's. Further, the estimated value count for each attribute is the smallest of its value counts among the R's. Similar statements apply to the S's.
>
> When we apply the rule for estimating the size of the join of two relations (from Section 16.4.4) to the two relations that are the join of the R's and the join of the S's, the estimate will be the product of the two estimates, divided by the larger of the value counts for each attribute that appears among both the R's and S's. Thus, this estimate will surely have one factor that is the size of each relation $R_1, \ldots, R_n, S_1, \ldots, S_m$. In addition, the estimate will have a divisor for each attribute value count that is *not* the smallest for its attribute. Either that divisor is already present in the estimate for the R's or the S's, or it is introduced at the last step, because its attribute A appears among both the R's and S's, and it is the larger of the two value counts that are the smallest of the $V(R_i, A)$'s and smallest of the $V(S_j, A)$'s, respectively.

Examples 16.23 and 16.25 form an illustration of this rule in action for the three groupings of a three-relation join, including the grouping where one of the "joins" is actually a product.

16.4.7   Estimating Sizes for Other Operations

We have seen two operations with an exact formula for the number of tuples in the result:

1. Projections do not change the number of tuples in a relation.

2. Products produce a result with a number of tuples equal to the product of the numbers of tuples in the argument relations.

There are two other operations — selection and join — where we have developed reasonable estimating techniques. However, for the remaining operations, the size of the result is not easy to determine. We shall review the other relational-algebra operators and give some suggestions as to how this estimation could be done.

Union

If the bag union is taken, then the size is exactly the sum of the sizes of the arguments. A set union can be as large as the sum of the sizes or as small as the larger of the two arguments. We suggest that something in the middle be chosen, e.g., the average of the sum and the larger (which is the same as the larger plus half the smaller).

Intersection

The result can have as few as 0 tuples or as many as the smaller of the two arguments, regardless of whether set- or bag-intersection is taken. One approach is to take the average of the extremes, which is half the smaller.

Another approach is to recognize that the intersection is an extreme case of the natural join and use the formula of Section 16.4.4. When a set intersection is meant, this formula is guaranteed to produce a result that is no greater than the smaller of the two relations. However, in the case of a bag intersection, there can be some anomalies, where the estimate is larger than either argument. For instance, consider $R(a, b) \cap_B S(a, b)$, where R consists of two copies of tuple $(0, 1)$ and S consists of three copies of the same tuple. Then

$$V(R, a) = V(S, a) = V(R, b) = V(S, b) = 1$$

$T(R) = 2$, and $T(S) = 3$. The estimate is $2 \times 3 / (\max(1, 1) \times \max(1, 1)) = 6$ from the rule for joins, but clearly there can be no more than $\min(T(R), T(S)) = 2$ tuples in the result.

Difference

When we compute $R - S$, the result can have between $T(R)$ and $T(R) - T(S)$ tuples. We suggest the average as an estimate: $T(R) - \frac{1}{2}T(S)$.

Duplicate Elimination

If $R(a_1, a_2, \ldots, a_n)$ is a relation, then $V(R, [a_1, a_2, \ldots, a_n])$ is the size of $\delta(R)$. However, often we shall not have this statistic available, so it must be approximated. In the extremes, the size of $\delta(R)$ could be the same as the size of R (no duplicates) or as small as 1 (all tuples in R are the same).[4] Another upper limit on the number of tuples in $\delta(R)$ is the maximum number of distinct tuples that could exist: the product of $V(R, a_i)$ for $i = 1, 2, \ldots, n$. That number could be

---

[4]Strictly speaking, if R is empty there are no tuples in either R or $\delta(R)$, so the lower bound is 0. However, we are rarely interested in this special case.

smaller than other estimates of $T(\delta(R))$. There are several rules that could be used to estimate $T(\delta(R))$. One reasonable one is to take the smaller of $\frac{1}{2}T(R)$ and the product of all the $V(R, a_i)$'s.

Grouping and Aggregation

Suppose we have an expression $\gamma_L(R)$, the size of whose result we need to estimate. If the statistic $V(R, [g_1, g_2, \ldots, g_k])$, where the g_i's are the grouping attributes in L, is available, then that is our answer. However, that statistic may well not be obtainable, so we need another way to estimate the size of $\gamma_L(R)$. The number of tuples in $\gamma_L(R)$ is the same as the number of groups. There could be as few as one group in the result or as many groups as there are tuples in R. As with δ, we can also upper-bound the number of groups by a product of $V(R, A)$'s, but here attribute A ranges over only the grouping attributes of L. We again suggest an estimate that is the smaller of $\frac{1}{2}T(R)$ and this product.

16.4.8 Exercises for Section 16.4

Exercise 16.4.1: Below are the vital statistics for four relations, W, X, Y, and Z:

$W(a, b)$	$X(b, c)$	$Y(c, d)$	$Z(d, e)$
$T(W) = 100$	$T(X) = 200$	$T(Y) = 300$	$T(Z) = 400$
$V(W, a) = 20$	$V(X, b) = 50$	$V(Y, c) = 50$	$V(Z, d) = 40$
$V(W, b) = 60$	$V(X, c) = 100$	$V(Y, d) = 50$	$V(Z, e) = 100$

Estimate the sizes of relations that are the results of the following expressions:

* a) $W \bowtie X \bowtie Y \bowtie Z$.

* b) $\sigma_{a=10}(W)$.

 c) $\sigma_{c=20}(Y)$.

 d) $\sigma_{c=20}(Y) \bowtie Z$.

 e) $W \times Y$.

 f) $\sigma_{d>10}(Z)$.

* g) $\sigma_{a=1 \text{ AND } b=2}(W)$.

 h) $\sigma_{a=1 \text{ AND } b>2}(W)$.

 i) $X \underset{X.c<Y.c}{\bowtie} Y$.

* **Exercise 16.4.2:** Here are the statistics for four relations E, F, G, and H:

$E(a, b, c)$	$F(a, b, d)$	$G(a, c, d)$	$H(b, c, d)$
$T(E) = 1000$	$T(F) = 2000$	$T(G) = 3000$	$T(H) = 4000$
$V(E, a) = 1000$	$V(F, a) = 50$	$V(G, a) = 50$	$V(H, b) = 40$
$V(E, b) = 50$	$V(F, b) = 100$	$V(G, c) = 300$	$V(H, c) = 100$
$V(E, c) = 20$	$V(F, d) = 200$	$V(G, d) = 500$	$V(H, d) = 400$

How many tuples does the join of these tuples have, using the techniques for estimation from this section?

! **Exercise 16.4.3:** How would you estimate the size of a semijoin?

!! **Exercise 16.4.4:** Suppose we compute $R(a, b) \bowtie S(a, c)$, where R and S each have 1000 tuples. The a attribute of each relation has 100 different values, and they are the *same* 100 values. If the distribution of values was uniform; i.e., each a-value appeared in exactly 10 tuples of each relation, then there would be 10,000 tuples in the join. Suppose instead that the 100 a-values have the same Zipfian distribution in each relation. Precisely, let the values be $a_1, a_2, \ldots, a_{100}$. Then the number of tuples of both R and S that have a-value a_i is proportional to $1/\sqrt{i}$. Under these circumstances, how many tuples does the join have? You should ignore the fact that the number of tuples with a given a-value may not be an integer.

16.5 Introduction to Cost-Based Plan Selection

Whether selecting a logical query plan or constructing a physical query plan from a logical plan, the query optimizer needs to estimate the cost of evaluating certain expressions. We study the issues involved in cost-based plan selection here, and in Section 16.6 we consider in detail one of the most important and difficult problems in cost-based plan selection: the selection of a join order for several relations.

As before, we shall assume that the "cost" of evaluating an expression is approximated well by the number of disk I/O's performed. The number of disk I/O's, in turn, is influenced by:

1. The particular logical operators chosen to implement the query, a matter decided when we choose the logical query plan.

2. The sizes of intermediate results, whose estimation we discussed in Section 16.4.

3. The physical operators used to implement logical operators, e.g., the choice of a one-pass or two-pass join, or the choice to sort or not sort a given relation; this matter is discussed in Section 16.7.

4. The ordering of similar operations, especially joins as discussed in Section 16.6.

5. The method of passing arguments from one physical operator to the next, which is also discussed in Section 16.7.

Many issues need to be resolved in order to perform effective cost-based plan selection. In this section, we first consider how the size parameters, which were so essential for estimating relation sizes in Section 16.4, can be obtained from the database efficiently. We then revisit the algebraic laws we introduced to find the preferred logical query plan. Cost-based analysis justifies the use of many of the common heuristics for transforming logical query plans, such as pushing selections down the tree. Finally, we consider the various approaches to enumerating all the physical query plans that can be derived from the selected logical plan. Especially important are methods for reducing the number of plans that need to be evaluated, while making it likely that the least-cost plan is still considered.

16.5.1 Obtaining Estimates for Size Parameters

The formulas of Section 16.4 were predicated on knowing certain important parameters, especially $T(R)$, the number of tuples in a relation R, and $V(R, a)$, the number of different values in the column of relation R for attribute a. A modern DBMS generally allows the user or administrator explicitly to request the gathering of statistics, such as $T(R)$ and $V(R, a)$. These statistics are then used in subsequent query optimizations to estimate the cost of operations. Changes in values for the statistics due to subsequent database modifications are considered only after the next statistics-gathering command.

By scanning an entire relation R, it is straightforward to count the number of tuples $T(R)$ and also to discover the number of different values $V(R, a)$ for each attribute a. The number of blocks in which R can fit, $B(R)$, can be estimated either by counting the actual number of blocks used (if R is clustered), or by dividing $T(R)$ by the number of tuples per block (or by the average number of tuples per block if tuples are of varying length). Note that these two estimates of $B(R)$ may not be the same, but they are usually "close enough" for comparisons of costs, as long as we consistently choose one approach or the other.

In addition, a DBMS may compute a *histogram* of the values for a given attribute. If $V(R, A)$ is not too large, then the histogram may consist of the number (or fraction) of the tuples having each of the values of attribute A. If there are a great many values of this attribute, then only the most frequent values may be recorded individually, while other values are counted in groups. The most common types of histograms are:

1. *Equal-width.* A width w is chosen, along with a constant v_0. Counts are provided of the number of tuples with values v in the ranges $v_0 \leq v < v_0 + w$, $v_0 + w \leq v < v_0 + 2w$, and so on. The value v_0 may be the lowest possible value or a lower bound on values seen so far. In the latter case, should a new, lower value be seen, we can lower the value of v_0 by w and add a new count to the histogram.

2. *Equal-height.* These are the common "percentiles." We pick some fraction p, and list the lowest value, the value that is fraction p from the lowest, the fraction $2p$ from the lowest, and so on, up to the highest value.

3. *Most-frequent-values.* We may list the most common values and their numbers of occurrences. This information may be provided along with a count of occurrences for all the other values as a group, or we may record frequent values in addition to an equal-width or equal-height histogram for the other values.

One advantage of keeping a histogram is that the sizes of joins can be estimated more accurately than by the simplified methods of Section 16.4. In particular, if a value of the join attribute appears explicitly in the histograms of both relations being joined, then we know exactly how many tuples of the result will have this value. For those values of the join attribute that do not appear explicitly in the histogram of one or both relations, we estimate their effect on the join as in Section 16.4. However, if we use an equal-width histogram, with the same bands for the join attributes of both relations, then we can estimate the size of the joins of corresponding bands, and sum those estimates. The result will be a good estimate, because only tuples in corresponding bands can join. The following examples will suggest how to carry out histogram-based estimation; we shall not use histograms in estimates subsequently.

Example 16.27: Consider histograms that mention the three most frequent values and their counts, and group the remaining values. Suppose we want to compute the join $R(a, b) \bowtie S(b, c)$. Let the histogram for $R.b$ be:

$$1: 200, \ 0: 150, \ 5: 100, \ \text{others}: 550$$

That is, of the 1000 tuples in R, 200 of them have b-value 1, 150 have b-value 0, and 100 have b-value 5. In addition, 550 tuples have b-values other than 0, 1, or 5, and none of these other values appears more than 100 times.

Let the histogram for $S.b$ be:

$$0: 100, \ 1: 80, \ 2: 70, \ \text{others}: 250$$

Suppose also that $V(R, b) = 14$ and $V(S, b) = 13$. That is, the 550 tuples of R with unknown b-values are divided among eleven values, for an average of 50 tuples each, and the 250 tuples of S with unknown b-values are divided among ten values, each with an average of 25 tuples each.

Values 0 and 1 appear explicitly in both histograms, so we can calculate that the 150 tuples of R with $b = 0$ join with the 100 tuples of S having the same b-value, to yield 15,000 tuples in the result. Likewise, the 200 tuples of R with $b = 1$ join with the 80 tuples of S having $b = 1$ to yield 16,000 more tuples in the result.

The estimate of the effect of the remaining tuples is more complex. We shall continue to make the assumption that every value appearing in the relation with the smaller set of values (S in this case) will also appear in the set of values of the other relation. Thus, among the eleven remaining b-values of S, we know one of those values is 2, and we shall assume another of the values is 5, since that is one of the most frequent values in R. We estimate that 2 appears 50 times in R, and 5 appears 25 times in S. These estimates are each obtained by assuming that the value is one of the "other" values for its relation's histogram. The number of additional tuples from b-value 2 is thus $70 \times 50 = 3500$, and the number of additional tuples from b-value 5 is $100 \times 25 = 2500$.

Finally, there are nine other b-values that appear in both relations, and we estimate that each of them appears in 50 tuples of R and 25 tuples of S. Each of the nine values thus contributes $50 \times 25 = 1250$ tuples to the result. The estimate of the output size is thus:

$$15000 + 16000 + 3500 + 2500 + 9 \times 1250$$

or 48,250 tuples. Note that the simpler estimate from Section 16.4 would be $1000 \times 500/14$, or 35,714, based on the assumptions of equal numbers of occurrences of each value in each relation. $\square$

Example 16.28: In this example, we shall assume an equal-width histogram, and we shall demonstrate how knowing that values of two relations are almost disjoint can impact the estimate of a join size. Our relations are:

```
Jan(day, temp)
July(day, temp)
```

and the query is:

```
SELECT Jan.day, July.day
FROM Jan, July
WHERE Jan.temp = July.temp;
```

That is, find pairs of days in January and July that had the same temperature. The query plan is to equijoin `Jan` and `July` on the temperature, and project onto the two `day` attributes.

Suppose the histogram of temperatures for the relations `Jan` and `July` are as given in the table of Fig. 16.24.[5] In general, if both join attributes have equal-width histograms with the same set of bands (perhaps with some bands empty for one of the relations), then we can estimate the size of the join by estimating the size of the join of each pair of corresponding bands and summing.

If two corresponding bands have T_1 and T_2 tuples, respectively, and the number of values in a band is V, then the estimate for the number of tuples in the join of those bands is T_1T_2/V, following the principles laid out in Section 16.4.4. For the histograms of Fig. 16.24, many of these products are 0, because one or the other of T_1 and T_2 is 0. The only bands for which neither

---

[5]Our friends south of the equator should reverse the columns for January and July.

Range	Jan	July
0–9	40	0
10–19	60	0
20–29	80	0
30–39	50	0
40–49	10	5
50–59	5	20
60–69	0	50
70–79	0	100
80–89	0	60
90–99	0	10

Figure 16.24: Histograms of temperature

Different Kinds of Cost Estimates

We have suggested estimating disk I/O's as a good way to predict the true cost of a query. Sometimes estimating disk I/O's may turn out to be too complex or error-prone, or may be impossible if we are estimating the cost of a logical (rather than physical) plan. In such cases, simply considering intermediate result sizes as discussed in Section 16.4 may be an effective approach to cost estimation. Remember that the query optimizer needs only to compare query plans, not to predict exact execution time. On the other hand, sometimes disk I/O's may be too *coarse* a predictor. A more detailed cost estimate would consider CPU time, and still more detailed would consider the motion of the disk head, taking into account the possible locality of blocks accessed on the disk.

---

is 0 are 40–49 and 50–59. Since $V = 10$ is the width of a band, the 40–49 band contributes $10 \times 5/10 = 5$ tuples, and the the 50–59 band contributes $5 \times 20/10 = 10$ tuples.

Thus our estimate for the size of this join is $5 + 10 = 15$ tuples. If we had no histogram, and knew only that each relation had 245 tuples distributed among 100 values from 0 to 99, then our estimate of the join size would be $245 \times 245/100 = 600$ tuples. □

16.5.2 Computation of Statistics

Periodic recomputation of statistics is the norm in most DBMS's, for several reasons. First, statistics tend not to change radically in a short time. Second, even somewhat inaccurate statistics are useful as long as they are applied consistently to all the plans. Third, the alternative of keeping statistics up-to-date can make the statistics themselves into a "hot-spot" in the database; because statistics are read frequently, we prefer not to update them frequently too.

The recomputation of statistics might be triggered automatically after some period of time, or after some number of updates. However, a database administrator noticing, that poor-performing query plans are being selected by the query optimizer on a regular basis, might request the recomputation of statistics in an attempt to rectify the problem.

Computing statistics for an entire relation R can be very expensive, particularly if we compute $V(R, a)$ for each attribute a in the relation (or even worse, compute histograms for each a). One common approach is to compute approximate statistics by sampling only a fraction of the data. For example, let us suppose we want to sample a small fraction of the tuples to obtain an estimate for $V(R, a)$. A statistically reliable calculation can be complex, depending on a number of assumptions, such as whether values for a are distributed uniformly, according to a Zipfian distribution, or according to some other distribution. However, the intuition is as follows. If we look at a small sample of R, say 1% of its tuples, and we find that most of the a-values we see are different, then it is likely that $V(R, a)$ is close to $T(R)$. If we find that the sample has very few different values of a, then it is likely that we have seen most of the a-values that exist in the current relation.

16.5.3   Heuristics for Reducing the Cost of Logical Query Plans

One important use of cost estimates for queries or subqueries is in the application of heuristic transformations of the query. We have already observed in Section 16.3.3 how certain heuristics applied independent of cost estimates can be expected almost certainly to improve the cost of a logical query plan. Pushing selections down the tree is the canonical example of such a transformation.

However, there are other points in the query optimization process where estimating the cost both before and after a transformation will allow us to apply a transformation where it appears to reduce cost and avoid the transformation otherwise. In particular, when the preferred logical query plan is being generated, we may consider a number of optional transformations and the costs before and after. Because we are estimating the cost of a *logical* query plan, so we have not yet made decisions about the physical operators that will be used to implement the operators of relational algebra, our cost estimate cannot be based on disk I/O's. Rather, we estimate the sizes of all intermediate results using the techniques of Section 16.4, and their sum is our heuristic estimate for the cost of the entire logical plan. One example will serve to illustrate the issues and process.

Example 16.29 : Consider the initial logical query plan of Fig. 16.25, and let

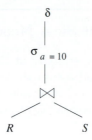

Figure 16.25: Logical query plan for Example 16.29

the statistics for the relations R and S be as follows:

$R(a,b)$	$S(b,c)$
$T(R) = 5000$	$T(S) = 2000$
$V(R,a) = 50$	
$V(R,b) = 100$	$V(S,b) = 200$
	$V(S,c) = 100$

To generate a final logical query plan from Fig. 16.25, we shall insist that the selection be pushed down as far as possible. However, we are not sure whether it makes sense to push the δ below the join or not. Thus, we generate from Fig. 16.25 the two query plans shown in Fig. 16.26; they differ in whether we have chosen to eliminate duplicates before or after the join. Notice that in plan (a) the δ is pushed down both branches of the tree. If R and/or S is known to have no duplicates, then the δ along its branch could be eliminated.

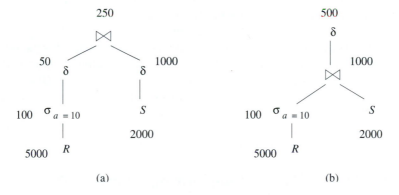

Figure 16.26: Two candidates for the best logical query plan

We know how to estimate the size of the result of the selections, from Section 16.4.3; we divide $T(R)$ by $V(R,a) = 50$. We also know how to estimate the size of the joins; we multiply the sizes of the arguments and divide by $\max\bigl(V(R,b), V(S,b)\bigr)$, which is 200. What we don't know is how to estimate the size of the relations with duplicates eliminated.

Estimates for Result Sizes Need Not Be the Same

Notice that in Fig. 16.26 the estimates at the roots of the two trees are different: 250 in one case and 500 in the other. Because estimation is an inexact science, these sorts of anomalies will occur. In fact, it is the exception when we can offer a guarantee of consistency, as we did in Section 16.4.6.

Intuitively, the estimate for plan (b) is higher because if there are duplicates in both R and S, these duplicates will be multiplied in the join; e.g., for tuples that appear 3 times in R and twice in S, their join will appear six times in $R \bowtie S$. Our simple formula for estimating the size of the result of a δ does not take into account the possibility that the effect of duplicates has been amplified by previous operations.

First, consider the size estimate for $\delta(\sigma_{a=10}(R))$. Since $\sigma_{a=10}(R)$ has only one value for a and up to 100 values for b, and there are an estimated 100 tuples in this relation, the rule from Section 16.4.7 tells us that the product of the value counts for each of the attributes is not a limiting factor. Thus, we estimate the size of the result of δ as half the tuples in $\sigma_{a=10}(R)$. Thus, Fig. 16.26(a) shows an estimate of 50 tuples for $\delta(\sigma_{a=10}(R))$.

Now, consider the estimate of the result of the δ in Fig. 16.26(b). The join has one value for a, an estimated $\min(V(R,b), V(S,b)) = 100$ values for b, and an estimated $V(S,c) = 100$ values for c. Thus again the product of the value counts does not limit how big the result of the δ can be. We estimate this result as 500 tuples, or half the number of tuples in the join.

To compare the two plans of Fig. 16.26, we add the estimated sizes for all the nodes except the root and the leaves. We exclude the root and leaves, because these sizes are not dependent on the plan chosen. For plan (a) this cost, the sum of the estimated sizes of the interior nodes, is $100 + 50 + 1000 = 1150$, while for plan (b) the sum is $100 + 1000 = 1100$. Thus, by a small margin we conclude that deferring the duplicate elimination to the end is a better plan. We would come to the opposite conclusion if, say, R or S had fewer b-values. Then the join size would be greater, making the cost of plan (b) greater. $\quad \Box$

16.5.4 Approaches to Enumerating Physical Plans

Now, let us consider the use of cost estimates in the conversion of a logical query plan to a physical query plan. The baseline approach, called *exhaustive*, is to consider all combinations of choices for each of the issues outlined at the beginning of Section 16.4 (order of joins, physical implementation of operators, and so on). Each possible physical plan is assigned an estimated cost, and the one with the smallest cost is selected.

However, there are a number of other approaches to selection of a physical plan. In this section, we shall outline various approaches that have been used, while Section 16.6 illustrates the major ideas in the context of the important problem of selecting a join order. Before proceeding, let us comment that there are two broad approaches to exploring the space of possible physical plans:

- *Top-down*: Here, we work down the tree of the logical query plan from the root. For each possible implementation of the operation at the root, we consider each possible way to evaluate its argument(s), and compute the cost of each combination, taking the best.[6]

- *Bottom-up*: For each subexpression of the logical-query-plan tree, we compute the costs of all possible ways to compute that subexpression. The possibilities and costs for a subexpression E are computed by considering the options for the subexpressions for E, and combining them in all possible ways with implementations for the root operator of E.

There is actually not much difference between the two approaches in their broadest interpretations, since either way, all possible combinations of ways to implement each operator in the query tree are considered. When limiting the search, a top-down approach may allow us to eliminate certain options that could not be eliminated bottom-up. However, bottom-up strategies that limit choices effectively have also been developed, so we shall concentrate on bottom-up methods in what follows.

You may, in fact, have noticed that there is an apparent simplification of the bottom-up method, where we consider only the *best* plan for each subexpression when we compute the plans for a larger subexpression. This approach, called *dynamic programming* in the list of methods below, is not guaranteed to yield the best plan, although often it does. The approach called *Selinger-style* (or *System-R-style*) optimization, also listed below, exploits additional properties that some of the plans for a subexpression may have, in order to produce optimal overall plans from plans that are not optimal for certain subexpressions.

Heuristic Selection

One option is to use the same approach to selecting a physical plan that is generally used for selecting a logical plan: make a sequence of choices based on heuristics. In Section 16.6.6, we shall discuss a "greedy" heuristic for join ordering, where we start by joining the pair of relations whose result has the smallest estimated size, then repeat the process for the result of that join and the other relations in the set to be joined. There are many other heuristics that may be applied; here are some of the most commonly used ones:

---

[6]Remember from Section 16.3.4 that a single node of the logical-query-plan tree may represent many uses of a single commutative and associative operator, such as join. Thus, the consideration of all possible plans for a single node may itself involve enumeration of very many choices.

1. If the logical plan calls for a selection $\sigma_{A=c}(R)$, and stored relation R has an index on attribute A, then perform an index-scan (as in Section 15.1.1) to obtain only the tuples of R with A-value equal to c.

2. More generally, if the selection involves one condition like $A = c$ above, and other conditions as well, we can implement the selection by an index-scan followed by a further selection on the tuples, which we shall represent by the physical operator *filter*. This matter is discussed further in Section 16.7.1.

3. If an argument of a join has an index on the join attribute(s), then use an index-join with that relation in the inner loop.

4. If one argument of a join is sorted on the join attribute(s), then prefer a sort-join to a hash-join, although not necessarily to an index-join if one is possible.

5. When computing the union or intersection of three or more relations, group the smallest relations first.

Branch-and-Bound Plan Enumeration

This approach, often used in practice, begins by using heuristics to find a good physical plan for the entire logical query plan. Let the cost of this plan be C. Then as we consider other plans for subqueries, we can eliminate any plan for a subquery that has a cost greater than C, since that plan for the subquery could not possibly participate in a plan for the complete query that is better than what we already know. Likewise, if we construct a plan for the complete query that has cost less than C, we replace C by the cost of this better plan in subsequent exploration of the space of physical query plans.

An important advantage of this approach is that we can choose when to cut off the search and take the best plan found so far. For instance, if the cost C is small, then even if there are much better plans to be found, the time spent finding them may exceed C, so it does not make sense to continue the search. However, if C is large, then investing time in the hope of finding a faster plan is wise.

Hill Climbing

This approach, in which we really search for a "valley" in the space of physical plans and their costs, starts with a heuristically selected physical plan. We can then make small changes to the plan, e.g., replacing one method for an operator by another, or reordering joins by using the associative and/or commutative laws, to find "nearby" plans that have lower cost. When we find a plan such that no small modification yields a plan of lower cost, we make that plan our chosen physical query plan.

Dynamic Programming

In this variation of the general bottom-up strategy, we keep for each subexpression only the plan of least cost. As we work up the tree, we consider possible implementations of each node, assuming the best plan for each subexpression is also used. We examine this approach extensively in Section 16.6.

Selinger-Style Optimization

This approach improves upon the dynamic-programming approach by keeping for each subexpression not only the plan of least cost, but certain other plans that have higher cost, yet produce a result that is sorted in an order that may be useful higher up in the expression tree. Examples of such *interesting* orders are when the result of the subexpression is sorted on one of:

1. The attribute(s) specified in a sort (τ) operator at the root.

2. The grouping attribute(s) of a later group-by (γ) operator.

3. The join attribute(s) of a later join.

   If we take the cost of a plan to be the sum of the sizes of the intermediate relations, then there appears to be no advantage to having an argument sorted. However, if we use the more accurate measure, disk I/O's, as the cost, then the advantage of having an argument sorted becomes clear if we can use one of the sort-based algorithms of Section 15.4, and save the work of the first pass for the argument that is sorted already.

16.5.5 Exercises for Section 16.5

Exercise 16.5.1: Estimate the size of the join $R(a, b) \bowtie S(b, c)$ using histograms for $R.b$ and $S.b$. Assume $V(R, b) = V(S, b) = 20$, and the histograms for both attributes give the frequency of the four most common values, as tabulated below:

	0	1	2	3	4	others
R.b	5	6	4	5		32
S.b	10	8	5		7	48

How does this estimate compare with the simpler estimate, assuming that all 20 values are equally likely to occur, with $T(R) = 52$ and $T(S) = 78$?

* **Exercise 16.5.2:** Estimate the size of the join $R(a, b) \bowtie S(b, c)$ if we have the following histogram information:

	$b < 0$	$b = 0$	$b > 0$
R	500	100	400
S	300	200	500

! **Exercise 16.5.3:** In Example 16.29 we suggested that reducing the number of values that either attribute named b had could make plan (a) better than plan (b) of Fig. 16.26. For what values of:

* a) $V(R, b)$

  b) $V(S, b)$

will plan (a) have a lower estimated cost than plan (b)?

! **Exercise 16.5.4:** Consider four relations R, S, T, and V. Respectively, they have 200, 300, 400, and 500 tuples, chosen randomly and independently from the same pool of 1000 tuples (e.g., the probabilities of a given tuple being in R is 1/5, in S is 3/10, and in both is 3/50).

* a) What is the expected size of $R \cup S \cup T \cup V$?

  b) What is the expected size of $R \cap S \cap T \cap V$?

* c) What order of unions gives the least cost (estimated sum of the sizes of the intermediate relations)?

  d) What order of intersections gives the least cost (estimated sum of the sizes of the intermediate relations)?

! **Exercise 16.5.5:** Repeat Exercise 16.5.4 if all four relations have 500 of the 1000 tuples, at random.[7]

!! **Exercise 16.5.6:** Suppose we wish to compute the expression

$$\tau_b\big(R(a, b) \bowtie S(b, c) \bowtie T(c, d)\big)$$

That is, we join the three relations and produce the result sorted on attribute b. Let us make the simplifying assumptions:

  i. We shall not "join" R and T first, because that is a product.

  ii. Any other join can be performed with a two-pass sort-join or hash-join, but in no other way.

  iii. Any relation, or the result of any expression, can be sorted by a two-phase, multiway merge-sort, but in no other way.

  iv. The result of the first join will be passed as an argument to the last join one block at a time and not stored temporarily on disk.

  v. Each relation occupies 1000 blocks, and the result of either join of two relations occupies 5000 blocks.

---

[7]Solutions to corresponding parts of this exercise are *not* published on the Web.

Answer the following based on these assumptions:

* a) What are all the subexpressions and orders that a Selinger-style optimization would consider?

  b) Which query plan uses the fewest disk I/O's?[8]

!! **Exercise 16.5.7:** Give an example of a logical query plan of the form $E \bowtie F$, for some expressions E and F (which you may choose), where using the best plans to evaluate E and F does not allow any choice of algorithm for the final join that minimizes the total cost of evaluating the entire expression. Make whatever assumptions you wish about the number of available main-memory buffers and the sizes of relations mentioned in E and F.

16.6 Choosing an Order for Joins

In this section we focus on a critical problem in cost-based optimization: selecting an order for the (natural) join of three or more relations. Similar ideas can be applied to other binary operations like union or intersection, but these operations are less important in practice, because they typically take less time to execute than joins, and they more rarely appear in clusters of three or more.

16.6.1 Significance of Left and Right Join Arguments

When ordering a join, we should remember that many of the join methods discussed in Chapter 15 are asymmetric. That is, the roles played by the two argument relations are different, and the cost of the join depends on which relation plays which role. Perhaps most important, the one-pass join of Section 15.2.3 reads one relation — preferably the smaller — into main memory, creating a structure such as a hash table to facilitate matching of tuples from the other relation. It then reads the other relation, one block at a time, to join its tuples with the tuples stored in memory.

For instance, suppose that when we select a physical plan we decide to use a one-pass join. Then we shall assume the left argument of the join is the smaller relation and store it in a main-memory data structure. This relation is called the *build relation*. The right argument of the join, called the *probe relation*, is read a block at a time and its tuples are matched in main memory with those of the build relation. Other join algorithms that distinguish between their arguments include:

1. Nested-loop join, where we assume the left argument is the relation of the outer loop.

2. Index-join, where we assume the right argument has the index.

---

[8] Notice that, because we have made some very specific assumptions about the join methods to be used, we can estimate disk I/O's, instead of relying on the simpler, but less accurate, counts of tuples as our cost measure.

16.6.2   Join Trees

When we have the join of two relations, we need to order the arguments. We shall conventionally select the one whose estimated size is the smaller as the left argument. Notice that the algorithms mentioned above — one-pass, nested-loop, and indexed — each work best if the left argument is the smaller. More precisely, one-pass and nested-loop joins each assign a special role to the smaller relation (build relation, or outer loop), and index-joins typically are reasonable choices only if one relation is small and the other has an index. It is quite common for there to be a significant and discernible difference in the sizes of arguments, because a query involving joins very often also involves a selection on at least one attribute, and that selection reduces the estimated size of one of the relations greatly.

Example 16.30 : Recall the query

```
SELECT movieTitle
FROM StarsIn, MovieStar
WHERE starName = name AND
    birthdate LIKE '%1960';
```

from Fig. 16.4, which leads to the preferred logical query plan of Fig. 16.21, in which we take the join of relation StarsIn and the result of a selection on relation MovieStar. We have not given estimates for the sizes of relations StarsIn or MovieStar, but we can assume that selecting for stars born in a single year will produce about 1/50th of the tuples in MovieStar. Since there are generally several stars per movie, we expect StarsIn to be larger than MovieStar to begin with, so the second argument of the join, $\sigma_{birthdate\ LIKE\ '%1960'}(\text{MovieStar})$, is much smaller than the first argument StarsIn. We conclude that the order of arguments in Fig. 16.21 should be reversed, so that the selection on MovieStar is the left argument.   □

There are only two choices for a join tree when there are two relations — take either of the two relations to be the left argument. When the join involves more than two relations, the number of possible join trees grows rapidly. For example, Fig. 16.27 shows three of the five shapes of trees in which four relations R, S, T, and U, are joined. However, each of these trees has the four relations in alphabetical order from the left. Since order of arguments matters, and there are $n!$ ways to order n things, each tree represents $4! = 24$ different trees when the possible labelings of the leaves are considered.

16.6.3   Left-Deep Join Trees

Figure 16.27(a) is an example of what is called a *left-deep* tree. In general, a binary tree is left-deep if all right children are leaves. Similarly, a tree like Fig. 16.27(c), all of whose left children are leaves, is called a *right-deep* tree. A tree like Fig. 16.27(b) that is neither left-deep nor right-deep is called *bushy*.

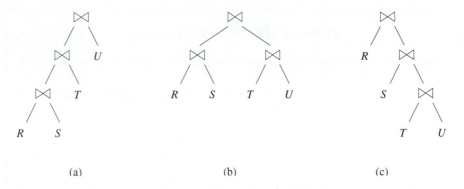

Figure 16.27: Ways to join four relations

We shall argue below that there is a two-fold advantage to considering only left-deep trees as possible join orders.

1. The number of possible left-deep trees with a given number of leaves is large, but not nearly as large as the number of all trees. Thus, searches for query plans can be used for larger queries if we limit the search to left-deep trees.

2. Left-deep trees for joins interact well with common join algorithms — nested-loop joins and one-pass joins in particular. Query plans based on left-deep trees plus these algorithms will tend to be more efficient than the same algorithms used with non-left-deep trees.

The "leaves" in a left- or right-deep join tree can actually be interior nodes, with operators other than a join. Thus, for instance, Fig. 16.21 is technically a left-deep join tree with one join operator. The fact that a selection is applied to the right operand of the join does not take the tree out of the left-deep join class.

The number of left-deep trees does not grow nearly as fast as the number of all trees for the multiway join of a given number of relations. For n relations, there is only one left-deep tree shape, to which we may assign the relations in $n!$ ways. There are the same number of right-deep trees for n relations. However, the total number of tree shapes $T(n)$ for n relations is given by the recurrence:

$$T(1) = 1$$
$$T(n) = \sum_{i=1}^{n-1} T(i)T(n-i)$$

The explanation for the second equation is that we may pick any number i between 1 and $n - 1$ to be the number of leaves in the left subtree of the root, and those leaves may be arranged in any of the $T(i)$ ways that trees with i leaves can be arranged. Similarly, the remaining $n - i$ leaves in the right subtree can be arranged in any of $T(n - i)$ ways.

Role of the Buffer Manager

The reader may notice a difference between our approach in the series of examples such as Example 15.4 and 15.7, where we assumed that there was a fixed limit on the number of main-memory buffers available for a join, and the more flexible assumption taken here, where we assume that as many buffers as necessary are available, but we try not to use "too many." Recall from Section 15.7 that the buffer manager has significant flexibility to allocate buffers to operations. However, if too many buffers are allocated at once, there will be thrashing, thus degrading the assumed performance of the algorithm being used.

The first few values of $T(n)$ are $T(1) = 1$, $T(2) = 1$, $T(3) = 2$, $T(4) = 5$, $T(5) = 14$, and $T(6) = 42$. To get the total number of trees once relations are assigned to the leaves, we multiply $T(n)$ by $n!$. Thus, for instance, the number of leaf-labeled trees of 6 leaves is $42 \times 6!$ or 30,240, of which 6!, or 720, are left-deep trees and another 720 are right-deep trees.

Now, let us consider the second advantage mentioned for left-deep join trees: their tendency to produce efficient plans. We shall give two examples:

1. If one-pass joins are used, and the build relation is on the left, then the amount of memory needed at any one time tends to be smaller than if we used a right-deep tree or a bushy tree for the same relations.

2. If we use nested-loop joins, with the relation of the outer loop on the left, then we avoid constructing any intermediate relation more than once.

Example 16.31 : Consider the left-deep tree in Fig. 16.27(a), and suppose that we use a simple one-pass join for each of the three $\bowtie$ operators. As always, the left argument is the build relation; i.e., it will be held in main memory. To compute $R \bowtie S$, we need to keep R in main memory, and as we compute $R \bowtie S$ we need to keep the result in main memory as well. Thus, we need $B(R) + B(R \bowtie S)$ main-memory buffers. If we pick R to be the smallest of the relations, and a selection has made R be rather small, then there is likely to be no problem making this number of buffers available.

Having computed $R \bowtie S$, we must join this relation with T. However, the buffers used for R are no longer needed and can be reused to hold (some of) the result of $(R \bowtie S) \bowtie T$. Similarly, when we join this relation with U, the relation $R \bowtie S$ is no longer needed, and its buffers can be reused for the result of the final join. In general, a left-deep join tree that is computed by one-pass joins requires main-memory space for at most two of the temporary relations any time.

Now, let us consider a similar implementation of the right-deep tree of Fig. 16.27(c). The first thing we need to do is load R into main-memory buffers, since left arguments are always the build relation. Then, we need to construct $S \bowtie (T \bowtie U)$ and use that as the probe relation for the join at the root. To compute $S \bowtie (T \bowtie U)$ we need to bring S into buffers and then compute $T \bowtie U$ as the probe relation for S. But $T \bowtie U$ requires that we first bring T into buffers. Now we have all three of R, S, and T in memory at the same time. In general, if we try to compute a right-deep join tree with n leaves, we shall have to bring $n - 1$ relations into memory simultaneously.

Of course it is possible that the total size $B(R) + B(S) + B(T)$ is less than the amount of space we need at either of the two intermediate stages of the computation of the left-deep tree, which are $B(R) + B(R \bowtie S)$ and $B(R \bowtie S) + B((R \bowtie S) \bowtie T)$, respectively.[9] However, as we pointed out in Example 16.30, queries with several joins often will have a small relation with which we can start as the leftmost argument in a left-deep tree. If R is small, we might expect $R \bowtie S$ to be significantly smaller than S and $(R \bowtie S) \bowtie T$ to be smaller than T, further justifying the use of a left-deep tree. □

Example 16.32: Now, let us suppose we are going to implement the four-way join of Fig. 16.27 by nested-loop joins, and that we use an iterator (as in Section 15.1.6) for each of the three joins involved. Also, assume for simplicity that each of the relations R, S, T, and U are stored relations, rather than expressions. If we use the left-deep tree of Fig. 16.27(a), then the iterator at the root gets a main-memory-sized chunk of its left argument $(R \bowtie S) \bowtie T$. It then joins the chunk with all of U, but as long as U is a stored relation, it is only necessary to scan U, not to construct it. When the next chunk of the left argument is obtained and put in memory, U will be read again, but nested-loop join requires that repetition, which cannot be avoided if both arguments are large.

Similarly, to get a chunk of $(R \bowtie S) \bowtie T$, we get a chunk of $R \bowtie S$ into memory and scan T. Several scans of T may eventually be necessary, but cannot be avoided. Finally, to get a chunk of $R \bowtie S$ requires reading a chunk of R and comparing it with S, perhaps several times. However, in all this action, only stored relations are read multiple times, and this repeated reading is an artifact of the way nested-loop join works when the main memory is insufficient to hold an entire relation.

Now, compare the behavior of iterators on the left-deep tree with the behavior of iterators on the right-deep tree of Fig. 16.27(c). The iterator at the root starts by reading a chunk of R. It must then construct the entire relation $S \bowtie (T \bowtie U)$ and compare it with that chunk of R. When we read the next chunk of R into memory, $S \bowtie (T \bowtie U)$ must be constructed again. Each subsequent chunk of R likewise requires constructing this same relation.

Of course, we could construct $S \bowtie (T \bowtie U)$ once and store it, either in memory or on disk. If we store it on disk, we are using extra disk I/O's compared with the left-deep tree's plan, and if we store it in memory, then we run into

---

[9]Note that as always we do not count the cost of storing the result of an expression tree when measuring costs.

the same problem with overuse of memory that we discussed in Example 16.31.
□

16.6.4 Dynamic Programming to Select a Join Order and Grouping

To pick an order for the join of many relations we have three choices:

1. Consider them all.

2. Consider a subset.

3. Use a heuristic to pick one.

We shall here consider a sensible approach to enumeration called *dynamic programming*. It can be used either to consider all orders, or to consider certain subsets only, such as orders restricted to left-deep trees. In Section 16.6.6 we consider a reasonable heuristic for selecting a single ordering. Dynamic programming is a common algorithmic paradigm.[10] The idea behind dynamic programming is that we fill in a table of costs, remembering only the minimum information we need to proceed to a conclusion.

Suppose we want to join $R_1 \bowtie R_2 \bowtie \cdots \bowtie R_n$. In a dynamic programming algorithm, we construct a table with an entry for each subset of one or more of the n relations. In that table we put:

1. The estimated size of the join of these relations. For this quantity we may use the formula of Section 16.4.6.

2. The least cost of computing the join of these relations. We shall use in our examples the sum of the sizes of the intermediate relations (not including the R_i's themselves or the join of the full set of relations associated with this table entry). Recall that the sizes of intermediate relations is the simplest measure we can use to estimate the true cost of disk I/O's, CPU utilization, or other factors. However, other, more complex estimates, such as total disk I/O's, could be used if we were willing and able to do the extra calculation involved. If we use disk I/O's or another measure of running time, then we also have to consider the algorithm used for the join in question, since different algorithms will have different costs. We shall discuss these issues after learning the basics of dynamic programming.

3. The expression that yields the least cost. This expression joins the set of relations in question, with some grouping. We can optionally restrict ourselves to left-deep expressions, in which case the expression is just an ordering of the relations.

---

[10]See Aho, Hopcroft and Ullman, *Data Structures and Algorithms*, Addison-Wesley, 1984, for a general treatment of dynamic programming.

The construction of this table is an induction on the subset size. There are two variations, depending on whether we wish to consider all possible tree shapes or only left-deep trees. We explain the difference when we discuss the inductive step of table construction.

BASIS: The entry for a single relation R consists of the size of R, a cost of 0, and an expression that is just R itself. The entry for a pair of relations $\{R_i, R_j\}$ is also easy to compute. The cost is 0, since there are no intermediate relations involved, and the size estimate is given by the rule of Section 16.4.6; it is the product of the sizes of R_i and R_j divided by the larger value-set size for each attribute shared by R_i and R_j, if any. The expression is either $R_i \bowtie R_j$ or $R_j \bowtie R_i$. Following the idea introduced in Section 16.6.1, we pick the smaller of R_i and R_j as the left argument.

INDUCTION: Now, we can build the table, computing entries for all subsets of size 3, 4, and so on, until we get an entry for the one subset of size n. That entry tells us the best way to compute the join of all the relations; it also gives us the estimated cost of that method, which is needed as we compute later entries. We need to see how to compute the entry for a set of k relations $\mathcal{R}$.

If we wish to consider only left-deep trees, then for each of the k relations R in $\mathcal{R}$ we consider the possibility that we compute the join for $\mathcal{R}$ by first computing the join of $\mathcal{R} - \{R\}$ and then joining it with R. The cost of the join for $\mathcal{R}$ is the cost of $\mathcal{R} - \{R\}$ plus the size of the latter join. We pick whichever R yields the least cost. The expression for $\mathcal{R}$ has the best join expression for $\mathcal{R} - \{R\}$ as the left argument of a final join, and R as the right argument. The size for $\mathcal{R}$ is whatever the formula from Section 16.4.6 gives.

If we wish to consider all trees, then computing the entry for a set of relations $\mathcal{R}$ is somewhat more complex. We need to consider all ways to partition $\mathcal{R}$ into disjoint sets $\mathcal{R}_1$ and $\mathcal{R}_2$. For each such subset, we consider the sum of:

1. The best costs of $\mathcal{R}_1$ and $\mathcal{R}_2$.

2. The sizes of $\mathcal{R}_1$ and $\mathcal{R}_2$.

For whichever partition gives the best cost, we use this sum as the cost for $\mathcal{R}$, and the expression for $\mathcal{R}$ is the join of the best join orders for $\mathcal{R}_1$ and $\mathcal{R}_2$.

Example 16.33 : Consider the join of four relations R, S, T, and U. For simplicity, we shall assume they each have 1000 tuples. Their attributes and the estimated sizes of values sets for the attributes in each relation are summarized in Fig. 16.28.

For the singleton sets, the sizes, costs and best plans are as in the table of Fig. 16.29. That is, for each single relation, the size is as given, 1000 for each, the cost is 0 since there are no intermediate relations needed, and the best (and only) expression is the relation itself.

Now, consider the pairs of relations. The cost for each is 0, since there are still no intermediate relations in a join of two. There are two possible plans,

$R(a,b)$	$S(b,c)$	$T(c,d)$	$U(d,a)$
$V(R,a)=100$			$V(U,a)=50$
$V(R,b)=200$	$V(S,b)=100$		
	$V(S,c)=500$	$V(T,c)=20$	
		$V(T,d)=50$	$V(U,d)=1000$

Figure 16.28: Parameters for Example 16.33

	$\{R\}$	$\{S\}$	$\{T\}$	$\{U\}$
Size	1000	1000	1000	1000
Cost	0	0	0	0
Best Plan	R	S	T	U

Figure 16.29: The table for singleton sets

since either of the two relations can be the left argument, but since the sizes happen to be the same for each relation we have no basis on which to choose between the plans. We shall take the first, in alphabetical order, to be the left argument in each case. The sizes of the resulting relations are computed by the usual formula. The results are summarized in Fig. 16.30. Note that 1M stands for 1,000,000, the size of those "joins" that are actually a product.

	$\{R,S\}$	$\{R,T\}$	$\{R,U\}$	$\{S,T\}$	$\{S,U\}$	$\{T,U\}$
Size	5000	1M	10,000	2000	1M	1000
Cost	0	0	0	0	0	0
Best Plan	$R \bowtie S$	$R \bowtie T$	$R \bowtie U$	$S \bowtie T$	$S \bowtie U$	$T \bowtie U$

Figure 16.30: The table for pairs of relations

Now, consider the table for joins of three out of the four relations. The only way to compute a join of three relations is to pick two to join first. The size estimate for the result is computed by the standard formula, and we omit the details of this calculation; remember that we'll get the same size regardless of which way we compute the join.

The cost estimate for each triple of relations is the size of the one intermediate relation — the join of the first two chosen. Since we want this cost to be as small as possible, we consider each pair of two out of the three relations and take the pair with the smallest size.

For the expression, we group the two chosen relations first, but these could be either the left or right argument. Let us suppose that we are only interested in left-deep trees, so we always use the join of the first two relations as the left argument. Since in all cases the estimated size for the join of two of our relations is at least 1000 (the size of each individual relation), were we to allow non-left-deep trees we would always select the single relation as the left argument in this example. The summary table for the triples is shown in Fig. 16.31.

	$\{R,S,T\}$	$\{R,S,U\}$	$\{R,T,U\}$	$\{S,T,U\}$
Size	10,000	50,000	10,000	2,000
Cost	2,000	5,000	1,000	1,000
Best Plan	$(S \bowtie T) \bowtie R$	$(R \bowtie S) \bowtie U$	$(T \bowtie U) \bowtie R$	$(T \bowtie U) \bowtie S$

Figure 16.31: The table for triples of relations

Let us consider $\{R,S,T\}$ as an example of the calculation. We must consider each of the three pairs in turn. If we start with $R \bowtie S$, then the cost is the size of this relation, which is 5000, as we learned from the table for the pairs in Fig. 16.30. Starting with $R \bowtie T$ gives us a cost of 1,000,000 for the intermediate relation, and starting with $S \bowtie T$ has a cost of 2000. Since the latter is the smallest cost of the three options, we choose that plan. The choice is reflected not only in the cost entry of the $\{R,S,T\}$ column, but in the best-plan row, where the plan that groups S and T first appears.

Now, we must consider the situation for the join of all four relations. The size estimate for this relation is 100 tuples, so the true cost is essentially all in the construction of intermediate relations. However, recall that we never charge for the size of the result anyway when comparing plans.

There are two general ways we can compute the join of all four:

1. Pick three to join in the best possible way, and then join in the fourth.

2. Divide the four relations into two pairs of two, join the pairs and then join the results.

Of course, if we only consider left-deep trees then the second type of plan is excluded, because it yields bushy trees. The table of Fig. 16.32 summarizes the seven possible ways to group the joins, based on the preferred groupings from Figs. 16.30 and 16.31.

For instance, consider the first expression in Fig. 16.32. It represents joining R, S, and T first, and then joining that result with U. From Fig. 16.31, we know that the best way to join R, S, and T is to join S and T first. We have used the left-deep form of this expression, and joined U on the right to continue the left-deep form. If we consider only left-deep trees, then this expression and relation order is the only option. If we allowed bushy trees, we would join U on the left, since it is smaller than the join of the other three. The cost of this join is 12,000, which is the sum of the cost and size of $(S \bowtie T) \bowtie R$, which are 2000 and 10,000, respectively.

Grouping	Cost
$((S \bowtie T) \bowtie R) \bowtie U$	12,000
$((R \bowtie S) \bowtie U) \bowtie T$	55,000
$((T \bowtie U) \bowtie R) \bowtie S$	11,000
$((T \bowtie U) \bowtie S) \bowtie R$	3,000
$(T \bowtie U) \bowtie (R \bowtie S)$	6,000
$(R \bowtie T) \bowtie (S \bowtie U)$	2,000,000
$(S \bowtie T) \bowtie (R \bowtie U)$	12,000

Figure 16.32: Join groupings and their costs

The last three expressions in Fig. 16.32 represent additional options if we include bushy trees. These are formed by joining relations first in two pairs. For example, the last line represents the strategy of joining $R \bowtie U$ and $S \bowtie T$, and then joining the result. The cost of this expression is the sum of the sizes and costs of the two pairs. The costs are 0, as must be the case for any pair, and the sizes are 10,000 and 2000, respectively. Since we generally select the smaller relation to be the left argument, we show the expression as $(S \bowtie T) \bowtie (R \bowtie U)$.

In this example, we see that the least of all costs is associated with the fourth expression: $((T \bowtie U) \bowtie S) \bowtie R$. This expression is the one we select for computing the join; its cost is 3000. Since it is a left-deep tree, it is the selected logical query plan regardless of whether our dynamic-programming strategy considers all plans or just left-deep plans. □

16.6.5 Dynamic Programming With More Detailed Cost Functions

Using relation sizes as the cost estimate simplifies the calculations in a dynamic-programming algorithm. However, a disadvantage of this simplification is that it does not involve the actual costs of the joins in the calculation. As an extreme example, if one possible join $R(a, b) \bowtie S(b, c)$ involves a relation R with one tuple and another relation S that has an index on the join attribute b, then the join takes almost no time. On the other hand, if S has no index, then we must scan it, taking $B(S)$ disk I/O's, even when R is a singleton. A cost measure that only involved the sizes of R, S, and $R \bowtie S$ cannot distinguish these two cases, so the cost of using $R \bowtie S$ in the grouping will be either overestimated or underestimated.

However, modifying the dynamic programming algorithm to take join algorithms into account is not hard. First, the cost measure we use becomes disk I/O's, or whatever running-time units we prefer. When computing the cost of $\mathcal{R}_1 \bowtie \mathcal{R}_2$, we sum the cost of $\mathcal{R}_1$, the cost of $\mathcal{R}_2$, and the least cost of joining these two relations using the best available algorithm. Since the latter cost usually depends on the sizes of $\mathcal{R}_1$ and $\mathcal{R}_2$, we must also compute estimates for these sizes as we did in Example 16.33.

An even more powerful version of dynamic programming is based on the Selinger-style optimization mentioned in Section 16.5.4. Now, for each set of relations that might be joined, we keep not only one cost, but several costs. Recall that Selinger-style optimization considers not only the least cost of producing the result of the join, but also the least cost of producing that relation sorted in any of a number of "interesting" orders. These interesting sorts include any that might be used to advantage in a later sort-join or that could be used to produce the output of the entire query in the sorted order desired by the user. When sorted relations must be produced, the use of sort-join, either one-pass or multipass, must be considered as an option, while without considering the value of sorting a result, hash-joins are always at least as good as the corresponding sort-join.

16.6.6 A Greedy Algorithm for Selecting a Join Order

As Example 16.33 suggests, even the carefully limited search of dynamic programming leads to a number of calculations that is exponential in the number of relations joined. It is reasonable to use an exhaustive method like dynamic programming or branch-and-bound search to find optimal join orders of five or six relations. However, when the number of joins grows beyond that, or if we choose not to invest the time necessary for an exhaustive search, then we can use a join-order heuristic in our query optimizer.

The most common choice of heuristic is a *greedy* algorithm, where we make one decision at a time about the order of joins and never backtrack or reconsider decisions once made. We shall consider a greedy algorithm that only selects a left-deep tree. The "greediness" is based on the idea that we want to keep the intermediate relations as small as possible at each level of the tree.

BASIS: Start with the pair of relations whose estimated join size is smallest. The join of these relations becomes the *current tree*.

INDUCTION: Find, among all those relations not yet included in the current tree, the relation that, when joined with the current tree, yields the relation of smallest estimated size. The new current tree has the old current tree as its left argument and the selected relation as its right argument.

Example 16.34 : Let us apply the greedy algorithm to the relations of Example 16.33. The basis step is to find the pair of relations that have the smallest join. Consulting Fig. 16.30, we see that this honor goes to the join $T \bowtie U$, with a cost of 1000. Thus, $T \bowtie U$ is the "current tree."

We now consider whether to join R or S into the tree next. Thus we compare the sizes of $(T \bowtie U) \bowtie R$ and $(T \bowtie U) \bowtie S$. Figure 16.31 tells us that the latter, with a size of 2000 is better than the former, with a size of 10,000. Thus, we pick as the new current tree $(T \bowtie U) \bowtie S$.

Now there is no choice; we must join R at the last step, leaving us with a total cost of 3000, the sum of the sizes of the two intermediate relations.

Join Selectivity

A useful way to view heuristics such as the greedy algorithm for selecting a left-deep join tree is that each relation R, when joined with the current tree, has a *selectivity*, which is the ratio

$$\frac{\text{size of the join result}}{\text{size of the current tree's result}}$$

Since we usually do not have the exact sizes of either relation, we estimate these sizes as we have done previously. A greedy approach to join ordering is to pick that relation with the smallest selectivity.

For example, if a join attribute is a key for R, then the selectivity is at most 1, which is usually a favorable situation. Notice that, judging from the statistics of Fig. 16.28, attribute d is a key for U, and there are no keys for other relations, which suggests why joining T with U is the best way to start the join.

Note that the tree resulting from the greedy algorithm is the same as that selected by the dynamic-programming algorithm in Example 16.33. However, there are examples where the greedy algorithm fails to find the best solution, while the dynamic-programming algorithm guarantees to find the best; see Exercise 16.6.4. $\square$

16.6.7 Exercises for Section 16.6

Exercise 16.6.1: For the relations of Exercise 16.4.1, give the dynamic-programming table entries that evaluates all possible join orders allowing: a) All trees   b) Left-deep trees only. What is the best choice in each case?

Exercise 16.6.2: Repeat Exercise 16.6.1 with the following modifications:

   i. The schema for Z is changed to $Z(d, a)$.

   ii. $V(Z, a) = 100$.

Exercise 16.6.3: Repeat Exercise 16.6.1 with the relations of Exercise 16.4.2.

* **Exercise 16.6.4:** Consider the join of relations $R(a, b)$, $S(b, c)$, $T(c, d)$, and $U(a, d)$, where R and U each have 1000 tuples, while S and T each have 100 tuples. Further, there are 100 values of all attributes of all relations, except for attribute c, where $V(S, c) = V(T, c) = 10$.

   a) What is the order selected by the greedy algorithm? What is its cost?

   b) What is the optimum join ordering and its cost?

Exercise 16.6.5: How many trees are there for the join of: *a) seven b) eight relations? How many of these are neither left-deep nor right-deep?

! **Exercise 16.6.6:** Suppose we wish to join the relations R, S, T, and U in one of the tree structures of Fig. 16.27, and we want to keep all intermediate relations in memory until they are no longer needed. Following our usual assumption, the result of the join of all four will be consumed by some other process as it is generated, so no memory is needed for that relation. In terms of the number of blocks required for the stored relations and the intermediate relations [e.g., $B(R)$ or $B(R \bowtie S)$], give a lower bound on M, the number of blocks of memory needed, for:

* a) The left-deep tree of Fig. 16.27(a).

  b) The bushy tree of Fig. 16.27(b).

  c) The right-deep of Fig. 16.27(c).

What assumptions let us conclude that one tree is certain to use less memory than another?

*! **Exercise 16.6.7:** If we use dynamic programming to select an order for the join of k relations, how many entries of the table do we have to fill?

16.7 Completing the Physical-Query-Plan

We have parsed the query, converted it to an initial logical query plan, and improved that logical query plan with transformations described in Section 16.3. Part of the process of selecting the physical query plan is enumeration and cost-estimation for all of our options, which we discussed in Section 16.5. Section 16.6 focused on the question of enumeration, cost estimation, and ordering for joins of several relations. By extension, we can use similar techniques to order groups of unions, intersections, or any associative/commutative operation.

There are still several steps needed to turn the logical plan into a complete physical query plan. The principal issues that we must yet cover are:

1. Selection of algorithms to implement the operations of the query plan, when algorithm-selection was not done as part of some earlier step such as selection of a join order by dynamic programming.

2. Decisions regarding when intermediate results will be *materialized* (created whole and stored on disk), and when they will be *pipelined* (created only in main memory, and not necessarily kept in their entirety at any one time).

3. Notation for physical-query-plan operators, which must include details regarding access methods for stored relations and algorithms for implementation of relational-algebra operators.

We shall not discuss the subject of selection of algorithms for operators in its entirety. Rather, we sample the issues by discussing two of the most important operators: selection in Section 16.7.1 and joins in Section 16.7.2. Then, we consider the choice between pipelining and materialization in Sections 16.7.3 through 16.7.5. A notation for physical query plans is presented in Section 16.7.6.

16.7.1 Choosing a Selection Method

One of the important steps in choosing a physical query plan is to pick algorithms for each selection operator. In Section 15.2.1 we mentioned the obvious implementation of a $\sigma_C(R)$ operator, where we access the entire relation R and see which tuples satisfy condition C. Then in Section 15.6.2 we considered the possibility that C was of the form "attribute equals constant," and we had an index on that attribute. If so, then we can find the tuples that satisfy condition C without looking at all of R. Now, let us consider the generalization of this problem, where we have a selection condition that is the AND of several conditions, some of which are of the form "attribute equals constant" or another comparison, such as $<$, between an attribute and a constant.

Assuming there are no multidimensional indexes on several of the attributes, then each physical plan uses some number of attributes that each:

a) Have an index, and

b) Are compared to a constant in one of the terms of the selection.

We then use these indexes to identify the sets of tuples that satisfy each of the conditions. Sections 13.2.3 and 14.1.5 discussed how we could use pointers obtained from these indexes to find only the tuples that satisfied all the conditions before we read these tuples from disk.

For simplicity, we shall not consider the use of several indexes in this way. Rather, we limit our discussion to physical plans that:

1. Use one comparison of the form $A\theta c$, where A is an attribute with an index, c is a constant, and θ is a comparison operator such as $=$ or $<$.

2. Retrieve all tuples that satisfy the comparison from (1), using the index-scan physical operator discussed in Section 15.1.1.

3. Consider each tuple selected in (2) to decide whether it satisfies the rest of the selection condition. We shall call the physical operator that performs this step `Filter`; it takes the condition used to select tuples as a parameter, much as the σ operator of relational algebra does.

In addition to physical plans of this form, we must also consider the plan that uses no index but reads the entire relation (using the table-scan physical operator) and passes each tuple to the `Filter` operator to check for satisfaction of the selection condition.

We decide among the physical plans with which to implement a given selection by estimating the cost of reading data for each possible option. To compare costs of alternative plans we cannot continue using the simplified cost estimate of intermediate-relation size. The reason is that we are now considering implementations of a single step of the logical query plan, and intermediate relations are independent of implementation.

Thus, we shall refocus our attention and resume counting disk I/O's, as we did when we discussed algorithms and their costs in Chapter 15. To simplify as before, we shall count only the cost of accessing the data blocks, not the index blocks. Recall that the number of index blocks needed is generally much smaller than the number of data blocks needed, so this approximation to disk I/O cost is usually accurate enough.

The following is an outline of how costs for the various plans are estimated. We assume that the operation is $\sigma_C(R)$, where condition C is the AND of one or more terms. We use the example terms $a = 10$ and $b < 20$ to represent equality conditions and inequality conditions, respectively.

1. The cost of the table-scan algorithm coupled with a filter step is:

   (a) $B(R)$ if R is clustered, and

   (b) $T(R)$ if R is not clustered.

2. The cost of a plan that picks an equality term such as $a = 10$ for which an index on attribute a exists, uses index-scan to find the matching tuples, and then filters the retrieved tuples to see if they satisfy the full condition C is:

   (a) $B(R)/V(R,a)$ if the index is clustering, and

   (b) $T(R)/V(R,a)$ if the index is not clustering.

3. The cost of a plan that picks an inequality term such as $b < 20$ for which an index on attribute b exists, uses index-scan to retrieve the matching tuples, and then filters the retrieved tuples to see if they satisfy the full condition C is:

   (a) $B(R)/3$ if the index is clustering,[11] and

   (b) $T(R)/3$ if the index is not clustering.

Example 16.35 : Consider selection $\sigma_{x=1 \text{ AND } y=2 \text{ AND } z<5}(R)$, where $R(x,y,z)$ has the following parameters: $T(R) = 5000$, $B(R) = 200$, $V(R,x) = 100$, and $V(R,y) = 500$. Further, suppose R is clustered, and there are indexes on all of x, y, and z, but only the index on z is clustering. The following are the options for implementing this selection:

---

[11] Recall that we assume the typical inequality retrieves only 1/3 the tuples, for reasons discussed in Section 16.4.3.

1. Table-scan followed by filter. The cost is $B(R)$, or 200 disk I/O's, since R is clustered.

2. Use the index on x and the index-scan operator to find those tuples with $x = 1$, then use the filter operator to check that $y = 2$ and $z < 5$. Since there are about $T(R)/V(R, x) = 50$ tuples with $x = 1$, and the index is not clustering, we require about 50 disk I/O's.

3. Use the index on y and index-scan to find those tuples with $y = 2$, then filter these tuples to see that $x = 1$ and $z < 5$. The cost for using this nonclustering index is about $T(R)/V(R, y)$, or 10 disk I/O's.

4. Use the clustering index on z and index-scan to find those tuples with $z < 5$, then filter these tuples to see that $x = 1$ and $y = 2$. The number of disk I/O's is about $B(R)/3 = 67$.

We see that the least cost plan is the third, with an estimated cost of 10 disk I/O's. Thus, the preferred physical plan for this selection retrieves all tuples with $y = 2$ and then filters for the other two conditions.   □

16.7.2   Choosing a Join Method

We saw in Chapter 15 the costs associated with the various join algorithms. On the assumption that we know (or can estimate) how many buffers are available to perform the join, we can apply the formulas in Section 15.4.8 for sort-joins, Section 15.5.7 for hash-joins, and Sections 15.6.3 and 15.6.4 for indexed joins.

However, if we are not sure of, or cannot know, the number of buffers that will be available during the execution of this query (because we do not know what else the DBMS is doing at the same time), or if we do not have estimates of important size parameters such as the $V(R, a)$'s, then there are still some principles we can apply to choosing a join method. Similar ideas apply to other binary operations such as unions, and to the full-relation, unary operators, γ and δ.

- One approach is to call for the one-pass join, hoping that the buffer manager can devote enough buffers to the join, or that the buffer manager can come close, so thrashing is not a major cost. An alternative (for joins only, not for other binary operators) is to choose a nested-loop join, hoping that if the left argument cannot be granted enough buffers to fit in memory at once, then that argument will not have to be divided into too many pieces, and the resulting join will still be reasonably efficient.

- A sort-join is a good choice when either:

  1. One or both arguments are already sorted on their join attribute(s), or

---

Materialization in Memory

One might imagine that there is an intermediate approach, between pipelining and materialization, where the entire result of one operation is stored in main-memory buffers (not on disk) before being passed to the consuming operation. We regard this possible mode of operation as pipelining, where the first thing that the consuming operation does is organize the entire relation, or a large portion of it, in memory. An example of this sort of behavior is a selection, whose result is pipelined as the left (build) argument to one of several join algorithms, including the simple one-pass join, multipass hash-join, or sort-join.

---

2. There are two or more joins on the same attribute, such as

$$\big(R(a,b) \bowtie S(a,c)\big) \bowtie T(a,d)$$

where sorting R and S on a will cause the result of $R \bowtie S$ to be sorted on a and used directly in a second sort-join.

- If there is an index opportunity such as a join $R(a,b) \bowtie S(b,c)$, where R is expected to be small (perhaps the result of a selection on a key that must yield only one tuple), and there is an index on the join attribute $S.b$, then we should choose an index-join.

- If there is no opportunity to use already-sorted relations or indexes, and a multipass join is needed, then hashing is probably the best choice, because the number of passes it requires depends on the size of the smaller argument rather than on both arguments.

16.7.3 Pipelining Versus Materialization

The last major issue we shall discuss in connection with choice of a physical query plan is pipelining of results. The naive way to execute a query plan is to order the operations appropriately (so an operation is not performed until the argument(s) below it have been performed), and store the result of each operation on disk until it is needed by another operation. This strategy is called *materialization*, since each intermediate relation is materialized on disk.

A more subtle, and generally more efficient, way to execute a query plan is to interleave the execution of several operations. The tuples produced by one operation are passed directly to the operation that uses it, without ever storing the intermediate tuples on disk. This approach is called *pipelining*, and it typically is implemented by a network of iterators (see Section 15.1.6), whose functions call each other at appropriate times. Since it saves disk I/O's, there is an obvious advantage to pipelining, but there is a corresponding disadvantage. Since several operations must share main memory at any time, there is a chance that algorithms with higher disk-I/O requirements must be chosen, or thrashing will occur, thus giving back all the disk-I/O savings that were gained by pipelining, and possibly more.

16.7.4 Pipelining Unary Operations

Unary operations — selection and projection — are excellent candidates for pipelining. Since these operations are tuple-at-a-time, we never need to have more than one block for input, and one block for the output. This mode of operation was suggested by Fig. 15.5.

We may implement a pipelined unary operation by iterators, as discussed in Section 15.1.6. The consumer of the pipelined result calls `GetNext()` each time another tuple is needed. In the case of a projection, it is only necessary to call `GetNext()` once on the source of tuples, project that tuple appropriately, and return the result to the consumer. For a selection σ_C (technically, the physical operator `Filter(C)`), it may be necessary to call `GetNext()` several times at the source, until one tuple that satisfies condition C is found. Figure 16.33 illustrates this process.

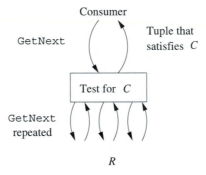

Figure 16.33: Execution of a pipelined selection using iterators

16.7.5 Pipelining Binary Operations

The results of binary operations can also be pipelined. We use one buffer to pass the result to its consumer, one block at a time. However, the number of other buffers needed to compute the result and to consume the result varies, depending on the size of the result and the sizes of other relations involved in the query. We shall use an extended example to illustrate the tradeoffs and opportunities.

Example 16.36: Let us consider physical query plans for the expression

$$\bigl(R(w,x) \bowtie S(x,y)\bigr) \bowtie U(y,z)$$

We make the following assumptions:

1. R occupies 5000 blocks; S and U each occupy 10,000 blocks.

2. The intermediate result $R \bowtie S$ occupies k blocks for some k. We can estimate k, based on the number of x-values in R and S and the size of (w, x, y) tuples compared to the (w, x) tuples of R and the (x, y) tuples of S. However, we want to see what happens as k varies, so we leave this constant open.

3. Both joins will be implemented as hash-joins, either one-pass or two-pass, depending on k.

4. There are 101 buffers available. This number, as usual, is set artificially low.

A sketch of the expression with key parameters is in Fig. 16.34.

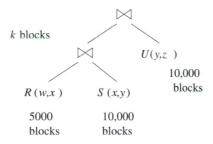

Figure 16.34: Logical query plan and parameters for Example 16.36

First, consider the join $R \bowtie S$. Neither relation fits in main memory, so we need a two-pass hash-join. If the smaller relation R is partitioned into the maximum-possible 100 buckets on the first pass, then each bucket for R occupies 50 blocks.[12] If R's buckets have 50 blocks, then the second pass of the hash-join $R \bowtie S$ uses 51 buffers, leaving 50 buffers to use for the join of the result of $R \bowtie S$ with U.

Now, suppose that $k \leq 49$; that is, the result of $R \bowtie S$ occupies at most 49 blocks. Then we can pipeline the result of $R \bowtie S$ into 49 buffers, organize them for lookup as a hash table, and we have one buffer left to read each block of U in turn. We may thus execute the second join as a one-pass join. The total number of disk I/O's is:

a) 45,000 to perform the two-pass hash join of R and S.

---

[12] We shall assume for convenience that all buckets wind up with exactly their fair share of tuples. If there are variations, as there surely will be, then some extra buffers will be needed occasionally, and we rely on the buffer manager to make them available, perhaps by moving some buffers to swap space on disk, temporarily. We do not, however, consider the additional cost of disk I/O's for swapping, as we can expect that cost to be a small fraction of the total cost.

   b) 10,000 to read U in the one-pass hash-join of $(R \bowtie S) \bowtie U$.

The total is 55,000 disk I/O's.

   Now, suppose $k > 49$, but $k \le 5000$. We can still pipeline the result of $R \bowtie S$, but we need to use another strategy, in which this relation is joined with U in a 50-bucket, two-pass hash-join.

1. Before we start on $R \bowtie S$, we hash U into 50 buckets of 200 blocks each.

2. Next, we perform a two-pass hash join of R and S using 51 buckets as before, but as each tuple of $R \bowtie S$ is generated, we place it in one of the 50 remaining buffers that is used to help form the 50 buckets for the join of $R \bowtie S$ with U. These buffers are written to disk when they get full, as is normal for a two-pass hash-join.

3. Finally, we join $R \bowtie S$ with U bucket by bucket. Since $k \le 5000$, the buckets of $R \bowtie S$ will be of size at most 100 blocks, so this join is feasible. The fact that buckets of U are of size 200 blocks is not a problem, since we are using buckets of $R \bowtie S$ as the build relation and buckets of U as the probe relation in the one-pass joins of buckets.

The number of disk I/O's for this pipelined join is:

   a) 20,000 to read U and write its tuples into buckets.

   b) 45,000 to perform the two-pass hash-join $R \bowtie S$.

   c) k to write out the buckets of $R \bowtie S$.

   d) $k + 10,000$ to read the buckets of $R \bowtie S$ and U in the final join.

The total cost is thus $75,000 + 2k$. Note that there is an apparent discontinuity as k grows from 49 to 50, since we had to change the final join from one-pass to two-pass. In practice, the cost would not change so precipitously, since we could use the one-pass join even if there were not enough buffers and a small amount of thrashing occurred.

   Last, let us consider what happens when $k > 5000$. Now, we cannot perform a two-pass join in the 50 buffers available if the result of $R \bowtie S$ is pipelined. We could use a three-pass join, but that would require an extra 2 disk I/O's per block of either argument, or $20,000 + 2k$ more disk I/O's. We can do better if we instead decline to pipeline $R \bowtie S$. Now, an outline of the computation of the joins is:

1. Compute $R \bowtie S$ using a two-pass hash join and store the result on disk.

2. Join $R \bowtie S$ with U, also using a two-pass hash-join. Note that since $B(U) = 10,000$, we can perform a two-pass hash-join using 100 buckets, regardless of how large k is. Technically, U should appear as the left argument of its join in Fig. 16.34 if we decide to make U the build relation for the hash join.

The number of disk I/O's for this plan is:

a) 45,000 for the two-pass join of R and S.

b) k to store $R \bowtie S$ on disk.

c) $30,000 + 3k$ for the two-pass hash-join of U with $R \bowtie S$.

The total cost is thus $75,000 + 4k$, which is less than the cost of going to a three-pass join at the final step. The three complete plans are summarized in the table of Fig. 16.35. □

Range of k	Pipeline or Materialize	Algorithm for final join	Total Disk I/O's
$k \leq 49$	Pipeline	one-pass	55,000
$50 \leq k \leq 5000$	Pipeline	50-bucket, two-pass	$75,000 + 2k$
$5000 < k$	Materialize	100-bucket, two-pass	$75,000 + 4k$

Figure 16.35: Costs of physical plans as a function of the size of $R \bowtie S$

16.7.6 Notation for Physical Query Plans

We have seen many examples of the operators that can be used to form a physical query plan. In general, each operator of the logical plan becomes one or more operators of the physical plan, and leaves (stored relations) of the logical plan become, in the physical plan, one of the scan operators applied to that relation. In addition, materialization would be indicated by a Store operator applied to the intermediate result that is to be materialized, followed by a suitable scan operator (usually TableScan, since there is no index on the intermediate relation unless one is constructed explicitly) when the materialized result is accessed by its consumer. However, for simplicity, in our physical-query-plan trees we shall indicate that a certain intermediate relation is materialized by a double line crossing the edge between that relation and its consumer. All other edges are assumed to represent pipelining between the supplier and consumer of tuples.

We shall now catalog the various operators that are typically found in physical query plans. Unlike the relational algebra, whose notation is fairly standard, each DBMS will use its own internal notation for physical query plans.

Operators for Leaves

Each relation R that is a leaf operand of the logical-query-plan tree will be replaced by a scan operator. The options are:

1. `TableScan(R)`: All blocks holding tuples of R are read in arbitrary order.

2. `SortScan(R,L)`: Tuples of R are read in order, sorted according to the attribute(s) on list L.

3. `IndexScan(R,C)`: Here, C is a condition of the form $A\theta c$, where A is an attribute of R, θ is a comparison such as $=$ or $<$, and c is a constant. Tuples of R are accessed through an index on attribute A. If the comparison θ is not $=$, then the index must be one, such as a B-tree, that supports range queries.

4. `IndexScan(R,A)`: Here A is an attribute of R. The entire relation R is retrieved via an index on $R.A$. This operator behaves like `TableScan`, but may be more efficient in certain circumstances, if R is not clustered and/or its blocks are not easily found.

Physical Operators for Selection

A logical operator $\sigma_C(R)$ is often combined, or partially combined, with the access method for relation R, when R is a stored relation. Other selections, where the argument is not a stored relation or an appropriate index is not available, will be replaced by the corresponding physical operator we have called `Filter`. Recall the strategy for choosing a selection implementation, which we discussed in Section 16.7.1. The notation we shall use for the various selection implementations are:

1. We may simply replace $\sigma_C(R)$ by the operator `Filter(C)`. This choice makes sense if there is no index on R, or no index on an attribute that condition C mentions. If R, the argument of the selection, is actually an intermediate relation being pipelined to the selection, then no other operator besides `Filter` is needed. If R is a stored or materialized relation, then we must use an operator, `TableScan` or perhaps `SortScan(R,L)`, to access R. We might prefer sort-scan if the result of $\sigma_C(R)$ will later be passed to an operator that requires its argument sorted.

2. If condition C can be expressed as $A\theta c$ AND D for some other condition D, and there is an index on $R.A$, then we may:

   (a) Use the operator `IndexScan(R,A`θ`c)` to access R, and

   (b) Use `Filter(D)` in place of the selection $\sigma_C(R)$.

Physical Sort Operators

Sorting of a relation can occur at any point in the physical query plan. We have already introduced the `SortScan(R,L)` operator, which reads a stored relation R and produces it sorted according to the list of attributes L. When we apply a sort-based algorithm for operations such as join or grouping, there is an initial phase in which we sort the argument according to some list of attributes. It is common to use an explicit physical operator Sort(L) to perform this sort on an operand relation that is not stored. This operator can also be used at the top of the physical-query-plan tree if the result needs to be sorted because of an ORDER BY clause in the original query, thus playing the same role as the τ operator of Section 5.4.6.

Other Relational-Algebra Operations

All other operations are replaced by a suitable physical operator. These operators can be given designations that indicate:

1. The operation being performed, e.g., join or grouping.

2. Necessary parameters, e.g., the condition in a theta-join or the list of elements in a grouping.

3. A general strategy for the algorithm: sort-based, hash-based, or in some joins, index-based.

4. A decision about the number of passes to be used: one-pass, two-pass, or multipass (recursive, using as many passes as necessary for the data at hand). Alternatively, this choice may be left until run-time.

5. An anticipated number of buffers the operation will require.

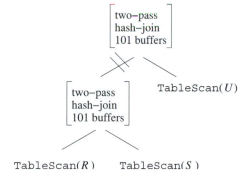

Figure 16.36: A physical plan from Example 16.36

Example 16.37: Figure 16.36 shows the physical plan developed in Example 16.36 for the case $k > 5000$. In this plan, we access each of the three relations by a table-scan. We use a two-pass hash-join for the first join, materialize it, and use a two-pass hash-join for the second join. By implication of the double-line symbol for materialization, the left argument of the top join is also obtained by a table-scan, and the result of the first join is stored using the Store operator.

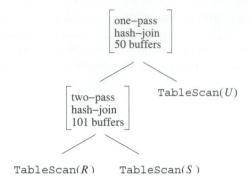

Figure 16.37: Another physical plan for the case where $R \bowtie S$ is expected to be very small

In contrast, if $k \leq 49$, then the physical plan developed in Example 16.36 is that shown in Fig. 16.37. Notice that the second join uses a different number of passes, a different number of buffers, and a left argument that is pipelined, not materialized. □

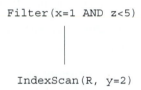

Figure 16.38: Annotating a selection to use the most appropriate index

Example 16.38 : Consider the selection operation in Example 16.35, where we decided that the best of options was to use the index on y to find those tuples with $y = 2$, then check these tuples for the other conditions $x = 1$ and $z < 5$. Figure 16.38 shows the physical query plan. The leaf indicates that R will be accessed through its index on y, retrieving only those tuples with $y = 2$. The filter operator says that we complete the selection by further selecting those of the retrieved tuples that have both $x = 1$ and $z < 5$. □

16.7.7   Ordering of Physical Operations

Our final topic regarding physical query plans is the matter of order of operations. The physical query plan is generally represented as a tree, and trees imply something about order of operations, since data must flow up the tree. However, since bushy trees may have interior nodes that are neither ancestors nor descendants of one another, the order of evaluation of interior nodes may not always be clear. Moreover, since iterators can be used to implement operations in a pipelined manner, it is possible that the times of execution for various nodes overlap, and the notion of "ordering" nodes makes no sense.

If materialization is implemented in the obvious store-and-later-retrieve way, and pipelining is implemented by iterators, then we may establish a fixed sequence of events whereby each operation of a physical query plan is executed. The following rules summarize the ordering of events implicit in a physical-query-plan tree:

1. Break the tree into subtrees at each edge that represents materialization. The subtrees will be executed one-at-a-time.

2. Order the execution of the subtrees in a bottom-up, left-to-right manner. To be precise, perform a preorder traversal of the entire tree. Order the subtrees in the order in which the preorder traversal exits from the subtrees.

3. Execute all nodes of each subtree using a network of iterators. Thus, all the nodes in one subtree are executed simultaneously, with `GetNext` calls among their operators determining the exact order of events.

Following this strategy, the query optimizer can now generate executable code, perhaps a sequence of function calls, for the query.

16.7.8 Exercises for Section 16.7

Exercise 16.7.1 : Consider a relation $R(a, b, c, d)$ that has a clustering index on a and nonclustering indexes on each of the other attributes. The relevant parameters are: $B(R) = 1000$, $T(R) = 5000$, $V(R, a) = 20$, $V(R, b) = 1000$, $V(R, c) = 5000$, and $V(R, d) = 500$. Give the best query plan (index-scan or table-scan followed by a filter step) and the disk-I/O cost for each of the following selections:

* a) $\sigma_{a=1 \text{ AND } b=2 \text{ AND } d=3}(R)$.

  b) $\sigma_{a=1 \text{ AND } b=2 \text{ AND } c \geq 3}(R)$.

  c) $\sigma_{a=1 \text{ AND } b \leq 2 \text{ AND } c \geq 3}(R)$.

! Exercise 16.7.2 : In terms of $B(R)$, $T(R)$, $V(R, x)$, and $V(R, y)$, express the following conditions about the cost of implementing a selection on R:

* a) It is better to use index-scan with a nonclustering index on x and a term that equates x to a constant than a nonclustering index on y and a term that equates y to a constant.

  b) It is better to use index-scan with a nonclustering index on x and a term that equates x to a constant than a clustering index on y and a term that equates y to a constant.

c) It is better to use index-scan with a nonclustering index on x and a term that equates x to a constant than a clustering index on y and a term of the form $y > C$ for some constant C.

Exercise 16.7.3: How would the conclusions about when to pipeline in Example 16.36 change if the size of relation R were not 5000 blocks, but:

a) 2000 blocks.

! b) 10,000 blocks.

! c) 100 blocks.

! **Exercise 16.7.4:** Suppose we want to compute $(R(a, b) \bowtie S(a, c)) \bowtie T(a, d)$ in the order indicated. We have $M = 101$ main-memory buffers, and $B(R) = B(S) = 2000$. Because the join attribute a is the same for both joins, we decide to implement the first join $R \bowtie S$ by a two-pass sort-join, and we shall use the appropriate number of passes for the second join, first dividing T into some number of sublists sorted on a, and merging them with the sorted and pipelined stream of tuples from the join $R \bowtie S$. For what values of $B(T)$ should we choose for the join of T with $R \bowtie S$:

* a) A one-pass join; i.e., we read T into memory, and compare its tuples with the tuples of $R \bowtie S$ as they are generated.

b) A two-pass join; i.e., we create sorted sublists for T and keep one buffer in memory for each sorted sublist, while we generate tuples of $R \bowtie S$.

16.8   Summary of Chapter 16

✦ *Compilation of Queries*: Compilation turns a query into a physical query plan, which is a sequence of operations that can be implemented by the query-execution engine. The principal steps of query compilation are parsing, semantic checking, selection of the preferred logical query plan (algebraic expression), and generation from that of the best physical plan.

✦ *The Parser*: The first step in processing an SQL query is to parse it, as one would for code in any programming language. The result of parsing is a parse tree with nodes corresponding to SQL constructs.

✦ *Semantic Checking*: A preprocessor examines the parse tree, checks that the attributes, relation names, and types make sense, and resolves attribute references.

✦ *Conversion to a Logical Query Plan*: The query processor must convert the semantically checked parse tree to an algebraic expression. Much of the conversion to relational algebra is straightforward, but subqueries present a problem. One approach is to introduce a two-argument selection that puts the subquery in the condition of the selection, and then apply appropriate transformations for the common special cases.

✦ *Algebraic Transformations*: There are many ways that a logical query plan can be transformed to a better plan by using algebraic transformations. Section 16.2 enumerates the principal ones.

✦ *Choosing a Logical Query Plan*: The query processor must select that query plan that is most likely to lead to an efficient physical plan. In addition to applying algebraic transformations, it is useful to group associative and commutative operators, especially joins, so the physical query plan can choose the best order and grouping for these operations.

✦ *Estimating Sizes of Relations*: When selecting the best logical plan, or when ordering joins or other associative-commutative operations, we use the estimated size of intermediate relations as a surrogate for the true running time. Knowing, or estimating, both the size (number of tuples) of relations and the number of distinct values for each attribute of each relation helps us get good estimates of the sizes of intermediate relations.

✦ *Histograms*: Some systems keep histograms of the values for a given attribute. This information can be used to obtain better estimates of intermediate-relation sizes than the simple methods stressed here.

✦ *Cost-Based Optimization*: When selecting the best physical plan, we need to estimate the cost of each possible plan. Various strategies are used to generate all or some of the possible physical plans that implement a given logical plan.

✦ *Plan-Enumeration Strategies*: The common approaches to searching the space of physical plans for the best include dynamic programming (tabularizing the best plan for each subexpression of the given logical plan), Selinger-style dynamic programming (which includes the sort-order of results as part of the table, giving best plans for each sort-order and for an unsorted result), greedy approaches (making a series of locally optimal decisions, given the choices for the physical plan that have been made so far), and branch-and-bound (enumerating only plans that are not immediately known to be worse than the best plan found so far).

✦ *Left-Deep Join Trees*: When picking a grouping and order for the join of several relations, it is common to restrict the search to left-deep trees, which are binary trees with a single spine down the left edge, with only leaves as right children. This form of join expression tends to yield efficient plans and also limits significantly the number of physical plans that need to be considered.

✦ *Physical Plans for Selection*: If possible, a selection should be broken into an index-scan of the relation to which the selection is applied (typically using a condition in which the indexed attribute is equated to a constant), followed by a filter operation. The filter examines the tuples retrieved by the index-scan and passes through only those that meet the portions of the selection condition other than that on which the index scan is based.

✦ *Pipelining Versus Materialization*: Ideally, the result of each physical operator is consumed by another operator, with the result being passed between the two in main memory ("pipelining"), perhaps using an iterator to control the flow of data from one to the other. However, sometimes there is an advantage to storing ("materializing") the result of one operator to save space in main memory for other operators. Thus, the physical-query-plan generator should consider both pipelining and materialization of intermediates.

16.9 References for Chapter 16

The surveys mentioned in the bibliographic notes to Chapter 15 also contain material relevant to query compilation. In addition, we recommend the survey [1], which contains material on the query optimizers of commercial systems.

Three of the earliest studies of query optimization are [4], [5], and [3]. Paper [6], another early study, incorporates the idea of pushing selections down the tree with the greedy algorithm for join-order choice. [2] is the source for "Selinger-style optimization" as well as describing the System R optimizer, which was one of the most ambitious attempts at query optimization of its day.

1. G. Graefe (ed.), *Data Engineering* **16**:4 (1993), special issue on query processing in commercial database management systems, IEEE.

2. P. Griffiths-Selinger, M. M. Astrahan, D. D. Chamberlin, R. A. Lorie, and T. G. Price, "Access path selection in a relational database system," *Proc. ACM SIGMOD Intl. Conf. on Management of Data* (1979), pp. 23–34.

3. P. A. V. Hall, "Optimization of a single relational expression in a relational database system," *IBM J. Research and Development* **20**:3 (1976), pp. 244–257.

4. F. P. Palermo, "A database search problem," in: J. T. Tou (ed.) *Information Systems COINS IV*, Plenum, New York, 1974.

5. J. M. Smith and P. Y. Chang, "Optimizing the performance of a relational algebra database interface," *Comm. ACM* **18**:10 (1975), pp. 568–579.

6. E. Wong and K. Youssefi, "Decomposition — a strategy for query processing," *ACM Trans. on Database Systems* **1**:3 (1976), pp. 223–241.

Chapter 17

Coping With System Failures

Starting with this chapter, we focus our attention on those parts of a DBMS that control access to data. There are two major issues to address:

1. Data must be protected in the face of a system failure. This chapter deals with techniques for supporting the goal of *resilience*, that is, integrity of the data when the system fails in some way.

2. Data must not be corrupted simply because several error-free queries or database modifications are being done at once. This matter is addressed in Chapters 18 and 19.

The principal technique for supporting resilience is a *log*, which records securely the history of database changes. We shall discuss three different styles of logging, called "undo," "redo," and "undo/redo." We also discuss *recovery*, the process whereby the log is used to reconstruct what has happened to the database when there has been a failure. An important aspect of logging and recovery is avoidance of the situation where the log must be examined into the distant past. Thus, we shall learn the important technique called "checkpointing," which limits the length of log that must be examined during recovery.

In a final section, we discuss "archiving," which allows the database to survive not only temporary system failures, but situations where the entire database is lost. Then, we must rely on a recent copy of the database (the archive) plus whatever log information survives, to reconstruct the database as it existed at some point in the recent past.

17.1 Issues and Models for Resilient Operation

We begin our discussion of coping with failures by reviewing the kinds of things that can go wrong, and what a DBMS can and should do about them. We

initially focus on "system failures" or "crashes," the kinds of errors that the
logging and recovery methods are designed to fix. We also introduce in Section 17.1.4 the model for buffer management that underlies all discussions of
recovery from system errors. The same model is needed in the next chapter as
we discuss concurrent access to the database by several transactions.

17.1.1 Failure Modes

There are many things that can go wrong as a database is queried and modified.
Problems range from the keyboard entry of incorrect data to an explosion in the
room where the database is stored on disk. The following items are a catalog
of the most important failure modes and what the DBMS can do about them.

Erroneous Data Entry

Some data errors are impossible to detect. For example, if a clerk mistypes one
digit of your phone number, the data will still look like a phone number that
could be yours. On the other hand, if the clerk omits a digit from your phone
number, then the data is evidently in error, since it does not have the form of
a phone number.

A modern DBMS provides a number of software mechanisms for catching
those data-entry errors that are detectable. For example, the SQL standard, as
well as all popular implementations of SQL, include a way for the database designer to introduce into the database schema constraints such as key constraints,
foreign key constraints, and constraints on values (e.g., a phone number must
be 10 digits long). Triggers, which are programs that execute whenever a modification of a certain type (e.g., insertion of a tuple into relation R) occurs, are
used to check that the data just entered meets any constraint that the database
designer believes it should satisfy.

Media Failures

A local failure of a disk, one that changes only a bit or a few bits, can normally
be detected by parity checks associated with the sectors of the disk, as we
discussed in Section 11.3.5. Major failures of a disk, principally head crashes,
where the entire disk becomes unreadable, are generally handled by one or both
of the following approaches:

1. Use one of the RAID schemes discussed in Section 11.7, so the lost disk
   can be restored.

2. Maintain an *archive*, a copy of the database on a medium such as tape
   or optical disk. The archive is periodically created, either fully or incrementally, and stored at a safe distance from the database itself. We shall
   discuss archiving in Section 17.5.

3. Instead of an archive, one could keep redundant copies of the database on-line, distributed among several sites. These copies are kept consistent by mechanisms we shall discuss in Section 19.6.

Catastrophic Failure

In this category are a number of situations in which the media holding the database is completely destroyed. Examples include explosions, fires, or vandalism at the site of the database. RAID will not help, since all the data disks and their parity check disks become useless simultaneously. However, the other approaches that can be used to protect against media failure — archiving and redundant, distributed copies — will also protect against a catastrophic failure.

System Failures

The processes that query and modify the database are called *transactions*. A transaction, like any program, executes a number of steps in sequence; often, several of these steps will modify the database. Each transaction has a *state*, which represents what has happened so far in the transaction. The state includes the current place in the transaction's code being executed and the values of any local variables of the transaction that will be needed later on.

System failures are problems that cause the state of a transaction to be lost. Typical system failures are power loss and software errors. To see why problems such as power outages cause loss of state, observe that, like any program, the steps of a transaction initially occur in main memory. Unlike disk, main memory is "volatile," as we discussed in Section 11.2.6. That is, a power failure will cause the contents of main memory to disappear, while a disk's (nonvolatile) data remains intact. Similarly, a software error may overwrite part of main memory, possibly including values that were part of the state of the program.

When main memory is lost, the transaction state is lost; that is, we can no longer tell what parts of the transaction, including its database modifications, were made. Running the transaction again may not fix the problem. For example, if the transaction must add 1 to a value in the database, we do not know whether to repeat the addition of 1 or not. The principal remedy for the problems that arise due to a system error is logging of all database changes in a separate, nonvolatile log, coupled with recovery when necessary. However, the mechanisms whereby such logging can be done in a fail-safe manner are surprisingly intricate, as we shall see starting in Section 17.2.

17.1.2 More About Transactions

We introduced the idea of transactions from the point of view of the SQL programmer in Section 8.6. Before proceeding to our study of database resilience and recovery from failures, we need to discuss the fundamental notion of a transaction in more detail.

The transaction is the unit of execution of database operations. For example, if we are issuing ad-hoc commands to an SQL system, then each query or database modification statement (plus any resulting trigger actions) is a transaction. When using an embedded SQL interface, the programmer controls the extent of a transaction, which may include several queries or modifications, as well as operations performed in the host language. In the typical embedded SQL system, transactions begin as soon as operations on the database are executed and end with an explicit COMMIT or ROLLBACK ("abort") command.

As we shall discuss in Section 17.1.3, a transaction must execute atomically, that is, all-or-nothing and as if it were executed at an instant in time. Assuring that transactions are executed correctly is the job of a *transaction manager*, a subsystem that performs several functions, including:

1. Issuing signals to the log manager (described below) so that necessary information in the form of "log records" can be stored on the log.

2. Assuring that concurrently executing transactions do not interfere with each other in ways that introduce errors ("scheduling"; see Section 18.1).

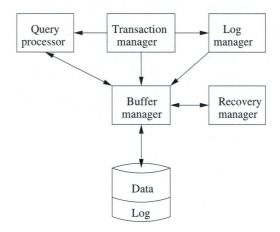

Figure 17.1: The log manager and transaction manager

The transaction manager and its interactions are suggested by Fig. 17.1. The transaction manager will send messages about actions of transactions to the log manager, to the buffer manager about when it is possible or necessary to copy the buffer back to disk, and to the query processor to execute the queries and other database operations that comprise the transaction.

The log manager maintains the log. It must deal with the buffer manager, since space for the log initially appears in main-memory buffers, and at certain times these buffers must be copied to disk. The log, as well as the data, occupies space on the disk, as we suggest in Fig. 17.1.

Finally, we show in Fig. 17.1 the role of the recovery manager. When there is a crash, the recovery manager is activated. It examines the log and uses it to repair the data, if necessary. As always, access to the disk is through the buffer manager.

17.1.3 Correct Execution of Transactions

Before we can deal with correcting system errors, we need to understand what it means for a transaction to be executed "correctly." To begin, we assume that the database is composed of "elements." We shall not specify precisely what an "element" is, except to say it has a value and can be accessed or modified by transactions. Different database systems use different notions of elements, but they are usually chosen from one or more of the following:

1. Relations, or their object-oriented equivalent: the extent of a class.

2. Disk blocks or pages.

3. Individual tuples of a relation, or their object-oriented equivalent: objects.

In examples to follow, one can imagine that database elements are tuples, or in many examples, simply integers. However, there are several good reasons in practice to use choice (2) — disk blocks or pages — as the database element. In this way, buffer-contents become single elements, allowing us to avoid some serious problems with logging and transactions that we shall explore periodically as we learn various techniques. Avoiding database elements that are bigger than disk blocks also prevents a situation where part but not all of an element has been placed in nonvolatile storage when a crash occurs.

A database has a *state*, which is a value for each of its elements.[1] Intuitively, we regard certain states as *consistent*, and others as inconsistent. Consistent states satisfy all constraints of the database schema, such as key constraints and constraints on values. However, consistent states must also satisfy implicit constraints that are in the mind of the database designer. The implicit constraints may be maintained by triggers that are part of the database schema, but they might also be maintained only by policy statements concerning the database, or warnings associated with the user interface through which updates are made.

A fundamental assumption about transactions is:

- *The Correctness Principle*: If a transaction executes in the absence of any other transactions or system errors, and it starts with the database in a consistent state, then the database is also in a consistent state when the transaction ends.

---

[1] We should not confuse the database state with the state of a transaction; the latter is values for the transaction's local variables, not database elements.

Is the Correctness Principle Believable?

Given that a database transaction could be an ad-hoc modification command issued at a terminal, perhaps by someone who doesn't understand the implicit constraints in the mind of the database designer, is it plausible to assume all transactions take the database from a consistent state to another consistent state? Explicit constraints are enforced by the database, so any transaction that violates them will be rejected by the system and not change the database at all. As for implicit constraints, one cannot characterize them exactly under any circumstances. Our position, justifying the correctness principle, is that if someone is given authority to modify the database, then they also have the authority to judge what the implicit constraints are.

There is a converse to the correctness principle that forms the motivation for both the logging techniques discussed in this chapter and the concurrency control mechanisms discussed in Chapter 18. This converse involves two points:

1. A transaction is *atomic*; that is, it must be executed as a whole or not at all. If only part of a transaction executes, then there is a good chance that the resulting database state will not be consistent.

2. Transactions that execute simultaneously are likely to lead to an inconsistent state unless we take steps to control their interactions, as we shall in Chapter 18.

17.1.4   The Primitive Operations of Transactions

Let us now consider in detail how transactions interact with the database. There are three address spaces that interact in important ways:

1. The space of disk blocks holding the database elements.

2. The virtual or main memory address space that is managed by the buffer manager.

3. The local address space of the transaction.

For a transaction to read a database element, that element must first be brought to a main-memory buffer or buffers, if it is not already there. Then, the contents of the buffer(s) can be read by the transaction into its own address space. Writing of a new value for a database element by a transaction follows the reverse route. The new value is first created by the transaction in its own space. Then, this value is copied to the appropriate buffer(s).

The buffer may or may not be copied to disk immediately; that decision is the responsibility of the buffer manager in general. As we shall soon see, one of the principal steps of using a log to assure resilience in the face of system errors is forcing the buffer manager to write the block in a buffer back to disk at appropriate times. However, in order to reduce the number of disk I/O's, database systems can and will allow a change to exist only in volatile main-memory storage, at least for certain periods of time and under the proper set of conditions.

In order to study the details of logging algorithms and other transaction-management algorithms, we need a notation that describes all the operations that move data between address spaces. The primitives we shall use are:

1. `INPUT(X)`: Copy the disk block containing database element X to a memory buffer.

2. `READ(X,t)`: Copy the database element X to the transaction's local variable t. More precisely, if the block containing database element X is not in a memory buffer then first execute `INPUT(X)`. Next, assign the value of X to local variable t.

3. `WRITE(X,t)`: Copy the value of local variable t to database element X in a memory buffer. More precisely, if the block containing database element X is not in a memory buffer then execute `INPUT(X)`. Next, copy the value of t to X in the buffer.

4. `OUTPUT(X)`: Copy the block containing X from its buffer to disk.

The above operations make sense as long as database elements reside within a single disk block, and therefore within a single buffer. That would be the case for database elements that *are* blocks. It would also be true for database elements that are tuples, as long as the relation schema does not allow tuples that are bigger than the space available in one block. If database elements occupy several blocks, then we shall imagine that each block-sized portion of the element is an element by itself. The logging mechanism to be used will assure that the transaction cannot complete without the write of X being atomic; i.e., either all blocks of X are written to disk, or none are. Thus, we shall assume for the entire discussion of logging that

- A database element is no larger than a single block.

It is important to observe that different DBMS components issue the various commands we just introduced. `READ` and `WRITE` are issued by transactions. `INPUT` and `OUTPUT` are issued by the buffer manager, although `OUTPUT` can also be initiated by the log manager under certain conditions, as we shall see.

Buffers in Query Processing and in Transactions

If you got used to the analysis of buffer utilization in the chapters on query processing, you may notice a change in viewpoint here. In Chapters 15 and 16 we were interested in buffers principally as they were used to compute temporary relations during the evaluation of a query. That is one important use of buffers, but there is never a need to preserve a temporary value, so these buffers do not generally have their values logged. On the other hand, those buffers that hold data retrieved from the database *do* need to have those values preserved, especially when the transaction updates them.

Example 17.1: To see how the above primitive operations relate to what a transaction might do, let us consider a database that has two elements, A and B, with the constraint that they must be equal in all consistent states.[2]

Transaction T consists logically of the following two steps:

```
A := A*2;
B := B*2;
```

Notice that if the only consistency requirement for the database is that $A = B$, and if T starts in a consistent state and completes its activities without interference from another transaction or system error, then the final state must also be consistent. That is, T doubles two equal elements to get new, equal elements.

Execution of T involves reading A and B from disk, performing arithmetic in the local address space of T, and writing the new values of A and B to their buffers. We could express T as the sequence of six relevant steps:

```
READ(A,t); t := t*2; WRITE(A,t);
READ(B,t); t := t*2; WRITE(B,t);
```

In addition, the buffer manager will eventually execute the OUTPUT steps to write these buffers back to disk. Figure 17.2 shows the primitive steps of T, followed by the two OUTPUT commands from the buffer manager. We assume that initially $A = B = 8$. The values of the memory and disk copies of A and B and the local variable t in the address space of transaction T are indicated for each step.

---

[2]One reasonably might ask why we should bother to have two different elements that are constrained to be equal, rather than maintaining only one element. However, this simple numerical constraint captures the spirit of many more realistic constraints, e.g., the number of seats sold on a flight must not exceed the number of seats on the plane by more than 10%, or the sum of the loan balances at a bank must equal the total debt of the bank.

Action	t	Mem A	Mem B	Disk A	Disk B
READ(A,t)	8	8		8	8
t := t*2	16	8		8	8
WRITE(A,t)	16	16		8	8
READ(B,t)	8	16	8	8	8
t := t*2	16	16	8	8	8
WRITE(B,t)	16	16	16	8	8
OUTPUT(A)	16	16	16	16	8
OUTPUT(B)	16	16	16	16	16

Figure 17.2: Steps of a transaction and its effect on memory and disk

At the first step, T reads A, which generates an INPUT(A) command for the buffer manager if A's block is not already in a buffer. The value of A is also copied by the READ command into local variable t of T's address space. The second step doubles t; it has no affect on A, either in a buffer or on disk. The third step writes t into A of the buffer; it does not affect A on disk. The next three steps do the same for B, and the last two steps copy A and B to disk.

Observe that as long as all these steps execute, consistency of the database is preserved. If a system error occurs before OUTPUT(A) is executed, then there is no effect to the database stored on disk; it is as if T never ran, and consistency is preserved. However, if there is a system error after OUTPUT(A) but before OUTPUT(B), then the database is left in an inconsistent state. We cannot prevent this situation from ever occurring, but we can arrange that when it does occur, the problem can be repaired — either both A and B will be reset to 8, or both will be advanced to 16. □

17.1.5 Exercises for Section 17.1

Exercise 17.1.1: Suppose that the consistency constraint on the database is $0 \le A \le B$. Tell whether each of the following transactions preserves consistency.

* a) A := A+B; B := A+B;

  b) B := A+B; A := A+B;

  c) A := B+1; B := A+1;

Exercise 17.1.2: For each of the transactions of Exercise 17.1.1, add the read- and write-actions to the computation and show the effect of the steps on main memory and disk. Assume that initially $A = 5$ and $B = 10$. Also, tell whether it is possible, with the appropriate order of OUTPUT actions, to assure that consistency is preserved even if there is a crash while the transaction is executing.

17.2   Undo Logging

We shall now begin our study of logging as a way to assure that transactions are atomic — they appear to the database either to have executed in their entirety or not to have executed at all. A *log* is a sequence of *log records*, each telling something about what some transaction has done. The actions of several transactions can "interleave," so that a step of one transaction may be executed and its effect logged, then the same happens for a step of another transaction, then for a second step of the first transaction or a step of a third transaction, and so on. This interleaving of transactions complicates logging; it is not sufficient simply to log the entire story of a transaction after that transaction completes.

If there is a system crash, the log is consulted to reconstruct what transactions were doing when the crash occurred. The log also may be used, in conjunction with an archive, if there is a media failure of a disk that does not store the log. Generally, to repair the effect of the crash, some transactions will have their work done again, and the new values they wrote into the database are written again. Other transactions will have their work undone, and the database restored so that it appears that they never executed.

Our first style of logging, which is called *undo logging*, makes only repairs of the second type. If it is not absolutely certain that the effects of a transaction have been completed and stored on disk, then any database changes that the transaction may have made to the database are undone, and the database state is restored to what existed prior to the transaction.

In this section we shall introduce the basic idea of log records, including the *commit* (successful completion of a transaction) action and its effect on the database state and log. We shall also consider how the log itself is created in main memory and copied to disk by a "flush-log" operation. Finally, we examine the undo log specifically, and learn how to use it in recovery from a crash. In order to avoid having to examine the entire log during recovery, we introduce the idea of "checkpointing," which allows old portions of the log to be thrown away. The checkpointing method for an undo log is considered explicitly in this section.

17.2.1   Log Records

Imagine the log as a file opened for appending only. As transactions execute, the *log manager* has the job of recording in the log each important event. One block of the log at a time is filled with log records, each representing one of these events. Log blocks are initially created in main memory and are allocated by the buffer manager like any other blocks that the DBMS needs. The log blocks are written to nonvolatile storage on disk as soon as is feasible; we shall have more to say about this matter in Section 17.2.2.

There are several forms of log record that are used with each of the types of logging we discuss in this chapter. These are:

1. $<$START $T>$: This record indicates that transaction T has begun.

Why Might a Transaction Abort?

One might wonder why a transaction would abort rather than commit. There are actually several reasons. The simplest is when there is some error condition in the code of the transaction itself, for example an attempted division by zero that is handled by "canceling" the transaction. The DBMS may also need to abort a transaction for one of several reasons. For instance, a transaction may be involved in a deadlock, where it and one or more other transactions each hold some resource (e.g., the privilege to write a new value of some database element) that the other wants. We shall see in Section 19.3 that in such a situation one or more transactions must be forced by the system to abort.

---

2. <COMMIT T>: Transaction T has completed successfully and will make no more changes to database elements. Any changes to the database made by T should appear on disk. However, because we cannot control when the buffer manager chooses to copy blocks from memory to disk, we cannot in general be sure that the changes are already on disk when we see the <COMMIT T> log record. If we insist that the changes already be on disk, this requirement must be enforced by the log manager (as is the case for undo logging).

3. <ABORT T>: Transaction T could not complete successfully. If transaction T aborts, no changes it made can have been copied to disk, and it is the job of the transaction manager to make sure that such changes never appear on disk, or that their effect on disk is cancelled if they do. We shall discuss the matter of repairing the effect of aborted transactions in Section 19.1.1.

For an undo log, the only other kind of log record we need is an *update record*, which is a triple <T, X, v>. The meaning of this record is: transaction T has changed database element X, and its former value was v. The change reflected by an update record normally occurs in memory, not disk; i.e., the log record is a response to a WRITE action, not an OUTPUT action (see Section 17.1.4 to recall the distinction between these operations). Notice also that an undo log does not record the new value of a database element, only the old value. As we shall see, should recovery be necessary in a system using undo logging, the only thing the recovery manager will do is cancel the possible effect of a transaction on disk by restoring the old value.

17.2.2 The Undo-Logging Rules

There are two rules that transactions must obey in order that an undo log allows us to recover from a system failure. These rules affect what the buffer manager

---

How Big Is an Update Record?

If database elements are disk blocks, and an update record includes the old value of a database element (or both the old and new values of the database element as we shall see in Section 17.4 for undo/redo logging), then it appears that a log record can be bigger than a block. That is not necessarily a problem, since like any conventional file, we may think of a log as a sequence of disk blocks, with bytes covering blocks without any concern for block boundaries. However, there are ways to compress the log. For instance, under some circumstances, we can log only the change, e.g., the name of the attribute of some tuple that has been changed by the transaction, and its old value. The matter of "logical logging" of changes is discussed in Section 19.1.7.

---

can do and also requires that certain actions be taken whenever a transaction commits. We summarize them here.

U_1: If transaction T modifies database element X, then the log record of the form $<T, X, v>$ must be written to disk *before* the new value of X is written to disk.

U_2: If a transaction commits, then its COMMIT log record must be written to disk only *after* all database elements changed by the transaction have been written to disk, but as soon thereafter as possible.

To summarize rules U_1 and U_2, material associated with one transaction must be written to disk in the following order:

a) The log records indicating changed database elements.

b) The changed database elements themselves.

c) The COMMIT log record.

However, the order of (a) and (b) applies to each database element individually, not to the group of update records for a transaction as a whole.

In order to force log records to disk, the log manager needs a *flush-log* command that tells the buffer manager to copy to disk any log blocks that have not previously been copied to disk or that have been changed since they were last copied. In sequences of actions, we shall show FLUSH LOG explicitly. The transaction manager also needs to have a way to tell the buffer manager to perform an OUTPUT action on a database element. We shall continue to show the OUTPUT action in sequences of transaction steps.

Preview of Other Logging Methods

In "redo logging" (Section 17.3), on recovery we redo any transaction that has a COMMIT record, and we ignore all others. Rules for redo logging assure that we may ignore transactions whose COMMIT records never reached the log. "Undo/redo logging" (Section 17.4) will, on recovery, undo any transaction that has not committed, and will redo those transactions that have committed. Again, log-management and buffering rules will assure that these steps successfully repair any damage to the database.

Example 17.2: Let us reconsider the transaction of Example 17.1 in the light of undo logging. Figure 17.3 expands on Fig. 17.2 to show the log entries and flush-log actions that have to take place along with the actions of the transaction T. Note we have shortened the headers to M-A for "the copy of A in a memory buffer" or D-B for "the copy of B on disk," and so on.

Step	Action	t	M-A	M-B	D-A	D-B	Log
1)							$<$START $T>$
2)	READ(A,t)	8	8		8	8	
3)	t := t*2	16	8		8	8	
4)	WRITE(A,t)	16	16		8	8	$<T, A, 8>$
5)	READ(B,t)	8	16	8	8	8	
6)	t := t*2	16	16	8	8	8	
7)	WRITE(B,t)	16	16	16	8	8	$<T, B, 8>$
8)	FLUSH LOG						
9)	OUTPUT(A)	16	16	16	16	8	
10)	OUTPUT(B)	16	16	16	16	16	
11)							$<$COMMIT $T>$
12)	FLUSH LOG						

Figure 17.3: Actions and their log entries

In line (1) of Fig. 17.3, transaction T begins. The first thing that happens is that the $<$START $T>$ record is written to the log. Line (2) represents the read of A by T. Line (3) is the local change to t, which affects neither the database stored on disk nor any portion of the database in a memory buffer. Neither lines (2) nor (3) require any log entry, since they have no affect on the database.

Line (4) is the write of the new value of A to the buffer. This modification to A is reflected by the log entry $<T, A, 8>$ which says that A was changed by T and its former value was 8. Note that the new value, 16, is not mentioned in an undo log.

Background Activity Affects the Log and Buffers

As we look at a sequence of actions and log entries like Fig. 17.3, it is tempting to imagine that these actions occur in isolation. However, the DBMS may be processing many transactions simultaneously. Thus, the four log records for transaction T may be interleaved on the log with records for other transactions. Moreover, if one of these transactions flushes the log, then the log records from T may appear on disk earlier than is implied by the flush-log actions of Fig. 17.3. There is no harm if log records reflecting a database modification appear earlier than necessary. The essential policy for undo logging is that we don't write the $<$COMMIT $T>$ record until the OUTPUT actions for T are completed.

A trickier situation occurs if two database elements A and B share a block. Then, writing one of them to disk writes the other as well. In the worst case, we can violate rule U_1 by writing one of these elements prematurely. It may be necessary to adopt additional constraints on transactions in order to make undo logging work. For instance, we might use a locking scheme where database elements are disk blocks, as described in Section 18.3, to prevent two transactions from accessing the same block at the same time. This and other problems that appear when database elements are fractions of a block motivate our suggestion that blocks *be* the database elements.

Lines (5) through (7) perform the same three steps with B instead of A. At this point, T has completed and must commit. It would like the changed A and B to migrate to disk, but in order to follow the two rules for undo logging, there is a fixed sequence of events that must happen.

First, A and B cannot be copied to disk until the log records for the changes are on disk. Thus, at step (8) the log is flushed, assuring that these records appear on disk. Then, steps (9) and (10) copy A and B to disk. The transaction manager requests these steps from the buffer manager in order to commit T.

Now, it is possible to commit T, and the $<$COMMIT $T>$ record is written to the log, which is step (11). Finally, we must flush the log again at step (12) to make sure that the $<$COMMIT $T>$ record of the log appears on disk. Notice that without writing this record to disk, we could have a situation where a transaction has committed, but for a long time a review of the log does not tell us that it has committed. That situation could cause strange behavior if there were a crash, because, as we shall see in Section 17.2.3, a transaction that appeared to the user to have committed and written its changes to disk would then be undone and effectively aborted. □

17.2.3 Recovery Using Undo Logging

Suppose now that a system failure occurs. It is possible that certain database changes made by a given transaction may have been written to disk, while other changes made by the same transaction never reached the disk. If so, the transaction was not executed atomically, and there may be an inconsistent database state. It is the job of the *recovery manager* to use the log to restore the database state to some consistent state.

In this section we consider only the simplest form of recovery manager, one that looks at the entire log, no matter how long, and makes database changes as a result of its examination. In Section 17.2.4 we consider a more sensible approach, where the log is periodically "checkpointed," to limit the distance back in history that the recovery manager must go.

The first task of the recovery manager is to divide the transactions into committed and uncommitted transactions. If there is a log record <COMMIT T>, then by undo rule U_2 all changes made by transaction T were previously written to disk. Thus, T by itself could not have left the database in an inconsistent state when the system failure occurred.

However, suppose that we find a <START T> record on the log but no <COMMIT T> record. Then there could have been some changes to the database made by T that got written to disk before the crash, while other changes by T either were not made, even in the main-memory buffers, or were made in the buffers but not copied to disk. In this case, T is an *incomplete transaction* and must be *undone*. That is, whatever changes T made must be reset to their previous value. Fortunately, rule U_1 assures us that if T changed X on disk before the crash, then there will be a <T, X, v> record on the log, and that record will have been copied to disk before the crash. Thus, during the recovery, we must write the value v for database element X. Note that this rule begs the question whether X had value v in the database anyway; we don't even bother to check.

Since there may be several uncommitted transactions in the log, and there may even be several uncommitted transactions that modified X, we have to be systematic about the order in which we restore values. Thus, the recovery manager must scan the log from the end (i.e., from the most recently written record to the earliest written). As it travels, it remembers all those transactions T for which it has seen a <COMMIT T> record or an <ABORT T> record. Also as it travels backward, if it sees a record <T, X, v>, then:

1. If T is a transaction whose COMMIT record has been seen, then do nothing. T is committed and must not be undone.

2. Otherwise, T is an incomplete transaction, or an aborted transaction. The recovery manager must change the value of X in the database to v, in case X had been altered just before the crash.

After making these changes, the recovery manager must write a log record <ABORT T> for each incomplete transaction T that was not previously aborted, and then flush the log. Now, normal operation of the database may resume, and new transactions may begin executing.

Example 17.3 : Let us consider the sequence of actions from Fig. 17.3 and Example 17.2. There are several different times that the system crash could have occurred; let us consider each significantly different one.

1. The crash occurs after step (12). Then we know the $<$COMMIT $T>$ record got to disk before the crash. When we recover, we do not undo the results of T, and all log records concerning T are ignored by the recovery manager.

2. The crash occurs between steps (11) and (12). It is possible that the log record containing the COMMIT got flushed to disk; for instance, the buffer manager may have needed the buffer containing the end of the log for another transaction, or some other transaction may have asked for a log flush. If so, then the recovery is the same as in case (1) as far as T is concerned. However, if the COMMIT record never reached disk, then the recovery manager considers T incomplete. When it scans the log backward, it comes first to the record $<T, B, 8>$. It therefore stores 8 as the value of B on disk. It then comes to the record $<T, A, 8>$ and makes A have value 8 on disk. Finally, the record $<$ABORT $T>$ is written to the log, and the log is flushed.

3. The crash occurs between steps (10) and (11). Now, the COMMIT record surely was not written, so T is incomplete and is undone as in case (2).

4. The crash occurs between steps (8) and (10). Again as in case (3), T is undone. The only difference is that now the change to A and/or B may not have reached disk. Nevertheless, the proper value, 8, is stored for each of these database elements.

5. The crash occurs prior to step (8). Now, it is not certain whether any of the log records concerning T have reached disk. However, it doesn't matter, because we know by rule U_1 that if the change to A and/or B reached disk, then the corresponding log record reached disk, and therefore if there were changes to A and/or B made on disk by T, then the corresponding log record will cause the recovery manager to undo those changes.

$\square$

17.2.4 Checkpointing

As we observed, recovery requires that the entire log be examined, in principle. When logging follows the undo style, once a transaction has its COMMIT log

---

Crashes During Recovery

Suppose the system again crashes while we are recovering from a previous crash. Because of the way undo-log records are designed, giving the old value rather than, say, the change in the value of a database element, the recovery steps are *idempotent*; that is, repeating them many times has exactly the same effect as performing them once. We have already observed that if we find a record $<T, X, v>$, it does not matter whether the value of X is already v — we may write v for X regardless. Similarly, if we have to repeat the recovery process, it will not matter whether the first, incomplete recovery restored some old values; we simply restore them again. Incidentally, the same reasoning holds for the other logging methods we discuss in this chapter. Since the recovery operations are idempotent, we can recover a second time without worrying about changes made the first time.

---

record written to disk, the log records of that transaction are no longer needed during recovery. We might imagine that we could delete the log prior to a COMMIT, but sometimes we cannot. The reason is that often many transactions execute at once. If we truncated the log after one transaction committed, log records pertaining to some other active transaction T might be lost and could not be used to undo T if recovery were necessary.

The simplest way to untangle potential problems is to *checkpoint* the log periodically. In a simple checkpoint, we:

1. Stop accepting new transactions.

2. Wait until all currently active transactions commit or abort and have written a COMMIT or ABORT record on the log.

3. Flush the log to disk.

4. Write a log record <CKPT>, and flush the log again.

5. Resume accepting transactions.

Any transaction that executed prior to the checkpoint will have finished, and by rule U_2 its changes will have reached the disk. Thus, there will be no need to undo any of these transactions during recovery. During a recovery, we scan the log backwards from the end, identifying incomplete transactions as in Section 17.2.3. However, when we find a <CKPT> record, we know that we have seen all the incomplete transactions. Since no transactions may begin until the checkpoint ends, we must have seen every log record pertaining to the incomplete transactions already. Thus, there is no need to scan prior to the

---

Finding the Last Log Record

The log is essentially a file, whose blocks hold the log records. A space in a block that has never been filled can be marked "empty." If records were never overwritten, then the recovery manager could find the last log record by searching for the first empty record and taking the previous record as the end of the file.

However, if we overwrite old log records, then we need to keep a serial number, which only increases, with each record, as suggested by:

~~1~~ 9	~~2~~ 10	~~3~~ 11	4	5	6	7	8

Then, we can find the record whose serial number is greater than that of the next record; the latter record will be the current end of the log, and the entire log is found by ordering the current records by their present serial numbers.

In practice, a large log may be composed of many files, with a "top" file whose records indicate the files that comprise the log. Then, to recover, we find the last record of the top file, go to the file indicated, and find the last record there.

<CKPT>, and in fact the log before that point can be deleted or overwritten safely.

Example 17.4: Suppose the log begins:

$$<\text{START } T_1>$$
$$<T_1, A, 5>$$
$$<\text{START } T_2>$$
$$<T_2, B, 10>$$

At this time, we decide to do a checkpoint. Since T_1 and T_2 are the active (incomplete) transactions, we shall have to wait until they complete before writing the <CKPT> record on the log.

A possible continuation of the log is shown in Fig. 17.4. Suppose a crash occurs at this point. Scanning the log from the end, we identify T_3 as the only incomplete transaction, and restore E and F to their former values 25 and 30, respectively. When we reach the <CKPT> record, we know there is no need to examine prior log records and the restoration of the database state is complete. □

17.2.5 Nonquiescent Checkpointing

A problem with the checkpointing technique described in Section 17.2.4 is that effectively we must shut down the system while the checkpoint is being made.

$$<\text{START } T_1>$$
$$<T_1, A, 5>$$
$$<\text{START } T_2>$$
$$<T_2, B, 10>$$
$$<T_2, C, 15>$$
$$<T_1, D, 20>$$
$$<\text{COMMIT } T_1>$$
$$<\text{COMMIT } T_2>$$
$$<\text{CKPT}>$$
$$<\text{START } T_3>$$
$$<T_3, E, 25>$$
$$<T_3, F, 30>$$

Figure 17.4: An undo log

Since the active transactions may take a long time to commit or abort, the system may appear to users to be stalled. Thus, a more complex technique known as *nonquiescent checkpointing*, which allows new transactions to enter the system during the checkpoint, is usually preferred. The steps in a nonquiescent checkpoint are:

1. Write a log record <START CKPT $(T_1, \ldots, T_k)$> and flush the log. Here, $T_1, \ldots, T_k$ are the names or identifiers for all the *active* transactions (i.e., transactions that have not yet committed and written their changes to disk).

2. Wait until all of $T_1, \ldots, T_k$ commit or abort, but do not prohibit other transactions from starting.

3. When all of $T_1, \ldots, T_k$ have completed, write a log record <END CKPT> and flush the log.

With a log of this type, we can recover from a system crash as follows. As usual, we scan the log from the end, finding all incomplete transactions as we go, and restoring old values for database elements changed by these transactions. There are two cases, depending on whether, scanning backwards, we first meet an <END CKPT> record or a <START CKPT $(T_1, \ldots, T_k)$> record.

- If we first meet an <END CKPT> record, then we know that all incomplete transactions began after the previous <START CKPT $(T_1, \ldots, T_k)$> record. We may thus scan backwards as far as the next START CKPT, and then stop; previous log is useless and may as well have been discarded.

- If we first meet a record <START CKPT $(T_1, \ldots, T_k)$>, then the crash occurred during the checkpoint. However, the only incomplete transactions are those we met scanning backwards before we reached the START CKPT and those of $T_1, \ldots, T_k$ that did not complete before the crash. Thus, we need scan no further back than the start of the earliest of these incomplete transactions. The previous START CKPT record is certainly prior to any of these transaction starts, but often we shall find the starts of the incomplete transactions long before we reach the previous checkpoint.[3] Moreover, if we use pointers to chain together the log records that belong to the same transaction, then we need not search the whole log for records belonging to active transactions; we just follow their chains back through the log.

As a general rule, once an <END CKPT> record has been written to disk, we can delete the log prior to the previous START CKPT record.

Example 17.5: Suppose that, as in Example 17.4, the log begins:

$$<\text{START } T_1>$$
$$<T_1, A, 5>$$
$$<\text{START } T_2>$$
$$<T_2, B, 10>$$

Now, we decide to do a nonquiescent checkpoint. Since T_1 and T_2 are the active (incomplete) transactions at this time, we write a log record

$$<\text{START CKPT } (T_1, T_2)>$$

Suppose that while waiting for T_1 and T_2 to complete, another transaction, T_3, initiates. A possible continuation of the log is shown in Fig. 17.5.

Suppose that at this point there is a system crash. Examining the log from the end, we find that T_3 is an incomplete transaction and must be undone. The final log record tells us to restore database element F to the value 30. When we find the <END CKPT> record, we know that all incomplete transactions began after the previous START CKPT. Scanning further back, we find the record $<T_3, E, 25>$, which tells us to restore E to value 25. Between that record, and the START CKPT there are no other transactions that started but did not commit, so no further changes to the database are made.

Now, let us consider a situation where the crash occurs during the checkpoint. Suppose the end of the log after the crash is as shown in Fig. 17.6. Scanning backwards, we identify T_3 and then T_2 as incomplete transactions and undo changes they have made. When we find the <START CKPT (T_1, T_2)> record, we know that the only other possible incomplete transaction is T_1. However, we have already scanned the <COMMIT T_1> record, so we know that T_1 is *not* incomplete. Also, we have already seen the <START T_3> record. Thus, we need only to continue backwards until we meet the START record for T_2, restoring database element B to value 10 as we go.   □

---

[3]Notice, however, that because the checkpoint is nonquiescent, one of the incomplete transactions could have begun between the start and end of the previous checkpoint.

$$<\text{START } T_1>$$
$$<T_1, A, 5>$$
$$<\text{START } T_2>$$
$$<T_2, B, 10>$$
$$<\text{START CKPT } (T_1, T_2)>$$
$$<T_2, C, 15>$$
$$<\text{START } T_3>$$
$$<T_1, D, 20>$$
$$<\text{COMMIT } T_1>$$
$$<T_3, E, 25>$$
$$<\text{COMMIT } T_2>$$
$$<\text{END CKPT}>$$
$$<T_3, F, 30>$$

Figure 17.5: An undo log using nonquiescent checkpointing

$$<\text{START } T_1>$$
$$<T_1, A, 5>$$
$$<\text{START } T_2>$$
$$<T_2, B, 10>$$
$$<\text{START CKPT } (T_1, T_2)>$$
$$<T_2, C, 15>$$
$$<\text{START } T_3>$$
$$<T_1, D, 20>$$
$$<\text{COMMIT } T_1>$$
$$<T_3, E, 25>$$

Figure 17.6: Undo log with a system crash during checkpointing

17.2.6 Exercises for Section 17.2

Exercise 17.2.1: Show the undo-log records for each of the transactions (call each T) of Exercise 17.1.1, assuming that initially $A = 5$ and $B = 10$.

Exercise 17.2.2: For each of the sequences of log records representing the actions of one transaction T, tell all the sequences of events that are legal according to the rules of undo logging, where the events of interest are the writing to disk of the blocks containing database elements, and the blocks of the log containing the update and commit records. You may assume that log records are written to disk in the order shown; i.e., it is not possible to write one log record to disk while a previous record is not written to disk.

* a) $<\text{START } T>$; $<T, A, 10>$; $<T, B, 20>$; $<\text{COMMIT } T>$;

b) <START T>; <$T, A, 10$>; <$T, B, 20$>; <$T, C, 30$><COMMIT T>;

! **Exercise 17.2.3:** The pattern introduced in Exercise 17.2.2 can be extended to a transaction that writes new values for n database elements. How many legal sequences of events are there for such a transaction, if the undo-logging rules are obeyed?

Exercise 17.2.4: The following is a sequence of undo-log records written by two transactions T and U: <START T>; <$T, A, 10$>; <START U>; <$U, B, 20$>; <$T, C, 30$>; <$U, D, 40$>; <COMMIT U>; <$T, E, 50$>; <COMMIT T>. Describe the action of the recovery manager, including changes to both disk and the log, if there is a crash and the last log record to appear on disk is:

a) <START U>.

* b) <COMMIT U>.

c) <$T, E, 50$>.

d) <COMMIT T>.

Exercise 17.2.5: For each of the situations described in Exercise 17.2.4, what values written by T and U *must* appear on disk? Which values *might* appear on disk?

*! **Exercise 17.2.6:** Suppose that the transaction U in Exercise 17.2.4 is changed so that the record <$U, D, 40$> becomes <$U, A, 40$>. What is the effect on the disk value of A if there is a crash at some point during the sequence of events? What does this example say about the ability of logging by itself to preserve atomicity of transactions?

Exercise 17.2.7: Consider the following sequence of log records: <START S>; <$S, A, 60$>; <COMMIT S>; <START T>; <$T, A, 10$>; <START U>; <$U, B, 20$>; <$T, C, 30$>; <START V>; <$U, D, 40$>; <$V, F, 70$>; <COMMIT U>; <$T, E, 50$>; <COMMIT T>; <$V, B, 80$>; <COMMIT V>. Suppose that we begin a nonquiescent checkpoint immediately after one of the following log records has been written (in memory):

a) <$S, A, 60$>.

* b) <$T, A, 10$>.

c) <$U, B, 20$>.

d) <$U, D, 40$>.

e) <$T, E, 50$>.

For each, tell:

i. When the <END CKPT> record is written, and

ii. For each possible point at which a crash could occur, how far back in the log we must look to find all possible incomplete transactions.

17.3   Redo Logging

While undo logging provides a natural and simple strategy for maintaining a log and recovering from a system failure, it is not the only possible approach. Undo logging has a potential problem that we cannot commit a transaction without first writing all its changed data to disk. Sometimes, we can save disk I/O's if we let changes to the database reside only in main memory for a while; as long as there is a log to fix things up in the event of a crash, it is safe to do so.

The requirement for immediate backup of database elements to disk can be avoided if we use a logging mechanism called *redo logging*. The principal differences between redo and undo logging are:

1. While undo logging cancels the effect of incomplete transactions and ignores committed ones during recovery, redo logging ignores incomplete transactions and repeats the changes made by committed transactions.

2. While undo logging requires us to write changed database elements to disk before the COMMIT log record reaches disk, redo logging requires that the COMMIT record appear on disk before any changed values reach disk.

3. While the old values of changed database elements are exactly what we need to recover when the undo rules U_1 and U_2 are followed, to recover using redo logging, we need the new values instead. Thus, although redo-log records have the same form as undo-log records, their interpretations, as described immediately below, are different.

17.3.1   The Redo-Logging Rule

In redo logging the meaning of a log record $<T, X, v>$ is "transaction T wrote new value v for database element X." There is no indication of the old value of X in this record. Every time a transaction T modifies a database element X, a record of the form $<T, X, v>$ must be written to the log.

For redo logging, the order in which data and log entries reach disk can be described by a single "redo rule," called the *write-ahead logging rule*.

R_1: Before modifying any database element X on disk, it is necessary that all log records pertaining to this modification of X, including both the update record $<T, X, v>$ and the $<$COMMIT $T>$ record, must appear on disk.

Since the COMMIT record for a transaction can only be written to the log when the transaction completes, and therefore the commit record must follow all the update log records, we can summarize the effect of rule R_1 by asserting that when redo logging is in use, the order in which material associated with one transaction gets written to disk is:

1. The log records indicating changed database elements.

2. The COMMIT log record.

3. The changed database elements themselves.

Example 17.6: Let us consider the same transaction T as in Example 17.2. Figure 17.7 shows a possible sequence of events for this transaction.

Step	Action	t	M-A	M-B	D-A	D-B	Log
1)							$<$START $T>$
2)	READ(A,t)	8	8		8	8	
3)	t := t*2	16	8		8	8	
4)	WRITE(A,t)	16	16		8	8	$<T, A, 16>$
5)	READ(B,t)	8	16	8	8	8	
6)	t := t*2	16	16	8	8	8	
7)	WRITE(B,t)	16	16	16	8	8	$<T, B, 16>$
8)							$<$COMMIT $T>$
9)	FLUSH LOG						
10)	OUTPUT(A)	16	16	16	16	8	
11)	OUTPUT(B)	16	16	16	16	16	

Figure 17.7: Actions and their log entries using redo logging

The major differences between Figs. 17.7 and 17.3 are as follows. First, we note in lines (4) and (7) of Fig. 17.7 that the log records reflecting the changes have the new values of A and B, rather than the old values. Second, we see that the $<$COMMIT $T>$ record comes earlier, at step (8). Then, the log is flushed, so all log records involving the changes of transaction T appear on disk. Only then can the new values of A and B be written to disk. We show these values written immediately, at steps (10) and (11), although in practice they might occur much later.   □

17.3.2   Recovery With Redo Logging

An important consequence of the redo rule R_1 is that unless the log has a $<$COMMIT $T>$ record, we know that no changes to the database made by transaction T have been written to disk. Thus, incomplete transactions may be treated during recovery as if they had never occurred. However, the committed transactions present a problem, since we do not know which of their database changes have been written to disk. Fortunately, the redo log has exactly the information we need: the new values, which we may write to disk regardless of whether they were already there. To recover, using a redo log, after a system crash, we do the following.

Order of Redo Matters

Since several committed transactions may have written new values for the same database element X, we have required that during a redo recovery, we scan the log from earliest to latest. Thus, the final value of X in the database will be the one written last, as it should be. Similarly, when describing undo recovery, we required that the log be scanned from latest to earliest. Thus, the final value of X will be the value that it had before any of the undone transactions changed it.

However, if the DBMS enforces atomicity, then we would not expect to find, in an undo log, two uncommitted transactions, each of which had written the same database element. In contrast, with redo logging we focus on the committed transactions, as these need to be redone. It is quite normal, for there to be two *committed* transactions, each of which changed the same database element at different times. Thus, order of redo is always important, while order of undo might not be if the right kind of concurrency control were in effect.

---

1. Identify the committed transactions.

2. Scan the log forward from the beginning. For each log record $<T, X, v>$ encountered:

   (a) If T is not a committed transaction, do nothing.

   (b) If T is committed, write value v for database element X.

3. For each incomplete transaction T, write an $<\texttt{ABORT}\ T>$ record to the log and flush the log.

Example 17.7: Let us consider the log written in Fig. 17.7 and see how recovery would be performed if the crash occurred after different steps in that sequence of actions.

1. If the crash occurs any time after step (9), then the $<\texttt{COMMIT}\ T>$ record has been flushed to disk. The recovery system identifies T as a committed transaction. When scanning the log forward, the log records $<T, A, 16>$ and $<T, B, 16>$ cause the recovery manager to write values 16 for A and B. Notice that if the crash occurred between steps (10) and (11), then the write of A is redundant, but the write of B had not occurred and changing B to 16 is essential to restore the database state to consistency. If the crash occurred after step (11), then both writes are redundant but harmless.

2. If the crash occurs between steps (8) and (9), then although the record <COMMIT T> was written to the log, it may not have gotten to disk (depending on whether the log was flushed for some other reason). If it did get to disk, then the recovery proceeds as in case (1), and if it did not get to disk, then recovery is as in case (3), below.

3. If the crash occurs prior to step (8), then <COMMIT T> surely has not reached disk. Thus, T is treated as an incomplete transaction. No changes to A or B on disk are made on behalf of T, and eventually an <ABORT T> record is written to the log.

☐

17.3.3 Checkpointing a Redo Log

We can insert checkpoints into a redo log as well as an undo log. However, redo logs present a new problem. Since the database changes made by a committed transaction can be copied to disk much later than the time at which the transaction commits, we cannot limit our concern to transactions that are active at the time we decide to create a checkpoint. Regardless of whether the checkpoint is quiescent (transactions are not allowed to begin) or nonquiescent, the key action we must take between the start and end of the checkpoint is to write to disk all database elements that have been modified by committed transactions but not yet written to disk. To do so requires that the buffer manager keep track of which buffers are *dirty*, that is, they have been changed but not written to disk. It is also required to know which transactions modified which buffers.

On the other hand, we can complete the checkpoint without waiting for the active transactions to commit or abort, since they are not allowed to write their pages to disk at that time anyway. The steps to be taken to perform a nonquiescent checkpoint of a redo log are as follows:

1. Write a log record <START CKPT $(T_1, \ldots, T_k)$>, where $T_1, \ldots, T_k$ are all the active (uncommitted) transactions, and flush the log.

2. Write to disk all database elements that were written to buffers but not yet to disk by transactions that had already committed when the START CKPT record was written to the log.

3. Write an <END CKPT> record to the log and flush the log.

Example 17.8 : Figure 17.8 shows a possible redo log, in the middle of which a checkpoint occurs. When we start the checkpoint, only T_2 is active, but the value of A written by T_1 may have reached disk. If not, then we must copy A to disk before the checkpoint can end. We suggest the end of the checkpoint occurring after several other events have occurred: T_2 wrote a value for database element C, and a new transaction T_3 started and wrote a value of D. After the end of the checkpoint, the only things that happen are that T_2 and T_3 commit.
☐

$$<\text{START } T_1>$$
$$<T_1, A, 5>$$
$$<\text{START } T_2>$$
$$<\text{COMMIT } T_1>$$
$$<T_2, B, 10>$$
$$<\text{START CKPT } (T_2)>$$
$$<T_2, C, 15>$$
$$<\text{START } T_3>$$
$$<T_3, D, 20>$$
$$<\text{END CKPT}>$$
$$<\text{COMMIT } T_2>$$
$$<\text{COMMIT } T_3>$$

Figure 17.8: A redo log

17.3.4 Recovery With a Checkpointed Redo Log

As for an undo log, the insertion of records to mark the start and end of a checkpoint helps us limit our examination of the log when a recovery is necessary. Also as with undo logging, there are two cases, depending on whether the last checkpoint record is START or END.

- Suppose first that the last checkpoint record on the log before a crash is <END CKPT>. Now, we know that every value written by a transaction that committed before the corresponding <START CKPT $(T_1, \ldots, T_k)$> has had its changes written to disk, so we need not concern ourselves with recovering the effects of these transactions. However, any transaction that is either among the T_i's or that started after the beginning of the checkpoint can still have changes it made not yet migrated to disk, even though the transaction has committed. Thus, we must perform recovery as described in Section 17.3.2, but may limit our attention to the transactions that are either one of the T_i's mentioned in the last <START CKPT $(T_1, \ldots, T_k)$> or that started after that log record appeared in the log. In searching the log, we do not have to look further back than the earliest of the <START T_i> records. Notice, however, that these START records could appear prior to any number of checkpoints. Linking backwards all the log records for a given transaction helps us to find the necessary records, as it did for undo logging.

- Now, let us suppose that the last checkpoint record on the log is a <START CKPT $(T_1, \ldots, T_k)$> record. We cannot be sure that committed transactions prior to the start of this checkpoint had their changes written to disk. Thus, we must search back to the previous <END CKPT> record,

find its matching <START CKPT $(S_1, \ldots, S_m)$> record,[4] and redo all those
committed transactions that either started after that START CKPT or are
among the S_i's.

Example 17.9: Consider again the log of Fig. 17.8. If a crash occurs at the
end, we search backwards, finding the <END CKPT> record. We thus know that
it is sufficient to consider as candidates to redo all those transactions that either
started after the <START CKPT (T_2)> record was written or that are on its list
(i.e., T_2). Thus, our candidate set is $\{T_2, T_3\}$. We find the records <COMMIT T_2>
and <COMMIT T_3>, so we know that each must be redone. We search the log as
far back as the <START T_2> record, and find the update records <$T_2, B, 10$>,
<$T_2, C, 15$>, and <$T_3, D, 20$> for the committed transactions. Since we don't
know whether these changes reached disk, we rewrite the values 10, 15, and 20
for B, C, and D, respectively.

Now, suppose the crash occurred between the records <COMMIT T_2> and
<COMMIT T_3>. The recovery is similar to the above, except that T_3 is no longer
a committed transaction. Thus, its change <$T_3, D, 20$> must *not* be redone,
and no change is made to D during recovery, even though that log record is in
the range of records that is examined. Also, we write an <ABORT T_3> record
to the log after recovery.

Finally, suppose that the crash occurs just prior to the <END CKPT> record.
In principal, we must search back to the next-to-last START CKPT record and
get its list of active transactions. However, in this case there is no previous
checkpoint, and we must go all the way to the beginning of the log. Thus, we
identify T_1 as the only committed transaction, redo its action <$T_1, A, 5$>, and
write records <ABORT T_2> and <ABORT T_3> to the log after recovery. □

Since transactions may be active during several checkpoints, it is convenient
to include in the <START CKPT $(T_1, \ldots, T_k)$> records not only the names of the
active transactions, but pointers to the place on the log where they started. By
doing so, we know when it is safe to delete early portions of the log. When we
write an <END CKPT>, we know that we shall never need to look back further
than the earliest of the <START T_i> records for the active transactions T_i. Thus,
anything prior to that START record may be deleted.

17.3.5 Exercises for Section 17.3

Exercise 17.3.1: Show the redo-log records for each of the transactions (call
each T) of Exercise 17.1.1, assuming that initially $A = 5$ and $B = 10$.

Exercise 17.3.2: Repeat Exercise 17.2.2 for redo logging.

Exercise 17.3.3: Repeat Exercise 17.2.4 for redo logging.

---

[4]There is a small technicality that there could be a START CKPT record that, because of a
previous crash, has no matching <END CKPT> record. Therefore, we must look not just for
the previous START CKPT, but first for an <END CKPT> and then the previous START CKPT.

Exercise 17.3.4: Repeat Exercise 17.2.5 for redo logging.

Exercise 17.3.5: Using the data of Exercise 17.2.7, answer for each of the positions (a) through (e) of that exercise:

  i. At what points could the <END CKPT> record be written, and

  ii. For each possible point at which a crash could occur, how far back in the log we must look to find all possible incomplete transactions. Consider both the case that the <END CKPT> record was or was not written prior to the crash.

17.4 Undo/Redo Logging

We have seen two different approaches to logging, differentiated by whether the log holds old values or new values when a database element is updated. Each has certain drawbacks:

- Undo logging requires that data be written to disk immediately after a transaction finishes, perhaps increasing the number of disk I/O's that need to be performed.

- On the other hand, redo logging requires us to keep all modified blocks in buffers until the transaction commits and the log records have been flushed, perhaps increasing the average number of buffers required by transactions.

- Both undo and redo logs may put contradictory requirements on how buffers are handled during a checkpoint, unless the database elements are complete blocks or sets of blocks. For instance, if a buffer contains one database element A that was changed by a committed transaction and another database element B that was changed in the same buffer by a transaction that has not yet had its COMMIT record written to disk, then we are required to copy the buffer to disk because of A but also forbidden to do so, because rule R_1 applies to B.

We shall now see a kind of logging called *undo/redo logging*, that provides increased flexibility to order actions, at the expense of maintaining more information on the log.

17.4.1 The Undo/Redo Rules

An undo/redo log has the same sorts of log records as the other kinds of log, with one exception. The update log record that we write when a database element changes value has four components. Record $<T, X, v, w>$ means that transaction T changed the value of database element X; its former value was v, and its new value is w. The constraints that an undo/redo logging system must follow are summarized by the following rule:

UR_1 Before modifying any database element X on disk because of changes
   made by some transaction T, it is necessary that the update record
   $<T, X, v, w>$ appear on disk.

Rule UR_1 for undo/redo logging thus enforces only the constraints enforced
by *both* undo logging and redo logging. In particular, the $<$COMMIT $T>$ log
record can precede or follow any of the changes to the database elements on
disk.

Example 17.10: Figure 17.9 is a variation in the order of the actions associated with the transaction T that we last saw in Example 17.6. Notice that the
log records for updates now have both the old and the new values of A and B.
In this sequence, we have written the $<$COMMIT $T>$ log record in the middle of
the output of database elements A and B to disk. Step (10) could also have
appeared before step (8) or step (9), or after step (11). □

Step	Action	t	M-A	M-B	D-A	D-B	Log
1)							$<$START $T>$
2)	READ(A,t)	8	8		8	8	
3)	t := t*2	16	8		8	8	
4)	WRITE(A,t)	16	16		8	8	$<T, A, 8, 16>$
5)	READ(B,t)	8	16	8	8	8	
6)	t := t*2	16	16	8	8	8	
7)	WRITE(B,t)	16	16	16	8	8	$<T, B, 8, 16>$
8)	FLUSH LOG						
9)	OUTPUT(A)	16	16	16	16	8	
10)							$<$COMMIT $T>$
11)	OUTPUT(B)	16	16	16	16	16	

Figure 17.9: A possible sequence of actions and their log entries using undo/redo
logging

17.4.2 Recovery With Undo/Redo Logging

When we need to recover using an undo/redo log, we have the information in
the update records either to undo a transaction T, by restoring the old values
of the database elements that T changed, or to redo T by repeating the changes
it has made. The undo/redo recovery policy is:

1. Redo all the committed transactions in the order earliest-first, and

2. Undo all the incomplete transactions in the order latest-first.

A Problem With Delayed Commitment

Like undo logging, a system using undo/redo logging can exhibit a behavior where a transaction appears to the user to have been completed (e.g., they booked an airline seat over the Web and disconnected), and yet because the <COMMIT T> record was not flushed to disk, a subsequent crash causes the transaction to be undone rather than redone. If this possibility is a problem, we suggest the use of an additional rule for undo/redo logging:

UR_2 A <COMMIT T> record must be flushed to disk as soon as it appears in the log.

For instance, we would add FLUSH LOG after step (10) of Fig. 17.9.

Notice that it is necessary for us to do both. Because of the flexibility allowed by undo/redo logging regarding the relative order in which COMMIT log records and the database changes themselves are copied to disk, we could have either a committed transaction with some or all of its changes not on disk, or an uncommitted transaction with some or all of its changes on disk.

Example 17.11 : Consider the sequence of actions in Fig. 17.9. Here are the different ways that recovery would take place on the assumption that there is a crash at various points in the sequence.

1. Suppose the crash occurs after the <COMMIT T> record is flushed to disk. Then T is identified as a committed transaction. We write the value 16 for both A and B to the disk. Because of the actual order of events, A already has the value 16, but B may not, depending on whether the crash occurred before or after step (11).

2. If the crash occurs prior to the <COMMIT T> record reaching disk, then T is treated as an incomplete transaction. The previous values of A and B, 8 in each case, are written to disk. If the crash occurs between steps (9) and (10), then the value of A was 16 on disk, and the restoration to value 8 is necessary. In this example, the value of B does not need to be undone, and if the crash occurs before step (9) then neither does the value of A. However, in general we cannot be sure whether restoration is necessary, so we always perform the undo operation.

□

17.4.3 Checkpointing an Undo/Redo Log

A nonquiescent checkpoint is somewhat simpler for undo/redo logging than for the other logging methods. We have only to do the following:

Strange Behavior of Transactions During Recovery

The astute reader may have noticed that we did not specify whether undo's or redo's are done first during recovery using an undo/redo log. In fact, whether we perform the redo's or undo's first, we are open to the following situation: A transaction T has committed and is redone. However, T read a value X written by some transaction U that has not committed and is undone. The problem is not whether we redo first, and leave X with its value prior to U, or we undo first and leave X with its value written by T. The situation makes no sense either way, because the final database state does not correspond to the effect of any sequence of atomic transactions.

In reality, the DBMS must do more than log changes. It must assure that such situations do not occur by some mechanisms. In Chapter 18, there is a discussion about the means to isolate transactions like T and U, so the interaction between them through database element X cannot occur. In Section 19.1, we explicitly address means for preventing this situation where T reads a "dirty" value of X — one that has not been committed.

---

1. Write a <START CKPT $(T_1, \ldots, T_k)$> record to the log, where $T_1, \ldots, T_k$ are all the active transactions, and flush the log.

2. Write to disk all the buffers that are *dirty*; i.e., they contain one or more changed database elements. Unlike redo logging, we flush all buffers, not just those written by committed transactions.

3. Write an <END CKPT> record to the log, and flush the log.

Notice in connection with point (2) that, because of the flexibility undo/redo logging offers regarding when data reaches disk, we can tolerate the writing to disk of data written by incomplete transactions. Therefore we can tolerate database elements that are smaller than complete blocks and thus may share buffers. The only requirement we must make on transactions is:

- A transaction must not write any values (even to memory buffers) until it is certain not to abort.

As we shall see in Section 19.1, this constraint is almost certainly needed anyway, in order to avoid inconsistent interactions between transactions. Notice that under redo logging, the above condition is not sufficient, since even if the transaction that wrote B is certain to commit, rule R_1 requires that the transaction's COMMIT record be written to disk before B is written to disk.

Example 17.12: Figure 17.10 shows an undo/redo log analogous to the redo log of Fig. 17.8. We have only changed the update records, giving them an old value as well as a new value. For simplicity, we have assumed that in each case the old value is one less than the new value.

$$<\text{START } T_1>$$
$$<T_1, A, 4, 5>$$
$$<\text{START } T_2>$$
$$<\text{COMMIT } T_1>$$
$$<T_2, B, 9, 10>$$
$$<\text{START CKPT } (T_2)>$$
$$<T_2, C, 14, 15>$$
$$<\text{START } T_3>$$
$$<T_3, D, 19, 20>$$
$$<\text{END CKPT}>$$
$$<\text{COMMIT } T_2>$$
$$<\text{COMMIT } T_3>$$

Figure 17.10: An undo/redo log

As in Example 17.8, T_2 is identified as the only active transaction when the checkpoint begins. Since this log is an undo/redo log, it is possible that T_2's new B-value 10 has been written to disk, which was not possible under redo logging. However, it is irrelevant whether or not that disk write has occurred. During the checkpoint, we shall surely flush B to disk if it is not already there, since we flush all dirty buffers. Likewise, we shall flush A, written by the committed transaction T_1, if it is not already on disk.

If the crash occurs at the end of this sequence of events, then T_2 and T_3 are identified as committed transactions. Transaction T_1 is prior to the checkpoint. Since we find the <END CKPT> record on the log, T_1 is correctly assumed to have both completed and had its changes written to disk. We therefore redo both T_2 and T_3, as in Example 17.8, and ignore T_1. However, when we redo a transaction such as T_2, we do not need to look prior to the <START CKPT (T_2)> record, even though T_2 was active at that time, because we know that T_2's changes prior to the start of the checkpoint were flushed to disk during the checkpoint.

For another instance, suppose the crash occurs just before the <COMMIT T_3> record is written to disk. Then we identify T_2 as committed but T_3 as incomplete. We redo T_2 by setting C to 15 on disk; it is not necessary to set B to 10 since we know that change reached disk before the <END CKPT>. However, unlike the situation with a redo log, we also undo T_3; that is, we set D to 19 on disk. If T_3 had been active at the start of the checkpoint, we would have had to look prior to the START-CKPT record to find if there were more actions by T_3 that may have reached disk and need to be undone. □

17.4.4 Exercises for Section 17.4

Exercise 17.4.1: Show the undo/redo-log records for each of the transactions (call each T) of Exercise 17.1.1, assuming that initially $A = 5$ and $B = 10$.

Exercise 17.4.2: For each of the sequences of log records representing the actions of one transaction T, tell all the sequences of events that are legal according to the rules of undo/redo logging, where the events of interest are the writing to disk of the blocks containing database elements, and the blocks of the log containing the update and commit records. You may assume that log records are written to disk in the order shown; i.e., it is not possible to write one log record to disk while a previous record is not written to disk.

* a) <START T>; <$T, A, 10, 11$>; <$T, B, 20, 21$>; <COMMIT T>;

  b) <START T>; <$T, A, 10, 21$>; <$T, B, 20, 21$>; <$T, C, 30, 31$>;
      <COMMIT T>;

Exercise 17.4.3: The following is a sequence of undo/redo-log records written by two transactions T and U: <START T>; <$T, A, 10, 11$>; <START U>; <$U, B, 20, 21$>; <$T, C, 30, 31$>; <$U, D, 40, 41$>; <COMMIT U>; <$T, E, 50, 51$>; <COMMIT T>. Describe the action of the recovery manager, including changes to both disk and the log, if there is a crash and the last log record to appear on disk is:

  a) <START U>.

* b) <COMMIT U>.

  c) <$T, E, 50, 51$>.

  d) <COMMIT T>.

Exercise 17.4.4: For each of the situations described in Exercise 17.4.3, what values written by T and U *must* appear on disk? Which values *might* appear on disk?

Exercise 17.4.5: Consider the following sequence of log records: <START S>; <$S, A, 60, 61$>; <COMMIT S>; <START T>; <$T, A, 61, 62$>; <START U>; <$U, B, 20, 21$>; <$T, C, 30, 31$>; <START V>; <$U, D, 40, 41$>; <$V, F, 70, 71$>; <COMMIT U>;   <$T, E, 50, 51$>; <COMMIT T>; <$V, B, 21, 22$>; <COMMIT V>. Suppose that we begin a nonquiescent checkpoint immediately after one of the following log records has been written (in memory):

  a) <$S, A, 60, 61$>.

* b) <$T, A, 61, 62$>.

  c) <$U, B, 20, 21$>.

d) $<U, D, 40, 41>$.

e) $<T, E, 50, 51>$.

For each, tell:

i. At what points could the $<\texttt{END CKPT}>$ record be written, and

ii. For each possible point at which a crash could occur, how far back in the log we must look to find all possible incomplete transactions. Consider both the case that the $<\texttt{END CKPT}>$ record was or was not written prior to the crash.

17.5 Protecting Against Media Failures

The log can protect us against system failures, where nothing is lost from disk, but temporary data in main memory is lost. However, as we discussed in Section 17.1.1, more serious failures involve the loss of one or more disks. We could, in principle, reconstruct the database from the log if:

a) The log were on a disk other than the disk(s) that hold the data,

b) The log were never thrown away after a checkpoint, and

c) The log were of the redo or the undo/redo type, so new values are stored on the log.

However, as we mentioned, the log will usually grow faster than the database, so it is not practical to keep the log forever.

17.5.1 The Archive

To protect against media failures, we are thus led to a solution involving *archiving* — maintaining a copy of the database separate from the database itself. If it were possible to shut down the database for a while, we could make a backup copy on some storage medium such as tape or optical disk, and store them remote from the database in some secure location. The backup would preserve the database state as it existed at this time, and if there were a media failure, the database could be restored to the state that existed then.

To advance to a more recent state, we could use the log, provided the log had been preserved since the archive copy was made, and the log itself survived the failure. In order to protect against losing the log, we could transmit a copy of the log, almost as soon as it is created, to the same remote site as the archive. Then, if the log as well as the data is lost, we can use the archive plus remotely stored log to recover, at least up to the point that the log was last transmitted to the remote site.

Why Not Just Back Up the Log?

We might question the need for an archive, since we have to back up the log in a secure place anyway if we are not to be stuck at the state the database was in when the previous archive was made. While it may not be obvious, the answer lies in the typical rate of change of a large database. While only a small fraction of the database may change in a day, the changes, each of which must be logged, will over the course of a year become much larger than the database itself. If we never archived, then the log could never be truncated, and the cost of storing the log would soon exceed the cost of storing a copy of the database.

Since writing an archive is a lengthy process if the database is large, one generally tries to avoid copying the entire database at each archiving step. Thus, we distinguish between two levels of archiving:

1. A *full dump*, in which the entire database is copied.

2. An *incremental dump*, in which only those database elements changed since the previous full or incremental dump are copied.

It is also possible to have several levels of dump, with a full dump thought of as a "level 0" dump, and a "level i" dump copying everything changed since the last dump at level i or below.

We can restore the database from a full dump and its subsequent incremental dumps, in a process much like the way a redo or undo/redo log can be used to repair damage due to a system failure. We copy the full dump back to the database, and then in an earliest-first order, make the changes recorded by the later incremental dumps. Since incremental dumps will tend to involve only a small fraction of the data changed since the last dump, they take less space and can be done faster than full dumps.

17.5.2 Nonquiescent Archiving

The problem with the simple view of archiving in Section 17.5.1 is that most databases cannot be shut down for the period of time (possibly hours) needed to make a backup copy. We thus need to consider *nonquiescent archiving*, which is analogous to nonquiescent checkpointing. Recall that a nonquiescent checkpoint attempts to make a copy on the disk of the (approximate) database state that existed when the checkpoint started. We can rely on a small portion of the log around the time of the checkpoint to fix up any deviations from that database state, due to the fact that during the checkpoint, new transactions may have started and written to disk.

Similarly, a nonquiescent dump tries to make a copy of the database that existed when the dump began, but database activity may change many database elements on disk during the minutes or hours that the dump takes. If it is necessary to restore the database from the archive, the log entries made during the dump can be used to sort things out and get the database to a consistent state. The analogy is suggested by Fig. 17.11.

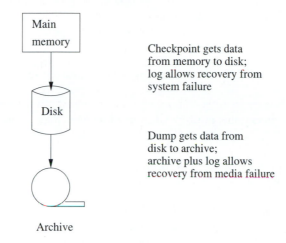

Figure 17.11: The analogy between checkpoints and dumps

A nonquiescent dump copies the database elements in some fixed order, possibly while those elements are being changed by executing transactions. As a result, the value of a database element that is copied to the archive may or may not be the value that existed when the dump began. As long as the log for the duration of the dump is preserved, the discrepancies can be corrected from the log.

Example 17.13: For a very simple example, suppose that our database consists of four elements, A, B, C, and D, which have the values 1 through 4, respectively when the dump begins. During the dump, A is changed to 5, C is changed to 6, and B is changed to 7. However, the database elements are copied in order, and the sequence of events shown in Fig. 17.12 occurs. Then although the database at the beginning of the dump has values $(1, 2, 3, 4)$, and the database at the end of the dump has values $(5, 7, 6, 4)$, the copy of the database in the archive has values $(1, 2, 6, 4)$, a database state that existed at no time during the dump. □

In more detail, the process of making an archive can be broken into the following steps. We assume that the logging method is either redo or undo/redo; an undo log is not suitable for use with archiving.

1. Write a log record <START DUMP>.

Disk	Archive
	Copy A
A := 5	
	Copy B
C := 6	
	Copy C
B := 7	
	Copy D

Figure 17.12: Events during a nonquiescent dump

2. Perform a checkpoint appropriate for whichever logging method is being used.

3. Perform a full or incremental dump of the data disk(s), as desired, making sure that the copy of the data has reached the secure, remote site.

4. Make sure that enough of the log has been copied to the secure, remote site that at least the prefix of the log up to and including the checkpoint in item (2) will survive a media failure of the database.

5. Write a log record <END DUMP>.

At the completion of the dump, it is safe to throw away log prior to the beginning of the checkpoint *previous* to the one performed in item (2) above.

Example 17.14: Suppose that the changes to the simple database in Example 17.13 were caused by two transactions T_1 (which writes A and B) and T_2 (which writes C) that were active when the dump began. Figure 17.13 shows a possible undo/redo log of the events during the dump.

<START DUMP>
<START CKPT (T_1, T_2)>
<$T_1, A, 1, 5$>
<$T_2, C, 3, 6$>
<COMMIT T_2>
<$T_1, B, 2, 7$>
<END CKPT>
Dump completes
<END DUMP>

Figure 17.13: Log taken during a dump

Notice that we did not show T_1 committing. It would be unusual that a transaction remained active during the entire time a full dump was in progress, but that possibility doesn't affect the correctness of the recovery method that we discuss next. $\square$

17.5.3   Recovery Using an Archive and Log

Suppose that a media failure occurs, and we must reconstruct the database from the most recent archive and whatever prefix of the log has reached the remote site and has not been lost in the crash. We perform the following steps:

1. Restore the database from the archive.

    (a) Find the most recent full dump and reconstruct the database from it (i.e., copy the archive into the database).

    (b) If there are later incremental dumps, modify the database according to each, earliest first.

2. Modify the database using the surviving log. Use the method of recovery appropriate to the log method being used.

Example 17.15: Suppose there is a media failure after the dump of Example 17.14 completes, and the log shown in Fig. 17.13 survives. Assume, to make the process interesting, that the surviving portion of the log does not include a <COMMIT T_1> record, although it does include the <COMMIT T_2> record shown in that figure. The database is first restored to the values in the archive, which is, for database elements A, B, C, and D, respectively, $(1, 2, 6, 4)$.

Now, we must look at the log. Since T_2 has completed, we redo the step that sets C to 6. In this example, C already had the value 6, but it might be that:

a) The archive for C was made before T_2 changed C, or

b) The archive actually captured a later value of C, which may or may not have been written by a transaction whose commit record survived. Later in the recovery, C will be restored to the value found in the archive *if* the transaction was committed.

Since T_1 does not have a COMMIT record, we must undo T_1. We use the log records for T_1 to determine that A must be restored to value 1 and B to 2. It happens that they had these values in the archive, but the actual archive value could have been different because the modified A and/or B had been included in the archive. $\square$

17.5.4   Exercises for Section 17.5

Exercise 17.5.1: If a redo log, rather than an undo/redo log, were used in Examples 17.14 and 17.15:

  a) What would the log look like?

*! b) If we had to recover using the archive and this log, what would be the consequence of T_1 not having committed?

  c) What would be the state of the database after recovery?

17.6   Summary of Chapter 17

✦ *Transaction Management*: The two principal tasks of the transaction manager are assuring recoverability of database actions through logging, and assuring correct, concurrent behavior of transactions through the scheduler (not discussed in this chapter).

✦ *Database Elements*: The database is divided into elements, which are typically disk blocks, but could be tuples, extents of a class, or many other units. Database elements are the units for both logging and scheduling.

✦ *Logging*: A record of every important action of a transaction — beginning, changing a database element, committing, or aborting — is stored on a log. The log must be backed up on disk at a time that is related to when the corresponding database changes migrate to disk, but that time depends on the particular logging method used.

✦ *Recovery*: When a system crash occurs, the log is used to repair the database, restoring it to a consistent state.

✦ *Logging Methods*: The three principal methods for logging are undo, redo, and undo/redo, named for the way(s) that they are allowed to fix the database during recovery.

✦ *Undo Logging*: This method logs the old value, each time a database element is changed. With undo logging, a new value of a database element can be written to disk only after the log record for the change has reached disk, but before the commit record for the transaction performing the change reaches disk. Recovery is done by restoring the old value for every uncommitted transaction.

✦ *Redo Logging*: Here, only the new value of database elements is logged. With this form of logging, values of a database element can be written to disk only after both the log record of its change and the commit record for its transaction have reached disk. Recovery involves rewriting the new value for every committed transaction.

◆ *Undo/Redo Logging* In this method, both old and new values are logged. Undo/redo logging is more flexible than the other methods, since it requires only that the log record of a change appear on the disk before the change itself does. There is no requirement about when the commit record appears. Recovery is effected by redoing committed transactions and undoing the uncommitted transactions.

◆ *Checkpointing*: Since all recovery methods require, in principle, looking at the entire log, the DBMS must occasionally checkpoint the log, to assure that no log records prior to the checkpoint will be needed during a recovery. Thus, old log records can eventually be thrown away and their disk space reused.

◆ *Nonquiescent Checkpointing*: To avoid shutting down the system while a checkpoint is made, techniques associated with each logging method allow the checkpoint to be made while the system is in operation and database changes are occurring. The only cost is that some log records prior to the nonquiescent checkpoint may need to be examined during recovery.

◆ *Archiving*: While logging protects against system failures involving only the loss of main memory, archiving is necessary to protect against failures where the contents of disk are lost. Archives are copies of the database stored in a safe place.

◆ *Incremental Backups*: Instead of copying the entire database to an archive periodically, a single complete backup can be followed by several incremental backups, where only the changed data is copied to the archive.

◆ *Nonquiescent Archiving*: We can create a backup of the data while the database is in operation. The necessary techniques involve making log records of the beginning and end of the archiving, as well as performing a checkpoint for the log during the archiving.

◆ *Recovery From Media Failures*: When a disk is lost, it may be restored by starting with a full backup of the database, modifying it according to any later incremental backups, and finally recovering to a consistent database state by using an archived copy of the log.

17.7 References for Chapter 17

The major textbook on all aspects of transaction processing, including logging and recovery, is by Gray and Reuter [5]. This book was partially fed by some informal notes on transaction processing by Jim Gray [3] that were widely circulated; the latter, along with [4] and [8] are the primary sources for much of the logging and recovery technology.

[2] is an earlier, more concise description of transaction-processing technology. [7] is a recent treatment of recovery.

Two early surveys, [1] and [6] both represent much of the fundamental work in recovery and organized the subject in the undo-redo-undo/redo tricotomy that we followed here.

1. P. A. Bernstein, N. Goodman, and V. Hadzilacos, "Recovery algorithms for database systems," *Proc. 1983 IFIP Congress*, North Holland, Amsterdam, pp. 799–807.

2. P. A. Bernstein, V. Hadzilacos, and N. Goodman, *Concurrency Control and Recovery in Database Systems*, Addison-Wesley, Reading MA, 1987.

3. J. N. Gray, "Notes on database operating systems," in *Operating Systems: an Advanced Course*, pp. 393–481, Springer-Verlag, 1978.

4. J. N. Gray, P. R. McJones, and M. Blasgen, "The recovery manager of the System R database manager," *Computing Surveys* **13**:2 (1981), pp. 223–242.

5. J. N. Gray and A. Reuter, *Transaction Processing: Concepts and Techniques*, Morgan-Kaufmann, San Francisco, 1993.

6. T. Haerder and A. Reuter, "Principles of transaction-oriented database recovery — a taxonomy," *Computing Surveys* **15**:4 (1983), pp. 287–317.

7. V. Kumar and M. Hsu, *Recovery Mechanisms in Database Systems*, Prentice-Hall, Englewood Cliffs NJ, 1998.

8. C. Mohan, D. J. Haderle, B. G. Lindsay, H. Pirahesh, and P. Schwarz, "ARIES: a transaction recovery method supporting fine-granularity locking and partial rollbacks using write-ahead logging," *ACM Trans. on Database Systems* **17**:1 (1992), pp. 94–162.

Chapter 18

Concurrency Control

Interactions among transactions can cause the database state to become inconsistent, even when the transactions individually preserve correctness of the state, and there is no system failure. Thus, the order in which the individual steps of different transactions occur needs to be regulated in some manner. The function of controlling these steps is given to the *scheduler* component of the DBMS, and the general process of assuring that transactions preserve consistency when executing simultaneously is called *concurrency control*. The role of the scheduler is suggested by Fig. 18.1.

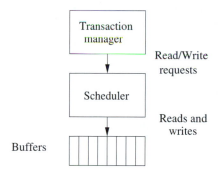

Figure 18.1: The scheduler takes read/write requests from transactions and either executes them in buffers or delays them

As transactions request reads and writes of database elements, these requests are passed to the scheduler. In most situations, the scheduler will execute the reads and writes directly, first calling on the buffer manager if the desired database element is not in a buffer. However, in some situations, it is not safe for the request to be executed immediately. The scheduler must delay the request; in some concurrency-control techniques, the scheduler may even abort the transaction that issued the request.

We begin by studying how to assure that concurrently executing transactions

917

preserve correctness of the database state. The abstract requirement is called *serializability*, and there is an important, stronger condition called *conflict-serializability* that most schedulers actually enforce. We consider the most important techniques for implementing schedulers: locking, timestamping, and validation.

Our study of lock-based schedulers includes the important concept of "two-phase locking," which is a requirement widely used to assure serializability of schedules. We also find that there are many different sets of lock modes that a scheduler can use, each with a different application. Among the locking schemes we study are those for nested and tree-structured collections of lockable elements.

18.1 Serial and Serializable Schedules

To begin our study of concurrency control, we must examine the conditions under which a collection of concurrently executing transactions will preserve consistency of the database state. Our fundamental assumption, which we called the "correctness principle" in Section 17.1.3, is: every transaction, if executed in isolation (without any other transactions running concurrently), will transform any consistent state to another consistent state. However, in practice, transactions often run concurrently with other transactions, so the correctness principle doesn't apply directly. Thus, we need to consider "schedules" of actions that can be guaranteed to produce the same result as if the transactions executed one-at-a-time. The major theme of this entire chapter is methods for forcing transactions to execute concurrently only in ways that make them appear to run one-at-a-time.

18.1.1 Schedules

A *schedule* is a time-ordered sequence of the important actions taken by one or more transactions. When studying concurrency control, the important read and write actions take place in the main-memory buffers, not the disk. That is, a database element A that is brought to a buffer by some transaction T may be read or written in that buffer not only by T but by other transactions that access A. Recall from Section 17.1.4 that the READ and WRITE actions first call INPUT to get a database element from disk if it is not already in a buffer, but otherwise READ and WRITE actions access the element in the buffer directly. Thus, only the READ and WRITE actions, and their orders, are important when considering concurrency, and we shall ignore the INPUT and OUTPUT actions.

Example 18.1 : Let us consider two transactions and the effect on the database when their actions are executed in certain orders. The important actions of the transactions T_1 and T_2 are shown in Fig. 18.2. The variables t and s are local variables of T_1 and T_2, respectively; they are *not* database elements.

T_1	T_2
READ(A,t)	READ(A,s)
t := t+100	s := s*2
WRITE(A,t)	WRITE(A,s)
READ(B,t)	READ(B,s)
t := t+100	s := s*2
WRITE(B,t)	WRITE(B,s)

Figure 18.2: Two transactions

We shall assume that the only consistency constraint on the database state is that $A = B$. Since T_1 adds 100 to both A and B, and T_2 multiplies both A and B by 2, we know that each transaction, run in isolation, will preserve consistency. □

18.1.2 Serial Schedules

We say a schedule is *serial* if its actions consist of all the actions of one transaction, then all the actions of another transaction, and so on, with no mixing of the actions. More precisely, a schedule S is serial if for any two transactions T and T', if any action of T precedes any action of T', then all actions of T precede all actions of T'.

T_1	T_2	A	B
		25	25
READ(A,t)			
t := t+100			
WRITE(A,t)		125	
READ(B,t)			
t := t+100			
WRITE(B,t)			125
	READ(A,s)		
	s := s*2		
	WRITE(A,s)	250	
	READ(B,s)		
	s := s*2		
	WRITE(B,s)		250

Figure 18.3: Serial schedule in which T_1 precedes T_2

Example 18.2 : For the transactions of Fig. 18.2, there are two serial schedules, one in which T_1 precedes T_2 and the other in which T_2 precedes T_1. Figure 18.3 shows the sequence of events when T_1 precedes T_2, and the initial state is $A = B = 25$. We shall take the convention that when displayed vertically, time proceeds down the page. Also, the values of A and B shown refer to their values in main-memory buffers, not necessarily to their values on disk.

T_1	T_2	A	B
		25	25
	READ(A,s)		
	s := s*2		
	WRITE(A,s)	50	
	READ(B,s)		
	s := s*2		
	WRITE(B,s)		50
READ(A,t)			
t := t+100			
WRITE(A,t)		150	
READ(B,t)			
t := t+100			
WRITE(B,t)			150

Figure 18.4: Serial schedule in which T_2 precedes T_1

Then, Fig. 18.4 shows another serial schedule in which T_2 precedes T_1; the initial state is again assumed to be $A = B = 25$. Notice that the final values of A and B are different for the two schedules; they both have value 250 when T_1 goes first and 150 when T_2 goes first. However, the final result is not the central issue, as long as consistency is preserved. In general, we would not expect the final state of a database to be independent of the order of transactions. □

We can represent a serial schedule as in Fig. 18.3 or Fig. 18.4, listing each of the actions in the order they occur. However, since the order of actions in a serial schedule depends only on the order of the transactions themselves, we shall sometimes represent a serial schedule by the list of transactions. Thus, the schedule of Fig. 18.3 is represented (T_1, T_2), and that of Fig. 18.4 is (T_2, T_1).

18.1.3 Serializable Schedules

The correctness principle for transactions tells us that every serial schedule will preserve consistency of the database state. But are there any other schedules that also are guaranteed to preserve consistency? There are, as the following example shows. In general, we say a schedule is *serializable* if its effect on the database state is the same as that of some serial schedule, regardless of what the initial state of the database is.

T_1	T_2	A	B
		25	25
READ(A,t)			
t := t+100			
WRITE(A,t)		125	
	READ(A,s)		
	s := s*2		
	WRITE(A,s)	250	
READ(B,t)			
t := t+100			
WRITE(B,t)			125
	READ(B,s)		
	s := s*2		
	WRITE(B,s)		250

Figure 18.5: A serializable, but not serial, schedule

Example 18.3 : Figure 18.5 shows a schedule of the transactions from Example 18.1 that is serializable but not serial. In this schedule, T_2 acts on A after T_1 does, but before T_1 acts on B. However, we see that the effect of the two transactions scheduled in this manner is the same as for the serial schedule (T_1, T_2) that we saw in Fig. 18.3. To convince ourselves of the truth of this statement, we must consider not only the effect from the database state $A = B = 25$, which we show in Fig. 18.5, but from any consistent database state. Since all consistent database states have $A = B = c$ for some constant c, it is not hard to deduce that in the schedule of Fig. 18.5, both A and B will be left with the value $2(c + 100)$, and thus consistency is preserved from any consistent state.

On the other hand, consider the schedule of Fig. 18.6. Clearly it is not serial, but more significantly, it is not serializable. The reason we can be sure it is not serializable is that it takes the consistent state $A = B = 25$ and leaves the database in an inconsistent state, where $A = 250$ and $B = 150$. Notice that in this order of actions, where T_1 operates on A first, but T_2 operates on B first, we have in effect applied different computations to A and B, that is $A := 2(A + 100)$ versus $B := 2B + 100$. The schedule of Fig. 18.6 is the sort of behavior that concurrency control mechanisms must avoid. $\Box$

18.1.4 The Effect of Transaction Semantics

In our study of serializability so far, we have considered in detail the operations performed by the transactions, to determine whether or not a schedule is serializable. The details of the transactions do matter, as we can see from the following example.

T_1	T_2	A	B
		25	25
READ(A,t)			
t := t+100			
WRITE(A,t)		125	
	READ(A,s)		
	s := s*2		
	WRITE(A,s)	250	
	READ(B,s)		
	s := s*2		
	WRITE(B,s)		50
READ(B,t)			
t := t+100			
WRITE(B,t)			150

Figure 18.6: A nonserializable schedule

Example 18.4 : Consider the schedule of Fig. 18.7, which differs from Fig. 18.6 only in the computation that T_2 performs. That is, instead of multiplying A and B by 2, T_2 multiplies them by 1.[1] Now, the values of A and B at the end of this schedule are equal, and one can easily check that regardless of the consistent initial state, the final state will be consistent. In fact, the final state is the one that results from either of the serial schedules (T_1, T_2) or (T_2, T_1). □

Unfortunately, it is not realistic for the scheduler to concern itself with the details of computation undertaken by transactions. Since transactions often involve code written in a general-purpose programming language as well as SQL or other high-level-language statements, it is sometimes very hard to answer questions like "does this transaction multiply A by a constant other than 1?" However, the scheduler does get to see the read and write requests from the transactions, so it can know what database elements each transaction reads, and what elements it *might* change. To simplify the job of the scheduler, it is conventional to assume that:

- Any database element A that a transaction T writes is given a value that depends on the database state in such a way that no arithmetic coincidences occur.

---

[1] One might reasonably ask why a transaction would behave that way, but let us ignore the matter for the sake of an example. In fact, there are many plausible transactions we could substitute for T_2 that would leave A and B unchanged; for instance, T_2 might simply read A and B and print their values. Or, T_2 might ask the user for some data, compute a factor F with which to multiply A and B, and find for some user inputs that $F = 1$.

T_1	T_2	A	B
		25	25
READ(A,t)			
t := t+100			
WRITE(A,t)		125	
	READ(A,s)		
	s := s*1		
	WRITE(A,s)	125	
	READ(B,s)		
	s := s*1		
	WRITE(B,s)		25
READ(B,t)			
t := t+100			
WRITE(B,t)			125

Figure 18.7: A schedule that is serializable only because of the detailed behavior of the transactions

Put another way, if there is something that T could have done to A that will make the database state inconsistent, then T will do that. We shall make this assumption more precise in Section 18.2, when we talk about sufficient conditions to guarantee serializability.

18.1.5   A Notation for Transactions and Schedules

If we accept that the exact computations performed by a transaction can be arbitrary, then we do not need to consider the details of local computation steps such as t := t+100. Only the reads and writes performed by the transaction matter. Thus, we shall represent transactions and schedules by a shorthand notation, in which the actions are $r_T(X)$ and $w_T(X)$, meaning that transaction T reads, or respectively writes, database element X. Moreover, since we shall usually name our transactions $T_1, T_2, \ldots$, we adopt the convention that $r_i(X)$ and $w_i(X)$ are synonyms for $r_{T_i}(X)$ and $w_{T_i}(X)$, respectively.

Example 18.5 : The transactions of Fig. 18.2 can be written:

$$T_1: r_1(A); w_1(A); r_1(B); w_1(B);$$
$$T_2: r_2(A); w_2(A); r_2(B); w_2(B);$$

Notice that there is no mention of the local variables t and s anywhere, and no indication of what has happened to A and B after they were read. Intuitively, we shall "assume the worst," regarding the ways in which these database elements change.

As another example, consider the serializable schedule of T_1 and T_2 from Fig. 18.5. This schedule is written:

$$r_1(A);\; w_1(A);\; r_2(A);\; w_2(A);\; r_1(B);\; w_1(B);\; r_2(B);\; w_2(B);$$

□

To make the notation precise:

1. An *action* is an expression of the form $r_i(X)$ or $w_i(X)$, meaning that transaction T_i reads or writes, respectively, the database element X.

2. A *transaction* T_i is a sequence of actions with subscript i.

3. A *schedule* S of a set of transactions $\mathcal{T}$ is a sequence of actions, in which for each transaction T_i in $\mathcal{T}$, the actions of T_i appear in S in the same order that they appear in the definition of T_i itself. We say that S is an *interleaving* of the actions of the transactions of which it is composed.

For instance, the schedule of Example 18.5 has all the actions with subscript 1 appearing in the same order that they have in the definition of T_1, and the actions with subscript 2 appear in the same order that they appear in the definition of T_2.

18.1.6   Exercises for Section 18.1

* Exercise 18.1.1: A transaction T_1, executed by an airline-reservation system, performs the following steps:

 i. The customer is queried for a desired flight time and cities. Information about the desired flights is located in database elements (perhaps disk blocks) A and B, which the system retrieves from disk.

 ii. The customer is told about the options, and selects a flight whose data, including the number of reservations for that flight is in B. A reservation on that flight is made for the customer.

 iii. The customer selects a seat for the flight; seat data for the flight is in database element C.

 iv. The system gets the customer's credit-card number and appends the bill for the flight to a list of bills in database element D.

 v. The customer's phone and flight data is added to another list on database element E for a fax to be sent confirming the flight.

Express transaction T_1 as a sequence of r and w actions.

*! Exercise 18.1.2: If two transactions consist of 4 and 6 actions, respectively, how many interleavings of these transactions are there?

18.2 Conflict-Serializability

We shall now develop a condition that is sufficient to assure that a schedule is serializable. Schedulers in commercial systems generally assure this stronger condition, which we shall call "conflict-serializability," when they want to assure that transactions behave in a serializable manner. It is based on the idea of a *conflict*: a pair of consecutive actions in a schedule such that, if their order is interchanged, then the behavior of at least one of the transactions involved can change.

18.2.1 Conflicts

To begin, let us observe that most pairs of actions do *not* conflict in the sense above. In what follows, we assume that T_i and T_j are different transactions; i.e., $i \neq j$.

1. $r_i(X); r_j(Y)$ is never a conflict, even if $X = Y$. The reason is that neither of these steps change the value of any database element.

2. $r_i(X); w_j(Y)$ is not a conflict provided $X \neq Y$. The reason is that should T_j write Y before T_i reads X, the value of X is not changed. Also, the read of X by T_i has no effect on T_j, so it does not affect the value T_j writes for Y.

3. $w_i(X); r_j(Y)$ is not a conflict if $X \neq Y$, for the same reason as (2).

4. Also similarly, $w_i(X); w_j(Y)$ is not a conflict as long as $X \neq Y$.

On the other hand, there are three situations where we may not swap the order of actions:

a) Two actions of the same transaction, e.g., $r_i(X); w_i(Y)$, conflict. The reason is that the order of actions of a single transaction are fixed and may not be reordered by the DBMS.

b) Two writes of the same database element by different transactions conflict. That is, $w_i(X); w_j(X)$ is a conflict. The reason is that as written, the value of X remains afterward as whatever T_j computed it to be. If we swap the order, as $w_j(X); w_i(X)$, then we leave X with the value computed by T_i. Our assumption of "no coincidences" tells us that the values written by T_i and T_j will be different, at least for some initial states of the database.

c) A read and a write of the same database element by different transactions also conflict. That is, $r_i(X); w_j(X)$ is a conflict, and so is $w_i(X); r_j(X)$. If we move $w_j(X)$ ahead of $r_i(X)$, then the value of X read by T_i will be that written by T_j, which we assume is not necessarily the same as the previous value of X. Thus, swapping the order of $r_i(X)$ and $w_j(X)$ affects the value T_i reads for X and could therefore affect what T_i does.

The conclusion we draw is that any two actions of different transactions may be swapped unless:

1. They involve the same database element, and

2. At least one is a write.

Extending this idea, we may take any schedule and make as many nonconflicting swaps as we wish, with the goal of turning the schedule into a serial schedule. If we can do so, then the original schedule is serializable, because its effect on the database state remains the same as we perform each of the nonconflicting swaps.

We say that two schedules are *conflict-equivalent* if they can be turned one into the other by a sequence of nonconflicting swaps of adjacent actions. We shall call a schedule *conflict-serializable* if it is conflict-equivalent to a serial schedule. Note that conflict-serializability is a sufficient condition for serializability; i.e., a conflict-serializable schedule is a serializable schedule. Conflict-serializability is not required for a schedule to be serializable, but it is the condition that the schedulers in commercial systems generally use when they need to guarantee serializability.

Example 18.6 : Consider the schedule

$$r_1(A); \; w_1(A); \; r_2(A); \; w_2(A); \; r_1(B); \; w_1(B); \; r_2(B); \; w_2(B);$$

from Example 18.5. We claim this schedule is conflict-serializable. Figure 18.8 shows the sequence of swaps in which this schedule is converted to the serial schedule (T_1, T_2), where all of T_1's actions precede all those of T_2. We have underlined the pair of adjacent actions about to be swapped at each step. $\Box$

$$r_1(A); \; w_1(A); \; r_2(A); \; \underline{w_2(A); \; r_1(B)}; \; w_1(B); \; r_2(B); \; w_2(B);$$
$$r_1(A); \; w_1(A); \; \underline{r_2(A); \; r_1(B)}; \; w_2(A); \; w_1(B); \; r_2(B); \; w_2(B);$$
$$r_1(A); \; w_1(A); \; r_1(B); \; r_2(A); \; \underline{w_2(A); \; w_1(B)}; \; r_2(B); \; w_2(B);$$
$$r_1(A); \; w_1(A); \; r_1(B); \; \underline{r_2(A); \; w_1(B)}; \; w_2(A); \; r_2(B); \; w_2(B);$$
$$r_1(A); \; w_1(A); \; r_1(B); \; w_1(B); \; r_2(A); \; w_2(A); \; r_2(B); \; w_2(B);$$

Figure 18.8: Converting a conflict-serializable schedule to a serial schedule by swaps of adjacent actions

18.2.2 Precedence Graphs and a Test for Conflict-Serializability

It is relatively simple to examine a schedule S and decide whether or not it is conflict-serializable. The idea is that when there are conflicting actions that

Why Conflict-Serializability is not Necessary for Serializability

One example has already been seen in Fig. 18.7. We saw there how the particular computation performed by T_2 made the schedule serializable. However, the schedule of Fig. 18.7 is not conflict-serializable, because A is written first by T_1 and B is written first by T_2. Since neither the writes of A nor the writes of B can be reordered, there is no way we can get all the actions of T_1 ahead of all actions of T_2, or vice-versa.

However, there are examples of serializable but not conflict-serializable schedules that do not depend on the computations performed by the transactions. For instance, consider three transactions T_1, T_2, and T_3 that each write a value for X. T_1 and T_2 also write values for Y before they write values for X. One possible schedule, which happens to be serial, is

$$S_1: w_1(Y); w_1(X); w_2(Y); w_2(X); w_3(X);$$

S_1 leaves X with the value written by T_3 and Y with the value written by T_2. However, so does the schedule

$$S_1: w_1(Y); w_2(Y); w_2(X); w_1(X); w_3(X);$$

Intuitively, the values of X written by T_1 and T_2 have no effect, since T_3 overwrites their values. Thus S_1 and S_2 leave both X and Y with the same value. Since S_1 is serial, and S_2 has the same effect as S_1 on any database state, we know that S_2 is serializable. However, since we cannot swap $w_1(Y)$ with $w_2(Y)$, and we cannot swap $w_1(X)$ with $w_2(X)$, therefore we cannot convert S_2 to any serial schedule by swaps. That is, S_2 is serializable, but not conflict-serializable.

appear anywhere in S, the transactions performing those actions must appear in the same order in any conflict-equivalent serial schedule as the actions appear in S. Thus, conflicting pairs of actions put constraints on the order of transactions in the hypothetical, conflict-equivalent serial schedule. If these constraints are not contradictory, we can find a conflict-equivalent serial schedule. If they are contradictory, we know that no such serial schedule exists.

Given a schedule S, involving transactions T_1 and T_2, perhaps among other transactions, we say that T_1 *takes precedence over* T_2, written $T_1 <_S T_2$, if there are actions A_1 of T_1 and A_2 of T_2, such that:

1. A_1 is ahead of A_2 in S,

2. Both A_1 and A_2 involve the same database element, and

3. At least one of A_1 and A_2 is a write action.

Notice that these are exactly the conditions under which we cannot swap the order of A_1 and A_2. Thus, A_1 will appear before A_2 in any schedule that is conflict-equivalent to S. As a result, if one of these schedules is a serial schedule, then it must have T_1 before T_2.

We can summarize these precedences in a *precedence graph*. The nodes of the precedence graph are the transactions of a schedule S. When the transactions are T_i for various i, we shall label the node for T_i by only the integer i. There is an arc from node i to node j if $T_i <_S T_j$.

Example 18.7: The following schedule S involves three transactions, T_1, T_2, and T_3.

$$S: r_2(A); r_1(B); w_2(A); r_3(A); w_1(B); w_3(A); r_2(B); w_2(B);$$

If we look at the actions involving A, we find several reasons why $T_2 <_S T_3$. For example, $r_2(A)$ comes ahead of $w_3(A)$ in S, and $w_2(A)$ comes ahead of both $r_3(A)$ and $w_3(A)$. Any one of these three observations is sufficient to justify the arc in the precedence graph of Fig. 18.9 from 2 to 3.

Figure 18.9: The precedence graph for the schedule S of Example 18.7

Similarly, if we look at the actions involving B, we find that there are several reasons why $T_1 <_S T_2$. For instance, the action $r_1(B)$ comes before $w_2(B)$. Thus, the precedence graph for S also has an arc from 1 to 2. However, these are the only arcs we can justify from the order of actions in schedule S.   □

There is a simple rule for telling whether a schedule S is conflict-serializable:

- Construct the precedence graph for S and ask if there are any cycles.

If so, then S is not conflict-serializable. But if the graph is acyclic, then S is conflict-serializable, and moreover, any topological order of the nodes[2] is a conflict-equivalent serial order.

Example 18.8: Figure 18.9 is acyclic, so the schedule S of Example 18.7 is conflict-serializable. There is only one order of the nodes or transactions consistent with the arcs of that graph: (T_1, T_2, T_3). Notice that it is indeed possible to convert S into the schedule in which all actions of each of the three transactions occur in this order; this serial schedule is:

$$S': r_1(B); w_1(B); r_2(A); w_2(A); r_2(B); w_2(B); r_3(A); w_3(A);$$

---

[2]A *topological order* of an acyclic graph is any order of the nodes such that for every arc $a \to b$, node a precedes node b in the topological order. We can find a topological order for any acyclic graph by repeatedly removing nodes that have no predecessors among the remaining nodes.

To see that we can get from S to S' by swaps of adjacent elements, first notice we can move $r_1(B)$ ahead of $r_2(A)$ without conflict. Then, by three swaps we can move $w_1(B)$ just after $r_1(B)$, because each of the intervening actions involves A and not B. We can then move $r_2(B)$ and $w_2(B)$ to a position just after $w_2(A)$, moving through only actions involving A; the result is S'. $\square$

Example 18.9: Consider the schedule

$$S_1: r_2(A); r_1(B); w_2(A); r_2(B); r_3(A); w_1(B); w_3(A); w_2(B);$$

which differs from S only in that action $r_2(B)$ has been moved forward three positions. Examination of the actions involving A still give us only the precedence $T_2 <_{S_1} T_3$. However, when we examine B we get not only $T_1 <_{S_1} T_2$ [because $r_1(B)$ and $w_1(B)$ appear before $w_2(B)$], but also $T_2 <_{S_1} T_1$ [because $r_2(B)$ appears before $w_1(B)$]. Thus, we have the precedence graph of Fig. 18.10 for schedule S_1.

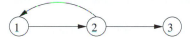

Figure 18.10: A cyclic precedence graph; its schedule is not conflict-serializable

This graph evidently has a cycle. We conclude that S_1 is not conflict-serializable. Intuitively, any conflict-equivalent serial schedule would have to have T_1 both ahead of and behind T_2, so therefore no such schedule exists. $\square$

18.2.3 Why the Precedence-Graph Test Works

As we have seen, a cycle in the precedence graph puts too many constraints on the order of transactions in a hypothetical conflict-equivalent serial schedule. That is, if there is a cycle involving n transactions $T_1 \to T_2 \to \ldots \to T_n \to T_1$, then in the hypothetical serial order, the actions of T_1 must precede those of T_2, which precede those of T_3, and so on, up to T_n. But the actions of T_n, which therefore come after those of T_1, are also required to precede those of T_1 because of the arc $T_n \to T_1$. Thus, we conclude that if there is a cycle in the precedence graph, then the schedule is not conflict-serializable.

The converse is a bit harder. We must show that if the precedence graph has no cycles, then we can reorder the schedule's actions using legal swaps of adjacent actions, until the schedule becomes a serial schedule. If we can do so, then we have our proof that every schedule with an acyclic precedence graph is conflict-serializable. The proof is an induction on the number of transactions involved in the schedule.

BASIS: If $n = 1$, i.e., there is only one transaction in the schedule, then the schedule is already serial, and therefore surely conflict-serializable.

INDUCTION: Let the schedule S consist of the actions of n transactions

$$T_1, T_2, \ldots, T_n$$

We suppose that S has an acyclic precedence graph. If a finite graph is acyclic, then there is at least one node that has no arcs in; let the node i corresponding to transaction T_i be such a node. Since there are no arcs into node i, there can be no action A in S that:

1. Involves any transaction T_j other than T_i,

2. Precedes some action of T_i, and

3. Conflicts with that action.

For if there were, we should have put an arc from node j to node i in the precedence graph.

It is thus possible to swap all the actions of T_i, keeping them in order, but moving them to the front of S. The schedule has now taken the form

$$(\text{Actions of } T_i)(\text{Actions of the other } n - 1 \text{ transactions})$$

Let us now consider the tail of S — the actions of all transactions other than T_i. Since these actions maintain the same relative order that they did in S, the precedence graph for the tail is the same as the precedence graph for S, except that the node for T_i and any arcs out of that node are missing.

Since the original precedence graph was acyclic, and deleting nodes and arcs cannot make it cyclic, we conclude that the tail's precedence graph is acyclic. Moreover, since the tail involves $n - 1$ transactions, the inductive hypothesis applies to it. Thus, we know we can reorder the actions of the tail using legal swaps of adjacent actions to turn it into a serial schedule. Now, S itself has been turned into a serial schedule, with the actions of T_i first and the actions of the other transactions following in some serial order. The induction is complete, and we conclude that every schedule with an acyclic precedence graph is conflict-serializable.

18.2.4   Exercises for Section 18.2

Exercise 18.2.1: Below are two transactions, described in terms of their effect on two database elements A and B, which we may assume are integers.

```
T₁: READ(A,t); t:=t+2; WRITE(A,t); READ(B,t); t:=t*3; WRITE(B,t);
T₂: READ(B,s); s:=s*2; WRITE(B,s); READ(A,s); s:=s+3; WRITE(A,s);
```

We assume that, whatever consistency constraints there are on the database, these transactions preserve them in isolation. Note that $A = B$ is *not* the consistency constraint.

a) It turns out that both serial orders have the same effect on the database; that is, (T_1, T_2) and (T_2, T_1) are equivalent. Demonstrate this fact by showing the effect of the two transactions on an arbitrary initial database state.

b) Give examples of a serializable schedule and a nonserializable schedule of the 12 actions above.

c) How many serial schedules of the 12 actions are there?

*!! d) How many serializable schedules of the 12 actions are there?

Exercise 18.2.2: The two transactions of Exercise 18.2.1 can be written in our notation that shows read- and write-actions only, as:

$$T_1: r_1(A); w_1(A); r_1(B); w_1(B);$$
$$T_2: r_2(B); w_2(B); r_2(A); w_2(A);$$

Answer the following:

*! a) Among the possible schedules of the eight actions above, how many are conflict-equivalent to the serial order (T_1, T_2)?

b) How many schedules of the eight actions are equivalent to the serial order (T_2, T_1)?

!! c) How many schedules of the eight actions are equivalent (not necessarily conflict-equivalent) to the serial schedule (T_1, T_2), assuming the transactions have the effect on the database described in Exercise 18.2.1?

! d) Why are the answers to (c) above and Exercise 18.2.1(d) different?

! **Exercise 18.2.3:** Suppose the transactions of Exercise 18.2.2 are changed to be:

$$T_1: r_1(A); w_1(A); r_1(B); w_1(B);$$
$$T_2: r_2(A); w_2(A); r_2(B); w_2(B);$$

That is, the transactions retain their semantics from Exercise 18.2.1, but T_2 has been changed so A is processed before B. Give:

a) The number of conflict-serializable schedules.

b) The number of serializable schedules, assuming the transactions have the same effect on the database state as in Exercise 18.2.1.

Exercise 18.2.4: For each of the following schedules:

* a) $r_1(A); r_2(A); r_3(B); w_1(A); r_2(C); r_2(B); w_2(B); w_1(C);$

b) $r_1(A)$; $w_1(B)$; $r_2(B)$: $w_2(C)$; $r_3(C)$; $w_3(A)$;

c) $w_3(A)$; $r_1(A)$; $w_1(B)$; $r_2(B)$: $w_2(C)$; $r_3(C)$;

d) $r_1(A)$; $r_2(A)$; $w_1(B)$; $w_2(B)$; $r_1(B)$; $r_2(B)$; $w_2(C)$; $w_1(D)$;

e) $r_1(A)$; $r_2(A)$; $r_1(B)$; $r_2(B)$; $r_3(A)$; $r_4(B)$; $w_1(A)$; $w_2(B)$;

Answer the following questions:

i. What is the precedence graph for the schedule?

ii. Is the schedule conflict-serializable? If so, what are all the equivalent serial schedules?

! *iii.* Are there any serial schedules that must be equivalent (regardless of what the transactions do to the data), but are not conflict-equivalent?

!! **Exercise 18.2.5 :** Say that a transaction T *precedes* a transaction U in a schedule S if every action of T precedes every action of U in S. Note that if T and U are the only transactions in S, then saying T precedes U is the same as saying that S is the serial schedule (T, U). However, if S involves transactions other than T and U, then S might not be serializable, and in fact, because of the effect of other transactions, might not even be conflict-serializable. Give an example of a schedule S such that:

i. In S, T_1 precedes T_2, and

ii. S is conflict-serializable, but

iii. In every serial schedule conflict-equivalent to S, T_2 precedes T_1.

! **Exercise 18.2.6 :** Explain how, for any $n > 1$, one can find a schedule whose precedence graph has a cycle of length n, but no smaller cycle.

18.3   Enforcing Serializability by Locks

Imagine a collection of transactions performing their actions in an unconstrained manner. These actions will form some schedule, but it is unlikely that the schedule will be serializable. It is the job of the scheduler to prevent orders of actions that lead to an unserializable schedule. In this section we consider the most common architecture for a scheduler, one in which "locks" are maintained on database elements to prevent unserializable behavior. Intuitively, a transaction obtains locks on the database elements it accesses to prevent other transactions from accessing these elements at roughly the same time and thereby incurring the risk of unserializability.

In this section, we introduce the concept of locking with an (overly) simple locking scheme. In this scheme, there is only one kind of lock, which transactions must obtain on a database element if they want to perform any operation whatsoever on that element. In Section 18.4, we shall learn more realistic locking schemes, with several kinds of lock, including the common shared/exclusive locks that correspond to the privileges of reading and writing, respectively.

18.3.1 Locks

In Fig. 18.11 we see a scheduler that uses a lock table to help perform its job. Recall that the responsibility of the scheduler is to take requests from transactions and either allow them to operate on the database or defer them until such time as it is safe to allow them to execute. A lock table will be used to guide this decision in a manner that we shall discuss at length.

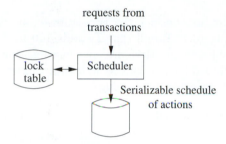

Figure 18.11: A scheduler that uses a lock table to guide decisions

Ideally, a scheduler would forward a request if and only if its execution cannot possibly lead to an inconsistent database state after all active transactions commit or abort. It is much too hard to decide this question in real time, however. Thus, all schedulers use a simple test that guarantees serializability but may forbid some actions that could not by themselves lead to inconsistency. A locking scheduler, like most types of scheduler, instead enforces conflict-serializability, which as we learned is a more stringent condition than serializability.

When a scheduler uses locks, transactions must request and release locks, in addition to reading and writing database elements. The use of locks must be proper in two senses, one applying to the structure of transactions, and the other to the structure of schedules.

- *Consistency of Transactions*: Actions and locks must relate in the expected ways:

  1. A transaction can only read or write an element if it previously requested a lock on that element and hasn't yet released the lock.

  2. If a transaction locks an element, it must later unlock that element.

- *Legality of Schedules*: Locks must have their intended meaning: no two transactions may have locked the same element without one having first released the lock.

We shall extend our notation for actions to include locking and unlocking actions:

$l_i(X)$: Transaction T_i requests a lock on database element X.

$u_i(X)$: Transaction T_i releases ("unlocks") its lock on database element X.

Thus, the consistency condition for transactions can be stated as: "Whenever a transaction T_i has an action $r_i(X)$ or $w_i(X)$, then there is a previous action $l_i(X)$ with no intervening action $u_i(X)$, and there is a subsequent $u_i(X)$." The legality of schedules is stated: "If there are actions $l_i(X)$ followed by $l_j(X)$ in a schedule, then somewhere between these actions there must be an action $u_i(X)$."

Example 18.10: Let us consider the two transactions T_1 and T_2 that we introduced in Example 18.1. Recall that T_1 adds 100 to database elements A and B, while T_2 doubles them. Here are specifications for these transactions, in which we have included lock actions as well as arithmetic actions to help us remember what the transactions are doing.[3]

T_1: $l_1(A)$; $r_1(A)$; `A := A+100`; $w_1(A)$; $u_1(A)$; $l_1(B)$; $r_1(B)$; `B := B+100`; $w_1(B)$; $u_1(B)$;

T_2: $l_2(A)$; $r_2(A)$; `A := A*2`; $w_2(A)$; $u_2(A)$; $l_2(B)$; $r_2(B)$; `B := B*2`; $w_2(B)$; $u_2(B)$;

Each of these transactions is consistent. They each release the locks on A and B that they take. Moreover, they each operate on A and B only in steps where they have previously requested a lock on that element and have not yet released the lock.

Figure 18.12 shows one legal schedule of these two transactions. To save space we have put several actions on one line. The schedule is legal because the two transactions never hold a lock on A at the same time, and likewise for B. Specifically, T_2 does not execute $l_2(A)$ until after T_1 executes $u_1(A)$, and T_1 does not execute $l_1(B)$ until after T_2 executes $u_2(B)$. As we see from the trace of the values computed, the schedule, although legal, is not serializable. We shall see in Section 18.3.3 the additional condition, "two-phase locking," that we need to assure that legal schedules are conflict-serializable. □

18.3.2 The Locking Scheduler

It is the job of a scheduler based on locking to grant requests if and only if the request will result in a legal schedule. To aid this decision, it has a lock table, which tells, for every database element, the transaction, if any, that currently holds a lock on that element. We shall discuss the structure of a

---

[3]Remember that the actual computations of the transaction usually are not represented in our current notation, since they are not considered by the scheduler when deciding whether to grant or deny transaction requests.

T_1	T_2	A	B
		25	25
$l_1(A); r_1(A);$			
`A := A+100;`			
$w_1(A); u_1(A);$		125	
	$l_2(A); r_2(A);$		
	`A := A*2;`		
	$w_2(A); u_2(A);$	250	
	$l_2(B); r_2(B);$		
	`B := B*2;`		
	$w_2(B); u_2(B);$		50
$l_1(B); r_1(B);$			
`B := B+100;`			
$w_1(B); u_1(B);$			150

Figure 18.12: A legal schedule of consistent transactions; unfortunately it is not serializable

lock table in more detail in Section 18.5.2. However, when there is only one kind of lock, as we have assumed so far, the table may be thought of as a relation `Locks(element, transaction)`, consisting of pairs (X, T) such that transaction T currently has a lock on database element X. The scheduler has only to query this relation and modify it with simple `INSERT` and `DELETE` statements.

Example 18.11: The schedule of Fig. 18.12 is legal, as we mentioned, so the locking scheduler would grant every request in the order of arrival shown. However, sometimes it is not possible to grant requests. Here are T_1 and T_2 from Example 18.10, with simple (but important, as we shall see in Section 18.3.3) changes, in which T_1 and T_2 each lock B before releasing the lock on A.

T_1: $l_1(A);$ $r_1(A);$ `A := A+100;` $w_1(A);$ $l_1(B);$ $u_1(A);$ $r_1(B);$ `B := B+100;` $w_1(B);$ $u_1(B);$

T_2: $l_2(A);$ $r_2(A);$ `A := A*2;` $w_2(A);$ $l_2(B);$ $u_2(A);$ $r_2(B);$ `B := B*2;` $w_2(B);$ $u_2(B);$

In Fig. 18.13, when T_2 requests a lock on B, the scheduler must deny the lock, because T_1 still holds a lock on B. Thus, T_2 stalls, and the next actions are from T_1. Eventually, T_1 executes $u_1(B)$, which unlocks B. Now, T_2 can get its lock on B, which is executed at the next step. Notice that because T_2 was forced to wait, it wound up multiplying B by 2 after T_1 added 100, resulting in a consistent database state. □

T_1	T_2	A	B
		25	25
$l_1(A)$; $r_1(A)$;			
A := A+100;			
$w_1(A)$; $l_1(B)$; $u_1(A)$;		125	
	$l_2(A)$; $r_2(A)$;		
	A := A*2;		
	$w_2(A)$;	250	
	$l_2(B)$ **Denied**		
$r_1(B)$; B := B+100;			
$w_1(B)$; $u_1(B)$;			125
	$l_2(B)$; $u_2(A)$; $r_2(B)$;		
	B := B*2;		
	$w_2(B)$; $u_2(B)$;		250

Figure 18.13: The locking scheduler delays requests that would result in an illegal schedule

18.3.3 Two-Phase Locking

There is a surprising condition under which we can guarantee that a legal schedule of consistent transactions is conflict-serializable. This condition, which is widely followed in commercial locking systems, is called *two-phase locking* or *2PL*. The 2PL condition is:

- In every transaction, all lock requests precede all unlock requests.

The "two phases" referred to by 2PL are thus the first phase, where locks are obtained and the second phase, where locks are relinquished. Two-phase locking is a condition, like consistency, on the order of actions in a transaction. A transaction that obeys the 2PL condition is said to be a *two-phase-locked transaction*, or 2PL transaction.

Example 18.12 : In Example 18.10, the transactions do not obey the two-phase locking rule. For instance, T_1 unlocks A before it locks B. However, the versions of the transactions found in Example 18.11 *do* obey the 2PL condition. Notice that T_1 locks both A and B within the first five actions and unlocks them within the next five actions; T_2 behaves similarly. If we compare Figs. 18.12 and 18.13, we see how the two-phase-locked transactions interact properly with the scheduler to assure consistency, while the non-2PL transactions allow inconsistent (and therefore not-conflict-serializable) behavior. □

18.3.4 Why Two-Phase Locking Works

It is true, but far from obvious, that the benefit from 2PL that we observed in our examples holds in general. Intuitively, each two-phase-locked transaction may be thought to execute in its entirety at the instant it issues its first unlock request, as suggested by Fig. 18.14. The conflict-equivalent serial schedule for a schedule S of 2PL transactions is the one in which the transactions are ordered in the same order as their first unlocks.[4]

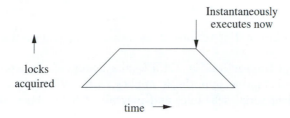

Figure 18.14: Every two-phase-locked transaction has a point at which it may be thought to execute instantaneously

We shall show how to convert any legal schedule S of consistent, two-phase-locked transactions to a conflict-equivalent serial schedule. The conversion is best described as an induction on n, the number of transactions in S. In what follows, it is important to remember that the issue of conflict-equivalence refers to the read and write actions only. As we swap the order of reads and writes, we ignore the lock and unlock actions. Once we have the read and write actions ordered serially, we can place the lock and unlock actions around them as the various transactions require. Since each transaction releases all locks before its end, we know that the serial schedule is legal.

BASIS: If $n = 1$, there is nothing to do; S is already a serial schedule.

INDUCTION: Suppose S involves n transactions $T_1, T_2, \ldots, T_n$, and let T_i be the transaction with the first unlock action in the entire schedule S, say $u_i(X)$. We claim it is possible to move all the read and write actions of T_i forward to the beginning of the schedule without passing any conflicting actions.

Consider some action of T_i, say $w_i(Y)$. Could it be preceded in S by some conflicting action, say $w_j(Y)$? If so, then in schedule S, actions $u_j(Y)$ and $l_i(Y)$ must intervene, in a sequence of actions

$$\cdots w_j(Y); \cdots; \ u_j(Y); \cdots; \ l_i(Y); \cdots: \ w_i(Y); \cdots$$

Since T_i is the first to unlock, $u_i(X)$ precedes $u_j(Y)$ in S; that is, S might look like:

$$\cdots; \ w_j(Y); \cdots; \ u_i(X); \cdots; \ u_j(Y); \cdots; \ l_i(Y); \cdots; \ w_i(Y); \cdots$$

---

[4]In some schedules, there are other conflict-equivalent serial schedules as well.

or $u_i(X)$ could even appear before $w_j(Y)$. In any case, $u_i(X)$ appears before $l_i(Y)$, which means that T_i is *not* two-phase-locked, as we assumed. While we have only argued the nonexistence of conflicting pairs of writes, the same argument applies to any pair of potentially conflicting actions, one from T_i and the other from another T_j.

We conclude that it is indeed possible to move all the actions of T_i forward to the beginning of S, using swaps of nonconflicting read and write actions, followed by restoration of the lock and unlock actions of T_i. That is, S can be written in the form

$$(\text{Actions of } T_i)(\text{Actions of the other } n-1 \text{ transactions})$$

The tail of $n-1$ transactions is still a legal schedule of consistent, 2PL transactions, so the inductive hypothesis applies to it. We convert the tail to a conflict-equivalent serial schedule, and now all of S has been shown conflict-serializable.

18.3.5   Exercises for Section 18.3

Exercise 18.3.1: Below are two transactions, with lock requests and the semantics of the transactions indicated. Recall from Exercise 18.2.1 that these transactions have the unusual property that they can be scheduled in ways that are not conflict-serializable, but, because of the semantics, are serializable.

T_1: $l_1(A)$; $r_1(A)$; A := A+2; $w_1(A)$; $u_1(A)$; $l_1(B)$; $r_1(B)$; B := B*3; $w_1(B)$; $u_1(B)$;

T_2: $l_2(B)$; $r_2(B)$; B := B*2; $w_2(B)$; $u_2(B)$; $l_2(A)$; $r_2(A)$; A := A+3; $w_2(A)$; $u_2(A)$;

In the questions below, consider only schedules of the read and write actions, not the lock, unlock, or assignment steps.

* a) Give an example of a schedule that is prohibited by the locks.

! b) Of the $\binom{8}{4} = 70$ orders of the eight read and write actions, how many are legal schedules (i.e., they are permitted by the locks)?

! c) Of the legal schedules, how many are serializable (according to the semantics of the transactions given)?

! d) Of those schedules that are legal and serializable, how many are conflict-serializable?

!! e) Since T_1 and T_2 are not two-phase-locked, we would expect that some nonserializable behaviors would occur. Are there any legal schedules that are unserializable? If so, give an example, and if not, explain why.

A Risk of Deadlock

One problem that is not solved by two-phase locking is the potential for deadlocks, where several transactions are forced by the scheduler to wait forever for a lock held by another transaction. For instance, consider the 2PL transactions from Example 18.11, but with T_2 changed to work on B first:

T_1: $l_1(A)$; $r_1(A)$; A := A+100; $w_1(A)$; $l_1(B)$; $u_1(A)$; $r_1(B)$; B := B+100; $w_1(B)$; $u_1(B)$;

T_2: $l_2(B)$; $r_2(B)$; B := B*2; $w_2(B)$; $l_2(A)$; $u_2(B)$; $r_2(A)$; A := A*2; $w_2(A)$; $u_2(A)$;

A possible interleaving of the actions of these transactions is:

T_1	T_2	A	B
		25	25
$l_1(A)$; $r_1(A)$;			
	$l_2(B)$; $r_2(B)$;		
A := A+100;			
	B := B*2;		
$w_1(A)$;		125	
	$w_2(B)$;		50
$l_1(B)$ **Denied**	$l_2(A)$ **Denied**		

Now, neither transaction can proceed, and they wait forever. In Section 19.3, we shall discuss methods to remedy this situation. However, observe that it is not possible to allow both transactions to proceed, since if we do so the final database state cannot possibly have $A = B$.

---

*! Exercise 18.3.2: Here are the transactions of Exercise 18.3.1, with all unlocks moved to the end so they are two-phase-locked.

T_1: $l_1(A)$; $r_1(A)$; A := A+2; $w_1(A)$; $l_1(B)$; $r_1(B)$; B := B*3; $w_1(B)$; $u_1(A)$; $u_1(B)$;

T_2: $l_2(B)$; $r_2(B)$; B := B*2; $w_2(B)$; $l_2(A)$; $r_2(A)$; A := A+3; $w_2(A)$; $u_2(B)$; $u_2(A)$;

How many legal schedules of all the read and write actions of these transactions are there?

Exercise 18.3.3: For each of the schedules of Exercise 18.2.4, assume that each transaction takes a lock on each database elements immediately before it reads or writes the element, and that each transaction releases its locks immediately after the last time it accesses an element. Tell what the locking scheduler would do with each of these schedules; i.e., what requests would get delayed, and when would they be allowed to resume?

! **Exercise 18.3.4:** For each of the transactions described below, suppose that we insert one lock and one unlock action for each database element that is accessed.

    * a) $r_1(A)$; $w_1(B)$;

    b) $r_2(A)$; $w_2(A)$; $w_2(B)$;

Tell how many orders of the lock, unlock, read, and write actions are:

    i. Consistent and two-phase locked.

   ii. Consistent, but not two-phase locked.

  iii. Inconsistent, but two-phase locked.

  iv. Neither consistent nor two-phase locked.

18.4   Locking Systems With Several Lock Modes

The locking scheme of Section 18.3 illustrates the important ideas behind locking, but it is too simple to be a practical scheme. The main problem is that a transaction T must take a lock on a database element X even if it only wants to read X and not write it. We cannot avoid taking the lock, because if we didn't, then another transaction might write a new value for X while T was active and cause unserializable behavior. On the other hand, there is no reason why several transactions could not read X at the same time, as long as none is allowed to write X.

We are thus motivated to introduce the first, and most common, locking scheme, where there are two different kinds of locks, one for reading (called a "shared lock" or "read lock"), and one for writing (called an "exclusive lock" or "write lock"). We then examine an improved scheme where transactions are allowed to take a shared lock and "upgrade" it to an exclusive lock later. We also consider "increment locks," which treat specially write actions that increment a database element; the important distinction is that increment operations commute, while general writes do not. These examples lead us to the general notion of a lock scheme described by a "compatibility matrix" that indicates what locks on a database element may be granted when other locks are held.

18.4.1 Shared and Exclusive Locks

Since two read actions on the same database element do not create a conflict, there is no need to use locking or any other concurrency-control mechanism to force the read actions to occur in one particular order. As suggested in the introduction, we still need to lock an element we are about to read, since a writer of that element must be inhibited. However, the lock we need for writing is "stronger" than the lock we need to read, since it must prevent both reads and writes.

Let us therefore consider a locking scheduler that uses two different kinds of locks: *shared locks* and *exclusive locks*. Intuitively, for any database element X there can be either one exclusive lock on X, or no exclusive locks but any number of shared locks. If we want to write X, we need to have an exclusive lock on X, but if we wish only to read X we may have either a shared or exclusive lock on X. Presumably, if we want to read X but not write it, then we prefer to take only a shared lock.

We shall use $sl_i(X)$ to mean "transaction T_i requests a shared lock on database element X" and $xl_i(X)$ for "T_i requests an exclusive lock on X." We continue to use $u_i(X)$ to mean that T_i unlocks X; i.e., it relinquishes whatever lock(s) it has on X.

The three kinds of requirements — consistency and 2PL for transactions, and legality for schedules — each have their counterpart for a shared/exclusive lock system. We summarize these requirements here:

1. *Consistency of transactions*: You may not write without holding an exclusive lock, and you may not read without holding some lock. More precisely, in any transaction T_i,

    (a) A read action $r_i(X)$ must be preceded by $sl_i(X)$ or $xl_i(X)$, with no intervening $u_i(X)$.

    (b) A write action $w_i(X)$ must be preceded by $xl_i(X)$, with no intervening $u_i(X)$.

   All locks must be followed by an unlock of the same element.

2. *Two-phase locking of transactions*: Locking must precede unlocking. To be more precise, in any two-phase locked transaction T_i, no action $sl_i(X)$ or $xl_i(X)$ can be preceded by an action $u_i(Y)$, for any Y.

3. *Legality of schedules*: An element may either be locked exclusively by one transaction or by several in shared mode, but not both. More precisely:

    (a) If $xl_i(X)$ appears in a schedule, then there cannot be a following $xl_j(X)$ or $sl_j(X)$, for some j other than i, without an intervening $u_i(X)$.

    (b) If $sl_i(X)$ appears in a schedule, then there cannot be a following $xl_j(X)$, for $j \neq i$, without an intervening $u_i(X)$.

Note that we *do* allow one transaction to request and hold both shared and exclusive locks on the same element, provided its doing so does not conflict with the lock(s) of other transactions. If transactions know in advance their needs for locks, then only the exclusive lock would have to be requested, but if lock needs are unpredictable, then it is possible that one transaction would request both shared and exclusive locks at different times.

Example 18.13: Let us examine a possible schedule of the following two transactions, using shared and exclusive locks:

$$T_1: sl_1(A); r_1(A); xl_1(B); r_1(B); w_1(B); u_1(A); u_1(B);$$
$$T_2: sl_2(A); r_2(A); sl_2(B); r_2(B); u_2(A); u_2(B);$$

Both T_1 and T_2 read A and B, but only T_1 writes B. Neither writes A.

In Fig. 18.15 is an interleaving of the actions of T_1 and T_2 in which T_1 begins by getting a shared lock on A. Then, T_2 follows by getting shared locks on both A and B. Now, T_1 needs an exclusive lock on B, since it will both read and write B. However, it cannot get the exclusive lock because T_2 already has a shared lock on B. Thus, the scheduler forces T_1 to wait. Eventually, T_2 releases the lock on B. At that time, T_1 may complete.   □

T_1	T_2
$sl_1(A); r_1(A);$	
	$sl_2(A); r_2(A);$
	$sl_2(B); r_2(B);$
$xl_1(B)$ **Denied**	
	$u_2(A); u_2(B)$
$xl_1(B); r_1(B); w_1(B);$	
$u_1(A); u_1(B);$	

Figure 18.15: A schedule using shared and exclusive locks

Notice that the resulting schedule in Fig 18.15 is conflict-serializable. The conflict-equivalent serial order is (T_2, T_1), even though T_1 started first. While we do not prove it here, the argument we gave in Section 18.3.4 to show that legal schedules of consistent, 2PL transactions are conflict-serializable applies to systems with shared and exclusive locks as well. In Fig. 18.15, T_2 unlocks before T_1, so we would expect T_2 to precede T_1 in the serial order. Equivalently, we may examine the read and write actions of Fig. 18.15 and notice that we can swap $r_1(A)$ back, past all the actions of T_2, while we cannot move $w_1(B)$ ahead of $r_2(B)$, which would be necessary if T_1 could precede T_2 in a conflict-equivalent serial schedule.

18.4.2 Compatibility Matrices

If we use several lock modes, then the scheduler needs a policy about when it can grant a lock request, given the other locks that may already be held on the same database element. While the shared/exclusive system is simple, we shall see that there are considerably more complex systems of lock modes in use. We shall therefore introduce the following notation for describing lock-granting policies in the context of the simple shared/exclusive system.

A *compatibility matrix* has a row and column for each lock mode. The rows correspond to a lock that is already held on an element X by another transaction, and the columns correspond to the mode of a lock on X that is requested. The rule for using a compatibility matrix for lock-granting decisions is:

- We can grant the lock in mode C if and only if for every row R such that there is already a lock on X in mode R by some other transaction, there is a "Yes" in column C.

		Lock requested	
		S	X
Lock held	S	Yes	No
in mode	X	No	No

Figure 18.16: The compatibility matrix for shared and exclusive locks

Example 18.14: Figure 18.16 is the compatibility matrix for shared (S) and exclusive (X) locks. The column for S says that we can grant a shared lock on an element if the only locks held on that element currently are shared locks. The column for X says that we can grant an exclusive lock only if there are no other locks held currently. Notice how these rules reflect the definition of legality of schedules for this system of locks. □

18.4.3 Upgrading Locks

A transaction T that takes a shared lock on X is being "friendly" toward other transactions, since they are allowed to read X at the same time T is. Thus, we might wonder whether it would be friendlier still if a transaction T that wants to read and write a new value of X were to first take a shared lock on X, and only later, when T was ready to write the new value, *upgrade* the lock to exclusive (i.e., request an exclusive lock on X in addition to its already held shared lock on X). There is nothing that prevents a transaction from issuing requests for locks on the same database element in different modes. We adopt the convention that $u_i(X)$ releases all locks on X held by transaction T_i, although we could introduce mode-specific unlock actions if there were a use for them.

Example 18.15: In the following example, transaction T_1 is able to perform its computation concurrently with T_2, which would not be possible had T_1 taken an exclusive lock on B initially. The two transactions are:

$$T_1: \; sl_1(A); \; r_1(A); \; sl_1(B); \; r_1(B); \; xl_1(B); \; w_1(B); \; u_1(A); \; u_1(B);$$
$$T_2: \; sl_2(A); \; r_2(A); \; sl_2(B); \; r_2(B); \; u_2(A); \; u_2(B);$$

Here, T_1 reads A and B and performs some (possibly lengthy) calculation with them, eventually using the result to write a new value of B. Notice that T_1 takes a shared lock on B first, and later, after its calculation involving A and B is finished, requests an exclusive lock on B. Transaction T_2 only reads A and B, and does not write.

T_1	T_2
$sl_1(A); \; r_1(A);$	
	$sl_2(A); \; r_2(A);$
	$sl_2(B); \; r_2(B);$
$sl_1(B); \; r_1(B);$	
$xl_1(B)$ **Denied**	
	$u_2(A); \; u_2(B)$
$xl_1(B); \; w_1(B);$	
$u_1(A); \; u_2(B);$	

Figure 18.17: Upgrading locks allows more concurrent operation

Figure 18.17 shows a possible schedule of actions. T_2 gets a shared lock on B before T_1 does, but on the fourth line, T_1 is also able to lock B in shared mode. Thus, T_1 has both A and B and can perform its computation using their values. It is not until T_1 tries to upgrade its lock on B to exclusive that the scheduler must deny the request and force T_1 to wait until T_2 releases its lock on B. At that time, T_1 gets its exclusive lock on B, writes B, and finishes.

Notice that had T_1 asked for an exclusive lock on B initially, before reading B, then the request would have been denied, because T_2 already had a shared lock on B. T_1 could not perform its computation without reading B, and so T_1 would have more to do after T_2 releases its locks. As a result, T_1 finishes later using only an exclusive lock on B than it would if it used the upgrading strategy. $\Box$

Example 18.16: Unfortunately, indiscriminate use of upgrading introduces a new and potentially serious source of deadlocks. Suppose, that T_1 and T_2 each read database element A and write a new value for A. If both transactions use an upgrading approach, first getting a shared lock on A and then upgrading it to exclusive, the sequence of events suggested in Fig. 18.18 will happen whenever T_1 and T_2 initiate at approximately the same time.

T_1	T_2
$sl_1(A)$	
	$sl_2(A)$
$xl_1(A)$ **Denied**	
	$xl_2(A)$ **Denied**

Figure 18.18: Upgrading by two transactions can cause a deadlock

T_1 and T_2 are both able to get shared locks on A. Then, they each try to upgrade to exclusive, but the scheduler forces each to wait because the other has a shared lock on A. Thus, neither can make progress, and they will each wait forever, or until the system discovers that there is a deadlock, aborts one of the two transactions, and gives the other the exclusive lock on A. □

18.4.4 Update Locks

There is a way to avoid the deadlock problem of Example 18.16 by using a third lock mode, called *update locks*. An update lock $ul_i(X)$ gives transaction T_i only the privilege to read X, not to write X. However, only the update lock can be upgraded to a write lock later; a read lock cannot be upgraded. We can grant an update lock on X when there are already shared locks on X, but once there is an update lock on X we prevent additional locks of any kind — shared, update, or exclusive — from being taken on X. The reason is that if we don't deny such locks, then the updater might never get a chance to upgrade to exclusive, since there would always be other locks on X.

This rule leads to an asymmetric compatibility matrix, because the update (U) lock looks like a shared lock when we are requesting it and looks like an exclusive lock when we already have it. Thus, the columns for U and S locks are the same, and the rows for U and X locks are the same. The matrix is shown in Fig. 18.19.[5]

Example 18.17: The use of update locks would have no effect on Example 18.15. As its third action, T_1 would take an update lock on B, rather than a shared lock. But the update lock would be granted, since only shared locks are held on B, and the same sequence of actions shown in Fig. 18.17 would occur.

---

[5] Remember, however, that there is an additional condition regarding legality of schedules that is not reflected by this matrix: a transaction holding a shared lock but not an update lock on an element X cannot be given an exclusive lock on X, even though we do not in general prohibit a transaction from holding multiple locks on an element.

	S	X	U
S	Yes	No	Yes
X	No	No	No
U	No	No	No

Figure 18.19: Compatibility matrix for shared, exclusive, and update locks

However, update locks fix the problem shown in Example 18.16. Now, both T_1 and T_2 first request update locks on A and only later take exclusive locks. Possible descriptions of T_1 and T_2 are:

$$T_1:\ ul_1(A);\ r_1(A);\ xl_1(A);\ w_1(A);\ u_1(A);$$
$$T_2:\ ul_2(A);\ r_2(A);\ xl_2(A);\ w_2(A);\ u_2(A);$$

The sequence of events corresponding to Fig. 18.18 is shown in Fig. 18.20. Now, T_2, the second to request an update lock on A, is denied. T_1 is allowed to finish, and then T_2 may proceed. The lock system has effectively prevented concurrent execution of T_1 and T_2, but in this example, any significant amount of concurrent execution will result in either a deadlock or an inconsistent database state. □

T_1	T_2
$ul_1(A);\ r_1(A);$	
	$ul_2(A)$ **Denied**
$xl_1(A);\ w_1(A);\ u_1(A);$	
	$ul_2(A);\ r_2(A);$
	$xl_2(A);\ w_2(A);\ u_2(A);$

Figure 18.20: Correct execution using update locks

18.4.5   Increment Locks

Another interesting kind of lock that is useful in some situations is an "increment lock." Many transactions operate on the database only by incrementing or decrementing stored values. Examples are:

1. A transaction that transfers money from one bank account to another.

2. A transaction that sells an airplane ticket and decrements the count of available seats on that flight.

The interesting property of increment actions is that they commute with each other, since if two transactions add constants to the same database element, it does not matter which goes first, as the diagram of database state transitions in Fig. 18.21 suggests. On the other hand, incrementation commutes with neither reading nor writing; If you read A before or after it is incremented, you get different values, and if you increment A before or after some other transaction writes a new value for A, you get different values of A in the database.

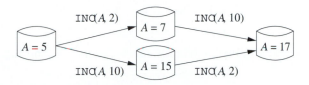

Figure 18.21: Two increment actions commute, since the final database state does not depend on which went first

Let us introduce as a possible action in transactions the *increment* action, written INC(A,c). Informally, this action adds constant c to database element A, which we assume is a single number. Note that c could be negative, in which case we are really decrementing A. In practice, we might apply INC to a component of a tuple, while the tuple itself, rather than one of its components, is the lockable element.

More formally, we use INC(A,c) to stand for the atomic execution of the following steps: READ(A,t); t := t+c; WRITE(A,t);. We shall not discuss the hardware and/or software mechanism that would be used to make this operation atomic, but we should note that this form of atomicity is on a lower level than the atomicity of transactions that we support by locking.

Corresponding to the increment action, we need an *increment lock*. We shall denote the action of T_i requesting an increment lock on X by $il_i(X)$. We also use shorthand $inc_i(X)$ for the action in which transaction T_i increments database element X by some constant; the exact constant doesn't matter.

The existence of increment actions and locks requires us to make several modifications to our definitions of consistent transactions, conflicts, and legal schedules. These changes are:

a) A consistent transaction can only have an increment action on X if it holds an increment lock on X at the time. An increment lock does not enable either read or write actions, however.

b) In a legal schedule, any number of transactions can hold an increment lock on X at any time. However, if an increment lock on X is held by some transaction, then no other transaction can hold either a shared or exclusive lock on X at the same time. These requirements are expressed by the compatibility matrix of Fig. 18.22, where I represents a lock in increment mode.

c) The action $inc_i(X)$ conflicts with both $r_j(X)$ and $w_j(X)$, for $j \neq i$, but does not conflict with $inc_j(X)$.

	S	X	I
S	Yes	No	No
X	No	No	No
I	No	No	Yes

Figure 18.22: Compatibility matrix for shared, exclusive, and increment locks

Example 18.18 : Consider two transactions, each of which read database element A and then increment B. Perhaps they add A to B, or the constant by which they increment B may depend in some other way on A.

$$T_1:\ sl_1(A);\ r_1(A);\ il_1(B);\ inc_1(B);\ u_1(A);\ u_1(B);$$
$$T_2:\ sl_2(A);\ r_2(A);\ il_2(B);\ inc_2(B);\ u_2(A);\ u_2(B);$$

Notice that the transactions are consistent, since they only perform an incrementation while they have an increment lock, and they only read while they have a shared lock. Figure 18.23 shows a possible interleaving of T_1 and T_2. T_1 reads A first, but then T_2 both reads A and increments B. However, T_1 is then allowed to get its increment lock on B and proceed.

T_1	T_2
$sl_1(A);\ r_1(A);$	
	$sl_2(A);\ r_2(A);$
	$il_2(B);\ inc_2(B);$
$il_1(B);\ inc_1(B);$	
	$u_2(A);\ u_2(B);$
$u_1(A);\ u_1(B);$	

Figure 18.23: A schedule of transactions with increment actions and locks

Notice that the scheduler did not have to delay any requests in Fig. 18.23. Suppose, for instance, that T_1 increments B by A, and T_2 increments B by $2A$. They can execute in either order, since the value of A does not change, and the incrementations may also be performed in either order.

Put another way, we may look at the sequence of non-lock actions in the schedule of Fig. 18.23; they are:

$$S:\ r_1(A);\ r_2(A);\ inc_2(B);\ inc_1(B);$$

We may move the last action, $inc_1(B)$, to the second position, since it does not conflict with another increment of the same element, and surely does not conflict with a read of a different element. This sequence of swaps shows that S is conflict-equivalent to the serial schedule $r_1(A)$; $inc_1(B)$; $r_2(A)$; $inc_2(B)$;. Similarly, we can move the first action, $r_1(A)$ to the third position by swaps, giving a serial schedule in which T_2 precedes T_1. $\square$

18.4.6 Exercises for Section 18.4

Exercise 18.4.1: For each of the schedules of transactions T_1, T_2, and T_3 below:

a) $r_1(A)$; $r_2(B)$; $r_3(C)$; $w_1(B)$; $w_2(C)$; $w_3(D)$;

b) $r_1(A)$; $r_2(B)$; $r_3(C)$; $w_1(B)$; $w_2(C)$; $w_3(A)$;

c) $r_1(A)$; $r_2(B)$; $r_3(C)$; $r_1(B)$; $r_2(C)$; $r_3(D)$; $w_1(C)$; $w_2(D)$; $w_3(E)$;

* d) $r_1(A)$; $r_2(B)$; $r_3(C)$; $r_1(B)$; $r_2(C)$; $r_3(D)$; $w_1(A)$; $w_2(B)$; $w_3(C)$;

e) $r_1(A)$; $r_2(B)$; $r_3(C)$; $r_1(B)$; $r_2(C)$; $r_3(A)$; $w_1(A)$; $w_2(B)$; $w_3(C)$;

do each of the following:

i. Insert shared and exclusive locks, and insert unlock actions. Place a shared lock immediately in front of each read action that is not followed by a write action of the same element by the same transaction. Place an exclusive lock in front of every other read or write action. Place the necessary unlocks at the end of every transaction.

ii. Tell what happens when each schedule is run by a scheduler that supports shared and exclusive locks.

iii. Insert shared and exclusive locks in a way that allows upgrading. Place a shared lock in front of every read, an exclusive lock in front of every write, and place the necessary unlocks at the ends of the transactions.

iv. Tell what happens when each schedule from (*iii*) is run by a scheduler that supports shared locks, exclusive locks, and upgrading.

v. Insert shared, exclusive, and update locks, along with unlock actions. Place a shared lock in front of every read action that is not going to be upgraded, place an update lock in front of every read action that will be upgraded, and place an exclusive lock in front of every write action. Place unlocks at the ends of transactions, as usual.

vi. Tell what happens when each schedule from (*v*) is run by a scheduler that supports shared, exclusive, and update locks.

! Exercise 18.4.2 : Consider the two transactions:

$$T_1:\ r_1(A);\ r_1(B);\ inc_1(A);\ inc_1(B);$$
$$T_2:\ r_2(A);\ r_2(B);\ inc_2(A);\ inc_2(B);$$

Answer the following:

* a) How many interleavings of these transactions are serializable?

  b) If the order of incrementation in T_2 were reversed [i.e., $inc_2(B)$ followed by $inc_2(A)$], how many serializable interleavings would there be?

Exercise 18.4.3 : For each of the following schedules, insert appropriate locks (read, write, or increment) before each action, and unlocks at the ends of transactions. Then tell what happens when the schedule is run by a scheduler that supports these three types of locks.

  a) $r_1(A);\ r_2(B);\ inc_1(B);\ inc_2(C);\ w_1(C);\ w_2(D);$

  b) $r_1(A);\ r_2(B);\ inc_1(B);\ inc_2(A);\ w_1(C);\ w_2(D);$

  c) $inc_1(A);\ inc_2(B);\ inc_1(B);\ inc_2(C);\ w_1(C);\ w_2(D);$

Exercise 18.4.4 : In Exercise 18.1.1, we discussed a hypothetical transaction involving an airline reservation. If the transaction manager had available to it shared, exclusive, update, and increment locks, what lock would you recommend for each of the steps of the transaction?

Exercise 18.4.5 : The action of multiplication by a constant factor can be modeled by an action of its own. Suppose `MC(X,c)` stands for an atomic execution of the steps `READ(X,t); t := c*t; WRITE(X,t);`. We can also introduce a lock mode that allows only multiplication by a constant factor.

  a) Show the compatibility matrix for read, write, and multiplication-by-a-constant locks.

  ! b) Show the compatibility matrix for read, write, incrementation, and multiplication-by-a-constant locks.

! Exercise 18.4.6 : Suppose for sake of argument that database elements are two-dimensional vectors. There are four operations we can perform on vectors, and each will have its own type of lock.

  i. Change the value along the x-axis (an X-lock).

  ii. Change the value along the y-axis (a Y-lock).

  iii. Change the angle of the vector (an A-lock).

  iv. Change the magnitude of the vector (an M-lock).

Answer the following questions.

* a) Which pairs of operations commute? For example, if we rotate the vector so it's angle is 120° and then change the x-coordinate to be 10, is that the same as first changing the x-coordinate to 10 and then changing the angle to 120°?

  b) Based on your answer to (a), what is the compatibility matrix for the four types of locks?

!! c) Suppose we changed the four operations so that instead of giving new values for a measure, the operations incremented the measure (e.g., "add 10 to the x-coordinate," or "rotate the vector 30° clockwise"). What would the compatibility matrix then be?

! **Exercise 18.4.7:** Here is a schedule with one action missing:

$$r_1(A); \; r_2(B); \; ???; \; w_1(C); \; w_2(A);$$

Your problem is to figure out what actions of certain types could replace the ??? and make the schedule not be serializable. Tell all possible nonserializable replacements for each of the following types of action: *a) Read   b) Write   c) Update   d) Increment.

18.5   An Architecture for a Locking Scheduler

Having seen a number of different locking schemes, we next need to consider how a scheduler that uses one of these schemes operates. We shall consider here only a simple scheduler architecture based on several principles:

1. The transactions themselves do not request locks, or cannot be relied upon to do so. It is the job of the scheduler to insert lock actions into the stream of reads, writes, and other actions that access data.

2. Transactions do not release locks. Rather, the scheduler releases the locks when the transaction manager tells it that the transaction will commit or abort.

18.5.1   A Scheduler That Inserts Lock Actions

Figure 18.24 shows a two-part scheduler that accepts requests such as read, write, commit, and abort, from transactions. The scheduler maintains a lock table, which, although it is shown as secondary-storage data, may be partially or completely in main memory. Normally, the main memory used by the lock table is not part of the buffer pool that is used for query execution and logging. Rather, the lock table is just another component of the DBMS, and will be

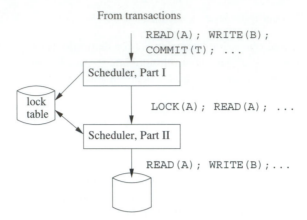

Figure 18.24: A scheduler that inserts lock requests into the transactions' request stream

allocated space by the operating system like other code and internal data of the DBMS.

Actions requested by a transaction are generally transmitted through the scheduler and executed on the database. However, under some circumstances a transaction is *delayed*, waiting for a lock, and its requests are not (yet) transmitted to the database. The two parts of the scheduler perform the following actions:

1. Part I takes the stream of requests generated by the transactions and inserts appropriate lock actions ahead of all database-access operations, such as read, write, increment, or update. The database access actions are then transmitted to Part II. Part I of the scheduler must select an appropriate lock mode from whatever set of lock modes the scheduler is using.

2. Part II takes the sequence of lock and database-access actions passed to it by Part I, and executes each appropriately. If a lock or database-access request is received by Part II, it determines whether the issuing transaction T is delayed because a lock has not been granted. If so, then the action is itself delayed and added to a list of actions that must eventually be performed for transaction T. If T is *not* delayed (i.e., all locks it previously requested have been granted already), then

   (a) If the action is a database access, it is transmitted to the database and executed.

   (b) If a lock action is received by Part II, it examines the lock table to see if the lock can be granted.

      i. If so, the lock table is modified to include the lock just granted.

  ii. If not, then an entry must be made in the lock table to indicate that the lock has been requested. Part II of the scheduler then delays further actions for transaction T, until such time as the lock is granted.

3. When a transaction T commits or aborts, Part I is notified by the transaction manager, and releases all locks held by T. If any transactions are waiting for any of these locks, Part I notifies Part II.

4. When Part II is notified that a lock on some database element X is available, it determines the next transaction or transactions that can now be given a lock on X. The transaction(s) that receive a lock are allowed to execute as many of their delayed actions as can execute, until either they complete or reach another lock request that cannot be granted.

Example 18.19: If there is only one kind of lock, as in Section 18.3, then the task of Part I of the scheduler is simple. If it sees any action on database element X, and it has not already inserted a lock request on X for that transaction, then it inserts the request. When a transaction commits or aborts, Part I can forget about that transaction after releasing its locks, so the memory required for Part I does not grow indefinitely.

  When there are several kinds of locks, the scheduler may require advance notice of what future actions on the same database element will occur. Let us reconsider the case of shared-exclusive-update locks, using the transactions of Example 18.15, which we now write without any locks at all:

$$T_1: r_1(A); r_1(B); w_1(B);$$
$$T_2: r_2(A); r_2(B);$$

The messages sent to Part I of the scheduler must include not only the read or write request, but an indication of future actions on the same element. In particular, when $r_1(B)$ is sent, the scheduler needs to know that there will be a later $w_1(B)$ action (or might be such an action, if transaction T_1 involves branching in its code). There are several ways the information might be made available. For example, if the transaction is a query, we know it will not write anything. If the transaction is an SQL database modification command, then the query processor can determine in advance the database elements that might be both read and written. If the transaction is a program with embedded SQL, then the compiler has access to all the SQL statements (which are the only ones that can write to the database) and can determine the potential database elements written.

  In our example, suppose that events occur in the order suggested by Fig. 18.17. Then T_1 first issues $r_1(A)$. Since there will be no future upgrading of this lock, the scheduler inserts $sl_1(A)$ ahead of $r_1(A)$. Next, the requests from T_2 — $r_2(A)$ and $r_2(B)$ — arrive at the scheduler. Again there is no future upgrade, so the sequence of actions $sl_2(A); r_2(A); sl_2(B); r_2(B)$ are issued by Part I.

Then, the action $r_1(B)$ arrives at the scheduler, along with a warning that this lock may be upgraded. The scheduler Part I thus emits $ul_1(B); r_1(B)$ to Part II. The latter consults the lock table and finds that it can grant the update lock on B to T_1, because there are only shared locks on B.

When the action $w_1(B)$ arrives at the scheduler, Part I emits $xl_1(B); w_1(B)$. However, Part II cannot grant the $xl_1(B)$ request, because there is a shared lock on B for T_2. This and any subsequent actions from T_1 are delayed, stored by Part II for future execution. Eventually, T_2 commits, and Part I releases the locks on A and B that T_2 held. At that time, it is found that T_1 is waiting for a lock on B. Part II of the scheduler is notified, and it finds the lock $xl_1(B)$ is now available. It enters this lock into the lock table and proceeds to execute stored actions from T_1 to the extent possible. In this case, T_1 completes. □

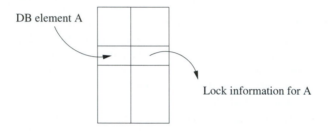

Figure 18.25: A lock table is a mapping from database elements to their lock information

18.5.2 The Lock Table

Abstractly, the lock table is a relation that associates database elements with locking information about that element, as suggested by Fig. 18.25. The table might, for instance, be implemented with a hash table, using (addresses of) database elements as the hash key. Any element that is not locked does not appear in the table, so the size is proportional to the number of locked elements only, not to the size of the entire database.

In Fig. 18.26 is an example of the sort of information we would find in a lock-table entry. This example structure assumes that the shared-exclusive-update lock scheme of Section 18.4.4 is used by the scheduler. The entry shown for a typical database element A is a tuple with the following components:

1. The *group mode* is a summary of the most stringent conditions that a transaction requesting a new lock on A faces. Rather than comparing the lock request with every lock held by another transaction on the same element, we can simplify the grant/deny decision by comparing the request with only the group mode.[6] For the shared-exclusive-update (SXU) lock scheme, the rule is simple: a group mode of

_____
[6]The lock manager must, however, deal with the possibility that the requesting transaction

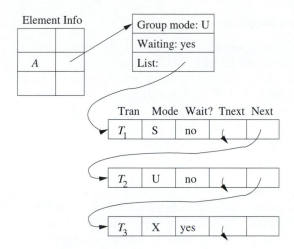

Figure 18.26: Structure of lock-table entries

(a) S means that only shared locks are held.

(b) U means that there is one update lock and perhaps one or more shared locks.

(c) X means there is one exclusive lock and no other locks.

For other lock schemes, there is usually an appropriate system of summaries by a group mode; we leave examples as exercises.

2. The *waiting* bit tells that there is at least one transaction waiting for a lock on A.

3. A list describing all those transactions that either currently hold locks on A or are waiting for a lock on A. Useful information that each list entry has might include:

(a) The name of the transaction holding or waiting for a lock.

(b) The mode of this lock.

(c) Whether the transaction is holding or waiting for the lock.

We also show in Fig. 18.26 two links for each entry. One links the entries themselves, and the other links all entries for a particular transaction (Tnext in the figure). The latter link would be used when a transaction commits or aborts, so that we can easily find all the locks that must be released.

---

already has a lock in another mode on the same element. For instance, in the SXU lock system discussed, the lock manager may be able to grant an X-lock request if the requesting transaction is the one that holds a U lock on the same element. For systems that do not support multiple locks held by one transaction on one element, the group mode always tells what the lock manager needs to know.

Handling Lock Requests

Suppose transaction T requests a lock on A. If there is no lock-table entry for A, then surely there are no locks on A, so the entry is created and the request is granted. If the lock-table entry for A exists, we use it to guide the decision about the lock request. We find the group mode, which in Fig. 18.26 is U, or "update." Once there is an update lock on an element, no other lock can be granted (except in the case that T itself holds the U lock and other locks are compatible with T's request). Thus, this request by T is denied, and an entry will be placed on the list saying T requests a lock (in whatever mode was requested), and `Wait? = 'yes'`.

If the group mode had been X (exclusive), then the same thing would happen, but if the group mode were S (shared), then another shared or update lock could be granted. In that case, the entry for T on the list would have `Wait? = 'no'`, and the group mode would be changed to U if the new lock were an update lock; otherwise, the group mode would remain S. Whether or not the lock is granted, the new list entry is linked properly, through its `Tnext` and `Next` fields. Notice that whether or not the lock is granted, the entry in the lock table tells the scheduler what it needs to know without having to examine the list of locks.

Handling Unlocks

Now suppose transaction T unlocks A. T's entry on the list for A is deleted. If the lock held by T is not the same as the group mode (e.g., T held an S lock, while the group mode was U), then there is no reason to change the group mode. On the other hand, if T's lock is in the group mode, we may have to examine the entire list to find the new group mode. In the example of Fig. 18.26, we know there can be only one U lock on an element, so if that lock is released, the new group mode could be only S (if there are shared locks remaining) or nothing (if no other locks are currently held).[7] If the group mode is X, we know there are no other locks, and if the group mode is S, we need to determine whether there are other shared locks.

If the value of `Waiting` is `'yes'`, then we need to grant one or more locks from the list of requested locks. There are several different approaches, each with its advantages:

1. *First-come-first-served*: Grant the lock request that has been waiting the longest. This strategy guarantees no *starvation*, the situation where a transaction can wait forever for a lock.

2. *Priority to shared locks*: First grant all the shared locks waiting. Then, grant one update lock, if there are any waiting. Only grant an exclusive lock if no others are waiting. This strategy can allow starvation, if a transaction is waiting for a U or X lock.

---

[7]We would never actually see a group mode of "nothing," since if there are no locks and no lock requests on an element, then there is no lock-table entry for that element.

3. *Priority to upgrading*: If there is a transaction with a U lock waiting to upgrade it to an X lock, grant that first. Otherwise, follow one of the other strategies mentioned.

18.5.3 Exercises for Section 18.5

Exercise 18.5.1: What are suitable group modes for a lock table if the lock modes used are:

a) Shared and exclusive locks.

*! b) Shared, exclusive, and increment locks.

!! c) The lock modes of Exercise 18.4.6.

Exercise 18.5.2: For each of the schedules of Exercise 18.2.4, tell the steps that the locking scheduler described in this section would execute.

18.6 Managing Hierarchies of Database Elements

Let us now return to the exploration of different locking schemes that we began in Section 18.4. In particular, we shall focus on two problems that come up when there is a tree structure to our data.

1. The first kind of tree structure we encounter is a hierarchy of lockable elements. We shall discuss in this section how to allow locks on both large elements, e.g., relations, and smaller elements contained within these, such as blocks holding several tuples of the relation, or individual tuples.

2. The second kind of hierarchy that is important in concurrency-control systems is data that is itself organized in a tree. A major example is B-tree indexes. We may view nodes of the B-tree as database elements, but if we do, then as we shall see in Section 18.7, the locking schemes studied so far perform poorly, and we need to use a new approach.

18.6.1 Locks With Multiple Granularity

Recall that the term "database element" was purposely left undefined, because different systems use different sizes of database elements to lock, such as tuples, pages or blocks, and relations. Some applications profit from small database elements, such as tuples, while others are best off with large elements.

Example 18.20: Consider a database for a bank. If we treated relations as database elements, and therefore had only one lock for an entire relation such as the one giving account balances, then the system would allow very little concurrency. Since most transactions will change the account balance either positively or negatively, most transactions would need an exclusive lock on the accounts relation. Thus, only one deposit or withdrawal could take place at any time, no matter how many processors we had available to execute these transactions. A better approach is to lock individual pages or data blocks. Thus, two accounts whose tuples are on different blocks can be updated at the same time, offering almost all the concurrency that is possible in the system. The extreme would be to provide a lock for every tuple, so any set of accounts whatsoever could be updated at once, but this fine a grain of locks is probably not worth the extra effort.

In contrast, consider a database of documents. These documents may be edited from time to time, but most transactions will retrieve whole documents. The sensible choice of database element is a complete document. Since most transactions are *read-only* (i.e., they do not perform any write actions), locking is only necessary to avoid the reading of a document that is in the middle of being edited. Were we to use smaller-granularity locks, such as paragraphs, sentences, or words, there would be essentially no benefit but added expense. The only activity a smaller granularity lock would support is the ability to read parts of a document during the time that other parts of the same document are being edited. □

Some applications could use both large- and small-grained locks. For instance, the bank database discussed in Example 18.20 clearly needs block- or tuple-level locking, but might also at some time need a lock on the entire accounts relation in order to audit accounts (e.g., check that the sum of the accounts is correct). However, taking a shared lock on the accounts relation, in order to compute some aggregation on the relation, while at the same time there are exclusive locks on individual account tuples can easily lead to unserializable behavior, because the relation is actually changing while a supposedly frozen copy of it is being read by the aggregation query.

18.6.2 Warning Locks

The solution to the problem of managing locks at different granularities involves a new kind of lock called a "warning." These locks are useful when the database elements form a nested or hierarchical structure, as suggested in Fig. 18.27. There, we see three levels of database elements:

1. Relations are the largest lockable elements.

2. Each relation is composed of one or more block or pages, on which its tuples are stored.

3. Each block contains one or more tuples.

The rules for managing locks on a hierarchy of database elements constitute the *warning protocol*, which involves both "ordinary" locks and "warning" locks.

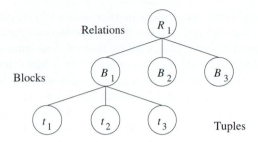

Figure 18.27: Database elements organized in a hierarchy

We shall describe the lock scheme where the ordinary locks are S and X (shared and exclusive). The warning locks will be denoted by prefixing I (for "intention to") to the ordinary locks; for example IS represents the intention to obtain a shared lock on a subelement. The rules of the warning protocol are:

1. To place an ordinary S or X lock on any element, we must begin at the root of the hierarchy.

2. If we are at the element that we want to lock, we need look no further. We request an S or X lock on that element.

3. If the element we wish to lock is further down the hierarchy, then we place a warning at this node; that is, if we want to get a shared lock on a subelement we request an IS lock at this node, and if we want an exclusive lock on a subelement, we request an IX lock on this node. When the lock on the current node is granted, we proceed to the appropriate child (the one whose subtree contains the node we wish to lock). We then repeat step (2) or step (3), as appropriate, until we reach the desired node.

	IS	IX	S	X
IS	Yes	Yes	Yes	No
IX	Yes	Yes	No	No
S	Yes	No	Yes	No
X	No	No	No	No

Figure 18.28: Compatibility matrix for shared, exclusive, and intention locks

In order to decide whether or not one of these locks can be granted, we use the compatibility matrix of Fig. 18.28. To see why this matrix makes sense, consider first the IS column. When we request an IS lock on a node N, we intend to read a descendant of N. The only time this intent could create a problem is if some other transaction has already claimed the right to write a new copy of the entire database element represented by N; thus we see "No" in the row for X. Notice that if some other transaction plans to write only a subelement, indicated by an IX lock at N, then we can afford to grant the IS lock at N, and allow the conflict to be resolved at a lower level, if indeed the intent to write and the intent to read happen to involve a common element.

Now consider the column for IX. If we intend to write a subelement of node N, then we must prevent either reading or writing of the entire element represented by N. Thus, we see "No" in the entries for lock modes S and X. However, per our discussion of the IS column, another transaction that reads or writes a subelement can have potential conflicts dealt with at that level, so IX does not conflict with another IX at N or with an IS at N.

Next, consider the column for S. Reading the element corresponding to node N cannot conflict with either another read lock on N or a read lock on some subelement of N, represented by IS at N. Thus, we see "Yes" in the rows for both S and IS. However, either an X or an IX means that some other transaction will write at least a part of the element represented by N. Thus, we cannot grant the right to read all of N, which explains the "No" entries in the column for S.

Finally, the column for X has only "No" entries. We cannot allow writing of all of node N if any other transaction already has the right to read or write N, or to acquire that right on a subelement.

Example 18.21: Consider the relation

```
Movie(title, year, length, studioName)
```

Let us postulate a lock on the entire relation and locks on individual tuples. Then transaction T_1, which consists of the query

```
SELECT *
FROM Movie
WHERE title = 'King Kong';
```

starts by getting an IS lock on the entire relation. It then moves to the individual tuples (there are two movies with the title *King Kong*), and gets S locks on each of them.

Now, suppose that while we are executing the first query, transaction T_2, which changes the year component of a tuple, begins:

```
UPDATE Movie
SET year = 1939
WHERE title = 'Gone With the Wind';
```

T_2 needs an IX lock on the relation, since it plans to write a new value for one of the tuples. T_1's IS lock on the relation is compatible, so the lock is granted. When T_2 goes to the tuple for *Gone With the Wind*, it finds no lock there, and so gets its X lock and rewrites the tuple. Had T_2 tried to write a new value in

---

Group Modes for Intention Locks

The compatibility matrix of Fig. 18.28 exhibits a situation we have not seen before regarding the power of lock modes. In prior lock schemes, whenever it was possible for a database element to be locked in both modes M and N at the same time, one of these modes *dominates* the other, in the sense that its row and column each has "No" in whatever positions the other mode's row or column, respectively, has "No." For example, in Fig. 18.19 we see that U dominates S, and X dominates both S and U. An advantage of knowing that there is always one dominant lock on an element is that we can summarize the effect of many locks with a "group mode," as discussed in Section 18.5.2.

As we see from Fig. 18.28, neither of modes S and IX dominate the other. Moreover, it is possible for an element to be locked in both modes S and IX at the same time, provided the locks are requested by the same transaction (recall that the "No" entries in a compatibility matrix only apply to locks held by some *other* transaction). A transaction might request both locks if it wanted to read an entire element and then write a small subset of its subelements. If a transaction has both S and IX locks on an element, then it restricts other transactions to the extent that either lock does. That is, we can imagine another lock mode SIX, whose row and column have "No" everywhere except in the entry for IS. The lock mode SIX serves as the group mode if there is a transaction with locks in S and IX modes, but not X mode.

Incidentally, we might imagine that the same situation occurs in the matrix of Fig 18.22 for increment locks. That is, one transaction could hold locks in both S and I modes. However, this situation is equivalent to holding a lock in X mode, so we could use X as the group mode in that situation.

---

the tuple for one of the *King Kong* movies, it would have had to wait until T_1 released its S lock, since S and X are not compatible. The collection of locks is suggested by Fig. 18.29. □

18.6.3 Phantoms and Handling Insertions Correctly

When transactions create new subelements of a lockable element, there are some opportunities to go wrong. The problem is that we can only lock existing items; there is no easy way to lock database elements that do not exist but might later be inserted. The following example illustrates the point.

Example 18.22: Suppose we have the same `Movie` relation as in Example 18.21, and the first transaction to execute is T_3, which is the query

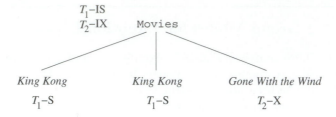

Figure 18.29: Locks granted to two transactions accessing `Movie` tuples

```
SELECT SUM(length)
FROM Movie
WHERE studioName = 'Disney';
```

T_3 needs to read the tuples of all the Disney movies, so it might start by getting an IS lock on the relation and S locks on each of the tuples for Disney movies.[8]

Now, a transaction T_4 comes along and inserts a new Disney movie. It seems that T_4 needs no locks, but it has made the result of T_3 incorrect. That fact by itself is not a concurrency problem, since the serial order (T_3, T_4) is equivalent to what actually happened. However, there could also be some other element X that both T_3 and T_4 write, with T_4 writing first, so there *could* be an unserializable behavior of more complex transactions.

To be more precise, suppose that D_1 and D_2 are pre-existing Disney movies, and D_3 is the new Disney movie inserted by T_4. Let L be the sum of the lengths of the Disney movies computed by T_3, and assume the consistency constraint on the database is that L should be equal to the sum of all the lengths of the Disney movies that existed the last time L was computed. Then the following is a sequence of events that is legal under the warning protocol:

$$r_3(D_1); \ r_3(D_2); \ w_4(D_3); \ w_4(X); \ w_3(L); \ w_3(X);$$

Here, we have used $w_4(D_3)$ to represent the creation of D_3 by transaction T_4. The schedule above is not serializable. In particular, the value of L is not the sum of the lengths of D_1, D_2, and D_3, which are the current Disney movies. Moreover, the fact that X has the value written by T_3 and not T_4 rules out the possibility that T_3 was ahead of T_4 in a supposed equivalent serial order.   □

The problem in Example 18.22 is that the new Disney movie has a *phantom* tuple, one that should have been locked but wasn't, because it didn't exist at the time the locks were taken. There is, however, a simple way to avoid the occurrence of phantoms. We must regard the insertion or deletion of a tuple as a write operation on the relation as a whole. Thus, transaction T_4 in Example 18.22 must obtain an X lock on the relation `Movie`. Since T_3 has already locked this relation in mode IS, and that mode is not compatible with mode X, T_4 would have to wait until after T_3 completes.

---

[8]However, if there were many Disney movies, it might be more efficient just to get an S lock on the entire relation.

18.6.4 Exercises for Section 18.6

Exercise 18.6.1: Consider, for variety, an object-oriented database. The objects of class C are stored on two blocks, B_1 and B_2. Block B_1 contains objects O_1 and O_2, while block B_2 contains objects O_3, O_4, and O_5. Class extents, blocks, and objects form a hierarchy of lockable database elements. Tell the sequence of lock requests and the response of a warning-protocol-based scheduler to the following sequences of requests. You may assume all requests occur just before they are needed, and all unlocks occur at the end of the transaction.

* a) $r_1(O_1)$; $w_2(O_2)$; $r_2(O_3)$; $w_1(O_4)$;

  b) $r_1(O_5)$; $w_2(O_5)$; $r_2(O_3)$; $w_1(O_4)$;

  c) $r_1(O_1)$; $r_1(O_3)$; $r_2(O_1)$; $w_2(O_4)$; $w_2(O_5)$;

  d) $r_1(O_1)$; $r_2(O_2)$; $r_3(O_1)$; $w_1(O_3)$; $w_2(O_4)$; $w_3(O_5)$; $w_1(O_2)$;

Exercise 18.6.2: Change the sequence of actions in Example 18.22 so that the $w_4(D_3)$ action becomes a write by T_4 of the entire relation `Movie`. Then, show the action of a warning-protocol-based scheduler on this sequence of requests.

!! **Exercise 18.6.3:** Show how to add increment locks to a warning-protocol-based scheduler.

18.7 The Tree Protocol

In this section we consider another problem involving trees of elements. Section 18.6 dealt with trees that are formed by the nesting structure of the database elements, with the children being subparts of the parent. Now, we deal with tree structures that are formed by the link pattern of the elements themselves. Database elements are disjoint pieces of data, but the only way to get to a node is through its parent; B-trees are an important example of this sort of data. Knowing that we must traverse a particular path to an element gives us some important freedom to manage locks differently from the two-phase locking approaches we have seen so far.

18.7.1 Motivation for Tree-Based Locking

Let us consider a B-tree index, in a system that treats individual nodes (i.e., blocks) as lockable database elements. The node is the right level of lock granularity, because treating smaller pieces as elements offers no benefit, and treating the entire B-tree as one database element prevents the sort of concurrent use of the index that can be achieved via the mechanisms that form the subject of Section 18.7.

If we use a standard set of lock modes, like shared, exclusive, and update locks, and we use two-phase locking, then concurrent use of the B-tree is almost impossible. The reason is that every transaction using the index must begin by locking the root node of the B-tree. If the transaction is 2PL, then it cannot unlock the root until it has acquired all the locks it needs, both on B-tree nodes and other database elements.[9] Moreover, since in principle any transaction that inserts or deletes could wind up rewriting the root of the B-tree, the transaction needs at least an update lock on the root node, or an exclusive lock if update mode is not available. Thus, only one transaction that is not read-only can access the B-tree at any time.

However, in most situations, we can deduce almost immediately that a B-tree node will not be rewritten, even if the transaction inserts or deletes a tuple. For example, if the transaction inserts a tuple, but the child of the root that we visit is not completely full, then we know the insertion cannot propagate up to the root. Similarly, if the transaction deletes a single tuple, and the child of the root we visit has more than the minimum number of keys and pointers, then we can be sure the root will not change.

Thus, as soon as a transaction moves to a child of the root and observes the (quite usual) situation that rules out a rewrite of the root, we would like to release the lock on the root. The same observation applies to the lock on any interior node of the B-tree, although most of the opportunity for concurrent B-tree access comes from releasing locks on the root early. Unfortunately, releasing the lock on the root early will violate 2PL, so we cannot be sure that the schedule of several transactions accessing the B-tree will be serializable. The solution is a specialized protocol for transactions that access tree-structured data like B-trees. The protocol violates 2PL, but uses the fact that accesses to elements must proceed down the tree to assure serializability.

18.7.2 Rules for Access to Tree-Structured Data

The following restrictions on locks form the *tree protocol*. We assume that there is only one kind of lock, represented by lock requests of the form $l_i(X)$, but the idea generalizes to any set of lock modes. We assume that transactions are consistent, and schedules must be legal (i.e., the scheduler will enforce the expected restrictions by granting locks only when they do not conflict with locks already at a node), but there is no two-phase locking requirement on transactions.

1. A transaction's first lock may be at any node of the tree.[10]

2. Subsequent locks may only be acquired if the transaction currently has a lock on the parent node.

3. Nodes may be unlocked at any time.

---

[9] Additionally, there are good reasons why a transaction will hold all its locks until it is ready to commit; see Section 19.1.

[10] In the B-tree example of Section 18.7.1, the first lock would always be at the root.

4. A transaction may not relock a node on which it has released a lock, even if it still holds a lock on the node's parent.

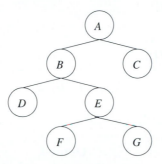

Figure 18.30: A tree of lockable elements

Example 18.23: Figure 18.30 shows a hierarchy of nodes, and Fig. 18.31 indicates the action of three transactions on this data. T_1 starts at the root A, and proceeds downward to B, C, and D. T_2 starts at B and tries to move to E, but its move is initially denied because of the lock by T_3 on E. Transaction T_3 starts at E and moves to F and G. Notice that T_1 is not a 2PL transaction, because the lock on A is relinquished before the lock on D is acquired. Similarly, T_3 is not a 2PL transaction, although T_2 happens to be 2PL. □

18.7.3 Why the Tree Protocol Works

The tree protocol forces a serial order on the transactions involved in a schedule. We can define an order of precedence as follows. Say that $T_i <_S T_j$ if in schedule S, the transactions T_i and T_j lock a node in common, and T_i locks the node first.

Example 18.24: In the schedule S of Fig 18.31, we find T_1 and T_2 lock B in common, and T_1 locks it first. Thus, $T_1 <_S T_2$. We also find that T_2 and T_3 lock E in common, and T_3 locks it first; thus $T_3 <_S T_2$. However, there is no precedence between T_1 and T_3, because they lock no node in common. Thus, the precedence graph derived from these precedence relations is as shown in Fig. 18.32. □

If the precedence graph drawn from the precedence relations that we defined above has no cycles, then we claim that any topological order of the transactions is an equivalent serial schedule. For example, either (T_1, T_3, T_2) or (T_3, T_1, T_2) is an equivalent serial schedule for Fig. 18.31. The reason is that in such a serial schedule, all nodes are touched in the same order as they are in the original schedule.

To understand why the precedence graph described above must always be acyclic, let us first observe the following:

T_1	T_2	T_3
$l_1(A); r_1(A);$		
$l_1(B); r_1(B);$		
$l_1(C); r_1(C);$		
$w_1(A); u_1(A);$		
$l_1(D); r_1(D);$		
$w_1(B); u_1(B);$		
	$l_2(B); r_2(B);$	
		$l_3(E); r_3(E);$
$w_1(D); u_1(D);$		
$w_1(C); u_1(C);$		
	$l_2(E)$ **Denied**	
		$l_3(F); r_3(F);$
		$w_3(F); u_3(F);$
		$l_3(G); r_3(G)$
		$w_3(E); u_3(E);$
	$l_2(E); r_2(E);$	
		$w_3(G); u_3(G)$
	$w_2(B); u_2(B);$	
	$w_2(E); u_2(E);$	

Figure 18.31: Three transactions following the tree protocol

- If two transactions lock several elements in common, then they are all locked in the same order.

Consider some transactions T and U, which lock two or more items in common. First, notice that each transaction locks a set of elements that form a tree, and the intersection of two trees is itself a tree. Thus, there is some one highest element X that both T and U lock. Suppose that T locks X first, but that there is some other element Y that U locks before T. Then there is a path in the tree of elements from X to Y, and both T and U must lock each element along the path, because neither can lock a node without having a lock on its

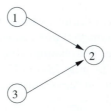

Figure 18.32: Precedence graph derived from the schedule of Fig. 18.31

parent.

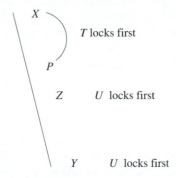

Figure 18.33: A path of elements locked by two transactions

Consider the first element along this path, say Z, that U locks first, as suggested by Fig. 18.33. Then T locks the parent P of Z before U does. But then T is still holding the lock on P when it locks Z, so U has not yet locked P when it locks Z. It cannot be that Z is the first element U locks in common with T, since they both lock ancestor X (which could also be P, but not Z). Thus, U cannot lock Z until after it has acquired a lock on P, which is after T locks Z. We conclude that T precedes U at every node they lock in common.

Now, consider an arbitrary set of transactions $T_1, T_2, \ldots, T_n$ that obey the tree protocol and lock some of the nodes of a tree according to schedule S. First, among those that lock the root, they do so in some order, and by the rule just observed:

- If T_i locks the root before T_j, then T_i locks every node in common with T_j before T_j does. That is, $T_i <_S T_j$, but not $T_j <_S T_i$.

We can show by induction on the number of nodes of the tree that there is some serial order equivalent to S for the complete set of transactions.

BASIS: If there is only one node, the root, then as we just observed, the order in which the transactions lock the root serves.

INDUCTION: If there is more than one node in the tree, consider for each subtree of the root the set of transactions that lock one or more nodes in that subtree. Note that transactions locking the root may belong to more than one subtree, but a transaction that does not lock the root will belong to only one of the subtrees. For instance, among the transactions of Fig. 18.31, only T_1 locks the root, and it belongs to both subtrees — the tree rooted at B and the tree rooted at C. However, T_2 and T_3 belong only to the tree rooted at B.

By the inductive hypothesis, there is a serial order for all the transactions that lock nodes in any one subtree. We have only to blend the serial orders for the various subtrees. Since the only transactions these lists of transactions have in common are the transactions that lock the root, and we established that these transactions lock every node in common in the same order that they lock the root, it is not possible that two transactions locking the root appear in different orders in two of the sublists. Specifically, if T_i and T_j appear on the list for some child C of the root, then they lock C in the same order as they lock the root and therefore appear on the list in that order. Thus, we can build a serial order for the full set of transactions by starting with the transactions that lock the root, in their appropriate order, and interspersing those transactions that do not lock the root in any order consistent with the serial order of their subtrees.

Example 18.25 : Suppose there are 10 transactions $T_1, T_2, \ldots, T_{10}$, and of these, T_1, T_2, and T_3 lock the root in that order. Suppose also that there are two children of the root, the first locked by T_1 through T_7 and the second locked by T_2, T_3, T_8, T_9, and T_{10}. Hypothetically, let the serial order for the first subtree be $(T_4, T_1, T_5, T_2, T_6, T_3, T_7)$; note that this order must include T_1, T_2, and T_3 in that order. Also, let the serial order for the second subtree be $(T_8, T_2, T_9, T_{10}, T_3)$. As must be the case, the transactions T_2 and T_3, which locked the root, appear in this sequence in the order in which they locked the root.

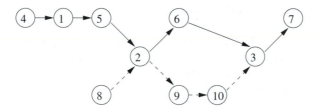

Figure 18.34: Combining serial orders for the subtrees into a serial order for all transactions

The constraints imposed on the serial order of these transactions are as shown in Fig. 18.34. Solid lines represent constraints due to the order at the first child of the root, while dashed lines represent the order at the second child. $(T_4, T_8, T_1, T_5, T_2, T_9, T_6, T_{10}, T_3, T_7)$ is one of the many topological sorts of this graph. □

18.7.4   Exercises for Section 18.7

Exercise 18.7.1 : Suppose we perform the following actions on the B-tree of Fig. 13.23. If we use the tree protocol, when can we release a write-lock on each of the nodes searched?

* a) Insert 10.

  b) Insert 20.

  c) Delete 5.

    d) Delete 23.

! Exercise 18.7.2: Consider the following transactions that operate on the tree of Fig. 18.30.

$$T_1: r_1(A); r_1(B); r_1(E);$$
$$T_2: r_2(A); r_2(C); r_2(B);$$
$$T_3: r_3(B); r_3(E); r_3(F);$$

If schedules follow the tree protocol, in how many ways can we interleave: *a) T_1 and T_2 b) T_1 and T_3 !! c) all three?

! Exercise 18.7.3: Suppose there are eight transactions $T_1, T_2, \ldots, T_8$, of which the odd-numbered transactions, T_1, T_3, T_5, and T_7, lock the root of a tree, in that order. There are three children of the root, the first locked by T_1, T_2, T_3, and T_4 in that order. The second child is locked by T_3, T_6, and T_5, in that order, and the third child is locked by T_8 and T_7, in that order. How many serial orders of the transactions are consistent with these statements?

!! Exercise 18.7.4: Suppose we use the tree protocol with shared and exclusive locks for reading and writing, respectively. Rule (2), which requires a lock on the parent to get a lock on a node, must be changed to prevent unserializable behavior. What is the proper rule (2) for shared and exclusive locks? *Hint*: Does the lock on the parent have to be of the same type as the lock on the child?

18.8 Concurrency Control by Timestamps

Next, we shall consider two methods other than locking that are used in some systems to assure serializability of transactions:

1. *Timestamping.* We assign a "timestamp" to each transaction, record the timestamps of the transactions that last read and write each database element, and compare these values to assure that the serial schedule according to the transactions' timestamps is equivalent to the actual schedule of the transactions. This approach is the subject of the present section.

2. *Validation.* We examine timestamps of the transaction and the database elements when a transaction is about to commit; this process is called "validation" of the transaction. The serial schedule that orders transactions according to their validation time must be equivalent to the actual schedule. The validation approach is discussed in Section 18.9.

Both these approaches are *optimistic*, in the sense that they assume that no unserializable behavior will occur and only fix things up when a violation is apparent. In contrast, all locking methods assume that things will go wrong unless transactions are prevented in advance from engaging in nonserializable behavior. The optimistic approaches differ from locking in that the only remedy when something does go wrong is to abort and restart a transaction that tries to engage in unserializable behavior. In contrast, locking schedulers delay transactions, but do not abort them.[11] Generally, optimistic schedulers are better than locking when many of the transactions are read-only, since those transactions can never by themselves cause unserializable behavior.

18.8.1 Timestamps

In order to use timestamping as a concurrency-control method, the scheduler needs to assign to each transaction T a unique number, its *timestamp* $\text{TS}(T)$. Timestamps must be issued in ascending order, at the time that a transaction first notifies the scheduler that it is beginning. Two approaches to generating timestamps are:

a) One possible way to create timestamps is to use the system clock, provided the scheduler does not operate so fast that it could assign timestamps to two transactions on one tick of the clock.

b) Another approach is for the scheduler to maintain a counter. Each time a transaction starts, the counter is incremented by 1, and the new value becomes the timestamp of the transaction. In this approach, timestamps have nothing to do with "time," but they have the important property that we need for any timestamp-generating system: a transaction that starts later has a higher timestamp than a transaction that starts earlier.

Whatever method of generating timestamps is used, the scheduler must maintain a table of currently active transactions and their timestamps.

To use timestamps as a concurrency-control method, we need to associate with each database element X two timestamps and an additional bit:

1. $\text{RT}(X)$, the *read time* of X, which is the highest timestamp of a transaction that has read X.

2. $\text{WT}(X)$, the *write time* of X, which is the highest timestamp of a transaction that has written X.

3. $\text{C}(X)$, the *commit bit* for X, which is true if and only if the most recent transaction to write X has already committed. The purpose of this bit is to avoid a situation where one transaction T reads data written by another transaction U, and U then aborts. This problem, where T makes a "dirty read" of uncommitted data, certainly can cause the database

---

[11]That is not to say that a system using a locking scheduler will never abort a transaction; for instance, Section 19.3 discusses aborting transactions to fix deadlocks. However, a locking scheduler never uses a transaction abort simply as a response to a lock request that it cannot grant.

state to become inconsistent, and any scheduler needs a mechanism to prevent dirty reads.[12]

18.8.2 Physically Unrealizable Behaviors

In order to understand the architecture and rules of a timestamp-based scheduler, we need to remember that the scheduler assumes that the timestamp order of transactions is also the serial order in which they must appear to execute. Thus, the job of the scheduler, in addition to assigning timestamps and updating RT, WT, and C for the database elements, is to check that whenever a read or write occurs, what happens in real time *could* have happened if each transaction had executed instantaneously at the moment of its timestamp. If not, we say the behavior is *physically unrealizable*. There are two kinds of problems that can occur:

1. *Read too late*: Transaction T tries to read database element X, but the write time of X indicates that the current value of X was written after T theoretically executed; that is, $\text{TS}(T) < \text{WT}(X)$. Figure 18.35 illustrates the problem. The horizontal axis represents the real time at which events occur. Dotted lines link the actual events to the times at which they theoretically occur — the timestamp of the transaction that performs the event. Thus, we see a transaction U that started after transaction T, but wrote a value for X before T reads X. T should not be able to read the value written by U, because theoretically, U executed after T did. However, T has no choice, because U's value of X is the one that T now sees. The solution is to abort T when the problem is encountered.

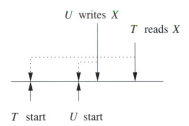

Figure 18.35: Transaction T tries to read too late

2. *Write too late*: Transaction T tries to write database element X, but the read time of X indicates that some other transaction should have read the value written by T but read some other value instead. That is, $\text{WT}(X) < \text{TS}(T) < \text{RT}(X)$. The problem is shown in Fig. 18.36. There we see a transaction U that started after T, but read X before T got a chance to write X. When T tries to write X, we find $\text{RT}(X) > \text{TS}(T)$, meaning that X has already been read by a transaction U that theoretically executed

---

[12]Although commercial systems generally give the user an option to allow dirty reads.

later than T. We also find $\text{WT}(X) < \text{TS}(T)$, which means that no other transaction wrote into X a value that would have overwritten T's value, thus, negating T's responsibility to get its value into X so transaction U could read it.

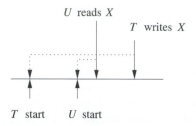

Figure 18.36: Transaction T tries to write too late

18.8.3 Problems With Dirty Data

There is a class of problems that the commit bit is designed to help deal with. One of these problems, a "dirty read," is suggested in Fig. 18.37. There, transaction T reads X, and X was last written by U. The timestamp of U is less than that of T, and the read by T occurs after the write by U in real time, so the event seems to be physically realizable. However, it is possible that after T reads the value of X written by U, transaction U will abort; perhaps U encounters an error condition in its own data, such as a division by 0, or as we shall see in Section 18.8.4, the scheduler forces U to abort because it tries to do something physically unrealizable. Thus, although there is nothing physically unrealizable about T reading X, it is better to delay T's read until U commits or aborts. We can tell that U is not committed because the commit bit $\text{C}(X)$ will be false.

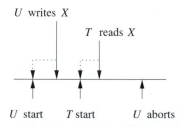

Figure 18.37: T could perform a dirty read if it reads X when shown

A second potential problem is suggested by Fig. 18.38. Here, U, a transaction with a later timestamp than T, has written X first. When T tries to write, the appropriate action is to do nothing. Evidently no other transaction V that should have read T's value of X got U's value instead, because if V

tried to read X it would have aborted because of a too-late read. Future reads of X will want U's value or a later value of X, not T's value. This idea, that writes can be skipped when a write with a later write-time is already in place, is called the *Thomas write rule*.

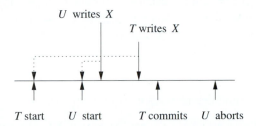

Figure 18.38: A write is cancelled because of a write with a later timestamp, but the writer then aborts

There is a potential problem with the Thomas write rule, however. If U later aborts, as is suggested in Fig. 18.38, then its value of X should be removed and the previous value and write-time restored. Since T is committed, it would seem that the value of X should be the one written by T for future reading. However, we already skipped the write by T and it is too late to repair the damage.

While there are many ways to deal with the problems just described, we shall adopt a relatively simple policy based on the following assumed capability of the timestamp-based scheduler.

- When a transaction T writes a database element X, the write is "tentative" and may be undone if T aborts. The commit bit $C(X)$ is set to false, and the scheduler makes a copy of the old value of X and its previous WT(X).

18.8.4 The Rules for Timestamp-Based Scheduling

We can now summarize the rules that a scheduler using timestamps must follow to make sure that nothing physically unrealizable may occur. The scheduler, in response to a read or write request from a transaction T has the choice of:

a) Granting the request,

b) Aborting T (if T would violate physical reality) and restarting T with a new timestamp (abort followed by restart is often called *rollback*), or

c) Delaying T and later deciding whether to abort T or to grant the request (if the request is a read, and the read might be dirty, as in Section 18.8.3).

The rules are as follows:

1. Suppose the scheduler receives a request $r_T(X)$.

   (a) If $\text{TS}(T) \geq \text{WT}(X)$, the read is physically realizable.

       i. If $C(X)$ is true, grant the request. If $\text{TS}(T) > \text{RT}(X)$, set $\text{RT}(X) := \text{TS}(T)$; otherwise do not change $\text{RT}(X)$.
       ii. If $C(X)$ is false, delay T until $C(X)$ becomes true or the transaction that wrote X aborts.

   (b) If $\text{TS}(T) < \text{WT}(X)$, the read is physically unrealizable. Rollback T; that is, abort T and restart it with a new, larger timestamp.

2. Suppose the scheduler receives a request $w_T(X)$.

   (a) If $\text{TS}(T) \geq \text{RT}(X)$ and $\text{TS}(T) \geq \text{WT}(X)$, the write is physically realizable and must be performed.

       i. Write the new value for X,
       ii. Set $\text{WT}(X) := \text{TS}(T)$, and
       iii. Set $C(X) := \texttt{false}$.

   (b) If $\text{TS}(T) \geq \text{RT}(X)$, but $\text{TS}(T) < \text{WT}(X)$, then the write is physically realizable, but there is already a later value in X. If $C(X)$ is true, then the previous writer of X is committed, and we simply ignore the write by T; we allow T to proceed and make no change to the database. However, if $C(X)$ is false, then we must delay T as in point 1(a)ii.

   (c) If $\text{TS}(T) < \text{RT}(X)$, then the write is physically unrealizable, and T must be rolled back.

3. Suppose the scheduler receives a request to commit T. It must find (using a list the scheduler maintains) all the database elements X written by T, and set $C(X) := \texttt{true}$. If any transactions are waiting for X to be committed (found from another scheduler-maintained list), these transactions are allowed to proceed.

4. Suppose the scheduler receives a request to abort T or decides to rollback T as in 1b or 2c. Then any transaction that was waiting on an element X that T wrote must repeat its attempt to read or write, and see whether the action is now legal after the aborted transaction's writes are cancelled.

Example 18.26 : Figure 18.39 shows a schedule of three transactions, T_1, T_2, and T_3 that access three database elements, A, B, and C. The real time at which events occur increases down the page, as usual. However, we have also indicated the timestamps of the transactions and the read and write times of the elements. We assume that at the beginning, each of the database elements has both a read and write time of 0. The timestamps of the transactions are acquired when they notify the scheduler that they are beginning. Notice that even though T_1 executes the first data access, it does not have the least

T_1	T_2	T_3	A	B	C
200	150	175	RT=0	RT=0	RT=0
			WT=0	WT=0	WT=0
$r_1(B)$;				RT=200	
	$r_2(A)$;		RT=150		
		$r_3(C)$;			RT=175
$w_1(B)$;				WT=200	
$w_1(A)$;			WT=200		
	$w_2(C)$;				
	Abort;				
		$w_3(A)$;			

Figure 18.39: Three transactions executing under a timestamp-based scheduler

timestamp. Presumably T_2 was the first to notify the scheduler of its start, and T_3 did so next, with T_1 last to start.

In the first action, T_1 reads B. Since the write time of B is less than the timestamp of T_1, this read is physically realizable and allowed to happen. The read time of B is set to 200, the timestamp of T_1. The second and third read actions similarly are legal and result in the read time of each database element being set to the timestamp of the transaction that read it.

At the fourth step, T_1 writes B. Since the read time of B is not bigger than the timestamp of T_1, the write is physically realizable. Since the write time of B is no larger than the timestamp of T_1, we must actually perform the write. When we do, the write time of B is raised to 200, the timestamp of the writing transaction T_1.

Next, T_2 tries to write C. However, C was already read by transaction T_3, which theoretically executed at time 175, while T_2 would have written its value at time 150. Thus, T_2 is trying to do something that would result in physically unrealizable behavior, and T_2 must be rolled back.

The last step is the write of A by T_3. Since the read time of A, 150, is less than the timestamp of T_3, 175, the write is legal. However, there is already a later value of A stored in that database element, namely the value written by T_1, theoretically at time 200. Thus, T_3 is not rolled back, but neither does it write its value. □

18.8.5 Multiversion Timestamps

An important variation of timestamping maintains old versions of database elements in addition to the current version that is stored in the database itself. The purpose is to allow reads $r_T(X)$ that otherwise would cause transaction T to abort (because the current version of X was written in T's future) to proceed by reading the version of X that is appropriate for a transaction with

T's timestamp. The method is especially useful if database elements are disk blocks or pages, since then all that must be done is for the buffer manager to keep in memory certain blocks that might be useful for some currently active transaction.

Example 18.27: Consider the set of transactions accessing database element A shown in Fig. 18.40. These transactions are operating under an ordinary timestamp-based scheduler, and when T_3 tries to read A, it finds $\text{WT}(A)$ to be greater than its own timestamp, and must abort. However, there is an old value of A written by T_1 and overwritten by T_2 that would have been suitable for T_3 to read; this version of A had a write time of 150, which is less than T_3's timestamp of 175. If this old value of A were available, T_3 could be allowed to read it, even though it is not the "current" value of A. □

T_1	T_2	T_3	T_4	A
150	200	175	225	RT=0
				WT=0
$r_1(A)$				RT=150
$w_1(A)$				WT=150
	$r_2(A)$			RT=200
	$w_2(A)$			WT=200
		$r_3(A)$		
		Abort		
			$r_4(A)$	RT=225

Figure 18.40: T_3 must abort because it cannot access an old value of A

A multiversion timestamping scheduler differs from the scheduler described in Section 18.8.4 in the following ways:

1. When a new write $w_T(X)$ occurs, if it is legal, then a new version of database element X is created. Its write time is $\text{TS}(T)$, and we shall refer to it as X_t, where $t = \text{TS}(T)$.

2. When a read $r_T(X)$ occurs, the scheduler finds the version X_t of X such that $t \leq \text{TS}(T)$, but there is no other version $X_{t'}$ with $t < t' \leq \text{TS}(T)$. That is, the version of X written immediately before T theoretically executed is the version that T reads.

3. Write times are associated with *versions* of an element, and they never change.

4. Read times are also associated with versions. They are used to reject certain writes, namely one whose time is less than the read time of the

previous version. Figure 18.41 suggests the problem, where X has versions X_{50} and X_{100}, the former was read at time 80, and a new write by a transaction T whose timestamp is 60 occurs. This write must cause T to abort, because its value of X should have been read by the transaction with timestamp 80, had T been allowed to execute.

5. When a version X_t has a write time t such that no active transaction has a timestamp less than t, then we may delete any version of X *previous* to X_t.

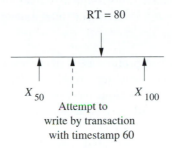

Figure 18.41: A transaction tries to write a version of X that would make events physically unrealizable

Example 18.28: Let us reconsider the actions of Fig. 18.40 if multiversion timestamping is used. First, there are three versions of A: A_0, which exists before these transactions start, A_{150}, written by T_1, and A_{200}, written by T_2. Figure 18.42 shows the sequence of events, when the versions are created, and when they are read. Notice in particular that T_3 does not have to abort, because it can read an earlier version of A.   □

T_1	T_2	T_3	T_4	A_0	A_{150}	A_{200}
150	200	175	225			
$r_1(A)$				Read		
$w_1(A)$					Create	
	$r_2(A)$				Read	
	$w_2(A)$					Create
		$r_3(A)$			Read	
			$r_4(A)$			Read

Figure 18.42: Execution of transactions using multiversion concurrency control

18.8.6   Timestamps and Locking

Generally, timestamping is superior in situations where either most transactions are read-only, or it is rare that concurrent transactions will try to read and write the same element. In high-conflict situations, locking performs better. The argument for this rule-of-thumb is:

- Locking will frequently delay transactions as they wait for locks, and can even lead to deadlocks, where several transactions wait for a long time, and then one has to be rolled back.

- But if concurrent transactions frequently read and write elements in common, then rollbacks will be frequent, introducing even more delay than a locking system.

There is an interesting compromise used in several commercial systems. The scheduler divides the transactions into read-only transactions and read/write transactions. Read/write transactions are executed using two-phase locking, to keep both each other and read-only transactions from accessing the elements they lock.

Read-only transactions are executed using multiversion timestamping. As the read/write transactions create new versions of a database element, those versions are managed as in Section 18.8.5. A read-only transaction is allowed to read whatever version of a database element is appropriate for its timestamp. A read-only transaction thus never has to abort, and will only rarely be delayed.

18.8.7   Exercises for Section 18.8

Exercise 18.8.1 : Below are several sequences of events, including *start* events, where st_i means that transaction T_i starts. These sequences represent real time, and the timestamp-based scheduler will allocate timestamps to transactions in the order of their starts. Tell what happens as each executes.

* a) st_1; st_2; $r_1(A)$; $r_2(B)$; $w_2(A)$; $w_1(B)$;

  b) st_1; $r_1(A)$; st_2; $w_2(B)$; $r_2(A)$; $w_1(B)$;

  c) st_1; st_2; st_3; $r_1(A)$; $r_2(B)$; $w_1(C)$; $r_3(B)$; $r_3(C)$; $w_2(B)$; $w_3(A)$;

  4) st_1; st_3; st_2; $r_1(A)$; $r_2(B)$; $w_1(C)$; $r_3(B)$; $r_3(C)$; $w_2(B)$; $w_3(A)$;

Exercise 18.8.2 : Tell what happens during the following sequences of events if a multiversion, timestamp-based scheduler is used. What happens instead, if the scheduler does not maintain multiple versions?

* a) st_1; st_2; st_3; st_4; $w_1(A)$; $w_2(A)$; $w_3(A)$; $r_2(A)$; $r_4(A)$;

  b) st_1; st_2; st_3; st_4; $w_1(A)$; $w_3(A)$; $r_4(A)$; $r_2(A)$;

c) st_1; st_2; st_3; st_4; $w_1(A)$; $w_4(A)$; $r_3(A)$; $w_2(A)$;

!! **Exercise 18.8.3 :** We observed in our study of lock-based schedulers that there are several reasons why transactions that obtain locks could deadlock. Can a timestamp-based scheduler using the commit bit $C(X)$ have a deadlock?

18.9 Concurrency Control by Validation

Validation is another type of optimistic concurrency control, where we allow transactions to access data without locks, and at the appropriate time we check that the transaction has behaved in a serializable manner. Validation differs from timestamping principally in that the scheduler maintains a record of what active transactions are doing, rather than keeping read and write times for all database elements. Just before a transaction starts to write values of database elements, it goes through a "validation phase," where the sets of elements it has read and will write are compared with the write sets of other active transactions. Should there be a risk of physically unrealizable behavior, the transaction is rolled back.

18.9.1 Architecture of a Validation-Based Scheduler

When validation is used as the concurrency-control mechanism, the scheduler must be told for each transaction T the set of database elements T reads and the set of elements T writes. These sets are the *read set*, RS(T), and the *write set*, WS(T), respectively. Transactions are executed in three phases:

1. *Read.* In the first phase, the transaction reads from the database all the elements in its read set. The transaction also computes in its local address space all the results it is going to write.

2. *Validate.* In the second phase, the scheduler validates the transaction by comparing its read and write sets with those of other transactions. We shall describe the validation process in Section 18.9.2. If validation fails, then the transaction is rolled back; otherwise it proceeds to the third phase.

3. *Write.* In the third phase, the transaction writes to the database its values for the elements in its write set.

Intuitively, we may think of each transaction that successfully validates as executing at the moment that it validates. Thus, the validation-based scheduler has an assumed serial order of the transactions to work with, and it bases its decision to validate or not on whether the transactions' behaviors are consistent with this serial order.

To support the decision whether to validate a transaction, the scheduler maintains three sets:

1. *START*, the set of transactions that have started, but not yet completed validation. For each transaction T in this set, the scheduler maintains START(T), the time at which T started.

2. *VAL*, the set of transactions that have been validated but not yet finished the writing of phase 3. For each transaction T in this set, the scheduler maintains both START(T) and VAL(T), the time at which T validated. Note that VAL(T) is also the time at which T is imagined to execute in the hypothetical serial order of execution.

3. *FIN*, the set of transactions that have completed phase 3. For these transactions T, the scheduler records START(T), VAL(T), and FIN(T), the time at which T finished. In principle this set grows, but as we shall see, we do not have to remember transaction T if FIN(T) < START(U) for any active transaction U (i.e., for any U in *START* or *VAL*). The scheduler may thus periodically purge the *FIN* set to keep its size from growing beyond bounds.

18.9.2 The Validation Rules

If maintained by the scheduler, the information of Section 18.9.1 is enough for it to detect any potential violation of the assumed serial order of the transactions — the order in which the transactions validate. To understand the rules, let us first consider what can be wrong when we try to validate a transaction T.

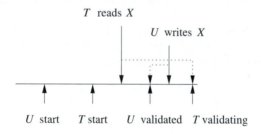

Figure 18.43: T cannot validate if an earlier transaction is now writing something that T should have read

1. Suppose there is a transaction U such that:

   (a) U is in *VAL* or *FIN*; that is, U has validated.

   (b) FIN(U) > START(T); that is, U did not finish before T started.[13]

---

[13]Note that if U is in *VAL*, then U has not yet finished when T validates. In that case, FIN(U) is technically undefined. However, we know it must be larger than START(T) in this case.

(c) $\text{RS}(T) \cap \text{WS}(U)$ is not empty; in particular, let it contain database element X.

Then it is possible that U wrote X after T read X. In fact, U may not even have written X yet. A situation where U wrote X, but not in time is shown in Fig. 18.43. To interpret the figure, note that the dotted lines connect the events in real time with the time at which they would have occurred had transactions been executed at the moment they validated. Since we don't know whether or not T got to read U's value, we must rollback T to avoid a risk that the actions of T and U will not be consistent with the assumed serial order.

2. Suppose there is a transaction U such that:

   (a) U is in *VAL*; i.e., U has successfully validated.

   (b) $\text{FIN}(U) > \text{VAL}(T)$; that is, U did not finish before T entered its validation phase.

   (c) $\text{WS}(T) \cap \text{WS}(U) \neq \emptyset$; in particular, let X be in both write sets.

Then the potential problem is as shown in Fig. 18.44. T and U must both write values of X, and if we let T validate, it is possible that it will write X before U does. Since we cannot be sure, we rollback T to make sure it does not violate the assumed serial order in which it follows U.

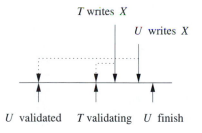

Figure 18.44: T cannot validate if it could then write something ahead of an earlier transaction

The two problems described above are the only situations in which a write by T could be physically unrealizable. In Fig. 18.43, if U finished before T started, then surely T would read the value of X that either U or some later transaction wrote. In Fig. 18.44, if U finished before T validated, then surely U wrote X before T did. We may thus summarize these observations with the following rule for validating a transaction T:

- Check that $\text{RS}(T) \cap \text{WS}(U) = \emptyset$ for any previously validated U that did not finish before T started, i.e., if $\text{FIN}(U) > \text{START}(T)$.

- Check that $\text{WS}(T) \cap \text{WS}(U) = \emptyset$ for any previously validated U that did not finish before T validated, i.e., if $\text{FIN}(U) > \text{VAL}(T)$.

Example 18.29: Figure 18.45 shows a time line during which four transactions T, U, V, and W attempt to execute and validate. The read and write sets for each transaction are indicated on the diagram. T starts first, although U is the first to validate.

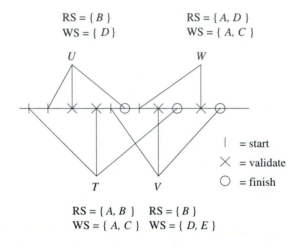

Figure 18.45: Four transactions and their validation

1. Validation of U: When U validates there are no other validated transactions, so there is nothing to check. U validates successfully and writes a value for database element D.

2. Validation of T: When T validates, U is validated but not finished. Thus, we must check that neither the read nor write set of T has anything in common with $\text{WS}(U) = \{D\}$. Since $\text{RS}(T) = \{A, B\}$, and $\text{WS}(T) = \{A, C\}$, both checks are successful, and T validates.

3. Validation of V: When V validates, U is validated and finished, and T is validated but not finished. Also, V started before U finished. Thus, we must compare both $\text{RS}(V)$ and $\text{WS}(V)$ against $\text{WS}(T)$, but only $\text{RS}(V)$ needs to be compared against $\text{WS}(U)$. we find:

   - $\text{RS}(V) \cap \text{WS}(T) = \{B\} \cap \{A, C\} = \emptyset$.
   - $\text{WS}(V) \cap \text{WS}(T) = \{D, E\} \cap \{A, C\} = \emptyset$.
   - $\text{RS}(V) \cap \text{WS}(U) = \{B\} \cap \{D\} = \emptyset$.

Thus, V also validates successfully.

Just a Moment

You may have been concerned with a tacit notion that validation takes place in a moment, or indivisible instant of time. For example, we imagine that we can decide whether a transaction U has already validated before we start to validate transaction T. Could U perhaps finish validating while we are validating T?

If we are running on a uniprocessor system, and there is only one scheduler process, we can indeed think of validation and other actions of the scheduler as taking place in an instant of time. The reason is that if the scheduler is validating T, then it cannot also be validating U, so all during the validation of T, the validation status of U cannot change.

If we are running on a multiprocessor, and there are several scheduler processes, then it might be that one is validating T while the other is validating U. If so, then we need to rely on whatever synchronization mechanism the multiprocessor system provides to make validation an atomic action.

---

4. Validation of W: When W validates, we find that U finished before W started, so no comparison between W and U is performed. T is finished before W validates but did not finish before W started, so we compare only $RS(W)$ with $WS(T)$. V is validated but not finished, so we need to compare both $RS(W)$ and $WS(W)$ with $WS(T)$. These tests are:

- $RS(W) \cap WS(T) = \{A, D\} \cap \{A, C\} = \{A\}$.
- $RS(W) \cap WS(V) = \{A, D\} \cap \{D, E\} = \{D\}$.
- $WS(W) \cap WS(V) = \{A, C\} \cap \{D, E\} = \emptyset$.

Since the intersections are not all empty, W is not validated. Rather, W is rolled back and does not write values for A or C.

□

18.9.3 Comparison of Three Concurrency-Control Mechanisms

The three approaches to serializability that we have considered — locks, timestamps, and validation — each have their advantages. First, they can be compared for their storage utilization:

- *Locks*: Space in the lock table is proportional to the number of database elements locked.

- *Timestamps*: In a naive implementation, space is needed for read- and write-times with every database element, whether or not it is currently accessed. However, a more careful implementation will treat all timestamps that are prior to the earliest active transaction as "minus infinity" and not record them. In that case, we can store read- and write-times in a table analogous to a lock table, in which only those database elements that have been accessed recently are mentioned at all.

- *Validation*: Space is used for timestamps and read/write sets for each currently active transaction, plus a few more transactions that finished after some currently active transaction began.

Thus, the amounts of space used by each approach is approximately proportional to the sum over all active transactions of the number of database elements the transaction accesses. Timestamping and validation may use slightly more space because they keep track of certain accesses by recently committed transactions that a lock table would not record. A potential problem with validation is that the write set for a transaction must be known before the writes occur (but after the transaction's local computation has been completed).

We can also compare the methods for their effect on the ability of transactions to complete without delay. The performance of the three methods depends on whether *interaction* among transactions (the likelihood that a transaction will access an element that is also being accessed by a concurrent transaction) is high or low.

- Locking delays transactions but avoids rollbacks, even when interaction is high. Timestamps and validation do not delay transactions, but can cause them to rollback, which is a more serious form of delay and also wastes resources.

- If interference is low, then neither timestamps nor validation will cause many rollbacks, and may be preferable to locking because they generally have lower overhead than a locking scheduler.

- When a rollback is necessary, timestamps catch some problems earlier than validation, which always lets a transaction do all its internal work before considering whether the transaction must rollback.

18.9.4 Exercises for Section 18.9

Exercise 18.9.1: In the following sequences of events, we use $R_i(X)$ to mean "transaction T_i starts, and its read set is the list of database elements X." Also, V_i means "T_i attempts to validate," and $W_i(X)$ means that "T_i finishes, and its write set was X." Tell what happens when each sequence is processed by a validation-based scheduler.

* a) $R_1(A, B)$; $R_2(B, C)$; V_1; $R_3(C, D)$; V_3; $W_1(A)$; V_2; $W_2(A)$; $W_3(B)$;

b) $R_1(A, B)$; $R_2(B, C)$; V_1; $R_3(C, D)$; V_3; $W_1(A)$; V_2; $W_2(A)$; $W_3(D)$;

c) $R_1(A, B)$; $R_2(B, C)$; V_1; $R_3(C, D)$; V_3; $W_1(C)$; V_2; $W_2(A)$; $W_3(D)$;

d) $R_1(A, B)$; $R_2(B, C)$; $R_3(C)$; V_1; V_2; V_3; $W_1(A)$; $W_2(B)$; $W_3(C)$;

e) $R_1(A, B)$; $R_2(B, C)$; $R_3(C)$; V_1; V_2; V_3; $W_1(C)$; $W_2(B)$; $W_3(A)$;

f) $R_1(A, B)$; $R_2(B, C)$; $R_3(C)$; V_1; V_2; V_3; $W_1(A)$; $W_2(C)$; $W_3(B)$;

18.10 Summary of Chapter 18

✦ *Consistent Database States*: Database states that obey whatever implied or declared constraints the designers intended are called consistent. It is essential that operations on the database preserve consistency, that is, they turn one consistent database state into another.

✦ *Consistency of Concurrent Transactions*: It is normal for several transactions to have access to a database at the same time. Transactions, run in isolation, are assumed to preserve consistency of the database. It is the job of the scheduler to assure that concurrently operating transactions also preserve the consistency of the database.

✦ *Schedules*: Transactions are broken into actions, mainly reading and writing from the database. A sequence of these actions from one or more transactions is called a schedule.

✦ *Serial Schedules*: If transactions execute one at a time, the schedule is said to be serial.

✦ *Serializable Schedules*: A schedule that is equivalent in its effect on the database to some serial schedule is said to be serializable. Interleaving of actions from several transactions is possible in a serializable schedule that is not itself serial, but we must be very careful what sequences of actions we allow, or an interleaving will leave the database in an inconsistent state.

✦ *Conflict-Serializability*: A simple-to-test, sufficient condition for serializability is that the schedule can be made serial by a sequence of swaps of adjacent actions without conflicts. Such a schedule is called conflict-serializable. A conflict occurs if we try to swap two actions of the same transaction, or to swap two actions that access the same database element, at least one of which actions is a write.

✦ *Precedence Graphs*: An easy test for conflict-serializability is to construct a precedence graph for the schedule. Nodes correspond to transactions, and there is an arc $T \rightarrow U$ if some action of T in the schedule conflicts with a later action of U. A schedule is conflict-serializable if and only if the precedence graph is acyclic.

✦ *Locking*: The most common approach to assuring serializable schedules is to lock database elements before accessing them, and to release the lock after finishing access to the element. Locks on an element prevent other transactions from accessing the element.

✦ *Two-Phase Locking*: Locking by itself does not assure serializability. However, two-phase locking, in which all transactions first enter a phase where they only acquire locks, and then enter a phase where they only release locks, will guarantee serializability.

✦ *Lock Modes*: To avoid locking out transactions unnecessarily, systems usually use several lock modes, with different rules for each mode about when a lock can be granted. Most common is the system with shared locks for read-only access and exclusive locks for accesses that include writing.

✦ *Compatibility Matrices*: A compatibility matrix is a useful summary of when it is legal to grant a lock in a certain lock mode, given that there may be other locks, in the same or other modes, on the same element.

✦ *Update Locks*: A scheduler can allow a transaction that plans to read and then write an element first to take an update lock, and later to upgrade the lock to exclusive. Update locks can be granted when there are already shared locks on the element, but once there, an update lock prevents other locks from being granted on that element.

✦ *Increment Locks*: For the common case where a transaction wants only to add or subtract a constant from an element, an increment lock is suitable. Increment locks on the same element do not conflict with each other, although they conflict with shared and exclusive locks.

✦ *Locking Elements With a Granularity Hierarchy*: When both large and small elements — relations, disk blocks, and tuples, perhaps — may need to be locked, a warning system of locks enforces serializability. Transactions place intention locks on large elements to warn other transactions that they plan to access one or more of its subelements.

✦ *Locking Elements Arranged in a Tree*: If database elements are only accessed by moving down a tree, as in a B-tree index, then a non-two-phase locking strategy can enforce serializability. The rules require a lock to be held on the parent while obtaining a lock on the child, although the lock on the parent can then be released and additional locks taken later.

✦ *Optimistic Concurrency Control*: Instead of locking, a scheduler can assume transactions will be serializable, and abort a transaction if some potentially nonserializable behavior is seen. This approach, called optimistic, is divided into timestamp-based, and validation-based scheduling.

♦ *Timestamp-Based Schedulers*: This type of scheduler assigns timestamps to transactions as they begin. Database elements have associated read- and write-times, which are the timestamps of the transactions that most recently performed those actions. If an impossible situation, such as a read by one transaction of a value that was written in that transaction's future is detected, the violating transaction is rolled back, i.e., aborted and restarted.

♦ *Validation-Based Schedulers*: These schedulers validate transactions after they have read everything they need, but before they write. Transactions that have read, or will write, an element that some other transaction is in the process of writing, will have an ambiguous result, so the transaction is not validated. A transaction that fails to validate is rolled back.

♦ *Multiversion Timestamps*: A common technique in practice is for read-only transactions to be scheduled by timestamps, but with multiple versions, where a write of an element does not overwrite earlier values of that element until all transactions that could possibly need the earlier value have finished. Writing transactions are scheduled by conventional locks.

18.11 References for Chapter 18

The book [6] is an important source for material on scheduling, as well as locking. [3] is another important source. Two recent surveys of concurrency control are [12] and [11].

Probably the most significant paper in the field of transaction processing is [4] on two-phase locking. The warning protocol for hierarchies of granularity is from [5]. Non-two-phase locking for trees is from [10]. The compatibility matrix was introduced to study behavior of lock modes in [7].

Timestamps as a concurrency control method appeared in [2] and [1]. Scheduling by validation is from [8]. The use of multiple versions was studied by [9].

1. P. A. Bernstein and N. Goodman, "Timestamp-based algorithms for concurrency control in distributed database systems," *Proc. Intl. Conf. on Very Large Databases* (1980), pp. 285–300.

2. P. A. Bernstein, N. Goodman, J. B. Rothnie, Jr., and C. H. Papadimitriou, "Analysis of serializability in SDD-1: a system of distributed databases (the fully redundant case)," *IEEE Trans. on Software Engineering* **SE-4**:3 (1978), pp. 154–168.

3. P. A. Bernstein, V. Hadzilacos, and N. Goodman, *Concurrency Control and Recovery in Database Systems*, Addison-Wesley, Reading MA, 1987.

4. K. P. Eswaran, J. N. Gray, R. A. Lorie, and I. L. Traiger, "The notions of consistency and predicate locks in a database system," *Comm. ACM* **19**:11 (1976), pp. 624–633.

5. J. N. Gray, F. Putzolo, and I. L. Traiger, "Granularity of locks and degrees of consistency in a shared data base," in G. M. Nijssen (ed.), *Modeling in Data Base Management Systems*, North Holland, Amsterdam, 1976.

6. J. N. Gray and A. Reuter, *Transaction Processing: Concepts and Techniques*, Morgan-Kaufmann, San Francisco, 1993.

7. H. F. Korth, "Locking primitives in a database system," *J. ACM* **30**:1 (1983), pp. 55–79.

8. H.-T. Kung and J. T. Robinson, "Optimistic concurrency control," *ACM Trans. on Database Systems* **6**:2 (1981), pp. 312–326.

9. C. H. Papadimitriou and P. C. Kanellakis, "On concurrency control by multiple versions," *ACM Trans. on Database Systems* **9**:1 (1984), pp. 89–99.

10. A. Silberschatz and Z. Kedem, "Consistency in hierarchical database systems," *J. ACM* **27**:1 (1980), pp. 72–80.

11. A. Thomasian, "Concurrency control: methods, performance, and analysis," *Computing Surveys* **30**:1 (1998), pp. 70–119.

12. B. Thuraisingham and H.-P. Ko, "Concurrency control in trusted database management systems: a survey," *SIGMOD Record* **22**:4 (1993), pp. 52–60.

Chapter 19

More About Transaction Management

In this chapter we cover several issues about transaction management that were not addressed in Chapters 17 or 18. We begin by reconciling the points of view of these two chapters: how do the needs to recover from errors, to allow transactions to abort, and to maintain serializability interact? Then, we discuss the management of deadlocks among transactions, which typically result from several transactions each having to wait for a resource, such as a lock, that is held by another transaction.

This chapter also includes an introduction to distributed databases. We focus on how to lock elements that are distributed among several sites, perhaps with replicated copies. We also consider how the decision to commit or abort a transaction can be made when the transaction itself involves actions at several sites.

Finally, we consider the problems that arise due to "long transactions." There are applications, such as CAD systems or "workflow" systems, in which human and computer processes interact, perhaps over a period of days. These systems, like short-transaction systems such as banking or airline reservations, need to preserve consistency of the database state. However, the concurrency-control methods discussed in Chapter 18 do not work reasonably when locks are held for days, or decisions to validate are based on events that happened days in the past.

19.1 Serializability and Recoverability

In Chapter 17 we discussed the creation of a log and its use to recover the database state when a system crash occurs. We introduced the view of database computation in which values move between nonvolatile disk, volatile main-memory, and the local address space of transactions. The guarantee the various

989

logging methods give is that, should a crash occur, it will be able to reconstruct the actions of the committed transactions (and only the committed transactions) on the disk copy of the database. A logging system makes no attempt to support serializability; it will blindly reconstruct a database state, even if it is the result of a nonserializable schedule of actions. In fact, commercial database systems do not always insist on serializability, and in some systems, serializability is enforced only on explicit request of the user.

On the other hand, Chapter 18 talked about serializability only. Schedulers designed according to the principles of that chapter may do things that the log manager cannot tolerate. For instance, there is nothing in the serializability definition that forbids a transaction with a lock on an element A from writing a new value of A into the database before committing, and thus violating a rule of the logging policy. Worse, a transaction might write into the database and then abort without undoing the write, which could easily result in an inconsistent database state, even though there is no system crash and the scheduler theoretically maintains serializability.

19.1.1   The Dirty-Data Problem

Recall from Section 8.6.5 that data is "dirty" if it has been written by a transaction that is not yet committed. The dirty data could appear either in the buffers, or on disk, or both; either can cause trouble.

T_1	T_2	A	B
		25	25
$l_1(A); r_1(A);$			
A := A+100;			
$w_1(A); l_1(B); u_1(A);$		125	
	$l_2(A); r_2(A);$		
	A := A*2;		
	$w_2(A);$	250	
	$l_2(B)$ **Denied**		
$r_1(B);$			
Abort; $u_1(B);$			
	$l_2(B); u_2(A); r_2(B);$		
	B := B*2;		
	$w_2(B); u_2(B);$		50

Figure 19.1: T_1 writes dirty data and then aborts

Example 19.1 : Let us reconsider the serializable schedule from Fig. 18.13, but suppose that after reading B, T_1 has to abort for some reason. Then the sequence of events is as in Fig. 19.1. After T_1 aborts, the scheduler releases the lock on B that T_1 obtained; that step is essential, or else the lock on B would be unavailable to any other transaction, forever.

However, T_2 has now read data that does not represent a consistent state of the database. That is, T_2 read the value of A that T_1 changed, but read the value of B that existed prior to T_1's actions. It doesn't matter in this case whether or not the value 125 for A that T_1 created was written to disk or not; T_2 gets that value from a buffer, regardless. As a result of reading an inconsistent state, T_2 leaves the database (on disk) with an inconsistent state, where $A \neq B$.

The problem in Fig. 19.1 is that A written by T_1 is dirty data, whether it is in a buffer or on disk. The fact that T_2 read A and used it in its own calculation makes T_2's actions questionable. As we shall see in Section 19.1.2, it is necessary, if such a situation is allowed to occur, to abort and roll back T_2 as well as T_1. □

T_1	T_2	T_3	A	B	C
200	150	175	RT=0	RT=0	RT=0
			WT=0	WT=0	WT=0
	$w_2(B)$;			WT=150	
$r_1(B)$;					
	$r_2(A)$;		RT=150		
		$r_3(C)$;			RT=175
	$w_2(C)$;				
	Abort;			WT=0	
		$w_3(A)$;	WT=175		

Figure 19.2: T_1 has read dirty data from T_2 and must abort when T_2 does

Example 19.2 : Now, consider Fig. 19.2, which shows a sequence of actions under a timestamp-based scheduler as in Section 18.8. However, we imagine that this scheduler does not use the commit bit that was introduced in Section 18.8.1. Recall that the purpose of this bit is to prevent a value that was written by an uncommitted transaction to be read by another transaction. Thus, when T_1 reads B at the second step, there is no commit-bit check to tell T_1 to delay. T_1 can proceed and could even write to disk and commit; we have not shown further details of what T_1 does.

Eventually, T_2 tries to write C in a physically unrealizable way, and T_2 aborts. The effect of T_2's prior write of B is cancelled; the value and write-time of B is reset to what it was before T_2 wrote. Yet T_1 has been allowed to use this cancelled value of B and can do anything with it, such as using it to compute new values of A, B, and/or C and writing them to disk. Thus, T_1, having read a dirty value of B, can cause an inconsistent database state. Note that, had the commit bit been recorded and used, the read $r_1(B)$ at step (2) would have been delayed, and not allowed to occur until after T_2 aborted and the value of B had been restored to its previous (presumably committed) value. $\square$

19.1.2   Cascading Rollback

As we see from the examples above, if dirty data is available to transactions, then we sometimes have to perform a *cascading rollback*. That is, when a transaction T aborts, we must determine which transactions have read data written by T, abort them, and recursively abort any transactions that have read data written by an aborted transaction. That is, we must find each transaction U that read dirty data written by T, abort U, find any transaction V that read dirty data from U, abort V, and so on. To cancel the effect of an aborted transaction, we can use the log, if it is one of the types (undo or undo/redo) that provides former values. We may also be able to restore the data from the disk copy of the database, if the effect of the dirty data has not migrated to disk. These approaches are considered in the next section.

As we have noted, a timestamp-based scheduler with a commit bit prevents a transaction that may have read dirty data from proceeding, so there is no possibility of cascading rollback with such a scheduler. A validation-based scheduler avoids cascading rollback, because writing to the database (even in buffers) occurs only after it is determined that the transaction will commit.

19.1.3   Recoverable Schedules

In order for any of the logging methods we have discussed in Chapter 17 to allow recovery, the set of transactions that are regarded as committed *after* recovery must be consistent. That is, if a transaction T_1 is, after recovery, regarded as committed, and T_1 used a value written by T_2, then T_2 must also remain committed, after recovery. Thus, we define:

- A schedule is *recoverable* if each transaction commits only after each transaction from which it has read has committed.

Example 19.3: In this and several subsequent examples of schedules with read- and write-actions, we shall use c_i for the action "transaction T_i commits." Here is an example of a recoverable schedule:

$$S_1:\ w_1(A);\ w_1(B);\ w_2(A);\ r_2(B);\ c_1;\ c_2;$$

Note that T_2 reads a value (B) written by T_1, so T_2 must commit after T_1 for the schedule to be recoverable.

Schedule S_1 above is evidently serial (and therefore serializable) as well as recoverable, but the two concepts are orthogonal. For instance, the following variation on S_1 is still recoverable, but not serializable.

$$S_2:\ w_2(A);\ w_1(B);\ w_1(A);\ r_2(B);\ c_1;\ c_2;$$

In schedule S_2, T_2 must precede T_1 in a serial order because of the writing of A, but T_1 must precede T_2 because of the writing and reading of B.

Finally, observe the following variation on S_1, which is serializable but not recoverable:

$$S_3:\ w_1(A);\ w_1(B);\ w_2(A);\ r_2(B);\ c_2;\ c_1;$$

In schedule S_3, T_1 precedes T_2, but their commitments occur in the wrong order. If before a crash, the commit record for T_2 reached disk, but the commit record for T_1 did not, then regardless of whether undo, redo, or undo/redo logging were used, T_2 would be committed after recovery, but T_1 would not. ☐

In order for recoverable schedules to be truly recoverable under any of the three logging methods, there is one additional assumption we must make regarding schedules:

- The log's commit records reach disk in the order in which they are written.

As we observed in Example 19.3 concerning schedule S_3, should it be possible for commit records to reach disk in the wrong order, then consistent recovery might be impossible. We shall return to and exploit this principle in Section 19.1.6.

19.1.4 Schedules That Avoid Cascading Rollback

Recoverable schedules sometimes require cascading rollback. For instance, if after the first four steps of schedule S_1 in Example 19.3 T_1 had to roll back, it would be necessary to roll back T_2 as well. To guarantee the absence of cascading rollback, we need a stronger condition than recoverability. We say that:

- A schedule *avoids cascading rollback* (or "is an *ACR schedule*") if transactions may read only values written by committed transactions.

Put another way, an ACR schedule forbids the reading of dirty data. As for recoverable schedules, we assume that "committed" means that the log's commit record has reached disk.

Example 19.4: The schedules of Example 19.3 are not ACR. In each case, T_2 reads B from the uncommitted transaction T_1. However, consider:

$$S_4:\ w_1(A);\ w_1(B);\ w_2(A);\ c_1;\ r_2(B);\ c_2;$$

Now, T_2 reads B only after T_1, the transaction that last wrote B, has committed, and its log record written to disk. Thus, schedule S_4 is ACR, as well as recoverable. ☐

Notice that should a transaction such as T_2 read a value written by T_1 after T_1 commits, then surely T_2 either commits or aborts after T_1 commits. Thus:

- Every ACR schedule is recoverable.

19.1.5 Managing Rollbacks Using Locking

Our prior discussion applies to schedules that are generated by any kind of scheduler. In the common case that the scheduler is lock-based, there is a simple and commonly used way to guarantee that there are no cascading rollbacks:

- *Strict Locking*: A transaction must not release any exclusive locks (or other locks, such as increment locks that allow values to be changed) until the transaction has either committed or aborted, and the commit or abort log record has been flushed to disk.

A schedule of transactions that follow the strict-locking rule is called a *strict schedule*. Two important properties of these schedules are:

1. *Every strict schedule is ACR*. The reason is that a transaction T_2 cannot read a value of element X written by T_1 until T_1 releases any exclusive lock (or similar lock that allows X to be changed). Under strict locking, the release does not occur until after commit.

2. *Every strict schedule is serializable*. To see why, observe that a strict schedule is equivalent to the serial schedule in which each transaction runs instantaneously at the time it commits.

With these observations, we can now picture the relationships among the different kinds of schedules we have seen so far. The containments are suggested in Fig.19.3.

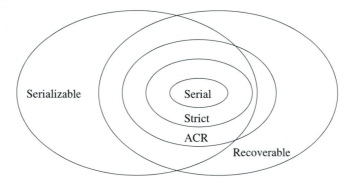

Figure 19.3: Containments an noncontainments among classes of schedules

Clearly, in a strict schedule, it is not possible for a transaction to read dirty data, since data written to a buffer by an uncommitted transaction remains locked until the transaction commits. However, we still have the problem of fixing the data in buffers when a transaction aborts, since these changes must have their effects cancelled. How difficult it is to fix buffered data depends on whether database elements are blocks or something smaller. We shall consider each.

Rollback for Blocks

If the lockable database elements are blocks, then there is a simple rollback method that never requires us to use the log. Suppose that a transaction T has obtained an exclusive lock on block A, written a new value for A in a buffer, and then had to abort. Since A has been locked since T wrote its value, no other transaction has read A. It is easy to restore the old value of A provided the following rule is followed:

- Blocks written by uncommitted transactions are pinned in main memory; that is, their buffers are not allowed to be written to disk.

In this case, we "roll back" T when it aborts by telling the buffer manager to ignore the value of A. That is, the buffer occupied by A is not written anywhere, and its buffer is added to the pool of available buffers. We can be sure that the value of A on disk is the most recent value written by a committed transaction, which is exactly the value we want A to have.

There is also a simple rollback method if we are using a multiversion system as in Sections 18.8.5 and 18.8.6. We must again assume that blocks written by uncommitted transactions are pinned in memory. Then, we simply remove the value of A that was written by T from the list of available values of A. Note that because T was a writing transaction, its value of A was locked from the time the value was written to the time it aborted (assuming the timestamp/lock scheme of Section 18.8.6 is used).

Rollback for Small Database Elements

When lockable database elements are fractions of a block (e.g., tuples or objects), then the simple approach to restoring buffers that have been modified by aborted transactions will not work. The problem is that a buffer may contain data changed by two or more transactions; if one of them aborts, we still must preserve the changes made by the other. We have several choices when we must restore the old value of a small database element A that was written by the transaction that has aborted:

1. We can read the original value of A from the database stored on disk and modify the buffer contents appropriately.

2. If the log is an undo or undo/redo log, then we can obtain the former value from the log itself. The same code used to recover from crashes may be used for "voluntary" rollbacks as well.

3. We can keep a separate main-memory log of the changes made by each transaction, preserved for only the time that transaction is active. The old value can be found from this "log."

None of these approaches is ideal. The first surely involves a disk access. The second (examining the log) might not involve a disk access, if the relevant

---

When is a Transaction Really Committed?

The subtlety of group commit reminds us that a completed transaction can be in several different states between when it finishes its work and when it is truly "committed," in the sense that under no circumstances, including the occurrence of a system failure, will the effect of that transaction be lost. As we noted in Chapter 17, it is possible for a transaction to finish its work and even write its COMMIT record to the log in a main-memory buffer, yet have the effect of that transaction lost if there is a system crash and the COMMIT record has not yet reached disk. Moreover, we saw in Section 17.5 that even if the COMMIT record is on disk but not yet backed up in the archive, a media failure can cause the transaction to be undone and its effect to be lost.

In the absence of failure, all these states are equivalent, in the sense that each transaction will surely advance from being finished to having its effects survive even a media failure. However, when we need to take failures and recovery into account, it is important to recognize the differences among these states, which otherwise could all be referred to informally as "committed."

---

portion of the log is still in a buffer. However, it could also involve extensive examination of portions of the log on disk, searching for the update record that tells the correct former value. The last approach does not require disk accesses, but may consume a large fraction of memory for the main-memory "logs."

19.1.6   Group Commit

Under some circumstances, we can avoid reading dirty data even if we do not flush every commit record on the log to disk immediately. As long as we flush log records in the order that they are written, we can release locks as soon as the commit record is written to the log in a buffer.

Example 19.5 : Suppose transaction T_1 writes X, finishes, writes its COMMIT record on the log, but the log record remains in a buffer. Even though T_1 has not committed in the sense that its commit record can survive a crash, we shall release T_1's locks. Then T_2 reads X and "commits," but its commit record, which follows that of T_1, also remains in a buffer. Since we are flushing log records in the order written, T_2 cannot be perceived as committed by a recovery manager (because its commit record reached disk) unless T_1 is also perceived as committed. Thus, there are three cases that the recovery manager could find:

1. Neither T_1 nor T_2 has its commit record on disk. Then both are aborted by the recovery manager, and the fact that T_2 read X from an uncommitted

T_1 is irrelevant.

2. T_1 is committed, but T_2 is not. There is no problem for two reasons: T_2 did not read X from an uncommitted transaction, and it aborted anyway, with no effect on the database.

3. Both are committed. Then the read of X by T_2 was not dirty.

On the other hand, suppose that the buffer containing T_2's commit record got flushed to disk (say because the buffer manager decided to use the buffer for something else), but the buffer containing T_1's commit record did not. If there is a crash at that point, it will look to the recovery manager that T_1 did not commit, but T_2 did. The effect of T_2 will be permanently reflected in the database, but this effect was based on the dirty read of X by T_2. □

Our conclusion from Example 19.5 is that we can release locks earlier than the time that the transaction's commit record is flushed to disk. This policy, often called *group commit*, is:

- Do not release locks until the transaction finishes, and the commit log record at least appears in a buffer.

- Flush log blocks in the order that they were created.

Group commit, like the policy of requiring "recoverable schedules" as discussed in Section 19.1.3, guarantees that there is never a read of dirty data.

19.1.7 Logical Logging

We saw in Section 19.1.5 that dirty reads are easier to fix up when the unit of locking is the block or page. However, there are at least two problems presented when database elements are blocks.

1. All logging methods require either the old or new value of a database element, or both, to be recorded in the log. When the change to a block is small, e.g., a rewritten attribute of one tuple, or an inserted or deleted tuple, then there is a great deal of redundant information written on the log.

2. The requirement that the schedule be recoverable, releasing its locks only after commit, can inhibit concurrency severely. For example, recall our discussion in Section 18.7.1 of the advantage of early lock release as we access data through a B-tree index. If we require that locks be held until commit, then this advantage cannot be obtained, and we effectively allow only one writing transaction to access a B-tree at any time.

Both these concerns motivate the use of *logical logging*, where only the changes to the blocks are described. There are several degrees of complexity, depending on the nature of the change.

1. A small number of bytes of the database element are changed, e.g., the update of a fixed-length field. This situation can be handled in a straight-forward way, where we record only the changed bytes and their positions. Example 19.6 will show this situation and an appropriate form of update record.

2. The change to the database element is simply described, and easily re-stored, but it has the effect of changing most or all of the bytes in the database element. One common situation, discussed in Example 19.7, is when a variable-length field is changed and much of its record, and even other records must slide within the block. The new and old values of the block look very different unless we realize and indicate the simple cause of the change.

3. The change affects many bytes of a database element, and further changes can prevent this change from ever being undone. This situation is true "logical" logging, since we cannot even see the undo/redo process as occur-ring on the database elements themselves, but rather on some higher-level "logical" structure that the database elements represent. We shall, in Ex-ample 19.8, take up the matter of B-trees, a logical structure represented by database elements that are disk blocks, to illustrate this complex form of logical logging.

Example 19.6 : Suppose database elements are blocks that each contain a set of tuples from some relation. We can express the update of an attribute by a log record that says something like "tuple t had its attribute a changed from value v_1 to v_2." An insertion of a new tuple into empty space on the block can be expressed as "a tuple t with value $(a_1, a_2, \ldots, a_k)$ was inserted beginning at offset position p." Unless the attribute changed or the tuple inserted are comparable in size to a block, the amount of space taken by these records will be much smaller than the entire block. Moreover, they serve for both undo and redo operations.

Notice that both these operations are idempotent; if you perform them sev-eral times on a block, the result is the same as performing them once. Likewise, their implied inverses, where the value of $t[a]$ is restored from v_2 back to v_1, or the tuple t is removed, are also idempotent. Thus, records of these types can be used for recovery in exactly the same way that update log records were used throughout Chapter 17. □

Example 19.7 : Again assume database elements are blocks holding tuples, but the tuples have some variable-length fields. If a change to a field such as was described in Example 19.6 occurs, we may have to slide large portions of the block to make room for a longer field, or to preserve space if a field becomes smaller. In extreme cases, we could have to create an overflow block (recall Section 12.5) to hold part of the contents of the original block, or we could remove an overflow block if a shorter field allows us to combine the contents of two blocks into one.

As long as the block and its overflow block(s) are considered part of one database element, then it is straightforward to use the old and/or new value of the changed field to undo or redo the change. However, the block-plus-overflow-block(s) must be thought of as holding certain tuples at a "logical" level. We may not even be able to restore the bytes of these blocks to their original state after an undo or redo, because there may have been reorganization of the blocks due to other changes that varied the length of other fields. However, if we think of a database element as being a collection of blocks that together represent certain tuples, then a redo or undo can indeed restore the logical "state" of the element. □

However, it may not be possible, as we suggested in Example 19.7, to treat blocks as expandable through the mechanism of overflow blocks. We may thus be able to undo or redo actions only at a level higher than blocks. The next example discusses the important case of B-tree indexes, where the management of blocks does not permit overflow blocks, and we must think of undo and redo as occurring at the "logical" level of the B-tree itself, rather than the blocks.

Example 19.8: Let us consider the problem of logical logging for B-tree nodes. Instead of writing the old and/or new value of an entire node (block) on the log, we write a short record that describes the change. These changes include:

1. Insertion or deletion of a key/pointer pair for a child.

2. Change of the key associated with a pointer.

3. Splitting or merging of nodes.

Each of these changes can be indicated with a short log record. Even the splitting operation requires only telling where the split occurs, and where the new nodes are. Likewise, merging requires only a reference to the nodes involved, since the manner of merging is determined by the B-tree management algorithms used.

Using logical update records of these types allows us to release locks earlier than would otherwise be required for a recoverable schedule. The reason is that dirty reads of B-tree blocks are never a problem for the transaction that reads them, provided its only purpose is to use the B-tree to locate the data the transaction needs to access.

For instance, suppose that transaction T reads a leaf node N, but the transaction U that last wrote N later aborts, and some change made to N (e.g., the insertion of a new key/pointer pair into N due to an insertion of a tuple by U) needs to be undone. If T has also inserted a key/pointer pair into N, then it is not possible to restore N to the way it was before U modified it. However, the effect of U on N can be undone; in this example we would delete the key/pointer pair that U had inserted. The resulting N is not the same as that which existed before U operated; it has the insertion made by T. However, there is no database inconsistency, since the B-tree as a whole continues to reflect only the changes made by committed transactions. That is, we have restored the B-tree at a logical level, but not at the physical level.   □

19.1.8   Recovery From Logical Logs

If the logical actions are idempotent — i.e., they can be repeated any number of times without harm — then we can recover easily using a logical log. For instance, we discussed in Example 19.6 how a tuple insertion could be represented in the logical log by the tuple and the place within a block where the tuple was placed. If we write that tuple in the same place two or more times, then it is as if we had written it once. Thus, when recovering, should we need to redo a transaction that inserted a tuple, we can repeat the insertion into the proper block at the proper place, without worrying whether we had already inserted that tuple.

In contrast, consider a situation where tuples can move around within blocks or between blocks, as in Examples 19.7 and 19.8. Now, we cannot associate a particular place into which a tuple is to be inserted; the best we can do is place in the log an action such as "the tuple t was inserted somewhere on block B." If we need to redo the insertion of t during recovery, we may wind up with two copies of t in block B. Worse, we may not know whether the block B with the first copy of t made it to disk. Another transaction writing to another database element on block B may have caused a copy of B to be written to disk, for example.

To disambiguate situations such as this when we recover using a logical log, a technique called *log sequence numbers* has been developed.

- Each log record is given a number one greater than that of the previous log record.[1] Thus, a typical logical log record has the form $<L, T, A, B>$, where:

  - L is the log sequence number, an integer.

  - T is the transaction involved.

  - A is the action performed by T, e.g., "insert of tuple t."

  - B is the block on which the action was performed.

- For each action, there is a *compensating action* that logically undoes the action. As discussed in Example 19.8, the compensating action may not restore the database to exactly the same state S it would have been in had the action never occurred, but it restores the database to a state that is logically equivalent to S. For instance, the compensating action for "insert tuple t" is "delete tuple t."

---

[1] Eventually the log sequence numbers must restart at 0, but the time between restarts of the sequence is so large that no ambiguity can occur.

- If a transaction T aborts, then for each action performed on the database by T, the compensating action is performed, and the fact that this action was performed is also recorded in the log.

- Each block maintains, in its header, the log sequence number of the last action that affected that block.

Suppose now that we need to use the logical log to recover after a crash. Here is an outline of the steps to take.

1. Our first step is to reconstruct the state of the database at the time of the crash, including blocks whose current values were in buffers and therefore got lost. To do so:

   (a) Find the most recent checkpoint on the log, and determine from it the set of transactions that were active at that time.

   (b) For each log entry $<L, T, A, B>$, compare the log sequence number N on block B with the log sequence number L for this log record. If $N < L$, then redo action A; that action was never performed on block B. However, if $N \geq L$, then do nothing; the effect of A was already felt by B.

   (c) For each log entry that informs us that a transaction T started, committed, or aborted, adjust the set of active transactions accordingly.

2. The set of transactions that remain active when we reach the end of the log must be aborted. To do so:

   (a) Scan the log again, this time from the end back to the previous checkpoint. Each time we encounter a record $<L, T, A, B>$ for a transaction T that must be aborted, perform the compensating action for A on block B and record in the log the fact that that compensating action was performed.

   (b) If we must abort a transaction that began prior to the most recent checkpoint (i.e., that transaction was on the active list for the checkpoint), then continue back in the log until the start-records for all such transactions have been found.

   (c) Write abort-records in the log for each of the transactions we had to abort.

19.1.9 Exercises for Section 19.1

* **Exercise 19.1.1:** Consider all ways to insert locks (of a single type only, as in Section 18.3) into the sequence of actions

$$r_1(A); \; r_1(B); \; w_1(A); \; w_1(B);$$

so that the transaction T_1 is:

a) Two-phase locked, and strict.

b) Two-phase locked, but not strict.

Exercise 19.1.2: Suppose that each of the sequences of actions below is followed by an abort action for transaction T_1. Tell which transactions need to be rolled back.

* a) $r_1(A)$; $r_2(B)$; $w_1(B)$; $w_2(C)$; $r_3(B)$; $r_3(C)$; $w_3(D)$;

b) $r_1(A)$; $w_1(B)$; $r_2(B)$; $w_2(C)$; $r_3(C)$; $w_3(D)$;

c) $r_2(A)$; $r_3(A)$; $r_1(A)$; $w_1(B)$; $r_2(B)$; $r_3(B)$; $w_2(C)$; $r_3(C)$;

d) $r_2(A)$; $r_3(A)$; $r_1(A)$; $w_1(B)$; $r_3(B)$; $w_2(C)$; $r_3(C)$;

Exercise 19.1.3: Consider each of the sequences of actions in Exercise 19.1.2, but now suppose that all three transactions commit and write their commit record on the log immediately after their last action. However, a crash occurs, and a tail of the log was not written to disk before the crash and is therefore lost. Tell, depending on where the lost tail of the log begins:

i. What transactions could be considered uncommitted?

ii. Are any dirty reads created during the recovery process? If so, what transactions need to be rolled back?

iii. What additional dirty reads could have been created if the portion of the log lost was not a tail, but rather some potions in the middle?

! **Exercise 19.1.4:** Consider the following two transactions:

$$T_1: w_1(A); w_1(B); r_1(C); c_1;$$
$$T_2: w_2(A); r_2(B); w_2(C); c_2;$$

* a) How many schedules of T_1 and T_2 are recoverable?

b) Of these, how many are ACR schedules?

c) How many are both recoverable and serializable?

d) How many are both ACR and serializable?

Exercise 19.1.5: Give an example of an ACR schedule with shared and exclusive locks that is not strict.

19.2 View Serializability

Recall our discussion in Section 18.1.4 of how our true goal in the design of a scheduler is to allow only schedules that are serializable. We also saw how differences in what operations transactions apply to the data can affect whether or not a given schedule is serializable. We also learned in Section 18.2 that schedulers normally enforce "conflict serializability," which guarantees serializability regardless of what the transactions do with their data.

However, there are weaker conditions than conflict-serializability that also guarantee serializability. In this section we shall consider one such condition, called "view-serializability." Intuitively, view-serializability considers all the connections between transactions T and U such that T writes a database element whose value U reads. The key difference between view- and conflict-serializability appears when a transaction T writes a value A that no other transaction reads (because some other transaction later writes its own value for A). In that case, the $w_T(A)$ action can be placed in certain other positions of the schedule (where A is likewise never read) that would not be permitted under the definition of conflict-serializability. In this section, we shall define view-serializability precisely and give a test for it.

19.2.1 View Equivalence

Suppose we have two schedules S_1 and S_2 of the same set of transactions. Imagine that there is a hypothetical transaction T_0 that wrote initial values for each database element read by any transaction in the schedules, and another hypothetical transaction T_f that reads every element written by one or more transactions after each schedule ends. Then for every read action $r_i(A)$ in one of the schedules, we can find the write action $w_j(A)$ that most closely preceded the read in question.[2] We say T_j is the *source* of the read action $r_i(A)$. Note that transaction T_j could be the hypothetical initial transaction T_0, and T_i could be T_f.

If for every read action in one of the schedules, its source is the same in the other schedule, we say that S_1 and S_2 are *view-equivalent*. Surely, view-equivalent schedules are truly equivalent; they each do the same when executed on any one database state. If a schedule S is view-equivalent to a serial schedule, we say S is *view-serializable*.

Example 19.9: Consider the schedule S defined by:

T_1:			$r_1(A)$		$w_1(B)$		
T_2:	$r_2(B)$	$w_2(A)$				$w_2(B)$	
T_3:				$r_3(A)$			$w_3(B)$

---

[2]While we have not previously prevented a transaction from writing an element twice, there is generally no need for it to do so, and in this study it is useful to assume that a transaction only writes a given element once.

Notice that we have separated the actions of each transaction vertically, to indicate better which transaction does what; you should read the schedule from left-to-right, as usual.

In S, both T_1 and T_2 write values of B that are lost; only the value of B written by T_3 survives to the end of the schedule and is "read" by the hypothetical transaction T_f. S is not conflict-serializable. To see why, first note that T_2 writes A before T_1 reads A, so T_2 must precede T_1 in a hypothetical conflict-equivalent serial schedule. The fact that the action $w_1(B)$ precedes $w_2(B)$ also forces T_1 to precede T_2 in any conflict-equivalent serial schedule. Yet neither $w_1(B)$ nor $w_2(B)$ has any long-term affect on the database. It is these sorts of irrelevant writes that view-serializability is able to ignore, when determining the true constraints on an equivalent serial schedule.

More precisely, let us consider the sources of all the reads in S:

1. The source of $r_2(B)$ is T_0, since there is no prior write of B in S.

2. The source of $r_1(A)$ is T_2, since T_2 most recently wrote A before the read.

3. Likewise, the source of $r_3(A)$ is T_2.

4. The source of the hypothetical read of A by T_f is T_2.

5. The source of the hypothetical read of B by T_f is T_3, the last writer of B.

Of course, T_0 appears before all real transactions in any schedule, and T_f appears after all transactions. If we order the real transactions (T_2, T_1, T_3), then the sources of all reads are the same as in schedule S. That is, T_2 reads B, and surely T_0 is the previous "writer." T_1 reads A, but T_2 already wrote A, so the source of $r_1(A)$ is T_2, as in S. T_3 also reads A, but since the prior T_2 wrote A, that is the source of $r_3(A)$, as in S. Finally, the hypothetical T_f reads A and B, but the last writers of A and B in the schedule (T_2, T_1, T_3) are T_2 and T_3 respectively, also as in S. We conclude that S is a view-serializable schedule, and the schedule represented by the order (T_2, T_1, T_3) is a view-equivalent schedule. □

19.2.2 Polygraphs and the Test for View-Serializability

There is a generalization of the precedence graph, which we used to test conflict serializability in Section 18.2.2, that reflects all the precedence constraints required by the definition of view serializability. We define the *polygraph* for a schedule to consist of the following:

1. A node for each transaction and additional nodes for the hypothetical transactions T_0 and T_f.

2. For each action $r_i(X)$ with source T_j, place an arc from T_j to T_i.

3. Suppose T_j is the source of a read $r_i(X)$, and T_k is another writer of X. It is not allowed for T_k to intervene between T_j and T_i, so it must appear either before T_j or after T_i. We represent this condition by an *arc pair* (shown dashed) from T_k to T_j and from T_i to T_k. Intuitively, one or the other of an arc pair is "real," but we don't care which, and when we try to make the polygraph acyclic, we can pick whichever of the pair helps to make it acyclic. However, there are important special cases where the arc pair becomes a single arc:

   (a) If T_j is T_0, then it is not possible for T_k to appear before T_j, so we use an arc $T_i \rightarrow T_k$ in place of the arc pair.

   (b) If T_i is T_f, then T_k cannot follow T_i, so we use an arc $T_k \rightarrow T_j$ in place of the arc pair.

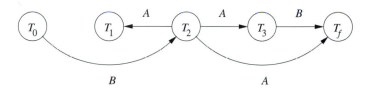

Figure 19.4: Beginning of polygraph for Example 19.10

Example 19.10: Consider the schedule S from Example 19.9. We show in Fig. 19.4 the beginning of the polygraph for S, where only the nodes and the arcs from rule (2) have been placed. We have also indicated the database element causing each arc. That is, A is passed from T_2 to T_1, T_3, and T_f, while B is passed from T_0 to T_2 and from T_3 to T_f.

Now, we must consider what transactions might interfere with each of these five connections by writing the same element between them. These potential interferences are ruled out by the arc pairs from rule (3), although as we shall see, in this example each of the arc pairs involves a special case and becomes a single arc.

Consider the arc $T_2 \rightarrow T_1$ based on element A. The only writers of A are T_0 and T_2, and neither of them can get in the middle of this arc, since T_0 cannot move its position, and T_2 is already an end of the arc. Thus, no additional arcs are needed. A similar argument tells us no additional arcs are needed to keep writers of A outside the arcs $T_2 \rightarrow T_3$ and $T_2 \rightarrow T_f$.

Now consider the arcs based on B. Note that T_0, T_1, T_2, and T_3 all write B. Consider the arc $T_0 \rightarrow T_2$ first. T_1 and T_3 are other writers of B; T_0 and T_2 also write B, but as we saw, the arc ends cannot cause interference, so we need not consider them. As we cannot place T_1 between T_0 and T_2, in principle we need the arc pair ($T_1 \rightarrow T_0$, $T_2 \rightarrow T_1$). However, nothing can precede T_0, so the option $T_1 \rightarrow T_0$ is not possible. We may in this special case just add the arc $T_2 \to T_1$ to the polygraph. But this arc is already there because of A, so in effect, we make no change to the polygraph to keep T_1 outside the arc $T_0 \to T_2$.

We also cannot place T_3 between T_0 and T_2. Similar reasoning tells us to add the arc $T_2 \to T_3$, rather than an arc pair. However, this arc too is already in the polygraph because of A, so we make no change.

Next, consider the arc $T_3 \to T_f$. Since T_0, T_1, and T_2 are other writers of B, we must keep them each outside the arc. T_0 cannot be moved between T_3 and T_f, but T_1 or T_2 could. Since neither could be moved after T_f, we must constrain T_1 and T_2 to appear before T_3. There is already an arc $T_2 \to T_3$, but we must add to the polygraph the arc $T_1 \to T_3$. This change is the only arc we must add to the polygraph, whose final set of arcs is shown in Fig. 19.5. $\square$

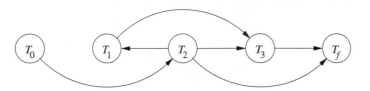

Figure 19.5: Complete polygraph for Example 19.10

Example 19.11 : In Example 19.10, all the arc pairs turned out to be single arcs as a special case. Figure 19.6 is an example of a schedule of four transactions where there is a true arc pair in the polygraph.

T_1	T_2	T_3	T_4
	$r_2(A);$		
$r_1(A); w_1(C);$			
		$r_3(C);$	
$w_1(B);$			
			$r_4(B);$
		$w_3(A);$	$r_4(C);$
	$w_2(D); r_2(B);$		
			$w_4(A); w_4(B);$

Figure 19.6: Example of transactions whose polygraph requires an arc pair

Figure 19.7 shows the polygraph, with only the arcs that come from the source-to-reader connections. As in Fig. 19.4 we label each arc by the element(s) that require it. We must then consider the possible ways that arc pairs could be added. As we saw in Example 19.10, there are several simplifications we can make. When avoiding interference with the arc $T_j \to T_i$, the only transactions that need be considered as T_k (the transaction that cannot be in the middle) are:

- Writers of an element that caused this arc $T_j \rightarrow T_i$,

- But not T_0 or T_f, which can never be T_k, and

- Not T_i or T_j, the ends of the arc itself.

With these rules in mind, let us consider the arcs due to database element A, which is written by T_0, T_3, and T_4. We need not consider T_0 at all. T_3 must not get between $T_4 \rightarrow T_f$, so we add arc $T_3 \rightarrow T_4$; remember that the other arc in the pair, $T_f \rightarrow T_3$ is not an option. Likewise, T_3 must not get between $T_0 \rightarrow T_1$ or $T_0 \rightarrow T_2$, which results in the arcs $T_1 \rightarrow T_3$ and $T_2 \rightarrow T_3$.

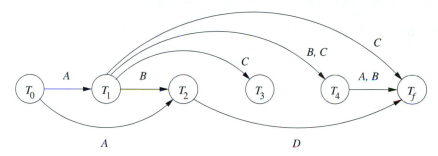

Figure 19.7: Beginning of polygraph for Example 19.11

Now, consider the fact that T_4 also must not get in the middle of an arc due to A. It is an end of $T_4 \rightarrow T_f$, so that arc is irrelevant. T_4 must not get between $T_0 \rightarrow T_1$ or $T_0 \rightarrow T_2$, which results in the arcs $T_1 \rightarrow T_4$ and $T_2 \rightarrow T_4$.

Next, let us consider the arcs due to B, which is written by T_0, T_1, and T_4. Again we need not consider T_0. The only arcs due to B are $T_1 \rightarrow T_2$, $T_1 \rightarrow T_4$, and $T_4 \rightarrow T_f$. T_1 cannot get in the middle of the first two, but the third requires arc $T_1 \rightarrow T_4$.

T_4 can get in the middle of $T_1 \rightarrow T_2$ only. This arc has neither end at T_0 or T_f, so it really requires an arc pair: $(T_4 \rightarrow T_1, T_2 \rightarrow T_4)$. We show this arc pair, as well as all the other arcs added, in Fig. 19.8.

Next, consider the writers of C: T_0 and T_1. As before, T_0 cannot present a problem. Also, T_1 is part of every arc due to C, so it cannot get in the middle. Similarly, D is written only by T_0 and T_2, so we can determine that no more arcs are necessary. The final polygraph is thus the one in Fig. 19.8.   □

19.2.3 Testing for View-Serializability

Since we must choose only one of each arc pair, we can find an equivalent serial order for schedule S if and only if there is some selection from each arc pair that turns S's polygraph into an acyclic graph. To see why, notice that if there

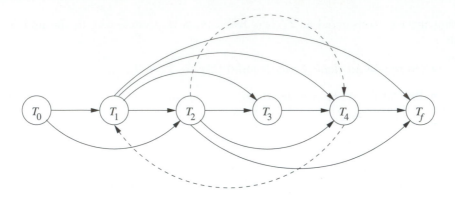

Figure 19.8: Complete polygraph for Example 19.11

is such an acyclic graph, then any topological sort of the graph gives an order in which no writer may appear between a reader and its source, and every writer appears before its readers. Thus, the reader-source connections in the serial order are exactly the same as in S; the two schedules are view-equivalent, and therefore S is view-serializable.

Conversely, if S is view-serializable, then there is a view-equivalent serial order S'. Every arc pair $(T_k \rightarrow T_j, T_i \rightarrow T_k)$ in S's polygraph must have T_k either before T_j or after T_i in S'; otherwise the writing by T_k breaks the connection from T_j to T_i, which means that S and S' are not view-equivalent. Likewise, every arc in the polygraph must be respected by the transaction order of S'. We conclude that there is a choice of arcs from each arc pair that makes the polygraph into a graph for which the serial order S' is consistent with each arc of the graph. Thus, this graph is acyclic.

Example 19.12: Consider the polygraph of Fig. 19.5. It is already a graph, and it is acyclic. The only topological order is (T_2, T_1, T_3), which is therefore a view-equivalent serial order for the schedule of Example 19.10.

Now consider the polygraph of Fig. 19.8. We must consider each choice from the one arc pair. If we choose $T_4 \rightarrow T_1$, then there is a cycle. However, if we choose $T_2 \rightarrow T_4$, the result is an acyclic graph. The sole topological order for this graph is (T_1, T_2, T_3, T_4). This order yields a view-equivalent serial order and shows that the original schedule is view-serializable. □

19.2.4   Exercises for Section 19.2

Exercise 19.2.1: Draw the polygraph and find all view-equivalent serial orders for the following schedules:

* a) $r_1(A); r_2(A); r_3(A); w_1(B); w_2(B); w_3(B);$

   b) $r_1(A); r_2(A); r_3(A); r_4(A); w_1(B); w_2(B); w_3(B); w_4(B);$

c) $r_1(A)$; $r_3(D)$; $w_1(B)$; $r_2(B)$; $w_3(B)$; $r_4(B)$; $w_2(C)$; $r_5(C)$; $w_4(E)$; $r_5(E)$; $w_5(B)$;

d) $w_1(A)$; $r_2(A)$; $w_3(A)$; $r_4(A)$; $w_5(A)$; $r_6(A)$;

! **Exercise 19.2.2:** Below are some serial schedules. Tell how many schedules are (i) conflict-equivalent and (ii) view-equivalent to these serial schedules.

* a) $r_1(A)$; $w_1(B)$; $r_2(A)$; $w_2(B)$; $r_3(A)$; $w_3(B)$; that is, three transactions each read A and then write B.

b) $r_1(A)$; $w_1(B)$; $w_1(C)$; $r_2(A)$; $w_2(B)$; $w_2(C)$; that is, two transactions each read A and then write B and C.

19.3 Resolving Deadlocks

Several times we have observed that concurrently executing transactions can compete for resources and thereby reach a state where there is a *deadlock*: each of several transactions is waiting for a resource held by one of the others, and none can make progress.

- In Section 18.3.4 we saw how ordinary operation of two-phase-locked transactions can still lead to a deadlock, because each has locked something that another transaction also needs to lock.

- In Section 18.4.3 we saw how the ability to upgrade locks from shared to exclusive can cause a deadlock because each transaction holds a shared lock on the same element and wants to upgrade the lock.

There are two broad approaches to dealing with deadlock. We can detect deadlocks and fix them, or we can manage transactions in such a way that deadlocks are never able to form.

19.3.1 Deadlock Detection by Timeout

When a deadlock exists, it is generally impossible to repair the situation so that all transactions involved can proceed. Thus, at least one of the transactions will have to be rolled back — aborted and restarted.

The simplest way to detect and resolve deadlocks is with a *timeout*. Put a limit on how long a transaction may be active, and if a transaction exceeds this time, roll it back. For example, in a simple transaction system, where typical transactions execute in milliseconds, a timeout of one minute would affect only transactions that are caught in a deadlock. If some transactions are more complex, we might want the timeout to occur after a longer interval, however.

Notice that when one transaction involved in the deadlock times out, it releases its locks or other resources. Thus, there is a chance that the other transactions involved in the deadlock will complete before reaching their timeout limits. However, since transactions involved in a deadlock are likely to have started at approximately the same time (or else, one would have completed before another started), it is also possible that spurious timeouts of transactions that are no longer involved in a deadlock will occur.

19.3.2   The Waits-For Graph

Deadlocks that are caused by transactions waiting for locks held by another can be addressed by a *waits-for graph*, indicating which transactions are waiting for locks held by another transaction. This graph can be used either to detect deadlocks after they have formed or to prevent deadlocks from ever forming. We shall assume the latter, which requires us to maintain the waits-for graph at all times, refusing to allow an action that creates a cycle in the graph.

Recall from Section 18.5.2 that a lock table maintains for each database element X a list of the transactions that are waiting for locks on X, as well as transactions that currently hold locks on X. The waits-for graph has a node for each transaction that currently holds a lock or is waiting for one. There is an arc from node (transaction) T to node U if there is some database element A such that:

1. U holds a lock on A,

2. T is waiting for a lock on A, and

3. T cannot get a lock on A in its desired mode unless U first releases its lock on A.[3]

If there are no cycles in the waits-for graph, then each transaction can eventually complete. There will be at least one transaction waiting for no other transaction, and this transaction surely can complete. At that time, there will be at least one other transaction that is not waiting, which can complete, and so on.

However, if there is a cycle, then no transaction in the cycle can ever make progress, so there is a deadlock. Thus, a strategy for deadlock avoidance is to roll back any transaction that makes a request that would cause a cycle in the waits-for graph.

Example 19.13: Suppose we have the following four transactions, each of which reads one element and writes another:

T_1: $l_1(A); r_1(A); l_1(B); w_1(B); u_1(A); u_1(B);$

---

[3]In common situations, such as shared and exclusive locks, every waiting transaction will have to wait until *all* current lock holders release their locks, but there are examples of systems of lock modes where a transaction can get its lock after only some of the current locks are released; see Exercise 19.3.6.

T_2: $l_2(C)$; $r_2(C)$; $l_2(A)$; $w_2(A)$; $u_2(C)$; $u_2(A)$;

T_3: $l_3(B)$; $r_3(B)$; $l_3(C)$; $w_3(C)$; $u_3(B)$; $u_3(C)$;

T_4: $l_4(D)$; $r_4(D)$; $l_4(A)$; $w_4(A)$; $u_4(D)$; $u_4(A)$;

We use a simple locking system with only one lock mode, although the same effect would be noted if we were to use a shared/exclusive system and took locks in the appropriate mode: shared for a read and exclusive for a write.

	T_1	T_2	T_3	T_4
1)	$l_1(A)$; $r_1(A)$;			
2)		$l_2(C)$; $r_2(C)$;		
3)			$l_3(B)$; $r_3(B)$;	
4)				$l_4(D)$; $r_4(D)$;
5)		$l_2(A)$; **Denied**		
6)			$l_3(C)$; **Denied**	
7)				$l_4(A)$; **Denied**
8)	$l_1(B)$; **Denied**			

Figure 19.9: Beginning of a schedule with a deadlock

In Fig. 19.9 is the beginning of a schedule of these four transactions. In the first four steps, each transaction obtains a lock on the element it wants to read. At step (5), T_2 tries to lock A, but the request is denied because T_1 already has a lock on A. Thus, T_2 waits for T_1, and we draw an arc from the node for T_2 to the node for T_1.

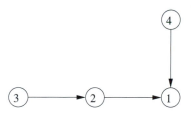

Figure 19.10: Waits-for graph after step (7) of Fig. 19.9

Similarly, at step (6) T_3 is denied a lock on C because of T_2, and at step (7), T_4 is denied a lock on A because of T_1. The waits-for graph at this point is as shown in Fig. 19.10. There is no cycle in this graph.

At step (8), T_1 must wait for the lock on B held by T_3. If we allowed T_1 to wait, then there would be a cycle in the waits-for graph involving T_1, T_2, and T_3, as suggested by Fig. 19.11. Since they are each waiting for another to finish, none can make progress, and therefore there is a deadlock involving these three

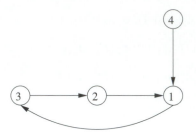

Figure 19.11: Waits-for graph with a cycle caused by step (8) of Fig. 19.9

Figure 19.12: Waits-for graph after T_1 is rolled back

transactions. Incidentally, T_4 could not finish either, although it is not in the cycle, because T_4's progress depends on T_1 making progress.

Since we roll back any transaction that would cause a cycle, then T_1 must be rolled back, yielding the waits-for graph of Fig. 19.12. T_1 relinquishes its lock on A, which may be given to either T_2 or T_4. Suppose it is given to T_2. Then T_2 can complete, whereupon it relinquishes its locks on A and C. Now T_3, which needs a lock on C, and T_4, which needs a lock on A, can both complete. At some time, T_1 is restarted, but it cannot get locks on A and B until T_2, T_3, and T_4 have completed. $\square$

19.3.3   Deadlock Prevention by Ordering Elements

Now, let us consider several more methods for deadlock prevention. The first requires us to order database elements in some arbitrary but fixed order. For instance, if database elements are blocks, we could order them lexicographically by their physical address. Recall from Section 8.3.4 that the physical address of a block is normally represented by a sequence of bytes describing its location within the storage system.

If every transaction is required to request locks on elements in order (a condition that is not realistic in most applications), then there can be no deadlock due to transactions waiting for locks. For suppose T_2 is waiting for a lock on A_1 held by T_1; T_3 is waiting for a lock on A_2 held by T_2, and so on, while T_n is waiting for a lock on A_{n-1} held by T_{n-1}, and T_1 is waiting for a lock on A_n held by T_n. Since T_2 has a lock on A_2 but is waiting for A_1, it must be that $A_2 < A_1$ in the order of elements. Similarly, $A_i < A_{i-1}$ for $i = 3, 4, \ldots, n$. But since T_1 has a lock on A_1 while it is waiting for A_n, it also follows that $A_1 < A_n$. We now have $A_1 < A_n < A_{n-1} < \cdots < A_2 < A_1$, which is impossible, since it implies $A_1 < A_1$.

Example 19.14 : Let us suppose elements are ordered alphabetically. Then if the four transactions of Example 19.13 are to lock elements in alphabetical order, T_2 and T_4 must be rewritten to lock elements in the opposite order. Thus, the four transactions are now:

T_1: $l_1(A)$; $r_1(A)$; $l_1(B)$; $w_1(B)$; $u_1(A)$; $u_1(B)$;

T_2: $l_2(A)$; $l_2(C)$; $r_2(C)$; $w_2(A)$; $u_2(C)$; $u_2(A)$;

T_3: $l_3(B)$; $r_3(B)$; $l_3(C)$; $w_3(C)$; $u_3(B)$; $u_3(C)$;

T_4: $l_4(A)$; $l_4(D)$; $r_4(D)$; $w_4(A)$; $u_4(D)$; $u_4(A)$;

Figure 19.13 shows what happens if the transactions execute with the same timing as Fig. 19.9. T_1 begins and gets a lock on A. T_2 tries to begin next by getting a lock on A, but must wait for T_1. Then, T_3 begins by getting a lock on B, but T_4 is unable to begin because it too needs a lock on A, for which it must wait.

	T_1	T_2	T_3	T_4
1)	$l_1(A)$; $r_1(A)$;			
2)		$l_2(A)$; **Denied**		
3)			$l_3(B)$; $r_3(B)$;	
4)				$l_4(A)$; **Denied**
5)			$l_3(C)$; $w_3(C)$;	
6)			$u_3(B)$; $u_3(C)$;	
7)	$l_1(B)$; $w_1(B)$;			
8)	$u_1(A)$; $u_1(B)$;			
9)		$l_2(A)$; $l_2(C)$;		
10)		$r_2(C)$; $w_2(A)$;		
11)		$u_2(A)$; $u_2(C)$;		
12)				$l_4(A)$; $l_4(D)$;
13)				$r_4(D)$; $w_4(A)$;
14)				$u_4(A)$; $u_4(D)$;

Figure 19.13: Locking elements in alphabetical order prevents deadlock

Since T_2 is stalled, it cannot proceed, and following the order of events in Fig. 19.9, T_3 gets a turn next. It is able to get its lock on C, whereupon it completes at step (6). Now, with T_3's locks on B and C released, T_1 is able to complete, which it does at step (8). At this point, the lock on A becomes available, and we suppose that it is given on a first-come-first-served basis to T_2. Then, T_2 can get both locks that it needs and completes at step (11). Finally, T_4 can get its locks and completes.   □

19.3.4 Detecting Deadlocks by Timestamps

We can detect deadlocks by maintaining the waits-for graph, as we discussed in Section 19.3.2. However, this graph can be large, and analyzing it for cycles each time a transaction has to wait for a lock can be time-consuming. An alternative to maintaining the waits-for graph is to associate with each transaction a timestamp. This timestamp:

- Is for deadlock detection only; it is not the same as the timestamp used for concurrency control in Section 18.8, even if timestamp-based concurrency control is in use.

- In particular, if a transaction is rolled back, it restarts with a new, later concurrency timestamp, but its timestamp for deadlock detection never changes.

The timestamp is used when a transaction T has to wait for a lock that is held by another transaction U. Two different things happen, depending on whether T or U is *older* (has the earlier timestamp). There are two different policies that can be used to manage transactions and detect deadlocks.

1. The *Wait-Die Scheme*:

    (a) If T is older than U (i.e., the timestamp of T is smaller than U's timestamp), then T is allowed to wait for the lock(s) held by U.

    (b) If U is older than T, then T "dies"; it is rolled back.

2. The *Wound-Wait Scheme*:

    (a) If T is older than U, it "wounds" U. Usually, the "wound" is fatal: U must roll back and relinquish to T the lock(s) that T needs from U. There is an exception if, by the time the "wound" takes effect, U has already finished and released its locks. In that case, U survives and need not be rolled back.

    (b) If U is older than T, then T waits for the lock(s) held by U.

Example 19.15 : Let us consider the wait-die scheme, using the transactions of Example 19.14. We shall assume that T_1, T_2, T_3, T_4 is the order of times; i.e., T_1 is the oldest transaction. We also assume that when a transaction rolls back, it does not restart soon enough to become active before the other transactions finish.

Figure 19.14 shows a possible sequence of events under the wait-die scheme. T_1 gets the lock on A first. When T_2 asks for a lock on A, it dies, because T_1

	T_1	T_2	T_3	T_4
1)	$l_1(A); r_1(A);$			
2)		$l_2(A);$ **Dies**		
3)			$l_3(B); r_3(B);$	
4)				$l_4(A);$ **Dies**
5)			$l_3(C); w_3(C);$	
6)			$u_3(B); u_3(C);$	
7)	$l_1(B); w_1(B);$			
8)	$u_1(A); u_1(B);$			
9)				$l_4(A); l_4(D);$
10)		$l_2(A);$ **Waits**		
11)				$r_4(D); w_4(A);$
12)				$u_4(A); u_4(D);$
13)		$l_2(A); l_2(C);$		
14)		$r_2(C); w_2(A);$		
15)		$u_2(A); u_2(C);$		

Figure 19.14: Actions of transactions detecting deadlock under the wait-die scheme

	T_1	T_2	T_3	T_4
1)	$l_1(A); r_1(A);$			
2)		$l_2(A);$ **Waits**		
3)			$l_3(B); r_3(B);$	
4)				$l_4(A);$ **Waits**
5)	$l_1(B); w_1(B);$		**Wounded**	
6)	$u_1(A); u_1(B);$			
7)		$l_2(A); l_2(C);$		
8)		$r_2(C); w_2(A);$		
9)		$u_2(A); u_2(C);$		
10)				$l_4(A); l_4(D);$
11)				$r_4(D); w_4(A);$
12)				$u_4(A); u_4(D);$
13)			$l_3(B); r_3(B);$	
14)			$l_3(C); w_3(C);$	
15)			$u_3(B); u_3(C);$	

Figure 19.15: Actions of transactions detecting deadlock under the wound-wait scheme

---

Why Timestamp-Based Deadlock Detection Works

We claim that in either the wait-die or wound-wait scheme, there can be no cycle in the waits-for graph, and hence no deadlock. Suppose otherwise; that is, there is a cycle such as $T_1 \to T_2 \to T_3 \to T_1$. One of the transactions is the oldest, say T_2.

In the wait-die scheme, you can only wait for younger transactions. Thus, it is not possible that T_1 is waiting for T_2, since T_2 is surely older than T_1. In the wound-wait scheme, you can only wait for older transactions. Thus, there is no way T_2 could be waiting for the younger T_3. We conclude that the cycle cannot exist, and therefore there is no deadlock.

---

is older than T_2. In step (3), T_3 gets a lock on B, but in step (4), T_4 asks for a lock on A and dies because T_1, the holder of the lock on A, is older than T_4. Next, T_3 gets its lock on C and completes. When T_1 continues, it finds the lock on B available and also completes at step (8).

Now, the two transactions that rolled back — T_2 and T_4 — start again. Their timestamps as far as deadlock is concerned, do not change; T_2 is still older than T_4. However, we assume that T_4 restarts first, at step (9), and when the older transaction T_2 requests a lock on A at step (10), it is forced to wait, but does not abort. T_4 completes at step (12), and then T_2 is allowed to run to completion, as shown in the last three steps. □

Example 19.16 : Next, let us consider the same transactions running under the wound-wait policy, as shown in Fig. 19.15. As in Fig. 19.14, T_1 begins by locking A. When T_2 requests a lock on A at step (2), it waits, since T_1 is older than T_2. After T_3 gets its lock on B at step (3), T_4 is also made to wait for the lock on A.

Then, suppose that T_1 continues at step (5) with its request for the lock on B. That lock is already held by T_3, but T_1 is older than T_3. Thus, T_1 "wounds" T_3. Since T_3 is not yet finished, the wound is fatal: T_3 relinquishes its lock and rolls back. Thus, T_1 is able to complete.

When T_1 makes the lock on A available, suppose it is given to T_2, which is then able to proceed. After T_2, the lock is given to T_4, which proceeds to completion. Finally, T_3 restarts and completes without interference. □

19.3.5 Comparison of Deadlock-Management Methods

In both the wait-die and wound-wait schemes, older transactions kill off newer transactions. Since transactions restart with their old timestamp, eventually each transaction becomes the oldest in the system and is sure to complete. This guarantee, that every transaction eventually completes, is called *no starvation*. Notice that other schemes described in this section do not necessarily prevent starvation; if extra measures are not taken, a transaction could repeatedly start, get involved in a deadlock, and be rolled back. See Exercise 19.3.7.

There is, however, a subtle difference in the way wait-die and wound-wait behave. In wound-wait, a newer transaction is killed whenever an old transaction asks for a lock held by the newer transaction. If we assume that transactions take their locks near the time that they begin, it will be rare that an old transaction was beaten to a lock by a new transaction. Thus, we expect rollback to be rare in wound-wait.

On the other hand, when a rollback does occur, wait-die rolls back a transaction that is still in the stage of gathering locks, presumably the earliest phase of the transaction. Thus, although wait-die may roll back more transactions than wound-wait, these transactions tend to have done little work. In contrast, when wound-wait does roll back a transaction, it is likely to have acquired its locks and for substantial processor time to have been invested in its activity. Thus, either scheme may turn out to cause more wasted work, depending on the population of transactions processed.

We should also consider the advantages and disadvantages of both wound-wait and wait-die when compared with a straightforward construction and use of the waits-for graph. The important points are:

- Both wound-wait and wait-die are easier to implement than a system that maintains or periodically constructs the waits-for graph. The disadvantage of constructing the waits-for graph is even more extreme when the database is distributed, and the waits-for graph must be constructed from a collection of lock tables at different sites. See Section 19.6 for a discussion.

- Using the waits-for graph minimizes the number of times we must abort a transaction because of deadlock. We never abort a transaction unless there really is a deadlock. On the other hand, either wound-wait or wait-die will sometimes roll back a transaction when there was no deadlock, and no deadlock would have occurred had the transaction been allowed to survive.

19.3.6 Exercises for Section 19.3

Exercise 19.3.1: For each of the sequences of actions below, assume that shared locks are requested immediately before each read action, and exclusive locks are requested immediately before every write action. Also, unlocks occur immediately after the final action that a transaction executes. Tell what actions are denied, and whether deadlock occurs. Also tell how the waits-for graph evolves during the execution of the actions. If there are deadlocks, pick a transaction to abort, and show how the sequence of actions continues.

* a) $r_1(A)$; $r_2(B)$; $w_1(C)$; $r_3(D)$; $r_4(E)$; $w_3(B)$; $w_2(C)$; $w_4(A)$; $w_1(D)$;

 b) $r_1(A)$; $r_2(B)$; $r_3(C)$; $w_1(B)$; $w_2(C)$; $w_3(D)$;

c) $r_1(A); r_2(B); r_3(C); w_1(B); w_2(C); w_3(A);$

d) $r_1(A); r_2(B); w_1(C); w_2(D); r_3(C); w_1(B); w_4(D); w_2(A);$

Exercise 19.3.2: For each of the action sequences in Exercise 19.3.1, tell what happens under the wound-wait deadlock avoidance system. Assume the order of deadlock-timestamps is the same as the order of subscripts for the transactions, that is, T_1, T_2, T_3, T_4. Also assume that transactions that need to restart do so in the order that they were rolled back.

Exercise 19.3.3: For each of the action sequences in Exercise 19.3.1, tell what happens under the wait-die deadlock avoidance system. Make the same assumptions as in Exercise 19.3.2.

! **Exercise 19.3.4:** Can one have a waits-for graph with a cycle of length n, but no smaller cycle, for any integer $n > 1$? What about $n = 1$, i.e., a loop on a node?

!! **Exercise 19.3.5:** One approach to avoiding deadlocks is to require each transaction to announce all the locks it wants at the beginning, and to either grant all those locks or deny them all and make the transaction wait. Does this approach avoid deadlocks due to locking? Either explain why, or give an example of a deadlock that can arise.

! **Exercise 19.3.6:** Consider the intention-locking system of Section 18.6. Describe how to construct the waits-for graph for this system of lock modes. Especially, consider the possibility that a database element A is locked by different transactions in modes IS and also either S or IX. If a request for a lock on A has to wait, what arcs do we draw?

*! **Exercise 19.3.7:** In Section 19.3.5 we pointed out that deadlock-detection methods other than wound-wait and wait-die do not necessarily prevent starvation, where a transaction is repeatedly rolled back and never gets to finish. Give an example of how using the policy of rolling back any transaction that would cause a cycle can lead to starvation. Does requiring that transactions request locks on elements in a fixed order necessarily prevent starvation? What about timeouts as a deadlock-resolution mechanism?

19.4   Distributed Databases

We shall now consider the elements of distributed database systems. In a distributed system, there are many, relatively autonomous processors that may participate in database operations. Distributed databases offer several opportunities:

1. Since many machines can be brought to bear on a problem, the opportunities for parallelism and speedy response to queries are increased.

2. Since data may be replicated at several sites, the system may not have to stop processing just because one site or component has failed.

On the other hand, distributed processing increases the complexity of every aspect of a database system, so we need to rethink how even the most basic components of a DBMS are designed. In many distributed environments, the cost of communicating may dominate the cost of processing, so a critical issue becomes how many messages are sent. In this section we shall introduce the principal issues, while the next sections concentrate on solutions to two important problems that come up in distributed databases: distributed commit and distributed locking.

19.4.1 Distribution of Data

One important reason to distribute data is that the organization is itself distributed among many sites, and the sites each have data that is germane primarily to that site. Some examples are:

1. A bank may have many branches. Each branch (or the group of branches in a given city) will keep a database of accounts maintained at that branch (or city). Customers can choose to bank at any branch, but will normally bank at "their" branch, where their account data is stored. The bank may also have data that is kept in the central office, such as employee records and policies such as current interest rates. Of course, a backup of the records at each branch is also stored, probably in a site that is neither a branch office nor the central office.

2. A chain of department stores may have many individual stores. Each store (or a group of stores in one city) has a database of sales at that store and inventory at that store. There may also be a central office with data about employees, chain-wide inventory, credit-card customers, and information about suppliers such as unfilled orders, and what each is owed. In addition, there may be a copy of all the stores' sales data in a "data warehouse," which is used to analyze and predict sales through ad-hoc queries issued by analysts; see Section 20.4.

3. A digital library may consist of a consortium of universities that each hold on-line books and other documents. Search at any site will examine the catalog of documents available at all sites and deliver an electronic copy of the document to the user if any site holds it.

In some cases, what we might think of logically as a single relation has been partitioned among many sites. For example, the chain of stores might be imagined to have a single sales relation, such as

```
Sales(item, date, price, purchaser)
```

Factors in Communication Cost

As bandwidth cost drops rapidly, one might wonder whether communication cost needs to be considered when designing a distributed database system. Now certain kinds of data are among the largest objects managed electronically, so even with very cheap communication the cost of sending a terabyte-sized piece of data cannot be ignored. However, communication cost generally involves not only the shipping of the bits, but several layers of protocol that prepare the data for shipping, reconstitute them at the receiving end, and manage the communication. These protocols each require substantial computation. While computation is also getting cheaper, the computation needed to perform the communication is likely to remain significant, compared to the needs for conventional, single-processor execution of key database operations.

However, this relation does not exist physically. Rather, it is the union of a number of relations with the same schema, one at each of the stores in the chain. These local relations are called *fragments*, and the partitioning of a logical relation into physical fragments is called *horizontal decomposition* of the relation Sales. We regard the partition as "horizontal" because we may visualize a single Sales relation with its tuples separated, by horizontal lines, into the sets of tuples at each store.

In other situations, a distributed database appears to have partitioned a relation "vertically," by decomposing what might be one logical relation into two or more, each with a subset of the attributes, and with each relation at a different site. For instance, if we want to find out which sales at the Boston store were made to customers who are more than 90 days in arrears on their credit-card payments, it would be useful to have a relation (or view) that included the item, date, and purchaser information from Sales, along with the date of the last credit-card payment by that purchaser. However, in the scenario we are describing, this relation is decomposed vertically, and we would have to join the credit-card-customer relation at the central headquarters with the fragment of Sales at the Boston store.

19.4.2 Distributed Transactions

A consequence of the distribution of data is that a transaction may involve processes at several sites. Thus, our model of what a transaction is must change. No longer is a transaction a piece of code executed by a single processor communicating with a single scheduler and a single log manager at a single site. Rather, a transaction consists of communicating *transaction components*, each at a different site and communicating with the local scheduler and logger. Two important issues that must thus be looked at anew are:

1. How do we manage the commit/abort decision when a transaction is distributed? What happens if one component of the transaction wants to abort the whole transaction, while others encountered no problem and want to commit? We discuss a technique called "two-phase commit" in Section 19.5; it allows the decision to be made properly and also frequently allows sites that are up to operate even if some other site(s) have failed.

2. How do we assure serializability of transactions that involve components at several sites? We look at locking in particular, in Section 19.6 and see how local lock tables can be used to support global locks on database elements and thus support serializability of transactions in a distributed environment.

19.4.3 Data Replication

One important advantage of a distributed system is the ability to *replicate* data, that is, to make copies of the data at different sites. One motivation is that if a site fails, there may be other sites that can provide the same data that was at the failed site. A second use is in improving the speed of query answering by making a copy of needed data available at the sites where queries are initiated. For example:

1. A bank may make copies of current interest-rate policy available at each branch, so a query about rates does not have to be sent to the central office.

2. A chain store may keep copies of information about suppliers at each store, so local requests for information about suppliers (e.g., the manager needs the phone number of a supplier to check on a shipment) can be handled without sending messages to the central office.

3. A digital library may temporarily cache a copy of a popular document at a school where students have been assigned to read the document.

However, there are several problems that must be faced when data is replicated.

a) How do we keep copies identical? In essence, an update to a replicated data element becomes a distributed transaction that updates all copies.

b) How do we decide where and how many copies to keep? The more copies, the more effort is required to update, but the easier queries become. For example, a relation that is rarely updated might have copies everywhere for maximum efficiency, while a frequently updated relation might have only one or two copies.

c) What happens when there is a communication failure in the network, and different copies of the same data have the opportunity to evolve separately and must then be reconciled when the network reconnects?

19.4.4   Distributed Query Optimization

The existence of distributed data also affects the complexity and options available in the design of a physical query plan (see Section 16.7). Among the issues that must be decided as we choose a physical plan are:

1. If there are several copies of a needed relation R, from which do we get the value of R?

2. If we apply an operator, say join, to two relations R and S, we have several options and must choose one. Some of the possibilities are:

   (a) We can copy S to the site of R and do the computation there.

   (b) We can copy R to the site of S and do the computation there.

   (c) We can copy both R and S to a third site and do the computation at that site.

   Which is best depends on several factors, including which site has available processing cycles, and whether the result of the operation will be combined with data at a third site. For example, if we are computing $(R \bowtie S) \bowtie T$, we may choose to ship both R and S to the site of T and take both joins there.

   If a relation R is in fragments $R_1, R_2, \ldots, R_n$ distributed among several sites, we should also replace a use of R in the query by a use of

$$R_1 \cup R_2 \cup \cdots \cup R_n$$

as we select a logical query plan. The query may then allow us to simplify the expression significantly. For instance, if the R_i's each represent fragments of the `Sales` relation discussed in Section 19.4.1, and each fragment is associated with a single store, then a query about sales at the Boston store might allow us to remove all R_i's except the fragment for Boston from the union.

19.4.5   Exercises for Section 19.4

*!! Exercise 19.4.1: The following exercise will allow you to address some of the problems that come up when deciding on a replication strategy for data. Suppose there is a relation R that is accessed from n sites. The ith site issues q_i queries about R and u_i updates to R per second, for $i = 1, 2, \ldots, n$. The cost of executing a query if there is a copy of R at the site issuing the query is c, while if there is no copy there, and the query must be sent to some remote site, then the cost is $10c$. The cost of executing an update is d for the copy of R at the issuing site and $10d$ for every copy of R that is not at the issuing site. As a function of these parameters, how would you choose, for large n, a set of sites at which to replicate R.

19.5 Distributed Commit

In this section, we shall address the problem of how a distributed transaction that has components at several sites can execute atomically. The next section discusses another important property of distributed transactions: executing them serializably. We shall begin with an example that illustrates the problems that might arise.

Example 19.17: Consider our example of a chain of stores mentioned in Section 19.4. Suppose a manager of the chain wants to query all the stores, find the inventory of toothbrushes at each, and issue instructions to move toothbrushes from store to store in order to balance the inventory. The operation is done by a single global transaction T that has component T_i at the ith store and a component T_0 at the office where the manager is located. The sequence of activities performed by T are summarized below:

1. Component T_0 is created at the site of the manager.

2. T_0 sends messages to all the stores instructing them to create components T_i.

3. Each T_i executes a query at store i to discover the number of toothbrushes in inventory and reports this number to T_0.

4. T_0 takes these numbers and determines, by some algorithm we shall not discuss, what shipments of toothbrushes are desired. T_0 then sends messages such as "store 10 should ship 500 toothbrushes to store 7" to the appropriate stores (stores 7 and 10 in this instance).

5. Stores receiving instructions update their inventory and perform the shipments.

□

19.5.1 Supporting Distributed Atomicity

There are a number of things that could go wrong in Example 19.17, and many of these result in violations of the atomicity of T. That is, some of the actions comprising T get executed, but others do not. Mechanisms such as logging and recovery, which we assume are present at each site, will assure that each T_i is executed atomically, but do not assure that T itself is atomic.

Example 19.18: Suppose a bug in the algorithm to redistribute toothbrushes might cause store 10 to be instructed to ship more toothbrushes than it has. T_{10} will therefore abort, and no toothbrushes will be shipped from store 10; neither will the inventory at store 10 be changed. However, T_7 detects no problems and commits at store 7, updating its inventory to reflect the supposedly shipped toothbrushes. Now, not only has T failed to execute atomically (since T_{10} never completes), but it has left the distributed database in an inconsistent state: the toothbrush inventory does not equal the number of toothbrushes on hand. □

Another source of problems is the possibility that a site will fail or be disconnected from the network while the distributed transaction is running.

Example 19.19 : Suppose T_{10} replies to T_0's first message by telling its inventory of toothbrushes. However, the machine at store 10 then crashes, and the instructions from T_0 are never received by T_{10}. Can distributed transaction T ever commit? What should T_{10} do when its site recovers?   □

19.5.2 Two-Phase Commit

In order to avoid the problems suggested in Section 19.5.1, distributed DBMS's use a complex protocol for deciding whether or not to commit a distributed transaction. In this section, we shall describe the basic idea behind these protocols, called *two-phase commit*.[4] By making a global decision about committing, each component of the transaction will commit, or none will. As usual, we assume that the atomicity mechanisms at each site assure that either the local component commits or it has no effect on the database state at that site; i.e., components of the transaction are atomic. Thus, by enforcing the rule that either all components of a distributed transaction commit or none does, we make the distributed transaction itself atomic.

Several salient points about the two-phase commit protocol follow:

- In a two-phase commit, we assume that each site logs actions at that site, but there is no global log.

- We also assume that one site, called the *coordinator*, plays a special role in deciding whether or not the distributed transaction can commit. For example, the coordinator might be the site at which the transaction originates, such as the site of T_0 in the examples of Section 19.5.1.

- The two-phase commit protocol involves sending certain messages between the coordinator and the other sites. As each message is sent, it is logged at the sending site, to aid in recovery should it be necessary.

With these points in mind, we can describe the two phases in terms of the messages sent between sites.

Phase I

In phase 1 of the two-phase commit, the coordinator for a distributed transaction T decides when to attempt to commit T. Presumably the attempt to commit occurs after the component of T at the coordinator site is ready to

---

[4]Do not confuse two-phase commit with two-phase locking. They are independent ideas, designed to solve different problems.

commit, but in principle the steps must be carried out even if the coordinator's component wants to abort (but with obvious simplifications as we shall see). The coordinator polls all the sites with components of the transaction T to determine their wishes regarding the commit/abort decision.

1. The coordinator places a log record <Prepare T> on the log at its site.

2. The coordinator sends to each component's site (in principle including itself) the message prepare T.

3. Each site receiving the message prepare T decides whether to commit or abort its component of T. The site can delay if the component has not yet completed its activity, but must eventually send a response.

4. If a site wants to commit its component, it must enter a state called *precommitted*. Once in the precommitted state, the site cannot abort its component of T without a directive to do so from the coordinator. The following steps are done to become precommitted:

   (a) Perform whatever steps are necessary to be sure the local component of T will not have to abort, even if there is a system failure followed by recovery at the site. Thus, not only must all actions associated with the local T be performed, but the appropriate actions regarding the log must be taken so that T will be redone rather than undone in a recovery. The actions depend on the logging method, but surely the log records associated with actions of the local T must be flushed to disk.

   (b) Place the record <Ready T> on the local log and flush the log to disk.

   (c) Send to the coordinator the message ready T.

   However, the site does not commit its component of T at this time; it must wait for phase 2.

5. If, instead, the site wants to abort its component of T, then it logs the record <Don't commit T> and sends the message don't commit T to the coordinator. It is safe to abort the component at this time, since T will surely abort if even one component wants to abort.

The messages of phase 1 are summarized in Fig. 19.16.

Phase II

The second phase begins when responses ready or don't commit are received from each site by the coordinator. However, it is possible that some site fails to respond; it may be down, or it has been disconnected by the network. In that case, after a suitable timeout period, the coordinator will treat the site as if it had sent don't commit.

Figure 19.16: Messages in phase 1 of two-phase commit

1. If the coordinator has received **ready** T from all components of T, then it decides to commit T. The coordinator

   (a) Logs <Commit T> at its site, and

   (b) Sends message **commit** T to all sites involved in T.

2. If the coordinator has received **don't commit** T from one or more sites, it:

   (a) Logs <Abort T> at its site, and

   (b) Sends **abort** T messages to all sites involved in T.

3. If a site receives a **commit** T message, it commits the component of T at that site, logging <Commit T> as it does.

4. If a site receives the message **abort** T, it aborts T and writes the log record <Abort T>.

The messages of phase 2 are summarized in Fig. 19.17.

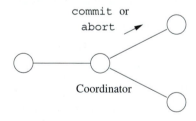

Figure 19.17: Messages in phase 2 of two-phase commit

19.5.3 Recovery of Distributed Transactions

At any time during the two-phase commit process, a site may fail. We need to make sure that what happens when the site recovers is consistent with the global decision that was made about a distributed transaction T. There are several cases to consider, depending on the last log entry for T.

1. If the last log record for T was <Commit T>, then T must have been committed by the coordinator. Depending on the log method used, it may be necessary to redo the component of T at the recovering site.

2. If the last log record is <Abort T>, then similarly we know that the global decision was to abort T. If the log method requires it, we undo the component of T at the recovering site.

3. If the last log record is <Don't commit T>, then the site knows that the global decision must have been to abort T. If necessary, effects of T on the local database are undone.

4. The hard case is when the last log record for T is <Ready T>. Now, the recovering site does not know whether the global decision was to commit or abort T. This site must communicate with at least one other site to find out the global decision for T. If the coordinator is up, the site can ask the coordinator. If the coordinator is not up at this time, some other site may be asked to consult its log to find out what happened to T. In the worst case, no other site can be contacted, and the local component of T must be kept active until the commit/abort decision is determined.

5. It may also be the case that the local log has no records about T that come from the actions of the two-phase commit protocol. If so, then the recovering site may unilaterally decide to abort its component of T, which is consistent with all logging methods. It is possible that the coordinator already detected a timeout from the failed site and decided to abort T. If the failure was brief, T may still be active at other sites, but it will never be inconsistent if the recovering site decides to abort its component of T and responds with don't commit T if later polled in phase 1.

The above analysis assumes that the failed site is not the coordinator. When the coordinator fails during a two-phase commit, new problems arise. First, the surviving participant sites must either wait for the coordinator to recover or elect a new coordinator. Since the coordinator could be down for an indefinite period, there is good motivation to elect a new leader, at least after a brief waiting period to see if the coordinator comes back up.

The matter of *leader election* is in its own right a complex problem of distributed systems, beyond the scope of this book. However, a simple method will work in most situations. For instance, we may assume that all participant sites have unique identifying numbers; IP addresses will work in many situations. Each participant sends messages announcing its availability as leader to all the other sites, giving its identifying number. After a suitable length of time, each participant acknowledges as the new coordinator the lowest-numbered site from which it has heard, and sends messages to that effect to all the other sites. If all sites receive consistent messages, then there is a unique choice for new coordinator, and everyone knows about it. If there is inconsistency, or a surviving site has failed to respond, that too will be universally known, and the election starts over.

Now, the new leader polls the sites for information about each distributed transaction T. Each site reports the last record on its log concerning T, if there is one. The possible cases are:

1. Some site has <Commit T> on its log. Then the original coordinator must have wanted to send commit T messages everywhere, and it is safe to commit T.

2. Similarly, if some site has <Abort T> on its log, then the original coordinator must have decided to abort T, and it is safe for the new coordinator to order that action.

3. Suppose now that no site has <Commit T> or <Abort T> on its log, but at least one site does *not* have <Ready T> on its log. Then since actions are logged before the corresponding messages are sent, we know that the old coordinator never received ready T from this site and therefore could not have decided to commit. It is safe for the new coordinator to decide to abort T.

4. The hard case is when there is no <Commit T> or <Abort T> to be found, but every surviving site has <Ready T>. Now, we cannot be sure whether the old coordinator found some reason to abort T or not; it could have decided to do so because of actions at its own site, or because of a don't commit T message from another failed site, for example. Or the old coordinator may have decided to commit T and already committed its local component of T. Thus, the new coordinator is not able to decide whether to commit or abort T and must wait until the original coordinator recovers. In real systems, the database administrator has the ability to intervene and manually force the waiting transaction components to finish. The result is a possible loss of atomicity, but the person executing the blocked transaction will be notified to take some appropriate compensating action.

19.5.4 Exercises for Section 19.5

! **Exercise 19.5.1:** Consider a transaction T initiated at a home computer that asks bank B to transfer $10,000 from an account at B to an account at another bank C.

 * a) What are the components of distributed transaction T? What should the components at B and C do?

   b) What can go wrong if there is not $10,000 in the account at B?

   c) What can go wrong if one or both banks' computers crash, or if the network is disconnected?

   d) If one of the problems suggested in (c) occurs, how could the transaction resume correctly when the computers and network resume operation?

Exercise 19.5.2: In this exercise, we need a notation for describing sequences of messages that can take place during a two-phase commit. Let (i, j, M) mean that site i sends the message M to site j, where the value of M and its meaning can be P (prepare), R (ready), D (don't commit), C (commit), or A (abort). We shall discuss a simple situation in which site 0 is the coordinator, but not otherwise part of the transaction, and sites 1 and 2 are the components. For instance, the following is one possible sequence of messages that could take place during a successful commit of the transaction:

$$(0, 1, P), \ (0, 2, P), \ (2, 0, R), \ (1, 0, R), \ (0, 2, C), \ (0, 1, C)$$

 * a) Give an example of a sequence of messages that could occur if site 1 wants to commit and site 2 wants to abort.

 *! b) How many possible sequences of messages such as the above are there, if the transaction successfully commits?

 ! c) If site 1 wants to commit, but site 2 does not, how many sequences of messages are there, assuming no failures occur?

 ! d) If site 1 wants to commit, but site 2 is down and does not respond to messages, how many sequences are there?

!! Exercise 19.5.3: Using the notation of Exercise 19.5.2, suppose the sites are a coordinator and n other sites that are the transaction components. As a function of n, how many sequences of messages are there if the transaction successfully commits?

19.6 Distributed Locking

In this section we shall see how to extend a locking scheduler to an environment where transactions are distributed and consist of components at several sites. We assume that lock tables are managed by individual sites, and that the component of a transaction at a site can only request a lock on the data elements at that site.

    When data is replicated, we must arrange that the copies of a single element X are changed in the same way by each transaction. This requirement introduces a distinction between locking the *logical* database element X and locking one or more of the copies of X. In this section, we shall offer a cost model for distributed locking algorithms that applies to both replicated and nonreplicated data. However, before introducing the model, let us consider an obvious (and sometimes adequate) solution to the problem of maintaining locks in a distributed database — centralized locking.

19.6.1   Centralized Lock Systems

Perhaps the simplest approach is to designate one site, the *lock site*, to maintain a lock table for logical elements, whether or not they have copies at that site. When a transaction wants a lock on logical element X, it sends a request to the lock site, which grants or denies the lock, as appropriate. Since obtaining a global lock on X is the same as obtaining a local lock on X at the lock site, we can be sure that global locks behave correctly as long as the lock site administers locks conventionally. The usual cost is three messages per lock (request, grant, and release), unless the transaction happens to be running at the lock site.

The use of a single lock site can be adequate in some situations, but if there are many sites and many simultaneous transactions, the lock site could become a bottleneck. Further, if the lock site crashes, no transaction at any site can obtain locks. Because of these problems with centralized locking, there are a number of other approaches to maintaining distributed locks, which we shall introduce after discussing how to estimate the cost of locking.

19.6.2   A Cost Model for Distributed Locking Algorithms

Suppose that each data element exists at exactly one site (i.e., there is no data replication) and that the lock manager at each site stores locks and lock requests for the elements at its site. Transactions may be distributed, and each transaction consists of components at one or more sites.

While there are several costs associated with managing locks, many of them are fixed, independent of the way transactions request locks over a network. The one cost factor over which we have control is the number of messages sent between sites when a transaction obtains and releases its locks. We shall thus count the number of messages required for various locking schemes on the assumption that all locks are granted when requested. Of course, a lock request may be denied, resulting in an additional message to deny the request and a later message when the lock is granted. However, since we cannot predict the rate of lock denials, and this rate is not something we can control anyway, we shall ignore this additional requirement for messages in our comparisons.

Example 19.20: As we mentioned in Section 19.6.1, in the central locking method, the typical lock request uses three messages, one to request the lock, one from the central site to grant the lock, and a third to release the lock. The exceptions are:

1. The messages are unnecessary when the requesting site is the central lock site, and

2. Additional messages must be sent when the initial request cannot be granted.

However, we assume that both these situations are relatively rare; i.e., most lock requests are from sites other than the central lock site, and most lock requests can be granted. Thus, three messages per lock is a good estimate of the cost of the centralized lock method. □

Now, consider a situation more flexible than central locking, where each database element X can maintain its locks at its own site. It might seem that, since a transaction wanting to lock X will have a component at the site of X, there are no messages between sites needed. The local component simply negotiates with the lock manager at that site for the lock on X. However, if the distributed transaction needs locks on several elements, say X, Y, and Z, then the transaction cannot complete its computation until it has locks on all three elements. If X, Y, and Z are at different sites, then the components of the transactions at those sites must at least exchange synchronization messages to prevent the transaction from "getting ahead of itself."

Rather than deal with all the possible variations, we shall take a simple model of how transactions gather locks. We assume that one component of each transaction, the *lock coordinator*, has the responsibility to gather all the locks that all components of the transaction require. The lock coordinator locks elements at its own site without messages, but locking an element X at any other site requires three messages:

1. A message to the site of X requesting the lock.

2. A reply message granting the lock (recall we assume all locks are granted immediately; if not, a denial message followed by a granting message later will be sent).

3. A message to the site of X releasing the lock.

Since we only wish to compare distributed locking protocols, rather than give absolute values for their average number of messages, this simplification will serve our purposes.

If we pick as the lock coordinator the site where the most locks are needed by the transaction, then we minimize the requirement for messages. The number of messages required is three times the number of database elements at the other sites.

19.6.3 Locking Replicated Elements

When an element X has replicas at several sites, we must be careful how we interpret the locking of X.

Example 19.21: Suppose there are two copies, X_1 and X_2, of a database element X. Suppose also that a transaction T gets a shared lock on the copy X_1 at the site of that copy, while transaction U gets an exclusive lock on the copy X_2 at its site. Now, U can change X_2 but cannot change X_1, resulting in the two copies of the element X becoming different. Moreover, since T and U may lock other elements as well, and the order in which they read and write

X is not forced by the locks they hold on the copies of X, there is also an opportunity for T and U to engage in unserializable behavior.   □

The problem illustrated by Example 19.21 is that when data is replicated, we must distinguish between getting a shared or exclusive lock on the logical element X and getting a local lock on a copy of X at the site of that copy. That is, in order to assure serializability, we need for transactions to take global locks on the logical elements. But the logical elements don't exist physically — only their copies do — and there is no global lock table. Thus, the only way that a transaction can obtain a global lock on X is to obtain local locks on one or more copies of X at the site(s) of those copies. We shall now consider methods for turning local locks into global locks that have the required properties:

- No two transactions can have a global exclusive lock on a logical element X at the same time.

- If a transaction has a global exclusive lock on logical element X, then no transaction can have a global shared lock on X.

- Any number of transactions can have global shared locks on X, as long as no transaction has a global exclusive lock.

19.6.4 Primary-Copy Locking

An improvement on the centralized locking approach is to distribute the function of the lock site, but still maintain the principle that each logical element has a single site responsible for its global lock. This distributed-lock method is called the *primary copy* method. This change avoids the possibility that the central lock site will become a bottleneck, while still maintaining the simplicity of the centralized method.

In the primary copy lock method, each logical element X has one of its copies designated the "primary copy." In order to get a lock on logical element X, a transaction sends a request to the site of the primary copy of X. The site of the primary copy maintains an entry for X in its lock table and grants or denies the request as appropriate. Again, global (logical) locks will be administered correctly as long as each site administers the locks for the primary copies correctly.

Also as with a centralized lock site, most lock requests generate three messages, except for those where the transaction and the primary copy are at the same site. However, if we choose primary copies wisely, then we expect that these sites will frequently be the same.

Example 19.22: In the chain-of-stores example, we should make each store's sales data have its primary copy at the store. Other copies of this data, such as at the central office or at a data warehouse used by sales analysts, are not primary copies. Probably, the typical transaction is executed at a store and updates only sales data for that store. No messages are needed when this type

---

Distributed Deadlocks

There are many opportunities for transactions to get deadlocked as they try to acquire global locks on replicated data. There are also many ways to construct a global waits-for graph and thus detect deadlocks. However, in a distributed environment, it is often simplest and also most effective to use a timeout. Any transaction that has not completed after an appropriate amount of time is assumed to have gotten deadlocked and is rolled back.

---

of transaction takes its locks. Only if the transaction examined or modified data at another store would lock-related messages be sent. □

19.6.5 Global Locks From Local Locks

Another approach is to synthesize global locks from collections of local locks. In these schemes, no copy of a database element X is "primary"; rather they are symmetric, and local shared or exclusive locks can be requested on any of these copies. The key to a successful global locking scheme is to require transactions to obtain a certain number of local locks on copies of X before the transaction can assume it has a global lock on X.

Suppose database element A has n copies. We pick two numbers:

1. s is the number of copies of A that must be locked in shared mode in order for a transaction to have a global shared lock on A.

2. x is the number of copies of A that must be locked in exclusive mode in order for a transaction to have an exclusive lock on A.

As long as $2x > n$ and $s + x > n$, we have the desired properties: there can be only one global exclusive lock on A, and there cannot be both a global shared and global exclusive lock on A. The explanation is as follows. Since $2x > n$, if two transactions had global exclusive locks on A, there would be at least one copy that had granted local exclusive locks to both (because there are more local exclusive locks granted than there are copies of A). However, then the local locking method would be incorrect. Similarly, since $s + x > n$, if one transaction had a global shared lock on A and another had a global exclusive lock on A, then some copy granted both local shared and exclusive locks at the same time.

In general, the number of messages needed to obtain a global shared lock is $3s$, and the number to obtain a global exclusive lock is $3x$. That number seems excessive, compared with centralized methods that require 3 or fewer messages per lock on the average. However, there are compensating arguments, as the following two examples of specific (s, x) choices shows.

- *Read-Locks-One; Write-Locks-All.* Here, $s = 1$ and $x = n$. Obtaining a global exclusive lock is very expensive, but a global shared lock requires three messages at the most. Moreover, this scheme has an advantage over the primary-copy method: while the latter allows us to avoid messages when we read the primary copy, the read-locks-one scheme allows us to avoid messages whenever the transaction is at the site of *any copy* of the database element we desire to read. Thus, this scheme can be superior when most transactions are read-only, but transactions to read an element X initiate at different sites. An example would be a distributed digital library that caches copies of documents where they are most frequently read.

- *Majority Locking.* Here, $s = x = \lceil (n+1)/2 \rceil$. It seems that this system requires many messages no matter where the transaction is. However, there are several other factors that may make this scheme acceptable. First, many network systems support *broadcast*, where it is possible for a transaction to send out one general request for local locks on an element X, which will be received by all sites. Similarly, the release of locks may be achieved by a single message. However, this selection of s and x provides an advantage others do not: it allows partial operation even when the network is disconnected. As long as there is one component of the network that contains a majority of the sites with copies of X, then it is possible for a transaction to obtain a lock on X. Even if other sites are active while disconnected, we know that they cannot even get a shared lock on X, and thus there is no risk that transactions running in different components of the network will engage in behavior that is not serializable.

19.6.6 Exercises for Section 19.6

! **Exercise 19.6.1 :** We showed how to create global shared and exclusive locks from local locks of that type. How would you create:

* a) Global shared, exclusive, and increment locks.

  b) Global shared, exclusive, and update locks.

!! c) Global shared, exclusive, and intention locks for each type.

from local locks of the same types?

Exercise 19.6.2 : Suppose there are five sites, each with a copy of a database element X. One of these sites P is the dominant site for X and will be used as X's primary site in a primary-copy distributed-lock system. The statistics regarding accesses to X are:

  i. 50% of all accesses are read-only accesses originating at P.

ii. Each of the other four sites originates 10% of the accesses, and these are read-only.

iii. The remaining 10% of accesses require exclusive access and may originate at any of the five sites with equal probability (i.e., 2% originate at each).

For each of the lock methods below, give the average number of messages needed to obtain a lock. Assume that all requests are granted, so no denial messages are needed.

* a) Read-locks-one; write-locks-all.

  b) Majority locking.

  c) Primary-copy locking, with the primary copy at P.

19.7 Long-Duration Transactions

There is a family of applications for which a database system is suitable for maintaining data, but the model of many short transactions on which database concurrency-control mechanisms are predicated, is inappropriate. In this section we shall examine some examples of these applications and the problems that arise. We then discuss a solution based on "compensating transactions" that negate the effects of transactions that were committed, but shouldn't have been.

19.7.1 Problems of Long Transactions

Roughly, a *long transaction* is one that takes too long to be allowed to hold locks that another transaction needs. Depending on the environment, "too long" could mean seconds, minutes, or hours; we shall assume that at least several minutes, and probably hours, are involved in "long" transactions. Three broad classes of applications that involve long transactions are:

1. *Conventional DBMS Applications.* While common database applications run mostly short transactions, many applications require occasional long transactions. For example, one transaction might examine all of a bank's accounts to verify that the total balance is correct. Another application may require that an index be reconstructed occasionally to keep performance at its peak.

2. *Design Systems.* Whether the thing being designed is mechanical like an automobile, electronic like a microprocessor, or a software system, the common element of design systems is that the design is broken into a set of components (e.g., files of a software project), and different designers work on different components simultaneously. We do not want two designers taking a copy of a file, editing it to make design changes, and then writing

the new file versions back, because then one set of changes would overwrite the other. Thus, a *check-out-check-in* system allows a designer to "check out" a file and check it in when the changes are finished, perhaps hours or days later. Even if the first designer is changing the file, another designer might want to look at the file to learn something about its contents. If the check-out operation were tantamount to an exclusive lock, then some reasonable and sensible actions would be delayed, possibly for days.

3. *Workflow Systems.* These systems involve collections of processes, some executed by software alone, some involving human interaction, and perhaps some involving human action alone. We shall give shortly an example of office paperwork involving the payment of a bill. Such applications may take days to perform, and during that entire time, some database elements may be subject to change. Were the system to grant an exclusive lock on data involved in a transaction, other transactions could be locked out for days.

Example 19.23 : Consider the problem of an employee vouchering travel expenses. The intent of the traveler is to be reimbursed from account A123, and the process whereby the payment is made is shown in Fig. 19.18. The process begins with action A_1, where the traveler's secretary fills out an on-line form describing the travel, the account to be charged, and the amount. We assume in this example that the account is A123, and the amount is $1000.

The traveler's receipts are sent physically to the departmental authorization office, while the form is sent on-line to an automated action A_2. This process checks that there is enough money in the charged account (A123) and reserves the money for expenditure; i.e., it tentatively deducts $1000 from the account but does not issue a check for that amount. If there is not enough money in the account, the transaction aborts, and presumably it will restart when either enough money is in the account or after changing the account to be charged.[5]

Action A_3 is performed by the departmental administrator, who examines the receipts and the on-line form. This action might take place the next day. If everything is in order, the form is approved and sent to the corporate administrator, along with the physical receipts. If not, the transaction is aborted. Presumably the traveler will be required to modify the request in some way and resubmit the form.

In action A_4, which may take place several days later, the corporate administrator either approves or denies the request, or passes the form to an assistant, who will then make the decision in action A_5. If the form is denied, the transaction again aborts and the form must be resubmitted. If the form is approved, then at action A_6 the check is written, and the deduction of $1000 from account A123 is finalized.

---

[5]Of course the traveler (who does not work for Stanford anyway) would *never* charge the travel inappropriately to another government contract, but would use an appropriate source of funds. We have to say this because government auditors, who have no clue about how a university should operate, are still swarming all over Stanford.

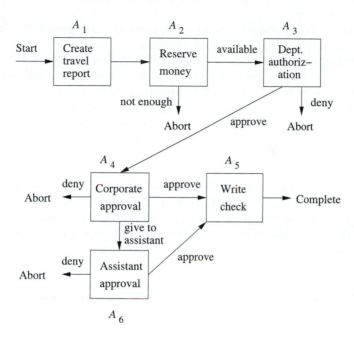

Figure 19.18: Workflow diagram for a traveler requesting expense reimbursement

However, suppose that the only way we could implement this workflow is by conventional locking. In particular, since the balance of account A123 may be changed by the complete transaction, it has to be locked exclusively at action A_2 and not unlocked until either the transaction aborts or action A_6 completes. This lock may have to be held for days, while the people charged with authorizing the payment get a chance to look at the matter. If so, then there can be no other charges made to account A123, even tentatively. On the other hand, if there are no controls at all over how account A123 can be accessed, then it is possible that several transactions will reserve or deduct money from the account simultaneously, leading to an overdraft. Thus, some compromise between rigid, long-term locks on one hand, and anarchy on the other, must be used. □

19.7.2 Sagas

A *saga* is a collection of actions, such as those of Example 19.23, that together form a long-duration "transaction." That is, a saga consists of:

1. A collection of actions.

2. A graph whose nodes are either actions or the special *Abort* and *Complete* nodes, and whose arcs link pairs of nodes. No arcs leave the two special nodes, which we call *terminal* nodes.

3. An indication of the node at which the action starts, called the *start node*.

The paths through the graph, from the start node to either of the terminal nodes, represent possible sequences of actions. Those paths that lead to the *Abort* node represent sequences of actions that cause the overall transaction to be rolled back, and these sequences of actions should leave the database unchanged. Paths to the *Complete* node represent successful sequences of actions, and all the changes to the database system that these actions perform will remain in the database.

Example 19.24: The paths in the graph of Fig. 19.18 that lead to the *Abort* node are: A_1A_2, $A_1A_2A_3$, $A_1A_2A_3A_4$, and $A_1A_2A_3A_4A_5$. The paths that lead to the *Complete* node are $A_1A_2A_3A_4A_6$, and $A_1A_2A_3A_4A_5A_6$. Notice that in this case the graph has no cycles, so there are a finite number of paths leading to a terminal node. However, in general, a graph can have cycles, in which case there may be an infinite number of paths. □

Concurrency control for sagas is managed by two facilities:

1. Each action may be considered itself a (short) transaction, that when executed uses a conventional concurrency-control mechanism, such as locking. For instance, A_2 may be implemented to (briefly) obtain a lock on account A123, decrement the amount indicated on the travel voucher, and release the lock. This locking prevents two transactions from trying to write new values of the account balance at the same time, thereby losing the effect of the first to write and making money "appear by magic."

2. The overall transaction, which can be any of the paths to a terminal node, is managed through the mechanism of "compensating transactions," which are inverses to the transactions at the nodes of the saga. Their job is to roll back the effect of a committed action in a way that does not depend on what has happened to the database between the time the action was executed and the time the compensating transaction is executed. We discuss compensating transactions in the next section.

19.7.3   Compensating Transactions

In a saga, each action A has a *compensating transaction*, which we denote A^{-1}. Intuitively, if we execute A, and later execute A^{-1}, then the resulting database state is the same as if neither A nor A^{-1} had executed. More formally:

- If D is any database state, and $B_1B_2\cdots B_n$ is any sequence of actions and compensating transactions (whether from the saga in question or any other saga or transaction that may legally execute on the database) then the same database states result from running the sequences $B_1B_2\cdots B_n$ and $AB_1B_2\cdots B_nA^{-1}$ on the database state D.

When are Database States "The Same"?

When discussing compensating transactions, we should be careful about what it means to return the database to "the same" state that it had before. We had a taste of the problem when we discussed logical logging for B-trees in Example 19.8. There we saw that if we "undid" an operation, the state of the B-tree might not be identical to the state before the operation, but would be equivalent to it as far as access operations on the B-tree were concerned. More generally, executing an action and its compensating transaction might not restore the database to a state literally identical to what existed before, but the differences must not be detectable by whatever application programs the database supports.

If a saga execution leads to the *Abort* node, then we roll back the saga by executing the compensating transactions for each executed action, in the reverse order of those actions. By the property of compensating transactions stated above, the effect of the saga is negated, and the database state is the same as if it had never happened. An explanation why the effect is guaranteed to be negated is given in Section 19.7.4

Example 19.25: Let us consider the actions in Fig. 19.18 and see what the compensating transactions for A_1 through A_6 might be. First, A_1 creates an on-line document. If the document is stored in the database, then A_1^{-1} must remove it from the database. Notice that this compensation obeys the fundamental property for compensating transactions: If we create the document, do any sequence of actions α (including deletion of the document if we wish), then the effect of $A_1 \alpha A_1^{-1}$ is the same as the effect of α.

A_2 must be implemented carefully. We "reserve" the money by deducting it from the account. The money will stay removed unless restored by the compensating transaction A_2^{-1}. We claim that this A_2^{-1} is a correct compensating transaction if the usual rules for how accounts may be managed are followed. To appreciate the point, it is useful to consider a similar transaction where the obvious compensation will not work; we consider such a case in Example 19.26, next.

The actions A_3, A_4, and A_5 each involve adding an approval to a form. Thus, their compensating transactions can remove that approval.[6]

Finally, A_6, which writes the check, does not have an obvious compensating transaction. In practice none is needed, because once A_6 is executed, this saga cannot be rolled back. However, technically A_6 does not affect the database

---

[6]In the saga of Fig. 19.18, the only time these actions are compensated is when we are going to delete the form anyway, but the definition of compensating transactions require that they work in isolation, regardless of whether some other compensating transaction was going to make their changes irrelevant.

anyway, since the money for the check was deducted by A_2. Should we need to consider the "database" as the larger world, where effects such as cashing a check affected the database, then we would have to design A_6^{-1} to first try to cancel the check, next write a letter to the payee demanding the money back, and if all remedies failed, restoring the money to the account by declaring a loss due to a bad debt. □

Next, let us take up the example, alluded to in Example 19.25, where a change to an account cannot be compensated by an inverse change. The problem is that accounts normally are not allowed to go negative.

Example 19.26: Suppose B is a transaction that adds $1000 to an account that has $2000 in it initially, and B^{-1} is the compensating transaction that removes the same amount of money. Also, it is reasonable to assume that transactions may fail if they try to delete money from an account and the balance would thereby become negative. Let C be a transaction that deletes $2500 from the same account. Then $BCB^{-1} \not\equiv C$. The reason is that C by itself fails, and leaves the account with $2000, while if we execute B then C, the account is left with $500, whereupon B^{-1} fails.

Our conclusion that a saga with arbitrary transfers among accounts and a rule about accounts never being allowed to go negative cannot be supported simply by compensating transactions. Some modification to the system must be done, e.g., allowing negative balances in accounts. □

19.7.4   Why Compensating Transactions Work

Let us say that two sequences of actions are *equivalent* ($\equiv$) if they take any database state D to the same state. The fundamental assumption about compensating transactions can be stated:

- If A is any action and α is any sequence of legal actions and compensating transactions, then $A\alpha A^{-1} \equiv \alpha$.

Now, we need to show that if a saga execution $A_1 A_2 \cdots A_n$ is followed by its compensating transactions in reverse order, $A_n^{-1} \cdots A_2^{-1} A_1^{-1}$, with any intervening actions whatsoever, then the effect is as if neither the actions nor the compensating transactions executed. The proof is an induction on n.

BASIS: If $n = 1$, then the sequence of all actions between A_1 and its compensating transaction A_1^{-1} looks like $A_1 \alpha A_1^{-1}$. By the fundamental assumption about compensating transactions, $A_1 \alpha A_1^{-1} \equiv \alpha$; i.e., there is no effect on the database state by the saga.

INDUCTION: Assume the statement for paths of up to $n - 1$ actions, and consider a path of n actions, followed by its compensating transactions in reverse order, with any other transactions intervening. The sequence looks like

$$A_1 \alpha_1 A_2 \alpha_2 \cdots \alpha_{n-1} A_n \beta A_n^{-1} \gamma_{n-1} \cdots \gamma_2 A_2^{-1} \gamma_1 A_1^{-1} \qquad (19.1)$$

where all Greek letters represent sequences of zero or more actions. By the definition of compensating transaction, $A_n\beta A_n^{-1} \equiv \beta$. Thus, (19.1) is equivalent to

$$A_1\alpha_1 A_2\alpha_2 \cdots A_{n-1}\alpha_{n-1}\beta\gamma_{n-1}A_{n-1}^{-1}\gamma_{n-2}\cdots\gamma_2 A_2^{-1}\gamma_1 A_1^{-1} \tag{19.2}$$

By the inductive hypothesis, expression (19.2) is equivalent to

$$\alpha_1\alpha_2 \cdots \alpha_{n-1}\beta\gamma_{n-1}\cdots\gamma_2\gamma_1$$

since there are only $n - 1$ actions in (19.2). That is, the saga and its compensation leave the database state the same as if the saga had never occurred.

19.7.5 Exercises for Section 19.7

*! **Exercise 19.7.1:** The process of "uninstalling" software can be thought of as a compensating transaction for the action of installing the same software. In a simple model of installing and uninstalling, suppose that an action consists of *loading* one or more files from the source (e.g., a CD-ROM) onto the hard disk of the machine. To load a file f, we copy f from CD-ROM, replacing the file with the same path name f, if there was one. To distinguish files with the same path name, we may assume each file has a timestamp.

    a) What is the compensating transaction for the action that loads file f? Consider both the case where no file with that path name existed, and where there was a file f' with the same path name.

    b) Explain why your answer to (a) is guaranteed to compensate. *Hint*: Consider carefully the case where after replacing f' by f, a later action replaces f by another file with the same path name.

! **Exercise 19.7.2:** Describe the process of booking an airline seat as a saga. Consider the possibility that the customer will query about a seat but not book it. The customer may book the seat, but cancel it, or not pay for the seat within the required time limit. The customer may or may not show up for the flight. For each action, describe the corresponding compensating transaction.

19.8 Summary of Chapter 19

    ✦ *Dirty Data*: Data that has been written, either into main-memory buffers or on disk, by a transaction that has not yet committed is called "dirty."

    ✦ *Cascading Rollback*: A combination of logging and concurrency control that allows a transaction to read dirty data may have to roll back transactions that read such data from a transaction that later aborts.

✦ *Strict Locking*: The strict locking policy requires transactions to hold their locks (except for shared-locks) until not only have they committed, but the commit record on the log has been flushed to disk. Strict locking guarantees that no transaction can read dirty data, even retrospectively after a crash and recovery.

✦ *Group Commit*: We can relax the strict-locking condition that requires commit records to reach disk if we assure that log records are written to disk in the order that they are written. There is still then a guarantee of no dirty reads, even if a crash and recovery occurs.

✦ *Restoring Database State After an Abort*: If a transaction aborts but has written values to buffers, then we can restore old values either from the log or from the disk copy of the database. If the new values have reached disk, then the log may still be used to restore the old value.

✦ *Logical Logging*: For large database elements such as disk blocks, it saves much space if we record old and new values on the log incrementally, that is, by indicating only the changes. In some cases, recording changes logically, that is, in terms of an abstraction of what blocks contain, allows us to restore state logically after a transaction abort, even if it is impossible to restore the state literally.

✦ *View Serializability*: When transactions may write values that are overwritten without being read, conflict serializability is too strong a condition on schedules. A weaker condition, called view serializability requires only that in the equivalent serial schedule, each transaction reads the value from the same source as in the original schedule.

✦ *Polygraphs*: The test for view serializability involves constructing a polygraph, with arcs representing writer-to-reader passing of values, and arc pairs that represent requirements that a certain write not intervene between a writer-reader connection. The schedule is view serializable if and only if selection of one arc from each pair results in an acyclic graph.

✦ *Deadlocks*: These may occur whenever transactions have to wait for a resource, such as a lock, held by another transaction. The risk is that, without proper planning, a cycle of waits may occur, and no transaction in the cycle is able to make progress.

✦ *Waits-For Graphs*: Create a node for each waiting transaction, with an arc to the transaction it is waiting for. The existence of a deadlock is the same as the existence of one or more cycles in the waits-for graph. We can avoid deadlocks if we maintain the waits-for graph and abort any transaction whose waiting would cause a cycle.

✦ *Deadlock Avoidance by Ordering Resources*: Requiring transactions to acquire resources according to some lexicographic order of the resources will prevent a deadlock from arising.

◆ *Timestamp-Based Deadlock Avoidance*: Other schemes maintain a time-stamp and base their abort/wait decision on whether the requesting transaction is newer or older than the one with the resource it wants. In the wait-die scheme, an older requesting transaction waits, and a newer one is rolled back with the same timestamp. In the wound-wait scheme, a newer transaction waits and an older one forces the transaction with the resource to roll back and give up the resource.

◆ *Distributed Data*: In a distributed database, data may be partitioned horizontally (one relation has its tuples spread over several sites) or vertically (a relation's schema is decomposed into several schemas whose relations are at different sites). It is also possible to replicate data, so presumably identical copies of a relation exist at several sites.

◆ *Distributed Transactions*: In a distributed database, one logical transaction may consist of components, each executing at a different site. To preserve consistency, these components must all agree on whether to commit or abort the logical transaction.

◆ *Two-Phase Commit*: This approach supports an agreement among transaction components whether to commit or abort, often allowing a resolution even in the face of a system crash. In the first phase, a coordinator component polls the components whether they want to commit or abort. In the second phase, the coordinator tells the components to commit if and only if all have expressed a willingness to commit.

◆ *Distributed Locks*: If transactions must lock database elements found at several sites, a method must be found to coordinate these locks. In the centralized-site method, one site maintains locks on all elements. In the primary-copy method, the home site for an element maintains its locks.

◆ *Locking Replicated Data*: When database elements are replicated at several sites, global locks on an element must be obtained through locks on one or more replicas. The majority locking method requires a read- or write-lock on a majority of the replicas to obtain a global lock. Alternatively, we may allow a global read lock by obtaining a read lock on any copy, while allowing a global write lock only through write locks on every copy.

◆ *Sagas*: When transactions involve long-duration steps that may take hours or days, conventional locking mechanisms may limit concurrency too much. A saga consists of a network of actions, each of which may lead to one or more other actions, to the completion of the entire saga, or to a requirement that the saga abort.

◆ *Compensating Transactions*: For a saga to make sense, each action must have a compensating action that will undo the effects of the first action on the database state, while leaving intact any other actions that have been made by other sagas that have completed or are currently in operation. If a saga aborts, the appropriate sequence of compensating actions is executed.

19.9   References for Chapter 19

Some useful general sources for topics covered here are [2], [1], and [10]. The material on logical logging follows [9]. View serializability and the polygraph test is from [11].

Deadlock-prevention was surveyed in [7]; the waits-for graph is from there. The wait-die and wound-wait schemes are from [12].

The two-phase commit protocol was proposed in [8]. A more powerful scheme (not covered here) called three-phase commit is from [13]. The leader-election aspect of recovery was examined in [4].

Distributed locking methods have been proposed by [3] (the centralized locking method) [14] (primary-copy) and [15] (global locks from locks on copies).

Long transactions were introduced by [6]. Sagas were described in [5].

1. N. S. Barghouti and G. E. Kaiser, "Concurrency control in advanced database applications," *Computing Surveys* **23**:3 (Sept., 1991), pp. 269–318.

2. S. Ceri and G. Pelagatti, *Distributed Databases: Principles and Systems*, McGraw-Hill, New York, 1984.

3. H. Garcia-Molina, "Performance comparison of update algorithms for distributed databases," TR Nos. 143 and 146, Computer Systems Laboratory, Stanford Univ., 1979.

4. H. Garcia-Molina, "Elections in a distributed computer system," *IEEE Trans. on Computers* **C-31**:1 (1982), pp. 48–59.

5. H. Garcia-Molina and K. Salem, "Sagas," *Proc. ACM SIGMOD Intl. Conf. on Management of Data* (1987), pp. 249–259.

6. J. N. Gray, "The transaction concept: virtues and limitations," *Proc. Intl. Conf. on Very Large Databases* (1981), pp. 144–154.

7. R. C. Holt, "Some deadlock properties of computer systems," *Computing Surveys* **4**:3 (1972), pp. 179–196.

8. B. Lampson and H. Sturgis, "Crash recovery in a distributed data storage system," Technical report, Xerox Palo Alto Research Center, 1976.

9. C. Mohan, D. J. Haderle, B. G. Lindsay, H. Pirahesh, and P. Schwarz, "ARIES: a transaction recovery method supporting fine-granularity locking and partial rollbacks using write-ahead logging," *ACM Trans. on Database Systems* **17**:1 (1992), pp. 94–162.

10. M. T. Ozsu and P. Valduriez, *Principles of Distributed Database Systems*, Prentice-Hall, Englewood Cliffs NJ, 1999.

11. C. H. Papadimitriou, "The serializability of concurrent updates," *J. ACM* **26**:4 (1979), pp. 631–653.

12. D. J. Rosenkrantz, R. E. Stearns, and P. M. Lewis II, "System-level concurrency control for distributed database systems," *ACM Trans. on Database Systems* **3**:2 (1978), pp. 178–198.

13. D. Skeen, "Nonblocking commit protocols," *Proc. ACM SIGMOD Intl. Conf. on Management of Data* (1981), pp. 133–142.

14. M. Stonebraker, "Retrospection on a database system," *ACM Trans. on Database Systems* **5**:2 (1980), pp. 225–240.

15. R. H. Thomas, "A majority consensus approach to concurrency control," *ACM Trans. on Database Systems* **4**:2 (1979), pp. 180–219.

Chapter 20

Information Integration

While there are many directions in which modern database systems are evolving, a large family of new applications fall under the general heading of *information integration*. Such applications take data that is stored in two or more databases (*information sources*) and build from them one large database, possibly virtual, containing information from all the sources, so the data can be queried as a unit. The sources may be conventional databases or other types of information, such as collections of Web pages.

In this chapter, we shall introduce important aspects of information integration. We begin with an outline of the principal approaches to integration: federation, warehousing, and mediation. Then, we examine wrappers, the sofware that allows information sources to conform to some shared schema. Information-integration systems require special kinds of query optimization techniques for their efficient operation, and we briefly examine capability-based optimization, an important technique not often found in conventional DBMS's.

We look at the kinds of applications that make use of integrated information. Especially important are "OLAP" (on-line analytic processing) queries and "data-mining" queries; these types of queries are among the most complex queries that are run on databases of any kind. A specialized database architecture, called the "data cube," is introduced as a way to organize the integrated data in some applications and help support OLAP and data-mining queries.

20.1 Modes of Information Integration

There are several ways that databases or other distributed information sources can be made to work together. In this section, we consider the three most common approaches:

1. *Federated databases.* The sources are independent, but one source can call on others to supply information.

2. *Warehousing.* Copies of data from several sources are stored in a single database, called a (*data*) *warehouse*. Possibly, the data stored at the warehouse is first processed in some way before storage; e.g., data may be filtered, and relations may be joined or aggregated. The warehouse is updated periodically, perhaps overnight. As the data is copied from the sources, it may need to be transformed in certain ways to make all data conform to the schema at the warehouse.

3. *Mediation.* A mediator is a software component that supports a *virtual database*, which the user may query as if it were *materialized* (physically constructed, like a warehouse). The mediator stores no data of its own. Rather, it translates the user's query into one or more queries to its sources. The mediator then synthesizes the answer to the user's query from the responses of those sources, and returns the answer to the user.

We shall introduce each of these approaches in turn. One of the key issues for all approaches is the way that data is transformed when it is extracted from an information source. We discuss the architecture of such transformers, called *wrappers* or *extractors*, in Section 20.2. Section 20.1.1 first introduces some of the problems that wrappers are designed to solve.

20.1.1 Problems of Information Integration

Whatever integration architecture we choose, there are subtle problems that come up when trying to attach meaning to the raw data in the various sources. We refer to (collections of) sources that deal with the same kind of data, yet differ in various subtle ways, as *heterogeneous* sources. An extended example will help expose the issues.

Example 20.1 : The Aardvark Automobile Co. has 1000 dealers, each of which maintains a database of their cars in stock. Aardvark wants to create an integrated database containing the information of all 1000 sources.[1] The integrated database will help dealers locate a particular model if they don't have one in stock. It also can be used by corporate analysts to predict the market and adjust production to provide the models most likely to sell.

However, the 1000 dealers do not all use the same database schema. For example, one dealer might store cars in a single relation that looks like:

```
Cars(serialNo, model, color, autoTrans, cdPlayer,...)
```

with one boolean-valued attribute for every possible option. Another dealer might use a schema in which options are separated out into a second relation, such as:

---

[1]Most real automobile companies have similar facilities in place, and the history of their development may be different from our example; e.g., the centralized database may have come first, with dealers later able to download relevant portions to their own database. However, this scenario serves as an example of what companies in many industries are attempting today.

```
Autos(serial, model, color)
Options(serial, option)
```

Notice that not only is the schema different, but apparently equivalent names have changed: `Cars` becomes `Autos`, and `serialNo` becomes `serial`.

To make matters worse, the data in the various databases, while having the same meaning, can be represented in many different ways.

1. *Data type differences.* Serial numbers might be represented by character strings of varying length at one source and fixed length at another. The fixed lengths could differ, and some sources might use integers rather than character strings.

2. *Value differences.* The same concept might be represented by different constants at different sources. The color black might be represented by an integer code at one source, the string `BLACK` at another, and the code `BL` at a third. The code `BL` might stand for "blue" at yet another source.

3. *Semantic differences.* Terms may be given different interpretations at different sources. One dealer might include trucks in the `Cars` relation, while another puts only automobile data in the `Cars` relation. One dealer might distinguish station wagons from minivans, while another doesn't.

4. *Missing values.* A source might not record information of a type that all or most of the other sources provide. For instance, one dealer might not record colors at all. To deal with missing values, sometimes we can use `NULL`'s or default values. However, a modern trend is to use "semistructured" data, as described in Section 4.6, to represent integrated data that may not conform exactly.

Each of these inconsistencies among sources requires a form of translation that must be implemented before the integrated database can be built. □

20.1.2 Federated Database Systems

Perhaps the simplest architecture for integrating several databases is to implement one-to-one connections between all pairs of databases that need to talk to one another. These connections allow one database system D_1 to query another D_2 in terms that D_2 can understand. The problem with this architecture is that if n databases each need to talk to the $n-1$ other databases, then we must write $n(n-1)$ pieces of code to support queries between systems. The situation is suggested in Fig. 20.1. There, we see four databases in a federation. Each of the four needs three components, one to access each of the other three databases.

Nevertheless, a federated system may be the easiest to build in some circumstances, especially when the communications between databases are limited in nature. An example will show how the translation components might work.

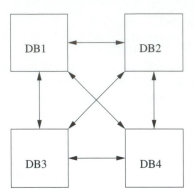

Figure 20.1: A federated collection of four databases needs 12 components to translate queries from one to another

Example 20.2 : Suppose the Aardvark Automobile dealers want to share inventory, but each dealer only needs to query the database of a few local dealers to see if they have a needed car. To be specific, consider Dealer 1, who has a relation

        NeededCars(model, color, autoTrans)

whose tuples represent cars that customers have requested, by model, color, and whether or not they want an automatic transmission. Dealer 2 stores inventory in the two-relation schema discussed in Example 20.1:

        Autos(serial, model, color)
        Options(serial, option)

Dealer 1 writes an application program that queries Dealer 2 remotely for cars that match each of the cars described in NeededCars. Figure 20.2 is a sketch of a program with embedded SQL that would find the desired cars. The intent is that the embedded SQL represents remote queries to the Dealer 2 database, with results returned to Dealer 1. We use the convention from standard SQL of prefixing a colon to variables that represent constants retrieved from a database.

    These queries address the schema of Dealer 2. If Dealer 1 also wants to ask the same question of Dealer 3, who uses the first schema discussed in Example 20.1, with a single relation

        Cars(serialNo, model, color, autoTrans,...)

the query would look quite different. But each query works properly for the database to which it is addressed.   □

```
for(each tuple (:m, :c, :a) in NeededCars) {
    if(:a= TRUE) { /* automatic transmission wanted */
        SELECT serial
        FROM Autos, Options
        WHERE Autos.serial = Options.serial AND
              Options.option = 'autoTrans' AND
              Autos.model = :m AND
              Autos.color = :c;
    }
    else { /* automatic transmission not wanted */
        SELECT serial
        FROM Autos
        WHERE Autos.model = :m AND
              Autos.color = :c AND
              NOT EXISTS (
                  SELECT *
                  FROM Options
                  WHERE serial = Autos.serial AND
                        option = 'autoTrans'
              );
    }
}
```

Figure 20.2: Dealer 1 queries Dealer 2 for needed cars

20.1.3 Data Warehouses

In the *data warehouse* integration architecture, data from several sources is extracted and combined into a *global* schema. The data is then stored at the warehouse, which looks to the user like an ordinary database. The arrangement is suggested by Fig. 20.3, although there may be many more than the two sources shown.

Once the data is in the warehouse, queries may be issued by the user exactly as they would be issued to any database. On the other hand, user updates to the warehouse generally are forbidden, since they are not reflected in the underlying sources, and can make the warehouse inconsistent with the sources.

There are at least three approaches to constructing the data in the warehouse:

1. The warehouse is periodically reconstructed from the current data in the sources. This approach is the most common, with reconstruction occurring once a night (when the system can be shut down so queries aren't issued while the warehouse is being constructed), or at even longer intervals. The main disadvantages are the requirement of shutting down

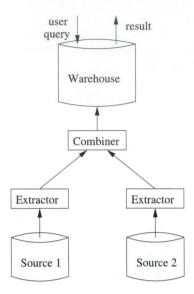

Figure 20.3: A data warehouse stores integrated information in a separate database

the warehouse, and the fact that sometimes reconstructing the warehouse can take longer than a typical "night." For some applications, another disadvantage is that the data in the warehouse can become seriously out of date.

2. The warehouse is updated periodically (e.g., each night), based on the changes that have been made to the sources since the last time the warehouse was modified. This approach can involve smaller amounts of data, which is very important if the warehouse needs to be modified in a short period of time, and the warehouse is large (multigigabyte and terabyte warehouses are in use). The disadvantage is that calculating changes to the warehouse, a process called *incremental update*, is complex, compared with algorithms that simply construct the warehouse from scratch.

3. The warehouse is changed immediately, in response to each change or a small set of changes at one or more of the sources. This approach requires too much communication and processing to be practical for all but small warehouses whose underlying sources change slowly. However, it is a subject of research, and a successful warehouse implementation of this type would have a number of important applications.

Example 20.3 : Suppose for simplicity that there are only two dealers in the Aardvark system, and they respectively use the schemas

```
Cars(serialNo, model, color, autoTrans, cdPlayer,...)
```

and

```
Autos(serial, model, color)
Options(serial, option)
```

We wish to create a warehouse with the schema

```
AutosWhse(serialNo, model, color, autoTrans, dealer)
```

That is, the global schema is like that of the first dealer, but we record only the option of having an automatic transmission, and we include an attribute that tells which dealer has the car.

The software that extracts data from the two dealers' databases and populates the global schema can be written as SQL queries. The query for the first dealer is simple:

```
INSERT INTO AutosWhse(serialNo, model, color,
        autoTrans, dealer)
    SELECT serialNo, model, color, autoTrans, 'dealer1'
    FROM Cars;
```

The extractor for the second dealer is more complex, since we have to decide whether or not a given car has an automatic transmission. We use the strings 'yes' and 'no' as values of the attribute autoTrans, with the obvious meanings. The SQL code for this extractor is shown in Fig. 20.4.

In this simple example, the combiner, shown in Fig. 20.3, for the data extracted from the sources is not needed. Since the warehouse is the union of the relations extracted from each source, the data may be loaded directly into the warehouse. However, many warehouses perform operations on the relations that they extract from each source. For instance relations extracted from two sources might be joined, and the result put at the warehouse. Or we might take the union of relations extracted from several sources and then aggregate the data of this union. More generally, several relations may be extracted from each source, and different relations combined in different ways. □

20.1.4 Mediators

A mediator supports a virtual view, or collection of views, that integrates several sources in much the same way that the materialized relation(s) in a warehouse integrate sources. However, since the mediator doesn't store any data, the mechanics of mediators and warehouses are rather different. Figure 20.5 shows a mediator integrating two sources; as for warehouses. there would typically be more than two sources. To begin, the user issues a query to the mediator. Since the mediator has no data of its own, it must get the relevant data from its sources and use that data to form the answer to the user's query.

Thus, we see in Fig. 20.5 the mediator sending a query to each of its wrappers, which in turn send queries to their corresponding sources. The mediator

```
INSERT INTO AutosWhse(serialNo, model, color,
        autoTrans, dealer)
    SELECT serial, model, color, 'yes', 'dealer2'
    FROM Autos, Options
    WHERE Autos.serial = Options.serial AND
            option = 'autoTrans';

INSERT INTO AutosWhse(serialNo, model, color,
        autoTrans, dealer)
    SELECT serial, model, color, 'no', 'dealer2'
    FROM Autos
    WHERE NOT EXISTS (
        SELECT *
        FROM Options
        WHERE serial = Autos.serial AND
                option = 'autoTrans'
    );
```

Figure 20.4: Extractor for translating Dealer-2 data to the warehouse

may send several queries to a wrapper, and may not query all wrappers. The results come back and are combined at the mediator; we do not show an explicit combiner component as we did in the warehouse diagram, Fig. 20.3, because in the case of the mediator, the combining of results from the sources is one of the tasks performed by the mediator.

Example 20.4: Let us consider a scenario similar to that of Example 20.3, but use a mediator. That is, the mediator integrates the same two automobile sources into a view that is a single relation with schema:

```
AutosMed(serialNo, model, color, autoTrans, dealer)
```

Suppose the user asks the mediator about red cars, with the query:

```
SELECT serialNo, model
FROM AutosMed
WHERE color = 'red';
```

The mediator, in response to this user query, can forward the same query to each of the two wrappers. The way that wrappers can be designed and implemented to handle queries like this one is the subject of Section 20.2, and for more complex scenarios, translation and distribution of query components by the mediator could be necessary. However, in this case, the translation work can be done by the wrappers alone.

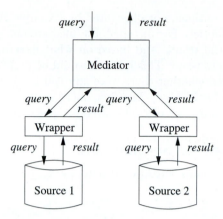

Figure 20.5: A mediator and wrappers translate queries into the terms of the sources and combine the answers

The wrapper for Dealer 1 translates the query into the terms of that dealer's schema, which we recall is

```
Cars(serialNo, model, color, autoTrans, cdPlayer,...)
```

A suitable translation is:

```
SELECT serialNo, model
FROM Cars
WHERE color = 'red';
```

An answer, which is a set of `serialNo-model` pairs, will be returned to the mediator by the first wrapper.

At the same time, the wrapper for Dealer 2 translates the same query into the schema of that dealer, which is:

```
Autos(serial, model, color)
Options(serial, option)
```

A suitable translated query for Dealer 2 is almost the same:

```
SELECT serial, model
FROM Autos
WHERE color = 'red';
```

It differs from the query at Dealer 1 only in the name of the relation queried, and in one attribute. The second wrapper returns to the mediator a set of `serial-model` pairs, which the mediator interprets as `serialNo-model` pairs.

The mediator takes the union of these sets and returns the result to the user. Since we expect the serial number to be a "global key," with no two cars, even in different databases, having the same serial number, we may take the bag union, assuming that there will not be duplicates anyway. □

There are several options, not illustrated by Example 20.4, that a mediator may use to answer queries. For instance, the mediator may issue one query to one source, look at the result, and based on what is returned, decide on the next query or queries to issue. This method would be appropriate, for instance, if the user query asked whether there were any Aardvark "Gobi" model sport-utility vehicles available in blue. The first query could ask Dealer 1, and only if the result was an empty set of tuples would a query be sent to Dealer 2.

20.1.5 Exercises for Section 20.1

! **Exercise 20.1.1:** Computer company A keeps data about the PC models it sells in the schema:

```
Computers(number, proc, speed, memory, hd)
Monitors(number, screen, maxResX, maxResY)
```

For instance, the tuple $(123, \mathtt{PIII}, 1000, 128, 40)$ in `Computers` means that model 123 has a Pentium-III processor running at 1000 megahertz, with 128M of memory and a 40G hard disk. The tuple $(456, 19, 1600, 1200)$ in `Monitors` means that model 456 has a 19-inch screen with a maximum resolution of 1600×1200.

Computer company B only sells complete systems, consisting of a computer and monitor. Its schema is

```
Systems(id, processor, mem, disk, screenSize)
```

The attribute `processor` is an integer speed; the type of processor (e.g., Pentium-III) is not recorded. Neither is the maximum resolution of the monitor recorded. Attributes `id`, `mem`, and `disk` are analogous to `number`, `memory`, and `hd` from company A, but the disk size is measured in megabytes instead of gigabytes.

a) If company A wants to insert into its relations information about the corresponding items from B, what SQL insert statements should it use?

* b) If Company B wants to insert into `Systems` as much information about the systems that can be built from computers and monitors made by A, what SQL statements best allow this information to be obtained?

*! **Exercise 20.1.2:** Suggest a global schema that would allow us to maintain as much information as we could about the products sold by companies A and B of Exercise 20.1.1.

Exercise 20.1.3: Write SQL queries to gather the information from the data at companies A and B and put it in a warehouse with your global schema of Exercise 20.1.2. You may consult the solutions for the global schema if you wish.

Exercise 20.1.4: Suppose your global schema from Exercise 20.1.2 (or the schema in the solutions if you don't like your own answer) is used at a mediator. How would the mediator process the query that asks for the maximum amount of hard-disk available with any computer with a 1500 megahertz processor speed?

! **Exercise 20.1.5:** Suggest two other schemas that computer companies might use to hold data like that of Exercise 20.1.1. How would you integrate your schemas into your global schema from Exercise 20.1.2?

! **Exercise 20.1.6:** In Example 20.3 we talked about a relation `Cars` at Dealer 1 that conveniently had an attribute `autoTrans` with only the values "yes" and "no." Since these were the same values used for that attribute in the global schema, the construction of relation `AutosWhse` was especially easy. Suppose instead that the attribute `Cars.autoTrans` has values that are integers, with 0 meaning no automatic transmission, and $i > 0$ meaning that the car has an i-speed automatic transmission. Show how the translation from `Cars` to `AutosWhse` could be done by an SQL query.

Exercise 20.1.7: How would the mediator of Example 20.4 translate the following queries?

* a) Find the serial numbers of cars with automatic transmission.

   b) Find the serial numbers of cars without automatic transmission.

! c) Find the serial numbers of the blue cars from Dealer 1.

Exercise 20.1.8: Go to the Web pages of several on-line booksellers, and see what information about this book you can find. How would you combine this information into a global schema suitable for a warehouse or mediator?

20.2 Wrappers in Mediator-Based Systems

In a data warehouse system like that of Fig. 20.3, the source extractors consist of:

1. One or more queries built-in that are executed at the source to produce data for the warehouse.

2. Suitable communication mechanisms, so the wrapper (extractor) can:

   (a) Pass ad-hoc queries to the source,

   (b) Receive responses from the source, and

   (c) Pass information to the warehouse.

The built-in queries to the source could be SQL queries if the source is an SQL database as in our examples of Section 20.1. Queries could also be operations in whatever language was appropriate for a source that was not a database system; e.g., the wrapper could fill out an on-line form at a Web page, issue a query to an on-line bibliography service in that system's own, specialized language, or use myriad other notations to pose the queries.

However, mediator systems require more complex wrappers than do most warehouse systems. The wrapper must be able to accept a variety of queries from the mediator and translate any of them to the terms of the source. Of course, the wrapper must then communicate the result to the mediator, just as a wrapper in a warehouse system communicates with the warehouse. In the balance of this section, we study the construction of flexible wrappers that are suitable for use with a mediator.

20.2.1 Templates for Query Patterns

A systematic way to design a wrapper that connects a mediator to a source is to classify the possible queries that the mediator can ask into *templates*, which are queries with parameters that represent constants. The mediator can provide the constants, and the wrapper executes the query with the given constants. An example should illustrate the idea; it uses the notation T => S to express the idea that the template T is turned by the wrapper into the source query S.

Example 20.5 : Suppose we want to build a wrapper for the source of Dealer 1, which has the schema

```
Cars(serialNo, model, color, autoTrans, cdPlayer,...)
```

for use by a mediator with schema

```
AutosMed(serialNo, model, color, autoTrans, dealer)
```

Consider how the mediator could ask the wrapper for cars of a given color. Whatever the color was, if we denote the code representing that color by the parameter $c, then we can use the template shown in Fig. 20.6.

Similarly, the wrapper could have another template that specified only the parameter $m representing a model, yet another template in which it was only specified whether an automatic transmission was wanted, and so on. In this case, there are eight choices, if queries are allowed to specify any of three attributes: model, color, and autoTrans. In general, there would be 2^n templates if we have the option of specifying n attributes.[2] Other templates would

---

[2] If the source is a database that can be queried in SQL, as in our example, you would rightly expect that one template could handle any number of attributes equated to constants, simply by making the WHERE clause a parameter. While that approach will work for SQL sources and queries that only bind attributes to constants, we could not necessarily use the same idea with an arbitrary source, such as a Web site that allowed only certain forms as an interface. In the general case, we cannot assume that the way we translate one query resembles at all the way similar queries are translated.

```
SELECT *
FROM AutosMed
WHERE color = '$c';
    =>
SELECT serialNo, model, color, autoTrans, 'dealer1'
FROM Cars
WHERE color = '$c';
```

Figure 20.6: A wrapper template describing queries for cars of a fixed color

be needed to deal with queries that asked for the total number of cars of certain types, or whether there exists a car of a certain type. The number of templates could grow unreasonably large, but some simplifications are possible by adding more sophistication to the wrapper, as we shall discuss starting in Section 20.2.3. □

20.2.2 Wrapper Generators

The templates defining a wrapper must be turned into code for the wrapper itself. The software that creates the wrapper is called a *wrapper generator*; it is similar in spirit to the parser generators (e.g., YACC) that produce components of a compiler from high-level specifications. The process, suggested in Fig. 20.7, begins when a specification, that is, a collection of templates, is given to the wrapper generator.

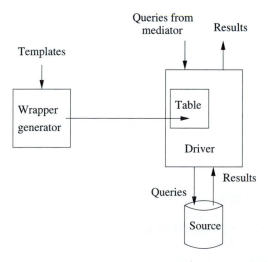

Figure 20.7: A wrapper generator produces tables for a driver; the driver and tables constitute the wrapper

The wrapper generator creates a table that holds the various query patterns contained in the templates, and the source queries that are associated with each. A *driver* is used in each wrapper; in general the driver can be the same for each generated wrapper. The task of the driver is to:

1. Accept a query from the mediator. The communication mechanism may be mediator-specific and is given to the driver as a "plug-in," so the same driver can be used in systems that communicate differently.

2. Search the table for a template that matches the query. If one is found, then the parameter values from the query are used to instantiate a source query. If there is no matching template, the wrapper responds negatively to the mediator.

3. The source query is sent to the source, again using a "plug-in" communication mechanism. The response is collected by the wrapper.

4. The response is processed by the wrapper, if necessary, and then returned to the mediator. The next sections discuss how wrappers can support a larger class of queries by processing results.

20.2.3 Filters

Suppose that a wrapper on a car dealer's database has the template shown in Fig. 20.6 for finding cars by color. However, the mediator is asked to find cars of a particular model *and* color. Perhaps the wrapper has been designed with a more complex template such as that of Fig. 20.8, which handles queries that specify both model and color. Yet, as we discussed at the end of Example 20.5, it is not always realistic to write a template for every possible form of query.

```
SELECT *
FROM AutosMed
WHERE model = '$m' AND color = '$c';
     =>
SELECT serialNo, model, color, autoTrans, 'dealer1'
FROM Cars
WHERE model = '$m' AND color = '$c';
```

Figure 20.8: A wrapper template that gets cars of a given model and color

Another approach to supporting more queries is to have the wrapper *filter* the results of queries that it poses to the source. As long as the wrapper has a template that (after proper substitution for the parameters) returns a superset of what the query wants, then it is possible to filter the returned tuples at the wrapper and pass only the desired tuples to the mediator. The decision

---

Position of the Filter Component

We have, in our examples, supposed that the filtering operations take place at the wrapper. It is also possible that the wrapper passes raw data to the mediator, and the mediator filters the data. However, if most of the data returned by the template does not match the mediator's query, then it is best to filter at the wrapper and avoid the cost of shipping unneeded tuples.

---

whether a mediator query asks for a subset of what the pattern of some wrapper template returns is a hard problem in general, although in simple cases such as the examples we have seen, the theory is well-developed. The references contain some pointers for further study.

Example 20.6: Suppose the only template we have is the one in Fig. 20.6 that finds cars given a color. However, the mediator needs to find blue 'Gobi' model cars, as with the query:

```
SELECT *
FROM AutosMed
WHERE color = 'blue' and model = 'Gobi';
```

A possible way to answer the query is to:

1. Use the template of Fig. 20.6 with $c = $ 'blue' to find all the blue cars.

2. Store the result in a temporary relation

    ```
    TempAutos(serialNo, model, color, autoTrans, dealer)
    ```

3. Select from TempAutos the Gobis and return the result, as with the query

    ```
    SELECT *
    FROM TempAutos
    WHERE model = 'Gobi';
    ```

The result is the desired set of automobiles. In practice, the tuples of TempAutos would be produced one-at-a-time and filtered one-at-a-time, in a pipelined fashion, rather than having the entire relation TempAutos materialized at the wrapper and then filtered. □

20.2.4 Other Operations at the Wrapper

It is possible to transform data in other ways at the wrapper, as long as we are sure that the source-query part of the template returns to the wrapper all the data needed in the transformation. For instance, columns may be projected out of the tuples before transmission to the mediator. It is even possible to take aggregations or joins at the wrapper and transmit the result to the mediator.

Example 20.7: Suppose the mediator wants to know about blue Gobis at the various dealers, but only asks for the serial number, dealer, and whether or not there is an automatic transmission, since the value of the `model` and `color` fields are obvious from the query. The wrapper could proceed as in Example 20.6, but at the last step, when the result is to be returned to the mediator, the wrapper performs a projection in the `SELECT` clause as well as the filtering for the Gobi model in the `WHERE clause`. The query

```
SELECT serialNo, autoTrans, dealer
FROM TempAutos
WHERE model = 'Gobi';
```

does this additional filtering, although as in Example 20.6 relation `TempAutos` would probably be pipelined into the projection operator, rather than materialized at the wrapper. □

Example 20.8: For a more complex example, suppose the mediator is asked to find dealers and models such that the dealer has two red cars, of the same model, one with and one without an automatic transmission. Suppose also that the only useful template for Dealer 1 is the one about colors from Fig. 20.6. That is, the mediator asks the wrapper for the answer to the query of Fig. 20.9. Note that we do not have to specify a dealer for either `A1` or `A2`, because this wrapper can only access data belonging to Dealer 1. The wrappers for all the other dealers will be asked the same query by the mediator.

```
SELECT A1.model A1.dealer
FROM AutosMed A1, AutosMed A2
WHERE A1.model = A2.model AND
      A1.color = 'red' AND
      A2.color = 'red' AND
      A1.autoTrans = 'no' AND
      A2.autoTrans = 'yes';
```

Figure 20.9: Query from mediator to wrapper

A cleverly designed wrapper could discover that it is possible to answer the mediator's query by first obtaining from the Dealer-1 source a relation with all the red cars at that dealer:

```
RedAutos(serialNo, model, color, autoTrans, dealer)
```

To get this relation, the wrapper uses its template from Fig. 20.6, which handles queries that specify a color only. In effect, the wrapper acts as if it were given the query:

```
SELECT *
FROM AutosMed
WHERE color = 'red';
```

The wrapper can then create the relation `RedAutos` from Dealer 1's database by using the template of Fig. 20.6 with $c = $ 'red'. Next, the wrapper joins `RedAutos` with itself, and performs the necessary selection, to get the relation asked for by the query of Fig. 20.9. The work performed by the wrapper[3] for this step is shown in Fig. 20.10. □

```
SELECT DISTINCT A1.model, A1.dealer
FROM RedAutos A1, RedAutos A2
WHERE A1.model = A2.model AND
      A1.autoTrans = 'no' AND
      A2.autoTrans = 'yes';
```

Figure 20.10: Query performed at the wrapper (or mediator) to complete the answer to the query of Fig. 20.9

20.2.5 Exercises for Section 20.2

* **Exercise 20.2.1:** In Fig. 20.6 we saw a simple wrapper template that translated queries from the mediator for cars of a given color into queries at the dealer with relation `Cars`. Suppose that the color codes used by the mediator in its schema were different from the color codes used at this dealer, and there was a relation `GtoL(globalColor, localColor)` that translated between the two sets of codes. Rewrite the template so the correct query would be generated.

Exercise 20.2.2: In Exercise 20.1.1 we spoke of two computer companies, A and B, that used different schemas for information about their products. Suppose we have a mediator with schema

```
PCMed(manf, speed, mem, disk, screen)
```

---

[3]In some information-integration architectures, this task might actually be performed by the mediator instead.

with the intuitive meaning that a tuple gives the manufacturer (A or B), processor speed, main-memory size, hard-disk size, and screen size for one of the systems you could buy from that company. Write wrapper templates for the following types of queries. Note that you need to write two templates for each query, one for each of the manufacturers.

* a) Given a speed, find the tuples with that speed.

   b) Given a screen size, find the tuples with that size.

   c) Given memory and disk sizes, find the matching tuples.

Exercise 20.2.3: Suppose you had the wrapper templates described in Exercise 20.2.2 available in the wrappers at each of the two sources (computer manufacturers). How could the mediator use these capabilities of the wrappers to answer the following queries?

* a) Find the manufacturer, memory size, and screen size of all systems with a 1000 megahertz speed and a 40 gigabyte disk.

! b) Find the maximum amount of hard disk available on a system with a 1500 megahertz processor.

   c) Find all the systems with 128M memory and a screen size (in inches) that exceeds the disk size (in gigabytes).

20.3   Capability-Based Optimization in Mediators

In Section 16.5 we introduced the idea of cost-based optimization. A typical DBMS estimates the cost of each query plan and picks what it believes to be the best. When a mediator is given a query to answer, it often has little knowledge of how long its sources will take to answer the queries it sends them. Furthermore, most sources are not SQL databases, and often they will answer only a small subset of the kinds of queries that the mediator might like to pose. As a result, optimization of mediator queries cannot rely on cost measures alone to select a query plan.

Optimization by a mediator usually follows the simpler strategy known as *capability-based optimization*. The central issue is not what a query plan costs, but whether the plan can be executed at all. Only among plans found to be executable ("feasible") do we try to estimate costs.

In this section, we shall examine why capability of sources is an important issue. Then we describe a notation for describing capabilities. Finally, we examine strategies for discovering feasible mediator query plans.

20.3.1 The Problem of Limited Source Capabilities

Today, many useful sources have only Web-based interfaces, even if they are, behind the scenes, an ordinary database. Web sources usually permit querying only through a query form, which does not accept arbitrary SQL queries. Rather, we are invited to enter values for certain attributes and can receive a response that gives values for other attributes.

Example 20.9 : The Amazon.com interface allows us to query about books in many different ways. We can specify an author and get all their books, or we can specify a book title and receive information about that book. We can specify keywords and get books that match the keywords. However, there is also information we can receive in answers but cannot specify. For instance, Amazon ranks books by sales, but we cannot ask "give me the top 10 sellers." Moreover, we cannot ask questions that are too general. For instance, the query:

```
SELECT * FROM Books;
```

"tell me everything you know about books," cannot be asked or answered through the Amazon Web interface, although it could be answered behind the scenes if we were able to access the Amazon database directly. □

There are a number of other reasons why a source may limit the ways in which queries can be asked. Among them are:

1. *Legacy* sources are places where data is kept in an archaic or unique system. Many of the earliest databases did not use a DBMS, surely not a relational DBMS that supports SQL queries. Many of these systems were designed to be queried in certain very specific ways only. It is almost impossible to migrate the data to a more modern system, because people rely on applications that run only on the legacy system. This problem of being "locked in" to an old system that no one likes is called the *legacy database problem*, and it is unlikely to be solved any time soon.

2. For reasons of security, a source may limit the kinds of queries that it will accept. Amazon's unwillingness to answer the query "tell me about all your books" is a rudimentary example; it protects against a rival exploiting the Amazon database. As another instance, a medical database may answer queries about averages, but won't disclose (to unauthorized users) the details of a particular patient's medical history.

3. Indexes on large databases may make certain kinds of queries feasible and others too expensive to execute. For instance, if a books database were relational, and one of the attributes were `author`, then without an index on that attribute, it would be infeasible to answer queries that specified only an author. Such queries would require examining millions of tuples each.[4]

---

[4]We should be aware, however, that information like Amazon's about products is not accessed as if it were a relational database. Rather, the information about books is stored

20.3.2   A Notation for Describing Source Capabilities

If data is relational, or may be thought of as relational, then we can describe the legal forms of queries by *adornments*,[5] which are sequences of codes that represent the requirements for the attributes of the relation, in their standard order. The codes we shall use for adornments reflect the most common capabilities of sources. They are:

1. f (free) means that the attribute can be specified or not, as we choose.

2. b (bound) means that we must specify a value for the attribute, but any value is allowed.

3. u (unspecified) means that we are not permitted to specify a value for the attribute.

4. $c[S]$ (choice from set S) means that a value must be specified, and that value must be one of the values in the finite set S. This option corresponds, for instance, to values that are specified from a pulldown menu in a Web interface.

5. $o[S]$ (optional, from set S) means that we either do not specify a value, or we specify one of the values in the finite set S.

In addition, we place a prime (e.g., f') on a code if the attribute is not part of the output of the query.

A *capabilities specification* for a source is a set of adornments. The intent is that in order to query the source successfully, the query must match one of the adornments in its capabilities specification. Note that, if an adornment has free or optional components, then queries with different sets of attributes specified may match that adornment.

Example 20.10 : Suppose we have two sources like those of the two dealers in Example 20.4. Dealer 1 is a source of data in the form:

```
Cars(serialNo, model, color, autoTrans, cdPlayer)
```

Note that in the original, we suggested relation `Cars` could have additional attributes representing options, but for simplicity in this example, let us limit our thinking to automatic transmissions and CD players only. Here are two possible ways that Dealer 1 might allow this data to be queried:

---

as text, with an inverted index, as we discussed in Section 13.2.4. Thus, queries about any aspect of books — authors, titles, words in titles, and perhaps words in descriptions of the book — are supported by this index.

[5]This term comes from the practice of attaching the capabilities of a relation as a superscript "adorning" the name of the relation.

1. The user specifies a serial number, and all the information about the car with that serial number (i.e., the other four attributes) is produced as output. The adornment for this query form is *b'uuuu*. That is, the first attribute, `serialNo` must be specified and is not part of the output. The other attributes must *not* be specified and *are* part of the output.

2. The user specifies a model and color, and perhaps whether or not automatic transmission and CD player are wanted. All five attributes are printed for all matching cars. An appropriate adornment is

$$ubbo[\text{yes, no}]o[\text{yes, no}]$$

   This adornment says we must not specify the serial number; we must specify a model and color, but are allowed to give any possible value in these fields/ Also, we may, if we wish, specify whether we want automatic transmission and/or a CD player, but must do so by using only the values "yes" and "no" in those fields.

As an alternative to adornment (2), we might suppose that queries limit the `model` and/or `color` attributes to have values that are valid; that is, the model is chosen from one of the models that Aardvark actually makes, and the color is chosen from one of the available colors. If so, then an adornment such as *uc*[Gobi, . . .]*c*[red, blue, . . .]*bo*[yes, no]*o*[yes, no] would be more appropriate. ☐

20.3.3 Capability-Based Query-Plan Selection

Given a query at the mediator, a capability-based query optimizer first considers what queries it can ask at the sources that will help answer the query. If we imagine those queries asked and answered, then we have bindings for some more attributes, and these bindings may make some more queries at the sources possible. We repeat this process until either:

1. We have asked enough queries at the sources to resolve all the conditions of the mediator query, and therefore we may answer that query. Such a plan is called *feasible*.

2. We can construct no more valid forms of source queries, yet we still cannot answer the mediator query, in which case the mediator must give up; it has been given an impossible query.

The simplest form of mediator query for which we need to apply the above strategy is a join of relations, each of which is available, with certain adornments, at one or more sources. If so, then the search strategy is to try to get tuples for each relation in the join, by providing enough argument bindings that some source allows a query about that relation to be asked and answered. A simple example will illustrate the point.

What Do Adornments Guarantee?

It would be wonderful if a source that supported queries matching a given adornment would return all possible answers to the query. However, sources normally have only a subset of the possible answers to a query. For instance, Amazon does not stock every book that has ever been written, and the two dealers of our running automobiles example each have distinct sets of cars in their database. Thus, a more proper interpretation of an adornment is: "I will answer a query in the form described by this adornment, and every answer I give will be a true answer, but I do not guarantee to provide all true answers."

Now, consider what happens if several sources provide data for the same relation R. Instead of a mediator selecting only one query plan for a query involving R, the mediator should select one plan that uses each of the sources for R. If the adornments for these sources are different, then these plans may have to be quite different. Further, if several relations mentioned in the query have alternative sources, then the number of different plans multiplies exponentially in the number of such relations.

Example 20.11: Let us suppose we have sources like the relations of Dealer 2 in Example 20.4:

```
Autos(serial, model, color)
Options(serial, option)
```

However, let us assume that `Autos` and `Options` are relations representing the data at two different sources.[6] Suppose that *ubf* is the sole adornment for `Autos`, while `Options` has two adornments, *bu* and *uc*[autoTrans, cdPlayer], representing two different kinds of queries that we can ask at that source. Let the query be "find the serial numbers and colors of Gobi models with a CD player."

Here are three different query plans that the mediator must consider:

1. Specifying that the model is Gobi, query `Autos` and get the serial numbers and colors of all Gobis. Then, using the *bu* adornment for `Options`, for each such serial number, find the options for that car and filter to make sure it has a CD player.

2. Specifying the CD-player option, query `Options` using the

$$uc[autoTrans, cdPlayer]$$

---

[6]Alternatively, we may suppose that the wrapper for Dealer 2 supports mediator features that allow it to optimize the queries sent to Dealer 2 using capability-based techniques.

adornment and get all the serial numbers for cars with CD player. Then query `Autos` as in (1), to get all the serial numbers and colors of Gobis, and intersect the two sets of serial numbers.

3. Query `Options` as in (2) to get the serial numbers for cars with a CD player. Then use these serial numbers to query `Autos` and see which of these cars are Gobis.

Either of the first two plans are acceptable. However, the third plan is one of several plans that will not work; the system does not have the capability to execute this plan because the second part — the query to `Autos` — does not have a matching adornment. A capability-based optimizer examines plans such as these and the adornments of the relations involved and eliminates infeasible plans such as the third above. □

20.3.4 Adding Cost-Based Optimization

The mediator's query optimizer is not done when the capabilities of the sources are examined. Having found the feasible plans, it must choose among them. Making an intelligent, cost-based optimization requires that the mediator know a great deal about the costs of the queries involved. Since the sources are usually independent of the mediator, it is difficult to estimate the cost. For instance, a source may take less time during periods when it is lightly loaded, but when are those periods? Long-term observation by the mediator is necessary for the mediator even to guess what the response time might be.

In Example 20.11, we might simply count the number of queries to sources that must be issued. Plan (2) uses only two source queries, while plan (1) uses one plus the number of Gobis found in the `Autos` relation. Thus, it appears that plan (2) has lower cost. On the other hand, if the queries of `Options`, one with each serial number, could be combined into one query, then plan (1) might turn out to be the superior choice.

20.3.5 Exercises for Section 20.3

Exercise 20.3.1: Suppose each relation from Exercise 20.1.1:

```
Computers(number, proc, speed, memory, hd)
Monitors(number, screen, maxResX, maxResY)
```

is an information source. Using the notation from Section 20.3.2, write one or more adornments that express the following capabilities:

* a) We can query for computers having a given processor, which must be one of "P-IV," "G4," or "Athlon," a given speed, and (optionally) a given amount of memory.

 b) We can query for computers having any specified hard-disk size and/or any given memory size.

c) We can query for monitors if we specify either the number of the monitor, the screen size, or the maximum resolution in both dimensions.

d) We can query for monitors if we specify the screen size, which must be either 15, 17, 19, or 21 inches. All attributes except the screen size are returned.

! e) We can query for computers if we specify any two of the processor type, processor speed, memory size, or disk size.

Exercise 20.3.2: Suppose we have the two sources of Exercise 20.3.1, but understand the attribute `number` of both relations to refer to the number of a complete system, some of whose attributes are found in one source and some in the other. Suppose also that the adornments describing access to the `Computers` relation are *buuuu*, *ubbff*, and *uuubb*, while the adornments for `Monitors` are *bfff* and *ubbb*. Tell what plans are feasible for the following queries (exclude any plans that are obviously more expensive than other plans on your list):

* a) Find the systems with 128 megabytes of memory, an 80-gigabyte hard disk, and a 19-inch monitor.

 b) Find the systems with a Pentium-IV processor running at 2000 megahertz, with a 21-inch monitor and a maximum resolution of 1600-by-1200.

! c) Find all systems with a G4 processor running at 750 megahertz with 256 megabytes of memory, a 40 gigabyte disk, and a 17-inch monitor.

20.4 On-Line Analytic Processing

We shall now take up an important class of applications for integrated information systems, especially data warehouses. Companies and organizations create a warehouse with a copy of large amounts of their available data and assign analysts to query this warehouse for patterns or trends of importance to the organization. This activity, called *OLAP* (standing for *On-Line Analytic Processing* and pronounced "oh-lap"), generally involves highly complex queries that use one or more aggregations. These queries are often termed *OLAP queries* or *decision-support queries*. Some examples will be given in Section 20.4.1; a typical example is to search for products with increasing or decreasing overall sales.

Decision-support queries used in OLAP applications typically examine very large amounts of data, even if the query results are small. In contrast, common database operations, such as bank deposits or airline reservations, each touch only a tiny portion of the database; the latter type of operation is often referred to as *OLTP* (*On-Line Transaction Processing*, spoken "oh-ell-tee-pee").

Recently, new query-processing techniques have been developed that are especially good at executing OLAP queries effectively. Furthermore, because of

---

Warehouses and OLAP

There are several reasons why data warehouses play an important role in OLAP applications. First, the warehouse may be necessary to organize and centralize corporate data in a way that supports OLAP queries; the data may initially be scattered across many different databases. But often more important is the fact that OLAP queries, being complex and touching much of the data, take too much time to be executed in a transaction-processing system with high throughput requirements. OLAP queries often can be considered "long transactions" in the sense of Section 19.7.

Long transactions locking the entire database would shut down the ordinary OLTP operations (e.g., recording new sales as they occur could not be permitted if there were a concurrent OLAP query computing average sales). A common solution is to make a copy of the raw data in a warehouse, run OLAP queries only at the warehouse, and run the OLTP queries and data modifications at the data sources. In a common scenario, the warehouse is only updated overnight, while the analysts work on a frozen copy during the day. The warehouse data thus gets out of date by as much as 24 hours, which limits the timeliness of its answers to OLAP queries, but the delay is tolerable in many decision-support applications.

---

the distinct nature of a certain class of OLAP queries, special forms of DBMS's have been developed and marketed to support OLAP applications. The same technology is beginning to migrate to standard SQL systems, as well. We shall discuss the architecture of these systems in Section 20.5.

20.4.1 OLAP Applications

A common OLAP application uses a warehouse of sales data. Major store chains will accumulate terabytes of information representing every sale of every item at every store. Queries that aggregate sales into groups and identify significant groups can be of great use to the company in predicting future problems and opportunities.

Example 20.12: Suppose the Aardvark Automobile Co. builds a data warehouse to analyze sales of its cars. The schema for the warehouse might be:

```
Sales(serialNo, date, dealer, price)
Autos(serialNo, model, color)
Dealers(name, city, state, phone)
```

A typical decision-support query might examine sales on or after April 1, 2001 to see how the recent average price per vehicle varies by state. Such a query is shown in Fig. 20.11.

```
SELECT state, AVG(price)
FROM Sales, Dealers
WHERE Sales.dealer = Dealers.name AND
      date >= '2001-01-04'
GROUP BY state;
```

Figure 20.11: Find average sales price by state

Notice how the query of Fig. 20.11 touches much of the data of the database, as it classifies every recent `Sales` fact by the state of the dealer that sold it. In contrast, common OLTP queries, such as "find the price at which the auto with serial number 123 was sold," would touch only a single tuple of the data. □

For another OLAP example, consider a credit-card company trying to decide whether applicants for a card are likely to be credit-worthy. The company creates a warehouse of all its current customers and their payment history. OLAP queries search for factors, such as age, income, home-ownership, and zip-code, that might help predict whether customers will pay their bills on time. Similarly, hospitals may use a warehouse of patient data — their admissions, tests administered, outcomes, diagnoses, treatments, and so on — to analyze for risks and select the best modes of treatment.

20.4.2   A Multidimensional View of OLAP Data

In typical OLAP applications there is a central relation or collection of data, called the *fact table*. A fact table represents events or objects of interest, such as sales in Example 20.12. Often, it helps to think of the objects in the fact table as arranged in a multidimensional space, or "cube." Figure 20.12 suggests three-dimensional data, represented by points within the cube; we have called the dimensions car, dealer, and date, to correspond to our earlier example of automobile sales. Thus, in Fig. 20.12 we could think of each point as a sale of a single automobile, while the dimensions represent properties of that sale.

A data space such as Fig. 20.12 will be referred to informally as a "data cube," or more precisely as a *raw-data cube* when we want to distinguish it from the more complex "data cube" of Section 20.5. The latter, which we shall refer to as a *formal* data cube when a distinction from the raw-data cube is needed, differs from the raw-data cube in two ways:

1. It includes aggregations of the data in all subsets of dimensions, as well as the data itself.

2. Points in the formal data cube may represent an initial aggregation of points in the raw-data cube. For instance, instead of the "car" dimension

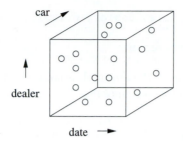

Figure 20.12: Data organized in a multidimensional space

representing each individual car (as we suggested for the raw-data cube), that dimension might be aggregated by model only, and a point of a formal data cube could represent the total sales of all cars of a given model by a given dealer on a given day.

The distinctions between the raw-data cube and the formal data cube are reflected in the two broad directions that have been taken by specialized systems that support cube-structured data for OLAP:

1. *ROLAP*, or *Relational OLAP*. In this approach, data may be stored in relations with a specialized structure called a "star schema," described in Section 20.4.3. One of these relations is the "fact table," which contains the *raw*, or unaggregated, data, and corresponds to what we called the raw-data cube. Other relations give information about the values along each dimension. The query language and other capabilities of the system may be tailored to the assumption that data is organized this way.

2. *MOLAP*, or *Multidimensional OLAP*. Here, a specialized structure, the formal "data cube" mentioned above, is used to hold the data, including its aggregates. Nonrelational operators may be implemented by the system to support OLAP queries on data in this structure.

20.4.3 Star Schemas

A *star schema* consists of the schema for the fact table, which links to several other relations, called "dimension tables." The fact table is at the center of the "star," whose points are the dimension tables. A fact table normally has several attributes that represent *dimensions*, and one or more *dependent* attributes that represent properties of interest for the point as a whole. For instance, dimensions for sales data might include the date of the sale, the place (store) of the sale, the type of item sold, the method of payment (e.g., cash or a credit card), and so on. The dependent attribute(s) might be the sales price, the cost of the item, or the tax, for instance.

Example 20.13: The `Sales` relation from Example 20.12

```
Sales(serialNo, date, dealer, price)
```

is a fact table. The dimensions are:

1. `serialNo`, representing the automobile sold, i.e., the position of the point in the space of possible automobiles.

2. `date`, representing the day of the sale, i.e., the position of the event in the time dimension.

3. `dealer`, representing the position of the event in the space of possible dealers.

The one dependent attribute is `price`, which is what OLAP queries to this database will typically request in an aggregation. However, queries asking for a count, rather than sum or average price would also make sense, e.g., "list the total number of sales for each dealer in the month of May, 2001." □

Supplementing the fact table are *dimension tables* describing the values along each dimension. Typically, each dimension attribute of the fact table is a foreign key, referencing the key of the corresponding dimension table, as suggested by Fig. 20.13. The attributes of the dimension tables also describe the possible groupings that would make sense in an SQL GROUP BY query. An example should make the ideas clearer.

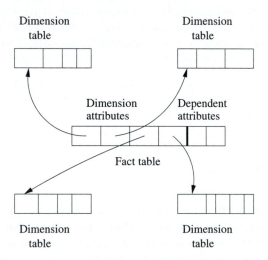

Figure 20.13: The dimension attributes in the fact table reference the keys of the dimension tables

Example 20.14 : For the automobile data of Example 20.12, two of the three dimension tables are obvious:

```
Autos(serialNo, model, color)
Dealers(name, city, state, phone)
```

Attribute `serialNo` in the fact table

```
Sales(serialNo, date, dealer, price)
```

is a foreign key, referencing `serialNo` of dimension table `Autos`.[7] The attributes `Autos.model` and `Autos.color` give properties of a given auto. We could have added many more attributes in this relation, such as boolean attributes indicating whether the auto has an automatic transmission. If we join the fact table `Sales` with the dimension table `Autos`, then the attributes `model` and `color` may be used for grouping sales in interesting ways. For instance, we can ask for a breakdown of sales by color, or a breakdown of sales of the Gobi model by month and dealer.

Similarly, attribute `dealer` of `Sales` is a foreign key, referencing `name` of the dimension table `Dealers`. If `Sales` and `Dealers` are joined, then we have additional options for grouping our data; e.g., we can ask for a breakdown of sales by state or by city, as well as by dealer.

One might wonder where the dimension table for time (the `date` attribute of `Sales`) is. Since time is a physical property, it does not make sense to store facts about time in a database, since we cannot change the answer to questions such as "in what year does the day July 5, 2000 appear?" However, since grouping by various time units, such as weeks, months, quarters, and years, is frequently desired by analysts, it helps to build into the database a notion of time, as if there were a time dimension table such as

```
Days(day, week, month, year)
```

A typical tuple of this "relation" would be

```
(5, 27, 7, 2000)
```

representing July 5, 2000. The interpretation is that this day is the fifth day of the seventh month of the year 2000; it also happens to fall in the 27th full week of the year 2000. There is a certain amount of redundancy, since the week is calculable from the other three attributes. However, weeks are not exactly commensurate with months, so we cannot obtain a grouping by months from a grouping by weeks, or vice versa. Thus, it makes sense to imagine that both weeks and months are represented in this "dimension table."   □

---

[7]It happens that `serialNo` is also a key for the `Sales` relation, but there need not be an attribute that is both a key for the fact table and a foreign key for some dimension table.

20.4.4 Slicing and Dicing

We can think of the points of the raw-data cube as partitioned along each dimension at some level of granularity. For example, in the time dimension, we might partition ("group by" in SQL terms) according to days, weeks, months, years, or not partition at all. For the cars dimension, we might partition by model, by color, by both model and color, or not partition. For dealers, we can partition by dealer, by city, by state, or not partition.

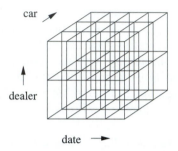

Figure 20.14: Dicing the cube by partitioning along each dimension

A choice of partition for each dimension "dices" the cube, as suggested by Fig. 20.14. The result is that the cube is divided into smaller cubes that represent groups of points whose statistics are aggregated by a query that performs the partitioning in its GROUP BY clause. Through the WHERE clause, a query also has the option of focusing on particular partitions along one or more dimensions (i.e., on a particular "slice" of the cube).

Example 20.15: Figure 20.15 suggests a query in which we ask for a slice in one dimension (the date), and dice in two other dimensions (car and dealer). The date is divided into four groups, perhaps the four years over which data has been accumulated. The shading in the diagram suggests that we are only interested in one of these years.

The cars are partitioned into three groups, perhaps sedans, SUV's, and convertibles, while the dealers are partitioned into two groups, perhaps the eastern and western regions. The result of the query is a table giving the total sales in six categories for the one year of interest.   □

The general form of a so-called "slicing and dicing" query is thus:

```
SELECT grouping attributes and aggregations
FROM fact table joined with zero or more dimension tables
WHERE certain attributes are constant
GROUP BY grouping attributes;
```

Example 20.16: Let us continue with our automobile example, but include the conceptual Days dimension table for time discussed in Example 20.14. If

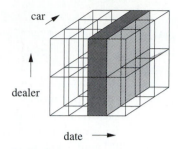

Figure 20.15: Selecting a slice of a diced cube

the Gobi isn't selling as well as we thought it would, we might try to find out which colors are not doing well. This query uses only the Autos dimension table and can be written in SQL as:

```
SELECT color, SUM(price)
FROM Sales NATURAL JOIN Autos
WHERE model = 'Gobi'
GROUP BY color;
```

This query dices by color and then slices by model, focusing on a particular model, the Gobi, and ignoring other data.

Suppose the query doesn't tell us much; each color produces about the same revenue. Since the query does not partition on time, we only see the total over all time for each color. We might suppose that the recent trend is for one or more colors to have weak sales. We may thus issue a revised query that also partitions time by month. This query is:

```
SELECT color, month, SUM(price)
FROM (Sales NATURAL JOIN Autos) JOIN Days ON date = day
WHERE model = 'Gobi'
GROUP BY color, month;
```

It is important to remember that the Days relation is not a conventional stored relation, although we may treat it as if it had the schema

```
Days(day, week, month, year)
```

The ability to use such a "relation" is one way that a system specialized to OLAP queries could differ from a conventional DBMS.

We might discover that red Gobis have not sold well recently. The next question we might ask is whether this problem exists at all dealers, or whether only some dealers have had low sales of red Gobis. Thus, we further focus the query by looking at only red Gobis, and we partition along the dealer dimension as well. This query is:

```
SELECT dealer, month, SUM(price)
FROM (Sales NATURAL JOIN Autos) JOIN Days ON date = day
WHERE model = 'Gobi' AND color = 'red'
GROUP BY month, dealer;
```

At this point, we find that the sales per month for red Gobis are so small that we cannot observe any trends easily. Thus, we decide that it was a mistake to partition by month. A better idea would be to partition only by years, and look at only the last two years (2001 and 2002, in this hypothetical example). The final query is shown in Fig. 20.16. □

```
SELECT dealer, year, SUM(price)
FROM (Sales NATURAL JOIN Autos) JOIN Days ON date = day
WHERE model = 'Gobi' AND
      color = 'red' AND
      (year = 2001 OR year = 2002)
GROUP BY year, dealer;
```

Figure 20.16: Final slicing-and-dicing query about red Gobi sales

20.4.5 Exercises for Section 20.4

* **Exercise 20.4.1:** An on-line seller of computers wishes to maintain data about orders. Customers can order their PC with any of several processors, a selected amount of main memory, any of several disk units, and any of several CD or DVD readers. The fact table for such a database might be:

```
Orders(cust, date, proc, memory, hd, rd, quant, price)
```

We should understand attribute `cust` to be an ID that is the foreign key for a dimension table about customers, and understand attributes `proc`, `hd` (hard disk), and `rd` (removable disk: CD or DVD, typically) similarly. For example, an `hd` ID might be elaborated in a dimension table giving the manufacturer of the disk and several disk characteristics. The `memory` attribute is simply an integer: the number of megabytes of memory ordered. The `quant` attribute is the number of machines of this type ordered by this customer, and the `price` attribute is the total cost of each machine ordered.

   a) Which are dimension attributes, and which are dependent attributes?

   b) For some of the dimension attributes, a dimension table is likely to be needed. Suggest appropriate schemas for these dimension tables.

Drill-Down and Roll-Up

Example 20.16 illustrates two common patterns in sequences of queries that slice-and-dice the data cube.

1. *Drill-down* is the process of partitioning more finely and/or focusing on specific values in certain dimensions. Each of the steps except the last in Example 20.16 is an instance of drill-down.

2. *Roll-up* is the process of partitioning more coarsely. The last step, where we grouped by years instead of months to eliminate the effect of randomness in the data, is an example of roll-up.

! Exercise 20.4.2 : Suppose that we want to examine the data of Exercise 20.4.1 to find trends and thus predict which components the company should order more of. Describe a series of drill-down and roll-up queries that could lead to the conclusion that customers are beginning to prefer a DVD drive to a CD drive.

20.5 Data Cubes

In this section, we shall consider the "formal" data cube and special operations on data presented in this form. Recall from Section 20.4.2 that the formal data cube (just "data cube" in this section) precomputes all possible aggregates in a systematic way. Surprisingly, the amount of extra storage needed is often tolerable, and as long as the warehoused data does not change, there is no penalty incurred trying to keep all the aggregates up-to-date.

In the data cube, it is normal for there to be some aggregation of the raw data of the fact table before it is entered into the data-cube and its further aggregates computed. For instance, in our cars example, the dimension we thought of as a serial number in the star schema might be replaced by the model of the car. Then, each point of the data cube becomes a description of a model, a dealer and a date, together with the sum of the sales for that model, on that date, by that dealer. We shall continue to call the points of the (formal) data cube a "fact table," even though the interpretation of the points may be slightly different from fact tables in a star schema built from a raw-data cube.

20.5.1 The Cube Operator

Given a fact table F, we can define an augmented table $\text{CUBE}(F)$ that adds an additional value, denoted $*$, to each dimension. The $*$ has the intuitive meaning "any," and it represents aggregation along the dimension in which it appears. Figure 20.17 suggests the process of adding a border to the cube in each dimension, to represent the ∗ value and the aggregated values that it implies. In this figure we see three dimensions, with the lightest shading representing aggregates in one dimension, darker shading for aggregates over two dimensions, and the darkest cube in the corner for aggregation over all three dimensions. Notice that if the number of values along each dimension is reasonably large, but not so large that most points in the cube are unoccupied, then the "border" represents only a small addition to the volume of the cube (i.e., the number of tuples in the fact table). In that case, the size of the stored data CUBE(F) is not much greater than the size of F itself.

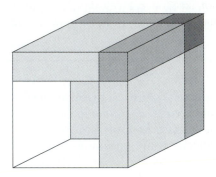

Figure 20.17: The cube operator augments a data cube with a border of aggregations in all combinations of dimensions

A tuple of the table CUBE(F) that has ∗ in one or more dimensions will have for each dependent attribute the sum (or another aggregate function) of the values of that attribute in all the tuples that we can obtain by replacing the ∗'s by real values. In effect, we build into the data the result of aggregating along any set of dimensions. Notice, however, that the CUBE operator does not support aggregation at intermediate levels of granularity based on values in the dimension tables. For instance, we may either leave data broken down by day (or whatever the finest granularity for time is), or we may aggregate time completely, but we cannot, with the CUBE operator alone, aggregate by weeks, months, or years.

Example 20.17: Let us reconsider the Aardvark database from Example 20.12 in the light of what the CUBE operator can give us. Recall the fact table from that example is

        Sales(serialNo, date, dealer, price)

However, the dimension represented by serialNo is not well suited for the cube, since the serial number is a key for Sales. Thus, summing the price over all dates, or over all dealers, but keeping the serial number fixed has no effect; we would still get the "sum" for the one auto with that serial number. A more useful data cube would replace the serial number by the two attributes — model and color — to which the serial number connects `Sales` via the dimension table `Autos`. Notice that if we replace `serialNo` by `model` and `color`, then the cube no longer has a key among its dimensions. Thus, an entry of the cube would have the total sales price for all automobiles of a given model, with a given color, by a given dealer, on a given date.

There is another change that is useful for the data-cube implementation of the `Sales` fact table. Since the CUBE operator normally sums dependent variables, and we might want to get average prices for sales in some category, we need both the sum of the prices for each category of automobiles (a given model of a given color sold on a given day by a given dealer) and the total number of sales in that category. Thus, the relation `Sales` to which we apply the CUBE operator is

> `Sales(model, color, date, dealer, val, cnt)`

The attribute `val` is intended to be the total price of all automobiles for the given model, color, date, and dealer, while `cnt` is the total number of automobiles in that category. Notice that in this data cube, individual cars are not identified; they only affect the value and count for their category.

Now, let us consider the relation CUBE(`Sales`). A hypothetical tuple that would be in both `Sales` and CUBE(`Sales`), is

> `('Gobi', 'red', '2001-05-21', 'Friendly Fred', 45000, 2)`

The interpretation is that on May 21, 2001, dealer Friendly Fred sold two red Gobis for a total of $45,000. The tuple

> `('Gobi', *, '2001-05-21', 'Friendly Fred', 152000, 7)`

says that on May 21, 2001, Friendly Fred sold seven Gobis of all colors, for a total price of $152,000. Note that this tuple is in CUBE(`Sales`) but not in `Sales`.

Relation CUBE(`Sales`) also contains tuples that represent the aggregation over more than one attribute. For instance,

> `('Gobi', *, '2001-05-21', *, 2348000, 100)`

says that on May 21, 2001, there were 100 Gobis sold by all the dealers, and the total price of those Gobis was $2,348,000.

> `('Gobi', *, *, *, 1339800000, 58000)`

Says that over all time, dealers, and colors, 58,000 Gobis have been sold for a total price of $1,339,800,000. Lastly, the tuple

> `(*, *, *, *, 3521727000, 198000)`

tells us that total sales of all Aardvark models in all colors, over all time at all dealers is 198,000 cars for a total price of $3,521,727,000. □

Consider how to answer a query in which we specify conditions on certain attributes of the Sales relation and group by some other attributes, while asking for the sum, count, or average price. In the relation CUBE(Sales), we look for those tuples t with the following properties:

1. If the query specifies a value v for attribute a, then tuple t has v in its component for a.

2. If the query groups by an attribute a, then t has any non-* value in its component for a.

3. If the query neither groups by attribute a nor specifies a value for a, then t has * in its component for a.

Each tuple t has the sum and count for one of the desired groups. If we want the average price, a division is performed on the sum and count components of each tuple t.

Example 20.18: The query

```
SELECT color, AVG(price)
FROM Sales
WHERE model = 'Gobi'
GROUP BY color;
```

is answered by looking for all tuples of CUBE(Sales) with the form

$$(\text{'Gobi'}, c, *, *, v, n)$$

where c is any specific color. In this tuple, v will be the sum of sales of Gobis in that color, while n will be the number of sales of Gobis in that color. The average price, although not an attribute of Sales or CUBE(Sales) directly, is v/n. The answer to the query is the set of $(c, v/n)$ pairs obtained from all $(\text{'Gobi'}, c, *, *, v, n)$ tuples. □

20.5.2 Cube Implementation by Materialized Views

We suggested in Fig. 20.17 that adding aggregations to the cube doesn't cost much in terms of space, and saves a lot in time when the common kinds of decision-support queries are asked. However, our analysis is based on the assumption that queries choose either to aggregate completely in a dimension or not to aggregate at all. For some dimensions, there are many degrees of granularity that could be chosen for a grouping on that dimension.

We have already mentioned the case of time, where numerous options such as aggregation by weeks, months, quarters, or years exist, in addition to the all-or-nothing choices of grouping by day or aggregating over all time. For another example based on our running automobile database, we could choose to aggregate dealers completely or not aggregate them at all. However, we could also choose to aggregate by city, by state, or perhaps by other regions, larger or smaller. Thus, there are at least six choices of grouping for time and at least four for dealers.

When the number of choices for grouping along each dimension grows, it becomes increasingly expensive to store the results of aggregating by every possible combination of groupings. Not only are there too many of them, but they are not as easily organized as the structure of Fig. 20.17 suggests for the all-or-nothing case. Thus, commercial data-cube systems may help the user to choose some *materialized views* of the data cube. A materialized view is the result of some query, which we choose to store in the database, rather than reconstructing (parts of) it as needed in response to queries. For the data cube, the views we would choose to materialize will typically be aggregations of the full data cube.

The coarser the partition implied by the grouping, the less space the materialized view takes. On the other hand, if we want to use a view to answer a certain query, then the view must not partition any dimension more coarsely than the query does. Thus, to maximize the utility of materialized views, we generally want some large views that group dimensions into a fairly fine partition. In addition, the choice of views to materialize is heavily influenced by the kinds of queries that the analysts are likely to ask. An example will suggest the tradeoffs involved.

```
INSERT INTO SalesV1
    SELECT model, color, month, city,
        SUM(val) AS val, SUM(cnt) AS cnt
    FROM Sales JOIN Dealers ON dealer = name
    GROUP BY model, color, month, city;
```

Figure 20.18: The materialized view `SalesV1`

Example 20.19 : Let us return to the data cube

```
Sales(model, color, date, dealer, val, cnt)
```

that we developed in Example 20.17. One possible materialized view groups dates by month and dealers by city. This view, which we call `SalesV1`, is constructed by the query in Fig. 20.18. This query is not strict SQL, since we imagine that dates and their grouping units such as months are understood by the data-cube system without being told to join `Sales` with the imaginary relation representing days that we discussed in Example 20.14.

```
INSERT INTO SalesV2
    SELECT model, week, state,
        SUM(val) AS val, SUM(cnt) AS cnt
    FROM Sales JOIN Dealers ON dealer = name
    GROUP BY model, week, state;
```

Figure 20.19: Another materialized view, `SalesV2`

Another possible materialized view aggregates colors completely, aggregates time into weeks, and dealers by states. This view, `SalesV2`, is defined by the query in Fig. 20.19. Either view `SalesV1` or `SalesV2` can be used to answer a query that partitions no more finely than either in any dimension. Thus, the query

```
Q1: SELECT model, SUM(val)
    FROM Sales
    GROUP BY model;
```

can be answered either by

```
SELECT model, SUM(val)
FROM SalesV1
GROUP BY model;
```

or by

```
SELECT model, SUM(val)
FROM SalesV2
GROUP BY model;
```

On the other hand, the query

```
Q2: SELECT model, year, state, SUM(val)
    FROM Sales JOIN Dealers ON dealer = name
    GROUP BY model, year, state;
```

can only be answered from `SalesV1`, as

```
SELECT model, year, state, SUM(val)
FROM SalesV1
GROUP BY model, year, state;
```

Incidentally, the query immediately above, like the queries that aggregate time units, is not strict SQL. That is, `state` is not an attribute of `SalesV1`; only `city` is. We must assume that the data-cube system knows how to perform the aggregation of cities into states, probably by accessing the dimension table for dealers.

We cannot answer $Q2$ from `SalesV2`. Although we could roll-up cities into states (i.e., aggregate the cities into their states) to use `SalesV1`, we cannot roll-up weeks into years, since years are not evenly divided into weeks, and data from a week beginning, say, Dec. 29, 2001, contributes to years 2001 and 2002 in a way we cannot tell from the data aggregated by weeks.

Finally, a query like

```
Q3: SELECT model, color, date, SUM(val)
       FROM Sales
       GROUP BY model, color, date;
```

can be answered from neither `SalesV1` nor `SalesV2`. It cannot be answered from `SalesV1` because its partition of days by months is too coarse to recover sales by day, and it cannot be answered from `SalesV2` because that view does not group by color. We would have to answer this query directly from the full data cube. □

20.5.3 The Lattice of Views

To formalize the observations of Example 20.19, it helps to think of a lattice of possible groupings for each dimension of the cube. The points of the lattice are the ways that we can partition the values of a dimension by grouping according to one or more attributes of its dimension table. We say that partition P_1 is below partition P_2, written $P_1 \leq P_2$ if and only if each group of P_1 is contained within some group of P_2.

Figure 20.20: A lattice of partitions for time intervals

Example 20.20 : For the lattice of time partitions we might choose the diagram of Fig. 20.20. A path from some node P_2 down to P_1 means that $P_1 \leq P_2$. These are not the only possible units of time, but they will serve as an example of what units a system might support. Notice that days lie below both weeks and months, but weeks do not lie below months. The reason is that while a group of events that took place in one day surely took place within one week and within one month, it is not true that a group of events taking place in one week necessarily took place in any one month. Similarly, a week's group need not be contained within the group corresponding to one quarter or to one year. At the top is a partition we call "all," meaning that events are grouped into a single group; i.e., we make no distinctions among different times.

All

State

City

Dealer

Figure 20.21: A lattice of partitions for automobile dealers

Figure 20.21 shows another lattice, this time for the dealer dimension of our automobiles example. This lattice is simpler; it shows that partitioning sales by dealer gives a finer partition than partitioning by the city of the dealer, which is in turn finer than partitioning by the state of the dealer. The top of the lattice is the partition that places all dealers in one group. □

Having a lattice for each dimension, we can now define a lattice for all the possible materialized views of a data cube that can be formed by grouping according to some partition in each dimension. If V_1 and V_2 are two views formed by choosing a partition (grouping) for each dimension, then $V_1 \leq V_2$ means that in each dimension, the partition P_1 that we use in V_1 is at least as fine as the partition P_2 that we use for that dimension in V_2; that is, $P_1 \leq P_2$.

Many OLAP queries can also be placed in the lattice of views. In fact, frequently an OLAP query has the same form as the views we have described: the query specifies some partitioning (possibly none or all) for each of the dimensions. Other OLAP queries involve this same sort of grouping, and then "slice" the cube to focus on a subset of the data, as was suggested by the diagram in Fig. 20.15. The general rule is:

- We can answer a query Q using view V if and only if $V \leq Q$.

Example 20.21: Figure 20.22 takes the views and queries of Example 20.19 and places them in a lattice. Notice that the `Sales` data cube itself is technically a view, corresponding to the finest possible partition along each dimension. As we observed in the original example, Q_1 can be answered from either `SalesV1` or

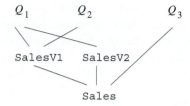

Figure 20.22: The lattice of views and queries from Example 20.19

SalesV2; of course it could also be answered from the full data cube Sales, but there is no reason to want to do so if one of the other views is materialized. Q_2 can be answered from either SalesV1 or Sales, while Q_3 can only be answered from Sales. Each of these relationships is expressed in Fig. 20.22 by the paths downward from the queries to their supporting views. □

Placing queries in the lattice of views helps design data-cube databases. Some recently developed design tools for data-cube systems start with a set of queries that they regard as "typical" of the application at hand. They then select a set of views to materialize so that each of these queries is above at least one of the views, preferably identical to it or very close (i.e., the query and the view use the same grouping in most of the dimensions).

20.5.4 Exercises for Section 20.5

Exercise 20.5.1: What is the ratio of the size of CUBE(F) to the size of F if fact table F has the following characteristics?

* a) F has ten dimension attributes, each with ten different values.

 b) F has ten dimension attributes, each with two different values.

Exercise 20.5.2: Let us use the cube CUBE(Sales) from Example 20.17, which was built from the relation

        Sales(model, color, date, dealer, val, cnt)

Tell what tuples of the cube we would use to answer the following queries:

* a) Find the total sales of blue cars for each dealer.

 b) Find the total number of green Gobis sold by dealer "Smilin' Sally."

 c) Find the average number of Gobis sold on each day of March, 2002 by each dealer.

*! Exercise 20.5.3: In Exercise 20.4.1 we spoke of PC-order data organized as a cube. If we are to apply the CUBE operator, we might find it convenient to break several dimensions more finely. For example, instead of one processor dimension, we might have one dimension for the type (e.g., AMD Duron or Pentium-IV), and another dimension for the speed. Suggest a set of dimensions and dependent attributes that will allow us to obtain answers to a variety of useful aggregation queries. In particular, what role does the customer play? Also, the price in Exercise 20.4.1 referred to the price of one machine, while several identical machines could be ordered in a single tuple. What should the dependent attribute(s) be?

Exercise 20.5.4: What tuples of the cube from Exercise 20.5.3 would you use to answer the following queries?

a) Find, for each processor speed, the total number of computers ordered in each month of the year 2002.

b) List for each type of hard disk (e.g., SCSI or IDE) and each processor type the number of computers ordered.

c) Find the average price of computers with 1500 megahertz processors for each month from Jan., 2001.

! Exercise 20.5.5: The computers described in the cube of Exercise 20.5.3 do not include monitors. What dimensions would you suggest to represent monitors? You may assume that the price of the monitor is included in the price of the computer.

Exercise 20.5.6: Suppose that a cube has 10 dimensions, and each dimension has 5 options for granularity of aggregation, including "no aggregation" and "aggregate fully." How many different views can we construct by choosing a granularity in each dimension?

Exercise 20.5.7: Show how to add the following time units to the lattice of Fig. 20.20: hours, minutes, seconds, fortnights (two-week periods), decades, and centuries.

Exercise 20.5.8: How would you change the dealer lattice of Fig. 20.21 to include "regions," if:

a) A region is a set of states.

* b) Regions are not commensurate with states, but each city is in only one region.

c) Regions are like area codes; each region is contained within a state, some cities are in two or more regions, and some regions have several cities.

! **Exercise 20.5.9:** In Exercise 20.5.3 we designed a cube suitable for use with the CUBE operator. However, some of the dimensions could also be given a nontrivial lattice structure. In particular, the processor type could be organized by manufacturer (e.g., SUN, Intel, AMD, Motorola), series (e.g., SUN UltraSparc, Intel Pentium or Celeron, AMD Athlon, or Motorola G-series), and model (e.g., Pentium-IV or G4).

   a) Design the lattice of processor types following the examples described above.

   b) Define a view that groups processors by series, hard disks by type, and removable disks by speed, aggregating everything else.

   c) Define a view that groups processors by manufacturer, hard disks by speed, and aggregates everything else except memory size.

   d) Give examples of queries that can be answered from the view of (b) only, the view of (c) only, both, and neither.

*!! **Exercise 20.5.10:** If the fact table F to which we apply the CUBE operator is sparse (i.e., there are many fewer tuples in F than the product of the number of possible values along each dimension), then the ratio of the sizes of CUBE(F) and F can be very large. How large can it be?

20.6 Data Mining

A family of database applications called *data mining* or *knowledge discovery in databases* has captured considerable interest because of opportunities to learn surprising facts from existing databases. Data-mining queries can be thought of as an extended form of decision-support query, although the distinction is informal (see the box on "Data-Mining Queries and Decision-Support Queries"). Data mining stresses both the query-optimization and data-management components of a traditional database system, as well as suggesting some important extensions to database languages, such as language primitives that support efficient sampling of data. In this section, we shall examine the principal directions data-mining applications have taken. We then focus on the problem called "frequent itemsets," which has received the most attention from the database point of view.

20.6.1 Data-Mining Applications

Broadly, data-mining queries ask for a useful summary of data, often without suggesting the values of parameters that would best yield such a summary. This family of problems thus requires rethinking the way database systems are to be used to provide such insights about the data. Below are some of the applications and problems that are being addressed using very large amounts

---

Data-Mining Queries and Decision-Support Queries

While decision-support queries may need to examine and aggregate large portions of the data in a database, the analyst posing the query usually tells the system exactly what query to execute; i.e., on which portion of the data to focus. A data-mining query goes a step beyond, inviting the system to decide where the focus should be. For example, a decision-support query might ask to "aggregate the sales of Aardvark automobiles by color and year," while a data-mining query might ask "what are the factors that have had the most influence over Aardvark sales?" Naive implementations of data-mining queries will result in execution of large numbers of decision-support queries, and may therefore take so much time to complete that the naive approach is completely infeasible.

---

of data. Since the best use of a DBMS in many of these problems is open, we shall not discuss the solutions to these problems, merely suggesting why they are hard. In Section 20.6.2 we shall discuss a problem where measurable progress has been made, and there we shall see a nontrivial, database-oriented solution.

Decision Tree Construction

Example 14.7 introduced us to what could be the basis for an interesting data-mining problem: "who buys gold jewelry?" In that example, we were only concerned with two properties of customers: their age and income. However, customer databases today can record much more about the customer or obtain the information from legitimate sources that are then integrated with the customer data into a warehouse. Examples of such properties could include the customer's zip code, marital status, own-or-rent-home, and information about any number of other items that he or she purchased recently.

Unlike the data in Example 14.7, which includes only data about people known to buy gold jewelry, a *decision tree* is a tree designed to guide the separation of data into two sets, which we might think of as "accept" and "reject." In the case of gold jewelry, the data would be information about people. The accept-set would be those we think would be likely to buy gold jewelry and the reject-set those we think are not likely to buy gold jewelry. If our predictions are reliable, then we have a good target population for direct-mail advertising of gold jewelry, for instance.

The decision tree itself would look something like Fig. 14.13, but without the actual data at the leaves. That is, the interior nodes each have an attribute and a value that serves as a threshold. The children of a node are either other interior nodes, or leaves representing a decision: accept or reject. A given tuple, representing data to be classified, is passed down the tree, going left or right at each step according to the value the tuple has in the attribute mentioned at the node, until a decision node is reached.

The tree is constructed by a *training set* of tuples whose outcome is known. In the case of gold jewelry, we take the database of customers, including information about which customers bought gold jewelry and which did not. The data-mining problem is to design from this data the decision tree that most reliably decides for a new customer, whose characteristics (age, salary, etc.) we know, whether or not they are likely to buy gold jewelry. That is, we must decide the best attribute A to put at the root and the best threshold value v for that attribute. Then, for the left child we find the best attribute and threshold for those customers who have $A < v$, and we do the same for the right child and those customers that have $A \geq v$. The same problem is faced at each level, until we can no longer profitably add nodes to the tree (because too few instances of the training data reach a given node for us to make a useful decision). The query asked as we design each node involves aggregating much of the data, so we can decide which attribute-threshold pair divides the data so the greatest fraction of "accepts" go to one side and "rejects" to the other side.

Clustering

Another class of data-mining problems involves "clustering," where we try to group our data items into some small number of groups such that the groups each have something substantial in common. Figure 20.23 suggests a clustering of two-dimensional data, although in practice the number of dimensions may be very large. In this figure we have shown the approximate outlines of the best three clusters, while some points are far from the center of any cluster; they would be considered "outliers" or grouped with the nearest cluster.

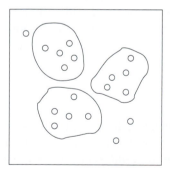

Figure 20.23: Three clusters in two-dimensional data

As an example application, Web search engines often find hundreds of thousands of documents that match a given query. To help organize these documents, the search engine may cluster them according to the words they use. For example, the search engine could place documents in a space that has one dimension for each possible word, perhaps excluding the most common words (*stop words*) such as "and" or "the," which tend to be present in all documents and tell us nothing about the content. A document is placed in this space according to the fraction of its word occurrences that are any particular word. For instance, if the document has 1000 word occurrences, two of which are "database," then the document would be placed at the .002 coordinate in the dimension corresponding to "database." By clustering documents in this space, we tend to get groups of documents that talk about the same thing. For instance, documents that talk about databases might have occurrences of words like "data," "query," "lock," and so on, while documents about baseball are unlikely to have occurrences of these words.

The data-mining problem here is to take the data and select the "means" or centers of the clusters. Often the number of clusters is given in advance, although that number may be selectable by the data-mining process as well. Either way, a naive algorithm for choosing the centers so that the average distance from a point to its nearest center is minimized involves many queries, each of which does a complex aggregation.

20.6.2 Finding Frequent Sets of Items

Now, we shall see a data-mining problem for which algorithms using secondary storage effectively have been developed. The problem is most easily described in terms of its principal application: the analysis of *market-basket* data. Stores today often hold in a data warehouse a record of what customers have bought together. That is, a customer approaches the checkout with a "market basket" full of the items he or she has selected. The cash register records all of these items as part of a single transaction. Thus, even if we don't know anything about the customer, and we can't tell if the customer returns and buys additional items, we *do* know certain items that a single customer buys together.

If items appear together in market baskets more often than would be expected, then the store has an opportunity to learn something about how customers are likely to traverse the store. The items can be placed in the store so that customers will tend to take certain paths through the store, and attractive items can be placed along these paths.

Example 20.22 : A famous example, which has been claimed by several people, is the discovery that people who buy diapers are unusually likely also to buy beer. Theories have been advanced for why that relationship is true, including the possibility that people who buy diapers, having a baby at home, are less likely to go out to a bar in the evening and therefore tend to drink beer at home. Stores may use the fact that many customers will walk through the store from where the diapers are to where the beer is, or vice versa. Clever marketers place beer and diapers near each other, with potato chips in the middle. The claim is that sales of all three items then increase. □

We can represent market-basket data by a fact table:

```
Baskets(basket, item)
```

where the first attribute is a "basket ID," or unique identifier for a market basket, and the second attribute is the ID of some item found in that basket. Note that it is not essential for the relation to come from true market-basket data; it could be any relation from which we want to find associated items. For instance, the "baskets" could be documents and the "items" could be words, in which case we are really looking for words that appear in many documents together.

The simplest form of market-basket analysis searches for sets of items that frequently appear together in market baskets. The *support* for a set of items is the number of baskets in which all those items appear. The problem of finding *frequent sets of items* is to find, given a support threshold s, all those sets of items that have support at least s.

If the number of items in the database is large, then even if we restrict our attention to small sets, say pairs of items only, the time needed to count the support for all pairs of items is enormous. Thus, the straightforward way to solve even the frequent pairs problem — compute the support for each pair of items i and j, as suggested by the SQL query in Fig. 20.24 — will not work. This query involves joining `Baskets` with itself, grouping the resulting tuples by the two items found in that tuple, and throwing away groups where the number of baskets is below the support threshold s. Note that the condition `I.item < J.item` in the `WHERE`-clause is there to prevent the same pair from being considered in both orders, or for a "pair" consisting of the same item twice from being considered at all.

```
SELECT I.item, J.item, COUNT(I.basket)
FROM Baskets I, Baskets J
WHERE I.basket = J.basket AND
      I.item < J.item
GROUP BY I.item, J.item
HAVING COUNT(I.basket) >= s;
```

Figure 20.24: Naive way to find all high-support pairs of items

20.6.3 The A-Priori Algorithm

There is an optimization that greatly reduces the running time of a query like Fig. 20.24 when the support threshold is sufficiently large that few pairs meet it. It is reasonable to set the threshold high, because a list of thousands or millions of pairs would not be very useful anyway; we want the data-mining query to focus our attention on a small number of the best candidates. The *a-priori* algorithm is based on the following observation:

Association Rules

A more complex type of market-basket mining searches for *association rules* of the form $\{i_1, i_2, \ldots, i_n\} \Rightarrow j$. Two possible properties that we might want in useful rules of this form are:

1. *Confidence*: the probability of finding item j in a basket that has all of $\{i_1, i_2, \ldots, i_n\}$ is above a certain threshold, e.g., 50%, e.g., "at least 50% of the people who buy diapers buy beer."

2. *Interest*: the probability of finding item j in a basket that has all of $\{i_1, i_2, \ldots, i_n\}$ is significantly higher or lower than the probability of finding j in a random basket. In statistical terms, j correlates with $\{i_1, i_2, \ldots, i_n\}$, either positively or negatively. The discovery in Example 20.22 was really that the rule $\{$diapers$\} \Rightarrow$ beer has high interest.

Note that even if an association rule has high confidence or interest, it will tend not to be useful unless the set of items involved has high support. The reason is that if the support is low, then the number of instances of the rule is not large, which limits the benefit of a strategy that exploits the rule.

- If a set of items X has support s, then each subset of X must also have support at least s.

In particular, if a pair of items, say $\{i, j\}$ appears in, say, 1000 baskets, then we know there are at least 1000 baskets with item i and we know there are at least 1000 baskets with item j.

The converse of the above rule is that if we are looking for pairs of items with support at least s, we may first eliminate from consideration any item that does not by itself appear in at least s baskets. The *a-priori algorithm* answers the same query as Fig. 20.24 by:

1. First finding the set of *candidate items* — those that appear in a sufficient number of baskets by themselves — and then

2. Running the query of Fig. 20.24 on only the candidate items.

The a-priori algorithm is thus summarized by the sequence of two SQL queries in Fig. 20.25. It first computes `Candidates`, the subset of the `Baskets` relation whose items have high support by themselves, then joins `Candidates` with itself, as in the naive algorithm of Fig. 20.24.

```
INSERT INTO Candidates
    SELECT *
    FROM Baskets
    WHERE item IN (
        SELECT item
        FROM Baskets
        GROUP BY item
        HAVING COUNT(*) >= s
    );

SELECT I.item, J.item, COUNT(I.basket)
FROM Candidates I, Candidates J
WHERE I.basket = J.basket AND
        I.item < J.item
GROUP BY I.item, J.item
HAVING COUNT(*) >= s;
```

Figure 20.25: The a-priori algorithm first finds frequent items before finding frequent pairs

Example 20.23 : To get a feel for how the a-priori algorithm helps, consider a supermarket that sells 10,000 different items. Suppose that the average market-basket has 20 items in it. Also assume that the database keeps 1,000,000 baskets as data (a small number compared with what would be stored in practice). Then the Baskets relation has 20,000,000 tuples, and the join in Fig. 20.24 (the naive algorithm) has 190,000,000 pairs. This figure represents one million baskets times $\binom{20}{2}$, which is 190, pairs of items. These 190,000,000 tuples must all be grouped and counted.

However, suppose that s is 10,000, i.e., 1% of the baskets. It is impossible that more than $20,000,000/10,000 = 2000$ items appear in at least 10,000 baskets, because there are only 20,000,000 tuples in Baskets, and any item appearing in 10,000 baskets appears in at least 10,000 of those tuples. Thus, if we use the a-priori algorithm of Fig. 20.25, the subquery that finds the candidate items cannot produce more than 2000 items, and will probably produce many fewer than 2000.

We cannot be sure how large Candidates is, since in the worst case *all* the items that appear in Baskets will appear in at least 1% of them. However, in practice Candidates will be considerably smaller than Baskets, if the threshold s is high. For sake of argument, suppose Candidates has on the average 10 items per basket; i.e., it is half the size of Baskets. Then the join of Candidates with itself in step (2) has 1,000,000 times $\binom{10}{2} = 45,000,000$ tuples, less than $1/4$ of the number of tuples in the join of Baskets with itself. We would thus expect the a-priori algorithm to run in about $1/4$ the time of the naive algorithm. In common situations, where `Candidates` has much less than half the tuples of `Baskets`, the improvement is even greater, since running time shrinks quadratically with the reduction in the number of tuples involved in the join.   □

20.6.4   Exercises for Section 20.6

Exercise 20.6.1: Suppose we are given the eight "market baskets" of Fig. 20.26.

$$B_1 = \{\text{milk, coke, beer}\}$$
$$B_2 = \{\text{milk, pepsi, juice}\}$$
$$B_3 = \{\text{milk, beer}\}$$
$$B_4 = \{\text{coke, juice}\}$$
$$B_5 = \{\text{milk, pepsi, beer}\}$$
$$B_6 = \{\text{milk, beer, juice, pepsi}\}$$
$$B_7 = \{\text{coke, beer, juice}\}$$
$$B_8 = \{\text{beer, pepsi}\}$$

Figure 20.26: Example market-basket data

* a) As a percentage of the baskets, what is the support of the set {beer, juice}?

  b) What is the support of the set {coke, pepsi}?

* c) What is the confidence of milk given beer (i.e., of the association rule {beer} ⇒ milk)?

  d) What is the confidence of juice given milk?

  e) What is the confidence of coke, given beer and juice?

* f) If the support threshold is 35% (i.e., 3 out of the eight baskets are needed), which pairs of items are frequent?

  g) If the support threshold is 50%, which pairs of items are frequent?

! **Exercise 20.6.2:** The a-priori algorithm also may be used to find frequent sets of more than two items. Recall that a set X of k items cannot have support at least s unless every proper subset of X has support at least s. In particular, the subsets of X that are of size $k - 1$ must all have support at least s. Thus, having found the frequent itemsets (those with support at least s) of size $k - 1$, we can define the *candidate sets* of size k to be those sets of k items, all of whose subsets of size $k - 1$ have support at least s. Write SQL queries that, given the frequent itemsets of size $k - 1$ first compute the candidate sets of size k, and then compute the frequent sets of size k.

Exercise 20.6.3: Using the baskets of Exercise 20.6.1, answer the following:

a) If the support threshold is 35%, what is the set of candidate triples?

b) If the support threshold is 35%, what sets of triples are frequent?

20.7 Summary of Chapter 20

✦ *Integration of Information*: Frequently, there exist a variety of databases or other information sources that contain related information. We have the opportunity to combine these sources into one. However, heterogeneities in the schemas often exist; these incompatibilities include differing types, codes or conventions for values, interpretations of concepts, and different sets of concepts represented in different schemas.

✦ *Approaches to Information Integration*: Early approaches involved "federation," where each database would query the others in the terms understood by the second. More recent approaches involve warehousing, where data is translated to a global schema and copied to the warehouse. An alternative is mediation, where a virtual warehouse is created to allow queries to a global schema; the queries are then translated to the terms of the data sources.

✦ *Extractors and Wrappers*: Warehousing and mediation require components at each source, called extractors and wrappers, respectively. A major function is to translate queries and results between the global schema and the local schema at the source.

✦ *Wrapper Generators*: One approach to designing wrappers is to use templates, which describe how a query of a specific form is translated from the global schema to the local schema. These templates are tabulated and interpreted by a driver that tries to match queries to templates. The driver may also have the ability to combine templates in various ways, and/or perform additional work such as filtering, to answer more complex queries.

✦ *Capability-Based Optimization*: The sources for a mediator often are able or willing to answer only limited forms of queries. Thus, the mediator must select a query plan based on the capabilities of its sources, before it can even think about optimizing the cost of query plans as conventional DBMS's do.

✦ *OLAP*: An important application of data warehouses is the ability to ask complex queries that touch all or much of the data, at the same time that transaction processing is conducted at the data sources. These queries, which usually involve aggregation of data, are termed on-line analytic processing, or OLAP, queries.

✦ *ROLAP and MOLAP*: It is frequently useful when building a warehouse for OLAP, to think of the data as residing in a multidimensional space, with dimensions corresponding to independent aspects of the data represented. Systems that support such a view of data take either a relational point of view (ROLAP, or relational OLAP systems), or use the specialized data-cube model (MOLAP, or multidimensional OLAP systems).

✦ *Star Schemas*: In a star schema, each data element (e.g., a sale of an item) is represented in one relation, called the fact table, while information helping to interpret the values along each dimension (e.g., what kind of product is item 1234?) is stored in a dimension table for each dimension.

✦ *The Cube Operator*: A specialized operator called CUBE pre-aggregates the fact table along all subsets of dimensions. It may add little to the space needed by the fact table, and greatly increases the speed with which many OLAP queries can be answered.

✦ *Dimension Lattices and Materialized Views*: A more powerful approach than the CUBE operator, used by some data-cube implementations, is to establish a lattice of granularities for aggregation along each dimension (e.g., different time units like days, months, and years). The warehouse is then designed by materializing certain views that aggregate in different ways along the different dimensions, and the view with the closest fit is used to answer a given query.

✦ *Data Mining*: Warehouses are also used to ask broad questions that involve not only aggregating on command, as in OLAP queries, but searching for the "right" aggregation. Common types of data mining include clustering data into similar groups, designing decision trees to predict one attribute based on the value of others, and finding sets of items that occur together frequently.

✦ *The A-Priori Algorithm*: An efficient way to find frequent itemsets is to use the a-priori algorithm. This technique exploits the fact that if a set occurs frequently, then so do all of its subsets.

20.8   References for Chapter 20

Recent surveys of warehousing and related technologies are in [9], [3], and [7]. Federated systems are surveyed in [12]. The concept of the mediator comes from [14].

Implementation of mediators and wrappers, especially the wrapper-generator approach, is covered in [5]. Capabilities-based optimization for mediators was explored in [11, 15].

The cube operator was proposed in [6]. The implementation of cubes by materialized views appeared in [8].

[4] is a survey of data-mining techniques, and [13] is an on-line survey of data mining. The a-priori algorithm was developed in [1] and [2].

1. R. Agrawal, T. Imielinski, and A. Swami, "Mining association rules between sets of items in large databases," *Proc. ACM SIGMOD Intl. Conf. on Management of Data* (1993), pp. 207–216.

2. R. Agrawal, and R. Srikant, "Fast algorithms for mining association rules," *Proc. Intl. Conf. on Very Large Databases* (1994), pp. 487–499.

3. S. Chaudhuri and U. Dayal, "An overview of data warehousing and OLAP technology," *SIGMOD Record* **26**:1 (1997), pp. 65–74.

4. U. M. Fayyad, G. Piatetsky-Shapiro, P. Smyth, and R. Uthurusamy, *Advances in Knowledge Discovery and Data Mining*, AAAI Press, Menlo Park CA, 1996.

5. H. Garcia-Molina, Y. Papakonstantinou, D. Quass, A. Rajaraman, Y. Sagiv, V. Vassalos, J. D. Ullman, and J. Widom) The TSIMMIS approach to mediation: data models and languages, *J. Intelligent Information Systems* **8**:2 (1997), pp. 117–132.

6. J. N. Gray, A. Bosworth, A. Layman, and H. Pirahesh, "Data cube: a relational aggregation operator generalizing group-by, cross-tab, and subtotals," *Proc. Intl. Conf. on Data Engineering* (1996), pp. 152–159.

7. A. Gupta and I. S. Mumick, *Materialized Views: Techniques, Implementations, and Applications*, MIT Press, Cambridge MA, 1999.

8. V. Harinarayan, A. Rajaraman, and J. D. Ullman, "Implementing data cubes efficiently," *Proc. ACM SIGMOD Intl. Conf. on Management of Data* (1996), pp. 205–216.

9. D. Lomet and J. Widom (eds.), Special issue on materialized views and data warehouses, *IEEE Data Engineering Bulletin* **18**:2 (1995).

10. Y. Papakonstantinou, H. Garcia-Molina, and J. Widom, "Object exchange across heterogeneous information sources," *Proc. Intl. Conf. on Data Engineering* (1995), pp. 251–260.

11. Y. Papakonstantinou, A. Gupta, and L. Haas, "Capabilities-base query rewriting in mediator systems," *Conference on Parallel and Distributed Information Systems* (1996). Available as:

    `http://dbpubs.stanford.edu/pub/1995-2`

12. A. P. Sheth and J. A. Larson, "Federated databases for managing distributed, heterogeneous, and autonomous databases," *Computing Surveys* **22**:3 (1990), pp. 183–236.

13. J. D. Ullman,

    `http://www-db.stanford.edu/~ullman/mining/mining.html`

14. G. Wiederhold, "Mediators in the architecture of future information sys-
    tems," *IEEE Computer* **C-25**:1 (1992), pp. 38–49.

15. R. Yerneni, C. Li, H. Garcia-Molina, and J. D. Ullman, "Computing capa-
    bilities of mediators," *Proc. ACM SIGMOD Intl. Conf. on Management
    of Data* (1999), pp. 443–454.

Index